THE REAL ACT® PREP GUIDE

THIRD EDITION

The **ONLY** Official Prep Guide
from the Makers of the ACT

ACT®

WILEY

THE REAL ACT® PREP GUIDE, THIRD EDITION

Published by John Wiley & Sons, Inc., Hoboken, New Jersey.

ACT endorses the *Code of Fair Testing Practices in Education* and the *Code of Professional Responsibilities in Educational Measurement,* guides to the conduct of those involved in educational testing. ACT is committed to ensuring that each of its testing programs upholds the guidelines in each *Code.* A copy of each *Code* may be obtained free of charge from ACT Customer Services (70), P.O. Box 1008, Iowa City, IA 52243-1008, 319-337-1429.

ACT Publications
P.O. Box 168
Iowa City, Iowa 52243-0168

The publisher and the author make no representations or warranties with respect to the accuracy or completeness of the contents of this work and specifically disclaim all warranties, including without limitation warranties of fitness for a particular purpose. No warranty may be created or extended by sales or promotional materials. The advice and strategies contained herein may not be suitable for every situation. This work is sold with the understanding that the publisher is not engaged in rendering legal, accounting, or other professional services. If professional assistance is required, the services of a competent professional person should be sought. Neither the publisher nor the author shall be liable for damages arising here from. The fact that an organization or Website is referred to in this work as a citation and/or a potential source of further information does not mean that the author or the publisher endorses the information the organization or Website may provide or recommendations it may make. Further, readers should be aware that Internet Websites listed in this work may have changed or disappeared between when this work was written and when it is read.

For general information on our other products and services or to obtain technical support please contact our Customer Care Department within the U.S. at (877) 762-2974, outside the U.S. at (317) 572-3993 or fax (317) *572-4002.*

ISBN 978-1-119-23641-2
Printed in the United States of America
Third Edition

Contents

Contents

Preface

You want to do your best on the ACT, and this book can help. It supplements our free booklet *Preparing for the ACT* and our *ACT Online Prep*™ (a Web-based preparation program for the ACT). This book features five actual ACTs—including the optional Writing Test—which you can use for practice, and it gives detailed explanatory answers to every question to help you review. Using this book will make you familiar with:

- the content of the ACT

- the procedures you'll follow when you're actually taking the ACT

- the types of questions you can expect to find on the ACT

- suggestions on how you might approach the questions

- general test-taking strategies

This book is intended to help you **know what to expect** when you take the ACT so you can relax and concentrate on doing your best. The more you know about what to expect on **any** test you take, the more likely it is that your performance on that test will accurately reflect your overall preparation and achievement in the areas it measures. Knowing what to expect can help reduce any nervousness you may feel as you approach the test. Not only will this information make you more comfortable, it can also help keep your performance on the test from being unfairly hampered by outside factors, like worrying about what's going to happen next.

The ACT measures your understanding of what you've been taught in courses that you are expected to have completed by the time you enter college. It has taken you years to learn all this material, and it will take you some time to review for the ACT. You can't expect to cram for the ACT in a night or two. However, any review should be helpful to you, even if it just makes you more comfortable when you actually sit down to take the ACT. We hope this book helps you to gauge how much reviewing you feel you need to do.

How This Book Is Arranged

This book is divided into five chapters:

Chapter 1:   About the ACT. This chapter describes the purpose of the ACT, how to register for it, and what to expect at the test center.

Chapter 2:   General Test-Taking Strategies. This chapter provides general test-taking strategies that apply to the ACT overall.

Chapter 3:   Test Format and Content. This chapter takes you step-by-step through each of the individual tests of the ACT (English, Mathematics, Reading, Science, and Writing) and includes sample questions.

Chapter 4:   Practice ACT Tests. Five complete ACT tests with answer explanations for every question are included.

Chapter 5:   Interpreting Your ACT Test Scores. This chapter gives instructions on how to score your practice tests and interpret your test scores.

The chapters are identified by bars on the edge of their right-hand pages.

Before You Begin

There is no standardized way to prepare for the ACT. Everyone learns and studies differently. Some people study best when they are by themselves. Others need to work with fellow students to do their best. Still others function best in a structured class with a teacher leading them through their studies. You should use whatever method works best for you. Keep in mind, though, that when you actually take the ACT, it will be just you and the test.

We recommend that as you use this book to help you prepare for the ACT you break your study time into one-hour segments (except when you're taking the timed practice tests, of course). If you want to study for more than one hour in a day, that's fine, but you may want to take a break each half hour, even if it's only to stretch and give your mind a chance to absorb what you've learned.

Chapter 1:
About the ACT

The ACT measures your achievement in core academic areas important for success in college. There are four multiple-choice tests—English, Mathematics, Reading, and Science—and an optional Writing Test. Topics covered on these five tests correspond very closely to topics covered in typical high school classes. Each test is described in detail in chapter 3.

The ACT isn't an IQ test—it doesn't measure your basic intelligence. It's an **achievement** test that's been carefully designed—using surveys of classroom teachers, reviews of curriculum guides for schools all over the country, and advice from curriculum specialists and college faculty—to be one of several effective tools for evaluating your readiness for college work.

The individual tests that make up the ACT consist of questions that measure your skills and knowledge. You're **not** required to memorize facts or vocabulary to do well on the ACT. Of course, all the terms, formulas, and other information you have learned in your classes will be useful to you when you take the ACT. However, last-minute cramming (like memorizing 5,000 vocabulary words or the entire periodic table of elements) won't directly improve your performance on the ACT.

What you **can** do to improve your performance on the ACT is to find out ahead of time what you'll be expected to know or do, and then to think about and use that information to your best advantage.

Registering for the ACT

Selecting a Test Date

One of the first decisions you'll need to make is **when** to take the ACT. There are several factors to consider:

- When is the ACT being offered near your home?

- When does each college or scholarship agency you're interested in need to have your ACT scores?

- Where do you stand in your high school coursework?

- Are you planning to take the ACT more than once?

Let's look in turn at each of these considerations.

The ACT is offered nationally several times a year, between September and June. However, it's not offered at every test center on each test date. If you need to take the ACT on a day other than Saturday because of religious reasons, you'll want to be especially attentive in selecting a test date when a test center near you is open on a non-Saturday date.

One of the first things you should find out, then, is where and when the ACT is being offered in your area. A quick and easy way to get that information is by accessing ACT's website at **www.actstudent.org**. Select a test date and location that is convenient for you. Often, your own or a neighboring school will serve as a test center.

One important decision you need to make is how early in your junior year to take the ACT. A number of factors will affect this decision. First, you should find out when colleges you're interested in need to have your test scores. Is there a particular program or scholarship for which you want to apply? If so, is there a deadline by which you need to have test scores submitted to the college or agency? Score reports are normally ready about 3–8 weeks after the test date. If you take the ACT Plus Writing, your reports will be ready only after all your scores are available, normally 5–8 weeks after the test date. So be sure to allow enough time. You may not be certain yet which school or program you'll decide on. That's okay. Just be sure you're doing everything, including taking the ACT, early enough to keep all your options open.

Another consideration in deciding when to take the ACT is where you stand in your high school coursework. If you're in a college-prep program and taking a lot of courses in English, mathematics, and science in your sophomore and junior years, it would be best for you to take the ACT in your junior year, while those subjects are still fresh in your memory. Perhaps you'll decide to take the ACT more than once, in hopes of improving your score. In that case, it's better to take the exam early in the spring of your junior year to allow time for a second try. If you find you're studying a significant amount of material covered on the ACT during your senior year, it's reasonable to assume that your performance on the ACT might be better and you may want to consider retaking the ACT in your senior year.

There are several advantages to taking the ACT in your junior year:

- You probably will have completed much of the coursework corresponding to the material covered on the ACT.

- You'll have your ACT scores and other information in time to help make decisions about your final year of high school coursework. (For example, you may decide to take additional classes in an area in which your test score was lower than you wanted it to be.)

- Colleges will know of your interest and have your scores in time to contact you during the summer before your senior year, when many of them like to send information about such things as admissions, scholarships, advanced placement, and special programs to prospective students.

- You'll have your ACT scores and information from colleges in time to make decisions about visiting campuses or contacting schools.

- You'll have the opportunity to take the ACT again if you feel your scores don't accurately reflect your achievement.

Test Information Release

On certain test dates, you may request and pay for a copy of the test questions used to determine your score, a copy of your answers, a list of the correct answers to the multiple-choice questions, and a copy of the table used to convert raw scores (the number of questions you answered correctly on each multiple-choice test) to reported scores (the scores that appear on your score report). If you take the Writing Test, you will also receive a copy of the prompt, the scoring rubric, and the scores assigned by the two raters. You'll also get information about requesting an actual copy of your answer document for an additional fee. The service isn't offered for all test dates, so if you're interested in receiving this information, you'll need to check the dates on ACT's website (**www.actstudent.org**) to be sure you're choosing a test date on which the service is available.

Selecting a Test Option

When you register, you must choose one of two test options—the ACT (No Writing) (which includes the four multiple-choice tests: English, Mathematics, Reading, and Science), or the ACT Plus Writing (which includes the four multiple-choice tests plus a 30-minute Writing Test). Taking the ACT Plus Writing will provide you with two additional scores: a Writing Test subscore and a Combined English/Writing score. Taking the Writing Test does **not** affect your subject area scores on the ACT or your Composite score.

Not all institutions require or recommend taking the ACT Writing Test. You should check directly with the institutions you are considering to find out their requirements, or ask your high school counselor which test option you should take. You can also use the search tool on ACT's website (**www.actstudent.org**) for a list of institutions that have provided information to ACT about their policies—whether they require, recommend, or do not need results from the ACT Writing Test.

Registering

The fastest and easiest way to register for the ACT is online at **www.actstudent.org**. When you register on the Web, you will know immediately if your preferred test center has space for you and you can print your admission ticket. Read all the information on your admission ticket carefully to make sure all the information is correct.

You are guaranteed a seat and test booklet at a test center **only** if you register by the deadline for a test date. If you miss the late registration deadline but need to test on the next test date, you can try to test as a "standby" examinee. Testing as a standby is more costly, and you are **not** guaranteed a seat or test booklet. If you decide to take your chance as a standby, be sure to follow the instructions for standby testing on the website. You must bring a completed standby request with you to the test center, along with acceptable identification. Standby examinees will be admitted only after all registered students have been seated for their test option.

Creating Your ACT Web Account. No matter how you register, you are encouraged to create your free ACT Web account. You can use your ACT Web account to:

- view your scores and score report on the Web at no charge
- send your scores to additional colleges
- receive e-mail updates from ACT about changes to your registration
- make changes to your student profile
- print your admission ticket

Registering Under Special Circumstances

See the website or our online registration brochure for instructions if special circumstances apply to you—for example, if your religious beliefs prevent you from taking the exam on Saturday and there are no non-Saturday test centers in your area or if you have a diagnosed disability and require test accommodations.

If you have a diagnosed disability and documentation of extended time accommodations in school, you *may* be eligible to test on national test dates with extended time. Details about the procedures for applying to test with extended time and the amount of time provided are on the website. To test with extended time, you **must** register by the deadline for the desired test date so your documentation may be reviewed and arrangements made. (Extended time is **not** available for standby examinees.)

At the Test Center

Arriving at the Test Center

You'll be asked to report to the test center by 8:00 a.m. on your test date. Under no circumstances will you be admitted after the test booklets have been distributed so **be sure** to arrive on time.

You may need to walk a few blocks to get to the test center, or you may need to drive several hours, perhaps to an unfamiliar city. Whatever your situation, be certain to allow plenty of time. If the test is being administered in a place that's new to you, you might consider finding the location the night before the test or even a few days in advance.

Test centers vary considerably. You may be taking the ACT in your own high school, at a local community college, or in a large building on a nearby university campus. Your surroundings may be quite familiar, or they may be uncomfortably new. If they're new, allow yourself a few extra minutes to get used to the place. Then try to forget about your surroundings so that you can concentrate on the test.

It's best to bring with you **only** the things you'll need that morning, because other materials will just be in your way and you may not be allowed to have them in the test room. Be sure to bring:

- several sharpened **No. 2 pencils with good erasers** (test the erasers to make sure they erase cleanly and leave no residue),
- your **admission ticket** (you will need it to complete your answer document),
- **acceptable photo identification** (see **www.actstudent.org** for details), and
- a **permitted calculator** if you wish to use one on the Mathematics Test (permitted calculators are described in detail at **www.actstudent.org**).

Because you will probably want to pace yourself, bring a **watch** with the alarm function turned off. Although the test supervisor will announce when there are 5 minutes remaining on each test, not all test rooms have wall clocks.

What to wear? Try making this decision ahead of time so you'll have one less thing to think about on the morning of the test. Keep in mind that the building used for administering the ACT is often one not normally used on a Saturday. As a result, you may find that the heat or air-conditioning has been turned down or off. It's a good idea to dress in layers so that you can adjust to the temperature you find in your testing room.

Remember, too, that you're going to be sitting in the same place for more than three hours. Wearing something you're especially comfortable in may make you better able to relax and concentrate on the test. For many people, what they're wearing can make a difference in how they feel about themselves. Picking something you like and feel good wearing may give you a little extra boost of confidence.

What to Expect at the Test Center

The way **check-in procedures** are handled at a particular test center depends on such things as how many students are taking the ACT at that center. You may find that all students are met at a central location and directed from there to different classrooms. You may find signs posted, telling you that everyone whose last name falls between certain letters should report directly to a particular room. However this part of the check-in is handled at your center, you can anticipate that certain things will be done, including verification of your identity.

You will be asked for your admission ticket and acceptable identification. To be admitted to take the ACT, you **must** present acceptable identification or be personally recognized by one of the test center personnel. Examples of acceptable identification include current identification issued by your school or city/state/federal government on which both your name and current photograph appear (for example, driver's license or passport); a recognizable *individual* photograph of you in a school yearbook or other publication, printed within the last year and with your first and last name in the caption; or an individually completed school letter of identification, which must include your name and full physical description and be on school letterhead with a raised or inked school seal, signed in ink by you in the presence of a school official (not a relative), and signed in ink by that official. Complete explanations of acceptable forms of identification appear on the website. **Be sure** that you have one of the acceptable forms of identification before you go to the test center. Otherwise, you will not be allowed to test.

In the room you'll be directed to a seat by a member of the testing staff. If you are left-handed, let the testing staff know so that an appropriate desk or table can be made available to you. If there is any problem with your desk, let the staff know.

You'll be asked to put away **everything** except your identification, admission ticket, pencils, and erasers. You'll be allowed to have your calculator on your desk only during the Mathematics Test. Nothing else will be allowed in the test room—no dictionaries, no books or other reading materials, no scratch paper or notes, no highlight pens, no radios or earphones, no electronic devices of any kind. You are encouraged to leave your cell phone at home or in the car. If you bring your cell phone, it must be turned completely off; silencing it is not sufficient. If your watch has an alarm, you'll be asked to turn the alarm off so it won't disturb others. If your phone, watch alarm, or any device goes off during testing, or you use your cell phone at any time (including break), you will be dismissed and your answer document will not be scored.

Eating, drinking, and the use of tobacco are not allowed in the test room. You may bring a snack to eat or drink before the test or during the break, but any food or beverage you bring must be put away during testing and must be consumed **outside** the test room.

Even though every room is different, you should expect an environment that is quiet, well lighted, and reasonably comfortable. If you have problems with the testing environment, let the testing staff know immediately.

While you're waiting for the test to begin, you may find yourself getting anxious or jittery. That's perfectly normal. Most of us get nervous in new situations. People handle this nervousness in different ways.

Some people find it helpful to practice **mental and physical relaxation techniques.** If this appeals to you, try alternately flexing and relaxing your muscles, beginning at your toes and moving up through your shoulders, neck, and arms. Meanwhile, imagine yourself in a quiet, peaceful place: at the beach, in the mountains, or just in your favorite lounge chair. Breathe deeply and smoothly.

Other people like to **control that nervous energy** and turn it to their advantage. For them, concentrating on the task at hand and shutting everything else out of their minds is the most helpful strategy. If this is your style, you may even want to close your eyes and imagine yourself already working on the exam, thinking about how it will feel to move confidently and smoothly through the tests.

If you have the chance, try out the two approaches on some classroom tests and see which one works better for you. The important thing is to keep the ACT in perspective. Try not to let it become "larger than life." Remember, it's just one part of a long academic career.

You will have the opportunity to read the **instructions** for each of the five ACT tests, but it's helpful to know them in advance. You'll find the test directions in the sample tests in this book.

Be sure to ask about any aspect of the test-taking procedure that is not perfectly clear to you. After all, how can you expect to do your best if you're worrying about a procedural detail? Testing staff will be available throughout the exam. In fact, they'll be moving quietly around the room while you're working. If you have a question about the administration of the test (not about any of the test questions), raise your hand and quietly ask for information.

During the exam, **you may find yourself getting tired.** If so, check your posture to make sure you're sitting up straight. It's difficult to get enough air in your lungs when you're slouching. You'll stay more alert and confident if you have a steady supply of fresh oxygen going to your brain.

You might want to practice those relaxation techniques again, too, because tension contributes to fatigue. As you start a new test, you might find it helpful to stretch your neck and shoulder muscles, rotate your shoulders, stretch back in your chair, and take some long, deep breaths.

You can expect a short break (approximately 10–15 minutes) after the second test. During this break, it's a good idea to stand up, walk around a little, stretch, and relax. You may wish to get a drink, go to the restroom, or have a snack. It's important to keep in mind, though, that you still have work requiring concentration ahead of you. It's also important to return to the room quickly. The third test will start promptly, and you'll need to be back at your desk and ready to go on time.

If you become ill during the test, you certainly may turn in your test materials and leave if you need to. Let the testing staff know that you are ill and whether you wish to have your answer document scored. One caution: once you leave the test center, you won't be allowed to return and continue—so **be sure** that leaving is what you want to do. You might try simply closing your eyes or putting your head on the desk for a minute first; then if you feel better, you'll be able to continue.

Summary

This book should help you to understand how to get ready to take the ACT. Knowing the basics should get you started. By now, you should have a fair idea of what to expect at the test center and know where to find more information: on ACT's website at **www.actstudent.org** and in *Preparing for the ACT*. Now that you know the basic information, you should be ready to move on to the ACT itself.

Chapter 2: General Test-Taking Strategies

You've already been preparing for the ACT for **years**. The best possible preparation for a college admission test is active, thoughtful high school coursework. If you've been taking challenging courses, paying attention in class, doing your homework, and thinking about the assignments, you've already done most of the preparation you need to take the ACT.

Getting Ready

It might be helpful to compare taking the ACT (or any other important exam) to playing an important match in tennis, performing in a music concert, facing another team in debate, or acting in a play. The best way to get ready for a game or performance is to prepare actively: practice the skills required, learn strategies to enable you to demonstrate your strengths, exercise your mind and body, and learn how to deal with the stress of the moment in order to turn it to your advantage.

To get ready for an important test, you need to prepare in much the same way. You need to exercise your mind (for example, through discussion, reading, problem solving), take care of your body (it's difficult for your mind to function well when your body is hungry or tired), and develop strategies (for example, find out in advance as much as you can about the test so you'll know what to expect).

It's a good idea to think about how you'll use what you know in order to do your best on the ACT. What kind of approach and preparation for this exam will allow you to best demonstrate the abilities and skills you've developed over the years? How can you make sure that you'll do your best?

The suggestions in this chapter are designed to help you build on the preparation that you have already completed. They're taken from advice gathered over years—from education specialists, from testing specialists, and from people who, like you, have taken lots of tests. Read the advice, try it out, and see how it fits with what you already know about the way you take tests. Realize that **you can choose how you will take the ACT.** Then make intelligent choices about what will work for you.

Mental Preparation

As we've said before, the best mental preparation for the ACT is solid schoolwork. However, there are some things you can do to prepare for the test and to boost your confidence as well. The following tips will help make you feel calm and mentally confident so that you'll do your very best on the ACT.

Get Organized

If you know that you are going to be taking the ACT, you should begin preparing well in advance. Don't leave preparation to the last minute. As the test date moves closer, organize a plan to help you do your best. Getting organized involves everything from assembling the materials you need to take the test to practicing specific test-taking strategies that will help you do your best. This chapter outlines many different aspects of successful test preparation.

Keep the Test in Perspective

Remembering that the ACT is only a small part of the long process of your education and training will help you keep it in perspective. So will remembering that the ACT and tests like it are designed to provide **you** with information. When you have completed the ACT, you will receive valuable information that you can use to help make decisions about your future educational plans.

Another way to keep the ACT in perspective is to remind yourself that it's you taking the test, not the test taking you. **Put yourself in charge** as you go into the test. That's the best way to ensure that you do as well on the test as you can.

Learn as Much as You Can About the ACT

Before you take the ACT, the first thing you should do is find out as much about the exam as you can. This advice may seem obvious, but it's surprising how many people just walk into the test and take their chances. Surprises may be fine sometimes, but they can be very upsetting when they turn up on tests. The more you know about the ACT in advance, the more confident you can feel.

Where can you find information about the ACT? The best place to get up-to-date information about the ACT is by accessing ACT's website (**www.actstudent.org**). Another good place to look for information is right in your school. Talk to other students who have taken the test and ask them for their impressions. Talk to **several** students, so you're not swayed by only one person's experience. Talk to your **teachers and school counselors**, too. Very often they can give you excellent advice based not only on their knowledge of the test but also on what they know about your abilities. You can also ask your school counselor for a copy of *Preparing for the ACT*, a free booklet published by ACT, or you can access it on our website. Another potential source of information is your public or school library.

Familiarize yourself with the content and format of the individual ACT tests (English, Mathematics, Reading, Science, and the optional Writing Test). Review the information about these tests provided in this book. Note which skills and knowledge are measured on each test. Know what to expect on test day. Familiarize yourself with the information in this book, the ACT website for students (**www.actstudent.org**), and the free booklet *Preparing for the ACT*.

Once you know **what** to expect, you can concentrate on **how** to do the work. For instance, once you know that the ACT Mathematics Test covers trigonometry skills, you can focus attention on the properties of triangles, if you need review in that area.

Maybe this seems obvious to you, but focusing attention on the task at hand is often harder than it sounds. Don't let preparing for the ACT seem like an overwhelming job. Cutting that large task into smaller pieces will make preparing much more manageable. Training yourself to concentrate your mental energies on small, manageable jobs instead of letting yourself be distracted by all sorts of other interesting things will have long-term benefits, including making it easier for you to prepare mentally for the ACT or any test.

Refresh Your Knowledge and Skills in the Content Areas

Once you have a good idea of the content of the individual ACT tests, review those content areas you have studied but do not have fresh in your mind. You also may want to spend time refreshing your knowledge in the content areas that make up large portions of the individual tests.

Identify the Content Areas You Have Not Studied

If you find that the individual ACT tests contain many unfamiliar content areas, consider taking courses to help you gain knowledge in those areas before you take the ACT. Because the ACT measures knowledge acquired over a period of time, it is unlikely that a "cram" course covering material that is unfamiliar to you will help you improve your scores. Longer, full-term courses in the subject matter will be most helpful to you because they aim to improve your knowledge in a subject area.

Plan Your Study Time

When an exam like the ACT is far in the future, it's pretty easy to put off preparing for it. Something else always seems to come up: going out, seeing a movie, watching your favorite television show, even cleaning your room may seem more interesting than studying for a test that's still in the hazy future. Somehow the days disappear, though, and you find yourself frantically cramming the night before the test, overwhelmed by just how much material you have to cover.

If this sounds familiar, try setting up a reasonable schedule for studying for the ACT. **Set aside small amounts of time** for studying over an extended period—days, weeks, or even months—so you won't have so much to do at the end that you feel swamped. Sometimes it's too easy to scrap the whole plan once there's a small change in it, so **make your schedule flexible** enough to allow for a surprise homework assignment or some unexpected fun. And find a way to **reward yourself** as you get the work done, even if it's just a checklist you can mark to show your progress.

Develop a Positive Mental Attitude

In addition to learning the material you'll be tested on and reviewing it to make sure it's fresh in your mind, it's important to go into the ACT with a good mental attitude, confident that you can do your best. While confidence obviously isn't enough by itself to ensure good performance on a test, a real lack of confidence can hurt your performance. Be confident in your ability to do well on the ACT. **You can do well!** You just need to be prepared to work hard.

Some small changes can make a surprising difference. For example, how you imagine yourself taking the exam may affect how well you actually do. Negative thoughts have a way of turning into negative actions. So **practice positive thinking:** imagine yourself meeting the challenge of the exam with ease, successfully. The day of the test, tell yourself you intend to do your best, and act as if you mean it. You probably won't get a perfect score, but that's not the point. You want to be sure you do as well as you can against the most important measure: your own capabilities. The real satisfaction doesn't lie in meeting somebody else's expectations for you, but in knowing that you've met your own expectations—that you've done your personal best.

Physical Preparation

You may wonder why physical preparation is important for an exam such as the ACT. After all, taking an exam isn't exactly like playing a game of soccer. So why should you prepare yourself physically?

Think of the body as the mind's support system. Being sure that your body is at peak performance the morning you take the ACT will help your mind work at its peak too.

Exercise

This is not the time to neglect your usual exercise. Be sure you get plenty of physical activity in the days before the exam. Hiking, running, walking, wheelchair exercising, biking, swimming, basketball, soccer—any aerobic exercises you regularly enjoy will improve your body's performance.

Diet

Diet is also important. You've probably heard the standard advice: "Be sure to **eat a good breakfast** before you take the test." That sounds like sensible advice, but what exactly is a "good breakfast"? Different people have different opinions.

On test day, you should probably select the healthiest breakfast **you** are accustomed to. If you routinely eat a very light breakfast, choose your **best** light breakfast—don't switch to something entirely new. If you usually have a bowl of cereal and juice, for example, you probably shouldn't have a huge stack of pancakes the morning of the ACT. On the other hand, if you're accustomed to a substantial breakfast, it would be a mistake to skip breakfast altogether or to eat significantly less than you're used to. A sugary breakfast will probably work against you. While it may give you an initial charge of energy to start the morning, that energy will most likely burn off before you're halfway through.

When planning what to eat the morning of the test, you may want to consider that, while eating and drinking are not allowed in the testing room, you can have a snack before the test or during the break. (You can expect a 10-minute break at the end of the second test.)

Somebody may suggest to you that you'll do better on the test if you "take something." This simply isn't true. The effect on your body of taking drugs not prescribed for you by a medical doctor is negative. Period.

Rest

Get plenty of sleep the night before the test so you will be in good physical condition for taking it. How much sleep is "plenty"? Again, keep in mind **your** typical schedule. If you routinely go to bed at 11:00 p.m., this is probably not the time to stay up until 2:30 a.m. On the other hand, going to bed at 8:00 p.m. may also be a mistake. If you suddenly go to bed much earlier than your body is used to, you may find yourself tossing and turning for hours, and you'll be more tired than you would have been if you'd watched television or read or shot baskets during that time.

Advice you hear about physical preparation for tests often focuses on just the day before a test. You'll find, however, that the amount of sleep and exercise you get—not just the day before the test, but for days and even weeks before—will make a difference in how you feel and how you are able to perform on the test. Similarly, it's not just what you eat for breakfast the morning of test day, but what you've eaten for several days before that gives you the power you need to perform well.

Test-Taking Strategies

As with most skills, test-taking skill varies from person to person. In this chapter we list some basic test-taking strategies that apply to nearly every test you take, as well as to the ACT. You've probably used most of these strategies before. Recognizing that you know how to use them—and that they are valuable—should help you approach the ACT with confidence.

Take a Practice Test

The best way to anticipate what it will be like to take the ACT is to take a sample version of it. You'll find a practice ACT in the free booklet *Preparing for the ACT*. You'll also find five complete ACTs in this book. (See chapter 4 for the tests and chapter 5 for suggestions on how to score them.) You may want to practice some of the strategies outlined in this section when you take the practice tests.

Learn to Pace Yourself

The ACT, like many tests, **must** be completed within a specific and limited amount of time. Working quickly and efficiently is one of the skills necessary for conveying how much you've learned on the topic being tested.

Pacing yourself on a test can be quite simple. For example, on the Mathematics Test, which consists of 60 multiple-choice questions, one possibility is to simply divide the amount of time available for the test by the number of questions you'll have to answer. One problem with this, on some tests, is that you may come up with a length of time that doesn't mean much. Do you have any clear idea of how long 80 seconds is, for example? Another problem may be that the amount of time sounds so short it's scary, and you can talk yourself into feeling panicky.

Another option is to divide the total number of questions into smaller groups and figure out how much time you have for each group. If you prefer this approach, try to keep the math simple. For example, if you have a total of 30 questions to answer in one hour, think of it as either two groups of 15 questions at 30 minutes for each group, or three groups of 10 questions at 20 minutes for each group. Then check your watch to see how closely you're keeping to that schedule as you take the practice ACTs. If after 10 questions you've used only 18 minutes, you'll know that you're doing well. On the other hand, if those first 10 questions have taken 23 minutes, you'll probably want to pick up the pace if you can. You will probably also want to set aside several minutes at the end of each individual test for a quick review of your work.

On the English, Reading, and Science tests, you may want to pace yourself by figuring out a certain amount of time to spend reading each passage and then determining how much time you have left to spend on the associated questions. For example, if you have four passages to cover in 40 minutes, you would allow yourself roughly 10 minutes for each passage and the related questions. If you spend 5 minutes reading a passage, then you would know that you have roughly 5 minutes to spend on the questions associated with the passage.

For the Writing Test, you will want to pace yourself in the way that best suits your personal writing strategy. Many writers choose to devote some time to planning their essay, and most of their time to writing it. Keep in mind that you probably won't have enough time to fully draft, revise, and then recopy your essay. So, taking a few minutes to plan your essay is a better strategy than writing a first draft with the intention of copying it over for your final essay. Overall, you should budget your time in a way that has been most effective for you as you have taken other essay exams in school, or whenever you have had to produce writing within a time limit.

No matter how you choose to pace yourself while taking the ACT, don't let your concern about time get in the way of your work. Don't try to push yourself to work so fast that you begin to feel out of control or to make careless errors. After all, answering 60 questions so quickly that, through carelessness, you miss 20 doesn't give you a better score than answering 50 more slowly and missing only 10.

The ACT has been designed so that most people taking it are able to finish each individual test. Many people have time to go back and check their work on each test too. So, while you won't want to lose time by being distracted, you shouldn't worry unnecessarily about time either. Use all of the time available so you can do your very best on the test.

We've included the time available for each individual test of the ACT in the information in chapter 3. Use the practice tests in this book to check your own working pace and see if you, like most people, will have time to finish each ACT test and go back and check your work. Perhaps working through the practice tests will let you know at what pace you need to work in order to finish within the available time. If so, you'll want to keep that in mind when you take the actual test.

If you wish to keep track of your pace while taking the ACT, bring a watch. Not all testing centers have wall clocks. The test supervisor will announce when there are 5 minutes left on each test.

Know the Directions and Understand the Answer Document

It's easy to ignore directions, no matter what we're doing. Many of us are more likely to just forge ahead—do whatever we're doing the way we think it ought to be done, regardless of what the designer had in mind.

Putting the instructions aside and "winging it" might be all right at home, but it is not a good strategy when you are taking the ACT. At home, if something goes wrong or doesn't make sense, you can often undo what you've done and start over. With an exam such as the ACT, you need to get it right the first time.

On the day that you take the ACT, you can read the directions for each test. However, it is helpful to know them in advance—it will save you time and worry. For example, the ACT English, Reading, and Science tests ask for the "best" answer, while the Mathematics Test asks for the "correct" answer. This simple difference in the instructions signals an important distinction you need to keep in mind as you're working through those tests. Because only one answer is "correct" in the Mathematics Test, you'll want to be sure your understanding of the question and your calculations are precise—so that your answer matches one, and only one, of the possible answers. In the other areas, more than one of the possible answers may arguably be "correct," and you'll need to be careful to select the "best" answer among those potentially "correct" ones. You'll find the directions for each test in the practice ACTs in this book.

The directions for the Writing Test are also very important. The directions spell out the aspects of writing that will be evaluated. They also tell you where in the test booklet you can write to *plan* your essay, and where you should write your final version. The directions for the Writing Test and a sample answer document appear in the practice ACTs in this book.

Before you take the ACT, you should become familiar with the answer document. Knowing in advance how to use the answer document will save you time and worry when you take the actual ACT.

Read Carefully and Thoroughly

Just as it's important to read and understand the **directions** for a test, it's also important to read and understand each **question** on the test. As you've probably discovered somewhere along the line, you can miss even the simplest test question by reading carelessly and overlooking an important word or detail. Some questions on the ACT, for instance, require more than one step, and the answer to each preliminary step may be included as an answer choice. If you read these questions too quickly, you can easily make the mistake of choosing a plausible answer that relates to a preliminary step but is the incorrect answer to the question.

Take the time to read each question carefully and thoroughly before deciding on your answer. Make sure you understand **exactly** what the question asks and what you are to do to answer it. You may want to underline or circle key words in the test booklet (see the section "Write Notes in Your Test Booklet If Allowed" on page 20). Reread the item if you are confused.

Watch the question's wording. Look for words such as *not* or *least*, especially when they are not clearly set off with underlining, capital letters, or bold type. Don't make careless errors because you only skimmed the question or the options. Pay close attention to qualifying words such as *all, most, some, none—always, usually, seldom, sometimes, never—best, worst—highest, lowest— smaller, larger*. (There are many other qualifying words; these are only a few examples of related groups.) When you find a qualifier in one of the responses to a question, a good way to determine whether or not the response is the best answer is to substitute related qualifiers and see which makes the best statement. For example, if a response says "Tests are always difficult," you might test the truth of the word *always* by substituting *sometimes* and the other words related to *always*. If any of the words other than the one in the answer makes the best statement, then the response is not the best answer.

Pay close attention to modifying or limiting phrases in the statement. For instance, a question in the Reading Test might have the following as a possible answer: "Lewis and Clark, the great British explorers, began their historic trip to the West Coast by traveling up the Mississippi." The answer is incorrect because Lewis and Clark were not British, but were U.S. citizens. (You would not be expected to know from memory that Lewis and Clark were U.S. citizens; that information would be included in the passage.)

Read all the answer choices before selecting one. Questions on the ACT often include answer choices that seem plausible but that aren't quite correct. Even though the first answer choice may appeal to you, the correct or best answer may be farther down the list.

When taking the Writing Test, reading the writing prompt carefully is extremely important. It is important that you understand exactly what the writing prompt asks you to do. Before you start to plan your essay, make sure you understand the writing prompt and the issue it asks you to respond to.

Mark Your Answer Document Carefully

Only answers marked on the answer document during the time allowed for a particular test will count. Carefully mark your answers on the answer document as you work through the questions on each test. Remember that during an actual test you may not fill in answers or alter answers on your answer document after "stop" is called.

For the Writing Test, writing (or printing) legibly in English in the correct place in the answer document is vital. If readers cannot make out what you have written, they will not be able to score your essay. You are allowed to write or print your essay; however, you must do so clearly. Keep in mind, you must write your essay **using a soft-lead pencil (not a mechanical pencil)**. You must write on the lined pages in the answer folder. If you make corrections, do so very thoroughly. You may write corrections or additions neatly between the lines of your essay, but you may not write in the margins.

Decide on Strategies for Answering Easier and Harder Questions

Many people work quickly through an entire individual test (English, Mathematics, Reading, or Science), answering only those questions they're pretty sure about the first time and skipping the others. Then they go back and work more slowly through the questions they found difficult at first. There are several advantages to this approach:

- You have the satisfaction of moving along quickly, accomplishing a lot in a short period of time.

- When you return to a tough question, you may have remembered something important in the meantime. (It's like putting part of your brain "on special assignment" while you go on to the rest of the test.)

- You can be sure you'll get to **all** the questions you can answer easily before you run out of time.

The biggest possible disadvantage to this approach is that you have to be **very careful** about where you're marking your answers on your answer document. If you skip a question in your test booklet, be sure to skip the question on your answer document too. You'll probably want to put a check or a star by each of these questions in your test booklet—**not on your answer document**—so that you can find them easily later on, when you're ready to return to them. (Remember: unless you're instructed otherwise, **you can write in the ACT test booklet** as much as you like. See the section "Write Notes in Your Test Booklet If Allowed" on page 20.)

Decide on a Strategy for Guessing on Multiple-Choice Questions

Should you guess or not? On some standardized tests, you're penalized for each incorrect answer. On the ACT multiple-choice tests, however, your raw score is based on the number of questions you get right—there's no deduction for wrong answers.

Because **you're not penalized for guessing on the ACT,** it's to your advantage to answer each question. Here's a good way to proceed:

1. When you come to a question that stumps you, see if you can eliminate at least a couple of the choices.

2. If you still aren't sure about the answer, take your best guess.

If you can rule out one or two of the possible answers, the odds are better that you'll select the right response. You don't need a perfect reason to eliminate one answer and choose another. Sometimes an intelligent guess is based on a hunch—on something you may know but don't have time to consciously recognize in a timed-test situation.

Maybe you've heard some advice about how to answer questions when you don't know the correct answer, such as "When in doubt, choose C," or "When in doubt, select the longest (or shortest) alternative," or "If NONE OF THE ABOVE (or a similar response) is among the answer choices, select it." While these bits of advice may hold true now and then, you should know that the questions on the ACT have been carefully written to make these strategies ineffective. The best advice is to rule out any of the possible answers you can on the basis of your knowledge and then, if necessary, make your best guess.

Decide on a Strategy for Changing Your Answer

You think that you might have marked the wrong answer choice on a certain question. Do you go with your original answer or change it to the new answer? People may tell you to always go with your first response. And surely everyone has had the experience of agonizing over a response, trying to decide whether to change it, then doing so only to find out later that the first answer was the right one.

However, some research by education and testing specialists suggests that you **should** change your answer when you change your mind. If you're like the people tested in that research, your second answer is more likely to be the correct one.

So, how can you decide what you should do? Unfortunately, there's no easy advice that will suit every test taker and every situation. What you should do depends upon **you** and your test-taking methods. Before you change an answer, think about how you approached the question in the first place. Give some weight to the reasons why you now believe another answer is better. Don't mechanically follow an arbitrary rule just because it works for somebody else. Know yourself; then trust yourself to make intelligent, informed decisions.

Plan to Check Your Work

When you get to the end of one of the individual ACT tests with several minutes to spare, you may feel you've done quite enough. After all, you've just spent from 30 to 55 minutes hassling with questions that didn't seem to want to be answered or writing about a topic you didn't get to choose. You're tired, and you just want to use that extra 5 minutes for a nap.

Hard as it may be, try to keep your energy going until time is called so you can go back through that test and check your answers or written response. (Remember: you're allowed to work on only one test at a time.)

Here are some suggestions for checking your answers before time is called on a test:

- For the multiple-choice tests, be sure you've marked all your answers in the proper places on the answer document.

- Be certain you've answered **all** the questions on your answer document, even the ones you weren't sure about. (Of course, you must be very careful to stop marking ovals when time is called.)

- When you reach the end of the Mathematics Test, check your calculations. You may check your calculations using the test booklet as scratch paper (if allowed) or using a permitted calculator. (Calculators are allowed for use **only** on the Mathematics Test.)

- Check your answer document for stray pencil marks that may be misread by the scoring machine. Erase any such marks cleanly and completely.

- Be sure you've marked only one answer on your answer document for each question.

- If there are too many questions for you to check all of your answers, be sure to check those that you feel most uncertain about first, then any others that you have time for on that test.

- At the end of the Writing Test, take a few minutes to read over your essay. Correct any mistakes in spelling, grammar, usage, or punctuation. If you see any words that are hard to read, recopy them so that the scorers can read them easily. Make any revisions neatly between the lines (but do not write in the margins).

Have a Panic Strategy

When you're under pressure during a test, an unexpected question or something small like breaking a pencil can be very upsetting. For many students, the natural tendency at such times is to panic. Panic detracts from test performance by causing students to become confused and discouraged and to have trouble recalling information that they know.

It's a good idea to have a strategy ready for dealing with panic that might arise while you take the ACT. One good panic strategy is to give yourself a brief "time out." To do this, take slow, deep breaths and let yourself relax. Put the test temporarily out of mind. Close your eyes if you want. Visualize yourself confidently resuming work on the test, turning in a completed test paper, and leaving the room with a feeling of having done your best work. Allow 20 to 30 seconds for your time out. That's probably all you'll need to get your panic under control and start back to work on the test.

Write Notes in Your Test Booklet If Allowed

As you will see in chapter 3, it can be helpful to jot notes (or underline, sketch, calculate, etc.) in your test booklet. Under most test conditions, that's allowed and the testing staff will tell you so. However, in a few circumstances you are not permitted to write in your test booklet. In such circumstances, you'll be given scratch paper to use.

Summary

All the strategies outlined in this chapter are merely suggestions intended to give you ideas about good preparation habits and strategies for getting through the ACT in the best, most efficient manner possible. Some of the strategies will work for you, others won't. Feel free to pick and choose from among all the strategies in this chapter, and the more specific strategies in chapter 3, so that you have a test-taking plan that works best for **you**.

3

Chapter 3:
Test Format and Content

The ACT consists of four multiple-choice tests and an optional Writing Test; each test is designed to measure academic achievement in a major area of high school study: English, mathematics, reading, science, and writing. This chapter contains five sections; each section describes one of the five tests in detail, gives examples of the kinds of questions you're likely to find on that test, and suggests how to approach those questions and that test as a whole.

The sample questions in each section of this chapter are taken from actual ACT tests, but the way they're presented and discussed varies from section to section.

The English section discusses sample questions relating to the sample passages and questions found at the end of the section. (Note that while there are 45 sample English questions in this section, there are 75 English questions in an actual test.) Not all of the sample questions with each of the passages in the English section are used as examples in the discussion; therefore, a complete answer key is provided on the last page of the section for you to check your answers.

Each sample question in the Mathematics section is followed immediately by a discussion of the question.

The Reading section discusses sample questions relating to the seven sample passages found at the end of the section.

In the Science section, you'll find three sample passages, each accompanied by five sample questions followed by a discussion of those five questions.

The section on the optional ACT Writing Test includes one sample prompt. This is followed by six student sample essays, each scored based on the six-point rubric for the Writing Test. The discussions of the scores for each essay should help you understand how to evaluate your own practice Writing Test essay.

However you approach this chapter, before you begin you may find it helpful to look at the following charts to give yourself an idea of the makeup of the ACT as a whole and of its individual tests.

ACT English Test
75 questions, 45 minutes

Content/Skills	Percent of Test	Number of Questions
Usage/Mechanics	**53%**	**40**
Punctuation	13%	10
Grammar and Usage	16%	12
Sentence Structure	24%	18
Rhetorical Skills	**47%**	**35**
Strategy	16%	12
Organization	15%	11
Style	16%	12
Total	**100%**	**75**

Scores reported:

Total English Test score based on all 75 questions

Usage/Mechanics subscore based on 40 questions

Rhetorical Skills subscore based on 35 questions

ACT Mathematics Test
60 questions, 60 minutes

Content Area	Percent of Test	Number of Questions
Pre-Algebra	23%	14
Elementary Algebra	17%	10
Intermediate Algebra	15%	9
Coordinate Geometry	15%	9
Plane Geometry	23%	14
Trigonometry	7%	4
Total	**100%**	**60**

Scores reported:

Total Mathematics Test score based on all 60 questions

Pre-Algebra/Elementary Algebra subscore based on 24 questions

Intermediate Algebra/Coordinate Geometry subscore based on 18 questions

Plane Geometry/Trigonometry subscore based on 18 questions

ACT Reading Test
40 questions, 35 minutes

Reading Content	Percent of Test	Number of Questions
Prose Fiction	25%	10
Humanities	25%	10
Social Studies	25%	10
Natural Sciences	25%	10
Total	**100%**	**40**

Scores reported:

Total Reading Test score based on all 40 questions

Arts/Literature subscore based on 20 questions (Prose Fiction, Humanities)

Social Studies/Sciences subscore based on 20 questions (Social Studies, Natural Sciences)

ACT Science Test
40 questions, 35 minutes

Content Area*	Format	Percent of Test	Number of Questions
Biology	Data Representation	38%	15
Chemistry			
Earth/Space Sciences	Research Summaries	45%	18
Physics	Conflicting Viewpoints	17%	7
Total		100%	40

Scores reported:

Total Science Test score based on all 40 questions

*Content areas are distributed over the different formats in such a way that at least one passage-question set, and no more than two passage-question sets, represents each content area.

ACT Writing Test (Optional)
1 writing prompt, 30 minutes

Content Area	Format	Number of Prompts
Writing	Essay Response	1
Total		1

Scores reported:

Writing Test subscore

Combined English/Writing score

ACT English Test

On the ACT English Test, you have 45 minutes to read five passages, or essays, and answer 75 multiple-choice questions about them—an average of 15 questions per essay. The essays on the English Test cover a variety of subjects; the sample passages that follow this discussion range from a personal essay about different ways of figuring one's age to an informative essay about the legal history of school dress codes.

Content of the ACT English Test

The ACT English Test is designed to measure your ability to accomplish the wide variety of decisions involved in revising and editing a given piece of writing. An important part of revision and editing decisions is a good understanding of the conventions of standard written English. You may not always use standard written English in casual writing (for instance, when you're e-mailing a friend) or in conversation. In casual writing or conversation, we often use slang expressions that have special meanings with friends our own age or in our part of the country. Because slang can become outdated (Does anybody say "groovy" anymore?) and regional terms might not be familiar to students everywhere (Do you and your friends say "soda" or "soft drink" or "pop"?), this test emphasizes the standard written English that is taught in schools around the country.

Questions on the English Test fall into two categories:

- **Usage/Mechanics** (punctuation, grammar and usage, sentence structure)

- **Rhetorical Skills** (writing strategy, organization, style)

You'll receive a score for all 75 questions, and two subscores—one based on 40 Usage/Mechanics questions and the other based on 35 Rhetorical Skills questions. If you choose to take the Writing Test, you will also receive a Combined English/Writing score.

You will **not** be tested on spelling, vocabulary, or on rote recall of the rules of grammar. Grammar and usage are tested only within the context of the essay, not by questions like "Must an appositive always be set off by commas?" Likewise, you won't be tested directly on your vocabulary, although the better your vocabulary is, the better equipped you'll be to answer questions that involve choosing the most appropriate word.

Like the other tests on the ACT, the English Test doesn't require you to memorize what you read. The questions and essays are side-by-side for easy reference. This is **not** a memorization test.

The questions discussed on the following pages are taken from the sample passages and questions that follow on pages 42–48. If you prefer, you can work through the sample passages and questions before you read the rest of this discussion. On the other hand, if you wish to better understand the English Test, you may want to first read the discussion, then work through the sample passages and questions.

Types of Questions on the ACT English Test

Usage/Mechanics questions always refer to an underlined portion of the essay. You must decide on the best choice of words and punctuation for that underlined portion. Usually, your options include NO CHANGE, which means that the essay is best as it's written. Sometimes, you'll also have the option of deleting the underlined portion. For example, the following question (from Sample Passage II on pages 44–46) offers you the option of removing the word *to* from the sentence.

Otherwise, this difference points <u>to</u> significant underlying cultural values. <u>22</u> ‾21	**22. F.** NO CHANGE
	     G. on
	     H. at
	     J. OMIT the underlined portion.

In this example, the best answer is not to delete the underlined portion but to leave it as it is (**F**).

Rhetorical Skills questions may refer to an underlined portion, or they may ask about a section of the essay or an aspect of the essay as a whole. For example, in the following question (from Sample Passage I on pages 42–44), you're given a sentence to be added to the essay, and then you're asked to decide the most logical place in the essay to add that sentence.

	15. Upon reviewing this essay and finding that some information has been left out, the writer composes the following sentence incorporating that information:
	
	Those same German influences helped spawn a similar musical form in northern Mexico known as *norteño*.
	
	The sentence would most logically be placed after the last sentence in Paragraph:
	
	  A. 1.
	  B. 2.
	  C. 3.
	  D. 4.

In this example, the best answer is **C**, because Paragraph 3 focuses on the European musical influences on the O'odham people of Arizona, and the last sentence of the paragraph specifically refers to the musical influences of German immigrants.

Let's look at some additional examples of the kinds of questions you're likely to find on the ACT English Test. If you want to know what an individual question looks like in the context of the passage it appears in, turn to the pages indicated. You can also use those sample passages and questions for practice, either before or after reading this discussion.

Usage/Mechanics

Usage/Mechanics questions focus on the conventions of punctuation, grammar and usage, and sentence structure and formation.

Punctuation questions involve identifying and correcting the following misplaced, missing, or unnecessary punctuation marks:

- commas

- apostrophes

- colons, semicolons, and dashes

- periods, question marks, and exclamation points

These questions address not only the "rules" of punctuation but also the use of punctuation to express ideas clearly. For example, you should be prepared to show how punctuation can be used to indicate possession or to set off a parenthetical element.

In many punctuation questions, the words in every choice will be identical but the commas or other punctuation will vary. It's important to read the choices carefully in order to notice the presence or absence of commas, semicolons, colons, periods, and other punctuation. The following example of a punctuation question comes from Sample Passage I on pages 42–44.

Around this time the polka music and button

accordion played by German immigrant rail-

road workers; left their mark on waila.
___
14

14. **F.** NO CHANGE
G. workers
H. workers:
J. workers,

It may help you to read through this sentence without paying attention to the punctuation so you can identify the grammatical construction of it. The subject of this sentence is "the polka music and button accordion." What follows that might seem like the predicate verb of the sentence, but it's not. The phrase "played by German immigrant railroad workers" is a dependent or subordinate clause (a clause that cannot stand on its own). More specifically, this type of dependent clause is known as an adjective clause because it modifies the noun it follows. This is a little tricky to figure out because the relative pronoun that normally introduces this clause (*that*) and the helping verb for *played* (*were*) are missing; they're understood but not expressed. If we stick them into the sentence, we'll notice that its meaning doesn't change:

Around this time the polka music and button accordion that were played by German immigrant railroad <u>workers;</u> left their mark on waila.

After the adjective clause is the predicate verb of the main clause, "left." Then, there's a phrase that explains what was left (the direct object "their mark") and a prepositional phrase that explains where it was left ("on waila").

Now we can deal with the question about what kind of punctuation should follow that adjective clause. Sometimes, these clauses are set off from the main clause with commas to indicate that the adjective clause is parenthetical or provides information not essential to the meaning of the sentence. That's not the case here for two reasons. First, there's no comma at the beginning of the adjective clause. Second, the adjective clause is essential to the sentence; the sentence is not referring to just any polka music and button accordion but to the music and accordion played by those German immigrant railroad workers (presumably, not while they were working on the railroad).

Ignoring the adjective clause for a minute, we need to ask ourselves what kind of punctuation we would normally place between the subject "the polka music and button accordion" and the predicate "left." Our answer should be no punctuation at all, making **G** the best answer. Of course, you could answer this question without this rather tedious analysis of the parts of the sentence. You might simply decide that if there's no other punctuation in the sentence, you would never insert a single punctuation mark between the subject and the predicate of the main clause. Or you might just plug in each of the four punctuation choices—semicolon, no punctuation, colon, comma—and choose the one that looks or sounds best to you.

Grammar and usage questions involve choosing the best word or words in a sentence based on considerations of the conventions of grammar and usage. Some examples of poor and better phrases are given below.

- Grammatical agreement

   (Subject and verb)
   "The owner of the bicycles *are* going to sell them."
   should be:
   "The owner of the bicycles *is* going to sell them."

   (Pronoun and antecedent)
   "Susan and Mary left *her* briefcases in the office."
   should be:
   "Susan and Mary left *their* briefcases in the office."

   (Adjectives and adverbs with corresponding nouns and verbs)
   "Danielle spread frosting *liberal* on the cat."
   should be:
   "Danielle spread frosting *liberally* on the cat."

- Verb forms

  "Fritz had just *began* to toast Lydia's marshmallows when the rabbits stampeded."
  should be:
  "Fritz had just *begun* to toast Lydia's marshmallows when the rabbits stampeded."

- Pronoun forms and cases

  "Seymour and Svetlana annoyed *there* parents all the time."
  should be:
  "Seymour and Svetlana annoyed *their* parents all the time."

  "After the incident with the peanut butter, the zebra and *me* were never invited back."
  should be:
  "After the incident with the peanut butter, the zebra and *I* were never invited back."

- Comparative and superlative modifiers

  "My goldfish is *more smarter* than your brother."
  should be:
  "My goldfish is *smarter* than your brother."

  "Your brother, however, has the *cuter* aardvark that I've ever seen."
  should be:
  "Your brother, however, has the *cutest* aardvark that I've ever seen."

- Idioms

  "An idiom is an established phrase that has a unique or special meaning that can be looked *down* in the dictionary."
  should be:
  "An idiom is an established phrase that has a unique or special meaning that can be looked *up* in the dictionary."

Questions dealing with pronouns often have to do with using the proper form and case of the pronoun. Sometimes they address a pronoun's agreement with its antecedent, or referent. In such cases, it's important to consider the entire sentence, and sometimes the preceding sentence, in order to make sure you know what the antecedent is. Consider the following question (from Sample Passage I on pages 42–44).

As the dancers step to

the music, they <u>were also stepping</u> in time to a

                   8

sound that embodies <u>their</u> unique history and

                9

suggests the influence of outside cultures on

their music.

9. **A.** NO CHANGE
   B. they're
   C. it's
   D. its'

Here, the possessive pronoun in question refers back to the subject of the main clause (*they*), which in turn refers back to the subject of the introductory subordinate clause (*the dancers*). Thus, the best answer is the third-person plural possessive pronoun (*their*, **A**). Choice **B** might seem like a possibility because *they're* sounds like *their* (that is, they're homonyms). However, *they're* is a contraction for *they are*. We can rule out **C** and **D** because of the pronoun-antecedent agreement problem and also because *it's* is not a possessive pronoun but a contraction for *it is* while *its'* is not even a word.

Sentence structure questions involve the effective formation of sentences, including dealing with relationships between and among clauses, placement of modifiers, and shifts in construction. Below are some examples:

- Subordinate or dependent clauses
  "These hamsters are excellent pets *because providing* hours of cheap entertainment."
  This sentence could be rewritten as:
  "These hamsters are excellent pets *providing* hours of cheap entertainment."
  It could also be revised as:
  "These hamsters are excellent pets *because they provide* hours of cheap entertainment."

- Run-on or fused sentences
  "We discovered that the entire family had been devoured by *anteaters it* was horrible."
  This sentence should actually be two:
  "We discovered that the entire family had been devoured by *anteaters. It* was horrible."

- Comma splices
  "The anteaters had terrible *manners, they* just ate and ran."
  This sentence could be rewritten as:
  "The anteaters had terrible *manners. They* just ate and ran."
  It could also be rewritten as:
  "The anteaters had terrible *manners; they* just ate and ran."

- Sentence fragments
  "*When he* found scorpions in his socks."
  This needs a subject to let us know who "he" is and what he did:
  "*Julio didn't lose his temper when he* found scorpions in his socks."

- Misplaced modifiers

  "*Snarling and snapping, Juanita attempted to control her pet turtle.*"

  Unless Juanita was doing the snarling and snapping, the sentence should be rewritten:

  "Snarling and snapping, *the pet turtle resisted Juanita's attempt to control it.*"

  It could also be rewritten this way:

  "Juanita attempted to control her pet turtle, which snarled and snapped."

- Shifts in verb tense or voice

  "We sat down to the table to eat, but before we began, John *says* grace."

  This should be rewritten as:

  "We sat down to the table to eat, but before we began, John *said* grace."

- Shifts in pronoun person or number

  "Hamsters should work at the most efficient pace that *one* can."

  This should be rewritten as:

  "Hamsters should work at the most efficient pace that *they* can."

Many questions about sentence structure and formation will ask you about how clauses and phrases are linked. This means that you may have to consider punctuation or the lack of punctuation, which can create problems like comma splices, run-on sentences, or sentence fragments. You also may have to consider various words that can be used to link clauses and phrases: conjunctions like *and*, *but*, *because*, and *when*, and pronouns like *who*, *whose*, *which*, and *that*. The following question (from Sample Passage I on pages 42–44) is a good example of a sentence structure question.

It is a social

<u>music that performed</u> at weddings, birthday

    4

parties, and feasts.

4. **F.** NO CHANGE
    G. music in which it is performed
    H. music, performing
    J. music, performed

What would be the best way to link the clause "It is a social music" and the phrase "performed [or performing] at weddings, birthday parties, and feasts"? Relative pronouns such as *that* and *which* stand in for the noun that the relative clause modifies. (They relate the clause to the noun.) One way to try out choices such as **F** and **G** is to replace the relative pronoun with the noun and then decide if the resulting statement makes sense:

Social music performed at weddings, birthday parties, and feasts. (**F**)

This does not make sense. Musicians perform, but the music itself does not. Music *is* performed.

In social music it is performed at weddings, birthday parties, and feasts. (**G**)

This also seems nonsensical. What does *it* refer to—social music?

The other two choices offer a different approach to connecting information in a sentence. The phrases "performing at weddings, birthday parties, and feasts" (H) and "performed at weddings, birthday parties, and feasts" (J) are participial phrases. Like adjective clauses, these phrases modify a noun. We can rule out H for the same reason that we rejected F: it doesn't make sense to think of "social music" as "performing." On the other hand, it sounds fine to refer to "social music" as "performed" (J).

Rhetorical Skills

Rhetorical Skills questions focus on writing strategy, organization, and style.

Writing strategy questions focus on the choices made and strategies used by a writer in the act of composing or revising an essay. These questions may ask you to make decisions concerning the appropriateness of a sentence or essay in relation to purpose, audience, unity, or focus, or the effect of adding, revising, or deleting supporting material.

The following question (from Sample Passage I on pages 42–44) is a fairly typical example of the kinds of writing decisions that strategy questions ask you to make.

In the early 1900s the O'odham became acquainted with marching bands and woodwind instruments (which explains the presence of saxophones in waila).
13

13. Given that all of the choices are true, which one is most relevant to the focus of this paragraph?

   A. NO CHANGE
   B. (although fiddles were once widely used in waila bands).
   C. (even though they're now often constructed of metal).
   D. (which are frequently found in jazz bands also).

It's important to read these questions carefully and, sometimes, to reread the essay or parts of the essay. This question is fairly clear-cut, but it does suggest that you need a pretty good sense of what Paragraph 3 is about. A quick review of the paragraph indicates that it is focused on how the O'odham and their music were influenced by the musical styles and instrumentation of the European immigrants they encountered.

Which of these parenthetical statements is most relevant to that focus? Choice **D**, which states that woodwind instruments are frequently found in jazz bands, is not. Likewise, choice **C**, which indicates that woodwind instruments are now often constructed of metal, strays from the paragraph's topic. Choice **B**, which points out that fiddles were once widely used in waila bands, is getting closer, but this too seems a diversion, unconnected to the other information in this paragraph. Guitars, woodwinds, and button accordions are mentioned, but not fiddles or violins.

Choice **A**, however, provides an appropriate and relevant elaboration. It draws the connection between the O'odhams' introduction to marching bands and woodwinds in the early 1900s and the eventual inclusion of saxophones in a typical waila band.

Organization questions deal with the order and coherence of ideas in an essay and the effective choice of opening, transitional, and closing statements. For example, you may be asked about the organization of ideas (the most logical order for sentences within a paragraph or paragraphs within an essay) or about the most logical transitional phrase or statement.

The following question (from Sample Passage II on pages 44–46) is a good example of the kind of organization question you might encounter.

Today, after many birthdays and New Year's Days, I now find meaningful the difference I once found confusing. Otherwise, 21 this difference points to significant underlying 22 cultural values.	**21. A.** NO CHANGE **B.** Though, **C.** In fact, **D.** Then,

The choices in this question are sometimes referred to as conjunctive adverbs or transitional words or phrases because their main job is to connect or link the statement in one sentence with the statement in a preceding sentence. These are often little words—*so*, *thus*, *soon*, *yet*, *also*—that do a lot of work to make an essay logical.

In order to answer such questions correctly, it helps to think about the logical relationship between the sentences, as well as the logical relationships expressed by the choices. The main statement of the opening sentence of this paragraph is "I now find meaningful the difference [in computing one's age] I once found confusing." The second sentence states, "This difference points to significant underlying cultural values." The writer then goes on to explain those cultural values.

Which of these four choices enables readers to move most easily from the opening sentence into the rest of this paragraph? Choice **A** suggests that the second statement contrasts with the first statement. A typical dictionary definition for *Otherwise* is "in different circumstances." Similarly, choice **B**, *Though*, suggests that the statement to follow is contrary to or in opposition to the preceding statement. Neither of those adverbs works well here. Nor does *Then* (choice **D**), which usually expresses a time relationship—meaning "next" or "soon after in time."

The best choice here is **C**. The phrase "In fact" is often used to introduce a statement that builds on the preceding statement. We can pare down these opening sentences to their bare essentials to show that the phrase works well here: I now find the difference in computing one's age meaningful. In fact, the difference points to important cultural values about life experience and longevity.

Style questions involve effective word choices in terms of writing style, tone, clarity, and economy. Sometimes, a phrase or sentence that isn't technically ungrammatical is nevertheless confusing because it's poorly written. Sometimes, there's a word or phrase that clashes with the tone of the essay. Good writing also involves eliminating ambiguous pronoun references, excessively wordy or redundant material, and vague or awkward expressions.

Like most writing strategy and organization questions, style questions require a general understanding of the essay as a whole. The following style question (from Sample Passage III on pages 46–48) focuses on the issues of economy and consistency of tone.

The school board members believed that wearing "play clothes" to school made the students inefficient toward their
<u>32</u>
school work, while more formal attire established a positive educational climate.

32. F. NO CHANGE
G. lazy and bored to tears with
H. blow off
J. lax and indifferent toward

You will be better able to recognize the appropriateness of choice **J** if you know that *lax* means "lacking necessary strictness, severity, or precision" and *indifferent* means "lacking interest, enthusiasm, or concern." These terms touch on two related but distinct concerns—academic laziness and apathy. One could imagine school board members using these very words in their meetings. And the words are consistent with the overall style and tone of this straightforward, informative essay about a legal case.

Choices **G** and **H** are fairly easy to rule out if you think about the generally formal tone of the essay. It's not that one should never use slang phrases such as "bored to tears" or "blow off" in one's writing; it's just that this particular essay is not the place to use them. When we consider that this statement is describing the school board members' belief, these phrases are even more inappropriate.

It seems more in character for school board members to be concerned about student inefficiency, but **F** is a weak choice because the phrase "inefficient toward their school work" sounds odd or awkward. Perhaps it's the preposition that trips us up. The word *toward* works fine in **J** when describing attitudes (lax, indifferent) toward school work, but the word *inefficient* is describing an ability or skill.

* * *

The questions provided here are a small sample of the kinds of questions that might be on the test. The previous question, for example, is only one kind of style question; it doesn't cover all the territory of "style" that might be addressed on the test. The sample passages and questions at the end of this section have all the examples referred to in this chapter as they would appear in a test. These sample passages and questions and the practice tests in chapter 4 will provide you with a thorough understanding of the ACT English Test.

Strategies for Taking the ACT English Test

Pace Yourself

The ACT English Test contains 75 questions to be completed in 45 minutes, which works out to exactly 36 seconds per question. Spending $1\frac{1}{2}$ minutes skimming through each essay leaves you about 30 seconds to respond to each question. If you spend less time than that on each question, you can use the remaining time allowed for this test to review your work and to return to the questions that were most difficult for you. Another way to think of it is that you have 45 minutes to read and answer the questions for five essays, giving you a maximum of 9 minutes for each essay and its questions.

Be Aware of the Writing Style Used in the Essay

The five essays cover a variety of topics and are written in a variety of styles. It's important that you take into account the writing style used in each essay as you respond to the questions.

Some of the essays will be anecdotes or narratives written from an informal, first-person point of view. Others will be more formal essays, scholarly or informative in nature, often written in the third person. Some questions will ask you to choose the best answer based not on its grammatical correctness but on its consistency with the style and tone of the essay as a whole. For example, an expression that's too breezy for an essay on the life of President Herbert Hoover might be just right for a personal narrative about a writer's attempt at learning to skateboard.

Be Sure to Consider a Question's Context Before You Choose an Answer

Some people find it helpful to skim an essay and its questions before trying to answer those questions. It can help to have a general sense of the essay in mind before you begin to answer questions involving writing strategy or style. If there are questions about the order of sentences within a paragraph, or the order of paragraphs within an essay, or where to add a sentence in an essay, you may want to answer those questions first to make sure that the major elements of the essay are arranged logically. Understanding the order of the passage may make it easier for you to answer some of the other questions.

As you're answering each question, be sure to read at least a sentence or two **beyond** the sentence containing the portion being questioned. You may need to read even more than that to make sure you understand what the writer is trying to say.

Be Aware of the Connotations of Words

Vocabulary isn't tested in an isolated way on the ACT English Test. Nevertheless, a good vocabulary and an awareness of not only the dictionary definitions of words but also the connotations (feelings and associations) suggested by those words will help you do well on the test.

The following question (from Sample Passage II on pages 44–46) asks you to think about how certain words and their connotations can function in terms of the rest of the essay.

Many people might be surprised to learn that the American way of computing a person's age differs from the traditional Korean way. In Korean tradition, a person is considered to be already one year old at the time of his or her birth.

As a child growing up in two cultures, I found this contest a bit confusing.
16

16. F. NO CHANGE
    G. change
    H. dispute
    J. difference

Which word best captures or summarizes what has been described in the preceding paragraph? The word *contest* (**F**) doesn't seem right because it suggests a competition between opposing sides or teams. In a similar vein, the word *dispute* (**H**) doesn't fit here because it generally refers to a verbal debate or argument. The word *change* (**G**) is a little off because it expresses the idea of transformation, making something or someone different, which doesn't accurately summarize that opening paragraph. The word *difference* (**J**), however, seems just right. It echoes the verb in the first sentence of the preceding paragraph, but more importantly, it accurately reflects the writer's perspective up to this point in the essay that the American way and Korean way of computing a person's age are not competing or arguing with each other. They are simply unlike each other (and because of that mismatch, a bit confusing).

In questions such as this one, you have to focus on what the words mean and what associations the words have for the typical reader.

Examine the Underlined Portions and Then See If There's a Stated Question

Before responding to a question identified by an underlined portion, check for a stated question preceding the options. If there is one, it will provide you with some guidelines for deciding on the best choice. Some questions will ask you to choose the alternative to the underlined portion that is NOT or LEAST acceptable. Here's an example from Sample Passage I on pages 42–44.

The music is

mainly instrumental—the bands generally consist of guitar, bass guitar, saxophones, accordion, and drums.

3. Which of the following alternatives to the underlined portion would NOT be acceptable?
   A. instrumental; in general, the bands
   B. instrumental, the bands generally
   C. instrumental. The bands generally
   D. instrumental; the bands generally

For these types of questions, it is good to look closely at the underlined portion, because the question has told you that it *is* acceptable. Likewise, three of the alternative choices are acceptable. The best answer, in this case, is the one that is *not* acceptable. In the underlined portion, a dash is used between two independent clauses: "The music is mainly instrumental" and "the bands generally consist of guitar, bass guitar, saxophones, accordion, and drums." The dash is sometimes thought of as a less formal type of punctuation, but it can work quite well to provide emphasis or to signal that an explanation will follow.

It would also be acceptable to place a period (**C**) or a semicolon (**D**) between these two independent clauses. Likewise, choice **A** is acceptable because it too places a semicolon between the two clauses, using the phrase "in general" rather than the adverb "generally." Choice **B** is not acceptable and is, therefore, the best answer. A comma is not normally a strong enough punctuation mark between two independent clauses not joined by a conjunction. Notice that there are other commas in this sentence, used to distinguish nouns in a series. How would a reader know that the comma between the clauses is a much stronger break than those other commas?

Whether there is a stated question or not, you should carefully examine what is underlined in the essay. Consider the features of writing that are included in the underlined portion. The options for each question will contain changes in one or more aspects of writing.

Note the Differences in the Answer Choices

Many of the questions that refer to underlined portions will involve more than one aspect of writing. Examine each choice and note how it differs from the others. Consider **all** the features of writing that are included in each option.

Avoid Making New Mistakes

Beware of correcting mistakes in the essay and, in your haste, picking a response that creates a new mistake. Be observant, especially in questions where the responses have similar wording. One comma or apostrophe can make all the difference, as the following question (from Sample Passage III on pages 46–48) illustrates.

His challenge

initiated a <u>review, of students' rights and admin-</u> istrative responsibility <u>in public education.</u>
    43   44

43. **A.** NO CHANGE
    B. review, of students' rights,
    C. review of students' rights
    D. review of students' rights,

It perhaps only took you a moment to reject choice **A** because of the unnecessary comma between the noun "review" and the prepositional phrase "of students' rights." And if you were able to make that call, you might have ruled out choice **B** for the same reason. It is probably more difficult to recognize that the comma between the noun *rights* and the conjunction *and* (**D**) is unnecessary and misleading. Because you were thinking about how the underlined portion should be punctuated, you might also have wondered about the plural apostrophe in the word *students'* but then realized that the apostrophe is in the same place in all four choices. (The best answer is **C**.)

Determine the Best Answer

There are at least two approaches you can take to determine the best answer to a question about an underlined portion. One approach is to reread the sentence or sentences containing the underlined portion, substitute each of the answer choices in turn, and decide which is best. Another approach is to decide how the underlined portion might best be phrased and then look for your phrasing among the choices offered. If the underlined portion is correct as it is, select the "NO CHANGE" option.

If you can't decide which option is best, you may want to mark the question in your test booklet so you can return to it later. Remember: you're not penalized for guessing, so after you've eliminated as many options as you can, take your best guess.

Reread the Sentence Using Your Selected Answer

Once you have selected the answer you feel is best, reread the corresponding sentence or sentences in the essay, substituting the answer you've selected for the underlined portion or for the boxed numeral. Sometimes an answer that sounds fine out of context doesn't "fit" within the sentence or essay. Be sure to keep in mind both the punctuation marks and words in each possible response; sometimes just the omission of a comma can make an important difference.

Watch for Questions About the Entire Essay or a Section of the Essay

Some questions ask about a section of the essay. They are identified by a question number in a box at the appropriate point in the essay, rather than by an underlined portion. Here's an example from Sample Passage II on pages 44–46.

> Perhaps the celebration of New Year's Day in Korean culture is <u>heightened</u>
> ___
>   19
> because it is thought of as everyone's birthday party. 20
>
> 20. Upon reviewing this paragraph, the writer considers deleting the preceding sentence. If the writer were to delete the sentence, the paragraph would primarily lose:
> F. a comment on the added significance of the Korean New Year celebration.
> G. a repetitive reminder of what happens every birthday.
> H. a defense of the case for celebrating every birthday.
> J. an illustration of the Korean counting system.

This question asks you to think about the role this sentence plays in terms of the paragraph as a whole. If the sentence were deleted, the paragraph would lose the elaboration on the point that Korean tradition indicates that everyone becomes a year older on New Year's Day, regardless of when they were actually born. Without the sentence, the point about the "added significance of the Korean New Year celebration" (**F**) would have been unstated.

Some other questions ask about an aspect of the essay as a whole. These are placed at the end of the essay, following boxed instructions like these:

> Question 15 asks about the preceding passage as a whole.

You may want to read any questions that ask about the essay as a whole first so you can keep them in mind while you're reading through the essay. For questions about a section of the essay or the essay as a whole, you must decide the best answer on the basis of the particular writing or revision problem presented in the question.

Be Careful with Two-Part Questions

Some questions require extra thought because you have to decide not only which option is best but also which supporting reason for an option is most appropriate or convincing. The following question occurs at the end of Sample Passage III on pages 46–48. Each option begins with either a yes or no response, followed by a supporting reason for that response.

> Question 45 asks about the preceding passage as a whole.

45. Suppose the writer's goal had been to write a brief persuasive essay urging students to exercise their constitutional rights. Would this essay fulfill that goal?

A. Yes, because the essay focuses on how Kevin encouraged other students to exercise their constitutional rights.

B. Yes, because the essay focuses on various types of clothing historically worn by students as a freedom of expression.

C. No, because the essay suggests that the right to wear blue jeans was not a substantial constitutional right in the 1970s.

D. No, because the essay objectively reports on one case of a student exercising a particular constitutional right.

Once you decide whether the essay would or would not fulfill the writer's goal, as described in the question, you need to decide which reason or explanation provides the most appropriate support for the answer and is most accurate in terms of the essay. Sometimes, the supporting reason does not accurately reflect the essay (the explanations in **B** and **C**, for example). Sometimes, the reason accurately reflects the essay but doesn't logically support the answer to the question. And sometimes, the reason might logically support the question (that is, the writer's goal) but that reason overstates the focus of the essay. It may be fair to say that Kevin Bannister's case led to a review of student rights, but this essay does not at any point describe Kevin encouraging other students to exercise their rights, as **A** states. The best answer is **D**: This essay is more an objective reporting on a legal case about student rights (and that case's historical significance) than it is a persuasive argument or call to students to exercise those rights.

Watch for Interrelated Questions

As was pointed out earlier, you'll sometimes find that the best way to answer questions about a passage is not necessarily in their numbered order. Occasionally, you'll find it easier to answer a question after you've answered the one that follows it. Or you might find two questions about different elements of the same sentence, in which case it may help you to consider them both together.

In the following example (from Sample Passage III on pages 46–48), it may be helpful to consider questions 40 and 41 together, because they're contained in the same sentence. First, answer the question that seems easier to you. Once you've solved that problem in the sentence, turn to the other question.

The court remained unconvinced, <u>therefore, that</u>

40

when <u>wearing jeans</u> would actually impair the

41

learning process of Kevin or of his fellow class-

mates.

40. **F.** NO CHANGE
    G. thus,
    H. moreover,
    J. however,

41. **A.** NO CHANGE
    B. by wearing
    C. wearing
    D. having worn

Questions 40 and 41 deal with different kinds of writing problems. Question 40 is about choosing the most logical transitional word, and question 41 is about the correct use in this sentence of the gerund (a verb form with an *ing* ending that's used as a noun). You might find that answering question 41 helps you to figure out the answer to question 40. The best answer to question 41 is C—the noun phrase "wearing jeans" works as the subject of the dependent clause "wearing jeans would actually impair the learning process of Kevin or of his fellow classmates." Try penciling in your answer choice for 41 (that is, edit the essay) so that you can more easily read the sentence while responding to question 40. Does this approach make it easier for you to decide that the most logical answer to question 40 is **J** (*however*)?

* * *

Remember that this section is only an overview of the English Test. Directly or indirectly, a question may test you in more than one of the areas mentioned, so it's important not to become overly concerned with categorizing a question before you answer it. And, while awareness of the types of questions can help you be a more critical and strategic test taker, just remember: The **type** of question you're answering isn't important. The most important thing is to focus on what the question asks and do your best to pick out the best answer, given the rest of the essay.

SAMPLE PASSAGE I

The Music of the O'odham

[1]

For some people, traditional American Indian music
is <u>associated and connected</u> with high penetrating vocals
accompanied by a steady drumbeat. In tribal communities
in the southwestern United States, however, one is likely to
hear something similar to the polka-influenced dance
music of northern Mexico. The music is called "waila."
Among the O'odham tribes of Arizona, waila has been
<u>popular for</u> more than a century. The music is mainly

<u>instrumental—the bands generally</u> consist of guitar, bass
guitar, saxophones, accordion, and drums.

[2]

Unlike some traditional tribal music, waila does
not serve a religious or spiritual purpose. It is a social
<u>music that performed</u> at weddings, birthday parties,

and feasts. The <u>word itself</u> comes from the Spanish

word for dance, *baile*. <u>Cheek to cheek, the dance is
performed to the relaxed two-step tempo, and the bands</u>

often <u>play long past</u> midnight. As the dancers step to the

music, they <u>were also stepping</u> in time to a sound that

1. **A.** NO CHANGE
   B. connected by some of them
   C. linked by association
   D. associated

2. **F.** NO CHANGE
   G. popular, one might say, for
   H. really quite popular for
   J. popular for the duration of

3. Which of the following alternatives to the underlined
   portion would NOT be acceptable?

   A. instrumental; in general, the bands
   B. instrumental, the bands generally
   C. instrumental. The bands generally
   D. instrumental; the bands generally

4. **F.** NO CHANGE
   G. music in which it is performed
   H. music, performing
   J. music, performed

5. **A.** NO CHANGE
   B. word, itself,
   C. word, itself
   D. word itself,

6. **F.** NO CHANGE
   G. Couples dance cheek to cheek to the relaxed two-
   step tempo,
   H. A relaxed two-step tempo, the couples dance
   cheek to cheek,
   J. Cheek to cheek, the two-step tempo relaxes dancing couples,

7. **A.** NO CHANGE
   B. play long, past,
   C. play, long past,
   D. play, long past

8. **F.** NO CHANGE
   G. are also stepping
   H. have also stepped
   J. will also step

embodies their unique history and suggests the influence
9

of outside cultures on their music. [10]

9. **A.** NO CHANGE
   B. they're
   C. it's
   D. its'

10. At this point, the writer is considering adding the following true statement:

    The agricultural practices of the O'odham are similar to those of the Maya.

    Should the writer make this addition here?

    F. Yes, because the sentence establishes that the O'odham often borrowed ideas from other groups.
    G. Yes, because the sentence provides important information about the O'odham people.
    H. No, because the sentence is not supported by evidence of a connection between the O'odham and the Maya.
    J. No, because the sentence distracts from the paragraph's focus on waila's uses and influences.

[3]

The O'odham in the 1700s first encountered the
11
guitars of Spanish missionaries. In the 1850s the O'odham

11. All of the following would be acceptable placements for the underlined portion EXCEPT:

    A. where it is now.
    B. at the beginning of the sentence (revising the capitalization accordingly).
    C. after the word *guitars.*
    D. after the word *missionaries* (ending the sentence with a period).

have borrowed from the waltzes and mazurkas of
12
people of European descent on their way to California.

12. **F.** NO CHANGE
    G. have been borrowing
    H. were borrowed
    J. borrowed

In the early 1900s the O'odham became acquainted

with marching bands and woodwind instruments

(which explains the presence of saxophones in waila).
13
Around this time the polka music and button accordion

13. Given that all of the choices are true, which one is most relevant to the focus of this paragraph?

    A. NO CHANGE
    B. (although fiddles were once widely used in waila bands).
    C. (even though they're now often constructed of metal).
    D. (which are frequently found in jazz bands also).

played by German immigrant railroad workers; left their
14
mark on waila.

14. **F.** NO CHANGE
    G. workers
    H. workers:
    J. workers,

[4]

It should be no surprise that musicians these days are adding touches of rock, country, and reggae to waila. Some listeners fear that an American musical form may soon be lost. But the O'odham are playing waila with as much energy and devotion as ever. A unique blend of traditions, waila will probably continue changing for as long as the O'odham use it to express their own sense of harmony and tempo.

> Question 15 asks about the preceding passage as a whole.

15. Upon reviewing this essay and finding that some information has been left out, the writer composes the following sentence incorporating that information:

> Those same German influences helped spawn a similar musical form in northern Mexico known as *norteño*.

This sentence would most logically be placed after the last sentence in Paragraph:

- A. 1.
- B. 2.
- C. 3.
- D. 4.

SAMPLE PASSAGE II

How Old Am I?

Many people might be surprised to learn that the American way of computing a person's age differs from the traditional Korean way. In Korean tradition, a person is considered to be already one year old at the time of his or her birth.

As a child growing up in two cultures, I found this <u>contest</u> a bit confusing. When I was in the fifth
16
grade, was I ten or eleven years old? To add to the

confusion, every New Year's Day a <u>person</u> according
17
to this Korean counting system, becomes a year older, regardless of his or her actual birthday.

<u>Birthdays are important throughout the world.</u> A person
18
who is sixteen years old on his or her birthday in March would become seventeen years old on the following New Year's Day, even though he or she isn't expected to turn seventeen (in "American" years) until that next birthday in March. Perhaps the celebration of New Year's Day in Korean culture is <u>heightened</u> because it is thought of as
19

16. F. NO CHANGE
    G. change
    H. dispute
    J. difference

17. A. NO CHANGE
    B. person,
    C. person;
    D. person who,

18. F. NO CHANGE
    G. Most cultures celebrate birthdays.
    H. Birthdays focus attention on a culture's youth.
    J. OMIT the underlined portion.

19. A. NO CHANGE
    B. raised
    C. lifted
    D. lighted

everyone's birthday party. [20]

Today, after many birthdays and New Year's Days, I now find meaningful the difference I once found confusing. Otherwise, this difference points
21

to significant underlying cultural values. The practice of
22

advancing a person's age seems to me to reflect the value a
23

society places on life experience and longevity. Their idea
24

was demonstrated often when my elderly relatives, who
25
took pride in reminding younger folk of their "Korean

age." With great enthusiasm, they added on a year every
26
New Year's Day. By contrast American society has often

been described as one that values the vibrant energy of
27

youth over the wisdom and experience gained with age. [28]
After a certain age, many Americans I know would

balk, refuse, and hesitate at the idea of adding a year or
29
two to what they regard as their actual age.

20. Upon reviewing this paragraph, the writer considers deleting the preceding sentence. If the writer were to delete the sentence, the paragraph would primarily lose:
F. a comment on the added significance of the Korean New Year celebration.
G. a repetitive reminder of what happens every birthday.
H. a defense of the case for celebrating every birthday.
J. an illustration of the Korean counting system.

21. A. NO CHANGE
B. Though,
C. In fact,
D. Then,

22. F. NO CHANGE
G. on
H. at
J. OMIT the underlined portion.

23. A. NO CHANGE
B. persons' age
C. persons age
D. person's age,

24. F. NO CHANGE
G. One's
H. Its
J. This

25. A. NO CHANGE
B. by
C. while
D. as if

26. Which choice would most clearly communicate the elderly relatives' positive attitude toward this practice?
F. NO CHANGE
G. Duplicating an accepted practice,
H. Living with two birthdays themselves,
J. Obligingly,

27. A. NO CHANGE
B. whose
C. this
D. whom

28. If the writer were to delete the phrases "the vibrant energy of" and "the wisdom and experience gained with" from the preceding sentence, the sentence would primarily lose:
F. its personal and reflective tone.
G. an element of humor.
H. details that illustrate the contrast.
J. the preference expressed by the writer.

29. A. NO CHANGE
B. balk and hesitate
C. refuse and balk
D. balk

Even something as <u>visibly</u> simple or natural as
₃₀
computing a person's age can prove to be not so clear-cut.
Traditions like celebrating birthdays reveal how deeply we
are affected by the culture we live in.

30. **F.** NO CHANGE
    G. apparently
    H. entirely
    J. fully

SAMPLE PASSAGE III

Wearing Jeans in School

In 1970, the school board in Pittsfield,
New Hampshire, approved a dress code that
prohibited students from wearing certain types
of <u>clothing.</u> The school board members believed that
₃₁
wearing "play clothes" to school made the students

31. Given that all of the choices are true, which one would best illustrate the term *dress code* as it is used in this sentence?
    A. NO CHANGE
    B. clothing that was inappropriate.
    C. clothing, including sandals, bell-bottom pants, and "dungarees" (blue jeans).
    D. clothing that is permitted in some schools today.

<u>inefficient toward</u> their school work, while more formal
₃₂
attire established a positive educational climate. When
twelve-year-old Kevin Bannister wore a pair of blue jeans
to school, he was sent home for violating the dress code.

32. **F.** NO CHANGE
    G. lazy and bored to tears with
    H. blow off
    J. lax and indifferent toward

<u>Kevin and his parents believed that his constitutional</u>
₃₃
<u>rights had been violated.</u> The United States District
₃₃

33. Given that all of the choices are true, which one would most effectively introduce the main idea of this paragraph?
    A. NO CHANGE
    B. The principal said dungarees and blue jeans were the same thing, so Kevin should have known better.
    C. If Kevin's jeans had been dirty and torn, the principal might have been justified in expelling him.
    D. These events occurred in a time of social unrest, and emotions were running high.

Court of New <u>Hampshire; agreed</u> to hear Kevin's case.
₃₄
His claim was based on the notion of personal liberty—the
right of every individual to the control of his or her own

34. **F.** NO CHANGE
    G. Court, of New Hampshire
    H. Court of New Hampshire
    J. Court of New Hampshire,

person—protected by the Constitution's Fourteenth Amendment. The court agreed with Kevin that a person's right for wearing clothing of his or her own choosing is, in fact, protected by the Fourteenth Amendment.

35. A. NO CHANGE
    B. of wearing
    C. to wear
    D. wearing

The court noted, however that restrictions may be justified in some circumstances, such as in the school setting.

36. F. NO CHANGE
    G. court noted, however,
    H. court, noted however,
    J. court noted however,

So did Kevin have a right to wear blue jeans to school? The court determined that the school board had failed to show that wearing jeans actually inhibited the educational process, which is guided by authority figures.

37. A. NO CHANGE
    B. process, which has undergone changes since the 1970s.
    C. process, a process we all know well.
    D. process.

Furthermore, the board offered no evidence to back up it's

38. F. NO CHANGE
    G. they're
    H. its
    J. ones

claim that such clothing created a negative educational environment. Certainly the school board would be justified in prohibiting students from wearing clothing that was unsanitary, revealing, or obscene. The court remained unconvinced, therefore, that

39. A. NO CHANGE
    B. where
    C. which
    D. in which

40. F. NO CHANGE
    G. thus,
    H. moreover,
    J. however,

when wearing jeans would actually impair the learning process of Kevin or of his fellow classmates.

41. A. NO CHANGE
    B. by wearing
    C. wearing
    D. having worn

Kevin Bannister's case was significant in that it was the first in the United States to address clothing prohibitions of a school dress code. His challenge

42. Which choice would most effectively open this paragraph and convey the importance of this case?
    F. NO CHANGE
    G. Therefore, Kevin's case reminds us that you should stand up for your rights, no matter how old you are.
    H. The case for personal liberty means the right to speak up must be taken seriously by the courts.
    J. All in all, clothing is an important part of our identity.

initiated a <u>review, of students' rights</u> and administrative
₄₃

responsibility <u>in</u> public education.
₄₄

43. A. NO CHANGE
B. review, of students' rights,
C. review of students' rights
D. review of students' rights,

44. F. NO CHANGE
G. on
H. with
J. about

Question 45 asks about the preceding passage as a whole.

---

45. Suppose the writer's goal had been to write a brief persuasive essay urging students to exercise their constitutional rights. Would this essay fulfill that goal?

A. Yes, because the essay focuses on how Kevin encouraged other students to exercise their constitutional rights.
B. Yes, because the essay focuses on various types of clothing historically worn by students as a freedom of expression.
C. No, because the essay suggests that the right to wear blue jeans was not a substantial constitutional right in the 1970s.
D. No, because the essay objectively reports on one case of a student exercising a particular constitutional right.

Answer Key for English Test Sample Questions

1.	D	16.	J	31.	C
2.	F	17.	B	32.	J
3.	B	18.	J	33.	A
4.	J	19.	A	34.	H
5.	A	20.	F	35.	C
6.	G	21.	C	36.	G
7.	A	22.	F	37.	D
8.	G	23.	A	38.	H
9.	A	24.	J	39.	A
10.	J	25.	B	40.	J
11.	C	26.	F	41.	C
12.	J	27.	A	42.	F
13.	A	28.	H	43.	C
14.	G	29.	D	44.	F
15.	C	30.	G	45.	D

ACT Mathematics Test

The ACT Mathematics Test asks you to answer 60 multiple-choice questions in 60 minutes. The questions are designed to measure your mathematical achievement—the knowledge, skills, and reasoning techniques that are taught in high school mathematics courses and needed for college mathematics courses. Therefore, the questions cover a wide variety of concepts, techniques, and procedures. Naturally, some questions will require computation, but you are allowed to use a calculator on the Mathematics Test. You'll need to understand basic mathematical terminology and to recall some basic mathematical principles and formulas. However, the questions on the test are designed to emphasize your ability to reason mathematically, not to focus on your computation ability or your ability to recall definitions, theorems, or formulas.

Content of the ACT Mathematics Test

As you saw in the chart on page 23, the questions on the ACT Mathematics Test are drawn from the following six categories, which are explained later in this section. These six content categories represent areas of mathematics commonly taught by the end of grade 11 that are important to success in entry-level college mathematics courses:

- Pre-Algebra

- Elementary Algebra

- Intermediate Algebra

- Coordinate Geometry

- Plane Geometry

- Trigonometry

You will receive a score for all 60 questions, and three subscores: a Pre-Algebra/Elementary Algebra subscore based on 24 questions, an Intermediate Algebra/Coordinate Geometry subscore based on 18 questions, and a Plane Geometry/Trigonometry subscore based on 18 questions.

Pre-Algebra questions involve solving problems using the mathematics that you probably learned before you took your first math course in high school—things like operations using whole numbers, fractions, decimals, and integers; numbers raised to positive integer powers and square roots of numbers; ratio, proportion, and percent; multiples and factors of integers; absolute value; ordering numbers from least to greatest or greatest to least; simple linear equations with one variable; simple probability and counting the number of ways something can happen; representing and interpreting data in charts, tables, and graphs; and simple descriptive statistics like mean, median, and mode.

Elementary Algebra questions involve topics like using variables to express relationships, substituting the value of a variable in an expression, performing basic operations on polynomials, factoring polynomials, solving simple quadratic equations (the kind that can be solved by factoring), solving linear inequalities with one variable, and applying properties of integer exponents and square roots.

Intermediate Algebra questions ask you to apply your knowledge, skills, and reasoning ability to solve problems that involve more advanced topics of algebra like the quadratic formula, radical and rational expressions, inequalities and absolute value equations, sequences, systems of equations, quadratic inequalities, functions, matrices, roots of polynomials, and complex numbers.

Coordinate Geometry questions deal with the real number line and the standard (x,y) coordinate plane. They cover number line graphs as well as graphs of points, lines, polynomials, circles, and other curves in the standard (x,y) coordinate plane. They also cover relationships between equations and graphs, slope, parallel and perpendicular lines, distance, midpoints, transformations, and conics.

Plane Geometry questions test your grasp of topics that are usually part of high school geometry, though some topics are introduced in earlier coursework. Included are the properties and relations of plane figures (triangles, rectangles, parallelograms, trapezoids, and circles); angles, parallel lines, and perpendicular lines; translations, rotations, and reflections; proof techniques; simple three-dimensional geometry; and measurement concepts like perimeter, area, and volume. Justification, proof, and logical conclusions are a part of this area.

Trigonometry questions cover the trigonometric ratios defined for right triangles; the values, properties, and graphs of the trigonometric functions; trigonometric identities; trigonometric equations; and modeling with trigonometric functions.

Types of Questions on the ACT Mathematics Test

The content of the questions on the ACT Mathematics Test varies; the questions also vary in their complexity and in the amount of thinking you have to do in order to answer them. The rest of this section gives you examples of questions—of various types and complexities—from all six content areas. All of the questions used in the examples are from actual ACT Mathematics Tests that have been taken by students from across the country. A solution strategy is given for each question. As you read and work through each example, please keep in mind that the strategy given is just one way to solve the problem. A variety of other strategies will also work for each question.

Basic Math Problems

The type of question you're probably the most familiar with (and probably find the easiest) is the stripped-down, bare-bones, basic math problem. Problems of this type are simple and straightforward. They test readily identifiable skills in the six content areas, usually have very few words and no extra information, ask the very question you'd expect them to ask, and usually have a numeric answer.

Question 1 is a good example of a basic math problem from pre-algebra.

> **1.** What is 4% of 1,100 ?
>
>   **A.**   4
>   **B.**   4.4
>   **C.**   40
>   **D.**   44
>   **E.** 440

This problem has very few words, asks a direct question, and has a numeric answer. The solution is simple: convert 4% to a decimal and multiply by 1,100 to get $(0.04)(1,100) = 44$ (**D**). You probably wouldn't need your calculator on this problem, but remember that you may use it if you wish. If you got answer **B** or **E**, you may have used rules about moving decimal points and moved the wrong number of places.

Question 2 is a basic elementary algebra problem.

> **2.** For all x, $(x + 4)(x - 5) = ?$
>
>   **F.** $x^2 - 20$
>   **G.** $x^2 - x - 20$
>   **H.** $2x - 1$
>   **J.** $2x^2 - 1$
>   **K.** $2x^2 - x + 20$

You should know what to do to answer the question the instant you read the problem—use the distributive property (FOIL—Firsts, Outside, Inside, Lasts) and get $x(x - 5) + 4(x - 5) = x^2 - 5x + 4x + 4(-5) = x^2 - x - 20$ (**G**). On this problem, you probably wouldn't use your calculator. If you got answer **F**, you probably just multiplied the first terms and the last terms. Check your answer by substituting a number (try 6) into the original expression and into your answer. If the results are not equal, then the expressions cannot be equivalent.

Question 3 is an example of a basic problem from intermediate algebra.

> **3.** If $x + y = 1$, and $x - y = 1$, then $y = ?$
>
>   **A.** -1
>   **B.**   0
>   **C.** $\frac{1}{2}$
>   **D.**   1
>   **E.**   2

This problem gives you a system of linear equations with unknowns x and y and asks for the value of y. You might be able to solve this problem intuitively—the only number that can be added to and subtracted from another number and give the same result for the problem ($x + y$ and $x - y$ both give 1) is 0, so y must be 0 (**B**). Or, you could use algebra and reason that, because $x + y$ and $x - y$ both equal 1, they equal each other, and $x + y = x - y$ gives $2y = 0$, so $y = 0$. Although some calculators have graphing or matrix functions for solving problems of this type, using a calculator on this problem would probably take most students longer than solving it with one of the strategies given here. If you chose answer **D**, you probably found the value of x rather than the value of y.

Question 4 is an example of a basic problem in coordinate geometry.

---

4. What is the slope of the line containing the points $(-2,7)$ and $(3,-3)$?

F.   4

G. $\dfrac{1}{4}$

H.   0

J. $-\dfrac{1}{2}$

K. -2

This problem has a few more words than some of the other examples of basic problems you've seen so far, but the most important word is "slope." Seeing that you are given two points, you would probably think of the formula that defines the slope of a line through two points:

$$\frac{y_1 - y_2}{x_1 - x_2}.$$

Applying the formula gives $\frac{7 - (-3)}{-2 - 3}$, or -2 (**K**). If you chose answer **J**, you probably got the expression for slope upside down. The change in y goes on top.

There are also some basic plane geometry problems on the ACT Mathematics Test. Question 5 is a good example.

5. If the measure of an angle is $37\frac{1}{2}°$, what is the measure of its supplement, shown in the figure below?

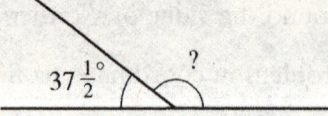

A. $52\frac{1}{2}°$

B. $62\frac{1}{2}°$

C. $127\frac{1}{2}°$

D. $142\frac{1}{2}°$

E. Cannot be determined from the given information

Like many geometry problems, this problem has a figure. The figure tells you what you are given (an angle of $37\frac{1}{2}°$) and what you're asked to find (its supplement, marked by "?"). There really isn't anything you need to mark on the figure because all the important information is already there. If you know that the sum of the measure of an angle and the measure of its supplement equals 180°, a simple subtraction gives the correct answer ($180° - 37\frac{1}{2}° = 142\frac{1}{2}°$), or **D**. If you answered **A**, you found the complement, not the supplement.

A word of caution is in order here. You probably noticed that "Cannot be determined from the given information" is one of the options for question 5. Statistics gathered over the years for the ACT Mathematics Test show that "Cannot be determined from the given information" is chosen by many students even when it is not the correct option. You should **not** think that whenever "Cannot be determined from the given information" is an option, it is automatically the correct answer. It isn't, as question 5 demonstrates. Later in this section, there's a question for which the correct answer is "Cannot be determined from the given information." Be sure to think carefully about problems with this answer choice.

You'll find basic trigonometry problems, like question 6, on the ACT Mathematics Test.

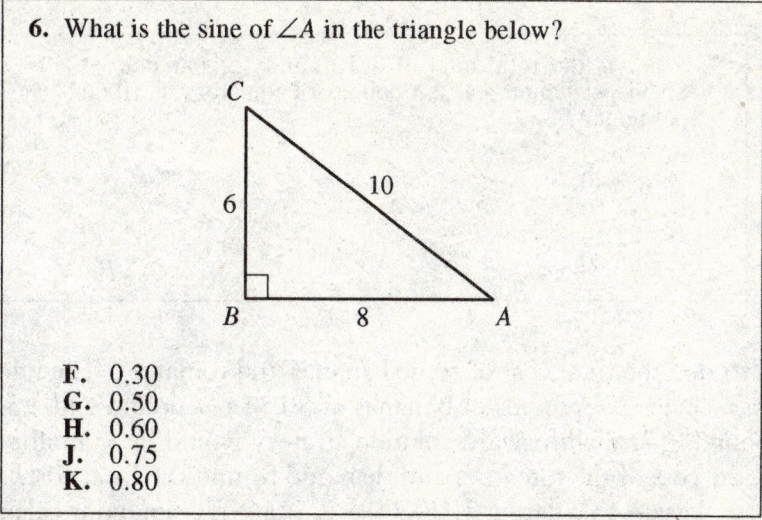

6. What is the sine of ∠A in the triangle below?

    F. 0.30
    G. 0.50
    H. 0.60
    J. 0.75
    K. 0.80

This question asks you to find the sine of ∠A in the triangle that is shown in the figure. If you have studied trigonometry, you've seen questions like this before. The lengths of all three sides of the triangle are given on the figure, even though only two are actually needed for finding sin ∠A. The extra information is there not to confuse you, but rather to test your ability to sort out the information that you need from the information that you are given. Picking 6 (the length of the side opposite ∠A) and 10 (the length of the hypotenuse) and forming the ratio $\frac{6}{10}$ gives the correct answer, 0.60 (**H**). The cosine and the tangent of ∠A are also present in the answer choices. In order to do well on problems like this one, you need to be able to tell which trigonometric function is which.

Basic Math Problems in Settings

Basic math problems in settings are what people often call "word problems" or "story problems." They typically describe situations from everyday life where you need to apply mathematics in order to find the answer to a question. The major difference between this type of problem and the basic math problems that you've seen in the examples so far is that the problem isn't set up for you— you have to set it up yourself. Most people find this to be the most difficult part of word problems. The key steps are reading the problem carefully, deciding what you're trying to find, sorting out what you really need from what's given, and then devising a strategy for finding the answer. Once the problem is set up, finding the answer is not much different than solving a basic math problem.

You can find basic math problems in settings in all of the content areas. Question 7 is an example from pre-algebra.

> **7.** What is the total cost of 2.5 pounds of bananas at $0.34 per pound and 2.5 pounds of tomatoes at $0.66 per pound?
>
> **A.** $1.00
> **B.** $2.40
> **C.** $2.50
> **D.** $3.50
> **E.** $5.00

Here, you're asked to find the total cost of some bananas and tomatoes. The important information is that the total cost includes 2.5 pounds of bananas at $0.34 per pound and 2.5 pounds of tomatoes at $0.66 per pound. A straightforward solution strategy would be to multiply to find the cost of the bananas and the cost of the tomatoes and then add to find the total cost. Now, the problem you're left with is very basic—calculating $2.5(0.34) + 2.5(0.66)$. Using your calculator might save time and avoid computation errors, but if you see that $2.5(0.34) + 2.5(0.66) = 2.5(0.34 + 0.66) = 2.5(1.00) = 2.50$, answer C, you might be able to do the computation more quickly in your head.

Basic elementary algebra problems can be in settings also. Question 8 is an example.

> **8.** The relationship between temperature expressed in degrees Fahrenheit (F) and degrees Celsius (C) is given by the formula
>
> $$F = \frac{9}{5}C + 32$$
>
> If the temperature is 14 degrees Fahrenheit, what is it in degrees Celsius?
>
> **F.** −10°
> **G.** −12°
> **H.** −14°
> **J.** −16°
> **K.** −18°

In this problem, you're given a relationship (in the form of an equation) between temperatures expressed in degrees Fahrenheit (F) and degrees Celsius (C). You're also given a temperature of 14 degrees Fahrenheit and asked what the corresponding temperature would be in degrees Celsius. Your strategy would probably be to substitute 14 into the equation in place of the variable F. This leaves you with a basic algebra problem—solving the equation $14 = \frac{9}{5}C + 32$ for C. Before going on to the next problem, it would probably be a good idea to check your answer, which should be $C = -10°$ (F), by substituting −10 for C, multiplying by $\frac{9}{5}$, and adding 32 to see if the result is 14. Checking doesn't take long, and you might catch an error.

Question 9 is an example of an intermediate algebra problem in a setting.

> **9.** Amy drove the 200 miles to New Orleans at an average speed 10 miles per hour faster than her usual average speed. If she completed the trip in 1 hour less than usual, what is her usual driving speed, in miles per hour?
>
> **A.** 20
> **B.** 30
> **C.** 40
> **D.** 50
> **E.** 60

After reading the problem, you know that it is about travel and that the basic formula "distance equals the rate multiplied by the time" ($D = rt$) or one of its variations ($r = \frac{D}{t}$ or $t = \frac{D}{r}$) will probably be useful. For travel problems, a table is often an efficient way to organize the information. Because the problem asks for Amy's usual speed (rate), it would probably be wise to let the variable r represent her usual speed in miles per hour (mph). You might organize your table like this:

	Distance (miles)	Rate (mph)	Time (hours)
Usual trip	200	r	$\frac{200}{r}$
This trip	200	$r + 10$	$\frac{200}{r+10}$

Then, because the time for this trip $\left(\frac{200}{r+10}\right)$ is 1 hour less than the time for the usual trip $\left(\frac{200}{r}\right)$, solving $\frac{200}{r+10} = \frac{200}{r} - 1$ will give the answer. Solving this equation is a matter of using routine algebra skills and procedures. The solution, $r = 40$ (C), answers the question, "What is her usual driving speed?" A quick check that driving 200 miles at 40 mph takes 5 hours and that driving 200 miles at 50 mph (which is 10 mph faster) takes 4 hours (which is 1 hour less) should convince you that your answer is correct.

Coordinate geometry problems can be in settings too. Question 10 is an example.

> **10.** A map is laid out in the standard (x,y) coordinate plane. How long, in units, is an airplane's path on the map as the airplane flies along a straight line from City A located at (20,14) to City B located at (5,10) ?
>
> **F.** $\sqrt{1{,}201}$
> **G.** $\sqrt{241}$
> **H.** $\sqrt{209}$
> **J.** 7
> **K.** $\sqrt{19}$

In this problem, you're told that you will be working with the standard (x,y) coordinate plane and that you will need to find a distance. The distance formula should immediately come to mind. All you need is two points, and those are given. The problem now becomes a basic math problem—applying the distance formula:

$$\sqrt{\left(x_1 - x_2\right)^2 + \left(y_1 - y_2\right)^2} = \sqrt{(20 - 5)^2 + (14 - 10)^2} = \sqrt{241}\ \textbf{(G)}.$$

Your calculator might be useful in finding $(20 - 5)^2 + (14 - 10)^2$, but you should not press the square root key because most of the answer choices are in radical form.

A geometry problem in a setting is illustrated by question 11.

> **11.** A person 2 meters tall casts a shadow 3 meters long. At the same time, a telephone pole casts a shadow 12 meters long. How many meters tall is the pole?
> **A.** 4
> **B.** 6
> **C.** 8
> **D.** 11
> **E.** 18

Question 11 has no figure, which is sometimes the case with geometry problems. It might be wise to draw your own figure and label it with the appropriate numbers from the problem. "A person 2 meters tall casts a shadow 3 meters long" is a pretty good clue that you should draw a right triangle with the vertical leg labeled 2 and the horizontal leg labeled 3. And, "a telephone pole casts a shadow 12 meters long" suggests that you should draw another right triangle with the horizontal leg labeled 12. Finding the height of the pole amounts to finding the length of the other leg of your second triangle, which you would label with a variable, say h. Your figure would be similar to this:

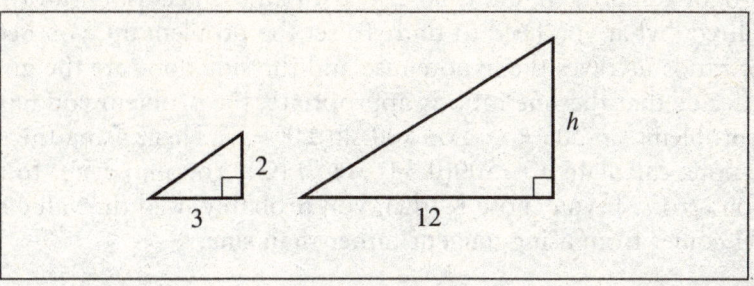

The triangles are similar (they're both right triangles and the angle that the sun's rays make with the ground is the same for both because the shadows were measured at the same time), so finding the height of the pole amounts to setting up and solving a proportion between corresponding sides of the triangles—a basic math problem. Your proportion might be $\frac{3}{12} = \frac{2}{h}$. Cross multiply to get $3(h) = 12(2)$, or $3h = 24$, and solve to get $h = 8$ (C). Because the numbers are quite simple to work with, you probably wouldn't use your calculator on this problem.

Last (but not least), question 12 shows an example of a trigonometry problem in a setting.

12. The hiking path to the top of a mountain makes, at the steepest place, an angle of 20° with the horizontal, and it maintains this constant slope for 500 meters, as illustrated below. Which of the following is the closest approximation to the change in elevation, in meters, over this 500-meter section?

(Note: You may use the following values, which are correct to 2 decimal places:
$\cos 20° \approx 0.94$; $\sin 20° \approx 0.34$; $\tan 20° \approx 0.36$)

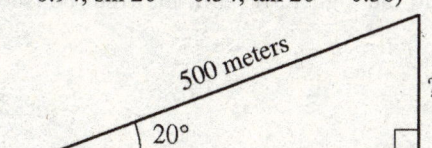

F. 20
G. 170
H. 180
J. 250
K. 470

This problem has a figure, and the figure is labeled with all the necessary information, including a question mark to tell you what you need to find. To set the problem up, you need to decide which of the trigonometric ratios involves the hypotenuse and the side opposite the given angle of a right triangle. Once you decide that the sine ratio is appropriate, the problem you have left to solve is a basic trigonometry problem: $\sin 20° = \frac{h}{500}$, or $500 \sin 20° = h$. Then, using the approximation for $\sin 20°$ given in the note, calculate $h \approx 500(0.34) = 170$ (**G**). You may want to use your calculator to avoid computation errors. If you chose **K**, then you probably used the value for cosine rather than sine. Answer **H** comes from using tangent rather than sine.

Very Challenging Problems

The ACT Mathematics Test emphasizes reasoning ability, so it naturally has problems that can be very challenging. Because these problems are designed to test your understanding of mathematical concepts and your ability to pull together what you have learned in your math classes, they will probably be unlike problems you usually see. Some will be in settings, and some won't. Some will have figures, and some won't. Some will have extra information that you'll have to sort out, and some won't have enough information, so the correct answer will be "Cannot be determined from the given information." Some will have numeric answers, some will have answers that are expressions or equations that you have to set up, and some will have answers that are statements for you to interpret and judge. On some questions your calculator will be helpful, and on others it will be better not to use it. All of the questions will share one important characteristic, however—they will challenge you to think hard and plan a strategy before you start to solve them.

These challenging problems come from all six content areas. Question 13 is one such pre-algebra problem.

---

13. If 537^{102} were calculated, it would have 279 digits. What would the digit farthest to the right be (the ones digit)?

   A. 1
   B. 3
   C. 4
   D. 7
   E. 9

You certainly wouldn't want to calculate 537^{102} by hand, and your calculator doesn't display enough digits for you to be able to read off the ones digit for this very large number, so you have to figure out another way to "see" the ones digit. A good place to start might be to look at the ones digit for powers of 7 because 7 is the ones digit of 537. Maybe there will be a pattern: $7^0 = 1$, $7^1 = 7$, $7^2 = 49$, $7^3 = 343$, $7^4 = 2{,}401$, $7^5 = 16{,}807$, $7^6 = 117{,}649$, $7^7 = 823{,}543$. It looks like the pattern of the ones digits is 1, 7, 9, 3, 1, 7, 9, 3, $\cdots$, with the sequence of these 4 digits repeating over and over. Now, if you can decide where in this pattern the ones digit of 537^{102} falls, you'll have the problem solved. You might organize a chart like this:

Ones digit	1	7	9	3
Power of 7	0	1	2	3
	4	5	6	7

The next row would read "8 9 10 11" to show that the ones digits of 7^8, 7^9, 7^{10}, and 7^{11}, respectively, are 1, 7, 9, and 3. You could continue the chart row after row until you got up to 102, but that would take a lot of time. Instead, think about where 102 would fall. The numbers in the first column are the multiples of 4, so 100 would fall there because it is a multiple of 4. Then 101 would be in the second column, and 102 would fall in the third column. Therefore, the ones digit of 537^{102} is 9 (E).

Question 14 is an elementary algebra problem designed to challenge your ability to think mathematically and use what you've learned.

> **14.** If $a < -1$, which of the following best describes a general relationship between a^3 and a^2 ?
>
> **F.** $a^3 > a^2$
>
> **G.** $a^3 < a^2$
>
> **H.** $a^3 = a^2$
>
> **J.** $a^3 = -a^2$
>
> **K.** $a^3 = \dfrac{1}{a^2}$

Here you are told that $a < -1$. Then you are asked for the relationship between a^3 and a^2. By stopping to think for a moment before trying to manipulate the given inequality or experimenting with numbers plugged into the answer choices, you might realize that if $a < -1$, then a is a negative number, so its cube is a negative number. Squaring a negative number, however, gives a positive number. Every negative number is less than every positive number, so the correct relationship between a^3 and a^2 is $a^3 < a^2$ (**G**). Of course, there are other ways to approach the problem.

> **15.** If $\left(\frac{4}{5}\right)^n = \sqrt{\left(\frac{5}{4}\right)^3}$, then $n = ?$
>
> A. $-\frac{3}{2}$
>
> B. -1
>
> C. $-\frac{2}{3}$
>
> D. $\frac{2}{3}$
>
> E. $\frac{3}{2}$

For a very challenging intermediate algebra problem, look at question 15.

In this problem, you're asked to find the value of a variable, but the variable is in the exponent. After some thought you might decide to try to rewrite $\sqrt{\left(\frac{5}{4}\right)^3}$ so that it is $\frac{5}{4}$ raised to a power. You should remember that the square root is the same as the $\frac{1}{2}$ power, so, after using some properties of exponents, $\sqrt{\left(\sqrt{\frac{5}{4}}\right)^3} = \left(\left(\sqrt{\frac{5}{4}}\right)^3\right)^{\frac{1}{2}} = \left(\frac{5}{4}\right)^{\frac{3}{2}}$. Now at least the left side and the right side of the equation have the same form, but the bases of the two expressions aren't the same—they're reciprocals. In thinking about the connection between reciprocals and exponents, it is good to realize that taking the opposite of the exponent (that is, making it have the opposite sign) will "flip" the base, because $a^{-k} = \frac{1}{a^k}$. That means $\left(\frac{5}{4}\right)^{\frac{3}{2}} = \left(\frac{4}{5}\right)^{-\frac{3}{2}}$. So now, with $\left(\frac{4}{5}\right)^n = \left(\frac{4}{5}\right)^{-\frac{3}{2}}, n = -\frac{3}{2}$ (**A**).

There are also coordinate geometry problems that are very challenging. Question 16 is an example.

> **16.** In the standard (x,y) coordinate plane, the triangle with vertices at $(0,0)$, $(0,k)$, and $(2,m)$, where m is constant, changes shape as k changes. What happens to the triangle's area, expressed in square coordinate units, as k increases starting from 2 ?
>
> F. The area increases as k increases.
> G. The area decreases as k increases.
> H. The area always equals 2.
> J. The area always equals m.
> K. The area always equals $2m$.

This problem might seem confusing at first because there are two different variables and there is no figure to help you sort things out. You're told that *m* is a constant but that *k* changes. So, to help get you started, you could pick a value for *m*, say *m* = 1. Then, at least you can start sketching a figure. The point (0,*k*) is on the *y*-axis and *k* increases starting with 2, so you could start by drawing a figure similar to this:

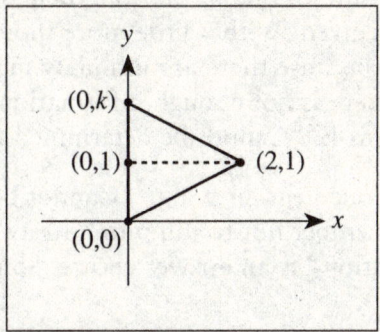

You can see the triangle that the problem mentions. If you think of the segment from (0,0) to (0,*k*) as the base and the segment from (2,1) to (0,1) as the height, you can see that as *k* increases, the base of the triangle gets longer but the height remains the same. From geometry, you know that the area of a triangle is given by $\frac{1}{2}$ (base)(height). Therefore, the area will increase as the base gets longer. So, the area will increase as *k* increases (**F**). You should be able to reason that for any value of *m*, the result would have been the same, and you can feel confident that the correct answer is the first answer choice.

Question 17 is an example of a very challenging geometry problem.

17. In the figure below, $\overline{AB} \cong \overline{AC}$ and $\overline{BC}$ is 10 units long. What is the area, in square inches, of $\triangle ABC$?

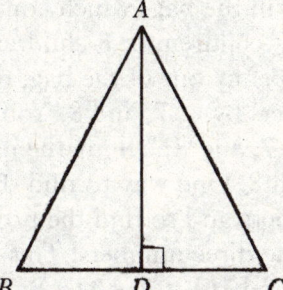

A. 12.5
B. 25
C. $25\sqrt{2}$
D. 50
E. Cannot be determined from the given information

This problem has a figure, but none of the information given is marked on the figure. It would probably be wise to mark the figure yourself to indicate which sides are congruent and which side is 10 units long. You need to find the area of $\triangle ABC$, and you know that the base $\overline{BC}$ is 10 units long. You need the measure of the height $\overline{AD}$ before you can apply the formula for the area of a triangle. You might ask yourself, "Is there any way to get the height?" If you were given the measure of one of the angles or the measure of one of the congruent sides, you might be able to find the height, but no other information is given. With a little more thought, you should realize that the height can be any positive number because there are infinitely many isosceles triangles with bases 10 units long. You conclude that there is not enough information to allow you to solve this problem, and the correct answer choice is E: "Cannot be determined from the given information."

This is the example that was mentioned earlier where "Cannot be determined from the given information" is the correct answer. Remember not to jump to a hasty conclusion when "Cannot be determined from the given information" is an answer choice. Sometimes it is the right answer, but sometimes it isn't.

Very challenging problems can be in settings, too. Question 18 is an example from pre-algebra.

> **18.** A bag of pennies could be divided among 6 children, or 7 children, or 8 children, with each getting the same number, and with 1 penny left over in each case. What is the smallest number of pennies that could be in the bag?
>
> **F.**   22
> **G.**   43
> **H.**   57
> **J.**   169
> **K.**   337

In this problem, whenever the pennies in the bag (which contains an unknown number of pennies) are divided evenly among 6 children, 7 children, or 8 children, there is always 1 penny left over. This means that if you take the extra penny out of the bag, then the number of pennies left in the bag will be divisible (with no remainder) by 6, 7, and 8. You should ask yourself, "What is the smallest number that is divisible by 6, 7, and 8?" In mathematical terminology, you're looking for the least common multiple of 6, 7, and 8. One way to find the least common multiple is to use the prime factorizations of the three numbers and to find the product of the highest power of each prime that occurs in one or more of the three numbers. This process will yield $2^3 \cdot 3 \cdot 7 = 168$. (As a check: $168 \div 6 = 28$, $168 \div 7 = 24$, and $168 \div 8 = 21$.) But wait! You're not quite finished. Remember to add back in the penny that you took out of the bag originally to make the divisions come out even. Thus, your answer is 169 (J).

Question 19 is an example of an elementary algebra word problem that is very challenging.

---

19. There are n students in a class. If, among those students, $p\%$ play at least 1 musical instrument, which of the following general expressions represents the number of students who play NO musical instrument?

A. np

B. $.01np$

C. $\dfrac{(100-p)n}{100}$

D. $\dfrac{(1-p)n}{.01}$

E. $100(1-p)n$

This is an example of a problem that has a mathematical expression as its answer. Finding an expression to answer a question usually makes you think more than finding a numerical answer because the variables require you to think abstractly. In this problem, you are told that out of a class of n students, $p\%$ play 1 or more musical instruments. Finding the percent of students who play no musical instrument is simple: $(100-p)\%$. To find the number of students who play no musical instrument, you'd probably want to convert $(100-p)\%$ to a decimal and multiply by n. If $100-p$ were a number, you'd automatically move the decimal point two places to the left. But, because there's no decimal point to move in $100-p$, you have to think about what you need to do to convert $(100-p)\%$ to a decimal. Moving the decimal point two places to the left is the same as dividing by 100, so $(100-p)\%$ as a decimal is $\frac{100-p}{100}$, and the number of students who play no musical instrument is $\frac{(100-p)n}{100}$ (C).

Question 20 is an example of a very challenging coordinate geometry problem that has a setting.

20. Starting at her doorstep, Ramona walked down the sidewalk at 1.5 feet per second for 4 seconds. Then she stopped for 4 seconds, realizing that she had forgotten something. Next she returned to her doorstep along the same route at 1.5 feet per second. The graph of Ramona's distance (*d*) from her doorstep as a function of time (*t*) would most resemble which of the following?

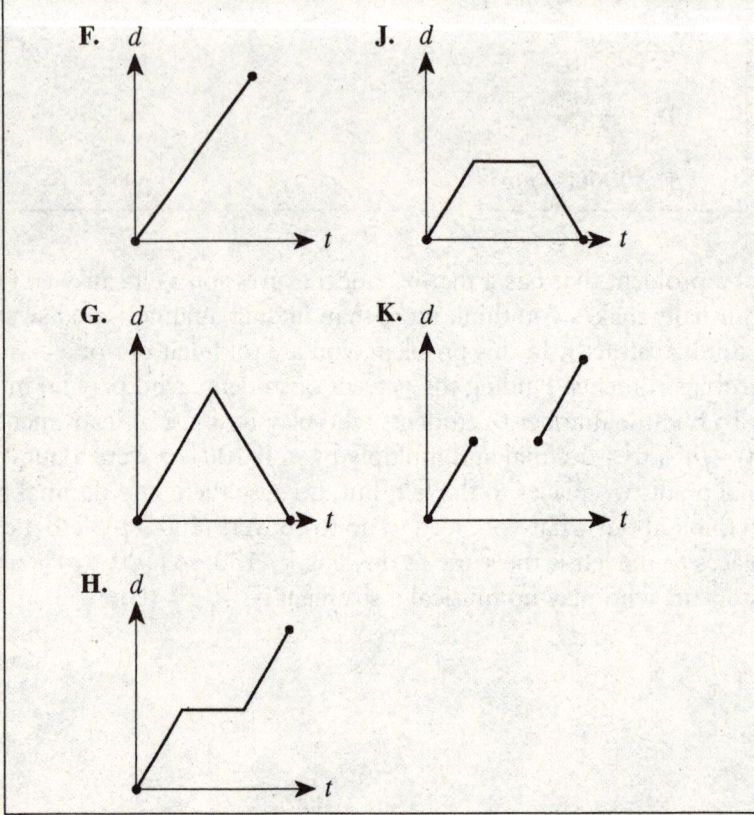

This problem is different from any of the problems you've seen so far because its answer is a graph. And, instead of giving you an equation and asking you to identify the equation's graph, this problem describes a situation and asks you to decide which graph represents the situation. You need to think about what the description of each of Ramona's activities says in terms of distance as a function of time and what each activity would translate into graphically. For example, at first Ramona walked at a constant rate down the sidewalk. Therefore, she moved farther away from her doorstep as time elapsed, and her distance from her doorstep increased at a constant rate as time increased. So, the first part of the graph should be a line segment with a positive slope. Unfortunately, all five graphs start out this way, so none of the options can be eliminated at this point. The next thing Ramona did was stop for 4 seconds. If she stood still, her distance from her doorstep would not change even though time was still elapsing. This part of the graph should then reflect a constant value for *d* as time increases. It should be a horizontal line segment. This information allows you to eliminate options **F, G,** and **K,** because they do not have a horizontal segment. Ramona's next activity helps you decide between **H** and **J.** Ramona walked back home at the same rate along the same route as before. On her way back home, her distance from her doorstep decreased at a constant rate as elapsed time increased. This would be graphed as a line segment with a negative slope, and therefore **J** is the correct graph.

Another word problem that challenges you to think mathematically is question 21.

> **21.** An object detected on radar is 5 miles to the east, 4 miles to the north, and 1 mile above the tracking station. Among the following, which is the closest approximation to the distance, in miles, that the object is from the tracking station?
>
> **A.** 6.5
> **B.** 7.2
> **C.** 8.3
> **D.** 9.0
> **E.** 10.0

This problem is about computing a distance, but it's a distance in three-dimensional space and there isn't a picture to help you. For this problem, it might be helpful for you to draw a sketch of the situation. Your sketch might be a "box" like this:

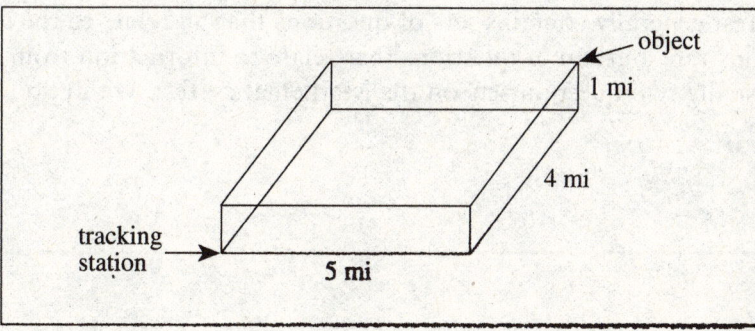

You need to find the length of the diagonal from the lower left corner of the front of the box to the top right corner of the back of the box. This is the hypotenuse of a right triangle ($\triangle OBT$ on the figure redrawn below) that has its right angle at B. One leg of this triangle has length 1, but the other leg is $\overline{BT}$, and you don't know the length of $\overline{BT}$.

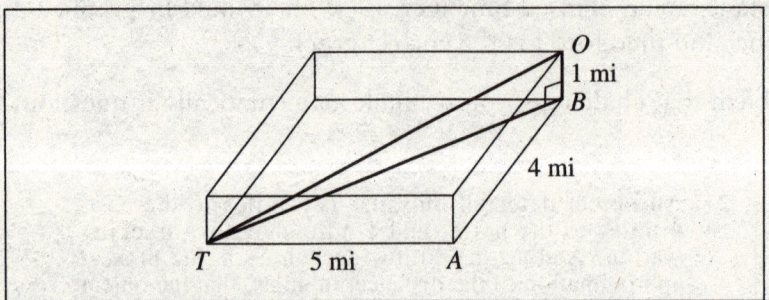

A closer look shows that $\overline{BT}$ is the hypotenuse of $\triangle TAB$, which has its right angle at A and legs that measure 5 and 4. Using the Pythagorean theorem gives $BT = \sqrt{5^2 + 4^2} = \sqrt{41}$.

Now you can use the Pythagorean theorem again to get $OT = \sqrt{BT^2 + OB^2} = \sqrt{\left(\sqrt{41}\right)^2 + 1^2} = \sqrt{42}$, which is about 6.5 (**A**).

Question Sets

The Mathematics Test generally contains sets of questions that all relate to the same information. Questions 22–24 illustrate a group of questions that relate to information from a paragraph and a graph. There are usually two question sets on the Mathematics Test, with two to four questions in each set.

Use the following information to answer questions 22–24.

At both Quick Car Rental and Speedy Car Rental, the cost, in dollars, of renting a full-size car depends on a fixed daily rental fee and a fixed charge per mile that the car is driven. However, the daily rental fee and the charge per mile are not the same for the 2 companies. In the graph below, line Q represents the total cost for Quick Car Rental and line S represents the total cost for Speedy Car Rental.

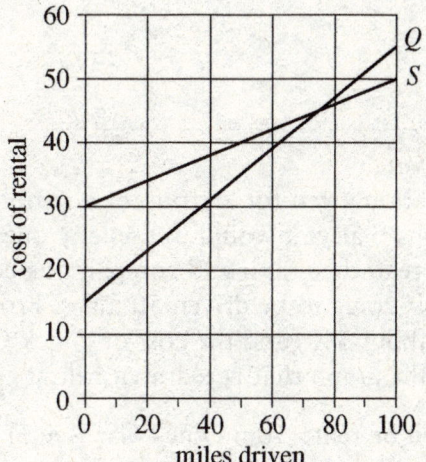

22. Robert plans to rent a full-size car for 1 day and drive only 50 miles. If his only consideration is to incur the least cost, which company should he choose?

  F. Quick Car Rental, because the cost is $5.00 less.
  G. Quick Car Rental, because the cost is $15.00 less.
  H. Either company, because the costs are equal.
  J. Speedy Car Rental, because the cost is $5.00 less.
  K. Speedy Car Rental, because the cost is $15.00 less.

23. If you rent a full-size car from Quick Car Rental for 1 day, how much more would the total rental cost be if you drove the car 78 miles than if you drove it 77 miles?

    A. $0.10
    B. $0.15
    C. $0.20
    D. $0.40
    E. $0.55

24. What would be the total cost of renting a full-size car from Speedy Car Rental for 1 day and driving the car 150 miles?

    F. $ 60
    G. $ 75
    H. $ 85
    J. $ 90
    K. $120

Once you've looked at the information given for a group of questions, you can use the same sorts of strategies to answer the questions that you would use on any question on the ACT Mathematics Test. Question 22 requires you to read the graph and compare the costs of renting a car from the 2 companies, assuming that the car is going to be driven 50 miles. From the graph, the cost for Speedy Car Rental appears to be about $40, and the cost of Quick Car Rental appears to be about $35. These points are marked on the graph that is redrawn below.

So Robert will incur the least cost if he rents from Quick Car Rental because that cost is $5 less (**F**).

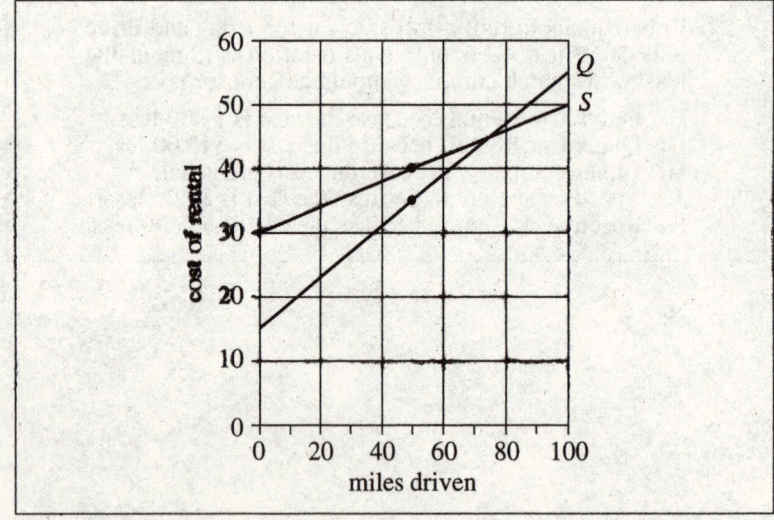

Question 23 requires you to determine how much more Robert would pay if he rented a car from Quick Car Rental and drove 78 miles than if he drove 77 miles. Using mathematical concepts might be a better approach than trying to read the graph, because you might not be able to read the graph accurately enough. You know from coordinate geometry that, in the standard (x,y) coordinate plane, the slope of a line gives the rate of change in y per unit change in x, which is exactly what you want to find in this problem—how much the cost at Quick Car Rental changes when the car is driven 1 more mile. Two points that are easy to read accurately off the graph are $(0,15)$ and $(50,35)$, labeled on the redrawn graph below.

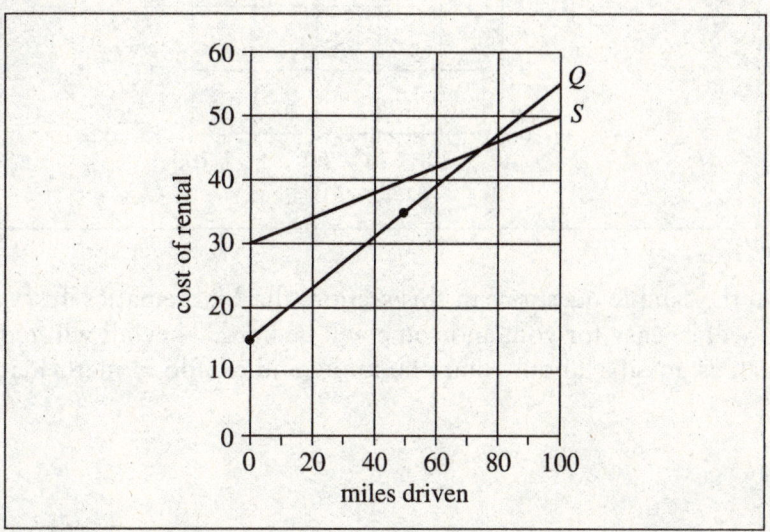

Using the formula for finding the slope of a line from two given points, you calculate the slope and get 0.4. So, the difference for driving 78 miles instead of 77 miles (that is, for driving 1 more mile) is $0.40 (**D**).

In question 24, you are asked for the cost of renting a car from Speedy Car Rental and driving it 150 miles. You can't simply read the cost off the graph, because 150 isn't on the graph, but you can find an equation of the line for Speedy Car Rental and then plug 150 into the equation. Recall that if you know two points (x_1, y_1) and (x_2, y_2) on a line, you can find an equation for the line using the two-point form: $y - y_1 = (x - x_1)$. Here, you can use two points that are easy to read off the graph, like $(0,30)$ and $(100,50)$, shown on the redrawn graph on the next page, to get $y - 30 = (x - 0)$, or $y = 0.20x + 30$. Then when $x = 150$, $y = 0.20(150) + 30 = 60$. So, $60 is the answer (**F**).

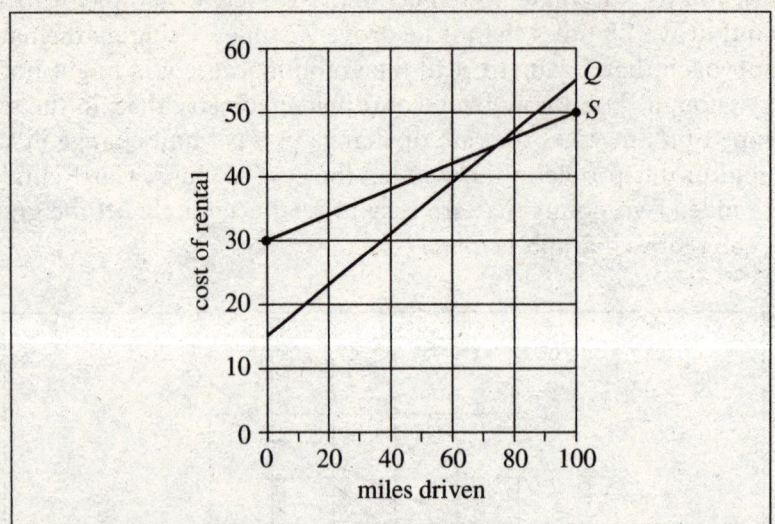

As you have seen in the sample questions in this section, the Mathematics Test includes many types of questions. Some will be easy for you, and some will be hard. They all will require you to demonstrate as much as possible about what you know and can do in mathematics.

Answer Key for Mathematics Test Sample Questions

1.	D	9.	C	17.	E
2.	G	10.	G	18.	J
3.	B	11.	C	19.	C
4.	K	12.	G	20.	J
5.	D	13.	E	21.	A
6.	H	14.	G	22.	F
7.	C	15.	A	23.	D
8.	F	16.	F	24.	F

Strategies for Taking the ACT Mathematics Test

Pace Yourself

There are 60 questions for you to answer in 60 minutes, which allows you an average of 1 minute per problem. Some problems will take you less than 1 minute, and some will take you more. Don't spend too much time on any one question. You should keep a close eye on your watch to make sure you work at a pace that will allow you to finish the test in the 60 minutes allotted. When determining your pace, be aware that the questions are arranged approximately in order of difficulty: the question that ACT predicts will be the easiest for most students is first and the question predicted to be the hardest is last.

Answer All the Easy Questions First, Then Go Back to Answer the Hard Ones

Easy and *hard* are relative terms. What might be easy for one student might be hard for another. You know which math topics are easy for you and which are hard. Answer all the questions that are easy for you and then go back to the hard ones. Remember that you don't get more points for answering hard questions. All questions, no matter how easy or hard, count equally toward your Mathematics total score. If you don't see a way to solve a problem, or if the method you're using seems to be taking a lot of time, skip the question and move on to questions that you can answer more easily. Don't forget, however, to mark in the test booklet (never on the answer document) all those questions that you skip so that you can find them easily when you go back to them later. (Note: In some circumstances you are not permitted to write in your test booklet. In those circumstances, you'll be given scratch paper, and you can use it to jot down the numbers of the questions you skip.)

Answer All Questions

Answer all questions even if you have no idea how to solve some of them. If you're stumped and have time, eliminate as many of the options as you can and then guess from among the ones that remain. If time is running out and you don't have time to eliminate any of the options, guess anyway. Even a wild guess has a 20% chance of being correct, but a blank has no chance of being correct. Remember, your score is based solely on the number of questions you answer correctly—there is no penalty for guessing and no penalty for wrong answers. Scores are most comparable if everyone answers every question.

Read Each Problem Carefully

Read carefully enough so you know what you're trying to find before you start looking for it, and so you know what you have to work with to help you find it. Remember that you don't necessarily have to use all the information you're given. Watch for cases where the information given is insufficient for solving the problem, but be fairly certain before you mark "Cannot be determined from the given information" that you haven't missed some information or that there isn't an alternate strategy that would enable you to solve the problem from the given information.

Look for Information in the Options

Sometimes looking at the answer choices will provide valuable information about the form of the answer. For example, you might be able to judge whether your answer should be left in radical form or converted to a decimal approximation, whether your polynomial answer should be left in factored form or multiplied out, or whether you should spend time reducing a probability to lowest terms. For some problems, you have to analyze the options as part of your solution strategy. For example, when a question asks, "Which of the following statements is true?" and the statements are the five options, there is often no way to proceed except by examining each option in turn. Sometimes, using the options gives you an alternate way to solve a problem. For example, suppose you're trying to solve a quadratic equation and you can't get the quadratic expression to factor and can't remember the quadratic formula. You might be able to get the correct answer by substituting the options, in turn, into the equation until one works. This strategy should be used very sparingly, however, because it can be more time-consuming than other strategies.

Use Figures Wisely and Whenever You Can

Whether the figure is given or you sketch your own, for visual learners there is truth in the old saying, "A picture is worth a thousand words." The marks you add to given figures (for example, dimensions that are given in the question but aren't on the figure or that you calculate in the process of solving the problem, marks to show congruences, auxiliary lines like perpendiculars and diagonals) and the figures you draw yourself often help you see the relationships more clearly. (Note: In some circumstances you are not permitted to write in your test booklet. In those circumstances, you'll be given scratch paper to use.)

Use Your Calculator Wisely

Each problem on the Mathematics Test can be solved in a reasonable amount of time without a calculator. A calculator will be most helpful if you are very familiar with the one you bring to the test and you use it wisely during the test. Trying to use a calculator that you are not very familiar with or trying to use a calculator on every problem can have disastrous effects. Experimenting with the capabilities of a new calculator during the testing session or using a calculator in situations where a non-calculator approach would be better can cost you precious time. Bring the calculator that you are most familiar with—the one you use in your math classes or at home. Don't worry that other students have more sophisticated calculators than yours; the type of calculator that students use should not make a difference in their scores. Use your calculator wisely; remember that a non-calculator strategy is often better than a calculator strategy. And don't believe everything your calculator tells you. Make sure the numbers it gives you are reasonable and make sense.

Think!

Your head is by far a more powerful and efficient problem-solving tool than your pencil or your calculator. Think before you plunge in and begin working on a problem. Don't panic if you suddenly can't remember a formula or all of the steps of a procedure you've been taught. There might be another way to do the problem that will work just as well. For example, you don't have to write and solve an equation for every algebra word problem. You might be able to reason through such a problem and get the correct answer without an equation. Sometimes it's best to let your common sense about numbers take over.

Show Your Work

You have certainly heard this before—probably in every math class you've ever taken. Of course, you're not going to have time during the test to write down every step for every problem the way you might on a homework assignment, but writing down at least some of what you are thinking and doing as you solve a problem will be worth the time it takes. It may be important, as a way of record keeping, to write down numbers that you plug into your calculator, and the intermediate results it gives you, in the process of solving a problem. If you don't write anything down and your answer for a problem doesn't match any of the answer choices, your only alternative is to start over. But, if you have at least something written down, you may be able to go back over your work and find your mistake. Also, if you have time at the end of the test to go back and check your answers, having something written down will enable you to check over your work more quickly.

Check Your Answers

Before you leave a question, make sure your answer makes sense. Don't believe everything your calculator tells you; make sure that the answer your calculator displays makes sense to you and that your answer actually answers the question. For example, if a problem about oranges and apples asks for the number of apples, make sure your answer doesn't give the number of oranges, or if a problem asks for the altitude of a triangle, make sure your answer isn't the hypotenuse. Remember, if you have time left after answering all of the questions on the Mathematics Test, use it wisely and go back and check your work. That's a skill that will help you in college, too.

ACT Reading Test

Designed to measure your skill in reading, the ACT Reading Test asks you to answer 40 questions—10 questions about each of four passages—in 35 minutes. The passages in the Reading Test come from published materials, such as books and magazines, that are like those a first-year college student can expect to read for a class.

Content of the ACT Reading Test

The ACT Reading Test contains one passage from each of the following four categories:

- **Prose Fiction** (passages from short stories or novels)

- **Humanities** (architecture, art, dance, ethics, film, language, literary criticism, memoir, music, personal essays, philosophy, radio, television, theater)

- **Social Studies** (anthropology, archaeology, biography, business, economics, education, geography, history, political science, psychology, sociology)

- **Natural Sciences** (anatomy, astronomy, biology, botany, chemistry, ecology, geology, medicine, meteorology, microbiology, natural history, physiology, physics, technology, zoology)

Your Reading Test score will tell you how you did on all 40 questions of the Reading Test. You'll also receive a Social Studies/Sciences subscore (based on how you do on the 20 questions in the social studies and natural sciences sections of the test) and an Arts/Literature subscore (based on how you do on the 20 questions in the prose fiction and humanities sections of the test).

You'll have 35 minutes to read the Reading Test's four passages and answer the 40 multiple-choice questions. This means you'll have about 8 to $8\frac{1}{2}$ minutes to read each passage and answer the questions that follow. That's not a lot of time, but it's more than you might think. Once you've read through this section, you'll have a better idea of what the Reading Test is all about and what you need to do in order to do your best on it.

The Reading Test evaluates your ability to understand the passages that appear in the test. It does **not** test your ability to remember relevant facts from outside the passage. You don't need to be knowledgeable about the subject area that a passage covers in order to do well on the questions, but you do need to read attentively and to think carefully about what you read. The passages may deal with subjects you're familiar with, or you may know almost nothing about the subjects of the passages. It doesn't matter, though: the passages contain all the information you need to answer the questions.

Types of Passages on the ACT Reading Test

Just as going to see the latest action movie is different from watching a wildlife special on public television, reading a novel or short story is a different experience from reading a scientific essay. As you read the different passages in the Reading Test, you may find it helpful to keep their essential differences in mind.

Prose Fiction

Prose fiction passages generally include a narration of events and revelation of character. Think about how you read fiction. What do you look for? Do you read fiction hoping to find facts, or to be entertained? Although we learn a great deal when we read fiction, most of us read for the story—to "find out what happens"—or because we're interested in the characters. The questions on prose fiction passages ask about the kinds of things you pay attention to when you read a short story or novel—plot, characters, and mood, among other things.

As you read a prose fiction passage, don't just note events. Try to be aware of the passage's mood or tone, the relationships of the characters, and the emotion implied by what the characters say as well as how they say it. An author often uses dialogue not only to explain a situation to a reader, but also to reveal character. Refer to the sample passages on pages 91 and 92 for examples of the type of prose fiction passage you can expect on the ACT Reading Test.

Humanities

Humanities passages describe or analyze ideas or works of art. Although some humanities passages taken from memoirs or personal essays may seem a bit like prose fiction passages, there is one important difference: the memoirs and personal essays are written as fact, and prose fiction is, well, fiction.

Humanities passages present information, but you'll also need to pay attention to the author and his or her point of view. Sometimes, a question will ask you to project the author's likely response to a hypothetical argument or situation based on what the passage tells you about the author's opinions and what the language implies.

These passages might have characters, but they're not characters like those in a short story. Rather, they're historical figures or contemporary people—people who have actually lived. In these passages, the kinds of relationships you'll be asked to infer or identify are those between events, ideas, people, trends, or modes of thought. Refer to the sample passage on page 95 for an example of the type of humanities passage you can expect on the ACT Reading Test.

Social Studies

Social studies passages typically present information gathered by research. A social studies passage might be about Japanese history or political action committees or a psychological experiment. You'll find names, dates, and concepts in these passages. You'll also need to pay close attention to what name goes with what concept in a discussion of political systems and to keep track of who said what in a passage discussing different views of a constitutional amendment. Watch for cause-effect relationships, comparisons, and sequences of events. Pay careful attention to the specifics, especially the way in which they help you shape an idea of the passage's subject. Refer to the sample passages on pages 93 and 94 for examples of the type of social studies passage you can expect on the ACT Reading Test.

Natural Sciences

This kind of passage usually presents a science topic and an explanation of the topic's significance. A natural sciences passage requires a different sort of analysis than a prose fiction passage. For instance, in a natural sciences passage, the author is typically concerned with the relationships between natural phenomena, not the relationships between characters. As with social studies passages, you should pay special attention to cause-effect relationships, comparisons, and sequences of events. Keep track of any specific laws, rules, and theories that are mentioned, but don't try to memorize them.

Many of the Reading Test's nonfiction passages, especially natural sciences passages, will include some specialized or technical language. Don't let new words throw you. If knowing the meaning of a word is necessary to answer a question, the passage will provide clues to the word's meaning. Do your best to figure out the meaning from the context, and then go on. Don't devote extra time to a single word unless it comes up later in one of the questions. Refer to the sample passages on pages 96 and 97 for examples of the type of natural sciences passage you can expect on the ACT Reading Test.

Types of Questions on the ACT Reading Test

On the Reading Test, all of the questions fall into one of two basic categories: referring and reasoning. **Referring** questions ask you to find or use information that is clearly stated in the passage. **Reasoning** questions ask you to do more: they ask you to take information that's either stated or implied in the passage and use it to answer more complex questions.

You shouldn't worry about these categories while you're taking the Reading Test. It's most important that you focus on the questions themselves and on what they ask you about a given passage. Because each passage is different, the kinds of questions you see will vary from passage to passage. Still, there are some general types of questions you're likely to encounter. Most questions will ask you to do one of the following:

- identify and interpret details

- determine the main idea of a paragraph, paragraphs, or a passage

- understand comparative relationships (comparisons and contrasts)

- understand cause-effect relationships

- make generalizations

- determine the meaning of words from context

- understand sequences of events

- draw conclusions about the author's voice and method

This list gives you an idea of what kinds of questions are asked most frequently on the Reading Test. Sometimes, the Reading Test contains other types of questions, but don't worry. Just make sure you read each passage and its questions carefully. You'll find that the information you need to determine the best answer for a question is always available in the passage. Questions that illustrate each of the most common types of questions on the Reading Test follow.

Representative ACT Reading Test Questions

Details. Some test questions ask you to pick out a detail from a passage. A detail can be something as seemingly simple as a characteristic of a person, place, or thing, or a particular date. Other questions of this type require you to do a bit more interpreting of minor or subtly stated details, as in the following example, based on a social studies passage on Eleanor Roosevelt (ER), which is found on page 93:

---

1. The passage states that ER believed the relationship between a people and their government should be:
   - **A.** begun and carried out as if it were an isolated, individualist adventure.
   - **B.** formed and modeled by the White House.
   - **C.** based on organized, widespread citizen participation.
   - **D.** controlled through radio broadcasts and formal channels.

You'll have to look around the passage for the information you need—not unusual for this kind of question. According to the author, ER's "abiding conviction . . . was that nothing good would happen to promote the people's interest unless the people themselves organized to demand government responses" (lines 55–58). Because ER felt "a people's movement required active citizen participation" (lines 58–59), it's clear that C is the best answer. A, B, and D violate the spirit of the quoted lines: ER wanted collective action and active citizen participation, not isolated individualism (**A**), White House domination (**B**), or control through radio broadcasts and formal channels (**D**).

Questions about details sometimes ask you to find the one detail that does **not** support a particular point. Such questions are usually signaled by words such as NOT and EXCEPT. You need to pay careful attention to these questions. When you answer them, remember that the usual question format is being reversed. Here's an example of this kind of "reverse" question, based on a prose fiction passage about a girl and her friend Eugene (page 91):

> **2.** Which of the following questions is NOT answered by information in the passage?
>   **F.** Has the narrator ever walked around inside Eugene's house?
>   **G.** What hobby or interest do Eugene and the narrator share?
>   **H.** What makes Eugene's house different from other houses on the block?
>   **J.** What careers other than teaching has the narrator considered pursuing?

Three of the questions presented in the answer choices are answered by the passage, while the fourth one—the one you're looking for—isn't. Of the four, the only question **not** answered by the passage is **J**: we never learn what other careers besides teaching the narrator has considered pursuing. All three of the other questions are answered in the passage. We learn from lines 81–82 that although the narrator has watched the house "for so many years," she only dreams about going inside, ruling out **F**. We know from lines 39–40 and lines 63–66 that Eugene and the narrator are both interested in books, so **G** is out. According to the narrator, Eugene's house is "the only house on the block that had a yard and trees" (lines 5–6), so **H**, too, is incorrect.

Detail questions aren't the only kind of question that can make use of the "reverse" format. Don't worry, though—just watch for words such as NOT and EXCEPT in questions, and you'll be fine.

Main Ideas. To answer this kind of question, you need to be able to determine the focus of a passage or of a paragraph or paragraphs in a passage. You shouldn't count on finding this information summed up in the first paragraph of a passage or in the first sentence of a paragraph. You may have been advised to make the first sentence of each paragraph the "topic sentence" in your own writing, but not every writer does that. You'll need to figure out what the author's main point is in one or more paragraphs or in an entire passage by reading the paragraph(s) or passage carefully.

Main idea questions can be fairly straightforward. The following question, based on a social studies passage about the development of perceptual abilities (page 94), is pretty direct:

> **3.** The main point of the passage is that:
>   **A.** during the first four to seven months of life, babies learn at an accelerated pace.
>   **B.** organisms deprived of critical life experiences may or may not develop normal sensory performance.
>   **C.** the development of perceptual abilities is the result of the interaction between nature and experience.
>   **D.** research concerned with physical skills and abilities adds little to our knowledge of the growth of the mind.

The idea that the interaction between nature and experience shapes the development of perceptual abilities (C) is the clear focus of the entire passage. In the first paragraph, the author says that "the ancient central question of psychology" is "how much is due to nature and how much to nurture (or, in developmental terms, to maturation and to learning)" (lines 5–8). The second through eighth paragraphs (lines 9–85) describe research designed to help answer this question as it relates to the development of perceptual abilities in children. The last paragraph sums up the passage by saying that this research helps us "catch the first glimpse of how mind is constructed out of matter by experience" (lines 88–89). Though in lines 50–53 the author describes the rapid development of infants between four and seven months old, this is only a minor part of the passage, so **A** is incorrect. The seventh paragraph (lines 61–73) does mention that organisms can be permanently harmed if they miss critical life experiences, but this, also, isn't the main point of the passage, making **B** incorrect. **D** is just plain wrong: the whole passage deals with how research on physical skills and abilities has added to our knowledge of the growth of the mind.

As that example shows, you may have to rule out answer choices that are either supporting (rather than main) ideas or that simply misstate what the passage says. Both types of wrong answers appear in this next example, based on the natural sciences passage about lightning and fire (page 96):

---

4. One of the main points of the third paragraph (lines 41–61) is that:

   F. Arizona researchers record tree mortality by volume.
   G. tree mortality rates fail to capture the true extent of lightning-inflicted damage.
   H. ponderosa pine trees are resistant to secondary diseases.
   J. pine tree forests draw fewer lightning strikes than many other habitat types in Arizona.

G is the best answer here. Tree mortality rates "describe only direct injury" to trees (line 56), but lightning can also kill trees indirectly by making them vulnerable to insects, wind, and mistletoe and by causing fires. While F is true, according to lines 54–56, the fact that Arizona researchers record tree mortality by volume is a minor point. The paragraph never says that ponderosa pine trees are resistant to secondary diseases or that pine tree forests draw fewer lightning strikes than do many other habitat types in Arizona, so both **H** and **J** are incorrect.

Some questions for prose fiction or humanities passages will use phrases such as "main conflict" or "main theme" instead of "main idea," but you should approach the questions in the same way as you would other main idea questions. Here's an example based on a prose fiction passage about a young woman, Cally Roy (page 92):

---

5. The main conflict in this passage could best be described as the:

   A. tension between the narrator's mother and Frank.
   B. hostility expressed between the narrator and her mother.
   C. narrator's efforts to break her ties to her mother and grandmothers.
   D. narrator's internal struggle to connect with her past and find her future.

You have to read the whole passage carefully to sort out what the main conflict is because there's at least some truth to all of the answer choices. **D** turns out to be the best of the four choices because the main conflict is within the narrator herself. She journeys away from home and "into the city's bloody heart" (lines 18–19), she wonders "about the meaning of [her] spirit name" (line 22), she feels out of place in her too-big "Frankenstein body" (line 76), and she ends the passage torn between her "city corner" and her life "back home" (lines 82–83). The narrator says her mother loves Frank "too much to live with" him (lines 36–37) and also that Frank "can't drag himself away from the magnetic field of mother's voice" (lines 68–69), but the tension between the narrator's mother and Frank isn't the main conflict of the passage, making **A** wrong. There could be some hostility between the narrator and her mother because the narrator doesn't seem to want to go to the tribal college like her mother wants her to (see lines 79–82), but the narrator also wants to "curl next to her and be a small girl again" (lines 74–75), so mother-daughter hostility isn't the main conflict, either, ruling out **B**. **C** misses the mark because while the narrator has left her home and her mother, her grandmothers are only briefly talked about in the passage (see lines 24–33), so the main conflict can't revolve around them.

Comparative Relationships. You're likely to find questions asking you to make comparisons and contrasts in passages that contain a lot of information or that feature multiple characters or points of view. This kind of test question can make you process a lot of information—you may be asked to weigh one concept against another and identify a significant difference between the two. But comparison and contrast questions aren't always overly complicated. In the following example, based on a humanities passage about the nature of work (page 95), the comparison is directly made in a few lines in the passage:

---

6. According to the author, the significant difference between a bread-maker and a bread pan is that only one:
   F. was used by previous generations.
   G. came on the market in recent years.
   H. goes in the oven when the dough is prepared.
   J. diminishes the human role in making bread.

Lines 1–3 state, "The difference between a machine and a tool—between a bread-maker and a bread pan—is that a tool extends human skills, a machine replaces them." Thus, **J** is the best answer. None of the other three answer choices is mentioned in the passage: the author never says that the significant difference between a bread-maker and a bread pan is that one was used by previous generations (**F**), came on the market in recent years (**G**), or goes in the oven when the dough is prepared (**H**).

Not all comparative relationships questions are this direct, however. This next example, based on the same passage, shows that this type of question can get more complicated, especially when the question is in the "reverse" format discussed in the Details section:

> **7.** In the third paragraph (lines 24–42), the author alludes to but apparently does NOT share the point of view of which of the following?
>
> **A.** Neighbors who live as if work is a kind of celebration
> **B.** The official who wants to shrink welfare rolls
> **C.** Those who believe that "the creation is a sacred gift"
> **D.** One who mends rather than replaces torn clothing

Here you have to not only determine the author's point of view, but also compare his perspective to those of other people mentioned in the third paragraph. The author thinks that the idea of a work ethic "has lost its edge from tumbling over the lips of too many cynical bosses and politicians" (lines 26–27). It's reasonable to conclude that the author doesn't agree with these bosses and politicians, including "the official who wants to shrink the welfare rolls" (lines 30–31), so **B** is the best answer. It's also reasonable to conclude from the paragraph that the author shares the point of view of the people mentioned in **A**, **C**, and **D**. In lines 34–39, the author identifies himself with neighbors and others who share "a belief that the creation is a sacred gift, and that by working we express our gratitude and celebrate our powers" (**A** and **C**). In lines 39–42, he says that part of honoring that gift is "patching clothes" (**D**).

Cause-Effect Relationships. Cause-effect questions can be asked about prose fiction passages—sometimes one character's actions cause another character to react a certain way. Cause-effect questions also can arise in natural sciences passages in which a process is described. Sometimes the answer to a cause-effect question is stated in the passage; sometimes you have to put together the information you've read and work out the answer on your own.

Here's an example of a fairly direct cause-effect question, based on the prose fiction passage about Cally Roy:

> **8.** The narrator implies that losing her indis has caused her to:
>
> **F.** cling to her family.
> **G.** leave her home.
> **H.** remember its every detail.
> **J.** fight with her family.

The information needed to answer this question is in the first paragraph: once the narrator lost her indis, she says, she "began to wander from home, first in my thoughts, then my feet took after" (lines 11–13). **G** is therefore the best answer. **F** is pretty much the opposite of the truth, in the sense that the narrator decided to leave home. While the narrator says she "remember[s] every detail" of her indis (line 5), this isn't because she lost it but because "the turtle hung near my crib, then off my belt, and was my very first play toy" (lines 5–7). So **H** can't be the best answer. **J** is incorrect because the narrator never really implies that losing her indis has caused her to fight with her family. While her mother was "in a panic" (line 27) over the narrator's decision to leave, this seems more out of concern for the narrator than the result of a fight.

Below is an example of a somewhat more complex cause-effect question, this time based on the natural sciences passage on lightning and fire:

---

9. The third paragraph (lines 41–61) suggests that if lightning did not fix atmospheric nitrogen, then:
   A. rain could not fall to earth, leaving nitrogen in the atmosphere.
   B. less nitrogen would be found on earth.
   C. electrical current could not be conducted by air.
   D. lightning bolts would strike the earth with less frequency.

Although the question lets you know to look in the third paragraph, the wording of that paragraph is subtle and requires close reading. The relevant information is in lines 45–46: "Lightning helps to fix atmospheric nitrogen into a form that rain can bring to earth." This matches nicely with B, which says that less nitrogen would be found on earth. Although nitrogen would remain in the atmosphere if lightning didn't fix it, the paragraph never suggests that rain wouldn't fall to earth, making A tempting but wrong. The paragraph doesn't suggest that if lightning didn't fix atmospheric nitrogen, electrical current couldn't be conducted by air or that lightning bolts would strike the earth with less frequency, making C and D incorrect.

Generalizations. This type of question usually asks you to take a lot of information—sometimes the whole passage—and boil it down into a more concise form. A generalization question may involve interpreting mood, tone, or character, or it may ask you to make some kind of general observation or draw a conclusion about the nature of an argument the author is making. The following example, based on the social studies passage about Eleanor Roosevelt, focuses on personality or character:

---

10. As she is revealed in the passage, ER is best described as:
   F. socially controversial but quietly cooperative.
   G. politically courageous and socially concerned.
   H. morally strong and deeply traditional.
   J. personally driven but calmly moderate.

This question requires you to sum up the complex personality of Eleanor Roosevelt in just a few short words. The best answer is G, because examples of ER being politically courageous and socially concerned are found all over the passage. The fourth paragraph (lines 20–25), for instance, reveals that as First Lady, "she upset race traditions, championed a New Deal for women, and on certain issues actually ran a parallel administration" to the one her husband, Franklin Delano Roosevelt, ran as president of the United States. While ER "is the most controversial First Lady in United States history" (lines 1–2) and though she believed in collective action and "united democratic movements for change" (lines 61–62), it would be wrong to say, as F does, that "socially controversial but quietly cooperative" is the best description of ER. The passage implies that there was very little quiet about ER. She clearly wasn't deeply traditional, so H is out. Like F, J is a tempting choice because it's in some ways true but, again, not the best description of ER. Although she was personally driven and supported the idea of a "middle way" (line 54) between fascism and communism, **J** wrongly states that ER was calmly moderate. She was, in fact, someone who challenged long-held traditions and created great controversy by doing so.

Meanings of Words. Questions about meanings of words ask you to determine from context what a particular word, phrase, or statement most nearly means. In some cases, the word or words will probably be unfamiliar to you, but even when familiar words are tested, you'll have to look at the context in which they appear to determine the closest synonym or paraphrase. Sometimes, looking at a single sentence of the passage is enough to figure this out, but other times, you'll have to look at sentences ahead of or after the given word, phrase, or statement in order to determine the closest meaning.

Many meanings of words questions will focus on a single word or a short phrase. The answer choices will include synonyms for the word or phrase that you might find in a dictionary or thesaurus, but only one of the choices will truly reflect how the word or phrase is used in this particular case. Look at the following example, based on the natural sciences passage about lightning and fire:

---

11. The *process of "electrocution"* mentioned in line 62 most nearly refers to:
   A. the ignition of rotten wood and pine needles.
   B. accidental death by electrical current.
   C. a lightning strike of a tree.
   D. the scorching of plants by lightning.

If you just looked at the question without looking at the passage, **B** might be an attractive choice because this is how the word *electrocution* is often used in everyday life. But **B** makes little sense in the context of the fourth paragraph (lines 62–70), which discusses how lightning scorches plants, so the best answer is **D**. Scorching isn't the same thing as igniting, and the paragraph doesn't mention rotten wood or pine needles, so **A** is incorrect. **C** isn't the best answer, either, because lines 64–65 state that the process of "electrocution" isn't "limited to trees."

Sometimes meanings of words questions will ask you to paraphrase an entire statement, as in the following example, taken from the prose fiction passage about a girl and her friend Eugene:

---

12. When the narrator says, "I begin to think of the present more than of the future" (lines 80–81), she most likely means that meeting Eugene led her to:
   F. shift some of her attention away from her career plans and onto the developing friendship.
   G. think more about her own work interests than about the career her parents thought she should pursue.
   H. put off her plans of returning to Puerto Rico for a visit in favor of continuing to prepare for college.
   J. want to spend more time with him instead of helping her parents plan a vacation to Puerto Rico.

All of the answer choices describe possible shifts from the future to the present, but only one, **F**, fits the context of the passage. While in the sixth paragraph (lines 67–79) the narrator discusses her parents' dreams and her own plans to go to college and become a teacher ("the future"), the last paragraph shows the narrator shifting some of her attention to her friendship with Eugene ("the present"). She wants to go into Eugene's house and sit at the kitchen table with him "like two adults" (lines 85–86). **G** is wrong because she's shifting attention away from her work interests and because we don't know what career her parents thought she should pursue. **H**, too, is incorrect: the narrator doesn't say she's had plans to return to Puerto Rico, and she's thinking less, not more, about preparing for college. While the narrator does want to spend more time with Eugene, she hasn't been helping her parents plan a vacation to Puerto Rico—the sixth paragraph only says that her parents would like to retire there someday—so **J** is incorrect.

Sequence of Events. In some passages, the order, or sequence, in which events happen is important. Sequence of events questions ask you to determine when, for example, a character in a prose fiction passage did something or to figure out the order in which the researchers described in a natural sciences passage performed certain steps in a biology experiment.

Speaking of natural sciences, the following question, based on a passage about the small-comet theory (page 97), requires a pretty straightforward ordering of events:

---

13. According to the passage, the research that led to the development of the small-comet theory began with a project originally intended to study:
    A. the electrical activity accompanying sunspots.
    B. water entering Earth's upper atmosphere.
    C. static in satellite transmissions.
    D. specks in satellite images.

The author indicates that Frank and Sigwarth were analyzing "photos of the electrical phenomena that accompany sunspots" when "they noted dark specks appearing in several images from NASA's Dynamics Explorer 1 satellite" (lines 46–48). These specks started Frank and Sigwarth toward their small-comet theory, as the rest of the passage reveals. Thus, **A** is the best answer. The other answer choices are related to Frank and Sigwarth's research, but none of them names the original study. Lines 55–58 show that **B** is incorrect: the two scientists decided that water was entering Earth's upper atmosphere in the form of small comets only after they'd examined photos of the electrical phenomena accompanying sunspots. The author says that static in the satellite transmission was the first hypothesis Frank and Sigwarth came up with to explain the dark specks (lines 49–50), but the photos in which the specks appeared were originally taken to study sunspot-related activity, so **C** is incorrect. **D** is likewise incorrect because the specks Frank and Sigwarth found were in photos originally taken as part of a study of sunspot-related activity.

The social studies passage on the development of perceptual abilities is challenging in part because you have to keep clear in your mind when certain abilities develop in infants. The following question, based on that passage, deals with that very point:

> **14.** It is reasonable to infer from the passage that one-month-old babies will demonstrate which of the following skills?
>
> **F.** Noticing the difference between a pale yellow rattle and a bright yellow rattle
> **G.** Recognizing each of their older brothers and sisters as individuals
> **H.** Glancing from their father's face to their mother's face and back to their father again
> **J.** Following a wooden butterfly on a slow-moving mobile hanging above their bed

What makes this question harder is that the examples provided in the answer choices aren't specifically found in the passage. You have to infer from the information given in the passage which of the four answer choices is most likely, given the age of the child. In this case, the best answer is **J**. Lines 39–40 state that "during the first month [infants] begin to track slowly moving objects." It's reasonable to infer from this that a one-month-old baby would be able to follow a wooden butterfly on a slow-moving mobile hanging above his or her head. **F**, **G**, and **J** are perceptual abilities that develop later. The ability to "differentiate among hues and levels of brightness" (lines 42–43) doesn't begin to develop until "the second month" (lines 40–41), meaning a one-month-old is unlikely to be able to note the difference between a pale yellow rattle and a bright yellow rattle (**F**). The ability to "glance from one object to another, and . . . distinguish among family members" (lines 44–45) doesn't emerge until three months, so a one-month-old couldn't recognize each of his or her older siblings as individuals (**G**) or glance from father to mother and back again (**H**).

Author's Voice and Method. Finally, there are questions that deal with the author's voice and method. *Voice* relates to such things as the author's style, attitude, and point of view, while *method* focuses on the craft of writing—the main purpose of a piece of writing, what role parts of a piece (such as a paragraph) play in the whole work, and so on.

A couple of examples should help clear up what this category is about. The first, taken from the social studies passage on Eleanor Roosevelt, asks you to consider what hypothetical statement the author would most likely agree with:

> **15.** According to the last paragraph, which of the following statements would the author most likely make with regard to ER's vision and ideals?
>
> **A.** ER considered politics a game and played only when she knew she could win.
> **B.** ER worked with agitators and remained dedicated to the pursuit of justice and peace in victory and defeat.
> **C.** ER placed herself in the position of president, making decisions that determined White House policy.
> **D.** ER saw herself as the country's role model and personally responsible for bringing about change.

All of the ideas in **B**—though not quite in those words—can be found in the last paragraph: ER "brought her network of agitators and activists into the White House" (lines 90–91), "worked with movements for justice and peace" (lines 87–88), and "never considered a political setback a permanent defeat" (lines 91–92). **A** is incorrect because although ER "enjoyed the game" (line 93), she saw defeat as only temporary, meaning she stuck with politics, win or lose. **C** goes well beyond what the last paragraph (or the rest of the passage, for that matter) says about ER. She never placed herself in the position of the president, even if, as the author pointed out earlier, "ER made decisions and engineered policy" (line 25) in some areas. **D** is incorrect for the same kind of reason: neither the last paragraph nor the passage as a whole says that ER saw herself as the country's role model and personally responsible for bringing about change. Though she lobbied for her views "in countless auditoriums, as a radio broadcaster, and in monthly, weekly, and, by 1936, daily columns" (lines 41–43), she also strongly believed in "active citizen participation" (line 59) in government.

A second example, based on the prose fiction passage about a girl and her friend Eugene, deals with the contribution two paragraphs make to the story:

---

16. In terms of developing the narrative, the last two paragraphs (lines 67–87) primarily serve to:
    F. provide background details about the narrator and her family in order to highlight the narrator's unique and shifting perspective.
    G. describe the narrator's family in order to establish a contrast between her parents and Eugene's parents.
    H. portray the narrator's family in order to show how her friendship with Eugene affected the various members of her family.
    J. depict the hopes and dreams of the narrator's parents in order to show how her parents' aspirations changed over time.

To answer this question correctly, you have to consider not only what the last two paragraphs of the passage say, but also their role in advancing the story. **F** is the best answer here. We learn in the sixth paragraph (lines 67–79) about the parents' dreams and how narrator's plans (going to college and becoming a teacher) differ, suggesting she has a unique perspective. The last paragraph emphasizes how the narrator's perspective has shifted from focusing on "the future" to focusing on "the present." **F** is easier to see when you consider the place of the last two paragraphs in the whole passage—lines 67–87 help shift the focus from the narrator's meetings with Eugene to her reflection on how her friendship with Eugene has changed her life. **G** is incorrect because while the second paragraph (lines 27–42) describes Eugene's parents and the sixth paragraph describes the narrator's parents, no direct contrast is made between the two sets of parents. There's also no indication in the passage that the narrator's friendship with Eugene affects her family at all (or that they even know about it), making **H** a poor choice. **J** is wrong because the only discussion of the narrator's parents' aspirations is in the sixth paragraph, and there's no suggestion that these aspirations changed over time.

Strategies for Taking the ACT Reading Test

Pace Yourself

Before you read the first passage of the Reading Test, you may want to take a quick look through the entire Reading Test. If you choose to do this, flip through the pages and look at each of the passages and their questions. (Note that the passages begin on the pages to your left, and the questions follow.) You don't need to memorize anything—you can look at any of the Reading Test passages and questions during the time allotted for that test.

Some readers find that looking quickly at the questions first gives them a better idea of what to look for as they're reading the passage. If you're a slow reader, though, this may not be a good strategy. If you do decide to preview the questions, don't spend too much time on them—just scan for a few key words or ideas that you can watch for when you read the passage. To see what approach works best for you, you might want to try alternating between previewing the questions and not previewing the questions as you work through the practice tests in this book. Remember that when you take the ACT for real, a clock will be running. Plan your approach for the Reading Test before you take the actual ACT.

Before you begin your careful reading of each passage, here are some more things you'll want to remember:

Use the Time Allotted

You have 35 minutes to read four passages and answer 40 questions. You'll want to pace yourself so you don't spend too much time on any one passage or question. If you take 2 to 3 minutes to read each passage, you'll have about 35 seconds to answer each question associated with the passage. Some of the questions will take less time, which will allow you more time for the more challenging ones.

Because time is limited, you should be very careful in deciding whether to skip more difficult questions. If you skip the difficult questions from the first passage until you work through the entire Reading Test, for example, you may find that you've forgotten so much of the first passage that you have to reread it before you can answer the questions that puzzled you the first time through. It will probably work better for you to think of the test as four $8\frac{1}{2}$-minute units and to try to complete all the questions for a passage within its allotted time. Answer all the questions; you're not penalized for guessing.

Think of an Overall Strategy That Works for You

Are you the kind of person who likes to get the big picture first, then carefully go over your work? Do you like to answer the questions you're sure of right away and then go back and puzzle out the tougher ones? Or are you something of a perfectionist? (Do you find it hard to concentrate on a question until you know you got the one before it right?) There isn't any right way or wrong way to approach the Reading Test—just make sure the way you choose is the way that works best for you.

Keep the Passage as a Whole in Mind

Your initial look at the whole Reading Test should give you some ideas about how to approach each passage. Notice that there are short paragraphs with subject headings in front of each passage. These "advance organizers" tell you the subject matter of the passage, where the passage comes from, who wrote it, and sometimes a little information about the passage. Occasionally, an advance organizer will define a difficult word, explain a concept, or provide background information. Reading the advance organizers carefully should help you be more prepared as you approach each passage.

Always remember that the Reading Test asks you to refer and reason on the basis of the passage. You may know a lot about the subject of some of the passages you read, but try not to let what you already know influence the way you answer the questions, as the author may have a different perspective than you. There's a reason why many questions begin with "According to the passage" or "It can reasonably be inferred from the passage." If you read and understand the passage well, the rest will take care of itself. During the Reading Test, you can refer back to the passages as often as you like.

Find a Strategy for Approaching Each Question

First, you should read each question carefully so you know what it asks. Look for the best answer, but read and consider all the options, even though you may feel you've identified the best one. Ask yourself whether you can justify your choice as the best answer.

Some people find it useful to answer the easy questions first and skip the difficult ones (being careful, of course, to mark the answer document correctly and to mark in the test booklet the questions they skipped). Then they go back and consider the difficult questions. When you're working on a test question and aren't certain about the answer, try to eliminate choices you're sure are incorrect. If you can rule out a couple of choices, you'll improve your chances of getting the question right. Keep referring back to the passage for information.

Reading Strategies Summary

The sample passages used as examples in this section can be found on the following pages. They come from ACTs that thousands of students have already taken. Remember, the passages in this section don't represent every type you're likely to see, but they should give you a good idea of the kinds of questions you'll see when you take the ACT Reading Test. If you want a more complete picture of what the ACT Reading Test will look like, there are five complete Reading Tests included in the five practice ACTs in chapter 4. And remember that the best way to do well on the ACT Reading Test is to have a solid understanding of each passage—so read quickly but carefully.

Sample Passage I

PROSE FICTION: This passage is adapted from the short story "American History" by Judith Ortiz-Cofer (©1992 by Judith Ortiz-Cofer). The story appeared in the anthology *Iguana Dreams: New Latino Fiction.*

There was only one source of beauty and light for me my ninth grade year. The only thing I had antici-pated at the start of the semester. That was seeing Eugene. In August, Eugene and his family had moved
5 into the only house on the block that had a yard and trees. I could see his place from my bedroom window in El Building. In fact, if I sat on the fire escape I was liter-ally suspended above Eugene's backyard. It was my favorite spot to read my library books in the summer.
10 Until that August the house had been occupied by an old couple. Over the years I had become part of their family, without their knowing it, of course. I had a view of their kitchen and their backyard, and though I could not hear what they said, I knew when they were arguing,
15 when one of them was sick, and many other things. I knew all this by watching them at mealtimes. I could see their kitchen table, the sink, and the stove. During good times, he sat at the table and read his newspapers while she fixed the meals. If they argued, he would leave and
20 the old woman would sit and stare at nothing for a long time. When one of them was sick, the other would come and get things from the kitchen and carry them out on a tray. The old man had died in June. The house had stood empty for weeks. I had had to resist the temptation to
25 climb down into the yard and water the flowers the old lady had taken such good care of.

By the time Eugene's family moved in, the yard was a tangled mass of weeds. The father had spent sev-eral days mowing, and when he finished, from where I
30 sat, I didn't see the red, yellow, and purple clusters that meant flowers to me. I didn't see this family sit down at the kitchen table together. It was just the mother, a red-headed tall woman who wore a white uniform; the father was gone before I got up in the morning and was
35 never there at dinner time. I only saw him on weekends when they sometimes sat on lawn-chairs under the oak tree, each hidden behind a section of the newspaper; and there was Eugene. He was tall and blond, and he wore glasses. I liked him right away because he sat at
40 the kitchen table and read books for hours. That summer, before we had even spoken one word to each other, I kept him company on my fire escape.

Once school started I looked for him in all my classes, but P. S. 13 was a huge place and it took me
45 days and many discreet questions to discover Eugene. After much maneuvering I managed "to run into him" in the hallway where his locker was—on the other side of the building from mine—and in study hall at the library where he first seemed to notice me, but did not
50 speak; and finally, on the way home after school one day when I decided to approach him directly, though my stomach was doing somersaults.

I was ready for rejection, snobbery, the worst. But when I came up to him and blurted out: "You're

55 Eugene. Right?" he smiled, pushed his glasses up on his nose, and nodded. I saw then that he was blushing deeply. Eugene liked me, but he was shy. I did most of the talking that day. He nodded and smiled a lot. In the weeks that followed, we walked home together. He
60 would linger at the corner of El Building for a few min-utes then walk down to his house.

I did not tell Eugene that I could see inside his kitchen from my bedroom. I felt dishonest, but I liked my secret sharing of his evenings, especially now that I
65 knew what he was reading since we chose our books together at the school library.

I also knew my mother was unhappy in Paterson, New Jersey, but my father had a good job at the blue-jeans factory in Passaic and soon, he kept assuring us,
70 we would be moving to our own house there. I had learned to listen to my parents' dreams, which were spoken in Spanish, as fairy tales, like the stories about life in Puerto Rico before I was born. I had been to the island once as a little girl. We had not been back there
75 since then, though my parents talked constantly about buying a house on the beach someday, retiring on the island—that was a common topic among the residents of El Building. As for me, I was going to go to college and become a teacher.

80 But after meeting Eugene I began to think of the present more than of the future. What I wanted now was to enter that house I had watched for so many years. I wanted to see the other rooms where the old people had lived, and where the boy spent his time. Most of all, I
85 wanted to sit at the kitchen table with Eugene like two adults, like the old man and his wife had done, maybe drink some coffee and talk about books.

Sample Passage II

PROSE FICTION: This passage is adapted from *The Antelope Wife* by Louise Erdrich (©1998 by Louise Erdrich).

My mother sewed my birth cord, with dry sage and sweet grass, into a turtle holder of soft white buckskin. She beaded that little turtle using precious old cobalts and yellows and Cheyenne pinks and greens in a careful
5 design. I remember every detail of it, me, because the turtle hung near my crib, then off my belt, and was my very first play toy. I was supposed to have it on me all my life, bury it with me on reservation land, but one day I came in from playing and my indis was gone.
10 I thought nothing of it, at first and for many years, but slowly over time the absence . . . it will tell. I began to wander from home, first in my thoughts, then my feet took after, so at last at the age of eighteen, I walked the road that led from the front of our place to the wider
15 spaces and then the country beyond that, where that one road widened into two lanes, then four, then six, past the farms and service islands, into the dead wall of the suburbs and still past that, finally, into the city's bloody heart.

20 My name is Cally Roy. Ozhawashkwamashkodeykway is what the spirits call me. All my life so far I've wondered about the meaning of my spirit name but nobody's told it, seen it, got ahold of my history flying past. Mama has asked, she has offered tobacco, even
25 blankets, but my grandmas Mrs. Zosie Roy and Mary Shawano only nod at her, holding their tongues as they let their eyes wander. In a panic, once she knew I was setting out, not staying home, Mama tried to call up my grandmas and ask if I could live at their apartment in
30 the city. But once they get down to the city, it turns out they never stop moving. They are out, and out again. Impossible to track down. It's true, they are extremely busy women.

So my mom sends me to Frank.

35 Frank Shawano. Famous Indian bakery chef. My Mama's eternal darling, the man she loves too much to live with.

I'm weary and dirty and sore when I get to Frank's bakery shop, but right away, walking in and the bell
40 dinging with a cheerful alertness, I smell those good bakery smells of yeasty bread and airy sugar. Behind the counter, lemony light falls on Frank. He is big, strong, pale brown like a loaf of light rye left to rise underneath a towel. His voice is muffled and weak, like
45 it is squeezed out of the clogged end of a pastry tube. He greets me with gentle pleasure.

"Just as I'm closing." His smile is very quiet. He cleans his hands on a towel and beckons me into the back of the bakery shop, between swinging steel doors.
50 I remember him as a funny man, teasing and playing games and rolling his eyes at us, making his pink sugar-cookie dogs bark and elephants trumpet. But now he is serious, and frowns slightly as I follow him up the back

stairs and into the big top-floor apartment with the
55 creaky floors, the groaning pipes, odd windows that view the yard. My little back room, no bigger than a closet, overlooks this space.

I'm so beat, though, I just want to crawl into my corner and sleep.

60 "Not too small, this place?" He sounds anxious.

I shake my head. The room seems okay, the mattress on the floor, the blankets, and the shelves for my things.

"Call your mom?" Frank gives orders in the form
65 of a question. He acts all purposeful, as though he is going back downstairs to close up the store, but as I dial the number on the kitchen wall phone he lingers. He can't drag himself away from the magnetic field of my mother's voice, muffled, far off, but on the other
70 end of the receiver. He stands in the doorway with that same towel he brought from downstairs, folding and refolding it in his hands.

"Mama," I say, and her voice on the phone suddenly hurts. I want to curl next to her and be a small
75 girl again. My body feels too big, electric, like a Frankenstein body enclosing a tiny child's soul.

We laugh at some corny joke and Frank darts a glance at me, then stares at his feet and frowns. Reading between my Mama's pauses on the phone, I
80 know she is hoping I'll miss the real land, and her, come back and resume my brilliant future at the tribal college. In spite of how I want to curl up in my city corner, I picture everything back home. On the wall of my room up north, there hang a bundle of sage and
85 Grandma Roy's singing drum. On the opposite wall, I taped up posters and photos. Ever since I was little, I slept with a worn bear and a new brown dog. And my real dog, too, curled at my feet sometimes, if Mama didn't catch us. I never liked dolls. I made good scores
90 in math. I get to missing my room and my dog and I lose track of Mama's voice.

Sample Passage III

SOCIAL SCIENCE: This passage is adapted from volume 2 of Blanche Wiesen Cook's biography *Eleanor Roosevelt* (©1999 by Blanche Wiesen Cook).

Eleanor Roosevelt [ER] is the most controversial First Lady in United States history. Her journey to greatness, her voyage out beyond the confines of good wife and devoted mother, involved determination and
5 amazing courage. It also involved one of history's most unique partnerships. Franklin Delano Roosevelt [FDR] admired his wife, appreciated her strengths, and depended on her integrity.

However, ER and FDR had different priorities,
10 occasionally competing goals, and often disagreed. In the White House they ran two distinct and separate courts.

By 1933 [her first year as First Lady], ER was an accomplished woman who had achieved several of her
15 life's goals. With her partners, ER was a businesswoman who co-owned the Val-Kill crafts factory, a political leader who edited and copublished the *Women's Democratic News,* and an educator who co-owned and taught at a New York school for girls.

20 As First Lady, Eleanor Roosevelt did things that had never been done before. She upset race traditions, championed a New Deal for women, and on certain issues actually ran a parallel administration. On housing and the creation of model communities, for
25 example, ER made decisions and engineered policy.

At the center of a network of influential women who ran the Women's Committee of the Democratic Party led by Molly Dewson, ER worked closely with the women who had dominated the nation's social
30 reform struggles for decades. With FDR's election, the goals of the great progressive pioneers, Jane Addams, Florence Kelley, and Lillian Wald, were at last at the forefront of the country's agenda. ER's mentors since 1903, they had battled on the margins of national poli-
35 tics since the 1880s for public health, universal education, community centers, sanitation programs, and government responsibility for the welfare of the nation's poor and neglected people.

Now their views were brought directly into the
40 White House. ER lobbied for them personally with her new administrative allies, in countless auditoriums, as a radio broadcaster, and in monthly, weekly, and, by 1936, daily columns. Called "Eleanor Everywhere," she was interested in everyone.

45 Every life was sacred and worthy, to be improved by education, employment, health care, and affordable housing. Her goal was simple, a life of dignity and decency for all. She was uninterested in complex theories, and demanded action for betterment. She feared
50 violent revolution, but was not afraid of socialism—and she courted radicals.

As fascism and communism triumphed in Europe and Asia, ER and FDR were certain that there was a middle way, what ER called an American "revolution
55 without bloodshed." Her abiding conviction, however, was that nothing good would happen to promote the people's interest unless the people themselves organized to demand government responses. A people's movement required active citizen participation, and
60 ER's self-appointed task was to agitate and inspire community action, encourage united democratic movements for change.

Between 1933 and 1938, while the Depression raged and the New Deal unfolded, ER worked with the
65 popular front. She called for alliances of activists to fight poverty and racism at home, and to oppose isolationism internationally.

Active with the women's peace movement, ER spoke regularly at meetings of the Women's Inter-
70 national League for Peace and Freedom, and the Conference on the Cause and Cure of War. She departed, however, from pacifist and isolationist positions and encouraged military preparedness, collective security, and ever-widening alliances.

75 Between 1933 and 1938 ER published countless articles and six books. She wrote in part for herself, to clear her mind and focus her thoughts. But she also wrote to disagree with her husband. From that time to this, no other First Lady has actually rushed for her pen
80 to jab her husband's public decisions. But ER did so routinely, including in her 1938 essay *This Troubled World,* which was a point-by-point rejection of FDR's major international decisions.

To contemplate ER's life of example and responsi-
85 bility is to forestall gloom. She understood, above all, that politics is not an isolated individualist adventure. She sought alliances, created community, worked with movements for justice and peace. Against great odds, and under terrific pressure, she refused to withdraw
90 from controversy. She brought her network of agitators and activists into the White House, and never considered a political setback a permanent defeat. She enjoyed the game, and weathered the abuse.

Sample Passage IV

SOCIAL SCIENCE: This passage is adapted from Morton Hunt's *The Story of Psychology* (©1993 by Morton Hunt). In the passage, the term *maturation* refers to the process of growth and development, and the term *perceptual ability* refers to the capacity to recognize something through the senses (sight, smell, touch, etc.).

Much maturation research is concerned with physical skills and physical attributes, and adds little to our knowledge of the growth of the mind. But research on the development of perceptual abilities begins to pro-
5 vide solid factual answers to the ancient central question of psychology: How much is due to nature and how much to nurture (or, in developmental terms, to maturation and to learning)?

The work has been focused on early infancy, when
10 perceptual abilities evolve rapidly; its aim is to discover when each new ability first appears, the assumption being that at its first appearance, the new ability arises not from learning but from maturation of the optic nervous structures and especially of that part of
15 the brain cortex where visual signals are received and interpreted.

Much has been learned by simply watching infants. What, exactly, do very young infants see? Since we cannot ask them what they see, how can we
20 find out?

In 1961, the psychologist Robert Fantz devised an ingenious method of doing so. He designed a stand in which, on the bottom level, the baby lies on her back, looking up. A few feet above is a display area where
25 the experimenter puts two large cards, each containing a design—a white circle, a yellow circle, a bull's-eye, a simple sketch of a face. The researcher, peering down through a tiny peephole, can watch the movement of the baby's eyes and time how long they are directed at
30 one or the other of each pair of patterns. Fantz found that at two months babies looked twice as long at a bull's-eye as at a circle of solid color, and twice as long at a sketch of a face as at a bull's-eye. Evidently, even a two-month-old can distinguish major differences and
35 direct her gaze toward what she finds more interesting.

Using this technique, developmental psychologists have learned a great deal about what infants see and when they begin to see it. In the first week infants distinguish light and dark patterns; during the first month
40 they begin to track slowly moving objects; by the second month they begin to have depth perception, coordinate the movement of the eyes, and differentiate among hues and levels of brightness; by three months they can glance from one object to another, and can dis-
45 tinguish among family members; by four months they focus at varying distances, make increasingly fine distinctions, and begin to recognize the meaning of what they see (they look longer at a normal sketch of a face than at one in which the features have been scrambled);
50 and from four to seven months they achieve stereopsis, recognize that a shape held at different angles is still the same shape, and gain near-adult ability to focus at varying distances.

Exactly how maturation and experience interact in
55 the brain tissues to produce such developmental changes is becoming clear from neuroscience research. Microscopic examination of the brains of infants shows that as the brain triples in size during the first two years of life, a profusion of dendrites (branches) grow from
60 its neurons and make contact with one another.

By the time a human is twelve, the brain has an estimated hundred trillion synapses (connections between nerve cells). Those connections are the wiring plan that establishes the brain's capabilities. Some of
65 the synaptic connections are made automatically by chemical guidance, but others are made by the stimulus of experience during the period of rapid dendrite growth. Lacking such stimulus, the dendrites wither away without forming the needed synapses. Mice
70 reared in the dark develop fewer dendritic spines and synaptic connections in the visual cortex than mice reared in the light, and even when exposed to light never attain normal vision.

Why should nature have done that? Why should
75 perceptual development be possible only at a critical period and not later? It does not make evolutionary sense for the organism to be permanently impaired in sensory performance just because it fails to have the proper experiences at specific times in its development.
80 But some brain researchers say that there is an offsetting advantage: the essential experiences are almost always available at the right time, and they fine-tune the brain structure so as to provide far more specific perceptual powers than could result from genetic con-
85 trol of synapse formation.

With that, the vague old terms nature and nurture take on precise new meaning. Now, after so many centuries of speculation, we catch the first glimpse of how mind is constructed out of matter by experience.

Sample Passage V

HUMANITIES: This passage is adapted from the essay "Faith and Work" by Scott Russell Sanders (©1995 by Scott Russell Sanders).

The difference between a machine and a tool—between a bread-maker and a bread pan—is that a tool extends human skills, a machine replaces them. When the freedom and craft have been squeezed out of work
5 it becomes toil, without mystery or meaning, and that is why many people hate their jobs. You can measure the drudgery of a job by the number of layers of supervision required to keep the wheels spinning or the cash registers ringing. Toil drains us; but good work may
10 renew us, by giving expression to our powers.

A generation or two ago it would have seemed less strange to relish hard work. My grandparents might smile at the laziness of Tom Sawyer, who fooled others into doing his chores, but they would remind you that
15 Tom was a child. Grown-ups do their own chores, unless they are idlers, good-for-nothings, ne'er-do-wells. Grown-ups look after their own needs, provide for their families, help their neighbors, do something useful. So my grandparents taught by word and
20 example. Any job worth doing is worth doing right, they used to say. To try sliding by with the least effort, my grandparents believed, was to be guilty of a sin called sloth.

I knew this cluster of values by experience long
25 before I heard it referred to as the work ethic, a phrase that has lost its edge from tumbling over the lips of too many cynical bosses and politicians. Whatever happened to the work ethic? laments the manager who wishes to squeeze more profit from his employees.
30 Whatever happened to the work ethic? groans the official who wants to shrink the welfare rolls. As I understand it, a regard for the necessity and virtue of work has nothing to do with productivity or taxes, and everything to do with fulfilling one's humanity. As I have
35 seen it embodied in the lives not only of grandparents but of parents and neighbors and friends, this ethic arises from a belief that the creation is a sacred gift, and that by working we express our gratitude and celebrate our powers. To honor that gift, we should live
40 simply, honestly, conservingly, saving money and patching clothes and fixing what breaks, sharing what we have.

Those values are under assault every minute of the day in a consumer economy—from advertising, from
45 the glittering goodies in stores, from the luxurious imagery of television, magazines, and films, and from a philosophy that views the universe not as a gift to be honored but as a warehouse to be ransacked. If money is meaning, if winning the lottery or beating the stock
50 market defines success, if the goal of life is easy sensation, then why lift a finger so long as you can force someone or something else to do it for you?

I can think of many reasons to lift a finger, among them the delight in exercising skill, in sharing labor

55 with companions, in planning a task and carrying it through, in bringing some benefit to the world. But the chief reason for relishing work is that it allows us to practice our faith, whatever that faith may be. The Buddha advised his followers to seek right livelihood,
60 to provide for their needs in a modest and responsible manner, with respect for other creatures, in harmony with the way of things. We show our understanding of the way of things by the quality of our work, whether or not we have heard the Buddha's teachings. The old theological debate as to whether salvation is to be gained
65 by works or by faith begins from a false dichotomy. Faith concerns our sense of what is real, what is valuable, what is holy; work is how we act out that faith.

The Shakers condensed their faith into the maxim,
70 "Hands to work, hearts to God." Anyone who has looked at their furniture or buildings can sense the clarity of their vision. "One feels that for the Shaker craftsmen," Thomas Merton observed, "love of God and love of truth in one's own work came to the same
75 thing, and that work itself was a prayer, a communion with the inmost spiritual reality of things and so with God." Mother Ann Lee, who launched the Shaker movement, counseled her followers to "Do all your work as if you had a thousand years to live, and as you
80 would if you knew you must die tomorrow."

If the purpose of life is not to acquire but to *inquire*, to seek understanding, to discover all we can about ourselves and the universe, to commune with the source of things, then we should care less about what
85 we earn—money, prestige, salvation—and more about what we learn. In light of all we have to learn, the difference between dying tomorrow and a hundred years from tomorrow is not very great.

Sample Passage VI

NATURAL SCIENCE: This passage is adapted from *Fire in America: A Cultural History of Wildland and Rural Fire* by Stephen J. Pyne (©1982 by Princeton University Press).

Lightning affects electrical equilibrium on the earth. Air is a poor conductor, but some electricity constantly leaks to the atmosphere, creating an electrical potential. Electricity moves back according to the gra-
5 dient [change in potential with distance]. During a thunderstorm, the gradient becomes very steep, and the electrical potential discharges as lightning. The discharge may move between any oppositely charged regions—from cloud to earth, from earth to cloud, or
10 from cloud to cloud. It was calculated as early as 1887 that the earth would lose almost all its charge in less than an hour unless the supply were replenished; that is, on a global scale, lightning will discharge to the earth every hour a quantity of electricity equal to the earth's
15 entire charge. Thunderstorms are thus an electromagnetic as well as a thermodynamic necessity. It has been reckoned that the earth experiences some 1,800 storms per hour, or 44,000 per day. Collectively, these storms produce 100 cloud-to-ground discharges per second, or
20 better than 8 million per day globally. And these estimates are probably low. The total energy in lightning bolts varies greatly, but about 250 kilowatt hours of electricity are packed into each stroke. Almost 75 percent of this total energy is lost to heat during discharge.

25 Two types of discharge patterns are commonly identified: the cold stroke, whose main return [ground-to-cloud] stroke is of intense current but of short duration, and the hot stroke, involving lesser currents of longer duration. Cold lightning, with its high voltage,
30 generally has mechanical or explosive effects; hot lightning is more apt to start fires. Studies in the Northern Rockies suggest that about one stroke in 25 has the electrical characteristics needed to start a fire. Whether it does or not depends strongly on the object it
35 strikes, the fuel properties of the object, and the local weather. Ignition requires both heat and kindling. Lightning supplies the one with its current and occasionally finds the other among the fine fuels of rotten wood, needles, grass, or dustlike debris blown from a
40 tree by the explosive shock of the bolt itself.

The consequences of lightning are complex. Any natural force of this magnitude will influence the biological no less than the geophysical environment, and the secondary effects of lightning are significant to life.
45 Lightning helps to fix atmospheric nitrogen into a form that rain can bring to earth. In areas of heavy thunderstorm activity, lightning can function as a major predator on trees, either through direct injury or by physiological damage. In the ponderosa pine forests of
50 Arizona, for example, one forester has estimated that lightning mortality runs between 0.7 and 1.0 percent per year. Other researchers have placed mortality as high as 25–33 percent. For southern pines, the figure may be even steeper. A study in Arkansas calculated
55 that 70 percent of mortality, by volume, was due to

lightning. These figures describe only direct injury, primarily the mechanical destruction of branches and bole; the other major causes of mortality—insects, wind, and mistletoe—are likely secondary effects brought about
60 in trees weakened by lightning. All of these effects, in turn, may be camouflaged by fire induced by lightning.

The process of "electrocution" is increasingly recognized. Lightning scorch areas of between 0.25 and 25 acres have been identified. Nor is the process lim-
65 ited to trees: it has been documented for grasses, tomatoes, potatoes, cabbages, tea, and other crops. Long attributed to inscrutable "die-offs" or to infestation by insects or diseases (often a secondary effect), such sites are now recognized worldwide as a product of physio-
70 logical trauma caused by lightning.

The most spectacular product of lightning is fire. Except in tropical rain forests and on ice-mantled land masses, lightning fire has occurred in every terrestrial environment on the globe, contributing to a natural
75 mosaic of vegetation types. Even in tropical landscapes lightning bombardment by itself may frequently be severe enough to produce a mosaic pattern similar to that resulting from lightning fire. Lightning fires have ignited desert grasslands, tundra, chaparral, swamp-
80 lands, marshes, grasslands, and, of course, forests. Though the intensity and frequency of these fires vary by region, their existence is undeniable.

Sample Passage VII

NATURAL SCIENCE: This passage is adapted from "Publish and Punish: Science's Snowball Effect" by Jon Van (©1997 by The Chicago Tribune Company).

It's a scientific finding so fundamental that it certainly will make the history books and maybe snag a Nobel Prize if it pans out, but the notion that cosmic snowballs are constantly pelting Earth is something
5 Louis Frank just as soon would have ducked.

Frank is the University of Iowa physicist whose research led him to declare more than a decade ago that Earth is being bombarded by hundreds of house-sized comets day after day that rain water on our planet and
10 are the reason we have oceans. That weather report caused the widely respected scientist to acquire a certain reputation among his colleagues as a bit unstable, an otherwise estimable fellow whose hard work may have pushed him over the edge.

15 Frank and his associate, John Sigwarth, probably went a way toward salvaging their reputations when they presented new evidence that leaves little doubt Earth is indeed being bombarded by *something* in a manner consistent with Frank's small-comet theory.
20 Rather than gloating or anticipating glory, Frank seemed relieved that part of a long ordeal was ending. "I knew we'd be in for it when we first put forth the small-comet theory," Frank conceded, "but I was naive about just how bad it would be. We were outvoted by
25 about 10,000 to 1 by our colleagues. I thought it would have been more like 1,000 to 1."

To the non-scientist this may seem a bit strange. After all, the point of science is to discover information and insights about how nature works. Shouldn't every
30 scientist be eager to overturn existing ideas and replace them with his or her own? In theory, that is the case, but in practice, scientists are almost as loath to embrace radically new ideas as the rest of us.

"Being a scientist puts you into a constant schizo-
35 phrenic existence," contends Richard Zare, chairman of the National Science Board. "You have to believe and yet question beliefs at the same time. If you are a complete cynic and believe nothing, you do nothing and get nowhere, but if you believe too much, you fool your-
40 self."

It was in the early 1980s when the small-comet theory started to haunt Frank and Sigwarth, who was Frank's graduate student studying charged particles called plasmas, which erupt from the sun and cause the
45 aurora borealis (northern lights). As they analyzed photos of the electrical phenomena that accompany sunspots, they noted dark specks appearing in several images from NASA's Dynamics Explorer 1 satellite. They assumed these were caused by static in the trans-
50 mission.

After a while their curiosity about the dark spots grew into a preoccupation, then bordered on obsession.

Try as they did, the scientists couldn't find any plausible explanation of the pattern of dark spots that
55 appeared on their images. The notion that the equipment was picking up small amounts of water entering Earth's upper atmosphere kept presenting itself as the most likely answer.

Based on their images, the Iowa scientists esti-
60 mated 20 comets an hour—each about 30 feet or so across and carrying 100 tons of water—were bombarding the Earth. At that rate, they would produce water vapor that would add about an inch of water to the planet every 10,000 years, Frank concluded. That may
65 not seem like much, but when talking about a planet billions of years old, it adds up.

Such intimate interaction between Earth and space suggests a fundamentally different picture of human evolution—which depends on water—than is com-
70 monly presented by scientists. Frank had great difficulty getting his ideas into a physics journal 11 years ago and was almost hooted from the room when he presented his theory at scientific meetings. Despite the derision, colleagues continued to respect Frank's main-
75 stream work on electrically charged particles in space and the imaging cameras he designed that were taken aboard recent NASA spacecraft to explore Earth's polar regions.

Unbeknown to most, in addition to gathering
80 information on the northern lights, Frank and Sigwarth designed the equipment to be able to snatch better views of any small comets the spacecraft might happen upon. It was those images from the latest flights that caused even harsh critics of the small-comet theory to
85 concede that some water-bearing objects appear to be entering Earth's atmosphere with regularity.

To be sure, it has not been proved that they are comets, let alone that they have anything to do with the oceans. But Frank's evidence opens the matter up to
90 study. Had he been a researcher of lesser standing, his theory probably would have died long ago.

ACT Science Test

The ACT Science Test asks you to answer 40 multiple-choice questions in 35 minutes. The questions measure the interpretation, analysis, evaluation, and problem-solving skills associated with science. The Science Test is made up of seven test units, each consisting of a passage with scientific information followed by several multiple-choice questions.

Content of the ACT Science Test

The content areas of the ACT Science Test parallel the content of courses commonly taught in grades 7 through 12 and at the entry level at colleges and universities. Each test unit consists of one of the following content areas (examples of subjects included in each content area are given in parentheses):

- **Biology** (cell biology, botany, zoology, microbiology, ecology, genetics, evolution)

- **Chemistry** (properties of matter, acids and bases, kinetics and equilibria, thermochemistry, organic chemistry, biochemistry, nuclear chemistry)

- **Earth/Space Sciences** (geology, meteorology, oceanography, astronomy, environmental science)

- **Physics** (mechanics, thermodynamics, electromagnetism, fluids, solids, optics)

You do not need advanced knowledge in these subjects, but you will need some knowledge—scientific terms or concepts—to answer some of the questions. The test assumes that students are in the process of taking the core science course of study (three years or more) that will prepare them for college-level work, and have completed two years of science coursework.

You do not need advanced mathematical skills for the Science Test, but you may need to make minimal arithmetic computations in order to answer some questions. The use of calculators is **not** permitted on the Science Test. The passages of the Science Test are concise and clear; you should have no trouble understanding them. The test emphasizes application of scientific reasoning skills rather than recall of scientific content, skill in mathematics, or reading ability.

Format of the ACT Science Test

The scientific information presented in each passage of the ACT Science Test is conveyed in one of three different formats. The **Data Representation** format requires you to understand, evaluate, and interpret information presented in graphic or tabular form. The **Research Summaries** format requires you to understand, evaluate, analyze, and interpret the design, execution, and results of one or more experiments. The **Conflicting Viewpoints** format requires you to evaluate several alternative theories, hypotheses, or viewpoints on a specific observable phenomenon. The approximate proportion of the ACT Science Test devoted to each of the three formats is given in the chart on page 24 at the beginning of this chapter.

You'll find examples of the kinds of passages that you're likely to find in each of the formats in the pages that follow.

The sample ACT Science Test passages and questions in this section are representative of those you'll encounter in the actual ACT. The following chart illustrates the content area, format, and topic covered by each sample passage given in the remainder of this section:

Passage	Content Area	Format	Topic of Passage
I	Chemistry	Data Representation	Calorimetry
II	Physics	Research Summaries	Illuminance
III	Biology	Conflicting Viewpoints	Conjugation

Data Representation Format

This type of format presents scientific information in charts, tables, graphs, and diagrams similar to those found in science journals and texts. Examples of tables used in an actual Data Representation passage administered to students are found in Sample Passage I on page 100.

The questions you'll find in the Data Representation format ask you to interpret charts and tables, read graphs, evaluate scatterplots, and analyze information presented in diagrams. There are five sample Data Representation questions presented with the sample Data Representation passage.

Sample Passage I

A *bomb calorimeter* is used to determine the amount of heat released when a substance is burned in oxygen (Figure 1). The heat, measured in kilojoules (kJ), is calculated from the change in temperature of the water in the bomb calorimeter. Table 1 shows the amounts of heat released when different foods were burned in a bomb calorimeter. Table 2 shows the amounts of heat released when different amounts of sucrose (table sugar) were burned. Table 3 shows the amounts of heat released when various chemical compounds were burned.

Table 2	
Amount of sucrose (g)	Heat released (kJ)
0.1	1.6
0.5	8.0
1.0	16.0
2.0	32.1
4.0	64.0

Table 3			
Chemical compound	Molecular formula	Mass (g)	Heat released (kJ)
Methanol	CH_3OH	0.5	11.4
Ethanol	C_2H_5OH	0.5	14.9
Benzene	C_6H_6	0.5	21.0
Octane	C_8H_{18}	0.5	23.9

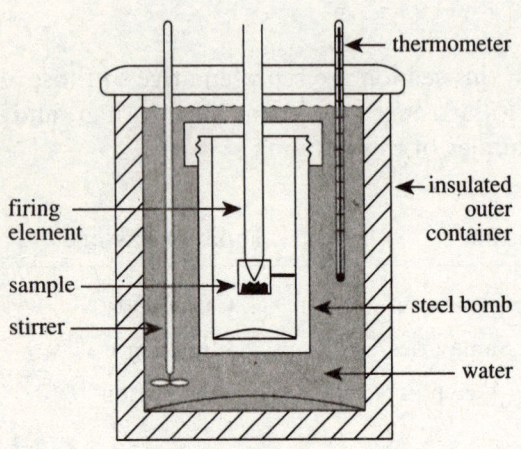

Figure 1

Figure 1 adapted from Antony C. Wilbraham, Dennis D. Staley, and Michael S. Matta, *Chemistry*. ©1995 by Addison-Wesley Publishing Company, Inc.

Table 1			
Food	Mass (g)	Change in water temperature (°C)	Heat released (kJ)
Bread	1.0	8.3	10.0
Cheese	1.0	14.1	17.0
Egg	1.0	5.6	6.7
Potato	1.0	2.7	3.2

Table 1 adapted from American Chemical Society, *ChemCom: Chemistry in the Community*. ©1993 by American Chemical Society.

1. According to Tables 1 and 2, as the mass of successive sucrose samples increased, the change in the water temperature produced when the sample was burned most likely:

    A. increased only.
    B. decreased only.
    C. increased, then decreased.
    D. remained the same.

2. Which of the following graphs best illustrates the relationship between the heat released by the foods listed in Table 1 and the change in water temperature?

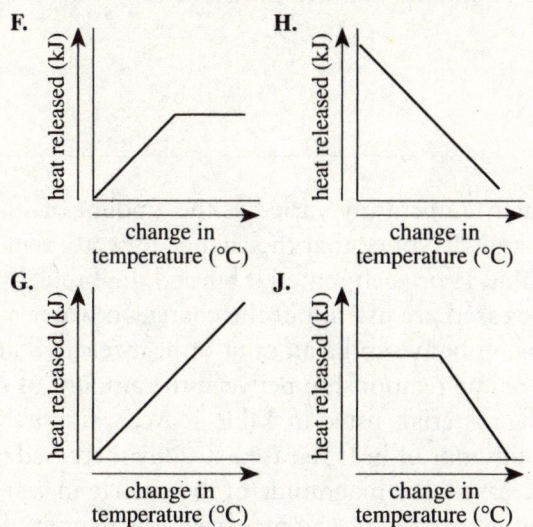

F.

heat released (kJ) vs change in temperature (°C)

H.

heat released (kJ) vs change in temperature (°C)

G.

heat released (kJ) vs change in temperature (°C)

J.

heat released (kJ) vs change in temperature (°C)

3. Based on the data in Table 2, one can conclude that when the mass of sucrose is decreased by one-half, the amount of heat released when it is burned in a bomb calorimeter will:

A. increase by one-half.
B. decrease by one-half.
C. increase by one-fourth.
D. decrease by one-fourth.

4. Which of the following lists the foods from Tables 1 and 2 in increasing order of the amount of heat released per gram of food?

F. Potato, egg, bread, sucrose, cheese
G. Sucrose, cheese, bread, egg, potato
H. Bread, cheese, egg, potato, sucrose
J. Sucrose, potato, egg, bread, cheese

5. Based on the information in Tables 1 and 2, the heat released from the burning of 5.0 g of potato in a bomb calorimeter would be closest to which of the following?

A. 5 kJ
B. 10 kJ
C. 15 kJ
D. 20 kJ

Discussion of Sample Passage I (Data Representation)

According to this Data Representation passage, the amount of heat generated when a material is burned in oxygen can be determined using a *bomb calorimeter*. The bomb calorimeter has an outer shell made of an insulating material. Inside this shell is a bomb (steel casing) immersed in a fixed amount of water. When a material is burned inside the bomb, the water absorbs heat generated by the combustion, causing the temperature of the water to increase. The amount of the increase in water temperature depends upon the amount of heat absorbed by the water. So, if we measure the increase in water temperature, we can calculate the amount of heat released when a material is burned inside the bomb.

Note that the passage contains 3 tables. Table 1 lists the temperature change of the water and the amount of heat generated when 1 g of each of 4 foods is burned in the calorimeter. Table 2 lists the amounts of heat released when various quantities of the sugar sucrose are burned. Table 3 lists several chemical compounds and their chemical formulas, as well as the amount of heat released for each compound when 0.5 g of the compound is burned in the calorimeter.

1. According to Tables 1 and 2, as the mass of successive sucrose samples increased, the change in the water temperature produced when the sample was burned most likely:

   A. increased only.
   B. decreased only.
   C. increased, then decreased.
   D. remained the same.

Question 1 asks you to determine how the change in water temperature varied as the amount of sucrose burned increased, based on the data in Tables 1 and 2. Notice that the change in water temperature and the amount of heat released are listed in Table 1 for each material burned. In Table 2, the amount of sucrose burned and the amount of heat released are listed, but the change in water temperature is not listed. Let us assume that the relationship between the amount of heat released and the change in water temperature for sucrose is the same as the relationship between the amount of heat released and the change in water temperature for the materials listed in Table 1. According to Table 2, as the amount of sucrose burned increased, the amount of heat released steadily increased. According to Table 1, as the amount of heat released increased, the magnitude of the change in water temperature steadily increased. Therefore, as the amount of sucrose burned increased, the magnitude of the change in the water temperature steadily increased. The best answer is **A**.

2. Which of the following graphs best illustrates the relationship between the heat released by the foods listed in Table 1 and the change in water temperature?

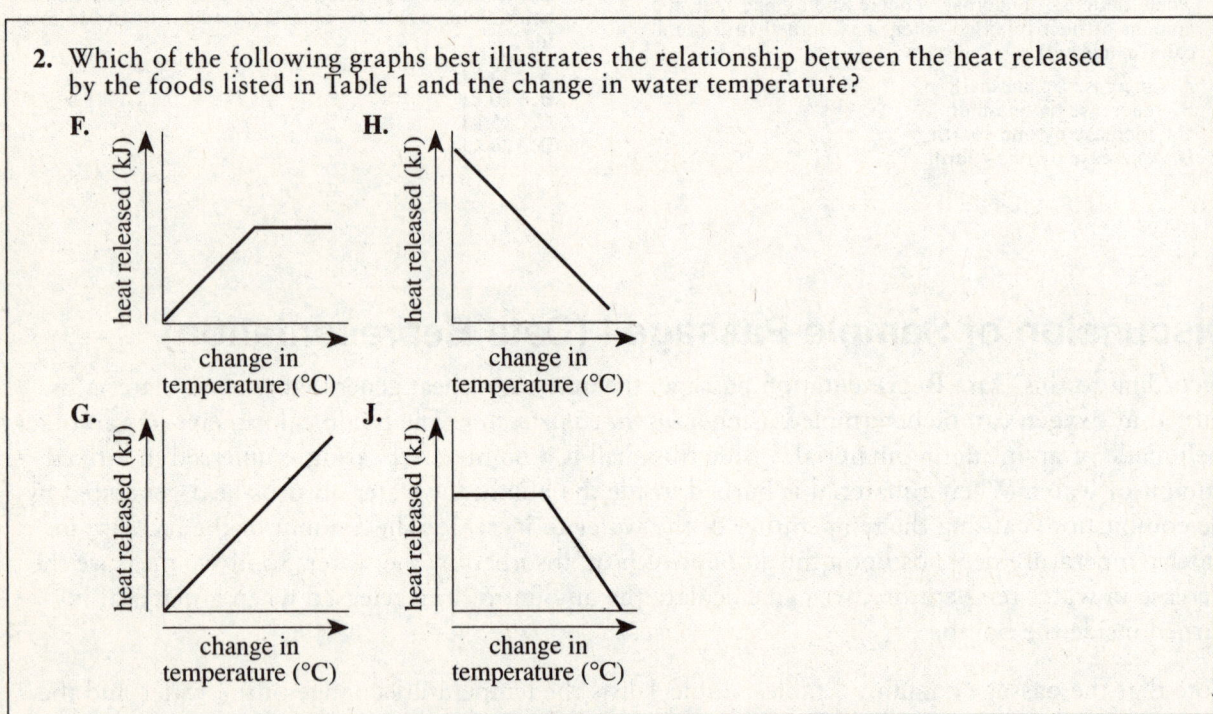

Question 2 asks you to choose a graph that best illustrates the relationship between the amount of heat released and the change in water temperature for the 4 substances listed in Table 1. According to the data in Table 1, as the change in water temperature increased, the amount of heat released steadily increased. There were no data in Table 1 to support the conclusion that as the change in water temperature increased, the amount of heat released decreased or remained constant. Therefore, **G** is the best answer.

---

3. Based on the data in Table 2, one can conclude that when the mass of sucrose is decreased by one-half, the amount of heat released when it is burned in a bomb calorimeter will:

A. increase by one-half.
B. decrease by one-half.
C. increase by one-fourth.
D. decrease by one-fourth.

Question 3 asks you to predict, based on the data in Table 2, the fractional change in the amount of heat released by sucrose when the amount of sucrose burned is decreased by half. An examination of the data in Table 2 shows that when the amount of sucrose burned was decreased by half, the amount of heat released decreased by half. For example, when the amount of sucrose burned was decreased from 4.0 g to 2.0 g, the amount of heat released decreased from 64.0 kJ to 32.1 kJ; that is, the amount of heat released also decreased by half. (The amount of heat released actually decreased by 31.9 kJ, which is not exactly half of 64.0 kJ, but the 0.1 kJ difference between 31.9 kJ and 32.0 kJ can be attributed to limitations in the precision of the measurements [the amount of heat released is rounded off to the nearest 0.1 kJ] and can be ignored.) The amount of heat released was also decreased by half when the amount of sucrose burned was decreased from 2.0 g to 1.0 g and again when the amount of sucrose burned was decreased from 1.0 g to 0.5 g. Therefore, one can conclude that when the amount of sucrose burned is decreased by half, the amount of heat released during the burning of sucrose is decreased by half, so **B** is the best answer.

---

4. Which of the following lists the foods from Tables 1 and 2 in increasing order of the amount of heat released per gram of food?

F. Potato, egg, bread, sucrose, cheese
G. Sucrose, cheese, bread, egg, potato
H. Bread, cheese, egg, potato, sucrose
J. Sucrose, potato, egg, bread, cheese

Question 4 asks you to list the foods from Tables 1 and 2 in increasing order, from the food that releases the least amount of heat per gram of food to the food that releases the greatest amount of heat per gram of food. According to Table 1, the amount of heat released was determined for 1 g samples of each of the foods listed. Therefore, the amount of heat listed in Table 1 for each food item is the amount of heat released per gram of food. In Table 2, the amount of heat released is given for various masses of sucrose. To get the amount of heat released per gram of sucrose we can divide the amount of heat released by the mass of sucrose that was burned. However, an easier method is to notice that a trial was conducted using 1.0 g of sucrose, and during that trial, the amount of heat released was 16.0 kJ. Therefore, the amount of heat released per g of sucrose was 16.0 kJ/g. (To be more sure that our result is correct, we can choose the results of another trial and divide the amount of heat released by the mass of sucrose burned during that trial. For example, when 4.0 g of sucrose was burned, 64.0 kJ of heat was released, and 64.0 kJ ÷ 4.0 g = 16 kJ/g, in agreement with our earlier finding.) An inspection of the heat released by the combustion of the foods in Table 1 shows that the potato sample released the least amount of heat (3.2 kJ/g), followed by the egg sample (6.7 kJ/g), the bread sample (10.0 kJ/g), and the cheese sample (17.0 kJ/g). The amount of heat per g released by sucrose, 16.0 kJ/g, places sucrose between the cheese sample and the bread sample. Therefore, the correct order is potato, egg, bread, sucrose, cheese. The best answer is **F**.

---

5. Based on the information in Tables 1 and 2, the heat released from the burning of 5.0 g of potato in a bomb calorimeter would be closest to which of the following?
   A. 5 kJ
   B. 10 kJ
   C. 15 kJ
   D. 20 kJ

Question 5 asks you to use Tables 1 and 2 to estimate the amount of heat released while 5.0 g of potato is burned. Notice that Table 1 provides you with the amount of heat released (3.2 kJ) when 1.0 g of potato is burned. You might guess that burning 5.0 g of potato in the calorimeter would cause the release of 5 times the amount of heat released when 1.0 g of potato is burned. Do you have any evidence to support this guess? Table 1 only lists the amount of heat released when 1.0 g of potato is burned. Table 2 provides the amount of heat released from various amounts of sucrose, but not potatoes. In the absence of information to the contrary, you might assume that the relationship between the amount of potato burned and the amount of heat released is similar to the relationship between the amount of sucrose burned and the amount of heat released. According to Table 2, the heat released in kJ equals 16 times the mass of sucrose burned in grams. Note that this relationship holds whether 0.1 g of sucrose is burned or 4.0 g of sucrose is burned. For example, if 0.1 g of sucrose is burned, 0.1 g × 16 kJ released per g of sucrose = 1.6 kJ of heat released. If 4.0 g of sucrose is burned, 4.0 g × 16 kJ released per g of sucrose = 64 kJ of heat released. This relationship is a linear relationship. If the relationship between the amount of potato burned and the amount of heat released is also linear, then burning 5 times the amount of potato will release 5 times the amount of heat. Because 3.2 kJ of heat was released when 1.0 g of potato was burned, 5 × 3.2 kJ = 16 kJ will be released when 5.0 g of potato is burned. The answer closest to 16 kJ is 15 kJ (**C**).

Research Summaries Format

This type of format provides descriptions of one or more related experiments or studies similar to those conducted by scientists or science students. The descriptions typically include the design, procedures, and results of the experiments or studies. The results are often depicted with graphs or tables. Sample Passage II provides an example of the Research Summaries format that shows the results of two different experiments with light bulbs. The questions you'll find in the Research Summaries format ask you to understand, evaluate, and interpret the design and procedures of the experiments or studies and to analyze the results. There are five sample Research Summaries questions in Sample Passage II.

Sample Passage II

A student studied illumination using the following equipment:

- 6 identical light bulbs (Bulbs A–F)
- Fixture 1, light fixture for Bulbs A–E
- Fixture 2, light fixture for Bulb F
- 2 identical paraffin blocks
- A sheet of aluminum foil having the same length and width as a paraffin block
- A meterstick

Light could pass through each paraffin block, and each block glowed when light passed through it. The aluminum foil was placed between the 2 blocks. The light fixtures, light bulbs, blocks, foil, and the meterstick were arranged as shown in Figure 1.

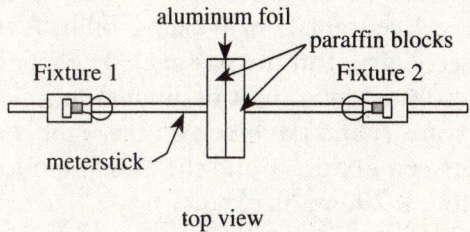

Figure 1

In the following experiments, the base of Fixture 2 was always 0.200 m from the aluminum foil, and L was the distance from the base of Fixture 1 to the aluminum foil. The distance between adjacent bulbs in Fixture 1 was the same for all of the bulbs.

Bulb F was always lit.

Experiment 1

The student turned the room lights off, lit Bulb A, and varied L until the 2 blocks looked equally bright. This process was repeated using Bulbs B–E. The results are shown in Table 1.

Table 1	
Bulb lit (in addition to Bulb F)	L (m) when the blocks looked equally bright
A	0.198
B	0.203
C	0.205
D	0.195
E	0.199

Experiment 2

The procedure from Experiment 1 was repeated using various combinations of Bulbs A–E. The results are shown in Table 2.

Table 2	
Bulbs lit (in addition to Bulb F)	L (m) when the blocks looked equally bright
A and B	0.281
A, B, and C	0.347
A, B, C, and D	0.400
A, B, C, D, and E	0.446

6. Which of the following best explains why the student turned off the room lights?

F. To ensure that only the light from Bulbs A–F illuminated the 2 paraffin blocks

G. To ensure that light from outside the room illuminated the 2 paraffin blocks unequally

H. To keep the 2 paraffin blocks from casting shadows, because shadows would make the meterstick harder to read

J. To keep the 2 light fixtures from casting shadows, because shadows would make the meterstick harder to read

7. During Experiment 2, suppose the student replaced Fixture 1 with a new fixture. The new fixture held 6 light bulbs, each bulb identical to Bulb F. When all 6 bulbs in the new fixture were lit and the paraffin blocks looked equally bright, L would probably have been closest to:

A. 0.262 m.
B. 0.331 m.
C. 0.415 m.
D. 0.490 m.

8. The main purpose of Experiment 1 was to:

F. calibrate the meterstick.
G. determine the relationship between L and the number of lit bulbs.
H. determine if L depended on a lit bulb's position in Fixture 1.
J. find the brightness of Bulb F.

9. Suppose that all of the light bulbs in Fixture 1 were replaced with a single bulb. Based on Experiments 1 and 2, if the 2 paraffin blocks looked equally bright when Fixture 2 was 0.200 m from the aluminum foil and $L = 0.446$ m, the brightness of the new light bulb was most likely:

A. $\frac{1}{6}$ the brightness of one of the original bulbs.

B. $\frac{1}{5}$ the brightness of one of the original bulbs.

C. 5 times the brightness of one of the original bulbs.

D. 6 times the brightness of one of the original bulbs.

10. In Experiment 2, suppose the student had replaced Bulb F with a much brighter light bulb, Bulb G. Compared to L when Bulb F was used, L when Bulb G was used would have been:

F. greater for every combination of lit bulbs.
G. smaller for every combination of lit bulbs.
H. smaller when Bulbs A–E were simultaneously lit and greater when other combinations of light bulbs were lit.
J. greater when both Bulbs A and B were simultaneously lit and smaller when other combinations of light bulbs were lit.

Discussion of Sample Passage II (Research Summaries)

This Research Summaries passage describes 2 experiments in which a student uses 2 identical paraffin blocks to compare the brightness of the light from one source (Fixture 1) with the brightness of the light from another source (Fixture 2). Fixture 1 contains 5 light bulbs, Bulbs A through E, while Fixture 2 contains only 1 light bulb, Bulb F (see Figure 1 in the passage). The 2 paraffin blocks are set between the fixtures. The 2 blocks are separated by a sheet of aluminum foil, so that the block on the left is only illuminated by bulbs in Fixture 1, and the block on the right is only illuminated by Bulb F in Fixture 2. The distance, L, between Fixture 1 and the aluminum foil can be varied, but the distance between Fixture 2 and the foil, 0.200 m, is fixed.

In Experiment 1, one bulb at a time is lit in Fixture 1, and Bulb F is lit in Fixture 2. For each combination of lit bulbs, L is varied until the 2 blocks glow equally brightly. This value of L is recorded in Table 1 along with the combination of lit bulbs used to obtain this value of L. In Experiment 2, two or more bulbs at a time are lit in Fixture 1, and Bulb F is lit in Fixture 2. For each combination of lit bulbs, L is varied until the 2 blocks glow equally brightly. This value of L is recorded in Table 2 along with the combination of lit bulbs.

6. Which of the following best explains why the student turned off the room lights?
    F. To ensure that only the light from Bulbs A–F illuminated the 2 paraffin blocks
    G. To ensure that light from outside the room illuminated the 2 paraffin blocks unequally
    H. To keep the 2 paraffin blocks from casting shadows, because shadows would make the meterstick harder to read
    J. To keep the 2 light fixtures from casting shadows, because shadows would make the meterstick harder to read

Question 6 asks you why the student turned off the room lights before making measurements of L. Recall that the student was to compare the brightness of the light produced by Fixture 1 to the brightness of the light produced by Fixture 2 under a variety of conditions. The presence of light sources other than Fixtures 1 and 2 could have introduced error into the measurements of L by making one fixture or the other seem brighter than it really was. The overhead lights were turned off so that all of the light on the blocks came from the light bulbs in Fixtures 1 and 2. Thus, **F** is the best answer.

7. During Experiment 2, suppose the student replaced Fixture 1 with a new fixture. The new fixture held 6 light bulbs, each bulb identical to Bulb F. When all 6 bulbs in the new fixture were lit and the paraffin blocks looked equally bright, L would probably have been closest to:
    A. 0.262 m.
    B. 0.331 m.
    C. 0.415 m.
    D. 0.490 m.

Question 7 proposes that Fixture 1 be replaced by a different fixture holding 6 light bulbs instead of 5. Each of the light bulbs in the new fixture is identical to Bulb F. The question asks you to estimate L for the case that all 6 light bulbs in the new fixture, as well as Bulb F, are lit. According to Table 2, as the number of lit bulbs in Fixture 1 increased from 2 to 5, L increased. So if the new fixture is used, increasing the number of lit bulbs from 5 to 6, one would expect L to be greater than the value of L given in Table 2 for 5 lit bulbs in Fixture 1, 0.446 m. Only **D** contains a value for L answer exceeding 0.446 m, so **D** must be the best answer.

8. The main purpose of Experiment 1 was to:
    F. calibrate the meterstick.
    G. determine the relationship between L and the number of lit bulbs.
    H. determine if L depended on a lit bulb's position in Fixture 1.
    J. find the brightness of Bulb F.

Question 8 asks you to determine the main purpose of Experiment 1. In Experiment 1, one bulb at a time was lit in Fixture 1, but the location of the lit bulb in Fixture 1 was varied. Thus, the main purpose of Experiment 1 must have been to determine the effect, if any, that the location of the lit bulb had on the value of L. Only **H** states that the purpose of Experiment 1 was to determine if the position of the lit bulb within Fixture 1 affected L, so **H** must be the best answer.

9. Suppose that all of the light bulbs in Fixture 1 were replaced with a single bulb. Based on Experiments 1 and 2, if the 2 paraffin blocks looked equally bright when Fixture 2 was 0.200 m from the aluminum foil and $L = 0.446$ m, the brightness of the new light bulb was most likely:

   A. $\frac{1}{6}$ the brightness of one of the original bulbs.

   B. $\frac{1}{5}$ the brightness of one of the original bulbs.

   C. 5 times the brightness of one of the original bulbs.

   D. 6 times the brightness of one of the original bulbs.

Question 9 proposes that the 5 light bulbs in Fixture 1 be replaced with a single light bulb, and that when the new bulb and Bulb F are lit, for the 2 blocks to glow equally brightly, L must equal 0.446 m. You are asked to compare the brightness of the new bulb to the brightness of 1 of the original bulbs in Fixture 1. According to Table 2, the 2 paraffin blocks glowed equally brightly when all 5 bulbs in Fixture 1 were lit and L was 0.446 m, the same as the L obtained with the new bulb. Thus, the brightness of the new bulb would have to equal the sum of the brightnesses of the 5 original bulbs. Because each of the 5 original bulbs had the same brightness, the new bulb would have to be 5 times as bright as one of the original bulbs. Only **C** is consistent with this conclusion, so the best answer is **C**.

10. In Experiment 2, suppose the student had replaced Bulb F with a much brighter light bulb, Bulb G. Compared to L when Bulb F was used, L when Bulb G was used would have been:

    F. greater for every combination of lit bulbs.
    G. smaller for every combination of lit bulbs.
    H. smaller when Bulbs A–E were simultaneously lit and greater when other combinations of light bulbs were lit.
    J. greater when both Bulbs A and B were simultaneously lit and smaller when other combinations of light bulbs were lit.

Question 10 proposes that in Experiment 2, Bulb F be replaced by a much brighter bulb, Bulb G. For each combination of lit bulbs in Fixture 1 and Bulb G lit in Fixture 2, when the 2 paraffin blocks are equally bright, how would the value of L compare to that obtained when Bulb F was used in Fixture 2? Because Bulb G is brighter than Bulb F and would be the same distance (0.200 m) away from the aluminum foil as Bulb F, the paraffin block closer to Bulb G would glow more brightly than it glowed when Bulb F was used. Thus, for each combination of lit bulbs in Fixture 1, to make the 2 blocks glow with equal brightness, Fixture 1 would have to be closer to the blocks than when Bulb F was used. That is, when Bulb G was used, L for each combination of lit bulbs in Fixture 1 would have to be less than when Bulb F was used for the 2 blocks to glow with equal brightness. Only **G** is consistent with this conclusion. The best answer is **G**.

Conflicting Viewpoints Format

This type of format provides several alternative theories, hypotheses, or viewpoints on a specific observable phenomenon. These conflicting viewpoints are based on differing premises or on incomplete data and are inconsistent with one another. Sample Passage III, a biology passage on gene replication, is an example of the Conflicting Viewpoints format. Notice that this passage presents the theories of four different students.

The questions you'll find in the Conflicting Viewpoints format ask you to understand, analyze, evaluate, and compare several theories, hypotheses, or viewpoints. There are five sample Conflicting Viewpoints questions presented with Sample Passage III.

Sample Passage III

Many bacteria contain *plasmids* (small, circular DNA molecules). Plasmids can be transferred from 1 bacterium to another. For this to occur, the plasmid *replicates* (produces a linear copy of itself). The relative position of the genes is the same on the original plasmid and on the linear copy, except that the 2 ends of the linear copy do not immediately connect.

While replication is occurring, 1 end of the linear copy leaves the donor bacterium and enters the recipient bacterium. Thus, the order in which the genes are replicated is the same as the order in which they are transferred. Unless this process is interrupted, the entire plasmid is transferred, and its 2 ends connect in the recipient bacterium.

Four students studied the way in which 6 genes (F, X, R, S, A, and G) on a specific plasmid were donated by a type of bacterium (see the figure). The students determined that the entire plasmid is transferred in 90 min and that the rate of transfer is constant. They also determined that the genes are evenly spaced around the plasmid, so 1 gene is transferred every 15 min. They disagreed, however, about the order in which the genes are replicated and thus transferred. Four models are presented.

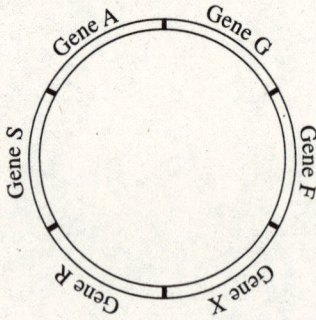

Student 1

Replication always begins between Gene F and Gene X. Gene X is replicated first and Gene F is replicated last.

Student 2

Replication always begins between Gene F and Gene X. However, the direction of replication varies. If Gene F is replicated first, Gene X is replicated last. Conversely, if Gene X is replicated first, Gene F is replicated last.

Student 3

Replication can begin between any 2 genes. Replication then proceeds around the plasmid in a clockwise direction (with respect to the figure). Thus, if Gene S is replicated first, Gene A is replicated second, and Gene R is replicated last.

Student 4

Replication can begin between any 2 genes. Likewise, replication can proceed in either direction. So the order of replication varies.

11. Based on the information presented, if the transfer of the linear copy was interrupted 50 min after transfer began, how many complete genes would have been transferred to the recipient bacterium?

   A. 2
   B. 3
   C. 4
   D. 5

12. Based on the model presented by Student 3, if all 6 genes are replicated and the first gene replicated is Gene G, the third gene replicated would be:

   F. Gene F.
   G. Gene A.
   H. Gene S.
   J. Gene X.

13. Which students believe that any of the 6 genes on the plasmid can be the first gene transferred to a recipient bacterium?

   A. Students 2 and 3
   B. Students 2 and 4
   C. Students 3 and 4
   D. Students 2, 3, and 4

14. Suppose that Student 2's model is correct and that the transfer of genes between 2 bacteria was interrupted after 30 min. Under these conditions, which of the following genes would definitely NOT be transferred from the donor bacterium to the recipient bacterium?

   F. Gene A
   G. Gene R
   H. Gene G
   J. Gene X

15. Suppose that the transfer of genes between 2 bacteria was interrupted, that the last gene transferred was Gene A, and that no incomplete copies of a gene were transferred. Based on this information, Student 1 would say that transfer was most likely interrupted how many minutes after the transfer began?

   A. 15
   B. 30
   C. 45
   D. 60

Discussion of Sample Passage III (Conflicting Viewpoints)

According to this Conflicting Viewpoints passage, plasmids (small DNA molecules, each molecule consisting of genes arranged in a circle) are found in bacteria. While a plasmid is replicating (producing an identical copy of itself) in one bacterium, the gene copies are being transferred to a second bacterium, the recipient bacterium, eventually forming a complete copy of the plasmid in the recipient bacterium.

Notice the diagram of a plasmid in the passage. The plasmid in the diagram contains 6 genes. The passage tells us that when the plasmid replicates, it produces a linear copy of itself; that is, the 6 genes in the copy are arranged in the same order as in the original plasmid, but the genes in the copy are first arranged in a row rather than in a circle. The plasmid copies 1 gene at a time, and, according to the passage, the gene copies are transferred to the recipient bacterium one at a time, in the order in which the copies are produced. For example, if the plasmid copies Gene F, followed by Gene X, Gene F will be transferred to the recipient bacterium first, followed by Gene X. Once all of the genes of the original plasmid have been copied and transferred to a recipient bacterium, the 2 ends of the linear plasmid copy connect to each other, forming a circle just like the one in the passage.

Four students agree that the rate of gene transfer between bacteria is constant and occurs at the rate of 1 gene every 15 minutes, so a complete plasmid is transferred between the bacteria in $6 \times 15 = 90$ minutes. However, the identity of the first gene to be replicated and the direction (clockwise or counterclockwise around the circle) in which replication proceeds are subjects of disagreement among the 4 students.

- According to Student 1, Gene X is always replicated and transferred first, and Gene F is always replicated and transferred last. That is, replication always starts with Gene X and proceeds in a clockwise direction around the plasmid.

- According to Student 2, replication always begins with either Gene F or Gene X. If Gene F is first, then Gene X is last; that is, if replication begins with Gene F, then replication proceeds in a counterclockwise direction around the plasmid. If Gene X is first, then Gene F is last; that is, if replication begins with Gene X, then replication proceeds in a clockwise direction around the plasmid.

- According to Student 3, replication can start with any gene but always proceeds in a clockwise direction around the plasmid.

- According to Student 4, replication can start with any gene and can proceed in either direction around the plasmid.

11. Based on the information presented, if the transfer of the linear copy was interrupted 50 min after transfer began, how many complete genes would have been transferred to the recipient bacterium?

    A. 2
    B. 3
    C. 4
    D. 5

Question 11 asks you to predict how many complete genes would have been transferred to the recipient bacterium if gene transfer had been interrupted 50 minutes after transfer had begun. According to the passage, 1 gene was transferred every 15 minutes. Therefore, 3 genes would have been transferred in $3 \times 15 = 45$ minutes. A partial gene transfer would have occurred in the remaining 5 minutes, but the question asks you about complete gene transfers, so we can ignore the partial gene transfer. The answer is 3 genes. Therefore, the best choice is **B**.

12. Based on the model presented by Student 3, if all 6 genes are replicated and the first gene replicated is Gene G, the third gene replicated would be:

    F. Gene F.
    G. Gene A.
    H. Gene S.
    J. Gene X.

Question 12 asks you to suppose that all 6 genes in a plasmid are replicated and that Gene G is the first gene replicated. You are asked to predict the third gene replicated, assuming that Student 3's model is correct. According to Student 3's model, replication can start with any gene but always proceeds around the plasmid in a clockwise direction. Therefore, starting with Gene G and proceeding in a clockwise direction, we find that Gene F would be the second gene replicated and Gene X would be the third gene replicated. The best answer is J.

13. Which students believe that any of the 6 genes on the plasmid can be the first gene transferred to a recipient bacterium?

    A. Students 2 and 3
    B. Students 2 and 4
    C. Students 3 and 4
    D. Students 2, 3, and 4

Question 13 asks which students believe that any of the 6 genes on the plasmid can be the first gene transferred to a recipient bacterium. According to the passage, the order in which genes are transferred is the same as the order in which genes are replicated. Student 1 asserts that replication always begins with Gene X, so Student 1 would agree that Gene X is always the first gene transferred. Thus, Student 1 would *disagree* with the statement that any of the 6 genes on the plasmid can be the first gene transferred. Student 2 asserts that replication always begins with either Gene X or Gene F, so Student 2 would agree that Gene F or Gene X is always the first gene transferred. Thus, Student 2 would *disagree* with the statement that any of the 6 genes on the plasmid can be the first gene transferred.

According to Student 3, replication can begin between any 2 genes on the plasmid and then proceeds in the clockwise direction around the plasmid. For example, replication can begin between Genes S and A, in which case Gene A will be the first gene replicated and transferred; replication can begin between Genes R and S, in which case Gene S will be the first gene replicated and transferred; and so on. Thus, according to Student 3, because replication can begin between any pair of genes and proceeds in the clockwise direction around the plasmid, any gene can be transferred first. According to Student 4, replication can begin between any 2 genes on the plasmid and then can proceed in either direction around the plasmid. For example, replication can begin between Genes S and A; if replication proceeds in a clockwise direction, Gene A will be the first gene transferred, but if replication proceeds in a counterclockwise direction, Gene S will be the first gene transferred; similarly, replication can begin between Genes R and S, in which case either Gene R or Gene S will be the first gene transferred, and so on. Thus, according to Student 4, because replication can begin between any pair of genes and can proceed in either direction around the plasmid, any gene can be transferred first. Because only Students 3 and 4 agree that any gene on the plasmid can be the first gene transferred, the best answer is **C**.

14. Suppose that Student 2's model is correct and that the transfer of genes between 2 bacteria was interrupted after 30 min. Under these conditions, which of the following genes would definitely NOT be transferred from the donor bacterium to the recipient bacterium?

F. Gene A
G. Gene R
H. Gene G
J. Gene X

Question 14 asks you to suppose that the transfer of genes between 2 bacteria was interrupted 30 minutes after the transfer began. You are asked to select from among a list of genes (A, R, G, and X) the gene that could NOT have been transferred to the recipient bacterium within the allotted 30 minutes, assuming that Student 2's model is correct. According to the passage, 1 complete gene transfer occurs every 15 minutes. Therefore, 2 complete gene transfers would have occurred after $2 \times 15 = 30$ minutes. Based on Student 2's model, gene transfer can start with Gene X and proceed around the plasmid in a clockwise direction, or transfer can start with Gene F and proceed around the plasmid in a counterclockwise direction. If transfer had started with Gene X, Gene R would have been the second gene transferred. If transfer had started with Gene F, Gene G would have been the second gene transferred. Therefore, we conclude Genes X, R, F, and G could have been transferred. The only gene in the list that could not have been transferred is Gene A. Based on Student 2's model, if Gene X had been the first gene transferred, then 4 × 15 = 60 minutes would have been required for Gene A to be transferred, because Gene A is the fourth gene in the clockwise direction from Gene X. If Gene F had been the first gene transferred, 3 × 15 = 45 minutes would have been required for Gene A to be transferred, because Gene A is the third gene in the counterclockwise direction from Gene F. The best answer is **F**.

---

15. Suppose that the transfer of genes between 2 bacteria was interrupted, that the last gene transferred was Gene A, and that no incomplete copies of a gene were transferred. Based on this information, Student 1 would say that transfer was most likely interrupted how many minutes after the transfer began?

   A. 15
   B. 30
   C. 45
   D. 60

Question 15 asks you to suppose that the transfer of genes between 2 bacteria was interrupted after the transfer of Gene A was completed, and that there was no incomplete transfer of a gene after the transfer of Gene A. You are asked to determine the number of minutes between the time that gene transfer began and the time at which gene transfer was interrupted, assuming that Student 1's model is correct. According to Student 1, Gene X is always transferred first, and Gene F is always transferred last. That is, transfer always starts with Gene X and proceeds in a clockwise direction around the plasmid. If we count genes in the clockwise direction, starting with Gene X, we find that Gene A is the fourth gene, so Gene A would have been the fourth gene transferred. According to the passage, each complete transfer of a gene requires 15 minutes. Thus, the number of minutes between the time at which the transfer of Gene X began and the time at which the transfer of Gene A was completed would have been 4 × 15 = 60 minutes. The best answer is **D**.

Answer Key for Science Test Sample Questions

1.	A	6.	F	11.	B
2.	G	7.	D	12.	J
3.	B	8.	H	13.	C
4.	F	9.	C	14.	F
5.	C	10.	G	15.	D

Strategies for Taking the ACT Science Test

Develop a Problem-Solving Method

Because you have only a limited time in which to take the Science Test, you may find it helpful to work out a general problem-solving method that you can use for all or most of the questions. The method described here is certainly not the only way to solve the problems, but it is one that works for most science problems. Whether you see a way to adapt this method, or you work out your own approach, use the method that works best for you.

One approach to solving problems is to break the process into a series of smaller steps. After you have read the passage, take a careful look at the question and restate it in your own words to make sure you have the problem clearly in mind. Next, decide what information you need to solve the problem. Examine the information given in the passage and decide what sort of information you have, including data and scientific concepts and assumptions underlying the experiments, arguments, or conclusions. If necessary, consider additional scientific information (terms or concepts) relevant to the problem. Sort and assemble the information necessary for a conclusion and logically think through your answer, then compare it to the possible answers. This problem-solving method may be described in five steps:

1. Restate the problem.

2. Decide what information is needed.

3. Find the needed information from the passage.

4. Supply additional scientific information (terms or concepts) if needed to solve the problem.

5. Organize the information and think through your answer.

General Strategies

It's important to read text, graphs, and tables carefully and thoughtfully so that you understand clearly what's being asked. Then you can determine the information needed to solve the problem and the information given in the passage that will help you find the answer. It may be helpful for you to underline important information or to make notes in the margins of your test booklet. (In some circumstances you are not permitted to write in your test booklet. In those circumstances, you'll be given scratch paper to use). For questions that ask you to compare viewpoints, these notes will help you answer more quickly.

Pace Yourself

Remember, you have 35 minutes to read seven passages and their accompanying questions. That's about 5 minutes for each passage and the accompanying questions. You can think of it as 40 questions in 35 minutes, or a little less than a minute per question. If you're like most people, you'll find some of the units more familiar and probably easier than some of the others, so it's a good idea to try to work fast enough to allow yourself time to come back to any questions you have trouble answering the first time.

Learn Specific Strategies for Data Representation Passages

When reading graphs and tables, you should be able to identify axis labels, find information in keys, identify the variables shown, determine relationships between variables (direct, inverse, or other relationships), interpolate between data points, extrapolate a data trend, make hypotheses or predictions from the data presented, translate data from one form of presentation into another, and determine if new information is consistent with presented data.

Learn Specific Strategies for Research Summaries Passages

When working with a Research Summaries passage, you should be able to understand scientific processes. This includes identifying the designs of experiments, identifying assumptions and hypotheses underlying the experiments, identifying controls and variables, determining the effects of altering the experiments, identifying similarities and differences between the experiments, identifying the strengths and weaknesses of the experiments, developing other experiments that will test the same hypothesis, making hypotheses or predictions from research results, and creating models from research results.

Learn Specific Strategies for Conflicting Viewpoints Passages

When working with a Conflicting Viewpoints passage, you should be able to interpret the viewpoints, theories, or hypotheses; determine their strengths and weaknesses; determine their similarities and differences; find out how new information affects the viewpoints; and determine how alternate viewpoints explain the same phenomenon.

Think About How You Can Use the Information in Graphs and Diagrams

Graphs and diagrams illustrate data in ways that can be very useful if you follow a few rules. First, it's important to identify what is being displayed in the graph or diagram (e.g., mass, volume, velocity). What unit or units of measurement is (are) used (e.g., grams, liters, kilometers per hour)? Graphs usually have captions or labels that provide this information; diagrams generally have a key or legend or other short explanation of the information presented. Many graphs consist of two axes (horizontal and vertical), both of which will be labeled. Remember, the first thing to find out about any graph or diagram is exactly what the numbers represent.

Once you've identified what is being presented in a graph or diagram, you can begin to look for trends in the data. The main reason for using a graph or diagram is to show how one characteristic of the data tends to influence one or more other characteristics.

For a coordinate graph, notice how a change on the horizontal axis (or x-axis) relates to the position of the variable on the vertical axis (or y-axis). If the curve shown angles upward from lower left to upper right (as in Figure 1a), then, as the variable shown on the x-axis increases, so does the variable on the y-axis (a direct relationship). An example of a direct relationship is that a person's weight increases as his or her height increases. If the curve goes from the upper left to the lower right (as in Figure 1b), then, as the variable on the x-axis increases, the variable on the y-axis decreases (an inverse relationship). An example of an inverse relationship is that the more players there are on a soccer team, the less time each of them gets to play (assuming everyone gets equal playing time). If the graph shows a vertical or horizontal line (as in Figure 1c), the variables are probably unrelated.

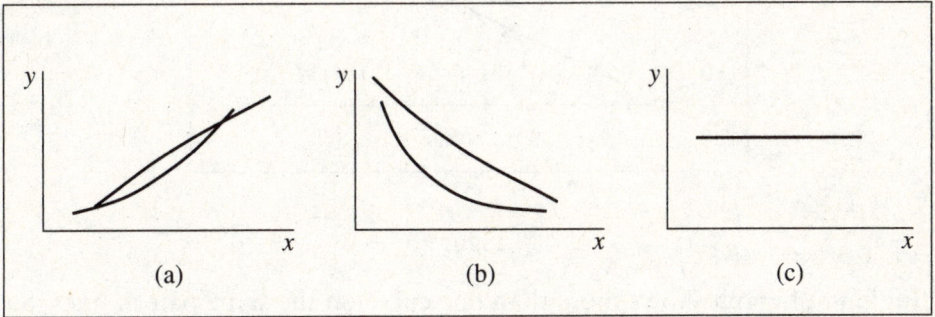

Figure 1

Sometimes, a question will ask you to estimate a value for one characteristic based on a given value of another characteristic that is beyond the limits of the curve shown on the graph. In this case, the solution will require you to *extrapolate*, or extend, the graph. If the curve is a relatively straight line, just use your pencil to extend that line far enough for the value called for to be included. If the graphed line is a curve, use your best judgment to extend the line to follow the apparent pattern. Figure 2 shows how to extend both types of graphs.

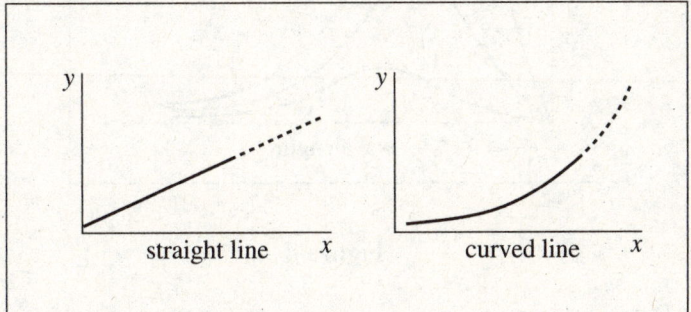

Figure 2

Another type of graph problem asks you to estimate a value that falls between two known values on a curve. This process is called *interpolation*. If the curve is shown, it amounts to finding a point on the curve that corresponds to a given value for one characteristic and reading the value for the other characteristic. (For example, "For a given x, find y.") If only scattered points are shown on the graph, draw a "best-fit line," a line that comes close to all of the points. Use this line to estimate the middle value. Figure 3 shows a best-fit line.

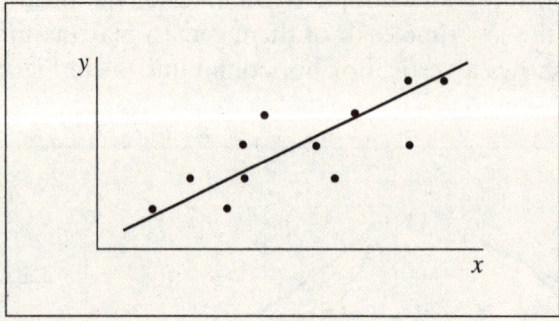

Figure 3

One very useful kind of graph shows more than one curve on the same pair of axes. Such a graph might be used when the results of a number of experiments are compared or when an experiment involves more than two variables. Analysis of this sort of graph requires that you determine the relationship shown by each curve and then determine how the curves are related to one another. Figure 4 shows a graph with multiple curves.

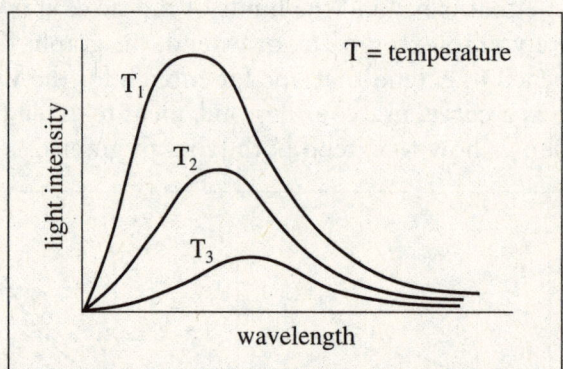

Figure 4

Think About How You Can Use the Information in Tables

While graphs and diagrams offer ways of illustrating data, sometimes you will have to work from raw data presented in a table. To understand what a table is showing you, you need to identify the information or data presented. You need to know two things about the information or data: the purpose it serves in the experiment, and the unit (or units) of measurement used to quantify it. Generally, experiments intentionally vary one characteristic (the independent variable) to see how it affects another (the dependent variable). Tables may report results for either or both.

Once you have identified the variables, it might be helpful to sketch a graph to illustrate the relationship between them. You might sketch an x-axis and a y-axis next to the table and decide which variable to represent on each axis. Mark off the axes with evenly spaced intervals that allow all of the numbers for a category to fit along each axis. Plot some points. Again, draw a best-fit line and characterize the relationship shown.

As with graphs and diagrams, you may be asked to look for trends in the data. For example, do the numbers representing the dependent variable increase or decrease as the numbers representing the independent variable increase or decrease? If no pattern is clear, you may want to sketch a rough graph as discussed above. You may also need to make predictions about values of quantities between the data points shown (interpolation), or beyond the limits of those shown on the table (extrapolation). Another type of problem may require you to compare data from multiple columns of a table. A simple examination of the numbers may be enough to see a relationship, but you may find it helpful to sketch a graph containing a curve for each category. The curves may be compared as described previously in "Think About How You Can Use the Information in Graphs and Diagrams" (page 116).

ACT Writing Test (Optional)

On the ACT Writing Test, you have 30 minutes to read a short prompt and to plan and write an essay in response to it. The prompts on the Writing Test cover a variety of subjects intended to reflect the interests and experiences of high school students, and they are designed to be appropriate for response in a 30-minute timed test.

The Writing Test is an optional test on the ACT. Should you decide to take the Writing Test, it will be administered after the four multiple-choice tests. Taking the Writing Test will **not** affect your scores on any of the multiple-choice tests or the Composite score. Rather, *in addition* to your scores from the multiple-choice tests and your Composite score, you will receive:

- two additional scores: a Combined English/Writing score on a scale from 1 through 36 (again, this score does **not** affect your score on the multiple-choice English Test), and a Writing Test subscore on a scale of 2 through 12

- between one and four narrative comments on your essay

- availability of your essay to your high school and colleges to which we report your scores from that test date

You will have a short break between the end of the last multiple-choice test and the beginning of the Writing Test.

Content of the ACT Writing Test

The ACT Writing Test is designed to measure your writing skills—specifically those writing skills taught in rigorous high school English and writing classes and expected of students entering first-year college composition courses.

The Writing Test consists of one writing prompt that briefly states an issue and describes two points of view on that issue. The prompt inquires about your opinion on the issue. You are asked to take a position and support that position with specific reasons and examples. The position you take does not affect your score. Your essay will be evaluated on the evidence it gives of your ability to do the following:

- express judgments by taking a position on the issue in the writing prompt

- maintain a focus on the topic throughout the essay

- develop a position by using logical reasoning and by supporting your ideas

- organize ideas in a logical way

- use language clearly and effectively according to the conventions of standard written English

The two different points of view provided in the writing prompt are designed to serve as examples of positions others have taken on the issue and to provide a starting place for your response. Should you choose to do so, you are welcome to adopt either point of view. If you adopt one of these points of view, you should state the position you're adopting and support the position with your own specific reasons and examples. If you choose not to adopt either of the points of view provided in the prompt, you should present a different point of view on the issue.

How Your Essay Will Be Scored

Your essay will be scored holistically (to see a copy of the actual Six-Point Holistic Scoring Rubric for the ACT Writing Test, please refer to page 141). In holistic scoring, no single aspect of writing is more important than any other—rather, it is the effectiveness of the writing as a whole that is most important. This means that your score will be assigned based on the overall impression created by all the elements of your writing. Two trained readers will separately score your essay, giving it a rating from 1 (low) to 6 (high). The sum of those ratings is your Writing Test subscore (2–12). If the readers' scores disagree by more than one point, a third reader will evaluate your essay and resolve the discrepancy.

Readers of your essay take into account that you had merely 30 minutes to compose and write your essay. Within that time limit, try to make your essay as polished as you can. Make sure that all words are written clearly and neatly so that the readers can read them easily. With careful planning, you should have time to briefly review your essay once you have finished writing it. Keep in mind that it is unlikely you will have time to rewrite or even recopy your essay within the time limit. Instead, you should take a few minutes to think through your essay and jot preliminary notes on the planning pages in the scoring booklet before you begin to write. Such preparatory work not only will help you organize your ideas and ensure that you don't forget anything, but also will help you pace your writing so that you finish your essay on time.

As we said earlier, taking the Writing Test will **not** affect your scores on any of the multiple-choice tests, nor will it affect your Composite score. Instead, if you take the Writing Test, you will receive two additional scores: one score for a combination of the English and Writing Tests (Combined English/Writing) on a scale of 1–36 and a Writing Test subscore on a scale of 2–12. Taking the Writing Test will **not** change your score on the English Test; the Combined English/Writing scale score and the Writing Test subscore will be reported *in addition to* the scores on the four multiple-choice tests. You will also receive between 1 and 4 coded narrative comments describing your essay. The comments will highlight strengths or weaknesses in your essay in relation to the scoring criteria in the Six-Point Holistic Scoring Rubric for the ACT Writing Test.

Types of Prompts on the ACT Writing Test

We've already mentioned that the prompts on the Writing Test cover a wide range of subjects, that these subjects are intended to reflect the interests and experiences of high school students, and that each prompt is designed to be appropriate for response in a 30-minute timed test. It's also important to note that the prompts do not require any specialized knowledge, so you should be able to use many things you have learned both in school and through your own experiences to support and explain the position you take in your essay.

Representative ACT Writing Test Prompt

Writing Test prompts are similar to the following example. The standard directions in the second paragraph will be a part of all prompts used in the Writing Test. You might want to practice by writing in response to this prompt for 30 minutes before you look ahead to the sample responses from other writers.

> In some high schools, many teachers and parents have encouraged the school to adopt a dress code that sets guidelines for what students can wear in the school building. Some teachers and parents support a dress code because they think it will improve the learning environment in the school. Other teachers and parents do not support a dress code because they think it restricts the individual student's freedom of expression. In your opinion, should high schools adopt dress codes for students?
>
> In your essay, take a position on this question. You may write about either one of the two points of view given, or you may present a different point of view on this question. Use specific reasons and examples to support your position.

Sample Essay Responses

The six essays that follow represent sample essays produced in response to the writing prompt given above. The essays illustrate how writing at different levels is evaluated and scored for the ACT Writing Test. The essays in no way represent a full range of ideas, approaches, or styles that could be used to fulfill this writing task. While we all can learn from reading other people's writing, you are encouraged to bring your own distinct, imaginative, personal writing skills to the test. You want to produce your own best essay writing for the Writing Test—not an imitation of someone else's essay writing.

The following essays have been evaluated using the Six-Point Holistic Scoring Rubric for the ACT Writing Test printed on page 141. This same rubric will be used to score the response that you write for the ACT Writing Test. Each essay is followed by a Scoring Explanation that comments on the essay.

Please enter the information at the right before beginning the Writing Test.

Use a soft lead No. 2 pencil only. Do NOT use a mechanical pencil, ink, ballpoint, or felt-tip pen.

WRITING TEST BOOKLET NUMBER

Print your 6-digit **Booklet Number** in the boxes at the right.

WRITING TEST FORM

Print your 3-character **Test Form** in the boxes above and fill in the corresponding oval at the right.

- ○ 40C
- ○ 41C
- ○ 42C
- ○ 43C
- ○ 44C
- ○ 45C
- ○ 46C
- ○ 47C
- ○ 48C
- ○ 49C
- ○ 50C
- ○ 51C
- ○ 52C
- ○ 53C
- ○ 54C
- ○ 55C
- ○ 56C
- ○ 57C
- ○ 58C
- ○ 59C
- ○ 60D

Begin WRITING TEST here.

Well I don't think they should have a dress code because, it takes away from the kids. We shouldn't be mindless drones. I thought this is America were you can express yourself. ~~By~~ The government should stay out of it. Next they will be telling us what we should eat and think. I think if they look good they should be able to wear what they want to. If they start to control how we dress. Next, they will control everything. I for one want to think and dress for myself. If we let them tell us what to do slowly our ~~freg~~ freedoms will reduced to nothing.

If you need more space, please continue on the next page.

Essay Example I (Score = 1)

Scoring Explanation

Essays that earn a score of 1 generally demonstrate little understanding of the purpose of the writing task, and this essay is a good example of that. The prompt indicates that the writing task is to take a position and support that position with specific reasons and examples. Essays in the 1 score range often fail to take a clear position. Or, if they do take a position, they fail to fulfill the second half of the task, which is to support that position. The writer of this essay takes a position on the issue in the prompt (*I don't think they should have a dress code*) and maintains focus on the general topic, but does not support his position. Although one reason is expressed for taking his position (*it takes away from the kids*), most of the essay seems to be discussing a different reason for taking that position (*If they start to control how we dress. Next, they will control everything*). Both ideas could be developed into strong support, if the writer explained and illustrated what he means. However, a lack of organization—or even of basic groupings of similar ideas—prevents either idea from being adequately expressed. Although a few transitions appear, they do not effectively link ideas. For the most part, word choice and sentence structure in this essay are very simple and riddled with frequently distracting errors. It is a very weak response.

Please enter the information at the right before beginning the Writing Test.

Use a soft lead No. 2 pencil only. Do NOT use a mechanical pencil, ink, ballpoint, or felt-tip pen.

WRITING TEST BOOKLET NUMBER

Print your 6-digit **Booklet Number** in the boxes at the right.

WRITING TEST FORM

Print your 3-character **Test Form** in the boxes above <u>and</u> fill in the corresponding oval at the right.

- 40C
- 41C
- 42C
- 43C
- 44C
- 45C
- 46C
- 47C
- 48C
- 49C
- 50C
- 51C
- 52C
- 53C
- 54C
- 55C
- 56C
- 57C
- 58C
- 59C
- 60D

Begin WRITING TEST here.

I agree with parents and teachers who say dress codes is needed. Dress codes sets guidelines for what students wear and helps the learning environment.

Uniforms encourage equality. They sets guidelines for what students wear so everyone looks the same. Uniforms encourage people to be equal by setting what all students wear at school.

Uniforms helps stops rivalry between groups and "clicks". Uniforms put an end to groups at school because everyone looks the same. If everyone looks the same than groups won't divide people by how they look because uniforms makes everyone equal. All students would be the same if they wear uniforms.

These is just a few of the many benefits to wearing a uniform. A dress code is only one ~~way~~ way of creating a good school environment, but it is a good one.

If you need more space, please continue on the next page.

Essay Example II (Score = 2)
Scoring Explanation

Essays that earn a score of 2 demonstrate either weak or inconsistent skill in responding to the task. This writer takes a clear position on the issue (*I agree with parents and teachers who say dress codes is needed*) and supplies a specific explanation for taking that position (*Dress codes sets guidelines for what students wear and helps the learning environment*). However, discussion focuses on an assumption (dress code = school uniform) that is not explained or made clear. This writer's inconsistency is apparent when comparing the content and form of her essay. There is no recognition of a counterargument to her position. Also, development of ideas is extremely minimal and repetitious: the second and third short paragraphs repeat the same idea. However, an organizational structure is in place, including a discernible introduction and conclusion. While the writer has written four distinct paragraphs, no transitional words or phrases are used. The essay's word choice and sentence structure are simple. Some errors, such as the lack of agreement between subjects and verbs, are very distracting. Overall, this is a weak response demonstrating a very few traits of developing skill.

Please enter the information at the right before beginning the Writing Test.

Use a soft lead No. 2 pencil only. Do NOT use a mechanical pencil, ink, ballpoint, or felt-tip pen.

WRITING TEST BOOKLET NUMBER

Print your 6-digit **Booklet Number** in the boxes at the right.

WRITING TEST FORM

Print your 3-character **Test Form** in the boxes above and fill in the corresponding oval at the right.

- ○ 40C
- ○ 41C
- ○ 42C
- ○ 43C
- ○ 44C
- ○ 45C
- ○ 46C
- ○ 47C
- ○ 48C
- ○ 49C
- ○ 50C
- ○ 51C
- ○ 52C
- ○ 53C
- ○ 54C
- ○ 55C
- ○ 56C
- ○ 57C
- ○ 58C
- ○ 59C
- ○ 60D

Begin WRITING TEST here.

In my opinion, teenagers should not have to have a dress code, because it restricts them and takes away a freedom they should have. I'm not talking about clothes that are tight or reveal a student's body, that kind of clothes should be restricted. But to enforce a code that tells them they can't wear kahkies or jeans, T-shirts or dress shirts, would clearly infringe upon their rights.

One of our rights is the right to express ourselves. Teenagers wear hats and T-shirts with sayings on them, and they wear clothes that show what group they belong to at school or to show they know whats trendy.

If we are restricted in what clothes we can wear, it is a clear violation of the basic rights America was built upon. If these rights are removed, who knows where it could lead next. Will schools start telling students what music they can listen to or what they have to eat for lunch?

If you need more space, please continue on the next page.

WRITING TEST

Dress codes are unfair because some families can't afford uniforms or proper clothes. If we had a dress code, some kids would need a whole new wardrobe—you would need regular clothes for outside of school, plus your uniform or better clothes for school. This is unfair to poorer students.

A dress code is a poor idea because it infringes on our right of freedom of expression and it can be a financial burden put upon students. It would be better if there was no dress code.

If you need more space, please continue on the back of this page.

Essay Example III (Score = 3)

Scoring Explanation

Essays that earn a score of 3 show developing skill in responding to the task. That is true of this essay, which demonstrates more awareness of writing choices than do the essays that scored lower than a 3. The essay takes a position on the issue in the prompt (*teenagers should not have to have a dress code*), gives reasoning for that position (*because it restricts them and takes away a freedom they should have*), and further explains the reasoning in order to make the writer's meaning clear (*I'm not talking about clothes that are tight or reveal a student's body, that kind of clothes should be restricted. But to enforce a code that tells them they can't wear kahkies or jeans, T-shirts or dress shirts, would clearly infringe upon their rights*). However, although the writer recognizes and acknowledges that there may be circumstances in which a dress code is appropriate, he offers no context for his discussion and does not clarify the apparent distinction between a dress code and school uniforms. There is no recognition of a counterargument.

The writer presents some relevant ideas in the second and third paragraphs, sequencing them appropriately. The fourth paragraph offers an additional idea (*Dress codes are unfair because some families can't afford uniforms or proper clothes*) which does not fit the essay's focus (*a dress code . . . restricts them and takes away a freedom they should have*) but which demonstrates the writer is trying to generate support for his position. Ultimately, all three paragraphs contain thoughts that are underdeveloped and examples that are too general to adequately support the writer's claims.

There is a simple organizational structure in this essay that indicates the developing skill of the writer. The organization and sequencing serve to tie ideas together somewhat, but the essay lacks transitions, and the conclusion is underdeveloped and lacks focus as a result of the new idea introduced in the fourth paragraph. Ideas are logically grouped, but there is little evidence of logical sequencing of ideas throughout the essay.

The essay demonstrates a writer beginning to craft language by exhibiting a little sentence variety and clear word choice. Spelling errors and unnecessary shifts of person ("teenagers" are referred to as "they," "we," and "you" in different parts of the essay) distract the reader, but these errors do not prevent understanding.

Please enter the information at the right before beginning the Writing Test.

Use a soft lead No. 2 pencil only. Do NOT use a mechanical pencil, ink, ballpoint, or felt-tip pen.

WRITING TEST BOOKLET NUMBER

Print your 6-digit **Booklet Number** in the boxes at the right.

WRITING TEST FORM

Print your 3-character **Test Form** in the boxes above and fill in the corresponding oval at the right.

- 40C
- 41C
- 42C
- 43C
- 44C
- 45C
- 46C
- 47C
- 48C
- 49C
- 50C
- 51C
- 52C
- 53C
- 54C
- 55C
- 56C
- 57C
- 58C
- 59C
- 60D

Begin WRITING TEST here.

I believe that it would be beneficial for our schools to adopt dress codes. Although some may argue that this action would restrict the individual student's freedom of expression, I do not agree. Our right to express ourselves is important, but in our society none of us has unrestricted freedom to do as we like at all times. We must all learn discipline, respect the feelings of others, and learn how to operate in the real world to be successful. Dress codes would not only create a better learning environment, but would also help prepare students for their futures.

Perhaps the most important benefit of adopting dress codes would be creating a better learning environment. Inappropriate clothing can be distracting to fellow students who are trying to concentrate. Short skirts, skimpy tops, and low pants are fine for after school, but not for the classroom. T-shirts with risky images or profanity may be offensive to certain groups. Students should express themselves through art or creative writing, not clothing. With fewer distractions, students can concentrate on getting a good education which

If you need more space, please continue on the next page.

WRITING TEST

can help them later on.

Another benefit of having a dress code is that it will prepare students to dress properly for different places. When you go to a party you do not wear the same clothes you wear to church. Likewise, when you dress for work you do not wear the same clothes you wear at the beach. Many professions even require uniforms. Having a dress code in high school will help students adjust to the real world.

Lastly, with all the peer pressure in school, many students worry about fitting in. If a dress code (or even uniforms) were required, there would be less emphasis on how you look, and more emphasis on learning.

In Conclusion, there are many important reasons our schools should adopt dress codes. Getting an education is hard enough without being distracted by inappropriate t-shirts or tight pants. Learning to dress for particular occasions prepares us for the real world. And teens have enough pressure already without having to worry about what they are wearing.

If you need more space, please continue on the back of this page.

Essay Example IV (Score = 4)

Scoring Explanation

Essays that earn a score of 4 demonstrate adequate skill in responding to the task. This essay takes a position on the issue in the prompt (*I believe that it would be beneficial for our schools to adopt dress codes*) but acknowledges the counterargument as well (*Although some may argue that this action would restrict the individual student's freedom of expression*).

Essays that earn a 4 tend to be fairly consistent and balanced, if predictable, responses. Most ideas in this essay are adequately developed, with the fourth paragraph being the least developed. The writer expands on her claims by developing each paragraph, supporting her ideas by using movement between general ideas (*Inappropriate clothing can be distracting to fellow students who are trying to concentrate*) and specific ideas (*Short shorts, skimpy tops, and low pants are fine for after school, but not for the classroom*). Focus is maintained on the specific issue of dress codes in high schools throughout the essay.

The essay is clearly, though predictably, organized. No credit is earned or lost specifically for using a familiar writing formula such as this one; in this case the basic structure worked adequately to help this writer develop her ideas logically. The introduction and conclusion are clear and somewhat developed, adding to the balance and consistency of the essay.

The writer demonstrates awareness of good writing choices through some logical sequencing of ideas and use of clear transitions to link paragraphs. Language control is adequate in this essay, with some sentence variety and appropriate word choice. There are few distracting errors.

PAGE 4

WRITING TEST BOOKLET NUMBER

Print your 6-digit **Booklet Number** in the boxes at the right.

WRITING TEST FORM

Print your 3-character **Test Form** in the boxes above and fill in the corresponding oval at the right.

○ 40C   ○ 52C
○ 41C   ○ 53C
○ 42C   ○ 54C
○ 43C   ○ 55C
○ 44C   ○ 56C
○ 45C   ○ 57C
○ 46C   ○ 58C
○ 47C   ○ 59C
○ 48C   ○ 60D
○ 49C
○ 50C
○ 51C

Begin WRITING TEST here.

Many teachers and parents are now debating whether or not a dress code should be adopted. They think that it will improve the learning environment in our schools, and I agree. I think that if we had a dress code, it would substantially improve the quality of our education. First, it would allow students to focus on academics rather than social aspects of school. Second, it would improve the appearance of school, and third, it will prepare students for the working world.

First, and most importantly, implementing a dress code will substantially reduce distractions in the classroom. It is important for our future success to be able to concentrate on what we are being taught, but it is difficult to do this when some students are whispering about what others are wearing, and others are admiring someone's Air Jordans. Too many young people today are more interested in style than substance. Plus, lots of kids think of school as a social club instead of a place to get

If you need more space, please continue on the next page.

WRITING TEST

an education.

Secondly, I believe that when students and faculty are well groomed, it improves the school esthetically. It is not necessary to dress formally to accomplish this. Requiring long pants (and an option of skirts for girls) and a collared shirt would be enough. Not only would the school and it's student body look more professional, I believe it would change the tone of the school. If a person is required to hold themselves to a certain standard, they will. Having to dress more maturely can make students act more maturely as well.

My final reason for supporting a standard of dress in high school is that it would prepare the youth of today for the workforce of tomorrow. The vast majority of jobs require some type of dress code or standard. Therefore I think that it is important to prepare students not only academically but also in conduct and grooming. Someone might have impressive qualifications, but if they look like a bum off the street, it is highly doubtful that they would be hired. Letting students dress any way they want might actually be hurting them in the long run.

Even though some teachers and parents think

If you need more space, please continue on the back of this page.

WRITING TEST

that establishing a dress code would restrict the individual student's freedom of expression. I still think having one is a good idea. Students aren't really ~~serious~~ trying to exercise their rights when they wear skimpy clothing, they just want to show off and be trendy. We have to look at what is most important. When students wear t-shirts with political slogans that might offend others or dress in skimpy outfits it can distract other students and detract from our learning environment. At this time in our lives the most important thing we have to do is get a good education so we can succeed in college and later life.

In conclusion, I am highly in favor of a dress code. Not only will it improve our learning environment by keeping classroom distractions to a minimum, it will also improve the tone of the school and prepare students to be successful in their future careers.

If you need more space, please continue on the next page.

Essay Example V (Score = 5)

Scoring Explanation

Essays that earn a score of 5 are clearly competent, and this essay is a good example. This writer has planned his essay well, which allowed him to make clear his position on the issue (*I think that if we had a dress code, it would substantially improve the quality of our education*) while also providing a context for the discussion (*Many teachers and parents are now debating whether or not a dress code should be adopted*) and setting up his support (*First, it would allow students to focus on academics. . . . Second, it would improve the appearance of school, and* [*Finally*], *it will prepare students for the working world*). In addition to supporting his own position, the writer addresses the complexity of the issue by responding to a counterargument in the fifth paragraph.

Although the essay is somewhat repetitious, development of ideas is specific and logical: the writer uses specific examples to illustrate each point (*Air Jordans and long pants . . . and a collared shirt*). The writer also maintains a clear focus on the specific issue of the impact of dress codes in high schools throughout the essay.

The essay is clearly organized. There is evidence of logical progression of ideas throughout the essay, although the transitions are predictable. The introduction and conclusion are well developed and successfully focus the essay.

The writer has good language control (*Therefore I think that it is important to prepare students not only academically but also in conduct and grooming*). There are only a few distracting errors in this writer's response.

Please enter the information at the right before beginning the Writing Test.

Use a soft lead No. 2 pencil only. Do NOT use a mechanical pencil, ink, ballpoint, or felt-tip pen.

WRITING TEST BOOKLET NUMBER

Print your 6-digit **Booklet Number** in the boxes at the right.

WRITING TEST FORM

Print your 3-character **Test Form** in the boxes above and fill in the corresponding oval at the right.

○ 40C   ○ 52C
○ 41C   ○ 53C
○ 42C   ○ 54C
○ 43C   ○ 55C
○ 44C   ○ 56C
○ 45C   ○ 57C
○ 46C   ○ 58C
○ 47C   ○ 59C
○ 48C   ○ 60D
○ 49C
○ 50C
○ 51C

Begin WRITING TEST here.

Parents and educators are increasingly concerned about the trend toward inappropriate dress in our schools. They feel that clothing that is too tight or too revealing may distract students and interfere with learning. They believe that a dress code should be adopted which would set guidelines for what students should wear in the school building. Others feel that a dress code should not be enacted because it would restrict individual students' freedom of expression.

Freedom of expression is important, but when inappropriate attire begins to interfere with the educational process, something needs to be done. Allowing students to wear whatever they want is clearly not working. Too many teens today seek to emulate rock stars and pick up fashion tips from MTV. In a culture that is inundated with sexual innuendo or worse, it is not surprising that kids show up at school in suggestive clothing. The educators are right. Short skirts and spandex tops can be extremely distracting to a population group driven largely by hormones. Establishing a dress code could help improve the learning environment in the school; unfortunately, dress codes can be extremely arbitrary and difficult to enforce. What is the solution? I think the answer is school uniforms. This option would be far easier to enforce and has several advantages.

If you need more space, please continue on the next page.

WRITING TEST

From a financial perspective, school uniforms could help even the playing field between poor and rich students. We live in a materialistic world and, for some, it is all about the label. They think that if its not Tommy, Levi, Gap, etc. that it is not good enough. Students can be cruel, and make fun of those who do not dress the same as they do. Wearing jeans with holes may be one student's form of expression but another's necessity. Mandating uniforms would dispense with this kind of descrimination. Purchasing a uniform would be far less expensive than a complete school wardrobe, and if there were some families that couldn't afford it, perhaps the school could provide one for them, or at least help defray the expense.

Another benefit of school uniforms is that they could help curb some of the gang-related violence in our schools. Gangs are associated with certain colors and members often hassle students who wear an opposing gang's color. Sporting the innocent-looking sweater Aunt Rose gave you for your birthday could be like waving a red flag in front of an angry bull. With uniforms, this problem would disappear.

From a personal perspective, I would enjoy the sheer effort-lessness of not having to rummage through my closet each morning trying to decide what to wear. Some may enjoy selecting their outfit for the day, but not me! Having a school uniform would make my morning routine go much faster, and maybe even leave a little extra time to finish up yesterday's homework.

While uniforms in high schools promise many benefits, we should not expect that they are a cure-all. Uniforms

If you need more space, please continue on the back of this page.

PAGE 6

WRITING TEST

alone will not raise student grades, confer equality, or make schools entirely safe for all students. Uniforms cannot learn math or earn high scores on state tests. Students must do these things for themselves. However, I do believe that uniforms in high schools can go a long way toward helping students succeed by providing a learning environment that supports achievement rather than one that is distracting, descriminating, and dangerous.

So, in conclusion, I strongly support not just a dress code, which would be difficult to enforce, but a resolution to adopt school uniforms for our entire district. Uniforms would not ~~solve~~ solve the problems associated with inappropriate dress and create a better learning environment, but could also serve to end inequality, help curb gang violence, and make our mornings a little less hectic.

If you need more space, please continue on the next page.

Essay Example VI (Score = 6)

Scoring Explanation

Essays that earn a score of 6 are effective essays that represent strong responses to the writing task. This essay is very strong and effective. It recognizes and addresses the complexity of the issue by dealing with several perspectives on the issue (parents and educators who are concerned about inappropriate dress, others who are protective of freedom of expression, the financial perspective, the author's personal perspective), by exploring some cultural dimensions of the issue (popular culture and gang violence), and by anticipating and responding to counterarguments (*Freedom of expression is important, but when inappropriate attire begins to interfere with the educational process, something needs to be done. . . . While uniforms in high schools promise many benefits, we should not expect that they are a cure-all*). Development of most ideas is thorough and logical, and the writer includes specific reasons and details for each of her arguments.

Organization is clear and ideas are logically sequenced both within and between paragraphs. Most transitions reflect the writer's logic and are integrated into the essay (Transitions between the first three paragraphs are particularly effective). The introduction offers a full context for the issue and segues into the writer's statement of position in the second paragraph very effectively. The conclusion is clear and adequately developed as well.

This writer's language is effective (*Sporting the innocent-looking sweater Aunt Rose gave you for your birthday could be like waving a red flag in front of an angry bull*) and shows good command: sentences are varied and word choice is varied and precise (*Mandating uniforms would dispense with this kind of discrimination*). Overall, this is a considered, eloquent and thorough response. The few errors present do not distract the reader.

Six-Point Holistic Scoring Rubric for the ACT Writing Test

Papers at each level exhibit *all* or *most* of the characteristics described at each score point.

Score = 6
Essays within this score range demonstrate effective skill in responding to the task.

The essay shows a clear understanding of the task. The essay takes a position on the issue and may offer a critical context for discussion. The essay addresses complexity by examining different perspectives on the issue, or by evaluating the implications and/or complications of the issue, or by fully responding to counterarguments to the writer's position. Development of ideas is ample, specific, and logical. Most ideas are fully elaborated. A clear focus on the specific issue in the prompt is maintained. The organization of the essay is clear: the organization may be somewhat predictable or it may grow from the writer's purpose. Ideas are logically sequenced. Most transitions reflect the writer's logic and are usually integrated into the essay. The introduction and conclusion are effective, clear, and well developed. The essay shows a good command of language. Sentences are varied and word choice is varied and precise. There are few, if any, errors to distract the reader.

Score = 5
Essays within this score range demonstrate competent skill in responding to the task.

The essay shows a clear understanding of the task. The essay takes a position on the issue and may offer a broad context for discussion. The essay shows recognition of complexity by partially evaluating the implications and/or complications of the issue, or by responding to counterarguments to the writer's position. Development of ideas is specific and logical. Most ideas are elaborated, with clear movement between general statements and specific reasons, examples, and details. Focus on the specific issue in the prompt is maintained. The organization of the essay is clear, although it may be predictable. Ideas are logically sequenced, although simple and obvious transitions may be used. The introduction and conclusion are clear and generally well developed. Language is competent. Sentences are somewhat varied and word choice is sometimes varied and precise. There may be a few errors, but they are rarely distracting.

Score = 4
Essays within this score range demonstrate adequate skill in responding to the task.

The essay shows an understanding of the task. The essay takes a position on the issue and may offer some context for discussion. The essay may show some recognition of complexity by providing some response to counterarguments to the writer's position. Development of ideas is adequate, with some movement between general statements and specific reasons, examples, and details. Focus on the specific issue in the prompt is maintained throughout most of the essay. The organization of the essay is apparent but predictable. Some evidence of logical sequencing of ideas is apparent, although most transitions are simple and obvious. The introduction and conclusion are clear and somewhat developed. Language is adequate, with some sentence variety and appropriate word choice. There may be some distracting errors, but they do not impede understanding.

Score = 3
Essays within this score range demonstrate some developing skill in responding to the task.

The essay shows some understanding of the task. The essay takes a position on the issue but does not offer a context for discussion. The essay may acknowledge a counterargument to the writer's position, but its development is brief or unclear. Development of ideas is limited and may be repetitious, with little, if any, movement between general statements and specific reasons, examples, and details. Focus on the general topic is maintained, but focus on the specific issue in the prompt may not be maintained. The organization of the essay is simple. Ideas are logically grouped within parts of the essay, but there is little or no evidence of logical sequencing of ideas. Transitions, if used, are simple and obvious. An introduction and conclusion are clearly discernible but underdeveloped. Language shows a basic control. Sentences show a little variety and word choice is appropriate. Errors may be distracting and may occasionally impede understanding.

Score = 2
Essays within this score range demonstrate inconsistent or weak skill in responding to the task.

The essay shows a weak understanding of the task. The essay may not take a position on the issue, or the essay may take a position but fail to convey reasons to support that position, or the essay may take a position but fail to maintain a stance. There is little or no recognition of a counterargument to the writer's position. The essay is thinly developed. If examples are given, they are general and may not be clearly relevant. The essay may include extensive repetition of the writer's ideas or of ideas in the prompt. Focus on the general topic is maintained, but focus on the specific issue in the prompt may not be maintained. There is some indication of an organizational structure, and some logical grouping of ideas within parts of the essay is apparent. Transitions, if used, are simple and obvious, and they may be inappropriate or misleading. An introduction and conclusion are discernible but minimal. Sentence structure and word choice are usually simple. Errors may be frequently distracting and may sometimes impede understanding.

Score = 1
Essays within this score range show little or no skill in responding to the task.

The essay shows little or no understanding of the task. If the essay takes a position, it fails to convey reasons to support that position. The essay is minimally developed. The essay may include excessive repetition of the writer's ideas or of ideas in the prompt. Focus on the general topic is usually maintained, but focus on the specific issue in the prompt may not be maintained. There is little or no evidence of an organizational structure or of the logical grouping of ideas. Transitions are rarely used. If present, an introduction and conclusion are minimal. Sentence structure and word choice are simple. Errors may be frequently distracting and may significantly impede understanding.

No Score
Blank, Off-Topic, Illegible, Not in English, or Void

Strategies for Taking the ACT Writing Test

Pace Yourself

The ACT Writing Test gives you 30 minutes to read and think about the issue in the prompt, and to plan and write your essay. When asked to write a timed essay, most writers find it useful to do some prewriting or planning before they write the essay, and to do a final check of the essay when it is finished. It is unlikely that you will have time to draft, revise, and recopy your essay. Therefore, taking a few minutes to plan your essay is a much better strategy than writing a first draft with the intent to copy it over for the final essay.

Prewrite

Some writers like to plunge right in, but this is seldom a good way to do well on a timed essay. Prewriting gets you acquainted with the issue, suggests patterns for presenting your thoughts, and gives you a little breathing room to come up with interesting ideas for introducing and concluding your essay. Before writing, then, carefully consider the prompt and make sure you understand it—reread it if you aren't sure. Decide how you want to answer the question in the prompt. Then jot down your ideas on the topic: this might simply be a list of ideas, reasons, and examples that you will use to explain your point of view on the issue. Write down what you think someone might say in opposition to your point of view and think about how you would refute their argument. Think of how best to organize the ideas in your essay. You should do your prewriting on the pages provided in your Writing Test booklet. You can refer back to these notes as you write the essay itself on the lined pages in your answer document.

Write

Once you're ready to write your essay, proceed with the confidence that you have prepared well and that you will have attentive and receptive readers who are interested in your ideas. At the beginning of your essay, make sure readers will see that you understand the issue. Explain your point of view in a clear and logical way. If possible, discuss the issue in a broader context or evaluate the implications or complications of the issue. Address what others might say to refute your point of view and present a counterargument. Use specific examples to explain and illustrate what you're saying. Vary the structure of your sentences, and use varied and precise word choices. Make logical relationships clear by using transitional words and phrases. Don't wander off the topic. End with a strong conclusion that summarizes or reinforces your position.

Is it advisable to organize the essay by using a formula, like "the five-paragraph essay"? Points are neither awarded nor deducted for following familiar formulas, so feel free to use one or not as best suits your preference. Some writers find formulas stifling, other writers find them a solid basis upon which to build a strong argument, and still other writers just keep them handy to use when needed. The exact numbers of words and paragraphs in your essay are less important than the clarity and development of your ideas. Writers who have something to say usually find that their ideas have a way of sorting themselves out at reasonable length and in an appropriate number of paragraphs.

Review Your Essay

Take a few minutes at the end of the testing session to read over your essay. Correct any mistakes in grammar, usage, punctuation, and spelling. If you find any words that are hard to read, recopy them so your readers can read them easily. Make any corrections and revisions neatly, between the lines (but not in the margins). Your readers take into account that you had merely 30 minutes to compose and write your essay. Within that time limit, try to make your essay as polished as you can.

Practice

There are many ways to prepare for the ACT Writing Test. You may be surprised that these include reading newspapers and magazines, listening to news analysis on television or radio, and participating in discussions and debates about issues and problems. These activities help you become more familiar with current issues, with different perspectives on those issues, and with strategies that skilled writers and speakers use to present their points of view.

Of course, one of the best ways to prepare for the ACT Writing Test is to practice writing. Practice writing different kinds of texts, for different purposes, with different audiences in mind. Writing you do in your English classes will help you. So will practice in writing essays, stories, poems, plays, editorials, reports, letters to the editor, a personal journal, or other kinds of writing that you do on your own. Strive for your writing to be well developed and well organized, using precise, clear and concise language. Because the ACT Writing Test asks you to explain your perspective on an issue in a convincing way, writing opportunities like editorials or letters to the editor of a newspaper are especially helpful. Practicing a variety of different kinds of writing will help make you a versatile writer able to adjust to different writing occasions and assignments.

Share your writing with others and get feedback. Feedback helps you anticipate how readers might interpret your writing and what types of questions they might have. It will also help you identify your strengths and weaknesses as a writer. Also, keep in mind what the readers will be looking for as they score your essay by examining the Six-Point Holistic Scoring Rubric for the ACT Writing Test (see page 141). Make sure your writing meets the criteria described for the high-scoring essays.

You should also get some practice writing within a time limit. This will help build skills that are important in college-level learning and in the world of work. Taking the practice ACT Writing Tests in this book will give you a good idea of what timed writing is like and how much additional practice you may need.

Moving to the Next Step

ACT. The example passages and questions in this chapter, taken from previous ACTs and representing each of the content areas that make up the ACT, were used to illustrate some of the different types of questions you can expect to see when you take the ACT. At this point, you may want to consider two different strategies for continuing to study for the ACT: studying in more depth some of the topics that have been covered in this chapter, perhaps with a study or a teacher, or continuing in this book and taking the practice tests in chapter 4 to see how you're progressing in your preparation for the ACT.

Note: The writing sections in this book do not represent enhancements to the design of the ACT writing test that will start with the September 12, 2015 ACT National test date. Read more about the most current information on the ACT writing test at www.actstudent.org/writing/enhancements.

Chapter 4:
Practice ACT Tests

In this chapter, you'll find five complete practice ACT tests, copies of real answer documents that you will use to record your answers, three complete sets of explanatory answers for the questions on all of the multiple-choice tests, and a description of the testing conditions under which you should take the practice tests.

Each practice test features the content tests in the same order as they will be on the ACT: the English Test, the Mathematics Test, the Reading Test, the Science Test, and the optional Writing Test. Following each complete practice test, you will find the explanatory answers for the multiple-choice questions on that test in the same pattern as the individual tests (English, Mathematics, Reading, and Science).

Two copies of answer documents that you can tear out and use to record your answers for the multiple-choice tests precede each practice test. (Two copies of these answer documents have been provided in case you make errors, or if you would like to retake a practice test. When you take the actual ACT, however, you will only be provided with one answer document.) One copy of the Writing Test answer document, which you can tear out (or photocopy) and use to write your essay, is provided for each practice Writing Test.

Testing Conditions

Taking the practice tests can help you become familiar with the ACT. It will be most helpful if you take the tests under conditions that are as similar as possible to those you will experience on the actual test day. The following tips will help you make the most of the practice tests:

- The four multiple-choice tests require a total of 2 hours and 55 minutes. Try an entire practice test in one sitting, with a 10-minute break between the Mathematics Test and the Reading Test. (If you are taking the Writing Test, you may also take a short break of roughly 5 minutes after the Science Test.)

- Sit at a desk with good lighting. You will need sharpened No. 2 pencils with good erasers. You may not use mechanical pencils or highlight pens. Remove all books and other aids from your desk. On test day, you will not be allowed to use references or notes. You won't need scratch paper because each page of the Mathematics Test has a blank column that you can use for scratch work.

- **If you plan to use a calculator on the Mathematics Test, review the details about permissible calculators on ACT's website, www.actstudent.org. Use a calculator with which you are familiar for both the practice test and on test day. You may use any four-function, scientific, or graphing calculator on the Mathematics Test, except as specified on ACT's website.**

- Use a digital timer or clock to time yourself on each test. Set your timer for five minutes less than the allotted time for each test so you can get used to the five-minute warning. (Students approved for extended-time should set a timer for 60-minute warnings up to the total time allowed—5 hours or 5 hours, 45 minutes.)

- Allow yourself only the time permitted for each test.

- Detach and use one sample multiple-choice answer document.

- Read the general test directions on the first page of the practice test. These are the same directions that will appear on your test booklet on the test day. After you have read the directions, start your timer and begin with the English Test. Continue through the Science Test, taking a short break between the Mathematics Test and the Reading Test. If you do not plan to take the ACT Writing Test, score your multiple-choice tests using the information in chapter 5.

- If you plan to take the Writing Test, take a short break after the Science Test. Detach (or photocopy) the Writing Test answer document that follows the Writing Test planning pages. Then read the test directions on the first page of the practice ACT Writing Test. These are the same directions that will appear on your test booklet on test day. After you have read the directions, start your timer, then carefully read the prompt. After you have considered what the prompt is asking you to do, use the unlined pages in your test booklet to plan your essay, and then write your essay on the lined pages of the answer document. When you have finished, score your essay using the information in chapter 5.

The ACT® *Sample Answer Sheet*

A   **NAME, MAILING ADDRESS, AND TELEPHONE**
(Please print.)

Last Name   First Name   MI (Middle Initial)

House Number & Street (Apt. No.); or PO Box & No.; or RR & No.

City   State/Province   ZIP/Postal Code

Area Code   Number   Country

ACT, Inc.—Confidential Restricted when data present.

ALL examinees must complete block A – please print.

REGISTERED examinees **MUST complete blocks B, C, and D.** Find the MATCHING INFORMATION on your admission ticket and enter it EXACTLY the same way, even if any of the information is missing or incorrect. Fill in the corresponding ovals. If you do not complete these blocks to match your admission ticket EXACTLY, your scores will be **delayed up to 8 weeks.** Leave blocks E and F blank.

STANDBY examinees **MUST complete blocks B, D, and F.** Enter your information in blocks B and D and fill in the corresponding ovals. Leave block C blank. **For block E,** if you provided your SSN when you created your Web account or completed your standby folder, enter it here. The SSN will be used to help match this document to your registration information and will be included on reports to your college choices. If you did not provide it earlier, do not know it, or do not wish to provide it, leave block E blank. Be sure to fill in the oval in block F.

Do NOT mark in this shaded area.

B   **MATCH NAME**
(First 5 letters of last name)

C   **MATCH NUMBER**
(Registered examinees only)

D   **DATE OF BIRTH**

Month	Day	Year
○ Jan.		
○ Feb.		
○ March		
○ April		
○ May		
○ June		
○ July		
○ Aug.		
○ Sept.		
○ Oct.		
○ Nov.		
○ Dec.		

↓ STANDBY TESTING ONLY ↓

E   **SOCIAL SECURITY NUMBER**
(Standby examinees only)

F   **STANDBY TESTING**

Fill in the oval below ONLY if you turned in a standby registration at the test center today.

○ Yes, I am testing as a standby.

USE A SOFT LEAD NO. 2 PENCIL ONLY.
(Do NOT use a mechanical pencil, ink, ballpoint, correction fluid, or felt-tip pen.)

EXAMINEE STATEMENT AND SIGNATURE

1. Read the following **Statement:** By submitting this answer sheet, I agree to the terms and conditions set forth in the ACT registration booklet or website for this exam, including the arbitration and dispute remedy provisions. I understand that ACT owns the test questions and responses and affirm that I will not share any test questions or responses with anyone by any form of communication.

2. Copy the **Certification** shown below (only the text in italics) on the lines provided. Write in your normal handwriting.

   Certification: *I agree to the Statement above and certify that I am the person whose name and address appear on this form.*

3. Sign your name as you would any official document and enter today's date.

Your Signature   Today's Date

ACT®

P.O. BOX 168, IOWA CITY, IOWA 52243-0168

PAGE 2

BOOKLET NUMBER

FORM

BE SURE TO FILL IN THE CORRECT FORM OVAL.

○ 1MC ○ 2MC ○ 3MC ○ 4MC
○ 5MC

Marking Directions: Mark only **one** oval for each question. Fill in response completely. Erase errors cleanly without smudging.

Correct mark: ○ ● ○ ○

- -

Do NOT use these *incorrect* or *bad* **marks.**

Incorrect marks: Ⓥ ⊗ ⊖ ⊙
Overlapping mark: ○○ ○● ○●
Cross-out mark: ● ● ○ ●
Smudged erasure: ○○○ ○
Mark is too light: ● ○ ○ ○

Print your 3-character **Test Form** in the boxes above and fill in the corresponding oval at the right.

TEST 1

1 Ⓐ Ⓑ Ⓒ Ⓓ 14 Ⓕ Ⓖ Ⓗ Ⓙ 27 Ⓐ Ⓑ Ⓒ Ⓓ 40 Ⓕ Ⓖ Ⓗ Ⓙ 53 Ⓐ Ⓑ Ⓒ Ⓓ 66 Ⓕ Ⓖ Ⓗ Ⓙ
2 Ⓕ Ⓖ Ⓗ Ⓙ 15 Ⓐ Ⓑ Ⓒ Ⓓ 28 Ⓕ Ⓖ Ⓗ Ⓙ 41 Ⓐ Ⓑ Ⓒ Ⓓ 54 Ⓕ Ⓖ Ⓗ Ⓙ 67 Ⓐ Ⓑ Ⓒ Ⓓ
3 Ⓐ Ⓑ Ⓒ Ⓓ 16 Ⓕ Ⓖ Ⓗ Ⓙ 29 Ⓐ Ⓑ Ⓒ Ⓓ 42 Ⓕ Ⓖ Ⓗ Ⓙ 55 Ⓐ Ⓑ Ⓒ Ⓓ 68 Ⓕ Ⓖ Ⓗ Ⓙ
4 Ⓕ Ⓖ Ⓗ Ⓙ 17 Ⓐ Ⓑ Ⓒ Ⓓ 30 Ⓕ Ⓖ Ⓗ Ⓙ 43 Ⓐ Ⓑ Ⓒ Ⓓ 56 Ⓕ Ⓖ Ⓗ Ⓙ 69 Ⓐ Ⓑ Ⓒ Ⓓ
5 Ⓐ Ⓑ Ⓒ Ⓓ 18 Ⓕ Ⓖ Ⓗ Ⓙ 31 Ⓐ Ⓑ Ⓒ Ⓓ 44 Ⓕ Ⓖ Ⓗ Ⓙ 57 Ⓐ Ⓑ Ⓒ Ⓓ 70 Ⓕ Ⓖ Ⓗ Ⓙ
6 Ⓕ Ⓖ Ⓗ Ⓙ 19 Ⓐ Ⓑ Ⓒ Ⓓ 32 Ⓕ Ⓖ Ⓗ Ⓙ 45 Ⓐ Ⓑ Ⓒ Ⓓ 58 Ⓕ Ⓖ Ⓗ Ⓙ 71 Ⓐ Ⓑ Ⓒ Ⓓ
7 Ⓐ Ⓑ Ⓒ Ⓓ 20 Ⓕ Ⓖ Ⓗ Ⓙ 33 Ⓐ Ⓑ Ⓒ Ⓓ 46 Ⓕ Ⓖ Ⓗ Ⓙ 59 Ⓐ Ⓑ Ⓒ Ⓓ 72 Ⓕ Ⓖ Ⓗ Ⓙ
8 Ⓕ Ⓖ Ⓗ Ⓙ 21 Ⓐ Ⓑ Ⓒ Ⓓ 34 Ⓕ Ⓖ Ⓗ Ⓙ 47 Ⓐ Ⓑ Ⓒ Ⓓ 60 Ⓕ Ⓖ Ⓗ Ⓙ 73 Ⓐ Ⓑ Ⓒ Ⓓ
9 Ⓐ Ⓑ Ⓒ Ⓓ 22 Ⓕ Ⓖ Ⓗ Ⓙ 35 Ⓐ Ⓑ Ⓒ Ⓓ 48 Ⓕ Ⓖ Ⓗ Ⓙ 61 Ⓐ Ⓑ Ⓒ Ⓓ 74 Ⓕ Ⓖ Ⓗ Ⓙ
10 Ⓕ Ⓖ Ⓗ Ⓙ 23 Ⓐ Ⓑ Ⓒ Ⓓ 36 Ⓕ Ⓖ Ⓗ Ⓙ 49 Ⓐ Ⓑ Ⓒ Ⓓ 62 Ⓕ Ⓖ Ⓗ Ⓙ 75 Ⓐ Ⓑ Ⓒ Ⓓ
11 Ⓐ Ⓑ Ⓒ Ⓓ 24 Ⓕ Ⓖ Ⓗ Ⓙ 37 Ⓐ Ⓑ Ⓒ Ⓓ 50 Ⓕ Ⓖ Ⓗ Ⓙ 63 Ⓐ Ⓑ Ⓒ Ⓓ
12 Ⓕ Ⓖ Ⓗ Ⓙ 25 Ⓐ Ⓑ Ⓒ Ⓓ 38 Ⓕ Ⓖ Ⓗ Ⓙ 51 Ⓐ Ⓑ Ⓒ Ⓓ 64 Ⓕ Ⓖ Ⓗ Ⓙ
13 Ⓐ Ⓑ Ⓒ Ⓓ 26 Ⓕ Ⓖ Ⓗ Ⓙ 39 Ⓐ Ⓑ Ⓒ Ⓓ 52 Ⓕ Ⓖ Ⓗ Ⓙ 65 Ⓐ Ⓑ Ⓒ Ⓓ

TEST 2

1 Ⓐ Ⓑ Ⓒ Ⓓ Ⓔ 11 Ⓐ Ⓑ Ⓒ Ⓓ Ⓔ 21 Ⓐ Ⓑ Ⓒ Ⓓ Ⓔ 31 Ⓐ Ⓑ Ⓒ Ⓓ Ⓔ 41 Ⓐ Ⓑ Ⓒ Ⓓ Ⓔ 51 Ⓐ Ⓑ Ⓒ Ⓓ Ⓔ
2 Ⓕ Ⓖ Ⓗ Ⓙ Ⓚ 12 Ⓕ Ⓖ Ⓗ Ⓙ Ⓚ 22 Ⓕ Ⓖ Ⓗ Ⓙ Ⓚ 32 Ⓕ Ⓖ Ⓗ Ⓙ Ⓚ 42 Ⓕ Ⓖ Ⓗ Ⓙ Ⓚ 52 Ⓕ Ⓖ Ⓗ Ⓙ Ⓚ
3 Ⓐ Ⓑ Ⓒ Ⓓ Ⓔ 13 Ⓐ Ⓑ Ⓒ Ⓓ Ⓔ 23 Ⓐ Ⓑ Ⓒ Ⓓ Ⓔ 33 Ⓐ Ⓑ Ⓒ Ⓓ Ⓔ 43 Ⓐ Ⓑ Ⓒ Ⓓ Ⓔ 53 Ⓐ Ⓑ Ⓒ Ⓓ Ⓔ
4 Ⓕ Ⓖ Ⓗ Ⓙ Ⓚ 14 Ⓕ Ⓖ Ⓗ Ⓙ Ⓚ 24 Ⓕ Ⓖ Ⓗ Ⓙ Ⓚ 34 Ⓕ Ⓖ Ⓗ Ⓙ Ⓚ 44 Ⓕ Ⓖ Ⓗ Ⓙ Ⓚ 54 Ⓕ Ⓖ Ⓗ Ⓙ Ⓚ
5 Ⓐ Ⓑ Ⓒ Ⓓ Ⓔ 15 Ⓐ Ⓑ Ⓒ Ⓓ Ⓔ 25 Ⓐ Ⓑ Ⓒ Ⓓ Ⓔ 35 Ⓐ Ⓑ Ⓒ Ⓓ Ⓔ 45 Ⓐ Ⓑ Ⓒ Ⓓ Ⓔ 55 Ⓐ Ⓑ Ⓒ Ⓓ Ⓔ
6 Ⓕ Ⓖ Ⓗ Ⓙ Ⓚ 16 Ⓕ Ⓖ Ⓗ Ⓙ Ⓚ 26 Ⓐ Ⓑ Ⓒ Ⓓ Ⓔ 36 Ⓕ Ⓖ Ⓗ Ⓙ Ⓚ 46 Ⓕ Ⓖ Ⓗ Ⓙ Ⓚ 56 Ⓕ Ⓖ Ⓗ Ⓙ Ⓚ
7 Ⓐ Ⓑ Ⓒ Ⓓ Ⓔ 17 Ⓐ Ⓑ Ⓒ Ⓓ Ⓔ 27 Ⓐ Ⓑ Ⓒ Ⓓ Ⓔ 37 Ⓐ Ⓑ Ⓒ Ⓓ Ⓔ 47 Ⓐ Ⓑ Ⓒ Ⓓ Ⓔ 57 Ⓐ Ⓑ Ⓒ Ⓓ Ⓔ
8 Ⓕ Ⓖ Ⓗ Ⓙ Ⓚ 18 Ⓕ Ⓖ Ⓗ Ⓙ Ⓚ 28 Ⓕ Ⓖ Ⓗ Ⓙ Ⓚ 38 Ⓕ Ⓖ Ⓗ Ⓙ Ⓚ 48 Ⓕ Ⓖ Ⓗ Ⓙ Ⓚ 58 Ⓕ Ⓖ Ⓗ Ⓙ Ⓚ
9 Ⓐ Ⓑ Ⓒ Ⓓ Ⓔ 19 Ⓐ Ⓑ Ⓒ Ⓓ Ⓔ 29 Ⓐ Ⓑ Ⓒ Ⓓ Ⓔ 39 Ⓐ Ⓑ Ⓒ Ⓓ Ⓔ 49 Ⓐ Ⓑ Ⓒ Ⓓ Ⓔ 59 Ⓐ Ⓑ Ⓒ Ⓓ Ⓔ
10 Ⓕ Ⓖ Ⓗ Ⓙ Ⓚ 20 Ⓕ Ⓖ Ⓗ Ⓙ Ⓚ 30 Ⓕ Ⓖ Ⓗ Ⓙ Ⓚ 40 Ⓕ Ⓖ Ⓗ Ⓙ Ⓚ 50 Ⓕ Ⓖ Ⓗ Ⓙ Ⓚ 60 Ⓕ Ⓖ Ⓗ Ⓙ Ⓚ

TEST 3

1 Ⓐ Ⓑ Ⓒ Ⓓ 8 Ⓕ Ⓖ Ⓗ Ⓙ 15 Ⓐ Ⓑ Ⓒ Ⓓ 22 Ⓕ Ⓖ Ⓗ Ⓙ 29 Ⓐ Ⓑ Ⓒ Ⓓ 36 Ⓕ Ⓖ Ⓗ Ⓙ
2 Ⓕ Ⓖ Ⓗ Ⓙ 9 Ⓐ Ⓑ Ⓒ Ⓓ 16 Ⓕ Ⓖ Ⓗ Ⓙ 23 Ⓐ Ⓑ Ⓒ Ⓓ 30 Ⓕ Ⓖ Ⓗ Ⓙ 37 Ⓐ Ⓑ Ⓒ Ⓓ
3 Ⓐ Ⓑ Ⓒ Ⓓ 10 Ⓕ Ⓖ Ⓗ Ⓙ 17 Ⓐ Ⓑ Ⓒ Ⓓ 24 Ⓕ Ⓖ Ⓗ Ⓙ 31 Ⓐ Ⓑ Ⓒ Ⓓ 38 Ⓕ Ⓖ Ⓗ Ⓙ
4 Ⓕ Ⓖ Ⓗ Ⓙ 11 Ⓐ Ⓑ Ⓒ Ⓓ 18 Ⓕ Ⓖ Ⓗ Ⓙ 25 Ⓐ Ⓑ Ⓒ Ⓓ 32 Ⓕ Ⓖ Ⓗ Ⓙ 39 Ⓐ Ⓑ Ⓒ Ⓓ
5 Ⓐ Ⓑ Ⓒ Ⓓ 12 Ⓕ Ⓖ Ⓗ Ⓙ 19 Ⓐ Ⓑ Ⓒ Ⓓ 26 Ⓕ Ⓖ Ⓗ Ⓙ 33 Ⓐ Ⓑ Ⓒ Ⓓ 40 Ⓕ Ⓖ Ⓗ Ⓙ
6 Ⓕ Ⓖ Ⓗ Ⓙ 13 Ⓐ Ⓑ Ⓒ Ⓓ 20 Ⓕ Ⓖ Ⓗ Ⓙ 27 Ⓐ Ⓑ Ⓒ Ⓓ 34 Ⓕ Ⓖ Ⓗ Ⓙ
7 Ⓐ Ⓑ Ⓒ Ⓓ 14 Ⓕ Ⓖ Ⓗ Ⓙ 21 Ⓐ Ⓑ Ⓒ Ⓓ 28 Ⓕ Ⓖ Ⓗ Ⓙ 35 Ⓐ Ⓑ Ⓒ Ⓓ

TEST 4

1 Ⓐ Ⓑ Ⓒ Ⓓ 8 Ⓕ Ⓖ Ⓗ Ⓙ 15 Ⓐ Ⓑ Ⓒ Ⓓ 22 Ⓕ Ⓖ Ⓗ Ⓙ 29 Ⓐ Ⓑ Ⓒ Ⓓ 36 Ⓕ Ⓖ Ⓗ Ⓙ
2 Ⓕ Ⓖ Ⓗ Ⓙ 9 Ⓐ Ⓑ Ⓒ Ⓓ 16 Ⓕ Ⓖ Ⓗ Ⓙ 23 Ⓐ Ⓑ Ⓒ Ⓓ 30 Ⓕ Ⓖ Ⓗ Ⓙ 37 Ⓐ Ⓑ Ⓒ Ⓓ
3 Ⓐ Ⓑ Ⓒ Ⓓ 10 Ⓕ Ⓖ Ⓗ Ⓙ 17 Ⓐ Ⓑ Ⓒ Ⓓ 24 Ⓕ Ⓖ Ⓗ Ⓙ 31 Ⓐ Ⓑ Ⓒ Ⓓ 38 Ⓕ Ⓖ Ⓗ Ⓙ
4 Ⓕ Ⓖ Ⓗ Ⓙ 11 Ⓐ Ⓑ Ⓒ Ⓓ 18 Ⓕ Ⓖ Ⓗ Ⓙ 25 Ⓐ Ⓑ Ⓒ Ⓓ 32 Ⓕ Ⓖ Ⓗ Ⓙ 39 Ⓐ Ⓑ Ⓒ Ⓓ
5 Ⓐ Ⓑ Ⓒ Ⓓ 12 Ⓕ Ⓖ Ⓗ Ⓙ 19 Ⓐ Ⓑ Ⓒ Ⓓ 26 Ⓕ Ⓖ Ⓗ Ⓙ 33 Ⓐ Ⓑ Ⓒ Ⓓ 40 Ⓕ Ⓖ Ⓗ Ⓙ
6 Ⓕ Ⓖ Ⓗ Ⓙ 13 Ⓐ Ⓑ Ⓒ Ⓓ 20 Ⓕ Ⓖ Ⓗ Ⓙ 27 Ⓐ Ⓑ Ⓒ Ⓓ 34 Ⓕ Ⓖ Ⓗ Ⓙ
7 Ⓐ Ⓑ Ⓒ Ⓓ 14 Ⓕ Ⓖ Ⓗ Ⓙ 21 Ⓐ Ⓑ Ⓒ Ⓓ 28 Ⓕ Ⓖ Ⓗ Ⓙ 35 Ⓐ Ⓑ Ⓒ Ⓓ

The **ACT**®

The ACT® *Sample Answer Sheet*

A NAME, MAILING ADDRESS, AND TELEPHONE
(Please print.)

Last Name   First Name   MI (Middle Initial)

House Number & Street (Apt. No.); or PO Box & No.; or RR & No.

City   State/Province   ZIP/Postal Code

Area Code   Number   Country

ACT, Inc.—Confidential Restricted when data present.

ALL examinees must complete block A – please print.

REGISTERED examinees **MUST complete blocks B, C, and D.** Find the MATCHING INFORMATION on your admission ticket and enter it EXACTLY the same way, even if any of the information is missing or incorrect. Fill in the corresponding ovals. If you do not complete these blocks to match your admission ticket EXACTLY, your scores will be **delayed up to 8 weeks.** Leave blocks E and F blank.

STANDBY examinees MUST complete blocks **B, D, and F.** Enter your information in blocks B and D and fill in the corresponding ovals. Leave block C blank. **For block E**, if you provided your SSN when you created your Web account or completed your standby folder, enter it here. The SSN will be used to help match this document to your registration information and will be included on reports to your college choices. If you did not provide it earlier, do not know it, or do not wish to provide it, leave block E blank. Be sure to fill in the oval in block F.

Do NOT mark in this shaded area.

B MATCH NAME
(First 5 letters of last name)

C MATCH NUMBER
(Registered examinees only)

D DATE OF BIRTH

Month	Day	Year
Jan.		
Feb.		
March		
April		
May		
June		
July		
Aug.		
Sept.		
Oct.		
Nov.		
Dec.		

↓ STANDBY TESTING ONLY ↓

E SOCIAL SECURITY NUMBER
(Standby examinees only)

F STANDBY TESTING

Fill in the oval below ONLY if you turned in a standby registration at the test center today.

○ Yes, I am testing as a standby.

USE A SOFT LEAD NO. 2 PENCIL ONLY.
(Do NOT use a mechanical pencil, ink, ballpoint, correction fluid, or felt-tip pen.)

EXAMINEE STATEMENT AND SIGNATURE

1. Read the following **Statement:** By submitting this answer sheet, I agree to the terms and conditions set forth in the ACT registration booklet or website for this exam, including the arbitration and dispute remedy provisions. I understand that ACT owns the test questions and responses and affirm that I will not share any test questions or responses with anyone by any form of communication.

2. Copy the **Certification** shown below (only the text in italics) on the lines provided. Write in your normal handwriting.

   Certification: *I agree to the Statement above and certify that I am the person whose name and address appear on this form.*

3. Sign your name as you would any official document and enter today's date.

Your Signature   Today's Date

ACT®
P.O. BOX 168, IOWA CITY, IOWA 52243-0168

Marking Directions: Mark only **one** oval for each question. Fill in response completely. Erase errors cleanly without smudging.

Correct mark: ⬭ ⬤ ⬭ ⬭

Do NOT use these *incorrect* or *bad* marks.

Incorrect marks: ⊘ ⊗ ⊜ ⊙
Overlapping mark: ⬭ ⬭ ⬬⬭
Cross-out mark: ⬤ ⊗ ⬭ ⬭
Smudged erasure: ⬤ ⬭ ⬮ ⬭
Mark is too light: ⬮ ⬭ ⬭ ⬭

BOOKLET NUMBER

① ① ① ① ① ①
② ② ② ② ② ②
③ ③ ③ ③ ③ ③
④ ④ ④ ④ ④ ④
⑤ ⑤ ⑤ ⑤ ⑤ ⑤
⑥ ⑥ ⑥ ⑥ ⑥ ⑥
⑦ ⑦ ⑦ ⑦ ⑦ ⑦
⑧ ⑧ ⑧ ⑧ ⑧ ⑧
⑨ ⑨ ⑨ ⑨ ⑨ ⑨
⓪ ⓪ ⓪ ⓪ ⓪ ⓪

FORM

Print your 3-character **Test Form** in the boxes above and fill in the corresponding oval at the right.

BE SURE TO FILL IN THE CORRECT FORM OVAL.

○ 1MC   ○ 2MC   ○ 3MC   ○ 4MC
○ 5MC

TEST 1

1 Ⓐ Ⓑ Ⓒ Ⓓ	14 Ⓕ Ⓖ Ⓗ Ⓙ	27 Ⓐ Ⓑ Ⓒ Ⓓ	40 Ⓕ Ⓖ Ⓗ Ⓙ	53 Ⓐ Ⓑ Ⓒ Ⓓ	66 Ⓕ Ⓖ Ⓗ Ⓙ
2 Ⓕ Ⓖ Ⓗ Ⓙ	15 Ⓐ Ⓑ Ⓒ Ⓓ	28 Ⓕ Ⓖ Ⓗ Ⓙ	41 Ⓐ Ⓑ Ⓒ Ⓓ	54 Ⓕ Ⓖ Ⓗ Ⓙ	67 Ⓐ Ⓑ Ⓒ Ⓓ
3 Ⓐ Ⓑ Ⓒ Ⓓ	16 Ⓕ Ⓖ Ⓗ Ⓙ	29 Ⓐ Ⓑ Ⓒ Ⓓ	42 Ⓕ Ⓖ Ⓗ Ⓙ	55 Ⓐ Ⓑ Ⓒ Ⓓ	68 Ⓕ Ⓖ Ⓗ Ⓙ
4 Ⓕ Ⓖ Ⓗ Ⓙ	17 Ⓐ Ⓑ Ⓒ Ⓓ	30 Ⓕ Ⓖ Ⓗ Ⓙ	43 Ⓐ Ⓑ Ⓒ Ⓓ	56 Ⓕ Ⓖ Ⓗ Ⓙ	69 Ⓐ Ⓑ Ⓒ Ⓓ
5 Ⓐ Ⓑ Ⓒ Ⓓ	18 Ⓕ Ⓖ Ⓗ Ⓙ	31 Ⓐ Ⓑ Ⓒ Ⓓ	44 Ⓕ Ⓖ Ⓗ Ⓙ	57 Ⓐ Ⓑ Ⓒ Ⓓ	70 Ⓕ Ⓖ Ⓗ Ⓙ
6 Ⓕ Ⓖ Ⓗ Ⓙ	19 Ⓐ Ⓑ Ⓒ Ⓓ	32 Ⓕ Ⓖ Ⓗ Ⓙ	45 Ⓐ Ⓑ Ⓒ Ⓓ	58 Ⓕ Ⓖ Ⓗ Ⓙ	71 Ⓐ Ⓑ Ⓒ Ⓓ
7 Ⓐ Ⓑ Ⓒ Ⓓ	20 Ⓕ Ⓖ Ⓗ Ⓙ	33 Ⓐ Ⓑ Ⓒ Ⓓ	46 Ⓕ Ⓖ Ⓗ Ⓙ	59 Ⓐ Ⓑ Ⓒ Ⓓ	72 Ⓕ Ⓖ Ⓗ Ⓙ
8 Ⓕ Ⓖ Ⓗ Ⓙ	21 Ⓐ Ⓑ Ⓒ Ⓓ	34 Ⓕ Ⓖ Ⓗ Ⓙ	47 Ⓐ Ⓑ Ⓒ Ⓓ	60 Ⓕ Ⓖ Ⓗ Ⓙ	73 Ⓐ Ⓑ Ⓒ Ⓓ
9 Ⓐ Ⓑ Ⓒ Ⓓ	22 Ⓕ Ⓖ Ⓗ Ⓙ	35 Ⓐ Ⓑ Ⓒ Ⓓ	48 Ⓕ Ⓖ Ⓗ Ⓙ	61 Ⓐ Ⓑ Ⓒ Ⓓ	74 Ⓕ Ⓖ Ⓗ Ⓙ
10 Ⓐ Ⓑ Ⓒ Ⓓ	23 Ⓐ Ⓑ Ⓒ Ⓓ	36 Ⓕ Ⓖ Ⓗ Ⓙ	49 Ⓕ Ⓖ Ⓗ Ⓙ	62 Ⓕ Ⓖ Ⓗ Ⓙ	75 Ⓐ Ⓑ Ⓒ Ⓓ
11 Ⓐ Ⓑ Ⓒ Ⓓ	24 Ⓕ Ⓖ Ⓗ Ⓙ	37 Ⓐ Ⓑ Ⓒ Ⓓ	50 Ⓕ Ⓖ Ⓗ Ⓙ	63 Ⓐ Ⓑ Ⓒ Ⓓ	
12 Ⓕ Ⓖ Ⓗ Ⓙ	25 Ⓐ Ⓑ Ⓒ Ⓓ	38 Ⓕ Ⓖ Ⓗ Ⓙ	51 Ⓐ Ⓑ Ⓒ Ⓓ	64 Ⓕ Ⓖ Ⓗ Ⓙ	
13 Ⓐ Ⓑ Ⓒ Ⓓ	26 Ⓕ Ⓖ Ⓗ Ⓙ	39 Ⓐ Ⓑ Ⓒ Ⓓ	52 Ⓕ Ⓖ Ⓗ Ⓙ	65 Ⓐ Ⓑ Ⓒ Ⓓ	

TEST 2

1 Ⓐ Ⓑ Ⓒ Ⓓ Ⓔ	11 Ⓐ Ⓑ Ⓒ Ⓓ Ⓔ	21 Ⓐ Ⓑ Ⓒ Ⓓ Ⓔ	31 Ⓐ Ⓑ Ⓒ Ⓓ Ⓔ	41 Ⓐ Ⓑ Ⓒ Ⓓ Ⓔ	51 Ⓐ Ⓑ Ⓒ Ⓓ Ⓔ
2 Ⓕ Ⓖ Ⓗ Ⓙ Ⓚ	12 Ⓕ Ⓖ Ⓗ Ⓙ Ⓚ	22 Ⓕ Ⓖ Ⓗ Ⓙ Ⓚ	32 Ⓕ Ⓖ Ⓗ Ⓙ Ⓚ	42 Ⓕ Ⓖ Ⓗ Ⓙ Ⓚ	52 Ⓕ Ⓖ Ⓗ Ⓙ Ⓚ
3 Ⓐ Ⓑ Ⓒ Ⓓ Ⓔ	13 Ⓐ Ⓑ Ⓒ Ⓓ Ⓔ	23 Ⓐ Ⓑ Ⓒ Ⓓ Ⓔ	33 Ⓐ Ⓑ Ⓒ Ⓓ Ⓔ	43 Ⓐ Ⓑ Ⓒ Ⓓ Ⓔ	53 Ⓐ Ⓑ Ⓒ Ⓓ Ⓔ
4 Ⓕ Ⓖ Ⓗ Ⓙ Ⓚ	14 Ⓕ Ⓖ Ⓗ Ⓙ Ⓚ	24 Ⓕ Ⓖ Ⓗ Ⓙ Ⓚ	34 Ⓕ Ⓖ Ⓗ Ⓙ Ⓚ	44 Ⓕ Ⓖ Ⓗ Ⓙ Ⓚ	54 Ⓕ Ⓖ Ⓗ Ⓙ Ⓚ
5 Ⓐ Ⓑ Ⓒ Ⓓ Ⓔ	15 Ⓐ Ⓑ Ⓒ Ⓓ Ⓔ	25 Ⓐ Ⓑ Ⓒ Ⓓ Ⓔ	35 Ⓐ Ⓑ Ⓒ Ⓓ Ⓔ	45 Ⓐ Ⓑ Ⓒ Ⓓ Ⓔ	55 Ⓐ Ⓑ Ⓒ Ⓓ Ⓔ
6 Ⓕ Ⓖ Ⓗ Ⓙ Ⓚ	16 Ⓕ Ⓖ Ⓗ Ⓙ Ⓚ	26 Ⓕ Ⓖ Ⓗ Ⓙ Ⓚ	36 Ⓕ Ⓖ Ⓗ Ⓙ Ⓚ	46 Ⓕ Ⓖ Ⓗ Ⓙ Ⓚ	56 Ⓕ Ⓖ Ⓗ Ⓙ Ⓚ
7 Ⓐ Ⓑ Ⓒ Ⓓ Ⓔ	17 Ⓐ Ⓑ Ⓒ Ⓓ Ⓔ	27 Ⓐ Ⓑ Ⓒ Ⓓ Ⓔ	37 Ⓐ Ⓑ Ⓒ Ⓓ Ⓔ	47 Ⓐ Ⓑ Ⓒ Ⓓ Ⓔ	57 Ⓐ Ⓑ Ⓒ Ⓓ Ⓔ
8 Ⓕ Ⓖ Ⓗ Ⓙ Ⓚ	18 Ⓕ Ⓖ Ⓗ Ⓙ Ⓚ	28 Ⓕ Ⓖ Ⓗ Ⓙ Ⓚ	38 Ⓕ Ⓖ Ⓗ Ⓙ Ⓚ	48 Ⓕ Ⓖ Ⓗ Ⓙ Ⓚ	58 Ⓕ Ⓖ Ⓗ Ⓙ Ⓚ
9 Ⓐ Ⓑ Ⓒ Ⓓ Ⓔ	19 Ⓐ Ⓑ Ⓒ Ⓓ Ⓔ	29 Ⓐ Ⓑ Ⓒ Ⓓ Ⓔ	39 Ⓐ Ⓑ Ⓒ Ⓓ Ⓔ	49 Ⓐ Ⓑ Ⓒ Ⓓ Ⓔ	59 Ⓐ Ⓑ Ⓒ Ⓓ Ⓔ
10 Ⓕ Ⓖ Ⓗ Ⓙ Ⓚ	20 Ⓕ Ⓖ Ⓗ Ⓙ Ⓚ	30 Ⓕ Ⓖ Ⓗ Ⓙ Ⓚ	40 Ⓕ Ⓖ Ⓗ Ⓙ Ⓚ	50 Ⓕ Ⓖ Ⓗ Ⓙ Ⓚ	60 Ⓕ Ⓖ Ⓗ Ⓙ Ⓚ

TEST 3

1 Ⓐ Ⓑ Ⓒ Ⓓ	8 Ⓕ Ⓖ Ⓗ Ⓙ	15 Ⓐ Ⓑ Ⓒ Ⓓ	22 Ⓕ Ⓖ Ⓗ Ⓙ	29 Ⓐ Ⓑ Ⓒ Ⓓ	36 Ⓕ Ⓖ Ⓗ Ⓙ
2 Ⓕ Ⓖ Ⓗ Ⓙ	9 Ⓐ Ⓑ Ⓒ Ⓓ	16 Ⓕ Ⓖ Ⓗ Ⓙ	23 Ⓐ Ⓑ Ⓒ Ⓓ	30 Ⓕ Ⓖ Ⓗ Ⓙ	37 Ⓐ Ⓑ Ⓒ Ⓓ
3 Ⓐ Ⓑ Ⓒ Ⓓ	10 Ⓕ Ⓖ Ⓗ Ⓙ	17 Ⓐ Ⓑ Ⓒ Ⓓ	24 Ⓕ Ⓖ Ⓗ Ⓙ	31 Ⓐ Ⓑ Ⓒ Ⓓ	38 Ⓕ Ⓖ Ⓗ Ⓙ
4 Ⓕ Ⓖ Ⓗ Ⓙ	11 Ⓐ Ⓑ Ⓒ Ⓓ	18 Ⓕ Ⓖ Ⓗ Ⓙ	25 Ⓐ Ⓑ Ⓒ Ⓓ	32 Ⓕ Ⓖ Ⓗ Ⓙ	39 Ⓐ Ⓑ Ⓒ Ⓓ
5 Ⓐ Ⓑ Ⓒ Ⓓ	12 Ⓕ Ⓖ Ⓗ Ⓙ	19 Ⓐ Ⓑ Ⓒ Ⓓ	26 Ⓕ Ⓖ Ⓗ Ⓙ	33 Ⓐ Ⓑ Ⓒ Ⓓ	40 Ⓕ Ⓖ Ⓗ Ⓙ
6 Ⓕ Ⓖ Ⓗ Ⓙ	13 Ⓐ Ⓑ Ⓒ Ⓓ	20 Ⓕ Ⓖ Ⓗ Ⓙ	27 Ⓐ Ⓑ Ⓒ Ⓓ	34 Ⓕ Ⓖ Ⓗ Ⓙ	
7 Ⓐ Ⓑ Ⓒ Ⓓ	14 Ⓕ Ⓖ Ⓗ Ⓙ	21 Ⓐ Ⓑ Ⓒ Ⓓ	28 Ⓕ Ⓖ Ⓗ Ⓙ	35 Ⓐ Ⓑ Ⓒ Ⓓ	

TEST 4

1 Ⓐ Ⓑ Ⓒ Ⓓ	8 Ⓕ Ⓖ Ⓗ Ⓙ	15 Ⓐ Ⓑ Ⓒ Ⓓ	22 Ⓕ Ⓖ Ⓗ Ⓙ	29 Ⓐ Ⓑ Ⓒ Ⓓ	36 Ⓕ Ⓖ Ⓗ Ⓙ
2 Ⓕ Ⓖ Ⓗ Ⓙ	9 Ⓐ Ⓑ Ⓒ Ⓓ	16 Ⓕ Ⓖ Ⓗ Ⓙ	23 Ⓐ Ⓑ Ⓒ Ⓓ	30 Ⓕ Ⓖ Ⓗ Ⓙ	37 Ⓐ Ⓑ Ⓒ Ⓓ
3 Ⓐ Ⓑ Ⓒ Ⓓ	10 Ⓕ Ⓖ Ⓗ Ⓙ	17 Ⓐ Ⓑ Ⓒ Ⓓ	24 Ⓕ Ⓖ Ⓗ Ⓙ	31 Ⓐ Ⓑ Ⓒ Ⓓ	38 Ⓕ Ⓖ Ⓗ Ⓙ
4 Ⓕ Ⓖ Ⓗ Ⓙ	11 Ⓐ Ⓑ Ⓒ Ⓓ	18 Ⓕ Ⓖ Ⓗ Ⓙ	25 Ⓐ Ⓑ Ⓒ Ⓓ	32 Ⓕ Ⓖ Ⓗ Ⓙ	39 Ⓐ Ⓑ Ⓒ Ⓓ
5 Ⓐ Ⓑ Ⓒ Ⓓ	12 Ⓕ Ⓖ Ⓗ Ⓙ	19 Ⓐ Ⓑ Ⓒ Ⓓ	26 Ⓕ Ⓖ Ⓗ Ⓙ	33 Ⓐ Ⓑ Ⓒ Ⓓ	40 Ⓕ Ⓖ Ⓗ Ⓙ
6 Ⓕ Ⓖ Ⓗ Ⓙ	13 Ⓐ Ⓑ Ⓒ Ⓓ	20 Ⓕ Ⓖ Ⓗ Ⓙ	27 Ⓐ Ⓑ Ⓒ Ⓓ	34 Ⓕ Ⓖ Ⓗ Ⓙ	
7 Ⓐ Ⓑ Ⓒ Ⓓ	14 Ⓕ Ⓖ Ⓗ Ⓙ	21 Ⓐ Ⓑ Ⓒ Ⓓ	28 Ⓕ Ⓖ Ⓗ Ⓙ	35 Ⓐ Ⓑ Ⓒ Ⓓ	

080658

Practice Test 1

Today's Date: _____

Your Signature: _____

Print Your Name Here: _____

Your Date of Birth:

Month	Day	Year

Form 1MC

The **ACT**® 2011|2012

Directions

This booklet contains tests in English, Mathematics, Reading, and Science. These tests measure skills and abilities highly related to high school course work and success in college. *CALCULATORS MAY BE USED ON THE MATHEMATICS TEST ONLY.*

The questions in each test are numbered, and the suggested answers for each question are lettered. On the answer document, the rows of ovals are numbered to match the questions, and the ovals in each row are lettered to correspond to the suggested answers.

For each question, first decide which answer is best. Next, locate on the answer document the row of ovals numbered the same as the question. Then, locate the oval in that row lettered the same as your answer. Finally, fill in the oval completely. Use a soft lead pencil and make your marks heavy and black. *DO NOT USE INK OR A MECHANICAL PENCIL.*

Mark only one answer to each question. If you change your mind about an answer, erase your first mark thoroughly before marking your new answer. For each question, make certain that you mark in the row of ovals with the same number as the question.

Only responses marked on your answer document will be scored. Your score on each test will be based only on the number of questions you answer correctly during the time allowed for that test. You will NOT be penalized for guessing. *IT IS TO YOUR ADVANTAGE TO ANSWER EVERY QUESTION EVEN IF YOU MUST GUESS.*

You may work on each test ONLY when your test supervisor tells you to do so. If you finish a test before time is called for that test, you should use the time remaining to reconsider questions you are uncertain about in that test. You may NOT look back to a test on which time has already been called, and you may NOT go ahead to another test. To do so will disqualify you from the examination.

Lay your pencil down immediately when time is called at the end of each test. You may NOT for any reason fill in or alter ovals for a test after time is called for that test. To do so will disqualify you from the examination.

Do not fold or tear the pages of your test booklet.

**DO NOT OPEN THIS BOOKLET
UNTIL TOLD TO DO SO.**

ENGLISH TEST
45 Minutes—75 Questions

DIRECTIONS: In the five passages that follow, certain words and phrases are underlined and numbered. In the right-hand column, you will find alternatives for the underlined part. In most cases, you are to choose the one that best expresses the idea, makes the statement appropriate for standard written English, or is worded most consistently with the style and tone of the passage as a whole. If you think the original version is best, choose "NO CHANGE." In some cases, you will find in the right-hand column a question about the underlined part. You are to choose the best answer to the question.

You will also find questions about a section of the passage, or about the passage as a whole. These questions do not refer to an underlined portion of the passage, but rather are identified by a number or numbers in a box.

For each question, choose the alternative you consider best and fill in the corresponding oval on your answer document. Read each passage through once before you begin to answer the questions that accompany it. For many of the questions, you must read several sentences beyond the question to determine the answer. Be sure that you have read far enough ahead each time you choose an alternative.

PASSAGE I

My "Sister" Ligia

Every year my high school hosts international exchange students, those teenagers join our senior class. Each student usually lives with the family of one of the seniors. I can recall students from Costa Rica, Italy, Norway, and Nigeria. Last year, one of our school's exchange students being Ligia Antolinez, who came from Bucaramanga, Colombia. I was a junior then. I wasn't in any of Ligia's classes and didn't know her, but I saw her at school events, which are sometimes supported financially by local businesses.

1. **A.** NO CHANGE
    B. students, he or she is invited to
    C. students who
    D. students they

2. **F.** NO CHANGE
    G. students was
    H. students, named
    J. students,

3. **A.** NO CHANGE
    B. whom
    C. which
    D. she who

4. **F.** NO CHANGE
    G. junior, therefore, so
    H. junior because
    J. junior, since

5. Given that all of the choices are true, which one provides the most relevant information with regard to the narrator's familiarity with Ligia?

    A. NO CHANGE
    B. had read a story about her in our school paper, which is written by students interested in journalism.
    C. saw her at school events and had read a story about her in our school paper.
    D. had read a story about her when I was checking our school paper for local movie listings.

GO ON TO THE NEXT PAGE.

About halfway through the school year, I learned that the exchange program was looking for a new home for Ligia. After a severe storm, the basement of her hosts house had flooded, leaving two bedrooms unusable. The two "little brothers" of Ligia's host family, who had volunteered to move, to those bedrooms for a year, had to

be moved upstairs to the room Ligia was using.

      I told my parents about Ligia's problem, which needed to be solved.

We agreed that it would be fun to host a student from another country. My older sister had gotten married the summer before, so not only did we have a room for Ligia,

and we all admitted that the house had seemed too quiet lately.

      The second half of my junior year was anything but quiet. Introduced by me to my favorite music, at top volume, I started being taught by Ligia the most popular Colombian dance steps. My father spoke fondly of the

days before two teenagers taken over the phone, the stereo, the kitchen—well, most of the house, really. My mother helped Ligia with her math homework, and Ligia taught Mom beginning Spanish. Both Ligia and I were studying French that year, and we practiced it at home. When we

---

6. **F.** NO CHANGE
   G. her hosts'
   H. Ligia's hosts
   J. Ligias hosts'

7. **A.** NO CHANGE
   B. volunteered to move to those bedrooms for a year
   C. volunteered to move to those bedrooms for a year,
   D. volunteered, to move to those bedrooms for a year,

8. **F.** NO CHANGE
   G. upstairs to the room Ligia was using, which had been freshly painted just that year.
   H. upstairs (it was a two-story house) to Ligia's room.
   J. OMIT the underlined portion and end the sentence with a period.

9. **A.** NO CHANGE
   B. problem, which was a dilemma.
   C. problem that needed a solution.
   D. problem.

10. Three of these choices indicate that the family felt confident about inviting Ligia to live in their home. Which choice does NOT do so?
   F. NO CHANGE
   G. decided
   H. knew
   J. supposed

11. **A.** NO CHANGE
   B. but
   C. while
   D. yet

12. **F.** NO CHANGE
   G. Introducing Ligia to my favorite music, at top volume, she started teaching me the most popular Colombian dance steps.
   H. Teaching me the most popular Colombian dance steps, Ligia was introduced by me to my favorite music, at top volume.
   J. I introduced Ligia to my favorite music, at top volume, and she started teaching me the most popular Colombian dance steps.

13. **A.** NO CHANGE
   B. took
   C. had took
   D. begun to take

GO ON TO THE NEXT PAGE.

planned a surprise anniversary party for my mom and dad,

we did it all right under their noses, in French.

At the end of the year, Ligia had gone home to
Colombia. This year I'm busy with senior activities and
with a part-time job. I'm trying to save enough to go see
my new sister next year. [15]

14. **F.** NO CHANGE
  G. will have gone
  H. went
  J. goes

15. Which of the following true sentences, if inserted here, would best conclude the essay as well as maintain the positive tone established earlier in the essay?
  A. I'm afraid of flying, but I think I'll be OK.
  B. I'm eager to eventually join the workforce full-time.
  C. I've been practicing my Spanish—and my dance steps.
  D. Senior activities are a lot of fun.

Down at the Laundromat

[1] Down the street from the college, I attend, the
Save-U Laundromat is always open, and someone is

always there. [2] It was on a corner, across the

street; from a drugstore on one side and a big park on the
other. [3] The park isn't really a park at all but part of the
grounds of a private boarding school. [4] But no one is
ever around to enforce the threats, and in the summer
everyone enjoys the benches, the grass, and the
coolly magnificence of the shade trees. [5] Signs are
posted all over the lawn threatening every sort of drastic
action against trespassers who wrongfully enter the
property. [21]

16. **F.** NO CHANGE
  G. college, I attend
  H. college I attend,
  J. college I attend

17. **A.** NO CHANGE
  B. is
  C. had been
  D. was located

18. **F.** NO CHANGE
  G. street from,
  H. street, from
  J. street from

19. **A.** NO CHANGE
  B. cool magnificence
  C. magnificently cool
  D. cool magnificent

20. **F.** NO CHANGE
  G. those who trespass by walking on private property.
  H. trespassers who ignore the signs and walk on the grass.
  J. trespassers.

21. For the sake of logic and coherence, Sentence 5 should be placed:
  A. where it is now.
  B. before Sentence 1.
  C. after Sentence 1.
  D. after Sentence 3.

GO ON TO THE NEXT PAGE.

The Save-U has a neon sign out front that says "Friendly 24-Hour Service," but as far as I can tell, no one really works there. The washers and dryers are lime green, and the paneling on the walls has been painted to match, although it was later varnished with some kind of artificial wood grain finish. [23] I often stare at that paneling when I don't have a magazine or newspaper to read and don't want to do my schoolwork. Deep in thought, I contemplate the competence of the laundromat's interior designer.

Some machines even provide a certain amount of sustenance and entertainment. This laundromat has three soda machines, two candy machines, two pinball machines, five video machines, and a machine that eats dollar bills and spits out too much or too few quarters.

There are many regular customers whose faces have become familiar—mostly older people from around the neighborhood. [26] Usually a crowd of thirteen-year-old kids that is gathered around the video machines, regardless of the time of day.

Imagining all these people, it is that I know they remain there even after I have left. I know that I could go in there anytime, and someone would look up from playing pinball

22. F. NO CHANGE
    G. have been
    H. were
    J. are

23. At this point, the writer wants to add a sentence that would further describe the laundromat's paneling. Which of the following sentences would best accomplish this?

    A. I guess the brush strokes are intended to resemble wood grain, but they don't.
    B. I know that the varnish provides some protection for the wood paneling.
    C. To me, it seems that lime green was a bizarre choice for an interior wall paint.
    D. I imagine that the person who chose that color scheme must be a unique individual.

24. Which choice most effectively guides the reader from the preceding paragraph into this new paragraph?

    F. NO CHANGE
    G. The Save-U has to have friendly service because it is across the street from a park.
    H. Maybe what the Save-U means by friendly service is an abundance of machines.
    J. Washing machines are the Save-U's version of 24-hour service.

25. A. NO CHANGE
    B. many or too fewer
    C. many or too few
    D. much or few

26. The writer is considering deleting the following phrase from the preceding sentence:

> —mostly older people from around the neighborhood

If the writer were to make this deletion, the essay would primarily lose:

    F. specific descriptive material.
    G. detail providing a logical transition.
    H. foreshadowing of the conclusion.
    J. an understatement of important information.

27. A. NO CHANGE
    B. kids who
    C. kids, and they
    D. kids

28. F. NO CHANGE
    G. It being that I imagine all these people, they
    H. Imagining all these people, they
    J. I imagine that all these people

GO ON TO THE NEXT PAGE.

or folding clothes and nods and smiles at me. It is
_____
29

comforting to know that the Save-U Laundromat. And its
_____
30

people are always nearby.

29. **A.** NO CHANGE
    B. nod and smile
    C. nodding and smiling
    D. nods to smile

30. **F.** NO CHANGE
    G. Laundromat. Its
    H. Laundromat and that its
    J. Laundromat and its

PASSAGE III

> The following paragraphs may or may not be in the most logical order. Each paragraph is numbered in brackets, and question 45 will ask you to choose where Paragraph 1 should most logically be placed.

Bill Williams Brings America Home to Dinner

[1]

You have to admire the honesty of a company

who's slogan is "Just About the Best." Glory Foods'
____
31

president, and founder Bill Williams, explains the unusual
_____
32

slogan by admitting that while he knows that his foods

can't beat the taste of real home cooking, it does come
_____
33

very close.

[2]

Even as a child, Williams loved to prepare food, and

as a young adult, he refined his cooking skills at the
_____
34

prestigiously acclaimed Culinary Institute of America.
_____
35

In 1989, he came up with his idea for a line of Southern-
_____
36

inspired cuisine, a time when there were no convenience
_____
36

foods designed for African American consumers. Over the

next three years, he developed a line of products that

31. **A.** NO CHANGE
    B. whose
    C. that's
    D. that the

32. **F.** NO CHANGE
    G. president, and founder Bill Williams
    H. president and founder Bill Williams,
    J. president and founder, Bill Williams,

33. **A.** NO CHANGE
    B. it has
    C. they do
    D. and that they

34. **F.** NO CHANGE
    G. his cooking skills were refined
    H. his skill in cooking was refined
    J. the refinement of his cooking skills occurred

35. **A.** NO CHANGE
    B. famed, renowned, and notable
    C. luscious
    D. prestigious

36. **F.** NO CHANGE
    G. He came up with his idea for a line of Southern-inspired cuisine in 1989,
    H. He came up in 1989, with his idea for a line of Southern-inspired cuisine,
    J. The idea came to him in 1989, that a line of Southern-inspired cuisine should be marketed,

GO ON TO THE NEXT PAGE.

included canned greens, sweet potatoes, beans, and okra, as well as bottled hot sauce and cornbread mixes.

[3]

Eventually, Williams was ready to launch his products in grocery stores. <u>Initially, Glory Foods were</u> first
₃₇
offered for sale in Ohio in 1992 and soon became available in neighboring states. Within a year, sales were twice the original projections. [38]

[4]

The company's African American focus is evident in all aspects of Glory Foods. The firm's headquarters are located in the same black neighborhood where Williams grew up, and the company helps to support several local community projects. The firm also employs African American <u>professional advisers</u> and subcontractors
₃₉
whenever possible and contracts African American farmers to grow much of the produce that goes into Glory Foods. [40]

[5]

The company's name reflects this African American focus as well. *Glory* is meant <u>to evoke</u>
₄₁
both the exultant spirit of gospel churches and the

37. A. NO CHANGE
   B. Glory Foods were
   C. They were originally
   D. At the outset, the earliest Glory Foods were

38. Given that all of the following sentences are true, which one would most effectively conclude this paragraph?
   F. Bill Williams's company continues to refine the recipes of its products.
   G. By 1995, Glory Foods were being distributed in twenty-two states.
   H. Today, there are several other companies that target their products to African American consumers.
   J. Bill Williams, however, sought the advice of food marketing experts.

39. A. NO CHANGE
   B. professional, advisers,
   C. professional advisers,
   D. professional advisers;

40. The writer is considering deleting the phrases "whenever possible" and "much of" from the preceding sentence. If the writer were to delete these phrases, would the meaning of the sentence change?
   F. Yes, because without these phrases, the reader would think that all of the subcontractors and farmers were African Americans.
   G. Yes, because without these phrases, the reader would not know that the company made an attempt to employ African American contractors in the production of its goods.
   H. No, because these phrases are examples of wordiness, and they can easily be eliminated from the sentence.
   J. No, because although these phrases describe the subcontractors and the farmers and provide interesting detail, they are not essential to the meaning of the sentence.

41. A. NO CHANGE
   B. at evoking
   C. in evoking of
   D. OMIT the underlined portion.

Practice ACT Tests

GO ON TO THE NEXT PAGE.

movie <u>during the Civil War of the same name</u>, which tells

        42

the story of a black regiment. ☐43

[6]

    With twenty full-time employees in its administrative offices, Glory Foods has come a long way from its beginnings. America's dinner tables <u>were</u> the beneficiaries

             44

of Bill Williams's drive, determination, and culinary expertise.

42. The best placement for the underlined portion would be:

F. where it is now.
G. after the word *name* (but before the comma).
H. after the word *story*.
J. after the word *regiment* (ending the sentence with a period).

43. At this point, the writer is considering adding the following sentence:

> The actor Denzel Washington starred in the film, which earned several awards.

Should the writer make this addition?

A. Yes, because the additional detail explains why the film *Glory* was so inspiring.
B. Yes, because if readers understand that the film *Glory* earned awards, they will also understand why the company was named "Glory Foods."
C. No, because the information distracts the reader from the focus of the essay.
D. No, because the essay does not say if Bill Williams had ever met the actor Denzel Washington.

44. F. NO CHANGE
G. had been
H. would have been
J. are

┌───┐
│ Question 45 asks about the preceding passage │
│ as a whole.   │
└───┘

45. For the sake of logic and coherence, Paragraph 1 should be placed:

A. where it is now.
B. after Paragraph 2.
C. after Paragraph 3.
D. after Paragraph 6.

PASSAGE IV

Pinball and Chance

[1]

    Doesn't anyone play pinball anymore? I was disappointed the other day when I took my kids to a game arcade. <u>Afterwards, I went to the movies.</u> Not one of the

          46

46. F. NO CHANGE
G. I made my way to the movie theater after that.
H. (The movie theater was my next stop.)
J. OMIT the underlined portion.

GO ON TO THE NEXT PAGE.

many colorful machines with flashing lights were a pinball
machine. Video games filled the room.

[2]

[1] I can understand why video games might
seem more attractive than pinball. [2] Video screens
which have been populated by movie stars, monsters, and
heroes. [3] You can blow up cities, escape from dungeons,
and battle all sorts of villains. [4] Pinball machines, on the
other hand, are essentially all the same. [5] Some machines
are bigger and fancier than others, but the object of pinball
never changes: you have to keep a steel ball in play long
enough to rack up a high score and win a free game. [49]

[3]

The attractions of video games, however, are
superficial and short-lived. As you guide your character
through the game's challenges, you come to know exactly
how the machine that's built to last will respond to your
every move. He or she learns where the hazards lurk and
the special weapons are hidden. Pinball, though, can't be
predicted with such accuracy. You never know when the
ball will drain straight down the middle, out of reach of
both flippers. Then again, you can sometimes get lucky,
and a ball you thought was lost, will inexplicably bounce
back into play.

47. A. NO CHANGE
    B. was a
    C. were an actual
    D. would have been an actual

48. F. NO CHANGE
    G. that are
    H. are
    J. OMIT the underlined portion.

49. For the sake of the logic and coherence of Paragraph 2,
    Sentence 4 should be:
    A. placed where it is now.
    B. placed after Sentence 1.
    C. placed after Sentence 5.
    D. OMITTED, because the paragraph focuses only on
       video games.

50. F. NO CHANGE
    G. machine, which is constructed durably,
    H. machine, which is built to last,
    J. machine

51. A. NO CHANGE
    B. We learn
    C. You learn
    D. People learned

52. Which of the following alternatives to the underlined
    portion would be LEAST acceptable?
    F. therefore,
    G. however,
    H. by contrast,
    J. on the contrary,

53. A. NO CHANGE
    B. lost will
    C. lost, will,
    D. lost will,

GO ON TO THE NEXT PAGE.

[4]

It is the element of chance that makes pinball more
interesting than video games. Most video games are

designed so that your main opponent in these video games
is a predictable computer program. Once you have

mastered a game, the challenge is gone, and you must look
for a new game to conquer. After you learn the new game,
you get bored again. The cycle keeps repeating. But in
pinball, you have three factors to consider: you, the
machine, and chance, which is sometimes your enemy
sometimes your ally. No matter how many games you play

on any pinball machine, the various times of each game is

different. That's what makes pinball a continually
challenge.

54. Which choice would most effectively and appropriately lead the reader from the topic of Paragraph 3 to that of Paragraph 4?
   F. NO CHANGE
   G. Pinball does share certain similarities with video games.
   H. Pinball, although less challenging than video games, can still be fun to play.
   J. Video games do generally evolve into subsequent editions or enhanced versions.

55. A. NO CHANGE
   B. during these video games
   C. in video games
   D. OMIT the underlined portion.

56. F. NO CHANGE
   G. you then looked
   H. one then looks
   J. one must look

57. A. NO CHANGE
   B. enemy,
   C. enemy;
   D. enemy, and,

58. F. NO CHANGE
   G. each
   H. each single unique
   J. every single time, each

59. A. NO CHANGE
   B. continuously
   C. continual
   D. continue

Question 60 asks about the preceding passage as a whole.

60. Suppose the writer had chosen to write an essay that indicates that pinball is superior to video games. Would this essay fulfill the writer's goal?
   F. No, because the writer admits that video games have become more popular than pinball machines.
   G. No, because the writer states that video games are designed to challenge the skills of the player.
   H. Yes, because the writer claims that pinball games require luck and are more visually attractive than video games.
   J. Yes, because the writer suggests that it is more difficult to become skilled at a pinball machine than at a video game.

GO ON TO THE NEXT PAGE.

PASSAGE V

When a Computer Gets Sick . . .

[1]

Imagine sitting in front of a computer monitor, filling the screen with your mind's jumbled thoughts. Tomorrow's assignment is slowly materializing before your eyes. Suddenly, without warning, each of the letters, in front of you tumbles to the bottom of the screen.
61
Is this a bad dream? Not exactly. The computer is probably sick, unless the diagnosis may be that the computer has a
62
virus.

[2]

Analogous to a biological virus that takes over a living cell, a computer virus is a program, or set of instructions, that invades a computer either to create mischief or do real damage. The type of computer virus mentioned above is more mischievous than harmful. Eventually, the letters reorder themselves on the screen. Not all viruses however, straighten themselves out.
63

[3]

Computer viruses range from being temporary
64
annoyances to permanently destroying data. Computer
64
vandals rig these viruses to go off at a preset time. These bombs can permanently destroy data, and that can be disastrous to the operation of a computer.
65

61. **A.** NO CHANGE
    B. letters in front of you tumbles,
    C. letters in front of you, tumbles
    D. letters in front of you tumbles

62. **F.** NO CHANGE
    G. except
    H. and
    J. as if

63. **A.** NO CHANGE
    B. viruses; however,
    C. viruses, howeror
    D. viruses, however,

64. Which choice is the most effective first sentence of Paragraph 3?
    F. NO CHANGE
    G. Among the more serious viruses are those referred to as "bombs."
    H. Most people would agree that they'd rather have a computer virus than a virus that puts them in bed for a week.
    J. Despite technological advances, computers are still fragile devices in many ways.

65. **A.** NO CHANGE
    B. a devastative disaster to the operation
    C. devastation to the operating
    D. possibly disastrous to operating

GO ON TO THE NEXT PAGE.

[4]

Detection programs are available that
<u>66</u>

searches for and then destroys computer viruses.
<u>67</u>

Evidence that some software writers have played

up the medical <u>analogy being found</u> in the names of their
<u>68</u>

<u>programs:</u> Vaccine, Checkup, Antitoxin, and Disinfectant.
<u>69</u>

[5]

As with all diseases, the best cure is prevention.
<u>70</u>

Experts suggest that you avoid borrowing computer

disks because they might contain viruses. They

<u>warn that many of these viruses are quite sophisticated in</u>

<u>their programming.</u> They also say that you should make
<u>71</u>

copies of your computer files, so that if a virus does strike

and you must delete your infected files, you will at least

have backup copies. Experts also point out that using the

Internet and World Wide Web has led to new risks of

infection in the form of viruses hidden in programs

downloaded, or copied, from these resources.

[6]

If there is a virus in your system, you had hope that it

<u>better responds</u> to the appropriate treatment and therapy.
<u>72</u>

Otherwise, you could be in for a long night at the

computer.

---

66. F. NO CHANGE
G. Detection programs that detect computer viruses
H. Computer viruses can be found by detection programs that
J. Detection programs that find computer viruses

67. A. NO CHANGE
B. searches for and destroys
C. search for and destroys
D. search for and destroy

68. F. NO CHANGE
G. analogy is
H. analogy, having been
J. analogy,

69. A. NO CHANGE
B. programs;
C. programs
D. programs,

70. F. NO CHANGE
G. Similarly to
H. In the same way as
J. According with

71. In this paragraph, the writer intends to recommend a number of specific ways to protect computer data against viruses. This is to be the second recommendation. Given that all of the choices are true, which one would best accomplish the writer's intention?

A. NO CHANGE
B. propose adding software that checks the spelling in the papers you write on your computer.
C. advise you to give your system frequent checkups with antivirus programs.
D. suggest that in order to protect your computer, you must be aware of the various ways to prevent viruses.

72. The best placement for the underlined portion would be:
F. where it is now.
G. after the word *your*.
H. after the word *had*.
J. after the word *responds*.

GO ON TO THE NEXT PAGE.

Questions 73–75 ask about the preceding passage as a whole.

73. Upon reviewing this essay and realizing that some information has been left out, the writer composes the following sentence, incorporating that information:

Names like these suggest that the problem is serious.

The most logical and effective place to add this sentence would be after the last sentence of Paragraph:

A. 2.
B. 3.
C. 4.
D. 5.

74. Paragraphs 1, 5, and 6 of this essay are written in the second person (*you, your*). If these paragraphs were revised so that the second-person pronouns were replaced with the pronouns *one* and *one's,* the essay would primarily:

F. gain a more polite and formal tone appropriate to the purpose of the essay.
G. gain accessibility by speaking to a broader and more inclusive audience.
H. lose the sense of directly addressing and advising the reader.
J. lose the immediacy of its setting in terms of time and place.

75. Suppose the writer had decided to write an essay discussing the moral and ethical consequences of programming a computer virus to tamper with a computer system. Would this essay successfully fulfill the writer's goal?

A. Yes, because the essay explains the moral and ethical consequences when a virus enters a computer system.
B. Yes, because the essay details the process of ridding a computer system of viruses, which helps the reader understand the consequences of programming computer viruses.
C. No, because the essay does not explain how to program a virus, so the reader has no basis for making a moral or ethical judgment.
D. No, because the essay limits itself to describing computer viruses and the basic precautions to be taken against them.

END OF TEST 1

STOP! DO NOT TURN THE PAGE UNTIL TOLD TO DO SO.

MATHEMATICS TEST

60 Minutes—60 Questions

DIRECTIONS: Solve each problem, choose the correct answer, and then fill in the corresponding oval on your answer document.

Do not linger over problems that take too much time. Solve as many as you can; then return to the others in the time you have left for this test.

You are permitted to use a calculator on this test. You may use your calculator for any problems you choose, but some of the problems may best be done without using a calculator.

Note: Unless otherwise stated, all of the following should be assumed.

1. Illustrative figures are NOT necessarily drawn to scale.
2. Geometric figures lie in a plane.
3. The word *line* indicates a straight line.
4. The word *average* indicates arithmetic mean.

---

1. Kaya ran $1\frac{2}{5}$ miles on Monday and $2\frac{1}{3}$ miles on Tuesday. What was the total distance, in miles, Kaya ran during those 2 days?

   A. $3\frac{2}{15}$

   B. $3\frac{3}{8}$

   C. $3\frac{2}{5}$

   D. $3\frac{7}{15}$

   E. $3\frac{11}{15}$

2. $3x^3 \cdot 2x^2y \cdot 4x^2y$ is equivalent to:

   F. $9x^7y^2$

   G. $9x^{12}y^2$

   H. $24x^7y^2$

   J. $24x^{12}y$

   K. $24x^{12}y^2$

3. Mr. Dietz is a teacher whose salary is $22,570 for this school year, which has 185 days. In Mr. Dietz's school district, substitute teachers are paid $80 per day. If Mr. Dietz takes a day off without pay and a substitute teacher is paid to teach Mr. Dietz's classes, how much less does the school district pay in salary by paying a substitute teacher instead of paying Mr. Dietz for that day?

   A. $ 42
   B. $ 80
   C. $ 97
   D. $105
   E. $122

4. So far, a student has earned the following scores on four 100-point tests this grading period: 65, 73, 81, and 82. What score must the student earn on the fifth and last 100-point test of the grading period to earn an average test grade of 80 for the 5 tests?

   F. 75
   G. 76
   H. 78
   J. 99
   K. The student cannot earn an average of 80.

DO YOUR FIGURING HERE.

GO ON TO THE NEXT PAGE.

DO YOUR FIGURING HERE.

5. The oxygen saturation level of a river is found by dividing the amount of dissolved oxygen the river water currently has per liter by the dissolved oxygen capacity per liter of the water and then converting to a percent. If the river currently has 7.3 milligrams of dissolved oxygen per liter of water and the dissolved oxygen capacity is 9.8 milligrams per liter, what is the oxygen saturation level, to the nearest percent?

- **A.** 34%
- **B.** 70%
- **C.** 73%
- **D.** 74%
- **E.** 98%

6. A rectangular lot that measures 150 ft by 200 ft is completely fenced. What is the approximate length, in feet, of the fence?

- **F.** 300
- **G.** 350
- **H.** 400
- **J.** 700
- **K.** 1,400

7. The expression $a[b + (c - d)]$ is equivalent to:

- **A.** $ab + ac - ad$
- **B.** $ab + ac + ad$
- **C.** $ab + ac - d$
- **D.** $ab + c + d$
- **E.** $ab + c - d$

8. If $4x + 3 = 9x - 4$, then $x = ?$

- **F.** $\dfrac{7}{5}$
- **G.** $\dfrac{5}{7}$
- **H.** $\dfrac{7}{13}$
- **J.** $\dfrac{1}{5}$
- **K.** $-\dfrac{1}{5}$

9. What 2 numbers should be placed in the blanks below so that the difference between consecutive numbers is the same?

$$17, \underline{\quad}, \underline{\quad}, 41$$

- **A.** 23, 29
- **B.** 24, 34
- **C.** 25, 33
- **D.** 26, 35
- **E.** 27, 31

GO ON TO THE NEXT PAGE.

Practice ACT Tests

10. If x is a real number such that $x^3 = 64$, then $x^2 + \sqrt{x} = ?$

F. 4
G. 10
H. 18
J. 20
K. 47

DO YOUR FIGURING HERE.

11. A formula for the volume V of a sphere with radius r is $V = \frac{4}{3}\pi r^3$. If the radius of a spherical rubber ball is $1\frac{1}{4}$ inches, what is its volume to the nearest cubic inch?

A. 5
B. 7
C. 8
D. 16
E. 65

12. If a marble is randomly chosen from a bag that contains exactly 8 red marbles, 6 blue marbles, and 6 white marbles, what is the probability that the marble will NOT be white?

F. $\frac{3}{4}$

G. $\frac{3}{5}$

H. $\frac{4}{5}$

J. $\frac{3}{10}$

K. $\frac{7}{10}$

13. The number of students participating in fall sports at a certain high school can be shown by the following matrix.

Tennis Soccer Cross-Country Football
$\begin{bmatrix} 40 & 60 & 80 & 80 \end{bmatrix}$

The athletic director estimates the ratio of the number of sports awards that will be earned to the number of students participating with the following matrix.

$\begin{matrix} \text{Tennis} \\ \text{Soccer} \\ \text{Cross-Country} \\ \text{Football} \end{matrix} \begin{bmatrix} 0.3 \\ 0.4 \\ 0.2 \\ 0.5 \end{bmatrix}$

Given these matrices, what is the athletic director's estimate for the number of sports awards that will be earned for these fall sports?

A. 80
B. 88
C. 91
D. 92
E. 99

GO ON TO THE NEXT PAGE.

DO YOUR FIGURING HERE.

Use the following information to answer questions 14–15.

The following chart shows the current enrollment in all the mathematics classes offered by Eastside High School.

Course title	Section	Period	Enrollment
Pre-Algebra	A	3	23
Algebra I	A	2	24
	B	3	25
	C	4	29
Geometry	A	1	21
	B	2	22
Algebra II	A	4	28
Pre-Calculus	A	6	19

14. What is the average number of students enrolled per section in Algebra I ?

F. 24
G. 25
H. 26
J. 27
K. 29

15. The school owns 2 classroom sets of 30 calculators each, which students are required to have during their mathematics class. There are 2 calculators from one set and 6 calculators from the other set that are not available for use by the students because these calculators are being repaired. For which of the following class periods, if any, are there NOT enough calculators available for each student to use a school-owned calculator without having to share?

A. Period 2 only
B. Period 3 only
C. Period 4 only
D. Periods 3 and 4 only
E. There are enough calculators for each class period.

16. What expression must the center cell of the table below contain so that the sums of each row, each column, and each diagonal are equivalent?

x	$8x$	$-3x$
$-2x$	?	$6x$
$7x$	$-4x$	$3x$

F. $6x$
G. $4x$
H. $2x$
J. $-2x$
K. $-4x$

GO ON TO THE NEXT PAGE.

17. Point *A* is to be graphed in a quadrant, not on an axis, of the standard (*x*,*y*) coordinate plane below.

DO YOUR FIGURING HERE.

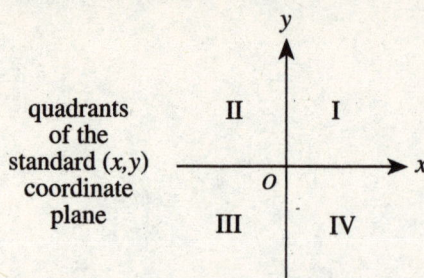

If the *x*-coordinate and the *y*-coordinate of point *A* are to have opposite signs, then point *A* *must* be located in:

A. Quadrant II only.
B. Quadrant IV only.
C. Quadrant I or III only.
D. Quadrant I or IV only.
E. Quadrant II or IV only.

18. Kareem has 4 sweaters, 6 shirts, and 3 pairs of slacks. How many distinct outfits, each consisting of a sweater, a shirt, and a pair of slacks, can Kareem select?

F. 13
G. 36
H. 42
J. 72
K. 216

19. At a refinery, 100,000 tons of sand are required to produce each 60,000 barrels of a tarry material. How many tons of sand are required to produce 3,000 barrels of this tarry material?

A. 5,000
B. 18,000
C. 20,000
D. 40,000
E. 50,000

20. If a rectangle measures 54 meters by 72 meters, what is the length, in meters, of the diagonal of the rectangle?

F. 48
G. 63
H. 90
J. 126
K. 252

GO ON TO THE NEXT PAGE.

21. For all positive integers x, y, and z, which of the following expressions is equivalent to $\frac{x}{y}$?

A. $\frac{x \cdot z}{y \cdot z}$

B. $\frac{x \cdot x}{y \cdot y}$

C. $\frac{y \cdot x}{x \cdot y}$

D. $\frac{x - z}{y - z}$

E. $\frac{x + z}{y + z}$

DO YOUR FIGURING HERE.

22. What is the slope-intercept form of $8x - y - 6 = 0$?

F. $y = -8x - 6$
G. $y = -8x + 6$
H. $y = 8x - 6$
J. $y = 8x + 6$
K. $y = 6x - 8$

23. Which of the following is a solution to the equation $x^2 - 36x = 0$?

A. 72
B. 36
C. 18
D. 6
E. −6

24. For right triangle $\triangle RST$ shown below, what is $\tan R$?

F. $\frac{r}{s}$

G. $\frac{r}{t}$

H. $\frac{t}{r}$

J. $\frac{t}{s}$

K. $\frac{s}{t}$

25. A chord 24 inches long is 5 inches from the center of a circle, as shown below. What is the radius of the circle, to the nearest tenth of an inch?

A. 29.0
B. 24.5
C. 16.9
D. 13.0
E. 10.9

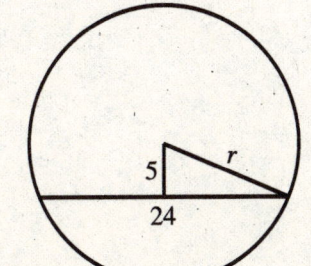

Practice ACT Tests

DO YOUR FIGURING HERE.

26. The length L, in meters, of a spring is given by the equation $L = \frac{2}{3}F + 0.03$, where F is the applied force in newtons. What force, in newtons, must be applied for the spring's length to be 0.18 meters?

   F. 0.13
   G. 0.15
   H. 0.225
   J. 0.255
   K. 0.27

27. After a snowstorm, city workers removed an estimated 10,000 cubic yards of snow from the downtown area. If this snow were spread in an even layer over the entire rectangular football field shown below, about how many yards deep would the layer of snow be?

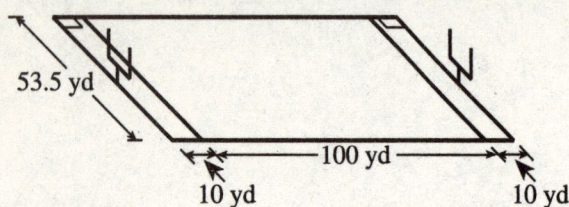

53.5 yd

100 yd

10 yd   10 yd

   A. Less than 1
   B. Between 1 and 2
   C. Between 2 and 3
   D. Between 3 and 4
   E. More than 4

28. The hypotenuse of the right triangle $\triangle PQR$ shown below is 16 feet long. The sine of $\angle P$ is $\frac{3}{5}$. About how many feet long is $\overline{QR}$?

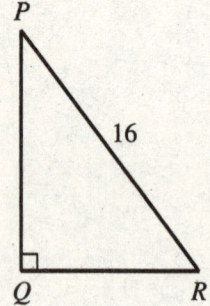

P

16

Q   R

   F. 8.0
   G. 9.6
   H. 12.4
   J. 14.3
   K. 15.4

GO ON TO THE NEXT PAGE.

DO YOUR FIGURING HERE.

29. The graph below shows the number of cars assembled last year in 4 cities, to the nearest 5,000 cars. According to the graph, what fraction of the cars assembled in all 4 cities were assembled in Coupeville?

	Key
🚗	= 10,000 cars

City	Cars assembled
Car Town	🚗 🚗 🚗 🚗
Coupeville	🚗 🚗 🚙
Truck City	🚗 🚗
Sedan Falls	🚗 🚙

A. $\frac{1}{5}$

B. $\frac{1}{4}$

C. $\frac{3}{11}$

D. $\frac{3}{10}$

E. $\frac{1}{3}$

30. Points B and C lie on $\overline{AD}$ as shown below. The length of $\overline{AD}$ is 30 units; $\overline{AC}$ is 16 units long; and $\overline{BD}$ is 20 units long. How many units long, if it can be determined, is $\overline{BC}$?

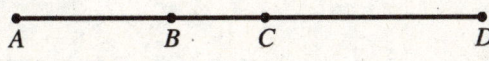

A   B   C   D

F. 4
G. 6
H. 10
J. 14
K. Cannot be determined from the given information

31. What is the x-coordinate of the point in the standard (x,y) coordinate plane at which the 2 lines $y = 2x + 6$ and $y = 3x + 4$ intersect?

A. 1
B. 2
C. 4
D. 6
E. 10

GO ON TO THE NEXT PAGE.

32. For all pairs of real numbers M and V where $M = 3V + 6$, $V = ?$

F. $\dfrac{M}{3} - 6$

G. $\dfrac{M}{3} + 6$

H. $3M - 6$

J. $\dfrac{M - 6}{3}$

K. $\dfrac{M + 6}{3}$

33. Parallelogram $ABCD$, with dimensions in inches, is shown in the diagram below. What is the area of the parallelogram, in square inches?

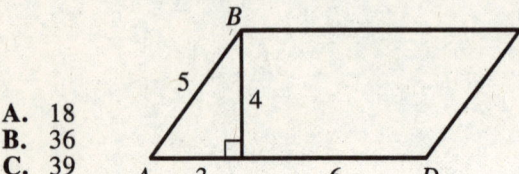

A. 18
B. 36
C. 39
D. 45
E. 72

34. If $a = b + 2$, then $(b - a)^4 = ?$
F. -16
G. -8
H. 1
J. 8
K. 16

35. A park has the shape and dimensions in blocks given below. A water fountain is located halfway between point B and point D. Which of the following is the location of the water fountain from point A ?

(Note: The park's borders run east-west or north-south.)

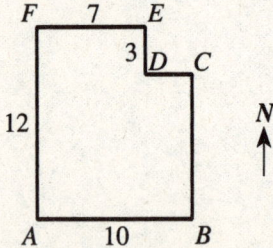

A. $3\frac{1}{2}$ blocks east and 6 blocks north

B. 5 blocks east and $4\frac{1}{2}$ blocks north

C. 5 blocks east and 6 blocks north

D. $8\frac{1}{2}$ blocks east and $4\frac{1}{2}$ blocks north

E. 9 blocks east and $7\frac{1}{2}$ blocks north

DO YOUR FIGURING HERE.

GO ON TO THE NEXT PAGE.

DO YOUR FIGURING HERE.

36. The larger of two numbers exceeds twice the smaller number by 8. The sum of twice the larger and 3 times the smaller number is 65. If x is the smaller number, which equation below determines the correct value of x ?

    F. $3(2x + 8) + 2x = 65$
    G. $3(2x - 8) + 2x = 65$
    H. $(4x + 8) + 3x = 65$
    J. $2(2x + 8) + 3x = 65$
    K. $2(2x - 8) + 3x = 65$

37. Members of the fire department lean a 30-foot ladder against a building. The side of the building is perpendicular to the level ground so that the base of the ladder is 10 feet away from the base of the building. To the nearest foot, how far up the building does the ladder reach?

    A. 10
    B. 20
    C. 28
    D. 31
    E. 40

38. A square is circumscribed about a circle of 7-foot radius, as shown below. What is the area of the square, in square feet?

    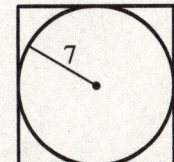

    F. 49
    G. 56
    H. 98
    J. 49π
    K. 196

39. The ratio of the side lengths for a triangle is exactly 12:14:15. In a second triangle similar to the first, the shortest side is 8 inches long. To the nearest tenth of an inch, what is the length of the longest side of the second triangle?

    A. 11.0
    B. 10.0
    C. 9.3
    D. 6.4
    E. Cannot be determined from the given information

40. In the figure below, $ABCD$ is a trapezoid, E lies on $\overleftrightarrow{AD}$, and angle measures are as marked. What is the measure of $\angle BDC$?

    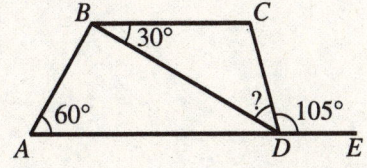

    F. 15°
    G. 25°
    H. 30°
    J. 35°
    K. 45°

Practice ACT Tests

GO ON TO THE NEXT PAGE.

DO YOUR FIGURING HERE.

41. In the figure shown below, each pair of intersecting line segments meets at a right angle, and all the lengths given are in inches. What is the perimeter, in inches, of the figure?

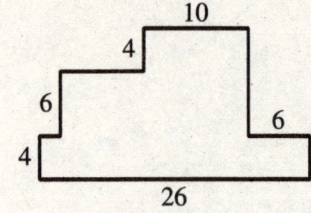

A. 40
B. 52
C. 56
D. 66
E. 80

42. Of the 804 graduating seniors in a certain high school, approximately $\frac{2}{5}$ are going to college and approximately $\frac{1}{4}$ of those going to college are going to a state university. Which of the following is the closest estimate for how many of the graduating seniors are going to a state university?

F. 80
G. 90
H. 160
J. 200
K. 320

43. If x and y are positive integers such that the greatest common factor of x^2y^2 and xy^3 is 45, then which of the following could y equal?

A. 45
B. 15
C. 9
D. 5
E. 3

44. If 115% of a number is 460, what is 75% of the number?

F. 280
G. 300
H. 320
J. 345
K. 400

45. What is the distance in the standard (x,y) coordinate plane between the points $(1,0)$ and $(0,5)$?

A. 4
B. 6
C. 16
D. 36
E. $\sqrt{26}$

GO ON TO THE NEXT PAGE.

DO YOUR FIGURING HERE.

46. The ratio of the radii of two circles is 4:9. What is the ratio of their circumferences?

F. 2:3
G. 4:9
H. 16:81
J. $4:8\pi$
K. $9:18\pi$

47. A circle in the standard (x,y) coordinate plane is tangent to the x-axis at 5 and tangent to the y-axis at 5. Which of the following is an equation of the circle?

A. $x^2 + y^2 = 5$
B. $x^2 + y^2 = 25$
C. $(x - 5)^2 + (y - 5)^2 = 5$
D. $(x - 5)^2 + (y - 5)^2 = 25$
E. $(x + 5)^2 + (y + 5)^2 = 25$

48. In the complex numbers, where $i^2 = -1$,

$$\frac{1}{1+i} \cdot \frac{1-i}{1-i} = ?$$

F. $i - 1$

G. $1 + i$

H. $1 - i$

J. $\frac{1-i}{2}$

K. $\frac{1+i}{2}$

49. Which of the following statements describes the total number of dots in the first n rows of the triangular arrangement illustrated below?

```
    •              1st row
   • • •           2nd row
  • • • • •         3rd row
 • • • • • • •      4th row
• • • • • • • • •   5th row
        ⋮
```

A. This total is always equal to 25 regardless of the number of rows.
B. This total is equal to twice the number of rows.
C. This total is equal to 5 times the number of rows.
D. This total is equal to the square of the number of rows.
E. There is no consistent relationship between this total and the number of rows.

GO ON TO THE NEXT PAGE.

50. After polling a class of 20 music students by a show of hands, you find that 8 students play the guitar and 9 students play the piano. Given that information, what is the minimum number of students in this music class who play both the guitar and the piano?

F.   0
G.   1
H.   8
J.   9
K.   17

51. Which of the following is the set of all real numbers x such that $x + 3 > x + 5$?

A.   The empty set
B.   The set containing all real numbers
C.   The set containing all negative real numbers
D.   The set containing all nonnegative real numbers
E.   The set containing only zero

52. Pentagons have 5 diagonals, as illustrated below.

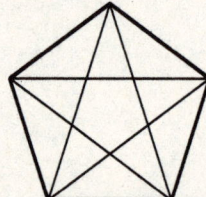

How many diagonals does the octagon below have?

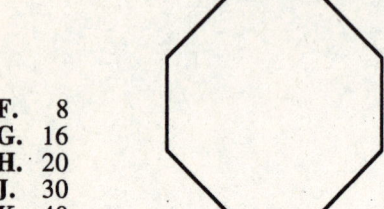

F.   8
G.   16
H.   20
J.   30
K.   40

53. Douglas wants to draw a circle graph showing the favorite colors of his friends. When he polled his friends asking each their favorite color, 25% of his friends said red; 30% of his friends said blue; 20% of his friends said green; 10% of his friends said purple; and the remaining friends said colors other than red, blue, green, and purple. The colors other than red, blue, green, and purple will be grouped together in an Other sector. What will be the degree measure of the Other sector?

A.   108°
B.   54°
C.   27°
D.   15°
E.   10°

GO ON TO THE NEXT PAGE.

54. If $\sin \theta = -\frac{3}{5}$ and $\pi < \theta < \frac{3\pi}{2}$, then $\tan \theta = ?$

DO YOUR FIGURING HERE.

   F. $-\frac{5}{4}$

   G. $-\frac{3}{4}$

   H. $-\frac{3}{5}$

   J. $\frac{3}{4}$

   K. $\frac{4}{5}$

55. Which of the following systems of inequalities is represented by the shaded region of the graph below?

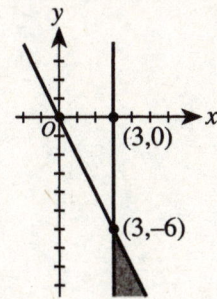

   A. $y \leq -2x$ and $x \geq 3$
   B. $y \leq -2x$ or $x \geq 3$
   C. $y \geq -2x$ and $x \geq 3$
   D. $y \geq -2x$ or $x \geq 3$
   E. $y \geq -2x$ and $x \leq 3$

56. If $f(x) = x^2 - 2$, then $f(x + h) = ?$

   F. $x^2 + h^2$
   G. $x^2 - 2 + h$
   H. $x^2 + h^2 - 2$
   J. $x^2 + 2xh + h^2$
   K. $x^2 + 2xh + h^2 - 2$

GO ON TO THE NEXT PAGE.

57. Which of the following is the graph, in the standard (x,y) coordinate plane, of $y = \dfrac{2x^2 + x}{x}$?

DO YOUR FIGURING HERE.

A.

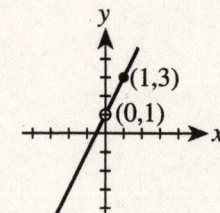

B.

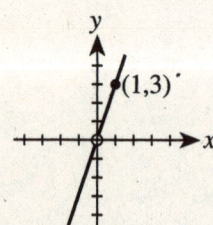

C.

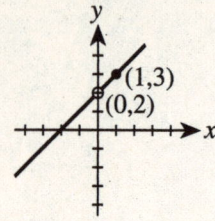

D.

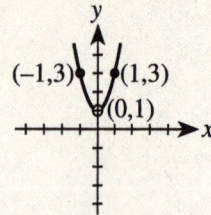

E.

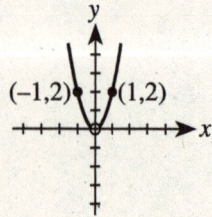

58. A triangle, $\triangle ABC$, is reflected across the x-axis to have the image $\triangle A'B'C'$ in the standard (x,y) coordinate plane; thus, A reflects to A'. The coordinates of point A are (c,d). What are the coordinates of point A' ?

F. $(\,c, -d)$
G. $(-c,\, d)$
H. $(-c, -d)$
J. $(\,d,\, c)$
K. Cannot be determined from the given information

59. If $x = 2t - 9$ and $y = 5 - t$, which of the following expresses y in terms of x ?

A. $y = \dfrac{1-x}{2}$

B. $y = \dfrac{19-x}{2}$

C. $y = 14 - 2x$

D. $y = 5 - x$

E. $y = 1 - x$

GO ON TO THE NEXT PAGE.

60. What is $\sin \frac{\pi}{12}$ given that $\frac{\pi}{12} = \frac{\pi}{3} - \frac{\pi}{4}$ and that $\sin(\alpha - \beta) = (\sin \alpha)(\cos \beta) - (\cos \alpha)(\sin \beta)$?

DO YOUR FIGURING HERE.

(Note: You may use the following table of values.)

θ	$\sin \theta$	$\cos \theta$
$\frac{\pi}{6}$	$\frac{1}{2}$	$\frac{\sqrt{3}}{2}$
$\frac{\pi}{4}$	$\frac{\sqrt{2}}{2}$	$\frac{\sqrt{2}}{2}$
$\frac{\pi}{3}$	$\frac{\sqrt{3}}{2}$	$\frac{1}{2}$

F. $\frac{1}{4}$

G. $\frac{1}{2}$

H. $\frac{\sqrt{3} - 2}{4}$

J. $\frac{\sqrt{3} - \sqrt{2}}{2}$

K. $\frac{\sqrt{6} - \sqrt{2}}{4}$

END OF TEST 2

STOP! DO NOT TURN THE PAGE UNTIL TOLD TO DO SO.

DO NOT RETURN TO THE PREVIOUS TEST.

Practice ACT Tests

READING TEST

35 Minutes—40 Questions

DIRECTIONS: There are four passages in this test. Each passage is followed by several questions. After reading a passage, choose the best answer to each question and fill in the corresponding oval on your answer document. You may refer to the passages as often as necessary.

Passage I

PROSE FICTION: This passage is adapted from the short story "Elba" by Marly Swick (©1991 by the University of Iowa). Fran is the narrator of the story.

Mother, who wanted to keep her, always thought of her as some wild little bird, but I knew she was a homing pigeon. I knew that at some point in her flight path, sooner or later, she would make a U-turn. A sort
5 of human boomerang. So even though I had long since stopped expecting it, I was not surprised when I walked down the gravel drive to the mailbox, which I'd painted papaya yellow to attract good news, and found the flimsy envelope with the Dallas postmark. I didn't
10 know a soul in Dallas, or Texas for that matter, but the handwriting reminded me of someone's. My own.

I walked back inside the house.

"Still raining?" Mother asked. She was sitting in her new electric wheelchair in front of the TV, painting
15 her fingernails a neon violet.

"Just let up," I said. "Sun's poking through. You know anyone in Dallas, Mother?"

"Not so as I recall." She dabbed at her pinky with a cottonball. Mother was vain about her hands. I was
20 used to how she looked now, but I noticed people staring in the doctor's waiting room. She had lost some weight and most of her hair to chemotherapy, and I guess people were startled to see these dragon-lady nails on a woman who looked as if she should be lying
25 in satin with some flowers on her chest.

"Why do you ask?" she said.

I opened the envelope and a picture fluttered into my lap. It was a Polaroid of a sweet-faced blond holding a newborn baby in a blue blanket. Before I
30 even read the letter I knew. I knew how those Nazis feel when suddenly, after twenty or thirty uneventful years, they are arrested walking down some sunny street in Buenos Aires. It's the shock of being found after waiting so long.

35 "What's that?" Mother said.

I wheeled her around to face me and handed her the Polaroid. She studied it for a minute and then

looked up, speechless for once, waiting for me to set the tone.

40 "That's her," I said. "Her name's Linda Rose Caswell."

We looked at the picture again. The blond woman was seated on a flowered couch, her wavy hair just grazing the edge of a dime-a-dozen seascape in a cheap
45 gilt frame.

Mother pointed to the envelope. "What's she say?"

I unfolded the letter, a single page neatly written.

"She says she's had my name and address for some time but wanted to wait to contact me until after
50 the birth. The baby's name is Blake and he weighs eight pounds, eight ounces, and was born by cesarean. She says they are waiting and hoping to hear back from me soon."

"That's it?"

55 I nodded and handed her the letter. It was short and businesslike, but I could see the ghosts of all the long letters she must have written and crumpled into the wastebasket.

"I guess that makes you a great-grandmother," I
60 said.

"What about you?" she snorted, pointing a Jungle Orchid fingernail at me. "You're a grandmother."

We shook our heads in disbelief. I sat silently, listening to my brain catch up with my history. Forty
65 years old and I felt as if I had just shaken hands with Death. I suppose it's difficult for any woman to accept that she's a grandmother, but in the normal order of things, you have ample time to adjust to the idea. You don't get a snapshot in the mail one day from a baby
70 girl you gave up twenty-four years ago saying, "Congratulations, you're a grandma!"

"It's not fair," I said. "I don't even feel like a *mother*."

"Well, here's the living proof." Mother tapped her
75 nail against the glossy picture. "She looks just like you. Only her nose is more aristocratic."

GO ON TO THE NEXT PAGE.

"I'm going to work." My knees cracked when I stood up. "You be all right here?"

Mother nodded, scrutinizing the picture in her lap. "You going to write to her?"

"Of course I am," I bristled. "I may be some things, but I am not rude."

"You going to invite them here? Her and the baby?" She swiveled her eyes sideways at me.

"I haven't thought that far," I said.

"Well, don't put it off." She slid her eyes back to the television. "She's been waiting twenty-five years. You worried she's going to be trouble or ask for money? For all we know, she's married to a brain surgeon with his and her Cadillacs."

"She didn't mention any husband at all," I said, getting drawn into it despite myself.

"Maybe you're worried she'll be disappointed in you," she said. "You know, that she's had this big fantasy for all these years that maybe you were Grace Kelly or Margaret Mead and who could live up to that? No one. But you don't have to, Fran, that's the thing. You're her flesh-and-blood mother and that's enough. That's all it'll take."

1. Fran would most likely agree with which of the following statements about her relationship with Linda Rose?

   A. Their lives are still connected despite long separations of time and distance.
   B. They have built up too much resentment toward each other to have a good relationship now.
   C. Fran's dreams of a perfect daughter will interfere with any real relationship she might have with Linda Rose.
   D. The two of them have enough in common that it won't be difficult for them to get close.

2. Fran's mother can most accurately be characterized as:

   F. arrogant and cruel.
   G. strong-willed and caring.
   H. friendly but withdrawn.
   J. loving but embittered.

3. Which of the following statements does NOT describe one of Fran's reactions to the news that she is a grandmother?

   A. She wishes she had had time to prepare for the news.
   B. She looks forward to inviting Linda Rose and her son, Blake, over for a visit.
   C. She feels suddenly older now that the label of grandmother applies to her.
   D. She protests that this change in her life is unfair.

4. The main point of the first paragraph is that:

   F. Fran believed Linda Rose would someday try to contact her.
   G. Linda Rose acted like a wild bird when she was young.
   H. Fran finds the arrival of a letter from Linda Rose surprising.
   J. Linda Rose's handwriting reminds Fran of her own handwriting.

5. The main point of the last paragraph is that Fran's mother believes:

   A. Linda Rose has few illusions about Fran.
   B. Linda Rose might cause trouble or ask for money.
   C. Fran shouldn't worry about disappointing Linda Rose.
   D. Fran shouldn't write to Linda Rose until Fran is emotionally prepared.

6. According to the passage, when Fran looks at her mother, Fran feels:

   F. surprised by how weak and old her mother looks.
   G. embarrassed by the gaudy colors of nail polish her mother uses.
   H. pity that so many people stare at her mother in public.
   J. accustomed to her mother's frailness and unusual fingernails.

7. Which of the following statements most accurately expresses Fran's feelings when she hands her mother the letter from Linda Rose?

   A. Fran is disappointed about getting such a short letter after so many years of no news from Linda Rose.
   B. Fran welcomes the good news about the birth of her grandson, Blake.
   C. Fran is offended by the letter's cold, businesslike tone.
   D. Fran knows how hard it must have been for Linda Rose to write the letter.

8. It can logically be inferred from the passage that the reason it has been a long time since Fran and Linda Rose have seen each other is because:

   F. Linda Rose left home to get married.
   G. arguments between Fran and Linda Rose drove Linda Rose away.
   H. Linda Rose chose to live with her father.
   J. as a child Linda Rose was adopted by another family.

9. A reasonable conclusion Fran and her mother draw about Linda Rose from her letter and picture is that Linda Rose:

   A. lives near the coast of Texas with her husband.
   B. enjoys and collects fine paintings.
   C. bears a strong resemblance to Fran.
   D. cares little about how she or her house looks.

GO ON TO THE NEXT PAGE.

10. According to the passage, the reason why Fran's mother warns Fran not to put off contacting Linda Rose is that Fran's mother:

F. wants before she dies to see her new great-grandson.

G. knows Fran tends to delay making hard decisions.

H. knows how long Linda Rose has been waiting to see Fran.

J. suspects Linda Rose is in some sort of trouble.

Passage II

SOCIAL SCIENCE: This passage is adapted from a book titled *How Courts Govern America* by Richard Neely (©1981 by Richard Neely).

Government is a technical undertaking, like the building of rocketships or the organizing of railroad yards. Except possibly on the local level, the issues which attract public notice usually involve raising
5 money (taxes), spending money (public works), foreign wars (preventing them or arguing for fighting easy ones), education, public morals, crime in the streets, and, most important of all, the economy. When times are bad, or there is a nationwide strike or disaster,
10 interest in the economy becomes all-consuming. However, the daily toiling of countless millions of civil servants in areas such as occupational health and safety, motor vehicle regulation, or control of navigable waterways escapes public notice almost completely.

15 Furthermore, even with regard to high-visibility issues, significant communication between the electorate and public officials is extremely circumscribed. Most serious political communication is limited to forty-five seconds on the network evening news. In
20 days gone by, when the only entertainment in town on a Wednesday night was to go to the county courthouse to listen to a prominent politician give a theatrical tirade against Herbert Hoover, an eloquent speaker could pack the courthouse and have five thousand people lined up
25 to the railroad tracks listening to the booming loud-speakers.

The political orator of yesteryear has been replaced by a flickering image on the tube unlocking the secrets of the government universe in forty-five-
30 second licks. Gone forever are Lincoln-Douglas type debates on courthouse steps. Newspapers take up the slack a little, but very little. Most of what one says to a local newspaper (maybe not the *New York Times*) gets filtered through the mind of an inexperienced
35 twenty-three-year-old journalism school graduate. Try sometime to explain the intricacies of a program budget, which basically involves solving a grand equation composed of numerous simultaneous differential functions, to a reporter whose journalism school cur-
40 riculum did not include advanced algebra, to say nothing of calculus.

But the electorate is as interested in the whys and wherefores of most technical, nonemotional political issues as I am in putting ships in bottles: they do not
45 particularly care. Process and personalities, the way decisions are made and by whom, the level of perquisites, extramarital sexual relations, and, in high offices, personal gossip dominate the public mind, while interest in the substance of technical decisions is
50 minimal. Reporters focus on what sells papers or gets a high Nielsen rating; neither newspapers nor television stations intend to lose their primary value as entertainment. Since the populace at large is more than willing to delegate evaluation of the technical aspects of gov-
55 ernment to somebody else, it inevitably follows that voting is a negative exercise, not a positive one. Angry voters turn the rascals out and, in the triumph of hope over experience, let new rascals in. What voters are unable to do—because they themselves do not under-
60 stand the technical questions—is tell the rascals how to do their jobs better.

Serious coverage of goings-on in government is deterred by the fact that government is so technical that even career civil servants cannot explain what is hap-
65 pening. In 1978 I attended a seminar on federal estate and gift tax, where the Internal Revenue Service lawyers responsible for this area frankly confessed that they did not understand the Tax Reform Act of 1976. Intricate technical issues such as taxation, arms control,
70 and nuclear power are difficult to understand for professionals, to say nothing of the most diligent layman.

That anything gets done by a political body at all is to be applauded as a miracle rather than accepted as a matter of course. When we recognize that in the federal
75 government, with its millions of employees, there are but five hundred and thirty-seven elected officials, put into office to carry out the "will" of a people who for the most part know little and care less about the technical functioning of their government, the absurdity of
80 the notion of rapid democratic responsiveness becomes clear. The widely held tenet of democratic faith that elected officials, as opposed to bureaucrats or the judiciary, are popularly selected and democratically responsive is largely a myth which gives a useful legiti-
85 macy to a system. In fact, however, far from democratic control, the two most important forces in political life are indifference and its direct byproduct, inertia.

11. One of the main points that the author seeks to make in the passage is that American citizens:

A. cannot understand government because they read too many newspapers and watch too much television.

B. have little chance of improving government because they do not understand the important details of government.

C. can control elected officials' technical decisions through elections, but have no control over the bureaucrats.

D. used to have a responsive government before television cut back on news and began to concentrate on entertainment.

GO ON TO THE NEXT PAGE.

12. The author asserts that local newspaper reporters are often:

   F. inexperienced and insufficiently educated.
   G. inexperienced but well educated.
   H. young but experienced.
   J. young and well educated.

13. The author uses the description of the tax seminar in 1978 to make the point that some governmental issues are:

   A. so technical that not even career civil servants can understand them.
   B. so technical that only career civil servants can understand them.
   C. more technical than they used to be before the passage of the Tax Reform Act.
   D. too technical for anyone other than an Internal Revenue Service tax lawyer to understand.

14. When the author asserts that *indifference* is a central fact of American political life (line 87), he most likely means that citizens are:

   F. not concerned about the technical, but important, details of government.
   G. completely taken in by the myth that government is responsive to democratic control.
   H. more responsive to elected government officials than to unelected bureaucrats.
   J. not prepared to concede legitimacy to a government unless it is democratically elected.

15. According to the passage, when is voter interest in the economy greatest?

   A. When national elections are held
   B. When interesting personalities are leaders
   C. When there are bad economic times
   D. When there are no other interesting issues

16. As it is used in line 17, the word *circumscribed* means:

   F. technical.
   G. limited.
   H. entertaining.
   J. serious.

17. According to the passage, the news story under which of the following headlines would attract the greatest number of readers?

   A. Department of Interior Announces End of National Park Fees
   B. New Accounting Procedures in Federal Budget
   C. New Federal Safety Regulations Due Out Today
   D. Senator Smith Claims 'I Never Made a Nickel On It'

18. The passage makes the claim that television news coverage is heavily influenced by Nielsen ratings because:

   F. those ratings place great emphasis on technical details.
   G. their competitors, the newspapers, get very high ratings.
   H. the Federal Communications Commission requires Nielsen ratings.
   J. television is primarily an entertainment medium.

19. In the fourth paragraph, the phrase "the triumph of hope over experience" (lines 57–58) is an expression of the belief that:

   A. newly elected officials will govern better than the ones just defeated.
   B. expertise in a technical field is a qualification for holding office.
   C. if the voters get angry enough, elected officials will do a better job.
   D. newspapers and television will eventually provide better news coverage.

20. In the passage, the argument is made that citizens are unable to tell government officials how to do their jobs better because citizens:

   F. don't vote in every election.
   G. have a tendency to elect rascals.
   H. don't read enough newspapers or see enough television.
   J. don't understand the technical details of government.

GO ON TO THE NEXT PAGE.

Passage III

HUMANITIES: This passage is adapted from Bharati Mukherjee's essay "A Four-Hundred-Year-Old Woman," which appears in the anthology *The Writer on Her Work* (©1991 by Janet Sternburg).

I was born into a class that did not live in its native language. I was born into a city that feared its future, and trained me for emigration. I attended a school run by Irish nuns, who regarded our walled-off school
5 compound in Calcutta as a corner of England. My "country"—called in Bengali *desh*—I have never seen. It is the ancestral home of my father and is now in Bangladesh. Nevertheless, I speak his dialect of Bengali, and think of myself as "belonging" to
10 Faridpur, the tiny village that was his birthplace. The larger political entity to which I gave my first allegiance—India—was not even a sovereign nation when I was born.

My horoscope, cast by a neighborhood astrologer
15 when I was a week-old infant, predicted that I would be a writer, that I would cross oceans and make my home among aliens. Brought up in a culture that places its faith in horoscopes, it never occurred to me to doubt it. The astrologer meant to offer me a melancholy future;
20 to be destined to leave India was to be banished from the sources of true culture. The nuns at school, on the other hand, insinuated that India had long outlived its glories, and that if we wanted to be educated, modern women, we'd better hit the trail westward. All my girl-
25 hood, I straddled the seesaw of contradictions.

I have found my way to the United States after many transit stops. The unglimpsed phantom Faridpur and the all too real Manhattan have merged as "desh." I am an American. I am an American writer, in the
30 American mainstream, trying to extend it. This is a vitally important statement for me—I am not an Indian writer, not an expatriate. I am an immigrant; my investment is in the American reality, not the Indian.

It took me ten painful years, from the early seven-
35 ties to the early eighties, to overthrow the smothering tyranny of nostalgia. The remaining struggle for me is to make the American readership, meaning the editorial and publishing industries as well, acknowledge the same fact. The foreign-born, the Third World immi-
40 grant with non-Western religions and non-European languages and appearance, can be as American as any steerage passenger from Ireland, Italy, or the Russian Pale.

My literary agenda begins by acknowledging that
45 America has transformed *me*. It does not end until I show how I (and the hundreds of thousands like me) have transformed America.

I've had to sensitize editors as well as readers to the richness of the lives I'm writing about. The most
50 moving form of praise I receive from readers can be summed up in three words: *I never knew.* Meaning, I see these people (call them Indians, Filipinos, Koreans,

Chinese) around me all the time and I never knew they had an inner life. I never knew they schemed and
55 cheated, suffered, cared so passionately. When even the forms of praise are so rudimentary, the writer knows she has an inexhaustible fictional population to enumerate. Perhaps even a mission.

I have been blessed with an enormity of material:
60 the rapid and dramatic transformation of the United States since the early 1970s. Within that perceived perimeter, however, I hope to wring surprises.

Yet my imaginative home is also in the tales told by my mother and grandmother, the world of the Hindu
65 epics. For all the hope and energy I have placed in the process of immigration and accommodation—I'm a person who couldn't ride a public bus when she first arrived, and now I'm someone who watches tractor pulls on obscure cable channels—there are parts of
70 me that remain Indian. The form that my stories and novels take inevitably reflects the resources of Indian mythology—shape-changing, miracles, godly perspectives. My characters can, I hope, transcend the straitjacket of simple psychologizing. The people I write
75 about are culturally and politically several hundred years old: consider the history they have witnessed (colonialism, technology, education, liberation, civil war). They have shed old identities, taken on new ones, and learned to hide the scars. They may sell you news-
80 papers, or clean your offices at night.

Writers (especially American writers weaned on affluence and freedom) often disavow the notion of a "literary duty" or "political consciousness," citing the all-too-frequent examples of writers ruined by their
85 shrill commitments. Glibness abounds on both sides of the argument, but finally I have to side with my "Third World" compatriots: I do have a duty, beyond telling a good story. My duty is to give voice to continents, but also to redefine the nature of *American.*

21. One of the main arguments the author is trying to make in the passage is that:

A. until recently, foreign-born residents have not wanted to be involved in defining the American reality.

B. non-Western immigrants are changing the definition of what it means to be an American.

C. the United States immigration policy is inherently unfair.

D. America has changed the political affiliations of most non-Western immigrants.

GO ON TO THE NEXT PAGE.

22. Considering the information given in the first three paragraphs (lines 1–33), which of the following is the most accurate description of the author's girlhood and early adulthood?

  F. She grew up and was educated in Calcutta, moved to the United States, and lived in Manhattan.

  G. She was born in Calcutta, was educated in England by Irish nuns, then moved to Manhattan.

  H. She was raised in Bangladesh, educated by Irish nuns in Calcutta, moved first to England and some time later arrived in the United States.

  J. She was born in Faridpur, was educated in Calcutta, then moved to Manhattan.

23. The author sees her "literary agenda" (line 44) and her "mission" (line 58) to be:

  A. raising the political consciousness of recent immigrants to the United States.

  B. creating characters whose cultural heritage is not easily identifiable.

  C. reinterpreting, through her stories, what it means to be an American.

  D. finding an audience for her stories and novels.

24. Which of the following statements from the passage is an acknowledgment by the author that she was changed by America?

  F. "The astrologer meant to offer me a melancholy future" (line 19).

  G. "All my girlhood, I straddled the seesaw of contradictions" (lines 24–25).

  H. "I'm someone who watches tractor pulls on obscure cable channels" (lines 68–69).

  J. "My characters can, I hope, transcend the straitjacket of simple psychologizing" (lines 73–74).

25. The author refers to the village of Faridpur as a "phantom" (line 27) because:

  A. it is a part of the Indian mythology her mother told her about.

  B. she considers Manhattan, not Bangladesh, to be her home.

  C. even though it was once part of India, it is now part of Bangladesh.

  D. even though she considers it to be her ancestral home, she has never been there.

26. When the author says that she is "trying to extend it" (line 30), she most likely means that she:

  F. wants to see people from non-European ethnicities included in what is considered mainstream American.

  G. prefers to be part of both the Indian and the American cultures.

  H. is trying to find a way to make her home in the United States permanent.

  J. is working to change regulations so that many more Indian immigrants can live in the United States.

27. The author implies that she had to "sensitize editors" (line 48) because those editors:

  A. did not understand that many Asian Americans were already reading her work.

  B. gave superficial praise to her work, but would not publish her novels.

  C. were overtly discriminatory when it came to non-Western writers.

  D. tended to view the people she wrote about as one-dimensional.

28. According to the passage, by reading her stories, many of the author's readers learned that:

  F. good fiction writing obscures cultural differences among characters.

  G. they have much more in common with the author's characters than they ever realized.

  H. stories about immigrants to the United States generally have many more characters than do other types of stories.

  J. because of their immigrant status, people from non-Western countries have developed a stronger inner life than have most native-born Americans.

29. The first paragraph states that, at the time of the author's birth, India was:

  A. engaged in a war with England.

  B. not an independent country.

  C. still part of Bangladesh.

  D. governed by the Irish.

30. When the author says that the people she writes about "are culturally and politically several hundred years old" (lines 75–76), she most likely means that her characters:

  F. have cultural and political viewpoints that are repressive and outdated.

  G. have rejected Bengali, British, Irish, and American values.

  H. have experienced an incredible amount of change in just one lifetime.

  J. are really her mother's and grandmother's ancestors.

GO ON TO THE NEXT PAGE.

Passage IV

NATURAL SCIENCE: This passage is adapted from the essay "Were Dinosaurs Dumb?" by Stephen Jay Gould (©1980 by Stephen Jay Gould).

The discovery of dinosaurs in the nineteenth century provided, or so it appeared, a quintessential case for the negative correlation of size and smarts. With their pea brains and giant bodies, dinosaurs became a
5 symbol of lumbering stupidity. Their extinction seemed only to confirm their flawed design.

Dinosaurs were not even granted the usual solace of a giant—great physical prowess. . . . Dinosaurs . . . have usually been reconstructed as slow and clumsy. In
10 the standard illustration, *Brontosaurus* wades in a murky pond because he cannot hold up his own weight on land. . . .

Dinosaurs have been making a strong comeback of late, in this age of "I'm OK, You're OK." Most paleon-
15 tologists are now willing to view them as energetic, active, and capable animals. The *Brontosaurus* that wallowed in its pond a generation ago is now running on land, while pairs of males have been seen twining their necks about each other in elaborate sexual combat
20 for access to females (much like the neck wrestling of giraffes). Modern anatomical reconstructions indicate strength and agility, and many paleontologists now believe that dinosaurs were warmblooded. . . .

The idea of warmblooded dinosaurs has captured
25 the public imagination and received a torrent of press coverage. Yet another vindication of dinosaurian capability has received very little attention, although I regard it as equally significant. I refer to the issue of stupidity and its correlation with size. The revisionist
30 interpretation, which I support, . . . does not enshrine dinosaurs as paragons of intellect, but it does maintain that they were not small brained after all. They had the "right-sized" brains for reptiles of their body size.

I don't wish to deny that the flattened, minuscule
35 head of large-bodied *Stegosaurus* houses little brain from our subjective, top-heavy perspective, but I do wish to assert that we should not expect more of the beast. First of all, large animals have relatively smaller brains than related, small animals. The correlation of
40 brain size with body size among kindred animals (all reptiles, all mammals for example) is remarkably regular. As we move from small to large animals, from mice to elephants or small lizards to Komodo dragons, brain size increases, but not so fast as body size. In
45 other words, bodies grow faster than brains, and large animals have low ratios of brain weight to body weight. In fact, brains grow only about two-thirds as fast as bodies. Since we have no reason to believe that large animals are consistently stupider than their smaller rel-
50 atives, we must conclude that large animals require relatively less brain to do as well as smaller animals. If we do not recognize this relationship, we are likely to underestimate the mental power of very large animals, dinosaurs in particular. . . .

55 If behavioral complexity is one consequence of mental power, then we might expect to uncover among dinosaurs some signs of social behavior that demand coordination, cohesiveness and recognition. Indeed we do, and it cannot be accidental that these signs were
60 overlooked when dinosaurs labored under the burden of a falsely imposed obtuseness. Multiple trackways have been uncovered, with evidence for more than twenty animals traveling together in parallel movement. Did some dinosaurs live in herds? At the Davenport Ranch
65 sauropod trackway, small footprints lie in the center and larger ones at the periphery. Could it be that some dinosaurs traveled much as some advanced herbivorous mammals do today, with large adults at the borders sheltering juveniles in the center? . . .

70 But the best illustration of dinosaurian capability may well be the fact most often cited against them—their demise. . . .

The remarkable thing about dinosaurs is not that they became extinct, but that they dominated the earth
75 for so long. Dinosaurs held sway for 100 million years while mammals, all the while, lived as small animals in the interstices of their world. After 70 million years on top, we mammals have an excellent track record and good prospects for the future, but we have yet to dis-
80 play the staying power of dinosaurs.

People, on this criterion, are scarcely worth mentioning—5 million years perhaps since *Australopithecus,* a mere 50,000 for our own species, *Homo sapiens.* Try the ultimate test within our system of values: Do you
85 know anyone who would wager a substantial sum even at favorable odds on the proposition that *Homo sapiens* will last longer than *Brontosaurus*?

---

31. In the context of the passage as a whole, it is most reasonable to infer that the phrase "the *Brontosaurus* that wallowed in its pond a generation ago is now running on land" (lines 16–18) means that:

A. the *Brontosaurus* evolved from living in the water to living on land.
B. scientists' understanding of the *Brontosaurus*'s lifestyle has changed within the last generation.
C. standard illustrations of dinosaurs still inaccurately depict their lifestyles.
D. the *Brontosaurus* eventually learned to hold up its own weight on land.

32. The passage suggests that some fossil evidence about dinosaur behavior has been overlooked in the past because scientists:

F. had preconceived ideas about the intelligence of dinosaurs.
G. believed that mammals were not capable of social formations.
H. did not have the current data about dinosaur brain size.
J. did not have the necessary equipment to discover the social patterns of dinosaurs.

GO ON TO THE NEXT PAGE.

33. What does the passage offer as evidence that dinosaurs may have exhibited complex behaviors?

A. Modern anatomical reconstructions indicating strength and agility

B. Fossils revealing that dinosaurs labored under severe burdens

C. Footprints of varying sizes indicating that dinosaurs traveled with advanced herbivorous mammals

D. Multiple trackways in which footprint size and location indicate social order

34. In the context of the passage, what does the author mean when he states that "people . . . are scarcely worth mentioning" (lines 81–82)?

F. Compared to the complex social behavior of dinosaurs, human behavior seems simple.

G. Compared to the longevity of dinosaurs, humans have been on earth a very short time.

H. Compared to the size of dinosaurs, humans seem incredibly small.

J. Compared to the amount of study done on dinosaurs, study of human behavior is severely lacking.

35. According to the passage, what is the revisionist interpretation concerning the relationship between intelligence and physical size?

A. Dinosaurs actually had relatively large brains.

B. Dinosaurs were paragons of intellect.

C. Dinosaurs were relatively small brained.

D. Dinosaurs' brains were appropriately sized.

36. What does the author suggest in lines 34–38 when he states that *Stegosaurus* has a small brain from "our subjective, top-heavy perspective"?

F. Humans are unusually smart in their judgment of other species.

G. The human physical construction is deformed by the largeness of the skull.

H. It is unfair to judge other species by human standards.

J. Not all species have a brain as small relative to body weight as do humans.

37. The passage states that the ratio of brain weight to body weight in larger animals, as compared to smaller animals, is:
A. higher.
B. lower.
C. the same.
D. overestimated.

38. According to the passage, which of the following correctly states the relationship of brain size to body size?

F. The brain grows at two-thirds the rate of body growth.

G. At maturity, the brain weighs an average of one-third of body weight.

H. Large animals are not consistently less intelligent than smaller animals.

J. Brain size is independent of body size.

39. The author states that the best illustration of dinosaurs' capability is their dominance of the earth for:

A. 100,000 years.
B. 5 million years.
C. 70 million years.
D. 100 million years.

40. As it is used in line 82, the term *Australopithecus* most nearly means:

F. the last of the dinosaurs, which became extinct 5 million years ago.

G. the first *Homo sapiens,* who appeared on earth 50,000 years ago.

H. an early version of humankind, but a different species.

J. a physically larger species of human with a much smaller brain.

END OF TEST 3

STOP! DO NOT TURN THE PAGE UNTIL TOLD TO DO SO.

DO NOT RETURN TO A PREVIOUS TEST.

Practice ACT Tests

SCIENCE TEST

35 Minutes—40 Questions

DIRECTIONS: There are seven passages in this test. Each passage is followed by several questions. After reading a passage, choose the best answer to each question and fill in the corresponding oval on your answer document. You may refer to the passages as often as necessary.

You are NOT permitted to use a calculator on this test.

Passage I

Flood basalt plateaus are large areas of Earth's surface covered with thick hardened lava. It has been hypothesized that the huge outpourings of lava that formed these plateaus were produced by *plumes* of molten material rising from deep within Earth.

Study 1

A model of a typical plume was created using a computer. It was hypothesized that the "head" of the plume produced the flood basalt plateaus when its molten material reached the surface. Figure 1 shows the computer-generated plume, its diameter, and how long, in millions of years (Myr), it would take the head of the plume to reach the surface.

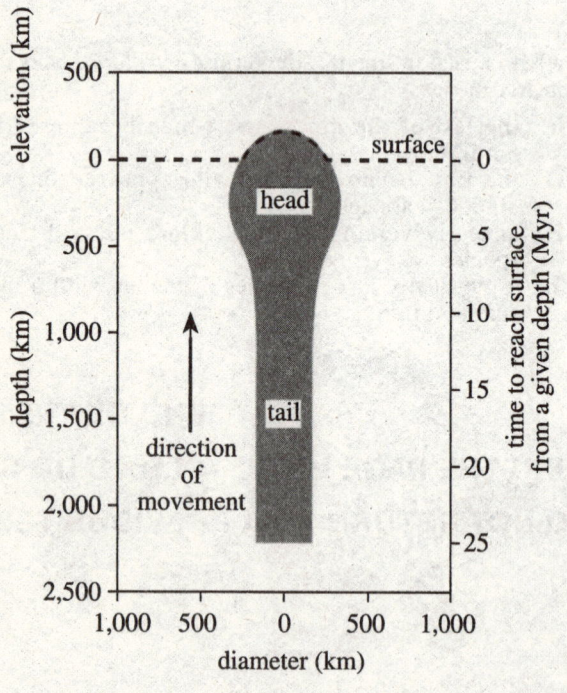

Figure 1

Figure adapted from R. I. Hill et al., *Mantle Plumes and Continental Tectonics.* ©1992 by the American Association for the Advancement of Science.

Study 2

Four flood basalt plateaus (A–D) were studied. The lava volume, in cubic kilometers (km³), was estimated for each plateau from the area of the plateau and the average thickness of the lava. The length of time lava was being produced at each plateau, and the rate of lava production, in km³ per year, were also estimated. The results are in Table 1.

			Length of time lava was produced (Myr)	Rate of lava production (km³/yr)
Table 1				
Plateau	Age (Myr)	Lava volume (km³)		
A	60	2,000,000	1.6	1.25
B	67	1,500,000	1.3	1.2
C	135	1,440,000	1.2	1.2
D	192	2,125,000	1.7	1.25

Table adapted from Mark A. Richards et al., *Flood Basalts and Hot-Spot Tracks: Plume Heads and Tails.* ©1989 by the American Association for the Advancement of Science.

Study 3

Scientists found that 3 large extinctions of marine organisms had ages similar to those of the formation of 3 of the flood basalt plateaus; 58 Myr, 66 Myr, and 133 Myr. It was hypothesized that the production of large amounts of lava and gases in the formation of plateaus may have contributed to those extinctions.

(Note: All of these ages have an error of ±1 Myr.)

GO ON TO THE NEXT PAGE.

1. If the plume model in Study 1 is typical of all mantle plumes, the scientists would generalize that the heads of plumes are:

   A. approximately half the diameter of the tail.
   B. approximately twice the diameter of the tail.
   C. the same diameter as the tail.
   D. half as dense as the tail.

2. The scientists in Study 3 hypothesized that the larger the volume of lava produced, the larger the number of marine organisms that would become extinct. If this hypothesis is correct, the formation of which of the following plateaus caused the largest number of marine organisms to become extinct?

   F. Plateau A
   G. Plateau B
   H. Plateau C
   J. Plateau D

3. Based on the results of Study 2, a flood basalt plateau that produced lava for a period of 1.8 Myr would most likely have a lava volume

   A. between 1,440,000 km^3 and 1,500,000 km^3.
   B. between 1,500,000 km^3 and 2,000,000 km^3.
   C. between 2,000,000 km^3 and 2,125,000 km^3.
   D. over 2,125,000 km^3.

4. According to Study 2, which of the following statements best describes the relationship, if any, between the age of a flood basalt plateau and the length of time lava was produced at that plateau?

   F. As the age of a plateau increases, the length of time lava was produced increases.
   G. As the age of a plateau increases, the length of time lava was produced decreases.
   H. As the age of a plateau increases, the length of time lava was produced increases, and then decreases.
   J. There is no apparent relationship between the age of a plateau and the length of time lava was produced.

5. Which of the following graphs best represents the relationship between the age of a flood basalt plateau and the rate of lava production?

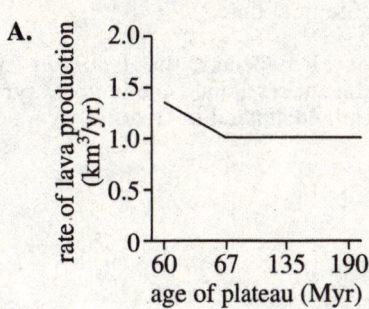

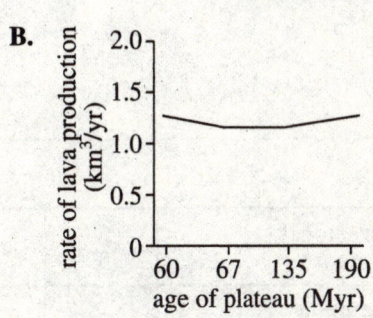

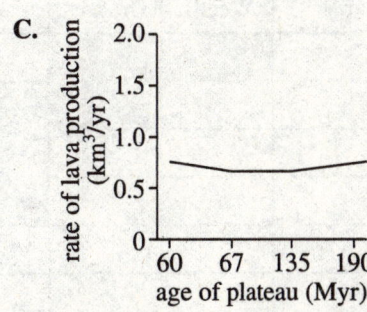

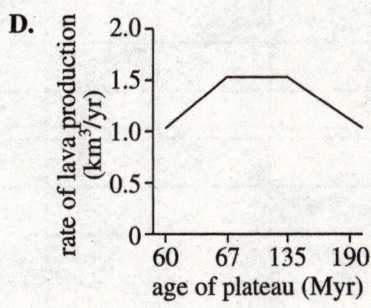

6. If the hypothesis made by the scientists in Study 3 is correct, evidence would most likely be found of another extinction of marine organisms that occurred around:

   F. 77 Myr ago.
   G. 192 Myr ago.
   H. 250 Myr ago.
   J. 314 Myr ago.

GO ON TO THE NEXT PAGE.

Passage II

Succession refers to the change in species composition in a given area over ecological time.

Table 1 shows the bird species, the *dominant* (most common) plants, and the successional time in years (yr) on plots of abandoned farmland studied in Georgia.

Table 1										
Bird species	Successional time (yr)	1	3	15	20	25	35	60	100	150
	Dominant plants	Weeds	Grasses	Shrubs		Pines				Oaks
Grasshopper sparrow		■	■							
Eastern meadowlark		┈	■	■						
Yellowthroat				■	■					
Field sparrow				■	■	■				
Yellow-breasted chat					■					
Rufous-sided towhee						■	■	■	■	
Pine warbler						■	■	■	■	
Cardinal							■	■	■	
Summer tanager							■	■	■	
Eastern wood pewee							■	■	■	
Blue-gray gnatcatcher								■	■	■
Crested flycatcher									■	■
Carolina wren									■	■
Ruby-throated hummingbird									■	■
Tufted titmouse									■	■
Hooded warbler									■	■
Red-eyed vireo									■	■
Wood thrush									■	■
Note: Shaded areas indicate bird species was present at a density of at least 1 pair per 10 acres.										

GO ON TO THE NEXT PAGE.

The estimated changes in *net productivity* (grams of organic mass produced per square meter per year [g/m²/yr]) and *biomass* (kilograms of organic material per square meter [kg/m²]) of plants on abandoned farmland in New York appear in Figures 1 and 2, respectively. Successional time is divided into 3 stages based on the dominant plants.

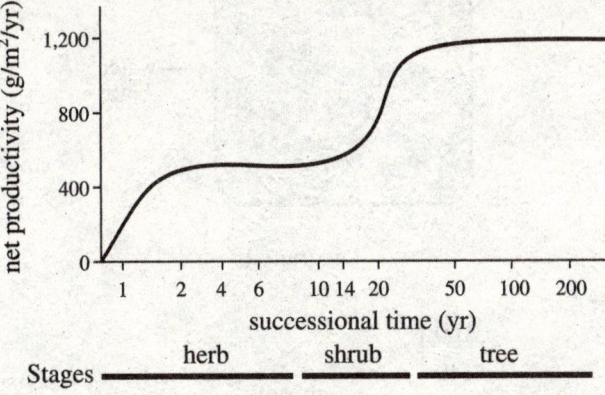

Figure 1

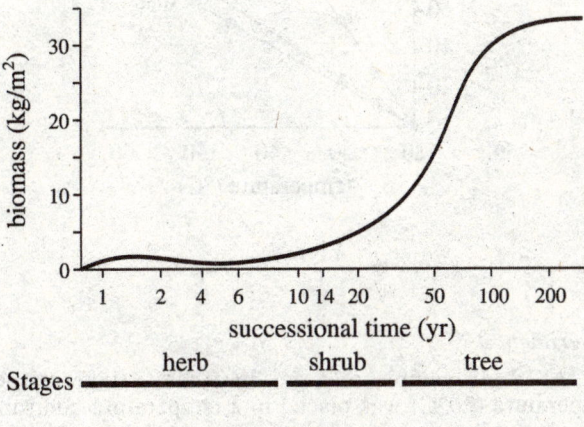

Figure 2

Figures and table adapted from William T. Keeton and James L. Gould, *Biological Science.* ©1986 by W.W. Norton & Company, Inc.

7. According to Figure 1, at the end of Year 50 the net productivity of the land was closest to:

   A.   15 g/m²/yr.
   B.   50 g/m²/yr.
   C.   425 g/m²/yr.
   D. 1,125 g/m²/yr.

8. Based on the data in Figures 1 and 2, the researchers should make which of the following conclusions about the overall change in net productivity and biomass over the 200 years studied?

   F. Both net productivity and biomass increased.
   G. Both net productivity and biomass decreased.
   H. Net productivity increased and biomass decreased.
   J. Net productivity decreased and biomass increased.

9. According to Figure 1, total net productivity increased the most during which of the following time periods?

   A. From the end of Year 2 to the end of Year   4
   B. From the end of Year 4 to the end of Year 14
   C. From the end of Year 14 to the end of Year 50
   D. From the end of Year 50 to the end of Year 200

10. Which of the following conclusions about net productivity is consistent with the results shown in Figure 1 ?

    F. Net productivity was lowest when shrubs were the dominant plants.
    G. Net productivity was lowest when trees were the dominant plants.
    H. Net productivity was highest when herbs were the dominant plants.
    J. Net productivity was highest when trees were the dominant plants.

11. A student learned that a particular plot of abandoned farmland in Georgia supported eastern meadowlarks, yellowthroats, and field sparrows at a density of at least 1 pair per 10 acres. Based on Table 1, the student would predict that the dominant plants on this plot of land were most likely:

    A. weeds.
    B. grasses.
    C. shrubs.
    D. pines.

GO ON TO THE NEXT PAGE.

Passage III

Solids, liquids, and gases usually expand when heated. Three experiments were conducted by scientists to study the expansion of different substances.

Experiment 1

The apparatus shown in Diagram 1 was used to measure the linear expansion of wires of the same length made from different metals. In each trial, a wire was connected to a voltage source, run through a series of pulleys, then attached to a weight. The temperature of the wire was varied by changing the amount of voltage applied. The amount of expansion is directly proportional to the rotation of the final pulley. The results are shown in Figure 1.

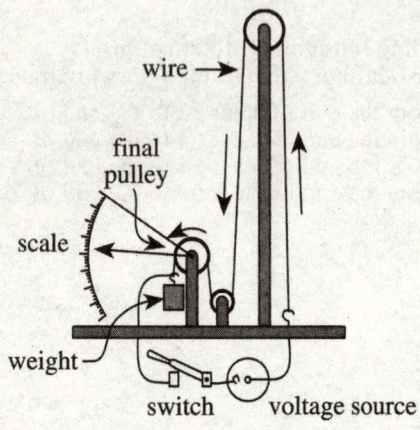

Diagram 1

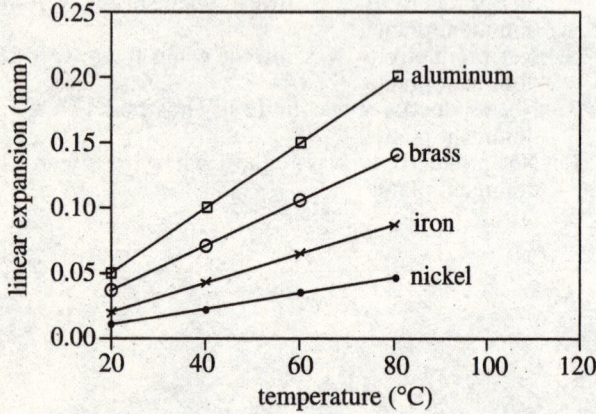

Figure 1

Experiment 2

A sample of liquid was placed in a stoppered test tube fitted with a graduated capillary tube and the test tube was then placed in a temperature-controlled water bath (Diagram 2). The rise of the liquid in the capillary tube was then measured at different temperatures. The results for 3 liquids are shown in Figure 2.

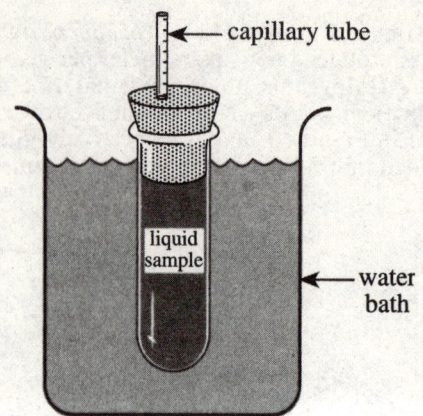

Diagram 2

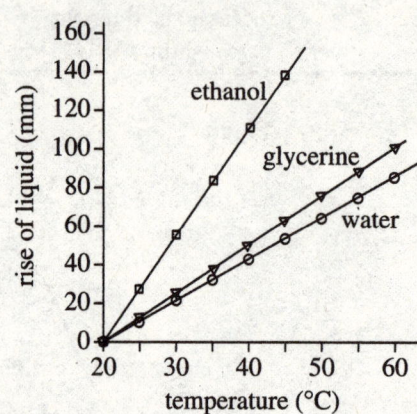

Figure 2

Experiment 3

A 20 mL sample of a gas in a gas syringe at room temperature (20°C) was placed in a temperature-controlled water bath (Diagram 3). Changes in gas volume as the temperature increased were measured for 3 gases. The results are shown in Figure 3.

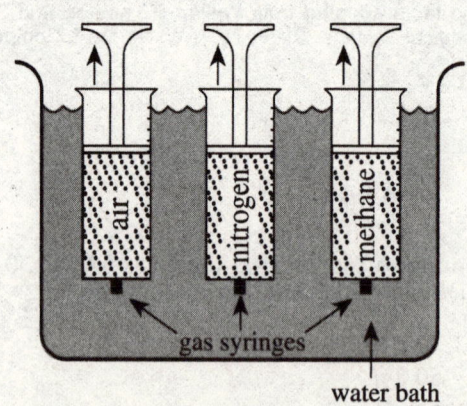

Diagram 3

GO ON TO THE NEXT PAGE.

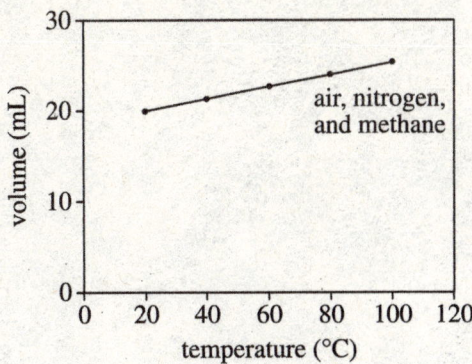

Figure 3

12. In Experiment 2, at which of the following temperatures did all of the liquids tested have the same volume?

F. 20°C
G. 30°C
H. 40°C
J. 50°C

13. A scientist has hypothesized that as the temperature of a gas is increased at constant pressure, the volume of the gas will also increase. Do the results of Experiment 3 support his hypothesis?

A. Yes; the volume of all of the gases tested in Experiment 3 increased as temperature increased.
B. Yes; although air decreased in volume when the temperature increased, nitrogen and methane volumes both increased.
C. No; the volume of all of the gases tested in Experiment 3 decreased as temperature increased.
D. No; although air increased in volume when the temperature increased, nitrogen and methane volumes both decreased.

14. Based on the results of Experiment 1, if an engineer needs a wire most resistant to stretching when it is placed under tension and heat, which of the following wires should she choose?

F. Aluminum
G. Brass
H. Iron
J. Nickel

15. Based on the results of Experiment 3, if a balloon was filled with air at room temperature and placed on the surface of a heated water bath, as the temperature of the water increased, the volume of the balloon would:

A. increase only.
B. decrease only.
C. decrease, then increase.
D. remain the same.

16. The scientists tested a copper wire of the same initial length as the wires tested in Experiment 1. At 80°C, the linear expansion of the wire was 0.12 mm. Based on the results of Experiment 1, which of the following correctly lists 5 wires by their length in the apparatus at 80°C from *shortest* to *longest*?

F. Aluminum, brass, copper, iron, nickel
G. Aluminum, copper, brass, iron, nickel
H. Nickel, iron, copper, brass, aluminum
J. Nickel, iron, brass, copper, aluminum

17. If Experiment 1 had been repeated using a heavier weight attached to the brass wire, which of the following figures best shows the comparison between the results of using the heavier weight and the original weight on the brass wire?

A.

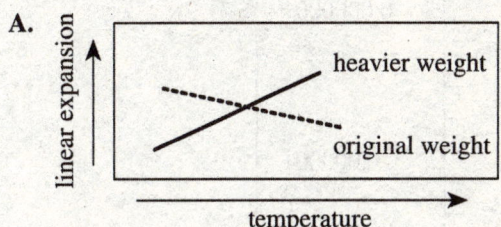

B.

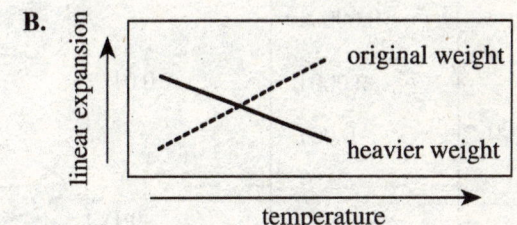

C.

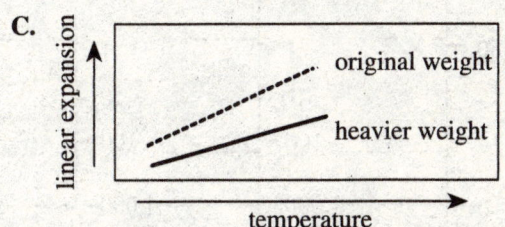

D.

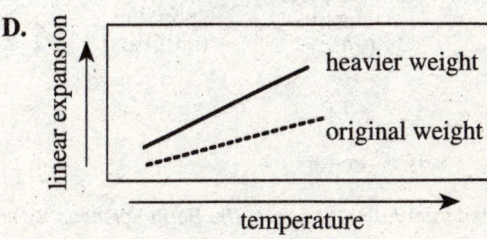

GO ON TO THE NEXT PAGE.

Passage IV

Certain layers of Earth's atmosphere absorb particular wavelengths of solar radiation while letting others pass through. Types of solar radiation include X rays, ultraviolet light, visible light, and infrared radiation. The cross section of Earth's atmosphere below illustrates the altitudes at which certain wavelengths are absorbed. The arrows point to the altitudes at which solar radiation of different ranges of wavelengths is absorbed. The figure also indicates the layers of the atmosphere and how atmospheric density, pressure, and temperature vary with altitude.

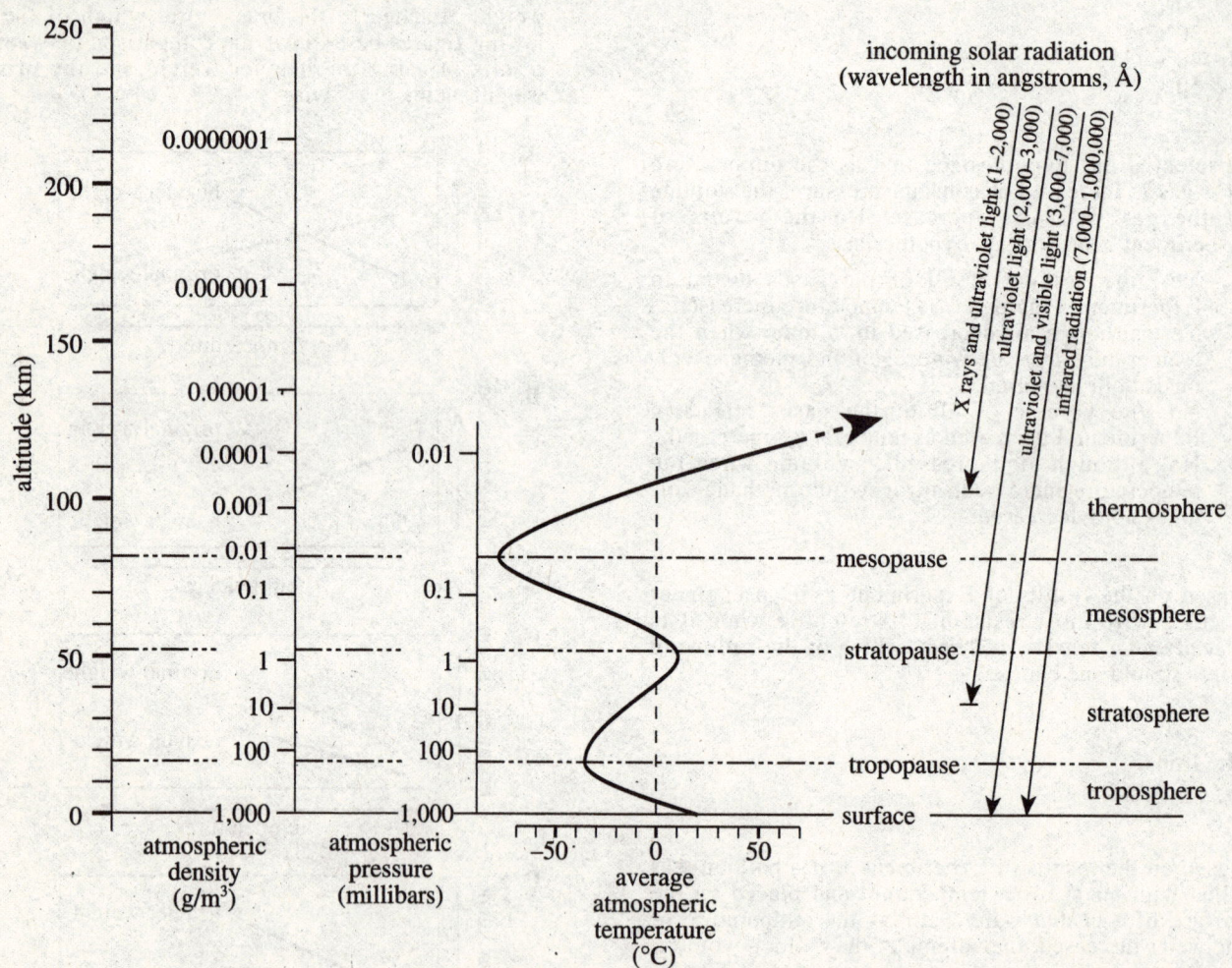

Note: 1 Å = 1 × 10⁻¹⁰ meters.

Figure adapted from Arthur Strahler, *The Earth Sciences*. ©1963 by Harper and Row.

GO ON TO THE NEXT PAGE.

18. According to the data provided, at what altitude is the upper boundary of the thermosphere located?

F. 150 km
G. 200 km
H. 250 km
J. The upper boundary is not included on the figure.

19. The ozone layer selectively absorbs ultraviolet radiation of 2,000–3,000 Å wavelengths. According to this information and the data, which atmospheric layer contains the ozone layer?

A. Troposphere
B. Stratosphere
C. Mesosphere
D. Thermosphere

20. The information provided in the figure indicates that the air temperature in the troposphere is LEAST likely to be influenced by which of the following wavelengths of energy?

F. 1,500 Å
G. 4,500 Å
H. 6,000 Å
J. 7,000 Å

21. On the basis of the information in the figure, one could generalize that atmospheric pressure in each atmospheric layer increases with:

A. decreasing temperature.
B. increasing temperature.
C. decreasing altitude.
D. increasing altitude.

22. Atmospheric boundaries are at a higher than usual altitude above areas that get more direct solar radiation. Based on this information and the data provided, which of the following predictions about atmospheric boundaries would most likely be true if Earth received *less* solar radiation than it presently does?

F. The tropopause, stratopause, and mesopause would all increase in altitude.
G. The tropopause, stratopause, and mesopause would all decrease in altitude.
H. The tropopause and stratopause would increase in altitude, but the mesopause would decrease in altitude.
J. The tropopause would decrease in altitude, but the stratopause and mesopause would increase in altitude.

GO ON TO THE NEXT PAGE.

Passage V

Some oceanic shrimp are vertical migrators. For vertically migrating species, most of the population is found at the bottom of their depth range during the day and at the top of their depth range at night. Table 1 shows the depth ranges and water, protein, lipid, and carbohydrate content of 3 vertically migrating (vm) species of shrimp and 3 nonmigrating (nm) species of deep-sea shrimp. Figure 1 shows water temperature and oxygen partial pressure at various ocean depths.

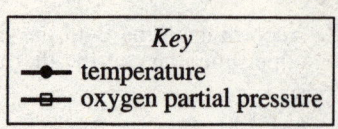

Key
● temperature
□ oxygen partial pressure

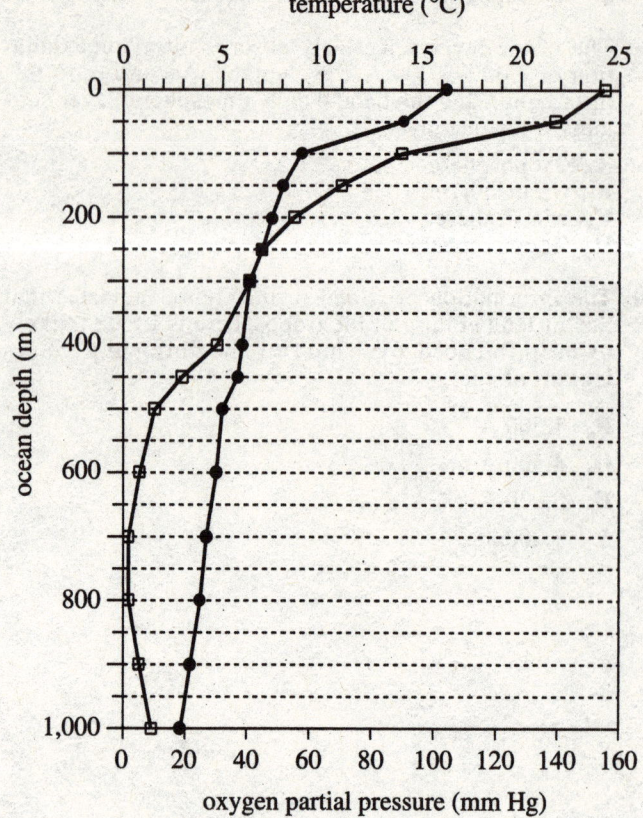

Figure 1

Table 1					
Species	Depth range (m)	Water content (% wet weight)	% ash-free dry weight		
			protein	lipid	carbohydrate
vm 1	300– 600	77.5	62.8	23.8	0.7
vm 2	10– 400	76.6	53.4	16.4	0.8
vm 3	75– 400	79.5	60.5	14.7	0.7
nm 1	500–1,100	75.9	36.9	36.1	0.5
nm 2	500–1,000	76.7	41.5	31.5	0.8
nm 3	650–1,100	72.8	35.8	49.0	0.5

GO ON TO THE NEXT PAGE.

23. Based on the information in Table 1, one would conclude that vertically migrating shrimp have a higher percent content of:

A. protein than lipid.
B. lipid than protein.
C. carbohydrate than lipid.
D. carbohydrate than protein.

24. On the basis of the information given, one would expect that, compared to the vertically migrating shrimp species, the nonmigrating shrimp species:

F. have a greater water content.
G. have a lower percent lipid content.
H. can tolerate higher water temperatures.
J. can tolerate lower oxygen partial pressures.

25. Assume that shrimp of a newly discovered species of vertically migrating shrimp were captured at night at a minimum depth of 200 m. Assume that only temperature limits the range of this species. Based on the information in Figure 1, one would predict that the maximum water temperature these shrimp could survive in would be:

A. 3.5°C.
B. 7.5°C.
C. 12.5°C.
D. 15.5°C.

26. Protein is a major component of muscle. Assume that shrimp that are strong swimmers tend to have a higher protein:lipid ratio than do shrimp that are weaker swimmers. On the basis of Table 1, one would conclude that which of the following shrimp species is the strongest swimmer?

F. vm 2
G. vm 3
H. nm 1
J. nm 3

27. Assume that only oxygen partial pressure limits the range of the shrimp species shown in Table 1. Accordingly, which of the following pieces of information supports the hypothesis that vm 2 and vm 3 cannot tolerate oxygen partial pressures below 25 mm Hg ?

A. They are not able to tolerate temperatures above 10°C.
B. They have unusually high water contents.
C. They are not found below a depth of 400 m.
D. They are not found above a depth of 100 m.

GO ON TO THE NEXT PAGE.

Passage VI

Two students explain why the *smoke* (a mixture of gases and carbon particles) from burning wood in a fireplace rises up the chimney from the fireplace. They also discuss how chimney *efficiency* (the volume of smoke flowing out the top of the chimney per second for a given temperature difference between inside and outside the chimney) is related to chimney height.

Student 1

Smoke rises because the gases from burning wood are less dense than the air that surrounds the fireplace. Because the gases are hotter than the air, the gas molecules have a higher average speed than the air molecules. Consequently, the average distance between adjacent gas molecules is greater than the average distance between adjacent air molecules, and so the gas *density* is less than the air density. As a result, the upward *buoyant force* acting on the gases is stronger than the downward *force of gravity* acting on the gases, and the gases rise, carrying the carbon particles with them. The upward flow of smoke is maintained as new air enters the fireplace, causing more wood to burn.

As chimney height increases, efficiency increases. The taller the chimney, the greater the volume of hot gas, the stronger the buoyant force compared with the force of gravity, and the more rapidly smoke rises.

Student 2

Smoke rises because wind blows across the top of the chimney. When no wind is blowing, the air pressure at the bottom of the chimney is slightly higher than the air pressure at the top of the chimney. However, when air at the top of the chimney moves at a higher speed than air at the bottom of the chimney, the pressure difference between the bottom and the top of the chimney is so great that air is forced upward, carrying smoke with it. The departure of air from the bottom of the chimney, in turn, creates a pressure difference that forces new air into the fireplace, causing further burning and an upward flow of smoke.

As chimney height increases, efficiency increases. Generally, wind speed increases with altitude. The taller the chimney, the greater the difference in air speed, the greater the difference in air pressure, and the more rapidly smoke rises.

28. According to Student 1, which of the following quantities is *less* for the gases from burning wood than for the air that surrounds the fireplace?

   F. Average speed of the molecules
   G. Average distance between adjacent molecules
   H. Density
   J. Temperature

29. When wood was burned in 2 fireplaces that differ only in the height of their chimneys (keeping the same temperature difference between inside and outside each chimney), Chimney Y was found to be more efficient than Chimney X. What conclusion would each student draw about which chimney is taller?

   A. Both Student 1 and Student 2 would conclude that Chimney X is taller.
   B. Both Student 1 and Student 2 would conclude that Chimney Y is taller.
   C. Student 1 would conclude that Chimney X is taller; Student 2 would conclude that Chimney Y is taller.
   D. Student 1 would conclude that Chimney Y is taller; Student 2 would conclude that Chimney X is taller.

30. Which student(s), if either, would predict that smoke from burning wood will rise up the chimney from a fireplace on a day when the air at the top of the chimney is NOT moving?

   F. Student 1 only
   G. Student 2 only
   H. Both Student 1 and Student 2
   J. Neither Student 1 nor Student 2

31. When wood is burned in a fireplace, air in the fireplace, as well as gases from the burning wood, rises up the chimney. Student 1 would most likely argue that the air in the fireplace rises because the air is:

   A. hotter than the gases from the burning wood.
   B. cooler than the gases from the burning wood.
   C. hotter than the air that surrounds the fireplace.
   D. cooler than the air that surrounds the fireplace.

32. When the air inside a particular hot-air balloon cooled, the balloon and its inside air descended. Based on Student 1's explanation, the reason the balloon and its inside air descended is most likely that the:

   F. downward buoyant force acting on the balloon and its inside air was stronger than the upward force of gravity acting on the balloon and its inside air.
   G. upward buoyant force acting on the balloon and its inside air was stronger than the downward force of gravity acting on the balloon and its inside air.
   H. downward force of gravity acting on the balloon and its inside air was stronger than the upward buoyant force acting on the balloon and its inside air.
   J. upward force of gravity acting on the balloon and its inside air was stronger than the downward buoyant force acting on the balloon and its inside air.

GO ON TO THE NEXT PAGE.

33. Based on Student 1's explanation, if the gases from burning wood lose heat while rising up a chimney, which of the following quantities pertaining to the gases simultaneously increases?

A. Density of the gases
B. Temperature of the gases
C. Average speed of the gas molecules
D. Average distance between adjacent gas molecules

34. Based on Student 2's explanation, the reason the wings of an airplane keep the airplane up in the air is that air moves at a higher speed:

F. above the wings than below the wings.
G. below the wings than above the wings.
H. in front of the wings than behind the wings.
J. behind the wings than in front of the wings.

GO ON TO THE NEXT PAGE.

Passage VII

Salts containing nitrite ions (NO_2^-) are often added to meats to prevent discoloration caused by air and bacterial growth. Use of NO_2^- is controversial because studies have linked NO_2^- with cancer. Students performed 2 experiments to measure NO_2^- levels.

Experiment 1

Four solutions, each containing a different amount of $NaNO_2$ (a salt) in H_2O were prepared. A coloring agent was added that binds with NO_2^- to form a purple compound that strongly absorbs light of a specific wavelength, and each solution was diluted to 100 mL. A *blank* solution was prepared in the same manner, but no $NaNO_2$ was added. A *colorimeter* (a device that measures how much light of a selected wavelength is absorbed by a sample) was used to measure the *absorbance* of each solution. The absorbances were corrected by subtracting the absorbance of the blank solution from each reading (see Table 1 and Figure 1).

Table 1		
Concentration of NO_2^- (ppm*)	Measured absorbance	Corrected absorbance
0.0	0.129	0.000
1.0	0.282	0.153
2.0	0.431	0.302
4.0	0.729	0.600
8.0	1.349	1.220
*ppm is parts per million		

Experiment 2

A 100 g meat sample was ground in a blender with 50 mL of H_2O and the mixture was filtered. The blender and remaining meat were then washed with H_2O, these washings were filtered, and the liquid was added to the sample solution. The coloring agent was added and the solution was diluted to 100 mL. The procedure was repeated for several meats, and the absorbances were measured (see Table 2).

Table 2		
Meat	Corrected absorbance	Concentration of NO_2^- (ppm)
Hot dog	0.667	4.4
Bologna	0.561	3.7
Ground turkey	0.030	0.2
Ham	0.940	6.2
Bacon	0.773	5.1

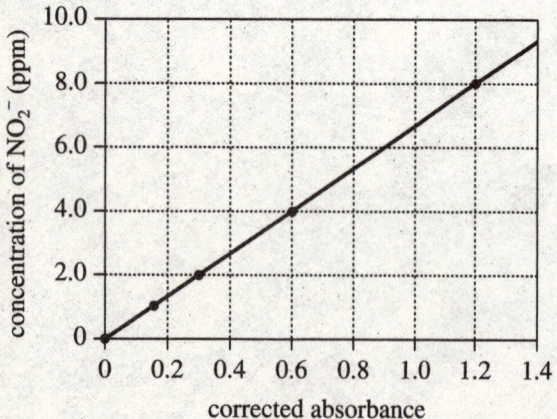

Figure 1

35. Based on the results of Experiment 1, if the concentration of NO_2^- in a solution is doubled, then the corrected absorbance of the solution will approximately:

A. remain the same.
B. halve.
C. double.
D. quadruple.

36. A sample of pastrami was also measured in Experiment 2 and its corrected absorbance was determined to be 0.603. Which of the following correctly lists bologna, bacon, and pastrami in *decreasing* order of NO_2^- concentration?

F. Bologna, bacon, pastrami
G. Pastrami, bacon, bologna
H. Bologna, pastrami, bacon
J. Bacon, pastrami, bologna

GO ON TO THE NEXT PAGE.

37. Based on the results of Experiment 1, if a solution with a concentration of 1.5 ppm NO_2^- had been tested, the corrected absorbance would have been closest to which of the following values?

   A. 0.15
   B. 0.23
   C. 0.30
   D. 0.36

38. If Experiments 1 and 2 were repeated using a different coloring agent that produces a different color when it binds with NO_2^-, then which of the following changes in procedure would be necessary?

   F. The new coloring agent should be added to the blank solution, but not to the sample solutions.
   G. Both of the coloring agents should be added to the blank solution and to all of the samples.
   H. The absorbance of the blank solution made with the new coloring agent should be added to the measured absorbances.
   J. The colorimeter should be set to measure at a different wavelength of light.

39. Based on the results of Experiments 1 and 2, if the measured absorbances for the meats tested in Experiment 2 were compared with their corrected absorbances, the measured absorbances would be:

   A. higher for all of the meats tested.
   B. lower for all of the meats tested.
   C. lower for some of the meats tested, higher for others.
   D. the same for all of the meats tested.

40. If some of the water-soluble contents found in all of the meats tested in Experiment 2 absorbed light of the same wavelength as the compound formed with NO_2^- and the coloring agent, how would the measurements have been affected? Compared to the actual NO_2^- concentrations, the NO_2^- concentrations apparently measured would be:

   F. higher.
   G. lower.
   H. the same.
   J. higher for some of the meats, lower for others.

END OF TEST 4

STOP! DO NOT RETURN TO ANY OTHER TEST.

Practice ACT Tests

Your Signature (do not print): _____

Print Your Name Here: _____

Your Date of Birth:

☐☐ – ☐☐ – ☐☐☐☐

Month   Day   Year

Form 1WT

The **ACT** WRITING TEST BOOKLET

You must take the multiple-choice tests before you take the Writing Test.

Directions

This is a test of your writing skills. You will have thirty (30) minutes to write an essay in English. Before you begin planning and writing your essay, read the writing prompt carefully to understand exactly what you are being asked to do. Your essay will be evaluated on the evidence it provides of your ability to express judgments by taking a position on the issue in the writing prompt; to maintain a focus on the topic throughout the essay; to develop a position by using logical reasoning and by supporting your ideas; to organize ideas in a logical way; and to use language clearly and effectively according to the conventions of standard written English.

You may use the unlined pages in this test booklet to plan your essay. These pages will not be scored. *You must write your essay in pencil on the lined pages in the answer folder.* Your writing on those lined pages will be scored. You may not need all the lined pages, but to ensure you have enough room to finish, do NOT skip lines. You may write corrections or additions neatly between the lines of your essay, but do NOT write in the margins of the lined pages. *Illegible essays cannot be scored, so you must write (or print) clearly.*

If you finish before time is called, you may review your work. Lay your pencil down immediately when time is called.

DO NOT OPEN THIS BOOKLET UNTIL TOLD TO DO SO.

P.O. BOX 168
IOWA CITY, IA 52243-0168   **ACT**®

Practice ACT Tests

Practice Writing Test Prompt 1

In some states, legislators have debated whether teenagers should be required to maintain a "C" grade average in school before receiving a driver's license. Some people think this would be a good policy because having passing grades shows that students are responsible enough to be good drivers. Other people think such a policy would not be appropriate because they see no relationship between grades in school and driving skills. In your opinion, should teenagers be required to maintain a "C" average in school before receiving a driver's license?

In your essay, take a position on this question. You may write about either one of the two points of view given, or you may present a different point of view on this question. Use specific reasons and examples to support your position.

Use this page to *plan* your essay.
Your work on this page will *not* be scored.

If you need more space to plan,
please continue on the back of this page.

Use this page to *plan* your essay.
Your work on this page will *not* be scored.

You may wish to photocopy these sample answer document pages to respond to the practice ACT Writing Test.

Please enter the information at the right before beginning the Writing Test.

Use a soft lead No. 2 pencil only. Do NOT use a mechanical pencil, ink, ballpoint, or felt-tip pen.

WRITING TEST BOOKLET NUMBER

Print your 6-digit **Booklet Number** in the boxes at the right.

WRITING TEST FORM

Print your 3-character **Test Form** in the boxes above <u>and</u> fill in the corresponding oval at the right.

○ 1WT ○ 2WT ○ 3WT
○ 4WT ○ 5WT

Begin WRITING TEST here.

_____

_____

_____

_____

_____

_____

_____

_____

_____

_____

_____

_____

_____

_____

_____

_____

_____

_____

_____

_____

_____

_____

If you need more space, please continue on the next page.

Practice ACT Tests

WRITING TEST

If you need more space, please continue on the next page.

WRITING TEST

_____

_____

_____

_____

_____

_____

_____

_____

_____

_____

_____

_____

_____

_____

_____

_____

_____

_____

_____

_____

_____

_____

_____

_____

_____

If you need more space, please continue on the back of this page.

0876008

WRITING TEST

STOP here with the Writing Test.

Passage I

Question 1. The best answer is **C** because it appropriately uses the relative pronoun *who* to introduce the clause that modifies *students*—"who join our senior class." Besides introducing that clause, the pronoun *who* also functions as the subject of the clause.

The best answer is NOT:

A because it creates a comma splice (two or more complete sentences separated only by a comma). The phrase "those teenagers" is the subject of the second complete sentence.

B because it, too, produces a comma splice. In addition, it creates grammatical disagreement between the plural *students* and the singular *he or she*.

D because it creates a run-on, or fused, sentence. There is no punctuation or conjunction (connecting word) between the two statements.

Question 2. The best answer is **G** because it provides the predicate *was*, which produces a complete sentence. Remember that a statement that has no predicate verb is a sentence fragment (an incomplete sentence).

The best answer is NOT:

F because it uses the verb form *being*, which is a participle. Because it is a verb form, a participle is often mistaken for the main verb in a sentence. This statement has no predicate, so it is a sentence fragment.

H because it has no predicate verb. Without a predicate, the statement is a sentence fragment and does not express a complete thought.

J because it lacks a verb and therefore creates another sentence fragment.

Question 3. The best answer is **A** because it correctly uses the pronoun *who* to introduce the clause that describes Ligia Antolinez. In this sentence, *who* is required because it refers to a person. The pronoun *who* is also appropriate because it functions as the subject of the clause.

The best answer is NOT:

B because it uses the object pronoun *whom* instead of the subject pronoun *who*.

C because it uses the pronoun *which* when the personal pronoun *who* is required. In general, *who* refers to people and *which* refers to objects, events, or animals.

D because it inserts an unnecessary pronoun, *she*. Because *who* is the subject of the descriptive clause, the pronoun *she* has no function in this sentence.

Question 4. The best answer is F because this short sentence expresses a complete thought and is clear, concise, and grammatically sound. It also logically fits between the preceding sentence and the sentence that follows.

The best answer is NOT:

G because it creates a statement that is not logical. The conjunction (connecting word) *therefore* suggests a cause-effect relationship that makes no sense. The fact that the narrator "was a junior then" was not the cause of her not being in classes with Ligia.

H because it makes no sense. It illogically suggests that the narrator was a junior because she "wasn't in any of Ligia's classes."

J because it creates the same error as H does by illogically suggesting that the narrator was a junior because she "wasn't in any of Ligia's classes."

Question 5. The best answer is C because it adds a relevant detail that fits with the point of the rest of the sentence. The narrator didn't know Ligia but knew of her. The narrator "saw her at school events and had read a story about her." Considering the other choices, C provides the most relevant information about the narrator's familiarity with Ligia.

The best answer is NOT:

A because the phrase "which are sometimes supported financially by local business" is not relevant with regard to the narrator's knowledge of Ligia.

B because the information that the school paper "is written by students interested in journalism" is irrelevant to the writer's purpose here.

D because information about the narrator checking the paper "for local movie listings" is a detail that distracts the reader from main point of the sentence.

Question 6. The best answer is G because the plural possessive form *hosts'* is the correct punctuation here. The phrase "her hosts' house" shows possession and requires an apostrophe.

The best answer is NOT:

F because it fails to use the required apostrophe to show possession.

H because again, it fails to use an apostrophe after the *s* in *hosts*.

J because although it does use the required apostrophe after *hosts*, it fails to use the required apostrophe to show possession in *Ligia's*.

ENGLISH ▪ PRACTICE TEST 1 ▪ EXPLANATORY ANSWERS

Question 7. The best answer is C because it correctly inserts a comma after the word *year*. Notice that this comma is necessary to set off the nonessential clause "who had volunteered to move." A nonessential clause adds information that is not necessary to the main idea. Nonessential clauses are set off with commas on both ends.

The best answer is NOT:

A because it inserts an unnecessary and confusing comma after *move*.

B because it fails to insert the required comma after *year*. This comma is necessary to set off the nonessential clause that begins with "who had volunteered. . . ."

D because it inserts an unnecessary and confusing comma after *volunteered*.

Question 8. The best answer is F because it provides the best explanation of the host family's situation and why Ligia needed a place to stay. This choice provides relevant information to show that after the storm, the two brothers needed their upstairs room back—the same room that Ligia had been using.

The best answer is NOT:

G because it adds irrelevant information. The detail that the upstairs room "had been freshly painted" distracts the reader from the main point of the sentence, which is to show why Ligia needed another place to live.

H because the statement in parentheses, "it was a two-story house," is also irrelevant to the writer's purpose here.

J because if the sentence simply ended with "had to be moved," it would not clearly explain why Ligia needed a new place to live.

Question 9. The best answer is D because, of the four choices, **D** makes the point in the clearest, most concise way.

The best answer is NOT:

A because it is redundant; that is, it repeats an idea that has already been stated. The sentence states that the narrator was aware of "Ligia's problem." Adding that this problem "needed to be solved" is overstating the obvious. It is better to end the sentence with the word *problem*.

B because it, too, is unnecessarily wordy. The word *problem* already implies a *dilemma*.

C because it is incorrect in the same way that **A** and **B** are. That Ligia's problem "needed a solution" overstates the obvious and lacks conciseness.

Question 10. **The best answer is J.** You need to pay close attention to the stated question. It asks you for the choice that does *not* show that the narrator's "family felt confident about inviting Ligia to live in their home." In other words, the question tells you that the best answer is the *worst* word choice with respect to the writer's purpose. The verb *supposed* is the only choice that does not show that "the family felt confident," so it is the best answer to this question.

The best answer is NOT:

F because it does indicate the family's confidence. Because the family *agreed* to host Ligia, they "felt confident about inviting Ligia to live in their home."

G because it, too, does indicate the family's confidence.

H because the word *knew* is appropriate in this context and, like **F** and **G**, does indicate confidence.

Question 11. **The best answer is B** because it correctly uses the correlative conjunctions *not only* and *but*. Correlative conjunctions connect similar ideas and are always used in pairs. In this sentence, the pair is "*not only* did we have a room . . . , *but* . . . the house had seemed too quiet." The conjunctions *not only* and *but* logically connect the two reasons that the family agreed to host Ligia.

The best answer is NOT:

A because "not only . . . and" does not logically connect the two reasons, and it is not idiomatic (it does not conform to standard written English).

C because it is incorrect in the same way that **A** is. It creates a statement that is not logical.

D because it is incorrect in the same way that **A** and **C** are. It also fails to use proper correlative conjunctions.

Question 12. **The best answer is J** because it is the clearest and most logical, and it is the most structurally sound. The two clauses in this sentence are parallel and logically follow one another. The second clause, "she started teaching me . . . dance steps," logically follows "I introduced Ligia to my favorite music."

The best answer is NOT:

F because using the passive voice ("I started being taught by Ligia") makes the sentence confusing. It is difficult for the reader to tell what the subject and object of this sentence are. The arrangement of the sentence elements is also confusing and garbled.

G because it has an incorrect modifier. When a modifying phrase containing a verbal comes at the beginning of a sentence, the phrase is followed by a comma. The word that the phrase modifies should immediately follow the comma. In this case, the modifying phrase "Introducing Ligia to my favorite music, at top volume," is followed by the pronoun *she*, instead of the pronoun *I* (to refer to the narrator).

H because the modifying word after the introductory phrase is correct, but the rest of the sentence is weak because it relies on the passive voice ("was introduced by me"). In addition, the phrase at the end of the sentence, "at top volume," is misplaced.

Question 13. The best answer is **B** because it uses the correct verb form. The entire essay is in the past tense, so the past tense *took* is required here.

The best answer is NOT:

A because it uses an incorrect verb form here—the past participle *taken* without an auxiliary verb (for example, *had*).

C because *had took* is an incorrect verb form.

D because it uses an incorrect verb form—the past participle *begun* without an auxiliary (helping) verb.

Question 14. The best answer is **H** because it appropriately uses the past tense verb form (*went*) to show that the event (Ligia's going home) occurred at a specific past time.

The best answer is NOT:

F because it inappropriately uses the past perfect tense. The perfect tenses are mainly used to show that one event happened before another event, which is not the case here.

G because it uses a future tense (in this case, the future perfect) to refer to a past event. You can tell that this is a past event by reading the sentence that follows.

J because it uses the present tense *goes* to refer to an event that happened in the past.

Question 15. The best answer is **C** because it concludes the essay by referring back to topics that were previously mentioned: that Ligia spoke Spanish and that she taught the narrator Colombian dance steps. In addition, it logically follows the preceding sentence by explaining how the narrator continues to make plans for a visit to Ligia.

The best answer is NOT:

A because it does somewhat follow the preceding sentence, but it does not refer back to any of the ideas mentioned in the essay. It is therefore a poor conclusion when compared with C.

B because this is a poor conclusion for the essay because it introduces an entirely new topic: joining the workforce.

D because although the essay does refer earlier to "senior activities," this is also a weak conclusion because it is a vague generalization. In addition, it does not logically follow the statement that the narrator is "trying to save enough to go see my new sister next year."

Passage II

Question 16. The best answer is **H** because it uses a comma after *attend* to appropriately set off the introductory phrase from the main clause. Without this comma, the reader might be confused and think that the narrator attended the laundromat.

The best answer is NOT:

F because it adds an unnecessary and confusing comma between *college* and *I*.

G because it, too, adds an unnecessary and confusing comma between *college* and *I*. In addition, it fails to add the appropriate comma after *attend*.

J because, like G, it omits the comma after *attend*, producing a potentially confusing statement for readers.

Question 17. The best answer is **B** because it appropriately uses the present tense to describe an event that is happening in the present time. Notice that the writer begins the essay in the present tense ("the Save-U Laundromat *is* always open").

The best answer is NOT:

A because it makes a confusing tense shift from present (*is*) to past (*was*).

C because it makes another confusing tense shift—this time from the present tense to the past perfect tense.

D because, like A, it makes a confusing tense shift from present to past.

Question 18. The best answer is **J** because no punctuation is needed here. The absence of punctuation creates the clearest and most understandable sentence.

The best answer is NOT:

F because it places a semicolon between two descriptive phrases, which is a misuse of the semicolon.

G because it inserts an unnecessary and confusing comma between a preposition and its object.

H because it places an unnecessary comma between the two descriptive phrases. There is no pause or separation between the phrases "across the street" and "from a drugstore." They belong together as one description.

Question 19. The best answer is **B** because it is grammatically correct. In this sentence, *cool* is used as an adjective to modify the noun *magnificence*.

The best answer is NOT:

A because *coolly* is an adverb, and an adverb cannot be used to modify a noun. (Adverbs generally modify verbs or adjectives.)

C because it uses an adjective phrase—"magnificently cool"—where a noun is required. The complete phrase "The magnificently cool of the shade trees" is both ungrammatical and confusing.

D because it uses an adjective phrase—"cool magnificent"—where a noun is called for. The phrase "the cool magnificent of the shade trees" is ungrammatical.

Question 20. The best answer is **J** because it states the idea most clearly and concisely. It does not repeat the same idea twice, and it does not add unnecessary words to the sentence.

The best answer is NOT:

F because it is redundant (repeats the same idea) and wordy (adds unnecessary words). The descriptive phrase "who wrongfully enter the property" is really a repetition of the same idea expressed by the use of the word *trespassers*. In other words, the descriptive phrase restates the obvious.

G because it has the same problem that F does. The phrase "who trespass by walking on private property" adds wordiness and redundancy.

H because it, too, is wordy. It is not necessary to state the obvious. It is already clear to readers that people "who ignore the signs and walk on the grass" are trespassers.

Question 21. The best answer is **D** because placing Sentence 5 after Sentence 3 makes the paragraph logical and coherent. If you read Sentences 3, 4, and 5 carefully, you will notice that Sentence 4 does not logically follow Sentence 3. The opening clause in Sentence 4, "But no one is ever around to enforce the threats," has no antecedent to connect it back to Sentence 3. The *threats* in Sentence 4 refer to the "signs . . . posted all over the lawn" that are referred to in Sentence 5. Therefore, Sentence 4 makes the best sense when it follows Sentence 5 rather than precedes it.

The best answer is NOT:

A because leaving Sentence 5 where it is now is not logical for the reasons explained above.

B because Sentence 5 would be a poor and illogical introduction to this paragraph because the reader would not know to what lawn the writer was referring. In addition, the paragraph would make no sense if Sentence 1 followed Sentence 5.

C because this arrangement of the sentences is also illogical and would confuse the reader. Placing Sentence 5 after the description of the laundromat in Sentence 1 makes no sense because the signs on the lawn are on the grounds of a school and are not part of the laundromat.

Question 22. The best answer is **F** because the singular verb *has* agrees with the singular noun *paneling*. Remember that the verb must agree in number with its subject (in this case, *paneling*) and not the object of the preposition (in this case, the plural noun *walls*).

The best answer is NOT:

G because the plural verb *have* does not agree in number with the singular noun *paneling*.

H because, like G, it has an agreement problem. The plural verb *were* does not agree in number with the singular noun *paneling*.

J because, like G and H, it has an agreement problem. The plural verb *are* does not agree in number with the singular noun *paneling*.

Question 23. **The best answer is A** because it provides the added detail asked for in the question. Pay close attention to the stated question. It asks for the sentence that would best accomplish the writer's wish to "further describe the laundromat's paneling." **A** is the only choice that accomplishes this goal. It further describes the "artificial wood grain finish" by showing that it was intended to resemble wood grain but doesn't.

The best answer is NOT:

B because it does *not* provide a detail that further describes the paneling. Although **B** mentions the paneling, it does not offer a further description of it. Rather, it adds a detail that is irrelevant to the paragraph.

C because it, too, fails to further describe the paneling. Instead, it offers an opinion about the color of the paneling.

D because it is incorrect in the same way that **C** is. It offers an opinion about the person who "chose that color scheme," but it does not further the description of the paneling.

Question 24. **The best answer is H** because it effectively links the new paragraph to the question implied by the preceding paragraph: Why does the neon sign promise friendly service? **H** also provides the most effective introduction to the information in the new paragraph.

The best answer is NOT:

F because it does not link the theme of friendly service that is questioned in the preceding paragraph to the description of the machines in this new paragraph. In addition, it shifts to a more formal tone.

G because it makes no sense. Being "across the street from a park" has nothing to do with friendly service. Besides, in the first paragraph, the writer states that "the park isn't really a park at all."

J because it misleads the reader into thinking that the topic of the new paragraph will be "washing machines."

Question 25. **The best answer is C** because it provides the correct adjectives (*many, few*) to describe the quarters. The phrase "too many or too few quarters" describes a relationship of number.

The best answer is NOT:

A because it is ungrammatical. It incorrectly uses an adjective of quantity (*much*) when an adjective of number (*many*) is required.

B because it incorrectly adds the modifier *too* to the comparative adjective *fewer*.

D because it is incorrect in the same way that **A** is. It incorrectly uses an adjective of quantity (*much*) when an adjective of number (*many*) is required.

Question 26. **The best answer is F** because the phrase "mostly older people from around the neighborhood" specifically describes the group of "regular customers" mentioned in the first part of the sentence. If the phrase were deleted, specific descriptive material would be lost.

The best answer is NOT:

G because the phrase is not a detail that provides a logical transition because the sentence that follows describes a different group of customers.

H because the phrase does not foreshadow the conclusion. The writer does not conclude the essay with "older people from around the neighborhood"; rather, the essay ends with all the people who frequent the laundromat.

J because this information is not understated. Also, it is not "important information"—essential to the essay—but, rather, an interesting and relevant side note.

Question 27. **The best answer is D** because it results in a complete sentence. The complete subject of the sentence is "a crowd of thirteen-year-old kids." The predicate *is* immediately follows this subject.

The best answer is NOT:

A because it creates an incomplete sentence. It improperly inserts the pronoun *that* between the subject and predicate, which results in a sentence fragment.

B because it is incorrect in the same way that **A** is. It inserts the relative pronoun *who* between the subject and the predicate and creates an incomplete sentence.

C because the use of the comma and the conjunction *and* generally indicates that the sentence contains two independent clauses, but in this case, there is only one independent clause. "Usually a crowd of thirteen-year-old kids" is a phrase, not a clause, because it has no verb. Meanwhile, in the main clause, the predicate *is* is disagreeing in number with the subject *they*.

Question 28. **The best answer is J** because it is clear, concise, and structurally sound. It clearly expresses the idea that it is the writer who is imagining.

The best answer is NOT:

F because it has an ineffective sentence structure that results in a dangling modifier. When a modifying phrase containing a verbal comes at the beginning of a sentence, the phrase is followed by a comma ("Imagining all these people,"). Following the comma is the word that this phrase modifies. Notice in this sentence that the pronoun *it* incorrectly follows the introductory phrase. The modifying word should be the pronoun *I*.

G because it creates a confusing and unclear statement. In the clause "It being that I imagine all these people," the reader does not know to what the pronoun *It* refers.

H because it has a dangling modifier. It has a problem that is similar to the one in **F**. The pronoun *I* should follow the introductory clause, not the pronoun *they*.

Question 29. The best answer is B because it is grammatically correct, and the verbs in the sentence are parallel (maintain the same verb tense). The appropriate verbs here are "nod and smile" because they correctly follow the auxiliary (helping) verb *would*: "someone *would* look up . . . and [would] nod and smile at me." Although the helping verb *would* is not repeated before "nod and smile," it is implied.

The best answer is NOT:

A because is ungrammatical. It incorrectly uses the third-person singular verb form ("nods and smiles") after the implied helping verb *would*.

C because the use of the present participle ("nodding and smiling") after the helping verb *would* is ungrammatical. Note also that that sentence lacks parallelism: "someone would look up . . . and nodding and smiling at me." There is an illogical tense shift from the present tense ("would look") to the present participle ("nodding and smiling").

D because it makes the same mistake as A. In addition, it results in an illogical statement.

Question 30. The best answer is J because it is the only choice that is a complete sentence with appropriate sentence structure. Notice that this sentence has a compound subject ("the Save-U Laundromat" and "its people"). This construction makes the subject of the sentence clear.

The best answer is NOT:

F because it inserts incorrect punctuation (a period) that results in two sentence fragments (incomplete sentences).

G because it also inserts incorrect punctuation. The clause after the period does create a complete sentence, but the opening phrase "It is comforting to know that the Save-U Laundromat" is *not* a complete sentence; the relative clause does not contain a predicate.

H because it has a confusing and ineffective sentence structure. Inserting the relative pronoun *that* between the conjunction *and* and the pronoun *its* results in a sentence with faulty parallelism. The first of these two relative clauses ("that the Save-U Laundromat") is incomplete.

Passage III

Question 31. The best answer is **B** because it correctly uses the relative pronoun *whose* to introduce the clause that describes the company that the narrator admires. The pronoun *whose* indicates possession and is appropriate here.

The best answer is NOT:

A because it uses a contraction (*who's*) instead of the required pronoun (*whose*). The contraction *who's* means "who is" and does not indicate possession.

C because it has a problem that is similar to the one in **A**. It incorrectly uses the contraction *that's*, which means "that is."

D because it is creates an unclear statement, and it fails to use the proper relative pronoun *whose* to indicate possession.

Question 32. The best answer is **J** because it provides the best punctuation to set off the appositive "Bill Williams." An appositive is a noun or pronoun that identifies and follows another noun or pronoun. In this sentence, "Bill Williams" identifies "Glory Foods' president and founder." Appositives are set off by commas (except when the apposition is restrictive, such as in the phrase "my sister Sue" when I have three sisters).

The best answer is NOT:

F because it inserts an unnecessary and confusing comma between *president* and *and*. In addition, it fails to set off the appositive with a necessary comma between *founder* and *Bill*.

G because, like **F**, it inserts an unnecessary and confusing comma between *president* and *and*.

H because it fails to set off the appositive by adding the necessary comma between *founder* and *Bill*.

Question 33. The best answer is **C** because the third-person plural pronoun *they* clearly refers back to the plural noun *foods*.

The best answer is NOT:

A because the singular pronoun *it* has no logical antecedent. An antecedent is the word or phrase to which a pronoun refers. In this sentence, the antecedent *foods* is plural and requires a plural pronoun (*they*).

B because it has the same problem described in **A**.

D because it creates faulty coordination and a confusing statement. The phrase "and that they" does not effectively coordinate with "that while he knows."

Question 34. The best answer is **F** because it provides the clearest, most concise statement, and it uses modifiers correctly. Note that the pronoun *he* directly follows and correctly modifies the adjective phrase "as a young adult."

The best answer is NOT:

G because it creates a dangling modifier. The phrase "as a young adult" does not logically refer to or modify the noun phrase it precedes ("his cooking skills"). This arrangement of sentence elements results in a confusing statement.

H because although the wording is somewhat different, the problem here, a dangling modifier, is the same as that in **G**. Here, "his skill" is not "a young adult."

J because the problem is much like that in both **G** and **H**. In this statement, "the refinement of his cooking skills" is not "a young adult."

Question 35. The best answer is **D** because it is the clearest and most concise statement. The writer logically describes the Culinary Institute of America as "prestigious."

The best answer is NOT:

A because it is redundant. That is, it repeats the same idea twice: *prestigious* and *acclaimed* mean the same thing.

B because it, too, is redundant. It repeats the same idea three times: *famed*, *renowned*, and *notable* all have similar meanings.

C because the adjective *luscious* makes no sense in this context. Food might be "luscious," but an institute would not be.

Question 36. The best answer is **G** because the sentence parts are arranged in a logical order so that they modify the appropriate elements. This results in the clearest word order for this sentence.

The best answer is NOT:

F because the clauses are put together in a way that confuses the reader. The noun phrase "a line of Southern-inspired cuisine" doesn't connect logically with the noun and the clause that immediately follows it—"a time when there were no convenience foods designed for African American consumers."

H because it is ambiguous. It is unclear what is meant by the opening clause "He came up in 1989."

J because, like **F**, it strings clauses together in a confusing way.

Question 37. The best answer is **B** because it creates the clearest, most logical, and most concise statement. This is another case (like question 35) where the least wordy choice is best.

The best answer is NOT:

A because it is redundant. It repeats the same idea twice. The introductory word *Initially* is redundant because the sentence later states that "Glory Foods were *first* offered for sale in Ohio in 1992."

C because it is redundant. In this case, the words *originally* and *first* mean the same thing.

D because it is both wordy and redundant. The phrases "At the outset" and "the earliest" both imply the same thing.

Question 38. The best answer is **G** because it most effectively concludes this paragraph by continuing the theme of Glory Foods' business success. That Glory Foods "were being distributed in twenty-two states" logically follows the information that "sales were twice the original projections."

The best answer is NOT:

F because it changes the topic by discussing recipes instead of the company's success.

H because it shifts to an entirely new topic, that of "several other companies."

J because the use of the word *however* makes this statement illogical. As it is used here, *however* indicates that this sentence is going to contradict the statement in the preceding sentence, but this sentence does not do that.

Question 39. The best answer is **A** because no punctuation is needed here. The absence of commas makes this the clearest sentence.

The best answer is NOT:

B because it adds unnecessary commas and incorrectly treats "professional, advisors, and subcontractors" as if they were items in a series, but *professional* functions as an adjective modifying the noun *advisors*.

C because the unnecessary comma between the two parts of the compound direct object "advisors and sub-contractors" adds confusion to the sentence.

D because it inserts an inappropriate and confusing semicolon between *advisors* and *and*.

Question 40. **The best answer is F** because without the qualifying phrases the sentence would give the impression that all the subcontractors and farmers were African Americans. These phrases clarify the writer's point that Glory Foods employs African Americans "whenever possible."

The best answer is NOT:

G because even without the phrases, Paragraph 4 clearly explains Glory Foods' attempt to employ African American contractors.

H because the phrases "whenever possible" and "much of" are not examples of wordiness; rather, they clearly inform the reader.

J because the phrases do not describe the subcontractors or farmers yet they are essential to the meaning of the sentence.

Question 41. **The best answer is A** because it correctly uses the infinitive form of the verb (*to evoke*) after the verb of intention (*is meant*).

The best answer is NOT:

B because the verb phrase "is meant at evoking" is not an idiom of standard written English and confuses the reader.

C because it is incorrect in a way that is similar to the problem in B. The verb phrase "is meant in evoking of" is not idiomatic English and results in an unclear statement.

D because omitting the infinitive *to evoke* also results in a phrase that is not standard written English. The verb *is meant* needs to be followed by an infinitive verb form—in this case *to evoke*.

Question 42. **The best answer is J** because it is the clearest, most logical statement. The prepositional phrase "during the Civil War" clearly modifies "a black regiment." Modifying phrases should be placed as near as possible to the words they modify, which is why "during the Civil War" is best placed at the end of this sentence.

The best answer is NOT:

F because the phrase "during the Civil War" appears to modify "the movie." This placement wrongly suggests that the movie was filmed and shown during the Civil War. In addition, the phrase "of the same name" appears to modify "the Civil War" instead of "the movie."

G because the phrase "during the Civil War" appears to modify "the same name," which makes no sense.

H because the phrase "during the Civil War" appears to modify "of a black regiment." Again, the resulting statement "which tells the story during the Civil War of a black regiment" reads as though the movie was shown during the war.

Question 43. **The best answer is** C because it clearly explains why the writer should not add the information about the actor who starred in the film *Glory*. This information is not in keeping with the main point of the paragraph, which is to explain how the company got its name. Adding information about an actor distracts the reader from the focus of the paragraph and the essay as a whole.

The best answer is NOT:

A because it suggests that the sentence belongs in the paragraph when it clearly does not. Information about the actor who starred in *Glory* is not relevant at this point in the essay.

B because it, too, wrongly suggests that the sentence belongs in the paragraph.

D because even though it does indicate that the writer should not add the sentence, the reason given for not making this addition makes no sense. Including additional information saying that Bill Williams had met the actor Denzel Washington would also be irrelevant to the essay.

Question 44. **The best answer is** J because it maintains the present tense (*are*). Notice that present tense is used throughout the essay. A tense shift here would be illogical.

The best answer is NOT:

F because it makes an illogical and confusing shift from present tense to past tense.

G because it makes an illogical and confusing shift from present tense to past perfect tense.

H because it makes an illogical and confusing shift from the present tense to the past conditional.

Question 45. **The best answer is** A because it provides the most effective introductory paragraph. This is the best opening for the essay because it introduces the main topic, which is Bill Williams and his company, Glory Foods.

The best answer is NOT:

B because Paragraph 2 would be an ineffective and confusing opening for this essay. Look at its first sentence: "Even as a child, Williams loved to prepare food." The clue that this is not a good opening sentence is that most essays would not begin this abruptly. The reader would not know who this Williams person was.

C because it has the same problem that B does. Placing Paragraph 1 after Paragraph 3 makes Paragraph 2 the opening paragraph, but that paragraph begins too abruptly to provide an effective introduction.

D because it is incorrect for the same basic reason that B and C are.

Passage IV

Question 46. **The best answer is J** because the paragraph is more focused when the underlined portion is omitted. Mentioning the writer's trip to the movies diverts the reader's attention from the focus of the paragraph, which is a description of the game arcade.

The best answer is NOT:

F because adding information about the writer's trip to the movies is irrelevant to this paragraph and should be omitted. If you read the entire paragraph, you will see that this information does not belong.

G because it is incorrect in the same way that F is. It adds information that distracts the reader from the main focus of this introductory paragraph.

H because it is incorrect in the same way that F and G are. Even though this information is set off by parentheses, it still distracts the reader and is irrelevant.

Question 47. **The best answer is B** because the past tense (*was*) is consistent with the rest of the paragraph. In addition, the singular verb *was* is in agreement with the singular subject *one*.

The best answer is NOT:

A because the subject and verb do not agree in number. The subject *one* is singular and therefore requires a singular verb. The verb *were* is plural.

C because, again, the subject and verb do not agree. The subject *one* is singular, and the verb *were* is plural and therefore incorrect.

D because the past conditional tense (*would have been*) is inappropriate and confusing. In addition, adding the adjective *actual* would make the sentence unnecessarily wordy.

Question 48. **The best answer is H** because it provides the predicate *are*, which produces a complete sentence. A statement that has no predicate is a sentence fragment (an incomplete sentence).

The best answer is NOT:

F because placing the relative pronoun *which* between the subject ("Video screens") and predicate ("have been populated") creates a sentence fragment.

G because it is incorrect in the same way that F is. In this case, the relative pronoun *that* is placed between the subject and predicate.

J because it fails to provide a predicate, which creates another incomplete sentence.

Question 49. The best answer is **A** because it provides the most logical sequence of sentences for this paragraph. Sentence 4 provides a necessary link between the description of the video games in Sentences 1 through 3 and the description of the pinball machines in Sentence 5. In Sentence 4, the phrase "on the other hand" signals that this sentence is going to provide a contrasting point of view. In this case, the writer contrasts video games and pinball machines.

The best answer is NOT:

B because if Sentence 4 were placed right after Sentence 1, the paragraph would be incoherent, illogical, and confusing. Placing Sentence 4 here would interrupt the description of the video games with a comment about pinball machines.

C because placing Sentence 4 after Sentence 5 would confuse readers. They would not understand that the phrase "Some machines" in Sentence 5 actually refers to pinball machines. Also, the transitional phrase "on the other hand" in Sentence 4 does not logically follow the information in Sentence 5.

D because omitting Sentence 4 would confuse readers. The transition that Sentence 4 provides is a necessary link between the description of the video games in Sentences 1 through 3 and the description of the pinball machines in Sentence 5.

Question 50. The best answer is **J** because information about the durability of video games is not relevant to the writer's argument in this paragraph. The main point of the paragraph is that video games are more predictable than pinball machines. Adding information about how video games are "built to last" or are "constructed durably" distracts the reader.

The best answer is NOT:

F because, as stated above, information about how the machines have been "built to last" diverts the reader from the main focus of the paragraph.

G because it is incorrect in the same way that **F** is. Adding the irrelevant information that the machine "is constructed durably" is distracting to the reader.

H because it is incorrect in the same way that **G** and **F** are.

Question 51. The best answer is **C** because it maintains the second-person (*You*) perspective that is used throughout this paragraph. It is important to note that the writer is using the second-person point of view in this paragraph to speak directly to and draw in the reader. Consider the sentence preceding this one: "As *you* guide *your* character through the game's challenges, *you* come to know how the machine will respond to *your* every move."

The best answer is NOT:

A because it fails to maintain a consistent viewpoint. It makes an illogical shift from the second person (*You*) to the third person singular (*He or she*).

B because it makes an illogical shift from the second person (*You*) to the first person plural (*We*).

D because it not only shifts from second person (*You*) to third person (*People*), but it also illogically shifts from present tense (*learn*) to past tense (*learned*).

Question 52. The best answer is **F.** Notice that this question asks for the *least* acceptable answer. In other words, the best answer is the weakest choice. If you read the paragraph carefully, you will see that the idea presented in this sentence (pinball is unpredictable) is meant to contrast with the idea in the preceding sentence (video games are predictable). Given this context, using the transitional word *therefore* at this point is illogical and confusing.

The best answer is NOT:

G because it is an acceptable alternative to *though*, providing the same logical transition.

H because it also provides an acceptable alternative to *though*.

J because, along with G and H, it provides an acceptable alternative to *though*.

Question 53. The best answer is **B** because the absence of a comma here creates the clearest and most understandable sentence.

The best answer is NOT:

A because it places an unnecessary and distracting comma between the subject clause ("a ball you thought was lost") and the predicate ("will . . . bounce").

C because it sets off the auxiliary (helping) verb *will* for no logical reason.

D because it places an unnecessary and distracting comma between the auxiliary verb *will* from the main verb *bounce*.

Question 54. The best answer is **F** because it most effectively links the topic of Paragraph 3 (pinball is less predictable than video games) and the topic of Paragraph 4 (the element of chance makes pinball more interesting than video games).

The best answer is NOT:

G because it fails to provide an effective link between the topics of the two paragraphs, as described above. This choice undermines the writer's argument by saying that pinball games are similar to video games.

H because it, too, fails to provide an effective transition from Paragraph 3 to Paragraph 4. H also contradicts the writer's previously stated point that pinball is challenging.

J because, like G and H, it provides an ineffective transition between the ideas presented in the two paragraphs. In addition, if you inserted this sentence at the beginning of Paragraph 4, the next sentence would not logically follow.

Question 55. The best answer is **D** because it results in the clearest and most concise response. In other words, it avoids redundancy (repeating the same idea) and wordiness.

The best answer is NOT:

A because it is redundant. At this point in the sentence, it is already clear that the writer is referring to "these video games."

B because it is incorrect for the same reason that A is.

C because it is incorrect in the same way that A and B are.

Question 56. The best answer is **F** because it maintains the second-person (*you*), present tense perspective that is used in the surrounding text. Notice that the preceding sentence establishes the second-person point of view: "Once *you* have mastered a game." (This question is similar to question 51.)

The best answer is NOT:

G because it makes a confusing tense shift in this sentence from the present perfect tense ("you have mastered") to the past tense ("you then looked").

H because it makes an illogical shift from the second-person plural (*you*) to the third person (*one*).

J because it, too, makes an illogical shift from the second-person plural (*you*) to the third person (*one*).

Question 57. The best answer is **B** because the comma between these two noun phrases ("sometimes your enemy" and "sometimes your ally") provides clarity for this sentence.

The best answer is NOT:

A because without the comma there, the statement becomes ambiguous and confusing. It's hard to tell whether the second *sometimes* is modifying *your enemy* or *your ally*.

C because it improperly uses a semicolon between these two noun phrases. By the way, those phrases are called "predicate nouns" because they follow the linking verb *is*.

D because even though the conjunction *and* could be used between these two sentence elements, setting off the conjunction with commas is inappropriate and confusing.

Question 58. The best answer is **G** because it provides the most concise way to make the writer's point.

The best answer is NOT:

F because it is vague and unnecessarily wordy. In addition, it creates a clause that lacks subject-verb agreement. The subject *times* is plural and requires a plural verb, not the singular verb *is*.

H because it is redundant (it repeats the same idea). In this sentence, *each*, *single*, and *unique* all mean the same thing.

J because the phrases "every single time" and "each" make this sentence wordy and repetitive.

Question 59. The best answer is **C** because it provides an adjective (*continual*) for the noun that it precedes (*challenge*).

The best answer is NOT:

A because the adverb *continually* lacks a neighboring sentence element that it can modify (a verb or an adjective).

B because the adverb *continuously* faces the same problem of lacking something to modify.

D because the verb form *continue* is simply out of place here between the article *a* and the noun *challenge*.

Question 60. The best answer is **J** because throughout the essay, the writer suggests that "pinball is superior" by making the argument that pinball requires more skill and is more challenging than video games. It is reasonable to conclude, then, that this essay fulfilled the writer's goal.

The best answer is NOT:

F because the writer does suggest in this essay that video games "might seem more attractive than pinball," but this has nothing to do with the writer's goal of writing an essay that shows pinball as being superior to video games.

G because this choice can be ruled out for two reasons: first, the essay does fulfill the writer's goal, and second, the writer does not say that video games challenge the skills of the player.

H because this answer states that the essay does fulfill the writer's goal, but the reason given is not accurate. The writer never states that pinball games "are more visually attractive than video games."

Passage V

Question 61. The best answer is **D** because the absence of commas here creates the clearest and most understandable sentence.

The best answer is NOT:

A because it inserts an unnecessary and confusing comma between the noun *letters* and the preposition *in*. The phrase "in front of you" modifies *letters*, and these elements should not be separated by any punctuation.

B because it inappropriately and confusingly inserts a comma between the verb *tumbles* and the preposition *to*.

C because it inserts an unnecessary and confusing comma between the complete subject phrase ("each of the letters in front of you") and the verb *tumbles*.

Question 62. The best answer is **H** because it effectively and logically uses the coordinating conjunction (linking word) *and* to connect the two independent clauses in this sentence.

The best answer is NOT:

F because the use of the conjunction *unless* here creates an illogical statement. It makes no sense to say, "The computer is probably sick, *unless* . . . [it] has a virus."

G because the use of the conjunction *except* also creates an illogical statement. A computer with a virus is *not* an exception to a computer being sick.

J because the use of the conjunction *as if* creates a confusing and ambiguous sentence.

Question 63. The best answer is **D** because it appropriately sets off the conjunctive adverb *however* with commas. When a conjunctive adverb or transitional expression interrupts a clause, as *however* does in this sentence, it should usually be set off with commas.

The best answer is NOT:

A because it places a comma after *however* but omits the corresponding comma before the word.

B because it inappropriately uses a semicolon instead of a comma before the adverb *however*.

C because it is incorrect because it places a comma before *however* but omits the corresponding comma after the word.

Question 64. The best answer is **G** because it provides the most effective introductory sentence for Paragraph 3. The topic of the paragraph is the serious computer viruses known as "bombs." Notice that the second sentence in this paragraph logically follows and further defines these "bombs."

The best answer is NOT:

F because the information is too broad. The topic of the paragraph is not all computer viruses; rather, it is the much narrower topic of viruses called "bombs." In addition, if this sentence opened the paragraph, the reader would not understand, later in the paragraph, what "these bombs" referred to.

H because it introduces a topic other than the "bombs." If you read the paragraph with this sentence as the introduction, the paragraph makes no sense.

J because it, too, strays from the main topic of the paragraph, which is the computer viruses referred to as "bombs."

Question 65. The best answer is **A** because it most clearly and concisely expresses the point being made in this sentence.

The best answer is NOT:

B because the phrase "devastative disaster" is redundant (repeating information). In this case, the use of the adjective *devastative* is redundant because the noun *disaster* expresses the same thought.

C because this phrasing is confusing if not nonsensical. How can something be "devastation to the operating of a computer"?

D because it is redundant and unclear. The redundancy occurs in the phrase "can be possibly." Also, the phrase "operating of a computer" is not idiomatic English; that is, it's not the way English speakers would normally say or write the phrase.

Question 66. The best answer is **F** because it is the clearest and most concise of the four choices given.

The best answer is NOT:

G because the phrase "that detect computer viruses" is redundant. The phrase is not necessary because the reader already knows that detection programs, by definition, "detect computer viruses." In addition, the phrase "computer viruses" appears a second time at the end of the sentence.

H because it is also unnecessarily wordy and redundant. The phrase "computer viruses" appears twice in this short sentence.

J because it, too, unnecessarily repeats the phrase "computer viruses."

Question 67. The best answer is **D** because both verbs in the subordinate, or dependent, clause of this sentence agree in number with the subject *programs*, which the clause modifies. The subject *programs* is plural, so the verbs *search* and *destroy* must also be plural.

The best answer is NOT:

A because the singular verb forms (*searches*, *destroys*) do not agree with their plural subject, *programs*.

B because it is incorrect in the same way that **A** is; the singular verb forms do not agree with their plural subject.

C because it is ungrammatical. Although the verb *search* is plural and agrees with the subject *programs*, the verb *destroys* is singular and does not agree.

Question 68. The best answer is **G** because it provides a predicate verb (*is found*) for the main clause of this sentence. ("Evidence . . . is found in the names of their programs.")

The best answer is NOT:

F because it creates an incomplete sentence, a fragment. The participle *being found* cannot function as the predicate verb of the main clause of this sentence.

H because, like **F**, it creates a fragment because the participle *having been found* cannot function as a predicate verb.

J because, in this case, the verb form *found* reads as if it were a past participle, not a predicate verb. This too is a sentence fragment because it lacks a predicate for the sentence's main clause.

Question 69. The best answer is **A** because it appropriately uses a colon to introduce the list of names of the programs. Introducing a list is one function of the colon.

The best answer is NOT:

B because it improperly uses the semicolon, which is generally used to separate two independent clauses.

C because it omits the necessary punctuation. The colon is needed here to signal to readers that a list of "the names of their programs" will follow.

D because the comma is not a "strong" enough punctuation mark here. Is this comma the same as or part of the series of commas that follow in this sentence?

Question 70. The best answer is **F** because it is the clearest and most logical of the four choices. It also provides a proper idiom of standard written English. The phrase "As with all diseases" indicates that the best cure for computer viruses is that same as that for all diseases: prevention.

The best answer is NOT:

G because it results in an ambiguous and illogical statement. It states that "the best cure" is "similarly to all diseases," which is illogical and ungrammatical.

H because it is unclear. The use of the phrase "In the same way as" suggests that the writer is trying to compare apples ("all diseases") and oranges ("the best cure").

J because "According with" is not an idiom of standard written English. Even if the sentence began "According to all diseases," which *is* idiomatic, the sentence still wouldn't make sense.

Question 71. The best answer is **C** because the question states that the writer's intention is to recommend "ways to protect computer data against viruses." **C** provides a recommendation by advising the reader to use antivirus programs frequently.

The best answer is NOT:

A because stating that many "viruses are quite sophisticated" does not provide a recommendation and, thus, does not accomplish the writer's stated intention.

B because it does provide a recommendation of sorts, but not the recommendation stated in the question. Adding software that checks spelling does not "protect computer data against viruses."

D because although this choice makes a broad recommendation ("be aware of the various ways to prevent viruses"), it does *not* recommend "specific ways to protect to protect computer data," which is the writer's stated intention.

Question 72. The best answer is **H** because placing the word *better* into the phrasing "you had better hope" provides the clearest statement and best clarifies the meaning of the sentence.

The best answer is NOT:

F because here, *better* inappropriately modifies *responds*, which confuses the meaning of the sentence. Also, the resultant phrase "you had hope" sounds wrong in this sentence along with its two present tense verbs (*is* and *responds*).

G because in this arrangement, *better* modifies *system* and implies a comparison that does not exist. "If there is a virus in your *better* system" wrongly suggests that there are two systems.

J because it is incorrect for the same reason that **F** is.

Question 73. The best answer is C because the most logical and effective placement for this sentence is after Paragraph 4. The last sentence of this paragraph lists the names of the virus detection programs; the new sentence, which refers to those names, logically follows. Also, this new sentence states that the "Names . . . suggest that the problem is serious." The names identified in Paragraph 4 (*Vaccine, Checkup, Antitoxin,* and *Disinfectant*) do imply a level of seriousness.

The best answer is NOT:

A because Paragraph 2 provides a description of what a computer virus can do and does not refer to any "names" of viruses. Adding the sentence here makes no sense.

B because the main topic of Paragraph 3 is computer "bombs." As with A, there is no reference to particular "names."

D because it, too, would be an illogical placement. Although there are "names" in the last sentence of Paragraph 5 (*Internet* and *World Wide Web*), these names do not suggest a serious problem in the way that the "names" in Paragraph 4 do.

Question 74. The best answer is H because the second-person pronouns (*you, your*) do directly address the reader. Revising the essay so that it used the third-person pronouns *one* and *one's* would sacrifice that sense of addressing and advising the reader.

The best answer is NOT:

F because, although shifting to the third-person pronouns *one* and *one's* may change the tone of the essay, a polite and formal tone is clearly not appropriate to the purpose of this piece.

G because changing the pronouns in the essay from second to third person would not suggest that the writer is "speaking to a broader and more inclusive audience."

J because, in this essay, the setting is not a prominent element, and a shift in pronouns from second to third person would not change the sense of that setting.

Question 75. The best answer is D because the essay does limit itself "to describing computer viruses and the basic precautions to be taken against them." The essay does not discuss the ethics of tampering with a computer system, so it would not meet the writer's goal as described in this question.

The best answer is NOT:

A because the essay does not explain any moral or ethical consequences resulting from computer viruses.

B because the process of ridding a computer system of viruses is not explained in detail.

C because a reader would not necessarily have to know how a virus is programmed in order to make a judgment about the morality or ethics of programming a virus.

Question 1. **The correct answer is E.** To find the total distance, in miles, Kaya ran, you need the sum of $1\frac{2}{5}$ and $2\frac{1}{3}$. To add mixed numbers together, each fraction must have a common denominator. Because 3 and 5 do not have any common factors besides 1, the least common denominator is 3(5), or 15. To convert $\frac{2}{5}$, you multiply by $\frac{3}{3}$. The result is $\frac{6}{15}$. To convert $\frac{1}{3}$, you multiply by $\frac{5}{5}$. The result is $\frac{5}{15}$. To add $1\frac{6}{15}$ and $2\frac{5}{15}$, you first add 1 and 2 and then $\frac{6}{15} + \frac{5}{15}$. The result is $3\frac{6+5}{15}$, or $3\frac{11}{15}$.

B is the most popular incorrect answer and comes from adding the whole number parts and adding the numerators and the denominators separately: $\frac{2+1}{5+3}$. If you chose **A**, you may have added the whole number parts and multiplied the fractions. If you chose **D**, you could have incorrectly converted $\frac{2}{5}$ to $\frac{2}{15}$ or $\frac{1}{3}$ to $\frac{1}{15}$ and then added.

Question 2. **The correct answer is H.** To find an equivalent expression, you can multiply the constants $(3 \cdot 2 \cdot 4)$, combine the x terms $(x^3 x^2 x^2 \Rightarrow x^{3+2+2} \Rightarrow x^7$, because when you have a common base you use the base and add the exponents), and combine the y terms $(y \cdot y \Rightarrow y^1 y^1 \Rightarrow y^{1+1} \Rightarrow y^2)$. The result is $24x^7 y^2$.

K is the most common incorrect answer and comes from multiplying the exponents on the x terms instead of adding. If you chose **F**, you probably added the constants instead of multiplying. If you chose **G**, you could have added the constants and multiplied the exponents on the x terms instead of adding. If you chose **J**, possibly you multiplied the exponents on the x terms and y terms instead of adding.

Question 3. **The correct answer is A.** To find Mr. Dietz's pay per day, you can divide his salary, \$22,570, by the number of days he works, 185. His pay per day is $\frac{22,570}{185}$, or \$122. When Mr. Dietz takes a day off without pay and the school pays a substitute \$80, the school district saves the difference in these amounts, $122 - 80$, or \$42.

If you chose **B**, you probably just picked a number from the problem. If you got **E**, you probably found Mr. Dietz's pay per day and stopped.

Question 4. **The correct answer is J.** To find what the student needs to score on the fifth 100-point test to average a score of 80, you need to find the point total for the student so far by adding 65, 73, 81, and 82. That sum is 301. Averaging 80 points on 5 tests means the student must earn 400 points $(80 \cdot 5)$. The score needed on the last test is the difference, $400 - 301$, or 99.

F is the average of the 4 scores, rounded to the nearest whole point. If you chose **H**, you probably took the average of 65, 73, 81, and 82, averaged that average with 80, and rounded to the nearest whole point. If you chose **K**, you possibly thought you needed 5(100), or 500, points total, and this total is not possible when adding a number 100 or less to 301.

Question 5. The correct answer is D. To find the oxygen saturation loss, you divide the current number of milligrams of dissolved oxygen per liter of water by the dissolved oxygen capacity in milligrams per liter of water, or $\frac{7.3}{9.8}$. Then, you approximate that fraction as a decimal, 0.7449, then convert to a percent, 74.49%, and round to 74%.

If you chose A, you probably divided 9.8 by 7.3, subtracted 1, converted to a percent, and rounded to the nearest whole percent. If you chose B, you probably rounded to the nearest 10%, that is, 74.49% to 70%. If you chose C, you probably just used numbers from the problem.

Question 6. The correct answer is J. To find the length of fence needed to fence a rectangular lot 150 ft by 200 ft, you need to find the perimeter. The formula for the perimeter of a rectangle is 2 times the sum of the length and width, or $P = 2(l + w)$. $2(150 + 200) = 2(350) = 700$.

If you chose G, you probably added the dimensions, but didn't double the sum. If you chose F or H, possibly you used only one dimension and doubled it.

Question 7. The correct answer is A. To find an equivalent expression, multiply a by $b + c - d$. This results in $a(b) + a(c) + a(-d)$, or $ab + ac - ad$.

If you chose E, you probably forgot to distribute the a to c and d.

Question 8. The correct answer is F. To solve for x in the equation $4x + 3 = 9x - 4$, you could subtract $4x$ and add 4 to both sides. That results in the equation $7 = 5x$. Then, dividing both sides by 5, the result is $\frac{7}{5} = x$.

If you chose G, you probably got to $7 = 5x$ and then divided 5 by 7. If you chose H, you probably added $4x$ to $9x$, resulting in $7 = 13x$, and then divided by 13. If you chose J, you might have combined the 3 and –4 and somehow got 1, then got to $1 = 5x$ and divided both sides by 5.

Question 9. The correct answer is C. These 4 numbers will be an arithmetic sequence. In an arithmetic sequence, each pair of successive terms differs by the same amount. To find the difference, you can define d as that difference and let 17 be the first term and 41 the fourth term. By definition, the second term is $17 + d$ and the third term is $(17 + d) + d$. The fourth term, 41, can also be written as $(17 + d + d) + d$. Using that expression you obtain the equation $41 = 17 + d + d + d$, or $41 = 17 + 3d$. After subtracting 17 from both sides, you can then divide by 3, resulting in $8 = d$. The difference is 8. Then, the second term is $17 + 8$, or 25. The third term is $17 + 8 + 8$, or 33.

If you chose A, you probably reasoned that because 41 is the fourth term, the relationship is $4d = 24$ (rather than $3d = 24$) and so the difference is 6. If you chose B, you probably added 7 to the first term and subtracted 7 from the fourth term. If you chose E, you probably added 10 to the first term and subtracted 10 from the fourth term.

Question 10. The correct answer is H. To find what $x^2 + \sqrt{x}$ equals, you need to solve $x^3 = 64$ for x. The solution is $\sqrt[3]{64}$, which is 4. Then, substituting into the original expression, you get $4^2 + \sqrt{4}$. This expression simplifies to $16 + 2$, or 18.

If you chose **F**, you probably solved $x^3 = 64$ for x and stopped. If you chose **G**, you could have gotten $x = 4$, used $4(2)$ for 4^2, and added $4(2)$ and 2 to get 10. If you chose **J**, possibly you got $x = 4$ and then simplified $\sqrt{4}$ to be 4.

Question 11. The correct answer is C. To find the volume, you substitute $\frac{5}{4}$ for r in the equation $V = \frac{4}{3}\pi r^3$. This yields $\frac{4}{3}\pi\left(\frac{5}{4}\right)^3$, or $\frac{125\pi}{48}$. This expression is about 8.18, or 8 to the nearest cubic inch.

If you chose **A**, you might have substituted to get $\frac{4}{3}\pi\left(\frac{5}{4}\right)$, yielding π, which is about 5. If you chose **B**, you probably substituted to get $\frac{4}{3}\pi\left(\frac{5}{4}\right)\left(\frac{5}{4}\right)$, yielding $\frac{25}{12}\pi$, or about 7. If you chose **D**, you probably substituted to get $\frac{4}{3}\pi\left(\frac{5}{4}\right)(3)$, yielding 5π, or about 16.

Question 12. The correct answer is K. The probability that the marble chosen will not be white when 8 marbles are red, 6 are blue, and 6 are white is the number of favorable outcomes divided by the total number of possible outcomes. The number of *favorable* outcomes is 14 because there are 8 red marbles and 6 blue marbles—a total of 14 marbles. The total number of *possible* outcomes is $8 + 6 + 6 = 20$, the total number of marbles. Thus, the probability of the marble NOT being white is $\frac{8+6}{8+6+6} = \frac{14}{20} = \frac{7}{10}$.

If you chose **G**, you probably added the number of blue marbles and the number of white marbles and divided by the total number of marbles: $\frac{6+6}{20} = \frac{12}{20} = \frac{3}{5}$. If you chose **H**, you probably found $\frac{8+8}{8+6+6} = \frac{16}{20} = \frac{4}{5}$. If you chose **J**, you probably found the probability of choosing a white marble: $\frac{6}{8+6+6} = \frac{6}{20} = \frac{3}{10}$.

Question 13. **The correct answer is D.** To find the number of sports awards earned, the number of participants in each sport is multiplied by the ratio for that sport and then the 4 products are added. This is a matrix multiplication.

$$[40 \ 60 \ 80 \ 80] \begin{bmatrix} 0.3 \\ 0.4 \\ 0.2 \\ 0.5 \end{bmatrix} = 40(0.3) + 60(0.4) + 80(0.2) + 80(0.5) = 12 + 24 + 16 + 40 = 92$$

If you chose B, you probably reversed the order on the first matrix to get $80(0.3) + 80(0.4) + 60(0.2) + 40(0.5) = 24 + 32 + 12 + 20 = 88$. If you chose C, you probably totaled the number of athletes and multiplied it by the average of the ratios, $260(0.35)$, which is 91.

Question 14. **The correct answer is H.** To find the average number of students enrolled per section of Algebra I, you add up the students in all the sections and divide by the number of sections. Thus, you add $24 + 25 + 29$ and get 78, then divide by 3. This results in an average of 26 students enrolled per section in Algebra I.

If you chose G, you could have found the median (or middle number) of 24, 25, and 29. Sometimes, *average* can mean the median or the mode. For this test, the directions say that, unless otherwise stated, "The word *average* indicates arithmetic mean." If you chose J, you likely found the average of 25 and 29.

Question 15. **The correct answer is C.** The total number of calculators available is $30 - 2 + 30 - 6 = 52$. To find the class periods for which there are not enough school calculators, find the total needed for each period, as given in the table below.

Period	1	2	3	4	6
Calculators needed	21	46	48	57	19

The only entry in the table more than 52 is 57 for Period 4.

If you chose D, possibly you looked at the Algebra I rows in the table and saw that Section B and Section C could not both be covered by the available calculators, and these sections are in Period 3 and Period 4. If you chose E, you probably used 60 for the available number of calculators and did not take into account the 8 calculators that are being repaired and are unavailable.

Question 16. **The correct answer is H.** Because the sum of each row is equivalent, the sum of Row 1 is the same as the sum of Row 2.

Row 1: $\qquad x + 8x + (-3x) \Rightarrow 6x$

Row 2: $\qquad -2x + \; ? \; + \; 6x \Rightarrow 4x + \;?$

The question mark must represent $2x$. You could have done this with other rows, columns, or diagonals.

If you chose **G**, you probably just added the first and last entries in either Row 2, Column 2, or one of the diagonals. If you chose **K**, you may have thought that each sum must be 0 and found that $-4x$ would make the sums of Row 2, of Column 2, and of both diagonals be 0.

Question 17. **The correct answer is E.** The x-coordinate is positive if A is to the right of the y-axis. The y-coordinate is positive if A is above the x-axis. The table below shows the sign of x and the sign of y in the four quadrants.

Quadrant	Sign of:	
	x	y
I	+	+
II	–	+
III	–	–
IV	+	–

Thus, the signs are opposite in Quadrants II and IV only.

If you chose **C** or **D**, you probably got confused about where x and y are positive and negative or about the order of the quadrants.

Question 18. The correct answer is J. To find the number of distinct outfits that Kareem can select from 4 sweaters, 6 shirts, and 3 pairs of slacks, multiply the numbers of the 3 different clothing pieces together. Thus, there are 4(6)(3), or 72, distinct outfits that Kareem can select. The figure below shows that for each sweater, there are 6 shirts, and for each shirt, there are 3 pairs of slacks.

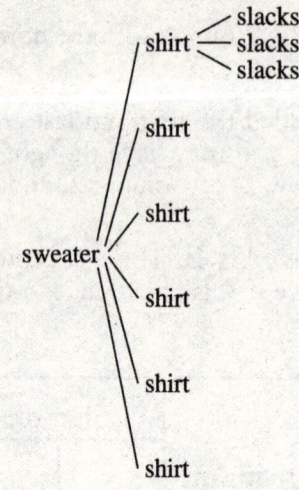

If you chose **F**, you probably added the 3 numbers together, getting 4 + 6 + 3 = 13.

Question 19. The correct answer is A. To find the number of tons of sand needed to produce 3,000 barrels of a tarry material that requires 100,000 tons of sand for 60,000 barrels, you can set up a proportion with ratios of tons of sand to barrels of tarry material, such as

$\frac{100,000}{60,000} = \frac{\text{tons of sand}}{3,000}$, which results in 5,000 tons of sand.

If you chose **B**, you probably calculated $\frac{60,000(30,000)}{100,000}$.

Question 20. The correct answer is H. The figure below shows the rectangle and a diagonal. To find the length of the diagonal, you could use the Pythagorean theorem because the sides of the rectangle are the legs of a right triangle and the diagonal of the rectangle is the hypotenuse of the right triangle. Then $h^2 = 72^2 + 54^2 \Rightarrow h = 90$.

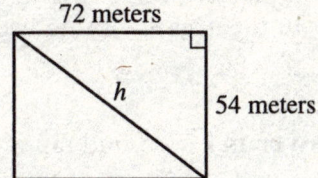

72 meters

h

54 meters

G is the average of 54 and 72. If you chose J, you probably added 54 and 72.

Question 21. The correct answer is A. To find an equivalent expression for $\frac{x}{y}$, you must either multiply or divide both the numerator and the denominator by the same value. Multiplying $\frac{x}{y}$ by $\frac{z}{z}$ yields $\frac{x \cdot z}{y \cdot z}$.

If you chose **B**, you probably thought you could multiply by the expression and obtain an equivalent expression, but if $\frac{x}{y} = \frac{2}{3}$, then $\frac{x^2}{y^2} = \frac{4}{9} \neq \frac{2}{3}$. If you chose **C**, you probably thought you could multiply by the reciprocal and obtain an equivalent expression, but if $\frac{x}{y} = \frac{2}{3}$, then $\frac{x \cdot y}{y \cdot x} = \frac{2 \cdot 3}{3 \cdot 2} = 1 \neq \frac{2}{3}$. If you chose **E**, you probably thought you could add the same number to both the numerator and the denominator and obtain an equivalent expression, but if $\frac{x}{y} = \frac{2}{3}$ and $z = 2$, then $\frac{x+2}{y+2} = \frac{2+2}{3+2} = \frac{4}{5} \neq \frac{2}{3}$.

Question 22. The correct answer is H. To find the slope-intercept form of the equation $8x - y - 6 = 0$, you could first add 6 and subtract $8x$ from both sides of the equation to get $-y = -8x + 6$. Then, multiply by -1 to get $y = 8x - 6$.

If you chose F, you probably forgot to switch the sign on $8x$ when you multiplied by -1. If you chose G, you probably just dropped the sign on $-y$. If you chose J, you probably forgot to multiply 6 by -1 in the last step.

Question 23. The correct answer is B. To solve the quadratic equation $x^2 - 36x = 0$ for x, you could factor the left side to $x(x - 36) = 0$ and apply the zero product rule. Thus, $x = 0$ or $x - 36 = 0$, which implies $x = 0$ or $x = 36$. The solution given as an answer choice is 36.

If you chose **C**, you probably divided 36 by 2. If you chose **D**, you probably dropped the x in the second term and solved $x^2 = 36$ for a positive value. If you chose **E**, you probably dropped the x in the second term and solved $x^2 = 36$ for negative value because there was a negative sign in the original equation.

Question 24. The correct answer is G. To find $\tan R$ in $\triangle RST$, take the ratio of the length of the opposite leg to the length of the adjacent leg, or ST to RS, or r to t, or $\frac{r}{t}$.

F is $\sin R$, **H** is $\cot R$, **J** is $\cos R$, and **K** is $\sec R$. If you did not get the correct answer, it would be wise to review trigonometric ratios in a right triangle.

Question 25. The correct answer is D. To find the radius, you can use the right triangle shown on the diagram. Half the length of the chord is 12 inches, which is the length of one leg. The other leg is 5 inches long, and the hypotenuse is r inches long. (This is a right triangle because the distance between a point and a line must be measured perpendicular to the line.) Using the Pythagorean theorem $r^2 = 12^2 + 5^2 \Rightarrow r^2 = 169 \Rightarrow r = 13$ inches.

A is $24 + 5$, which is clearly much longer than the radius. If you chose **B**, you probably used 24 and 5 for the leg lengths and got $r = \sqrt{601}$, which is about $r = 24.5$ inches. Choice **C** is closest to $5 + 12$. Going along the radius line must be shorter than going along the 2 legs of the triangle.

Question 26. The correct answer is H. To find the force F (in newtons) corresponding to a spring length, L, of 0.18 meters when the relationship is given by the equation $L = \frac{2}{3}F + 0.03$, you would substitute 0.18 for L to get $0.18 = \frac{2}{3}F + 0.03$. After subtracting 0.03 from both sides, you'd get $0.15 = \frac{2}{3}F$. Then, after multiplying by $\frac{3}{2}$, you'd get $0.225 = F$.

G is the result of replacing F by 0.18 and solving for L. If you chose **J**, possibly you got $0.225 = F$ and added 0.03.

Question 27. The correct answer is B. To find the uniform depth the 10,000 cubic yards of snow would be on the rectangular football field with dimensions 120 yards by 53.5 yards, you would substitute in the formula for volume, V, of a rectangular prism with the height h, length l, and width w, which is $V = lwh$. After substituting you should have $10,000 = 120(53.5)(h)$, or $10,000 = 6,420h$. Thus, $h = \frac{10,000}{6,420}$, or about 1.558. And 1.558 is between 1 and 2.

If you chose A, you probably took $\frac{6,420}{10,000}$ and got 0.642, which is less than 1. If you chose C or D, you probably used the wrong dimensions or made a mistake in calculations.

Question 28. The correct answer is G. To find the length of $\overline{QR}$ in $\triangle PQR$, where $\overline{PR}$ is 16 feet long and sin $\angle P = \frac{3}{5}$, use the definition of sine: the ratio of the length of the opposite side to the length of the hypotenuse. In $\triangle PQR$, sin $\angle P = \frac{QR}{PR}$. After substituting for sin $\angle P$ and PR, the length of the hypotenuse, you obtain $\frac{3}{5} = \frac{QR}{16} \Rightarrow 5 \cdot QR = 48 \Rightarrow QR = 9.6$ feet.

F is $\frac{1}{2}$ of PR. If you chose H, you probably found cos $\angle P = 0.8$ and then multiplied 16(0.8) to get 12.4.

Question 29. The correct answer is B. To find the fraction of cars assembled in Coupeville, you would divide the number assembled in Coupeville by the total number assembled. The table below shows the conversion of car symbols to numbers for the 4 cities and the total.

City	Number of cars assembled
Car Town	40,000
Coupeville	25,000
Truck City	20,000
Sedan Falls	15,000
All	100,000

The fraction assembled in Coupeville is $\frac{25,000}{100,000}$, or $\frac{1}{4}$.

If you chose A, you probably found the fraction for Truck City, $\frac{20,000}{100,000}$, or $\frac{1}{5}$. If you chose C, you may have thought a half car represented 10,000, so your fraction was $\frac{30,000}{110,000}$, or $\frac{3}{11}$. If you chose D, you probably used the fraction $\frac{30,000}{100,000}$, or $\frac{3}{10}$. If you chose E, you probably used the number in Coupeville divided by the total number from the other 3 cities, $\frac{25,000}{75,000}$, or $\frac{1}{3}$.

Question 30. The correct answer is G. To find BC when AD is 30 units, AC is 16 units, BD is 20 units, and the points are along $\overline{AD}$ as shown below, you must notice that $\overline{BC}$ is the intersection of $\overline{AC}$ and $\overline{BD}$.

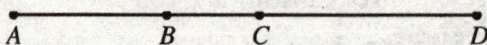

So, the sum of the lengths of $\overline{AC}$ and $\overline{BD}$ is the same as the sum of the lengths of $\overline{AD}$ and $\overline{BC}$. Because $AC = AB + BC$, $BD = BC + CD$, and $AD = AB + BC + CD$, by substitution $AC + BD = AB + BC + BC + CD = AB + BC + CD + BC = AD + BC$.

Using the actual lengths, $AC + BD = AD + BC \Rightarrow 16 + 20 = 30 + BC \Rightarrow 36 = 30 + BC \Rightarrow BC = 6$.

If you chose **F**, you probably subtracted 16 from 20. If you chose **K**, you probably thought you needed more information to solve the problem, which is not the case.

Question 31. The correct answer is B. To find the x-coordinate where the 2 lines $y = 2x + 6$ and $y = 3x + 4$ intersect, you could substitute $y = 2x + 6$ into $y = 3x + 4$ to get $2x + 6 = 3x + 4$. Subtracting $2x$ and 4 from both sides results in the equation $2 = x$.

Another strategy is to graph the equations and estimate the coordinates of the intersection point.

If you chose **C**, you probably used the constant from the second equation. If you chose **D**, you probably used the constant from the first equation. If you chose **E**, you probably found the y-coordinate instead of the x-coordinate.

Question 32. The correct answer is J. To solve the equation $M = 3V + 6$ for V, you could subtract 6 from both sides to get $M - 6 = 3V$, and then divide by 3 on both sides to get $\frac{M-6}{3} = V$.

If you chose **F**, you did not divide the 6 by 3. If you chose **G**, you might have moved the 6 from the right side to the left and also forgotten to divide it by 3. If you chose **H**, you possibly transferred the 3 from the V to the M. If you chose **K**, you probably made a sign error.

Question 33. The correct answer is B. The area is bh for a parallelogram with base b and corresponding height h. For parallelogram $ABCD$, base $\overline{AD}$ is $3 + 6$, or 9 inches long, and the corresponding height is 4 inches. So the area is $9(4)$, or 36 square inches.

The most common wrong answer is **D**, which comes from multiplying the two side lengths: $(3 + 6)(5) = 9(5) = 45$.

Question 34. The correct answer is K. To find $(b - a)^4$ given $a = b + 2$, you could solve the equation for $b - a$. By subtracting a and 2 from both sides, you get $-2 = b - a$. Substituting -2 for $b - a$ in $(b - a)^4$ yields $(-2)^4$, or 16.

If you got stuck working this one, you could try choosing a specific value for b, say $b = 3$. Then a must be $3 + 2 = 5$. And $(b - a)^4 = (3 - 5)^4 = (-2)^4 = 16$.

If you chose F, you probably got -2 for $b - a$ but then replaced $(-2)^4$ by -2^4, or -16. Be careful $(-2)^4 = (-2)(-2)(-2)(-2) = 16$, but $-2^4 = -(2 \cdot 2 \cdot 2 \cdot 2) = -16$.

If you chose H, you probably got $b - a = 1$ or $b - a = -1$, and either $(1)^4$ or $(-1)^4$ is 1. Choices G and J come from calculating 2^4 as $2 \cdot 4$ and, for G, making a minus sign mistake.

Because $(b - a)^4$ is an even power of the number $(b - a)$, you can eliminate any negative numbers (F and G). This kind of observation can help you catch mistakes even when your problem is not multiple-choice.

Question 35. The correct answer is D. To find the location of the water fountain located halfway between points B and D, it makes sense to give coordinates to the points relative to point A (see the diagram below). The first coordinate is the number of blocks east and the second coordinate is the number of blocks north.

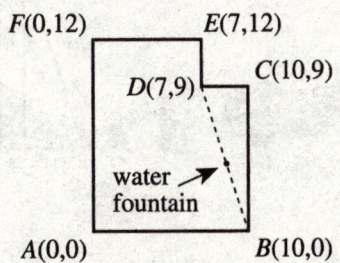

The water fountain is at the midpoint of $\overline{BD}$, and so the midpoint formula applies. For points with coordinates (x_1, y_1) and (x_2, y_2), the midpoint has coordinates $\left(\frac{x_1 + x_2}{2}, \frac{y_1 + y_2}{2}\right)$. For B (10,0) and D (7,9), the midpoint is $\left(\frac{10 + 7}{2}, \frac{0 + 9}{2}\right) \Rightarrow \left(\frac{17}{2}, \frac{9}{2}\right) \Rightarrow \left(8\frac{1}{2}, 4\frac{1}{2}\right)$.

B is halfway between A and C. Choice C is halfway between B and F. If you chose E, you may have found the wrong coordinates for C, D, or E.

Once you put coordinates on the picture, you can see that only one answer choice is reasonable.

Question 36. The correct answer is J. One strategy for solving this problem is to find equations. You can let y be the larger number and obtain the equation $y = 2x + 8$ from the first sentence. The second sentence says that $2y + 3x = 65 \Rightarrow 2(2x + 8) + 3x = 65$.

If you chose **F**, you probably took 3 times the larger number and added it to twice the smaller number to get 65, rather than the other way around. If you chose **G**, you probably defined y as $y = 2x - 8$ and then also made the same error as in **F**. Choice **H** can come from distributing the 2 in $2(2x + 8)$ as $2(2x) + 8$ and doing everything else correctly.

Question 37. The correct answer is C. To find out how far a 30-foot ladder 10 feet away from the base of a building reaches up the building, you can use the Pythagorean theorem. Let the length of the ladder be the hypotenuse, and let the legs be the distances away from the base of the building and from the ground to the top of the ladder along the building (see the figure below). This gives the equation $30^2 = 10^2 + d^2$, where d is the distance the ladder reaches up the building. Simplifying, you get $900 = 100 + d^2 \Rightarrow 800 = d^2 \Rightarrow d$ is about 28 feet.

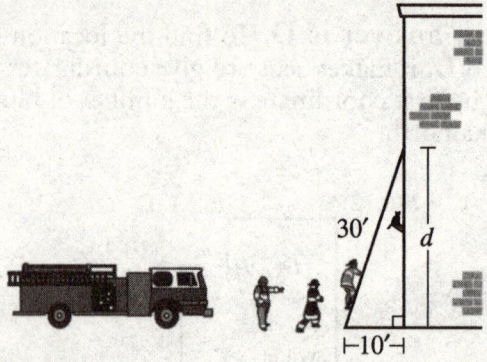

B comes from subtracting 10 from 30 or "simplifying" $\sqrt{900 - 100}$ to $\sqrt{900} - \sqrt{100}$.

Question 38. The correct answer is K. The most common way of finding the area of a square involves finding the side length of the square. If you draw radius lines in different positions, as shown below, you can see a relation between the radius of the circle and the side length of the square. The side length of the square is twice the radius, or $2(7) = 14$ feet. To find the area of the square, you square the side length, to get $14^2 = 196$ square feet.

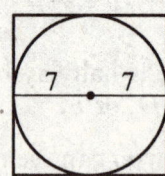

If you chose **F**, you probably thought 7 feet was the side length and squared 7 to get 49. If you chose **J**, you probably found the area of a circle, πr^2, where r is the radius, to get $\pi(7)^2 = 49\pi$.

Question 39. The correct answer is B. It might be good to sketch a picture, something like the diagram below. To find the length of the longest side of the second triangle, you can use the ratios of corresponding sides of each triangle. For example, $\frac{12}{8} = \frac{15}{x}$, where x is the length of the longest side of the second triangle. After cross multiplying, you get $12x = 120$. Then, you divide by 12 to get $x = 10$ inches.

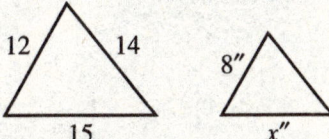

If you chose **A**, you probably noticed that the first triangle's longest side is 3 units longer than its shortest side. If this same relation held in the second triangle, its longest side would be $8 + 3 = 11$. This additive relation does not hold. If you chose **E**, you may have thought you needed the length of the middle side of the second triangle to solve the problem.

Question 40. The correct answer is K. To find the measure of $\angle BDC$ in the figure below, it is helpful to recognize that $\overline{AD}$ and $\overline{BC}$ are parallel and are connected by transversal $\overline{BD}$. Then $\angle CBD$ and $\angle ADB$ are alternate interior angles and so each measures 30°. (Go ahead and write in "30°" for $\angle ADB$ on the figure.)

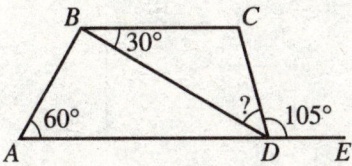

By definition, $\angle ADE$ is a straight angle and has a measure of 180°. Because $\angle ADE$ is made up of $\angle ADB$, $\angle BDC$, and $\angle CDE$, you know that the measures of those 3 angles add up to 180°. You might write this, using m to represent *measure*, as $m\angle ADB + m\angle BDC + m\angle CDE = 180°$. Substituting the measures you know gives $30° + m\angle BDC + 105° = 180° \Rightarrow m\angle BDC + 135° = 180° \Rightarrow m\angle BDC = 45°$.

If you chose **H**, you might have thought $\triangle BDC$ is isosceles. If you chose **J**, possibly you estimated the measure of $\angle BDC$ or made a subtraction error.

Question 41. The correct answer is E. This figure has 10 sides, but lengths are given for only 6 of the sides. Those lengths add up to 4 + 6 + 4 + 10 + 6 + 26 = 56 inches. The perimeter is longer than this because of the missing 4 sides.

Then you should find the lengths of the missing sides, right? The figure below focuses on the vertical sides. The vertical sides that face left have lengths 4, 6, and 4. The lengths of the sides that face right are unknown. But, the vertical distance that the left-facing sides cover is the same as the vertical distance that the right-facing sides cover.

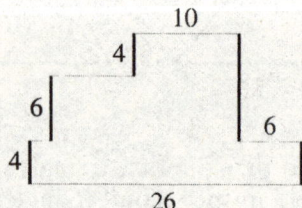

So, since the total length of the left-facing sides is 4 + 6 + 4 = 14 inches, the total length of the right-facing sides is also 14 inches.

Finding the lengths of the horizontal sides (see the figure below) is a similar process. The horizontal distance covered by the top-facing sides must be 26 inches because that's what's covered by the bottom-facing sides.

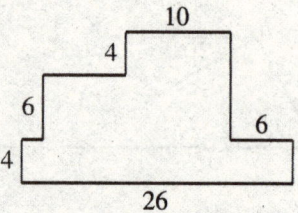

This makes the perimeter the sum of the lengths of the left-facing, right-facing, top-facing, and bottom-facing sides, which is 14 + 14 + 26 + 26 = 80 inches. You can't know the length of each side, but you can find the perimeter.

If you chose C, you probably just found the sum of the side lengths shown: 4 + 6 + 4 + 10 + 6 + 26 = 56. If you chose D, you may have left out the right-facing sides, or you may have estimated the lengths of the 4 missing sides and been too low. Estimation is a reasonable strategy for this question.

Question 42. **The correct answer is F.** To find out how many of the 804 seniors in a certain high school are going to a state university when approximately $\frac{2}{5}$ of the seniors are going to college, and when $\frac{1}{4}$ of those going to college are going to a state university, you could first find how many of the 804 seniors are going to college. This is $\frac{2}{5}(804)$, or almost 322 seniors. Then, find the number of those 322 seniors going to college who are going to a state university, which is $\frac{1}{4}(322)$, or about 80 seniors that are going to a state university.

J is closest to $\frac{1}{4}$ of 804.

Question 43. **The correct answer is E.** You could take a brute-force approach and test all the given values of y and see if you could find an x that worked. For example, if $y = 45$ from **A**, then the two numbers are $x^2 \cdot 45^2$ and $x \cdot (45)^3$. You can see that 45^2 is a common factor of these two numbers, so 45 can't be the *greatest* common factor.

Maybe it will be productive to be more general and avoid having to test all 5 values of y. Notice that xy^2 is a common factor of x^2y^2 and xy^3. Because it is a common factor, it must be a factor of 45 (the greatest common factor). Because 45 factors as $5 \cdot 3^2$, it seems natural to see whether $x = 5$ and $y = 3$ is a possible solution. In this case, the two numbers are $5^2 \cdot 3^2$ and $5 \cdot 3^3$, and then the greatest common factor is $5 \cdot 3^2 = 45$. It works.

B is a possible value of xy, C is a possible value of y^2, D is a possible value of x, and E is a possible value of x (when $y = 1$). If you don't see right away what to do, dig in and test some numbers to see what happens.

Question 44. **The correct answer is G.** Because 115% of "the number" is 460, then "the number" is $\frac{460}{1.15}$, which is 400. Next, 75% of "the number" 400 is 300.

You can also solve this with equations. Let n be "the number." Then $1.15n = 460$ and you want to find $0.75n$.

J is 75% of $460 \Rightarrow (0.75)460 \Rightarrow 345$. If you chose **K**, you probably found "the number" but not 75% of that.

Question 45. **The correct answer is E.** To find the distance between 2 points in the standard (x,y) coordinate plane, you can use the distance formula, $\sqrt{(x_2 - x_1)^2 + (y_2 - y_1)^2}$. So the distance is $\sqrt{(5-0)^2 + (0-1)^2} \Rightarrow \sqrt{5^2 + 1^2} \Rightarrow \sqrt{26}$ coordinate units.

A can come from mixing x and y coordinates: $\sqrt{(5-1)^2 + (0-0)^2}$. If you chose **B**, you probably added $1 + 5$ or simplified the radical expression incorrectly.

Question 46. **The correct answer is G.** To find the ratio of the circumferences of 2 circles for which the ratio of their radii is 4:9, you would recognize that both circumference and radius are 1-dimensional attributes of a circle. Because of that, the ratios should be the same, 4:9. Another way is to use the ratio of the radii and let $4x$ be the radius of the first circle and $9x$ be the radius of the second circle. Then, the circumferences would be $2\pi(4x)$ and $2\pi(9x)$, respectively. Setting them in a ratio, you get $8\pi x : 18\pi x$, which simplifies to 4:9.

If you chose **F**, you probably thought that you should take the ratio of the square roots, $\sqrt{4} : \sqrt{9}$, or 2:3. If you chose **H**, you probably thought that you should take the ratio of the squares, $4^2 : 9^2$, or 16:81 (which is the ratio of the circles' areas).

Question 47. **The correct answer is D.** You may want to have a picture of this situation in your mind, or even sketch it out in the space in your test booklet. Your picture might look something like this.

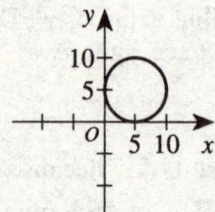

One way to find an equation for a circle is to know the coordinates of the center, (h,k), and the radius, r. Then, an equation is $(x - h)^2 + (y - k)^2 = r^2$. For this circle, the center is at $(5,5)$ and the radius is 5. (It's fairly easy to see that. If you needed to prove those are exactly right, you could use symmetry or you could use the fact that a tangent line is perpendicular to the radius that goes through the point of tangency.) Given center $(5,5)$ and radius 5, the circle has equation $(x - 5)^2 + (y - 5)^2 = 5^2$.

Another way to solve this problem is to find the coordinates of points on the circle and see which equation(s) each point satisfies. The points $(0,5)$, $(5,0)$, $(5,10)$, and $(10,5)$ are all on the circle. Testing these points in all the equations would probably take longer than the first method, but testing the points in the equation you think is correct would be a good check of your answer.

B is a circle centered at $(0,0)$ instead of $(5,5)$. If you chose **C**, you probably forgot to square the radius on the right side of the equation. If you chose **E**, you likely used $(x + h)$ and $(y + k)$ in the equation. Testing $(10,5)$ would have helped you eliminate these incorrect answers.

Question 48. The correct answer is J. To find an equivalent expression for $\frac{1}{1+i} \cdot \frac{1-i}{1-i}$, you can multiply and get $\frac{1(1-i)}{(1+i)(1-i)} = \frac{1-i}{1-i^2} = \frac{1-i}{1-(-1)} = \frac{1-i}{2}$.

If you chose **G**, possibly you thought $\frac{1}{1+i}$ was equivalent to $1 + i$ and canceled $1 - i$ in both places.

If you chose **H**, you probably simplified $1 - i^2$ as 1 and got $\frac{1-i}{1}$, or $1 - i$.

Question 49. The correct answer is D. You want to find which statement describes the total number of dots in the first n rows of the figure below.

```
        ·            1st row
       · · ·         2nd row
      · · · · ·       3rd row
     · · · · · · ·     4th row
    · · · · · · · · ·   5th row
              ⋮
```

You could make a table like the one below, showing the number of rows and the total number of dots.

Number of rows	1	2	3	4	5
Total number of dots	1	4	9	16	25

You would probably recognize that the total number of dots is the square of the number of rows. This seems like a consistent relationship (it works for all 5 columns in your table). You can rule out **A** because the total is not always 25. For **B**, the total would have to go 2, 4, 6, 8, 10. For **C**, the total would need to be 5, 10, 15, 20, 25.

B works for the total of the first 2 rows. If you chose **C**, that works for the total of the first 5 rows. If you chose **E**, you might have seen that the relationship was not linear and viewed this as inconsistent.

Question 50. The correct answer is F. If the first 8 students in the class play only guitar and the next 9 play only piano, that accounts for 17 of the 20 students in the class. The other 3 students could play only trombone. This describes a class where 0 students play both guitar and piano, and you can't get any less than this.

G is $9 - 8$ and **K** is $9 + 8$. If you chose **H**, that is the maximum rather than the minimum number.

Question 51. The correct answer is A. To find the real numbers x such that $x + 3 > x + 5$, you could subtract x and 3 from both sides. The result is $0 > 2$, and because that inequality is never true, there is no solution for x. The solution set is the empty set.

If you chose **B**, you probably got mixed up on the direction of the inequality and got $0 < 2$, which is true for all values of x. If you chose **C**, you probably got $0 > 2$ and then thought that a negative value for x would change the direction of the inequality.

Question 52. **The correct answer is H.** You can use symmetry to solve this problem. A picture might be useful. As shown below, there are 5 diagonals coming into each vertex point.

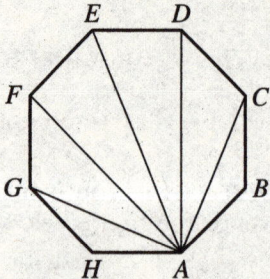

Because there are 8 vertex points, you might be tempted to conclude that there are $8 \cdot 5 = 40$ diagonals. But this method counts each diagonal exactly twice. (It counts $\overline{AD}$ as a diagonal coming into vertex A and counts $\overline{DA}$ as a diagonal coming into vertex D, but these are the same diagonal.) Because each diagonal is counted exactly twice, there are $\frac{40}{2} = 20$ diagonals.

If you like other kinds of patterns, you might choose a different solution path. You can list the diagonals. But, to be sure you list them all, organize them into a pattern such as the one below.

$$\overline{AC}$$
$$\overline{AD}\ \overline{BD}$$
$$\overline{AE}\ \overline{BE}\ \overline{CE}$$
$$\overline{AF}\ \overline{BF}\ \overline{CF}\ \overline{DF}$$
$$\overline{AG}\ \overline{BG}\ \overline{CG}\ \overline{DG}\ \overline{EG}$$
$$\overline{BH}\ \overline{CH}\ \overline{DH}\ \overline{EH}\ \overline{FH}$$
$$\overline{CA}\ \overline{DA}\ \overline{EA}\ \overline{FA}\ \overline{GA}$$
$$\overline{DB}\ \overline{EB}\ \overline{FB}\ \overline{GB}\ \overline{HB}$$
$$\overline{EC}\ \overline{FC}\ \overline{GC}\ \overline{HC}$$
$$\overline{FD}\ \overline{GD}\ \overline{HD}$$
$$\overline{GE}\ \overline{HE}$$
$$\overline{HF}$$

The ones that are light gray are already listed. You wouldn't have to write those down. Now you can tell there are $5 + 5 + 4 + 3 + 2 + 1 = 20$ diagonals.

Alternately, you could draw in every diagonal and count them. This method would work if you were careful to draw in every diagonal and to count every one you drew in. Try it below.

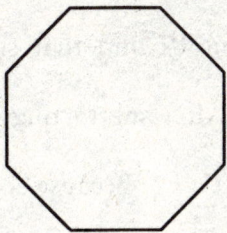

If you chose **F**, you probably reasoned that because the pentagon (a 5-sided figure) has 5 diagonals, then an octagon (an 8-sided figure) has 8 diagonals. As you can see from the picture above, this pattern doesn't hold. If you chose **G**, you may have tried to count all of the diagonals directly and missed a few. Choice **K** is the result of counting each diagonal twice.

Question 53. **The correct answer is B.** Douglas will count any color other than red, blue, green, and purple in the Other sector. The table below gives percentages of friends who picked red, blue, green, and purple.

Color	Red	Blue	Green	Purple	Other
Percentage	25%	30%	20%	10%	

The 4 known percentages add up to 85%. That leaves 15% for the Other sector. That means 15% of the 360° in the circle belong in the Other sector. This is $(0.15)(360°) = 54°$.

C is 15% of 180° rather than of 360°. If you chose **D**, you probably found the correct percent for the Other sector and then just labeled it degrees.

Question 54. **The correct answer is J.** One way to find tan θ, given that $\sin \theta = -\frac{3}{5}$ and $\pi < \theta < \frac{3\pi}{2}$, is to first find cos θ, then find $\frac{\sin \theta}{\cos \theta}$ (which is equivalent to tan θ). To find cos θ, use the facts that cos θ < 0 in Quadrant III and that $\sin^2\theta + \cos^2\theta = 1$. Substituting, you get $\left(-\frac{3}{5}\right)^2 + \cos^2\theta = 1$, or $\frac{9}{25} + \cos^2\theta = 1$. After subtracting $\frac{9}{25}$, you get $\cos^2\theta = \frac{16}{25}$. After taking the square root of both sides, you get $\cos^2\theta = \pm\frac{4}{5}$. Because cos θ < 0, $\cos \theta = -\frac{4}{5}$. Substituting into $\frac{\sin \theta}{\cos \theta}$ gives you $\frac{-\frac{3}{5}}{-\frac{4}{5}}$, which simplifies to $\frac{3}{4}$.

Another way you could do this problem is to construct an angle in Quadrant III with $\sin \theta = -\frac{3}{5}$. (Recall that sine is the ratio of opposite to hypotenuse.) Such an angle is shown below.

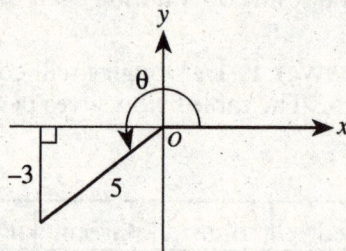

By the Pythagorean theorem, the missing side of the right triangle is 4 coordinate units long, and the directed distance along the side is –4. The figure below shows this.

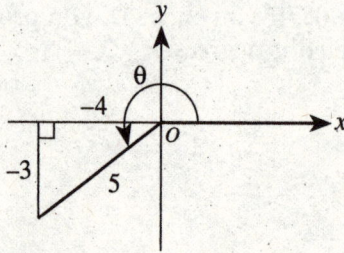

From this right triangle, knowing that tangent is $\frac{\text{opposite}}{\text{adjacent}}$, you can get $\tan \theta = \frac{-3}{-4} = \frac{3}{4}$.

G comes from using $\frac{4}{5}$ for cos θ instead of $-\frac{4}{5}$. If you chose **H**, you might have mixed up the definition of sine or tangent in the right triangle.

Question 55. The correct answer is A. To find the system of inequalities represented by the shaded region of the graph below,

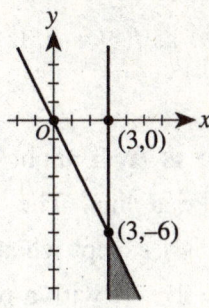

you could first find the equations of the line through (0,0) and (3,−6) and the line through (3,0) and (3,−6). Those are $y = -2x$ and $x = 3$. It is clear from the graph that the inequality that represents the shaded side of $x = 3$ is $x \geq 3$. For the other line, if you test (3,0), you find it satisfies $y > -2x$. Because (3,0) is on the wrong side (the unshaded side) of $y = -2x$, the correct inequality is $y \leq -2x$.

The graphs of the incorrect answer choices are shown below.

Choice **C** is the most popular incorrect answer (about as many people choose this as choose the correct answer). The inequality sign is backwards for the line $y = -2x$.

Choice **B** differs from the correct answer only in the "or" connector. The graph of **B** includes points that satisfy one of the inequalities but not necessarily the other inequality, while the "and" connector means the graph can only include points that satisfy both inequalities.

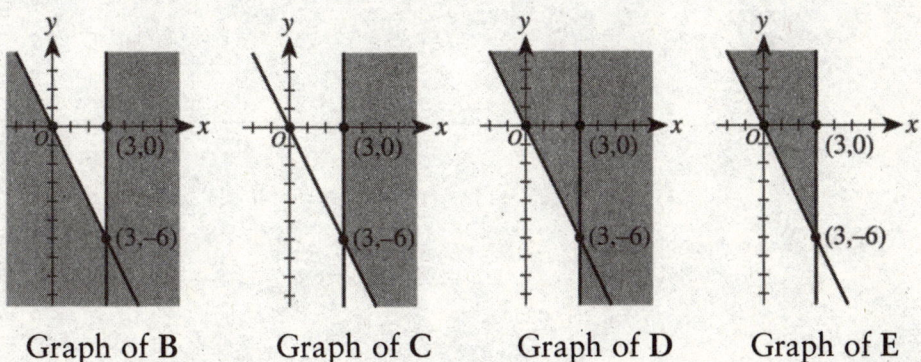

Graph of **B**   Graph of **C**   Graph of **D**   Graph of **E**

Question 56. The correct answer is K. To find $f(x + h)$ when $f(x) = x^2 - 2$, you would substitute $(x + h)$ for x in $f(x) = x^2 - 2$. The result is $(x + h)^2 - 2$. Multiplying out $(x + h)^2$ yields $x^2 + xh + xh + h^2$, or $x^2 + 2xh + h^2$. Then add -2 to the result.

If you chose **G**, you interpreted $f(x + h)$ as $f(x) + h$. If you chose **H**, you replaced $(x + h)^2$ with $x^2 + h^2$. If you chose **J**, you found $(x + h)^2$.

Question 57. The correct answer is A. It might be surprising to see that the graph of this complicated function looks almost like a line. The equation $y = \frac{2x^2 + x}{x}$ can be written as $y = \frac{x(2x + 1)}{x}$. This is equivalent to $y = 2x + 1$ except when $x = 0$. When $x = 0$, the original equation is undefined. So the correct graph is $y = 2x + 1$ with a point removed where $x = 0$.

If you noticed that the function was undefined when $x = 0$, you may have thought the open dot belonged at $(0,0)$. That leaves **B** as the only answer choice that also goes through $(1,3)$.

Choice **C** is the only one that involves $(0,2)$, and you may have gotten this by substituting $x = 0$ to get $y = \frac{2(0^2) + 0}{0}$, and decided all the zeros could be dropped to yield $y = 2$.

If you chose **D**, you may have "cancelled" x's as $y = \frac{2(x^2) + \cancel{x}}{\cancel{x}}$ to get $y = 2x^2 + 1$. You could have eliminated this answer by testing $(-1,3)$ in the original equation, but testing $(1,3)$ would not have been enough.

Choice **E** can come from "cancelling" x's as $y = \frac{2x^2 + \cancel{x}}{\cancel{x}}$ to get $y = 2x^2$. You could have eliminated this answer by testing $(1,2)$ in the original equation.

MATHEMATICS · PRACTICE TEST 1 · EXPLANATORY ANSWERS

Question 58. The correct answer is F. To find the coordinates of vertex A after it is reflected across the x-axis, notice that a reflection across the x-axis does not change the x-coordinate but does change the sign of the y-coordinate. You might sketch or imagine a figure like the one below. Thus, the reflection of $A(c,d)$ across the x-axis is $A'(c,-d)$.

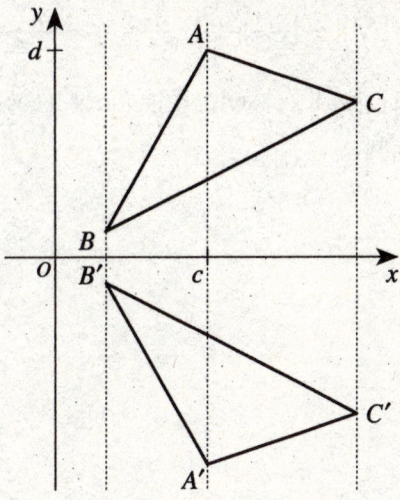

G gives A reflected across the y-axis. **H** gives A reflected across $(0,0)$. **J** gives A reflected over the line $y = x$ and is the most popular answer.

Question 59. The correct answer is A. To obtain an expression for y in terms of x when $x = 2t - 9$ and $y = 5 - t$, you can first solve $x = 2t - 9$ for t by adding 9 to both sides to get $x + 9 = 2t$. Then, divide both sides by 2 to get $\frac{x+9}{2} = t$. Substitute that expression for t into $y = 5 - t$ to get $y = 5 - \frac{x+9}{2}$. To simplify the right side, rewrite 5 as $\frac{10}{2}$ and then combine the 2 fractions together to get $y = \frac{10-(x+9)}{2}$. You can then distribute and combine like terms to get $y = \frac{1-x}{2}$.

If you chose **B**, you probably got $y = \frac{10-(x+9)}{2}$ and simplified it to $y = \frac{19-x}{2}$. If you chose **C**, you may have substituted $2x - 9$ for t in $y = 5 - t$, which results in $y = 5 - (2x - 9)$. After distributing, this would be $y = 5 - 2x + 9$, or $y = 14 - 2x$.

Question 60. **The correct answer is K.** To find $\sin \frac{\pi}{12}$ using $\sin(\alpha - \beta) = (\sin \alpha)(\cos \beta) - (\cos \alpha)(\sin \beta)$ given that $\frac{\pi}{12} = \frac{\pi}{3} - \frac{\pi}{4}$, you can first substitute $\frac{\pi}{3}$ for α and $\frac{\pi}{4}$ for β and get $\sin \frac{\pi}{12} = \sin\left(\frac{\pi}{3} - \frac{\pi}{4}\right) = \left(\sin \frac{\pi}{3}\right)\left(\cos \frac{\pi}{4}\right) - \left(\cos \frac{\pi}{3}\right)\left(\sin \frac{\pi}{4}\right)$. Using the table of values to substitute in that equation, you get $\sin \frac{\pi}{12} = \left(\frac{\sqrt{3}}{2}\right)\left(\frac{\sqrt{2}}{2}\right) - \left(\frac{1}{2}\right)\left(\frac{\sqrt{2}}{2}\right) = \frac{\sqrt{6}}{4} - \frac{\sqrt{2}}{4} = \frac{\sqrt{6} - \sqrt{2}}{4}$.

H comes from calculating $\left(\frac{\sqrt{3}}{2}\right)\left(\frac{1}{2}\right) - \left(\frac{\sqrt{2}}{2}\right)\left(\frac{\sqrt{2}}{2}\right)$, which is $\left(\sin \frac{\pi}{3}\right)\left(\cos \frac{\pi}{3}\right) - \left(\sin \frac{\pi}{4}\right)\left(\cos \frac{\pi}{4}\right)$. If you chose J, you probably just used $\sin \frac{\pi}{3} - \sin \frac{\pi}{4}$.

Passage I

Question 1. The best answer is **A** because Fran describes Linda Rose as "a homing pigeon" (lines 2–3) and "a sort of human boomerang" (lines 4–5) who'd "make a U-turn" (line 4) back to Fran despite a twenty-five-year wait. Though Fran had "long since stopped expecting" word from Linda Rose, she was still "not surprised" when she got it (lines 5–6). Fran experienced "the shock of being found after waiting so long" (lines 33–34), which again suggests she'd been expecting to hear from Linda Rose.

The best answer is NOT:

B because the passage doesn't support the idea that Fran and Linda Rose have built up resentment toward each other.

C because the passage doesn't support the idea that Fran has dreams of a perfect daughter. It's Fran's mother who brings up—and dismisses—the idea that Linda Rose has unrealistic expectations about Fran being "Grace Kelly or Margaret Mead" (lines 95–96).

D because there's no indication in the passage that Fran and Linda Rose share much of anything beyond a biological tie, similar handwriting (see lines 9–11), and physical appearance (see lines 75–76).

Question 2. The best answer is **G** because "strong-willed" and "caring" best describe Fran's mother. She has "dragon-lady nails" (lines 23–24) in defiance of her chemotherapy. She "snorted" (line 61) a response to Fran's comment about her being a great-grandmother. She also firmly tells Fran not to put off contacting Linda Rose, who's "been waiting for twenty-five years" (line 87) for a meeting. But Fran's mother also cares deeply about Fran and tries to reassure her by saying, "You're [Linda Rose's] flesh-and-blood mother and that's enough. That's all it'll take" (lines 98–99).

The best answer is NOT:

F because while Fran's mother might (with some difficulty) be described as arrogant, she isn't cruel. While Fran's mother "snorted" a response to Fran and though she firmly tells Fran not to put off contacting Linda Rose, her love for Fran and her concern for Linda Rose's feelings also come through.

H because while Fran's mother might be described as friendly, she isn't withdrawn, as revealed by her nails, her snort, and her firm warning to Fran.

J because while Fran's mother is loving, there's no evidence in the passage that she's embittered.

Question 3.

This is a NOT question, which asks you to find the answer choice that is *not* supported by the passage.

The best answer is B because Fran's reactions to learning she's a grandmother don't include looking forward to inviting Linda Rose and Blake over for a visit. When Fran's mother asks if Fran is going to invite Linda Rose and the baby, Fran replies, "I haven't thought that far" (line 85). The remainder of the passage suggests that Fran is nervous about such a visit. The other three answer choices are supported by the passage.

The best answer is NOT:

A because Fran notes that "in the normal order of things, you have ample time to adjust to the idea" of being a grandmother (lines 67–68). In Fran's case, however, she simply gets "a snapshot in the mail one day" (line 69) letting her know she's a grandmother.

C because Fran notes that upon getting the news about being a grandmother, she feels "as if I had just shaken hands with Death" (lines 65–66).

D because in lines 72–73, Fran says being a grandmother is "not fair" because she doesn't "even feel like a *mother*."

Question 4. **The best answer is F** because the first paragraph is built around Fran's lack of surprise that Linda Rose contacted her. Fran calls Linda Rose "a homing pigeon" (lines 2–3) and "a sort of human boomerang" (lines 4–5) who she knew "sooner or later . . . would make a U-turn" back to her (line 4). The paragraph closes with Fran's suspicion, based on the familiarity of the handwriting, that the letter in the mailbox is from Linda Rose. Fran claims that while she had "long stopped expecting" such a letter, she "was not surprised" when she got it (lines 5–6).

The best answer is NOT:

G because the first paragraph doesn't claim that Linda Rose acted like a wild bird, just that Fran's mother "always thought of her as some wild little bird" (lines 1–2). In any case, the first paragraph doesn't focus on Linda Rose's behavior as a child.

H because the passage states that Fran "was not surprised" when she got the letter from Linda Rose.

J because while Linda Rose's handwriting reminds Fran of her own, this isn't the main point of the last paragraph. It's just a detail supporting the paragraph's main idea.

Question 5. The best answer is C because the last paragraph focuses on Fran's mother's efforts to reassure Fran. Fran's mother brings up the idea of Linda Rose having a "big fantasy" (lines 94–95) that Fran is Grace Kelly or Margaret Mead and says "no one" (line 97) could live up to that. She goes on to say, though, that as Linda Rose's "flesh-and-blood mother," Fran has "all it'll take" to have a good relationship with Linda Rose (lines 98–99).

The best answer is NOT:

A because neither Fran nor her mother has seen Linda Rose for a quarter century, so they can only guess about what Linda Rose thinks.

B because the only reference to the idea that Linda Rose might cause trouble or ask for money occurs in the twenty-seventh paragraph (lines 86–90), not in the last paragraph.

D because in the last paragraph, Fran's mother tries to reassure Fran in an effort to encourage her to invite Linda Rose and Blake for a visit in the near future.

Question 6. The best answer is J because Fran says that while her mother "had lost some weight and most of her hair to chemotherapy" (lines 21–22), Fran "was used to how she looked now" (lines 19–20).

The best answer is NOT:

F because rather than being surprised, Fran says she "was used to" her mother's appearance (lines 19–20).

G because there's no support in the passage for the idea that Fran is embarrassed by the nail polish colors her mother uses. Fran merely notes that her mother "was vain about her hands" (line 19) and had painted her nails "Jungle Orchid" (lines 61–62).

H because while Fran says she's "noticed people staring" at her mother (lines 20–21), there's no evidence in the passage that Fran feels pity for her mother as a result.

Question 7. The best answer is D because in thinking about the letter she receives from Linda Rose, Fran notes, "I could see the ghosts of all the long letters she must have written and crumpled into the wastebasket" (lines 56–58), suggesting Fran sympathizes with Linda Rose.

The best answer is NOT:

A because while Fran acknowledges that the letter was "short" (line 55), she feels sympathy, not disappointment.

B because soon after handing her mother the letter from Linda Rose, Fran comments, "Forty years old and I felt as if I had just shaken hands with Death" (lines 64–66)—hardly a happy reaction.

C because while the letter was "businesslike" (line 56), Fran sympathizes with Linda Rose and doesn't feel offended.

Question 8. The best answer is **J** because details in the passage suggest Fran had put Linda Rose up for adoption a quarter century ago. Fran says her mother had "wanted to keep" Linda Rose (line 1), which implies that Fran didn't. More directly, Fran notes upon receiving the letter and photograph from Linda Rose that a person doesn't usually "get a snapshot in the mail one day from a baby girl you gave up twenty-four years ago saying, 'Congratulations, you're a grandma!'" (lines 69–71).

The best answer is NOT:

F, G, or **H** because there's no evidence in the passage that the reason it's been such a long time since Fran and Linda Rose have seen each other is that Linda Rose left home to get married (**F**), that arguments between the two drove Linda Rose away (**G**), or that Linda Rose chose to live with her father (**H**).

Question 9. The best answer is **C** because after looking at the picture Linda Rose sends, Fran's mother says to Fran, "She looks just like you. Only her nose is more aristocratic" (lines 75–76).

The best answer is NOT:

A because when Fran's mother suggests that Linda Rose may be "married to a brain surgeon with his and her Cadillacs" (lines 89–90), Fran replies, "She didn't mention any husband at all" (line 91) in the letter.

B because the passage's only reference to a piece of art is to the "dime-a-dozen seascape in a cheap gilt frame" (lines 44–45) behind Linda Rose in the picture.

D because there's no evidence in the passage that either the letter or the picture reveals that Linda Rose cares little about how she or her house looks.

Question 10. The best answer is **H** because after telling Fran not to put off contacting Linda Rose and inviting her and the baby for a visit, Fran's mother says Linda Rose has "been waiting twenty-five years" (line 87).

The best answer is NOT:

F because Fran's mother never directly expresses the desire to see her new great-grandson before she dies.

G because there's no evidence in the passage that Fran generally tends to delay making hard decisions.

J because while Fran's mother wonders aloud whether Linda Rose is "going to be trouble or ask for money" (lines 88–89), she only does this because she thinks Fran might use this as an excuse to put off contacting Linda Rose and inviting her and the baby for a visit. Fran's mother goes on to say, "For all we know, [Linda Rose is] married to a brain surgeon with his and her Cadillacs" (lines 89–90).

Passage II

Question 11. The best answer is B because the author argues throughout the passage, and particularly in the fourth paragraph (lines 42–61), that people's lack of understanding of important details about government keeps them from improving government. He contends that people "do not particularly care" (lines 44–45) about "the whys and wherefores of most technical, non-emotional political issues" (lines 42–44) and are "more than willing to delegate evaluation of the technical aspects of government to somebody else" (lines 53–55). For the author, this means that "angry voters turn the rascals out and, in the triumph of hope over experience, let new rascals in" (lines 56–58) but that the voters are unable to "tell the rascals how to do their jobs better" (lines 60–61) because the voters "themselves do not understand the technical questions" (lines 59–60).

The best answer is NOT:

A because the author doesn't argue that American citizens read too many newspapers or watch too much television.

C because while the author does contend that people have a certain control over elected officials through voting, he also claims that voters are unable to affect how officials do their jobs while in office because the voters "themselves do not understand the technical questions." The author also doesn't directly address whether people can control bureaucrats.

D because there's no evidence in the passage that television has cut back on news to focus on entertainment. Furthermore, the author undermines the idea that Americans ever had a truly responsive government when he repeats but dismisses "the widely held tenet of democratic faith that elected officials, as opposed to bureaucrats or the judiciary, are popularly selected and democratically responsive" (lines 81–84).

Question 12. The best answer is F because the author contends that a typical local newspaper reporter is "an inexperienced twenty-three-year-old journalism school graduate" (lines 34–35) whose "journalism school curriculum did not include advanced algebra, to say nothing of calculus" (lines 39–41)—leaving the reporter ill prepared to understand "the intricacies of a program budget, which basically involves solving a grand equation composed of numerous simultaneous differential functions" (lines 36–39).

The best answer is NOT:

G because while the author contends that the reporters are often inexperienced, he doesn't think they're well educated.

H or J because while the author contends that the reporters are often young, he also calls them "inexperienced" (ruling out H) and not well educated (ruling out J).

Question 13. The best answer is **A** because according to the author, even the "Internal Revenue Service lawyers" at the tax seminar who were experts on federal estate and gift tax laws "frankly confessed that they did not understand the Tax Reform Act of 1976" (lines 66–68). The author uses this example to make the point that "government is so technical that even career civil servants cannot explain what is happening" (lines 63–65).

The best answer is NOT:

B or **D** because even the civil servants couldn't understand the law.

C because the author doesn't use the example to make the broad claim that some governmental issues are more technical than they used to be before passage of the act, nor is the timing of the act relevant here.

Question 14. The best answer is **F** because the author contends that Americans "for the most part know little and care less about the technical functioning of their government" (lines 77–79). Such indifference helps reduce the idea of elected officials being "democratically responsive" (lines 83–84) to (more or less) the status of "a myth" (line 84).

The best answer is NOT:

G or **J** because the author doesn't specifically claim that people are completely taken in by the myth that government is responsive to democratic control (**G**) or that people are prepared to concede legitimacy only to a democratically elected government (**J**). In any case, he uses the word *indifference* to refer directly to the idea that Americans are largely ignorant of and unconcerned about technical governmental issues.

H because the idea that citizens are responsive to either elected officials or bureaucrats isn't discussed in the passage.

Question 15. The best answer is **C** because the author states that "interest in the economy becomes all-consuming" when "times are bad, or there is a nationwide strike or disaster" (lines 8–10).

The best answer is NOT:

A, B, or **D** because the author doesn't claim that voter interest in the economy is greatest when national elections are held (**A**), when interesting personalities are leaders (**B**), or when there are no other interesting issues (**D**).

Question 16. The best answer is G because *limited* is the best synonym for *circumscribed* in context. The author states that "most serious political communication" between public officials and voters "is limited to forty-five seconds on the network evening news" (lines 18–19) even when the issues are known to voters. Furthermore, in the third paragraph (lines 27–41), the author stresses the limited knowledge communicated by television and local newspapers on serious and complicated political issues.

The best answer is NOT:

F because *technical* makes no sense in context. Since people "for the most part know little and care less about the technical functioning of their government" (lines 77–79), it's not likely that communication between public officials and voters would be extremely technical.

H because *entertaining* makes no sense in context given the fact that people are largely ignorant of and unconcerned about technical governmental issues.

J because *serious* is not the best synonym in context. Lines 15–17 set up a contrast between the seriousness of the political issues and the "extremely circumscribed," or limited, communication between public officials and voters on those issues.

Question 17. The best answer is D because the author states, "Process and personalities, the way decisions are made and by whom, the level of perquisites, extramarital sexual relations, and, in high offices, personal gossip dominate the public mind" (lines 45–48). It can reasonably be inferred, then, that a news story with a headline about Senator Smith denying he improperly made money would attract the greatest number of readers.

The best answer is NOT:

A, B, or C because news stories with headlines about park fees (A), accounting procedures (B), and safety regulations (C)—"the substance of technical decisions" (line 49)—would, based on the passage, draw comparatively few readers.

Question 18. The best answer is J because the author claims that "reporters focus on what sells papers or gets a high Nielsen rating" (lines 50–51). Since "neither newspapers nor television stations intend to lose their primary value as entertainment" (lines 51–53), it's clear that Nielsen ratings in some way measure how "entertaining" television news coverage is to the public, which is why television news coverage is heavily influenced by them.

The best answer is NOT:

F or H because there's no evidence in the passage that Nielsen ratings place great emphasis on technical details (F) or that the Federal Communications Commission requires Nielsen ratings (H).

G because lines 50–51, which distinguish between selling newspapers and getting high Nielsen ratings, suggest that Nielsen ratings are relevant only to television.

Question 19. The best answer is A because the author states, "Angry voters turn the rascals out and, in the triumph of hope over experience, let new rascals in" (lines 56–58). The "new rascals" are newly elected officials who the angry voters hope will do a better job than the "rascals" they just voted out of office.

The best answer is NOT:

B or **D** because in context, the phrase "the triumph of hope over experience" has nothing to do with the belief that expertise in a technical field is a qualification for holding office (**B**) or that newspapers and television will eventually provide better news coverage (**D**).

C because in context, the phrase "the triumph of hope over experience" relates to the hope that new officials will outperform old officials, not to the hope that a sufficient amount of anger will make a given group of officials do a better job.

Question 20. The best answer is J because the author states, "What voters are unable to do—because they themselves do not understand the technical questions—is tell the rascals how to do their jobs better" (lines 58–61).

The best answer is NOT:

F or **H** because the passage never argues that citizens are unable to tell government officials how to do their jobs better because citizens don't vote in every election (**F**) or read enough newspapers or see enough television (**H**).

G because while the author does suggest that citizens have a tendency to elect rascals, he doesn't say that this tendency is why citizens can't tell government officials how to do their jobs better. The real reason is that citizens don't understand the technical questions.

Passage III

Question 21. The best answer is B because throughout the passage, the author makes the argument that non-Western immigrants are changing the definition of what it means to be an American. About herself, she says, "I am an American writer, in the American mainstream, trying to extend it" (lines 29–30). She says she's tried to make Americans aware that "the foreign-born, the Third World immigrant with non-Western religions and non-European languages and appearance, can be as American as any steerage passenger from Ireland, Italy, or the Russian Pale" (lines 39–43). The author feels it's part of her "literary agenda" (line 44) to "show how I (and the hundreds of thousands like me) have transformed America" (lines 46–47). She concludes, "I do have a duty, beyond telling a good story. My duty is to give voice to continents, but also to redefine the nature of *American*" (lines 87–89).

The best answer is NOT:

A or **C** because the author never argues in the passage that until recently, foreign-born residents haven't wanted to be involved in defining the American reality (**A**) or that the United States immigration policy is inherently unfair (**C**).

D because while the author does suggest that America can change immigrants—"America has transformed *me*" (line 45)—she doesn't make the stronger, more specific argument that America has changed the political affiliations of most non-Western immigrants.

Question 22. **The best answer is F** because lines 3–5 reveal that the author attended school in Calcutta, while lines 26–28 indicate she moved to the United States and lived in "the all too real Manhattan."

The best answer is NOT:

G because lines 3–5 indicate that the school run by Irish nuns was in Calcutta (even though the nuns considered it "a corner of England").

H because the passage doesn't say that the author was raised in Bangladesh or that she moved to England before moving to the United States.

J because the author says she's never been to Faridpur, her father's birthplace: "My 'country'—called in Bengali *desh*—I have never seen. It is the ancestral home of my father and is now in Bangladesh" (lines 5–8).

Question 23. **The best answer is C** because the author repeatedly claims that her agenda or mission is to reinterpret, through her stories, what it means to be an American. About herself, she says, "I am an American writer, in the American mainstream, trying to extend it" (lines 29–30). She says she's tried to make Americans aware that "the foreign-born, the Third World immigrant with non-Western religions and non-European languages and appearance, can be as American as any steerage passenger from Ireland, Italy, or the Russian Pale" (lines 39–43). The author feels it's part of her "literary agenda" (line 44) to "show how I (and the hundreds of thousands like me) have transformed America" (lines 46–47). She concludes, "I do have a duty, beyond telling a good story. My duty is to give voice to continents, but also to redefine the nature of *American*" (lines 87–89).

The best answer is NOT:

A or **B** because the author never says in the passages that her agenda and mission are to raise the political consciousness of recent immigrants to the United States (**A**) or to create characters whose cultural heritage isn't easily identifiable (**B**).

D because while the author undoubtedly wants to find an audience for her stories and novels, she says her agenda or mission is to reinterpret what it means to be an American.

Question 24. **The best answer is H** because the author notes that as part of her "process of immigration and accommodation" to the United States, she's gone from being "a person who couldn't ride a public bus when she first arrived" to being "someone who watches tractor pulls on obscure cable channels" (lines 66–69).

The best answer is NOT:

F because line 19 refers to a horoscope "cast by a neighborhood astrologer when [the author] was a week-old infant" living in Calcutta (lines 14–15).

G because lines 24–25 refer to the author's girlhood in Calcutta, where she had to deal with such "contradictions" as hearing native people praise India and the Irish nuns at her school condemn it (see lines 19–24).

J because lines 73–74 deal with how the author creates her fictional characters and thus have no direct relationship to the idea that she's been changed by America.

Question 25. The best answer is **D** because the author says, "My 'country'—called in Bengali *desh*—I have never seen. It is the ancestral home of my father and is now in Bangladesh. Nevertheless, I . . . think of myself as 'belonging' to Faridpur, the tiny village that was his birthplace" (lines 5–10).

The best answer is NOT:

A because Faridpur is a real place that, based on the passage at least, has no role in Indian mythology.

B because in lines 27–28, the author says, "The unglimpsed phantom Faridpur and the all too real Manhattan have merged as 'desh,'" meaning both Faridpur and Manhattan are in some sense her home now.

C because while it's true that Faridpur is now part of Bangladesh, this isn't why she refers to Faridpur as a "phantom"—it's a "phantom" because she's never seen it.

Question 26. The best answer is **F** because of the context in which the phrase "trying to extend it" appears. The author writes, "I am an American writer, in the American mainstream, trying to extend it" (lines 29–30), with *it* being the American mainstream. Soon after, she says her "remaining struggle" (line 36) as a writer is to convince American readers, editors, and publishers that "the foreign-born, the Third World immigrant with non-Western religions and non-European languages and appearance, can be as American as any steerage passenger from Ireland, Italy, or the Russian Pale" (lines 39–43). Thus, through her stories, she's trying to extend the boundaries of the American mainstream to include people of non-European ethnicities.

The best answer is NOT:

G because the author says she's not part of both Indian and American cultures: "I am an immigrant; my investment is in the American reality, not the Indian" (lines 32–33).

H or **J** because there's no evidence in the passage that the author is trying to find a way to make her home in the United States permanent (**H**)—she implies, in fact, that it already is—or is working to change immigration regulations (**J**).

Question 27. The best answer is **D** because when the author says she's "had to sensitize editors as well as readers to"—that is, make them aware of—"the richness of the lives I'm writing about" (lines 48–49), she's implying that these editors had previously tended to view the people she writes about in one-dimensional, stereotypical terms.

The best answer is NOT:

A, **B**, or **C** because there's no evidence in the passage that the author is implying that the editors didn't understand that many Asian Americans were already reading her work (**A**), that the editors gave her work superficial praise but refused to publish her novels (**B**), or that the editors were overtly (openly) discriminatory when it came to non-Western writers (**C**).

Question 28. The best answer is **G** because the author implies that many readers come unexpectedly to see themselves in her stories' characters. Adopting the voice of some of her readers, the author says, ". . . I see these people (call them Indians, Filipinos, Koreans, Chinese) around me all the time and I never knew they had an inner life. I never knew they schemed and cheated, suffered, cared so passionately" (lines 51–55). In other words, these readers gain from "the richness of the lives [she's] writing about" (line 49) a sense that "these people" have the same kinds of dreams, feelings, and experiences as the readers themselves do.

The best answer is NOT:

F because lines 51–55 show how readers come to see characters in the author's stories as distinct individuals from diverse cultural backgrounds.

H because there's no evidence in the passage that stories about immigrants to the United States generally have many more characters than other types of stories do.

J because the author never claims that immigrants from non-Western countries have developed a stronger inner life than have native-born Americans, only that non-Western immigrants have an inner life, just like everyone else.

Question 29. The best answer is **B** because the author states in the first paragraph that "the larger political entity to which I gave my first allegiance—India—was not even a sovereign [independent] nation when I was born" (lines 10–13).

The best answer is NOT:

A, C, or D because the first paragraph doesn't state that at the time of the author's birth, India was engaged in a war with England (A), still part of Bangladesh (C), or governed by the Irish (D).

Question 30. The best answer is **H** because immediately after the quoted phrase, the author writes, "Consider the history [the characters] have witnessed (colonialism, technology, education, liberation, civil war). They have shed old identities, taken on new ones, and learned to hide the scars" (lines 76–79).

The best answer is NOT:

F because the author isn't being critical of her characters' cultural and political viewpoints; rather, she's saying that the people she writes about have seen and experienced a great deal in a short amount of time, making them seem "older" than they actually are.

G or J because the author doesn't make the specific claim that her characters have rejected Bengali, British, Irish, and American values (G) or that her characters are really her mother's and grandmother's ancestors (J).

Passage IV

Question 31. The best answer is B because lines 16–18 are introduced by the author's claim that "most paleontologists are now willing to view [dinosaurs] as energetic, active, and capable animals" (lines 14–16) despite earlier theories that dinosaurs were stupid, slow, and clumsy. It's reasonable, then, that what follows in lines 16–18 is a description of scientists' changing understanding of *Brontosaurus* lifestyle.

The best answer is NOT:

A or **D** because the words "a generation ago" and "now" in lines 16–18 indicate that the author is describing the present and recent past, not the time when *Brontosaurus* lived.

C because there's no evidence in the passage that the author believes standard illustrations of dinosaurs still inaccurately depict their lifestyles. "The standard illustration" of *Brontosaurus* mentioned in line 10 refers to an outdated image based on earlier scientific beliefs. Lines 16–22 (especially the reference to "modern anatomical reconstructions") suggest that illustrations have changed along with scientists' beliefs about dinosaurs.

Question 32. The best answer is F because the author indicates that "signs of social behavior that demand coordination, cohesiveness and recognition" (lines 57–58) in dinosaurs "were overlooked when dinosaurs labored under the burden of a falsely imposed obtuseness" (lines 59–61). In other words, when scientists thought dinosaurs were unintelligent, they failed to see evidence of complex social behaviors, such as "multiple trackways" (line 61) and hints that adult dinosaurs flanked young, immature dinosaurs during travel in order to protect them.

The best answer is NOT:

G because there's no evidence in the passage that scientists ever believed mammals were incapable of social formations.

H because there's no indication in the passage that the information in the fifth paragraph (lines 34–54) about brain and body sizes is new to scientists.

J because the passage doesn't say that any particular equipment was needed to identify the "multiple trackways" and the evidence that adult dinosaurs protected young, immature ones while traveling. It was mainly a matter of looking at fossilized footprints without the preconceived notion that dinosaurs were unintelligent.

Question 33. The best answer is **D** because the author describes "signs of social behavior that demand coordination, cohesiveness and recognition" (lines 57–58) in dinosaurs. These include "multiple trackways . . . with evidence for more than twenty animals traveling together in parallel movement" (lines 61–63), suggesting some dinosaurs may have lived in herds, and "small footprints" in a sauropod trackway that "lie in the center" with "larger ones at the periphery" (lines 65–66), suggesting adult dinosaurs may have flanked young, immature dinosaurs during travel in order to protect them.

The best answer is NOT:

A because while the author mentions "modern anatomical reconstructions" that "indicate strength and agility" in dinosaurs (lines 21–22), he doesn't use these as evidence of complex behaviors in dinosaurs.

B because in lines 60–61, the author is referring to old scientific misinterpretations, not to fossil evidence, when he mentions that at one time "dinosaurs labored under the burden of a falsely imposed obtuseness."

C because the author doesn't say that dinosaurs traveled with advanced herbivorous mammals, only that some evidence suggests that some dinosaurs may have traveled "much as some advanced herbivorous mammals do today, with large adults at the borders sheltering juveniles in the center" (lines 67–69).

Question 34. The best answer is **G** because the author states that while "dinosaurs held sway for 100 million years" (line 75), people have a much shorter history: "5 million years perhaps since *Australopithecus*, a mere 50,000 for our own species, *Homo sapiens*" (lines 82–83).

The best answer is NOT:

F because while the author does see "signs of social behavior that demand coordination, cohesiveness and recognition" in dinosaurs (lines 57–58), he nowhere suggests that human behavior seems simple in comparison to the complexity of dinosaur social behavior.

H because while the author does call dinosaurs "very large animals" (line 53), he doesn't claim that humans seem incredibly small in comparison.

J because nowhere in the passage does the author contend that study on human behavior is severely lacking in comparison to the amount of study done on dinosaurs.

Question 35. The best answer is **D** because the author claims that the revisionist interpretation of the relationship between dinosaur intelligence and physical size is that dinosaurs "had the 'right-sized' brains for reptiles of their body size" (lines 32–33).

The best answer is NOT:

A because, according to the author, the revisionist position isn't that dinosaurs had relatively large brains, but rather that they had appropriately sized brains.

B because the author states, "The revisionist interpretation, which I support, . . . does not enshrine dinosaurs as paragons of intellect" (lines 29–31).

C because the author states that revisionists claim dinosaurs "were not small brained after all" (line 32).

Question 36. The best answer is **H** because the author says the revisionist position he endorses is that dinosaurs "had the 'right-sized' brains for reptiles of their body size" (lines 32–33), a point people are likely to miss if they judge dinosaurs by human standards of brain size, body size, and intelligence. In fact, people wrongly used to see dinosaurs as "a symbol of lumbering stupidity" (lines 4–5).

The best answer is NOT:

F because the author suggests just the opposite—that humans, with their "subjective, top-heavy perspective," are likely to misjudge dinosaurs and, by implication, other nonhuman species.

G because while the author does say that humans are "top-heavy," he never claims that the human physical construction is deformed by the largeness of the skull. Instead, he uses the idea of people being "top-heavy" to question humans' ability to judge dinosaurs and other nonhuman species.

J because the idea that humans are "top-heavy" undercuts the idea that humans have a small brain relative to their body weight.

Question 37. The best answer is **B** because the passage states that relative to smaller animals, "large animals have low ratios of brain weight to body weight" (lines 45–46).

The best answer is NOT:

A or **C** because lines 45–46 rule out the possibility that the ratio is higher in larger animals (**A**) or the same in both larger and smaller animals (**C**).

D because there's no evidence in the passage that the ratio is overestimated.

Question 38. The best answer is **F** because the passage states, "In fact, brains grow only about two-thirds as fast as bodies" (lines 47–48).

The best answer is NOT:

G because even though brains grow about two-thirds as fast as bodies, this doesn't mean that at maturity, the brain weighs an average of one-third of body weight.

H because while the passage does say that "we have no reason to believe that large animals are consistently stupider than their smaller relatives" (lines 48–50), this speaks to the relationship of intelligence to body size, not brain size to body size.

J because the passage does not say that brain size is independent of body size, but instead asserts that there is a relationship.

Question 39. **The best answer is D** because the author states, "Dinosaurs held sway for 100 million years" (line 75), which the author finds "remarkable" (line 73).

The best answer is NOT:

A, B, or C because dinosaurs dominated Earth for 100 million years, not just 100,000 years (**A**), 5 million years (**B**), or 70 million years (**C**).

Question 40. **The best answer is H** because the author begins the last paragraph by stating that compared to the longevity of dinosaurs, "people . . . are scarcely worth mentioning" (lines 81–82) and immediately after notes that it's been only 5 million years since the emergence of *Australopithecus* and only 50,000 years since "our own species, *Homo sapiens*," emerged (line 83). It's clear from this that *Australopithecus* was human (a "person"), but not a modern human (*H. sapiens*).

The best answer is NOT:

F because *Australopithecus* wasn't a dinosaur.

G because *Australopithecus* was different from *H. sapiens* and appeared on Earth 5 million years ago.

J because there's no evidence in the passage that *Australopithecus* was a physically larger species of human or that it had a much smaller brain.

Passage I

Question 1. The best answer is B. Figure 1 shows a model describing the relative proportions of a plume. In Figure 1, the head of the plume has a diameter of approximately 500 km, and the tail of the plume has a diameter of approximately 250 km. If the model is typical of all mantle plumes, then the heads of plumes are approximately twice the diameter of the tails.

The best answer is NOT:

A, C, or D because in Study 1, the head of the plume was approximately twice the diameter of the tail of the plume.

Question 2. The best answer is J. The scientists hypothesized that the larger the volume of lava produced, the larger the number of marine organisms that would become extinct. If larger lava volumes resulted in a larger number of marine organisms becoming extinct, then the plateau with the largest lava volume would result in the largest number of marine organisms becoming extinct. According to Table 1, Plateau D has the largest lava volume. So, based on the scientists' hypothesis, the formation of Plateau D caused the largest number of marine organisms to become extinct.

The best answer is NOT:

F, G, or H because Plateau D has the largest lava volume, so the formation of Plateau D most likely caused the largest number of marine organisms to become extinct.

Question 3. The best answer is D. Table 1 shows that as the length of time that lava was produced increased, lava volume increased. According to Table 1, Plateau D produced lava for 1.7 Myr and had a lava volume of 2,125,000 km³. Based on these results, if a flood basalt plateau produced lava for 1.8 Myr, then the lava volume associated with this plateau would likely exceed 2,125,000 km³.

The best answer is NOT:

A, B, or C because the lava volume would exceed 2,125,000 km³.

Question 4. The best answer is J. According to Table 1, the age of Plateau A is 60 Myr; of Plateau B, 67 Myr; of Plateau C, 135 Myr; and of Plateau D, 192 Myr. The length of time lava was produced at Plateau A is 1.6 Myr; at Plateau B, 1.3 Myr; at Plateau C, 1.2 Myr; and at Plateau D, 1.7 Myr. For these data, there is no apparent relationship between the age of a plateau and the length of time lava was produced.

The best answer is NOT:

F because as the age of a plateau increases, the length of time lava was produced does not increase only. Initially it decreases.

G because as the age of a plateau increases, the length of time lava was produced does not decrease only. It increases after it decreases.

H because as the age of a plateau increases, the length of time lava was produced does not increase and then decrease. It decreases, and then increases.

Question 5. The best answer is B. For each of the 4 plateaus, an ordered pair can be determined using Table 1, which relates the age of the plateau and the rate of lava production. If the *x*-value corresponds to the age of a plateau in Myr and the *y*-value corresponds to the rate of lava production in km³/yr, then the ordered pair for Plateau A is (60,1.25); for Plateau B, (67,1.2); for Plateau C, (135,1.2); and for Plateau D, (192,1.25). The graph in **B** best represents these 4 ordered pairs.

The best answer is NOT:

A because the *y*-value should decrease between 60 Myr and 67 Myr, remain constant between 67 Myr and 135 Myr, and then increase between 135 Myr and 192 Myr. In **A**, the *y*-value remains constant between 67 Myr and 192 Myr.

C because the *y*-value should exceed 1.0 km³/yr. However, in **C** the *y*-value is less than 1.0 km³/yr.

D because the *y*-value should decrease between 60 Myr and 67 Myr, remain constant between 67 Myr and 135 Myr, and then increase between 135 Myr and 192 Myr. In **D**, the *y*-value increases between 60 Myr and 67 Myr, remains constant between 67 Myr and 135 Myr, and then decreases between 135 Myr and 192 Myr.

Question 6. The best answer is G. The scientists in Study 3 hypothesized that the production of large amounts of lava and gases in the formation of plateaus may have contributed to large extinctions of marine organisms. They cite large extinctions associated with the formation of Plateaus A, B, and C. Based on their hypothesis, a large extinction of marine organisms also occurred when Plateau D was formed, about 192 Myr ago.

The best answer is NOT:

F, H, or **J** because there is no evidence of the production of large amounts of lava and gases at 77 Myr ago, 250 Myr ago, and 314 Myr ago, respectively.

Passage II

Question 7. The best answer is D. Figure 1 shows the net productivity of plants on abandoned farmland along the vertical axis and successional time along the horizontal axis. At Year 50, net productivity was between 1,000 g/m²/yr and 1,200 g/m²/yr.

The best answer is NOT:

A, B, or **C** because 1,125 g/m²/yr is closer to the value at Year 50 than are 15 g/m²/yr, 50 g/m²/yr, and 425 g/m²/yr, respectively.

Question 8. The best answer is F. Figure 1 shows how net productivity changed over the 200 years studied. During this time, net productivity increased from 0 g/m²/yr to about 1,200 g/m²/yr. Figure 2 shows how biomass changed over the 200 years studied. During this time, biomass increased from 0 kg/m² to about 35 kg/m². These data show that both net productivity and biomass increased over the 200 years studied.

The best answer is NOT:

G or H because biomass did not decrease.

J because net productivity did not decrease.

Question 9. The best answer is C. According to Figure 1, net productivity increased by less than 100 g/m²/yr from the end of Year 2 to the end of Year 4, from the end of Year 4 to the end of Year 14, and from the end of Year 50 to the end of Year 200. In contrast, from the end of Year 14 to the end of Year 50, net productivity increased by about 700 g/m²/yr.

The best answer is NOT:

A because net productivity increased more from the end of Year 14 to the end of Year 50 than it did from the end of Year 2 to the end of Year 4.

B because net productivity increased more from the end of Year 14 to the end of Year 50 than it did from the end of Year 4 to the end of Year 14.

D because net productivity increased more from the end of Year 14 to the end of Year 50 than it did from the end of Year 50 to the end of Year 200.

Question 10. The best answer is J. Figure 1 shows the net productivity of plants on abandoned farmland along the vertical axis and successional time along the horizontal axis. Successional time is subdivided into 3 stages—herb, shrub, and tree—based on the types of plants that were dominant at different times. According to Figure 1, net productivity was lowest when herbs were the dominant plants and highest when trees were the dominant plants.

The best answer is NOT:

F because net productivity was not lowest when shrubs were the dominant plants. Net productivity was lowest when herbs were the dominant plants.

G because net productivity was not lowest when trees were the dominant plants. Net productivity was lowest when herbs were the dominant plants.

H because net productivity was not highest when herbs were the dominant plants. Net productivity was highest when trees were the dominant plants.

Question 11. The best answer is C. Table 1 shows the bird species on plots of abandoned farmland in Georgia. Based on Table 1, if a plot of abandoned farmland in Georgia supported eastern meadowlarks, yellowthroats, and field sparrows at a density of at least 1 pair per 10 acres, then the successional time for that farmland would most likely be approximately 15 yr. At a successional time of 15 yr, shrubs were the dominant plants.

The best answer is NOT:

A, B, or D because the presence of eastern meadowlarks, yellowthroats, and field sparrows at a density of at least 1 pair per 10 acres indicates that successional time was approximately 15 years. At a successional time of 15 years, shrubs were the dominant plants. Thus, weeds, grasses, and pines, respectively, were not the dominant plants.

Passage III

Question 12. The best answer is F. Figure 2 shows the rise of liquid in the capillary tube. As the level of liquid in the capillary tube increased, the volume of liquid increased. All the liquids had the same volume when the level of each liquid was the same. This occurred when the temperature of the water bath was 20°C.

The best answer is NOT:

G, H, or J because the height of ethanol in the capillary tube was greater than the height of glycerine and of water in the capillary tube at 30°C, 40°C, and 50°C, respectively.

Question 13. The best answer is A. Figure 3 shows how the volume of the 3 gases varied with temperature. For each of the 3 gases, as temperature increased from 20°C to 100°C, the volume of each gas increased from about 20 mL to about 25 mL. The constant slope over this temperature interval indicates that the increase in volume was linear. These results support the hypothesis that as the temperature of a gas is increased at a constant pressure, the volume of the gas will also increase.

The best answer is NOT:

B because the volume of air increased as the temperature increased.

C because as the temperature increased from 20°C to 100°C, the volume of each gas increased from about 20 mL to about 25 mL.

D because the volumes of nitrogen and methane increased as the temperature increased.

Question 14. The best answer is J. Figure 1 shows the linear expansion of the 4 metals when the metals were stretched. At each of the 4 temperatures used in Experiment 1, aluminum had the greatest linear expansion and nickel had the smallest linear expansion. Because the engineer needs a wire that is resistant to stretching, the engineer should use the metal with the smallest linear expansion.

The best answer is NOT:

F, G, or H because the linear expansions of aluminum, brass, and iron, respectively, were greater than that of nickel.

Question 15. The best answer is A. If a balloon is placed on the surface of a heated water bath, the temperature of the gases within the balloon will increase. Figure 3 shows that the volume of air increases as the temperature of the air increases. Thus, the volume of the balloon would increase.

The best answer is NOT:

B or C because the volume of the balloon would increase only; it would not decrease.

D because the volume of the balloon would increase only; it would not remain the same.

Question 16. The best answer is H. In Experiment 1, each of the wires had the same initial length. After the wires were stretched in the apparatus, the final length of each wire was directly proportional to its linear expansion. According to Figure 1, at 80°C, the linear expansion of aluminum was 0.20 mm; of brass, 0.14 mm; of iron, 0.08 mm; and of nickel, 0.04 mm. Because the linear expansion of the copper wire at 80°C was 0.12 mm, the copper wire would be shorter than the brass wire and longer than the iron wire. Thus, the order of the wires from the longest wire to the shortest wire would be as follows: nickel, iron, copper, brass, and aluminum.

The best answer is NOT:

F or G because the nickel wire would be the shortest wire, not the longest wire.

J because the copper wire would be shorter than the brass wire.

Question 17. The best answer is D. If a heavier weight were used, the linear expansion would be greater, because the force exerted by the weight on the wire would be greater. Figure 1 shows that linear expansion increases as temperature increases. The correct figure should show linear expansion increasing with temperature and a greater linear expansion when the heavier weight was used.

The best answer is NOT:

A because in this figure, linear expansion decreases as temperature increases with the original weight. Linear expansion should increase as temperature increases.

B because in this figure, linear expansion decreases as temperature increases with the heavier weight. Linear expansion should increase as temperature increases.

C because in this figure, linear expansion is greater with the original weight than with the heavier weight. However, linear expansion should be greater with the heavier weight than with the original weight.

Passage IV

Question 18. **The best answer is J.** The figure shows the upper boundary of the troposphere, stratosphere, and mesosphere. It does not, however, show the upper boundary of the thermosphere.

The best answer is NOT:

F, G, or H because the figure does not indicate that the upper boundary of the thermosphere is located at 150 km, 200 km, and 250 km, respectively. Thus, one cannot conclude that the upper boundary of the thermosphere is located at any of these altitudes.

Question 19. **The best answer is B.** According to the figure, radiation with wavelengths between 2,000 Å and 3,000 Å is absorbed at an altitude of about 35 km. This absorption occurs within the stratosphere. If the ozone layer absorbs radiation with wavelengths between 2,000 Å and 3,000 Å, then the ozone layer must be located within the stratosphere.

The best answer is NOT:

A because the figure does not indicate that radiation with wavelengths between 2,000 Å and 3,000 Å is absorbed at altitudes between 0 km and 17 km (troposphere).

C because the figure does not indicate that radiation with wavelengths between 2,000 Å and 3,000 Å is absorbed at altitudes between 52 km and 82 km (mesosphere).

D because the figure does not indicate that radiation with wavelengths between 2,000 Å and 3,000 Å is absorbed at altitudes greater than 82 km (thermosphere).

Question 20. **The best answer is F.** Absorption of radiation within an atmospheric layer affects the air temperature of that layer. The troposphere absorbs radiation with wavelengths between 3,000 Å and 1,000,000 Å. Radiation with wavelengths outside this range will be less likely to affect the air temperature of the troposphere than will radiation with wavelengths within this range.

The best answer is NOT:

G because the troposphere absorbs radiation with wavelengths between 3,000 Å and 1,000,000 Å, including radiation with a wavelength of 4,500 Å. Because the troposphere absorbs radiation with a wavelength of 4,500 Å but does not absorb radiation with a wavelength of 1,500 Å, air temperature in the troposphere is less likely to be influenced by radiation with a wavelength of 1,500 Å than by radiation with a wavelength of 4,500 Å.

H because the troposphere absorbs radiation with wavelengths between 3,000 Å and 1,000,000 Å, including radiation with a wavelength of 6,000 Å. Because the troposphere absorbs radiation with a wavelength of 6,000 Å but does not absorb radiation with a wavelength of 1,500 Å, air temperature in the troposphere is less likely to be influenced by radiation with a wavelength of 1,500 Å than by radiation with a wavelength of 6,000 Å.

J because the troposphere absorbs radiation with wavelengths between 3,000 Å and 1,000,000 Å, including radiation with a wavelength of 7,000 Å. Because the troposphere absorbs radiation with a wavelength of 7,000 Å but does not absorb radiation with a wavelength of 1,500 Å, air temperature in the troposphere is less likely to be influenced by radiation with a wavelength of 1,500 Å than by radiation with a wavelength of 7,000 Å.

Question 21. The best answer is C. The figure shows that atmospheric pressure increases as altitude decreases. For example, at an altitude of 100 km, atmospheric pressure is less than 0.001 millibar. At an altitude of 50 km, atmospheric pressure is between 0.1 millibar and 1 millibar. At an altitude of 0 km, atmospheric pressure equals 1,000 millibars. In general, atmospheric pressure increases with decreasing altitude. This trend occurs within each atmospheric layer as well as between atmospheric layers. The figure also shows that the average atmospheric temperature varies with atmospheric pressure. As atmospheric pressure increases within the troposphere, average atmospheric temperature increases. However, as atmospheric pressure increases within the stratosphere, average atmospheric temperature decreases.

The best answer is NOT:

A or B because there is no simple relationship between atmospheric pressure in each atmospheric layer and average atmospheric temperature. In the troposphere, as atmospheric pressure increases, average atmospheric temperature increases. However, in the stratosphere, as atmospheric pressure increases, average atmospheric temperature decreases.

D because the atmospheric pressure in each atmospheric layer increases with decreasing altitude, not with increasing altitude.

Question 22. The best answer is G. If atmospheric boundaries are at a higher than usual altitude above areas that get more direct solar radiation, then atmospheric boundaries are at a lower than usual altitude above areas that get less direct solar radiation. Thus, if Earth received less solar radiation, the tropopause, stratopause, and mesopause would decrease in altitude.

The best answer is NOT:

F because the tropopause, stratopause, and mesopause would decrease in altitude; they would not increase in altitude.

H because the tropopause and stratopause would decrease in altitude; they would not increase in altitude.

J because the stratopause and mesopause would decrease in altitude; they would not increase in altitude.

Passage V

Question 23. The best answer is A. According to Table 1, for vertically migrating shrimp species, the percent dry weight composed of protein exceeds 50% for each of the 3 species. The percent dry weight composed of lipid ranges from 14.7% to 23.8% for each of the 3 species. The percent dry weight composed of carbohydrate is less than 1% for each of the 3 species. Based on these data, vertically migrating shrimp have a higher percent content of protein than lipid.

The best answer is NOT:

B because vertically migrating shrimp have a higher percent content of protein than lipid.

C because vertically migrating shrimp have a higher percent content of lipid than carbohydrate.

D because vertically migrating shrimp have a higher percent content of protein than carbohydrate.

Question 24. The best answer is J. According to Table 1, nonmigrating shrimp species are generally found at greater ocean depths than are vertically migrating shrimp species. According to Figure 1, at greater ocean depths, the water has a lower temperature and a lower oxygen partial pressure. Thus, Table 1 and Figure 1 support the conclusion that compared to vertically migrating shrimp species, nonmigrating shrimp species can tolerate lower oxygen partial pressures.

The best answer is NOT:

F because, according to Table 1, nonmigrating shrimp species tend to have slightly less water content than do vertically migrating shrimp species.

G because, according to Table 1, nonmigrating shrimp species have a higher lipid content than do vertically migrating shrimp species.

H because nonmigrating shrimp species are generally found at greater depths than are vertically migrating shrimp species. Because temperature decreases as depth increases, nonmigrating shrimp species are found at depths that have lower water temperatures than are vertically migrating shrimp species. Thus, it is likely that nonmigrating shrimp species cannot tolerate higher water temperatures than can vertically migrating shrimp species.

Question 25. The best answer is B. The passage notes that for vertically migrating shrimp species, most of the population are found at the top of their depth range at night. If the newly discovered species were captured at night at a depth of 200 m or lower, then the top of the species' range would most likely be at a depth of 200 m. According to Figure 1, the water temperature at this depth is about 7.5°C. Below 200 m, temperature decreases. Thus, if temperature limits the range of the species, then the maximum water temperature at which these shrimp could survive is most likely 7.5°C.

The best answer is NOT:

A because the discovery of the shrimp species at a depth of 200 m indicates that the species can tolerate temperatures as high as 7.5°C. If they could not tolerate temperatures as high as 7.5°C, then they would be found at lower depths, where temperatures are lower.

C or D because the passage indicates that for vertically migrating shrimp species, most of the population are found at the top of their depth range at night. If temperature limits the range of the species, then the species cannot tolerate temperatures found at depths of less than 200 m. The temperature at 200 m is about 7.5°C. Therefore, 7.5°C is most likely the maximum water temperature at which these shrimp can survive.

Question 26. The best answer is G. According to Table 1, the protein:lipid ratios for the 4 species listed in the 4 options are: 53.4:16.4 for vm 2, 60.5:14.7 for vm 3, 36.9:36.1 for nm 1, and 35.8:49.0 for nm 3. The question indicates that shrimp that are stronger swimmers tend to have a higher protein:lipid ratio than do shrimp that are weaker swimmers. Based on this information, the shrimp with the highest protein:lipid ratio are most likely the strongest swimmers.

The best answer is NOT:

F because vm 3 has a higher protein:lipid ratio (60.5:14.7) than does vm 2 (53.4:16.4).

H because vm 3 has a higher protein:lipid ratio (60.5:14.7) than does nm 1 (36.9:36.1).

J because vm 3 has a higher protein:lipid ratio (60.5:14.7) than does nm 3 (35.8:49.0).

Question 27. The best answer is C. According to Figure 1, oxygen partial pressure is greater than or equal to 25 mm Hg at depths of approximately 400 m or less. At depths greater than 400 m, oxygen partial pressure is less than 25 mm Hg. If only oxygen partial pressure limits the range of a species, then failure to observe a species at depths greater than 400 m would support the hypothesis that the species is unable to tolerate oxygen partial pressures below 25 mm Hg. According to Table 1, the depth range of vm 2 is 10–400 m and the depth range of vm 3 is 75–400 m. Thus, vm 2 and vm 3 are not observed at depths greater than 400 m.

The best answer is NOT:

A because temperatures above 10°C occur at depths of less than approximately 100 m. At these depths, oxygen partial pressures are above 80 mm Hg. Therefore, the inability of a species to tolerate temperatures above 10°C does not suggest that the species is unable to tolerate oxygen partial pressures below 25 mm Hg.

B because no evidence is provided that relates water content and the ability to tolerate specific oxygen partial pressures.

D because depths above 100 m have oxygen partial pressures that are above 80 mm Hg. An inability to survive in depths above 100 m would suggest that these species are unable to survive in oxygen partial pressures that are above 80 mm Hg. However, it would not indicate that these species are unable to survive in oxygen partial pressures that are below 25 mm Hg.

Passage VI

Question 28. The best answer is H. According to Student 1, gases from burning wood are less dense than the air that surrounds the fireplace.

The best answer is NOT:

F because, according to Student 1, gases from burning wood are hotter than the surrounding air and the molecules of hotter gases have a higher average speed than do the molecules of cooler gases.

G because, according to Student 1, gases from burning wood are hotter than the surrounding air and the average distance between molecules is greater for hotter gases than for cooler gases.

J because, according to Student 1, gases from burning wood are hotter than the surrounding air. Thus, they have a higher temperature.

Question 29. The best answer is B. Both Students 1 and 2 assert that as chimney height increases, efficiency increases. Therefore, according to both students, if Chimneys X and Y have the same temperature difference between the inside and the outside and Chimney Y is more efficient than Chimney X, then Chimney Y must be taller.

The best answer is NOT:

A because both students would conclude that Chimney Y is taller.

C because Student 1 would conclude that Chimney Y is taller.

D because Student 2 would conclude that Chimney Y is taller.

Question 30. The best answer is F. According to Student 2, smoke rises because wind blows across the top of the chimney. If the air at the top of the chimney is not moving, then the smoke from burning wood will not rise up the chimney. In contrast, Student 1 does not suggest that air movement above a chimney affects the rising of smoke. Student 1 asserts that smoke rises because of the buoyant force on hot gases inside the chimney. The buoyant force will be present whether or not wind blows across the chimney.

The best answer is NOT:

G or H because Student 2 would not predict that smoke from burning wood will rise up the chimney from a fireplace on a day when the air at the top of the chimney is not moving.

J because Student 1 would predict that smoke from burning wood will rise up the chimney from a fireplace on a day when the air at the top of the chimney is not moving.

Question 31. The best answer is C. According to Student 1, gases from burning wood rise because they are less dense than the air that surrounds the fireplace. Student 1 also asserts that the gases from burning wood are less dense than the air that surrounds the fireplace because the gases from the burning wood are hotter than the air that surrounds the fireplace. Thus, Student 1 would likely predict that if the air in the fireplace rises, then this air is less dense than the air that surrounds the fireplace. Student 1 would also conclude that the air in the fireplace is less dense than the air that surrounds the fireplace because the air in the fireplace is hotter than the air that surrounds the fireplace.

The best answer is NOT:

A because although Student 1 argues that the gases from the burning wood are hotter than the air that surrounds the fireplace, Student 1 does not suggest that other gases (air) in the fireplace must be hotter than the gases from the burning wood.

B or D because Student 1 argues that hotter gases rise. Thus, cooler gases do not rise.

Question 32. The best answer is H. Student 1 argues that heating a parcel of air makes it less dense. As the density of the parcel decreases, the buoyant force on the parcel increases. If the upward buoyant force exceeds the downward gravitational force, the parcel rises. Based on this line of reasoning, if the air inside a hot-air balloon cooled, then the density of the air would increase. As a result, the upward buoyant force on the balloon and its inside air would decrease. If the downward gravitational force exceeded the upward buoyant force, the balloon and its inside air would descend.

The best answer is NOT:

F or J because the buoyant force is upward and the force of gravity is downward.

G because for the balloon to descend, the downward force of gravity acting on the balloon and its inside air must be greater than the upward buoyant force on the balloon and its inside air.

Question 33. The best answer is A. According to Student 1, the average speed of the gas molecules that make up a gas increases as the average temperature of the gas increases. In addition, as the average speed of gas molecules increases, the average distance between adjacent gas molecules increases. As a result, the density of the gas decreases. Thus, if the temperature of a gas decreases, then the density of the gas increases, the average speed of the gas molecules decreases, and the average distance between adjacent gas molecules decreases.

The best answer is NOT:

B because the temperature of the gases decreases as the gases lose heat.

C because the average speed of the gas molecules decreases as the gases lose heat.

D because the average distance between adjacent gas molecules decreases as the gases lose heat.

Question 34. The best answer is F. According to Student 2, the gases inside a chimney rise because air blowing over the top of the chimney results in a lower pressure at the top of the chimney than at the bottom of the chimney. Likewise, if the air on top of a wing moves faster than the air below the wing, the pressure above the wings is less than the pressure below the wings. As a result, there is an upward force on the wings, keeping the airplane up in the air.

The best answer is NOT:

G because if the air moves at a higher speed below the wings than above the wings, then the pressure above the wings will be greater than the pressure below the wings. As a result, there will be a downward force on the wings, forcing the airplane down.

H or J because Student 2's explanation does not provide a means for evaluating the relative impact of the speed of the air in front of the wings and the speed of the air behind the wings.

Passage VII

Question 35. The best answer is C. Figure 1 shows that the corrected absorbance was directly proportional to the concentration of NO_2^-. Thus, if the concentration of NO_2^- doubled, the corrected absorbance doubled. For example, as the concentration of NO_2^- increased from 4.0 ppm to 8.0 ppm, the corrected absorbance increased from 0.6 to 1.2.

The best answer is NOT:

A, B, or D because the corrected absorbance was directly proportional to the concentration of NO_2^-. Thus, a doubling of the NO_2^- concentration will result in a doubling of the corrected absorbance.

Question 36. The best answer is J. In Experiment 1, the corrected absorbance was directly proportional to the concentration of NO_2^-. Therefore, the meat with the highest corrected absorbance had the highest concentration of NO_2^- and the meat with the lowest corrected absorbance had the lowest concentration of NO_2^-. According to the information provided, the corrected absorbance of bacon was 0.773; of pastrami, 0.603; and of bologna, 0.561.

The best answer is NOT:

F, G, or H because bacon had the highest corrected absorbance, so bacon has the highest concentration of NO_2^-. Therefore, bacon should be listed before pastrami and bologna.

Question 37. The best answer is B. According to Table 1, an NO_2^- concentration of 1.0 ppm resulted in a corrected absorbance of 0.153 and an NO_2^- concentration of 2.0 ppm resulted in a corrected absorbance of 0.302. Thus, an NO_2^- concentration of 1.5 ppm should result in a corrected absorbance greater than 0.153 and less than 0.302. In addition, Table 1 shows that the corrected absorbance was directly proportional to the concentration of NO_2^-. Based on this trend, the corrected absorbance for an NO_2^- concentration of 1.5 ppm should be about halfway between 0.153 and 0.302, or approximately 0.228.

The best answer is NOT:

A because 0.23 is closer to 0.228 than is 0.15.

C because 0.23 is closer to 0.228 than is 0.30.

D because 0.23 is closer to 0.228 than is 0.36.

Question 38. The best answer is J. According to the passage, a colorimeter is a device that measures how much light of a selected wavelength is absorbed by a sample. The colorimeter is typically set so that the wavelength measured corresponds to the wavelength associated with the color of the solution. If the color of the solution differed, then the wavelength measured would have to be changed. Apart from changing the wavelength measured, all other experimental procedures would be held constant.

The best answer is NOT:

F because the coloring agent must be added to the sample solutions before the absorbance of each solution can be determined. If the coloring agent is not added to the sample solutions, then all of the sample solutions would have the same absorbance and the NO_2^- concentration could not be determined.

G because the question supposes that Experiments 1 and 2 were repeated using a different coloring agent. Thus, the original coloring agent would not be added to the blank solution or to the samples.

H because the absorbances were corrected by subtracting the absorbance of the blank solution from each measured absorbance. This ensures that the corrected absorbance only reflects the concentration of the colored compound that is formed between the NO_2^- and the coloring agent.

Question 39. The best answer is A. Table 1 indicates that the measured absorbances of the NO_2^- solutions were higher than the corrected absorbances. To get the corrected absorbance, the absorbance of the blank was subtracted from each measured absorbance. Similarly, the absorbance for the blank is subtracted from each of the measured absorbances for the meats. So the measured absorbance is always higher than the corrected absorbance.

The best answer is NOT:

B, C, or D because for each of the meats, to get the corrected absorbance, the absorbance of the blank was subtracted from the measured absorbance. Because the absorbance of the blank was greater than zero, the measured absorbance was higher than the corrected absorbance. Thus, the measured absorbance would not be lower than or the same as the corrected absorbance for any of the meats.

Question 40. The best answer is F. If the water-soluble substances absorbed light at the wavelength being measured, then the measured absorbance would be higher. This would occur because the water-soluble substances would absorb light. As a result, the solution would appear to contain more NO_2^- than had actually been present in the solution. Therefore, the measured NO_2^- concentration would be higher than if the solution did not contain the water-soluble substances.

The best answer is NOT:

G or J because the water-soluble substances would increase the absorbance. Therefore, the measured NO_2^- concentration would be higher than the actual NO_2^- concentration for each of the meats. The measured NO_2^- concentration would not be lower than the actual NO_2^- concentration for any of the meats.

H because the water-soluble substance would increase the absorbance. Therefore, the measured NO_2^- concentration would be higher than the actual NO_2^- concentration for each of the meats. The measured NO_2^- concentration would not be the same as the actual NO_2^- concentration for any of the meats.

The ACT® *Sample Answer Sheet*

A — **NAME, MAILING ADDRESS, AND TELEPHONE**
(Please print.)

Last Name   First Name   MI (Middle Initial)

House Number & Street (Apt. No.); or PO Box & No.; or RR & No.

City   State/Province   ZIP/Postal Code

Area Code   Number   Country

ACT, Inc.—Confidential Restricted when data present.

ALL examinees must complete block A – please print.

REGISTERED examinees **MUST complete blocks B, C, and D.** Find the MATCHING INFORMATION on your admission ticket and enter it EXACTLY the same way, even if any of the information is missing or incorrect. Fill in the corresponding ovals. If you do not complete these blocks to match your admission ticket EXACTLY, your scores will be **delayed up to 8 weeks.** Leave blocks E and F blank.

STANDBY examinees **MUST complete blocks B, D, and F.** Enter your information in blocks B and D and fill in the corresponding ovals. Leave block C blank. **For block E,** if you provided your SSN when you created your Web account or completed your standby folder, enter it here. The SSN will be used to help match this document to your registration information and will be included on reports to your college choices. If you did not provide it earlier, do not know it, or do not wish to provide it, leave block E blank. Be sure to fill in the oval in block F.

Do NOT mark in this shaded area.

B — **MATCH NAME**
(First 5 letters of last name)

C — **MATCH NUMBER**
(Registered examinees only)

D — **DATE OF BIRTH**

	Month	Day	Year

Jan.
Feb.
March
April
May
June
July
Aug.
Sept.
Oct.
Nov.
Dec.

↓ STANDBY TESTING ONLY ↓

E — **SOCIAL SECURITY NUMBER**
(Standby examinees only)

F — **STANDBY TESTING**

Fill in the oval below ONLY if you turned in a standby registration at the test center today.

○ Yes, I am testing as a standby.

USE A SOFT LEAD NO. 2 PENCIL ONLY.
(Do NOT use a mechanical pencil, ink, ballpoint, correction fluid, or felt-tip pen.)

EXAMINEE STATEMENT AND SIGNATURE

1. Read the following **Statement:** By submitting this answer sheet, I agree to the terms and conditions set forth in the ACT registration booklet or website for this exam, including the arbitration and dispute remedy provisions. I understand that ACT owns the test questions and responses and affirm that I will not share any test questions or responses with anyone by any form of communication.

2. Copy the **Certification** shown below (only the text in italics) on the lines provided. Write in your normal handwriting.

   Certification: *I agree to the Statement above and certify that I am the person whose name and address appear on this form.*

3. Sign your name as you would any official document and enter today's date.

Your Signature   Today's Date

Marking Directions: Mark only **one** oval for each question. Fill in response completely. Erase errors cleanly without smudging.

Correct mark: ○ ● ○ ○

- -

Do NOT use these *incorrect* or *bad* marks.

Incorrect marks: ⊘ ⊗ ⊖ ⊙
Overlapping mark: ○ ○ ◐
Cross-out mark: ○ ✕ ○
Smudged erasure: ○ ● ○
Mark is too light: ◐ ○ ○

BOOKLET NUMBER

① ① ① ① ① ①
② ② ② ② ② ②
③ ③ ③ ③ ③ ③
④ ④ ④ ④ ④ ④
⑤ ⑤ ⑤ ⑤ ⑤ ⑤
⑥ ⑥ ⑥ ⑥ ⑥ ⑥
⑦ ⑦ ⑦ ⑦ ⑦ ⑦
⑧ ⑧ ⑧ ⑧ ⑧ ⑧
⑨ ⑨ ⑨ ⑨ ⑨ ⑨
⓪ ⓪ ⓪ ⓪ ⓪ ⓪

FORM

Print your 3-character **Test Form** in the boxes above and fill in the corresponding oval at the right.

BE SURE TO FILL IN THE CORRECT FORM OVAL.

○ 1MC   ○ 2MC   ○ 3MC   ○ 4MC
○ 5MC

TEST 1

1 Ⓐ Ⓑ Ⓒ Ⓓ	14 Ⓕ Ⓖ Ⓗ Ⓙ	27 Ⓐ Ⓑ Ⓒ Ⓓ	40 Ⓕ Ⓖ Ⓗ Ⓙ	53 Ⓐ Ⓑ Ⓒ Ⓓ	66 Ⓕ Ⓖ Ⓗ Ⓙ
2 Ⓕ Ⓖ Ⓗ Ⓙ	15 Ⓐ Ⓑ Ⓒ Ⓓ	28 Ⓕ Ⓖ Ⓗ Ⓙ	41 Ⓐ Ⓑ Ⓒ Ⓓ	54 Ⓕ Ⓖ Ⓗ Ⓙ	67 Ⓐ Ⓑ Ⓒ Ⓓ
3 Ⓐ Ⓑ Ⓒ Ⓓ	16 Ⓕ Ⓖ Ⓗ Ⓙ	29 Ⓐ Ⓑ Ⓒ Ⓓ	42 Ⓕ Ⓖ Ⓗ Ⓙ	55 Ⓐ Ⓑ Ⓒ Ⓓ	68 Ⓕ Ⓖ Ⓗ Ⓙ
4 Ⓕ Ⓖ Ⓗ Ⓙ	17 Ⓐ Ⓑ Ⓒ Ⓓ	30 Ⓕ Ⓖ Ⓗ Ⓙ	43 Ⓐ Ⓑ Ⓒ Ⓓ	56 Ⓕ Ⓖ Ⓗ Ⓙ	69 Ⓐ Ⓑ Ⓒ Ⓓ
5 Ⓐ Ⓑ Ⓒ Ⓓ	18 Ⓕ Ⓖ Ⓗ Ⓙ	31 Ⓐ Ⓑ Ⓒ Ⓓ	44 Ⓕ Ⓖ Ⓗ Ⓙ	57 Ⓐ Ⓑ Ⓒ Ⓓ	70 Ⓕ Ⓖ Ⓗ Ⓙ
6 Ⓕ Ⓖ Ⓗ Ⓙ	19 Ⓐ Ⓑ Ⓒ Ⓓ	32 Ⓕ Ⓖ Ⓗ Ⓙ	45 Ⓐ Ⓑ Ⓒ Ⓓ	58 Ⓕ Ⓖ Ⓗ Ⓙ	71 Ⓐ Ⓑ Ⓒ Ⓓ
7 Ⓐ Ⓑ Ⓒ Ⓓ	20 Ⓕ Ⓖ Ⓗ Ⓙ	33 Ⓐ Ⓑ Ⓒ Ⓓ	46 Ⓕ Ⓖ Ⓗ Ⓙ	59 Ⓐ Ⓑ Ⓒ Ⓓ	72 Ⓕ Ⓖ Ⓗ Ⓙ
8 Ⓕ Ⓖ Ⓗ Ⓙ	21 Ⓐ Ⓑ Ⓒ Ⓓ	34 Ⓕ Ⓖ Ⓗ Ⓙ	47 Ⓐ Ⓑ Ⓒ Ⓓ	60 Ⓕ Ⓖ Ⓗ Ⓙ	73 Ⓐ Ⓑ Ⓒ Ⓓ
9 Ⓐ Ⓑ Ⓒ Ⓓ	22 Ⓕ Ⓖ Ⓗ Ⓙ	35 Ⓐ Ⓑ Ⓒ Ⓓ	48 Ⓕ Ⓖ Ⓗ Ⓙ	61 Ⓐ Ⓑ Ⓒ Ⓓ	74 Ⓕ Ⓖ Ⓗ Ⓙ
10 Ⓕ Ⓖ Ⓗ Ⓙ	23 Ⓐ Ⓑ Ⓒ Ⓓ	36 Ⓕ Ⓖ Ⓗ Ⓙ	49 Ⓐ Ⓑ Ⓒ Ⓓ	62 Ⓕ Ⓖ Ⓗ Ⓙ	75 Ⓐ Ⓑ Ⓒ Ⓓ
11 Ⓐ Ⓑ Ⓒ Ⓓ	24 Ⓕ Ⓖ Ⓗ Ⓙ	37 Ⓐ Ⓑ Ⓒ Ⓓ	50 Ⓕ Ⓖ Ⓗ Ⓙ	63 Ⓐ Ⓑ Ⓒ Ⓓ	
12 Ⓕ Ⓖ Ⓗ Ⓙ	25 Ⓐ Ⓑ Ⓒ Ⓓ	38 Ⓕ Ⓖ Ⓗ Ⓙ	51 Ⓐ Ⓑ Ⓒ Ⓓ	64 Ⓕ Ⓖ Ⓗ Ⓙ	
13 Ⓐ Ⓑ Ⓒ Ⓓ	26 Ⓕ Ⓖ Ⓗ Ⓙ	39 Ⓐ Ⓑ Ⓒ Ⓓ	52 Ⓕ Ⓖ Ⓗ Ⓙ	65 Ⓐ Ⓑ Ⓒ Ⓓ	

TEST 2

1 Ⓐ Ⓑ Ⓒ Ⓓ Ⓔ	11 Ⓐ Ⓑ Ⓒ Ⓓ Ⓔ	21 Ⓐ Ⓑ Ⓒ Ⓓ Ⓔ	31 Ⓐ Ⓑ Ⓒ Ⓓ Ⓔ	41 Ⓐ Ⓑ Ⓒ Ⓓ Ⓔ	51 Ⓐ Ⓑ Ⓒ Ⓓ Ⓔ
2 Ⓕ Ⓖ Ⓗ Ⓙ Ⓚ	12 Ⓕ Ⓖ Ⓗ Ⓙ Ⓚ	22 Ⓕ Ⓖ Ⓗ Ⓙ Ⓚ	32 Ⓕ Ⓖ Ⓗ Ⓙ Ⓚ	42 Ⓕ Ⓖ Ⓗ Ⓙ Ⓚ	52 Ⓕ Ⓖ Ⓗ Ⓙ Ⓚ
3 Ⓐ Ⓑ Ⓒ Ⓓ Ⓔ	13 Ⓐ Ⓑ Ⓒ Ⓓ Ⓔ	23 Ⓐ Ⓑ Ⓒ Ⓓ Ⓔ	33 Ⓐ Ⓑ Ⓒ Ⓓ Ⓔ	43 Ⓐ Ⓑ Ⓒ Ⓓ Ⓔ	53 Ⓐ Ⓑ Ⓒ Ⓓ Ⓔ
4 Ⓕ Ⓖ Ⓗ Ⓙ Ⓚ	14 Ⓕ Ⓖ Ⓗ Ⓙ Ⓚ	24 Ⓕ Ⓖ Ⓗ Ⓙ Ⓚ	34 Ⓕ Ⓖ Ⓗ Ⓙ Ⓚ	44 Ⓕ Ⓖ Ⓗ Ⓙ Ⓚ	54 Ⓕ Ⓖ Ⓗ Ⓙ Ⓚ
5 Ⓐ Ⓑ Ⓒ Ⓓ Ⓔ	15 Ⓐ Ⓑ Ⓒ Ⓓ Ⓔ	25 Ⓐ Ⓑ Ⓒ Ⓓ Ⓔ	35 Ⓐ Ⓑ Ⓒ Ⓓ Ⓔ	45 Ⓐ Ⓑ Ⓒ Ⓓ Ⓔ	55 Ⓐ Ⓑ Ⓒ Ⓓ Ⓔ
6 Ⓕ Ⓖ Ⓗ Ⓙ Ⓚ	16 Ⓕ Ⓖ Ⓗ Ⓙ Ⓚ	26 Ⓕ Ⓖ Ⓗ Ⓙ Ⓚ	36 Ⓕ Ⓖ Ⓗ Ⓙ Ⓚ	46 Ⓕ Ⓖ Ⓗ Ⓙ Ⓚ	56 Ⓕ Ⓖ Ⓗ Ⓙ Ⓚ
7 Ⓐ Ⓑ Ⓒ Ⓓ Ⓔ	17 Ⓐ Ⓑ Ⓒ Ⓓ Ⓔ	27 Ⓐ Ⓑ Ⓒ Ⓓ Ⓔ	37 Ⓐ Ⓑ Ⓒ Ⓓ Ⓔ	47 Ⓐ Ⓑ Ⓒ Ⓓ Ⓔ	57 Ⓐ Ⓑ Ⓒ Ⓓ Ⓔ
8 Ⓕ Ⓖ Ⓗ Ⓙ Ⓚ	18 Ⓕ Ⓖ Ⓗ Ⓙ Ⓚ	28 Ⓕ Ⓖ Ⓗ Ⓙ Ⓚ	38 Ⓕ Ⓖ Ⓗ Ⓙ Ⓚ	48 Ⓕ Ⓖ Ⓗ Ⓙ Ⓚ	58 Ⓕ Ⓖ Ⓗ Ⓙ Ⓚ
9 Ⓐ Ⓑ Ⓒ Ⓓ Ⓔ	19 Ⓐ Ⓑ Ⓒ Ⓓ Ⓔ	29 Ⓐ Ⓑ Ⓒ Ⓓ Ⓔ	39 Ⓐ Ⓑ Ⓒ Ⓓ Ⓔ	49 Ⓐ Ⓑ Ⓒ Ⓓ Ⓔ	59 Ⓐ Ⓑ Ⓒ Ⓓ Ⓔ
10 Ⓕ Ⓖ Ⓗ Ⓙ Ⓚ	20 Ⓕ Ⓖ Ⓗ Ⓙ Ⓚ	30 Ⓕ Ⓖ Ⓗ Ⓙ Ⓚ	40 Ⓕ Ⓖ Ⓗ Ⓙ Ⓚ	50 Ⓕ Ⓖ Ⓗ Ⓙ Ⓚ	60 Ⓕ Ⓖ Ⓗ Ⓙ Ⓚ

TEST 3

1 Ⓐ Ⓑ Ⓒ Ⓓ	8 Ⓕ Ⓖ Ⓗ Ⓙ	15 Ⓐ Ⓑ Ⓒ Ⓓ	22 Ⓕ Ⓖ Ⓗ Ⓙ	29 Ⓐ Ⓑ Ⓒ Ⓓ	36 Ⓕ Ⓖ Ⓗ Ⓙ
2 Ⓕ Ⓖ Ⓗ Ⓙ	9 Ⓐ Ⓑ Ⓒ Ⓓ	16 Ⓕ Ⓖ Ⓗ Ⓙ	23 Ⓐ Ⓑ Ⓒ Ⓓ	30 Ⓕ Ⓖ Ⓗ Ⓙ	37 Ⓐ Ⓑ Ⓒ Ⓓ
3 Ⓐ Ⓑ Ⓒ Ⓓ	10 Ⓕ Ⓖ Ⓗ Ⓙ	17 Ⓐ Ⓑ Ⓒ Ⓓ	24 Ⓕ Ⓖ Ⓗ Ⓙ	31 Ⓐ Ⓑ Ⓒ Ⓓ	38 Ⓕ Ⓖ Ⓗ Ⓙ
4 Ⓕ Ⓖ Ⓗ Ⓙ	11 Ⓐ Ⓑ Ⓒ Ⓓ	18 Ⓕ Ⓖ Ⓗ Ⓙ	25 Ⓐ Ⓑ Ⓒ Ⓓ	32 Ⓕ Ⓖ Ⓗ Ⓙ	39 Ⓐ Ⓑ Ⓒ Ⓓ
5 Ⓐ Ⓑ Ⓒ Ⓓ	12 Ⓕ Ⓖ Ⓗ Ⓙ	19 Ⓐ Ⓑ Ⓒ Ⓓ	26 Ⓕ Ⓖ Ⓗ Ⓙ	33 Ⓐ Ⓑ Ⓒ Ⓓ	40 Ⓕ Ⓖ Ⓗ Ⓙ
6 Ⓕ Ⓖ Ⓗ Ⓙ	13 Ⓐ Ⓑ Ⓒ Ⓓ	20 Ⓕ Ⓖ Ⓗ Ⓙ	27 Ⓐ Ⓑ Ⓒ Ⓓ	34 Ⓕ Ⓖ Ⓗ Ⓙ	
7 Ⓐ Ⓑ Ⓒ Ⓓ	14 Ⓕ Ⓖ Ⓗ Ⓙ	21 Ⓐ Ⓑ Ⓒ Ⓓ	28 Ⓕ Ⓖ Ⓗ Ⓙ	35 Ⓐ Ⓑ Ⓒ Ⓓ	

TEST 4

1 Ⓐ Ⓑ Ⓒ Ⓓ	8 Ⓕ Ⓖ Ⓗ Ⓙ	15 Ⓐ Ⓑ Ⓒ Ⓓ	22 Ⓕ Ⓖ Ⓗ Ⓙ	29 Ⓐ Ⓑ Ⓒ Ⓓ	36 Ⓕ Ⓖ Ⓗ Ⓙ
2 Ⓕ Ⓖ Ⓗ Ⓙ	9 Ⓐ Ⓑ Ⓒ Ⓓ	16 Ⓕ Ⓖ Ⓗ Ⓙ	23 Ⓐ Ⓑ Ⓒ Ⓓ	30 Ⓕ Ⓖ Ⓗ Ⓙ	37 Ⓐ Ⓑ Ⓒ Ⓓ
3 Ⓐ Ⓑ Ⓒ Ⓓ	10 Ⓕ Ⓖ Ⓗ Ⓙ	17 Ⓐ Ⓑ Ⓒ Ⓓ	24 Ⓕ Ⓖ Ⓗ Ⓙ	31 Ⓐ Ⓑ Ⓒ Ⓓ	38 Ⓕ Ⓖ Ⓗ Ⓙ
4 Ⓕ Ⓖ Ⓗ Ⓙ	11 Ⓐ Ⓑ Ⓒ Ⓓ	18 Ⓕ Ⓖ Ⓗ Ⓙ	25 Ⓐ Ⓑ Ⓒ Ⓓ	32 Ⓕ Ⓖ Ⓗ Ⓙ	39 Ⓐ Ⓑ Ⓒ Ⓓ
5 Ⓐ Ⓑ Ⓒ Ⓓ	12 Ⓕ Ⓖ Ⓗ Ⓙ	19 Ⓐ Ⓑ Ⓒ Ⓓ	26 Ⓕ Ⓖ Ⓗ Ⓙ	33 Ⓐ Ⓑ Ⓒ Ⓓ	40 Ⓕ Ⓖ Ⓗ Ⓙ
6 Ⓕ Ⓖ Ⓗ Ⓙ	13 Ⓐ Ⓑ Ⓒ Ⓓ	20 Ⓕ Ⓖ Ⓗ Ⓙ	27 Ⓐ Ⓑ Ⓒ Ⓓ	34 Ⓕ Ⓖ Ⓗ Ⓙ	
7 Ⓐ Ⓑ Ⓒ Ⓓ	14 Ⓕ Ⓖ Ⓗ Ⓙ	21 Ⓐ Ⓑ Ⓒ Ⓓ	28 Ⓕ Ⓖ Ⓗ Ⓙ	35 Ⓐ Ⓑ Ⓒ Ⓓ	

The **ACT**®

The ACT® *Sample Answer Sheet*

A — NAME, MAILING ADDRESS, AND TELEPHONE
(Please print.)

Last Name   First Name   MI (Middle Initial)

House Number & Street (Apt. No.); or PO Box & No.; or RR & No.

City   State/Province   ZIP/Postal Code

Area Code   Number   Country

ACT, Inc.—Confidential Restricted when data present.

ALL examinees must complete block A – please print.

REGISTERED examinees **MUST complete blocks B, C, and D.** Find the MATCHING INFORMATION on your admission ticket and enter it EXACTLY the same way, even if any of the information is missing or incorrect. Fill in the corresponding ovals. If you do not complete these blocks to match your admission ticket EXACTLY, your scores will be **delayed up to 8 weeks.** Leave blocks E and F blank.

STANDBY examinees **MUST complete blocks B, D, and F.** Enter your information in blocks B and D and fill in the corresponding ovals. Leave block C blank. **For block E,** if you provided your SSN when you created your Web account or completed your standby folder, enter it here. The SSN will be used to help match this document to your registration information and will be included on reports to your college choices. If you did not provide it earlier, do not know it, or do not wish to provide it, leave block E blank. Be sure to fill in the oval in block F.

Do NOT mark in this shaded area.

B — MATCH NAME
(First 5 letters of last name)

C — MATCH NUMBER
(Registered examinees only)

D — DATE OF BIRTH

| Month | Day | Year |

○ Jan.
○ Feb.
○ March
○ April
○ May
○ June
○ July
○ Aug.
○ Sept.
○ Oct.
○ Nov.
○ Dec.

↓ STANDBY TESTING ONLY ↓

E — SOCIAL SECURITY NUMBER
(Standby examinees only)

F — STANDBY TESTING

Fill in the oval below ONLY if you turned in a standby registration at the test center today.

○ Yes, I am testing as a standby.

USE A SOFT LEAD NO. 2 PENCIL ONLY.
(Do NOT use a mechanical pencil, ink, ballpoint, correction fluid, or felt-tip pen.)

EXAMINEE STATEMENT AND SIGNATURE

1. Read the following **Statement:** By submitting this answer sheet, I agree to the terms and conditions set forth in the ACT registration booklet or website for this exam, including the arbitration and dispute remedy provisions. I understand that ACT owns the test questions and responses and affirm that I will not share any test questions or responses with anyone by any form of communication.

2. Copy the **Certification** shown below (only the text in italics) on the lines provided. Write in your normal handwriting.

   Certification: *I agree to the Statement above and certify that I am the person whose name and address appear on this form.*

   _____

   _____

   _____

   _____

3. Sign your name as you would any official document and enter today's date.

   _____   _____
   Your Signature   Today's Date

Marking Directions: Mark only **one** oval for each question. Fill in response completely. Erase errors cleanly without smudging.

Correct mark: ○ ● ○ ○

Do NOT use these *incorrect* or *bad* **marks.**

Incorrect marks: ⊘ ⊗ ○ ⊙
Overlapping mark: ○ ◉ ●
Cross-out mark: ● ⊗ ○ ○
Smudged erasure: ● ○ ◐ ◐
Mark is too light: ◌ ○ ○ ○

BOOKLET NUMBER

① ① ① ① ① ①
② ② ② ② ② ②
③ ③ ③ ③ ③ ③
④ ④ ④ ④ ④ ④
⑤ ⑤ ⑤ ⑤ ⑤ ⑤
⑥ ⑥ ⑥ ⑥ ⑥ ⑥
⑦ ⑦ ⑦ ⑦ ⑦ ⑦
⑧ ⑧ ⑧ ⑧ ⑧ ⑧
⑨ ⑨ ⑨ ⑨ ⑨ ⑨
⓪ ⓪ ⓪ ⓪ ⓪ ⓪

FORM

Print your 3-character **Test Form** in the boxes above and fill in the corresponding oval at the right.

BE SURE TO FILL IN THE CORRECT FORM OVAL.
○ 1MC   ○ 2MC   ○ 3MC   ○ 4MC
○ 5MC

TEST 1

(Answer grid, questions 1–75, options A B C D / F G H J)

TEST 2

(Answer grid, questions 1–60, options A B C D E / F G H J K)

TEST 3

(Answer grid, questions 1–40, options A B C D / F G H J)

TEST 4

(Answer grid, questions 1–40, options A B C D / F G H J)

The **ACT**

080659

Practice Test 2

Examinee Agreement and Signature: By testing today, I agree to the terms and conditions set forth in the ACT registration booklet or website for this exam, including the provisions about prohibited behaviors. I also certify that I am the person whose signature appears below.

Today's Date: _____

Your Signature: _____

Print Your Name Here: _____

Your Date of Birth:

☐☐ – ☐☐ – ☐☐☐☐
Month   Day   Year

Form 2MC

The ACT® 2011|2012

Directions

This booklet contains tests in English, Mathematics, Reading, and Science. These tests measure skills and abilities highly related to high school course work and success in college. *CALCULATORS MAY BE USED ON THE MATHEMATICS TEST ONLY.*

The questions in each test are numbered, and the suggested answers for each question are lettered. On the answer document, the rows of ovals are numbered to match the questions, and the ovals in each row are lettered to correspond to the suggested answers.

For each question, first decide which answer is best. Next, locate on the answer document the row of ovals numbered the same as the question. Then, locate the oval in that row lettered the same as your answer. Finally, fill in the oval completely. Use a soft lead pencil and make your marks heavy and black. *DO NOT USE INK OR A MECHANICAL PENCIL.*

Mark only one answer to each question. If you change your mind about an answer, erase your first mark thoroughly before marking your new answer. For each question, make certain that you mark in the row of ovals with the same number as the question.

Only responses marked on your answer document will be scored. Your score on each test will be based only on the number of questions you answer correctly during the time allowed for that test. You will NOT be penalized for guessing. *IT IS TO YOUR ADVANTAGE TO ANSWER EVERY QUESTION EVEN IF YOU MUST GUESS.*

You may work on each test ONLY when your test supervisor tells you to do so. If you finish a test before time is called for that test, you should use the time remaining to reconsider questions you are uncertain about in that test. You may NOT look back to a test on which time has already been called, and you may NOT go ahead to another test. To do so will disqualify you from the examination.

Lay your pencil down immediately when time is called at the end of each test. You may NOT for any reason fill in or alter ovals for a test after time is called for that test. To do so will disqualify you from the examination.

Do not fold or tear the pages of your test booklet.

**DO NOT OPEN THIS BOOKLET
UNTIL TOLD TO DO SO.**

ENGLISH TEST
45 Minutes—75 Questions

DIRECTIONS: In the five passages that follow, certain words and phrases are underlined and numbered. In the right-hand column, you will find alternatives for the underlined part. In most cases, you are to choose the one that best expresses the idea, makes the statement appropriate for standard written English, or is worded most consistently with the style and tone of the passage as a whole. If you think the original version is best, choose "NO CHANGE." In some cases, you will find in the right-hand column a question about the underlined part. You are to choose the best answer to the question.

You will also find questions about a section of the passage, or about the passage as a whole. These questions do not refer to an underlined portion of the passage, but rather are identified by a number or numbers in a box.

For each question, choose the alternative you consider best and fill in the corresponding oval on your answer document. Read each passage through once before you begin to answer the questions that accompany it. For many of the questions, you must read several sentences beyond the question to determine the answer. Be sure that you have read far enough ahead each time you choose an alternative.

PASSAGE I

Grandpa's Remote Control

[1]

My grandfather is not known for embracing technological change. He still drives his '59 Chevy
<u>technological change. He still drives his '59 Chevy</u>
₁

Impala. (He <u>says, he</u> can't imagine needing frivolous
₂
options like automatic transmission or power steering.)

So, when he <u>has went</u> to buy a new color television—
₃

<u>owing to the knowledge that</u> his old black-and-white
₄
model had finally quit—and the salesperson tried to talk him into buying a model with a remote control, he resisted. He said that he had two good legs and was perfectly capable of getting out of his chair. [5]

[2]

However, the salesperson was persistent and, appealing to Grandpa's TV-viewing habits, described the

1. **A.** NO CHANGE
   B. change he still drives
   C. change still driving,
   D. change, and still driving

2. **F.** NO CHANGE
   G. says
   H. says, that
   J. says, that,

3. **A.** NO CHANGE
   B. had went
   C. went
   D. goes

4. **F.** NO CHANGE
   G. due to the understandable fact that
   H. because
   J. so

5. Given that all are true, which of the following additions to the preceding sentence (replacing "chair.") would be most relevant?

   A. chair that was made of black leather.
   B. chair when he wanted to change the channel.
   C. chair by the south window in the family room.
   D. chair where he liked to sit.

GO ON TO THE NEXT PAGE.

various functions on the remote. However, my grandpa

could punch in the time, and the channel of his favorite

daily news program, and the TV would turn on that

program at the proper time. In the end, Grandpa did buy

the remote, and it has since become something he uses all

the time.

[3]

Grandpa is intrigued by the various uses for that

remote. He has confided in me that the volume control is

perfect for turning up the sound whenever Grandma asks

him to take out the garbage. For example, he says, the

button that mutes the sound lets him cut them off in

midsentence.

[4]

Grandpa's favorite feature on the remote is the sleep

function. This option automatically turns the TV off after a

preset amount of time, which is very convenient when he

falls asleep while watching a show. For him, Grandpa says

what he wants his TV doing, even when he sleeps, is to

know a source of both pleasure and power.

[5]

[1] As for the programming function, Grandpa not

only uses it for the news but also for playing jokes on his

6. **F.** NO CHANGE
   G. Additionally, Grandpa
   H. Conversely, my grandpa
   J. Grandpa

7. **A.** NO CHANGE
   B. time and, the channel,
   C. time and the channel
   D. time and the channel,

8. **F.** NO CHANGE
   G. To illustrate,
   H. On the one hand,
   J. On the other hand,

9. **A.** NO CHANGE
   B. advertisers
   C. it
   D. its function

10. **F.** NO CHANGE
    G. convenient, when
    H. convenient. When
    J. convenient; when

11. **A.** NO CHANGE
    B. Even when he sleeps, Grandpa says that to know
       his TV is doing what he wants is a source of both
       pleasure and power for him.
    C. Doing what he wants, even when he sleeps, is to
       know his TV is a source of both pleasure and
       power for him, Grandpa says.
    D. Grandpa says that to know his TV is doing what he
       wants, even when he sleeps, is a source of both
       pleasure and power for him.

GO ON TO THE NEXT PAGE.

youngest grandchildren. [2] Explaining to the unsuspecting child that he has a remote control implanted in his little finger, <u>Grandpa points</u> his finger at the TV and, to the
₁₂
child's amazement, seemingly turns it on. [3] I suppose Grandpa hasn't learned all the possible uses of the remote control, <u>but I don't doubt he will continue to discover new</u>
₁₃
<u>and creative ways of using it.</u> [14]
₁₃

12. **F.** NO CHANGE
    G. pointing
    H. having pointed
    J. Grandpa has pointed

13. Which of the choices would provide an ending most consistent with the essay as a whole?
    A. NO CHANGE
    B. and he probably won't bother learning them either.
    C. so the salesperson should explain how to interpret the 200-page manual.
    D. and Grandma gratefully acknowledges this.

14. Upon reviewing Paragraph 5 and realizing that some information has been left out, the writer composes the following sentence:

> He programs the TV to turn on at a time when a grandchild will be visiting.

The most logical placement for this sentence would be:
    F. before Sentence 1.
    G. after Sentence 1.
    H. after Sentence 2.
    J. after Sentence 3.

Question 15 asks about the preceding passage as a whole.

---

15. The writer is considering deleting the first sentence from Paragraph 3. If the writer removed this sentence, the essay would primarily lose:
    A. information about the intriguing uses of the remote.
    B. details supporting the fact that Grandpa liked using the remote.
    C. a humorous blend of descriptive details and relevant information.
    D. a transition from the first two paragraphs to the rest of the essay.

PASSAGE II

Tejano Music and Its Meadowlark

<u>One of the liveliest</u> folk music forms to develop
₁₆
in the twentieth century is Tejano music. Also known as

Tex-Mex or border music because of <u>it's having</u> origins on
₁₇
both sides of the Texas-Mexico border, this form combines

16. **F.** NO CHANGE
    G. One of the most liveliest
    H. The most lively
    J. The liveliest

17. **A.** NO CHANGE
    B. its
    C. it's
    D. its'

GO ON TO THE NEXT PAGE.

elements from Spanish, German, and English musical

traditions.

In the late nineteenth century, German immigrants to

south Texas and northern Mexico brought with them their

dance music [18] and the button accordion. The music and

the instrument were adopted by musicians in that region,

who began to use the accordion, in their own dance music,
                                    _____
                                            19

huapangos and *rancheras.* At the same time, the

Spanish and English folk ballad traditions took root

in Tejano music in the form of *corridos,* narrative

songs of bravery, romance, and tragedy set in the

towns and ranches of the region. Eventually, a unique

musical style developed; based on duet singing and
_____
              20

an instrumentation of accordion, drums, upright bass,

and *bajo sexto,* the Spanish twelve-string bass guitar.

It was *conjunto* and became the heart of Tejano music.
_____
          21

[1] The first Tejano musician to gain star status was

Lydia Mendoza. [2] She was born in Mexico in 1916, but

her family soon immigrated to the United States. [3] The

Mendoza family made their living working alternately as
                   _____
                         22

field hands and they were touring musicians. [4] Mendoza
                 _____
                    23

18. At this point, the writer is considering adding the following parenthetical phrase:

    —polkas and waltzes—

    Given that it is true, would this be a relevant addition to make here?

    F. Yes, because it can help the reader have a better understanding of the music being referred to.
    G. Yes, because it helps explain to the reader why this music became so popular.
    H. No, because it fails to explain the connection between this music and the button accordion.
    J. No, because it is inconsistent with the style of this essay to mention specific musical forms.

19. A. NO CHANGE
    B. accordion in their own dance music,
    C. accordion, in their own dance music
    D. accordion in their own dance music

20. F. NO CHANGE
    G. style developed based on
    H. style developed based on,
    J. style, developed based on

21. A. NO CHANGE
    B. This style, known as *conjunto,*
    C. Being known as *conjunto,* it
    D. It being *conjunto*

22. Which of the following alternatives to the underlined portion would NOT be acceptable?

    F. earned their living by
    G. made their living from
    H. made their living on
    J. earned their living

23. A. NO CHANGE
    B. as well
    C. being
    D. as

GO ON TO THE NEXT PAGE.

learned the words to many of her songs from bubble gum

wrappers, where music publishers had song lyrics printed

in the hope of making them popular. [24] [5] In 1928

in San Antonio, Texas, where Mendoza and her
                                   25

family made their first recording. [6] Her clear and

expressive singing style soon gained her widespread

popularity in the Spanish-speaking regions of
                                     26

North and South America. [27]

Others have followed Lydia Mendoza's lead

and have immigrated to the United States from Mexico.
                                      28
Like other folk music forms, Tejano music has an

intensity, literary richness, and rhythmic variety that

means it'll stick around a while.
       29

24. The writer is considering deleting the following clause from the preceding sentence (placing a period after the word *wrappers*):

> where music publishers had song lyrics printed in the hope of making them popular

Should the writer make this deletion?

F. Yes, because the information is unrelated to the topic addressed in this paragraph.
G. Yes, because the information diminishes the musical accomplishments and successes of Lydia Mendoza and her family.
H. No, because the information explains the reference to bubble gum wrappers, which might otherwise puzzle readers.
J. No, because the information shows how popular the songs were that Lydia Mendoza performed.

25. A. NO CHANGE
B. it was there that
C. was where
D. OMIT the underlined portion.

26. F. NO CHANGE
G. popularity: in the Spanish-speaking regions
H. popularity, in the Spanish-speaking regions,
J. popularity in the Spanish-speaking regions,

27. Upon reviewing this paragraph and finding that some information has been left out, the writer composes the following sentence incorporating that information:

> She became widely known as La Alondra de la Frontera (The Meadowlark of the Border).

This sentence would most logically be placed after Sentence:

A. 3.
B. 4.
C. 5.
D. 6.

28. Given that all of the choices are true, which one would most effectively tie together the two main subjects of this essay?

F. NO CHANGE
G. and have expanded the influence of Tejano music.
H. such as Santiago Jiménez and his son Flaco.
J. and have signed large recording contracts.

29. A. NO CHANGE
B. causes it to be one of those enduring things with a timeless appeal.
C. makes lots of people really like it.
D. ensures its continued vitality.

GO ON TO THE NEXT PAGE.

Question 30 asks about the preceding passage as a whole.

30. Suppose the writer's goal had been to write a brief essay focusing on the history and development of Tejano music. Would this essay successfully fulfill that goal?

F. Yes, because the essay describes the origins of Tejano music and one of its early important figures.
G. Yes, because the essay mentions the contributions that Tejano music has made to other folk music traditions.
H. No, because the essay refers to other musical forms besides Tejano music.
J. No, because the essay focuses on only one Tejano musician, Lydia Mendoza.

PASSAGE III

"Topping Out" the Gateway Arch

During the early morning hours of October 28, <u>1965, engineers</u> stationed 630 feet above the ground
₃₁

made careful measurements for the <u>days</u> work.
₃₂

The results indicated a problem that <u>threatened to</u>
₃₃

postpone <u>and delay</u> the topping-out ceremony marking
₃₄
the placement of the final section between the two

freestanding legs of the St. Louis Gateway Arch. [35]

31. A. NO CHANGE
    B. 1965, and engineers
    C. 1965. Engineers
    D. 1965; engineers

32. F. NO CHANGE
    G. days'
    H. day's
    J. days's

33. A. NO CHANGE
    B. had been threatened
    C. will have threatened
    D. threatens

34. F. NO CHANGE
    G. to a later time
    H. by delaying
    J. OMIT the underlined portion.

35. The writer is considering deleting the following from the preceding sentence:

    > marking the placement of the final section between the two freestanding legs of the St. Louis Gateway Arch

    If the writer were to delete this phrase, the essay would primarily lose:

    A. a minor detail in the essay's opening paragraph.
    B. an explanation of the term "topping-out ceremony."
    C. the writer's opinion about the significance of the topping-out ceremony.
    D. an indication of the topping-out ceremony's importance to the people of St. Louis.

GO ON TO THE NEXT PAGE.

Thirty-two years of planning and effort resulted in this moment. In 1933, attorney and civic leader Luther Ely Smith envisioned a memorial that would recognize St. Louis's major role in the westward expansion of the United States. [37] Architect

Eero Saarinen, who created the design that symbolized the memorial's theme of St. Louis as the "Gateway to the

West." Meanwhile, the arch would have a stainless steel exterior and interior structural supports made of concrete. Both legs of the arch would be built simultaneously using triangular sections. Those at the base of each arch leg would be the largest, with the higher sections progressively smaller.

After nearly three years of construction, the day had come to place the final section at the top of the arch and finish the project. But a problem had arisen. The engineers confirmed that the heat of the sun had caused the south leg of the arch to expand five inches. This small but critical deviation caused concern that the two legs and the final section might not connect properly. The engineers called in local firefighters in the hope that spraying the leg with water to cool it would make it contract. The firefighters, using 700 feet of hose, were able to reach as high as 550 feet on the south leg in

36. **F.** NO CHANGE
G. attorney, and civic leader
H. attorney and civic leader,
J. attorney, and civic leader,

37. If the writer were to delete the preceding sentence, the paragraph would primarily lose:
A. an explanation of why St. Louis had a major role in the westward expansion of the United States.
B. details about what Luther Ely Smith thought the memorial he envisioned should look like.
C. background information about the history leading to the Gateway Arch.
D. biographical information about Luther Ely Smith.

38. **F.** NO CHANGE
G. Saarinen, creator of
H. Saarinen created
J. Saarinen creating

39. **A.** NO CHANGE
B. Therefore, the
C. However, the
D. The

40. **F.** NO CHANGE
G. reduce.
H. decrease.
J. compress.

GO ON TO THE NEXT PAGE.

they're attempt to reduce its expansion.
   41

   The plan worked. By late morning,

the crowd cheered as, welded to the two legs of
                                              42
the arch, the final section was hoisted up. Over three
                                                   42

decades and more than thirty years of planning and
                              43

building had come to a conclusion, and the tallest
                              44
monument in the United States was now complete.

41. **A.** NO CHANGE
    B. they're attempt to reduce it's
    C. their attempt to reduce its
    D. their attempt to reduce it's

42. **F.** NO CHANGE
    G. as the crowd cheered, the final section was hoisted up and welded to the two legs of the arch.
    H. as the crowd cheered, welded to the two legs of the arch, the final section was hoisted up.
    J. the final section was hoisted up as the crowd cheered and welded to the two legs of the arch.

43. **A.** NO CHANGE
    B. decades amounting to more than thirty years
    C. decades—over thirty years—
    D. decades

44. Which of the following alternatives to the underlined portion would be LEAST acceptable in terms of the context of this sentence?

    F. reached completion,
    G. come to a halt,
    H. come to an end,
    J. ended,

Question 45 asks about the preceding passage as a whole.

---

45. Suppose the writer had intended to write a brief essay that describes the entire process of designing and building the St. Louis Gateway Arch. Would this essay successfully fulfill the writer's goal?

    A. Yes, because it offers such details as the materials used to make the exterior and the interior structural supports.
    B. Yes, because it explains in detail each step in the design and construction of the arch.
    C. No, because it focuses primarily on one point in the development of the arch rather than on the entire process.
    D. No, because it is primarily a historical essay about the early stages in the development of the arch.

GO ON TO THE NEXT PAGE.

PASSAGE IV

Our Place in the World

In the dusk of a late summer evening, I walked
46
quietly with a small gathering of people toward a

shelter at the edge of a field in northern Indiana.

Although I had never met more of the people who
47

walked with me, a few of them I did know quite well.
48
We were Miami Indians, and we had waited years to

make this journey across Miami land into a ceremonial
49

longhouse made of saplings and earth. ☐50

For years I had seen other Miami's pictures—
51
many of them the ancestors of the

people, who walked along with me,
52
to the longhouse that summer evening.

46. **F.** NO CHANGE
    G. On
    H. With
    J. From

47. **A.** NO CHANGE
    B. more of the people whom
    C. most of the people who
    D. most of the people whom

48. The writer wants to balance the statement made in the earlier part of this sentence with a related detail that suggests the unity of the people. Given that all of the choices are true, which one best accomplishes this goal?

    F. NO CHANGE
    G. we each had our own personal reasons for being there.
    H. I hoped I could get to know some of them.
    J. I felt a kinship with them.

49. Which of the following alternatives to the underlined portion would NOT be acceptable?

    A. among
    B. over
    C. on
    D. through

50. The writer is considering revising the preceding sentence by deleting the phrase "into a ceremonial longhouse made of saplings and earth" (placing a period after the word *land*). If the writer did this, the paragraph would primarily lose:

    F. information comparing the narrator's own journey to similar ones made by members of other tribes.
    G. details describing the destination of the people the narrator is traveling with.
    H. details that establish the time and place of the events in the essay.
    J. interesting but irrelevant information about the Miami.

51. **A.** NO CHANGE
    B. pictures in which other Miami were present—
    C. pictures of other Miami—
    D. other Miami whose pictures had been taken—

52. **F.** NO CHANGE
    G. people who, walked along with me
    H. people, who walked along, with me
    J. people who walked along with me

GO ON TO THE NEXT PAGE.

My mother and grandmother helped preserve tribal

history by collecting books and newspaper clippings.

Books describing the history and culture of the Miami

people lined the bookshelves, and framed photos of Miami

lined the walls of these rooms. While I was growing up I

often found my mother and grandmother each sitting

quietly in her own room, reading old letters or listening

to the music of Native American drums.

That room contained everything I knew about being a

Miami, and unlike the larger Plains tribes, the Miami had

retained no reservation lands. Once a year, the tribe held a

powwow that was always well attended. This social

gathering was the only tribal event that my grandmother or

mother had ever participated in. For generations, the tribe

had owned no land on which a longhouse could be built

and Miami religious ceremonies conducted. Because of

this, I had never attended a Miami religious ceremony,

never danced in front of a crowd of Miami. Still, I had

never known any other Miami children outside of my

own family.

When the tribal council was able to purchase land

and build a longhouse, my mother, grandmother, and I

traveled to the summer ceremony. As we walked together

through the open field that evening, hundreds of tiny

fireflies flashing softly from the tall grasses. The

insects lit our path like the spirits of ancestors

accompanying us home.

53. Given that all of the choices are true, which one would most effectively lead the reader from the first sentence of this paragraph to the description that follows in the next two sentences?
- **A.** NO CHANGE
- **B.** Some of those pictures had been reprinted in books my mother and grandmother collected.
- **C.** My grandmother and mother proudly displayed those pictures in their houses.
- **D.** Like many Miami, my grandmother and mother had each dedicated a room in her own house to the tribe.

54.
- **F.** NO CHANGE
- **G.** Her rooms
- **H.** Those rooms
- **J.** This room

55.
- **A.** NO CHANGE
- **B.** Miami unlike
- **C.** Miami, unlike
- **D.** Miami. Unlike

56. Given that all of the choices are true, which one provides information most relevant to the main focus of this paragraph?
- **F.** NO CHANGE
- **G.** notable for its exquisite dancing.
- **H.** on borrowed land.
- **J.** that lasted several days.

- **A.** NO CHANGE
- **B.** Miami ceremonies were conducted there.
- **C.** there were Miami ceremonies conducted there.
- **D.** the conducting of Miami ceremonies.

- **F.** NO CHANGE
- **G.** Meanwhile,
- **H.** In fact,
- **J.** On the other hand,

59.
- **A.** NO CHANGE
- **B.** fireflies, which flashed
- **C.** fireflies that flashed
- **D.** fireflies flashed

60.
- **F.** NO CHANGE
- **G.** just as
- **H.** as like
- **J.** such as

GO ON TO THE NEXT PAGE.

PASSAGE V

Why Wolves Howl

Why do wolves howl? Thanks to the work of naturalists and animal behaviorists, we know wolves are highly social animals that live in structured packs and that communicate using a variety of sounds, including whining, growling, and barking. Howling, the sound most often
₆₁

associated with wolves, by themselves perform several key
₆₂
social functions within wolf packs.

One of these, self-defense, which includes protecting
₆₃
territory. Packs claim sections of land as private hunting and living spaces and will howl to warn away potential intruders, those are usually other wolves. This "Keep Out"
₆₄

warning serves as a peacekeeping technique because it
₆₅
helps prevent competing packs from warring over prey, fighting for mates, or otherwise interfering with pack life.

Wolves also howl to locate and communicate with
₆₆
one another over long distances. Like their dog

descendants, wolves possess intense hearing, which
₆₇
makes it possible for them to pick up the sound of howling

from as far away as ten miles. Frequently, common
₆₈
activities, such as hunting for prey, often

61. A. NO CHANGE
   B. Howling has been
   C. While howling is
   D. Howling is

62. F. NO CHANGE
   G. on themselves perform
   H. by itself performs
   J. on itself performs

63. A. NO CHANGE
   B. One of these is
   C. One being
   D. One,

64. F. NO CHANGE
   G. most often these are
   H. and are typically
   J. usually

65. Which of the following alternatives to the underlined portion would be the LEAST acceptable?
   A. although
   B. in that
   C. since
   D. as

66. F. NO CHANGE
   G. It's also the case that howling is employed
   H. In addition, howling is a way
   J. Howling is also used

67. A. NO CHANGE
   B. cunning
   C. acute
   D. vivid

68. F. NO CHANGE
   G. Quite regularly, common
   H. Many times, common
   J. Common

GO ON TO THE NEXT PAGE.

call upon animals' sharp instincts; in order to reunite,
____
69

the separated wolves howl to one another.

Finally, wolves use howling in the pack's social
____
70

rituals. Upon waking, pack members howl morning

greetings while wagging their tails, they nuzzle each other,
____
71

and engaging in mock fights. Before leaving on a hunt, the

pack gathers for a "group sing" called chorus howling.

Usually begun by the alpha or, dominant, pair of wolves,
____
72

the pack is excited in preparation for the hunt partly by
____
73

chorus howling. The collective sound of wolves howling
____
73

in various keys also make the pack seem larger and more
____
74

powerful to potential enemies than it really is.

Further study of wolves will likely uncover still more

reasons for their howling. What's already clear, is that the
____
75

stereotypical image of the lone wolf howling at the full

moon obscures the importance howling has in the social

life of these animals.

69. Given that all of the choices are true, which one provides the most logical cause for the action described in the statement immediately following this underlined portion?
   A. NO CHANGE
   B. disperse a pack over large areas of land;
   C. require the pack to travel some distance;
   D. involve the entire pack;

70. F. NO CHANGE
   G. Nevertheless,
   H. Second,
   J. Thus,

71. A. NO CHANGE
   B. nuzzling
   C. nuzzled
   D. nuzzle

72. F. NO CHANGE
   G. alpha, or dominant, pair
   H. alpha or dominant pair,
   J. alpha or, dominant pair

73. A. NO CHANGE
   B. the purpose of chorus howling is to help excite the pack in preparation for the hunt.
   C. excitement in the pack is raised, in preparation for the hunt, by chorus howling.
   D. chorus howling helps excite the pack in preparation for the hunt.

74. F. NO CHANGE
   G. have the effect of making
   H. are intended to make
   J. makes

75. A. NO CHANGE
   B. clear is that,
   C. clear is, that
   D. clear is that

END OF TEST 1

STOP! DO NOT TURN THE PAGE UNTIL TOLD TO DO SO.

MATHEMATICS TEST

60 Minutes—60 Questions

DIRECTIONS: Solve each problem, choose the correct answer, and then fill in the corresponding oval on your answer document.

Do not linger over problems that take too much time. Solve as many as you can; then return to the others in the time you have left for this test.

You are permitted to use a calculator on this test. You may use your calculator for any problems you choose, but some of the problems may best be done without using a calculator.

Note: Unless otherwise stated, all of the following should be assumed.

1. Illustrative figures are NOT necessarily drawn to scale.
2. Geometric figures lie in a plane.
3. The word *line* indicates a straight line.
4. The word *average* indicates arithmetic mean.

1. A restaurant occupying the top floor of a skyscraper rotates as diners enjoy the view. Ling and Sarah notice that they began their meal at 7:00 P.M. looking due north. At 7:45 P.M. they had rotated 180° to a view that was due south. At this rate, how many degrees will the restaurant rotate in 1 hour?

   A. 90°
   B. 180°
   C. 240°
   D. 270°
   E. 400°

2. If 12 vases cost $18.00, what is the cost of 1 vase?

   F. $0.67
   G. $1.05
   H. $1.33
   J. $1.50
   K. $1.60

3. Your friend shows you a scale drawing of her apartment. The drawing of the apartment is a rectangle 4 inches by 6 inches. Your friend wants to know the length of the shorter side of the apartment. If she knows that the length of the longer side of the apartment is 30 feet, how many feet long is the shorter side of her apartment?

   A. 9
   B. 20
   C. 24
   D. 30
   E. 45

4. A company earned a profit of $8.0 million each year for 3 consecutive years. For each of the next 2 years the company earned a profit of $9.0 million. For this 5-year period, what was the company's average yearly profit, in millions of dollars?

   F. 8.2
   G. 8.25
   H. 8.4
   J. 8.5
   K. 8.6

DO YOUR FIGURING HERE.

GO ON TO THE NEXT PAGE.

DO YOUR FIGURING HERE.

5. A company rents moving vans for a rental fee of $25.00 per day with an additional charge of $0.30 per mile that the van is driven. Which of the following expressions represents the cost, in dollars, of renting a van for 1 day and driving it *m* miles?

A. $0.30m + 25$
B. $25m + 30$
C. $30m + 25$
D. $25.30m$
E. $55m$

6. The figure below shows quadrilateral *ABCD*. What is the measure of $\angle C$?

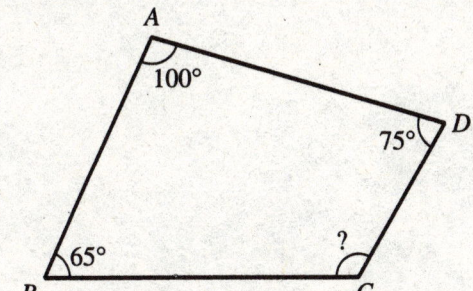

F. $120°$
G. $115°$
H. $105°$
J. $100°$
K. $80°$

7. In the figure below, $\triangle ABC$ and $\triangle DEF$ are similar triangles with the given side lengths in meters. What is the perimeter, in meters, of $\triangle DEF$?

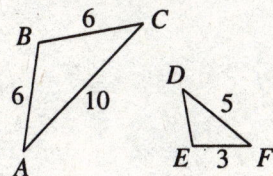

A. 3
B. 8
C. 11
D. 12
E. 13

8. The relationship between temperature in degrees Fahrenheit, F, and temperature in degrees Celsius, C, is expressed by the formula $F = \frac{9}{5}C + 32$. Calvin reads a temperature of $38°$ on a Celsius thermometer. To the nearest degree, what is the equivalent temperature on a Fahrenheit thermometer?

F. $36°$
G. $53°$
H. $68°$
J. $70°$
K. $100°$

GO ON TO THE NEXT PAGE.

DO YOUR FIGURING HERE.

9. Nick needs to order 500 pens from his supplier. The catalog shows that these pens come in cases of 24 boxes with 10 pens in each box. Nick knows that he may NOT order partial cases. What is the fewest number of cases he should order?

   A. 2
   B. 3
   C. 18
   D. 21
   E. 50

10. When $a + b = 6$, what is the value of

    $2(a + b) + \dfrac{a + b}{6} + (a + b)^2 - 2$?

    F. 23
    G. 37
    H. 38
    J. 43
    K. 47

11. The cost of a hamburger and a soft drink together is $2.10. The cost of 2 hamburgers and a soft drink together is $3.50. What is the cost of a soft drink?

    A. $0.50
    B. $0.55
    C. $0.70
    D. $1.05
    E. $1.40

12. If $12x = -8(10 - x)$, then $x = $?

    F. 20

    G. 8

    H. $7\frac{3}{11}$

    J. $6\frac{2}{13}$

    K. -20

13. Shannon is planning to tile a rectangular kitchen countertop that is 24 inches wide and 64 inches long. She determined that 1 tile will be needed for each 4-inch-by-4-inch region. What is the minimum number of tiles that will be needed to completely cover the countertop to its edges?

    A. 44
    B. 88
    C. 96
    D. 176
    E. 384

14. Which of the following lists gives 2 of the 3 interior angle measurements of a triangle for which the 3rd angle measurement would be equal to 1 of the 2 given measurements?

    F. 20°, 40°
    G. 30°, 60°
    H. 40°, 100°
    J. 45°, 120°
    K. 50°, 60°

GO ON TO THE NEXT PAGE.

DO YOUR FIGURING HERE.

15. A triangle with a perimeter of 66 inches has one side that is 16 inches long. The lengths of the other two sides have a ratio of 2:3. What is the length, in inches, of the *longest* side of the triangle?

A. 16
B. 20
C. 30
D. 40
E. 50

16. What is the *y*-intercept of the line in the standard (*x*,*y*) coordinate plane that goes through the points (–3,6) and (3,2) ?

F. 0
G. 2
H. 4
J. 6
K. 8

17. In the figure below, lines *m* and *n* are parallel, transversals *r* and *s* intersect to form an angle of measure *x*°, and 2 other angle measures are as marked. What is the value of *x* ?

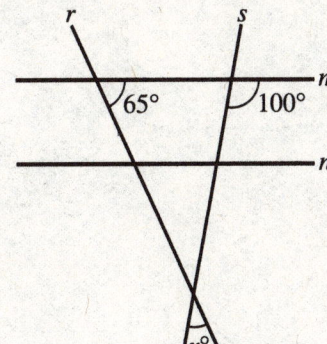

A. 15
B. 25
C. 35
D. 65
E. 80

18. The depth of a pond is 180 cm and is being reduced by 1 cm per week. The depth of a second pond is 160 cm and is being reduced by $\frac{1}{2}$ cm per week. If the depths of both ponds continue to be reduced at these constant rates, in about how many weeks will the ponds have the same depth?

F. 10
G. 20
H. 40
J. 80
K. 140

GO ON TO THE NEXT PAGE.

Practice ACT Tests

DO YOUR FIGURING HERE.

19. When graphed in the standard (x,y) coordinate plane, which of the following equations does NOT represent a line?

A. $x = 4$

B. $3y = 6$

C. $x - y = 1$

D. $y = \frac{3}{4}x - 2$

E. $x^2 + y = 5$

20. In the right triangle shown below, which of the following statements is true about $\angle A$?

F. $\cos A = \frac{12}{13}$

G. $\sin A = \frac{12}{13}$

H. $\tan A = \frac{12}{13}$

J. $\cos A = \frac{13}{12}$

K. $\sin A = \frac{13}{12}$

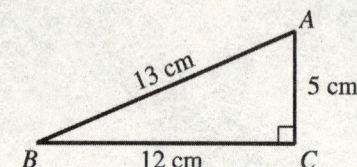

21. What is the slope of any line parallel to the line $7x + 9y = 6$?

A. -7

B. $-\frac{7}{9}$

C. $\frac{7}{6}$

D. 6

E. 7

22. The braking distance, y feet, for Damon's car to come to a complete stop is modeled by $y = \frac{3(x^2 + 10x)}{40}$, where x is the speed of the car in miles per hour. According to this model, which of the following is the maximum speed, in miles per hour, Damon can be driving so that the braking distance is less than or equal to 150 feet?

F. 10
G. 30
H. 40
J. 50
K. 60

GO ON TO THE NEXT PAGE.

DO YOUR FIGURING HERE.

23. If $f(x) = x^2 + x + 5$ and $g(x) = \sqrt{x}$, then what is the value of $\frac{g(4)}{f(1)}$?

   A. $\frac{2}{7}$

   B. $\frac{25}{7}$

   C. $\frac{2}{25}$

   D. 2

   E. 4

24. At a school picnic, 1 junior and 1 senior will be selected to lead the activities. If there are 125 juniors and 100 seniors at the picnic, how many different 2-person combinations of 1 junior and 1 senior are possible?

   F.   25
   G.   100
   H.   125
   J.   225
   K. 12,500

25. A ramp for wheelchair access to the gym has a slope of 5% (that is, the ramp rises 5 feet vertically for every 100 feet of horizontal distance). The entire ramp is built on level ground, and the entrance to the gym is 2 feet above the ground. What is the *horizontal* distance, in feet, between the ends of the ramp?

   A.   4
   B.   10
   C.   40
   D.   100
   E.   400

26. The temperature, t, in degrees Fahrenheit, in a certain town on a certain spring day satisfies the inequality $|t - 24| \le 30$. Which of the following temperatures, in degrees Fahrenheit, is NOT in this range?

   F. −10
   G.   −6
   H.   −5
   J.   0
   K.   54

27. If 5 times a number n is subtracted from 15, the result is negative. Which of the following gives the possible value(s) for n ?

   A.   0 only
   B.   3 only
   C. 10 only
   D. All $n > 3$
   E. All $n < 3$

GO ON TO THE NEXT PAGE.

28. $(x^2 - 4x + 3) - (3x^2 - 4x - 3)$ is equivalent to:

F. $2x^2 - 6$
G. $2x^2 - 8x$
H. $2x^2 - 8x - 6$
J. $-2x^2 + 6$
K. $-2x^2 - 8x$

DO YOUR FIGURING HERE.

29. The median of a set of data containing 9 items was found. Four data items were added to the set. Two of these items were greater than the original median, and the other 2 items were less than the original median. Which of the following statements *must* be true about the median of the new data set?

A. It is the average of the 2 new lower values.
B. It is the same as the original median.
C. It is the average of the 2 new higher values.
D. It is greater than the original median.
E. It is less than the original median.

30. The figure below shows 2 tangent circles such that the 10-centimeter diameter of the smaller circle is equal to the radius of the larger circle. What is the area, in square centimeters, of the shaded region?

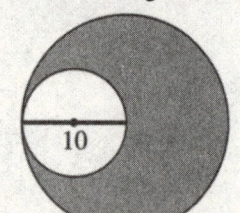

F. 10
G. 75
H. 5π
J. 10π
K. 75π

31. Which of the following sets of 3 numbers could be the side lengths, in meters, of a 30°-60°-90° triangle?

A. $1, 1, 1$
B. $1, 1, \sqrt{2}$
C. $1, \sqrt{2}, \sqrt{2}$
D. $1, \sqrt{2}, \sqrt{3}$
E. $1, \sqrt{3}, 2$

> Use the following information to answer questions 32–34.

The curve $y = 0.005x^2 - 2x + 200$ for $0 \le x \le 200$ and the line segment from $F(0,200)$ to $G(200,0)$ are shown in the standard (x,y) coordinate plane below.

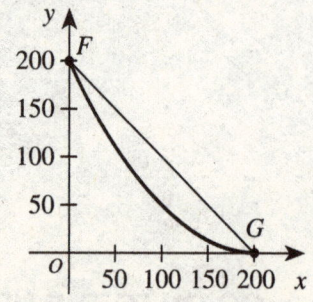

GO ON TO THE NEXT PAGE.

DO YOUR FIGURING HERE.

32. What is the *y*-coordinate for the point on the curve with *x*-coordinate 20 ?

   F. 160
   G. 162
   H. 164
   J. 166
   K. 168

33. The length of this curve is longer than $\overline{FG}$. About how many coordinate units long is $\overline{FG}$?

   A. 20
   B. 141
   C. 200
   D. 283
   E. 400

34. Tran wants to approximate the area underneath the curve $y = 0.005x^2 - 2x + 200$ for $0 \le x \le 200$, shown shaded in the graph below.

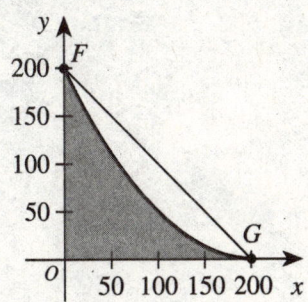

He finds an initial estimate, *A*, for the

shaded area by using $\overline{FG}$ and computing

$A = \frac{1}{2}$(200 units)(200 units) = 20,000 square units.

The area of the shaded region is:

   F. less than 20,000 square units, because the curve lies under $\overline{FG}$.
   G. less than 20,000 square units, because the curve lies over $\overline{FG}$.
   H. equal to 20,000 square units.
   J. greater than 20,000 square units, because the curve lies under $\overline{FG}$.
   K. greater than 20,000 square units, because the curve lies over $\overline{FG}$.

GO ON TO THE NEXT PAGE.

DO YOUR FIGURING HERE.

35. A cargo ship is 4.2 miles from a lighthouse, and a fishing boat is 5.0 miles from the lighthouse, as shown below. The angle between the straight lines from the lighthouse to the 2 vessels is 5°. The approximate distance, in miles, from the cargo ship to the fishing boat is given by which of the following expressions?

(Note: The law of cosines states that for any triangle with vertices A, B, and C and the sides opposite those vertices with lengths a, b, and c, respectively, $c^2 = a^2 + b^2 - 2ab \cos C$.)

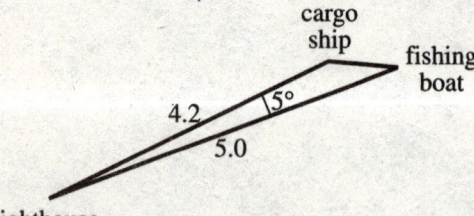

A. $\sqrt{(5.0)^2 - (4.2)^2}$

B. $\sqrt{(4.2)^2 + (5.0)^2 - 2 \cdot 4.2 \cdot 5.0 \cos 5°}$

C. $\sqrt{(4.2)^2 + (5.0)^2 + 2 \cdot 4.2 \cdot 5.0 \cos 5°}$

D. $\sqrt{(4.2)^2 + (5.0)^2 - 2 \cdot 4.2 \cdot 5.0 \cos 85°}$

E. $\sqrt{(4.2)^2 + (5.0)^2 + 2 \cdot 4.2 \cdot 5.0 \cos 85°}$

36. Which of the following equations expresses c in terms of a for all real numbers a, b, and c such that $a^3 = b$ and $b^2 = c$?

F. $c = a^6$

G. $c = a^5$

H. $c = 2a^3$

J. $c = \frac{1}{2}a$

K. $c = a$

37. Which of the following statements is NOT true about the arithmetic sequence 17, 12, 7, 2, ··· ?

A. The fifth term is -3.
B. The sum of the first 5 terms is 35.
C. The eighth term is −18.
D. The common difference of consecutive terms is −5.
E. The common ratio of consecutive terms is −5.

GO ON TO THE NEXT PAGE.

DO YOUR FIGURING HERE.

38. In the standard (x,y) coordinate plane below, the points $(0,0)$, $(10,0)$, $(13,6)$, and $(3,6)$ are the vertices of a parallelogram. What is the area, in square coordinate units, of the parallelogram?

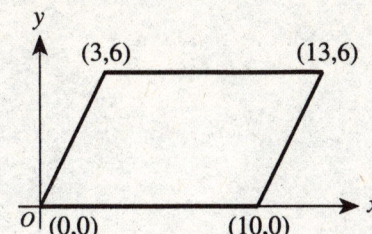

F. 30

G. 60

H. $30\sqrt{3}$

J. $30\sqrt{5}$

K. $60\sqrt{5}$

39. The normal amount of lead in a certain water supply is 1.5×10^{-5} milligrams per liter. Today, when the water was tested, the lead level found was exactly 100 times as great as the normal level, still well below the Environmental Protection Agency's action level. What concentration of lead, in milligrams per liter, was in the water tested today?

A. 1.5×10^{-105}

B. 1.5×10^{-10}

C. 1.5×10^{-7}

D. 1.5×10^{-3}

E. $1.5 \times 10^{-\frac{5}{2}}$

40. A certain perfect square has exactly 4 digits (that is, it is an integer between 1,000 and 9,999). The positive square root of the perfect square must have how many digits?

F. 1

G. 2

H. 3

J. 4

K. Cannot be determined from the given information

41. $\left(\frac{1}{2}x - y\right)^2 = ?$

A. $\frac{1}{4}x^2 + y^2$

B. $\frac{1}{4}x^2 - xy + y^2$

C. $\frac{1}{2}x^2 - xy + y^2$

D. $x^2 + y^2$

E. $x^2 - xy + y^2$

GO ON TO THE NEXT PAGE.

DO YOUR FIGURING HERE.

42. What is the matrix product $\begin{bmatrix} a \\ 2a \\ 3a \end{bmatrix} \begin{bmatrix} 1 & 0 & -1 \end{bmatrix}$?

F. $\begin{bmatrix} a & 0 & -a \\ 2a & 0 & -2a \\ 3a & 0 & -3a \end{bmatrix}$

G. $\begin{bmatrix} a & 2a & 3a \\ 0 & 0 & 0 \\ -a & -2a & -3a \end{bmatrix}$

H. $\begin{bmatrix} 2a & 0 & -2a \end{bmatrix}$

J. $\begin{bmatrix} 6a & 0 & -6a \end{bmatrix}$

K. $[0]$

43. What is the degree measure of the smaller of the 2 angles formed by the line and the ray shown in the figure below?

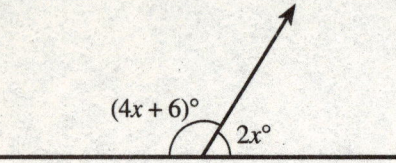

A. $14°$
B. $28°$
C. $29°$
D. $58°$
E. Cannot be determined from the given information

44. How many prime numbers are there between 30 and 50 ?
F. 4
G. 5
H. 6
J. 7
K. 8

45. The lengths, in feet, of the sides of right triangle $\triangle ABC$ are as shown in the diagram below, with $x > 0$. What is the cotangent of $\angle A$, in terms of x ?

A. $\sqrt{4 - x^2}$

B. $\dfrac{2}{x}$

C. $\dfrac{x}{2}$

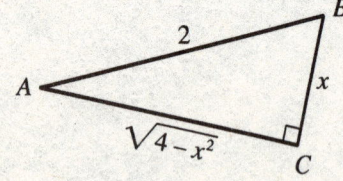

D. $\dfrac{x}{\sqrt{4 - x^2}}$

E. $\dfrac{\sqrt{4 - x^2}}{x}$

GO ON TO THE NEXT PAGE.

DO YOUR FIGURING HERE.

46. A restaurant has 10 booths that will seat up to 4 people each. If 20 people are seated in booths, and NO booths are empty, what is the greatest possible number of booths that could be filled with 4 people?

F. 0
G. 1
H. 2
J. 3
K. 5

47. The trapezoid below is divided into 2 triangles and 1 rectangle. Lengths are given in inches. What is the combined area, in square inches, of the 2 shaded triangles?

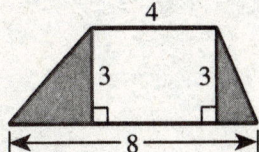

A. 4
B. 6
C. 9
D. 12
E. 18

48. In the figure below, *ABCD* is a square and *E*, *F*, *G*, and *H* are the midpoints of its sides. If *AB* = 12 inches, what is the perimeter of *EFGH*, in inches?

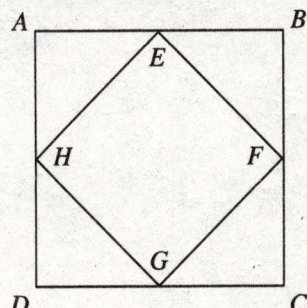

F. 24
G. $24\sqrt{2}$
H. $36\sqrt{2}$
J. $48\sqrt{2}$
K. 72

49. Which of the following expressions, if any, are equal for all real numbers *x* ?

   I. $\sqrt{(-x)^2}$
   II. $|-x|$
   III. $-|x|$

A. I and II only
B. I and III only
C. II and III only
D. I, II, and III
E. None of the expressions are equivalent.

GO ON TO THE NEXT PAGE.

50. In the figure below, A, C, F, and D are collinear; B, C, and E are collinear; and the angles at A, E, and F are right angles, as marked. Which of the following statements is NOT justifiable from the given information?

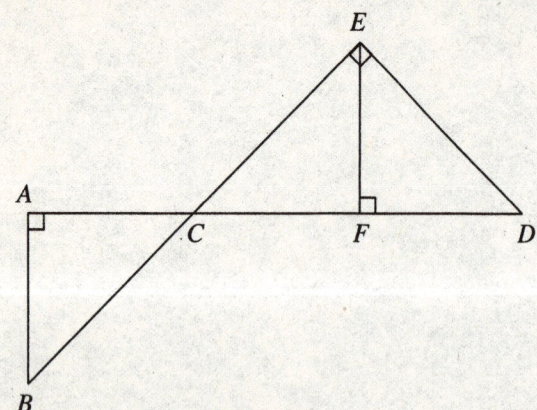

F. $\overleftrightarrow{AB}$ is parallel to $\overleftrightarrow{EF}$.

G. $\overline{DE}$ is perpendicular to $\overline{BE}$.

H. $\angle ACB$ is congruent to $\angle FCE$.

J. $\triangle BAC$ is similar to $\triangle EFC$.

K. $\overline{CE}$ is congruent to $\overline{ED}$.

51. In the figure below, all line segments are either horizontal or vertical and the dimensions given are in inches. What is the perimeter, in inches, of the figure?

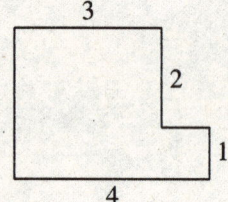

A. 10
B. 12
C. 13
D. 14
E. 16

52. A 6-inch-by-8-inch rectangle is inscribed in a circle as shown below. What is the area of the circle, in square inches?

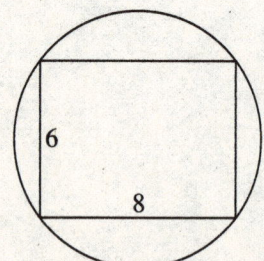

F. 5π
G. 16π
H. 25π
J. 48π
K. 96π

GO ON TO THE NEXT PAGE.

53. On his first day as a telemarketer, Marshall made 24 calls. His goal was to make 5 more calls on each successive day than he had made the day before. If Marshall met, but did not exceed, his goal, how many calls had he made in all after spending exactly 20 days making calls as a telemarketer?

A. 670
B. 690
C. 974
D. 1,430
E. 1,530

54. Which of the following is the graph of the function $f(x)$ defined below?

$$f(x) = \begin{cases} x^2 - 2 \text{ for } x \le 1 \\ x - 7 \text{ for } 1 < x < 5 \\ 4 - x \text{ for } x \ge 5 \end{cases}$$

F.
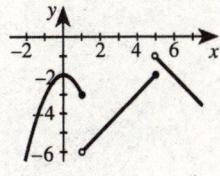

J.
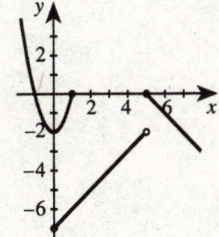

G.
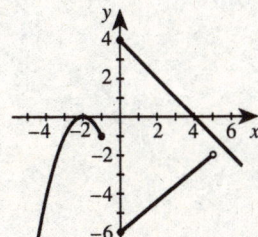

K.
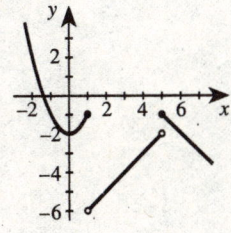

H.
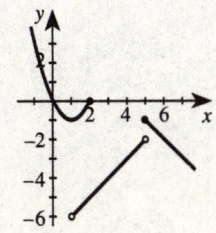

GO ON TO THE NEXT PAGE.

55. If the value, to the nearest thousandth, of $\cos\theta$ is -0.385, which of the following could be true about θ ?

A. $0 \le \theta < \frac{\pi}{6}$

B. $\frac{\pi}{6} \le \theta < \frac{\pi}{3}$

C. $\frac{\pi}{3} \le \theta < \frac{\pi}{2}$

D. $\frac{\pi}{2} \le \theta < \frac{2\pi}{3}$

E. $\frac{2\pi}{3} \le \theta \le \pi$

DO YOUR FIGURING HERE.

56. Which of the following quadratic equations has solutions $x = 6a$ and $x = -3b$?

F. $x^2 - 18ab = 0$

G. $x^2 - x(3b - 6a) - 18ab = 0$

H. $x^2 - x(3b + 6a) + 18ab = 0$

J. $x^2 + x(3b - 6a) - 18ab = 0$

K. $x^2 + x(3b + 6a) + 18ab = 0$

57. In the standard (x,y) coordinate plane below, the vertices of the square have coordinates $(0,0)$, $(6,0)$, $(6,6)$, and $(0,6)$. Which of the following is an equation of the circle that is inscribed in the square?

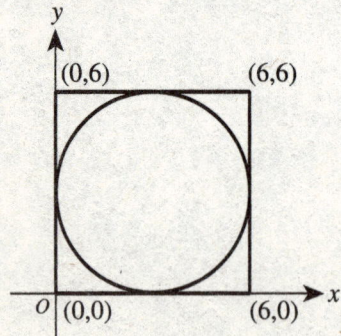

A. $(x - 3)^2 + (y - 3)^2 = 9$

B. $(x - 3)^2 + (y - 3)^2 = 3$

C. $(x + 3)^2 + (y + 3)^2 = 9$

D. $(x + 3)^2 + (y + 3)^2 = 6$

E. $(x + 3)^2 + (y + 3)^2 = 3$

GO ON TO THE NEXT PAGE.

DO YOUR FIGURING HERE.

58. A simple pendulum consists of a small mass suspended from a string that is fixed at its upper end and has negligible mass. The length of time, t seconds, for a complete swing of a simple pendulum can be modeled by the equation $t = 2\pi \sqrt{\dfrac{L}{32}}$, where L is the length, in feet, of the string. If the time required for a complete swing of Pendulum 1 is triple the time required for a complete swing of Pendulum 2, the length of Pendulum 1's string is how many times the length of Pendulum 2's string?

F. $\dfrac{1}{3}$

G. 3

H. 6

J. 9

K. 27

59. If $\log_a x = s$ and $\log_a y = t$, then $\log_a (xy)^2 = ?$

A. $2(s + t)$
B. $s + t$
C. $4st$
D. $2st$
E. st

60. Jennifer's best long jump distance increased by 10% from 1990 to 1991 and by 20% from 1991 to 1992. By what percent did her best long jump distance increase from 1990 to 1992 ?

F. 32%
G. 30%
H. 20%
J. 15%
K. 2%

END OF TEST 2

STOP! DO NOT TURN THE PAGE UNTIL TOLD TO DO SO.

DO NOT RETURN TO THE PREVIOUS TEST.

READING TEST
35 Minutes—40 Questions

DIRECTIONS: There are four passages in this test. Each passage is followed by several questions. After reading a passage, choose the best answer to each question and fill in the corresponding oval on your answer document. You may refer to the passages as often as necessary.

Passage I

PROSE FICTION: This passage is adapted from the novel *Monkey Bridge* by Lan Cao (©1997 by Lan Cao). The story is set in the late 1970s in Virginia, where the narrator and her mother have moved from Vietnam after the fall of Saigon.

I discovered soon after my arrival in Virginia that everything, even the simple business of shopping the American way, unsettled my mother's nerves. From the outside, it had been an ordinary building that held no
5 promises or threats. But inside, the A & P brimmed with unexpected abundance. Metal stands overflowed with giant oranges and meticulously arranged grapefruits. Columns of canned vegetables and fruits stood among multiple shelves as people well rehearsed to the
10 demands of modern shopping meandered through florescent aisles. I remembered the sharp chilled air against my face, the way the hydraulic door made a sucking sound as it closed behind.

My mother did not appreciate the exacting orderli-
15 ness of the A & P. She could not give in to the precision of previously weighed and packaged food, the bloodlessness of beef slabs in translucent wrappers, the absence of carcasses and pigs' heads. When we were in Saigon, there were only outdoor markets. "Sky mar-
20 kets," they were called, vast, prosperous expanses in the middle of the city where barrels of live crabs and yellow carps and booths of ducks and geese would be stacked side by side with cardboard stands of expensive silk fabric. It was always noisy there—a voluptuous
25 mix of animal and human sounds. The sharp acrid smell of gutters choked by the monsoon rain. The odor of horses, partially camouflaged by the scent of guavas and bananas.

My mother knew the vendors and the shoppers by
30 name and would take me from stall to stall to expose me to her skills. They were all addicted to each other's oddities. My mother would feign indifference and they would inevitably call out to her. She would heed their call and they would immediately retreat into sudden
35 apathy. They knew my mother's slick bargaining skills, and she, in turn, knew how to navigate with grace through their extravagant prices and rehearsed huffiness. Theirs had been a mating dance, a match of wills.

Every morning, we drifted from vendor to vendor.
40 Tables full of shampoo and toothpaste were pocketed among vegetable stands one day and jars of herbs the next. The market was randomly organized, and only the mighty and experienced like my mother could navigate its patternless paths.

45 But with a sense of neither drama nor calamity, my mother's ability to navigate and decipher simply became undone in our new life. She preferred the improvisation of haggling to the conventional certainty of discount coupons, the primordial messiness and fish-
50 mongers' stink of the open-air market to the aroma-free order of individually wrapped fillets.

Now, a mere three and a half years or so after her last call to the sky market, the dreadful truth was simply this: we were going through life in reverse, and I was
55 the one who would help my mother through the hard scrutiny of ordinary suburban life. I would have to forgo the luxury of adolescent experiments and temper tantrums, so that I could scoop my mother out of harm's way and give her sanctuary. Now, when we stepped into
60 the exterior world, I was the one who told my mother what was acceptable or unacceptable behavior.

All children of immigrant parents have experienced these moments. When it first occurs, when the parent first reveals the behavior of a child, is a defining
65 moment. Of course, all children eventually watch their parents' astonishing return to the vulnerability of childhood, but for us the process begins much earlier than expected.

"We don't have to pay the moment we decide to
70 buy the pork. We can put as much as we want in the cart and pay only once, at the checkout counter." It took a few moments' hesitation for my mother to succumb to the peculiarity of my explanation.

"I can take you in this aisle," a store clerk offered
75 as she unlocked a new register to accommodate the long line of customers. She gestured us to "come over here" with an upturned index finger, a disdainful hook we Vietnamese use to summon dogs. My mother did not understand the ambiguity of American hand
80 gestures. In Vietnam, we said "Come here" to humans differently, with our palm up and all four fingers waved in unison—the way people over here waved goodbye.

"Even the store clerks look down on us," my mother grumbled. This was a truth I was only begin-

GO ON TO THE NEXT PAGE.

85 ning to realize: it was not the enormous or momentous
event, but the gradual suggestion of irrevocable and
protracted change that threw us off balance and made
us know in no uncertain terms that we would not be
returning to the familiarity of our former lives.

1. At the time of the events of the story, the narrator is:

A. an adult remembering how hard it was on her
mother when the two of them visited the United
States from Saigon.
B. an adult planning to take her mother back to their
native Saigon after an unsuccessful trip to the
United States.
C. an adolescent imagining what it had been like
when her mother moved to the United States years
ago.
D. an adolescent trying to ease her mother's adjust-
ment to life in the United States.

2. It can reasonably be inferred from the passage as a
whole that the narrator views her mother's bargaining
skills as ones that were developed:

F. to a degree that was exceptional even in Saigon
but that have no apparent outlet in the United
States.
G. to a degree that is commonplace in the competitive
sky markets but that is exceptional in the United
States.
H. to a lesser degree than those of most sky market
shoppers in Saigon but to a degree that seems
exceptional in the United States.
J. solidly and irrevocably over years of shopping in
Saigon, putting her at an advantage in the chal-
lenging circumstances of her adopted home.

3. It can reasonably be inferred from the passage that
when shopping at the sky market the narrator's mother
viewed which of the following as something disagreeable to overcome?

A. The primordial messiness
B. The extravagant prices
C. The odors of animals
D. The other shoppers

4. The passage states that the narrator's mother finds all
of the following aspects of shopping at the A & P troubling EXCEPT the:

F. orderliness of the place.
G. absence of carcasses.
H. hurried shoppers.
J. system of paying for merchandise.

5. It can reasonably be inferred that the narrator views
her mother's approach to shopping at the sky market
with a mixture of:

A. anxiety and huffiness.
B. surprise and embarrassment.
C. impatience and amusement.
D. respect and nostalgia.

6. The passage states that the narrator became aware of
her mother's particular way of behaving in the sky
markets as a result of:

F. talking to the vendors who knew her mother years
ago.
G. her mother's vivid descriptions of the sky market
and the things she purchased there.
H. her mother's deliberate attempts to display her
shopping skills to her daughter.
J. tagging along defiantly on shopping trips against
the wishes of her strong-willed mother.

7. The distinction the narrator makes between children in
general and the children of immigrants in particular is
that:

A. children of immigrants inevitably have to watch
their parents return to a state of childlike vulnerability while other children may not.
B. the inevitable shift from being the vulnerable child
to protecting the vulnerable parent takes place
sooner for children of immigrants than for other
children.
C. children of immigrants anticipate assuming the
role of protectors of their parents, while other
children are taken by surprise by the inevitable
responsibility.
D. children of immigrants are misunderstood by their
parents to a greater degree than are other children.

8. Which of the following statements best describes the
way the seventh paragraph (lines 62–68) functions in
the passage as a whole?

F. It provides the first indication that making the
transition to another culture has been difficult for
the narrator and her mother.
G. It sets up a contrast between the narrator's view of
what it takes to adjust to a new culture and what
she thought it would take before she left Saigon.
H. It shows the narrator making connections between
the experiences she describes elsewhere in the passage and the experiences of the children of immigrants in general.
J. It divides the passage into two parts, one focused
on the narrator, the other focused on children of
immigrants in general.

9. The statement "They were all addicted to each other's
oddities" (lines 31–32) functions in the passage to support the narrator's view that:

A. there was a consistent dynamic between the sky
market vendors and her mother.
B. the sky markets were in some ways not as appealing as the American supermarkets.
C. sky market shoppers purchased items they didn't
need just for the enjoyment of bargaining.
D. people shopped at the sky markets because the
items for sale were so unusual.

GO ON TO THE NEXT PAGE.

10. The narrator refers to "temper tantrums" (lines 57–58) as behavior she would have to view as:

F. one of the best ways she could use to get her mother's undivided attention.

G. a luxury she could not afford in her new relationship with her mother.

H. a part of her character that she inherited from her headstrong mother.

J. an understandable reaction on her mother's part to a confusing new set of circumstances.

Passage II

SOCIAL SCIENCE: This passage is adapted from Joseph Ellis's biography *American Sphinx: The Character of Thomas Jefferson* (©1997 by Joseph J. Ellis).

The most famous section of the Declaration of Independence, which has become the most quoted statement of human rights in recorded history as well as the most eloquent justification of revolution on behalf
5 of them, went through the Continental Congress without comment and with only one very minor change. These are, in all probability, the best-known fifty-eight words in American history: "We hold these truths to be self-evident; that all men are created equal; that they
10 are endowed by their Creator with certain inherent and inalienable Rights; that among these are life, liberty and the pursuit of happiness; that to secure these rights, governments are instituted among men, deriving their just powers from the consent of the governed." This is
15 the seminal statement of the American Creed, the closest approximation to political poetry ever produced in American culture. In the nineteenth century Abraham Lincoln, who also knew how to change history with words, articulated with characteristic eloquence the
20 quasi-religious view of Thomas Jefferson as the original American oracle: "All honor to Jefferson—to the man who, in the concrete pressure of a struggle for national independence by a single people, had the coolness, forecaste, and capacity to introduce into a merely
25 revolutionary document, an abstract truth, and so to embalm it there, that today and in all coming days, it shall be a rebuke and a stumbling block to the very harbingers of reappearing tyranny and oppression."

No serious student of either Jefferson or the
30 Declaration of Independence has ever claimed that he foresaw all or even most of the ideological consequences of what he wrote. But the effort to explain what *was* in his head has spawned almost as many interpretations as the words themselves have generated
35 political movements. Jefferson himself was accused of plagiarism by enemies or jealous friends on so many occasions throughout his career that he developed a standard reply. "Neither aiming at originality of principle or sentiment, nor yet copied from any particular
40 and previous writing," he explained, he drew his ideas from "the harmonizing sentiments of the day, whether expressed in letters, printed essays or in the elementary books of public right, as Aristotle, Cicero, Locke, Sidney, etc."

45 This is an ingeniously double-edged explanation, for it simultaneously disavows any claims to originality and yet insists that he depended upon no specific texts or sources. The image it conjures up is that of a medium, sitting alone at the writing desk and making
50 himself into an instrument for the accumulated wisdom and "harmonizing sentiments" of the ages. It is only a short step from this image to Lincoln's vision of Jefferson as oracle or prophet, receiving the message from the gods and sending it on to us and then to the
55 ages. Given the character of the natural rights section of the Declaration, several generations of American interpreters have felt the irresistible impulse to bathe the scene in speckled light and cloudy mist, thereby implying that efforts to dispel the veil of mystery rep-
60 resent some vague combination of sacrilege and treason.

Any serious attempt to pierce through this veil must begin by recovering the specific conditions inside that room on Market and Seventh streets in June 1776.
65 Even if we take Jefferson at his word, that he did not copy sections of the Declaration from any particular books, he almost surely had with him copies of his own previous writings, to include *Summary View, Causes and Necessities* and his three drafts of the Virginia con-
70 stitution. This is not to accuse him of plagiarism, unless one wishes to argue that an author can plagiarize himself. It is to say that virtually all the ideas found in the Declaration and much of the specific language had already found expression in those earlier writings.

75 Recall the context. The Congress is being overwhelmed with military reports of imminent American defeat in New York and Canada. The full Congress is in session six days a week, and committees are meeting throughout the evenings. The obvious practical course
80 for Jefferson to take was to rework his previous drafts on the same general theme. While it seems almost sacrilegious to suggest that the creative process that produced the Declaration was a cut-and-paste job, it strains credulity and common sense to the breaking point to
85 believe that Jefferson did not have these items at his elbow and draw liberally from them when drafting the Declaration.

11. It can reasonably be inferred from the passage that the author believes that Jefferson was:

A. a mysterious character whose attempts at originality were very patriotic.

B. a brilliant yet practical man, neither plagiarizer nor prophet, writing under pressure.

C. a politician who deserves more attention for his writing than he gets.

D. an average man who has been represented as a quasi-religious leader by later generations.

GO ON TO THE NEXT PAGE.

12. Details in the passage suggest that the author's personal position on the question of Jefferson's alleged plagiarism is that the:

F. idea of Jefferson copying from his own writings is only common sense.
G. notion of Jefferson copying from past writings is in fact sacrilegious.
H. concept of the Declaration as a cut-and-paste job strains credulity.
J. claim that the Declaration is related in some way to *Causes and Necessities* strains common sense.

13. It can reasonably be inferred that one of the functions of the first sentence (lines 1–6) is to:

A. point out that Jefferson's words have been used to justify revolutions as well as to promote human rights.
B. establish that the author believes that the Continental Congress should have commented on and reworked the Declaration.
C. emphasize the author's surprise at the eventual fame achieved by this section of the Declaration.
D. suggest that equally eloquent works were probably produced before the beginning of recorded history.

14. Which of the following statements best summarizes Lincoln's thoughts about what Jefferson achieved when he wrote the Declaration (lines 21–28)?

F. Even during the fight for independence, Jefferson's cool intelligence allowed him to write a statement that has been used against revolutionaries ever since.
G. Even during a revolution, Jefferson was calm enough to change a merely political document into a statement that predicted the rise of future tyrants.
H. Even under pressure of war, Jefferson was able to write a document that not only announced a revolution but also spoke against oppression for all time.
J. Even under pressure of war, Jefferson was able to write a document that both proclaimed abstract truths and dared tyrants to continually reappear.

15. The main function of the second paragraph (lines 29–44) in relation to the passage as a whole is to:

A. redirect the passage toward a discussion of various interpretations of the Declaration.
B. establish the passage's claim that Jefferson receives a great deal of serious scholarly attention for many of his writings.
C. shift the passage's focus toward an inquiry into the sources of the ideas expressed in the Declaration.
D. emphasize the passage's point that interpreters disagree about why the Declaration was written.

16. In saying "Even if we take Jefferson at his word, that he did not copy sections of the Declaration from any particular books" (lines 65–67), the author implies that he thinks Jefferson:

F. may not have been totally honest when he said that no parts of the Declaration were copied from any previous writing.
G. may have in fact copied some of Abraham Lincoln's writings when drafting the Declaration.
H. should not be believed because his character has been hidden behind a veil of mystery for so long.
J. cannot be accused of plagiarizing parts of the Declaration because it was written so long ago.

17. Use of the phrase *characteristic eloquence* (line 19) to describe Abraham Lincoln's words indicates the author's:

A. use of irony to describe words written by Lincoln that the author finds difficult to believe.
B. belief that Lincoln was usually a persuasive, expressive speaker and writer.
C. notion that Lincoln was a bit of a character because of his controversial opinions.
D. feelings of regret that Lincoln's words are so often difficult for modern readers to understand.

18. According to lines 29–32, students of Jefferson and of the Declaration think that Jefferson:

F. carefully contrived to write ambiguously about freedom.
G. anticipated most of the ideological outcomes of what he wrote.
H. never foresaw most of the ideological outcomes of what he wrote.
J. wrote the Declaration from memory without consulting other works.

19. The author thinks Jefferson's reply to accusations of plagiarism was "ingeniously double-edged" (line 45) because Jefferson claimed that:

A. he wrote alone, while also implying that he copied from his own previous writings.
B. his work was prophetic, yet he made no claim to originality.
C. he was a prophet, and he later influenced Lincoln to agree with that claim.
D. his writing was not new, yet he maintained he had not copied from any particular text.

20. The author uses the description of what was happening in the country when Jefferson was writing the Declaration (lines 75–79) to suggest that Jefferson:

F. felt great urgency to get the Declaration written, and didn't have much time to do so.
G. was depressed by news of American defeats and so lacked energy to draft a new document.
H. knew the Declaration could solve the problems of the nation and finished it in a hurry.
J. worried that the war was moving closer to home and felt he should take his time writing the Declaration.

Practice ACT Tests

GO ON TO THE NEXT PAGE.

Passage III

HUMANITIES: This passage is adapted from the essay "Spaced Out: The *Star Trek* Literary Phenomenon: Where No TV Series Has Gone Before" by Michael M. Epstein, which appeared in *Television Quarterly* (©1996 by The National Academy of Television Arts and Sciences).

On September 8, 1966, when NBC premiered its new futuristic series, *Star Trek,* few were watching. Conceived by television writer Gene Roddenberry as part American Western, part science fiction, and part
5 contemporary morality play, *Star Trek* languished for two and a half years before being canceled as a ratings flop in January 1969.

Two years later, *Star Trek* somehow had captured the imagination and viewer loyalty of millions of
10 Americans who "discovered" the show anew in syndicated reruns. *Star Trek*'s meteoric rise to popularity was unprecedented for a television program. By January 1972, the show was airing in over one hundred local markets in America and seventy more around the
15 world.

Perhaps more than other television series, *Star Trek* benefited greatly from being the right show at the right time. In middle-class America, social and political change in the late 1960s made it increasingly
20 difficult for people to unite in common purpose. Civil rights struggles, the Vietnam War, and the rise of a culturally empowered youth movement, among other things, divided many Americans by race, gender, age, and politics.

25 Although television news programs helped focus the country on the rifts that had begun to percolate on campuses, in city streets, and around dining room tables, as a rule entertainment programming avoided conflict and controversy. Escapist comedy about sub-
30 urban witches, genies, and rural townspeople was standard fare. Network drama emphasized law, order, and conformity, whether on the police beat, in a courtroom, or out on the great Western frontier.

Star Trek was different. Created in the optimistic
35 afterglow of John F. Kennedy's inauguration of the space race, *Star Trek*'s exploration of the "final frontier" was a theme that resonated with millions of idealistic and awestruck Americans who looked at the Apollo moon landings as a crowning, positive achieve-
40 ment for humankind. Still, as Gene Roddenberry often claimed, *Star Trek* was less about the future than the present.

Indeed, it was precisely because of its futuristic storyline that *Star Trek* was able to address many of the
45 contemporary social problems that other programs shunned. *Star Trek*'s visionary episodes on race relations, nuclear deterrence, multiculturalism, and ecology (among others) were not threatening to those who saw it as fantastic science fiction. For those who saw the
50 program as a window into current controversy, *Star Trek* offered insight and added perspective to continued

American cultural and political change in the 1970s. Either way, the show's wide appeal in syndication was such that, by 1977, *Star Trek* had become the most-
55 watched off-network series drama of all time.

In nearly thirty years, Gene Roddenberry's fantasy space concept has spawned four prime-time series, continued syndication, a cartoon, eight major motion pictures, countless toys, games, and computer software.
60 Nearly overlooked, however, is the unparalleled impact *Star Trek* has had on an industry that has only recently become television friendly: publishing. Since the early 1970s, when the first novels hit bookshelves, the world of *Star Trek* has exploded in print like no other phe-
65 nomenon in American popular culture. *Star Trek* fan volumes, cast memoirs, and novels continue to appear—and in record numbers.

Of all the "classic" and contemporary shows available to a critic, none illustrates the scope of America's
70 cultural evolution as eloquently as the saga of *Star Trek* and its next-generation spin-offs. In a culture that has undergone dramatic and far-reaching change in the last thirty years, *Star Trek* sweetens the often bitter alienation of contemporary change with the type of famil-
75 iarity and constancy that only a show with a thirty-year history can offer.

Star Trek offers viewers the paradox of a program that combines provocative insight into changing cultural values with the reassuring comfort that the
80 "known" universe of Starfleet, Klingons, and phasers can nonetheless survive intact, and even grow.

Because of its active fandom, *Star Trek* has become a television phenomenon like no other in American culture. And just as the original *Star Trek* has
85 found new expression in series such as *The Next Generation, Deep Space Nine,* and *Voyager,* I suspect fans will find new ways to indulge or express their private affection for *Star Trek* by reading—and writing—books in greater numbers. As America goes boldly into
90 the next millennium, so will *Star Trek* in print, on television, and in formats yet to come.

21. The main purpose of the passage can best be described as an effort to:
   A. explain how and why *Star Trek* has endured.
   B. illustrate what American society was like at the time the original *Star Trek* series was created.
   C. discuss how *Star Trek*'s storyline has changed over its thirty-year history.
   D. describe the different forms that *Star Trek* has taken, such as television series, films, and novels.

GO ON TO THE NEXT PAGE.

22. The author's attitude toward the subject of the passage can best be characterized as:

- **F.** amused tolerance.
- **G.** detached interest.
- **H.** warm appreciation.
- **J.** mild skepticism.

23. It can be reasonably inferred that the author believes *Star Trek* first became a success in:

- **A.** 1966.
- **B.** 1969.
- **C.** 1971.
- **D.** 1977.

24. According to the fourth paragraph (lines 25–33), compared to television news programs of the time period, entertainment programming is described as:

- **F.** more willing to examine the rifts developing in American society.
- **G.** more willing to portray violent conflict and controversy.
- **H.** less willing to promote the principles of conformity and order.
- **J.** less willing to present a realistic picture of contemporary life.

25. As described in the passage, the effect *Star Trek* has had on the publishing industry can best be summarized by which of the following statements?

- **A.** *Star Trek*'s impact can be safely overlooked because the publishing industry remains unfriendly to television.
- **B.** *Star Trek* made an impact with its first novels, but that impact has lessened over time.
- **C.** *Star Trek*'s tremendous impact has been primarily limited to novels.
- **D.** *Star Trek* has had a deep impact with its extensive and popular range of books.

26. When the author states that *Star Trek* was "the right show at the right time" (lines 17–18), he most likely means that the series benefited from:

- **F.** the unsettled social and political conditions.
- **G.** the general popularity of syndicated reruns.
- **H.** an increasing appetite for escapist entertainment.
- **J.** the increasingly empowered middle class.

27. The passage indicates that *Star Trek* creator Gene Roddenberry's primary purpose in creating the series was to:

- **A.** show how different life would be in the future.
- **B.** promote the space program and the exploration of space.
- **C.** offer a lighthearted alternative to serious entertainment.
- **D.** comment on problems facing people in the present.

28. According to the author, the primary benefit of the original *Star Trek*'s futuristic storyline was that it allowed the series' writers to:

- **F.** offer perspectives and insights that were unthreatening.
- **G.** invent fantastic and entertaining science fiction worlds.
- **H.** easily develop related spin-offs, such as films and new series.
- **J.** avoid controversial topics, such as nuclear deterrence and multiculturalism.

29. The author calls some of the original *Star Trek*'s episodes "visionary" in line 46 most likely because they:

- **A.** presented issues that weren't problems at the time but that now are.
- **B.** dealt with complex themes with imagination and foresight.
- **C.** offered dreamy and unrealistic solutions to difficult problems.
- **D.** appealed to a wide audience through syndication.

30. The "paradox" mentioned in line 77 most directly refers to what the author sees as the conflicting ideas of:

- **F.** cultural values and entertainment.
- **G.** familiarity and change.
- **H.** comfort and the *Star Trek* universe.
- **J.** survival and being provocative.

GO ON TO THE NEXT PAGE.

Passage IV

NATURAL SCIENCE: This passage is adapted from *An Anthropologist on Mars* by Oliver Sacks (©1995 by Oliver Sacks). Johann Wolfgang von Goethe was an eighteenth-century German poet and philosopher; Hermann von Helmholtz was a nineteenth-century scientist and philosopher.

Goethe's color theory, his *Farbenlehre* (which he regarded as the equal of his entire poetic opus), was, by and large, dismissed by all his contemporaries and has remained in a sort of limbo ever since, seen as the
5 whimsy, the pseudoscience, of a very great poet. But science itself was not entirely insensitive to the "anomalies" that Goethe considered central, and Helmholtz, indeed, gave admiring lectures on Goethe and his science, on many occasions—the last in 1892. Helmholtz
10 was very conscious of "color constancy"—the way in which the colors of objects are preserved, so that we can categorize them and always know what we are looking at, despite great fluctuations in the wavelength of the light illuminating them. The actual wavelengths
15 reflected by an apple, for instance, will vary considerably depending on the illumination, but we consistently see it as red, nonetheless. This could not be, clearly, a mere translation of wavelength into color. There had to be some way, Helmholtz thought, of "discounting the
20 illuminant"—and this he saw as an "unconscious inference" or "an act of judgement" (though he did not venture to suggest where such judgement might occur). Color constancy, for him, was a special example of the way in which we achieve perceptual constancy gener-
25 ally, make a stable perceptual world from a chaotic sensory flux—a world that would not be possible if our perceptions were merely passive reflections of the unpredictable and inconstant input that bathes our receptors.

30 Helmholtz's great contemporary, James Clerk Maxwell, had also been fascinated by the mystery of color vision from his student days. He formalized the notions of primary colors and color mixing by the invention of a color top (the colors of which fused,
35 when it was spun, to yield a sensation of grey), and a graphic representation with three axes, a color triangle, which showed how any color could be created by different mixtures of the three primary colors. These prepared the way for his most spectacular demonstration,
40 the demonstration in 1861 that color photography was possible, despite the fact that photographic emulsions were themselves black and white. He did this by photographing a colored bow three times, through red, green, and violet filters. Having obtained three "color-
45 separation" images, as he called them, he now brought these together by superimposing them upon a screen, projecting each image through its corresponding filter (the image taken through the red filter was projected with red light, and so on). Suddenly, the bow burst
50 forth in full color. Clerk Maxwell wondered if this was how colors were perceived in the brain, by the addition of color-separation images or their neural correlates [what functions in the brain as a color-separation image], as in his magic-lantern demonstrations.

55 Clerk Maxwell himself was acutely aware of the drawback of this additive process: color photography had no way of "discounting the illuminant," and its colors changed helplessly with changing wavelengths of light.

60 In 1957, ninety-odd years after Clerk Maxwell's famous demonstration, Edwin Land—not merely the inventor of the instant Land camera and Polaroid, but an experimenter and theorizer of genius—provided a photographic demonstration of color perception even
65 more startling. Unlike Clerk Maxwell, he made only two black-and-white images (using a split-beam camera so they could be taken at the same time from the same viewpoint, through the same lens) and superimposed these on a screen with a double-lens projector. He used
70 two filters to make the images: one passing longer wavelengths (a red filter), the other passing shorter wavelengths (a green filter). The first image was then projected through a red filter, the second with ordinary white light, unfiltered. One might expect that this
75 would produce just an overall pale-pink image, but something "impossible" happened instead. The photograph of a young woman appeared instantly in full color—"blonde hair, pale blue eyes, red coat, bluegreen collar, and strikingly natural flesh tones," as Land later
80 described it. Where did these colors come from, how were they made? They did not seem to be "in" the photographs or the illuminants themselves. These demonstrations, overwhelming in their simplicity and impact, were color "illusions" in Goethe's sense, but illusions
85 that demonstrated a neurological truth—that colors are not "out there" in the world, nor (as classical theory held) an automatic correlate of wavelength, but, rather, are *constructed by the brain*.

31. According to the passage, regarding Goethe's color theory, Helmholtz expressed which of the following attitudes?

A. Disbelief
B. Respect
C. Amusement
D. Skepticism

32. It can be inferred that in Clerk Maxwell's 1861 demonstration a color image would not have been produced from black-and-white film emulsions without the use of color:

F. filters.
G. triangles.
H. tops.
J. slides.

GO ON TO THE NEXT PAGE.

33. As described in the passage, Goethe's contemporaries for the most part regarded him as a:

A. mediocre poet whose most important work was as a scientist.
B. theorist whose attempts at poetry were commendable but insignificant.
C. leading poet whose contributions to science were less noteworthy.
D. leading theorist who overturned previously standard approaches to scientific inquiry.

34. The tendency to perceive objects as having a given color, such as the perception of an apple as "red" even if it is "red" only in certain lighting, is an example of what Helmholtz refers to as:

F. split-beam filtering.
G. sensory flux.
H. color separation.
J. color constancy.

35. According to lines 14–17, the wavelengths reflected by the apple vary considerably as a result of:

A. the differences between the viewer's right and left eye.
B. the distance between the apple and the eyes.
C. a viewer's ability to perceive red in different light.
D. variations in the source of light reaching the apple.

36. The term *illuminant,* as it is used in line 20 and elsewhere in the passage, refers to which of the following?

F. Camera flash equipment
G. A color theorist
H. Light that makes an object visible
J. Light before it passes through a filter

37. What about the nature of color perception is described as a preoccupation of Helmholtz's? The way in which:

A. varying wavelengths of light stabilize the appearance of an object.
B. humans arrive at a notion of what the color of an object is.
C. humans undergo changes in color awareness as they age.
D. one color becomes another when images are superimposed.

38. According to the passage, the relationship between primary colors and other colors can be best described by which of the following statements?

F. All colors are either primary colors or can be created by a combination of primary colors.
G. The human eye perceives primary colors first, then other colors.
H. Primary colors were the first colors captured on film by the camera; other colors were captured by later, more sophisticated, equipment.
J. Primary colors emerge as a result of blending nonprimary colors along the axes of Clerk Maxwell's triangle.

39. Clerk Maxwell demonstrated that color photography was possible even though at the time of his demonstrations:

A. illuminants were thought to be stable rather than variable.
B. photographic emulsions were available only in black-and-white.
C. the general public rejected the new technology as stunts with no practical application.
D. professional photographers were reluctant to abandon the established black-and-white aesthetic.

40. The two images that became the single image in Land's photograph of a woman were obtained by using:

F. a screen lit from the front and back.
G. flickering light sources.
H. one lens in two cameras.
J. one camera with one divided lens.

END OF TEST 3

STOP! DO NOT TURN THE PAGE UNTIL TOLD TO DO SO.

DO NOT RETURN TO A PREVIOUS TEST.

SCIENCE TEST

35 Minutes—40 Questions

DIRECTIONS: There are seven passages in this test. Each passage is followed by several questions. After reading a passage, choose the best answer to each question and fill in the corresponding oval on your answer document. You may refer to the passages as often as necessary.

You are NOT permitted to use a calculator on this test.

Passage I

A team of researchers constructed a greenhouse, consisting of 3 artificially lighted and heated sections, to be used to grow food during a long space voyage. The researchers found the weekly average light intensity, in arbitrary units, and the weekly average air temperature, in degrees Celsius (°C), in each section. The results for the first 6 weeks of their measurements are given in Table 1 (weekly average light intensity) and Table 2 (weekly average air temperature).

Table 1			
	Weekly average light intensity (arbitrary units)		
Week	Section 1	Section 2	Section 3
1	289.3	84.4	120.7
2	305.5	79.2	80.8
3	313.4	76.2	77.0
4	314.9	73.6	69.4
5	304.5	68.8	74.6
6	311.1	68.5	68.4

Table 2			
	Weekly average air temperature (°C)		
Week	Section 1	Section 2	Section 3
1	19.68	19.10	18.66
2	20.12	19.22	18.47
3	20.79	19.21	18.61
4	20.98	19.49	18.95
5	21.04	19.91	19.09
6	21.13	19.60	18.59

1. The highest weekly average air temperature recorded during the first 6 weeks of the study was:
   A. 18.47°C.
   B. 21.13°C.
   C. 120.7°C.
   D. 314.9°C.

2. According to Table 2, weekly average air temperatures were recorded to the nearest:
   F. 0.01°C.
   G. 0.1°C.
   H. 1.0°C.
   J. 10°C.

GO ON TO THE NEXT PAGE.

3. A plot of weekly average air temperature versus weekly average light intensity for Section 1 is best represented by which of the following graphs?

A.
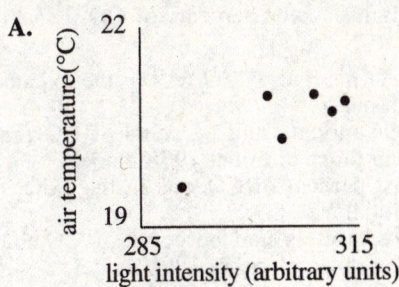

B.
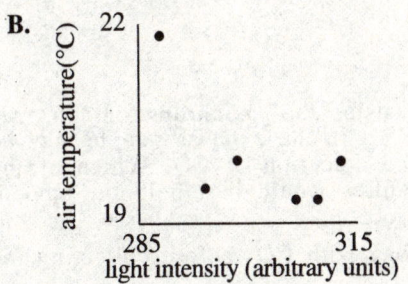

C.
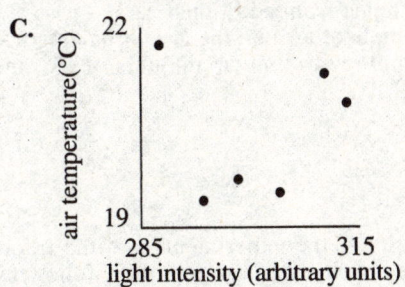

D.
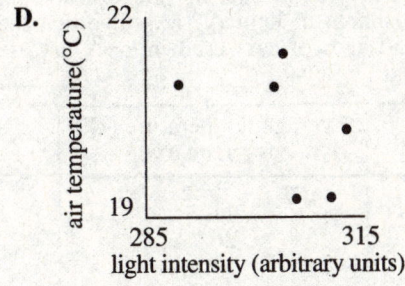

4. Which of the following statements best describes the changes in the weekly average air temperature in Section 1 during Weeks 1–6 ?

F. The weekly average air temperature increased between Weeks 1 and 3 and decreased between Weeks 4 and 6.

G. The weekly average air temperature decreased between Weeks 1 and 3 and increased between Weeks 4 and 6.

H. The weekly average air temperature always increased.

J. The weekly average air temperature always decreased.

5. Suppose the *efficiency of illumination* is defined as the intensity of light absorbed by the plants divided by the intensity of light provided to the plants. Based on the data, would one be justified in concluding that the efficiency of illumination was higher in Section 1 than in the other sections?

A. Yes, because the illumination provided to the plants was highest in Section 1.

B. Yes, because the amount of light not absorbed by the plants was highest in Section 1.

C. No, because the amount of light absorbed by the plants was lowest in Section 1.

D. No, because the information provided is insufficient to determine efficiency of illumination.

Practice ACT Tests

GO ON TO THE NEXT PAGE.

Passage II

Carbon monoxide gas (CO) is toxic in air at concentrations above 0.1% by volume. Cars are the major source of atmospheric CO in urban areas. Higher CO levels are observed during colder weather. A group of students proposed that cars emit more CO at colder air temperatures than at warmer air temperatures during the first 15 minutes after they are started. The students did the following experiments to investigate this hypothesis.

Experiment 1

A hose was connected to the tailpipe of a car. The engine was started and the exhaust was collected in a plastic bag. A 1 mL sample of the exhaust was taken from the bag with a syringe and injected into a *gas chromatograph*, an instrument that separates a mixture of gases into its individual components. Comparisons of the exhaust with mixtures of known CO concentrations were made to determine the percent by volume of CO in the exhaust. Exhaust was collected at 2-minute intervals. Samples of exhaust from each of 4 cars were tested at an external temperature of $-9°C$. The results are shown in Table 1.

Time after starting (min)	Percent of CO in the exhaust at $-9°C$:			
	1978 Model X	1978 Model Y	1996 Model X	1996 Model Y
1	3.5	3.2	1.2	0.3
3	4.0	3.7	1.0	1.2
5	4.5	7.5	1.5	2.5
7	3.6	10.0	1.0	3.0
9	3.2	9.1	0.5	2.6
11	3.1	8.0	0.5	2.0
13	3.0	7.0	0.5	2.0
15	2.9	7.0	0.4	1.8

Table 1

Experiment 2

The same 4 cars were tested at a temperature of $20°C$ using the procedure from Experiment 1. The results are shown in Table 2.

Time after starting (min)	Percent of CO in the exhaust at $20°C$:			
	1978 Model X	1978 Model Y	1996 Model X	1996 Model Y
1	2.0	0.8	0.3	0.2
3	2.8	2.0	0.5	1.0
5	3.4	6.0	0.5	1.5
7	1.5	7.0	0.3	0.8
9	1.3	7.0	0.3	0.5
11	1.0	6.5	0.1	0.3
13	1.0	5.0	0.1	0.3
15	0.9	4.8	0.1	0.2

Table 2

6. Do the results from Experiment 1 support the hypothesis that, at a given temperature and time, the exhaust of newer cars contains lower percents of CO than the exhaust of older cars?

F. Yes; the highest percent of CO was in the exhaust of the 1996 Model Y.
G. Yes; both 1996 models had percents of CO that were lower than those of either 1978 model.
H. No; the highest percent of CO was in the exhaust of the 1978 Model Y.
J. No; both 1978 models had percents of CO that were lower than those of either 1996 model.

7. A student, when using the gas chromatograph, was concerned that CO_2 in the exhaust sample may be interfering in the detection of CO. Which of the following procedures would best help the student investigate this problem?

A. Filling the bag with CO_2 before collecting the exhaust
B. Collecting exhaust from additional cars
C. Injecting a sample of air into the gas chromatograph
D. Testing a sample with known amounts of CO and CO_2

8. Based on the results of the experiments and the information in the table below, cars in which of the following cities would most likely contribute the greatest amount of CO to the atmosphere in January? (Assume that the types, numbers, and ages of cars used in each city are approximately equal.)

City	Average temperature (°F) for January
Minneapolis	11.2
Pittsburgh	26.7
Seattle	39.1
San Diego	56.8

F. Minneapolis
G. Pittsburgh
H. Seattle
J. San Diego

9. In Experiment 1, which of the following factors varied?

A. The method of sample collection
B. The volume of exhaust that was tested
C. The year in which the cars were made
D. The temperature at which the engine was started

GO ON TO THE NEXT PAGE.

10. Many states require annual testing of cars to determine the levels of their CO emissions. Based on the experiments, in order to determine the maximum percent of CO found in a car's exhaust, during which of the following times after starting a car would it be best to sample the exhaust?

F. 1–3 min
G. 5–7 min
H. 9–11 min
J. 13 min or longer

11. How would the results of the experiments be affected, if at all, if the syringe contents were contaminated with CO-free air? (The composition of air is 78% N_2, 21% O_2, 0.9% Ar, and 0.1% other gases.) The measured percents of CO in the exhaust would be:

A. higher than the actual percents at both –9°C and 20°C.
B. lower than the actual percents at –9°C, but higher than the actual percents at 20°C.
C. lower than the actual percents at both –9°C and 20°C.
D. the same as the actual percents at both –9°C and 20°C.

GO ON TO THE NEXT PAGE.

Passage III

A student performed 3 activities with a microscope that had 4 objective lenses.

Activity 1

The student viewed 4 slides (A, B, C, and D) through each objective lens. Each slide had 2 thin lines painted on it. For each objective lens, the student determined whether she could see the lines as separate or whether they blurred into 1 image. The results appear in Table 1.

	Table 1			
	Objective Lens:			
Slide	1	2	3	4
A	|	|	|	|
B	|	|	|	||
C	|	|	||	||
D	|	||	||	||

Note: ‖ indicates lines appeared separate; │ indicates lines blurred together.

Activity 2

The student was given a prepared slide with a line on it that was 0.1 mm in length. This length was defined as the *object size*. Next, she viewed the slide with each objective lens, estimating how long the line appeared. This estimated length was called the *image size*. Finally, she calculated the magnification (M) associated with each objective lens from the following formula:

$$M = \text{image size} \div \text{object size}.$$

The data appear in Table 2.

Table 2		
Objective Lens	Image size (mm)	M
1	4	40
2	10	100
3	20	200
4	40	400

Activity 3

The *numerical aperture* (NA) of each objective lens was printed on the microscope. NA determines how much detail can be seen and is related to *resolution* (R). R is defined as the smallest distance separating 2 objects such that the objects appear separate. Thus an objective lens with a small R shows a sample more clearly than does an objective lens with a large R. R is calculated from the following formula:

$$R = \lambda \div 2(NA)$$

where λ is the wavelength of the light, in nanometers (nm), used to view the objects.

The student calculated R for each objective lens, assuming a λ of 550 nm. The data appear in Table 3.

Table 3		
Objective Lens	NA	R (nm)
1	0.10	2,750
2	0.25	1,100
3	0.40	688
4	0.65	423

12. If the student had viewed the slide used in Activity 2 through a fifth objective lens and the image size with this objective lens was 30 mm, the M associated with this objective lens would have been:

F. 30.
G. 100.
H. 300.
J. 1,000.

13. Based on the results of Activity 2, the combination of which of the following lines and objective lenses would result in the greatest image size?

A. A 0.7 mm line viewed through Objective Lens 1
B. A 0.6 mm line viewed through Objective Lens 2
C. A 0.5 mm line viewed through Objective Lens 3
D. A 0.4 mm line viewed through Objective Lens 4

GO ON TO THE NEXT PAGE.

14. When viewing Slide C in Activity 1, the student was able to discern 2 distinct lines with how many of the objective lenses?

F. 1
G. 2
H. 3
J. 4

15. Which of the following equations correctly calculates R (in nm) for Objective Lens 2, using light with a wavelength of 425 nm ?

A. $R = 425 \div 2(0.10)$
B. $R = 425 \div 2(0.25)$
C. $R = 0.10 \div 2(425)$
D. $R = 0.25 \div 2(425)$

16. Another student calculated the R of a fifth objective lens as described in Activity 3. He determined that for this fifth objective lens, R = 1,830 nm. Accordingly, the NA of this lens was most likely closest to which of the following values?

F. 0.15
G. 0.25
H. 0.35
J. 0.45

17. Activity 1 and Activity 2 differed in that in Activity 1:

A. 4 different slides were used.
B. 4 different objective lenses were used.
C. the wavelength of the light was varied.
D. the object sizes were greater than the image sizes.

GO ON TO THE NEXT PAGE.

Passage IV

A *blackbody* is an object that absorbs all of the radiation that strikes it. The blackbody also emits radiation at all wavelengths; the emitted radiation is called *blackbody radiation*. The brightness of blackbody radiation at a given wavelength depends on the temperature of the blackbody. A graph of brightness versus wavelength for a blackbody is called a *blackbody curve*. Blackbody curves for the same blackbody at 3 different temperatures are shown in the figure below.

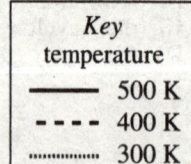

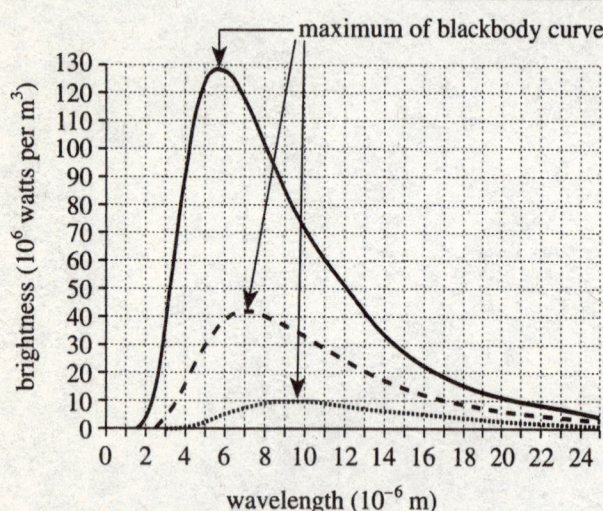

(Note: 1 watt = 1 joule per second; joule is a unit of energy. At wavelengths above 25×10^{-6} m, the brightness of the blackbody at each temperature continues to decrease.)

18. The area under each blackbody curve gives the total amount of energy emitted every second by 1 m² of the blackbody. Which of the following correctly ranks the 3 curves, from *greatest* to *least*, according to the total amount of energy emitted every second by 1 m² of the blackbody at the wavelengths shown?

F. 300 K, 400 K, 500 K
G. 300 K, 500 K, 400 K
H. 400 K, 500 K, 300 K
J. 500 K, 400 K, 300 K

19. Based on the figure, at a temperature of 300 K and a wavelength of 30×10^{-6} m, the brightness of a blackbody will most likely be:

A. less than 5×10^6 watts per m³.
B. between 5×10^6 watts per m³ and 40×10^6 watts per m³.
C. between 41×10^6 watts per m³ and 130×10^6 watts per m³.
D. greater than 130×10^6 watts per m³.

20. The radiation emitted by a star can be represented by the radiation from a blackbody having the same temperature as the star's visible surface. Based on the figure, which of the following sets of blackbody curves best represents stars of equal diameter with surface temperatures of 3,000 K, 6,000 K, and 9,000 K ?

F.

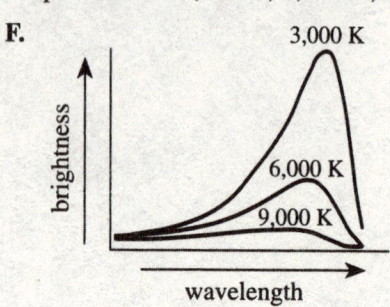

G.

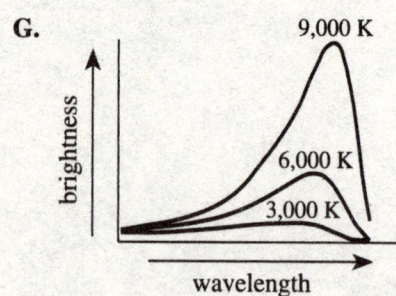

H.

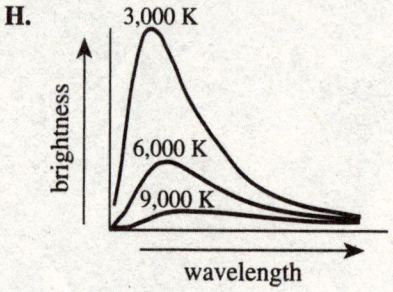

J.

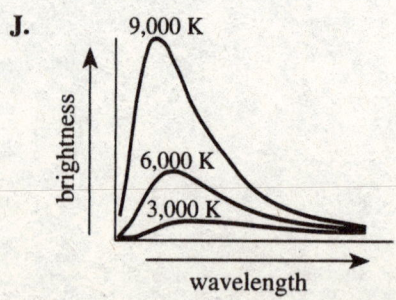

GO ON TO THE NEXT PAGE.

21. Based on the figure, the maximum of the blackbody curve will equal 75×10^6 watts per m^3 when the temperature of the blackbody is closest to:

A. 250 K.
B. 350 K.
C. 450 K.
D. 550 K.

22. The frequency of radiation increases as the radiation's wavelength decreases. Based on this information, over all wavelengths in the figure, as the frequency of the radiation from a blackbody increases, the brightness of the radiation:

F. increases only.
G. decreases only.
H. increases, then decreases.
J. decreases, then increases.

GO ON TO THE NEXT PAGE.

Passage V

Some of the liquid in a closed container evaporates, forming a vapor that condenses, reforming the liquid. The pressure of the vapor at *equilibrium* (when the rates of evaporation and condensation are equal) is the liquid's *vapor pressure*. A liquid in an open container boils when its vapor pressure equals the *external pressure*. The following experiments were performed to study vapor pressures.

Experiment 1

The apparatus shown in Figure 1 was assembled except for the tubing. The flask was placed in a 20°C H₂O bath. After 5 minutes the manometer was connected, and 2 mL of hexane was added to the flask from the dropper. Some of the hexane evaporated. The vapor pressure was determined by measuring the height of the mercury (Hg) after the Hg level had stabilized. Additional trials were performed at different temperatures and with other liquids in the flask. The results are shown in Table 1.

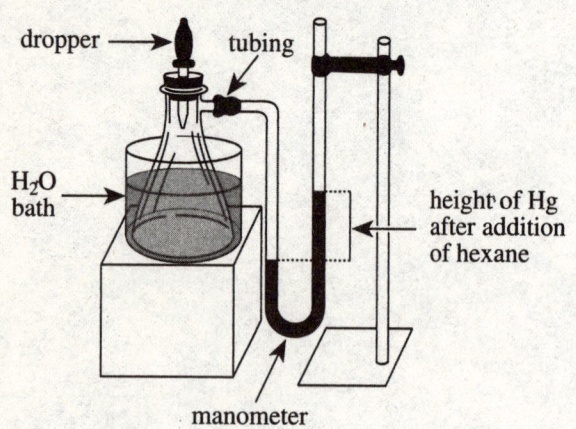

Figure 1

Figure 1 adapted from Henry Dorin, Peter E. Demmin, and Dorothy L. Gabel, *Chemistry: The Study of Matter.* ©1989 by Prentice-Hall, Inc.

Table 1

Liquid	Vapor pressure (mm Hg) at:		
	0°C	20°C	40°C
2-Butanone	35	75	200
Ethyl acetate	20	70	180
Hexane	40	110	250
Methanol	25	90	245
2-Propanol	9	35	100

Experiment 2

A test tube containing a thermometer and hexane was heated in an oil bath until the hexane boiled gently. The temperature was recorded. The external pressure was 760 mm Hg. This procedure was repeated in a chamber at pressures of 400 mm Hg and 100 mm Hg. The boiling points of other liquids were also determined. The results are shown in Table 2.

Table 2

Liquid	Boiling point (°C) at external pressure of:		
	760 mm Hg	400 mm Hg	100 mm Hg
2-Butanone	79.6	60.0	25.0
Ethyl acetate	77.1	59.3	27.0
Hexane	68.7	49.6	15.8
Methanol	64.7	49.9	21.2
2-Propanol	82.5	67.8	39.5

23. Which of the following bar graphs best represents the vapor pressures of the liquids from Experiment 1 at 20°C ?

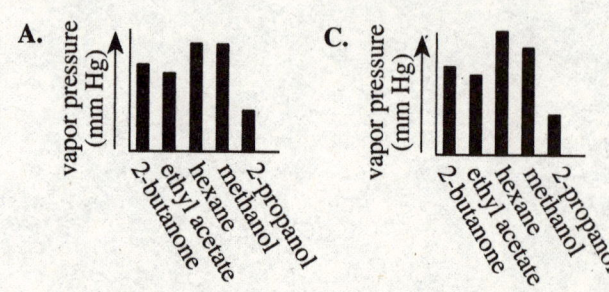

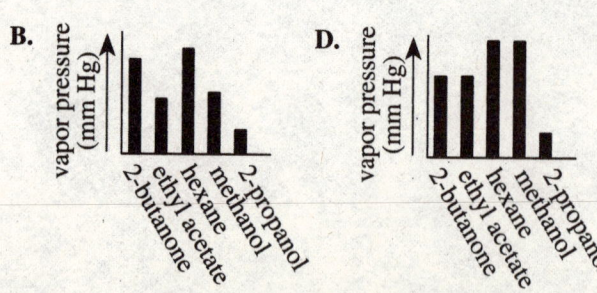

GO ON TO THE NEXT PAGE.

24. Which of the following figures best depicts the change in height of the Hg in the manometer in Experiment 1 ?

Hg height before liquid was added | Hg height after Hg level stabilized

F.

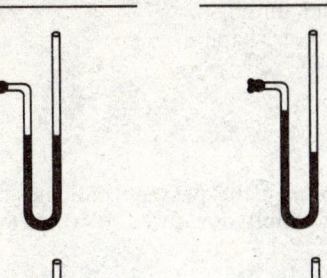

G.

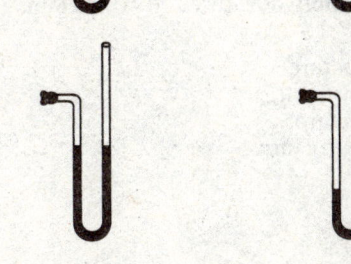

H.

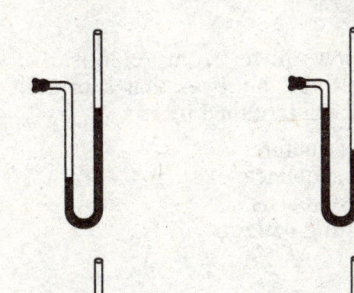

J.

25. A student hypothesized that, at a given external pressure, the higher a liquid's molecular weight, the higher the boiling point of that liquid. Do the results of Experiment 2 and all of the information in the table below support his hypothesis?

Liquid	Molecular weight (grams per mole)
2-Butanone	72
Ethyl acetate	88
Hexane	86
Methanol	32
2-Propanol	60

A. Yes; methanol has the lowest molecular weight and the lowest boiling point.
B. Yes; ethyl acetate has a higher molecular weight and boiling point than hexane.
C. No; the higher a liquid's molecular weight, the lower the liquid's boiling point.
D. No; there is no clear relationship in these data between boiling point and molecular weight.

26. According to the results of Experiment 2, as the external pressure increases, the boiling points of the liquids:

F. decrease only.
G. increase only.
H. decrease, then increase.
J. increase, then decrease.

27. Which of the following figures best illustrates the apparatus used inside the pressure chamber in Experiment 2 ?

A.

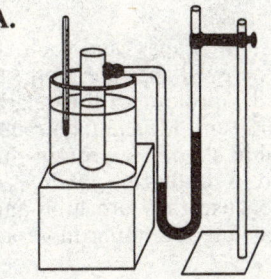

C.

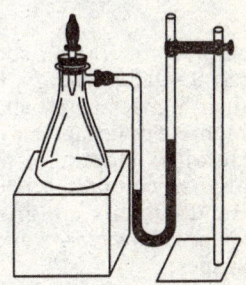

B.

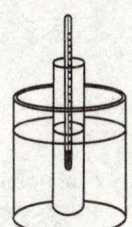

D.

28. Which of the following statements best explains why in Experiment 1 the experimenter waited 5 minutes before connecting the manometer to the flask with the tubing? The experimenter waited to allow:

F. all of the H_2O vapor to be removed from the flask.
G. time for the liquid in the flask to evaporate.
H. time for the height of the Hg in the manometer to stabilize.
J. the air in the flask to adjust to the temperature of the H_2O bath.

GO ON TO THE NEXT PAGE.

Passage VI

A *polypeptide* molecule is a chain of amino acids. A *protein* consists of 1 or more polypeptides. A protein's shape is described by 3 or 4 levels of structure.

1. The *primary structure* of a protein is the sequence of amino acids in each polypeptide.

2. The *secondary structure* of a protein is the local folding patterns within short segments of each polypeptide due to *hydrogen bonding* (weak chemical bonds).

3. The *tertiary structure* is the folding patterns that result from interactions between amino acid *side chains* (parts of an amino acid) in each polypeptide. These folding patterns generally occur across greater distances than those associated with the secondary structure.

4. The *quaternary structure* is the result of the clustering between more than 1 folded polypeptide.

A protein can adopt different shapes, and each shape has a relative energy. Lower-energy shapes are more stable than higher-energy shapes, and a protein with a relatively high-energy shape may *denature* (unfold) and then *renature* (refold), adopting a more stable shape. A protein that is almost completely denatured is called a *random coil*. Random coils are unstable because they are high-energy shapes; however, some can renature, adopting more stable shapes.

Two scientists discuss protein shape.

Scientist 1

The *active shape* (the biologically functional shape) of a protein is always identical to the protein's lowest-energy shape. Any other shape would be unstable. Because a protein's lowest-energy shape is determined by its primary structure, its active shape is determined by its primary structure.

Scientist 2

The active shape of a protein is dependent upon its primary structure. However, a protein's active shape may also depend on its *process of synthesis*, the order (in time) in which the amino acids were bonded together. As synthesis occurs, stable, local structures form within short segments of the polypeptide chain due to hydrogen bonding. These local structures may be different than the local structures associated with the protein's lowest-energy shape. After synthesis, these structures persist, trapping the protein in an active shape that has more energy than its lowest-energy shape.

29. According to the passage, protein shapes with relatively low energy tend to:

   A. be random coils.
   B. lack a primary structure.
   C. become denatured.
   D. maintain their shape.

30. The information in the passage indicates that when a protein is completely denatured, it still retains its original:

   F. primary structure.
   G. secondary structure.
   H. tertiary structure.
   J. quaternary structure.

31. Scientist 2's views differ from Scientist 1's views in that only Scientist 2 believes that a protein's active shape is partially determined by its:

   A. quaternary structure.
   B. amino acid sequence.
   C. process of synthesis.
   D. tertiary folding patterns.

32. A student has 100 balls. The balls are various colors. The student chooses 15 balls and aligns them in a row. The spatial order in which the balls were placed corresponds to which of the following levels of structure in a protein?

   F. Primary structure
   G. Secondary structure
   H. Tertiary structure
   J. Quaternary structure

33. Suppose proteins are almost completely denatured and then allowed to renature in a way that allows them to have their lowest-energy shapes. Which of the following statements about the proteins is most consistent with the information presented in the passage?

   A. If Scientist 1 is correct, all of the proteins will have their active shapes.
   B. If Scientist 1 is correct, all of the proteins will have shapes different than their active shapes.
   C. If Scientist 2 is correct, all of the proteins will have their active shapes.
   D. If Scientist 2 is correct, all of the proteins will have shapes different than their active shapes.

GO ON TO THE NEXT PAGE.

34. Which of the following diagrams showing the relationship between a given protein's shape and its relative energy is consistent with Scientist 2's assertions about the energy of proteins, but is NOT consistent with Scientist 1's assertions about the energy of proteins?

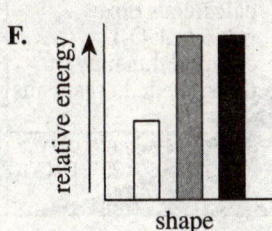

F.

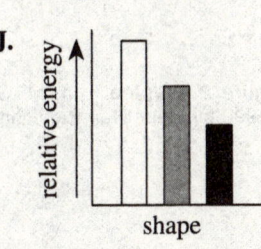

H.

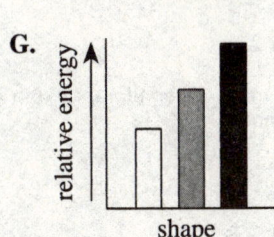

G.

J.

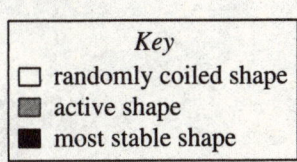

Key
- ☐ randomly coiled shape
- ▨ active shape
- ◼ most stable shape

35. Scientist 2 says that a protein may be trapped in a moderately high-energy shape. Which of the following findings, if true, could be used to *counter* this argument?

A. Once a protein has achieved its tertiary structure, all of the folding patterns at the local level are stable.

B. Enough energy is available in the environment to overcome local energy barriers, driving the protein to its lowest-energy shape.

C. During protein synthesis, the secondary structure of a protein is determined before the tertiary structure is formed.

D. Proteins that lose their tertiary structure or quaternary structure also tend to lose their biological functions.

Passage VII

Tiny marine organisms build shells from *calcite* ($CaCO_3$) dissolved in seawater. After the organisms' death, the shells sink. Some shells dissolve before they reach the seafloor, but some form layers of *calcareous ooze* ($CaCO_3$-rich sediment). Figure 1 shows how seawater's degree of saturation with respect to $CaCO_3$ and the rate at which $CaCO_3$ dissolves change with depth. The *CaCO₃ compensation depth* (CCD) represents the depth beneath which $CaCO_3$ dissolves faster than it precipitates. Figure 2 shows typical depths at which various seafloor sediments are found. Figure 3 shows the percent coverage for 2 seafloor sediments in 3 oceans.

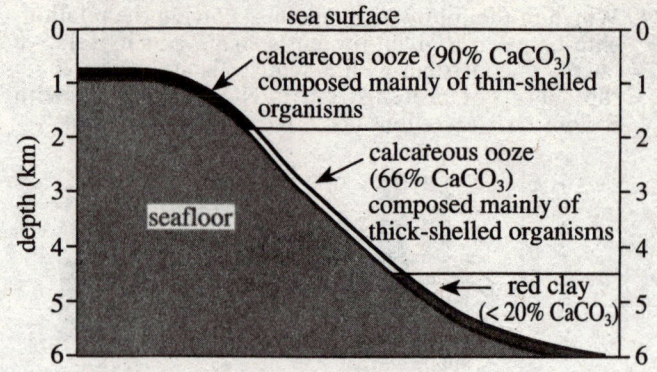

Figure 2

Figure 2 adapted from M. Grant Gross, *Oceanography*, 6th ed. ©1990 by Macmillan Publishing Company.

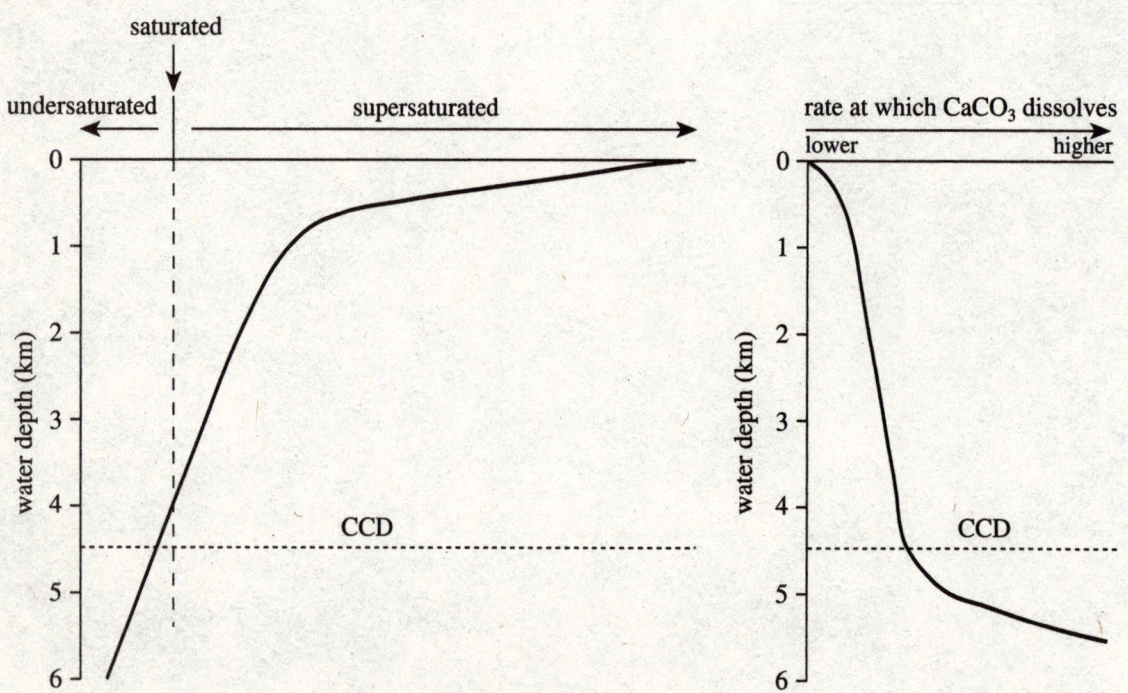

Figure 1

Figure 1 adapted from J. Andrews, P. Brimblecombe, T. Jickells, and P. Liss, *An Introduction to Environmental Chemistry*. ©1996 by Blackwell Science, Ltd.

GO ON TO THE NEXT PAGE.

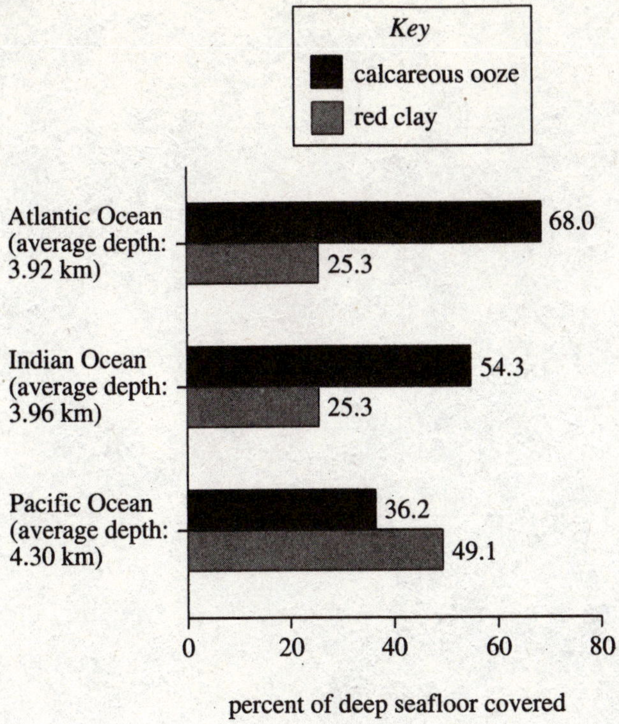

Key
■ calcareous ooze
▦ red clay

Atlantic Ocean
(average depth:
3.92 km)
68.0
25.3

Indian Ocean
(average depth:
3.96 km)
54.3
25.3

Pacific Ocean
(average depth:
4.30 km)
36.2
49.1

0 20 40 60 80

percent of deep seafloor covered

Figure 3

Figure 3 adapted from Harold Thurman, *Introductory Oceanography.*
©1991 by Macmillan Publishing Company.

36. Assume that the Arctic Ocean seafloor has an average depth of 4.9 km. According to Figures 2 and 3, the Arctic Ocean seafloor is most likely covered with:

F. calcareous ooze only.
G. nearly the same areas of calcareous ooze and red clay.
H. a greater area of calcareous ooze than of red clay.
J. a greater area of red clay than of calcareous ooze.

37. The data in Figure 2 support which of the following statements about the relative thickness of marine organism shells and the depths at which calcareous oozes composed of those shells are found? Calcareous oozes formed mainly from thick-shelled organisms are found:

A. at shallower depths than those formed mainly from thin-shelled organisms.
B. at greater depths than those formed mainly from thin-shelled organisms.
C. over the same depth range as those formed mainly from thin-shelled organisms.
D. in the same areas of a given ocean as those formed mainly from thin-shelled organisms.

38. $CaCO_3$ often precipitates out of seawater in areas where the seawater is shallow (less than 1 km deep). According to Figure 1, this most likely occurs because seawater in those locations:

F. is undersaturated with respect to $CaCO_3$.
G. is saturated with respect to $CaCO_3$.
H. is supersaturated with respect to $CaCO_3$.
J. contains no $CaCO_3$.

39. According to Figure 1, above what maximum depth is seawater supersaturated with respect to $CaCO_3$?

A. 3.0 km
B. 3.5 km
C. 4.0 km
D. 4.5 km

40. Figure 1 shows that the rate at which $CaCO_3$ dissolves increases the most between which of the following depths?

F. Between 3.5 km and 4.0 km
G. Between 4.0 km and 4.5 km
H. Between 4.5 km and 5.0 km
J. Between 5.0 km and 5.5 km

END OF TEST 4

STOP! DO NOT RETURN TO ANY OTHER TEST.

Practice ACT Tests

Your Signature (do not print): _____

Print Your Name Here: _____

Your Date of Birth:

☐☐ – ☐☐ – ☐☐☐☐
Month   Day   Year

Form 2WT

The ACT® WRITING TEST BOOKLET

You must take the multiple-choice tests before you take the Writing Test.

Directions

This is a test of your writing skills. You will have thirty (30) minutes to write an essay in English. Before you begin planning and writing your essay, read the writing prompt carefully to understand exactly what you are being asked to do. Your essay will be evaluated on the evidence it provides of your ability to express judgments by taking a position on the issue in the writing prompt; to maintain a focus on the topic throughout the essay; to develop a position by using logical reasoning and by supporting your ideas; to organize ideas in a logical way; and to use language clearly and effectively according to the conventions of standard written English.

You may use the unlined pages in this test booklet to plan your essay. These pages will not be scored. *You must write your essay in pencil on the lined pages in the answer folder.* Your writing on those lined pages will be scored. You may not need all the lined pages, but to ensure you have enough room to finish, do NOT skip lines. You may write corrections or additions neatly between the lines of your essay, but do NOT write in the margins of the lined pages. *Illegible essays cannot be scored, so you must write (or print) clearly.*

If you finish before time is called, you may review your work. Lay your pencil down immediately when time is called.

DO NOT OPEN THIS BOOKLET UNTIL TOLD TO DO SO.

P.O. BOX 168
IOWA CITY, IA 52243-0168   **ACT**®

Practice ACT Tests

Practice Writing Test Prompt 2

In some high schools, students are required to complete a certain number of community service hours prior to graduation. Some people think community service is a good requirement because they think students will benefit from this experience. Other people think schools should not require community service because students will resent the requirement and, as a result, will not benefit from the experience. In your opinion, should high schools require students to complete a certain number of hours of community service?

In your essay, take a position on this question. You may write about either one of the two points of view given, or you may present a different point of view on this question. Use specific reasons and examples to support your position.

Use this page to *plan* your essay.
Your work on this page will *not* be scored.

If you need more space to plan,
please continue on the back of this page.

Use this page to *plan* your essay.
Your work on this page will *not* be scored.

You may wish to photocopy these sample answer document pages to respond to the practice ACT Writing Test.

Please enter the information at the right before beginning the Writing Test.

Use a soft lead No. 2 pencil only. Do NOT use a mechanical pencil, ink, ballpoint, or felt-tip pen.

WRITING TEST BOOKLET NUMBER

Print your 6-digit **Booklet Number** in the boxes at the right.

WRITING TEST FORM

Print your 3-character **Test Form** in the boxes above and fill in the corresponding oval at the right.

○ 1WT ○ 2WT ○ 3WT
○ 4WT ○ 5WT

Begin WRITING TEST here.

If you need more space, please continue on the next page.

WRITING TEST

If you need more space, please continue on the next page.

WRITING TEST

_____

_____

_____

_____

_____

_____

_____

_____

_____

_____

_____

_____

_____

_____

_____

_____

_____

_____

_____

_____

_____

_____

_____

_____

_____

_____

_____

If you need more space, please continue on the back of this page.

0876008

WRITING TEST

STOP here with the Writing Test.

Passage I

Question 1. The best answer is **A** because it provides punctuation (in this case, a period) that appropriately separates these two complete thoughts or statements—"My grandfather is not known for embracing technological change" and "He still drives his '59 Chevy Impala."

The best answer is NOT:

B because it creates a run-on, or fused, sentence. There is no punctuation or conjunction (connecting word) between the two statements.

C because the phrase "still driving his '59 Chevy Impala" is not a complete statement (because there is no stated subject). It could work in this sentence if it were set off from the main clause with a comma. It would then modify "My grandfather," the subject of the main clause. But this answer doesn't provide that punctuation.

D because the conjunction *and* that connects the phrase "still driving his '59 Chevy Impala" to the main clause creates confusion by linking groups of words that are not grammatically parallel.

Question 2. The best answer is **G** because it correctly punctuates this sentence, which is actually a fairly simple subject–verb–direct object sentence except that the direct object is a noun clause. The sentence could also be written with the word *that* introducing the clause.

The best answer is NOT:

F because it inserts an unnecessary comma between the verb *says* and the direct object, which is what he says ("he can't imagine needing frivolous options like automatic transmission or power steering"). It's worth pointing out that the comma would be correct if what followed the verb were a direct quotation, as in speech: He says, "I can't imagine needing frivolous options."

H because it inserts an unnecessary comma between the verb and the direct object clause.

J because it adds the same unnecessary comma as H does, plus it places an unnecessary comma between the pronoun *that* and the clause it introduces.

Question 3. The best answer is **C** because it provides the correct past tense form of the irregular verb *go*.

The best answer is NOT:

A because the verb *has went* is grammatically incorrect. It should be *has gone* (which would still be incorrect here because it would create an awkward tense shift).

B because the verb *had went* is grammatically incorrect. It should be *had gone*.

D because it is in the present tense, creating a shift in verb tense in this sentence. The three verbs that follow this one in the sentence are all in the past tense—*had quit, tried,* and *resisted.*

Question 4. **The best answer is H** because the coordinating word *because* clearly and concisely links this parenthetical clause ("because his old black-and-white model had finally quit") to the preceding clause ("he went to buy a new color television").

The best answer is NOT:

F because it is excessively wordy and clunky. The phrase "owing to the knowledge that his old black-and-white model had finally quit" doesn't express anything that the clause "because his old black-and-white model had finally quit" doesn't express more clearly and more precisely.

G because it is unnecessarily wordy. The clause "due to the understandable fact that his old black-and-white model had finally quit" seems, on first glance, impressive. But it is empty, pretentious language, and not consistent with the style of the rest of this essay.

J because the coordinating word *so* does not logically link this parenthetical clause to the preceding clause.

Question 5. **The best answer is B** because it adds an appropriate and relevant detail here. In this sentence, the writer is expressing that the grandfather believed he was still healthy and had no need of a remote control for his television—"He said that he had two good legs and was perfectly capable of getting out of his chair." The addition of "when he wanted to change the channel" fits with the point of the rest of the sentence.

The best answer is NOT:

A because the fact that the chair "was made of black leather" is irrelevant to the writer's purpose here.

C because the fact that the chair is located "by the south window in the family room" is a pointless digression in this sentence.

D because, again, the fact that the grandfather "liked to sit" in his chair is an insignificant detail here. Since it was "his chair," he would presumably like to sit there.

Question 6. **The best answer is J** because, here, no adverb or phrase is needed to make a connection between these two sentences. The essay works fine here without that kind of help.

The best answer is NOT:

F because the adverb *however*, as it is used here, indicates that this sentence is going to contradict or contrast with the statement in the preceding sentence. This sentence does not do that.

G because the adverb *additionally* indicates that this sentence is going to add a point that builds on the statement in the preceding sentence. This sentence does not do that.

H because the adverb *conversely* expresses the same general idea that *however* does. This sentence does not provide a contrast to the statement in the preceding sentence.

Question 7. The best answer is **C** because the absence of commas here creates the clearest and most understandable sentence. This is another case (like question 6) where less is more.

The best answer is NOT:

A because it inserts a comma that confounds your ability to understand the sentence. The comma after the word *time* makes you think that Grandpa punched in the time and then he punched in the channel of his favorite news program, when actually he punched in the time that the program came on and the channel it was on.

B because it also inserts an unnecessary and confusing comma, this time after the conjunction *and* rather than just before it.

D because the comma after the word *channel* indicates that the phrase "of his favorite daily news program" is not essential. It's set off from the rest of the sentence with commas, as if it were parenthetical—a nice piece of information but not necessary to the meaning of the sentence. But if you try reading the sentence without this phrase, the meaning of the sentence is no longer clear.

Question 8. The best answer is **J** because the phrase *On the other hand* signals that this sentence is going to provide a contrasting point or a different perspective. Grandpa's logic goes like this: The remote control's volume button is great for drowning out someone he doesn't want to hear; on the other hand (from another perspective), the mute button is great for silencing the television when he doesn't want to hear it.

The best answer is NOT:

F because the phrase *For example* indicates that this sentence will offer an example of the statement expressed in the sentence before it. This sentence does not provide that payoff.

G because it is incorrect for the same reason that F is. The phrase *To illustrate* is fairly close in meaning to *For example*.

H because the phrase *On the one hand* suggests that the writer is going to make a point here and then make another point. But the other point never gets made here; this is the last sentence in this paragraph.

Question 9. The best answer is **B** because *advertisers* is a specific noun that clearly communicates who Grandpa wants to be able to cut off in midsentence.

The best answer is NOT:

A because the pronoun *them* does not have a clear antecedent (a noun that it refers to and stands in for).

C because the pronoun *it* seems to refer back to the noun *sound*, but that is nonsensical. How do you "cut sound off in midsentence"?

D because the possessive pronoun *its* might refer back to the noun *sound* or to the noun *button*, but both of those would be nonsensical. What do you make of "the button that mutes the sound lets him cut the button's function off in midsentence"?

Question 10. The best answer is **F** because it appropriately punctuates this complex sentence. A complex sentence, by definition, contains an independent clause ("This option automatically turns the TV off after a preset amount of time") and one or more dependent clauses ("which is very convenient" and "when he falls asleep while watching a show").

The best answer is NOT:

G because by inserting a comma before the clause "when he falls asleep while watching a show" and setting it off from the rest of the sentence, the writer is signaling that the clause is not essential to the meaning of the rest of the sentence. But that is not so. Try reading the sentence without that final clause. The option of automatically turning off the TV is not always convenient, but it's sure handy when Grandpa falls asleep in the middle of a show.

H because it creates a sentence fragment. "When he falls asleep while watching a show" cannot stand alone. It's not a complete thought. Readers want to know more.

J because it is incorrect for the same reason that H is wrong. As it is used here, the semicolon is signaling that the statements on either side of the semicolon should be independent clauses (complete thoughts).

Question 11. The best answer is **D.** Think of this sentence as a jigsaw puzzle. Each puzzle piece is a phrase or clause. In this version, all the pieces of this sentence fit together well. And the "picture" that results looks like something that we can understand.

The best answer is NOT:

A because the parts of this complex sentence are poorly arranged—to the point of nonsense. Perhaps the best way of answering this question is to listen carefully to each wording as you read it out loud to yourself. The clause "what he wants his TV doing . . . is to know a source of both pleasure and power" is pretty funny, but it's probably not what the writer meant to say here.

B because of a similarly flawed arrangement of the elements of this sentence. Placing the introductory clause "Even when he sleeps" directly before the statement "Grandpa says" gives readers the wrong impression that Grandpa is talking in his sleep.

C because of its clumsiness. The following makes little or no sense at all: "Doing what he wants . . . is to know his TV is a source of both pleasure and power for him."

Question 12. The best answer is **F** because it provides a main clause for this sentence: "Grandpa points his finger at the TV and . . . seemingly turns it on." Notice that the phrase introducing the sentence (which is often called a participial phrase) cannot be a main clause because it has no stated subject.

The best answer is NOT:

G because it creates a sentence fragment. There is no stated subject and no main clause.

H because it is incorrect for the same reason that G is incorrect—no subject, no main clause.

J—not because of a fragment problem but because of a tense shift problem. Both the verb in the preceding sentence (*uses*) and the second verb in the compound predicate in this sentence (*turns*) express action in the present. It doesn't make sense to place a verb here (*has pointed*) that expresses action that began in the past and continues in the present.

Question 13. The best answer is **A** because it provides a fitting ending for this personal essay because it refers to Grandpa's continuing discovery of creative ways of using his new television remote control.

The best answer is NOT:

B because it provides a description of Grandpa as uninterested in learning how to use his remote control. That's inconsistent with the rest of the essay's portrayal of him as embracing this new technology.

C because it introduces elements that are insignificant in terms of the rest of the essay. The 200-page manual had not been mentioned elsewhere in the story, and the salesperson had only a minor role early in the story.

D because it suggests that the grandmother's feelings or thoughts are central to the essay, but the rest of the essay has focused on the actions and opinions of the grandfather.

Question 14. The best answer is **G** because the placement that creates the most logical order is between Sentences 1 and 2. First, the statement that Grandpa likes to use the programming function to play jokes on his grandchildren. Then, the explanation of how he does it: He programs the TV to turn on at a certain time; in the grandchildren's presence, he points his finger at the TV when it's programmed to turn on.

The best answer is NOT:

F because it is not the most logical place to add this information. It doesn't make sense to explain Grandpa's TV programming trick before the reader even knows that Grandpa likes to use the programming function to play jokes on his grandchildren.

H because it reverses the chronological order of how Grandpa's joke works. He can't play the trick on the grandchildren and then program the TV to turn on at a certain time.

J because it is incorrect for the same reason that **H** is. The chronological order of the setup of the remote-control-finger joke is out of whack.

Question 15. The best answer is **D** because it provides an effective transition from the first part of the essay to the second part. The opening paragraphs focus on Grandpa's resistance to but eventual acquisition of a new TV with a remote control. The last sentence of Paragraph 2 indicates that Grandpa overcame his resistance to technology and began to use the remote. The first sentence of Paragraph 3 points out that Grandpa has actually grown interested in the uses of the remote, and this leads into the rest of the essay's description of the uses that he discovers, many of which wouldn't be found in that 200-page manual.

The best answer is NOT:

A because the first sentence of Paragraph 3 is "Grandpa is intrigued by the various uses for that remote." This sentence suggests that the remote control might have intriguing uses, but it doesn't provide any *information* about those uses.

B because, again, the sentence does suggest that Grandpa liked using the remote, but it doesn't provide any *details* that support that as a fact.

C because it would be a vast overstatement to say that this sentence is "a humorous blend of descriptive details and relevant information."

Passage II

Question 16. The best answer is F because it provides a correct superlative adjective form (*liveliest*) as well as a singular subject (*One*) to match the predicate found later in this sentence (*is*).

The best answer is NOT:

G because the superlative adjective *most liveliest* is redundant. The word *most* and the ending *-est* both signal a comparison of more than two items.

H because it creates a plural subject—"The most lively folk music forms"—which does not agree with the singular predicate *is*.

J because it also creates a plural subject—"The liveliest folk music forms."

Question 17. The best answer is B because it provides the correct form of the possessive pronoun *its*. The pronoun is standing in for "Tejano music's."

The best answer is NOT:

A because it proposes using the contraction *it's* (which means "it is") where the possessive pronoun *its* is required. If we take *it's* as a contraction here, then the clause reads as a sentence structure error: "because of it is having origins on both side of the Texas-Mexico border."

C because it proposes using the contraction *it's* where the possessive pronoun *its* is called for.

D because it proposes using *its'* where the possessive pronoun *its* is called for.

Question 18. The best answer is F because adding this parenthetical phrase does further the description of the dance music that the German immigrants brought to south Texas and northern Mexico. Maybe some readers might already know that the dance music of late-nineteenth-century German immigrants was polkas and waltzes. Probably many readers wouldn't know that. Stating it here does give most readers a better sense of this influence on Tejano music.

The best answer is NOT:

G because this brief addition does not in any way explain why German dance music became popular in south Texas and northern Mexico in the late nineteenth century.

H because this phrase *is* a relevant addition to the sentence. It does not explain the connection between the German dance music and the button accordion; however, that explanation is irrelevant to the essay.

J because this phrase *is* a relevant addition to the sentence. The essay does refer to other musical forms, besides Tejano of course, so this addition would *not* be inconsistent with the rest of the essay.

Question 19. The best answer is **B** because it correctly uses a comma to set off the appositive noun phrase "*huapangos* and *rancheras*" from the preceding noun phrase that it describes and renames, "their own dance music."

The best answer is NOT:

A because it inserts an unnecessary comma between the noun *accordion* and the prepositional phrase *in their own dance music*. This comma creates a confusing pause or break where none is needed.

C because it fails to place a comma between those two noun phrases. Occasionally, appositive nouns or noun phrases are *not* set off by commas, but only if they are essential to the basic meaning of the sentence. That is not the case here.

D because it also fails to place a comma between the noun phrase and the appositive phrase that further describes it.

Question 20. The best answer is **G** because it offers the most appropriate punctuation for this sentence. It might help you to think about words in this sentence that are not expressed even though their meaning is understood. We could also write this sentence as follows: Eventually, a unique musical style developed *that was* based on duet singing and an instrumentation of accordion, drums, etc.

The best answer is NOT:

F because it places a semicolon between the main clause—"a unique musical style developed"—and a modifying phrase—"based on duet singing and an instrumentation. . . ." A semicolon is normally placed only between independent clauses (that is, clauses that express complete thoughts).

H because it places an unnecessary and distracting comma between the preposition *on* and the object of that preposition, *duet singing*.

J because it places an unnecessary and distracting comma between the subject—*a unique musical style*—and that subject's predicate—*developed*.

Question 21. The best answer is **B** because it provides a wording that is clear and unambiguous. "This style" clearly refers the reader back to the phrase "a unique musical style" at the beginning of the preceding sentence. The clause "known as *conjunto*" (which could also have been written "which is known as *conjunto*") modifies the noun that precedes it.

The best answer is NOT:

A because the pronoun *It* has no clear antecedent. What noun is *It* standing in for? Spanish twelve-string bass guitar? Upright bass? Accordion? Instrumentation? Duet singing? Musical style? The reader is forced to guess. On top of that, the sentence itself is rather clumsy: "It was *conjunto* and became the heart of Tejano music."

C because of the unclear pronoun antecedent. The fact that "it" is "known as *conjunto*" doesn't help the reader. The Spanish twelve-string guitar is a *bajo sexto*. Maybe the upright bass is a *conjunto*? We really don't know.

D because of that same pronoun antecedent problem. In addition, the sentence "It being *conjunto* became the heart of Tejano music" doesn't work well, raising more questions for the reader than it answers.

Question 22. **The best answer is H.** You need to pay close attention to the stated question, because it tells you that the best answer in this case is the *worst* answer—the alternative to the underlined portion that is *not* acceptable. The preposition *on* in the clause "The Mendoza family made their living on working" is simply the wrong word to use here.

The best answer is NOT:

F because it *is* an acceptable alternative. The phrase "earned their living" means the same thing as "made their living." The word *by* sounds fine in the clause "The Mendoza family made their living by working."

G because it *is* an acceptable alternative. The word *from* sounds fine in the clause "The Mendoza family made their living from working."

J because it *is* an acceptable alternative to the underlined portion. As was stated earlier, the phrase "earned their living" means the same thing as "made their living."

Question 23. **The best answer is D** because the preposition *as* provides the parallel construction that is called for by the adverb *alternately* (meaning simply "by turns") and the connecting word *and*, resulting in the phrase "working alternately as field hands and as touring musicians."

The best answer is NOT:

A because of the lack of parallelism of "as field hands and they were touring musicians." For this sentence to flow smoothly and to make sense, the phrases on either side of the conjunction *and* should mirror or nearly mirror each other in terms of sentence structure.

B because of this same lack of parallelism. The phrase "as field hands and as well touring musicians" is clunky and raises doubt about whether the family worked alternately in these two roles.

C because it is, likewise, incorrect because of lack of parallelism: "working alternately as field hands and being touring musicians."

Question 24. **The best answer is H** because this clause should be kept in the essay. Although this information about music publishers printing song lyrics on bubble gum wrappers as a way to promote the songs seems irrelevant to this essay about Tejano music, it sure helps to explain that preceding statement: "Mendoza learned the words to many of her songs from bubble gum wrappers."

The best answer is NOT:

F because this clause should *not* be deleted from the essay. It's true that this information is rather unrelated to the main topic of the paragraph, but it is crucial to this particular sentence. Without this clause, the sentence would mystify most of us. Have you ever seen a bubble gum wrapper with entire song lyrics printed on it?

G because this clause should *not* deleted from the essay, and besides, the information in this clause does not diminish the musical accomplishments of Lydia Mendoza.

J because it's true that this clause should be kept in the essay, but the information presented in the clause does *not* show that the songs that Lydia Mendoza performed were popular, only that music publishers had hopes of popularizing many of the songs that she performed.

Question 25. The best answer is **D** because it creates a complete sentence. When we delete the underlined portion, the sentence reads, "In 1928 in San Antonio, Texas, Mendoza and her family made their first recording."

The best answer is NOT:

A because it creates a sentence fragment. There is a dependent clause—"where Mendoza and her family made their first recording"—but no independent clause.

B because it is needlessly wordy and because it provides a weak link between the two introductory prepositional phrases and the main clause: "it was there" seems to refer only to "in San Antonio, Texas" and not to "In 1928."

C because it creates a sentence fragment. The clause lacks a subject.

Question 26. The best answer is **F** because it appropriately and effectively punctuates this sentence. Sometimes, less punctuation is best.

The best answer is NOT:

G because it places an unnecessary and distracting colon between the noun phrase *her widespread popularity* and the prepositional phrase that follows and describes it.

H because it places unnecessary and distracting commas between the noun phrase *her widespread popularity* and the prepositional phrase that follows it, and between the prepositional phrase *in the Spanish-speaking regions* and the prepositional phrase that follows it.

J because it places an unnecessary and distracting comma between the noun phrase *the Spanish-speaking regions* and the prepositional phrase that follows and describes it.

Question 27. The best answer is **D** because this addition about how she became widely known as La Alondra de la Frontera fits best after the sentence that states that she "soon gained . . . widespread popularity" (Sentence 6).

The best answer is NOT:

A because of the chronological arrangement of the information in this paragraph; it doesn't make sense to insert this sentence about Lydia Mendoza's popularity right after a sentence about the Mendoza family working as field hands and touring musicians (Sentence 3).

B because it is incorrect for the same reason as that given for **A**. It doesn't make sense to insert this sentence right before the sentence about the Mendoza family making their first recording (Sentence 5).

C because it is incorrect for the same reason as that given for **A** and **B**. It doesn't make sense to insert this sentence about her established reputation right *before* the sentence about her singing style soon gaining her widespread popularity.

Question 28. The best answer is **G** because it ties together Tejano music and Lydia Mendoza, which are arguably the two main subjects of this essay. With the wording of **G**, the sentence reads, "Others have followed Lydia Mendoza's lead and have expanded the influence of Tejano music."

The best answer is NOT:

F because it brings in the issue of immigration from Mexico to the U.S. Although the immigration of Germans to Texas and Mexico is mentioned in the second paragraph and the Mendoza family's immigration to the U.S. is mentioned in the third paragraph, immigration is not one of the main topics of the essay.

H because it introduces Santiago and Flaco Jiménez, who are not mentioned elsewhere in this essay.

J because it focuses on large recording contracts. Although the preceding paragraph mentions that the Mendoza family made a recording, the essay makes no reference to large or lucrative recording contracts.

Question 29. The best answer is **D** because it provides wording that is most consistent with the overall style and tone of this straightforward informative essay.

The best answer is NOT:

A because the statement that Tejano music will "stick around a while" uses an informal or casual phrasing that is unlike anything else in this essay. That phrasing also suggests a less respectful attitude toward Tejano music than is expressed elsewhere in this piece.

B because it is unnecessarily wordy, vague, and repetitive. The phrase "causes it to be" could be more succinctly expressed by "results in," for example. Do we know what the writer means by "enduring things"? Besides, something that is "enduring" is, by definition, "timeless." What is gained by using both of these adjectives here?

C because, like **A**, it is more informal or casual than the rest of the essay. We might easily say "lots of people really like it" in conversation with friends, but would we use that phrasing in a school research paper or in a college admissions essay? At the very least, we can reasonably conclude that, in light of the rest of this essay, we would not do so here.

Question 30. The best answer is **F** because this essay has focused on the history and development of Tejano music, in part by describing the career of one of the earliest Tejano music stars.

The best answer is NOT:

G because although the essay does describe how various Spanish, German, and English musical traditions influenced the development of Tejano music, the essay makes no mention of Tejano music's contributions to other folk music traditions.

H because the essay does tell the story of Tejano music. Anyway, just because an essay mentions other folk music forms and traditions, that doesn't mean the essay can't also focus on describing the history of one particular folk music.

J because it's true that Lydia Mendoza is the only Tejano musician described in any detail, but she's not mentioned until halfway through the essay. The essay does not limit its focus to Mendoza and, in fact, uses the story of Mendoza's life as a way to continue the larger story of Tejano music.

Passage III

Question 31. The best answer is A because it provides the punctuation (a comma) that best indicates the relationship between the introductory prepositional phrases ("During the early morning hours of October 28, 1965") and the main clause ("engineers stationed 630 feet above the ground made careful measurements").

The best answer is NOT:

B because the connecting word *and* creates confusion here. A word like *and* usually connects similar kinds of grammatical units—nouns (Tom and Mary), verbs (wander and search), adverbs (high and low), etc. Here, the word tries to connect an introductory phrase and a main clause.

C because placing a period here creates a sentence fragment: "During the early morning hours of October 28, 1965."

D because it is incorrect for the same reason that C is wrong. A semicolon is normally used to connect two independent clauses (that is, clauses that could each stand alone as complete sentences).

Question 32. The best answer is H because it shows the correct use of the apostrophe in expressions of time. You're probably more familiar with the uses of the apostrophe to express possession or ownership or to indicate a contraction (letters left out when words are combined). But you've probably seen phrases such as "yesterday's news" and "tomorrow's headlines" and "an hour's delay"—they all follow the same punctuation rule as "the day's work."

The best answer is NOT:

F because it leaves out that necessary apostrophe. Without the apostrophe, a reader might misread "the days" as a subject and "work" as a predicate.

G because it places the apostrophe in the wrong location. The rest of this sentence makes it clear that this is *one* day's work.

J because one would never use an apostrophe like this—by adding *'s* to the end of a plural noun.

Question 33. The best answer is A because this story of the last step in the construction of the Gateway Arch is told in the past tense. The past tense verb *threatened* is consistent with the other predicate verbs used in this paragraph—*stationed, made, indicated.*

The best answer is NOT:

B because the passive voice of the verb *had been threatened* doesn't make sense in this sentence.

C because the future perfect tense verb *will have threatened* creates an awkward and confusing shift from the past tense used elsewhere in this essay.

D because the present tense verb *threatens* creates a similarly awkward and confusing shift in tense.

Question 34. **The best answer is J** because it provides the most concise wording for this sentence and avoids the pointless repetition of the other choices.

The best answer is NOT:

F because it is pointlessly repetitive. The word *delay* doesn't add any information here that's not already clearly expressed by the word *postpone*.

G because the phrase "postpone to a later time" is pointlessly wordy. Can you postpone something to an earlier time? The information "to a later time" is already clearly expressed by the word *postpone*.

H because it is incorrect for the same reason that **F** is. The phrase "postpone by delaying" is another example of verbal overkill. Readers can sometimes feel disrespected when an essay tells them the same thing over and over.

Question 35. **The best answer is B** because this sentence explains that the topping-out ceremony being referred to here is "the placement of the final section between the two freestanding legs of the St. Louis Gateway Arch." Without this phrase, we wouldn't be able to figure out what "topping out" meant until we were halfway into the essay.

The best answer is NOT:

A because the essay would *not* lose a minor detail if this phrase were deleted. This is a key piece of information.

C because the wording of this phrase is straightforward and factual—there's nothing to suggest that the writer is expressing his or her opinion on the significance of anything.

D because the phrase does not state the ceremony's importance to St. Louis residents. Readers might draw a conclusion about the ceremony's importance based on the essay as a whole, but that's something else entirely.

Question 36. **The best answer is F** because the phrase "Luther Ely Smith" is an appositive for (renames or explains) the phrase it follows, "attorney and civic leader." Most appositive phrases are set off by commas, but this one should not be, because it is essential to the meaning of the sentence. Try reading the sentence without "Luther Ely Smith"—doesn't it sound strange or clunky?

The best answer is NOT:

G because the comma between the nouns *attorney* and *civic leader* is unnecessary and distracting. The word *and* is linking up these two nouns; the comma just gets in the way of that.

H because there should not be a comma separating the noun phrase "attorney and civic leader" and the noun phrase that defines and specifies it, "Luther Ely Smith."

J because it is incorrect for the reasons given for **G** and **H** as well as the reason that the proliferation of commas just totally confuses things: "In 1933, attorney, and civic leader" starts looking like it might be a series of three items.

Question 37. The best answer is **C** because this sentence states, "In 1933, attorney and civic leader Luther Ely Smith envisioned a memorial that would recognize St. Louis's major role in the westward expansion of the United States." It does provide some helpful background about the history leading up to the construction of the Gateway Arch, and it's the only place in the essay where such background is provided.

The best answer is NOT:

A because the sentence does state that St. Louis played a role in the westward expansion, but it does not explain why St. Louis played that role.

B because the sentence does state that Smith envisioned a memorial, but it does not mention what the memorial that he envisioned might look like.

D because the sentence does provide some biographical facts about Smith—he was an attorney and a civic leader, and he had an idea about a memorial. However, this information is not particularly crucial. The information that is most relevant and meaningful to this paragraph is that a memorial to St. Louis's role in the U.S. westward expansion (that is, the Gateway Arch) was first envisioned in 1933.

Question 38. The best answer is **H** because it is the only choice that makes this a complete sentence.

The best answer is NOT:

F because it creates a sentence fragment—a noun phrase ("Architect Eero Saarinen") and a dependent clause that modifies the noun phrase ("who created the design that symbolized the memorial's theme").

G because it too creates a sentence fragment—that same noun phrase and an appositive phrase that renames the noun phrase ("creator of the design that symbolized the memorial's theme").

J because it too creates a sentence fragment—that same noun phrase and a participial phrase modifying the noun phrase ("creating the design that symbolized the memorial's theme").

Question 39. The best answer is **D** because this question asks you to decide which word would provide the most logical and effective transition from one sentence to another. The best decision here is to use no transitional adverb at all. The preceding sentence states that Saarinen designed the Gateway Arch. This sentence is the first of three that describe the details of that design.

The best answer is NOT:

A because the sense of *Meanwhile* is that this event takes place at the same time that the preceding event takes place. That sense doesn't work logically here.

B because the sense of *Therefore* is that this condition exists or event takes place as a result of the preceding condition or event. That sense would work here only if we'd already been told that Saarinen's designs always look like the description that follows.

C because the sense of *However* is that this condition exists or event takes place in contrast to the preceding condition or event. That sense would work only if we'd already been told that Saarinen's designs never look like the description that follows.

Question 40. The best answer is F. All of these word choices are similar in meaning, having something to do with "decreasing or reducing in size," but they are not interchangeable synonyms. The context of this sentence helps us to decide the best choice: "spraying the [metal and concrete] leg [of the Gateway Arch] with water to cool it would make it contract." *Merriam-Webster's Collegiate Dictionary* (11th ed.) supports the accuracy of this choice, stating that "CONTRACT applies to a drawing together of surfaces or particles or a reduction of area or length" (p. 271).

The best answer is NOT:

G because *reduce* has more of a sense of "bringing down or lowering in size or degree or intensity," which is not exactly the action being described in this sentence. It's a much less precise word choice than *contract* is.

H because *decrease* has more of a sense of "declining in size or number or amount," which is not exactly the action being described here. It's a much less precise word choice than *contract* is.

J because *compress* primarily means "to reduce in size by pressing or squeezing," which is not the action being described here.

Question 41. The best answer is C because this phrasing uses the correct forms of the possessive pronouns *their* and *its:* "in their attempt to reduce its expansion."

The best answer is NOT:

A because it uses the contraction *they're* (meaning "they are") where the possessive pronoun *their* is called for.

B because it uses the contraction *they're* and the contraction *it's* (meaning "it is") where the possessive pronouns *their* and *its* are called for.

D because it uses the contraction *it's* where the possessive pronoun *its* is called for.

Question 42. The best answer is G because it provides the most logical and fluent arrangement of the possible parts of this sentence: an introductory dependent clause ("as the crowd cheered") followed by a main clause with a compound predicate ("the final section was hoisted up and welded to the two legs of the arch").

The best answer is NOT:

F because this arrangement of the pieces of information provides us with the nonsensical image of the final section being hoisted up *after* it had been welded to the legs of the arch.

H because this arrangement of the pieces of information provides us with the absurd image of the crowd being welded to the legs of the arch.

J because this arrangement of the pieces of information provides us with the confusing image of the crowd either doing some of the welding or being welded to the legs of the arch.

Question 43. The best answer is D because it offers the most concise wording and avoids the redundancy of the other choices. (Have you ever heard of the Department of Redundancy Department? That might be a handy way to remember what the word *redundant* means.)

The best answer is NOT:

A because, since a decade is ten years and three decades are thirty years, the phrase "Over three decades and more than thirty years" is redundant.

B because its phrasing is redundant and pointless. "Over three decades" do amount to "more than thirty years," but there's no reason to inform readers of that here.

C because the parenthetical phrase "over thirty years" merely repeats the time span just reported in a different measure of time (decades).

Question 44. The best answer is G because this is the LEAST acceptable alternative to the underlined portion. The sentence with the underlined portion reads, "Over three decades of planning and building had come to a conclusion, and the tallest monument in the United States was now complete." Replacing the word *conclusion* with *halt* creates a meaning problem in the context of this sentence because "coming to a halt" expresses the idea of stopping or suspending before or without completion.

The best answer is NOT:

F because it provides an acceptable wording. The phrase "reached completion" works in the context of this sentence just as well as "come to a conclusion" does.

H because it provides an acceptable wording. The phrase "come to an end" works in this sentence just as well as "come to a conclusion" does.

J because it provides an acceptable wording. The word "ended" works in this sentence just as well as "come to a conclusion" does.

Question 45. The best answer is C because the title of this essay—"'Topping Out' the Gateway Arch"—is a fairly good summary of the piece and actually helps us to arrive at the answer. The essay does *not* do a good job of describing the entire process of designing and building the Gateway Arch because it focuses instead on telling the story of this one step in the process.

The best answer is NOT:

A because this essay does mention the materials used to make the exterior and interior structural supports, but that doesn't mean it has described the entire design and construction process.

B simply because it presents an inaccurate description of this essay. An essay that did do what B claims to do would indeed fulfill the intended goal.

D because it is incorrect for the same reason as B is—it inaccurately describes this essay. This essay devotes just a few sentences to the early stages in the development of the arch.

Passage IV

Question 46. The best answer is **F** because it provides the word that sounds right in this sentence. When we refer to periods of the day, such as "the dusk of a later summer evening," we generally use the preposition *in*: in the morning I got up; in the afternoon he took a nap; we went to a movie in the evening.

The best answer is NOT:

G because the preposition *On* sounds wrong here, especially when you combine this introductory phrase with the main clause: "On the dusk of a late summer evening, I walked." This wording makes the dusk sound like some sort of hard surface that can be walked upon.

H because the preposition *With* sounds wrong here. Try to imagine "walking with the dusk of a late summer evening"—maybe hand in hand? It just doesn't work.

J because the preposition *From* sounds wrong here. "From the dusk of a late summer evening, I walked . . . toward a shelter." This wording makes the dusk sound like a location rather than a period of time.

Question 47. The best answer is **C** because it provides the correct pronouns—*most* and *who*—in this context. The pronoun *most* carries the sense of "the greatest part"—not all of the people but not merely a few of them. The pronoun *who* is a relative pronoun; in an adjective or relative clause, it takes the place of the noun that precedes it. In this sentence, *who* is standing in for "the people" in the clause "who walked with me."

The best answer is NOT:

A because the pronoun *more* doesn't fit here. It calls for some sort of comparison: more of the people than you met or more of the people than I knew before this evening. But those comparisons are not being made in this sentence.

B because the pronoun *more* doesn't fit here. The pronoun *whom* is also wrong here: this pronoun is used only when it is functioning as the direct object or the object of a preposition in the adjective clause. In this clause, the pronoun is functioning as the subject.

D because the pronoun *whom* doesn't fit here. In this clause, the pronoun is serving as the subject. The pronoun *whom* is used only when it serves as the direct object or the object of a preposition in the clause. (Have you heard of Ernest Hemingway's war novel *For Whom the Bell Tolls*?)

Question 48. **The best answer is J** because it achieves exactly what the writer wants to achieve, according to the question. The clause "I felt a kinship with them" balances the statement made in the first part of this sentence with a detail that suggests the unity of these people.

The best answer is NOT:

F because, although this clause works well with the first half of the sentence, it's not successful at expressing a sense of unity among the people. It only mentions that the narrator knew a few of the people that he or she walked with.

G because it not only fails to suggest a sense of unity among the people, it expresses the somewhat contradictory sense of individualism: "we each had our own personal reasons for being there."

H because this clause expresses the narrator's hope of making friends with some of these people, which is not the same as expressing a feeling of unity that actually exists among a group of people.

Question 49. **The best answer is A** because this word is *not* an acceptable alternative to the underlined word. This writing issue is similar to the issue presented in question 46. These little prepositions can be hard to pin down and explain, but if we just listen to how they fit in a particular sentence, we often know what is right. Would you "make this journey *among* Miami land"? This preposition usually has the meaning of "in the midst of" or "surrounded by" objects or people.

The best answer is NOT:

B because this word is an acceptable alternative to the underlined word. In this sentence, the preposition *over* works just about as well as *across* does.

C because this word is an acceptable alternative to the underlined word. The preposition *on* does not give as strong a sense of traversing as *across* and *over* do, but it still makes sense here. The bottom line is this: one can travel across or over or on land, but one can't travel among land.

D because this word is an acceptable alternative to the underlined word. As with *over* and *on*, the preposition *through* works well here. When the narrator makes this journey across Miami land, he or she is also making it *through* that land.

Question 50. **The best answer is G** because, in the opening sentence of this paragraph, the reader is told that the people are walking "toward a shelter at the edge of a field in northern Indiana." But this phrase adds some important description about the shelter—that it's made of saplings and earth, that it's called a longhouse, and that it has a ceremonial function or purpose.

The best answer is NOT:

F because this phrase does not offer a comparison to the journeys made by the members of other American Indian tribes.

H because this phrase does help establish the place of the events described in this paragraph, but it doesn't contribute anything to establishing the time of those events.

J because this phrase provides relevant information; it introduces and explains the term *longhouse*, which is used elsewhere in the essay, as a ceremonial building made of saplings and earth.

Question 51. The best answer is C because it provides the clearest and most concise wording in this sentence. This wording ensures that the pronoun that follows in this sentence, *them*, has a clear antecedent (*other Miami*).

The best answer is NOT:

A because this wording leads to an ambiguity later in the sentence. The pronoun *them* in the phrase "many of them the ancestors of the people" would seem to be referring back to the nearest noun, *pictures*, even though that antecedent doesn't make sense.

B because it is clunky phrasing and needlessly wordy. Nothing meaningful is gained by stating that "other Miami were present" in the pictures that the narrator had seen for years.

D because it, too, is needlessly wordy. It also has the same sense problem that choice A has—this wording makes *pictures* the most likely antecedent for the pronoun *them* that appears later in the sentence.

Question 52. The best answer is J because it provides the correct punctuation for this clause. The relative clause "who walked along with me to the longhouse that summer evening" modifies or describes the noun *people*. This clause is not set off from the rest of the sentence with a comma because it is restrictive, or necessary: it provides information that the reader needs to know in order to make sense of the sentence.

The best answer is NOT:

F because the comma setting off the relative clause from the noun it describes is wrong, and the comma between the prepositional phrase "with me" and the prepositional phrase "to the longhouse" is unnecessary and distracting.

G because the comma between the relative pronoun (*who*, which is standing in for the noun *people*) and the predicate verb of this clause (*walked*) is wrong and distracting.

H because the commas setting off the relative clause from the noun it describes is wrong, and the comma between the adverb *along* and the prepositional phrase "with me" is unnecessary and distracting.

Question 53. The best answer is D because, by introducing the rooms that the narrator's grandmother and mother had dedicated to their tribe, this sentence effectively bridges the preceding sentence (about having seen pictures of the ancestors of many of the Miami walking with the narrator that evening) and the following two sentences (about the rooms and the framed photos lining their walls and what the grandmother and mother did there).

The best answer is NOT:

A because it makes no mention of the rooms that are referred to in the next two sentences. If this sentence were used here, how would we know what the writer meant by "these rooms" in the next sentence?

B because it is incorrect for the same reason that A is. This sentence does a good job of explaining the pictures mentioned in the preceding sentence, but it makes no mention of the rooms referred to in the following sentences.

C because it is incorrect for the same reason. This sentence also mentions the pictures and at least notes that they are displayed in the grandmother's and mother's houses, but the sentence still fails to mention any specific rooms, which makes the reference to "these rooms" in the next sentence a confusing one.

Question 54. The best answer is H because it provides the most logical referent in terms of the information already provided. The preceding two sentences refer to "these rooms" and "my mother and grandmother each sitting quietly in her own room." This sentence clearly continues that description of "those rooms."

The best answer is NOT:

F because we are not sure what "That room" refers to—the mother's room or the grandmother's room. It could be either one, and we readers are left to wonder.

G because we are not sure who *Her* refers to—the narrator's mother or grandmother. Each one has her own special room, so using the plural *rooms* with the singular *Her* also makes no sense.

J because it is incorrect for the same reason that F is. The phrase "This room" leaves us wondering whether the writer is referring to the mother's room or the grandmother's room.

Question 55. The best answer is D because it correctly and effectively punctuates these two clauses as separate sentences. Sometimes, combining clauses into one sentence can be a good writing decision. In this case, however, the statements in these two clauses are too different from each other—one is about the room; the other is about the tribe.

The best answer is NOT:

A because this sentence rambles. Sometimes we might talk this way, but we should try to avoid writing sentences in which clauses are randomly connected by the conjunction *and*. We might call this kind of sentence problem an "on-and-on sentence."

B because it creates a run-on, or fused, sentence. Where does one statement end and the other begin? As readers, we're not really sure what to do with that prepositional phrase "unlike the larger Plains tribes."

C because it creates a comma splice. As with the punctuation decision in **B**, this one doesn't give us a clue about where one statement ends and the other begins.

Question 56. The best answer is H because it provides relevant information in terms of the focus of this paragraph. The preceding sentence states that the Miami had not retained reservation lands. Later in the paragraph, we learn that the tribe owned no land where a tribal longhouse could be built or religious ceremonies held. Thus, the information provided by **H** that the Miami also had to hold their powwow "on borrowed land" builds on the point that the Miami were lacking because they had no tribal or communal land.

The best answer is NOT:

F because the information that the powwow "was always well attended" doesn't fit here. In the context of this paragraph, which is building a case for the tribe's need to own a piece of land, what is the point of sharing this detail?

G because the detail that the Miami powwow is "notable for its exquisite dancing" is pointless and peripheral in terms of the main focus and purpose of this paragraph.

J because the detail that the powwow "lasted several days" is random. As with the information provided in F and G, the writer makes no attempt to link this detail to the other statements being made in this paragraph.

Question 57. The best answer is A because this wording creates parallelism in verb form and clause structure. In this compound dependent clause, the two parts are introduced by the relative pronoun *which* and linked by the conjunction *and*, and the auxiliary verbs are understood (not stated) in the second part: "no land on which a longhouse could be built and Miami religious ceremonies [could be] conducted." Both verbs are in the passive voice. Using the passive a lot is often a bad move, but here it places emphasis on that which could be built (a longhouse) and conducted (religious ceremonies).

The best answer is NOT:

B because this wording causes the verbs in the two parts of the compound clause to shift from "could be built" to "were conducted." Also, the adverb *there* is confusing and unnecessary; the relative pronoun in the prepositional phrase "on which" has already communicated a sense of place or location.

C because this wording is awkward and unnecessarily wordy. Here, the parts of the compound clause shift from "a longhouse could be built" to "there were Miami ceremonies conducted." As in **B**, the adverb *there* is redundant.

D because the parts of the compound clause are not parallel in structure. The first part contains a passive voice verb; the second part consists of the participial phrase "the conducting of Miami ceremonies." Notice, for example, how the parallel verb forms and clause structures of **A** make it much easier to understand than **D**.

Question 58. The best answer is H because it logically connects the statements in these two sentences. The preceding sentence states that the narrator "had never attended a Miami religious ceremony, never danced in front of a crowd of Miami." The phrase "In fact" communicates to readers that the statement to follow will build on the preceding one, perhaps taking it one step further. The statement that the narrator "had never known any other Miami children outside of my own family" does that.

The best answer is NOT:

F because the word *Still*, when used as a transitional adverb, generally communicates a time relationship or a sense of contradiction (similar to *nevertheless*). Neither one of those meanings logically works to connect these two sentences.

G because the transitional adverb *Meanwhile* expresses a time relationship that doesn't make sense in terms of connecting the statements in these two sentences.

J because the transitional phrase "On the other hand" expresses a sense of contrast, which doesn't work logically to connect the statements in these two sentences.

Question 59. The best answer is D because it provides a verb form that makes this a complete sentence. The introductory clause "As we walked together through the open field that evening" is a subordinate, or dependent, clause. It cannot stand alone as a complete sentence. The verb *flashed* enables the second clause in this sentence to be an independent clause: "hundreds of tiny fireflies flashed softly from the tall grasses." This clause can stand alone or function as the main clause of a sentence.

The best answer is NOT:

A because inserting the participle verb *flashing* here makes this into a participial phrase instead of a clause. Because there is no main clause, this becomes a sentence fragment.

B because it creates a sentence fragment. There are two dependent clauses here—"As we walked together through the open field that evening" and "which flashed softly from the tall grasses"—but no main or independent clause.

C because it is incorrect for the same reason that B is. This choice creates two dependent clauses but no main clause.

Question 60. The best answer is F because the preposition *like* fits well here because it expresses the comparison of the fireflies and the ancestral spirits. In this setting, *like* means "in the manner of" or "similarly to" (definition 2 in *Merriam-Webster's Collegiate Dictionary*, 11th edition).

The best answer is NOT:

G because the phrase "just as" causes readers to stumble over various misreadings. The first misreading leads one to *as* in its role as a conjunction meaning "as if" or "in the way or manner that." The second misreading leads one to the most common meaning of the preposition *as*—"in the capacity, character, condition, or role of"—which makes no sense here. The preposition *as* can also mean "similarly to," but what do we make of the adverb *just* meaning "exactly, precisely"? Here, "just as" would mean "precisely similarly to," which sounds overstated if not redundant.

H because this combination of two prepositions ("as like") is not found in standard written English.

J because the phrase "such as" usually means "for example," which doesn't make sense in the context of this sentence.

Passage V

Question 61. The best answer is A because this choice provides a sentence structure that won't fall down on us. Here, the subject—"Howling"—is followed by an appositive—"the sound most often associated with wolves." Do you recall that an appositive renames or describes the noun it follows? The word *howling* may look more like a verb than a noun, but it's what's called a gerund, a verb form being used as a noun. The verb in this sentence shows up later and is either *perform* or *performs*, depending on how you answer question 62. You may already be thinking that the sentence will sound best like this: "Howling . . . by itself performs several social functions within wolf packs."

The best answer is NOT:

B because it creates an awkwardly constructed sentence: two verb phrases—"has been the sound most often associated with wolves" and "by itself performs several key social functions within wolf packs"—that are connected by a mere comma.

C because it creates an introductory dependent clause—"While howling is the sound most often associated with wolves"—which can serve as a wing or annex to this sentence structure. But the main clause is missing; there's no foundation.

D because it results in basically the same lopsided sentence construction that **B** does.

Question 62. The best answer is H because we've already been thinking about this problem while answering question 61. If the subject of this sentence is *Howling*, then the pronoun that refers back to it must agree with it in number (the singular *itself*), and the verb of this subject must also be in agreement (the third-person singular *performs*). The result, of course, is an agreeable sentence.

The best answer is NOT:

F because of its problems with pronoun-antecedent and subject-verb agreement. It's easier to see the problem with this sentence when we leave out the appositive: "Howling . . . by themselves perform several key social functions."

G because of the same pronoun-antecedent and subject-verb agreement problems described in **F**.

J because it is incorrect for a different reason. The phrase "by itself" expresses the meaning "alone" or "without help or company," which fits well in this sentence. The phrase "on itself" does not have that same sense. In fact, do we know what the phrase "howling on itself" might mean?

Question 63. The best answer is B because it creates a complete sentence. Here, the main clause is "One of these is self-defense," which is followed by a dependent clause that modifies the noun *self-defense* ("which includes protecting territory").

The best answer is NOT:

A because it's a sentence fragment. There's no verb in the main clause—it feels like all the action has been sucked out of the statement "One of these, self-defense."

C because, like A, it creates a sentence fragment. We start off with a noun ("One"), then a participial phrase ("being self-defense"), then a dependent clause ("which includes protecting territory").

D because it is incorrect for the same reason that A is. Those words posing as a main clause have now been pared down to less than their bare essentials: "One, self-defense." This might work when taking notes for oneself but not when communicating with someone else.

Question 64. The best answer is J because it wraps up this sentence in a way that is apt and correct. This phrase after the comma ("usually other wolves") becomes an appositive that renames or defines the preceding noun phrase ("potential intruders"). This wraps up a mini-run of questions about sentence structure (see questions 61 and 63).

The best answer is NOT:

F because it creates a confusing comma splice. When just a comma (without a conjunction word) connects two clauses, it's hard to tell what that connection means. The comma normally isn't strong enough to signal that these two clauses can each stand on their own.

G because it is incorrect for the same reason that F is—that pesky comma splice.

H because the phrase that wraps up the sentence—"and are typically other wolves"—is poorly attached to the main trunk of the sentence. Are the "potential intruders" (the closest noun) typically other wolves? Or are the "packs" (the main subject) typically other wolves? The structure of the sentence seems to suggest the latter is the case, but good sense suggests otherwise. And readers are left to scratch their heads.

Question 65. The best answer is A. This is one of those questions where you have to choose the wording that is *least* or *not* acceptable. The underlined word, *because*, is a conjunction linking two clauses. It expresses the idea that the statement to follow is a reason for or cause of the other statement in the sentence. The conjunction *although* expresses a relationship between these two clauses—one of counteraction or counterbalance—that is not logical here.

The best answer is NOT:

B because it is an acceptable alternative. The conjunctive phrase "in that" expresses the same kind of causal relationship that the underlined word does.

C because it is acceptable. The conjunction *since* is closely synonymous to the word *because*.

D because it, too, is acceptable. One of the meanings of the conjunction *as* is identical to the meaning of *because*.

Question 66. The best answer is **F** because it states this action in the active voice, thus providing an agent for the action—"Wolves"—which ensures that the pronoun that appears later in the sentence (in the phrase "with one another") has a noun to refer back to.

The best answer is NOT:

G because it is unnecessarily wordy and because the sentence that it creates offers no antecedent for the pronoun "one another." The reader is left asking the question, "One another what?"

H because, like G, it is wordy and doesn't provide a clear antecedent for the pronoun. That pronoun has to be standing in for some noun. The most likely candidate would be the subject of the sentence, but "howling" doesn't make sense. The reader then retreats to the last sentence of the preceding paragraph—could it be "mates" or "prey" or "packs"? At that point, he or she is lost.

J because it, too, fails to offer a noun that provides the pronoun "one another" with a clear and logical meaning.

Question 67. The best answer is **C** because the adjective *acute*, meaning "sensitive" or "sharp," is an appropriate word choice to describe the sense of hearing. The context of this sentence makes it clear that the hearing of the wolves is being described as very good.

The best answer is NOT:

A because the adjective *intense* doesn't fit here. One common meaning of this word is "deeply felt" or "profound," which doesn't make sense here. Another common meaning is "extreme in degree or size," which seems close but no cigar. Would it sound right to you to say that "wolves possess extreme hearing"?

B because the adjective *cunning*, which generally means "crafty" or "sly" or "having skill or keen insight," isn't the right word to describe the sense of hearing.

D because the adjective *vivid* is usually used to describe a color or graphic image. It can also mean "producing a strong impression on the senses," but this meaning wouldn't make sense when describing hearing.

Question 68. The best answer is **J** because it provides wording that is succinct and that avoids the pointless repetition of meaning that the other choices offer.

The best answer is NOT:

F because of the repetitiousness of "*Frequently*, common activities . . . *often*." Both of these adverbs mean the same thing. It's unnecessary to use them together in this sentence to describe the same action.

G because of the repetitiousness of "*Quite regularly*, common activities . . . *often*." Repetition can occasionally be used in writing to emphasize a point, but there's no need for that kind of emphasis here.

H because of the repetitiousness of "*Many times*, common activities . . . *often*." Sometimes in writing, less is more.

Question 69. The best answer is **B** because it describes a situation—"activities, such as hunting for prey, often disperse a pack over large areas of land"—that clearly and logically leads to the action described later in this sentence—"in order to reunite, the separated wolves howl to one another." Because the wolves become widely spread out over a hunting territory, howling serves a specific role in bringing the wolves back together.

The best answer is NOT:

A because the clause that follows this underlined portion states, "in order to reunite, the separated wolves howl to one another." As readers, we have to wonder why the pack became separated in the first place. This statement—"activities, such as hunting for prey, often call upon animals' sharp instincts"—doesn't give us a clue.

C because this statement that activities such as hunting often "require the pack to travel some distance" might seem to lead readers to the second statement in this sentence; however, that first statement suggests that the pack is traveling *together*. If so, why would they need to howl to be reunited?

D because this statement that activities such as hunting often "involve the entire pack" also seems to lead to that second statement, but it doesn't go far enough in providing a logical reason for the pack's howling. Through this statement, readers learn that the entire pack participates in activities such as hunting. But it at least suggests that they do these activities together. And if they do, then there's no need to reunite.

Question 70. The best answer is **F** because the adverb *Finally* provides an effective and logical transition from the preceding paragraph to this one. As the title suggests, this essay is attempting to explain "Why Wolves Howl." The second paragraph explains the purpose of self-defense and protecting territory. The third paragraph focuses on the purpose of communication among pack members. This paragraph addresses the role of howling in terms of the pack's social rituals. It's the third and final reason given for why wolves howl.

The best answer is NOT:

G because the adverb *Nevertheless* creates an odd logical shift here. This sentence and paragraph are not providing a contrast or counterbalance to what came before them. The movement of this essay is more clearly that of an accumulation of points.

H because the adverb *Second* doesn't logically fit here. The second paragraph begins with "One of these [key social functions]." The third paragraph begins with "Wolves also howl." If the writer wanted to count the functions of howling, then this paragraph would begin with "*Third*, wolves use howling."

J because the adverb *Thus* doesn't work logically here. This word normally introduces an effect that results from a previously stated condition or cause. There's no indication that the wolves' use of howling in pack social rituals has a cause-effect relationship with statements in the preceding paragraph about the wolf pack's use of howling to communicate with each other.

Question 71. The best answer is B because it provides a phrasing that is parallel in structure with the other two phrases in this series. This kind of parallel construction not only results in pleasant-sounding prose but also contributes to clear communication.

The best answer is NOT:

A because it upsets the parallelism suggested by the two phrases on either side of it—"wagging their tails" and "engaging in mock fights." This wording also creates a comma splice that makes the sentence confusing and difficult to read.

C because it, too, upsets the parallelism and confuses the meaning of the sentence. The verbs in the other two phrases in this series have -*ing* endings, suggesting ongoing action, while this middle one has an -*ed* ending, which causes an odd shift to action completed in the past.

D because it is incorrect for the same reason as **C** is. Here, the proposed wording creates a troubling shift in this series of actions from ongoing to present (*nuzzle*) and then back to ongoing.

Question 72. The best answer is G because it effectively uses commas to set off the appositive *or dominant* from the word it is explaining, *alpha*. The conjunction *or* gives readers a clue that this is an appositive, but the commas make it clear that the word *dominant* is actually restating what precedes it and not describing a separate item.

The best answer is NOT:

F because it places the first of two commas after the conjunction rather than before it. The commas used with an appositive signal that the appositive can be deleted without disturbing the sentence. Compare these two versions of this phrase: "Usually begun by the alpha pair of wolves" (**G**) and "Usually begun by the alpha or pair of wolves" (**F**).

H because the appositive is not set off with commas and an unnecessary and distracting comma has been placed between the noun *pair* and the prepositional phrase *of wolves*.

J because it places a single comma after the conjunction *or*, which does not set off the appositive from the word it restates or from the rest of the sentence.

Question 73. The best answer is D because it provides the best arrangement of the parts of this sentence. The participial phrase at the beginning of this sentence—"Usually begun by the alpha, or dominant, pair of wolves"—is modifying a noun. Such phrases should be placed as close as possible to the noun they modify. By making "chorus howling" the subject of the main clause, and placing it directly after the phrase that logically modifies it, **D** provides a good solution to this writing problem.

The best answer is NOT:

A because it results in a misplaced modifier. The prepositional phrase string "in preparation for the hunt," placed right after the verb phrase "is excited," weakly modifies that verb. The prepositional phrase that more effectively and more closely modifies the verb—"by chorus howling"—is placed farther away from the verb.

B because it results in a misplaced modifier. As the sentence reads, "the purpose of chorus howling" is usually begun by the alpha pair of wolves. This arrangement creates a nonsense sentence.

C because it results in misplaced modifiers. As the sentence reads, "excitement in the pack" is usually begun by the alpha pair of wolves. Furthermore, the prepositional phrase string "in preparation for the hunt," placed right after the verb phrase "is raised," weakly modifies that verb. Again, the phrase that more closely modifies the verb—"by chorus howling"—is located farther away from it.

Question 74. The best answer is J because it ensures that the verb "makes" agrees in number with the subject "the collective sound." Both are singular in number.

The best answer is NOT:

F because the plural verb "make" doesn't agree with the singular subject "the collective sound." One way to confirm that this is wrong is to take out all the words that come between the subject and its verb—"of wolves howling in various keys also." Now read the opening of this sentence: "The collective sound make the pack seem larger and more powerful." Does that sound right to you?

G because the plural verb "have" doesn't agree with the singular subject "the collective sound."

H because the plural verb "are intended" doesn't agree with the singular subject "the collective sound."

Question 75. The best answer is D because it effectively punctuates this sentence (by resisting the impulse to add a comma when one is not necessary).

The best answer is NOT:

A because it inserts an unnecessary and distracting comma between the subject clause "What's already clear" and the verb *is*.

B because it inserts an unnecessary and distracting comma between the relative pronoun *that* and the clause it introduces.

C because it inserts an unnecessary and distracting comma between the verb *is* and the predicate noun clause "that the stereotypical image of the lone wolf howling at the full moon obscures the importance howling has in the social life of these animals." (If you're not familiar with the term *predicate noun*, think of *is* or any other linking verb as an equal sign. In such cases, [the subject] = [the predicate noun].)

Question 1. **The correct answer is C.** The restaurant is rotating 180° in 45 minutes. That is 60° each 15 minutes. That is 240° every 60 minutes. You might want to sketch something like the drawing below.

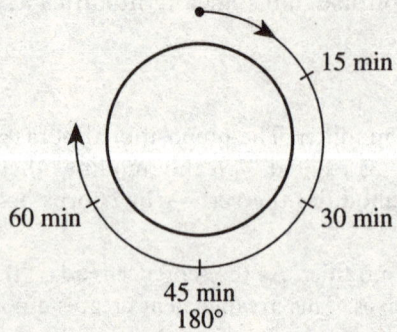

If you like an algebraic solution, you can set up a proportion $\frac{180°}{45 \text{ min}} = \frac{x°}{60 \text{ min}}$ and solve it: $x = \left(\frac{180}{45}\right) = 4 \cdot 60 = 240$.

Most people who do not get this question right choose **D**, which gives the number of degrees the restaurant would rotate in 45 minutes if it made 1 complete rotation each hour.

Question 2. **The correct answer is J.** The 12 vases cost $18, so each vase costs $\frac{\$18}{12} = \$1.50$.

If you chose **F**, you probably divided 12 by 18 rather than 18 by 12. If vases cost $0.67 each, then 12 vases would cost less than $12.

Question 3. **The correct answer is B.** The longer side of the apartment is 30 feet long, and it is 6 inches long on the scale drawing. So, the length of the room, in feet, is 5 times the length on the drawing, in inches. Using this relationship, the length of the shorter side of the apartment is 5 times the 4 inches from the scale drawing. This is 20 feet.

Alternately, you could notice that the length of the shorter side is $\frac{2}{3}$ the length of the longer side

on the drawing, and so the length of the shorter side of the room is $\frac{2}{3}$ of 30 feet, which is 20 feet.

These solutions are equivalent to using a proportion such as $\frac{6 \text{ in}}{30 \text{ ft}} = \frac{4 \text{ in}}{x \text{ ft}}$ and solving: $x = \frac{4 \cdot 30}{6} = 4 \cdot 5 = 20$ feet.

Question 4. **The correct answer is H.** The total profit for the 5 years was, in millions, $8 + $8 + $8 + $9 + $9 = $42. Then the average profit, in millions, was $\frac{\$42}{5} = \$8.4$.

The most common wrong answer was **J**, which is the average of 8 and 9. Because there were more years with a profit of $8 million than with $9 million, the average for the 5 years must be closer to $8 million than to $9 million.

Question 5. The correct answer is A. If the van were driven for 20 miles, the cost for those miles would be $0.30 \cdot 20 = \$6$. Then the daily charge of $25 would have to be added in, for a total of $31. Similarly, if the van were driven for m miles, the cost for those miles would be $0.30m$ dollars, and the daily charge would make the total $0.30m + 25$ dollars.

C comes from treating the 30 cents like it was 30 dollars.

Question 6. The correct answer is F. The sum of the measures of all four interior angles in any quadrilateral is always 360°. The given three angle measures add up to $65° + 100° + 75° = 240°$, so the missing angle measure is $360° - 240° = 120°$.

If $\overline{AB}$ were parallel to $\overline{CD}$, then the measure of $\angle B$ and the measure of $\angle C$ would add up to 180° and the answer would be G. But the problem does not say that those sides are parallel, and it turns out that they are not parallel.

If you chose K, you may have calculated the average of the three given angle measures or taken the supplement of $\angle A$.

Question 7. The correct answer is C. The shorter two sides are the same length in $\triangle ABC$, so the same thing has to happen in any triangle similar to it. That means that $\overline{DE}$ is the same length as $\overline{EF}$, which is 3 meters. Then, the perimeter of $\triangle DEF$ is $3 + 3 + 5 = 11$ meters.

The most common incorrect answer is A, correctly finding the length of $\overline{DE}$ and stopping there.

Question 8. The correct answer is K. This problem can be solved by substituting the Celsius temperature ($C = 38$) into the formula and solving for F. The substitution step gives $F = \frac{9}{5}(38) + 32$, which can be solved as follows: $F = 68.4 + 32 \Rightarrow F = 100.4$. It is appropriate to round this to the nearest degree Fahrenheit because the precision of the Celsius temperature was only to the nearest degree Celsius.

If you chose J, you may have added $38 + 32$ and missed the $\frac{9}{5}$. An answer of H might come from calculating $\frac{9}{5}(38)$ correctly and forgetting to add in 32.

Question 9. The correct answer is B. Nick can only order whole cases, which contain 24 boxes of pens with 10 pens per box, for a total of $24 \cdot 10 = 240$ pens per case. An order of 2 cases would be 480 pens, which falls short of the desired 500 pens. To get 500 pens from his supplier, Nick needs to order 3 cases, and he will get 720 pens.

If you got answer A, you may have correctly divided 500 by 240 to get approximately 2.08 cases, but you may have rounded that to the nearest integer, which does not give the correct answer in this context. Answer E represents the number of boxes (not cases) of pens needed if Nick could order any whole number of boxes.

Question 10. The correct answer is K. When $a + b = 6$, then $2(a + b) + \frac{a+b}{6} + (a + b)^2 - 2$ becomes $2(6) + \frac{6}{6} + (6)^2 - 2$, which simplifies to $12 + 1 + 36 - 2 = 47$.

Question 11. The correct answer is C. If you bought 1 hamburger and 1 soft drink, it would cost \$2.10. If you bought 1 hamburger more, your order would cost \$3.50. So, the cost of the additional hamburger was \$3.50 − \$2.10 = \$1.40. Because 1 hamburger and 1 soft drink cost \$2.10, a soft drink must cost \$2.10 − \$1.40 = \$0.70.

Alternatively, you could set up two equations with two unknowns. Let h dollars be the cost of each hamburger and s dollars be the cost of each soft drink. Then $h + s = 2.10$ and $2h + s = 3.50$. Subtraction gives:

$$
\begin{array}{rl}
2h + s &= 3.50 \\
-(h + s &= 2.10) \\
\hline
h\phantom{{}+s} &= 1.40
\end{array}
$$

And then, substituting 1.40 for h in $h + s = 2.10$ gives $s = 2.10 - 1.40 = 0.70$.

The most common wrong answer is E, which is the correct cost of a hamburger. However, the question asks for the cost of a soft drink. Answer choice D is half of \$2.10, which would only be correct if a soft drink cost the same as a hamburger.

Question 12. The correct answer is K. There are many ways to solve this equation. One solution is the following.

$$
\begin{array}{lrcl}
\text{start with} & 12x &=& -8(10 - x) \\
\text{divide both sides by } -8 \Rightarrow & -\tfrac{3}{2}x &=& 10 - x \\
\text{add } x \text{ to both sides} \Rightarrow & -\tfrac{1}{2}x &=& 10 \\
\text{multiply both sides by } -2 \Rightarrow & x &=& -20
\end{array}
$$

Another solution method would be to graph $y = 12x$ and $y = -8(10 - x)$ and see where the two graphs intersect. A calculator would produce these graphs, and you could find an approximate solution. That is good enough for this problem, because the answer choices are spread apart.

This is a problem where checking your answer is easy and can pay off. When $x = -20$, the left side of the original equation is $12(-20)$, which is −240. The right side is $-8(10 - (-20))$, which simplifies to $-8(10 + 20)$, then to $-8(30)$, then to −240. This solution checks. No other answer choice would satisfy the equation.

If you chose H or J, you may have multiplied out $-8(10 - x)$ to get $-80 + x$ or $-80 - x$ and done the rest of the steps correctly. You could have caught this by checking your answer. If you made an error with minus signs, you may have gotten one of the other answer choices.

Question 13. **The correct answer is C.** There would be 6 tiles along the 24″ side (6 · 4″ = 24″). There would be 16 tiles along the 64″ side (16 · 4″ = 64″). Then, 6 · 16 = 96 tiles are needed to completely cover the rectangular countertop:

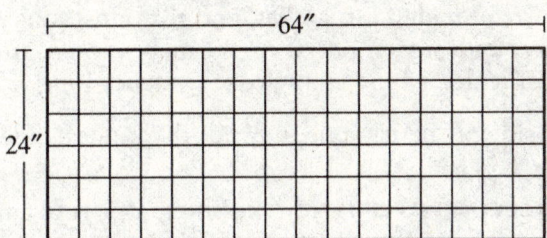

An alternate solution is to figure the area of the countertop in square inches, 24 · 64, which is 1,536 square inches. Then, divide that by the area of a tile, which is 16 square inches. The result is 96, which is the number of tiles needed. The tiles cover the area without being cut because the side lengths of the countertop are divisible by the side length of a tile.

The most common wrong answer is **E**, which comes from correctly calculating the area of the countertop (1,536 square inches), but dividing by the length of the side of the square (4 inches) rather than by 4 · 4 square inches. If you chose **A** or **B**, you may have confused perimeter and area.

Question 14. **The correct answer is H.** If the answer choices give 2 of the 3 interior angle measures in a triangle, then the third angle measure is 180° minus the sum of the given angle measures. The chart below shows this calculation.

	1st angle	2nd angle	Sum of 1st + 2nd angles	3rd angle (180° – sum of 1st + 2nd angles)
F.	20°	40°	60°	120°
G.	30°	60°	90°	90°
H.	40°	100°	140°	40°
J.	45°	120°	165°	15°
K.	50°	60°	110°	70°

The only place where the third angle has measure equal to one of the first two angles is in **H**, where there are two 40° angles.

Question 15. The correct answer is C. The perimeter of the triangle, 66 inches, is the length of the three sides added together. Because one side is 16 inches long, the lengths of the other two sides added together must be 66 − 16 = 50 inches. The ratio of the lengths of these two sides is 2:3. This ratio denotes 2 parts for the first side, 3 parts for the second side, and therefore 5 parts altogether. Because there are 50 inches altogether, and this must make up the 5 parts, each part is 10 inches long. That makes one side 2 parts, or 20 inches long, and the other side 3 parts, or 30 inches long. So the longest side of the triangle is 30 inches long.

B is the length of another side of the triangle, but not the longest side.

Question 16. The correct answer is H. Sketching a picture can be helpful.

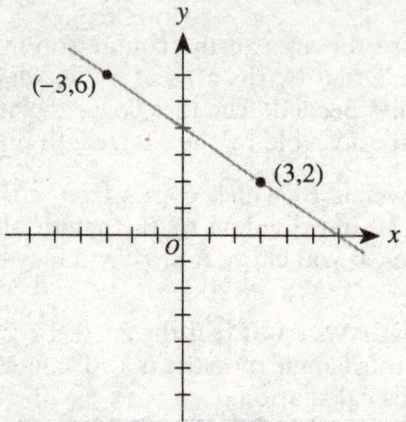

The points (−3,6) and (3,2) are on opposite sides of the y-axis, and an equal distance away from the y-axis, because the x-coordinates are 3 and −3. So, the midpoint will be the y-intercept of the line. The y-coordinate of the midpoint is $\frac{6+2}{2}$, which is 4.

If the points were not so nicely spaced with the y-axis, you could find the equation of the line through the two points and use it to identify the y-intercept. The slope of the line would be the change in y divided by the change in x, $\frac{6-2}{-3-3} = -\frac{2}{3}$. The point-slope form of the equation is then $y - 2 = -\frac{2}{3}(x - 3)$. To find the y-intercept, set $x = 0$ and solve for y, so $y - 2 = 2 \Rightarrow y = 4$. This shows that 4 is the y-intercept.

From the picture alone, you could deduce that the line had to cross the y-axis between 2 and 6. This observation eliminates all the answer choices except the correct one.

Question 17. The correct answer is C. In the figure below, the angles with measure $a°$ and $100°$ form a straight angle along line m. This means $a° + 100° = 180°$, or $a° = 80°$. Now, you know two of the three angles in the larger triangle. The sum of all three must be $180°$. So, $80° + b° + 65° = 180°$, which means that $b° = 35°$. The angle measure $b°$ is equal to angle measure $x°$ because vertical angles have the same measure. So, $x° = 35°$.

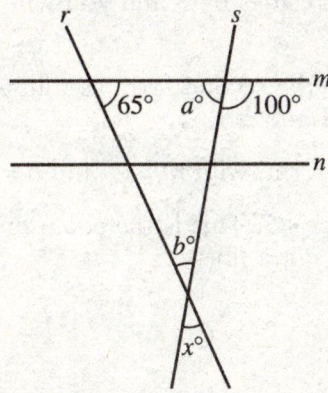

If you chose **A**, you may have calculated $180° - (65° + 100°)$. These three given angle measures, $x°$, $65°$, and $100°$, do not need to add to $180°$. They are not the measures of the three interior angles in the *same* triangle.

Question 18. The correct answer is H. Each week, both ponds get shallower. The table below shows what happens for the first few weeks.

	Now	1 week	2 weeks	3 weeks	4 weeks
First pond	180 cm	179 cm	178 cm	177 cm	176 cm
Second pond	160 cm	159.5 cm	159 cm	158.5 cm	158 cm
Difference	20 cm	19.5 cm	19 cm	18.5 cm	18 cm

The ponds are getting closer and closer to the same depth, at the rate of 0.5 cm per week. Because the ponds started out 20 cm different, it will take $20 ÷ 0.5 = 40$ weeks to bring them to the same depth.

You could also check the answer choices. Answer **F** is not correct because, after 10 weeks, the first pond would be $180 - 10 = 170$ cm deep and the second pond would be $160 - 5 = 155$ cm deep. The other incorrect answers can be eliminated in the same way.

The most common incorrect answer is **G**. If you chose that answer, you may have reasoned that it would take 20 weeks for the first pond to get down to the level of the second pond. And that is correct, except that the second pond has gotten shallower during that 20 weeks, so the ponds are not the same depth.

Question 19. The correct answer is **E.** A line will always have an equation of the form $x = a$ or $y = mx + b$, for suitable constants a, m, and b. And, if a graph has an equation that can be put into one of these forms, the graph is a line.

Equation **A** is already in the first form, where $a = 4$.

Starting with Equation **B**, divide both sides by 3 and you will get $y = 2$. This is the second form, with $m = 0$ and $b = 2$.

Equation **C** can be manipulated into the second form as follows: $x - y = 1 \Rightarrow -y = 1 - x \Rightarrow +y = -1 + x \Rightarrow y = x - 1$, which has $m = 1$ and $b = -1$.

Equation **D** is already in the second form, with $m = \frac{3}{4}$ and $b = -2$.

Equation **E** can be written as $y = -x^2 + 5$. This is the equation of a parabola, shown below. It is the only one of the equations that is not a line.

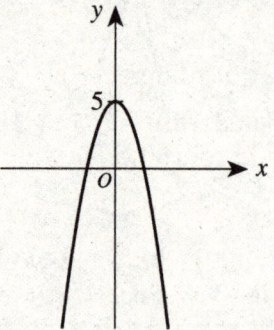

Question 20. The correct answer is **G.** All the answer choices are in terms of $\angle A$. Many people remember the trigonometric functions in the context of a right triangle, in terms of the lengths of the side opposite the angle, the side adjacent to the angle, and the hypotenuse. For the triangle given in the problem, the side opposite $\angle A$ has length 12 cm, the side adjacent to $\angle A$ has length 5 cm, and the hypotenuse has length 13 cm. The values of the trig functions are $\cos A = \frac{\text{adjacent}}{\text{hypotenuse}} = \frac{5}{13}$, $\sin A = \frac{\text{opposite}}{\text{hypotenuse}} = \frac{12}{13}$, and $\tan A = \frac{\text{opposite}}{\text{adjacent}} = \frac{5}{12}$.
The only answer choice that gives one of these is **G**.

If you chose **F**, you may have been expecting the angle to be at one end of the horizontal base of the triangle. The value of $\cos B$ is $\frac{12}{13}$. Triangles can be rotated to any position. The terms "opposite," "adjacent," and "hypotenuse" are chosen to apply when the triangle is in an arbitrary position.

Question 21. The correct answer is B. Parallel lines have the same slope, so any line parallel to this line has the same slope as this line. To find the slope of this line, you could put it into slope-intercept form, and then the slope is the coefficient of x. $7x + 9y = 6 \Rightarrow 9y = -7x + 6 \Rightarrow y = -\frac{7}{9x} + \frac{6}{9}$, and so the slope is $-\frac{7}{9}$.

If you chose **E**, you probably knew that the slope is the coefficient of x, but that only is true when the equation is in slope-intercept form.

If you chose **A**, you may have gotten the equation into the form $9y = -7x + 6$ and then read off the coefficient of x. You didn't quite have it in slope-intercept form.

If you chose **C**, you may have made a mistake putting the equation in slope-intercept form.

Answer choice **D** could be reading off the constant 6 from the original equation.

Question 22. The correct answer is H. While it may not be worth your time to sketch a graph during the ACT, you should at least have a general idea of the situation in your mind. This is the equation of a parabola. Common sense will tell you that if the car is going faster, it will take a longer distance to brake to a stop. So, the parabola is opening upward.

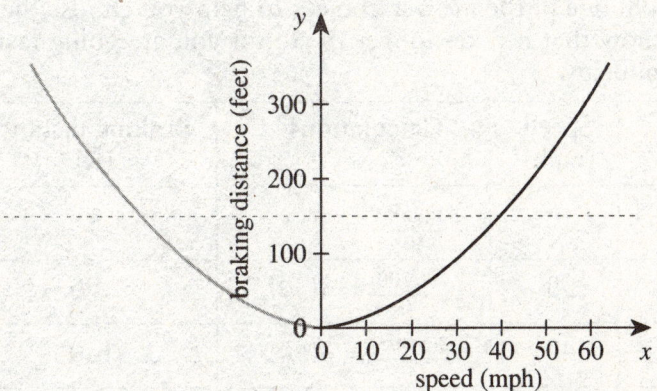

The horizontal dashed line on the graph is where the braking distance is 150 feet. There are two points where the parabola intersects this line. One is to the left of the y-axis, which represents a negative speed for the car. If you solve an equation to find the intersection points, you will have to discard the intersection point with a negative speed.

If you took the time to create a graph, perhaps even on a graphing calculator, you might be able to estimate closely enough to choose among the answer choices. The desired speed is the x-coordinate of the intersection point.

To get this speed algebraically, the desired braking distance is 150 feet, and the equation $y = \frac{3(x^2 + 10x)}{40}$ gives the relation between speed (x) and braking distance (y). So you can solve the equation $150 = \frac{3(x^2 + 10x)}{40}$. One solution path starts by multiplying both sides by 40 and continues as follows: $150 \cdot 40 = 3(x^2 + 10x) \Rightarrow \frac{6,000}{3} = x^2 + 10x \Rightarrow x^2 + 10x - 2,000 = 0 \Rightarrow (x + 50)(x - 40) = 0 \Rightarrow x = -50$ or $x = 40$. You must discard the first solution. The only remaining solution is $x = 40$, which represents a speed of 40 miles per hour.

If you chose **J**, you may have done everything correctly except that when you solved $(x + 50)(x - 40) = 0$, you thought $x = 50$ was a solution. If you substitute 50 for x in the equation $(x + 50)(x - 40) = 0$, you will see that it is not a solution.

If you chose **F**, you may have made a numerical mistake when you substituted $x = 10$ into the braking-distance equation. The value is $\frac{3(10^2 + 10 \cdot 10)}{40} = \frac{3(200)}{40}$. It might be tempting to reduce $\frac{200}{40}$ to 50 and then get $3(50) = 150$, which is what you are looking for. But $\frac{200}{40}$ is 5, not 50.

Substituting the answer choices into the equation is a reasonable strategy for this problem. You can use the results from one of the answer choices to help you choose the next one to substitute, since you probably know that it takes longer to stop if you are going faster. The results of these substitutions are given below.

	Speed (mph)	Calculations	Braking distance (ft)
F.	10	$\frac{3(200)}{40} = 3(5)$	15
G.	30	$\frac{3(1,200)}{40} = 3(30)$	90
H.	40	$\frac{3(2,000)}{40} = 3(50)$	150
J.	50	$\frac{3(3,000)}{40} = 3(75)$	225
K.	60	$\frac{3(4,200)}{40} = 3(105)$	315

Question 23. The correct answer is A. Substitution gives $g(4) = \sqrt{4} = 2$ and $f(1) = 1^2 + 1 + 5 = 7$. Then $\frac{g(4)}{f(1)} = \frac{2}{7}$.

If you chose **C**, you may have started substituting 4 into function g and then continued substituting 4 into function f. The value of $\frac{g(4)}{f(4)}$ is $\frac{2}{25}$.

Question 24. The correct answer is K. There are 125 juniors who could be chosen. For *each* of those 125 juniors, there are 100 seniors who could be chosen. That makes $125 \cdot 100 = 12{,}500$ different pairs of students who could be chosen.

If you chose **J**, you probably added 125 and 100. If you chose **G**, perhaps you were figuring that once 100 pairs were formed, there would be no seniors left to put into another pair. Only 1 pair will be chosen, but there are many more than 100 pairs that are possible choices.

Question 25. The correct answer is C. The figure below shows the ramp.

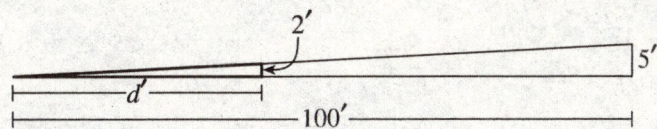

The slope is given as rising 5 feet for every 100 feet of horizontal run. The ramp's rise is 2 feet, and the horizontal run is unknown. Let the horizontal run be represented as d. Then there is a proportion $\frac{2}{d} = \frac{5}{100}$. Its solution is $d = \frac{2 \cdot 100}{5} = 40$ feet.

If you chose **A**, you might have simplified 5% to 0.5. Then the proportion $\frac{2}{d} = 0.5$ has the solution 4 feet.

The most popular incorrect choice was **B**, which happens when the run is 5 times the rise. This gives a reasonable-looking ramp. However, the slope of such a ramp is $\frac{1}{5}$. The required slope is $\frac{1}{20}$.

Question 26. The correct answer is F. You could certainly test all of the answer choices to solve this problem. The first choice, –10, leaves the left side of the relation as $|-10 - 24|$, which simplifies to $|-34|$, which is 34. And $-34 \le 30$ is false, so this is the correct answer.

Another way to solve this problem is to think about the interpretation of absolute value as a distance: $|t - 24| \le 30$ means that the distance on the number line between t and 24 is at most 30 units. This distance would be greater than 30 only when t was more than 30 above 24 or more than 30 below 24. That is when t is more than 54 or t is less than –6. Answer choices **G–K** are all closer to 24 than this.

The most common wrong answer is 54 (**K**), which is right at the limit of how far away it can get from 24.

Question 27. The correct answer is D. The phrase "5 times a number n" can be represented as $5n$. If this is subtracted from 15, the expression $15 - 5n$ represents the result. Saying that this result is negative can be represented as $15 - 5n < 0$. Subtracting 15 from both sides gives $-5n < -15$, and then dividing both sides by -5 gives $n > 3$ (remember to reverse the direction of the inequality).

Most people who missed this chose E. This could come from not reversing the inequality in the last step of the solution, or it could come from subtracting 15 from $5n$ rather than subtracting $5n$ from 15.

Answer choice B is the result of solving $15 - 5n = 0$. This would give the boundary where the expression changes from positive to negative, so it's closely related to the problem you were asked to solve. If you chose this, you would still need to find the values of n where the expression is negative, knowing that $n = 3$ is the only place the expression is zero.

Question 28. The correct answer is J. A quick scan of the answer choices should give you a clue that combining like terms is in order.

$$(x^2 - 4x + 3) - (3x^2 - 4x - 3)$$
$$= (x^2 - 4x + 3) + (-3x^2 + 4x + 3) \qquad \text{subtracting is adding the opposite}$$
$$= (x^2 + (-3x^2)) + (-4x + 4x) + (3 + 3) \qquad \text{reordering terms}$$
$$= -2x^2 + 0x + 6 \qquad \text{combining like terms}$$

If you chose K, you probably subtracted the $3x^2$ but *added* the $-4x$ and the -3. The solution above took care of this explicitly on the second line.

The other incorrect answers result from various combinations of errors with minus signs.

Question 29. The correct answer is B. Imagine the original 9 data items in order from smallest to largest. You might sketch a picture something like that shown below. The median is the 5th item in this list, because it is the middle value in the set.

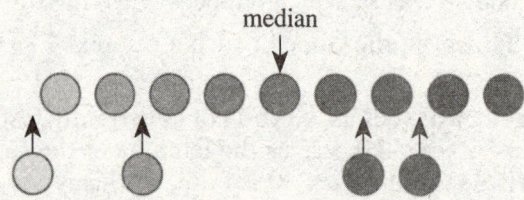

median

When the additional 4 data items are put into the list, there are $9 + 4 = 13$ items on the list. Because 2 of these items are greater than the original median, and 2 of these items are less than the original median, the original median is the middle value in the new set. That makes the original median the new median.

MATHEMATICS · PRACTICE TEST 2 · EXPLANATORY ANSWERS

Question 30. **The correct answer is K.** The shaded area is the area of the larger circle minus the area of the smaller circle. The area of the larger circle is $\pi r^2 = \pi(10)^2 = 100\pi$ square centimeters. The area of the smaller circle is $\pi(5)^2 = 25\pi$ square centimeters. The difference is 75π square centimeters.

If you chose **J**, you likely found the difference in the perimeters of the two circles. You may have used a perimeter formula when you wanted an area formula. (Another possibility is that you calculated 10^2 as $2 \cdot 10$ and 5^2 as $2 \cdot 5$. But, 10^2 is $10 \cdot 10$ and 5^2 is $5 \cdot 5$.)

Question 31. **The correct answer is E.** The side lengths of a 30°-60°-90° triangle are in the ratio $1 : \sqrt{3} : 2$. If you didn't remember this, you could view a 30°-60°-90° triangle as half of an equilateral triangle, as shown below.

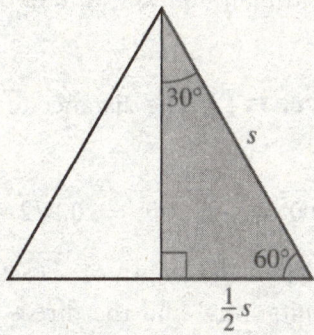

For the shaded triangle, you know that the base is half as long as the hypotenuse, because the base of the equilateral triangle is the same length as the other sides of the equilateral triangle. If the hypotenuse is s units long and the base is $\frac{1}{2}s$, then the Pythagorean theorem gives the height as

$$\sqrt{s^2 - \left(\frac{s}{2}\right)^2} = \sqrt{s^2 - \frac{s^2}{2^2}} = \sqrt{\frac{4s^2}{4} - \frac{s^2}{4}} = \sqrt{\frac{3s^2}{4}} = \sqrt{3\frac{s^2}{4}} = \sqrt{3}\sqrt{\frac{s^2}{4}} = \sqrt{3}\frac{s}{2} = \frac{\sqrt{3}}{2}s.$$

This shows that the ratios are $\frac{1}{2} : \frac{\sqrt{3}}{2} : 1$, which are equivalent to those given above, $1 : \sqrt{3} : 2$. (Obviously, it's quicker to know the ratios than to try to derive them each time you need them, but don't give up if you can't remember something—try to find it a different way.)

You could also use trigonometry to derive the side length ratios in a 30°-60°-90° triangle.

If you chose **B**, you might have been thinking of a 45°-45°-90° triangle, which has this ratio of side lengths.

If you chose **D**, you may have reasoned that because the angle measures are in the ratio 1:2:3, maybe the side lengths are in the ratio $\sqrt{1} : \sqrt{2} : \sqrt{3}$. This is a right triangle (it satisfies the Pythagorean theorem), but the angles are closer to 35°-55°-90°.

The triangles in **A** and **C** are not right triangles. You could have eliminated them because they do not satisfy the Pythagorean theorem. For **A**, $\sqrt{1^2 + 1^2} = \sqrt{2} \neq 1$. For **C**, $\sqrt{1^2 + \left(\sqrt{2}\right)^2} = \sqrt{1 + 2} \neq \sqrt{2}$.

Question 32. The correct answer is G. If the x-coordinate is 20, then the y-coordinate can be found by substituting 20 for x: $0.005(20)^2 - 2(20) + 200 = 0.005(400) - 40 + 200 = 0.5(4) + 160 = 2 + 160$.

In theory, you could read the value off the graph, but you would not be able to read it accurately enough.

Many incorrect answers are caused by mistakes with the first term, $0.005x^2$. If you chose **F**, you may have made a decimal error calculating $0.005(20)^2$ and gotten 0.2 rather than 2.0. Other errors in calculation lead to **H**, **J**, and **K**.

Question 33. The correct answer is D. The distance formula (or the Pythagorean theorem) gives this distance directly. It is

$$\sqrt{(200 - 0)^2 + (0 - 200)^2} = \sqrt{200^2 + 200^2} = \sqrt{2 \cdot 200^2} = 200\sqrt{2} \approx 200(1.414) = 282.8$$

Another way to solve this is to notice that the length of $\overline{FO}$ is 200 units, and $\overline{FG}$ is longer. Also, the path from F to O to G is 400 units long, and the direct path along $\overline{FG}$ is shorter than this path. So, **D** is the only reasonable answer among those given.

Question 34. The correct answer is F. The shaded region is entirely contained in the given triangle because the curve is below the hypotenuse of the triangle, $\overline{FG}$. The area of the triangle is made up of the shaded area plus the unshaded area above the curve and inside the triangle. So, the shaded area is less than the area of the triangle.

Question 35. The correct answer is B. With $a = 4.2$, $b = 5.0$, and a $5°$ measure for $\angle C$, then the law of cosines gives the length of the third side of the triangle (the distance between the cargo ship and the fishing boat) as:

$$\sqrt{(4.2)^2 + (5.0)^2 - 2 \cdot 4.2 \cdot 5.0 \cos 5°}$$

If you chose **C**, you probably missed the minus sign in the middle of the expression. About half the students who do not get the correct answer choose **C**.

The $85°$ angle in answer choices **D** and **E** would be the angle measure by the fishing boat, but only if the angle by the cargo ship was a right angle. It turns out that it isn't a right angle.

Question 36. **The correct answer is F.** Because $a^3 = b$, then $b^2 = (a^3)^2$. Substituting this into the equation $c = b^2$ gives $c = (a^3)^2$. Because $(a^3)^2 = a^6$, the result is $c = a^6$.

The most common incorrect answer is **G**. If you chose that answer, you probably wrote $(a^3)^2$ as a^5. If you write $(a^3)^2$ out as $(a^3)(a^3)$ and then $(a \cdot a \cdot a)(a \cdot a \cdot a)$, you can see that it is a^6.

If you chose **H**, perhaps you wrote $(a^3)^2$ as $2(a^3)$.

Question 37. **The correct answer is E.** This sequence decreases by $17 - 12 = 5$ each term. Here are some more terms:

Term #	1	2	3	4	5	6	7	8	9
Value	17	12	7	2	−3	−8	−13	−18	−23

Each of **A–D** can be verified from the chart. The common difference for **D** is defined so that it is positive if the sequence is increasing and negative if the sequence is decreasing. In symbols, if the sequence is represented by terms $a_1, a_2, a_3, \cdots$, then the difference between two terms is $a_{i+1} - a_i$ for all i. If this difference is constant for all i, then it is called the *common difference* and the sequence is called *arithmetic*.

That leaves only **E** that could be false. The ratio of consecutive terms is defined by $\frac{a_i + 1}{a_i}$ for all i. For the first two terms, the ratio is $\frac{12}{17}$, which is a bit more than 0.70. For the second and third terms, the ratio is $\frac{7}{12}$, which is a bit less than 0.59. That means the ratios are not equal for all terms, and so there is no common ratio. That means **E** is false.

The most common incorrect answer is **B**. If you chose this, perhaps you reasoned that, because the sum of the first 4 terms is 38, the sum of the first 5 terms cannot be anything less. Writing out more terms makes it clear that this can be so. Or, you may have made an arithmetic mistake finding the fifth term and so arrived at the wrong sum.

If you chose **C**, and had the correct sum for the first 5 terms, then perhaps you made an arithmetic mistake subtracting 5 for each term, or you miscounted terms. If you have a different sum for **B** and also have a different eighth term than **C**, you know that there is something amiss in your work and you should go back and try to find your mistake if there is time.

If you chose **D**, perhaps you did not understand the concepts of common difference and common ratio.

Question 38. **The correct answer is G.** The area of a parallelogram is given by bh, where b is the length of the base and h is the height (here, the distance between the bottom and the top). It sometimes helps to picture this formula geometrically.

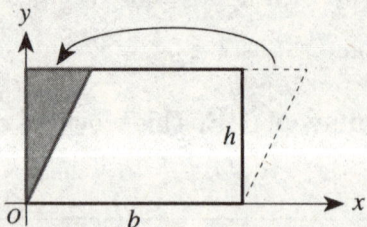

If you cut off the right triangle from the right side, it fits exactly onto the left side to form a rectangle. The rectangle has the same area as the parallelogram. The rectangle's area is bh, where b is the length of the base and h is the height. This is even the same formula as for the parallelogram. The difference is that h is the length of a side of the rectangle, but it is not the length of a side of the parallelogram.

And so, for either the rectangle or the parallelogram, $b = 10$ coordinate units and $h = 6$ coordinate units, making the area $bh = 10 \cdot 6 = 60$ square coordinate units.

The distance from $(0,0)$ to $(3,6)$ is $\sqrt{3^2 + 6^2} = 3\sqrt{1^2 + 2^2} = 3\sqrt{5}$ coordinate units. If you chose **J**, you probably multiplied this side length by the length of the base, 10 coordinate units. This is the stereotypical mistake when figuring the area of a parallelogram. The picture above shows why the height is the right thing to use, not the length of the side.

If you chose **H**, you may have calculated the length from $(0,0)$ to $(3,6)$ as $\sqrt{6^2 - 3^2} = 3\sqrt{2^2 - 1^2} = 3\sqrt{3}$ and multiplied by the length of the base.

Question 39. **The correct answer is D.** The normal amount of lead is 1.5×10^{-5} milligrams per liter. This can be written as 0.000015 milligrams per liter.

Today's level, 100 times the normal amount, is $100(1.5 \times 10^{-5}) = 1.5 \times 10^{-5} \times 10^2 = 1.5 \times 10^{-5+2} = 1.5 \times 10^{-3}$ milligrams per liter. This can be written as 0.0015 milligrams per liter. This is larger than the normal amount.

If you chose **A**, you likely added -100 to the exponent. This answer is 0.00000000···0000000015 milligrams per liter, where there are 104 zeros between the decimal point and the "15." This is smaller than the normal amount.

If you chose **B**, possibly you multiplied the exponent 2 from 10^2 by the exponent -5 from the normal amount. This is 0.00000000015 milligrams per liter, which is smaller than the normal amount.

If you chose **C**, you could have subtracted the exponent 2 from the exponent -5 in the normal amount. This gives 0.00000015 milligrams per liter, which is smaller than the normal amount.

Question 40. The correct answer is G. If you don't see a way to approach this problem right off, a useful general technique is to look for some concrete numbers that illustrate the conditions. One thought is to start checking numbers from 1,000 on up to find a perfect square. Using a calculator would be a good idea. $\sqrt{1,000} \approx 31.62$, $\sqrt{1,001} \approx 31.64$, $\sqrt{1,002} \approx 31.65$, . . . clearly, this will take a while. A perfect square between 1,000 and 9,999 would have to have its square root between $\sqrt{1,000}$ and $\sqrt{9,999}$ because the square root function is an increasing function. This will help you find examples more quickly: $25^2 = 625$ is too low, $35^2 = 1,225$ is in the interval. The smallest perfect square in this interval is $32^2 = 1,024$. Because $100^2 = 10,000$, the largest perfect square in this interval has to be $99^2 = 9,801$. The square roots of all of these perfect squares are the integers from 32 up to 99. All these square roots have 2 digits.

A quicker way is to find $\sqrt{1,000} \approx 31.62$ and $\sqrt{9,999} \approx 99.99$, which is a range that contains all possible square roots of the perfect squares. Any integer in this range (from 32 to 99) has 2 digits.

The most common incorrect answer is **K.** If you chose this answer, perhaps you made a calculation error that led you to believe you'd found a perfect square between 1,000 and 9,999 whose square root had 3 digits. And then you correctly found one whose square root had 2 digits. Your logic was correct. Some students probably choose **K** because they do not know how to solve the problem. Looking for concrete numbers would be a good strategy if you have time.

Question 41. The correct answer is B. This problem is in the general form $(a + b)^2$, which is equivalent to $a^2 + 2ab + b^2$ by the following derivation.

$$(a + b)^2 = (a + b)(a + b) = a \cdot a + a \cdot b + b \cdot a + b \cdot b = a^2 + 2ab + b^2$$

If $a = \frac{1}{2}x$ and $b = -y$, then $(a + b)^2 = (\frac{1}{2}x - y)^2$. This is equivalent to $a^2 + 2ab + b^2 = (\frac{1}{2}x)^2 + 2(\frac{1}{2}x)(-y) + (-y)^2 = \frac{1}{4}x^2 - xy + y^2$.

If you chose **A,** you probably squared the first term and squared the second term. This is the stereotypical error, and it's something that college math teachers (and high school math teachers) want you to know not to do. Something that might help you remember is to have a concrete example: $(1 + 3)^2 = 4^2 = 16$, but $1^2 + 3^2 = 1 + 9 = 10$.

If you chose **C,** you probably did everything correctly except remembering to square the $\frac{1}{2}$ to get $\frac{1}{4}$.

Question 42. The correct answer is F. To calculate a matrix product, you go across each row in the first matrix and down each column in the second matrix. You multiply the terms from a row by the corresponding terms from the column, and you add all of those terms together for the row-column combination and put the sum in that row-column of the result matrix. You do this for each row-column combination.

That explanation is all correct, but pretty abstract. Your math text might have some examples that you can look over to make things more concrete.

In this case, there is only 1 element in each row of the first matrix, and 1 element in each column in the second matrix. The matrix product is:

$$\begin{bmatrix} a \\ 2a \\ 3a \end{bmatrix} \begin{bmatrix} 1 & 0 & -1 \end{bmatrix} = \begin{bmatrix} a\cdot1 & a\cdot0 & a\cdot(-1) \\ 2a\cdot1 & 2a\cdot0 & 2a\cdot(-1) \\ 3a\cdot1 & 3a\cdot0 & 3a\cdot(-1) \end{bmatrix} = \begin{bmatrix} a & 0 & -a \\ 2a & 0 & -2a \\ 3a & 0 & -3a \end{bmatrix}$$

The computations in G are correct, but the terms were put in the wrong places.

If you chose K, you may have reasoned that whatever role the 1 played in the second matrix, the −1 would cancel it out, and the 0 would not change that. If all of the terms were combined, that would be the case. But a matrix can keep the terms separate.

Question 43. The correct answer is D. Because the base is a straight line, these two angle measures add up to 180°. In the language of algebra, this can be represented as $(4x + 6) + (2x) = 180$. Solving this for x gives $6x + 6 = 180$, then $x + 1 = 30$, then $x = 29$. This makes one angle measure $4(29) + 6 = 122$ degrees and the other angle measure $2(29) = 58$ degrees. (Check: Is 122° + 58° equal to 180°? Yes.)

The problem asks for the measure of the smallest of these two angles. That is 58°.

If you chose C, you probably just stopped as soon as you found the value of x. The problem asks for something different. The other popular incorrect answer is E.

Question 44. The correct answer is G. One way to solve this problem is to list out all the numbers in this range that you think might be prime, then check to see if any of them factor. You probably know that you don't have to check the even numbers. That leaves the following list:

31 33 35 37 39 41 43 45 47 49

If one of these does factor, it will have a prime factor of at most $\sqrt{49}$, which is 7. You have already eliminated all multiples of 2. If you eliminate all multiples of 3, 5, and 7, anything left on the list is a prime number. The multiples of 3 on the list are 33, 39, and 45. You can eliminate 35 because it is a multiple of 5. You can eliminate 49 because it is a multiple of 7. Then all the numbers remaining, namely 31, 37, 41, 43, and 47, are prime numbers.

If you chose H, you must have counted a number as prime that really isn't prime. You might want to figure out which one that was. People who miss this problem tend to count extra numbers as primes.

Question 45. **The correct answer is E.** The cotangent of $\angle A$ in this right triangle is the length of the leg adjacent to the angle divided by the length of the leg opposite the angle. That ratio is $\frac{\sqrt{4-x^2}}{x}$.

If you chose **D**, you chose the tangent of the angle. Answer choice **C** represents the sine of the angle. Answer choice **B** is the cosecant of the angle. If you want to get problems like this correct, you need to have a way to keep the trig functions straight.

Question 46. **The correct answer is J.**

Because no booths can be empty, imagine 1 person sitting in each booth. That leaves 10 people standing around waiting for you to tell them where to sit. How many booths can you fill up with another 3 people each? Well, you can get 3 groups of 3 people from the 10 who are still standing, with 1 person left over. That means that you can fill at most 3 booths with 4 people. There will be 1 booth with 2 people, and the other 6 booths will have 1 person. (Check: Are there 20 people? $3(4) + 0(3) + 1(2) + 6(1) = 12 + 2 + 6 = 20$. Yes. Are there 10 booths? $3 + 0 + 1 + 6 = 10$. Yes.)

If you chose **K**, you filled up 5 booths with 4 people each. But, you left the other 5 booths with no one sitting there. The problem specified that NO booths are empty. (This is the most common wrong answer.)

If you chose **H**, you may have just miscounted. Make sure you check your work. You might want to draw a diagram for problems like this so that you can check your work easily.

Question 47. The correct answer is **B.** The area of the trapezoid is $\frac{1}{2}(b_1 + b_2)h =$ $\frac{1}{2}(8 + 4)3 = 6 \cdot 3 = 18$ square inches. The area of the unshaded rectangle is $4 \cdot 3 = 12$ square inches. The triangles and the rectangle together form the trapezoid, so the area of the trapezoid minus the area of the rectangle is the area of the triangles. And this area is $18 - 12 = 6$ square inches.

Another way to solve this problem is to slide the two shaded triangles together and calculate the area of the new triangle. From the original figure, notice that the combined base of the triangles is the amount left over from the trapezoid's bottom base when the width of the rectangle is removed. That is $8 - 4 = 4$ inches. The figure below shows the combined triangles. Their combined area is $\frac{1}{2}bh = \frac{1}{2}(4)(3) = 6$ square inches.

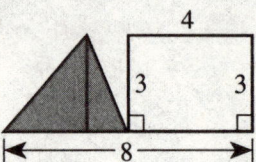

The most common incorrect answer is **D**, which could come up in a variety of ways. Many students have trouble finding the area of trapezoids and resort to calculating bh as if the trapezoid were a rectangle or parallelogram. The figure below shows the trapezoid inside a rectangle with base 8 inches and height 3 inches. The rectangle has area bh, which is clearly larger than the area of the trapezoid.

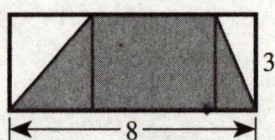

If you chose **E**, perhaps you calculated the area of the trapezoid and stopped. Perhaps you thought the problem was asking for the area of the triangles combined with the area of the rectangle, but it asks for the combined area of the triangles only.

The triangle on the left looks like it is half of a square. If so, it has base 3 inches and height 3 inches and then area $\frac{1}{2}(3)(3) = \frac{9}{2}$ square inches. If the other triangle has the same area, the combined area of the triangles is $\frac{9}{2} + \frac{9}{2} = 9$ square inches. Perhaps you reasoned this way if you chose **C**.

Question 48. **The correct answer is G.** Each of the corner triangles are right triangles because they share an angle with the square. Both legs of these right triangles are 6 inches long because they are half the length of the side of the square. So, the hypotenuse of each of these triangles is $\sqrt{6^2 + 6^2} = 6\sqrt{1^2 + 1^2} = 6\sqrt{2}$ inches. The perimeter of EFGH is made up of 4 of these hypotenuses, so the perimeter of EFGH is $4 \cdot 6\sqrt{2} = 24\sqrt{2}$ inches.

You could have used the ratio of sides in an isosceles right triangle, rather than the Pythagorean theorem, to get the hypotenuse of the corner triangles. The basic flow of the solution is the same.

If you chose F, perhaps you noticed that the area of EFGH is half the area of ABCD. That's a good observation. That does not mean, though, that the perimeter of EFGH is half the perimeter of ABCD. If that were true, then each side of EFGH would be 6 inches long, and the corner triangles would have 3 sides of length 6 inches. The triangle must then be equilateral and have a right angle. That can't happen. (The perimeter of a figure that is geometrically similar to the original and has area in the ratio 2:1 has perimeter in the ratio $\sqrt{2}$:1.)

Question 49. **The correct answer is A.** To see this, start with the statement $\sqrt{y^2} = |y|$, which is true for all real values of y. (If you wonder why there is an absolute value in this equation, test $y = -5$.) Substitute $-x$ for y in the equation. The result is $\sqrt{(-x)^2} = |-x|$, which is expression I.

On the other hand, II is always positive or zero, and III is always negative or zero, so the only time they are equal is when x is zero. For example, when $x = 1$, $|-1| = 1$ but $-|1| = -1$. So, II and III are not equivalent.

The most common incorrect answer is C. Even though expressions II and III look a lot alike—they have the exact same symbols in almost the same order—they are not equivalent. Expression II is never negative and III is never positive.

If you answered E, you likely saw that II and III are not equivalent. Expression I looks so much different than either of the others that it is tempting to just say it can't be the same. One approach would be to test a few numbers in the expressions. Be sure you test a positive number and a negative number. If you substitute these into I and into II correctly, you will find they match. Then, you should suspect that I and II could be equivalent and look for a way to convince yourself of this.

Question 50. **The correct answer is K.** Statement **F**, that $\overline{AB}$ and $\overline{EF}$ are parallel, is true because both are perpendicular to the same other line, $\overline{AD}$.

Because $\angle DEB$ is marked with a right angle, $\overline{DE}$ is perpendicular to $\overline{BE}$, and so **G** is true.

H is true because the two angles, $\angle ACB$ and $\angle FCE$, are vertical angles.

Statement **J** is true because the angles in $\triangle BAC$ are congruent to the angles in $\triangle EFC$. First, $\angle A$ is congruent to $\angle EFC$ because they are both right angles. Next, $\angle ACB$ and $\angle FCE$ are vertical angles. And third, the remaining angles have to have the same measure because the sum of the interior angle measures in any triangle is 180°.

Because all of the other statements are true, you should expect that statement **K** could be false. The following diagram shows such a case. (Only if $\angle ECF$ is congruent to $\angle EDF$ can $\overline{CE}$ be congruent to $\overline{DE}$.)

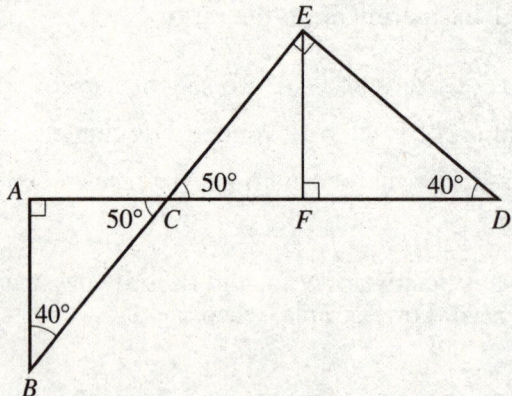

Question 51. **The correct answer is D.** This geometric figure has 6 sides, but you are only given the length of 4 of those sides. One of the slickest ways to find the perimeter is to move two of the sides to form a rectangle with the same perimeter. The drawing below shows the new rectangle.

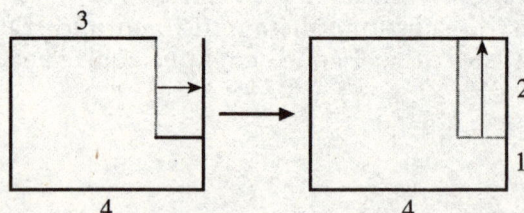

The bottom of this rectangle is 4 inches long, and the right side is 3 inches long. So, the perimeter is $4 + 3 + 4 + 3 = 14$ inches.

An alternate method is to deduce that the left side is 3 inches long because it is the same length as the vertical sides on the right. And, the last unknown side is 1 inch long because it is the difference between the horizontal 4-inch side on the bottom and the horizontal 3-inch side on the top. Then, the perimeter (going clockwise) is 4 + 3 + 3 + 2 + 1 + 1 = 14 inches.

If you chose C, you may have forgotten to add in the horizontal side that connects the vertical 2-inch side and the vertical 1-inch side.

If you chose A, you may have added just the numbers given directly on the figure. Or, you may have calculated the area instead of the perimeter.

Question 52. The correct answer is H. To find the area of the circle, all you need to know is the radius of the circle. If you drew in a diagonal of the rectangle, it would look something like the following.

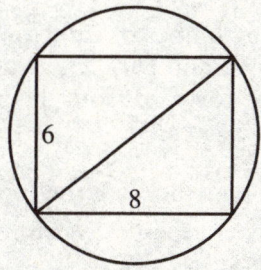

The diagonal of the rectangle is a diameter of the circle. By the Pythagorean theorem (do you see the right triangle?) the length of the diagonal is $= \sqrt{6^2 + 8^2} = \sqrt{100} = 10$ inches. So, the radius is 5 inches. That makes the area $\pi(5)^2 = 25\pi$ square inches.

The most common incorrect answer is J, which you might get by finding the area of the rectangle and multiplying by π.

If you chose G, you may have thought that the diameter of the circle was 8 inches because that is the longest segment drawn on the picture. Then, the radius would be 4 inches and the area would be $\pi(4)^2 = 16\pi$ square inches. The diameter is 10 inches, which is longer than the 8-inch side, as the diagram above shows.

Question 53. The correct answer is D. Marshall made 24 calls on the first day. He makes 5 more calls each day than he had the day before. That means he made 29 calls on the second day. The table below shows the number of calls he made on each of the 20 days.

day	1	2	3	4	5	6	7	8	9	10
# calls	24	29	34	39	44	49	54	59	64	69

day	11	12	13	14	15	16	17	18	19	20
# calls	74	79	84	89	94	99	104	109	114	119

You could try to add all of these up. You might make a mistake, even with a calculator. But, that method is straightforward and would work.

Another approach is to notice that the number of calls for the first day and the last day add up to 143, as do the number of calls for Day 2 and Day 19, as do the number for Day 3 and Day 18, as do all the other pairs of days, working forward from the beginning and backwards from the end. There are 10 pairs of days, each with 143 calls. That is 1,430 calls for the 20 days.

A third approach relies on accurately remembering the following formula for the sum of an arithmetic series: $S_n = \frac{n}{2}[2a + (n-1)d]$, where the first term in the series is a, the common difference between terms is d, there are n terms in the series, and the sum is S_n. Substituting the quantities you know gives $\frac{20}{2}[2 \cdot 24 + (20-1) \cdot 5] = 10[48 + 95] = 10[143] = 1,430$ calls.

If you chose **B**, you may have calculated the number of calls for Day 10 and multiplied this by 10.

If you chose **C**, you may have broken the problem into 2 parts, the base 24 calls and the additional calls. This is a good strategy. The additional calls now are a geometric series $(5 + 10 + 15 + \cdots + 95)$. This has 19 terms (remember that on Day 1 there are no additional calls). The sum of the series is $19 \cdot \frac{5+95}{2} = 950$. Great. Then $950 + 24 = 974$ calls. Unfortunately, you've only added in the base 24 calls for 1 day. Marshall made the base 24 calls on all 20 days. You'd need to add $20 \cdot 24 = 480$ instead of just 24. This gives $950 + 480 = 1,430$ calls, which is correct.

Question 54. The correct answer is K. This is called a *piecewise-defined function* because it is pieces of different functions put together to form a single function. When $x \le 1$, the equation is $f(x) = x^2 - 2$, so $f(1) = 1^2 - 2 = -1$ and $f(0) = 0^2 - 2 = -2$. (Actually, this information is enough to eliminate all the graphs except the correct one. But you might want to read the rest of this explanation anyhow.)

The graph of $y = x^2 - 2$ is a parabola, opening upward. Its graph is shown on the next page. The only part of the graph that applies for this piecewise defined function is the part where $x \le 1$. The rest of the graph is represented with dashes.

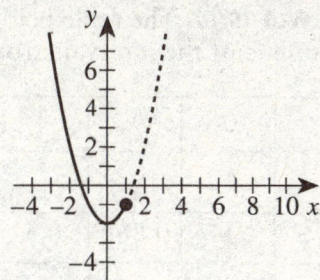

When $1 < x < 5$, then $f(x) = x - 7$, so $f(2) = 2 - 7 = -5$ and $f(4) = 4 - 7 = -3$. This is a straight line. A graph is shown below, with the parts outside $1 < x < 5$ shown with dashes and open circles.

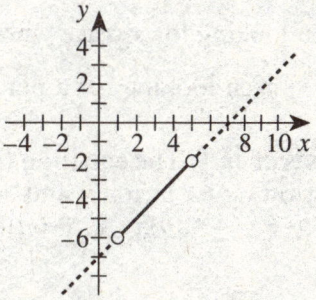

When $x \geq 5$, the equation is $f(x) = 4 - x$, so $f(5) = 4 - 5 = -1$ and $f(6) = 4 - 6 = -2$. This is also a straight line. Its graph is shown below, with the part outside $x \geq 5$ shown with dashes.

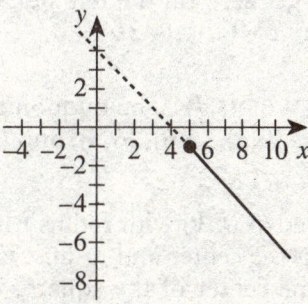

K puts all of these pieces together.

Question 55. The correct answer is D. The table below shows the value of the cosine function at values of θ that are the endpoints of the intervals from each of the answer choices.

θ	0	$\frac{\pi}{6}$	$\frac{\pi}{3}$	$\frac{\pi}{2}$	$\frac{2\pi}{3}$	π
$\cos\theta$	1	$\frac{\sqrt{3}}{\pi}$	$\frac{1}{2}$	0	$-\frac{1}{2}$	-1
approximation of $\cos\theta$	1	0.866	0.5	0	-0.5	-1

The value -0.385 is between 0 and -0.5, which is saying that the value of $\cos\theta$ is between $\cos\frac{\pi}{2}$ and $\cos\frac{2\pi}{3}$. Because $\cos\theta$ is continuous, that means there is a value of θ between $\frac{\pi}{2}$ and $\frac{2\pi}{3}$ that satisfies the conditions of the problem.

If you chose **C**, you might have been looking for a place where $\cos\theta = +0.385$ rather than -0.385.

If you chose **A** or **E**, you might have been looking for a place where $\sin\theta = 0.385$.

Question 56. The correct answer is J. The equation $(x - 6a)(x + 3b) = 0$ has these two solutions. (You can check this by substituting $6a$ in for x and substituting $-3b$ in for x.) Multiplying out this equation gives $x^2 + (-6a + 3b)x + (-6a)(3b) = 0$, which is the same as $x^2 + (-6a + 3b)x - 18ab = 0$.

If you chose **F**, you may have gotten the initial equation right, $(x - 6a)(x + 3b) = 0$, but then multiplied incorrectly to get $(x)(x) + (-6a)(3a) = 0$.

Most of the other incorrect answers could be due to mistakes with negative signs. **G** comes from the initial equation $(x + 6a)(x - 3b) = 0$, where the signs are opposite what they should be. (If you substitute $6a$ in for x, you will not get zero on the left side of the equation.) If you chose **H**, you may have started with the equation $(x - 6a)(x - 3b) = 0$.

Question 57. The correct answer is A. The midpoints of the sides of the square are on the circle. These points have coordinates $(0,3)$, $(3,6)$, $(6,3)$, and $(3,0)$. The first point, $(0,3)$, satisfies **A**, but none of the other equations.

Alternately, because the circle centered at (h,k) with radius r has the equation $(x - h)^2 + (y - k)^2 = r^2$, you can find the equation by finding the center and radius. From the diagram, you can see that the center of the circle is the same as the center of the square, which is $(3,3)$. Also, the radius of the circle is the distance from $(0,3)$ to $(3,3)$, which is 3 coordinate units. So, $(x - 3)^2 + (y - 3)^2 = 3^2$ is an equation of the circle.

One common mistake is to remember the equation of the circle incorrectly, with plus signs where there should be minus signs (**C**). Another common mistake is to not square the radius on the right side of the equation (**B**). Or, some people do both of these things (**E**). If you chose **D**, you may have used the diameter on the right side of the equation, or you may have used the largest coordinate from the figure (and used plus signs instead of minus).

Question 58. The correct answer is J. Let L_1 feet be the length of Pendulum 1 and t_1 seconds be the time for a complete swing of Pendulum 1. Let L_2 and t_2 describe Pendulum 2 in the same way. The time for a complete swing of Pendulum 1 is triple the time required for a complete swing of Pendulum 2. This means that $t_1 = 3t_2$.

The most common approaches to solving problems like this involve finding an equation that contains the two variables the question asks about, here L_1 and L_2, and solving for one variable or solving for the ratio of the variables.

By the equation that relates L to t, the equation $t_1 = 3t_2$ becomes $2\pi \sqrt{\frac{L_1}{32}} = 3 \cdot 2\pi \sqrt{\frac{L_2}{32}}$ (which is an equation that contains both L_1 and L_2). Dividing both sides by 2π gives the equation $\sqrt{\frac{L_1}{32}} = 3 \sqrt{\frac{L_2}{32}}$.

Squaring both sides gives $\sqrt{\frac{L_1}{32}} = 9 \cdot \sqrt{\frac{L_2}{32}}$. Multiplying both sides by 32 gives $L_1 = 9L_2$.

So, Pendulum 1's string is 9 times the length of Pendulum 2's string.

The most common incorrect answer is **G.** If you chose that, you might have reasoned that if one variable triples, then any other variable must also triple. This happens for some functions, notably linear functions, but the function in this problem is not linear. The value of L must go up by a factor of 9 so that the square root will go up by a factor of 3.

If you chose **H,** you may have reasoned that, in order for the square root to go up by a factor of 3, the quantity under the square root must go up by a factor of 6. That would mean that L would go up by a factor of 6. This turns out not to be enough, because if L goes up by a factor of 6, the square root will only go up by a factor of $\sqrt{6}$, which is less than 3.

Question 59. The correct answer is A. By properties of logarithms, $\log_a (xy)^2 = 2 \log_a (xy) = 2(\log_a x + \log_a y) = 2(s + t)$.

If you chose **D,** you may have done all of the steps above correctly, except for thinking that $\log_a (xy) = \log_a x \cdot \log_a y$ (using multiplication rather than addition on the right side).

Answer **C** can come from thinking that $\log_a (xy)^2 = \log_a (x^2 y^2) = \log_a x^2 \cdot \log_a y^2 = 2 \log_a x \cdot 2 \log_a y$. The first and last steps are correct, but not the middle one.

Question 60. **The correct answer is F.** Let d be Jennifer's distance in 1990. Her distance in 1991 would be $1.1 \cdot d$. And her distance in 1992 would be $1.2(1.1 \cdot d)$, which simplifies to $1.32 \cdot d$. This represents an increase of 32% from 1990 to 1992.

The most common incorrect answer is **G**. If you chose this, you probably added the 10% and the 20% to get 30%. This would work fine if the percents were percents of the same thing. But the first increase is a percent of the 1990 distance while the second is a percent of the 1991 distance.

One good strategy for investigating problems like this is to choose a specific number to represent the initial distance. Say you choose 10 feet for her 1990 distance. The 1991 distance would be the original 10 feet plus a 10% increase, which is 1 more foot, for a total of 11 feet. To find the 1992 distance, take the 11 feet and add 20% of this amount, which is 2.2 feet. Then, the 1992 distance is $11 + 2.2 = 13.2$ feet. The percent increase from the original 10 feet is $\left(\frac{13.2 - 10}{10}\right)(100\%) = (0.32)(100\%) = 32\%$. These are the exact same operations as were done in the first method, but the calculations are done with concrete numbers rather than abstract variables.

Passage I

Question 1. The best answer is D because the narrator indicates that "now" (line 52) she "would have to forgo the luxury of adolescent experiments and temper tantrums" (lines 56–58), which indicates that the narrator is an adolescent. She takes on adult responsibilities so that she "could scoop [her] mother out of harm's way and give her sanctuary" (lines 58–59) in the United States.

The best answer is NOT:

A because the narrator is not an adult and because she and her mother are not merely visiting the United States: it has been "three and a half years or so" (line 52) since the mother's last trip to the sky market.

B because the narrator is not an adult and because there's no indication in the passage that the narrator and her mother plan to return to Saigon.

C because rather than imagining her mother's move to the United States, the narrator relates her own and her mother's shared experiences in Vietnam and the United States.

Question 2. The best answer is F because in Saigon, vendors recognized the "slick bargaining skills" (line 35) of the narrator's mother, who could "navigate with grace through their extravagant prices and rehearsed huffiness" (lines 36–38) and who was "mighty and experienced" (line 43). The narrator says, however, that "my mother's ability to navigate and decipher simply became undone in our new life" (lines 46–47) in the United States.

The best answer is NOT:

G or H because the mother's skills were not commonplace (G) or below average (H) in the Saigon sky markets, nor were her skills exceptional in the United States.

J because the mother's skills didn't give her an advantage in the United States, her adopted home; in fact, they were of no use there.

Question 3. The best answer is B because the narrator says that in dealing with the Saigon sky market vendors, her mother "knew how to navigate with grace through their extravagant prices and rehearsed huffiness" (lines 36–38).

The best answer is NOT:

A or C because the narrator says that her mother preferred "the primordial messiness and fishmongers' stink of the open-air market to the aroma-free order of individually wrapped fillets" (lines 49–51) found at the A & P.

D because while the narrator's mother "knew . . . the shoppers by name" (lines 29–30), there's no evidence in the passage that she found her fellow sky market shoppers to be something disagreeable to overcome.

Question 4.

This is an EXCEPT question, which asks you to find the answer choice that is *not* supported by the passage.

The best answer is H because the narrator states that the other A & P shoppers "meandered" (line 10) rather than hurried through the store. The other three answer choices are supported by the passage.

The best answer is NOT:

F because lines 14–15 state, "My mother did not appreciate the exacting orderliness of the A & P."

G because the narrator states that at the A & P, her mother "could not give in to . . . the absence of carcasses and pigs' heads" (lines 15–18).

J because when the narrator explains to her mother that they don't need to pay for pork as soon as they decide to buy it, instead paying for everything at once at the checkout counter, the narrator says, "It took a few moments' hesitation for my mother to succumb to the peculiarity of my explanation" (lines 71–73).

Question 5. The best answer is D because the narrator views her mother's approach to sky market shopping with respect and nostalgia. The narrator describes her mother's "slick bargaining skills" (line 35) and calls her "mighty and experienced" (line 43). It has been "three and a half years or so after her [mother's] last call to the sky market" (lines 52–53), and the narrator is fondly looking back in order to set up a contrast with "the hard scrutiny of ordinary suburban life" (lines 55–56) in the United States through which she has to guide her mother.

The best answer is NOT:

A, B, or C because there's no evidence in the passage that the narrator views her mother's approach to sky market shopping with anxiety or huffiness (A), surprise or embarrassment (B), or impatience or amusement (C).

Question 6. The best answer is H because the narrator says her mother "would take me from stall to stall" in the sky markets "to expose me to her skills" (lines 30–31).

The best answer is NOT:

F because the passage doesn't state that the narrator talked to the vendors.

G because the narrator learned about her mother's sky market behavior directly, by accompanying her "from stall to stall" (line 30), and not through her mother's descriptions.

J because the narrator didn't have to tag along defiantly on shopping trips against her mother's wishes; her mother wanted her to come.

Question 7. The best answer is B because the narrator says, "Of course, all children eventually watch their parents' astonishing return to the vulnerability of childhood, but for us [children of immigrant parents] the process begins much earlier than expected" (lines 65–68). Having experienced this shift, the narrator took on adult responsibilities so that she "could scoop [her] mother out of harm's way and give her sanctuary" (lines 58–59) in the United States.

The best answer is NOT:

A because the narrator says that "all children," not just children of immigrants, "eventually watch their parents' astonishing return to the vulnerability of childhood."

C because the narrator contends that children of immigrants are taken by surprise when "the process" of parents reverting to childlike vulnerability "begins much earlier than expected."

D because the passage provides no evidence that children of immigrants are misunderstood by their parents to a greater degree than are other children.

Question 8. The best answer is H because the passage's first six paragraphs (lines 1–61) describe the narrator's disconcerting experiences shopping with her mother at the A & P, which leads into the assertion in the seventh paragraph (lines 62–68) that "all children of immigrant parents have experienced these moments" (lines 62–63) when a parent acts like a child. The seventh paragraph goes on to contend that for children of immigrant parents, the parents' return to childlike vulnerability "begins much earlier than expected" (lines 67–68).

The best answer is NOT:

F because the seventh paragraph is not the first place in which the narrator indicates that adjusting to another culture has been difficult for her and her mother. For example, the passage's opening sentence (lines 1–3) says, "I discovered soon after my arrival in Virginia that everything, even the simple business of shopping the American way, unsettled my mother's nerves."

G because neither the seventh paragraph nor the rest of the passage discusses what the narrator, before leaving Saigon, thought it would take to adjust to a new culture.

J because while the seventh paragraph does discuss children of immigrant parents in general, the narrator relates details about her experiences both before and after the seventh paragraph.

Question 9. The best answer is A because the third paragraph (lines 29–38), in which the quoted statement appears, illustrates a consistent relationship, or dynamic, between the sky market vendors and the narrator's mother. As an example of the "oddities" to which her mother and the vendors were "addicted," the narrator says, "My mother would feign indifference and they would inevitably call out to her" (lines 32–33). The paragraph concludes, "Theirs had been a mating dance, a match of wills" (line 38).

The best answer is NOT:

B because while "oddities" may seem negative, the quoted statement and the third paragraph as a whole reflect a positive relationship between the sky market vendors and the narrator's mother; in contrast, the mother found American supermarkets unappealing.

C because there's no evidence in the passage that sky market shoppers purchased items they didn't need at the markets.

D because "oddities" doesn't refer to the unusualness of the items for sale at the sky markets but rather to the behaviors of the sky market vendors and the narrator's mother.

Question 10. The best answer is **G** because the narrator says, "I would have to forgo the luxury of adolescent experiments and temper tantrums" (lines 56–58) in order to protect her mother.

The best answer is NOT:

F because the narrator says she had to "forgo" tantrums, not "use" tantrums.

H because there's no evidence in the passage that temper tantrums were a part of the narrator's character inherited from her mother.

J because the temper tantrums mentioned in lines 57–58 are ones that the narrator, not her mother, would have to "forgo."

Passage II

Question 11. The best answer is **B** because throughout the passage, the author reveals his belief that Jefferson was brilliant yet practical and writing under pressure. The author calls the natural rights section of Jefferson's Declaration "the seminal statement of the American Creed, the closest approximation to political poetry ever produced in American culture" (lines 15–17). He stresses Jefferson's practicality by mentioning that "virtually all the ideas found in the Declaration and much of the specific language had already found expression in those earlier writings" (lines 72–74) of Jefferson—but the author doesn't want to "accuse [Jefferson] of plagiarism" (line 70) for this borrowing. The author provides details highlighting the pressure under which Jefferson worked: "The Congress is being overwhelmed with military reports of imminent American defeat in New York and Canada. The full Congress is in session six days a week, and committees are meeting throughout the evenings" (lines 75–79). This led Jefferson to take "the obvious practical course" (line 79), which was to draw from his previous writings in composing the Declaration.

The best answer is NOT:

A because author tries to "pierce through" the "veil" (line 62) of mystery surrounding Jefferson. The author also presents a complex notion of Jefferson's originality, which isn't reflected in the idea of Jefferson merely making attempts at originality.

C because the author contends that Jefferson has received a great deal of deserved praise for the Declaration. Everyone from Abraham Lincoln to "several generations of American interpreters" (lines 56–57) has praised Jefferson and the Declaration.

D because the author views Jefferson as anything but ordinary and because the passage never identifies Jefferson as a quasi-religious leader.

Question 12. The best answer is **F** because in the last paragraph, the author reminds readers of the high-pressure circumstances under which the Declaration was written and says, "The obvious practical course for Jefferson to take was to rework his previous drafts on the same general theme" (lines 79–81). He dismisses the idea that Jefferson didn't draw from his older works, saying it "strains credulity and common sense to the breaking point" (lines 83–84).

The best answer is NOT:

G because while the author asserts that "it seems almost sacrilegious to suggest that the creative process that produced the Declaration was a cut-and-paste job" (lines 81–83), in trying to recover "the specific conditions inside that room on Market and Seventh streets in June 1776" (lines 63–64), the author shows he wants to question assumptions about how Jefferson composed the Declaration.

H because the idea that the Declaration was wholly original is what, in the author's mind, "strains credulity."

J because the author believes that in writing the Declaration, Jefferson "almost surely had with him copies of his own previous writings, to include *Summary View*, *Causes and Necessities* and his three drafts of the Virginia constitution" (lines 67–70).

Question 13. The best answer is **A** because in the passage's first sentence (lines 1–6), the author calls the natural rights section of the Declaration "the most quoted statement of human rights in recorded history as well as the most eloquent justification of revolution on behalf of them."

The best answer is NOT:

B because while the author notes in lines 1–6 that the Continental Congress made no comment and only one slight change to the natural rights section, he doesn't suggest in lines 1–6 or elsewhere in the passage that the Congress should have commented on or reworked the Declaration.

C because in neither lines 1–6 nor elsewhere in the passage does the author express surprise at the eventual fame of the natural rights section, which he calls "the seminal statement of the American Creed, the closest approximation to political poetry ever produced in American culture" (lines 15–17).

D because the author offers no indication in either lines 1–6 or elsewhere in the passage that equally eloquent works were probably produced before the beginning of recorded history.

Question 14. The best answer is **H** because in Lincoln's words, Jefferson wrote under "the concrete pressure of a struggle for national independence by a single people" (lines 22–23), yet he had the ability "to introduce into a merely revolutionary document, an abstract truth, and so to embalm it there" permanently, for "today and in all coming days" (lines 24–26). This truth forever serves as "a rebuke and a stumbling block to the very harbingers of reappearing tyranny and oppression" (lines 27–28).

The best answer is NOT:

F because Lincoln doesn't describe Jefferson's statement as having been used against revolutionaries ever since its writing. Indeed, the statement was itself part of a "revolutionary document."

G because Lincoln describes the natural rights section of the Declaration as a permanent "rebuke and a stumbling block to the very harbingers of reappearing tyranny and oppression," not as a predictor of the rise of future tyrants.

J because Lincoln mentions only a single "abstract truth" in the natural rights section and doesn't claim that the section dared tyrants to continually reappear, only that it acted as "a rebuke and a stumbling block" whenever the first signs of tyranny revealed themselves.

Question 15. The best answer is C because the author signals that the second paragraph (lines 29–44) and the rest of the passage will focus on "the effort to explain what *was* in [Jefferson's] head" (lines 32–33) as he wrote the Declaration. The rest of the second paragraph presents Jefferson's standard response to those who accused him of plagiarism, which reinforces the notion that sources of ideas will be the subject of the rest of the passage.

The best answer is NOT:

A because while the second paragraph does allude to numerous "interpretations" (line 34), these are interpretations of "what *was* in [Jefferson's] head" (line 33) when he wrote the Declaration.

B because while the second paragraph does mention that Jefferson receives a great deal of scholarly attention, the focus of the paragraph and passage is on the process Jefferson used to put together the Declaration.

D because, again, while the second paragraph does allude to numerous "interpretations," nowhere does the paragraph or passage suggest anyone has doubts about why the Declaration was written.

Question 16. The best answer is F because the phrase "even if" (line 65) implies that the author doubts Jefferson was being totally honest about not copying from any previous writing—an implication reinforced in lines 72–74 when the author says that "virtually all the ideas found in the Declaration and much of the specific language had already found expression in [Jefferson's] earlier writings."

The best answer is NOT:

G because Lincoln was a nineteenth-century political figure (see lines 17–28), while Jefferson wrote the Declaration in the late eighteenth century (see lines 62–64), making it impossible for Jefferson to have copied from Lincoln.

H because the phrase "even if" implies some doubt, but it isn't a clear-cut assertion that Jefferson shouldn't be believed. Furthermore, the author declines "to accuse [Jefferson] of plagiarism" (line 70).

J because while the author doesn't accuse Jefferson of plagiarism, this isn't because Jefferson wrote the Declaration so long ago but because the author thinks that at worst Jefferson "plagiarize[d] himself" (lines 71–72), something the author doubts is even truly possible.

Question 17. The best answer is B because, as used in line 19, *characteristic* most nearly means "usually," and *eloquence* translates to "persuasive" and "expressive." That the author is being sincere in his praise for Lincoln is made clear when he says that Lincoln, like Jefferson, "also knew how to change history with words" (lines 18–19).

The best answer is NOT:

A because there's nothing ironic or negative about the author's view of Lincoln, as expressed in the passage.

C because calling Lincoln "a bit of a character" would be patronizing, which is clearly not the author's intent. In addition, Lincoln's view of Jefferson "as the original American oracle" (lines 20–21) is the standard view of "several generations of American interpreters" (lines 56–57), which means, in this case anyway, that Lincoln's opinion is not controversial.

D because there's no evidence in the passage that the author feels Lincoln's words are often difficult for modern readers to understand.

Question 18. The best answer is H because lines 29–32 state, "No serious student of either Jefferson or the Declaration of Independence has ever claimed that he foresaw all or even most of the ideological consequences of what he wrote."

The best answer is NOT:

G because according to lines 29–32, students of Jefferson or of the Declaration do not claim that Jefferson anticipated most of the ideological outcomes of what he wrote.

F or J because there's no evidence in lines 29–32 that students of Jefferson or of the Declaration think Jefferson purposely wrote ambiguously about freedom (F) or that he wrote the Declaration from memory without consulting other works (J).

Question 19. The best answer is D because in lines 45–48, the author explains that by calling Jefferson's explanation "ingeniously double-edged," he means that the explanation "simultaneously disavows any claims to originality"—thus, the writing wasn't new—"and yet insists that he depended upon no specific texts or sources"—thus, the writing wasn't copied from any particular text.

The best answer is NOT:

A, B, or C because the phrase "ingeniously double-edged" doesn't mean that Jefferson claimed to have written alone and copied from his own previous writings (A), that Jefferson felt his work was prophetic (B), or that Jefferson claimed he was a prophet or an influence on Lincoln (C).

Question 20. The best answer is F because lines 75–79 help create a sense of urgency about the writing of the Declaration, with the Continental Congress "being overwhelmed with military reports of imminent American defeat in New York and Canada," being "in session six days a week" as a full group, and meeting in committees "throughout the evenings." This situation led Jefferson to take "the obvious practical course" (line 79) writing the Declaration, which "was to rework his previous drafts on the same general theme" (lines 80–81).

The best answer is NOT:

G because there's no evidence in lines 75–79 or elsewhere in the passage that Jefferson was depressed by news of American defeats or that he lacked energy to draft a new document.

H because while Jefferson finished the Declaration in a hurry, there's no evidence in lines 75–79 or elsewhere in the passage that Jefferson knew the Declaration could solve the problems of the nation.

J because while lines 75–79 suggest that the war was moving closer to home, they also describe an urgent situation that would have made it impossible for Jefferson to take his time writing the Declaration.

Passage III

Question 21. The best answer is A because claims and supporting details presented throughout the passage explain how and why *Star Trek* has endured: it "captured the imagination and viewer loyalty of millions of Americans" (lines 8–10), it was "the right show at the right time" (lines 17–18), and its space-exploration theme "resonated with millions of idealistic and awestruck Americans" (lines 37–38). The seventh paragraph (lines 56–67) and last paragraph highlight ways in which the show has endured. For instance, *Star Trek* "has spawned four prime-time series, continued syndication, a cartoon, eight major motion pictures, countless toys, games, and computer software" (lines 57–59), it has "exploded in print like no other phenomenon in American popular culture" (lines 64–65), and it "has become a television phenomenon like no other in American culture" (lines 82–84).

The best answer is NOT:

B because while the passage does describe what American society was like at the time the original *Star Trek* was created, particularly in the third paragraph (lines 16–24), the author only does this to put *Star Trek* into historical context.

C because the author doesn't discuss how *Star Trek*'s storyline has changed over its thirty-year history. The passage, in fact, suggests that little has changed in the "'known' universe of Starfleet, Klingons, and phasers" (line 80).

D because while the passage does mention the different forms *Star Trek* has taken, it doesn't describe any of these in detail.

Question 22. The best answer is H because the language the author uses throughout the passage—for example, "visionary episodes" (line 46), "eloquently" (line 70), and "provocative insight" (line 78)—shows his warm appreciation for *Star Trek*.

The best answer is NOT:

F because there's no evidence in the passage that the author is amused by *Star Trek*, and his appreciation for it goes well beyond tolerance.

G because the author's interest in *Star Trek* is not detached, but rather quite passionate.

J because there's no evidence in the passage that the author is mildly skeptical about *Star Trek*. On the contrary, the author is deeply enthusiastic about *Star Trek*, and he concludes with a strong note of optimism about *Star Trek*'s future: "As America goes boldly into the next millennium, so will *Star Trek* in print, on television, and in formats yet to come" (lines 89–91).

Question 23. The best answer is C because two years after *Star Trek*'s cancellation in 1969—in other words, 1971—"*Star Trek* somehow had captured the imagination and viewer loyalty of millions of Americans who 'discovered' the show anew in syndicated reruns" (lines 8–11).

The best answer is NOT:

A because "few were watching" (line 2) when *Star Trek* premiered in 1966.

B because *Star Trek* was "canceled as a ratings flop in January 1969" (lines 6–7).

D because while the passage states that "by 1977, *Star Trek* had become the most-watched off-network series drama of all time" (lines 54–55), the year 1977 was not when *Star Trek* first became a success—that was 1971.

Question 24. The best answer is J because the fourth paragraph (lines 25–33) indicates that entertainment programming during the time period was generally less willing than news programming to present a realistic picture of contemporary life. The author states, "Although television news programs helped focus the country on the rifts that had begun to percolate . . . as a rule entertainment programming avoided conflict and controversy" (lines 25–29). In addition, "Escapist comedy about suburban witches, genies, and rural townspeople was standard fare" (lines 29–31).

The best answer is NOT:

F or **G** because they reverse the actual relationship: entertainment programming was generally less, not more, willing than news programming to examine the rifts developing in American society (**F**) and to display violent conflict and controversy (**G**).

H because the fourth paragraph implies entertainment programming was generally more, not less, willing than news programming to promote the principles of conformity and order: "network drama emphasized law, order, and conformity" (lines 31–32), whereas "television news programs helped focus the country on the rifts that had begun to percolate."

Question 25. The best answer is D because the author claims *Star Trek* has had an "unparalleled impact" (line 60) on the publishing industry and that this impact has come in the diverse forms of "fan volumes, cast memoirs, and novels" (lines 65–66).

The best answer is NOT:

A because the author feels *Star Trek* has had an "unparalleled impact" on the publishing industry and that the industry has "recently become television friendly" (lines 61–62).

B because while the author traces the impact of *Star Trek* on publishing back to "the early 1970s, when the first novels hit bookshelves" (lines 62–63), the author contradicts the idea of a lessening impact by noting that *Star Trek* books "continue to appear—and in record numbers" (lines 66–67).

C because the author doesn't claim *Star Trek*'s impact on publishing has been primarily limited to novels.

Question 26. The best answer is F because the series, with its "visionary episodes on race relations, nuclear deterrence, multiculturalism, and ecology (among others)" (lines 46–48), came out during a period in which "social and political change" (lines 18–19) was not otherwise dealt with by most entertainment programming, which "avoided conflict and controversy" (lines 28–29).

The best answer is NOT:

G because while *Star Trek* had a "wide appeal in syndication" (line 53), there's no evidence in the passage that syndicated reruns in general were popular.

H because the author portrays *Star Trek*, with its "visionary episodes" on serious topics, as the opposite of escapist entertainment. The author does acknowledge that some people viewed *Star Trek* as "fantastic science fiction" (line 49), but the author himself believes *Star Trek* was "a window into current controversy" that "offered insight and added perspective to continued American cultural and political change in the 1970s" (lines 51–52).

J because the author makes no reference to an increasingly empowered middle class, only to "a culturally empowered youth movement" (lines 21–22) and to a middle class divided by "social and political change" (lines 18–19).

Question 27. The best answer is **D** because the author reports Roddenberry's claim that "*Star Trek* was less about the future than the present" (lines 41–42), which the author takes to mean that "precisely because of its futuristic storyline . . . *Star Trek* was able to address many of the contemporary social problems that other programs shunned" (lines 43–46).

The best answer is NOT:

A because, as the above quotations show, Roddenberry wasn't primarily concerned with showing how different life would be in the future.

B because while the author does note that *Star Trek* was "created in the optimistic afterglow of John F. Kennedy's inauguration of the space race" (lines 34–36), he doesn't claim that promoting the space program and the exploration of space was Roddenberry's main purpose in creating *Star Trek*.

C because with its "visionary episodes on race relations, nuclear deterrence, multiculturalism, and ecology (among others)" (lines 46–48), *Star Trek* was, in the author's view, anything but light entertainment.

Question 28. The best answer is **F** because the author states that "it was precisely because of its futuristic storyline that *Star Trek* was able to address many of the contemporary social problems that other programs shunned" (lines 43–46). The author claims that *Star Trek*'s episodes dealing with present-day social problems "were not threatening to those who saw it as fantastic science fiction" (lines 48–49); for those who wanted to see *Star Trek* as a commentary on social problems, the series "offered insight and added perspective" (line 51).

The best answer is NOT:

G because the passage indicates that the main benefit of the futuristic storyline wasn't to enable writers to invent fantastic and entertaining science fiction (even if some people saw the series as "fantastic science fiction") but rather to offer unthreatening perspectives and insights.

H because while *Star Trek* "has spawned . . . eight major motion pictures" (lines 57–59) and "series such as *The Next Generation*, *Deep Space Nine*, and *Voyager*" (lines 85–86), the author doesn't claim that the ease with which related spin-offs could be developed was the primary benefit of the original show's futuristic storyline.

J because the series addressed, rather than avoided, controversial topics such as multiculturalism and nuclear deterrence.

Question 29. The best answer is **B** because the original *Star Trek*'s "episodes on race relations, nuclear deterrence, multiculturalism, and ecology (among others)" (lines 46–48) were visionary because they dealt with contemporary social problems in a way that, like the series generally, "offered insight and added perspective" (line 51).

The best answer is NOT:

A because the passage indicates that the visionary episodes addressed "contemporary social problems" (line 45) and "current controversy" (line 50).

C because while the series did deal with difficult problems, nowhere does the author claim that the series offered solutions that were dreamy and unrealistic—a claim that would be inconsistent with the praiseful tone of the passage.

D because although the original *Star Trek* did have "wide appeal in syndication" (line 53), this fact is not directly relevant to the author's claim that some of the series' episodes were visionary.

Question 30. The best answer is **G** because the ideas of familiarity and change are at the heart of the paradox described by the author. He presents as conflicting the ideas of "changing cultural values" (lines 78–79) and the familiar, "'known' universe of Starfleet, Klingons, and phasers" (line 80).

The best answer is NOT:

F because although the author does mention "changing cultural values," he doesn't describe the ideas of cultural values and entertainment as conflicting.

H because the author sees the ideas of comfort and the *Star Trek* universe as compatible, not conflicting: in times of "changing cultural values," people can take "reassuring comfort" (line 79) in the fact that the familiar *Star Trek* universe "can nonetheless survive intact, and even grow" (line 81).

J because the author doesn't present the ideas of survival and being provocative as conflicting, as evidenced by *Star Trek*, whose universe "can . . . survive intact, and even grow" despite the fact that the series offers "provocative insight" (line 78).

Passage IV

Question 31. The best answer is **B** because, according to the passage, Helmholtz had respect for Goethe's color theory: "Helmholtz . . . gave admiring lectures on Goethe and his science, on many occasions" (lines 7–9) and he, like Goethe, was interested in the idea of "color constancy" (line 10). Helmholtz was unusual in his respect for Goethe's color theory, as it "was, by and large, dismissed by all [Goethe's] contemporaries and has remained in a sort of limbo ever since, seen as the whimsy, the pseudoscience, of a very great poet" (lines 2–5).

The best answer is NOT:

A, C, or **D** because the reference to Helmholtz's "admiring lectures on Goethe and his science" rules out disbelief (**A**), amusement (**C**), and skepticism (**D**) as Helmholtz's attitude.

Question 32. The best answer is **F** because Clerk Maxwell showed how color photography was possible despite black-and-white emulsions "by photographing a colored bow three times, through red, green, and violet filters" (lines 42–44), then superimposing the "three 'color-separation' images" (lines 44–45) on a screen, "projecting each image through its corresponding filter" (line 47), which allowed the bow to "burst forth in full color" (lines 49–50).

The best answer is NOT:

G because the passage doesn't indicate that Clerk Maxwell's color triangle—"a graphic representation with three axes" that "showed how any color could be created by different mixtures of the three primary colors" (lines 35–38)—had any role in his 1861 demonstration.

H because the passage doesn't indicate that Clerk Maxwell's color top—which helped formalize "the notions of primary colors and color mixing" (lines 32–33)—had any role in his 1861 demonstration.

J because the passage doesn't mention color slides as being part of Clerk Maxwell's 1861 demonstration. Clerk Maxwell used "three 'color-separation' images" and three color filters, but these aren't the same as color slides.

Question 33. The best answer is C because the passage says Goethe was generally viewed by his contemporaries as "a very great poet" whose attempt at a color theory was "whimsy" and "pseudoscience" (line 5).

The best answer is NOT:

A or B because in ranking Goethe's science above his poetry, they say essentially the opposite of what the passage says about the general view of Goethe among his contemporaries.

D because by noting that Goethe's color theory was widely dismissed, the passage contradicts the idea that Goethe was generally viewed as a leading theorist who overturned previously standard approaches to scientific inquiry.

Question 34. The best answer is J because the passage defines color constancy as "the way in which the colors of objects are preserved, so that we can categorize them and always know what we are looking at, despite great fluctuations in the wavelength of the light illuminating them" (lines 10–14). Color constancy means, in this case, that a "red" apple looks "red" regardless of the wavelength of the light reflected by the apple.

The best answer is NOT:

F because the only mention in the passage of "split-beam" is in reference to Land's "split-beam camera" (line 66).

G because the only mention in the passage of "sensory flux" is in reference to the "chaotic sensory flux" (lines 25–26) from which "a stable perceptual world" (line 25)—including stable perceptions of color—must somehow be drawn.

H because the idea of color separation relates to the multiple images, taken through red, green, and violet filters, that Clerk Maxwell "brought . . . together by superimposing them upon a screen, projecting each image through its corresponding filter" (lines 45–47), thus demonstrating that "color photography was possible, despite the fact that photographic emulsions were themselves black and white" (lines 40–42).

Question 35. The best answer is D because the passage states that "the actual wavelengths reflected by an apple, for instance, will vary considerably depending on the illumination" (lines 14–16), or light reaching the apple.

The best answer is NOT:

A or B because there's no evidence in lines 14–17 to support the idea that the wavelengths reflected by an apple vary considerably as a result of differences between a viewer's two eyes (A) or the distance between the apple and the eyes (B).

C because while a viewer has the ability to perceive an apple as red in different lights according to Helmholtz's idea of "color constancy" (line 10), this isn't the reason the wavelengths reflected by an apple vary considerably. This stable perception of color is possible despite considerable variance in the wavelengths reflected by an apple.

Question 36. The best answer is **H** because the word *illuminant*, as it is used in line 20, refers to light that makes an object visible. Lines 14–16 indicate that "the actual wavelengths reflected by an apple, for instance, will vary considerably depending on the illumination," or light reaching the apple. Helmholtz felt people had some way of "discounting the illuminant" (lines 19–20), by which he meant some way of seeing an apple as red regardless of the wavelength of the light reflected by the apple.

The best answer is NOT:

F or **G** because there's no evidence in the passage to support the idea that the word *illuminant*, as it is used in line 20, refers to camera flash equipment (**F**) or to a color theorist (**G**).

J because while the word *illuminant*, as it is used in line 20, does refer to light, it doesn't refer specifically to light before it passes through a filter; instead, it refers more generally to light that makes an object visible.

Question 37. The best answer is **B** because the passage describes Helmholtz as being interested in "'color constancy'—the way in which the colors of objects are preserved, so that we can categorize them and always know what we are looking at, despite great fluctuations in the wavelength of the light illuminating them" (lines 10–14).

The best answer is NOT:

A because although Helmholtz was interested in "color constancy," he believed that people continually saw an apple as red despite, not because of, varying wavelengths of light: "the actual wavelengths reflected by an apple, for instance, will vary considerably depending on the illumination, but we consistently see it as red, nonetheless" (lines 14–17).

C because there's no evidence in the passage that Helmholtz was preoccupied with the notion that humans undergo changes in color awareness as they age.

D because in the passage, Clerk Maxwell and Land—not Helmholtz—were the people interested in superimposing images.

Question 38. The best answer is **F** because the passage states that "any color could be created by different mixtures of the three primary colors" (lines 37–38).

The best answer is NOT:

G because there's no evidence in the passage that the human eye perceives primary colors first and then other colors.

H because the passage doesn't provide a sequence listing the order in which colors were first captured on film.

J because it's basically the opposite of what the passage says.

Question 39. The best answer is **B** because the passage says Clerk Maxwell's "most spectacular demonstration [was] the demonstration in 1861 that color photography was possible, despite the fact that photographic emulsions were themselves black and white" (lines 39–42).

The best answer is NOT:

A because there's no evidence in the passage that illuminants were thought to be stable rather than variable in Clerk Maxwell's time. On the contrary, Clerk Maxwell was Helmholtz's "great contemporary" (line 30), meaning he lived in Helmholtz's time, and Helmholtz knew there were "great fluctuations in the wavelength of the light illuminating" objects (lines 13–14).

C because there's no evidence in the passage that in Clerk Maxwell's time, the general public rejected the new technology of color photography as a stunt with no practical application.

D because there's no evidence in the passage that professional photographers in Clerk Maxwell's time were reluctant to abandon the established black-and-white aesthetic when presented with color photography.

Question 40. The best answer is **J** because for the demonstration, Land made "two black-and-white images (using a split-beam camera so they could be taken at the same time from the same viewpoint, through the same lens)" (lines 66–68).

The best answer is NOT:

F because although Land used a screen in the demonstration (see lines 65–69), there's no evidence in the passage that the screen was lit from the front and back.

G because there's no evidence in the passage that the light sources flickered in the demonstration.

H because while Land did use a single lens to obtain his two images, there's no evidence in the passage that this lens was in two cameras.

Passage I

Question 1. The best answer is B. Table 2 lists the weekly average air temperatures in each of the 3 greenhouse sections. According to Table 2, the highest weekly average air temperature recorded was 21.13°C. This weekly average air temperature occurred in Section 1 during Week 6.

The best answer is NOT:

A because 18.47°C is lower than 21.13°C.

C or D because 120.7°C and 314.9°C, respectively, do not correspond to any of the weekly average air temperatures in Table 2.

Question 2. The best answer is F. Table 2 lists the weekly average air temperatures. The values were recorded to the second decimal place. For example, in Section 1 during Week 1 the weekly average air temperature was 19.68°C. Therefore, weekly average air temperatures were recorded to the nearest 0.01°C.

The best answer is NOT:

G, H, or J because the weekly average air temperatures were recorded with greater precision than 0.1°C, 1.0°C, and 10°C, respectively.

Question 3. The best answer is A. According to Table 1, in Section 1, the weekly average light intensity for Week 1 was 289.3; for Week 2, 305.5; for Week 3, 313.4; for Week 4, 314.9; for Week 5, 304.5; and for Week 6, 311.1. According to Table 2, in Section 1, the weekly average air temperature, in °C, for Week 1 was 19.68; for Week 2, 20.12; for Week 3, 20.79; for Week 4, 20.98; for Week 5, 21.04; and for Week 6, 21.13. The weekly average light intensity and the weekly average air temperature for each of the 6 weeks correspond to the 6 ordered pairs that must be plotted. For example, during Week 1, the weekly average light intensity was 289.3 and the weekly average air temperature was 19.68°C. Thus, a plot of the data must include a point at 289.3 on the horizontal axis and 19.68 on the vertical axis. Likewise, during Week 2, the weekly average light intensity was 305.5 and the weekly average air temperature was 20.12°C. Thus, a plot of the data must include a point at 305.5 on the horizontal axis and 20.12 on the vertical axis. A is the only graph that has each of the 6 ordered pairs plotted correctly.

The best answer is NOT:

B, C, or D because the figures in these options do not contain the 6 ordered pairs. For example, none of the figures in B, C, and D has a point for the ordered pair that corresponds to a weekly average light intensity of 289.3 and a weekly average air temperature of 19.68°C.

Question 4. The best answer is H. According to Table 2, in Section 1, the weekly average air temperature, in °C, for Week 1 was 19.68; for Week 2, 20.12; for Week 3, 20.79; for Week 4, 20.98; for Week 5, 21.04; and for Week 6, 21.13. Thus, from week to week, the weekly average air temperature always increased.

The best answer is NOT:

F because the weekly average air temperature did not decrease between Weeks 4 and 6.

G because the weekly average air temperature did not decrease between Weeks 1 and 3.

J because the weekly average air temperature did not always decrease.

Question 5. The best answer is D. Efficiency of illumination is defined as the intensity of light absorbed by the plants divided by the intensity of light provided to the plants. Weekly average light intensities are listed in Table 1. However, the passage provides no information about the intensity of light absorbed by the plants. Without this information, the efficiency of illumination cannot be determined.

The best answer is NOT:

A because it is not possible to determine the efficiency of illumination based solely on the level of illumination. To determine the efficiency of illumination, the intensity of light absorbed must also be determined.

B because the amount of light not absorbed by the plants in Section 1 was not determined.

C because the amount of light absorbed by the plants in Section 1 was not determined.

Passage II

Question 6. The best answer is G. Table 1 lists the results from Experiment 1. According to Table 1, at –9°C (the only temperature measured) and at a given time after starting, the percent of CO in the exhaust was greater for the 1978 cars than for the 1996 cars. For example, 1 minute after starting, the percent of CO in the exhaust of the 1978 Model X car was 3.5% and the percent of CO in the exhaust of the 1978 Model Y car was 3.2%. In contrast, the percent of CO in the exhaust of the 1996 Model X car was 1.2% and the percent of CO in the exhaust of the 1996 Model Y car was 0.3%. Similar comparisons for each of the other 7 times after starting indicate that both of the 1996 cars had a lower CO percent than did either of the 1978 cars. The results support the hypothesis that the exhaust of newer cars contains lower percents of CO than does the exhaust of older cars.

The best answer is NOT:

F because the 1996 Model Y car did not have the highest percent of CO.

H or J because the results of Experiment 1 support the hypothesis.

Question 7. The best answer is D. The student was concerned that the presence of CO_2 in the exhaust may have affected the measurement of CO in the exhaust. To explore this issue, one could test the gas chromatograph with samples containing known amounts of CO_2 and CO. This would provide a means of determining whether the chromatograph is accurately reporting the amount of CO in a sample, even as the amount of CO_2 in the sample varies.

The best answer is NOT:

A because filling the bag with CO_2 before making measurements would not provide a means of determining whether the chromatograph was correctly reporting the CO in the sample, unless the percent of CO in the sample was already known.

B because collecting the exhaust from additional cars would merely provide more data like that in Tables 1 and 2 and would not address the relationship between the presence of CO_2 in a sample and the measurement of CO in the sample.

C because injecting air into the gas chromatograph would not help one determine whether the presence of CO_2 affects the measurement of CO by the gas chromatograph.

Question 8. The best answer is F. The results of Experiments 1 and 2 show that for each of the 4 cars, at any given time after starting, the percent of CO in the exhaust was greater at $-9°C$ than at $20°C$. These results are consistent with the hypothesis that the percent of CO in the exhaust of a car increases as temperature decreases. The question indicates that Minneapolis has a lower average temperature during January than do Pittsburgh, Seattle, and San Diego. Together, this information supports the conclusion that cars in Minneapolis would most likely contribute a greater amount of CO to the atmosphere in January than would cars in any of the other cities listed (Pittsburgh, Seattle, and San Diego).

The best answer is NOT:

G because the average temperature for Pittsburgh is greater than the average temperature for Minneapolis.

H because the average temperature for Seattle is greater than the average temperature for Minneapolis.

J because the average temperature for San Diego is greater than the average temperature for Minneapolis.

Question 9. The best answer is C. Some of the cars used in Experiment 1 were made in 1978 and some were made in 1996. That is, the year in which the cars were made varied.

The best answer is NOT:

A because the method of sample collection did not vary across the different trials and samples in Experiment 1.

B because the volume of exhaust that was tested was always 1 mL in Experiment 1.

D because the temperature at which the engine was started was always $-9°C$.

Question 10. The best answer is G. For the 4 cars used in Experiment 1, the maximum values for percent of CO in the exhaust were obtained at either 5 min or 7 min after starting. For the 4 cars used in Experiment 2, the maximum values for percent of CO in the exhaust were obtained at 5 min, 7 min, and 9 min after starting. In Experiment 2, the maximum occurred at 9 min only once (1978 Model Y); however, for this car, the same maximum value was found at 7 min after starting. The data support the conclusion that the maximum value for percent of CO in the exhaust is typically reached between 5 min and 7 min after starting.

The best answer is NOT:

F because the percent of CO in the exhaust was greater between 5 min and 7 min than it was between 1 min and 3 min.

H because the percent of CO in the exhaust was greater between 5 min and 7 min than it was between 9 min and 11 min.

J because the percent of CO in the exhaust was greater between 5 min and 7 min than it was after 13 or more min.

Question 11. The best answer is C. If the syringe contents were contaminated with air that did not contain CO, then the syringe would contain proportionately less CO than would a sample that had not been contaminated with CO-free air. This would occur because the amount of CO in the sample would remain constant, but the amounts of other gases in the sample would increase. As a result, the percent of CO would decrease. This effect would occur both at $-9°C$ and at $20°C$.

The best answer is NOT:

A or B because the measured percent of CO in the exhaust would be lower than the actual percents, rather than higher than the actual percents. This would be true for the measurements performed both at $-9°C$ and at $20°C$.

D because the measured percent of CO in the exhaust would be lower than the actual percents, rather than the same as the actual percents. This would be true for the measurements performed both at $-9°C$ and at $20°C$.

Passage III

Question 12. The best answer is H. The object viewed during Activity 2 had a length of 0.1 mm. The passage explains that magnification (M) can be calculated using the formula M = image size ÷ object size. If the image size was 30 mm, then M = 30 mm ÷ 0.1 mm = 300.

The best answer is NOT:

F, G, or J because, according to the formula provided, M = 300.

Question 13. The best answer is D. According to the passage, magnification (M) equals image size divided by object size. Therefore, image size equals M times object size. Table 2 lists the magnification associated with each objective lens. These values can be used to calculate the image size of each of the lines described in the 4 options. The question asks for the line with the greatest image size. In D, image size = 400 × 0.4 = 160 mm, which is the greatest image size yielded by the answer choices.

The best answer is NOT:

A because image size = 40 × 0.7 mm = 28 mm, which is less than the value in D.

B because image size = 100 × 0.6 mm = 60 mm, which is less than the value in D.

C because image size = 200 × 0.5 mm = 100 mm, which is less than the value in D.

Question 14. The best answer is G. Table 1 indicates whether the 2 lines appeared separate or whether the lines blurred together. For Slide C, the lines appeared separate with Objective Lenses 3 and 4. The lines appeared blurred with Objective Lenses 1 and 2. Based on Table 1, when viewing Slide C in Activity 1, the student was able to discern 2 distinct lines with 2 of the objective lenses.

The best answer is NOT:

F, H, or J because the student was able to discern 2 distinct lines with exactly 2 of the object lenses.

Question 15. The best answer is B. According to the passage, R (in nm) can be calculated using the formula $R = \lambda \div 2(NA)$. According to Table 3, for Objective Lens 2, the NA (numerical aperture) equals 0.25. The question requires that R be calculated for light with a wavelength (λ) of 425 nm. The correct equation for determining R is $R = \lambda \div 2(NA) = 425 \div 2(0.25)$.

The best answer is NOT:

A because NA for Objective Lens 2 is 0.25, not 0.10.

C or D because the equations used in these options do not correspond to the equation given in the passage. As noted above, $R = \lambda \div 2(NA)$. In C and D, an NA is being divided by 2 times the wavelength of the light (425 nm).

Question 16. The best answer is F. The equation used to calculate resolution R indicates that R is directly proportional to wavelength and inversely proportional to NA. In Activity 3, calculations were based on a wavelength of 550 nm. Thus, variability in R reflected variability in NA. Specifically, as NA decreased, R increased. R for Objective Lenses 1 and 2 equaled 2,750 nm and 1,100 nm, respectively. For the fifth objective lens, R equaled 1,830 nm. Based on these results, the NA of the fifth lens was greater than the NA of Lens 1 (0.10) and less than the NA of Lens 2 (0.25).

The best answer is NOT:

G because 0.25 is the NA that resulted in an R = 1,100 nm.

H or J because each of these values corresponds to an NA that would result in an R < 1,100 nm.

Question 17. The best answer is A. In Activity 1, the student used 4 different slides (A, B, C, and D). In Activity 2, the student used a single prepared slide.

The best answer is NOT:

B because in both Activity 1 and Activity 2, 4 different objective lenses were used.

C because the same light source was used in Activities 1 and 2.

D because the microscope magnified each image, so image sizes were greater than object sizes in both Activity 1 and Activity 2.

Passage IV

Question 18. The best answer is J. The figure shows that as the blackbody temperature increases, the area under the blackbody curve increases. The question indicates that as the area under a blackbody curve increases, the rate at which energy is emitted also increases. This information supports the conclusion that 1 m² of the blackbody with the highest temperature emits the greatest amount of energy per second at the wavelengths shown. This information also supports the conclusion that 1 m² of the blackbody with the lowest temperature emits the least amount of energy per second at the wavelengths shown. The correct order is 500 K, 400 K, 300 K.

The best answer is NOT:

F or G because the blackbody with the lowest temperature emits the least amount of energy per second at the wavelengths shown, not the greatest amount of energy per second at the wavelengths shown.

H because the blackbody with the highest temperature emits the greatest amount of energy per second at the wavelengths shown. Therefore, more energy will be emitted at 500 K than at 400 K.

Question 19. The best answer is A. According to the figure, at a temperature of 300 K and a wavelength equal to or greater than 11×10^{-6} m, brightness decreases as wavelength increases. The maximum wavelength included in the figure is 25×10^{-6} m. At this wavelength, brightness is about 1×10^6 watts per m³. Thus, for longer wavelengths, such as 30×10^{-6} m, brightness will be less than 1×10^6 watts per m³.

The best answer is NOT:

B, C, or D because all of the values for brightness in each of the ranges listed are greater than 5×10^6 watts per m³.

Question 20. The best answer is J. The figure shows that the area under a blackbody curve increases as the temperature of the blackbody increases. The figure also shows that the wavelength with the maximum brightness for a blackbody increases as the temperature of the blackbody decreases. Of the 4 options, only J shows both of these characteristics.

The best answer is NOT:

F or H because in these options, the area under the blackbody curve decreases as the temperature of the blackbody increases.

G because in this option, the wavelength with the maximum brightness for a blackbody decreases as the temperature of the blackbody decreases.

Question 21. **The best answer is C.** In the figure, the maximum of the blackbody curve increases as the temperature of the blackbody increases. At 300 K, the blackbody had a maximum brightness of about 10×10^6 watts per m^3. At 400 K, the blackbody had a maximum brightness of about 42×10^6 watts per m^3. At 500 K, the blackbody had a maximum brightness of about 128×10^6 watts per m^3. The temperature associated with a maximum brightness of 75×10^6 watts per m^3 can be determined through interpolation. This temperature must fall between 400 K and 500 K.

The best answer is NOT:

A or **B** because at 400 K, the blackbody had a maximum brightness of about 42×10^6 watts per m^3. Thus, if the blackbody has a maximum brightness of 75×10^6 watts per m^3, it must have a temperature greater than 400 K.

D because at 500 K, the blackbody had a maximum brightness of about 128×10^6 watts per m^3. Thus, if the blackbody has a maximum brightness of 75×10^6 watts per m^3, it must have a temperature less than 500 K.

Question 22. **The best answer is H.** According to the question, the frequency of radiation increases as the wavelength of the radiation decreases. In the figure, for each of the 3 temperatures, as wavelength decreases, the brightness of the blackbody increases, then decreases. Because frequency is inversely proportional to wavelength, as the frequency of the radiation from a blackbody increases, the brightness increases, then decreases.

The best answer is NOT:

F because as the frequency of the radiation from a blackbody increases, the brightness does not increase only.

G because as the frequency of the radiation from a blackbody increases, the brightness does not decrease only.

J because as the frequency of the radiation from a blackbody increases, the brightness increases before it decreases, not the other way around.

Passage V

Question 23. **The best answer is C.** In Experiment 1, at 20°C, the vapor pressure of 2-butanone was 75 mm Hg; of ethyl acetate, 70 mm Hg; of hexane, 110 mm Hg; of methanol, 90 mm Hg; and of 2-propanol, 35 mm Hg. Only the figure in C shows relative bar heights for the liquids that correctly correspond to these values.

The best answer is NOT:

A or **D** because the vapor pressure of hexane should be greater than the vapor pressure of methanol.

B because the vapor pressure of methanol should be greater than the vapor pressure of 2-butanone.

Question 24. The best answer is G. Before the liquid was added, the forces exerted by the gases in the 2 sections of the tubing were equal. As a result, the heights of the Hg in the 2 sections of the tubing were the same. When the liquid was added to the flask, some of the liquid evaporated. This increased the vapor pressure of the gases in the section of the tubing that was connected to the flask (the left side of the tubing in the figures). As a result, the force exerted by these gases increased, pushing down the column of Hg in the left side of the tubing. The correct figure should show the levels of Hg within the 2 sections of the tubing at the same height before the liquid was added and the level of Hg within the left section of the tubing lower than the level of Hg within the right section of the tubing after the liquid was added.

The best answer is NOT:

F because the figure shows the level of Hg within the left section of the tubing as being higher than the level of Hg within the right section of the tubing after the liquid was added.

H or J because the figures show the levels of Hg within the 2 sections of the tubing at different heights before the liquid was added.

Question 25. The best answer is D. The liquids used in Experiment 2 can be ordered based on their boiling points at a given external pressure. For example, if the liquids are ordered from the liquid with the lowest boiling point to the liquid with the highest boiling point at 760 mm Hg, the correct sequence is as follows: methanol, hexane, ethyl acetate, 2-butanone, and 2-propanol. Similarly, if the liquids are ordered from the liquid with the lowest boiling point to the liquid with the highest boiling point at 400 mm Hg, the correct sequence is as follows: hexane, methanol, ethyl acetate, 2-butanone, and 2-propanol. At 100 mm Hg, the correct sequence is as follows: hexane, methanol, 2-butanone, ethyl acetate, and 2-propanol. If these same liquids are ordered from the liquid with the lowest molecular weight to the liquid with highest molecular weight, the correct sequence is as follows: methanol, 2-propanol, 2-butanone, hexane, and ethyl acetate. These orderings are inconsistent with the hypothesis that at a given external pressure, the higher a liquid's molecular weight, the higher the boiling point of the liquid. The results are consistent with the conclusion that there is no relationship in these data between boiling point and molecular weight.

The best answer is NOT:

A or B because the data do not support the hypothesis. For example, hexane has one of the highest molecular weights, but its boiling point is lower than the boiling points of most of the other liquids. Likewise, ethyl acetate has the highest molecular weight, but it has an intermediate boiling point compared with the other liquids.

C because liquids with higher molecular weights do not have lower boiling points. For example, ethyl acetate has the highest molecular weight, but its boiling point is higher than the boiling point of both hexane and methanol at each of the 3 external pressures.

Question 26. **The best answer is G.** In Experiment 2, for each liquid, as the external pressure increased, the boiling point of the liquid increased. For example, at external pressures of 100 mm Hg, 400 mm Hg, and 760 mm Hg, the boiling points of 2-butanone were 25.0°C, 60.0°C, and 79.6°C, respectively. Likewise, at external pressures of 100 mm Hg, 400 mm Hg, and 760 mm Hg, the boiling points of ethyl acetate were 27.0°C, 59.3°C, and 77.1°C, respectively.

The best answer is NOT:

F, H, or J because as the external pressure increased, the boiling points never decreased. For each of the 5 liquids used in Experiment 2, the highest boiling point was obtained at a pressure 760 mm Hg and the lowest boiling point was obtained at a pressure of 100 mm Hg.

Question 27. **The best answer is B.** For Experiment 2, the apparatus was described as a test tube containing a thermometer. This test tube was heated in an oil bath. Of the 4 figures, only the figure in B shows a thermometer inside a test tube, which sits in an oil bath.

The best answer is NOT:

A because the test tube does not contain a thermometer.

C because the apparatus does not have a thermometer.

D because the apparatus does not have a test tube.

Question 28. **The best answer is J.** In Experiment 1, the procedure states that the manometer was connected 5 minutes after the flask was placed in an H_2O bath. This procedure indicates that the experimenter wanted the air in the flask to reach the temperature of the H_2O bath. The procedure is also consistent with the experimental design. For a gas, pressure varies with temperature. So the procedure helped to ensure that changes in pressure within the flask were due to the addition of the liquid added and not simply due to changes in air temperature.

The best answer is NOT:

F because at the temperatures that were used in the experiment, 5 minutes would not be enough time to remove all of the H_2O vapor from the flask.

G because the liquid was not added to the flask until after the manometer was connected to the flask.

H because at this point in the experiment, the manometer had not been connected to the flask.

Passage VI

Question 29. The best answer is D. According to the passage, all proteins have primary structures. In addition, proteins with lower-energy shapes are more stable than proteins with higher-energy shapes. Because of this, proteins with lower-energy shapes tend to maintain their shapes. In contrast, proteins with higher-energy shapes tend to denature. If a protein is almost completely denatured, it is a random coil and has a relatively high-energy shape.

The best answer is NOT:

A because random coils have relatively high-energy shapes.

B because all proteins have primary structures.

C because proteins with relatively low energy shapes tend to maintain their shapes. Therefore, they do not tend to become denatured.

Question 30. The best answer is F. The passage explains that the primary structure of a protein is the sequence of amino acids in each polypeptide of that protein. Because a protein is composed of a sequence of amino acids, it must have a primary structure. Otherwise, the protein does not exist. Higher levels of structure—secondary, tertiary, and quaternary—are all associated with the spatial relationships between different parts of the amino acid sequence. When a protein becomes a random coil, these relationships are destroyed. Thus, when a protein denatures, it loses its original secondary, tertiary, and quaternary structure.

The best answer is NOT:

G, H, or J because a protein that is completely denatured lacks its original secondary structure, tertiary structure, and quaternary structure, respectively.

Question 31. The best answer is C. Scientist 1 states that the active shape of a protein is always identical to the protein's lowest-energy shape. This shape is determined by the primary structure of the protein. Scientist 2 also states that the active shape of a protein is dependent upon the protein's primary structure. However, according to Scientist 2, a protein's active shape may also depend on its process of synthesis: the order (in time) in which the amino acids were bonded together as the protein was created. Both scientists believe that the active shape of a protein is dependent on the sequence of amino acids in the protein, but only Scientist 2 believes that the process of synthesis influences the active shape of the protein.

The best answer is NOT:

A because many proteins do not have quaternary structures. Only proteins with more than 1 polypeptide have quaternary structures.

B because both Scientists 1 and 2 believe that a protein's active shape is partially determined by its amino acid sequence.

D because Scientist 2 believes that a protein's active shape is determined by its primary structure and by its process of synthesis. Tertiary folding patterns are determined by these 2 factors.

Question 32. The best answer is F. The student selected 15 colored balls from a pool of 100 balls and aligned the 15 balls in a row. This is analogous to the primary structure of a protein, because the primary structure of a protein corresponds to the sequence of amino acids in the protein. Additional levels of structure reflect folding patterns between different parts of a polypeptide or between 2 or more polypeptides. These levels of structure do not correspond to the alignment of 15 balls into a row.

The best answer is NOT:

G because the secondary structure of a protein is the local folding patterns within short segments of each polypeptide. Because the balls lack a folding pattern, their arrangement does not correspond to the secondary structure of a protein.

H because the tertiary structure of a protein is the folding patterns that result from interactions between amino acid side chains. Because the balls lack a folding pattern, their arrangement does not correspond to the tertiary structure of a protein.

J because the quaternary structure of a protein is the result of the clustering between more than 1 folded polypeptide. The balls correspond to a single polypeptide, so their arrangement does not correspond to a structure that arises due to the clustering of more than 1 polypeptide.

Question 33. The best answer is A. Suppose a protein is almost completely denatured and then is allowed to renature so that the protein has its lowest-energy shape. According to Scientist 1, the protein will still be in its active shape, because the active shape is identical to the lowest-energy shape. Scientist 2 disagrees. According to Scientist 2, the active shape may be identical to the lowest-energy shape, but it also may not be identical to the lowest-energy shape. So if a protein is almost completely denatured and then is allowed to renature so that the protein is in its lowest-energy shape, the protein may, or may not, be in its active shape.

The best answer is NOT:

B because, according to Scientist 1, each protein will be in its active shape.

C because, according to Scientist 2, the active shape may be identical to the lowest-energy shape, but it also may not be identical to the lowest-energy shape. Thus, some of the proteins will not have their active shapes.

D because, according to Scientist 2, the active shape may be identical to the lowest-energy shape, but it also may not be identical to the lowest-energy shape. Thus, some of the proteins will have their active shapes.

Question 34. The best answer is J. According to the passage, the most stable shape of a protein corresponds to the protein's lowest-energy shape. The passage also explains that the randomly coiled shape is a high-energy shape. Therefore, in the correct figure, the randomly coiled shape should have a higher relative energy than does the most stable shape. In addition, Scientist 1 believes that the active shape is identical to the lowest-energy shape, while Scientist 2 believes the active shape of a protein may differ from the lowest-energy shape. Scientist 2's view is consistent with a higher relative energy for the active shape than for the most stable shape.

The best answer is NOT:

F or G because the randomly coiled shape should have a higher relative energy than do the active shape and the most stable shape.

H because it is consistent with Scientist 1's assertion that the active shape is identical with the lowest-energy shape and that this shape has a lower relative energy than the randomly coiled shape.

Question 35. The best answer is B. According to Scientist 2, the secondary structure of a protein can correspond to stable, local structures that are associated with a moderately high-energy shape rather than the lowest-energy shape. If, as B suggests, energy barriers that maintain the stability of these local structures could be overcome, the secondary structure of the protein would change such that the protein would no longer be trapped in a moderately high-energy shape, but would instead exist in its lowest-energy shape.

The best answer is NOT:

A because it is consistent with Scientist 2's viewpoint that during protein synthesis, stable local structures can form that are associated with a moderately high-energy shape. These stable, local structures correspond to the protein's secondary structure, which is formed prior to the formation of the tertiary structure.

C because it is consistent with Scientist 2's viewpoint that the secondary structure of a protein begins to form as the protein is constructed. That is why the active shape of the protein is affected by the protein's process of synthesis. The tertiary structure, however, corresponds to folding patterns that generally occur across greater distances than those associated with the secondary structure. Therefore, these folding patterns lag the formation of the secondary structure. Thus, according to Scientist 2, the secondary structure is determined before the tertiary structure is formed.

D because proteins that lose their tertiary structures or quaternary structures are no longer in their active shapes. Thus, proteins that lose their tertiary structure or quaternary structure also lose their biological functions. This observation is not inconsistent with Scientist 2's viewpoint, so it could not be used to counter Scientist 2's argument.

Passage VII

Question 36. The best answer is J. Figure 2 shows that at depths below 4.5 km the seafloor is typically covered with red clay sediment and at depths above 4.5 km the seafloor is typically covered with calcareous ooze. If the Arctic Ocean seafloor has an average depth of 4.9 km, it is likely that a majority of the seafloor will be at a depth of 4.5 km or greater. As a result, the Arctic Ocean seafloor will be covered with more red clay than calcareous ooze. Figure 3 is consistent with this view. As average depth increases, the relative proportion of the seafloor that is covered with red clay increases. In addition, in the Pacific Ocean, which has an average depth of 4.30 km, a greater proportion of the seafloor is covered with red clay than with calcareous ooze.

The best answer is NOT:

F, G, or H because a majority of the Arctic Ocean seafloor will be at a depth of more than 4.5 km. Thus, a greater proportion of the Arctic Ocean seafloor will be covered with red clay than with calcareous ooze.

Question 37. **The best answer is B.** Figure 2 shows that calcareous oozes composed mainly of thin-shelled organisms cover areas of the seafloor having depths up to 1.8 km. Between a depth of 1.8 km and a depth of 4.5 km, the seafloor is covered with calcareous oozes composed mainly of thick-shelled organisms. Therefore, calcareous oozes composed mainly of thick-shelled organisms are found at greater depths than those composed mainly of thin-shelled organisms.

The best answer is NOT:

A or **C** because calcareous oozes composed mainly of thick-shelled organisms are found at greater depths than those composed mainly of thin-shelled organisms.

D because calcareous oozes composed mainly of thick-shelled organisms are found at greater depths than those composed mainly of thin-shelled organisms. Thus, calcareous oozes composed mainly of thick-shelled organisms would occur in different locations than would calcareous oozes composed mainly of thin-shelled organisms.

Question 38. **The best answer is H.** Figure 1 shows that seawater in shallow areas (less than 1 km deep) is supersaturated with respect to $CaCO_3$. This means that the seawater contains more dissolved $CaCO_3$ than would be expected based simply on the solubility of $CaCO_3$ in seawater. When seawater is supersaturated with respect to $CaCO_3$, the $CaCO_3$ tends to precipitate out of the seawater.

The best answer is NOT:

F because in areas where the seawater is shallow (less than 1 km deep), the seawater is supersaturated with respect to $CaCO_3$; it is not undersaturated with respect to $CaCO_3$.

G because in areas where the seawater is shallow (less than 1 km deep), the seawater is supersaturated with respect to $CaCO_3$; it is not saturated with respect to $CaCO_3$.

J because in areas where the seawater is shallow (less than 1 km deep), the seawater is supersaturated with respect to $CaCO_3$; therefore, this seawater contains $CaCO_3$.

Question 39. **The best answer is C.** Figure 1 shows that seawater is supersaturated with respect to $CaCO_3$ between depths of 0 km and 4.0 km. At a depth greater than 4.0 km, seawater is undersaturated with $CaCO_3$. At a depth of 4.0 km, seawater is saturated with $CaCO_3$. Thus, 4.0 km is the maximum depth above which all the seawater is supersaturated with respect to $CaCO_3$.

The best answer is NOT:

A or **B** because at depths less than 4.0 km, seawater is supersaturated with respect to $CaCO_3$. Therefore, there are depths greater than 3.0 km and 3.5 km that are saturated with respect to $CaCO_3$.

D because at a depth of 4.5 km, the seawater is not supersaturated with respect to $CaCO_3$.

Question 40. **The best answer is J.** Figure 1 shows the rate at which $CaCO_3$ dissolves in seawater. From a depth of 3.5 km to a depth of 4.0 km, the increase in the rate at which $CaCO_3$ dissolves is relatively small. That is, the rate at which $CaCO_3$ dissolves in seawater at a depth of 3.5 km is similar to the rate at which $CaCO_3$ dissolves in seawater at a depth of 4.0 km. Likewise, from a depth of 4.0 km to a depth of 4.5 km, and from a depth of 4.5 km to a depth of 5.0 km, the increase in the rate at which $CaCO_3$ dissolves is relatively small. However, from a depth of 5.0 km to a depth of 5.5 km, the increase in the rate at which $CaCO_3$ dissolves is relatively large. Of the 4 options provided, the rate at which $CaCO_3$ dissolves increases the most between depths of 5.0 km and 5.5 km.

The best answer is NOT:

F because the change in the rate at which $CaCO_3$ dissolves in seawater between depths of 3.5 km and 4.0 km is less than the change in the rate at which $CaCO_3$ dissolves in seawater between depths of 5.0 km and 5.5 km.

G because the change in the rate at which $CaCO_3$ dissolves in seawater between depths of 4.0 km and 4.5 km is less than the change in the rate at which $CaCO_3$ dissolves in seawater between depths of 5.0 km and 5.5 km.

H because the change in the rate at which $CaCO_3$ dissolves in seawater between depths of 4.5 km and 5.0 km is less than the change in the rate at which $CaCO_3$ dissolves in seawater between depths of 5.0 km and 5.5 km.

The ACT® *Sample Answer Sheet*

A — NAME, MAILING ADDRESS, AND TELEPHONE
(Please print.)

Last Name   First Name   MI (Middle Initial)

House Number & Street (Apt. No.); or PO Box & No.; or RR & No.

City   State/Province   ZIP/Postal Code

Area Code   Number   Country

ACT, Inc.—Confidential Restricted when data present.

ALL examinees must complete block A – please print.

REGISTERED examinees **MUST complete blocks B, C, and D.** Find the MATCHING INFORMATION on your admission ticket and enter it EXACTLY the same way, even if any of the information is missing or incorrect. Fill in the corresponding ovals. If you do not complete these blocks to match your admission ticket EXACTLY, your scores will be **delayed up to 8 weeks.** Leave blocks E and F blank.

STANDBY examinees MUST complete blocks B, D, and F. Enter your information in blocks B and D and fill in the corresponding ovals. Leave block C blank. **For block E,** if you provided your SSN when you created your Web account or completed your standby folder, enter it here. The SSN will be used to help match this document to your registration information and will be included on reports to your college choices. If you did not provide it earlier, do not know it, or do not wish to provide it, leave block E blank. Be sure to fill in the oval in block F.

Do NOT mark in this shaded area.

B — MATCH NAME
(First 5 letters of last name)

A B C D E F G H I J K L M N O P Q R S T U V W X Y Z

C — MATCH NUMBER
(Registered examinees only)

1 2 3 4 5 6 7 8 9 0

D — DATE OF BIRTH

Month	Day	Year
Jan.		
Feb.		
March	1	1 1
April	2	2 2
May	3	3 3
June		4 4
July		5 5
Aug.		6 6
Sept.		7 7
Oct.		8 8
Nov.		9 9
Dec.		0 0

↓ STANDBY TESTING ONLY ↓

E — SOCIAL SECURITY NUMBER
(Standby examinees only)

1 2 3 4 5 6 7 8 9 0

F — STANDBY TESTING

Fill in the oval below ONLY if you turned in a standby registration at the test center today.

○ Yes, I am testing as a standby.

USE A SOFT LEAD NO. 2 PENCIL ONLY.
(Do NOT use a mechanical pencil, ink, ballpoint, correction fluid, or felt-tip pen.)

EXAMINEE STATEMENT AND SIGNATURE

1. Read the following **Statement:** By submitting this answer sheet, I agree to the terms and conditions set forth in the ACT registration booklet or website for this exam, including the arbitration and dispute remedy provisions. I understand that ACT owns the test questions and responses and affirm that I will not share any test questions or responses with anyone by any form of communication.

2. Copy the **Certification** shown below (only the text in italics) on the lines provided. Write in your normal handwriting.

   Certification: *I agree to the Statement above and certify that I am the person whose name and address appear on this form.*

3. Sign your name as you would any official document and enter today's date.

Your Signature   Today's Date

ACT®
P.O. BOX 168, IOWA CITY, IOWA 52243-0168

Marking Directions: Mark only **one** oval for each question. Fill in response completely. Erase errors cleanly without smudging.

Correct mark: ⊘ ● ⊘ ⊘

- -

Do NOT use these *incorrect* **or** *bad* **marks.**

Incorrect marks: ⊘ ⊗ ⊖ ⊙
Overlapping mark: ◯◯ ◯◯ ◯◉
Cross-out mark: ●● ●● ◉
Smudged erasure: ◯◯ ◯◯ ◯
Mark is too light: ◯◯ ◯◯ ◯

BOOKLET NUMBER

① ① ① ① ① ①
② ② ② ② ② ②
③ ③ ③ ③ ③ ③
④ ④ ④ ④ ④ ④
⑤ ⑤ ⑤ ⑤ ⑤ ⑤
⑥ ⑥ ⑥ ⑥ ⑥ ⑥
⑦ ⑦ ⑦ ⑦ ⑦ ⑦
⑧ ⑧ ⑧ ⑧ ⑧ ⑧
⑨ ⑨ ⑨ ⑨ ⑨ ⑨
⓪ ⓪ ⓪ ⓪ ⓪ ⓪

FORM

Print your 3-character **Test Form** in the boxes above and fill in the corresponding oval at the right.

BE SURE TO FILL IN THE CORRECT FORM OVAL.

◯ 1MC   ◯ 2MC   ◯ 3MC   ◯ 4MC
◯ 5MC

TEST 1

1 Ⓐ Ⓑ Ⓒ Ⓓ   14 Ⓕ Ⓖ Ⓗ Ⓙ   27 Ⓐ Ⓑ Ⓒ Ⓓ   40 Ⓕ Ⓖ Ⓗ Ⓙ   53 Ⓐ Ⓑ Ⓒ Ⓓ   66 Ⓕ Ⓖ Ⓗ Ⓙ
2 Ⓕ Ⓖ Ⓗ Ⓙ   15 Ⓐ Ⓑ Ⓒ Ⓓ   28 Ⓕ Ⓖ Ⓗ Ⓙ   41 Ⓐ Ⓑ Ⓒ Ⓓ   54 Ⓕ Ⓖ Ⓗ Ⓙ   67 Ⓐ Ⓑ Ⓒ Ⓓ
3 Ⓐ Ⓑ Ⓒ Ⓓ   16 Ⓕ Ⓖ Ⓗ Ⓙ   29 Ⓐ Ⓑ Ⓒ Ⓓ   42 Ⓕ Ⓖ Ⓗ Ⓙ   55 Ⓐ Ⓑ Ⓒ Ⓓ   68 Ⓕ Ⓖ Ⓗ Ⓙ
4 Ⓕ Ⓖ Ⓗ Ⓙ   17 Ⓐ Ⓑ Ⓒ Ⓓ   30 Ⓕ Ⓖ Ⓗ Ⓙ   43 Ⓐ Ⓑ Ⓒ Ⓓ   56 Ⓕ Ⓖ Ⓗ Ⓙ   69 Ⓐ Ⓑ Ⓒ Ⓓ
5 Ⓐ Ⓑ Ⓒ Ⓓ   18 Ⓕ Ⓖ Ⓗ Ⓙ   31 Ⓐ Ⓑ Ⓒ Ⓓ   44 Ⓕ Ⓖ Ⓗ Ⓙ   57 Ⓐ Ⓑ Ⓒ Ⓓ   70 Ⓕ Ⓖ Ⓗ Ⓙ
6 Ⓕ Ⓖ Ⓗ Ⓙ   19 Ⓐ Ⓑ Ⓒ Ⓓ   32 Ⓕ Ⓖ Ⓗ Ⓙ   45 Ⓐ Ⓑ Ⓒ Ⓓ   58 Ⓕ Ⓖ Ⓗ Ⓙ   71 Ⓐ Ⓑ Ⓒ Ⓓ
7 Ⓐ Ⓑ Ⓒ Ⓓ   20 Ⓕ Ⓖ Ⓗ Ⓙ   33 Ⓐ Ⓑ Ⓒ Ⓓ   46 Ⓕ Ⓖ Ⓗ Ⓙ   59 Ⓐ Ⓑ Ⓒ Ⓓ   72 Ⓕ Ⓖ Ⓗ Ⓙ
8 Ⓕ Ⓖ Ⓗ Ⓙ   21 Ⓐ Ⓑ Ⓒ Ⓓ   34 Ⓕ Ⓖ Ⓗ Ⓙ   47 Ⓐ Ⓑ Ⓒ Ⓓ   60 Ⓕ Ⓖ Ⓗ Ⓙ   73 Ⓐ Ⓑ Ⓒ Ⓓ
9 Ⓐ Ⓑ Ⓒ Ⓓ   22 Ⓕ Ⓖ Ⓗ Ⓙ   35 Ⓐ Ⓑ Ⓒ Ⓓ   48 Ⓕ Ⓖ Ⓗ Ⓙ   61 Ⓐ Ⓑ Ⓒ Ⓓ   74 Ⓕ Ⓖ Ⓗ Ⓙ
10 Ⓕ Ⓖ Ⓗ Ⓙ   23 Ⓐ Ⓑ Ⓒ Ⓓ   36 Ⓕ Ⓖ Ⓗ Ⓙ   49 Ⓐ Ⓑ Ⓒ Ⓓ   62 Ⓕ Ⓖ Ⓗ Ⓙ   75 Ⓐ Ⓑ Ⓒ Ⓓ
11 Ⓐ Ⓑ Ⓒ Ⓓ   24 Ⓕ Ⓖ Ⓗ Ⓙ   37 Ⓐ Ⓑ Ⓒ Ⓓ   50 Ⓕ Ⓖ Ⓗ Ⓙ   63 Ⓐ Ⓑ Ⓒ Ⓓ
12 Ⓕ Ⓖ Ⓗ Ⓙ   25 Ⓐ Ⓑ Ⓒ Ⓓ   38 Ⓕ Ⓖ Ⓗ Ⓙ   51 Ⓐ Ⓑ Ⓒ Ⓓ   64 Ⓕ Ⓖ Ⓗ Ⓙ
13 Ⓐ Ⓑ Ⓒ Ⓓ   26 Ⓕ Ⓖ Ⓗ Ⓙ   39 Ⓐ Ⓑ Ⓒ Ⓓ   52 Ⓕ Ⓖ Ⓗ Ⓙ   65 Ⓐ Ⓑ Ⓒ Ⓓ

TEST 2

1 Ⓐ Ⓑ Ⓒ Ⓓ Ⓔ   11 Ⓐ Ⓑ Ⓒ Ⓓ Ⓔ   21 Ⓐ Ⓑ Ⓒ Ⓓ Ⓔ   31 Ⓐ Ⓑ Ⓒ Ⓓ Ⓔ   41 Ⓐ Ⓑ Ⓒ Ⓓ Ⓔ   51 Ⓐ Ⓑ Ⓒ Ⓓ Ⓔ
2 Ⓕ Ⓖ Ⓗ Ⓙ Ⓚ   12 Ⓕ Ⓖ Ⓗ Ⓙ Ⓚ   22 Ⓕ Ⓖ Ⓗ Ⓙ Ⓚ   32 Ⓕ Ⓖ Ⓗ Ⓙ Ⓚ   42 Ⓕ Ⓖ Ⓗ Ⓙ Ⓚ   52 Ⓕ Ⓖ Ⓗ Ⓙ Ⓚ
3 Ⓐ Ⓑ Ⓒ Ⓓ Ⓔ   13 Ⓐ Ⓑ Ⓒ Ⓓ Ⓔ   23 Ⓐ Ⓑ Ⓒ Ⓓ Ⓔ   33 Ⓐ Ⓑ Ⓒ Ⓓ Ⓔ   43 Ⓐ Ⓑ Ⓒ Ⓓ Ⓔ   53 Ⓐ Ⓑ Ⓒ Ⓓ Ⓔ
4 Ⓕ Ⓖ Ⓗ Ⓙ Ⓚ   14 Ⓕ Ⓖ Ⓗ Ⓙ Ⓚ   24 Ⓕ Ⓖ Ⓗ Ⓙ Ⓚ   34 Ⓕ Ⓖ Ⓗ Ⓙ Ⓚ   44 Ⓕ Ⓖ Ⓗ Ⓙ Ⓚ   54 Ⓕ Ⓖ Ⓗ Ⓙ Ⓚ
5 Ⓐ Ⓑ Ⓒ Ⓓ Ⓔ   15 Ⓐ Ⓑ Ⓒ Ⓓ Ⓔ   25 Ⓐ Ⓑ Ⓒ Ⓓ Ⓔ   35 Ⓐ Ⓑ Ⓒ Ⓓ Ⓔ   45 Ⓐ Ⓑ Ⓒ Ⓓ Ⓔ   55 Ⓐ Ⓑ Ⓒ Ⓓ Ⓔ
6 Ⓕ Ⓖ Ⓗ Ⓙ Ⓚ   16 Ⓕ Ⓖ Ⓗ Ⓙ Ⓚ   26 Ⓕ Ⓖ Ⓗ Ⓙ Ⓚ   36 Ⓕ Ⓖ Ⓗ Ⓙ Ⓚ   46 Ⓕ Ⓖ Ⓗ Ⓙ Ⓚ   56 Ⓕ Ⓖ Ⓗ Ⓙ Ⓚ
7 Ⓐ Ⓑ Ⓒ Ⓓ Ⓔ   17 Ⓐ Ⓑ Ⓒ Ⓓ Ⓔ   27 Ⓐ Ⓑ Ⓒ Ⓓ Ⓔ   37 Ⓐ Ⓑ Ⓒ Ⓓ Ⓔ   47 Ⓐ Ⓑ Ⓒ Ⓓ Ⓔ   57 Ⓐ Ⓑ Ⓒ Ⓓ Ⓔ
8 Ⓕ Ⓖ Ⓗ Ⓙ Ⓚ   18 Ⓕ Ⓖ Ⓗ Ⓙ Ⓚ   28 Ⓕ Ⓖ Ⓗ Ⓙ Ⓚ   38 Ⓕ Ⓖ Ⓗ Ⓙ Ⓚ   48 Ⓕ Ⓖ Ⓗ Ⓙ Ⓚ   58 Ⓕ Ⓖ Ⓗ Ⓙ Ⓚ
9 Ⓐ Ⓑ Ⓒ Ⓓ Ⓔ   19 Ⓐ Ⓑ Ⓒ Ⓓ Ⓔ   29 Ⓐ Ⓑ Ⓒ Ⓓ Ⓔ   39 Ⓐ Ⓑ Ⓒ Ⓓ Ⓔ   49 Ⓐ Ⓑ Ⓒ Ⓓ Ⓔ   59 Ⓐ Ⓑ Ⓒ Ⓓ Ⓔ
10 Ⓕ Ⓖ Ⓗ Ⓙ Ⓚ   20 Ⓕ Ⓖ Ⓗ Ⓙ Ⓚ   30 Ⓕ Ⓖ Ⓗ Ⓙ Ⓚ   40 Ⓕ Ⓖ Ⓗ Ⓙ Ⓚ   50 Ⓕ Ⓖ Ⓗ Ⓙ Ⓚ   60 Ⓕ Ⓖ Ⓗ Ⓙ Ⓚ

TEST 3

1 Ⓐ Ⓑ Ⓒ Ⓓ   8 Ⓕ Ⓖ Ⓗ Ⓙ   15 Ⓐ Ⓑ Ⓒ Ⓓ   22 Ⓕ Ⓖ Ⓗ Ⓙ   29 Ⓐ Ⓑ Ⓒ Ⓓ   36 Ⓕ Ⓖ Ⓗ Ⓙ
2 Ⓕ Ⓖ Ⓗ Ⓙ   9 Ⓐ Ⓑ Ⓒ Ⓓ   16 Ⓕ Ⓖ Ⓗ Ⓙ   23 Ⓐ Ⓑ Ⓒ Ⓓ   30 Ⓕ Ⓖ Ⓗ Ⓙ   37 Ⓐ Ⓑ Ⓒ Ⓓ
3 Ⓐ Ⓑ Ⓒ Ⓓ   10 Ⓕ Ⓖ Ⓗ Ⓙ   17 Ⓐ Ⓑ Ⓒ Ⓓ   24 Ⓕ Ⓖ Ⓗ Ⓙ   31 Ⓐ Ⓑ Ⓒ Ⓓ   38 Ⓕ Ⓖ Ⓗ Ⓙ
4 Ⓕ Ⓖ Ⓗ Ⓙ   11 Ⓐ Ⓑ Ⓒ Ⓓ   18 Ⓕ Ⓖ Ⓗ Ⓙ   25 Ⓐ Ⓑ Ⓒ Ⓓ   32 Ⓕ Ⓖ Ⓗ Ⓙ   39 Ⓐ Ⓑ Ⓒ Ⓓ
5 Ⓐ Ⓑ Ⓒ Ⓓ   12 Ⓕ Ⓖ Ⓗ Ⓙ   19 Ⓐ Ⓑ Ⓒ Ⓓ   26 Ⓕ Ⓖ Ⓗ Ⓙ   33 Ⓐ Ⓑ Ⓒ Ⓓ   40 Ⓕ Ⓖ Ⓗ Ⓙ
6 Ⓕ Ⓖ Ⓗ Ⓙ   13 Ⓐ Ⓑ Ⓒ Ⓓ   20 Ⓕ Ⓖ Ⓗ Ⓙ   27 Ⓐ Ⓑ Ⓒ Ⓓ   34 Ⓕ Ⓖ Ⓗ Ⓙ
7 Ⓐ Ⓑ Ⓒ Ⓓ   14 Ⓕ Ⓖ Ⓗ Ⓙ   21 Ⓐ Ⓑ Ⓒ Ⓓ   28 Ⓕ Ⓖ Ⓗ Ⓙ   35 Ⓐ Ⓑ Ⓒ Ⓓ

TEST 4

1 Ⓐ Ⓑ Ⓒ Ⓓ   8 Ⓕ Ⓖ Ⓗ Ⓙ   15 Ⓐ Ⓑ Ⓒ Ⓓ   22 Ⓕ Ⓖ Ⓗ Ⓙ   29 Ⓐ Ⓑ Ⓒ Ⓓ   36 Ⓕ Ⓖ Ⓗ Ⓙ
2 Ⓕ Ⓖ Ⓗ Ⓙ   9 Ⓐ Ⓑ Ⓒ Ⓓ   16 Ⓕ Ⓖ Ⓗ Ⓙ   23 Ⓐ Ⓑ Ⓒ Ⓓ   30 Ⓕ Ⓖ Ⓗ Ⓙ   37 Ⓐ Ⓑ Ⓒ Ⓓ
3 Ⓐ Ⓑ Ⓒ Ⓓ   10 Ⓕ Ⓖ Ⓗ Ⓙ   17 Ⓐ Ⓑ Ⓒ Ⓓ   24 Ⓕ Ⓖ Ⓗ Ⓙ   31 Ⓐ Ⓑ Ⓒ Ⓓ   38 Ⓕ Ⓖ Ⓗ Ⓙ
4 Ⓕ Ⓖ Ⓗ Ⓙ   11 Ⓐ Ⓑ Ⓒ Ⓓ   18 Ⓕ Ⓖ Ⓗ Ⓙ   25 Ⓐ Ⓑ Ⓒ Ⓓ   32 Ⓕ Ⓖ Ⓗ Ⓙ   39 Ⓐ Ⓑ Ⓒ Ⓓ
5 Ⓐ Ⓑ Ⓒ Ⓓ   12 Ⓕ Ⓖ Ⓗ Ⓙ   19 Ⓐ Ⓑ Ⓒ Ⓓ   26 Ⓕ Ⓖ Ⓗ Ⓙ   33 Ⓐ Ⓑ Ⓒ Ⓓ   40 Ⓕ Ⓖ Ⓗ Ⓙ
6 Ⓕ Ⓖ Ⓗ Ⓙ   13 Ⓐ Ⓑ Ⓒ Ⓓ   20 Ⓕ Ⓖ Ⓗ Ⓙ   27 Ⓐ Ⓑ Ⓒ Ⓓ   34 Ⓕ Ⓖ Ⓗ Ⓙ
7 Ⓐ Ⓑ Ⓒ Ⓓ   14 Ⓕ Ⓖ Ⓗ Ⓙ   21 Ⓐ Ⓑ Ⓒ Ⓓ   28 Ⓕ Ⓖ Ⓗ Ⓙ   35 Ⓐ Ⓑ Ⓒ Ⓓ

The ACT®

The ACT® *Sample Answer Sheet*

A NAME, MAILING ADDRESS, AND TELEPHONE
(Please print.)

Last Name   First Name   MI (Middle Initial)

House Number & Street (Apt. No.); or PO Box & No.; or RR & No.

City   State/Province   ZIP/Postal Code

Area Code   Number   Country

ACT, Inc.—Confidential Restricted when data present.

ALL examinees must complete block A – please print.

REGISTERED examinees **MUST complete blocks B, C, and D.** Find the MATCHING INFORMATION on your admission ticket and enter it EXACTLY the same way, even if any of the information is missing or incorrect. Fill in the corresponding ovals. If you do not complete these blocks to match your admission ticket EXACTLY, your scores will be **delayed up to 8 weeks.** Leave blocks E and F blank.

STANDBY examinees **MUST complete blocks B, D, and F.** Enter your information in blocks B and D and fill in the corresponding ovals. Leave block C blank. **For block E,** if you provided your SSN when you created your Web account or completed your standby folder, enter it here. The SSN will be used to help match this document to your registration information and will be included on reports to your college choices. If you did not provide it earlier, do not know it, or do not wish to provide it, leave block E blank. Be sure to fill in the oval in block F.

Do NOT mark in this shaded area.

B MATCH NAME
(First 5 letters of last name)

C MATCH NUMBER
(Registered examinees only)

D DATE OF BIRTH

Month	Day	Year
○ Jan.		
○ Feb.		
○ March		
○ April		
○ May		
○ June		
○ July		
○ Aug.		
○ Sept.		
○ Oct.		
○ Nov.		
○ Dec.		

↓ STANDBY TESTING ONLY ↓

E SOCIAL SECURITY NUMBER
(Standby examinees only)

F STANDBY TESTING

Fill in the oval below ONLY if you turned in a standby registration at the test center today.

○ Yes, I am testing as a standby.

USE A SOFT LEAD NO. 2 PENCIL ONLY.
(Do NOT use a mechanical pencil, ink, ballpoint, correction fluid, or felt-tip pen.)

EXAMINEE STATEMENT AND SIGNATURE

1. Read the following **Statement:** By submitting this answer sheet, I agree to the terms and conditions set forth in the ACT registration booklet or website for this exam, including the arbitration and dispute remedy provisions. I understand that ACT owns the test questions and responses and affirm that I will not share any test questions or responses with anyone by any form of communication.

2. Copy the **Certification** shown below (only the text in italics) on the lines provided. Write in your normal handwriting.

   Certification: *I agree to the Statement above and certify that I am the person whose name and address appear on this form.*

3. Sign your name as you would any official document and enter today's date.

Your Signature   Today's Date

ACT®
P.O. BOX 168, IOWA CITY, IOWA 52243-0168

Marking Directions: Mark only **one** oval for each question. Fill in response completely. Erase errors cleanly without smudging.

Correct mark: ○ ● ○ ○

Do NOT use these *incorrect* or *bad* marks.

Incorrect marks: ⊘ ⊗ ⊖ ⊙
Overlapping mark: ○ ○ ◖ ◑
Cross-out mark: ● ● ◐ ○
Smudged erasure: ○ ○ ◑ ○
Mark is too light: ● ○ ○ ○

BOOKLET NUMBER

① ① ① ① ① ①
② ② ② ② ② ②
③ ③ ③ ③ ③ ③
④ ④ ④ ④ ④ ④
⑤ ⑤ ⑤ ⑤ ⑤ ⑤
⑥ ⑥ ⑥ ⑥ ⑥ ⑥
⑦ ⑦ ⑦ ⑦ ⑦ ⑦
⑧ ⑧ ⑧ ⑧ ⑧ ⑧
⑨ ⑨ ⑨ ⑨ ⑨ ⑨
⓪ ⓪ ⓪ ⓪ ⓪ ⓪

FORM

Print your 3-character **Test Form** in the boxes above and fill in the corresponding oval at the right.

BE SURE TO FILL IN THE CORRECT FORM OVAL.

○ 1MC   ○ 2MC   ○ 3MC   ○ 4MC
○ 5MC

TEST 1

1 Ⓐ Ⓑ Ⓒ Ⓓ	14 Ⓕ Ⓖ Ⓗ Ⓙ	27 Ⓐ Ⓑ Ⓒ Ⓓ	40 Ⓕ Ⓖ Ⓗ Ⓙ	53 Ⓐ Ⓑ Ⓒ Ⓓ	66 Ⓕ Ⓖ Ⓗ Ⓙ
2 Ⓕ Ⓖ Ⓗ Ⓙ	15 Ⓐ Ⓑ Ⓒ Ⓓ	28 Ⓕ Ⓖ Ⓗ Ⓙ	41 Ⓐ Ⓑ Ⓒ Ⓓ	54 Ⓕ Ⓖ Ⓗ Ⓙ	67 Ⓐ Ⓑ Ⓒ Ⓓ
3 Ⓐ Ⓑ Ⓒ Ⓓ	16 Ⓕ Ⓖ Ⓗ Ⓙ	29 Ⓐ Ⓑ Ⓒ Ⓓ	42 Ⓕ Ⓖ Ⓗ Ⓙ	55 Ⓐ Ⓑ Ⓒ Ⓓ	68 Ⓕ Ⓖ Ⓗ Ⓙ
4 Ⓕ Ⓖ Ⓗ Ⓙ	17 Ⓐ Ⓑ Ⓒ Ⓓ	30 Ⓕ Ⓖ Ⓗ Ⓙ	43 Ⓐ Ⓑ Ⓒ Ⓓ	56 Ⓕ Ⓖ Ⓗ Ⓙ	69 Ⓐ Ⓑ Ⓒ Ⓓ
5 Ⓐ Ⓑ Ⓒ Ⓓ	18 Ⓕ Ⓖ Ⓗ Ⓙ	31 Ⓐ Ⓑ Ⓒ Ⓓ	44 Ⓕ Ⓖ Ⓗ Ⓙ	57 Ⓐ Ⓑ Ⓒ Ⓓ	70 Ⓕ Ⓖ Ⓗ Ⓙ
6 Ⓕ Ⓖ Ⓗ Ⓙ	19 Ⓐ Ⓑ Ⓒ Ⓓ	32 Ⓕ Ⓖ Ⓗ Ⓙ	45 Ⓐ Ⓑ Ⓒ Ⓓ	58 Ⓕ Ⓖ Ⓗ Ⓙ	71 Ⓐ Ⓑ Ⓒ Ⓓ
7 Ⓐ Ⓑ Ⓒ Ⓓ	20 Ⓕ Ⓖ Ⓗ Ⓙ	33 Ⓐ Ⓑ Ⓒ Ⓓ	46 Ⓕ Ⓖ Ⓗ Ⓙ	59 Ⓐ Ⓑ Ⓒ Ⓓ	72 Ⓕ Ⓖ Ⓗ Ⓙ
8 Ⓕ Ⓖ Ⓗ Ⓙ	21 Ⓐ Ⓑ Ⓒ Ⓓ	34 Ⓕ Ⓖ Ⓗ Ⓙ	47 Ⓐ Ⓑ Ⓒ Ⓓ	60 Ⓕ Ⓖ Ⓗ Ⓙ	73 Ⓐ Ⓑ Ⓒ Ⓓ
9 Ⓐ Ⓑ Ⓒ Ⓓ	22 Ⓕ Ⓖ Ⓗ Ⓙ	35 Ⓐ Ⓑ Ⓒ Ⓓ	48 Ⓕ Ⓖ Ⓗ Ⓙ	61 Ⓐ Ⓑ Ⓒ Ⓓ	74 Ⓕ Ⓖ Ⓗ Ⓙ
10 Ⓕ Ⓖ Ⓗ Ⓙ	23 Ⓐ Ⓑ Ⓒ Ⓓ	36 Ⓕ Ⓖ Ⓗ Ⓙ	49 Ⓐ Ⓑ Ⓒ Ⓓ	62 Ⓕ Ⓖ Ⓗ Ⓙ	75 Ⓐ Ⓑ Ⓒ Ⓓ
11 Ⓐ Ⓑ Ⓒ Ⓓ	24 Ⓕ Ⓖ Ⓗ Ⓙ	37 Ⓐ Ⓑ Ⓒ Ⓓ	50 Ⓕ Ⓖ Ⓗ Ⓙ	63 Ⓐ Ⓑ Ⓒ Ⓓ	
12 Ⓕ Ⓖ Ⓗ Ⓙ	25 Ⓐ Ⓑ Ⓒ Ⓓ	38 Ⓕ Ⓖ Ⓗ Ⓙ	51 Ⓐ Ⓑ Ⓒ Ⓓ	64 Ⓕ Ⓖ Ⓗ Ⓙ	
13 Ⓐ Ⓑ Ⓒ Ⓓ	26 Ⓕ Ⓖ Ⓗ Ⓙ	39 Ⓐ Ⓑ Ⓒ Ⓓ	52 Ⓕ Ⓖ Ⓗ Ⓙ	65 Ⓐ Ⓑ Ⓒ Ⓓ	

TEST 2

1 Ⓐ Ⓑ Ⓒ Ⓓ Ⓔ	11 Ⓐ Ⓑ Ⓒ Ⓓ Ⓔ	21 Ⓐ Ⓑ Ⓒ Ⓓ Ⓔ	31 Ⓐ Ⓑ Ⓒ Ⓓ Ⓔ	41 Ⓐ Ⓑ Ⓒ Ⓓ Ⓔ	51 Ⓐ Ⓑ Ⓒ Ⓓ Ⓔ
2 Ⓕ Ⓖ Ⓗ Ⓙ Ⓚ	12 Ⓕ Ⓖ Ⓗ Ⓙ Ⓚ	22 Ⓕ Ⓖ Ⓗ Ⓙ Ⓚ	32 Ⓕ Ⓖ Ⓗ Ⓙ Ⓚ	42 Ⓕ Ⓖ Ⓗ Ⓙ Ⓚ	52 Ⓕ Ⓖ Ⓗ Ⓙ Ⓚ
3 Ⓐ Ⓑ Ⓒ Ⓓ Ⓔ	13 Ⓐ Ⓑ Ⓒ Ⓓ Ⓔ	23 Ⓐ Ⓑ Ⓒ Ⓓ Ⓔ	33 Ⓐ Ⓑ Ⓒ Ⓓ Ⓔ	43 Ⓐ Ⓑ Ⓒ Ⓓ Ⓔ	53 Ⓐ Ⓑ Ⓒ Ⓓ Ⓔ
4 Ⓕ Ⓖ Ⓗ Ⓙ Ⓚ	14 Ⓕ Ⓖ Ⓗ Ⓙ Ⓚ	24 Ⓕ Ⓖ Ⓗ Ⓙ Ⓚ	34 Ⓕ Ⓖ Ⓗ Ⓙ Ⓚ	44 Ⓕ Ⓖ Ⓗ Ⓙ Ⓚ	54 Ⓕ Ⓖ Ⓗ Ⓙ Ⓚ
5 Ⓐ Ⓑ Ⓒ Ⓓ Ⓔ	15 Ⓐ Ⓑ Ⓒ Ⓓ Ⓔ	25 Ⓐ Ⓑ Ⓒ Ⓓ Ⓔ	35 Ⓐ Ⓑ Ⓒ Ⓓ Ⓔ	45 Ⓐ Ⓑ Ⓒ Ⓓ Ⓔ	55 Ⓐ Ⓑ Ⓒ Ⓓ Ⓔ
6 Ⓕ Ⓖ Ⓗ Ⓙ Ⓚ	16 Ⓕ Ⓖ Ⓗ Ⓙ Ⓚ	26 Ⓕ Ⓖ Ⓗ Ⓙ Ⓚ	36 Ⓕ Ⓖ Ⓗ Ⓙ Ⓚ	46 Ⓕ Ⓖ Ⓗ Ⓙ Ⓚ	56 Ⓕ Ⓖ Ⓗ Ⓙ Ⓚ
7 Ⓐ Ⓑ Ⓒ Ⓓ Ⓔ	17 Ⓐ Ⓑ Ⓒ Ⓓ Ⓔ	27 Ⓐ Ⓑ Ⓒ Ⓓ Ⓔ	37 Ⓐ Ⓑ Ⓒ Ⓓ Ⓔ	47 Ⓐ Ⓑ Ⓒ Ⓓ Ⓔ	57 Ⓐ Ⓑ Ⓒ Ⓓ Ⓔ
8 Ⓕ Ⓖ Ⓗ Ⓙ Ⓚ	18 Ⓕ Ⓖ Ⓗ Ⓙ Ⓚ	28 Ⓕ Ⓖ Ⓗ Ⓙ Ⓚ	38 Ⓕ Ⓖ Ⓗ Ⓙ Ⓚ	48 Ⓕ Ⓖ Ⓗ Ⓙ Ⓚ	58 Ⓕ Ⓖ Ⓗ Ⓙ Ⓚ
9 Ⓐ Ⓑ Ⓒ Ⓓ Ⓔ	19 Ⓐ Ⓑ Ⓒ Ⓓ Ⓔ	29 Ⓐ Ⓑ Ⓒ Ⓓ Ⓔ	39 Ⓐ Ⓑ Ⓒ Ⓓ Ⓔ	49 Ⓐ Ⓑ Ⓒ Ⓓ Ⓔ	59 Ⓐ Ⓑ Ⓒ Ⓓ Ⓔ
10 Ⓕ Ⓖ Ⓗ Ⓙ Ⓚ	20 Ⓕ Ⓖ Ⓗ Ⓙ Ⓚ	30 Ⓕ Ⓖ Ⓗ Ⓙ Ⓚ	40 Ⓕ Ⓖ Ⓗ Ⓙ Ⓚ	50 Ⓕ Ⓖ Ⓗ Ⓙ Ⓚ	60 Ⓕ Ⓖ Ⓗ Ⓙ Ⓚ

TEST 3

1 Ⓐ Ⓑ Ⓒ Ⓓ	8 Ⓕ Ⓖ Ⓗ Ⓙ	15 Ⓐ Ⓑ Ⓒ Ⓓ	22 Ⓕ Ⓖ Ⓗ Ⓙ	29 Ⓐ Ⓑ Ⓒ Ⓓ	36 Ⓕ Ⓖ Ⓗ Ⓙ
2 Ⓕ Ⓖ Ⓗ Ⓙ	9 Ⓐ Ⓑ Ⓒ Ⓓ	16 Ⓕ Ⓖ Ⓗ Ⓙ	23 Ⓐ Ⓑ Ⓒ Ⓓ	30 Ⓕ Ⓖ Ⓗ Ⓙ	37 Ⓐ Ⓑ Ⓒ Ⓓ
3 Ⓐ Ⓑ Ⓒ Ⓓ	10 Ⓕ Ⓖ Ⓗ Ⓙ	17 Ⓐ Ⓑ Ⓒ Ⓓ	24 Ⓕ Ⓖ Ⓗ Ⓙ	31 Ⓐ Ⓑ Ⓒ Ⓓ	38 Ⓕ Ⓖ Ⓗ Ⓙ
4 Ⓕ Ⓖ Ⓗ Ⓙ	11 Ⓐ Ⓑ Ⓒ Ⓓ	18 Ⓕ Ⓖ Ⓗ Ⓙ	25 Ⓐ Ⓑ Ⓒ Ⓓ	32 Ⓕ Ⓖ Ⓗ Ⓙ	39 Ⓐ Ⓑ Ⓒ Ⓓ
5 Ⓐ Ⓑ Ⓒ Ⓓ	12 Ⓕ Ⓖ Ⓗ Ⓙ	19 Ⓐ Ⓑ Ⓒ Ⓓ	26 Ⓕ Ⓖ Ⓗ Ⓙ	33 Ⓐ Ⓑ Ⓒ Ⓓ	40 Ⓕ Ⓖ Ⓗ Ⓙ
6 Ⓕ Ⓖ Ⓗ Ⓙ	13 Ⓐ Ⓑ Ⓒ Ⓓ	20 Ⓕ Ⓖ Ⓗ Ⓙ	27 Ⓐ Ⓑ Ⓒ Ⓓ	34 Ⓕ Ⓖ Ⓗ Ⓙ	
7 Ⓐ Ⓑ Ⓒ Ⓓ	14 Ⓕ Ⓖ Ⓗ Ⓙ	21 Ⓐ Ⓑ Ⓒ Ⓓ	28 Ⓕ Ⓖ Ⓗ Ⓙ	35 Ⓐ Ⓑ Ⓒ Ⓓ	

TEST 4

1 Ⓐ Ⓑ Ⓒ Ⓓ	8 Ⓕ Ⓖ Ⓗ Ⓙ	15 Ⓐ Ⓑ Ⓒ Ⓓ	22 Ⓕ Ⓖ Ⓗ Ⓙ	29 Ⓐ Ⓑ Ⓒ Ⓓ	36 Ⓕ Ⓖ Ⓗ Ⓙ
2 Ⓕ Ⓖ Ⓗ Ⓙ	9 Ⓐ Ⓑ Ⓒ Ⓓ	16 Ⓕ Ⓖ Ⓗ Ⓙ	23 Ⓐ Ⓑ Ⓒ Ⓓ	30 Ⓕ Ⓖ Ⓗ Ⓙ	37 Ⓐ Ⓑ Ⓒ Ⓓ
3 Ⓐ Ⓑ Ⓒ Ⓓ	10 Ⓕ Ⓖ Ⓗ Ⓙ	17 Ⓐ Ⓑ Ⓒ Ⓓ	24 Ⓕ Ⓖ Ⓗ Ⓙ	31 Ⓐ Ⓑ Ⓒ Ⓓ	38 Ⓕ Ⓖ Ⓗ Ⓙ
4 Ⓕ Ⓖ Ⓗ Ⓙ	11 Ⓐ Ⓑ Ⓒ Ⓓ	18 Ⓕ Ⓖ Ⓗ Ⓙ	25 Ⓐ Ⓑ Ⓒ Ⓓ	32 Ⓕ Ⓖ Ⓗ Ⓙ	39 Ⓐ Ⓑ Ⓒ Ⓓ
5 Ⓐ Ⓑ Ⓒ Ⓓ	12 Ⓕ Ⓖ Ⓗ Ⓙ	19 Ⓐ Ⓑ Ⓒ Ⓓ	26 Ⓕ Ⓖ Ⓗ Ⓙ	33 Ⓐ Ⓑ Ⓒ Ⓓ	40 Ⓕ Ⓖ Ⓗ Ⓙ
6 Ⓕ Ⓖ Ⓗ Ⓙ	13 Ⓐ Ⓑ Ⓒ Ⓓ	20 Ⓕ Ⓖ Ⓗ Ⓙ	27 Ⓐ Ⓑ Ⓒ Ⓓ	34 Ⓕ Ⓖ Ⓗ Ⓙ	
7 Ⓐ Ⓑ Ⓒ Ⓓ	14 Ⓕ Ⓖ Ⓗ Ⓙ	21 Ⓐ Ⓑ Ⓒ Ⓓ	28 Ⓕ Ⓖ Ⓗ Ⓙ	35 Ⓐ Ⓑ Ⓒ Ⓓ	

The **ACT**®

080660

Practice Test 3

Examinee Agreement and Signature: By testing today, I agree to the terms and conditions set forth in the ACT registration booklet or website for this exam, including the provisions about prohibited behaviors. I also certify that I am the person whose signature appears below.

Today's Date: _____

Your Signature: _____

Print Your Name Here: _____

Your Date of Birth:

Month   Day   Year

Form 3MC

The ACT® 2011|2012

Directions

This booklet contains tests in English, Mathematics, Reading, and Science. These tests measure skills and abilities highly related to high school course work and success in college. *CALCULATORS MAY BE USED ON THE MATHEMATICS TEST ONLY.*

The questions in each test are numbered, and the suggested answers for each question are lettered. On the answer document, the rows of ovals are numbered to match the questions, and the ovals in each row are lettered to correspond to the suggested answers.

For each question, first decide which answer is best. Next, locate on the answer document the row of ovals numbered the same as the question. Then, locate the oval in that row lettered the same as your answer. Finally, fill in the oval completely. Use a soft lead pencil and make your marks heavy and black. *DO NOT USE INK OR A MECHANICAL PENCIL.*

Mark only one answer to each question. If you change your mind about an answer, erase your first mark thoroughly before marking your new answer. For each question, make certain that you mark in the row of ovals with the same number as the question.

Only responses marked on your answer document will be scored. Your score on each test will be based only on the number of questions you answer correctly during the time allowed for that test. You will NOT be penalized for guessing. *IT IS TO YOUR ADVANTAGE TO ANSWER EVERY QUESTION EVEN IF YOU MUST GUESS.*

You may work on each test ONLY when your test supervisor tells you to do so. If you finish a test before time is called for that test, you should use the time remaining to reconsider questions you are uncertain about in that test. You may NOT look back to a test on which time has already been called, and you may NOT go ahead to another test. To do so will disqualify you from the examination.

Lay your pencil down immediately when time is called at the end of each test. You may NOT for any reason fill in or alter ovals for a test after time is called for that test. To do so will disqualify you from the examination.

Do not fold or tear the pages of your test booklet.

**DO NOT OPEN THIS BOOKLET
UNTIL TOLD TO DO SO.**

P.O. BOX 168
IOWA CITY, IA 52243-0168

DIRECTIONS: In the five passages that follow, certain words and phrases are underlined and numbered. In the right-hand column, you will find alternatives for the underlined part. In most cases, you are to choose the one that best expresses the idea, makes the statement appropriate for standard written English, or is worded most consistently with the style and tone of the passage as a whole. If you think the original version is best, choose "NO CHANGE." In some cases, you will find in the right-hand column a question about the underlined part. You are to choose the best answer to the question.

You will also find questions about a section of the passage, or about the passage as a whole. These questions do not refer to an underlined portion of the passage, but rather are identified by a number or numbers in a box.

For each question, choose the alternative you consider best and fill in the corresponding oval on your answer document. Read each passage through once before you begin to answer the questions that accompany it. For many of the questions, you must read several sentences beyond the question to determine the answer. Be sure that you have read far enough ahead each time you choose an alternative.

PASSAGE I

A Literary Magazine

[1]

Whether or not wanting to work for *Fairground,*
———————————————————————
                                    1
you have to be willing to push yourself. The editors of

our triannual literary magazine is kept busy all year
                                    ——————
                                       2
with a wide variety of tasks.

[2]

Our year begins in July, with fund-raising and

promotion for the magazine, which presents a mixture of

poetry, short stories, and essays. Our office fills up with

subscription forms and fliers that we must sort, bundle,
                         ——————————————————
                                    3
and tote to the post office to be mailed.

[3]

In August, we send letters to our favorite

authors, inviting them to send manuscripts.

Meanwhile, we're receiving unsolicited submissions

from other writers. During September and October,

1. **A.** NO CHANGE
   B. If you want to work for *Fairground,*
   C. Wanting to work for *Fairground,* if you do,
   D. Having decided whether or not you want to work for *Fairground,*

2. **F.** NO CHANGE
   G. keeps
   H. are kept
   J. has been keeping

3. **A.** NO CHANGE
   B. fliers, these we must
   C. fliers these we have to
   D. fliers, we must

GO ON TO THE NEXT PAGE.

we read and evaluate hundreds of manuscripts.
___4___

[4]

Some offerings are scrawled in pencil; others, are
___5___
expertly typed. Some arrive with letters proclaiming the

writer's genius; others may be written even more illegibly.
___6___
We base our decisions only on the work itself.

Actual typesetting will come later. The editors
___7___

agree that every issue has to be good and has to
___8___

reflect and show the varied diversity of the United States.
___9___

Within they're policy that's plenty of room for discussion,
___10___

and editors have to be ready to sprint the distance favoring
___11___
their choices.

[5]

By November, we have selected enough material

to fill three issues. Once we've found artwork suitable

for the covers, editorial production, begins. We plan
___12___

4. Which choice should the writer use to create the clearest and most logical transition to Paragraph 4?
   F. NO CHANGE
   G. the leaves fall faster than the manuscripts piling up on our desks.
   H. you can imagine it's different from back in August.
   J. they see hundreds of manuscript readings and evaluations.

5. A. NO CHANGE
   B. pencil others
   C. pencil; others
   D. pencil so others,

6. Given that all are true, which of the choices creates the most logical and appropriate contrast in this sentence?
   F. NO CHANGE
   G. can't appreciate how much work our editors put in.
   H. come with apologies for taking up our time.
   J. arrive folded up and dog-eared.

7. A. NO CHANGE
   B. The typesetting comes in much later.
   C. Typesetting is handled later on.
   D. OMIT the underlined portion.

8. F. NO CHANGE
   G. more good
   H. positively well
   J. as well as we can make it

9. A. NO CHANGE
   B. reflect and show the cultural diversity of a multi-cultural
   C. mirror and reflect the diversity of a diverse
   D. reflect the cultural diversity of the

10. F. NO CHANGE
    G. our policy their is
    H. that policy theirs
    J. that policy there's

11. A. NO CHANGE
    B. argue spiritedly for
    C. contend the spirit of
    D. be argumentative to

12. F. NO CHANGE
    G. editorial production begin.
    H. we begin, editorial production.
    J. editorial production begins.

GO ON TO THE NEXT PAGE.

the contents of the year's issues, page by page.
13

It may snow just after New Year's Day; the first
14
issue is mailed to a typesetter. While that issue is

being set, we complete the next one's layout. Thus,

as soon as an issue comes back from the typesetter

for proofreading, the next can go in for typesetting.

By this time, there's plenty of material for three issues.
15
After the proofreading is done, each issue is sent to a

printer, who prints it, binds it, and delivers it to our door.

Our office fills up again with the printed copies, ready to

be mailed to subscribers, reviewers, and contributors.

Finally, in midsummer, we ship out our third and final

issue—just in time to begin another publishing year.

PASSAGE II

Are Wolves Making a Comeback?

[1]

[1] At dawn a hunter crept across a steep,

wooded, pine-covered slope in northwest Wyoming.
16

[2] He was searching for signs of elk when he noticed an
17

unusual track, broad as a human hand, in the fresher fallen
18

snow. [3] He thought it might have been made
19

13. **A.** NO CHANGE
    B. years issues,
    C. years issues
    D. issue's for the year,

14. **F.** NO CHANGE
    G. After what may be a snowy New Year's Day but not by much
    H. Shortly thereafter New Year's Day,
    J. Just after New Year's Day,

15. **A.** NO CHANGE
    B. Three issues' worth of material has already been selected.
    C. We have chosen material sufficient for all three issues.
    D. OMIT the underlined portion.

16. **F.** NO CHANGE
    G. sloping, pine-covered hill
    H. pine-covered slope
    J. slanting, pine-covered slope

17. **A.** NO CHANGE
    B. elk when noticing
    C. elk, when
    D. elk, when seeing

18. **F.** NO CHANGE
    G. freshly fallened
    H. newly fallen
    J. newer falling

19. **A.** NO CHANGE
    B. might of
    C. could of
    D. could

GO ON TO THE NEXT PAGE.

by <u>something.</u>
₂₀

[2]

[1] Even though <u>wolves supposedly</u> disappeared
₂₁
from the area years ago, the hunter's story was not

unusual. [2] Many <u>reports, most of them filed by hunters</u>
₂₂
have recounted howlings, tracks, and possible wolf kills

(that is, animals killed by wolves). [3] A few people even

claim to have stood face-to-face with wolves before the

animals faded into black timber. ⬚23 [4] The United States

Forest Service has verified thirty reports of wolf sightings

in the past decade in Wyoming's Bridger-Teton National

Forest.

[3]

According to Forest Service officials, the Rocky

Mountain gray wolf was common throughout most of

Wyoming in the 1860s and 1870s. However, ranchers

and government "wolfers" made a concerted effort to

eliminate the predators <u>by trapping</u> and poisoning
₂₄

them. ⬚25

[4]

Wolves are now classified as an endangered species

in all the lower forty-eight states except Minnesota,

<u>after which</u> the animals began migrating from Canada in
₂₆
the 1960s. There is also a sizable population of wolves just

north of the Montana border. Biologists believe that the

recent flurry of possible wolf sightings in Wyoming may

indicate that a few wolves are moving south.

---

20. Which choice provides the most specific transition to the next paragraph?
- **F.** NO CHANGE
- **G.** someone else.
- **H.** a wolf.
- **J.** a large animal.

21. A. NO CHANGE
- **B.** wolves, supposedly
- **C.** wolves supposedly,
- **D.** wolves' had

22. F. NO CHANGE
- **G.** reports—most of them filed by hunters—
- **H.** reports; most of them filed by hunters,
- **J.** reports, having been filing by hunters,

23. Which of the following true statements, if added here, would best strengthen the assertion that wolves are present in northwest Wyoming?
- **A.** Many other wolf sightings have no doubt gone unreported.
- **B.** Others have mentioned seeing garbage cans tipped over and food spilled on the ground.
- **C.** A camper's daughter imagined seeing wolf-shaped shadows near her tent at nightfall.
- **D.** Many rangers have reported hearing the soft cry of wolf cubs in the evening.

24. F. NO CHANGE
- **G.** through traps
- **H.** with traps
- **J.** in traps

25. Given that all of the following sentences are true, which one, if added here, would offer the best transition from Paragraph 3 to Paragraph 4?
- **A.** This caused some problems for the wolves.
- **B.** There were not too many "wolfers" employed in Wyoming, however.
- **C.** By the turn of the century, there was scarcely a wolf left in the state.
- **D.** The Rocky Mountain gray wolf was a majestic animal and, thus, not easily trapped.

26. F. NO CHANGE
- **G.** from which
- **H.** when
- **J.** into which

GO ON TO THE NEXT PAGE.

Practice ACT Tests

[5]

Although Forest Service officials consider the sightings to be honestly reported, they need to confirm the presence of wolf packs and breeding pairs in the Bridger-Teton area. So, biologists decided, to look for the wolves
<u>themselves</u>. They have flown to elk and deer wintering
₂₇
areas, ridden horses and snowmobiles through the mountains, and <u>throwing</u> back their heads and called out
₂₈

with low, moaning howls <u>in hopes of communicating</u> with
₂₉
the wolves. Occasionally, the wolves have answered back.

27. **A.** NO CHANGE
    B. So biologists decided
    C. So biologists decided,
    D. So biologists, decided

28. **F.** NO CHANGE
    G. throw
    H. threw
    J. even thrown

29. **A.** NO CHANGE
    B. to hope to communicate
    C. in hopes to communicate
    D. in hope's communication

Question 30 asks about the preceding passage as a whole.

---

30. In order to explain why it is not ordinarily dangerous for people to be near wolves, the writer is considering adding the following sentence to the essay:

    (Contrary to popular belief, wolves rarely attack humans.)

    If added, this sentence would most logically be placed after:

    F. Sentence 3 in Paragraph 1.
    G. Sentence 2 in Paragraph 2.
    H. Sentence 4 in Paragraph 2.
    J. the first sentence in Paragraph 3.

PASSAGE III

The Suzuki Method

In the early 1930s, <u>Dr. Shinichi Suzuki was teaching</u>
₃₁
violin at the Imperial Conservatory in Japan, a father

brought in his four-year-old son for lessons. <u>Although</u>
₃₂
<u>Suzuki had never taught anyone so young, he reluctantly</u>
₃₂
agreed to accept the tiny violin student.

As he pondered what training might work for this preschooler, Suzuki began to think about how young

31. **A.** NO CHANGE
    B. Dr. Shinichi Suzuki taught
    C. that Dr. Shinichi Suzuki was teaching
    D. while Dr. Shinichi Suzuki was teaching

32. At this point in the essay, the writer wants to show that Dr. Suzuki did not feel prepared to teach music at the preschool level. Given that all of the choices are true, which one best conveys that message?

    F. NO CHANGE
    G. Generally, conservatory students were between seventeen and twenty-five years of age, and he
    H. Given the fact that his music students were much older, he deliberately
    J. After conversing with the boy's parents, he

GO ON TO THE NEXT PAGE.

children learn to use language in very sophisticated

ways. He suspected that this miraculous-seeming process
_____
33

may or may not offer valuable insights into how all
_____
34
learning occurs, including learning to play a musical

instrument.

[1] Immersion was already understood to be a
_____
35
key to a child's language development by Suzuki.
_____
35

[2] Newborns are immersed in language. [3] Babies
_____
36
first attempts at speech generate excited responses

from adults who encourage and guide the children

toward more precise and complex speech. [4] Teachers

provide in-depth language understanding, and children

are rewarded for improving his or her communication
_____
37
skills. [5] Based on these realizations, Suzuki

developed an awareness of how children learn language.
_____
38
[6] His program has since grown into an internationally

acclaimed philosophy of music education. ▪39▪

In the Suzuki method, students are immersed in

music. Each day students and their families listen to
_____
40

33. A. NO CHANGE
    B. Nevertheless, he suspected
    C. He suspected, however,
    D. Instead, he suspected

34. F. NO CHANGE
    G. might offer
    H. could suggest important
    J. might indeed provide one with

35. A. NO CHANGE
    B. As Suzuki already understood, that immersion is a key to a child's language development.
    C. Suzuki already understood that immersion is a key to a child's language development.
    D. A key to a child's language development, Suzuki already understood that it was immersion.

36. F. NO CHANGE
    G. Baby's
    H. Babys
    J. Babies'

37. A. NO CHANGE
    B. one's
    C. there
    D. their

38. Given that all of the choices are true, which one would provide the most effective link between Sentences 4 and 6?
    F. NO CHANGE
    G. developed a unique approach to violin studies.
    H. transferred his knowledge into something positive.
    J. decided to see where this information might acquire more additional applications.

39. The writer is considering adding the following true statement to this paragraph:

    Babies begin to coordinate hand and eye movements early in life.

    Should the sentence be added to this paragraph, and if so, where should it be placed?
    A. Yes, after Sentence 1.
    B. Yes, after Sentence 2.
    C. Yes, after Sentence 3.
    D. The sentence should NOT be added.

40. F. NO CHANGE
    G. music, and that each
    H. music and that each
    J. music, each

GO ON TO THE NEXT PAGE.

recorded music that at a future date the students later
41
learn on an instrument. When the time comes to play a

composition, the student already feels intimately familiar

with it. The child's early musical accomplishments are

greeted with enthusiasm. Lessons provide expert

assistance; group sessions and concerts reward
42
students with opportunities to share music.

Even so, for a long time, Suzuki encouraged
43
students and teachers alike to strive toward lifelong

learning. Worldwide, he promoted the idea that

every child possesses the potential to develop

musical talent and for the joys of achievement.
44

All that his teaching inspired are enriched, who
45
hear the beautiful music.
45

41. **A.** NO CHANGE
    B. subsequently
    C. before long
    D. OMIT the underlined portion.

42. **F.** NO CHANGE
    G. rewarded
    H. had rewarded
    J. in rewarding

43. Given that all of the choices are true, which one would provide the most effective introductory phrase?
    A. NO CHANGE
    B. Recurrently with time,
    C. For many decades,
    D. For scores of years then,

44. **F.** NO CHANGE
    G. the joys of achievement can be experienced.
    H. for experiencing the joys of achievement.
    J. to experience the joys of achievement.

45. **A.** NO CHANGE
    B. that his teaching inspired who hear the beautiful music are enriched.
    C. who hear the beautiful music that his teaching inspired are enriched.
    D. are enriched by hearing the beautiful music of which his teaching inspired.

PASSAGE IV

The Beltway: Washington's Expressway

If you visit our nation's capital, recently, as I did, you
46
will probably plan trips to several of the famous memorials

there, many of which you have probably seen on television.
47
These celebrated landmarks were designed to inspire

feelings of patriotism and pride. Nevertheless, the structure
48
I remember most vividly from my trip was an expressway

46. **F.** NO CHANGE
    G. recently visit our nation's capital, as I did,
    H. visit recently, as I did, our nation's capital,
    J. visit our nation's capital, as I did recently,

47. Given that all of the choices are true, which one would conclude this sentence by providing the clearest examples of some of the attractions that are available in the nation's capital?
    A. NO CHANGE
    B. including the ones that are readily recognizable to us.
    C. including the Washington Monument and the Lincoln Memorial.
    D. those structures that potentially add to the history of the capital.

48. **F.** NO CHANGE
    G. Therefore,
    H. As a result,
    J. In addition,

GO ON TO THE NEXT PAGE.

called the Washington Beltway, which seems to be a

memorial to the frenzied and crazy lunacy of modern life.
<u>   </u>
                              49

     This expressway resembles an ordinary highway

about as much as a space shuttle resembles an airplane. At

ten lanes wide, they are much larger than the bypass loops
<u>   </u>
          50

I have driven around Indianapolis and Cincinnati. The

beltway is also far more busier, perhaps because it
<u>   </u>
              51

extends through two populous states—Virginia and

Maryland—and intersecting with many lesser highways.
<u>   </u>
        52

It's also fast, the thousands of Washingtonians who dash
<u>   </u>
        53

from home to work and back sometimes ignore the posted

speed limit. The one, redeeming, feature of the beltway is
<u>   </u>
                54

that it's impossible to get lost on it. If you keep driving

long enough, you will eventually circle the city and return

to the point where you began. ⬚55

     As I've already mentioned, I was on a visit to
<u>   </u>
                  56

Washington. I was staying with friends in their suburban
<u>   </u>
   56

Virginia home, and I asked them for help with alternate,

more scenic routes. But by their puzzled looks, I realized

---

49. A. NO CHANGE
B. frenzy of modern
C. frenzy of modern contemporary
D. confused disarray of

50. F. NO CHANGE
G. it is
H. it was
J. they were

51. A. NO CHANGE
B. far busier,
C. more busier,
D. most busiest,

52. F. NO CHANGE
G. but intersects
H. and intersects
J. and

53. A. NO CHANGE
B. It's also fast:
C. Its also fast:
D. Its also fast,

54. F. NO CHANGE
G. one redeeming, feature of the beltway
H. one redeeming feature of the beltway,
J. one redeeming feature of the beltway

55. At this point, the writer is considering adding the following true statement:

> Atlanta and Houston also are surrounded by such giant loop highways.

Should the writer make this addition here?

A. Yes, because it informs the reader that such highways are not unique to Washington, D.C.
B. Yes, because it helps the reader to better understand what the beltway looks like.
C. No, because it distracts the reader from the main focus of the paragraph.
D. No, because it is inconsistent with the tone and style of the essay.

56. Given that all of the choices are true, which one would most effectively introduce this paragraph?

F. NO CHANGE
G. Initially, I planned to avoid driving on the beltway.
H. The hustle and bustle was evident everywhere I went.
J. The beltway seems to turn official Washington into an island.

GO ON TO THE NEXT PAGE.

they had surrendered to the beltway long ago. Graciously, I
57

learned to navigate this expressway. I approach it as if it
58

were an unpredictable natural force that required careful

monitoring. Was it congested? Overcrowded? Moving
59

freely? Blocked completely? What about construction

zones? The radio provided me with frequent updates. Just

as some people on vacation like to keep a close watch on

the weather, I wanted to keep track of beltway conditions.

I'm not sure how much American history I learned on

my trip, as my powers of concentration were taxed merely

reading road signs. 60

57. A. NO CHANGE
    B. Carefully, however,
    C. So, unhappily,
    D. In fact,

58. F. NO CHANGE
    G. approached it,
    H. approached it
    J. approach it,

59. A. NO CHANGE
    B. Jammed with cars?
    C. Proceeding smoothly?
    D. OMIT the underlined portion.

60. Which of the following sentences, if added here, would
    provide the best conclusion to the paragraph and is
    most consistent with the main focus of the essay?

    F. However, my ability to merge in traffic improved
       immensely!
    G. Nevertheless, I did learn a lot about the Wash-
       ington Monument and the Jefferson Memorial.
    H. Washington's celebrated landmarks are truly
       inspirational.
    J. Opportunities, nevertheless, for learning this his-
       tory abound in our nation's capital.

Modern Uses for Old Ways

[1] At first glance, Jane Mt. Pleasant's

garden plots look a total mess. [2] The ground

being bumpy with mounds and covered with old leaves.
61

[3] Beans hang on the cornstalks, and squash vines

had sprawled everywhere. [4] But this apparent
62

chaos is the subject of scientific research. [5] Mt.
63

61. A. NO CHANGE
    B. was bumpy with mounds and is
    C. is bumpy with mounds and
    D. bumpy with mounds and

62. F. NO CHANGE
    G. sprawl
    H. sprawled
    J. could have sprawled

63. A. NO CHANGE
    B. chaos, is the subject
    C. chaos is the subject,
    D. chaos: is the subject

GO ON TO THE NEXT PAGE.

Pleasant's gardens are modeled for those grown by the
        ‾‾
64
Iroquois and other Native peoples. [6] The data the gardens

are yielding may provide evidence to support the use of

old methods to improve modern agriculture. ⬛65

A Cornell University agronomist and an Iroquois

herself, Jane Mt. Pleasant questions some of modern

agriculture's practices, and she has a Ph.D. degree. Many
                                    ‾‾‾‾‾‾‾‾‾‾‾‾‾‾‾‾‾‾
                                            66
farmers and agronomists believe that the recent boom in

crop production in the last few years—fueled by the
     ‾‾‾‾‾‾‾‾‾‾‾‾‾‾‾‾‾‾‾‾‾‾‾‾‾‾
                67
intensive use of farmland and increased dependence on

herbicides and pesticides—have come with hidden costs.
                          ‾‾‾‾
                           68
Soil erosion and pollution have put our food supply and

our health at risk. ⬛69

The Iroquois method begins with corn being planted

at three-foot intervals. Later, soil had been mounded
                                   ‾‾‾‾‾‾‾‾
                                      70
around the young stalks, enhancing drainage and warming
                       ‾‾‾‾‾‾‾‾‾‾‾‾‾‾‾‾‾‾‾‾‾‾‾‾‾‾‾‾‾‾‾
                                   71

64. F. NO CHANGE
    G. on
    H. as
    J. by

65. For the sake of the logic and coherence of this paragraph, Sentence 6 should be placed:

    A. where it is now.
    B. after Sentence 1.
    C. after Sentence 2.
    D. after Sentence 3.

66. At this point, the writer wants to add a statement that would lead into the sentence that follows it. Given that all of the choices are true, which one would best accomplish that purpose?

    F. NO CHANGE
    G. her concern is shared by others.
    H. she's enjoyed gardening since she was a.child.
    J. her opinions are based on scientific research.

67. A. NO CHANGE
    B. production of late—
    C. production lately—
    D. production—

68. F. NO CHANGE
    G. has
    H. are
    J. OMIT the underlined portion.

69. Which of the following sentences, if added at this point, would both reinforce the conclusions presented in the essay and create an effective transition to the next paragraph?

    A. Iroquois farming techniques, however, offer possible solutions to such problems.
    B. Many diseases have a direct link to these toxins in our air, land, and water.
    C. Certain farming practices have been employed by the Iroquois people.
    D. These social problems must be resolved one way or another.

70. F. NO CHANGE
    G. has been
    H. was
    J. is

71. Which of the following alternatives to the underlined portion would NOT be acceptable?

    A. stalks because of enhancing drainage and warming
    B. stalks in order to enhance drainage and warm
    C. stalks, which enhances drainage and warms
    D. stalks. This enhances drainage and warms

GO ON TO THE NEXT PAGE.

the soil. Beans are then planted on the mounds, and squash
is planted between the mounds.

Corn, beans, and squash—
all of which might be grown in your garden—
work as a team. The corn stalks support the bean vines, the
nitrogen-fixing roots of the beans enrich the soil, and the
squashes' broad leaves stifle the weeds. After the harvest,
the remains of the plants are left to rot, further enriching
the soil and reducing the potential for erosion. Mt. Pleasant
has found that total crop production in her experimental
plots rivals that of high-tech, single-crop farming. Her
research is helping farmers make better decisions about
planting soil-protecting cover crops.

Perhaps the best endorsement of the Iroquois
"three-sisters" system is that it has worked for over four
centuries. Mt. Pleasant notes, "It is a balance between
production and soil protection."

72. Which of the following alternatives to the underlined portion would NOT be acceptable?
   F. mounds, while squash
   G. mounds. Squash
   H. mounds; squash
   J. mounds squash

73. Given that all of the choices are true, which one would provide information that is most relevant and meaningful to the essay as a whole?
   A. NO CHANGE
   B. which could make a nice vegetarian dish—
   C. the Iroquois "three sisters"—
   D. representing various food families—

74. F. NO CHANGE
   G. system, is
   H. system is,
   J. system is:

Question 75 asks about the preceding passage as a whole.

75. Suppose the writer had chosen to write a brief essay about an example of how the past can inform the present. Would this essay successfully fulfill the writer's goal?

   A. Yes, because the essay compares the traditional techniques of three-sisters farming to the high-tech methods of modern farming.
   B. Yes, because the essay describes how the traditional farming practices of the Iroquois people can offer ways to improve modern agriculture.
   C. No, because the essay presents the theories of Jane Mt. Pleasant, who is currently an agronomist at Cornell University and, therefore, not a reflection of the past.
   D. No, because the essay describes the planting of cover crops, which has always been a common practice among farmers.

END OF TEST 1

STOP! DO NOT TURN THE PAGE UNTIL TOLD TO DO SO.

MATHEMATICS TEST
60 Minutes—60 Questions

DIRECTIONS: Solve each problem, choose the correct answer, and then fill in the corresponding oval on your answer document.

Do not linger over problems that take too much time. Solve as many as you can; then return to the others in the time you have left for this test.

You are permitted to use a calculator on this test. You may use your calculator for any problems you choose, but some of the problems may best be done without using a calculator.

Note: Unless otherwise stated, all of the following should be assumed.

1. Illustrative figures are NOT necessarily drawn to scale.
2. Geometric figures lie in a plane.
3. The word *line* indicates a straight line.
4. The word *average* indicates arithmetic mean.

---

1. Kalino earned 85, 95, 93, and 80 points on the 4 tests, each worth 100 points, given so far this term. How many points must he earn on his fifth test, also worth 100 points, to average 90 points for the 5 tests given this term?

   A. 87
   B. 88
   C. 90
   D. 92
   E. 97

2. What is the value of the expression $g \cdot (g + 1)^2$ for $g = 2$?

   F. 10
   G. 12
   H. 18
   J. 20
   K. 36

3. Company A sells 60 pens for $15.00, while Company B sells the same type of pens 40 for $8.00. Which company's price per pen is cheaper, and what is that price?

   A. Company A, at $0.20
   B. Company A, at $0.23
   C. Company A, at $0.25
   D. Company B, at $0.20
   E. Company B, at $0.25

4. A ladder is 10 ft long and reaches 8 ft up a wall, as shown below. How many feet is the bottom of the ladder from the base of the wall?

   F. 2
   G. 3
   H. 6
   J. $\sqrt{2}$
   K. $\sqrt{164}$

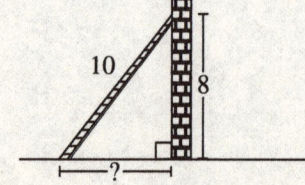

DO YOUR FIGURING HERE.

GO ON TO THE NEXT PAGE.

DO YOUR FIGURING HERE.

5. Consider the 3 statements below to be true.

All insects that are attracted to honey are ants.
Insect I is not an ant.
Insect J is attracted to honey.

Which of the following statements is necessarily true?

A. Insect I is an ant not attracted to honey.
B. Insect I is an ant attracted to honey.
C. Insect I is attracted to honey.
D. Insect J is not attracted to honey.
E. Insect J is an ant.

6. A city utility department charges residential customers $2.50 per 1,000 gallons of water and $16.00 per month for trash pickup. Which of the following expressions gives a residential customer's total monthly charges, in dollars, for use of g thousand gallons of water and trash pickup?

F. $2.50g +$ 16.00
G. $2.50g + 1,016.00$
H. $16.00g +$ 2.50
J. $18.50g$
K. $2,500.00g +$ 16.00

7. What is the value of x that satisfies the equation $2(x + 4) = 5x - 7$?

A. -1

B. $\dfrac{1}{3}$

C. $\dfrac{11}{3}$

D. 5

E. $\dfrac{43}{3}$

8. In the figure below, B is on $\overline{AC}$, E is on $\overline{DF}$, $\overline{AC}$ is parallel to $\overline{DF}$, and $\overline{BE}$ is congruent to $\overline{BF}$. What is the measure of $\angle DEB$?

F. $35°$
G. $135°$
H. $145°$
J. $155°$
K. $215°$

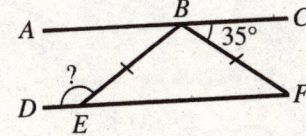

9. What is the least common denominator when adding the fractions $\dfrac{a}{2}$, $\dfrac{b}{3}$, $\dfrac{c}{9}$, and $\dfrac{d}{15}$?

A.   45
B.   90
C. 135
D. 270
E. 810

GO ON TO THE NEXT PAGE.

10. Which of the following expressions is equivalent to $3x(x^2y + 2xy^2)$?

F. $3x^2y + 6xy^2$

G. $3x^3y + 2xy^2$

H. $3x^3y + 6x^2y^2$

J. $5x^4y^3$

K. $9x^4y^3$

DO YOUR FIGURING HERE.

11. A certain type of notebook costs $2.50 before sales tax is added. When you buy 9 of these notebooks you receive 1 additional notebook free. What is the average cost per notebook for the 10 notebooks before sales tax is added?

A. $2.78

B. $2.50

C. $2.30

D. $2.25

E. $2.15

12. For all x, $(3x + 1)^2 = $?

F. $6x + 2$

G. $6x^2 + 2$

H. $9x^2 + 1$

J. $9x^2 + 3x + 1$

K. $9x^2 + 6x + 1$

13. Mark and Juanita own a sandwich shop. They offer 3 kinds of bread, 5 kinds of meat, and 3 kinds of cheese. Each type of sandwich has a combination of exactly 3 ingredients: 1 bread, 1 meat, and 1 cheese. How many types of sandwiches are possible?

A. 11

B. 15

C. 30

D. 45

E. 120

14. If $a^2 = 49$ and $b^2 = 64$, which of the following CANNOT be a value of $a + b$?

F. −15

G. −1

H. 1

J. 15

K. 113

GO ON TO THE NEXT PAGE.

DO YOUR FIGURING HERE.

15. On the real number line, what is the midpoint of –5 and 17 ?

A. –11
B. 6
C. 11
D. 12
E. 22

16. If $3\frac{3}{5} = x + 2\frac{2}{3}$, then x = ?

F. $\frac{4}{5}$
G. $\frac{14}{15}$
H. $1\frac{1}{2}$
J. $1\frac{6}{15}$
K. $6\frac{4}{15}$

17. A system of linear equations is shown below.

$$3y = -2x + 8$$
$$3y = 2x + 8$$

Which of the following describes the graph of this system of linear equations in the standard (x,y) coordinate plane?

A. Two distinct intersecting lines
B. Two parallel lines with positive slope
C. Two parallel lines with negative slope
D. A single line with positive slope
E. A single line with negative slope

18. Which real number satisfies $(2^x)(4) = 8^3$?

F. 2
G. 3
H. 4
J. 4.5
K. 7

Practice ACT Tests

GO ON TO THE NEXT PAGE.

DO YOUR FIGURING HERE.

19. The graph shown in the standard (x,y) coordinate plane below is to be rotated in the plane 180° about the origin.

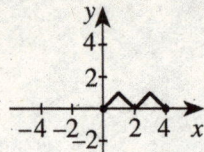

One of the following graphs is the result of this rotation. Which one is it?

A.
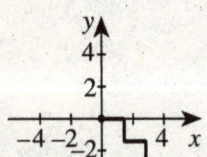

D.
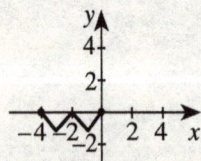

B.
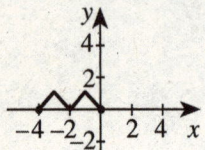

E.
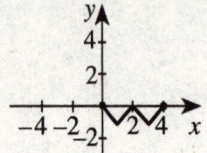

C.
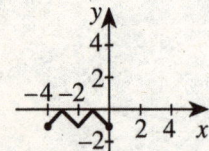

20. What are the values for x that satisfy the equation $(x + a)(x + b) = 0$?

   F. $-a$ and $-b$
   G. $-a$ and b
   H. $-ab$
   J. a and $-b$
   K. a and b

21. On the real number line below, with coordinates as labeled, an object moves according to the following set of instructions: From point P the object moves right to Q, then left to R, then right to S, and finally left until it returns to its original position at P. What is the closest estimate of the total length, in coordinate units, of the movements this object makes?

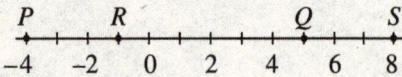

   A.   0
   B.   4
   C. 12
   D. 22
   E. 36

GO ON TO THE NEXT PAGE.

DO YOUR FIGURING HERE.

22. By definition, the determinant $\begin{vmatrix} a & b \\ c & d \end{vmatrix}$ equals $ad - bc$.

What is the value of $\begin{vmatrix} 2x & 3y \\ 5x & 4y \end{vmatrix}$ when $x = -3$ and $y = 2$?

F. −138
G. −42
H.   12
J.   42
K. 138

23. When Angela was cleaning her refrigerator, she found 2 bottles of catsup. Looking at the labels, she noticed that the capacity of the larger bottle was twice the capacity of the smaller bottle. She estimated that the smaller bottle was about $\frac{1}{3}$ full of catsup and the larger bottle was about $\frac{2}{3}$ full of catsup. She poured all the catsup from the smaller bottle into the larger bottle. Then, about how full was the larger bottle?

A. $\frac{2}{9}$ full

B. $\frac{1}{2}$ full

C. $\frac{5}{6}$ full

D. Completely full

E. Overflowing

24. When Jeff starts a math assignment, he spends 5 minutes getting out his book and a sheet of paper, sharpening his pencil, looking up the assignment in his assignment notebook, and turning to the correct page in his book. The equation $t = 10p + 5$ models the time, t minutes, Jeff budgets for a math assignment with p problems. Which of the following statements is necessarily true according to Jeff's model?

F. He budgets 15 minutes per problem.
G. He budgets 10 minutes per problem.
H. He budgets 5 minutes per problem.
J. He budgets 10 minutes per problem for the hard problems and 5 minutes per problem for the easy problems.
K. He budgets a 5-minute break after each problem.

GO ON TO THE NEXT PAGE.

DO YOUR FIGURING HERE.

25. Kaya drove 200 miles in 5 hours of actual driving time. By driving an average of 10 miles per hour faster, Kaya could have saved how many hours of actual driving time?

  A. $\frac{1}{6}$

  B. $\frac{2}{3}$

  C. $\frac{7}{10}$

  D. 1

  E. 4

26. What number can you add to the numerator and denominator of $\frac{7}{9}$ to get $\frac{1}{2}$?

  F. -11

  G. -5

  H. $-2\frac{1}{2}$

  J. $-1\frac{2}{3}$

  K. 5

27. If the inequality $|a| > |b|$ is true, then which of the following *must* be true?
  A. $a = b$
  B. $a \neq b$
  C. $a < b$
  D. $a > b$
  E. $a > 0$

28. What is the slope of the line given by the equation $14x - 11y + 16 = 0$?

  F. -11

  G. $-\frac{14}{11}$

  H. $-\frac{11}{14}$

  J. $\frac{14}{11}$

  K. 14

29. Which of the following is a value of x that satisfies $\log_x 36 = 2$?
  A. 4
  B. 6
  C. 8
  D. 16
  E. 18

GO ON TO THE NEXT PAGE.

30. In △ABC below, D, E, and F are points on $\overline{AB}$, $\overline{BC}$, and $\overline{AC}$, respectively, and $\overline{DF}$ is congruent to $\overline{EF}$. What is the *sum* of the measures of the angles marked x and y ?

DO YOUR FIGURING HERE.

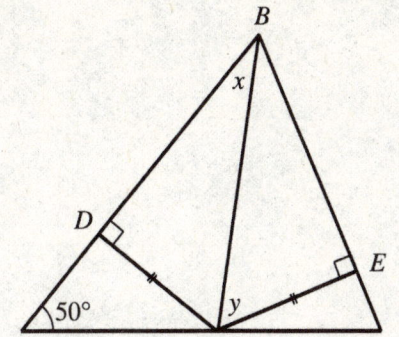

F. 40°
G. 80°
H. 90°
J. 100°
K. 130°

31. Which of the following expressions is equivalent to $(-2x^5y^2)^4$?

A. $-16x^{20}y^8$
B. $-8x^{20}y^8$
C. $-8x^9y^6$
D. $16x^9y^6$
E. $16x^{20}y^8$

32. A line contains the points A, B, C, and D. Point B is between points A and C. Point D is between points C and B. Which of the following inequalities *must* be true about the lengths of these segments?

F. $BC < AB$
G. $BD < AB$
H. $BD < CD$
J. $CD < AB$
K. $CD < BC$

33. Which of the following inequalities defines the solution set for the inequality $16 - 5x \leq 8$?

A. $x \geq \dfrac{8}{5}$

B. $x \geq \dfrac{5}{8}$

C. $x \geq -\dfrac{8}{5}$

D. $x \leq -\dfrac{5}{8}$

E. $x \leq -\dfrac{8}{5}$

GO ON TO THE NEXT PAGE.

DO YOUR FIGURING HERE.

34. The electrical resistance, *r* ohms, of 1,000 ft of solid copper wire at 77°F can be approximated by the model $r = \dfrac{10,770}{d^2} - 0.37$ for any wire diameter, *d* mils (1 mil = 0.001 inch), such that $5 \le d \le 100$. What is the approximate resistance, in ohms, for such a wire with a diameter of 50 mils ?

F. 1
G. 4
H. 17
J. 215
K. 430

35. In the figure below, points *A*, *C*, *E*, and *G* are collinear; *B*, *C*, and *D* are collinear; and *D*, *E*, and *F* are collinear. Angle measures are as marked. What is the measure of $\angle EFG$?

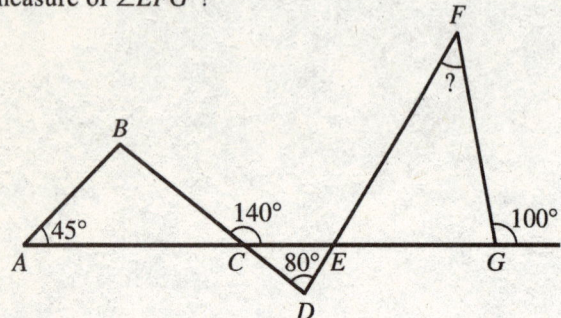

A. 40°
B. 45°
C. 60°
D. 80°
E. Cannot be determined from the given information

36. The solution set of $\sqrt{x-1} > 5$ is the set of all real numbers *x* such that:

F. $x > 4$
G. $x > 6$
H. $x > 24$
J. $x > 25$
K. $x > 26$

37. The measure of each interior angle of a regular polygon with *n* sides is $\left[\dfrac{(n-2)180}{n}\right]$ degrees. What is the measure of each interior angle of a regular polygon with *n* sides, in *radians* ?

A. $\dfrac{(n-2)\pi}{4n}$

B. $\dfrac{(n-2)\pi}{2n}$

C. $\dfrac{(n-2)\pi}{n}$

D. $\dfrac{(n-2)2\pi}{n}$

E. $\dfrac{(n-2)4\pi}{n}$

GO ON TO THE NEXT PAGE.

DO YOUR FIGURING HERE.

38. What is the distance, in coordinate units, between the points $(-3,5)$ and $(4,-1)$ in the standard (x,y) coordinate plane?

F. $\sqrt{13}$

G. $\sqrt{17}$

H. $\sqrt{85}$

J. 13

K. 85

Use the following information to answer questions 39–41.

The end-on view of a cylindrical milk tank on its support is shown in the figure below. The interior radius of the tank's circular end is 4 feet. The interior length of the tank is 25 feet.

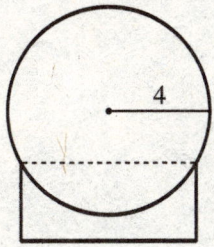

39. Which of the following is closest to the tank's volume, in cubic feet?

A. 310

B. 630

C. 1,300

D. 2,500

E. 5,000

40. The tank currently holds 5,000 gallons of milk. Each gallon of milk weighs about 8 pounds. About how many pounds does this milk weigh?

F. 625

G. 4,000

H. 4,992

J. 5,008

K. 40,000

41. The center of the circular end of the tank is 2 feet above the top level of the support. What is the width, in feet, of the support?

A. $2\sqrt{3}$

B. $4\sqrt{3}$

C. $4\sqrt{5}$

D. 12

E. 24

GO ON TO THE NEXT PAGE.

DO YOUR FIGURING HERE.

42. The tent illustrated below is in the shape of a right triangular prism and is made of nylon. How many square feet of nylon is required for the front, rear, and 2 sides of the tent?

(Note: Please ignore the extra nylon for seams.)

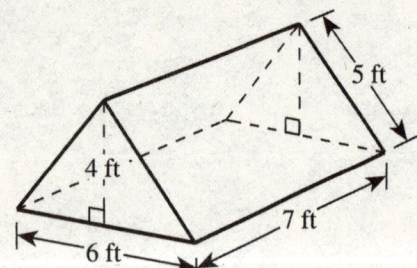

- F.   47
- G.   59
- H.   82
- J.   94
- K. 118

43. Points M and N are the endpoints of the diameter of a circle with center at O, as shown below. Point P is on the circle, and $\angle MOP$ measures 60°. The shortest distance along the circle from M to P is what percent of the distance along the circle from M to N?

- A. 75%
- B. 60%
- C. 50%
- D. $33\frac{1}{3}\%$
- E. $16\frac{2}{3}\%$

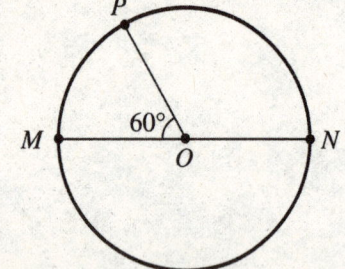

44. Traveling at approximately 186,000 miles per second, about how many miles does a beam of light travel in 2 hours?

- F. 3.72×10^5
- G. 2.23×10^6
- H. 2.68×10^7
- J. 6.70×10^8
- K. 1.34×10^9

45. Barb is going to cover a rectangular area 8 feet by 10 feet with rectangular paving blocks that are 4 inches by 8 inches by 2 inches to make a flat patio. What is the minimum number of paving blocks she will need if all the paving blocks will face the same direction?

(Note: Barb will not cut any of the paving blocks.)

- A.   80
- B.   360
- C.   601
- D.   960
- E.   1,213

GO ON TO THE NEXT PAGE.

46. A right triangle that has its sides measured in the same unit of length is shown below. For any such triangle, $(\tan A)(\sin B)$ is equivalent to:

DO YOUR FIGURING HERE.

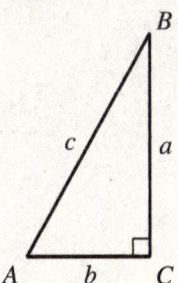

F. $\dfrac{a}{c}$

G. $\dfrac{ab}{c^2}$

H. $\dfrac{a^2}{bc}$

J. $\dfrac{b^2}{ac}$

K. $\dfrac{c}{a}$

47. A swimming pool of uniform depth is being filled. When the pool started filling, its drain was closed. The graph below shows the depth of the water in the pool as a function of the length of time that water has been flowing into the pool.

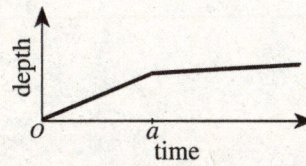

Exactly 1 event occurred at time a that changed the rate at which the depth was increasing. Which of the following could have been that event?

    I. The flow of water into the pool was increased.
    II. The flow of water into the pool was decreased.
    III. The drain was opened.

A. I only
B. II only
C. III only
D. I or II only
E. II or III only

GO ON TO THE NEXT PAGE.

48. Shown below is the graph of the equation $y = 2x + 3$ for values of x such that $0 \le x \le 4$.

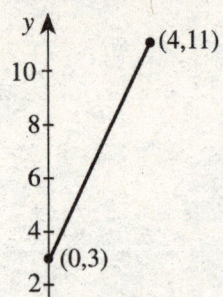

Which of the following statements is(are) true?

    I. The graph has constant slope 2.
    II. The range of the graph consists of all values of y such that $3 \le y \le 11$.
    III. The polynomial $2x + 3$ has a zero of $x = 3$.

F. I only
G. I and II only
H. I and III only
J. I, II, and III
K. None of the statements is true.

49. If $\tan A = \dfrac{a}{b}$, $a > 0$, $b > 0$, and $0 < A < \dfrac{\pi}{2}$, then what is $\cos A$?

A. $\dfrac{a}{b}$

B. $\dfrac{b}{a}$

C. $\dfrac{a}{\sqrt{a^2 + b^2}}$

D. $\dfrac{b}{\sqrt{a^2 + b^2}}$

E. $\dfrac{\sqrt{a^2 + b^2}}{b}$

GO ON TO THE NEXT PAGE.

DO YOUR FIGURING HERE.

50. The 3 parabolas graphed in the standard (x,y) coordinate plane below are from a family of parabolas. A general equation that defines this family of parabolas contains the variable n in addition to x and y. For one of the parabolas shown, $n = 1$; for another, $n = 2$; and for the third, $n = 3$. Which of the following could be a general equation that defines this family of parabolas for all $n \geq 1$?

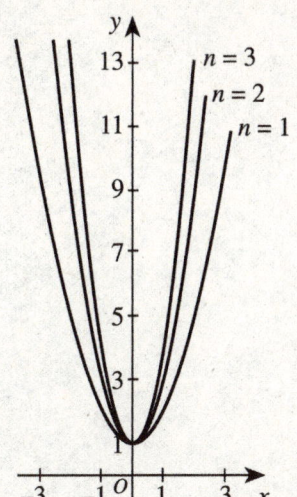

F. $y = nx^2 + 1$

G. $y = \frac{1}{n}x^2 + 1$

H. $y = x^2 + n$

J. $y = -nx^2 + 1$

K. $y = -\frac{1}{n}x^2 + 1$

51. Thomas and Jonelle are playing darts in their garage using the board with the point values for each region shown below. The radius of the outside circle is 10 inches, and each of the other circles has a radius 2 inches smaller than the next larger circle. All of the circles have the same center. Thomas has only 1 dart left to throw and needs at least 30 points to win the game. Assuming that his last dart hits at a random point within a single region on the board, what is the percent chance that Thomas will win the game?

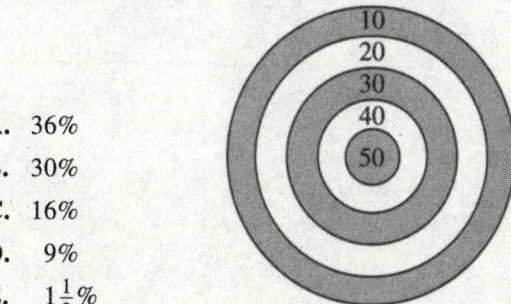

A. 36%

B. 30%

C. 16%

D. 9%

E. $1\frac{1}{2}$%

52. The ratio of a to b is 3 to 4, and the ratio of c to b is 1 to 2. What is the ratio of a to c ?

F. 1 to 1
G. 3 to 1
H. 3 to 2
J. 3 to 8
K. 6 to 1

GO ON TO THE NEXT PAGE.

DO YOUR FIGURING HERE.

53. For the function graphed below, the x-axis can be partitioned into intervals, each of length p radians, and the curve over any one interval is a repetition of the curve over each of the other intervals. What is the least possible value for p, the period of the function?

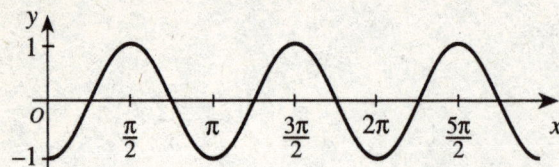

A. $\dfrac{\pi}{2}$

B. π

C. $\dfrac{3\pi}{2}$

D. 2π

E. 3π

54. Which of the following graphs represents the solution set of the inequality $|x| < 2$ on the real number line?

F.
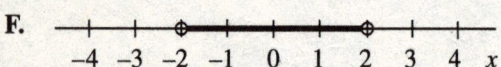

G.

-4 -3 -2 -1 0 1 2 3 4 x

H.

-4 -3 -2 -1 0 1 2 3 4 x

J.

-4 -3 -2 -1 0 1 2 3 4 x

K.

-4 -3 -2 -1 0 1 2 3 4 x

55. If $(x - 7)$ is a factor of $2x^2 - 11x + k$, what is the value of k ?

A. -21
B. -17
C. -7
D. 7
E. 28

56. Let a equal $2b + 3c - 5$. What happens to the value of a if the value of b decreases by 1 and the value of c increases by 2 ?

F. It increases by 4.
G. It increases by 2.
H. It increases by 1.
J. It is unchanged.
K. It decreases by 2.

GO ON TO THE NEXT PAGE.

57. A large cube has edges that are twice as long as those of a small cube. The volume of the large cube is how many times the volume of the small cube?

A. 2
B. 4
C. 6
D. 8
E. 16

58. The center of the unit circle shown below is O. Points A, B, C, and D are points on the circle. When $\angle COA$ is measured in the direction of the arrow shown, its measure is α. Similarly, when $\angle COB$ is measured in the direction of the arrow shown, its measure is β. Both α and β are positive. The length of $\overarc{BA}$ is the same as the length of $\overarc{DC}$. What is the measure of $\angle COD$ measured in the direction of the arrow shown?

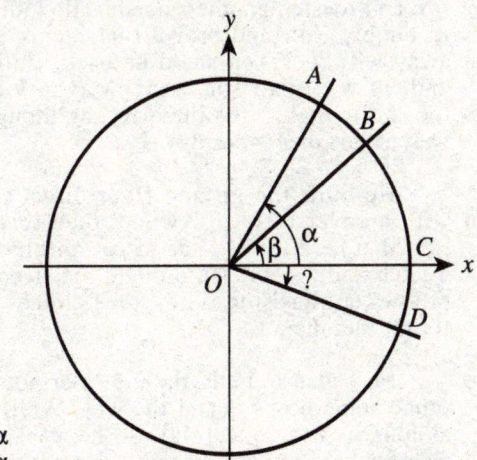

F. $-\beta$
G. $-\beta - \alpha$
H. $\beta - \alpha$
J. $-\alpha$
K. Cannot be determined from the given information

59. In a town of 500 people, the 300 males have an average age of 45 and the 200 females have an average age of 35. To the nearest year, what is the average age of the town's entire population?

A. 40
B. 41
C. 42
D. 43
E. 44

60. On September 1, a dress was priced at $90. On October 1, the price was reduced by 20%. On November 1, the price was further reduced by 25% of the October 1 price and marked FINAL. What percent of the original price was the FINAL price?

F. 40%
G. 45%
H. 55%
J. 60%
K. 77.5%

END OF TEST 2

STOP! DO NOT TURN THE PAGE UNTIL TOLD TO DO SO.

DO NOT RETURN TO THE PREVIOUS TEST.

Practice ACT Tests

READING TEST
35 Minutes—40 Questions

DIRECTIONS: There are four passages in this test. Each passage is followed by several questions. After reading a passage, choose the best answer to each question and fill in the corresponding oval on your answer document. You may refer to the passages as often as necessary.

Passage I

PROSE FICTION: This passage is adapted from the short story "Golden Glass" by Alma Villanueva (©1982 by Bilingual Press).

It was his fourteenth summer. He was thinning out, becoming angular and clumsy, but the cautiousness, the old-man seriousness he'd had as a baby, kept him contained, ageless and safe. His humor, always dry
5 and to the bone since a small child, let you know he was watching everything.

He seemed always to be at the center of his own universe, so it was no surprise to his mother to hear Ted say: "I'm building a fort and sleeping out in it all
10 summer, and I won't come in for anything, not even food. Okay?"

This had been their silent communion, the steady presence of love that flowed regularly, daily—food. The presence of his mother preparing it, his great
15 appetite and obvious enjoyment of it—his nose smelling everything, seeing his mother more vividly than with his eyes.

He watched her now for signs of offense, alarm, and only saw interest. "Where will you put the fort?"
20 Vida asked.

She trusted him to build well and not ruin things, but of course she had to know where.

"I'll build it by the redwoods, in the cypress trees. Okay?"

25 "Make sure you keep your nails together and don't dig into the trees. I'll be checking. If the trees get damaged, it'll have to come down."

The cypress was right next to the redwoods, making it seem very remote. Redwoods do that—they
30 suck up sound and time and smell like another place. So he counted the footsteps, when no one was looking, from the fort to the house. He couldn't believe it was so close; it seemed so separate, alone—especially in the dark, when the only safe way of travel seemed flight
35 (invisible at best).

Ted had seen his mother walk out to the bridge at night, looking into the water, listening to it. He knew

she loved to see the moon's reflection in the water. She'd pointed it out to him once by a river where they
40 camped, her face full of longing. Then, she swam out into the water, at night, as though trying to touch the moon. He wouldn't look at her. He sat and glared at the fire and roasted another marshmallow the way he liked it: bubbly, soft and brown (maybe six if he could get
45 away with it). Then she'd be back, chilled and bright, and he was glad she went. Maybe I like the moon too, he thought, involuntarily, as though the thought weren't his own—but it was.

He built the ground floor directly on the earth,
50 with a cover of old plywood, then scattered remnant rugs that he'd asked Vida to get for him. He concocted a latch and a door. He brought his sleeping bag, some pillows, a transistor radio, some clothes, and moved in for the summer.

55 He began to build the top floor now but he had to prune some limbs out of the way. Well, that was okay as long as he was careful. So he stacked them to one side for kindling and began to brace things in place. It felt weird going up into the tree, not as safe as his
60 small, contained place on the ground.

Vida noticed Ted had become cheerful and would stand next to her, to her left side, talking sometimes. But she realized she mustn't face him or he'd become silent and wander away. So she stood listening, in the
65 same even breath and heart beat she kept when she spotted the wild pheasants with their long, lush tails trailing the grape arbor, picking delicately and greedily at the unpicked grapes in the early autumn light. So sharp, so perfect, so rare to see a wild thing at peace.

70 Ted was taking a makeup course and one in stained glass. There, he talked and acted relaxed; no one expected any more or less. The colors of the stained glass were deep and beautiful, and special—you couldn't waste this glass. The sides were sharp, the cuts
75 were slow and meticulous with a steady pressure. The design's plan had to be absolutely followed or the beautiful glass would go to waste, and he'd curse himself.

The stained glass was finished and he decided to place it in his fort facing the back fields. In fact, it
80 looked like the back fields—trees and the sun in a dark sky. During the day the glass sun shimmered a beautiful

GO ON TO THE NEXT PAGE.

yellow, the blue a much better color than the sky outside: deeper, like night.

He was so used to sleeping outside now he didn't
85 wake up during the night, just like in the house. One
night, toward the end when he'd have to move back
with everyone (school was starting, frost was coming
and the rains), Ted woke up to see the stained glass full
of light. The little sun was a golden moon and the
90 inside glass sky and the outside sky matched.

In a few days he'd be inside, and he wouldn't
mind at all.

1. The passage establishes that Vida and Ted have all of
the following traits in common EXCEPT:

A. a willingness to accommodate the requests each
makes of the other.
B. a response to elements of nature.
C. a perception of others that surfaces in humor.
D. an awareness of what delights the other.

2. Which of the following is NOT an accurate description
of the passage?

F. A story about a teenager whose summer experiences building and occupying a fort near his house
have a positive effect on his relationship with his
mother
G. A glimpse at what connects a mother and son and
what separates them as the boy tests his own limits
with a summer project
H. A look at how two characters—one grown, one
young—behave when each perceives the fragility
of someone or something he or she holds dear
J. A portrait of two family members whose painful
disagreements force one to seek shelter outside the
home until they reach an understanding

3. In both the twelfth paragraph (lines 61–69) and the
thirteenth paragraph (lines 70–77) the author is por-
traying characters who:

A. feel compelled to act carefully in order to avoid
shattering something precious.
B. are frustrated to the point of indignation that success seems always slightly out of reach.
C. are at first excited by a project but later lose interest as others get involved.
D. discover that a personal weakness in some situations can be a personal strength in others.

4. It can most reasonably be inferred that as it is used in
line 69 the term *wild thing* refers not only to a pheasant
but also to:

F. Ted as Vida somewhat reverently sees him.
G. Vida as seen by Ted when she visits the fort.
H. Ted as he imagines himself to be.
J. what Vida wishes Ted would cease to be.

5. Which of the following best describes the difference
between Ted as a little boy and Ted at the time he
builds and occupies the fort?

A. By the time Ted builds the fort he has lost the
lighthearted manner he had as a child and has
become more of a brooder who avoids the company of others.
B. As a teenager Ted is physically clumsier and more
angular than he was as a child, but he retains the
humor, cautiousness, and seriousness that distinguished him at an early age.
C. As a child Ted was constantly observing others for
indications of how he should behave, but as a
teenager he looks more to nature for guidance.
D. As a child Ted was outgoing in a way that
appealed to adults, but as a teenager he was intro-
spective in a way that alarmed them.

6. The passage indicates that Vida was not surprised by
Ted's decision to build a fort because she:

F. knew that more often than not he was inclined to
take projects she had started a step farther.
G. sensed that it fit with his tendency to approach life
as if he were self-contained.
H. had noticed that ever since their camping trip he
had been putting more and more distance between
himself and her.
J. had noticed that he no longer worried that his fascination with nature would interfere with his longstanding craving for the company of others.

7. As it is used in the passage, the term *silent communion*
(line 12) refers to the:

A. way that without using words Ted communicates
his disappointments to Vida.
B. promise Ted made to himself that he would not
return to the house all summer, even for food.
C. way a thought shifted in Ted's mind from feeling
like someone else's to feeling like his own.
D. exchange of warm emotions between Ted and
Vida during the preparation and sharing of food.

8. Which of the following best describes the way the seventh paragraph (lines 25–27) functions in the passage?

F. It reinforces the image of Vida established elsewhere in the passage as someone whose skeptical
nature disheartens Ted on the brink of new projects.
G. It foreshadows events described later in the passage that lead to the dismantling of the tree house
once Ted is back in school.
H. It reveals that Vida takes an interest in Ted's project to the extent that she determines ways in
which he needs to carry it out to avoid problems.
J. It reveals that Vida's willingness to shift responsibility to her son for his actions is greater than his
willingness to accept such responsibility.

GO ON TO THE NEXT PAGE.

Practice ACT Tests

9. According to the passage, Ted attributes which of the following characteristics to the redwoods?

A. They make ideal supports for a fort because they are strong and tall.
B. They create a sense of remoteness by absorbing time and sound and by smelling like another place.
C. They lend a feeling of danger to whatever surrounds them because they themselves are endangered.
D. They grace their surroundings with a serenity that softens disturbing emotions like fear of the dark.

10. Ted felt that in comparison to the ground floor of the fort, going up into the tree to build the top floor seemed:

F. safer because the top floor was less accessible to intruders.
G. safer because the branches provided him with a sense of privacy.
H. less safe because the place felt bigger and more exposed.
J. less safe because the top floor was made of cypress instead of redwood.

Passage II

SOCIAL SCIENCE: This passage is adapted from *Biomimicry: Innovation Inspired by Nature* by Janine M. Benyus (©1997 by Janine M. Benyus).

If anybody's growing biomass, it's us. To keep our system from collapsing on itself, industrial ecologists are attempting to build a "no-waste economy." Instead of a linear production system, which binges on virgin
5 raw materials and spews out unusable waste, they envision a web of closed loops in which a minimum of raw materials comes in the door, and very little waste escapes. The first examples of this no-waste economy are collections of companies clustered in an ecopark
10 and connected in a food chain, with each firm's waste going next door to become the other firm's raw material or fuel.

In Denmark, the town of Kalundborg has the world's most elaborate prototype of an ecopark. Four
15 companies are co-located, and all of them are linked, dependent on one another for resources or energy. The Asnaesverket Power Company pipes some of its waste steam to power the engines of two companies: the Statoil Refinery and Novo Nordisk (a pharmaceutical
20 plant). Another pipeline delivers the remaining waste steam to heat thirty-five hundred homes in the town, eliminating the need for oil furnaces. The power plant also delivers its cooling water, now toasty warm, to fifty-seven ponds' worth of fish. The fish revel in the
25 warm water, and the fish farm produces 250 tons of sea trout and turbot each year.

Waste steam from the power company is used by Novo Nordisk to heat the fermentation tanks that produce insulin and enzymes. This process in turn creates
30 700,000 tons of nitrogen-rich slurry a year, which used

to be dumped into the fjord. Now, Novo bequeaths it free to nearby farmers—a pipeline delivers the fertilizer to the growing plants, which are in turn harvested to feed the bacteria in the fermentation tanks.

35 Meanwhile, back at the Statoil Refinery, waste gas that used to go up a smokestack is now purified. Some is used internally as fuel, some is piped to the power company, and the rest goes to Gyproc, the wallboard maker next door. The sulfur squeezed from the gas
40 during purification is loaded onto trucks and sent to Kemira, a company that produces sulfuric acid. The power company also squeezes sulfur from its emissions, but converts most of it to calcium sulfate (industrial gypsum), which it sells to Gyproc for wallboard.

45 Although Kalundborg is a cozy co-location, industries need not be geographically close to operate in a food web as long as they are connected by a mutual desire to use waste. Already, some companies are designing their processes so that any waste that falls on
50 the production-room floor is valuable and can be used by someone else. In this game of "designed offal," a process with lots of waste, as long as it's "wanted waste," may be better than one with a small amount of waste that must be landfilled or burned. As author
55 Daniel Chiras says, more companies are recognizing that "technologies that produce by-products society cannot absorb are essentially failed technologies."

So far, we've talked about recycling within a circle of companies. But what happens when a product
60 leaves the manufacturer and passes to the consumer and finally to the trash can? Right now, a product visits one of two fates at the end of its useful life. It can be buried in a landfill or incinerated, or it can be recaptured through recycling or reuse.

65 Traditionally, manufacturers haven't had to worry about what happens to a product after it leaves their gates. But that is starting to change, thanks to laws now in the wings in Europe (and headed for the United States) that will require companies to take back their
70 durable goods such as refrigerators, washers, and cars at the end of their useful lives. In Germany, the take-back laws start with the initial sale. Companies must take back all their packaging or hire middlemen to do the recycling. Take-back laws mean that manufacturers
75 who have been saying, "This product can be recycled," must now say, "*We* recycle our products and packaging."

When the onus shifts in this way, it's suddenly in the company's best interest to design a product that will
80 either last a long time or come apart easily for recycling or reuse. Refrigerators and cars will be assembled using easy-open snaps instead of glued-together joints, and for recyclability, each part will be made of one material instead of twenty. Even simple things, like the snack
85 bags for potato chips, will be streamlined. Today's bags, which have nine thin layers made of *seven* different materials, will no doubt be replaced by one material that can preserve freshness and can easily be remade into a new bag.

GO ON TO THE NEXT PAGE.

11. According to the passage, waste emissions from the Asnaesverket Power Company are used to help produce all of following EXCEPT:

A. insulin.
B. heating oil.
C. plant fertilizer.
D. industrial gypsum.

12. When the author says "our system" (lines 1–2), she is most likely referring to a production system in:

F. Denmark in which four companies are co-located in one small town and are linked by their dependence on energy resources.
G. the United States that produces recyclable durable goods such as refrigerators, washers, and cars.
H. the United States and Europe in which products are developed with few virgin raw materials and leave little or no waste.
J. the United States and Europe that uses too many virgin raw materials and produces too much unused waste.

13. The main purpose of the second, third, and fourth paragraphs (lines 13–44) is to show:

A. how four companies depend on each other for resources and the recycling of waste.
B. that Denmark is one of the world's leaders in developing new sources of energy.
C. that one town's need for energy can be eliminated through recycling.
D. that a no-waste economy saves money.

14. It is reasonable to infer that the author's proposed solution to what she sees as the problem of an increasing amount of biomass is to:

F. change the process by which manufacturers produce their products.
G. make consumers responsible for recycling the products they buy.
H. encourage traditional businesses to compete with new, innovative businesses.
J. encourage companies that produce similar products to cluster together in ecoparks.

15. Based on the passage, which of the following pairs of industries is shown to depend directly on one another for the production of their products?

A. Statoil and Gyproc
B. Asnaesverket and fish farmers
C. Novo Nordisk and plant farmers
D. Statoil and Novo Nordisk

16. The main function of the sixth paragraph (lines 58–64) in relation to the passage as a whole is most likely to provide:

F. evidence to support Daniel Chiras's statement in lines 54–57.
G. a transition between the two main points discussed in the passage.
H. a conclusion to the author's discussion about a no-waste economy.
J. a summary of the author's main argument.

17. According to the passage, take-back laws in Germany shift the responsibility for recycling from the:

A. local government to the manufacturer.
B. manufacturer to the local government.
C. manufacturer to the consumer.
D. consumer to the manufacturer.

18. According to the passage, the common element for companies that want to be part of a food web is their mutual interest in:

F. relocating their operations to a common geographic area in Europe.
G. providing industrial waste to private homes and farming operations.
H. eliminating the need for raw materials.
J. using industrial waste as raw materials.

19. The author uses the term "designed offal" (line 51) to indicate that:

A. companies can design ways in which their waste products can be used.
B. industrial ecologists have designed ways to reduce waste products.
C. technology has not kept pace with how to dispose of waste products.
D. companies can learn to design more efficient landfill spaces.

20. According to Daniel Chiras, a failed technology is one that:

F. cannot reuse its own waste.
G. produces more waste than it uses.
H. produces waste that is unusable.
J. makes durable goods such as refrigerators.

Practice ACT Tests

GO ON TO THE NEXT PAGE.

Passage III

HUMANITIES: This passage is adapted from the article "What Light Through Yonder Windows Breaks?" by Stephen Greenblatt, which appeared in *Civilization* (©1995 by L.O.C. Associates, L.P.). The CD-ROMs referred to in this passage are discs that, when inserted into a computer, provide the user with multimedia information on a given subject.

Shakespeare on CD-ROM is potentially the most important thing to happen to the texts of Shakespeare's plays since the 18th century, when they were first given the serious scholarly attention reserved for cultural
5　treasures. It is important to understand why the innovations represented by these CDs—the BBC Shakespeare Series' *Romeo and Juliet* and Voyager's *Macbeth*—are so significant.

What exactly is a printed play by Shakespeare?
10　Where it was once thought that Shakespeare's plays sprang from his noble brow in definitive and final form, it is now widely recognized that many of them were repeatedly revised. Some of these early alterations were likely made by the theater company to adapt a play to a
15　particular occasion, others by a collaborator, others for the government censors, still others by the printer, but many of the most significant changes seem to bear the mark of Shakespeare himself. For example, there are two strikingly distinct versions of *King Lear*, three of
20　*Hamlet* and two of *Romeo and Juliet*. The point is not simply that Shakespeare had second or third thoughts but rather that he apparently regarded his plays as open and unfinished; he intended them to be repeatedly performed, and this meant that they would be continually
25　cut, revised or even radically reconceived according to the ideas of the players and the demands of the public. The words were not meant to remain on the page. They were destined for the beauty and mutability of the human voice.

30　Nevertheless, even today most editors silently stitch together the different versions of *Hamlet* or *King Lear* in an attempt to present the "final" version Shakespeare supposedly meant to leave behind. These printed editions also hide or at least de-emphasize the
35　presentation of the play on stage.

The CD-ROM is a radical departure. The words of the play appear on the screen, synchronized with a complete audio performance. It has long been possible to read the text of the play while listening to a recorded
40　version, but now it is wonderfully easy to locate particular scenes and instantly hear them, to go back and listen again, and to stop and look at the glosses keyed to difficult words and phrases. Each CD includes video clips of some of the most famous scenes, so that the
45　pleasure of listening and reading can be supplemented with glimpses of a full production.

These video clips are at once among the most promising and the most frustrating aspects of the current technology. The quality of both the sound and the
50　visual effects is mediocre, and, to make matters worse, in the BBC's *Romeo and Juliet* the actors on the video are not the same as the actors reading the words. The dubbing is inevitably imperfect, and it is disconcerting to hear Albert Finney's unmistakable voice as Romeo
55　coming from Patrick Ryecart's mouth. Still, there is considerable pleasure in the brief glimpses of performance, a pleasure quite distinct from watching the play on stage or film, since it is here linked so intimately and effortlessly with the words on the screen.

60　Let me be clear: These Shakespeare CDs are not principally interesting as performances. Rather, they are remarkable because they change our experience of what it is to read a play, insistently recalling for us that the words were meant for our ears as well as our eyes.
65　Texts on CD-ROM have, in effect, recovered something of the magic that books possessed in the late Middle Ages, when they were still rare enough to seem slightly eerie, as if they were haunted by spirits.

One stunning moment on the *Romeo and Juliet*
70　CD-ROM is a brief audio clip of an interview with the actress Gwen Ffrangcon-Davies, who had played Juliet in 1924. The interviewer asks her to recite some lines from the balcony scene, and after a brief demurral, she begins to speak the enchanting lines in a lush style
75　completely different from Claire Bloom's quietly restrained rendition. For a minute or so we get a glimpse of what the technology can do. If a stage performance at its best makes us experience a certain inevitability, leading us to think of the actors' interpre-
80　tation of the play, "This *must* be so," then a CD-ROM has the power to make us think, "It could be so different." We could compare three or four radically different performances of the same scene, just as we could for the first time easily compare differences in the text.
85　In one version of Juliet's death scene, for example, she stabs herself with a dagger and says, "There rest." In another version she says, "There rust."

21. Which of the following statements best characterizes the author's attitude toward the CD-ROMs he reviews in the passage?

   A. He welcomes them as a means of experiencing the works of Shakespeare in a way that is closer to the playwright's original intent.
   B. He applauds them as the first technology to verify that Shakespeare's plays were revised by countless individuals.
   C. He bemoans their arrival as further evidence that the magic of books has been lost in the feverish pursuit of technological advances.
   D. He is skeptical of their potential to reach the audience for whom they are intended: those who are intimidated by Shakespeare in the first place.

GO ON TO THE NEXT PAGE.

22. Without the last paragraph, the passage would contain no specific examples of:

F. how CD-ROM technology enhances appreciation for Shakespeare centuries after his death.

G. actors and actresses who have performed roles in Shakespeare plays.

H. what caused scholars to view Shakespeare's plays as cultural treasures.

J. inconsistencies in the text of Shakespeare plays as well known as *Romeo and Juliet.*

23. In the first paragraph, the author compares the dawning of the age of CD-ROM Shakespeare to the dawning of scholarly attention to Shakespeare's work in the eighteenth century. This comparison supports the author's point that:

A. since books became widely available, the magic of the theater has diminished.

B. academics have long regarded Shakespeare as too sophisticated for the general public.

C. each generation identifies with a different one of Shakespeare's plays.

D. CD-ROMs of Shakespeare plays represent a profound shift in the treatment of his work.

24. According to the passage, the CD-ROMs offer a combination of:

F. complete text and full-length video of a production.

G. selections from the text and selected scenes on video from a production.

H. selections from the text and a full-length video of a production.

J. complete audio and written text and selected scenes on video from a production.

25. It can be reasonably inferred that one of the author's concerns is that his praise for the Shakespeare CD-ROMs will be misunderstood as:

A. support of CD-ROMs in general.

B. praise of well-meaning but mediocre actors.

C. a suggestion that they are a substitute for live performances.

D. support for more than one interpretation of a Shakespeare play.

26. It is most reasonable to infer that in line 77 the phrase "what the technology can do" refers to the capacity of CD-ROMs to:

F. interfere with the playwright's original intent.

G. reduce a play to the level of a television program.

H. invite an appreciation for the immense possibilities contained in a Shakespeare play.

J. simplify Shakespeare's complex messages by conveying them in modern English.

27. The passage refers to efforts today by editors to assemble a final version of one Shakespeare play or another. These efforts are most closely aligned in spirit with which of the following?

A. Shakespeare's concept of the adaptable nature of his plays

B. Previously held beliefs "that Shakespeare's plays sprang from his noble brow in definitive and final form" (lines 10–11)

C. The form and spirit of the new versions of Shakespeare's plays on CD-ROM

D. The view expressed in the passage of how Shakespeare's plays should be treated

28. The author is bothered by Albert Finney's voice on the BBC's *Romeo and Juliet* CD-ROM because the actor's words:

F. don't match the original script.

G. are muddled by static interference.

H. accompany the performance of another actor.

J. conjure up the tragic fate of Romeo.

29. It is the author's opinion that CD-ROMs' primary advantage over printed versions of Shakespeare's plays is that a CD-ROM appeals to more senses in making the connection between:

A. original and contemporary set designs.

B. the themes of *Hamlet* and *King Lear.*

C. the eighteenth century and today.

D. the written and the spoken word.

30. In line 80, the statement "This *must* be so" is intended as an example of:

F. an audience member's response to a high quality theater performance.

G. a line from a Shakespeare play that appears slightly altered in another version of the same play.

H. the author quoting a director who sees only one possible interpretation of a Shakespeare play.

J. an audio clip from the CD-ROM version of Shakespeare's *Romeo and Juliet.*

GO ON TO THE NEXT PAGE.

Passage IV

NATURAL SCIENCE: This passage is adapted from the article "The Mars Model" by Bridget Mintz Testa, which appears in *Discover Magazine* (©1995 by The Walt Disney Company).

The first close-up images of Mars, captured in 1972 by the probe *Mariner 9,* were a planetary scientist's dream: they revealed networks of valleys that looked uncannily like drainage basins and streambeds
5 back here on Earth and thus implied that there had once been water freely flowing over the surface of Mars. The images also implied that Mars had once had a thick atmosphere. Our planet is blessed with liquid water on its surface only because it has a thick atmosphere to
10 maintain a high pressure and trap the sun's heat. So planetary scientists proposed that when Mars formed 4.6 billion years ago, it too had a dowry of a heat-trapping atmosphere, composed of carbon dioxide and water vapor. With warmth, water, and air, they specu-
15 lated, Mars might once have been a garden world, a paradise among planets.

But, as they also discovered, the garden didn't last long. None of the streambeds were younger than 3.7 billion years. Something happened to Mars, some-
20 thing that stripped nearly all of its atmosphere, killed its streams, and froze the garden forever.

Researchers have suggested many scenarios for the Martian apocalypse. Some have proposed that the sun gradually whittled away Mars' atmosphere with its
25 wind of charged particles. Others have hypothesized that the planet itself absorbed most of its atmosphere, turning carbon dioxide into carbonate rocks. For the past seven years, however, Ann Vickery and Jay Melosh, two planetary scientists from the University of
30 Arizona, have been exploring a far more spectacular ending: most of Mars' atmosphere, they suggest, was blasted away by a succession of asteroids and comets.

"The basic idea," Melosh says, "is that an impact doesn't just open a crater. With high velocities, the
35 projectile vaporizes and expands into the atmosphere." This superheated expanding plume shoves the atmosphere above it like a snowplow pushing snow to the heavens. How high a vapor plume goes depends on the mass and velocity of the object that crashed into the
40 planet. If it is big enough and fast enough, it can drive its plume straight back up into space. The portion of the atmosphere it plows away is then stripped from the planet forever.

To see if this process could account for Mars'
45 missing atmosphere, Vickery and Melosh essentially ran a film of the Red Planet in reverse, starting with today's wispy atmosphere and adding back the air that might have been removed by impacts over the eons. First they derived a mathematical expression relating
50 time to the rates of both impacts and atmosphere loss. Using this expression, they then ran the clock backward to find out how long it would take to "grow" an ancient, Earth-like atmosphere from Mars' current tiny one. If

their model was right, it would produce the original,
55 early Mars. And the time it took to "grow" a thick atmosphere by going backward would be the same as the time it took to lose a thick atmosphere, traveling forward. Using an impact rate that prevailed 3.7 billion years ago—one impact every 10,000 years—Vickery
60 and Melosh were able to start with a virtually dead planet and grow a thick atmosphere in only 600 or 700 million years.

However, now that an attractive explanation finally exists for how the young paradise of Mars was
65 destroyed, some researchers are questioning whether that paradise ever existed in the first place. Studies of other stars suggest that the young sun was 25 to 30 percent dimmer than it is today. Mars, which is 49 million miles farther from the sun than is Earth, would have
70 been receiving less than a third of the sunlight we now enjoy. Some scientists have calculated that given so little sunlight, Mars' atmosphere wouldn't be able to trap enough heat to keep water from freezing and that under such conditions, carbon dioxide would form
75 frozen clouds. What little sunlight Mars received would bounce off the clouds, and the planet would cool even further. As to how the Martian valleys we see today might have formed without a warm atmosphere, it is suggested that the planet might have been covered by
80 large expanses of ice and that the heat from Mars' interior could have thawed out hidden channels.

Vickery, however, is sticking by her original assumptions. "There exist on Mars valley networks that look like terrestrial river valley networks and don't
85 look like any other kind of feature found anywhere else in the solar system," she points out. "The first, obvious interpretation is that these networks were formed more or less the same way as similar terrestrial networks."

31. The author's purpose in writing this passage is most likely to:

A. point out irreconcilable differences between contending theories concerning the early history of Mars.
B. examine why the early history of Mars is important in understanding other aspects of planetary science.
C. illustrate the differences in atmospheric pressure between Mars and Earth.
D. report on recent theories and controversies in research concerning the early history of Mars.

32. The last paragraph supports the general hypothesis provided earlier in the passage that:

F. a series of comets and asteroids repeatedly struck Mars.
G. Mars formed about 4.6 billion years ago.
H. Mars once had warmth, water, and air.
J. large expanses of ice once covered Mars.

GO ON TO THE NEXT PAGE.

33. Which of the following findings, if true, would best support the idea that Mars once was "a garden world, a paradise among planets" (lines 15–16)?

A. Images of Mars revealed networks of drainage basins and streambeds.
B. When the sun was young, it was 25 to 30 percent dimmer than it is today.
C. A succession of asteroids and comets struck Mars about every 10,000 years.
D. Large expanses of ice on Mars were thawed by a heat source deep within the planet.

34. It is reasonable to conclude from the passage that the amount of solar heat a planet retains is most directly related to its distance from the sun and to:

F. the amount of liquid water it has.
G. its distance from other planets.
H. the thickness of its atmosphere.
J. the volume and mass of its underground ice.

35. The main purpose of the third paragraph (lines 22–32) is to point out that there are several theories about:

A. why Mars now has a thin atmosphere.
B. how carbon dioxide turns into rock.
C. how the wind on Mars became charged with particles.
D. why the sun gradually took away the atmosphere of Mars.

36. The central idea of the hypothesis proposed by Vickery and Melosh is that:

F. a series of asteroid and comet impacts pushed away the atmosphere of Mars.
G. the atmosphere of Mars trapped too much heat and burned away a layer of carbon dioxide.
H. the water vapor once prevalent on Mars was blown away by a wind of charged particles.
J. carbon dioxide on Mars was absorbed into the atmosphere and changed into carbonate rocks.

37. Based on the passage, which of the following statements, if true, would most WEAKEN the hypothesis made by Vickery and Melosh?

A. The network of valleys on Mars was made up of drainage basins and streambeds.
B. Asteroids collided with Mars at a much higher frequency than was previously thought.
C. Most of the comets and asteroids that struck Mars were very small.
D. The atmosphere around Mars was once as thick as Earth's atmosphere.

38. If it could be proved "that the young sun was 25 to 30 percent dimmer than it is today" (lines 67–68), then, according to the passage, it might also be shown that Mars:

F. has always had an Earth-like atmosphere.
G. has never had an Earth-like atmosphere.
H. once had liquid water.
J. has been routinely hit by large asteroids.

39. The word *projectile* in line 35 refers to:

A. a large mass of charged particles carried by the wind.
B. a large mass of carbonate rock.
C. a plume of water vapor.
D. an asteroid or comet.

40. According to Vickery and Melosh, about how long did it take Mars to go from a planet with an Earth-like atmosphere to a planet with the atmosphere it has today?

F. 10,000 years
G. 600–700 million years
H. 3.7 billion years
J. 4.6 billion years

END OF TEST 3

STOP! DO NOT TURN THE PAGE UNTIL TOLD TO DO SO.

DO NOT RETURN TO A PREVIOUS TEST.

SCIENCE TEST

35 Minutes—40 Questions

DIRECTIONS: There are seven passages in this test. Each passage is followed by several questions. After reading a passage, choose the best answer to each question and fill in the corresponding oval on your answer document. You may refer to the passages as often as necessary.

You are NOT permitted to use a calculator on this test.

Passage I

Students used 2 methods to calculate D, a car's *total stopping distance*; D is the distance a car travels from the time a driver first reacts to an emergency until the car comes to a complete stop.

In Method 1, R is the distance a car travels during a driver's assumed reaction time of 0.75 sec, and B is the average distance traveled once the brakes are applied. Method 2 assumes that D = initial speed in ft/sec × 2 sec. Table 1 lists R, B, and D for various initial speeds, where D was computed using both methods. Figure 1 contains graphs of D versus initial speed for Method 1 and Method 2.

Table 1					
		Method 1			Method 2
Initial speed (mi/hr)	Initial speed (ft/sec)	R (ft)	B (ft)	D (ft)	D (ft)
20	29	22	20	42	58
40	59	44	80	124	118
60	88	66	180	246	176
80	118	88	320	408	236

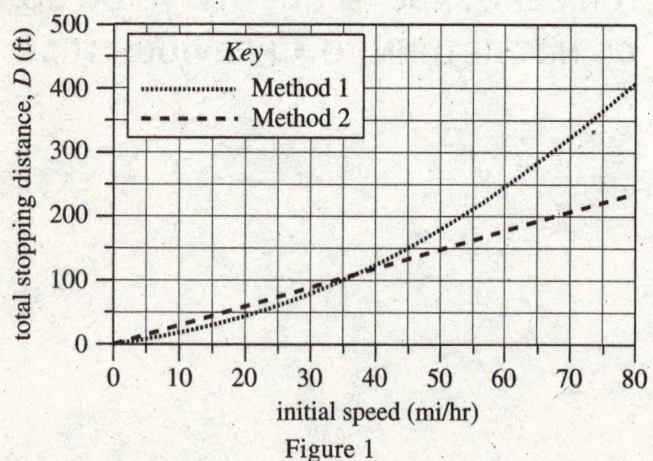

Figure 1

Table 1 and Figure 1 adapted from Edwin F. Meyer III, *Multiple-Car Pileups and the Two-Second Rule.* ©1994 by The American Association of Physics Teachers.

1. Compared to R at an initial speed of 20 mi/hr, R at an initial speed of 80 mi/hr is:

   A. $\frac{1}{4}$ as great.

   B. $\frac{1}{2}$ as great.

   C. 2 times as great.

   D. 4 times as great.

2. In Method 1, D equals:

   F. $R + B$.
   G. $R - B$.
   H. $R \times B$.
   J. $R \div B$.

3. According to Figure 1, the 2 methods yield the same value for D when the initial speed is closest to:

   A. 20 mi/hr.
   B. 40 mi/hr.
   C. 60 mi/hr.
   D. 80 mi/hr.

4. A driver was traveling 60 mi/hr when she spotted an accident and immediately applied her brakes. It took her 2 sec from the time she spotted the accident until she brought her car to a complete stop. According to Method 2, how far did her car travel during the 2 sec interval?

   F. 58 ft
   G. 118 ft
   H. 176 ft
   J. 234 ft

5. Based on Table 1 or Figure 1, if the initial speed of a car is 90 mi/hr, D, according to Method 2, will be:

   A. less than 90 ft.
   B. between 95 ft and 150 ft.
   C. between 150 ft and 250 ft.
   D. greater than 250 ft.

GO ON TO THE NEXT PAGE.

Passage II

Urine samples were collected from 4 students on 1 day at 8:00 A.M. and 8:00 P.M. The samples were then analyzed. Tables 1 and 2 show the volume, color, specific gravity, and the concentration of suspended solids of the 8:00 A.M. and 8:00 P.M. urine samples, respectively. *Specific gravity* was calculated as follows:

$$specific\ gravity = \frac{density\ of\ sample}{density\ of\ water}$$

The normal range for the specific gravity of urine is 1.0001–1.0350.

Table 1				
8:00 A.M. urine samples				
Student	Volume (mL)	Color*	Specific gravity	Suspended solids (g/L)
A	100	8	1.028	74.48
B	260	5	1.016	42.56
C	270	4	1.027	71.82
D	385	2	1.006	15.96

*Note: Color was assigned using the following scale: 0 = very pale; 10 = very dark.

Table 2				
8:00 P.M. urine samples				
Student	Volume (mL)	Color*	Specific gravity	Suspended solids (g/L)
A	150	7	1.024	63.84
B	300	4	1.015	39.90
C	305	3	1.020	53.20
D	400	0	1.001	2.66

*Note: Color was assigned using the following scale: 0 = very pale; 10 = very dark.

6. Based on the information presented, which of the following urine samples most likely had the highest water content per milliliter?

F. The 8:00 A.M. urine sample from Student A
G. The 8:00 A.M. urine sample from Student B
H. The 8:00 P.M. urine sample from Student C
J. The 8:00 P.M. urine sample from Student D

7. Do the data in Tables 1 and 2 support the conclusion that as urine volume increases, urine color darkens?

A. Yes, because urine samples with the greatest volumes had the highest color values.
B. Yes, because urine samples with the greatest volumes had the lowest color values.
C. No, because urine samples with the greatest volumes had the highest color values.
D. No, because urine samples with the greatest volumes had the lowest color values.

8. Based on the results provided, as the concentration of suspended solids in urine increase, the specific gravity of the urine:

F. increases only.
G. decreases only.
H. increases, then decreases.
J. decreases, then increases.

9. One of the 4 students had the flu on the 2 days preceding the collection of the urine samples. During these 2 days, the student experienced a net fluid loss due to vomiting and diarrhea. Based on the information provided, the student with the flu was most likely:

A. Student A.
B. Student B.
C. Student C.
D. Student D.

10. A volume of 1 mL from which of the following urine samples would weigh the most?

F. The 8:00 A.M. urine sample from Student B
G. The 8:00 A.M. urine sample from Student D
H. The 8:00 P.M. urine sample from Student A
J. The 8:00 P.M. urine sample from Student C

GO ON TO THE NEXT PAGE.

Passage III

The following experiments were performed to investigate the effects of adding various *solutes* (substances that are dissolved in a solution), in varying amounts, on the boiling points and freezing points of H_2O solutions. Pure H_2O freezes at 0°C and boils at 100°C at standard atmospheric pressure.

Experiment 1

A student dissolved 0.01 mole of sodium chloride (NaCl) in 100 g of H_2O. Each mole of NaCl produces 2 moles of solute particles (1 mole of sodium ions and 1 mole of chloride ions in solution). After the NaCl dissolved, the freezing point of the solution was determined. This procedure was repeated using different amounts of NaCl and table sugar (sucrose). Each mole of sucrose produces 1 mole of solute particles (sucrose molecules). The results are shown in Table 1.

Solution	Substance added to H_2O	Amount added (mole)	Freezing point (°C)
		Table 1	
1	NaCl	0.01	−0.3
2	NaCl	0.05	−1.7
3	NaCl	0.1	−3.4
4	NaCl	0.2	−6.9
5	sucrose	0.01	−0.2
6	sucrose	0.05	−1.0
7	sucrose	0.1	−2.1
8	sucrose	0.2	−4.6

Note: Freezing points were measured at standard atmospheric pressure.

Experiment 2

A student dissolved 0.01 mole of NaCl in 100 g of H_2O. After the NaCl dissolved, the boiling point of the solution was determined. The procedure was repeated using various amounts of NaCl. The results are shown in Table 2.

	Table 2	
Solution	Amount of NaCl added (mole)	Boiling point (°C)
9	0.01	100.1
10	0.05	100.5
11	0.1	101.0
12	0.2	102.0

Note: Boiling points were measured at standard atmospheric pressure.

11. A solution containing 100 g of H_2O and an unknown amount of NaCl boils at 104°C. Based on the results of Experiment 2, the number of moles of NaCl dissolved in the solution is closest to:

   A. 0.2.
   B. 0.3.
   C. 0.4.
   D. 0.5.

12. Which of the following factors was NOT directly controlled by the student in Experiment 2 ?

   F. The substance added to the H_2O
   G. The amount of H_2O used
   H. The amount of solute added to the H_2O
   J. The boiling points of the H_2O solutions

13. From the results of Experiment 2, what would one hypothesize, if anything, about the effect of the number of solute particles dissolved in H_2O on the boiling point of a solution?

   A. The more solute particles that are present, the higher the boiling point.
   B. The more solute particles that are present, the lower the boiling point.
   C. No hypothesis can be made because only 1 solute was tested.
   D. The number of solute particles produced does not affect the boiling point.

14. According to the results of Experiments 1 and 2, which of the following conclusions can be made about the magnitudes of the changes in the boiling point and freezing point of H_2O solutions when 0.2 mole of NaCl is added to 100 g of H_2O ? The freezing point is:

   F. raised less than the boiling point is lowered.
   G. raised more than the boiling point is raised.
   H. lowered less than the boiling point is lowered.
   J. lowered more than the boiling point is raised.

GO ON TO THE NEXT PAGE.

15. Based on the results of Experiment 1, as the number of sodium particles and chloride particles in 100 g of H_2O increased, the freezing point of the solution:

   A. increased only.
   B. decreased only.
   C. decreased, then increased.
   D. remained the same.

16. $CaCl_2$ produces 3 moles of solute particles per mole when dissolved. Experiment 1 was repeated using a solution containing 100 g of H_2O and 0.1 mole $CaCl_2$. Assuming that $CaCl_2$ has the same effect on the freezing point of H_2O as does NaCl per particle produced when dissolved, the freezing point of the solution would most likely be:

   F. between 0°C and –2.1°C.
   G. between –2.1°C and –3.4°C.
   H. between –3.4°C and –6.9°C.
   J. below –6.9°C.

Practice ACT Tests

Passage IV

The study of oxygen isotopes present in water can give us clues to the climate of a certain location. The ratio of the isotopes ^{18}O and ^{16}O in a sample of rain, snow, or ice is compared to the $^{18}O/^{16}O$ ratio in a *standard sample*. A standard sample has a known value for the parameter being measured. The comparison of a sample's ratio to that of the standard is called the *O-18 index* ($\delta^{18}O$). The $\delta^{18}O$ is calculated using the following formula:

$$\delta^{18}O = \frac{\left(^{18}O/^{16}O\right)_{sample} - \left(^{18}O/^{16}O\right)_{standard}}{\left(^{18}O/^{16}O\right)_{standard}} \times 1{,}000$$

Scientists conducted 3 studies to examine the $\delta^{18}O$ of glacial ice in Arctic and Antarctic locations and learn about the past climates there.

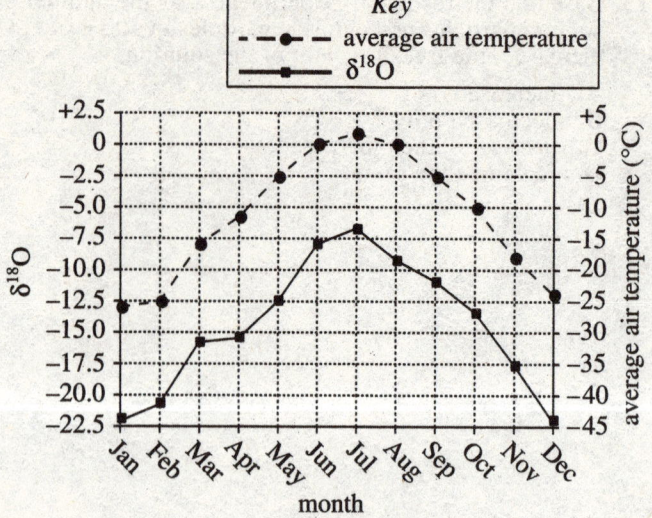

Figure 1

Study 1

Containers were placed on glaciers at 25 locations in the Arctic to collect snowfall. The containers' contents were collected every 2 weeks during a 1-year period and analyzed for ^{16}O and ^{18}O. Figure 1 shows the calculated monthly $\delta^{18}O$ and air temperature averages.

Study 2

At the 25 Arctic locations from Study 1, a 500 m deep vertical ice core was drilled. Each core represented the past 100,000 years of glacial ice accumulation at the site. Starting at the surface, samples were taken every 10 m along the length of the cores. These samples were analyzed for ^{18}O and ^{16}O. Larger $\delta^{18}O$ values indicate that a relatively warmer climate existed at the time the ice was formed than do smaller $\delta^{18}O$ values. The calculated average $\delta^{18}O$ values for the samples are shown in Figure 2.

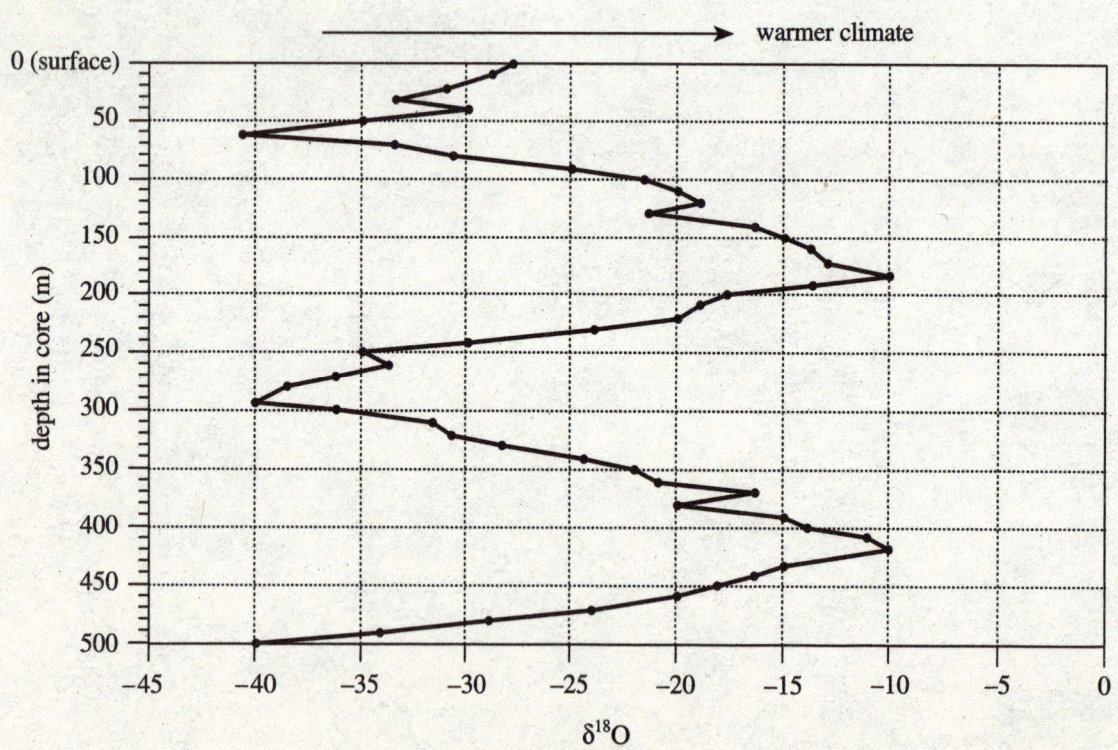

Figure 2

GO ON TO THE NEXT PAGE.

Study 3

The procedures of Study 2 were repeated at 25 Antarctic locations. The past 100,000 years of glacial ice accumulation at the site was represented by a 300 m ice core. The calculated average $\delta^{18}O$ values for the samples are shown in Figure 3.

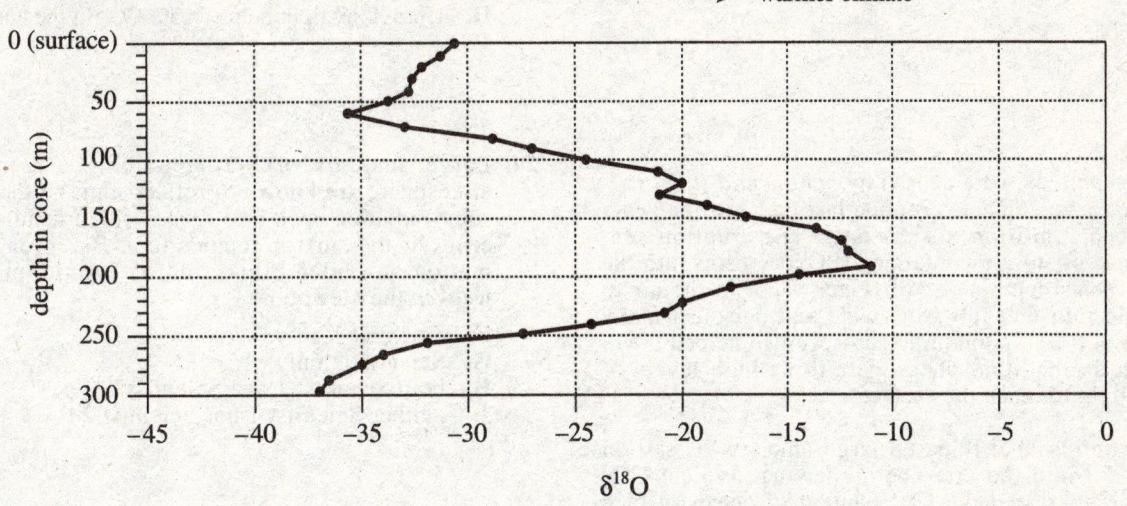

Figure 3

17. According to Study 1, average air temperatures in the Arctic were closest for which of the following pairs of months?

A. January and March
B. March and September
C. May and September
D. October and December

18. According to Study 1, which of the following best describes the relationship between the $\delta^{18}O$ of the Arctic snow samples and the average monthly air temperatures? As the average monthly air temperatures increased, then decreased, the $\delta^{18}O$:

F. increased only.
G. increased, then decreased.
H. decreased only.
J. decreased, then increased.

19. Which of the following statements best describes why sites in the Arctic and Antarctic were chosen for these studies? These sites had to have:

A. average air temperatures below –25°C year-round.
B. glaciers present at many different locations.
C. several months during the year in which no precipitation fell.
D. large areas of bare soil and rock present.

20. According to Study 2, the ice found in the Arctic core at depths between 150 m and 200 m was formed during a period when the climate in the Arctic was most likely:

F. somewhat cooler than the present climate in the Arctic.
G. the same as the present climate in the Arctic.
H. the same as the present climate in the Antarctic.
J. somewhat warmer than the present climate in the Arctic.

21. According to Studies 2 and 3, 100,000 years of ice accumulation was represented by a 500 m core in the Arctic and a 300 m core in the Antarctic. Which of the following statements best explains why the ice cores were different lengths? The average rate of glacial ice accumulation over that time period in the Arctic:

A. was greater than the rate in the Antarctic.
B. was the same as the rate in the Antarctic.
C. was less than the rate in the Antarctic.
D. could not be determined with any accuracy.

22. According to the information provided, a sample that had a calculated $\delta^{18}O$ of zero had a $^{18}O/^{16}O$ value that compared in which of the following ways to the $^{18}O/^{16}O$ value of the standard sample? The sample's $^{18}O/^{16}O$ ratio was:

F. $\frac{1}{2}$ of the $^{18}O/^{16}O$ ratio of the standard.

G. the same as the $^{18}O/^{16}O$ ratio of the standard.

H. $1\frac{1}{2}$ times larger than the $^{18}O/^{16}O$ ratio of the standard.

J. twice as large as the $^{18}O/^{16}O$ ratio of the standard.

GO ON TO THE NEXT PAGE.

Passage V

Scientists discuss 2 possible causes of an event 250 million years ago (Ma) in which 90% of all marine species became extinct.

Scientist 1

The extinctions were caused by *continental flood vulcanism*, a massive volcanic eruption lasting 1 million years that produced 2 million km^3 of lava. The eruption sent large amounts of sulfate-containing (SO_4) aerosols into the air. The aerosols combined with water vapor in the air to produce acid rain that fell worldwide and poisoned many bodies of water. SO_4-containing aerosols also helped break down ozone in the atmosphere, permitting high levels of ultraviolet light to reach the surface.

The eruption also released large amounts of carbon dioxide (CO_2) into the air. The higher-than-typical CO_2 levels in the air raised the CO_2 content of ocean surface waters to levels that were toxic to many marine organisms. The increased levels of CO_2 also caused climatic warming that decreased the temperature difference between the poles and the equator, thus slowing ocean circulation and causing ocean water to become oxygen-poor.

Scientist 2

The extinctions were caused by an overturning of deep, CO_2-rich ocean waters.

No continental ice sheets were present on Earth just prior to 250 Ma. Today, continental ice sheets help cool ocean surface waters, which then sink and drive the ocean's vertical circulation. Since this circulation was absent 250 Ma, the ocean water was stagnant and oxygen-poor.

Photosynthetic organisms living in ocean surface waters removed CO_2 from the atmosphere, converting it to organic matter. This organic matter sank to the ocean bottom, where it was oxidized to CO_2. As a result, the CO_2 levels in the deep ocean waters rose dramatically, while atmospheric CO_2 levels continued to drop, causing climatic cooling. Glaciers and ice sheets grew rapidly, cooling the ocean surface waters such that vertical circulation of the ocean began. Deep ocean water was brought to the surface, where it released the accumulated CO_2, dramatically increasing atmospheric and surface water concentrations of CO_2. This excess CO_2 was toxic to many marine organisms.

23. Which of the following statements best explains why Scientist 1 mentioned ultraviolet light?

   A. High levels of ultraviolet light are beneficial to many living things.
   B. High levels of ultraviolet light are harmful to many living things.
   C. Ultraviolet light helps create ozone in the atmosphere.
   D. Ultraviolet light helps create CO_2 in the atmosphere.

24. Large amounts of SO_4-containing aerosols in the atmosphere are known to reflect some of the incoming solar radiation back into space, which results in a lowering of the surface temperature. Based on the information provided, this finding would most likely *weaken* the viewpoint(s) of:

   F. Scientist 1 only.
   G. Scientist 2 only.
   H. both Scientist 1 and Scientist 2.
   J. neither Scientist 1 nor Scientist 2.

25. Scientist 2 would most likely state that the vertical circulation that is present in most of the oceans today is maintained, at least in part, by the presence of:

   A. high levels of CO_2 in the air.
   B. active volcanoes around the Pacific Ocean rim.
   C. ice sheets in Earth's polar regions.
   D. marine organisms in deep ocean waters.

26. Both scientists would most likely agree that the ocean water was, or became, oxygen-poor when which of the following events occurred?

   F. Ocean water circulation reversed its usual direction.
   G. Ocean water circulation slowed, stopped, or was absent.
   H. Oceanic organisms dramatically increased the available oxygen in the ocean water.
   J. Oceanic organisms used up all the available CO_2 in the ocean water.

27. According to the information provided, radioactive dating of volcanic rocks created during the continental flood vulcanism described by Scientist 1 would show the rocks to be about how many million years old?

   A. 1
   B. 50
   C. 100
   D. 250

GO ON TO THE NEXT PAGE.

28. SO_4-containing aerosols are produced today in large quantities by human activity. Scientist 1 would most likely predict that the climatic effect in an area where large amounts of SO_4-containing aerosols are put into the atmosphere would be a *decrease* in the:

F. amount of ultraviolet light reaching Earth's surface in that area.

G. average pH of rainfall in that area.

H. amount of rainfall in that area.

J. average wind speed in that area.

29. *Inorganic carbonates* are rocks formed from calcium carbonate ($CaCO_3$) that precipitate out of ocean surface waters which have much higher than normal levels of dissolved CO_2. If scientists found large deposits of inorganic carbonates that had formed around 250 Ma, this discovery would most likely support the viewpoint(s) of:

A. Scientist 1 only.

B. Scientist 2 only.

C. both Scientist 1 and Scientist 2.

D. neither Scientist 1 nor Scientist 2.

GO ON TO THE NEXT PAGE.

Passage VI

When hydrogen and oxygen are mixed under certain conditions, H_2O will form. Students did the following experiments to study how H_2O forms.

Experiment 1

A thick-walled gas syringe fitted with a sparking device was filled with 20 mL of hydrogen gas (H_2) and 10 mL of oxygen gas (O_2), as shown in Figure 1.

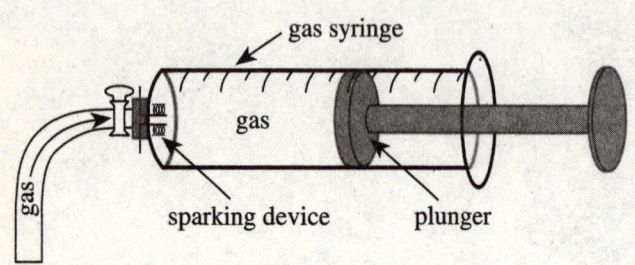

gas syringe

gas

gas

sparking device   plunger

Figure 1

The syringe plunger was then locked in place and the gases were sparked. A reaction took place, forming droplets of water. The plunger was then released. The gas in the syringe was allowed to adjust to room temperature and pressure, and the final volume of gas was recorded. The remaining gas, if any, was then analyzed to determine its composition. The procedure was repeated with different volumes of gases, and the results were recorded in Table 1.

		Table 1		
	Volume (mL)			
Trial	Initial H_2	Initial O_2	Final H_2	Final O_2
1	20	10	0	0
2	20	20	0	10
3	20	30	0	20
4	10	20	0	15
5	40	20	0	0
6	50	20	10	0

Since it is known that equal numbers of molecules of different gases occupy equal volumes at the same pressure and temperature, the following equation was suggested:

$$2 H_2 + O_2 \rightarrow 2 H_2O$$

Experiment 2

In the apparatus shown in Figure 2, a stream of H_2 was passed over hot copper oxide (CuO), producing H_2O vapor. The vapor was then absorbed by calcium chloride ($CaCl_2$).

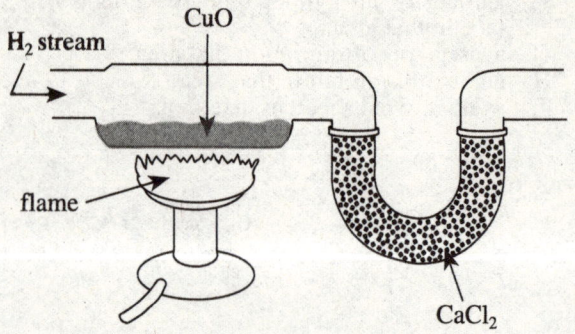

H_2 stream

CuO

flame

$CaCl_2$

Figure 2

The changes in the masses of the tube sections containing the CuO and $CaCl_2$ were used to calculate the mass of CuO reacted and the mass of H_2O formed. It was determined that 1 molecule of H_2O was produced for every CuO reacted:

$$CuO + H_2 \rightarrow Cu + H_2O$$

30. When an electric current is passed through H_2O, the H_2O decomposes to form H_2 and O_2. Which of the following correctly represents this reaction?

F. $2 H_2 + O_2 \rightarrow 2 H_2O$

G. $H_2 + 2 O_2 \rightarrow 2 H_2O$

H. $2 H_2O \rightarrow 2 H_2 + O_2$

J. $2 H_2O \rightarrow H_2 + 2 O_2$

31. In Trial 1 of Experiment 1, after the reaction had taken place, but before the syringe plunger was unlocked, one would predict that, compared to the pressure in the syringe before the spark, the pressure in the syringe after the spark was:

A. lower, because the overall amount of gas decreased.

B. lower, because the overall amount of gas increased.

C. higher, because the overall amount of gas decreased.

D. higher, because the overall amount of gas increased.

GO ON TO THE NEXT PAGE.

32. If 50 mL of H_2 and 50 mL of O_2 were reacted using the procedure from Experiment 1, the final volume of O_2 would most likely be:

F. 0 mL.
G. 10 mL.
H. 15 mL.
J. 25 mL.

33. Which of the following assumptions about the chemical reactions in Experiment 1 were made before the final measurements were taken?

A. Excess O_2 must be present for water to form.
B. Only hot CuO will react with H_2.
C. H_2 is not absorbed by $CaCl_2$.
D. Each reaction had run to completion.

34. When nitrogen gas (N_2) is reacted with H_2 under certain conditions, the following reaction occurs:

$$N_2 + 3 H_2 \rightarrow 2 NH_3$$

Based on the results of Experiment 1, if 10 mL of N_2 were completely reacted with 40 mL of H_2 at the same pressure and temperature, what volume of H_2 would remain unreacted?

F. 0 mL
G. 10 mL
H. 20 mL
J. 30 mL

35. Which of the following, if it had occurred, would probably NOT have caused an error in interpreting the results of Experiment 2 ?

A. Using H_2 contaminated with nonreactive impurities
B. Using CuO contaminated with reactive impurities
C. H_2O escaping without being absorbed by the $CaCl_2$
D. Other reactions occurring between CuO and H_2 that produced different products

GO ON TO THE NEXT PAGE.

Passage VII

A heavy chain was positioned on a frictionless tabletop with a length of the chain, Y_0, hanging over the edge of the table, as shown in Figure 1.

Figure 1

The total length of the chain was L. When the chain was released it slid off the table, as shown in Figure 2.

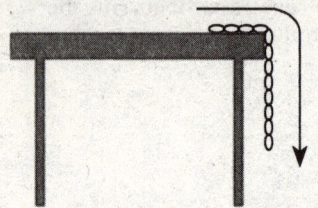

Figure 2

The *fall time* was the time required for the chain to slide completely off the table. The fall time is graphed in Figure 3 for a fixed L and various Y_0 on the surfaces of Jupiter, Earth, and the Moon. The fall time is graphed in Figure 4 for $Y_0 = 20$ cm and various L on the same 3 surfaces. The acceleration due to gravity at these surfaces is shown in Table 1.

Table 1	
Planet or moon	Acceleration due to gravity at surface of planet or moon (m/sec^2)
Jupiter	24.9
Earth	9.8
Moon	1.6

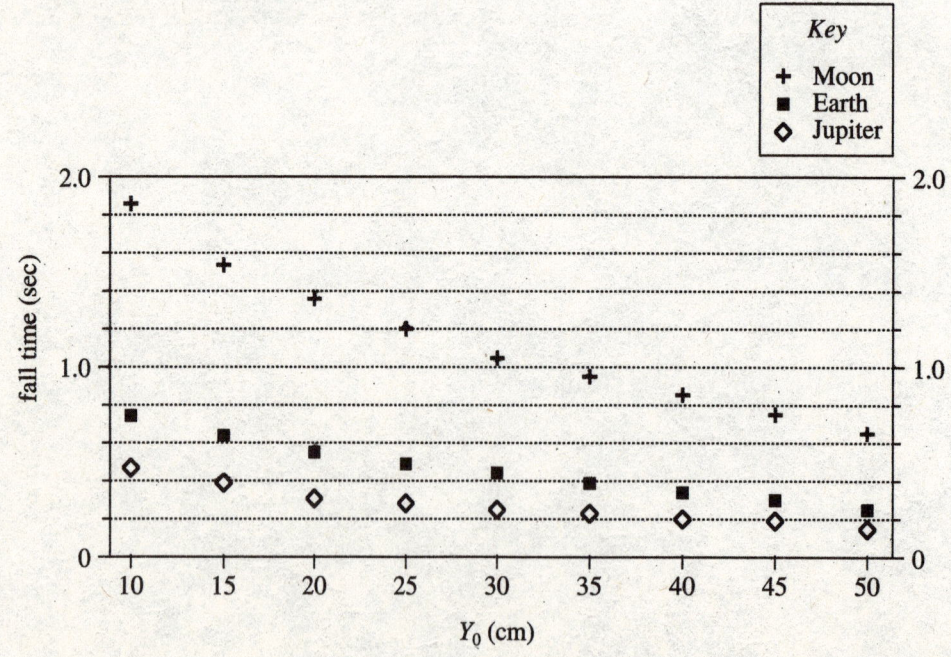

Figure 3

GO ON TO THE NEXT PAGE.

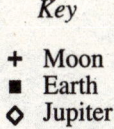

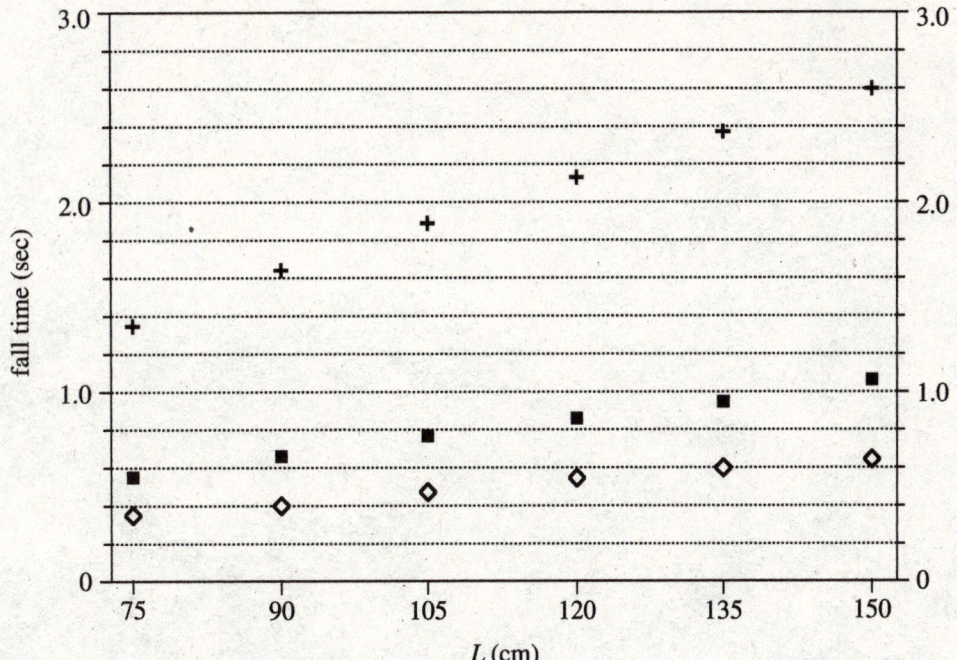

Figure 4

36. Based on Figure 3, if Y_0 were 5 cm, the fall time on the Moon would be closest to:

F. 0.4 sec.
G. 0.8 sec.
H. 1.9 sec.
J. 2.3 sec.

37. According to Figure 4, the chain with $Y_0 = 20$ cm will have a fall time on the Moon of 2.0 sec if L is approximately:

A. 75 cm.
B. 94 cm.
C. 113 cm.
D. 135 cm.

38. Before the chain was released, the horizontal length of the chain on the tabletop equaled:

F. $L + Y_0$.
G. $L - Y_0$.
H. Y_0.
J. L.

39. Suppose the chain represented in Figure 3 has a 0.7 sec fall time at Earth's surface. For the same chain to have a 0.7 sec fall time at the Moon's surface, Y_0 at the Moon's surface would have to be approximately:

A. 35 cm greater than at Earth's surface.
B. 35 cm less than at Earth's surface.
C. 47 cm greater than at Earth's surface.
D. 47 cm less than at Earth's surface.

40. The acceleration due to gravity on the surface at the planet Neptune is approximately 11.7 m/sec². Based on Figure 3, a chain's fall time, calculated for Neptune's surface and a given Y_0, would be:

F. less than its fall time at Jupiter's surface.
G. greater than its fall time at Jupiter's surface, and less than its fall time at Earth's surface.
H. greater than its fall time at Earth's surface, and less than its fall time at the Moon's surface.
J. greater than its fall time at the Moon's surface.

END OF TEST 4

STOP! DO NOT RETURN TO ANY OTHER TEST.

Practice ACT Tests

Your Signature (do not print): _____

Print Your Name Here: _____

Your Date of Birth:

☐☐ –	☐☐ –	☐☐☐☐
Month	Day	Year

Form 3WT

The **ACT®** WRITING TEST BOOKLET

You must take the multiple-choice tests before you take the Writing Test.

Directions

This is a test of your writing skills. You will have thirty (30) minutes to write an essay in English. Before you begin planning and writing your essay, read the writing prompt carefully to understand exactly what you are being asked to do. Your essay will be evaluated on the evidence it provides of your ability to express judgments by taking a position on the issue in the writing prompt; to maintain a focus on the topic throughout the essay; to develop a position by using logical reasoning and by supporting your ideas; to organize ideas in a logical way; and to use language clearly and effectively according to the conventions of standard written English.

You may use the unlined pages in this test booklet to plan your essay. These pages will not be scored. *You must write your essay in pencil on the lined pages in the answer folder.* Your writing on those lined pages will be scored. You may not need all the lined pages, but to ensure you have enough room to finish, do NOT skip lines. You may write corrections or additions neatly between the lines of your essay, but do NOT write in the margins of the lined pages. *Illegible essays cannot be scored, so you must write (or print) clearly.*

If you finish before time is called, you may review your work. Lay your pencil down immediately when time is called.

DO NOT OPEN THIS BOOKLET UNTIL TOLD TO DO SO.

P.O. BOX 168
IOWA CITY, IA 52243-0168   **ACT®**

Practice Writing Test Prompt 3

Some high schools in the United States have considered creating separate classrooms for male and female students in subjects such as mathematics and science. Some educators think separate classes will be beneficial because students will be less distracted from learning. Other educators think having separate classes for females and males will not be beneficial because it seems to support false stereotypes about differences in ability between males and females. In your opinion, should high schools create separate classes for male and female students?

In your essay, take a position on this question. You may write about either one of the two points of view given, or you may present a different point of view on this question. Use specific reasons and examples to support your position.

**Use this page to *plan* your essay.
Your work on this page will *not* be scored.**

**If you need more space to plan,
please continue on the back of this page.**

Use this page to *plan* your essay.
Your work on this page will *not* be scored.

You may wish to photocopy these sample answer document pages to respond to the practice ACT Writing Test.

Please enter the information at the right before beginning the Writing Test.

Use a soft lead No. 2 pencil only. Do NOT use a mechanical pencil, ink, ballpoint, or felt-tip pen.

WRITING TEST BOOKLET NUMBER

Print your 6-digit **Booklet Number** in the boxes at the right.

Print your 3-character **Test Form** in the boxes above and fill in the corresponding oval at the right.

WRITING TEST FORM

○ 1WT ○ 2WT ○ 3WT
○ 4WT ○ 5WT

Begin WRITING TEST here.

_____

_____

_____

_____

_____

_____

_____

_____

_____

_____

_____

_____

_____

_____

_____

_____

_____

_____

_____

_____

_____

If you need more space, please continue on the next page.

Practice ACT Tests

491

WRITING TEST

If you need more space, please continue on the next page.

WRITING TEST

_____

_____

_____

_____

_____

_____

_____

_____

_____

_____

_____

_____

_____

_____

_____

_____

_____

_____

_____

_____

_____

_____

_____

_____

_____

_____

If you need more space, please continue on the back of this page.

0876008

Practice ACT Tests

WRITING TEST

STOP here with the Writing Test.

Passage I

Question 1. The best answer is B because the subordinate (dependent) clause "If you want to work for *Fairground*," logically precedes the independent clause and provides sound sentence structure. The result is the clearest, most logical, most concise sentence to open this essay.

The best answer is NOT:

A because the phrase "Whether or not wanting to work" is unclear and confusing. The inappropriate use of the participle (*wanting*) instead of the appropriate verb form (*you want*) makes the information in this sentence ambiguous.

C because it also inappropriately uses the participle *wanting* and sets up a confusing independent-dependent clause relationship. In addition, the phrase "if you do" is unnecessarily wordy.

D because it creates an illogical and ambiguous statement. If you read the entire sentence carefully, you will see that it makes no sense to say, "you have to be willing to push yourself" if you have already decided whether or not you want to work for a literary magazine.

Question 2. The best answer is H because it provides a verb that is in agreement with the subject of this sentence. The plural verb form *are kept* is required because the subject *editors* is plural.

The best answer is NOT:

F because the verb *is kept* is singular, but a plural form is required to maintain subject-verb agreement.

G because *keeps* is also a singular verb and does not agree with the plural subject *editors*.

J because the singular verb *has been keeping* does not agree with the plural subject *editors*.

Question 3. The best answer is A because the relative pronoun *that* appropriately introduces the essential clause that begins "that we must sort, bundle, and tote." This clause modifies and appropriately follows the compound noun "subscription forms and fliers."

The best answer is NOT:

B because it creates a comma splice (two independent clauses separated only by a comma). The pronoun *these* is the subject of the second independent clause.

C because it creates a run-on, or fused, sentence (two independent clauses that run together with no conjunction or punctuation between them). The second sentence should begin with the pronoun *these*.

D because it is incorrect in the same way that **B** is. It creates a comma splice.

Question 4. The best answer is F because it creates the clearest and most logical transition to the next paragraph by referring to the process of evaluating manuscripts, a topic that is introduced in Paragraph 3 and is also the subject of Paragraph 4.

The best answer is NOT:

G because even though it refers to manuscripts, it fails to pass the "clearest . . . transition to Paragraph 4" test. The use of the falling-leaves metaphor to describe the manuscripts that are arriving at the magazine's office is never explained and makes no sense in the context of either paragraph.

H because the shift from the first-person point of view (*we*) to the second person (*you*) is illogical and distracting to the reader. In addition, this choice is a poor transition because it is a vague generalization that adds no new information to the essay.

J because it makes an illogical shift in number from the first-person plural *we* to the third-person plural *they*. Notice that the text in the first two sentences of Paragraph 3 clearly establishes the first-person viewpoint: "In August, we send letters" and "Meanwhile, we're receiving unsolicited submissions."

Question 5. The best answer is C because it correctly uses a semicolon to separate these two independent but related clauses. A semicolon is used between independent clauses unless they are joined by a conjunction (*and, but, or,* etc.).

The best answer is NOT:

A because even though it uses a semicolon to separate the clauses, it inserts an unnecessary and confusing comma between the subject *others* and the verb *are typed* in the second clause.

B because it creates a run-on, or fused, sentence. There is no punctuation or conjunction (connecting word) between the two independent clauses.

D because it inserts an unnecessary and confusing comma between the subject *others* and the verb *are typed*. In addition, the conjunction *so* creates an illogical connection between the two independent clauses.

Question 6. The best answer is H because the question asks for the "most logical and appropriate contrast in this sentence." H meets this criterion because it contrasts submission letters in which the writer expresses overconfidence ("proclaiming the writer's genius") with letters in which the writer expresses lack of confidence ("apologies for taking up our time").

The best answer is NOT:

F because it attempts to make a contrast, but the attempted contrast—letters proclaiming genius with manuscripts that are illegible—is not logical.

G because it does not make a contrast; rather, it adds a second, but unrelated, description of the types of letters that arrive on the editors' desks.

J because the problem here is similar to the problem in F. There is an attempt to make a contrast, but it is a weak contrast because the second clause of the sentence focuses on the physical appearance of the submission letters and not on their content.

Question 7. The best answer is D because the other choices do not logically fit in this paragraph and distract the reader. Leaving out the information about typesetting here provides for a more unified, better-focused paragraph.

The best answer is NOT:

A because the proposed sentence does not logically fit with the other sentences in this paragraph. Information about how the magazine will be typeset is irrelevant to the paragraph, which focuses on the submissions and editorial decisions.

B because it is incorrect for the same reason that A is. It adds irrelevant and distracting information.

C because it is incorrect for the same reasons that A and B are.

Question 8. The best answer is F because it provides the correct adjective form (*good*). Because no comparison is implied here and a predicate adjective (an adjective occurring after a linking verb) is required, *good* is the best word to use.

The best answer is NOT:

G because *more good* is not a correct comparative adjective form. *Better* would be the appropriate word to use if there were a comparison, but in this sentence, there is no comparison.

H because "positively well" is an adverb, but an adjective is required here to modify the noun *issue*.

J because *well* is an adverb and the adjective *good* is needed here. In addition, this choice is unnecessarily wordy.

Question 9. The best answer is D because it states the idea most clearly and concisely. It does not repeat the same idea twice, and it does not add unnecessary words to the sentence.

The best answer is NOT:

A because it is redundant (repeats an idea) and wordy (adds unnecessary words). The verbs *reflect* and *show* mean about the same thing, and the phrase "varied diversity" is also redundant.

B because it, too, is redundant. The verbs *reflect* and *show* mean about the same thing. In addition, the phrase "the cultural diversity of a multicultural United States" is pointlessly repetitive.

C because it is incorrect in a way that is similar to the problems in A and B. In this case, the phrase "mirror and reflect" is redundant, as is "diversity of a diverse United States."

Question 10. **The best answer is J** because the contraction *there's*, which means *there is*, is required here. Also, in the sentence's opening phrase, "Within that policy," the demonstrative pronoun *that* is appropriate because it refers to a particular thing (*policy*).

The best answer is NOT:

F because *they're* is a contraction that means *they are*, while a possessive pronoun (*their*) is needed here. One way to check to see if a contraction is misused is to read the sentence, inserting the meaning of the contraction. In this case, if we begin the sentence "Within *they are* policy," we can quickly see why **F** is an incorrect choice.

G because *their* is a possessive pronoun, but a contraction (*there's*) is required in this sentence.

H because it is incorrect in the same way that **G** is. The possessive pronoun *theirs* is mistakenly used in place of the contraction *there's*.

Question 11. **The best answer is B** because it uses the clearest language to make the writer's point. By saying that the "editors have to be ready to argue spiritedly for their choices," the writer clearly describes the process of making editorial decisions at the magazine. This choice also maintains the style and tone of this essay.

The best answer is NOT:

A because it is ambiguous and unclear. Given the text that precedes this sentence, the reader cannot know what is meant by the statement "editors have to be ready to sprint the distance favoring their choices."

C because it is incoherent. The phrase "contend the spirit of their choices" makes no sense.

D because it also results in an incoherent statement. The problem here is the misuse of the preposition *to*: "editors have to be ready to be argumentative *to* their choices." It is doubtful that the editors would be making an argument *to* something inanimate.

Question 12. **The best answer is J** because it provides appropriate subject-verb agreement and removes all unnecessary commas.

The best answer is NOT:

F because it inserts an unnecessary and confusing comma between the subject *editorial production* and the predicate *begins*.

G because the plural verb *begin* does not agree with the singular subject of this sentence (*editorial production*).

H because it places an unnecessary and confusing comma between the predicate verb *begin* and its direct object (*editorial production*).

Question 13. **The best answer is A** because it provides the required punctuation. The issues are "of the year," so the apostrophe with the singular noun—"the *year's* issues"—is appropriate.

The best answer is NOT:

B because the word *years* lacks the necessary apostrophe.

C because it is incorrect in the same way that B is. The apostrophe in *years* is missing. Also, in this sentence a comma after *issues* is needed to avoid ambiguity.

D because an apostrophe in the plural *issues* is not appropriate.

Question 14. **The best answer is J** because it is the clearest, most logical, and most concise wording for this sentence. It provides a clear time marker ("Just after New Year's Day") for the action described in the main clause ("the first issue is mailed to a typesetter").

The best answer is NOT:

F because it adds information that is irrelevant to this sentence and the paragraph. Information suggesting that "It may snow just after New Year's Day" is not relevant to process of getting the magazines ready for subscribers.

G because it, too, contains irrelevant information about the weather. It is also unnecessarily wordy.

H because it is unclear and confusing. The phrase "Shortly thereafter New Year's Day" is not grammatical.

Question 15. **The best answer is D** because it makes the paragraph coherent and concise. Adding information at this point about there being three issues' worth of material would disrupt the flow of this narrative about putting together an issue.

The best answer is NOT:

A because it is redundant (that is, it repeats a statement). The first sentence in Paragraph 5 explains that there is "enough material to fill three issues," and there is no need to restate this.

B because it is incorrect for the same reason that A is. It is repetitive. This same information has already appeared in the first sentence of this paragraph.

C because it is incorrect in the same way that A and B are. Adding the sentence here would create a redundancy.

Passage II

Question 16. **The best answer is H** because it uses the clearest, most concise language for this description. The phrase "a steep, pine-covered slope" provides a clear and precise image with no unnecessary words.

The best answer is NOT:

F because it contains a redundancy. (It repeats information.) The word *wooded* doesn't add any information that's not already provided by the word *pine-covered*.

G because it also creates a redundancy. In this choice, the hill is described as both *steep* and *sloping*. Because these words have similar meanings, the sentence is unnecessarily repetitious.

J because it, too, is redundant. The phrase "a steep, slanting, pine-covered slope" is wordy and repetitious. The words *steep*, *slanting*, and *slope* all provide the same information for the reader.

Question 17. **The best answer is A** because the verb in the subordinate, or dependent, clause is in the past tense (*noticed*) and logically follows the verb (*was searching*) in the main clause.

The best answer is NOT:

B because it is not clear who is doing the *noticing*. Because the dependent clause has no subject, the reader does not know if the hunter or the elk was "noticing an unusual track."

C because the dependent clause, which begins with *when*, has neither a subject nor a verb. The result is an unclear, illogical statement.

D because it is incorrect in the same way that B is. The reader does not know who is *seeing*.

Question 18. **The best answer is H** because it provides the correct adverb and adjective (*newly fallen*) combination to describe the *snow*. An adverb modifies a verb or an adjective; an adjective generally modifies a noun. In this sentence, the adverb *newly* modifies the adjective *fallen*, which then modifies the noun *snow*.

The best answer is NOT:

F because the comparative adjective *fresher* is inappropriate because no comparison is suggested in the sentence.

G because although the adverb *freshly* is used properly, the word *fallened* is not grammatically acceptable. The correct past participle verb form (which can be used as an adjective) is *fallen*.

J because while *falling* is an appropriate way to describe *snow*, the comparative adjective *newer* is inappropriate because no comparison is suggested in this sentence.

Question 19. **The best answer is A** because it provides the correct verb form ("might have been made") for this subordinate (dependent) clause.

The best answer is NOT:

B because "might of been made" is not an acceptable verb form, although "might've been made" is. *Of* is not an auxiliary (helping) verb.

C because it is incorrect in the same way that B is. "Could *of* been made" is not an acceptable verb form.

D because "could been made" has no auxiliary (helping) verb and is therefore not an acceptable verb form.

Question 20. **The best answer is H.** Notice that the question asks for the word or phrase that provides "the most specific transition." Of the four choices, "a wolf" is the only one that is specific and precise. This choice logically and effectively leads in to Paragraph 2, which focuses on wolf sightings.

The best answer is NOT:

F because it is vague and unspecific and does not provide a reasonable transition to the paragraph that follows.

G because it is unspecific and illogical. To say that the hunter thought the unusual track "might have been made by someone else" is so obvious as not to need saying.

J because even though "a large animal" might be logical in this context, this choice does not provide "the most specific transition to the next paragraph."

Question 21. **The best answer is A** because the absence of punctuation in the opening clause of this sentence creates the clearest and most understandable sentence.

The best answer is NOT:

B because placing an unnecessary comma between the subject *wolves* and the adverb *supposedly* introduces a pause that makes this sentence difficult to understand.

C because it inserts an unnecessary and confusing comma, this time between the adverb *supposedly* and the verb it modifies, *disappeared*.

D because it places an apostrophe after the plural noun *wolves'*. An apostrophe here signals that this is a possessive noun, but in this context there is no possession.

Question 22. The best answer is G because it appropriately sets off the parenthetical phrase "most of them filed by hunters" with dashes. Often, a phrase such as this one is set off from the main clause with commas, but dashes will also do the job.

The best answer is NOT:

F because it provides one comma only and therefore does not set off or separate this phrase from the rest of the sentence.

H because instead of using two commas (or two dashes), it wrongly uses a semicolon after the noun *reports*.

J because the verb participle form "having been filing" is unacceptable. A correct form here would have been "having been filed."

Question 23. The best answer is D because, of the four choices, it best strengthens "the assertion that wolves are present in northwest Wyoming." That "many rangers" heard the cries of wolf cubs does provide evidence that wolves are present in the area.

The best answer is NOT:

A because it offers an assumption that does not provide reasonable evidence to support the existence of wolves in the region.

B because it suggests an action (tipping over garbage cans) that could easily be attributed to other wild animals, such as bears or raccoons, or vandalizing humans for that matter.

C because it describes one individual's imagined sighting. It does not provide solid evidence that wolves were actually seen.

Question 24. The best answer is F because the two coordinate elements in this sentence (*trapping* and *poisoning*) are parallel. Parallelism means that sentence elements that have the same function—in this case, *trapping* and *poisoning*—share the same grammatical form. Here, they are both present participles (verb forms ending in *-ing*).

The best answer is NOT:

G because the sentence elements in the phrase "through traps and poisoning" are not parallel. In addition, the phrase "through traps" is unclear in this context.

H because it, too, lacks parallelism. The two coordinate elements do not share the same grammatical form.

J because it is incorrect in the same way as G and H are.

Question 25. The best answer is **C** because providing information that the wolves were nearly wiped out "by the turn of the century" is a logical conclusion to Paragraph 3, which describes how the wolves were eliminated. **C** also provides a logical link to Paragraph 4, which explains that wolves "are now classified as an endangered species."

The best answer is NOT:

A because it is a vague generalization that fails to provide a strong conclusion to Paragraph 3 and doesn't offer any information that creates a link to Paragraph 4.

B because it focuses on "wolfers" and not on the systematic elimination of the wolves.

D because it provides a weak if not illogical transition to Paragraph 4. It's hard to follow the connection between the gray wolf being "a majestic animal . . . not easily trapped" and wolves becoming an endangered species.

Question 26. The best answer is **J** because it is idiomatic, and it provides the wording that logically introduces the subordinate (dependent) clause in this sentence. If you read the independent clause carefully, you will see that this is the only choice that provides a clear meaning. The wolves began migrating from Canada *into* Minnesota.

The best answer is NOT:

F because it is unclear and confusing. The use of the phrase "after which" to introduce the dependent clause suggests that "the animals began migrating from Canada" *after* they were "now classified as an endangered species."

G because the statement "from which the animals began migrating from Canada" is confusing. The reader cannot tell where the migration began.

H because it is incorrect in a way similar to that of **F**. This statement is illogical because it implies that "the animals began migrating from Canada" at the same time (*when*) they were "now classified as an endangered species."

Question 27. The best answer is **B** because the absence of commas in this sentence provides the clearest statement.

The best answer is NOT:

A because the unnecessary commas that set off the subject and verb in this sentence confuse the reader into thinking that "biologists decided" is a parenthetical or nonessential clause, which is clearly not the case here.

C because it inserts an unnecessary and confusing comma between the verb *decided* and the infinitive phrase "to look for the wolves themselves."

D because it inserts an unnecessary and confusing comma between the subject *biologists* and the predicate verb *decided*.

Question 28. The best answer is **J** because it makes the three verbs in this sentence (*have flown*, *[have] ridden*, and *[have] thrown*) parallel. The auxiliary (helping) verb *have* is implied in the last two verbs in the series. Parallelism means that sentence elements that have the same function—in this case, *flown, ridden, thrown*—share the same grammatical form.

The best answer is NOT:

F because it has faulty parallelism. In this series of compound verbs, *throwing* is not parallel with *have flown* and *[have] ridden*.

G because it, too, has faulty parallelism. Here, *throw* is not parallel with *have flown* and *[have] ridden*.

H because it is ungrammatical. In this case, *[have] threw* is an incorrect verb form.

Question 29. The best answer is **A** because it results in the clearest statement by using prepositions that are idiomatically correct in this context ("in hopes of communicating").

The best answer is NOT:

B because it creates an ambiguous and confusing statement. Read the phrase carefully: "moaning howls to hope to communicate with the wolves" suggests that the howls have the ability to hope. The infinitives *to hope* and *to communicate* are used when prepositional phrases are better suited.

C because it, too, uses an infinitive (*to communicate*) when a prepositional phrase is more appropriate.

D because it is unclear and illogical. The phrase "in hope's communication" makes no sense because *hope* does not possess the ability to communicate.

Question 30. The best answer is **G** because inserting it right after Sentence 2 in Paragraph 2 is the most logical placement for this new information. Sentence 2 mentions the issue of "possible wolf kills." Adding information that "wolves rarely attack humans" logically follows.

The best answer is NOT:

F because the main focus of Paragraph 1 is a hunter noticing an unusual track. It would not make sense to follow this up with information about whether or not wolves attack humans.

H because the information in the new sentence does not logically follow information about "wolf sightings," which is the topic of Sentence 4.

J because it results in a poorly organized paragraph. The two sentences in Paragraph 3 logically follow each other. Inserting another sentence on a different topic here would interrupt the flow of the paragraph.

Passage III

Question 31. The best answer is D because it sets up a logical relationship between the clauses in this sentence. The subordinate (dependent) clause "while Dr. Shinichi Suzuki was teaching violin at the Imperial Conservatory in Japan" clarifies a time relationship. It shows that "a father brought in his . . . son for lessons" during the time that Dr. Suzuki was teaching.

The best answer is NOT:

A because it creates a comma splice (two independent clauses separated only by a comma). The phrase "a father" is the subject of the second clause.

B because it is incorrect in the same way that A is. It creates a comma splice.

C because there is no logical referent to the relative pronoun *that*.

Question 32. The best answer is F. Notice that the question asks you to choose the sentence that shows that Dr. Suzuki "did not feel prepared to teach music at the preschool level." F is the only choice that does this because it indicates that Suzuki had never before taught a four-year-old.

The best answer is NOT:

G because although it states that Suzuki's students "were between seventeen and twenty-five," this choice does not say that Suzuki felt unprepared to teach someone younger.

H because it indicates that Suzuki "deliberately agreed to accept" a four-year-old, so it would be illogical to assume that he "did not feel prepared" to teach at the preschool level.

J because it makes no reference to Suzuki's lack of preparedness to teach a preschool music student.

Question 33. The best answer is A because it provides the clearest, most logical transition from the preceding sentence to the idea expressed in this new sentence. The statement in this sentence follows logically from the statement in the preceding sentence without the help of a transitional word or phrase.

The best answer is NOT:

B because the transitional word *Nevertheless* sets up a contrast between this sentence and the preceding sentence. However, the statement in this sentence does not contrast with or oppose the statement in the preceding sentence, so this creates an illogical transition.

C because it is incorrect in the same way that B is. The transitional word *however* sets up an opposition between ideas, but no opposition exists.

D because it is incorrect because the transitional word *Instead* sets up an opposition that is illogical and nonexistent.

Question 34. The best answer is G because it provides the clearest, most concise wording for this sentence.

The best answer is NOT:

F because it is unnecessarily wordy. The phrase "or may not" adds nothing to the meaning of this sentence and should be deleted.

H because it repeats information to no good effect. In the phrase "important valuable insights," the adjectives *important* and *valuable* mean about the same thing. Besides, it's hard to imagine how a "process could suggest . . . insights."

J because the phrase "might indeed provide one with valuable insights" is an unnecessarily wordy and stilted phrasing that is inconsistent with the style and tone of the rest of the essay.

Question 35. The best answer is C because it provides the clearest sentence, one that is free of errors in sentence structure and logic. In this sentence *Suzuki* is the subject because he is one who has completed the action (*understood*).

The best answer is NOT:

A because the prepositional phrase at the end of the sentence, "by Suzuki," is misplaced. This misplacement implausibly suggests that Suzuki developed "a child's language." In addition, the passive voice ("Immersion was already understood") is ineffectively used here.

B because using the pronoun *that* in the phrase "*that* immersion" is confusing, whether one reads it as a relative pronoun (introducing a relative clause) or a demonstrative pronoun (like *this* or *those*).

D because it contains a dangling modifier. When a modifying phrase introduces a sentence, the word that the phrase modifies should follows. In this sentence the introductory phrase "A key to a child's development" is not followed by the word it modifies, which is *immersion*. Placing the proper noun *Suzuki* after the phrase creates a dangling modifier.

Question 36. The best answer is J because it appropriately uses the apostrophe with a plural noun to signal possession (*Babies'*). You know that *Babies'* must be plural because the sentence later refers to "the children," which is also plural. *Babies'* needs to apostrophe to show that the "first attempts" belong to the babies.

The best answer is NOT:

F because the apostrophe after *Babies* is missing.

G because the singular *Baby's* does not agree with the plural noun *children* that appears later in the sentence.

H because it lacks the necessary apostrophe and forms the plural incorrectly.

Question 37. The best answer is D because the possessive plural pronoun *their* agrees with its plural referent *children*.

The best answer is NOT:

A because "his or her" are singular pronouns and therefore do not agree with the preceding plural noun *children*.

B because the possessive noun *one's* is also singular and does not agree with the preceding plural noun *children*.

C because *there* is an adverb used to indicate place, which is clearly not what is called for here. The possessive pronoun *their* is required.

Question 38. The best answer is G. Notice that the question asks you to connect the information in Sentence 4 with the information in Sentence 6. Sentence 6 refers to Suzuki's "philosophy of music education." This philosophy came from Suzuki's "unique approach to violin studies," which is explained in this sentence and which connects back to the information in Sentence 4.

The best answer is NOT:

F because it makes no reference to music or music education, so it fails to provide an effective link to Sentence 6.

H because it is too vague and, like F, does not refer directly to Suzuki's developing a "philosophy of music education."

J because it is unnecessarily wordy and, at the same time, so vague as to be meaningless. In this way, it fails as an effective connecting sentence.

Question 39. The best answer is D because this information about infant development is not relevant to the topic of this paragraph, which is the development of musical ability in children. Adding this sentence would only distract the reader.

The best answer is NOT:

A because information about babies' hand and eye movements does not logically follow from the statement in Sentence 1 about "a child's language development."

B because it does not logically fit at this, or any, point in the paragraph.

C because information about coordinating "hand and eye movements" does not logically follow from the statement in Sentence 3.

Question 40. The best answer is F because it separates two complete, independent clauses with the appropriate punctuation (a period).

The best answer is NOT:

G because it creates faulty subordination. It inserts the relative pronoun *that*, which creates an awkward and flawed sentence.

H because it is incorrect in the same way that G is. There are two independent clauses here with a subject and predicate for each. Inserting the pronoun *that* makes the second clause a subordinate (dependent) clause.

J because it creates a comma splice (two independent clauses separated by a comma). Independent clauses should be separated by a period or a semicolon.

Question 41. The best answer is D because it provides a clear, concise statement that is free from redundancies (repeated information).

The best answer is NOT:

A because it is redundant. The phrase *at a future date* means the same thing as *later*, so it should be omitted from the sentence.

B because it is incorrect in the same way that A is. The words *subsequently* and *later* are unnecessarily repetitious.

C because it, too, is redundant. In this case, *before long* and *later* have essentially the same function.

Question 42. The best answer is F because the use of the present tense (*reward*) is consistent with the use of the present tense elsewhere in this paragraph.

The best answer is NOT:

G because it creates an illogical tense shift from the present (the verb *provide* in the first clause in this sentence) to the past (*rewarded*).

H because it also creates an illogical tense shift—from the present to the past perfect (*had rewarded*).

J because a present tense verb (*reward*) is required, not a present participle (*rewarding*).

Question 43. The best answer is C because it is the clearest, most understandable phrase to introduce this sentence. The phrase "For many decades" provides a specific time frame for Suzuki's work.

The best answer is NOT:

A because it is vague and meaningless. The phrase "for a long time" does not give the reader any sense of the true time involved.

B because it is confusing, vague, and meaningless. The phrase "Recurrently with time" defies explanation.

D because the phrase "For scores of years then" is imprecise. In addition, the word *then* suggests a relationship with preceding information, but no such relationship exists.

Question 44. The best answer is **J** because the two coordinate elements in this sentence ("*to develop* musical talent" and "*to experience* the joys of achievement") are parallel. Parallelism means that sentence elements that serve the same function share the same grammatical form. In this case both *to develop* and *to experience* are infinitive verb forms.

The best answer is NOT:

F because the sentence elements do not have a parallel structure. The phrase "for the joys of achievement" is not parallel with "to develop musical talent."

G because it, too, has faulty parallelism, which confuses the reader.

H because it is incorrect in the same way that F and G are.

Question 45. The best answer is **C** because the sentence elements are ordered in a way that creates the clearest, most understandable statement, and the modifiers are placed so that they modify the appropriate element.

The best answer is NOT:

A because the clause "who hear the beautiful music" is misplaced. This phrase modifies and should be placed after the noun *All*, which is the subject of this sentence.

B because once again the clause "who hear the beautiful music" is not placed next to the element that it modifies. The correct placement would be "All who hear the beautiful music."

D because the relative pronoun phrase "of which" does not relate or connect the clause "his teaching inspired" to the preceding noun phrase "the beautiful music."

Passage IV

Question 46. The best answer is **J** because the sentence elements are ordered in a way that creates the clearest, most understandable statement. In addition, the modifiers are placed so that they modify the appropriate element.

The best answer is NOT:

F because the adverb *recently* is misplaced and creates confusion. The narrator cannot reasonably propose that you may "visit our nation's capital" in the future if that action has already happened in the past (*recently*).

G because once again *recently* is misplaced. This sentence results in an illogical statement: "If you recently visit our nation's capital." This makes no sense in terms of time because *recently* is a reference to a past event, but the verb *visit* is in the present tense.

H because it is incorrect in the same way that G is. The phrase "If you visit recently" is implausible.

Question 47. **The best answer is C** because it clearly answers the terms of the question by naming specific monuments in the nation's capital. Pay close attention to the question, which asks for "the clearest examples."

The best answer is NOT:

A because it is vague and unspecific and therefore does not provide the clear examples asked for in the question.

B because it is yet another vague and imprecise statement. The wording "the ones that are readily recognizable" does not provide clear examples.

D because "structures that potentially add to the history of the capital" could be any of hundreds of buildings in the nation's capital.

Question 48. **The best answer is F** because it provides the transitional word that most effectively links the information in this sentence to the information in the preceding sentence. *Nevertheless* indicates that the writer is going to oppose or contrast something from his or her prior statement. In this case, the writer is saying that even though the famous memorials were inspirational, a trip on an expressway was more vivid.

The best answer is NOT:

G because *Therefore* is used to show a cause-effect relationship, not a contrasting one.

H because the phrase "As a result" is used to link cause and effect, but in these two sentences no cause-effect relationship exists.

J because the phrase "In addition" indicates that the writer will provide additional information on the same topic, but in this sentence, the writer is shifting topics.

Question 49. **The best answer is B** because it provides the clearest, most concise, and most understandable statement. It avoids redundancies or confusing word choices.

The best answer is NOT:

A because it is redundant. (It repeats information.) The words *frenzied* and *crazy* imply the same thing in this context. The phrase "crazy lunacy" is also redundant.

C because it, too, is redundant. The adjectives *modern* and *contemporary* have the same meaning.

D because in the phrase "confused disarray," the adjective *confused* could be deleted without changing the meaning of the sentence. The word *disarray* already suggests confusion.

Question 50. The best answer is **G** because the third-person singular pronoun *it* agrees with its singular antecedent *expressway*.

The best answer is NOT:

F because it lacks pronoun-antecedent agreement. The pronoun *they* is plural but the antecedent *expressway* is singular.

H because it creates an illogical and confusing tense shift from the present tense in the surrounding text to the past tense (*was*).

J because it lacks pronoun-antecedent agreement, and it makes an inappropriate tense shift.

Question 51. The best answer is **B** because it uses the correct comparative adjective form (*busier*).

The best answer is NOT:

A because *more busier* is an inappropriate and redundant form. The word *more* and the ending -*er* both signal a comparison.

C because it is incorrect in the same way that **A** is.

D because it uses the superlative form (*busiest*) when the comparative is called for here. Also, the wording *most busiest* is a redundant and incorrect form.

Question 52. The best answer is **H** because it creates a coherent sentence that is structurally sound. The subordinate (dependent) clause in this sentence has a compound verb ("extends . . . and intersects"). In this choice, these two verbs appropriately function in the same way.

The best answer is NOT:

F because the two verbs are not parallel. The participle *intersecting* does not function in the same way as the verb *extends*.

G because the conjunction (connecting word) *but* signals a contrast. However, the fact that the beltway "intersects with many lesser highways" does not contrast with "it extends through two populous states."

J because it results in a confusing statement. It is nonsensical to say that "it extends through two populous states . . . and [extends] with many lesser highways."

Question 53. The best answer is **B** because it provides the correct punctuation for this sentence. A colon is best here because it links two independent clauses where the second clause defines the first clause ("It's also fast").

The best answer is NOT:

A because it creates a comma splice (two independent clauses separated by a comma).

C because the apostrophe in *Its* is missing. An apostrophe is needed here to show that *It's* is a contraction meaning *It is*, not a possessive pronoun.

D because it, too, uses the possessive pronoun *Its* when the contraction *It's* is required. In addition, it creates a comma splice.

Question 54. The best answer is J because it avoids unnecessary punctuation and creates the clearest sentence.

The best answer is NOT:

F because it adds two confusing and unnecessary commas. There should not be a comma between *one* and *redeeming* because *one* describes *redeeming feature*. With the comma, the sentence reads as though there is only one feature, when in fact there is "one redeeming feature." In addition, there is a second inappropriate comma between the adjective *redeeming* and the noun *feature*.

G because here, as in F, the comma between the adjective *redeeming* and the noun *feature* is inappropriate and distracting.

H because in this case, the unnecessary comma is between the noun *beltway* and the verb *is*.

Question 55. The best answer is C. The writer should not make this addition because the proposed sentence takes the reader away from the main topic, which is the Washington Beltway, not loop highways in other parts of the country.

The best answer is NOT:

A because it recommends adding a sentence that is irrelevant to this essay.

B because the proposed new sentence does not help the reader "to better understand what the beltway looks like."

D because although this answer does state that the proposed sentence not be added, the reason for not adding the sentence is inaccurate. The proposed sentence *is* consistent in style and tone with the rest of the essay.

Question 56. The best answer is G because it is the most effective way to introduce the topic of this new paragraph. It gives background on the narrator's initial attitude toward using the beltway, and the actions described in the paragraph arise out of that attitude.

The best answer is NOT:

F because it repeats information given earlier in the essay, and it fails to show why the narrator would ask "for help with alternate, more scenic routes."

H because it has no connection to the ideas expressed in this paragraph.

J because it introduces a new topic and idea, but the rest of the paragraph does not in any way support this information.

Question 57. The best answer is C. Because the narrator had hoped to drive scenic routes, as evidenced by information provided earlier in this paragraph, it makes sense that the narrator would be unhappy about learning "to navigate this expressway."

The best answer is NOT:

A because the narrator might have been gracious with friends, but it is hard to imagine that someone "graciously" learned to drive on the expressway when he or she found such highways so unpleasant.

B because although the transitional word *Carefully* might fit here, the use of the word *however* is illogical in this context. It suggests that the narrator's careful driving is somehow at odds with something else.

D because the phrase "In fact" is generally used to emphasize something that was stated previously, which is not the case here.

Question 58. The best answer is H because the past tense (*approached*) is consistent with the surrounding text. Past tense is appropriate here because the events have already taken place.

The best answer is NOT:

F because the use of the present tense (*approach*) is an illogical shift from the past tense.

G because it inserts a confusing and unnecessary comma after the pronoun *it*.

J because it creates an illogical tense shift from past to present, as F does, and it inserts a confusing and unnecessary comma after the pronoun *it*, as G does.

Question 59. The best answer is D because it avoids the repetition of a question and provides for the clearest and most concise paragraph.

The best answer is NOT:

A because it is redundant. The first two questions in this series—"Was it congested?" and "Overcrowded?"—mean essentially the same thing, so the essay would be more effective if one of them were deleted.

B because it is incorrect for the same reason that A is. In this case, "Was it congested?" and "Jammed with cars?" mean the same thing.

C because it, too, is redundant. Here the questions "Proceeding smoothly?" and "Moving freely?" have about the same meaning.

Question 60. The best answer is **F** because it is the most effective conclusion for the essay, and it logically follows the preceding sentence. The narrator may not have learned much history, but by driving on the beltway, he or she did learn "to merge in traffic."

The best answer is NOT:

G because it does not logically follow the preceding sentence. In fact, **G** contradicts the preceding sentence. Learning about the Washington Monument and the Jefferson Memorial *is* learning about history.

H because it strays completely from the topic of the essay, which is the Washington Beltway, not Washington's landmarks.

J because an effective concluding sentence should reinforce the ideas presented in the essay, and this sentence clearly fails to mention the narrator's experience with the beltway.

Passage V

Question 61. The best answer is **C** because it provides a complete sentence that is structurally sound and consistent in verb tense with the rest of the paragraph.

The best answer is NOT:

A because it creates a sentence fragment. There is no predicate verb, so the sentence is not complete.

B because it makes a tense shift from present to past tense. Notice that the essay begins in the present tense (*look*). Changing to the past tense (*was*) in the second sentence is illogical and confusing.

D because it creates a sentence fragment. Like **A**, it has no predicate.

Question 62. The best answer is **G** because it appropriately and consistently uses the present tense to describe an event that is happening in the present time ("Beans hang . . . and squash vines sprawl").

The best answer is NOT:

F because it makes an illogical and confusing shift from the present tense (*hang*) to the past perfect tense (*had sprawled*).

H because it makes an illogical and confusing shift from the present tense (*hang*) to the past tense (*sprawled*).

J because it makes an illogical shift from the present tense to the past conditional.

Question 63. The best answer is **A** because the absence of commas here creates the clearest and most understandable sentence.

The best answer is NOT:

B because it inserts a confusing and unnecessary comma between the subject of the sentence (*chaos*) and the predicate verb (*is*).

C because it inserts an unnecessary comma and sets off the prepositional phrase "of scientific research" as if it were not essential. If you read this sentence without this phrase, you discover that it is essential to the meaning.

D because it wrongly inserts a colon between the subject *chaos* and the verb *is*. A colon is used to link the words that follow it to the words that precede it, which is clearly not the case here.

Question 64. The best answer is **G** because the verb phrase "modeled on" is idiomatically correct English. Jane Mt. Pleasant's gardens are designed to resemble and imitate those grown by the Iroquois. The phrase "modeled on" most clearly conveys this idea.

The best answer is NOT:

F because the phrase "modeled for" is confusing and illogical. Mt. Pleasant's gardens were not modeled *for* the Iroquois gardens.

H because the verb phrase "modeled as" does not adequately convey the idea that Mt. Pleasant used the Iroquois gardens as her model.

J because it is unclear and illogical. It makes no sense to say that Mt. Pleasant's gardens were modeled *by* Iroquois gardens.

Question 65. The best answer is **A** because it provides the most logical organization for the sentences in this paragraph. Information about "the data the gardens are yielding" is a direct reference to the "scientific research" in Sentence 4. Placing Sentence 6 anywhere before Sentence 4 would create confusion for the reader.

The best answer is NOT:

B because it would be confusing to refer to the data before the point had been made that scientific research on the gardens was under way.

C because it is incorrect for the same reason that **B** is. Placing Sentence 6 after Sentence 2 in this paragraph would not provide a logical order.

D because it is incorrect for the same reason that **B** and **C** are.

Question 66. The best answer is **G** because it is the most effective link to the sentence that follows. The sentence that follows supports Mt. Pleasant's assertion that her concern about some of modern agriculture's practices "is shared by others." The others are the "many farmers and agronomists."

The best answer is NOT:

F because while Mt. Pleasant's education (her Ph.D. degree) might be relevant to the essay in general, this information does not lead into the sentence that follows and therefore does not accomplish the writer's purpose.

H because, like **F**, this information has some connection to the topic, but it is not relevant at this point in the essay, and it provides a poor transition to the sentence that follows it.

J because this information does not effectively lead into the statement about the "farmers and agronomists" in the next sentence.

Question 67. The best answer is **D** because it results in the clearest, most concise statement, and it avoids repeating information.

The best answer is NOT:

A because it creates a redundancy. The phrase "in the last few years" repeats information given earlier in the sentence ("the recent boom").

B because it is redundant. The words "of late" and "recent" repeat information for no good reason or purpose.

C because it is incorrect in the same way that **A** and **B** are.

Question 68. The best answer is **G** because the singular verb *has come* agrees with its singular subject *boom*. Notice that in this sentence the subject *boom* is separated from the predicate *has come* by a prepositional phrase and a parenthetical phrase.

The best answer is NOT:

F because the plural verb *have come* does not agree with the singular subject *boom*.

H because *are come* is not a proper verb form.

J because the plural verb *come* does not agree with the singular subject *boom*.

Question 69. The best answer is **A** because it reinforces the conclusions presented in the essay—that Iroquois farming methods offer solutions to the problems created by herbicides and pesticides. It also creates an effective transition to the next paragraph, which explains what the Iroquois farming methods are.

The best answer is NOT:

B because while it does offer some support for the preceding sentence, it is not an effective transition to the information about Iroquois farming methods.

C because although it does mention "certain farming practices . . . by the Iroquois people," it is a vague generalization when compared to **A**. This vagueness makes it an weak concluding sentence for this paragraph and a weak lead-in to the next paragraph.

D because it is a poor conclusion—the phrase "these social problems" is an inaccurate and imprecise description of the problems with modern agriculture—and because it does not provide a logical link to the next paragraph.

Question 70. The best answer is **J** because it ensures a consistency of verb tense in this essay. The present tense (*is*) in this sentence is consistent and logical with the present tense (*begins*) in the first sentence of this paragraph.

The best answer is NOT:

F because it inappropriately shifts from the present tense (*begins*) to the past perfect tense (*had been*).

G because it creates an illogical statement and confuses the reader with regard to time. It makes no sense to say, "Later, soil has been mounded." The reader is confused about when the action occurred.

H because it inappropriately and illogically shifts from the present tense (*begins*) to the past tense (*was*).

Question 71. The best answer is A. Pay close attention to the stated question, because it tells you that the best answer to this question is actually the *worst* answer. You are looking for the choice that is *not* an acceptable alternative to the underlined portion. **A** is not acceptable because it creates an illogical cause-effect relationship. Soil is mounded around stalks to enhance drainage and warming, not "*because of* enhancing drainage and warming."

The best answer is NOT:

B because it is an acceptable alternative to the underlined portion. Here, the cause-effect relationship is logical.

C because it is an acceptable and logical alternative. Mounding the soil does enhance drainage.

D because it is an acceptable alternative. This choice creates two complete sentences that explain the cause-effect relationship. Mounding the soil is the cause; drainage and warmth are the effect.

Question 72. The best answer is J. Once again, pay close attention to the stated question, because it tells you that the best answer here is actually the *worst* answer. You are looking for the choice that is *not* an acceptable alternative to the underlined portion. **J** is not acceptable because it results in a run-on sentence (because there is no punctuation and/or conjunction between two independent clauses).

The best answer is NOT:

F because it is an acceptable alternative to the underlined portion. In this sentence, the two independent clauses are appropriately separated by a comma and a conjunction. Here, *while* functions as a coordinating conjunction.

G because it is an acceptable alternative. The two sentences are separated by a period.

H because it is an acceptable alternative. A semicolon is appropriate punctuation to use to separate two independent clauses.

Question 73. The best answer is C because it provides the most relevant information to the essay as a whole. The phrase "three sisters" refers to the three vegetables corn, beans, and squash and the Iroquois method of planting them so that they help each other to grow. In addition, **C** clears up confusion that might otherwise result from the reference in the last paragraph to "the Iroquois 'three-sisters' system."

The best answer is NOT:

A because it fails to provide meaningful information and makes a confusing shift to the second person (*your*).

B because vegetarian cooking has no relevance to this essay, which focuses on Iroquois farming methods.

D because it is so vague that it is almost meaningless.

Question 74. **The best answer is F** because the absence of punctuation here results in the clearest, most understandable sentence.

The best answer is NOT:

G because it inserts an unnecessary comma between the subject *system* and the predicate verb *is*. A pause here would confuse the reader.

H because it inserts a comma between the verb *is* and the relative clause that functions as a predicate noun. This comma interferes with the flow of ideas in this sentence.

J because it inserts an inappropriate and distracting colon between the verb *is* and the relative clause functioning as a predicate noun.

Question 75. **The best answer is B.** Pay close attention to this question, which asks if this essay could be said to provide an example of how the past can provide information to people today. Because this essay shows how Iroquois farming practices from the past offer ways to improve problems in farming today, it does provide such an example.

The best answer is NOT:

A because its reason is off the mark. This essay does not address "high-tech methods of modern farming."

C because it contains faulty logic. Just because Mt. Pleasant is a practicing agronomist, that fact does not prevent her from having ties to the past.

D because it distorts the essay. The focus of the essay is on how old farming methods can be applied to modern agriculture; it does not focus on "the planting of cover crops."

MATHEMATICS · PRACTICE TEST 3 · EXPLANATORY ANSWERS

Question 1. **The correct answer is E.** If you knew the unknown score, you could check to see that it was correct by adding up all 5 scores, dividing by 5 to get the average, and checking to see that the result was 90. Let x be the unknown score. Then the sum of all of the scores is $85 + 95 + 93 + 80 + x$, and the average is $\frac{85 + 95 + 93 + 80 + x}{5}$. For the average to be 90, that means $\frac{85 + 95 + 93 + 80 + x}{5} = 90$. To solve, you can multiply both sides by 5 to get $85 + 95 + 93 + 80 + x = 450$, and then subtract 353 from both sides to get $x = 97$.

If you chose B, that is closest to the average of the four given scores, $\frac{85 + 95 + 93 + 80}{4} = 88.25$. To raise an average of 88.25 up to 90 would take a raise of about 2 points, but a single new score of 92 (answer choice D) would not raise the average much. You can check your answer to see that it is too low: $\frac{85 + 95 + 93 + 80 + 92}{5} = \frac{445}{5} = 89$. You can check any of the answer choices to see whether it is correct.

Question 2. **The correct answer is H.** When $g = 2$, the value of $g \cdot (g + 1)^2$ is $2 \cdot (2 + 1) = 2 \cdot (3)^2 = 2 \cdot 9 = 18$.

If you chose F, you might have thought of $(g + 1)^2$ as equivalent to the alternate expression $g^2 + 1^2$. But, when $g = 2$, the original has the value $(2 + 1)^2 = (3)^2 = 9$, while the alternate has the value $2^2 + 1^2 = 5$.

Question 3. **The correct answer is D.** Company A sells at $15 for 60 pens, which is $\frac{\$15}{60}$ per pen. That reduces to $\frac{\$1}{4}$, or $0.25 per pen. Company B sells at $8 for 40 pens, which is $\frac{\$8}{40} = \frac{\$1}{5} = \$0.20$ per pen. Company B is a nickel cheaper.

If you chose A, possibly you found the minimum cost correctly but identified it with the wrong company. Choice C is the average for Company A.

Question 4. **The correct answer is H.** The Pythagorean theorem applies here, so that $a^2 + 8^2 = 10^2$, where a is the distance from the base of the ladder to the wall, in feet. That means $a^2 = 10^2 - 8^2 = 36$ and then $a = 6$.

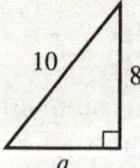

K comes from adding $10^2 + 8^2$, which is 164. If you had noticed that the longest side of the triangle is 10 feet long, and $\sqrt{164}$ is more than 10, you could have eliminated this answer choice. **F** (2 feet) cannot be true. If it were, the path along the two shorter sides of the triangle (ground and wall) would be the same length as a path along the longest side of the triangle (ladder). This is impossible because the shortest path between points must go along a straight line, not over and then up.

Question 5. **The correct answer is E.** While you could try out various combinations of the given three statements and try to make a conclusion, it might be more straightforward to look at each of the answer choices to see whether it contradicts one of the given three statements or whether it could be deduced from the given three statements.

A and **B** each say that Insect I is an ant. This directly contradicts the second given statement. So, **A** and **B** are false.

Consider **C**: if it is true (Insect I is attracted to honey), then the first given statement implies that Insect I is an ant. This contradicts the second given statement. So, **C** is false.

D directly contradicts the third given statement. So, **D** is false.

For **E**, consider Insect J. The third given statement tells you that Insect J is attracted to honey. And then because of the first given statement (all insects attracted to honey are ants), Insect J must be an ant. So, **E** must be true.

Question 6. **The correct answer is F.** Each 1,000 gallons of water costs $2.50, so g of these "1,000 gallons of water" cost $g \cdot (\$2.50)$. On top of this, there is a $16 charge that is added for trash pickup. The result is $2.50g + 16$.

Answer choice **K** represents a cost of $2.50 per gallon rather than per 1,000 gallons.

Question 7. The correct answer is D. The left side of the equation, $2(x + 4)$, can be written as $2x + 8$. Then, the equation becomes $2x + 8 = 5x - 7$. One way to solve this is to first add 7 to both sides (resulting in $2x + 15 = 5x$) and then subtracting $2x$ from both sides (resulting in $15 = 3x$). Dividing both sides by 3 gives the result $5 = x$.

It's a good idea to check this answer: does $2(5 + 4)$ equal $5(5) - 7$? The left side simplifies to $2(9)$, which is 18. The right side simplifies to $25 - 7$, which is also 18. Yes!

Some students will write $2(x + 4)$ as $2x + 4$, but it isn't. That mistake would lead to answer choice **C**. Note that $2(x + 4)$ is two $(x + 4)$s added together, or $x + 4 + x + 4$.

Question 8. The correct answer is H. $\overline{BF}$ is a transversal between the two parallel lines. Therefore, because $\angle CBF$ and $\angle BFE$ are alternate interior angles, their measures are equal, and so $f°$ in the figure below is 35°. You can also see that $\triangle BEF$ is isosceles, which makes the base angles equal in measure, so $e°$ is also 35°. The angle the problem asks you to find is the supplement of $\angle BEF$, which makes its measure $180° - 35°$, or 145°.

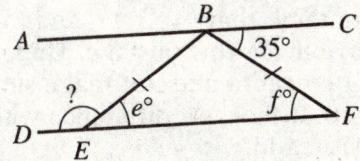

Question 9. The correct answer is B. The least common denominator is the smallest positive multiple of 2, 3, 9, and 15. These four numbers can be written in prime-power form as 2, 3, 3^2, and $3 \cdot 5$. The least common denominator must have all of these as factors. The number $2 \cdot 3^2 \cdot 5$ is divisible by 2, by 3, by 3^2, and by $3 \cdot 5$, and it has no extra prime factors, so it is the smallest of all of the common multiples. $2 \cdot 3^2 \cdot 5 = 2 \cdot 9 \cdot 5 = 10 \cdot 9 = 90$.

The most popular incorrect answer is **A**, which is divisible by 15, by 9, and by 3, but not by 2.

Question 10. The correct answer is H. $3x(x^2y + 2xy^2) = 3x \cdot x^2y + 3x \cdot 2xy^2 = 3x^3y + 6x^2y^2$.

F is $3(x^2y + 2xy^2)$, dropping the x multiplier in $3x$. If you chose **G**, you probably correctly multiplied $3x$ and x^2y but forgot to multiply $3x$ by $2xy^2$.

Question 11. **The correct answer is D.** The 10 notebooks would cost 9($2.50), which is $22.50. The average price for one of the 10 notebooks would be $\frac{\$22.50}{10}$, which is $2.25.

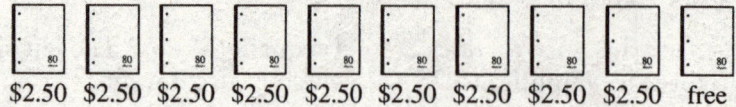

$2.50 $2.50 $2.50 $2.50 $2.50 $2.50 $2.50 $2.50 $2.50 free

If you chose **B**, you may not have understood that notebook 10 was free, so you only had to pay for 9 notebooks.

Question 12. **The correct answer is K.** $(3x + 1)^2 = (3x + 1)(3x + 1)$ because that's what the power 2 means. There are several methods for continuing from this point, such as FOIL (first, outer, inner, last). The solution shown below uses the distributive property.

$(3x + 1)(3x + 1) = 3x(3x + 1) + 1(3x + 1) = 3x(3x) + 3x(1) + 3x + 1 = 9x^2 + 6x + 1$

It is fairly common for students to think that $(3x + 1)^2$ and $(3x)^2 + (1)^2$ are equivalent, but they're not. If you chose **H**, you may have made this mistake. Understanding why this is a mistake can help you understand other parts of algebra and not make similar mistakes. If you let $x = 1$, then $(3x + 1)^2 = 16$ but $(3x)^2 + (1)^2 = 10$. It makes a difference whether you add first and then square, or whether you square first and then add.

Question 13. **The correct answer is D.** For each kind of bread, there are 5 kinds of meat, so that is $3 \cdot 5$ combinations of bread and meat. For each of these 15 combinations of bread and meat, there are 3 kinds of cheese. That makes $15 \cdot 3 = 45$ combinations of bread, meat, and cheese.

The tree diagram on the next page shows all 45 combinations. It would take a lot of time to list all of these cases, but you can imagine what the tree looks like without having to write it all out. You can see that parts of the tree repeat many times, and so you can use multiplication to help you count.

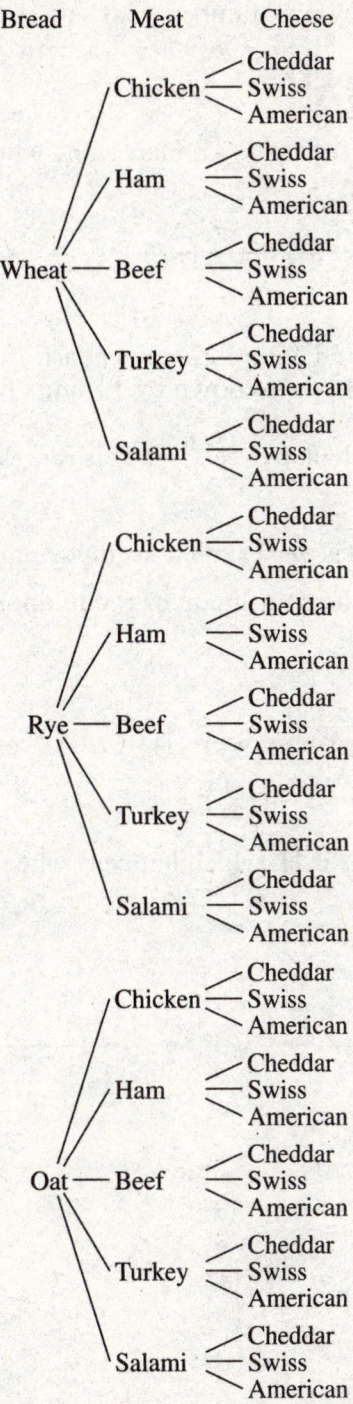

Question 14. The correct answer is K. Because the only real numbers that satisfy $a^2 = 49$ are 7 and –7, and the only real numbers that satisfy $b^2 = 64$ are 8 and –8, the only possibilities for $a + b$ are $7 + 8$, $7 + (-8)$, $-7 + 8$, and $-7 + (-8)$. These possibilities are 15, –1, 1, and –15. The only answer choice left is 113.

Question 15. The correct answer is B. Here's one where drawing a picture might help you avoid some mistakes.

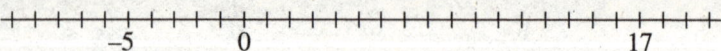

The points with coordinates –5 and 17 are 22 units apart. If you go up by 11 units from –5, you should get to the same place as if you go down by 11 units from 17. This is 6.

If you chose **C**, you may have calculated $\frac{17 - (-5)}{2}$. This represents the distance from the midpoint

to an endpoint. This expression is very similar to the average of the two coordinates, $\frac{17 + (-5)}{2}$ (notice the plus sign), which is the coordinate of the midpoint. That's why drawing a picture is a good idea.

Question 16. The correct answer is G. $3\frac{3}{5} = x + 2\frac{2}{3} \Rightarrow x = 3\frac{3}{5} - 2\frac{2}{3} = (3 - 2) + \left(\frac{3}{5} - \frac{2}{3}\right) = 1 + \left(\frac{9}{15} - \frac{10}{15}\right) = 1 + \left(-\frac{1}{15}\right) = \frac{14}{15}$.

The most common wrong answer is **H**, which happens when someone tries to reduce $\left(\frac{3}{5} - \frac{2}{3}\right)$ to $\left(\frac{3-2}{5-3}\right)$.

MATHEMATICS · PRACTICE TEST 3 · EXPLANATORY ANSWERS

Question 17. The correct answer is A. Although you could deduce some things the way the equations are given, you might be more comfortable with the equations in slope-intercept form. The system would then be:

$$y = -\frac{2}{3}x + \frac{8}{3}$$
$$y = \frac{2}{3}x + \frac{8}{3}$$

The slopes of the two lines are different (the first is $\frac{2}{3}$, the second $-\frac{2}{3}$). That, by itself, means **A** is correct. The graph below shows what this system looks like. You can see that none of the other answer choices is correct.

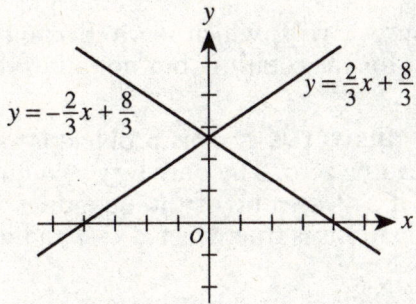

Question 18. The correct answer is K. Properties of exponents make this straightforward to solve. All of the *bases* (2, 4, and 8) are powers of 2. The equation can be rewritten as $(2^x)(2^2) = (2^3)^3$. Properties of exponents lead to the equation $2^{x+2} = 2^{3 \cdot 3}$, which simplifies to $2^{x+2} = 2^9$. If the two exponents are the same, then the left and right sides are equal. This happens when $x + 2 = 9$, which is when $x = 7$.

You can check this answer (or whatever answer you got). When $x = 7$, the left side of the equation is $(2^7)(4)$, which simplifies to $(128)(4)$, and then to 512. The right side is 8^3, which is also 512.

The most common wrong answer for this problem is **G**, which happens when people combine $(2^x)(4)$ and get (8^x). These are not equivalent (check $x = 2$). Another common mistake is to write $(2^3)^3$ as 2^6, which leads to **H**.

Question 19. The correct answer is D. A rotation of 180° goes halfway around a circle. The graph below illustrates this rotation. Because it is halfway, it does not matter whether you rotate clockwise or counterclockwise.

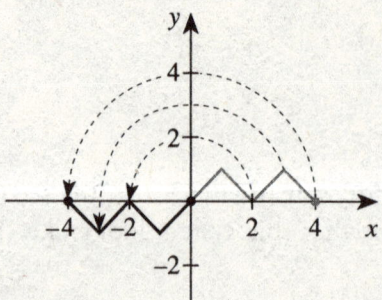

The most common incorrect answer is **B**, which is a reflection across the *y*-axis. Several of the points on this graph are correct for the rotation, but not all of them.

Question 20. The correct answer is F. This problem is asking you to figure out when two quantities multiplied together can be zero. The only way two quantities can be multiplied together to get an answer of zero is if at least one of the quantities is zero. So, either $(x + a) = 0$ or $(x + b) = 0$. The first of these equations is true when $x = -a$ and the second when $x = -b$. These are the two solution values for *x*.

As a check, substitute $-a$ in for *x*. The original equation becomes $(-a + a)(-a + b)$, which simplifies to $(0)(-a + b)$, and zero times anything is zero, so the original equation holds when $x = -a$. You could check $x = -b$ in the same manner.

If you chose **K**, you may have solved the two equations incorrectly, or you may have just looked at the quantities and chosen the $+a$ and $+b$ that appeared in the problem.

If you missed this problem, you might try substituting a value of *x* from your answer into the original equation to see what happens.

Question 21. The correct answer is E. To go from *P* to *Q* is 9 units. From *Q* to *R* is 6 units. From *R* to *S* is 9 units. From *S* back to *P* is 12 units. The total length is 9 + 6 + 9 + 12 = 36 units.

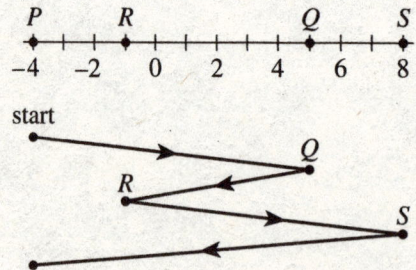

Question 22. **The correct answer is J.** The determinant $\begin{vmatrix} 2x & 3y \\ 5x & 4y \end{vmatrix}$ has the value $(2x)(4y) - (3y)(5x)$, which simplifies to $8xy - 15xy = -7xy$. When $x = -3$ and $y = 2$, the value of the expression is $-7(-3)(2) = 42$.

Another approach is to substitute $x = -3$ and $y = 2$ first, giving the determinant $\begin{vmatrix} -6 & 6 \\ -15 & 8 \end{vmatrix}$, which has the value $(-6)(8) - (6)(-15) = (-48) - (-90) = -48 + 90 = 42$.

If you got answer **G**, you probably made a mistake with a minus sign. If you got answers **F** or **K**, you probably used the second approach and made an error with a minus sign.

Question 23. **The correct answer is C.** Let the capacity of the larger bottle be B ounces. Then, the capacity of the smaller bottle is $\frac{1}{2}B$ ounces. The larger bottle starts with $\frac{2}{3}B$ ounces of catsup. The smaller bottle starts with $\frac{1}{3}(\frac{1}{2}B) = \frac{1}{6}B$ ounces of catsup. When this catsup is poured into the larger bottle (when you pour, be sure to get it all out of the smaller bottle), the larger bottle now contains $\frac{2}{3}B + \frac{1}{6}B$ ounces of catsup, which is $\frac{5}{6}B$ ounces of catsup. This means the bottle is $\frac{5}{6}$ full.

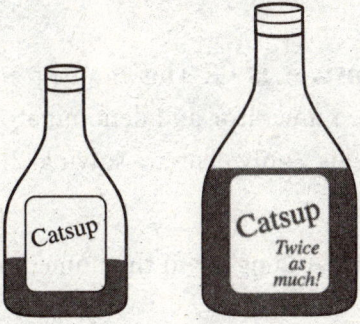

If you find it hard to follow the steps with the abstract "B ounces" for the larger bottle's capacity, try thinking of a particular size of bottle, say a 12-ounce bottle. Then the smaller bottle's capacity is 6 ounces. The larger bottle contains $\frac{2}{3}(12) = 8$ ounces of catsup. The smaller bottle contains $\frac{1}{3}(6) = 2$ ounces of catsup. When poured together, the larger bottle would now contain 10 ounces of catsup, which is $\frac{10}{12} = \frac{5}{6}$ of its capacity.

The most common wrong answer is **D**. If one catsup bottle is $\frac{2}{3}$ full and another is $\frac{1}{3}$ full, then together they would be a whole bottle of catsup—if the bottles were the same size. Because the $\frac{1}{3}$ of the smaller bottle is smaller than the missing $\frac{1}{3}$ of the larger bottle, the larger bottle won't be full.

Question 24. The correct answer is G. In the given equation, $t = 10p + 5$, the 10 represents the number of minutes that the time changes when the number of problems increases by 1. That's the slope. So, Jeff is budgeting 10 minutes per problem. The 5 minutes for getting set up is not budgeted on a per-problem basis.

For 1 problem, the total time budgeted is $10(1) + 5 = 15$ minutes. This may lead you to believe that **F** is the correct answer, but consider an assignment with 2 problems. Using the given equation, that would be budgeted at $10(2) + 5 = 25$ minutes. Using **F**, it would be budgeted at 30 minutes. Some of the other answer choices could be true, but they do not have to be true. For example, Jeff could budget a 5-minute break after each problem, which would fit into the 10 minutes he budgets per problem. But, he would not have to schedule any breaks between problems, or he could schedule 2-minute breaks.

Question 25. The correct answer is D. Because Kaya drove 200 miles in 5 hours, she was averaging $\frac{200}{5} = 40$ miles per hour. If she drove 10 miles per hour faster, that would be 50 miles per hour. To complete the 200 miles at 50 miles per hour would take a driving time of $\frac{200}{50} = 4$ hours. That's a savings of 1 hour.

The most common wrong answer was **E**, which is the number of hours the faster trip would take. That isn't what the question asks for.

Question 26. The correct answer is G. This can be translated to algebraic language. Let x be the number that is added to the numerator and denominator. Then, you want to find the number x that satisfies $\frac{7+x}{9+x} = \frac{1}{2}$. This is equivalent to solving $2(7 + x) = 1(9 + x) \Rightarrow 14 + 2x = 9 + x \Rightarrow x = 9 - 14 = -5$.

You can always check your answer. Adding -5 to the numerator of $\frac{7}{9}$ gives 2, and to the denominator gives 4, and $\frac{2}{4}$ is $\frac{1}{2}$.

The result is $\frac{1}{2}$ when **H** is added to the numerator but not to the denominator, that is, $\frac{7+\left(-2\frac{1}{2}\right)}{9}$. For this problem, you can check each of the answers to see whether it works.

Question 27. The correct answer is B. If $a = b$, then $|a| = |b|$. (This is a property of a *function*, that if you start with the same number then you will get the same result. Absolute value is a function.) This shows that **A** is false, and it also shows that **B** must be true.

You can eliminate **C** by checking $a = 2$ and $b = 1$. You can eliminate **D** and **E** by checking $a = -2$ and $b = 1$. The most common wrong answer is **D**.

MATHEMATICS · PRACTICE TEST 3 · EXPLANATORY ANSWERS

Question 28. The correct answer is J. One way to solve this is to put the equation into slope-intercept form (solve for y). This can be accomplished as follows: $14x - 11y + 16 = 0 \Rightarrow$ $-11y = -14x - 16 \Rightarrow y = \frac{14}{11}x + \frac{16}{11}$. The slope is the coefficient of x, which is $\frac{14}{11}$. The most common errors are making a sign mistake (**G**) or getting the fraction upside down (**H**).

Question 29. The correct answer is B. By definition, $\log_x 36$ is the power of x that it takes to get 36. That power is 2 because $\log_x 36 = 2$. So, $x^2 = 36$. This equation is satisfied when $x = 6$.

The most common wrong answer is **E**, which is the solution to $2x = 36$.

Question 30. The correct answer is H. $\triangle DFB$ and $\triangle EFB$ are congruent, which can be seen by using side-side-side congruence and the following steps. First, $\overline{DF} \cong \overline{EF}$ is given. Second, the triangles share a common side, $\overline{FB}$, so certainly $\overline{FB} \cong \overline{FB}$. And, the third sides are congruent ($\overline{DB} \cong \overline{EB}$) because the length of the third side in each triangle is determined from the other two sides by the Pythagorean theorem—the calculation is the same in both cases.

Because $\triangle DFB$ and $\triangle CFB$ are congruent, $\angle DFB$ is congruent to $\angle EFB$. Then, the three angles within $\triangle DFB$ are a right angle, $\angle x$, and an angle congruent to $\angle y$. That means that the measures of the angles add up to 180°, and so the measures of $\angle x$ and $\angle y$ add up to 90°. It really didn't matter that the given angle at A measured 50°. You can't tell the measure of $\angle x$ or $\angle y$, but you can find the sum.

Question 31. The correct answer is E. $(-2x^5y^2)^4 = (-2)^4 (x^5)^4 (y^2)^4 = 16x^{5 \cdot 4} y^{2 \cdot 4} = 16x^{20}y^8$.

If you chose **D**, you likely wrote $(x^5)^4$ as x^{5+4} and $(y^2)^4$ as y^{2+4}. If you chose **A**, you likely multiplied exponents properly but wrote $(-2)^4$ as -16 when it is really $(-2)(-2)(-2)(-2) = +16$.

Question 32. The correct answer is K. As the diagrams below show, there are many different arrangements of points that satisfy the conditions. But, in all of these, the order of points starting from point A is A, B, D, C.

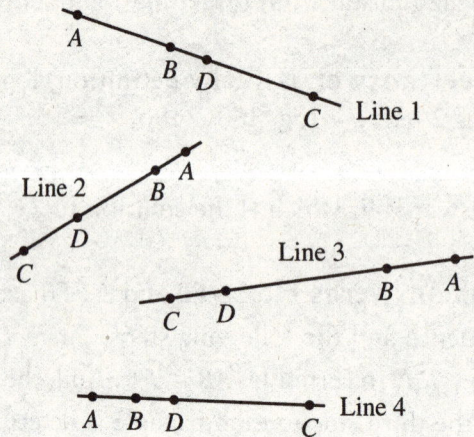

Because D is between C and B, that means that distance CD is always shorter than distance BC. So, answer choice **K** is always true.

The other answer choices can each be true for particular arrangements of the points, but they can also each be false for particular arrangements. Line 1 shows that **F** is sometimes false, Line 2 that **G** is sometimes false, Line 3 that **H** is sometimes false, and Line 4 that **J** is sometimes false. If you got an incorrect answer, you probably did not consider enough cases.

Question 33. The correct answer is A. $16 - 5x \leq 8$ is equivalent (meaning it has the same solutions) as $-5x \leq 8 - 16$, where 16 has been subtracted from both sides. This chain continues with $-5x \leq -8 \Rightarrow x \geq \frac{-8}{-5} \Rightarrow x \geq \frac{8}{5}$.

Most mistakes on this problem involve minus signs.

Question 34. The correct answer is G. Here, d is given as 50 mils and $r = \frac{10,770}{(50)^2} - 0.37$, which is approximately $\frac{10,000}{2,500} = 4$ ohms. A calculator would give 3.938, and you would have to decide that it is closest to answer choice **G**.

If you got **H**, you may have divided by the radius squared rather than dividing by the diameter squared. If you got **J**, you may have divided by 50 rather than by 50^2.

Question 35. The correct answer is A. Because the measures of the interior angles in a triangle add to 180°, you can find the measure of $\angle F$ if you find the measures of $\angle FEG$ and $\angle EGF$ in $\triangle EFG$. Notice that $\angle EGF$ makes a straight angle with the angle marked 100°, so $\angle EGF$ measures 180° − 100° = 80°. Second, notice that $\angle FEG$ has the same measure as $\angle CED$ because they are vertical angles. So, consider $\triangle CDE$. In that triangle, $\angle ECD$ forms a straight angle with the angle marked 140°, so $\angle ECD$ measures 180° − 140° = 40°. Then, $\angle CED$ measures 180° − 40° − 80° = 60°, which is the same as the measure of $\angle FEG$. In $\triangle EFG$, $\angle F$ measures 180° − 60° − 80° = 40°.

The most common wrong answer is "Cannot be determined from the given information" (**E**).

Question 36. The correct answer is K. Although you don't necessarily need to draw a graph to solve this question, the following graph might be helpful in explaining what is going on.

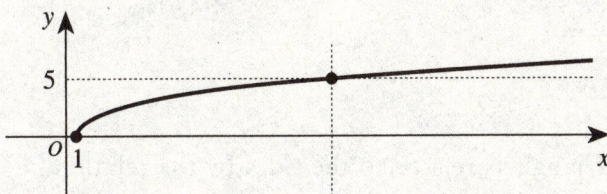

You are supposed to find the x-values of all points on the curve that are above 5 (above the horizontal dashed line). That is all of the x-values that are to the right of the vertical dashed line. The point on the curve where the dashed lines meet has y-coordinate 5. What is its x-coordinate? To get that, solve $\sqrt{x-1} = 5$. All solutions of this equation satisfy $\left(\sqrt{x-1}\right)^2 = 5^2$, which is equivalent to $x − 1 = 25 \Rightarrow x = 26$. Now you know that the points to the right of the vertical dashed line have x-coordinates that satisfy $x > 26$.

If you chose **G**, you may have solved $x − 1 \geq 5$ rather than $\sqrt{x-1} \geq 5$. If you chose **F**, you may have solved $x − 1 \geq 5$ incorrectly by adding 1 to the left side but subtracting 1 from the right side.

If you chose **H** or **J**, you probably did not account for the −1 quite correctly under the square root sign.

Question 37. The correct answer is C. 180° is the same as π radians. Multiplying the expression by the conversion factor of $\frac{\pi}{180}$ gives $\left[\frac{(n-2)\pi}{n}\right]$.

If you chose **D**, you may have thought there were 2π radians in 180°. If you chose **B**, you may have thought that there were π radians in 360°.

Question 38. The correct answer is H. This can be solved by using the distance formula, or by using the Pythagorean theorem directly. Look at the graph below to see the right triangle where the Pythagorean theorem applies.

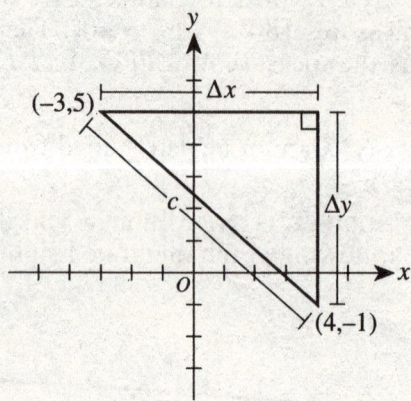

The hypotenuse of this triangle is related to the sides by the relation $c^2 = (\Delta x)^2 + (\Delta y)^2$. The value of Δx is $4 - (-3) = 4 + 3 = 7$. The value of Δy is $-1 - 5 = -6$. So, $c^2 = (7)^2 + (-6)^2 = 49 + 36 = 85$. Then, $c = \sqrt{85}$.

J represents the distance along the horizontal and vertical sides of the triangle rather than taking the direct route along the hypotenuse of the triangle. If you subtracted $(\Delta y)^2$ from $(\Delta x)^2$ instead of adding, you would get $c^2 = 13$, which leads to **F**. Choice **G** comes from adding instead of subtracting when finding Δx and Δy.

Question 39. The correct answer is C. The volume of this cylinder is the area of the circular end times the length of the tank. The area of the end is $\pi \cdot 4^2 = 16\pi$ square feet. So, the volume is $16\pi \cdot 25 = 400\pi$ cubic feet. This number is approximately $1{,}256.637\cdots$, which is closest to 1,300 among the choices.

The most common wrong answer is **B**, which you would get if you used the perimeter of the circular end rather than the area.

Question 40. The correct answer is K. 5,000 gallons that each weigh about 8 pounds would be about $5{,}000 \cdot 8 = 40{,}000$ pounds.

The most common mistake on this problem is dividing by 8 rather than multiplying (**F**).

MATHEMATICS · PRACTICE TEST 3 · EXPLANATORY ANSWERS

Question 41. The correct answer is B. The center of the circle is 2 feet above the top level of the support, which is shown as the dashed line. Drawing a picture might be helpful on this problem.

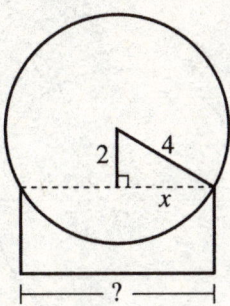

Once you see the right triangle, you can apply the Pythagorean theorem to find x. It is given by

$x = \sqrt{4^2 - 2^2} = \sqrt{16 - 4} = \sqrt{12} = \sqrt{4 \cdot 3} = \sqrt{4}\sqrt{3} = 2\sqrt{3}$. And the full width of the support is

double this, or $4\sqrt{3}$.

If you stopped after finding half the width of the support, you would have gotten **A**. If you got mixed up on the Pythagorean theorem and calculated $x = \sqrt{4^2 + 2^2}$ (note the plus sign), you would have gotten **C**.

From the diagram, you can see that the width of the brace must be shorter than the distance across the circle, which is 8 feet. This eliminates **C**, **D**, and **E**.

Question 42. The correct answer is J. The front and rear of the tent are each triangles and have the same area. That area is $\frac{1}{2}(6)(4) = 12$ square feet. The two tent sides are rectangles, and have the same area. That area is $(5)(7) = 35$ square feet. So, the total of all four of these areas is $2(12) + 2(35) = 2(47) = 94$ square feet.

If you got **K**, possibly you calculated the area of each triangle as $(6)(4)$. This would be the area of a rectangle with length 6 and height 4; the triangle would fit inside this rectangle and have space left over. In fact, it would take up exactly $\frac{1}{2}$ the rectangle. If you chose **F**, you probably only counted one end and one side, not two of each. Answer **G** represents two ends and one side (or one end computed incorrectly as $(6)(4)$ and one side). Answer **H** represents one end and two sides.

Question 43. The correct answer is D. There are 180° along the circle from M to N, as shown below. Arc $\overparen{MP}$ has the same length as $\overparen{PQ}$ and as $\overparen{QN}$, so each of those has $\frac{1}{3}$ the length of $\overparen{MN}$. That means $\overparen{MP}$ is $\frac{1}{3}$ the length of $\overparen{MN}$, or $33\frac{1}{3}\%$ the length.

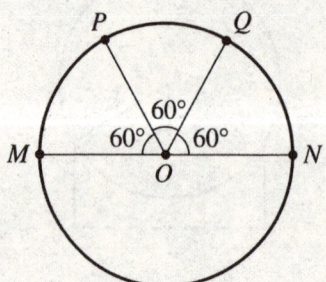

If you chose C, you might have been using the distance directly from M to N rather than the distance along the circle from M to N. That would give you about 52.3%, which is closest to 50%.

Question 44. The correct answer is K. In 2 hours, there are $2(60)(60) = 7,200 = 7.2 \times 10^3$ seconds. In each of those seconds, light travels about $186,000 = 1.86 \times 10^5$ miles. Light would travel about $(7.2 \times 10^3)(1.86 \times 10^5)$ miles in those 2 hours. That is $(7.2)(1.86) \times 10^{3+5} = 13.392 \times 10^8 \approx 1.34 \times 10^9$ miles.

If you chose J, you could have calculated the distance for 1 hour and then did not double it. If you chose G, you likely figured the distance for 120 seconds rather than 120 minutes. You need another factor of 60 to account for the 60 seconds per minute. Answer F is simply $(2)(186,000)$ and is approximately the distance light travels in 2 seconds.

Question 45. The correct answer is B. The way to use the minimum number of blocks is to have a side of the block with the largest area face upward. That is the side that is 4″ by 8″. The 4″ width of the blocks will fit 3 to each foot. The 8″ length of the blocks will fit 3 to each 2 feet. The blocks could be arranged as shown, with 24 block widths in one direction and 15 block lengths in the other direction. That makes $15 \cdot 24 = 360$ blocks. The blocks could be arranged in different patterns, but the top area of all of the blocks has to equal the $(8)(10) = 80$-square-foot area Barb is covering.

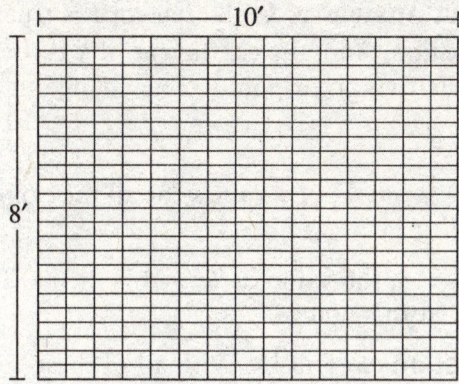

Because a whole number of blocks fits exactly along each edge, you can use area to solve this problem. You can calculate the total area, 80 square feet, and divide by the largest area a single block can cover, 32 square inches. The area to be covered is (8)(12) = 96 inches in one direction and (10)(12) = 120 inches in the other direction, which makes the total area (96)(120) = 11,520 square inches. If you divide this by the area of a single block, 32 square inches, you will get $\frac{11,520}{32}$ = 360 blocks.

If you got answer **A**, you may have calculated the area of the patio in square feet and stopped, or you may have multiplied and divided that by 12.

Question 46. The correct answer is **F**. For $\triangle ABC$, tan A is $\frac{\text{opposite}}{\text{adjacent}} = \frac{a}{b}$ and sin B is $\frac{\text{opposite}}{\text{hypotenuse}} = \frac{b}{c}$. Their product is $\frac{a}{b} \cdot \frac{b}{c} = \frac{a}{c}$.

If you chose **H**, you probably used sin A rather than sin B. Answer **G** is (sin A)(sin B). Answer **J** is (tan B)(sin B).

Question 47. The correct answer is **E**. The rate at which the water depth was increasing changed at time a. The depth was increasing faster before time a than after time a. Event I would have caused the depth to increase faster after it happened than before it happened, so that cannot be the event that happened at time a. Event II would slow down the rate at which the water depth was increasing. Event III would cause water to start draining from the pool even as the pool was filling, and that would keep the depth from rising as fast as it had been rising. The amount of water coming into the pool would be greater than the amount being drained out. Either II or III would explain the change in the graph at time a.

The most common wrong answer is **A**, which could be due to misunderstanding what the graph shows. Even though the depth increases after time a, it is the rate at which the depth increases that is important. The rate has slowed down (it takes a longer time to increase the depth by 1 inch after time a than before time a). This corresponds to the slope of the graph being less after time a than before time a.

Question 48. **The correct answer is G.** Statement I is true: The slope of the graph is constant because it is a linear function. And, the coefficient of x is the slope, which is 2. You can also calculate the slope between the two given points. The change in y is $11 - 3 = 8$. The change in x is $4 - 0 = 4$. The slope is $\frac{8}{4} = 2$.

Statement II is true: The range is the set of y-values for all the points on the graph. Those y-values cover the whole range from 3 to 11.

Statement III is false: When $x = 3$, the value of $2x + 3$ is $2(3) + 3 = 9$, which is not zero. So, the function does not have a zero at this point.

Question 49. **The correct answer is D.** With all of these conditions, angle A is an angle in a right triangle with legs of length a and b, as illustrated below.

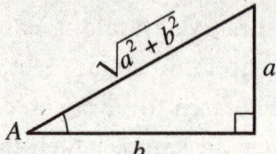

The hypotenuse of the triangle will have length $\sqrt{a^2 + b^2}$. So $\cos A = \frac{\text{adjacent}}{\text{hypotenuse}} = \frac{b}{\sqrt{a^2 + b^2}}$.

Most errors are due to not associating the correct ratio of sides with the correct trigonometric function.

Question 50. **The correct answer is F.** All of the parabolas open upward. This rules out answer choices J and K. All of the parabolas have the same y-intercept, $(0,1)$. This rules out answer choice H, which has y-intercept equal to n, which varies. The parabolas in the family go up more quickly as the value of n increases. This means the coefficient of x must get larger as n gets larger. That happens in F, but not in G.

The most common incorrect answer is H. A graph of that family is shown below.

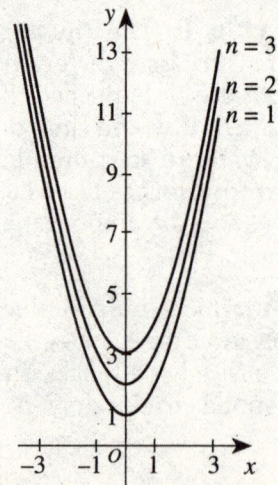

Question 51. **The correct answer is A.** The area of the whole board is $\pi r^2 = \pi \cdot 10^2 = 100\pi$ square inches. The radius of the outside of the 20-ring is $10 - 2 = 8$ inches. The radius of the outside of the 30-ring is $8 - 2 = 6$ inches, so the area of the circle that includes 30, 40, and 50 points is $\pi \cdot 6^2 = 36\pi$ square inches. If a dart hits at a random spot on the board, the chance of it hitting in a certain region is proportional to the area of that region. So, the percent chance of hitting inside a region that is worth at least 30 points is $\frac{36\pi}{100\pi} \cdot 100\% = 36\%$.

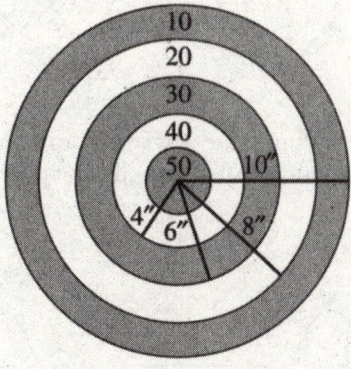

If you chose C, this is the percent chance of getting *more* than 30 points, using the 4-inch radius of the inside of the 30-ring.

Question 52. **The correct answer is H.** The ratio $\frac{a}{b}$ is $\frac{3}{4}$. The ratio $\frac{c}{b}$ is $\frac{1}{2}$. You want to get the ratio $\frac{a}{c}$. Note that $\frac{a}{c} = \frac{a}{b} \cdot \frac{b}{c}$. This is the same as $\frac{3}{4} \cdot \frac{2}{1} = \frac{3}{2}$.

The most common wrong answer is **G**, where people assume a is 3 and c is 1. The problem here is that b would have to be both 4 (from the first ratio) and also 2 (from the second ratio). Numbers that satisfy the conditions are $a = 3$, $b = 4$, and $c = 2$, or any nonzero multiple of these 3 numbers.

Question 53. **The correct answer is B.** The figure below divides the *x*-axis into intervals of length π units. You can see that the function in one interval is the same as the function in any other interval.

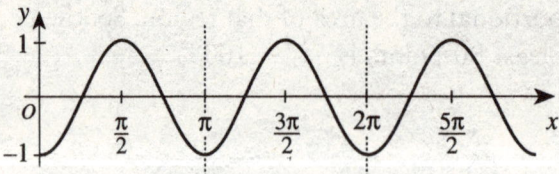

Note that it doesn't really matter where the divisions are made as long as the length is always π units (see the graph below). The function in one interval is a repetition of the curve in each of the other intervals.

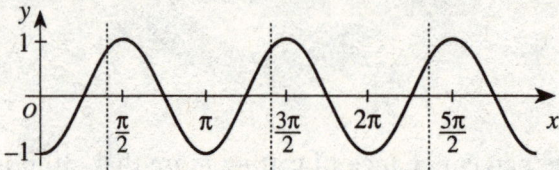

If there were smaller intervals, each interval would each have to contain a maximum value of the function (1) and a minimum value of the function (−1). The only way that can happen is if the spacing is $\frac{\pi}{2}$, as shown below. But, the function is not a repetition in each of those intervals. It is increasing in one of the intervals and decreasing in the next.

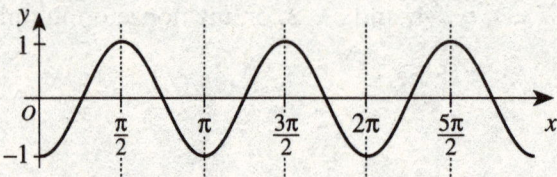

Being familiar with trigonometric functions and the concept of *period* would be useful for solving a problem like this.

Question 54. The correct answer is F. A geometric interpretation of $|x|$ is the distance from x to zero. So, this question is asking for a graph of all the values of x that are less than 2 units from zero. That is graph **F**.

Another way to solve this question is to check values and eliminate all but one graph. For example, $x = 0$ is a solution of the inequality because $|0| < 2$, and that eliminates **G** and **H**. Because $|3| < 2$ is false, $x = 3$ is not a solution, which eliminates **J**. Similarly, $|-3| < 2$ is false, so $x = -3$ is not a solution, which eliminates **K**.

The most common wrong answer is **K**, which is a graph of $x < 2$ (note no absolute value). The graph of $|x| > 2$ is also popular (**H**), being the places that are farther than 2 units from zero.

Question 55. The correct answer is A. If $(x - 7)$ is a factor, then there would have to be another factor $(2x + b)$ where $(x - 7)(2x + b) = 2x^2 - 11x + k$. The product $(x - 7)$ $(2x + b)$ can be expanded to $x \cdot 2x + x \cdot b + (-7) \cdot 2x + (-7) \cdot b = 2x^2 + (b - 14)x - 7b$. In order for this to be equivalent to the original polynomial, $2x^2 + (b - 14)x - 7b = 2x^2 - 11x + k$, which means that $b - 14 = -11$ and $-7b = k$. So, $b = -11 + 14 = 3$, and then $k = -7b = -7(3) = -21$.

Another way to solve the problem is to use a relationship between factors and zeros of polynomials. If $(x - r)$ is a factor of a polynomial, then r is a zero of the polynomial. So, if 7 is a zero of the polynomial $2x^2 - 11x + k$, you know that $2 \cdot 7^2 - 11 \cdot 7 + k = 0$. This can be solved for k as follows: $2 \cdot 49 - 77 + k = 0 \Rightarrow 98 - 77 + k = 0 \Rightarrow 21 + k = 0 \Rightarrow k = -21$.

Question 56. The correct answer is F. The new value of b is $(b - 1)$, and the new value of c is $(c + 2)$. Substituting into the expression for a gives $2(b - 1) + 3(c + 2) - 5$, which simplifies to $2b - 2 + 3c + 6 - 5 \Rightarrow 2b + 3c - 1$. Because you are looking for the change in a, try to write this expression in terms of the original expression for a. You can do this as $(2b + 3c - 5) + 4$. And that is the old value of a increased by 4.

If you got **H**, you may have reasoned that a decrease of 1 followed by an increase of 2 is a net increase of 1. That would work if you were finding the change in $(b + c)$. But in $2b + 3c - 5$, the change in b is doubled and the change in c is tripled. So the net change is $2(-1) + 3(2) \Rightarrow -2 + 6 \Rightarrow 4$. If you got stuck on this question, you could try substituting specific numbers for b and c. For example, if $b = 2$ and $c = 5$, then $a = 2b + 3c - 5 = 14$. And then if b decreased by 1 and c increased by 2, the new values are $b = 1$ and $c = 7$. Then, the new value of $a = 2(-1) + 3(7) - 5 = 18$. The new value of a is 4 more than the old value.

Question 57. The correct answer is D. Let s be the edge length of the small cube. Then, its volume is s^3. The large cube has edges twice as long as those of the small cube, and so the edge length of the large cube can be represented as $2s$. The volume of the large cube is $(2s)^3 = (2s)(2s)(2s) = (2)(2)(2)(s)(s)(s) = 8s^3$. So, the large cube has 8 times the volume of the small cube.

These two cubes are similar geometric figures, with a scale factor of 2. A theorem about scaling says that the surface area of the figures has a scale factor of 2^2 and the volume has a scale factor of 2^3. If you chose **B**, you may have remembered the area part of this theorem.

Answer **A** is popular, which may come from reasoning that if the side is twice as long, then everything else will be twice as big. The picture below shows that 8 copies of the small cube would fit inside the large cube, not just 2 copies. That means that the volume of the large cube is 8 times the volume of the small cube.

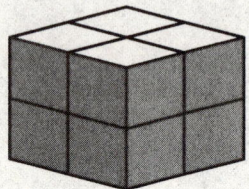

Question 58. The correct answer is H. In this setting, it might be clearest to think of an angle measure as the amount the first side of the angle must be rotated (relative to the counterclockwise direction) in order to line up with the second side of the angle. For example, the measure of $\angle COB$ is β (beta) because rotating $\overrightarrow{OC}$ by β will move it to line up with $\overrightarrow{OB}$. The measure of $\angle COA$ is α (alpha).

Let γ (gamma) be the measure of $\angle BOA$. You could work the problem without giving this angle a name, but naming it might make it simpler to keep track of quantities. The figure below includes γ. Now, starting from $\overrightarrow{OC}$, if you rotate it by β, it will line up with $\overrightarrow{OB}$. If you rotate further by γ, it will line up with $\overrightarrow{OA}$. This is the same as a single rotation of α, which shows that $\beta + \gamma = \alpha$, or $\gamma = \alpha - \beta$.

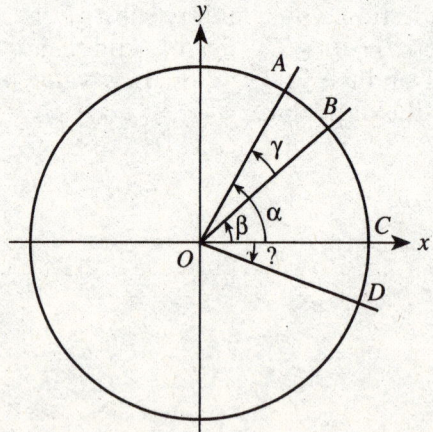

Because the arc length of $\overset{\frown}{BA}$ is the same as the arc length of $\overset{\frown}{DC}$, the measure of $\angle BOA$ is the same as the measure of $\angle DOC$. This means the measure of $\angle DOC$ is also γ. In terms of rotation, $\overrightarrow{OD}$ would need to rotate counterclockwise by γ in order to line up with $\overrightarrow{OC}$. This, in turn, means that $\overrightarrow{OC}$ would need to rotate by γ in a *clockwise* direction in order to line up with $\overrightarrow{OD}$. This is equivalent to rotating $\overrightarrow{OC}$ by $-\gamma$ in a counterclockwise direction. And, that means the measure of $\angle COD$ is $-(\alpha - \beta)$, which can be written $\beta - \alpha$.

Question 59. The correct answer is B. Because the 300 males have an average age of 45, the sum of their ages is (approximately) $300 \cdot 45 = 13{,}500$ years. Similarly, the sum of the females' ages is (approximately) $200 \cdot 35 = 7{,}000$ years. Then, the sum of the ages of all 500 people in the town is about $13{,}500 + 7{,}000 = 20{,}500$ years, which means the average age is about $\frac{20{,}500}{500} = 41$ years.

The most common wrong answer is **A**, which is the average of the two averages. This would only be correct if the number of males was equal to the number of females. Because the number of males is higher, the average of all 500 people is closer to the male average than to the female average.

Question 60. The correct answer is J. On September 1, the dress was priced at $90. On October 1, this price was reduced by 20%. That made its new price $90 − (20%)($90) = $90 − $18 = $72.

On November 1, this new price was reduced by 25% of the $72. The FINAL price was then $72 − (25%)($72) = $72 − $18 = $54.

The FINAL price of $54 is what percent of $90? That is $\frac{54}{90} \cdot 100\% = \frac{6}{10} \cdot 100\% = 60\%$.

If you chose **F**, you may have calculated the FINAL $54 price correctly, but figured the percent discount needed to get from $90 to $54 rather than the percent that $54 was of $90.

If you chose **H**, you likely calculated 100% − 20% − 25% = 55%. This only works when the percents are percents of the *same thing*. In this problem, the 100% and the 20% are of the $90, but the 25% is of the $72. Answer choice **G** is 20% + 25%.

Passage I

Question 1.

This is an EXCEPT question, which asks you to find the answer choice that is *not* supported by the passage.

The best answer is C because neither Vida nor Ted has a perception of others that surfaces in humor. The other three answer choices are supported by the passage.

The best answer is NOT:

A because Vida and Ted share a willingness to accommodate each other's requests. When Ted asks Vida if it's OK if he builds and moves into a fort for the summer, she doesn't respond with "offense" or "alarm," but only with "interest" (lines 18–19). Vida sets the rules Ted has to follow: "Make sure you keep your nails together and don't dig into the trees" (lines 25–26). Though Ted never directly says he'll obey, the fact that he builds and is allowed to keep the fort suggests that he does.

B because Vida and Ted share a response to elements of nature. For example, the eighth paragraph (lines 28–35) illustrates Ted's response to the redwoods, while the ninth paragraph (lines 36–48) shows Ted's and Vida's responses to the moon.

D because Vida and Ted know what delights the other. They have a "silent communion" (line 12) through food, which Vida prepares knowing Ted's "great appetite and obvious enjoyment of it" (lines 14–15). Ted, for his part, knows Vida "loved to see the moon's reflection in the water" (line 38) and that she seemed to want to "touch the moon" (lines 41–42).

Question 2.

This is a NOT question, which asks you to find the answer choice that is *not* supported by the passage.

The best answer is J because nothing in the passage indicates Ted and Vida have painful disagreements that force Ted to move out. When Ted asks Vida if it's OK if he builds and moves into a fort for the summer, she doesn't respond with "offense" or "alarm," but only with "interest" (lines 18–19). The passage lists the reasons why Ted moves back into the house—"school was starting, frost was coming and the rains" (lines 87–88)—but these reasons don't include reaching an understanding with Vida. The other three answer choices are supported by the passage.

The best answer is NOT:

F because the passage shows Ted's relationship with Vida improving after he builds and occupies the fort: "Vida noticed Ted had become cheerful and would stand next to her, to her left side, talking sometimes" (lines 61–62), which leads Vida to think of him as "a wild thing at peace" (line 69).

G because the passage shows what connects and separates Vida and Ted and how Ted tests his limits. Ted and Vida are connected by, among other things, food (see lines 12–17) and their fondness for the moon (see lines 36–48). They're separated by physical distance, when Ted moves out into the fort, and by emotional distance, since Vida "realized she mustn't face [Ted] or he'd become silent and wander away" (lines 63–64). The passage implies in many ways that Ted is testing his limits, such as by showing him asking for privacy and privileges from Vida (see, for example, lines 9–11) and working on the upper floor of the fort (see lines 55–60).

H because the passage shows how Vida and Ted behave when each sees the fragility of someone or something held dear. To observe Ted, Vida "stood listening, in the same even breath and heart beat she kept when she spotted the wild pheasants" (lines 64–66). Ted would "curse himself" if he wasted the "beautiful glass" (lines 76–77).

Question 3. The best answer is A because in the twelfth paragraph (lines 61–69), the author says Vida avoided facing Ted and remained still to keep from disturbing "a wild thing at peace" (line 69), while in the thirteenth paragraph (lines 70–77), the author describes Ted making cuts in glass that "were slow and meticulous with a steady pressure" (line 75) and carefully following the design in order to avoid wasting the glass.

The best answer is NOT:

B because Vida is neither frustrated nor unsuccessful in the twelfth paragraph, while the thirteenth paragraph only says Ted became frustrated when he failed, not that success was always slightly out of reach for him.

C or **D** because neither the twelfth nor the thirteenth paragraph shows a character losing interest in a project as others get involved (C) or discovering a personal weakness in some situations becoming a personal strength in others (D).

Question 4. The best answer is F because the twelfth paragraph (lines 61–69) shows Vida carefully and reverently observing Ted in the same way she used with the wild pheasants. She "realized she mustn't face him or he'd become silent and wander away" (lines 63–64). She "stood listening" to Ted "in the same even breath and heart beat she kept when she spotted the wild pheasants" (lines 64–66) in order to avoid disturbing Ted. When the paragraph concludes, "So sharp, so perfect, so rare to see a wild thing at peace" (lines 68–69), it's clear the phrase *wild thing* refers both to the pheasants and to Ted.

The best answer is NOT:

G because the phrase refers to Ted, not Vida.

H because the phrase refers to how Vida sees Ted, not to how Ted sees himself.

J because the twelfth paragraph shows Vida appreciates how Ted "had become cheerful and would stand next to her, to her left side, talking sometimes" (lines 61–62), and she respects that Ted is like a wild thing, even though it means she has to act carefully around him.

Question 5. The best answer is B because the passage describes the teenage Ted as "thinning out, becoming angular and clumsy" and retaining "the cautiousness, the old-man seriousness he'd had as a baby" (lines 1–3) as well as his sense of humor, "always dry and to the bone since a small child" (lines 4–5).

The best answer is NOT:

A because Ted had always been cautious and serious, not lighthearted, and because Ted "had become cheerful" (line 61) and more talkative, not brooding and isolated, since moving into the fort.

C because while the passage says Ted even as a small child "let you know he was watching everything" (lines 5–6), it doesn't say that he watched others for indications of how he should behave or that as a teenager he looked to nature for such guidance.

D because Ted was cautious and serious, not outgoing, as a child, and because no adult, including Vida, is alarmed by Ted's introspection as a teenager. When Ted watches Vida "for signs of offense, alarm," he "only saw interest" in his plan for building and moving into a fort for the summer (lines 18–19).

Question 6. The best answer is G because the passage states that to Vida, Ted "seemed always to be at the center of his own universe, so it was no surprise to his mother" to hear Ted's plan to build and move into a fort for the summer (lines 7–11).

The best answer is NOT:

F because the passage presents the fort as Ted's project, not as something Vida started.

H or J because there's no evidence in the passage that Ted had put more and more distance between himself and Vida since the camping trip (H) or that he had a longstanding craving for the company of others (J).

Question 7. The best answer is D because the passage describes the *silent communion* as "the steady presence of love that flowed regularly, daily" (lines 12–13) through food: "the presence of his mother preparing it, his great appetite and obvious enjoyment of it—his nose smelling everything, seeing his mother more vividly than with his eyes" (lines 14–17).

The best answer is NOT:

A because Ted isn't disappointed but instead pleased by the food and his mother's preparation of it.

B because while Ted does promise not to return to the house all summer, even for food (see lines 9–11), he makes this promise aloud to Vida, and in any case this promise isn't what the phrase *silent communion* refers to.

C because while Ted's thought about liking the moon does shift from seeming like someone else's to seeming like his own (see lines 46–48), this shift isn't what the phrase *silent communion* refers to.

Question 8. The best answer is H because the seventh paragraph (lines 25–27) illustrates both Vida's interest in Ted's project and her concerns about it. Earlier, the passage says Vida showed "interest" (line 19) in Ted's plan and that "she trusted him to build well and not ruin things" (line 21). The seventh paragraph shows Vida anticipating possible problems with the proposed fort and indicating how to avoid them: "Make sure you keep your nails together and don't dig into the trees. I'll be checking. If the trees get damaged, it'll have to come down."

The best answer is NOT:

F or J because there's no evidence in the passage that Vida has a skeptical nature or that Ted feels disheartened (F) or that Vida wants to give Ted more responsibility than Ted himself wants to take on (J).

G because the passage never says the fort was dismantled, only that Ted would have to move back inside "in a few days" (line 91).

Question 9. The best answer is B because in Ted's view, redwoods "suck up sound and time and smell like another place" (line 30), making the cypress near the redwoods seem like a "very remote" location (line 29) for the fort.

The best answer is NOT:

A because the passage doesn't say that Ted will use the redwoods as supports for the fort, only that Ted will build the fort "by the redwoods, in the cypress trees" (line 23).

C because while the passage does say that the site for the fort "seemed so separate, alone—especially in the dark, when the only safe way of travel seemed flight (invisible at best)" (lines 33–35), it doesn't say that this was because redwoods are endangered.

D because as lines 33–35 show, the redwoods increased, rather than softened, disturbing emotions such as fear of the dark.

Question 10. The best answer is H because lines 58–60 state, "It felt weird going up into the tree, not as safe as his small, contained place on the ground."

The best answer is NOT:

F or G because Ted feels less, not more, safe going up into the tree to build the top floor.

J because there's no evidence in the passage that Ted built any of the fort from redwood or cypress; the only building material mentioned by name is plywood (see lines 49–51).

Passage II

Question 11.

This is an EXCEPT question, which asks you to find the answer choice that is *not* supported by the passage.

The best answer is B because the passage doesn't mention waste emissions from the Asnaesverket Power Company being used to help produce heating oil. The other three answer choices are supported by the passage.

The best answer is NOT:

A because lines 27–29 state, "Waste steam from the power company is used by Novo Nordisk to heat the fermentation tanks that produce insulin and enzymes."

C because the process described in lines 27–29 "creates 700,000 tons of nitrogen-rich slurry a year" (lines 29–30), which Novo Nordisk gives to farmers for use as plant fertilizer.

D because lines 41–44 state, "The power company also squeezes sulfur from its emissions, but converts most of it to calcium sulfate (industrial gypsum), which it sells to Gyproc for wallboard."

Question 12. The best answer is J because "our system" (lines 1–2) is "a linear production system, which binges on virgin raw materials and spews out unusable waste" (lines 4–5). That "our system" is the system of the United States and Europe is implied in the seventh paragraph (lines 65–77) when the author mentions that environmental reform in the form of take-back laws is coming to these two regions.

The best answer is NOT:

F because while the passage does discuss four linked, co-located Denmark companies (see lines 13–44), the phrase "our system" refers to a wasteful system found in the United States and Europe.

G because the author implies that a system that produces recyclable durable goods such as refrigerators, washers, and cars is only "headed for the United States" (lines 68–69) via take-back laws yet to be passed. In any case, the phrase "our system" refers to a wasteful system found in both the United States and Europe.

H because it's the opposite of "our system," as described in the passage.

Question 13. **The best answer is A** because the second, third, and fourth paragraphs (lines 13–44) are mainly a case study of an ecopark in Kalundborg, Denmark. The three paragraphs show how the four companies in the ecopark depend on each other for resources and the recycling of waste. For example, the Asnaesverket Power Company sends waste steam to the Statoil Refinery and Novo Nordisk for use as a power source (see lines 16–20), while Statoil sends purified waste gas to Asnaesverket and Gyproc (see lines 35–39).

The best answer is NOT:

B because nowhere in the three paragraphs does the author indicate Denmark is one of the world's leading developers of new sources of energy or even that the sources of energy being used by the four companies in the ecopark are new.

C because while the passage does say that waste steam from the power company is used "to heat thirty-five hundred homes in the town, eliminating the need for oil furnaces" (lines 21–22), this isn't the same as saying that the town's need for energy can be eliminated through recycling. The town still needs energy; it just gets some of its energy needs met by an unusual source.

D because the three paragraphs aren't clear on whether a no-waste economy saves money, so saving money can't be their main focus.

Question 14. **The best answer is F** because the author says, "To keep our system from collapsing on itself" due to increasing amounts of biomass, "industrial ecologists are attempting to build a 'no-waste economy'" (lines 1–3), which she describes as "a web of closed loops in which a minimum of raw materials comes in the door, and very little waste escapes" (lines 6–8).

The best answer is NOT:

G because through her description in the seventh and last paragraphs (lines 65–89) of take-back laws and their impact, the author suggests that manufacturers, not consumers, should be held responsible for recycling many kinds of products.

H because the notion of having traditional businesses compete with new, innovative businesses doesn't directly come up in the passage. Instead, the author focuses on changes that can take place in all kinds of companies, traditional and new.

J because while the four Kalundborg companies described in the second, third, and fourth paragraphs (lines 13–44) are co-located in an ecopark, the author says that "industries need not be geographically close to operate in a food web as long as they are connected by a mutual desire to use waste" (lines 45–48). Also, the four Kalundborg companies aren't producing similar products.

Question 15. The best answer is C because Novo Nordisk's fermentation process produces "700,000 tons of nitrogen-rich slurry a year" (line 30), which is given free as fertilizer to farmers, whose plants "are in turn harvested to feed the bacteria in the fermentation tanks" (lines 33–34).

The best answer is NOT:

A because while purified waste gas from Statoil Refinery is sent to Gyproc (see lines 35–39), the passage doesn't show how, if at all, Statoil depends directly on Gyproc.

B because while the Asnaesverket Power Company "delivers its cooling water, now toasty warm, to fifty-seven ponds' worth of fish" (lines 23–24), the passage doesn't show how, if at all, Asnaesverket depends directly on fish farmers.

D because the passage doesn't show any direct relationship between Statoil and Novo Nordisk.

Question 16. The best answer is G because in the sixth paragraph (lines 58–64), the author uses phrases such as "so far" (line 58), "but what happens" (line 59), and "right now" (line 61) to signal a transition between the two main points in the passage: "recycling within a circle of companies" (lines 58–59) and the final fate of products once they leave the manufacturer.

The best answer is NOT:

F because the sixth paragraph doesn't provide any evidence to support Daniel Chiras's statement in lines 54–57: the discussion in the sixth paragraph is on products, not by-products.

H because the sixth paragraph offers no conclusion to the author's discussion about a no-waste economy; instead, the paragraph shifts gears between two points related to the idea of a no-waste economy.

J because while the sixth paragraph does provide something of a summary ("so far . . ."), the paragraph goes on to introduce the passage's second main point, which concerns the final fate of products once they leave the manufacturer.

Question 17. The best answer is D because the author says the German take-back laws "start with the initial sale," meaning "companies must take back all their packaging or hire middlemen to do the recycling" (lines 72–74). This fits in with the author's general discussion in the seventh paragraph (lines 65–77) of take-back laws, which "will require companies to take back their durable goods such as refrigerators, washers, and cars at the end of their useful lives" (lines 69–71).

The best answer is NOT:

A or B because there's no evidence in the passage that German take-back laws shift the responsibility of recycling from the local government to the manufacturer (A) or from the manufacturer to the local government (B).

C because it reverses the actual relationship.

Question 18. The best answer is J because lines 45–48 state that "industries need not be geographically close to operate in a food web as long as they are connected by a mutual desire to use waste."

The best answer is NOT:

F because, as the above quotation shows, companies need not relocate their operations to a common geographic area in Europe to be part of a food web.

G because while the Asnaesverket Power Company and Novo Nordisk do provide industrial waste to private homes and farming operations (see lines 16–34), the passage doesn't say that all companies that want to be part of a food web have to do this.

H because food webs, as described in the passage, don't eliminate the need for raw materials. Instead, one company's waste becomes another company's raw material, as when sulfur removed from Statoil Refinery's waste gas during purification is sent to Kemira for use in sulfuric acid production (see lines 35–41).

Question 19. The best answer is A because the author says "designed offal" results when companies design their processes in such a way that "any waste that falls on the production-room floor is valuable and can be used by someone else" (lines 49–51).

The best answer is NOT:

B because "designed offal" doesn't necessarily involve reducing waste products: "in this game of 'designed offal,' a process with lots of waste, as long as it's 'wanted waste,' may be better than one with a small amount of waste that must be landfilled or burned" (lines 51–54).

C because "designed offal" is a success story, not a failure of technology to keep pace with how to dispose of waste products.

D because while the author does mention landfills (see lines 51–54 and 62–64), she never discusses the idea of making landfill spaces more efficient. Her focus is on keeping products out of landfills.

Question 20. The best answer is H because in lines 56–57, Daniel Chiras is quoted as saying that "technologies that produce by-products society cannot absorb are essentially failed technologies."

The best answer is NOT:

F or G because Chiras's quotation deals with whether society as a whole, and not a particular technology, can make use of waste. The "designed offal" example described in lines 48–54 suggests that how much waste a particular technology produces isn't the most important factor in evaluating the environmental impact of the technology: a technology might produce more waste than it uses but still be environmentally sound so long as someone can use the waste.

J because Chiras doesn't say in the passage that a failed technology is one that produces durable goods such as refrigerators. The passage, on the contrary, indicates that durable goods can be produced with a greatly reduced environmental impact (see lines 59–84).

Passage III

Question 21. The best answer is A because the author praises Shakespeare on CD-ROM, calling it "potentially the most important thing to happen to the texts of Shakespeare's plays since the 18th century" (lines 1–3). The CD-ROM is, for the author, "a radical departure" (line 36) from the standard approach to presenting Shakespeare's works, which is to "silently stitch together the different versions of *Hamlet* or *King Lear* in an attempt to present the 'final' version Shakespeare supposedly meant to leave behind" (lines 30–33). The standard approach ignores the notion that Shakespeare "apparently regarded his plays as open and unfinished" (lines 22–23), to be "continually cut, revised or even radically reconceived according to the ideas of the players and the demands of the public" (lines 24–26). The author contends that "a CD-ROM has the power to make us think, 'It could be so different'" (lines 80–82), meaning that it allows users to, for example, "compare three or four radically different performances of the same scene, just as we could for the first time easily compare differences in the text" (lines 82–84).

The best answer is NOT:

B because while the author claims that "it is now widely recognized" that many of Shakespeare's plays "were repeatedly revised" (lines 12–13), he doesn't claim that the CD-ROMs he reviews were the first technology to verify this fact (though the CD-ROMs do allow people to easily see such revisions).

C because the author feels that "texts on CD-ROM have, in effect, recovered something of the magic that books possessed in the late Middle Ages" (lines 65–67).

D because the author never claims that the CD-ROMs are targeted to those who are intimidated by Shakespeare.

Question 22.

Note that this question is similar to a NOT or EXCEPT question in that you have to find the element of the passage that would be lost if the last paragraph had been omitted.

The best answer is J because only the last paragraph contains a specific example of an inconsistency in the text of a well-known Shakespeare play, such as *Romeo and Juliet*: the rest/rust example in lines 85–87.

The best answer is NOT:

F because several places in the passage other than the last paragraph contain examples of how CD-ROM technology enhances appreciation for Shakespeare centuries after his death. For example, the fourth paragraph (lines 36–46) mentions how easy it is for CD-ROM users to find and repeatedly listen to selected scenes as well as to look at glosses.

G because the fifth paragraph (lines 47–59), and not just the last paragraph, gives specific examples of people (Albert Finney and Patrick Ryecart) who have performed roles in Shakespeare plays.

H because not even the last paragraph gives specific examples of what caused scholars to view Shakespeare's plays as cultural treasures, although the first paragraph mentions that this first happened in the eighteenth century (see lines 1–5).

Question 23. **The best answer is D** because in the first paragraph, the author states, "Shakespeare on CD-ROM is potentially the most important thing to happen to the texts of Shakespeare's plays since the 18th century, when they were first given the serious scholarly attention reserved for cultural treasures" (lines 1–5). He then goes on, in the first paragraph and elsewhere, to explain what the shift is and how profound it is.

The best answer is NOT:

A because the author never claims that the magic of the theater has diminished since books became widely available, although he implies that books themselves have lost the magic they had in the late Middle Ages (see lines 65–68).

B because while the author does say that scholars see Shakespeare's works as "cultural treasures," he never says that scholars have long regarded Shakespeare as too sophisticated for the general public.

C because the author never claims that each generation identifies with a different one of Shakespeare's plays.

Question 24. **The best answer is J** because lines 36–38 state, "The words of the play appear on the screen, synchronized with a complete audio performance," while lines 43–44 state, "Each CD includes video clips of some of the most famous scenes."

The best answer is NOT:

F because while the CD-ROMs do contain complete text, they don't contain full-length video of a production.

G because while the CD-ROMs contain selected scenes on video from a production, they also contain complete text, not just selections.

H because the CD-ROMs contain complete text, not just selections, and because they don't contain full-length video of a production.

Question 25. **The best answer is C** because in lines 60–61, the author states, "Let me be clear: These Shakespeare CDs are not principally interesting as performances."

The best answer is NOT:

A or B because nowhere in the passage does the author worry that his praise for the Shakespeare CD-ROMs will be misunderstood as support of CD-ROMs in general (A) or as praise for well-meaning but mediocre actors (B). The author seems to appreciate the value of CD-ROMs generally, and he has nothing but praise for the actors he mentions.

D because the author supports having more than one interpretation of a Shakespeare play. He considers it a mistake for editors to try to "silently stitch together the different versions of *Hamlet* or *King Lear* in an attempt to present the 'final' version Shakespeare supposedly meant to leave behind" (lines 30–33), and he's excited that Shakespeare on CD-ROM can allow people to "compare three or four radically different performances of the same scene" and easily see "differences in the text" (lines 82–84).

Question 26. The best answer is H because the phrase "what the technology can do" (line 77) is preceded by a contrast, illustrated by the *Romeo and Juliet* CD-ROM, between Gwen Ffrangcon-Davies's and Claire Bloom's performances as Juliet; the phrase is then followed by the claim that "a CD-ROM has the power to make us think, 'It could be so different'" (lines 80–82), meaning the CD-ROM can easily illustrate how vastly different performances and interpretations can be inspired by Shakespeare's rich plays.

The best answer is NOT:

F because while the author criticizes the CD-ROMs he reviews for poor video clips and for problems with dubbing (see lines 47–55), the author feels Shakespeare CD-ROMs can support rather than interfere with the playwright's original intent by reminding users that Shakespeare's plays were "continually cut, revised or even radically reconceived" (lines 24–25) and that his words "were destined for the beauty and mutability of the human voice" (lines 28–29).

G or J because there's no evidence in the passage that the phrase "what the technology can do" refers to the capacity of CD-ROMs to reduce a play to the level of a television program (G) or simplify Shakespeare's complex messages by conveying them in modern English (J).

Question 27. The best answer is B because the author writes that although "it is now widely recognized that many of [Shakespeare's plays] were repeatedly revised" (lines 12–13), editors today generally still "silently stitch together the different versions of *Hamlet* or *King Lear* in an attempt to present the 'final' version Shakespeare supposedly meant to leave behind" (lines 30–33). This editing practice artificially tries to create the "definitive and final form" that people used to believe sprang from Shakespeare's "noble brow" (line 11).

The best answer is NOT:

A because the effort by editors to produce a "final" version is inconsistent with Shakespeare's concept of the adaptable nature of his plays: since in Shakespeare's mind the plays were "open and unfinished" (lines 22–23), there could be no "final" version.

C because the CD-ROM emphasizes the multiple versions of Shakespeare's plays (as in the rest/rust example in lines 85–87) rather than try to hide them, as most editors still try to do.

D because the effort by editors to produce a "final" version is inconsistent with the author's view of how Shakespeare's plays should be treated: he feels excited that, through CD-ROM technology, people could "compare three or four radically different performances of the same scene" and "easily compare differences in the text" (lines 82–84).

Question 28. The best answer is H because in lines 53–55, the author writes that "it is disconcerting to hear Albert Finney's unmistakable voice as Romeo coming from Patrick Ryecart's mouth."

The best answer is NOT:

F because while the author does say that "the dubbing is inevitably imperfect" (lines 52–53) on the *Romeo and Juliet* CD-ROM, this isn't the same as saying that Finney's words don't match the original script.

G because while the author does say that the audio accompanying the video clips is "mediocre" (line 50) in quality, he never mentions static interference.

J because there's no evidence in the passage that the author is bothered by Finney's voice on the *Romeo and Juliet* CD-ROM because the actor's words conjure up the tragic fate of Romeo.

Question 29. The best answer is D because the author asserts that the Shakespeare CD-ROMs' primary advantage is their ability to remind us that "the words were meant for our ears"—the spoken word—"as well as our eyes"—the written word (line 64).

The best answer is NOT:

A or B because there's no evidence in the passage that the author feels the CD-ROMs' primary advantage is their ability to make connections between original and contemporary set designs (A) or the themes of *Hamlet* and *King Lear* (B).

C because while the author does mention the eighteenth century, he does this only in passing to note when Shakespeare's plays "were first given the serious scholarly attention reserved for cultural treasures" (lines 3–5).

Question 30. The best answer is F because the author states that "a stage performance at its best [can make] us experience a certain inevitability, leading us to think of the actors' interpretation of the play, 'This *must* be so'" (lines 77–80).

The best answer is NOT:

G, H, or J because there's no evidence in the passage that the statement "It *must* be so" is an example of a line from a Shakespeare play (G), a quotation from a director (H), or an audio clip from the CD-ROM version of Shakespeare's *Romeo and Juliet* (J).

Passage IV

Question 31. The best answer is D because throughout the passage, the author reports on recent theories and controversies related to Mars's early history. The first paragraph describes the theory that Mars was once a "garden world" (line 15); the second through fifth paragraphs (lines 17–62) present theories about the "Martian apocalypse" (line 23), focusing on the work of Vickery and Melosh; and the last two paragraphs (lines 63–88) discuss criticism of the "garden world" theory and Vickery and Melosh's response to that criticism.

The best answer is NOT:

A because while the author does present contending theories about the early history of Mars, she doesn't claim that these differences are irreconcilable, and she spends at least as much time on a single theory (Vickery and Melosh's) as she does on the differences.

B because the author never suggests that early Martian history is important to understanding other aspects of planetary science.

C because a comparison between the atmospheric pressure of Earth and Mars is only a relatively small aspect of the passage, and even when the two are directly compared, as in lines 8–14, the comparison suggests they were likely similar (long ago, at least), not different.

Question 32. The best answer is H because in the last paragraph, Vickery asserts that the "valley networks" on Mars "look like terrestrial river valley networks" (lines 83–84), which leads her to conclude that "these networks were formed more or less the same way as similar terrestrial networks" (lines 87–88)—that is, by liquid water. The first paragraph also mentions these valleys, which "implied that there had once been water freely flowing over the surface of Mars" (lines 5–6). As lines 8–10 point out, "Our planet is blessed with liquid water on its surface only because it has a thick atmosphere to maintain a high pressure and trap the sun's heat," leading scientists to hypothesize that Mars at one time also had "warmth, water, and air" (line 14).

The best answer is NOT:

F because while Vickery and Melosh propose that "most of Mars' atmosphere . . . was blasted away by a succession of asteroids and comets" (lines 31–32), the information in the last paragraph is about what Mars would have been like when it was a "garden world" (line 15) with liquid water on its surface, not about "the Martian apocalypse" (line 23).

G because while scientists believe Mars formed about 4.6 billion years ago (see lines 10–14), the information in the last paragraph isn't directly related to this hypothesis.

J because the hypothesis that large expanses of ice once covered Mars is part of a theory Vickery and Melosh dispute about how the Martian valley networks were formed. The last paragraph says that despite this alternative explanation, involving surface ice and Mars's interior heat, "Vickery . . . is sticking by her original assumptions" (lines 82–83) that liquid water created the valley networks.

Question 33. **The best answer is A** because while the idea of the Martian valleys being drainage basins and streambeds is just a hypothesis, if the hypothesis were correct, it would support the idea of Mars having once been a "garden world" (line 15). The author indicates that *Mariner 9*'s images of Mars "revealed networks of valleys that looked uncannily like drainage basins and streambeds back here on Earth" (lines 3–5). These images "implied that there had once been water freely flowing over the surface of Mars" and that "Mars had once had a thick atmosphere" (lines 5–8) to hold in the sun's heat. "Warmth, water, and air" could have made Mars "a paradise among planets" (lines 14–16).

The best answer is NOT:

B because the possibility that the young sun was 25 to 30 percent dimmer than it is today would reduce the likelihood that Mars was once a "garden world" since Mars would have had less of the "warmth" needed for such a world.

C because while Vickery and Melosh assumed that a succession of asteroids and comets struck Mars about every 10,000 years (see lines 58–62), this rate of impact, even if correct, wouldn't by itself prove that Mars was once a "garden world"—the asteroids and comments would presumably have struck Mars whether or not it had Earthlike conditions.

D because lines 77–81 present the idea that large expanses of ice on Mars were thawed by a heat source deep within the planet in order to show how Mars might have come by its valleys without ever having been a "garden world" with liquid water on its surface.

Question 34. **The best answer is H** because the author repeatedly links the amount of solar heat a planet retains to the thickness of its atmosphere. In lines 8–10, she says, "Our planet is blessed with liquid water on its surface only because it has a thick atmosphere to maintain a high pressure and trap the sun's heat." She suggests that Mars also once may have had "a dowry of a heat-trapping atmosphere" (lines 12–13). In the third paragraph (lines 22–32), she discusses several theories of the "Martian apocalypse" (line 23); all of which center on Mars losing its thick atmosphere.

The best answer is NOT:

F because, according to the passage, the amount of liquid water a planet has (on its surface, anyway) is in part a consequence of the amount of solar heat the planet's atmosphere retains. The passage doesn't say that the liquid water itself retains the heat.

G or **J** because the passage never links the amount of solar heat a planet retains to the planet's distance from other planets (**G**) or to the volume and mass of its underground ice (**J**).

Question 35. The best answer is **A** because the third paragraph (lines 22–32) presents three theories attempting to account for how Mars lost its thick atmosphere: it could have been worn away by the solar wind, absorbed into carbonate rocks, or "blasted away by a succession of asteroids and comets" (line 32).

The best answer is NOT:

B because the third paragraph doesn't indicate that there are several theories about how carbon dioxide turns into rock.

C because the third paragraph mentions the solar wind but not the wind on Mars.

D because only one of the three theories mentioned in the third paragraph has anything to do with the sun gradually taking away Mars's atmosphere.

Question 36. The best answer is **F** because Vickery and Melosh contend that "most of Mars' atmosphere . . . was blasted away by a succession of asteroids and comets" (lines 31–32). Each high-speed object crashing into Mars "vaporizes and expands into the atmosphere" (line 35), according to Melosh, "shov[ing] the atmosphere above it" (lines 36–37). If the object "is big enough and fast enough, it can drive its plume straight back up into space" (lines 40–41), pushing a portion of the planet's atmosphere out with it.

The best answer is NOT:

G because there's no evidence in the passage that Vickery and Melosh think the atmosphere of Mars trapped too much heat and burned away a layer of carbon dioxide.

H or J because the only reference to a wind of charged particles (H) or to carbonate rocks (J) is in relation to theories rejected by Vickery and Melosh about how Mars lost its thick atmosphere (see lines 23–27). These two answer choices also misstate the theories in lines 23–27.

Question 37. The best answer is **C** because Vickery and Melosh's hypothesis depends in part on the impacting comets and asteroids being "big enough and fast enough" to drive their vapor plumes "straight back up into space," taking with them portions of Mars's atmosphere that are "then stripped from the planet forever" (lines 40–43). If the majority of the comets and asteroids were very small, they would lack sufficient mass to drive their plumes into space. Vickery and Melosh's hypothesis wouldn't be weakened if any of the other answer choices were true.

The best answer is NOT:

A because the last paragraph shows that Vickery and Melosh already assume that the network of valleys on Mars was made up of drainage basins and streambeds.

B because the rate of asteroid impact isn't central to Vickery and Melosh's hypothesis, and a much higher rate would presumably only have accelerated the destruction of Mars's atmosphere.

D because Vickery and Melosh's hypothesis already assumes that Mars once had a thick, Earth-like atmosphere that "was blasted away by a succession of asteroids and comets" (lines 31–32).

Question 38. The best answer is **G** because the passage suggests that if "the young sun was 25 to 30 percent dimmer than it is today" (lines 67–68), then Mars "would have been receiving less than a third of the sunlight we now enjoy" (lines 69–71). This has led some scientists to conclude that "Mars' atmosphere wouldn't be able to trap enough heat to keep water from freezing and that under such conditions, carbon dioxide would form frozen clouds" (lines 72–75) that would cool the planet further by reflecting sunlight.

The best answer is NOT:

F because at some point in the past, something happened to Mars "that stripped nearly all of its atmosphere" (line 20).

H because a dimmer sun would make it less, not more, likely that liquid water once existed on Mars.

J because the passage doesn't show a connection between a dimmer sun and large asteroids routinely hitting Mars.

Question 39. The best answer is **D** because Vickery and Melosh's hypothesis is that "most of Mars' atmosphere . . . was blasted away by a succession of asteroids and comets" (lines 31–32). "The basic idea" of the hypothesis is that an asteroid or comet "impact doesn't just open a crater. With high velocities, the projectile"—the comet or asteroid—"vaporizes and expands into the atmosphere" (lines 33–35), driving atmosphere ahead of it, possibly into space if the projectile has sufficient mass and velocity.

The best answer is NOT:

A because the passage never mentions a large mass of charged particles carried by the wind; it only mentions the solar wind, which is made up of charged particles (see lines 23–25).

B because while the passage does refer to carbonate rocks in lines 25–27, such rocks aren't the same as the asteroids and comets referred to by the word *projectile*.

C because a "superheated expanding plume" (line 36)—and not a plume of water vapor—is created by the impact of the projectile, so the plume itself isn't the projectile.

Question 40. The best answer is **G** because lines 59–62 state, "Vickery and Melosh were able to start with a virtually dead planet and grow a thick atmosphere in only 600 or 700 million years."

The best answer is NOT:

F because the figure 10,000 is related to the rate of asteroid and comet impact that "prevailed 3.7 billion years ago—one impact every 10,000 years" (lines 58–59).

H because 3.7 billion years is both the age of the youngest Martian streambed (see lines 18–19) and the number of years backward in time that Vickery and Melosh's model goes (see lines 58–62).

J because "Mars formed 4.6 billion years ago" (lines 11–12).

Passage I

Question 1. The best answer is D. Table 1 lists R for each of the 4 initial speeds. At an initial speed of 20 mi/hr, $R = 22$ ft. At an initial speed of 80 mi/hr, $R = 88$ ft. Compared to R at an initial speed of 20 mi/hr, R at an initial speed of 80 mi/hr is 4 times as great.

The best answer is NOT:

A because compared to R at an initial speed of 20 mi/hr, R at an initial speed of 80 mi/hr is 4 times as great, not one-fourth as great.

B because compared to R at an initial speed of 20 mi/hr, R at an initial speed of 80 mi/hr is 4 times as great, not one-half as great.

C because compared to R at an initial speed of 20 mi/hr, R at an initial speed of 80 mi/hr is 4 times as great, not 2 times as great.

Question 2. The best answer is F. Table 1 lists R, B, and D. At 20 mi/hr, $R = 22$ ft, $B = 20$ ft, and $D = 42$ ft. At 40 mi/hr, $R = 44$ ft, $B = 80$ ft, and $D = 124$ ft. At 60 mi/hr, $R = 66$ ft, $B = 180$ ft, and $D = 246$ ft. At 80 mi/hr, $R = 88$ ft, $B = 320$ ft, and $D = 408$ ft. So, for each initial speed, $D = R + B$.

The best answer is NOT:

G because $D \neq R - B$.

H because $D \neq R \times B$. Note that if $D = R \times B$, the unit of measure for D would be ft^2. However, the unit of measure for D is ft.

J because $D \neq R \div B$. Note that if $D = R \div B$, then D would not have a unit of measure. However, the unit of measure for D is ft.

Question 3. The best answer is B. In Figure 1, the 2 methods give the same value for D where the 2 curves intersect. The curves intersect at an initial speed of about 37 mi/hr. Of the speeds listed in the 4 options, 37 mi/hr is closest to 40 mi/hr.

The best answer is NOT:

A because at 20 mi/hr, Method 2 yields a larger value for D than does Method 1.

C or D because at 60 mi/hr and 80 mi/hr, respectively, Method 1 yields a larger value for D than does Method 2.

Question 4. The best answer is **H.** According to Method 2, the total stopping distance (D) equals the initial speed in ft/sec multiplied by 2 sec. The question specifies that the initial speed is 60 mi/hr, which, according to Table 1, is 88 ft/sec. So, D = 88 ft/sec × 2 sec = 176 ft, as given in Table 1. The answer can also be determined using Figure 1. In Figure 1, along the curve for Method 2, an x-value of 60 mi/hr corresponds to a y-value of approximately 176 ft for D.

The best answer is NOT:

F or G because the car would travel more than 58 ft and 118 ft, respectively, during the 2 sec interval.

J because the car would travel less than 234 ft during the 2 sec interval.

Question 5. The best answer is **D.** According to Table 1, for every 20 mi/hr increase in the initial speed, D increases approximately 60 ft. Because an initial speed of 90 mi/hr represents a 10 mi/hr increase over an initial speed of 80 mi/hr, D for an initial speed of 90 mi/hr must be about 30 ft longer than D for an initial speed of 80 mi/hr. Based on this analysis, D for an initial speed of 90 mi/hr is 236 ft + 30 ft = 266 ft. In Figure 1, note that the slope of the straight line representing Method 2 is approximately equal to 150 ft per 50 mi/hr, or 3 ft per 1 mi/hr. For an initial speed of 80 mi/hr, D is greater than 230 ft. For an initial speed of 90 mi/hr, D will be greater than 230 ft + (10 mi/hr × 3 ft per mi/hr) = 260 ft.

The best answer is NOT:

A, B, or C because, as noted above, for an initial speed of 90 mi/hr, D will be greater than 260 ft, not less than 260 ft.

Passage II

Question 6. The best answer is **J.** The urine sample with the highest water content per milliliter will most likely be the urine sample with the lowest concentration of suspended solids. In addition, because the specific gravity of a urine sample equals the density of the urine sample divided by the density of water, the urine sample with a specific gravity closest to 1.0 is the urine sample with the highest water content per milliliter. According to Tables 1 and 2, of the 4 options provided, the urine sample from Student D at 8:00 P.M. had the lowest concentration of suspended solids and had a specific gravity closest to 1.0.

The best answer is NOT:

F because the urine sample from Student D at 8:00 P.M. had a lower concentration of suspended solids and a specific gravity closer to 1.0 than did the 8:00 A.M. urine sample from Student A.

G because the urine sample from Student D at 8:00 P.M. had a lower concentration of suspended solids and a specific gravity closer to 1.0 than did the 8:00 A.M. urine sample from Student B.

H because the urine sample from Student D at 8:00 P.M. had a lower concentration of suspended solids and a specific gravity closer to 1.0 than did the 8:00 P.M. urine sample from Student C.

Question 7. **The best answer is D.** Table 1 shows that as the urine volume increases from 100 mL to 385 mL, the color value decreases from 8 to 2. The note in the table indicates that the values for color range from 0 for very pale urine to 10 for very dark urine. These data do not support the conclusion that as urine volume increases, urine color darkens. Table 2 shows that as the urine volume increases from 150 mL to 400 mL, the color value decreases from 7 to 0. These data do not support the conclusion that as urine volume increases, urine color darkens. The urine samples with the greatest volume had the lightest color (for example, Student D at 8:00 A.M. and Student D at 8:00 P.M.).

The best answer is NOT:

A or B because the data do not support the conclusion that as urine volume increases, urine color darkens.

C because in each of the 2 tables the urine sample with the greatest volume had the lowest color value, not the highest color value. For example, in Table 2 the 8:00 P.M. urine sample from Student D had the greatest volume and the lowest color value.

Question 8. **The best answer is F.** If the urine samples are listed in order from the urine sample with the lowest concentration of suspended solids (Student D at 8:00 P.M.) to the urine sample with the highest concentration of suspended solids (Student A at 8:00 A.M.), then the urine samples will also be ordered from the urine sample with the lowest specific gravity to the urine sample with the highest specific gravity. This result supports the conclusion that as the concentration of suspended solids in urine increases, the specific gravity of the urine increases.

The best answer is NOT:

G, H, or J because as the concentration of suspended solids in the urine samples increases, the specific gravity of the urine samples never decreases.

Question 9. **The best answer is A.** If 1 of the 4 students experienced a net fluid loss prior to providing urine samples, then this student would most likely have urine samples of low volume. In addition, compared to the other urine samples, these urine samples would have higher specific gravities, because they would contain higher concentrations of suspended solids. For both sets (8:00 A.M. and 8:00 P.M.) of urine samples, Student A's urine sample had the lowest volume and the highest specific gravity.

The best answer is NOT:

B, C, or D because for both sets of urine samples, Student A's urine sample had a lower volume and a higher specific gravity than did Student B's urine sample, Student C's urine sample, and Student D's urine sample, respectively.

Question 10. The best answer is H. If volume is held constant across urine samples, then the urine sample with the greatest density will weigh the most. Because the specific gravity of a urine sample equals the density of the urine sample divided by the density of water, the urine sample with the highest specific gravity will have the highest density. Of the 4 options provided, the urine sample with the highest specific gravity was the 8:00 P.M. urine sample from Student A. Therefore, per unit volume, this urine sample weighed the most.

The best answer is NOT:

F, G, or J because the 8:00 P.M. urine sample from Student A had a higher specific gravity than did the 8:00 A.M. urine sample from Student B, the 8:00 A.M. urine sample from Student D, and the 8:00 P.M. urine sample from Student C, respectively.

Passage III

Question 11. The best answer is C. Table 2 shows that the boiling point of an NaCl solution made with 100 g of H_2O increases by 1°C for every 0.1 moles of NaCl in the solution. Because the boiling point of pure H_2O is 100°C, if the solution boils at 104°C, the solution must contain 0.4 moles of NaCl.

The best answer is NOT:

A because a solution containing 100 g of H_2O and 0.2 moles of NaCl will boil at 102°C.

B because a solution containing 100 g of H_2O and 0.3 moles of NaCl will boil at 103°C.

D because a solution containing 100 g of H_2O and 0.5 moles of NaCl will boil at 105°C.

Question 12. The best answer is J. In Experiment 2, the student kept the amount of H_2O constant at 100 g, kept the substance added (NaCl) the same in each trial, and intentionally varied the amount of NaCl added in each trial, while measuring the boiling point of the resulting solutions. Thus, boiling point was not directly controlled. (Boiling point was the dependent variable.)

The best answer is NOT:

F because the student always added NaCl to the solution.

G because the student always used 100 g of H_2O to make each solution.

H because the student determined the amount of solute added to the H_2O by controlling the amount of NaCl added to the H_2O.

Question 13. The best answer is A. The passage explains that each mole of NaCl dissolves to produce 2 moles of solute particles. So, as the amount of NaCl dissolved increases, the number of solute particles increases. Table 2 shows that as the amount of NaCl dissolved in the H_2O increased, the boiling point increased. This information supports the hypothesis that as the number of solute particles increases, the boiling point of a solution increases.

The best answer is NOT:

B because more solute particles resulted in a higher boiling point.

C because as the concentration of NaCl was varied, the concentration of solute particles varied. Thus, a hypothesis *can* be made about the relationship between the number of solute particles in a solution and the boiling point of the solution.

D because as the number of solute particles increases, the boiling point of a solution increases. Thus, the number of solute particles *does* affect the boiling point of the solution.

Question 14. The best answer is J. Solutions 4 and 12 each contained 0.2 mole of NaCl and 100 g of H_2O. The NaCl resulted in a 6.9°C decrease in the freezing point (from 0°C for H_2O to –6.9°C for Solution 4) and a 2.0°C increase in the boiling point (from 100°C for H_2O to 102.0°C for Solution 12). Thus, the freezing point was lowered more than the boiling point was raised.

The best answer is NOT:

F or G because the freezing point was lowered.

H because the freezing point was lowered more than the boiling point was raised.

Question 15. The best answer is B. According to the passage, each mole of NaCl dissolved to form a mole of sodium ions and a mole of chloride ions. Accordingly, as the amount of NaCl increased, the number of sodium particles and chloride particles in solution also increased. In addition, Table 1 shows that as the amount of NaCl increased, the freezing point decreased. Thus, as the number of sodium particles and chloride particles in solution increased, the freezing point decreased.

The best answer is NOT:

A or C because as the number of sodium particles and chloride particles in solution increased, the freezing point decreased only.

D because as the number of sodium particles and chloride particles in solution increased, the freezing point did not remain the same.

Question 16. The best answer is H. The passage states that each mole of NaCl produces 2 moles of solute particles. Because each mole of $CaCl_2$ produces 3 moles of solute particles, the addition of 0.1 mole of $CaCl_2$ will result in 0.3 mole of solute particles. Solution 3 contained 0.2 mole of solute particles. Solution 4 contained 0.4 mole of solute particles. Because $CaCl_2$ affects the freezing point of H_2O in the same way that NaCl affects the freezing point of H_2O, the effect of 0.3 mole of $CaCl_2$ will be greater than the effect of 0.2 mole of NaCl and less than the effect of 0.1 mole of NaCl. That is, 0.1 mole of $CaCl_2$ will decrease the freezing point by more than 3.4°C and less than 6.9°C. As a result, the freezing point will be less than –3.4°C and more than –6.9°C.

The best answer is NOT:

F or G because 0.1 mole of $CaCl_2$ will decrease the freezing point by more than 3.4°C. Thus, the freezing point will be lower than –3.4°C.

J because 0.1 mole of $CaCl_2$ will decrease the freezing point by less than 6.9°C. Thus, the freezing point will be greater than –6.9°C.

Passage IV

Question 17. The best answer is C. According to Figure 1, the average air temperature was –26°C for January and –16°C for March. The average air temperature was –16°C for March and –5°C for September. The average air temperature was –5°C for May and –5°C for September. The average air temperature was –10°C for October and –24°C for December.

The best answer is NOT:

A, B, or D because the average air temperatures in the Arctic were identical in May and September. For each of the other pairs of months, the average air temperatures in the Arctic were not identical.

Question 18. The best answer is G. Figure 1 shows that from January to July, the average monthly air temperature increased and $\delta^{18}O$ increased. Figure 1 also shows that from July to December, the average monthly air temperature decreased and $\delta^{18}O$ decreased. In general, Figure 1 is most consistent with the conclusion that as the average monthly air temperature increased (from January to July), then decreased (from July to December), $\delta^{18}O$ increased, then decreased.

The best answer is NOT:

F because as the average monthly air temperature increased, then decreased, $\delta^{18}O$ did not increase only.

H because as the average monthly air temperature increased, then decreased, $\delta^{18}O$ did not decrease only.

J because as the average monthly air temperature increased, then decreased, $\delta^{18}O$ did not decrease, then increase.

Question 19. The best answer is B. The passage explains that the scientists wanted to examine $\delta^{18}O$ in glacial ice. The Arctic and Antarctic were chosen because many locations in the Arctic and Antarctic have had glaciers for thousands of years. Thus, ice cores could be collected from these locations.

The best answer is NOT:

A because Figure 1 shows that the Arctic does not have average monthly air temperatures below $-25°C$ year-round.

C because the experimenters wanted to collect precipitation during each month so they could calculate $\delta^{18}O$.

D because though it may be true that the sites had large areas of bare soil and rock present, the researchers were doing studies on areas where glaciers were present. The areas of bare soil and rock would not provide a reason to choose these locations for the studies.

Question 20. The best answer is J. Figure 2 shows $\delta^{18}O$ along the bottom of the graph and climate along the top of the graph. As the climate warms, $\delta^{18}O$ increases. In Figure 2, at depths between 150 and 200 m, $\delta^{18}O$ ranges from -17.5 to -10.0. The $\delta^{18}O$ value at the surface (a depth of 0 m) corresponds to the present-day climate. The $\delta^{18}O$ values for the portion of the ice cores at depths of 150 m and 200 m are all higher than the value for the present day. This indicates that compared to the present-day climate, the climate was warmer at the time the ice that is currently located at depths of 150 m to 200 m was forming.

The best answer is NOT:

F or G because compared to the present-day climate, the climate was warmer at the time the ice that is currently located at depths of 150 m to 200 m was forming.

H because Study 2 did not examine ice cores from the Antarctic.

Question 21. The best answer is A. The ice cores in Studies 2 and 3 correspond to 100,000 years of glacial ice accumulation. If 100,000 years resulted in 500 m of ice in the Arctic and 300 m of ice in the Antarctic, then the rate of ice accumulation was greater in the Arctic (0.005 m/year) than in the Antarctic (0.003 m/year).

The best answer is NOT:

B or C because 100,000 years resulted in more glacial ice accumulation in the Arctic than in the Antarctic. Thus, the rate of glacial ice accumulation was greater in the Arctic than in the Antarctic.

D because the rate could be determined by dividing the ice core length by the time of accumulation.

Question 22. The best answer is G. Based on the formula provided in the passage, $\delta^{18}O$ equals zero if and only if the $^{18}O/^{16}O$ of the sample equals the $^{18}O/^{16}O$ of the standard. When this occurs, the numerator equals zero, so $\delta^{18}O$ equals zero.

The best answer is NOT:

F, H, or J because each of these options results in a nonzero numerator. If the numerator in the formula is nonzero, then $\delta^{18}O$ is also nonzero.

Passage V

Question 23. The best answer is B. The scientists discuss the extinction of most marine species 250 million years ago. Scientist 1 states that volcanic eruptions sent large amounts of SO_4-containing aerosols into the air. This contributed to the breakdown of the ozone layer, which allowed higher levels of ultraviolet light to reach Earth's surface. Scientist 1 argues that this process may have contributed to the extinction of many species. This is most consistent with the conclusion that high levels of ultraviolet light are harmful to many species.

The best answer is NOT:

A because Scientist 1 provides no reason to conclude that high levels of ultraviolet light are beneficial to many living things. In fact, this conclusion would weaken Scientist's 1 argument, because Scientist 1 is trying to explain why most marine species became extinct.

C because Scientist 1 does not suggest that ultraviolet light helps create ozone in the atmosphere.

D because Scientist 1 does not suggest that ultraviolet light helps create CO_2 in the atmosphere. Instead, Scientist 1 argues that volcanic eruptions released large amounts of CO_2 into the air.

Question 24. The best answer is F. Scientist 1 states that volcanic eruptions sent large quantities of SO_4-containing aerosols and CO_2 into the atmosphere. Scientist 1 then argues that the increase in atmospheric CO_2 led to climatic warming. However, if SO_4-containing aerosols in the atmosphere result in a lowering of the surface temperature, then Scientist 1's viewpoint would be weakened, because the SO_4-containing aerosols would tend to counteract the climatic warming caused by the increase in atmospheric CO_2. In contrast, Scientist 2 did not mention SO_4-containing aerosols as a part of the sequence of events that caused the extinctions. Therefore, the finding would not weaken Scientist 2's viewpoint.

The best answer is NOT:

G or H because the finding that SO_4-containing aerosols in the atmosphere result in a lowering of the surface temperature would weaken Scientist 1's viewpoint, but would not weaken Scientist 2's viewpoint.

J because the finding that SO_4-containing aerosols in the atmosphere result in a lowering of the surface temperature would weaken Scientist 1's viewpoint.

Question 25. The best answer is C. Scientist 2 explains that a cooling of the ocean surface contributed to vertical circulation of the ocean. This explanation indicates that Scientist 2 would most likely predict that vertical circulation requires cooling of the ocean surface. Of the 4 options provided, only C is associated with a cooling of the ocean surface. Ice sheets in Earth's polar region contribute to the cooling of the ocean surface.

The best answer is NOT:

A because high levels of CO_2 would tend to raise atmospheric and ocean surface temperatures.

B because Scientist 2 does not suggest that active volcanoes around the Pacific Ocean rim affect ocean surface temperatures or vertical circulation.

D because Scientist 2 does not suggest that marine organisms in deep ocean waters affect ocean surface temperatures or vertical circulation.

Question 26. The best answer is G. Scientist 1 states that the ocean water became oxygen-poor when ocean circulation slowed. Scientist 2 states that ocean water was stagnant and oxygen-poor because vertical circulation of the ocean was absent. Both scientists agree that a lack of ocean circulation contributes to an oxygen-poor environment.

The best answer is NOT:

F because Scientists 1 and 2 do not discuss the reversal of ocean water circulation.

H because an increase in the available oxygen in ocean waters would make the ocean water oxygen-rich, not oxygen-poor.

J because a change in the available CO_2 in the ocean water would not affect the abundance of oxygen in ocean waters.

Question 27. The best answer is D. The extinctions addressed by the scientists happened about 250 million years ago. Scientist 1 states that these extinctions were caused by massive volcanic eruptions. The lava produced by these eruptions would have solidified into rock. If these rocks were dated, they would be approximately 250 million years old.

The best answer is NOT:

A, B, or C because the lava produced by the volcanic eruptions would have solidified into rock soon after the eruptions occurred. The age of a rock is determined by the time at which the rock solidifies, so the rocks produced by the volcanic eruptions would be approximately 250 million years old.

Question 28. The best answer is G. Scientist 1 describes how large amounts of SO_4-containing aerosols were sent into the air. According to Scientist 1, these compounds combined with water vapor to produce acid rain. Acid rain is more acidic than is normal rain. Thus, acid rain has a lower pH than does normal rain.

The best answer is NOT:

F because, according to Scientist 1, SO_4-containing aerosols help break down ozone in the atmosphere, and this breakdown in ozone leads to an *increase* in the amount of ultraviolet light reaching Earth's surface.

H because Scientist 1 does not suggest a link between SO_4-containing aerosols and rainfall.

J because Scientist 1 does not suggest a link between SO_4-containing aerosols and wind speed.

Question 29. The best answer is C. Scientist 1 states that high levels of CO_2 in the atmosphere raised the CO_2 content of ocean surface waters to levels that were toxic to many marine organisms. Scientist 2 states that deep, CO_2-rich ocean waters came to the surface and dramatically increased the CO_2 content of surface waters. Both explanations identify higher levels of CO_2 in ocean surface waters as a contributory factor to the mass extinctions. The presence of large deposits of inorganic carbonates that had formed around 250 Ma would, therefore, support both hypotheses.

The best answer is NOT:

A, B, or D for the reason just stated: the discovery of large deposits of inorganic carbonates would indicate higher levels of CO_2 in ocean surface waters, which both scientists claim contributed to the mass extinctions.

Passage VI

Question 30. The best answer is H. The passage shows a reaction for the formation of water: $2 H_2 + O_2 \rightarrow 2 H_2O$. The decomposition of H_2O results in the reverse of this reaction: $2 H_2O \rightarrow 2 H_2 + O_2$.

The best answer is NOT:

F or G because the decomposition of H_2O does not result in the production of H_2O.

J because the decomposition of H_2O results in 2 molecules of H_2 and 1 molecule of O_2, rather than 1 molecule of H_2 and 2 molecules of O_2.

Question 31. The best answer is A. In Trial 1, when the mixture of gases was sparked, the gases were consumed and liquid water formed. Because the reactants were gases, they had a greater volume than did the product, which was a liquid. Because of this change in volume, the pressure in the syringe should have decreased. Thus, a decrease in the overall amount of gas in the syringe caused a decrease in the volume of the contents of the syringe and a decrease in the pressure in the syringe.

The best answer is NOT:

B because the overall amount of gas did not increase; the overall amount of gas decreased.

C or D because the pressure in the syringe after the spark was lower than before the spark. This decrease in pressure occurred because the gases were consumed and liquid water was formed. The liquid water had a lower volume than did the gases, so the pressure decreased.

Question 32. The best answer is J. The reaction provided in the passage and the data in Table 1 show that H_2 and O_2 react in a ratio of 2:1 to form H_2O. If 50 mL of H_2 reacts with 50 mL of O_2, all 50 mL of H_2 reacts, but only 25 mL of O_2 reacts, so the final volume of O_2 remaining in the syringe will be 25 mL.

The best answer is NOT:

F, G, or H for the reason just stated: the syringe would still contain 25 mL of unreacted O_2.

Question 33. The best answer is D. To properly interpret the results of Experiment 1 and arrive at the conclusion that the reaction given in the passage is correct, one must assume that each of the reactions ran to completion. If the reactions had not run to completion, then the researchers would not have been able to draw conclusions about the reaction that occurred in the syringe. Because the researchers provide an equation based on the results of the trials, it is most likely that they assumed the reaction had run to completion.

The best answer is NOT:

A because the reaction would occur whether or not excess O_2 was present. For example, in Trials 1, 5, and 6, no excess O_2 was present, but the reaction still occurred.

B because CuO was not used in Experiment 1.

C because $CaCl_2$ was not used in Experiment 1.

Question 34. The best answer is G. The chemical coefficients for a reaction involving gases correspond to the ratio of the volumes of the gases that will react to form a product. For the reaction provided, the coefficient of N_2 is 1 and the coefficient of H_2 is 3. So, N_2 and H_2 will react in a 1:3 ratio of volumes. Therefore, 10 mL of N_2 will react with 30 mL of H_2, leaving 10 mL of H_2 that has not reacted.

The best answer is NOT:

F, H, or J because the reaction consumes 10 mL of N_2 and 30 mL of H_2. Thus, if 10 mL of N_2 and 40 mL of H_2 were completely reacted, 10 mL of H_2 would remain unreacted.

Question 35. The best answer is A. In Experiment 2, there was a steady stream of H_2 used in the reaction, so H_2 was in excess for the reaction. If nonreactive impurities had been present, these impurities would not have affected the amount of H_2 used, nor would these impurities have caused any side reactions that could have changed the results.

The best answer is NOT:

B because if the CuO contained reactive impurities, the initial and final masses of CuO would not have been correctly determined, and consequently, the mass of CuO reacted would not have been correctly determined. In addition, if the impurities were reactive, they might have produced other products that would have been absorbed by the $CaCl_2$, affecting the final mass of the $CaCl_2$.

C because if the H_2O escaped without being absorbed by the $CaCl_2$, the final mass of the $CaCl_2$ would not have indicated the actual amount of H_2O that was produced.

D because if CuO reacted with H_2 to produce products other than H_2O, then one could not have used this experiment to determine the validity of the reaction given in the passage. One could not have determined whether or not the increase in the mass of the $CaCl_2$ was caused only by H_2O.

Passage VII

Question 36. The best answer is J. Figure 3 shows fall time as a function of Y_0 for the Moon, Earth, and Jupiter. On the Moon's surface, as Y_0 decreases, fall time increases. When Y_0 decreases from 25 cm to 20 cm, fall time increases from about 1.20 sec to about 1.35 sec, a change of about 0.15 sec. When Y_0 decreases from 20 cm to 15 cm, fall time increases from about 1.35 sec to about 1.55 sec, a change of about 0.20 sec. When Y_0 decreases from 15 cm to 10 cm, fall time increases from about 1.55 sec to about 1.85 sec, a change of about 0.30 sec. These results indicate that as Y_0 decreases, the magnitude of the change in fall time increases. Therefore, if Y_0 decreases from 10 cm to 5 cm, fall time will likely increase by more than 0.30 sec. At $Y_0 = 5$ cm, fall time will most likely be greater than 2.15 sec (1.85 sec + 0.30 sec).

The best answer is NOT:

F, G, or H because if Y_0 were 5 cm, fall time would be greater than 2.15 sec. Of the 4 values listed—0.4 sec, 0.8 sec, 1.9 sec, and 2.3 sec—2.3 sec is closest to 2.15 sec.

Question 37. **The best answer is C.** Figure 4 shows fall time for chains of length L. For each of these fall times, $Y_0 = 20$ cm. If $L = 105$ cm, the fall time on the Moon's surface is about 1.9 sec. If $L = 120$ cm, the fall time on the Moon's surface is about 2.15 sec. Thus, a fall time of 2.0 sec will occur if L is greater than 105 cm and less than 120 cm.

The best answer is NOT:

A or **B** because Figure 4 shows that if $Y_0 = 20$ cm, L must be greater than 105 cm if the fall time on the Moon's surface is 2.0 sec.

D because Figure 4 shows that if $Y_0 = 20$ cm, L must be less than 120 cm if the fall time on the Moon's surface is 2.0 sec.

Question 38. **The best answer is G.** The total length of the chain is L. This length can be separated into 2 components: the vertical section of the chain (the section hanging over the edge of the table) and the horizontal section of the chain (the section on top of the table). The vertical section equals Y_0. So, the horizontal section equals $L - Y_0$.

The best answer is NOT:

F because L is the length of the chain. Thus, the horizontal section of the chain must be less than L, not greater than L.

H because Y_0 equals the vertical section of the chain, not the horizontal section of the chain.

J because L is the length of the chain. Because the chain has a vertical section, the horizontal section of the chain must be less than the entire length of the chain.

Question 39. **The best answer is A.** Based on Figure 3, if the chain has a fall time of 0.7 sec at Earth's surface, then Y_0 is approximately 13 cm. This result follows from the observation that a Y_0 of 10 cm results in a fall time of about 0.75 sec at Earth's surface and a Y_0 of 15 cm results in a fall time of about 0.65 sec at Earth's surface. Similarly, if the chain has a fall time of 0.7 sec at the Moon's surface, then Y_0 is approximately 48 cm. This result follows from the observation that a Y_0 of 45 cm results in a fall time of about 0.75 sec at the Moon's surface and a Y_0 of 50 cm results in a fall time of about 0.65 sec at the Moon's surface. Based on these calculations, Y_0 must be approximately 35 cm longer if the chain is at the Moon's surface.

The best answer is NOT:

B or **D** because, for a given chain and a given fall time, Y_0 must be longer at the Moon's surface than at Earth's surface. For example, Figure 3 shows that a fall time of 0.8 sec is obtained if Y_0 is about 45 cm at the Moon's surface or if Y_0 is about 10 cm at Earth's surface.

C because, according to Figure 3, if the fall time is 0.7 sec at Earth's surface, then Y_0 is approximately 13 cm, and if the fall time is 0.7 sec at the Moon's surface, then Y_0 is approximately 48 cm. So, Y_0 must be about 35 cm longer if the chain is at the Moon's surface than at Earth's surface.

Question 40. The best answer is G. Figure 3 and Table 1 show that as the acceleration due to gravity increases, fall time decreases. For example, in Figure 3, when $Y_0 = 10$ cm, fall time is greatest at the Moon's surface, and in Table 1, the acceleration due to gravity is least at the Moon's surface. Likewise, fall time is least at Jupiter's surface and the acceleration due to gravity is greatest at Jupiter's surface. Because the acceleration due to gravity at Neptune's surface is about 11.7 m/sec^2, the fall time at Neptune's surface would be greater than the fall time at Jupiter's surface and less than the fall time at Earth's surface.

The best answer is NOT:

F because the acceleration due to gravity at Neptune's surface is less than the acceleration due to gravity at Jupiter's surface. Fall time decreases as the acceleration due to gravity increases, so fall time would be less at Jupiter's surface than at Neptune's surface.

H because the acceleration due to gravity at Neptune's surface is greater than the acceleration due to gravity at Earth's surface. Fall time decreases as the acceleration due to gravity increases, so fall time would be greater at Earth's surface than at Neptune's surface.

J because the acceleration due to gravity at Neptune's surface is greater than the acceleration due to gravity at the Moon's surface. Fall time decreases as the acceleration due to gravity increases, so fall time would be greater at the Moon's surface than at Neptune's surface.

The ACT® *Sample Answer Sheet*

A NAME, MAILING ADDRESS, AND TELEPHONE
(Please print.)

Last Name   First Name   MI (Middle Initial)

House Number & Street (Apt. No.); or PO Box & No.; or RR & No.

City   State/Province   ZIP/Postal Code

Area Code   Number   Country

ACT, Inc.—Confidential Restricted when data present.

ALL examinees must complete block A – please print.

REGISTERED examinees **MUST complete blocks B, C, and D.** Find the MATCHING INFORMATION on your admission ticket and enter it EXACTLY the same way, even if any of the information is missing or incorrect. Fill in the corresponding ovals. If you do not complete these blocks to match your admission ticket EXACTLY, your scores will be **delayed up to 8 weeks.** Leave blocks E and F blank.

STANDBY examinees **MUST complete blocks B, D, and F.** Enter your information in blocks B and D and fill in the corresponding ovals. Leave block C blank. **For block E,** if you provided your SSN when you created your Web account or completed your standby folder, enter it here. The SSN will be used to help match this document to your registration information and will be included on reports to your college choices. If you did not provide it earlier, do not know it, or do not wish to provide it, leave block E blank. Be sure to fill in the oval in block F.

Do NOT mark in this shaded area.

B MATCH NAME
(First 5 letters of last name)

C MATCH NUMBER
(Registered examinees only)

D DATE OF BIRTH

Month	Day	Year
Jan.		
Feb.		
March		
April		
May		
June		
July		
Aug.		
Sept.		
Oct.		
Nov.		
Dec.		

↓ STANDBY TESTING ONLY ↓

E SOCIAL SECURITY NUMBER
(Standby examinees only)

F STANDBY TESTING

Fill in the oval below ONLY if you turned in a standby registration at the test center today.

○ Yes, I am testing as a standby.

USE A SOFT LEAD NO. 2 PENCIL ONLY.
(Do NOT use a mechanical pencil, ink, ballpoint, correction fluid, or felt-tip pen.)

EXAMINEE STATEMENT AND SIGNATURE

1. Read the following **Statement:** By submitting this answer sheet, I agree to the terms and conditions set forth in the ACT registration booklet or website for this exam, including the arbitration and dispute remedy provisions. I understand that ACT owns the test questions and responses and affirm that I will not share any test questions or responses with anyone by any form of communication.

2. Copy the **Certification** shown below (only the text in italics) on the lines provided. Write in your normal handwriting.

   Certification: *I agree to the Statement above and certify that I am the person whose name and address appear on this form.*

   _____

   _____

   _____

   _____

3. Sign your name as you would any official document and enter today's date.

   _____   _____
   Your Signature   Today's Date

ACT®
P.O. BOX 168, IOWA CITY, IOWA 52243-0168

Marking Directions: Mark only **one** oval for each question. Fill in response completely. Erase errors cleanly without smudging.

Correct mark: ○ ● ○ ○

- -

Do NOT use these *incorrect* or *bad* **marks.**

Incorrect marks: ○ ○ ○ ○
Overlapping mark: ○ ○ ○ ○
Cross-out mark: ● ● ○ ○
Smudged erasure: ○ ○ ○ ○
Mark is too light: ○ ○ ○ ○

BOOKLET NUMBER

①	①	①	①	①	①
②	②	②	②	②	②
③	③	③	③	③	③
④	④	④	④	④	④
⑤	⑤	⑤	⑤	⑤	⑤
⑥	⑥	⑥	⑥	⑥	⑥
⑦	⑦	⑦	⑦	⑦	⑦
⑧	⑧	⑧	⑧	⑧	⑧
⑨	⑨	⑨	⑨	⑨	⑨
⓪	⓪	⓪	⓪	⓪	⓪

FORM

Print your 3-character **Test Form** in the boxes above and fill in the corresponding oval at the right.

BE SURE TO FILL IN THE CORRECT FORM OVAL.

○ 1MC   ○ 2MC   ○ 3MC   ○ 4MC
○ 5MC

TEST 1

1 Ⓐ Ⓑ Ⓒ Ⓓ	14 Ⓕ Ⓖ Ⓗ Ⓙ	27 Ⓐ Ⓑ Ⓒ Ⓓ	40 Ⓕ Ⓖ Ⓗ Ⓙ	53 Ⓐ Ⓑ Ⓒ Ⓓ	66 Ⓕ Ⓖ Ⓗ Ⓙ
2 Ⓕ Ⓖ Ⓗ Ⓙ	15 Ⓐ Ⓑ Ⓒ Ⓓ	28 Ⓕ Ⓖ Ⓗ Ⓙ	41 Ⓐ Ⓑ Ⓒ Ⓓ	54 Ⓕ Ⓖ Ⓗ Ⓙ	67 Ⓐ Ⓑ Ⓒ Ⓓ
3 Ⓐ Ⓑ Ⓒ Ⓓ	16 Ⓕ Ⓖ Ⓗ Ⓙ	29 Ⓐ Ⓑ Ⓒ Ⓓ	42 Ⓕ Ⓖ Ⓗ Ⓙ	55 Ⓐ Ⓑ Ⓒ Ⓓ	68 Ⓕ Ⓖ Ⓗ Ⓙ
4 Ⓕ Ⓖ Ⓗ Ⓙ	17 Ⓐ Ⓑ Ⓒ Ⓓ	30 Ⓕ Ⓖ Ⓗ Ⓙ	43 Ⓐ Ⓑ Ⓒ Ⓓ	56 Ⓕ Ⓖ Ⓗ Ⓙ	69 Ⓐ Ⓑ Ⓒ Ⓓ
5 Ⓐ Ⓑ Ⓒ Ⓓ	18 Ⓕ Ⓖ Ⓗ Ⓙ	31 Ⓐ Ⓑ Ⓒ Ⓓ	44 Ⓕ Ⓖ Ⓗ Ⓙ	57 Ⓐ Ⓑ Ⓒ Ⓓ	70 Ⓕ Ⓖ Ⓗ Ⓙ
6 Ⓕ Ⓖ Ⓗ Ⓙ	19 Ⓐ Ⓑ Ⓒ Ⓓ	32 Ⓕ Ⓖ Ⓗ Ⓙ	45 Ⓐ Ⓑ Ⓒ Ⓓ	58 Ⓕ Ⓖ Ⓗ Ⓙ	71 Ⓐ Ⓑ Ⓒ Ⓓ
7 Ⓐ Ⓑ Ⓒ Ⓓ	20 Ⓕ Ⓖ Ⓗ Ⓙ	33 Ⓐ Ⓑ Ⓒ Ⓓ	46 Ⓕ Ⓖ Ⓗ Ⓙ	59 Ⓐ Ⓑ Ⓒ Ⓓ	72 Ⓕ Ⓖ Ⓗ Ⓙ
8 Ⓕ Ⓖ Ⓗ Ⓙ	21 Ⓐ Ⓑ Ⓒ Ⓓ	34 Ⓕ Ⓖ Ⓗ Ⓙ	47 Ⓐ Ⓑ Ⓒ Ⓓ	60 Ⓕ Ⓖ Ⓗ Ⓙ	73 Ⓐ Ⓑ Ⓒ Ⓓ
9 Ⓐ Ⓑ Ⓒ Ⓓ	22 Ⓕ Ⓖ Ⓗ Ⓙ	35 Ⓐ Ⓑ Ⓒ Ⓓ	48 Ⓕ Ⓖ Ⓗ Ⓙ	61 Ⓐ Ⓑ Ⓒ Ⓓ	74 Ⓕ Ⓖ Ⓗ Ⓙ
10 Ⓕ Ⓖ Ⓗ Ⓙ	23 Ⓐ Ⓑ Ⓒ Ⓓ	36 Ⓕ Ⓖ Ⓗ Ⓙ	49 Ⓐ Ⓑ Ⓒ Ⓓ	62 Ⓕ Ⓖ Ⓗ Ⓙ	75 Ⓐ Ⓑ Ⓒ Ⓓ
11 Ⓐ Ⓑ Ⓒ Ⓓ	24 Ⓕ Ⓖ Ⓗ Ⓙ	37 Ⓐ Ⓑ Ⓒ Ⓓ	50 Ⓕ Ⓖ Ⓗ Ⓙ	63 Ⓐ Ⓑ Ⓒ Ⓓ	
12 Ⓕ Ⓖ Ⓗ Ⓙ	25 Ⓐ Ⓑ Ⓒ Ⓓ	38 Ⓕ Ⓖ Ⓗ Ⓙ	51 Ⓐ Ⓑ Ⓒ Ⓓ	64 Ⓕ Ⓖ Ⓗ Ⓙ	
13 Ⓐ Ⓑ Ⓒ Ⓓ	26 Ⓕ Ⓖ Ⓗ Ⓙ	39 Ⓐ Ⓑ Ⓒ Ⓓ	52 Ⓕ Ⓖ Ⓗ Ⓙ	65 Ⓐ Ⓑ Ⓒ Ⓓ	

TEST 2

1 Ⓐ Ⓑ Ⓒ Ⓓ Ⓔ	11 Ⓐ Ⓑ Ⓒ Ⓓ Ⓔ	21 Ⓐ Ⓑ Ⓒ Ⓓ Ⓔ	31 Ⓐ Ⓑ Ⓒ Ⓓ Ⓔ	41 Ⓐ Ⓑ Ⓒ Ⓓ Ⓔ	51 Ⓐ Ⓑ Ⓒ Ⓓ Ⓔ
2 Ⓕ Ⓖ Ⓗ Ⓙ Ⓚ	12 Ⓕ Ⓖ Ⓗ Ⓙ Ⓚ	22 Ⓕ Ⓖ Ⓗ Ⓙ Ⓚ	32 Ⓕ Ⓖ Ⓗ Ⓙ Ⓚ	42 Ⓕ Ⓖ Ⓗ Ⓙ Ⓚ	52 Ⓕ Ⓖ Ⓗ Ⓙ Ⓚ
3 Ⓐ Ⓑ Ⓒ Ⓓ Ⓔ	13 Ⓐ Ⓑ Ⓒ Ⓓ Ⓔ	23 Ⓐ Ⓑ Ⓒ Ⓓ Ⓔ	33 Ⓐ Ⓑ Ⓒ Ⓓ Ⓔ	43 Ⓐ Ⓑ Ⓒ Ⓓ Ⓔ	53 Ⓐ Ⓑ Ⓒ Ⓓ Ⓔ
4 Ⓕ Ⓖ Ⓗ Ⓙ Ⓚ	14 Ⓕ Ⓖ Ⓗ Ⓙ Ⓚ	24 Ⓕ Ⓖ Ⓗ Ⓙ Ⓚ	34 Ⓕ Ⓖ Ⓗ Ⓙ Ⓚ	44 Ⓕ Ⓖ Ⓗ Ⓙ Ⓚ	54 Ⓕ Ⓖ Ⓗ Ⓙ Ⓚ
5 Ⓐ Ⓑ Ⓒ Ⓓ Ⓔ	15 Ⓐ Ⓑ Ⓒ Ⓓ Ⓔ	25 Ⓐ Ⓑ Ⓒ Ⓓ Ⓔ	35 Ⓐ Ⓑ Ⓒ Ⓓ Ⓔ	45 Ⓐ Ⓑ Ⓒ Ⓓ Ⓔ	55 Ⓐ Ⓑ Ⓒ Ⓓ Ⓔ
6 Ⓕ Ⓖ Ⓗ Ⓙ Ⓚ	16 Ⓕ Ⓖ Ⓗ Ⓙ Ⓚ	26 Ⓕ Ⓖ Ⓗ Ⓙ Ⓚ	36 Ⓕ Ⓖ Ⓗ Ⓙ Ⓚ	46 Ⓕ Ⓖ Ⓗ Ⓙ Ⓚ	56 Ⓕ Ⓖ Ⓗ Ⓙ Ⓚ
7 Ⓐ Ⓑ Ⓒ Ⓓ Ⓔ	17 Ⓐ Ⓑ Ⓒ Ⓓ Ⓔ	27 Ⓐ Ⓑ Ⓒ Ⓓ Ⓔ	37 Ⓐ Ⓑ Ⓒ Ⓓ Ⓔ	47 Ⓐ Ⓑ Ⓒ Ⓓ Ⓔ	57 Ⓐ Ⓑ Ⓒ Ⓓ Ⓔ
8 Ⓕ Ⓖ Ⓗ Ⓙ Ⓚ	18 Ⓕ Ⓖ Ⓗ Ⓙ Ⓚ	28 Ⓕ Ⓖ Ⓗ Ⓙ Ⓚ	38 Ⓕ Ⓖ Ⓗ Ⓙ Ⓚ	48 Ⓕ Ⓖ Ⓗ Ⓙ Ⓚ	58 Ⓕ Ⓖ Ⓗ Ⓙ Ⓚ
9 Ⓐ Ⓑ Ⓒ Ⓓ Ⓔ	19 Ⓐ Ⓑ Ⓒ Ⓓ Ⓔ	29 Ⓐ Ⓑ Ⓒ Ⓓ Ⓔ	39 Ⓐ Ⓑ Ⓒ Ⓓ Ⓔ	49 Ⓐ Ⓑ Ⓒ Ⓓ Ⓔ	59 Ⓐ Ⓑ Ⓒ Ⓓ Ⓔ
10 Ⓕ Ⓖ Ⓗ Ⓙ Ⓚ	20 Ⓕ Ⓖ Ⓗ Ⓙ Ⓚ	30 Ⓕ Ⓖ Ⓗ Ⓙ Ⓚ	40 Ⓕ Ⓖ Ⓗ Ⓙ Ⓚ	50 Ⓕ Ⓖ Ⓗ Ⓙ Ⓚ	60 Ⓕ Ⓖ Ⓗ Ⓙ Ⓚ

TEST 3

1 Ⓐ Ⓑ Ⓒ Ⓓ	8 Ⓕ Ⓖ Ⓗ Ⓙ	15 Ⓐ Ⓑ Ⓒ Ⓓ	22 Ⓕ Ⓖ Ⓗ Ⓙ	29 Ⓐ Ⓑ Ⓒ Ⓓ	36 Ⓕ Ⓖ Ⓗ Ⓙ
2 Ⓕ Ⓖ Ⓗ Ⓙ	9 Ⓐ Ⓑ Ⓒ Ⓓ	16 Ⓕ Ⓖ Ⓗ Ⓙ	23 Ⓐ Ⓑ Ⓒ Ⓓ	30 Ⓕ Ⓖ Ⓗ Ⓙ	37 Ⓐ Ⓑ Ⓒ Ⓓ
3 Ⓐ Ⓑ Ⓒ Ⓓ	10 Ⓕ Ⓖ Ⓗ Ⓙ	17 Ⓐ Ⓑ Ⓒ Ⓓ	24 Ⓕ Ⓖ Ⓗ Ⓙ	31 Ⓐ Ⓑ Ⓒ Ⓓ	38 Ⓕ Ⓖ Ⓗ Ⓙ
4 Ⓕ Ⓖ Ⓗ Ⓙ	11 Ⓐ Ⓑ Ⓒ Ⓓ	18 Ⓕ Ⓖ Ⓗ Ⓙ	25 Ⓐ Ⓑ Ⓒ Ⓓ	32 Ⓕ Ⓖ Ⓗ Ⓙ	39 Ⓐ Ⓑ Ⓒ Ⓓ
5 Ⓐ Ⓑ Ⓒ Ⓓ	12 Ⓕ Ⓖ Ⓗ Ⓙ	19 Ⓐ Ⓑ Ⓒ Ⓓ	26 Ⓕ Ⓖ Ⓗ Ⓙ	33 Ⓐ Ⓑ Ⓒ Ⓓ	40 Ⓕ Ⓖ Ⓗ Ⓙ
6 Ⓕ Ⓖ Ⓗ Ⓙ	13 Ⓐ Ⓑ Ⓒ Ⓓ	20 Ⓕ Ⓖ Ⓗ Ⓙ	27 Ⓐ Ⓑ Ⓒ Ⓓ	34 Ⓕ Ⓖ Ⓗ Ⓙ	
7 Ⓐ Ⓑ Ⓒ Ⓓ	14 Ⓕ Ⓖ Ⓗ Ⓙ	21 Ⓐ Ⓑ Ⓒ Ⓓ	28 Ⓕ Ⓖ Ⓗ Ⓙ	35 Ⓐ Ⓑ Ⓒ Ⓓ	

TEST 4

1 Ⓐ Ⓑ Ⓒ Ⓓ	8 Ⓕ Ⓖ Ⓗ Ⓙ	15 Ⓐ Ⓑ Ⓒ Ⓓ	22 Ⓕ Ⓖ Ⓗ Ⓙ	29 Ⓐ Ⓑ Ⓒ Ⓓ	36 Ⓕ Ⓖ Ⓗ Ⓙ
2 Ⓕ Ⓖ Ⓗ Ⓙ	9 Ⓐ Ⓑ Ⓒ Ⓓ	16 Ⓕ Ⓖ Ⓗ Ⓙ	23 Ⓐ Ⓑ Ⓒ Ⓓ	30 Ⓕ Ⓖ Ⓗ Ⓙ	37 Ⓐ Ⓑ Ⓒ Ⓓ
3 Ⓐ Ⓑ Ⓒ Ⓓ	10 Ⓕ Ⓖ Ⓗ Ⓙ	17 Ⓐ Ⓑ Ⓒ Ⓓ	24 Ⓕ Ⓖ Ⓗ Ⓙ	31 Ⓐ Ⓑ Ⓒ Ⓓ	38 Ⓕ Ⓖ Ⓗ Ⓙ
4 Ⓕ Ⓖ Ⓗ Ⓙ	11 Ⓐ Ⓑ Ⓒ Ⓓ	18 Ⓕ Ⓖ Ⓗ Ⓙ	25 Ⓐ Ⓑ Ⓒ Ⓓ	32 Ⓕ Ⓖ Ⓗ Ⓙ	39 Ⓐ Ⓑ Ⓒ Ⓓ
5 Ⓐ Ⓑ Ⓒ Ⓓ	12 Ⓕ Ⓖ Ⓗ Ⓙ	19 Ⓐ Ⓑ Ⓒ Ⓓ	26 Ⓕ Ⓖ Ⓗ Ⓙ	33 Ⓐ Ⓑ Ⓒ Ⓓ	40 Ⓕ Ⓖ Ⓗ Ⓙ
6 Ⓕ Ⓖ Ⓗ Ⓙ	13 Ⓐ Ⓑ Ⓒ Ⓓ	20 Ⓕ Ⓖ Ⓗ Ⓙ	27 Ⓐ Ⓑ Ⓒ Ⓓ	34 Ⓕ Ⓖ Ⓗ Ⓙ	
7 Ⓐ Ⓑ Ⓒ Ⓓ	14 Ⓕ Ⓖ Ⓗ Ⓙ	21 Ⓐ Ⓑ Ⓒ Ⓓ	28 Ⓕ Ⓖ Ⓗ Ⓙ	35 Ⓐ Ⓑ Ⓒ Ⓓ	

The **ACT**®

The ACT® *Sample Answer Sheet*

A — NAME, MAILING ADDRESS, AND TELEPHONE
(Please print.)

Last Name   First Name   MI (Middle Initial)

House Number & Street (Apt. No.); or PO Box & No.; or RR & No.

City   State/Province   ZIP/Postal Code

Area Code   Number   Country

ACT, Inc.—Confidential Restricted when data present.

ALL examinees must complete block A – please print.

REGISTERED examinees MUST complete blocks B, C, and D. Find the MATCHING INFORMATION on your admission ticket and enter it EXACTLY the same way, even if any of the information is missing or incorrect. Fill in the corresponding ovals. If you do not complete these blocks to match your admission ticket EXACTLY, your scores will be **delayed up to 8 weeks**. Leave blocks E and F blank.

STANDBY examinees MUST complete blocks B, D, and F. Enter your information in blocks B and D and fill in the corresponding ovals. Leave block C blank. **For block E**, if you provided your SSN when you created your Web account or completed your standby folder, enter it here. The SSN will be used to help match this document to your registration information and will be included on reports to your college choices. If you did not provide it earlier, do not know it, or do not wish to provide it, leave block E blank. Be sure to fill in the oval in block F.

Do **NOT** mark in this shaded area.

B — MATCH NAME
(First 5 letters of last name)

C — MATCH NUMBER
(Registered examinees only)

D — DATE OF BIRTH

Month	Day	Year
Jan.		
Feb.		
March		
April		
May		
June		
July		
Aug.		
Sept.		
Oct.		
Nov.		
Dec.		

↓ STANDBY TESTING ONLY ↓

E — SOCIAL SECURITY NUMBER
(Standby examinees only)

F — STANDBY TESTING

Fill in the oval below ONLY if you turned in a standby registration at the test center today.

○ Yes, I am testing as a standby.

USE A SOFT LEAD NO. 2 PENCIL ONLY.
(Do NOT use a mechanical pencil, ink, ballpoint, correction fluid, or felt-tip pen.)

EXAMINEE STATEMENT AND SIGNATURE

1. Read the following **Statement:** By submitting this answer sheet, I agree to the terms and conditions set forth in the ACT registration booklet or website for this exam, including the arbitration and dispute remedy provisions. I understand that ACT owns the test questions and responses and affirm that I will not share any test questions or responses with anyone by any form of communication.

2. Copy the **Certification** shown below (only the text in italics) on the lines provided. Write in your normal handwriting.

   Certification: *I agree to the Statement above and certify that I am the person whose name and address appear on this form.*

3. Sign your name as you would any official document and enter today's date.

Your Signature   Today's Date

ACT®
P.O. BOX 168, IOWA CITY, IOWA 52243-0168

Marking Directions: Mark only **one** oval for each question. Fill in response completely. Erase errors cleanly without smudging.

Correct mark: ⬭ ⬛ ⬭ ⬭

Do NOT use these *incorrect* or *bad* marks.

Incorrect marks: ⊘ ⊗ ⊖ ⊙
Overlapping mark: ⬭ ⬭
Cross-out mark: ⬛ ⬛ ⬭
Smudged erasure: ⬭ ⬭ ⬭
Mark is too light: ⬭ ⬭ ⬭ ⬭

BOOKLET NUMBER

① ① ① ① ① ①
② ② ② ② ② ②
③ ③ ③ ③ ③ ③
④ ④ ④ ④ ④ ④
⑤ ⑤ ⑤ ⑤ ⑤ ⑤
⑥ ⑥ ⑥ ⑥ ⑥ ⑥
⑦ ⑦ ⑦ ⑦ ⑦ ⑦
⑧ ⑧ ⑧ ⑧ ⑧ ⑧
⑨ ⑨ ⑨ ⑨ ⑨ ⑨
⓪ ⓪ ⓪ ⓪ ⓪ ⓪

FORM

Print your 3-character **Test Form** in the boxes above and fill in the corresponding oval at the right.

BE SURE TO FILL IN THE CORRECT FORM OVAL.

○ 1MC   ○ 2MC   ○ 3MC   ○ 4MC
○ 5MC

TEST 1

1 Ⓐ Ⓑ Ⓒ Ⓓ	14 Ⓕ Ⓖ Ⓗ Ⓙ	27 Ⓐ Ⓑ Ⓒ Ⓓ	40 Ⓕ Ⓖ Ⓗ Ⓙ	53 Ⓐ Ⓑ Ⓒ Ⓓ	66 Ⓕ Ⓖ Ⓗ Ⓙ
2 Ⓕ Ⓖ Ⓗ Ⓙ	15 Ⓐ Ⓑ Ⓒ Ⓓ	28 Ⓕ Ⓖ Ⓗ Ⓙ	41 Ⓐ Ⓑ Ⓒ Ⓓ	54 Ⓕ Ⓖ Ⓗ Ⓙ	67 Ⓐ Ⓑ Ⓒ Ⓓ
3 Ⓐ Ⓑ Ⓒ Ⓓ	16 Ⓕ Ⓖ Ⓗ Ⓙ	29 Ⓐ Ⓑ Ⓒ Ⓓ	42 Ⓕ Ⓖ Ⓗ Ⓙ	55 Ⓐ Ⓑ Ⓒ Ⓓ	68 Ⓕ Ⓖ Ⓗ Ⓙ
4 Ⓕ Ⓖ Ⓗ Ⓙ	17 Ⓐ Ⓑ Ⓒ Ⓓ	30 Ⓕ Ⓖ Ⓗ Ⓙ	43 Ⓐ Ⓑ Ⓒ Ⓓ	56 Ⓕ Ⓖ Ⓗ Ⓙ	69 Ⓐ Ⓑ Ⓒ Ⓓ
5 Ⓐ Ⓑ Ⓒ Ⓓ	18 Ⓕ Ⓖ Ⓗ Ⓙ	31 Ⓐ Ⓑ Ⓒ Ⓓ	44 Ⓕ Ⓖ Ⓗ Ⓙ	57 Ⓐ Ⓑ Ⓒ Ⓓ	70 Ⓕ Ⓖ Ⓗ Ⓙ
6 Ⓕ Ⓖ Ⓗ Ⓙ	19 Ⓐ Ⓑ Ⓒ Ⓓ	32 Ⓕ Ⓖ Ⓗ Ⓙ	45 Ⓐ Ⓑ Ⓒ Ⓓ	58 Ⓕ Ⓖ Ⓗ Ⓙ	71 Ⓐ Ⓑ Ⓒ Ⓓ
7 Ⓐ Ⓑ Ⓒ Ⓓ	20 Ⓕ Ⓖ Ⓗ Ⓙ	33 Ⓐ Ⓑ Ⓒ Ⓓ	46 Ⓕ Ⓖ Ⓗ Ⓙ	59 Ⓐ Ⓑ Ⓒ Ⓓ	72 Ⓕ Ⓖ Ⓗ Ⓙ
8 Ⓕ Ⓖ Ⓗ Ⓙ	21 Ⓐ Ⓑ Ⓒ Ⓓ	34 Ⓕ Ⓖ Ⓗ Ⓙ	47 Ⓐ Ⓑ Ⓒ Ⓓ	60 Ⓕ Ⓖ Ⓗ Ⓙ	73 Ⓐ Ⓑ Ⓒ Ⓓ
9 Ⓐ Ⓑ Ⓒ Ⓓ	22 Ⓕ Ⓖ Ⓗ Ⓙ	35 Ⓐ Ⓑ Ⓒ Ⓓ	48 Ⓕ Ⓖ Ⓗ Ⓙ	61 Ⓐ Ⓑ Ⓒ Ⓓ	74 Ⓕ Ⓖ Ⓗ Ⓙ
10 Ⓕ Ⓖ Ⓗ Ⓙ	23 Ⓐ Ⓑ Ⓒ Ⓓ	36 Ⓕ Ⓖ Ⓗ Ⓙ	49 Ⓐ Ⓑ Ⓒ Ⓓ	62 Ⓕ Ⓖ Ⓗ Ⓙ	75 Ⓐ Ⓑ Ⓒ Ⓓ
11 Ⓐ Ⓑ Ⓒ Ⓓ	24 Ⓕ Ⓖ Ⓗ Ⓙ	37 Ⓐ Ⓑ Ⓒ Ⓓ	50 Ⓕ Ⓖ Ⓗ Ⓙ	63 Ⓐ Ⓑ Ⓒ Ⓓ	
12 Ⓕ Ⓖ Ⓗ Ⓙ	25 Ⓐ Ⓑ Ⓒ Ⓓ	38 Ⓕ Ⓖ Ⓗ Ⓙ	51 Ⓐ Ⓑ Ⓒ Ⓓ	64 Ⓕ Ⓖ Ⓗ Ⓙ	
13 Ⓐ Ⓑ Ⓒ Ⓓ	26 Ⓕ Ⓖ Ⓗ Ⓙ	39 Ⓐ Ⓑ Ⓒ Ⓓ	52 Ⓕ Ⓖ Ⓗ Ⓙ	65 Ⓐ Ⓑ Ⓒ Ⓓ	

TEST 2

1 Ⓐ Ⓑ Ⓒ Ⓓ Ⓔ	11 Ⓐ Ⓑ Ⓒ Ⓓ Ⓔ	21 Ⓐ Ⓑ Ⓒ Ⓓ Ⓔ	31 Ⓐ Ⓑ Ⓒ Ⓓ Ⓔ	41 Ⓐ Ⓑ Ⓒ Ⓓ Ⓔ	51 Ⓐ Ⓑ Ⓒ Ⓓ Ⓔ
2 Ⓕ Ⓖ Ⓗ Ⓙ Ⓚ	12 Ⓕ Ⓖ Ⓗ Ⓙ Ⓚ	22 Ⓕ Ⓖ Ⓗ Ⓙ Ⓚ	32 Ⓕ Ⓖ Ⓗ Ⓙ Ⓚ	42 Ⓕ Ⓖ Ⓗ Ⓙ Ⓚ	52 Ⓕ Ⓖ Ⓗ Ⓙ Ⓚ
3 Ⓐ Ⓑ Ⓒ Ⓓ Ⓔ	13 Ⓐ Ⓑ Ⓒ Ⓓ Ⓔ	23 Ⓐ Ⓑ Ⓒ Ⓓ Ⓔ	33 Ⓐ Ⓑ Ⓒ Ⓓ Ⓔ	43 Ⓐ Ⓑ Ⓒ Ⓓ Ⓔ	53 Ⓐ Ⓑ Ⓒ Ⓓ Ⓔ
4 Ⓕ Ⓖ Ⓗ Ⓙ Ⓚ	14 Ⓕ Ⓖ Ⓗ Ⓙ Ⓚ	24 Ⓕ Ⓖ Ⓗ Ⓙ Ⓚ	34 Ⓕ Ⓖ Ⓗ Ⓙ Ⓚ	44 Ⓕ Ⓖ Ⓗ Ⓙ Ⓚ	54 Ⓕ Ⓖ Ⓗ Ⓙ Ⓚ
5 Ⓐ Ⓑ Ⓒ Ⓓ Ⓔ	15 Ⓐ Ⓑ Ⓒ Ⓓ Ⓔ	25 Ⓐ Ⓑ Ⓒ Ⓓ Ⓔ	35 Ⓐ Ⓑ Ⓒ Ⓓ Ⓔ	45 Ⓐ Ⓑ Ⓒ Ⓓ Ⓔ	55 Ⓐ Ⓑ Ⓒ Ⓓ Ⓔ
6 Ⓕ Ⓖ Ⓗ Ⓙ Ⓚ	16 Ⓕ Ⓖ Ⓗ Ⓙ Ⓚ	26 Ⓕ Ⓖ Ⓗ Ⓙ Ⓚ	36 Ⓕ Ⓖ Ⓗ Ⓙ Ⓚ	46 Ⓕ Ⓖ Ⓗ Ⓙ Ⓚ	56 Ⓕ Ⓖ Ⓗ Ⓙ Ⓚ
7 Ⓐ Ⓑ Ⓒ Ⓓ Ⓔ	17 Ⓐ Ⓑ Ⓒ Ⓓ Ⓔ	27 Ⓐ Ⓑ Ⓒ Ⓓ Ⓔ	37 Ⓐ Ⓑ Ⓒ Ⓓ Ⓔ	47 Ⓐ Ⓑ Ⓒ Ⓓ Ⓔ	57 Ⓐ Ⓑ Ⓒ Ⓓ Ⓔ
8 Ⓕ Ⓖ Ⓗ Ⓙ Ⓚ	18 Ⓕ Ⓖ Ⓗ Ⓙ Ⓚ	28 Ⓕ Ⓖ Ⓗ Ⓙ Ⓚ	38 Ⓕ Ⓖ Ⓗ Ⓙ Ⓚ	48 Ⓕ Ⓖ Ⓗ Ⓙ Ⓚ	58 Ⓕ Ⓖ Ⓗ Ⓙ Ⓚ
9 Ⓐ Ⓑ Ⓒ Ⓓ Ⓔ	19 Ⓐ Ⓑ Ⓒ Ⓓ Ⓔ	29 Ⓐ Ⓑ Ⓒ Ⓓ Ⓔ	39 Ⓐ Ⓑ Ⓒ Ⓓ Ⓔ	49 Ⓐ Ⓑ Ⓒ Ⓓ Ⓔ	59 Ⓐ Ⓑ Ⓒ Ⓓ Ⓔ
10 Ⓕ Ⓖ Ⓗ Ⓙ Ⓚ	20 Ⓕ Ⓖ Ⓗ Ⓙ Ⓚ	30 Ⓕ Ⓖ Ⓗ Ⓙ Ⓚ	40 Ⓕ Ⓖ Ⓗ Ⓙ Ⓚ	50 Ⓕ Ⓖ Ⓗ Ⓙ Ⓚ	60 Ⓕ Ⓖ Ⓗ Ⓙ Ⓚ

TEST 3

1 Ⓐ Ⓑ Ⓒ Ⓓ	8 Ⓕ Ⓖ Ⓗ Ⓙ	15 Ⓐ Ⓑ Ⓒ Ⓓ	22 Ⓕ Ⓖ Ⓗ Ⓙ	29 Ⓐ Ⓑ Ⓒ Ⓓ	36 Ⓕ Ⓖ Ⓗ Ⓙ
2 Ⓕ Ⓖ Ⓗ Ⓙ	9 Ⓐ Ⓑ Ⓒ Ⓓ	16 Ⓕ Ⓖ Ⓗ Ⓙ	23 Ⓐ Ⓑ Ⓒ Ⓓ	30 Ⓕ Ⓖ Ⓗ Ⓙ	37 Ⓐ Ⓑ Ⓒ Ⓓ
3 Ⓐ Ⓑ Ⓒ Ⓓ	10 Ⓕ Ⓖ Ⓗ Ⓙ	17 Ⓐ Ⓑ Ⓒ Ⓓ	24 Ⓕ Ⓖ Ⓗ Ⓙ	31 Ⓐ Ⓑ Ⓒ Ⓓ	38 Ⓕ Ⓖ Ⓗ Ⓙ
4 Ⓕ Ⓖ Ⓗ Ⓙ	11 Ⓐ Ⓑ Ⓒ Ⓓ	18 Ⓕ Ⓖ Ⓗ Ⓙ	25 Ⓐ Ⓑ Ⓒ Ⓓ	32 Ⓕ Ⓖ Ⓗ Ⓙ	39 Ⓐ Ⓑ Ⓒ Ⓓ
5 Ⓐ Ⓑ Ⓒ Ⓓ	12 Ⓕ Ⓖ Ⓗ Ⓙ	19 Ⓐ Ⓑ Ⓒ Ⓓ	26 Ⓕ Ⓖ Ⓗ Ⓙ	33 Ⓐ Ⓑ Ⓒ Ⓓ	40 Ⓕ Ⓖ Ⓗ Ⓙ
6 Ⓕ Ⓖ Ⓗ Ⓙ	13 Ⓐ Ⓑ Ⓒ Ⓓ	20 Ⓕ Ⓖ Ⓗ Ⓙ	27 Ⓐ Ⓑ Ⓒ Ⓓ	34 Ⓕ Ⓖ Ⓗ Ⓙ	
7 Ⓐ Ⓑ Ⓒ Ⓓ	14 Ⓕ Ⓖ Ⓗ Ⓙ	21 Ⓐ Ⓑ Ⓒ Ⓓ	28 Ⓕ Ⓖ Ⓗ Ⓙ	35 Ⓐ Ⓑ Ⓒ Ⓓ	

TEST 4

1 Ⓐ Ⓑ Ⓒ Ⓓ	8 Ⓕ Ⓖ Ⓗ Ⓙ	15 Ⓐ Ⓑ Ⓒ Ⓓ	22 Ⓕ Ⓖ Ⓗ Ⓙ	29 Ⓐ Ⓑ Ⓒ Ⓓ	36 Ⓕ Ⓖ Ⓗ Ⓙ
2 Ⓕ Ⓖ Ⓗ Ⓙ	9 Ⓐ Ⓑ Ⓒ Ⓓ	16 Ⓕ Ⓖ Ⓗ Ⓙ	23 Ⓐ Ⓑ Ⓒ Ⓓ	30 Ⓕ Ⓖ Ⓗ Ⓙ	37 Ⓐ Ⓑ Ⓒ Ⓓ
3 Ⓐ Ⓑ Ⓒ Ⓓ	10 Ⓕ Ⓖ Ⓗ Ⓙ	17 Ⓐ Ⓑ Ⓒ Ⓓ	24 Ⓕ Ⓖ Ⓗ Ⓙ	31 Ⓐ Ⓑ Ⓒ Ⓓ	38 Ⓕ Ⓖ Ⓗ Ⓙ
4 Ⓕ Ⓖ Ⓗ Ⓙ	11 Ⓐ Ⓑ Ⓒ Ⓓ	18 Ⓕ Ⓖ Ⓗ Ⓙ	25 Ⓐ Ⓑ Ⓒ Ⓓ	32 Ⓕ Ⓖ Ⓗ Ⓙ	39 Ⓐ Ⓑ Ⓒ Ⓓ
5 Ⓐ Ⓑ Ⓒ Ⓓ	12 Ⓕ Ⓖ Ⓗ Ⓙ	19 Ⓐ Ⓑ Ⓒ Ⓓ	26 Ⓕ Ⓖ Ⓗ Ⓙ	33 Ⓐ Ⓑ Ⓒ Ⓓ	40 Ⓕ Ⓖ Ⓗ Ⓙ
6 Ⓕ Ⓖ Ⓗ Ⓙ	13 Ⓐ Ⓑ Ⓒ Ⓓ	20 Ⓕ Ⓖ Ⓗ Ⓙ	27 Ⓐ Ⓑ Ⓒ Ⓓ	34 Ⓕ Ⓖ Ⓗ Ⓙ	
7 Ⓐ Ⓑ Ⓒ Ⓓ	14 Ⓕ Ⓖ Ⓗ Ⓙ	21 Ⓐ Ⓑ Ⓒ Ⓓ	28 Ⓕ Ⓖ Ⓗ Ⓙ	35 Ⓐ Ⓑ Ⓒ Ⓓ	

080661

Practice Test 4

Examinee Agreement and Signature: By testing today, I agree to the terms and conditions set forth in the ACT registration booklet or website for this exam, including the provisions about prohibited behaviors. I also certify that I am the person whose signature appears below.

Today's Date: _____

Your Signature: _____

Print Your Name Here: _____

Your Date of Birth:

☐☐ – ☐☐ – ☐☐☐☐
Month   Day   Year

Form 4MC

The **ACT**® 2011|2012

Directions

This booklet contains tests in English, Mathematics, Reading, and Science. These tests measure skills and abilities highly related to high school course work and success in college. *CALCULATORS MAY BE USED ON THE MATHEMATICS TEST ONLY.*

The questions in each test are numbered, and the suggested answers for each question are lettered. On the answer document, the rows of ovals are numbered to match the questions, and the ovals in each row are lettered to correspond to the suggested answers.

For each question, first decide which answer is best. Next, locate on the answer document the row of ovals numbered the same as the question. Then, locate the oval in that row lettered the same as your answer. Finally, fill in the oval completely. Use a soft lead pencil and make your marks heavy and black. *DO NOT USE INK OR A MECHANICAL PENCIL.*

Mark only one answer to each question. If you change your mind about an answer, erase your first mark thoroughly before marking your new answer. For each question, make certain that you mark in the row of ovals with the same number as the question.

Only responses marked on your answer document will be scored. Your score on each test will be based only on the number of questions you answer correctly during the time allowed for that test. You will NOT be penalized for guessing. *IT IS TO YOUR ADVANTAGE TO ANSWER EVERY QUESTION EVEN IF YOU MUST GUESS.*

You may work on each test ONLY when your test supervisor tells you to do so. If you finish a test before time is called for that test, you should use the time remaining to reconsider questions you are uncertain about in that test. You may NOT look back to a test on which time has already been called, and you may NOT go ahead to another test. To do so will disqualify you from the examination.

Lay your pencil down immediately when time is called at the end of each test. You may NOT for any reason fill in or alter ovals for a test after time is called for that test. To do so will disqualify you from the examination.

Do not fold or tear the pages of your test booklet.

DO NOT OPEN THIS BOOKLET
UNTIL TOLD TO DO SO.

P.O. BOX 168
IOWA CITY, IA 52243-0168

ENGLISH TEST
45 Minutes—75 Questions

DIRECTIONS: In the five passages that follow, certain words and phrases are underlined and numbered. In the right-hand column, you will find alternatives for the underlined part. In most cases, you are to choose the one that best expresses the idea, makes the statement appropriate for standard written English, or is worded most consistently with the style and tone of the passage as a whole. If you think the original version is best, choose "NO CHANGE." In some cases, you will find in the right-hand column a question about the underlined part. You are to choose the best answer to the question.

You will also find questions about a section of the passage, or about the passage as a whole. These questions do not refer to an underlined portion of the passage, but rather are identified by a number or numbers in a box.

For each question, choose the alternative you consider best and fill in the corresponding oval on your answer document. Read each passage through once before you begin to answer the questions that accompany it. For many of the questions, you must read several sentences beyond the question to determine the answer. Be sure that you have read far enough ahead each time you choose an alternative.

PASSAGE I

Antarctic Adventure

In February 2001, polar adventurers Liv Arnesen of Norway, and Ann Bancroft of
₁
Minnesota became the first women to climb and ski across the continent of Antarctica. The two former schoolteachers completed their 2,400-mile journey
₂
in 96 days.

[1] Months before their expedition, Arnesen and Bancroft began training by learning to ski behind sails—parachute-like devices that can pull a skier loaded with supplies about six miles per hour in steady winds. [2] On November 13, 2000, the pair boarded a small plane in South Africa and took a six-hour flight to Blue One Runway, it is a solid-ice airstrip on the Atlantic coast of
₃
Antarctica. [3] They set out soon after landing. [4] Hiking unassisted up the 10,000-foot-high Sygyn Glacier, and
₄
each woman pulled a sled that weighed more than

1. **A.** NO CHANGE
   B. Arnesen, of Norway, and Ann Bancroft,
   C. Arnesen, of Norway and Ann Bancroft,
   D. Arnesen of Norway and Ann Bancroft

2. **F.** NO CHANGE
   G. achieved
   H. finalized
   J. implemented

3. **A.** NO CHANGE
   B. Runway,
   C. Runway
   D. Runway, being

4. **F.** NO CHANGE
   G. when
   H. while
   J. DELETE the underlined portion.

GO ON TO THE NEXT PAGE.

260 pounds. [5] The sleds carried all the women's supplies, including a tent, a one-burner camp stove, diaries, two sets of skis, a laptop computer, and a snow shovel. [5]

By December 1, the adventurers had skied onto the Polar Plateau, stretching for 1,000 miles a high, frozen
                                    6
desert. The first week, strong winds had blew daily, and
                                      7
the team sailed 210 miles in just five days. For the next
 8
five days, accordingly, there was almost no wind, and the
              9
pair sailed only 34 miles. No matter how hard the women skied, daily mileage typically depended upon wind direction and intensity.

On January 16, Arnesen and Bancroft reached the South Pole, where they visited with scientists and replenished their food supply. In order
                        10
to safely descend the glacier's sharp ice, the women attached mountaineer spikes to their boots. Two days later, they were again in bitter cold, and while climbing
                                                      11
over a 10,200-foot-high glacier named Titan Dome.

5. If the writer were to delete Sentence 5, the essay would primarily lose details that:

A. reveal why Arnesen and Bancroft were each limited to carrying about 260 pounds of supplies.
B. expand upon information provided in Sentence 4 and also give readers a sense of what the women needed for their journey.
C. suggest that the women brought more supplies than they thought they would need for their journey.
D. contradict the information provided in Sentence 4 about the weight of Arnesen and Bancroft's supplies.

6. The best placement for the underlined phrase would be:

F. where it is now.
G. before the word *By* (revising the capitalization accordingly).
H. after the word *adventurers*.
J. after the word *desert* (ending the sentence with a period).

7. A. NO CHANGE
B. blow
C. blew
D. blown

8. Which of the following alternatives to the underlined portion would be LEAST acceptable?

F. the two
G. Arnesen and Bancroft
H. the women
J. these

9. A. NO CHANGE
B. otherwise,
C. consequently,
D. however,

10. F. NO CHANGE
G. scientists and, replenished their
H. scientists and replenished there
J. scientists, and replenished there

11. A. NO CHANGE
B. they climbed
C. climbing
D. to climb

GO ON TO THE NEXT PAGE.

Fortunately, the wind was with them the final few miles, and during those last miles of the trip, they were able to
12

ski off the continent itself and onto the Ross Ice Shelf. 13

Although the adventurers had planned to continue across the ice shelf to McMurdo Station, 460 miles away on the Pacific coast, the winds did not cooperate. To avoid becoming stranded when winter arrived, the women called a ski plane prudently to airlift them to McMurdo.
14

12. **F.** NO CHANGE
G. and during those fortunate moments,
H. so the wind carried them and
J. and

13. Which of the following true statements, if added here, would most effectively and specifically emphasize the women's main accomplishment as described in this essay?
A. It had been a long journey.
B. They had crossed the Antarctic landmass.
C. They were relieved to have safely descended Titan Dome.
D. These final miles were some of the speediest of Arnesen and Bancroft's trip.

14. The best placement for the underlined word would be:
F. where it is now.
G. before the word *becoming*.
H. before the word *stranded*.
J. before the word *called*.

Question 15 asks about the preceding passage as a whole.

15. If the writer were to delete the final paragraph of this essay, the essay would primarily lose information that:
A. explains why Arnesen and Bancroft were unable to ski to McMurdo Station, their final destination.
B. explains why skiing to McMurdo Station was part of Arnesen and Bancroft's original plan.
C. describes the specific weather conditions at different times of the year on the Ross Ice Shelf.
D. indicates Arnesen and Bancroft's reaction to having to be airlifted to McMurdo Station.

PASSAGE II

Working at the Bait & Tackle Shop

[1]

Most folks who live in our little bayside village work at a job having something to do with fishing or tourism, and I'm no different.

[2]

The shop opens at six in the morning, I arrive thirty
16
minutes early to set up. On many mornings, the sky

16. **F.** NO CHANGE
G. morning, however,
H. morning, but
J. morning

GO ON TO THE NEXT PAGE.

is adorned with peach-and-melon-colored ribbons as
17

a blazing solar sun begins to peek over the
18
horizon. Walking toward the docks,

the seagulls are wheeling and swooping. Their
19
high-pitched cries sound like rusty door hinges.

[3]

Usually, as I'm opening the door,
Carney, the night security guard at the marina, walks
20
by on his way home and offers me a sleepy hello.

[4]

The shop smells salty, like the bay, itself
21
and the creaky oak floor is gritty with sand. I

turn on the lights in the middle of the shop
22

sits wooden bins filled with sinkers, floats, and
23

lures. The wide variety of fishing equipment attracts both
24
the serious angler and the casual vacationer. If I notice any
24

merchandise out of place, I straighten it up.
25

17. Which of the following alternatives to the underlined portion would be LEAST acceptable?
A. ribbons at the same time that
B. ribbons in order that
C. ribbons while
D. ribbons, and

18. Which choice would be most consistent with the figurative description provided elsewhere in this sentence?
F. NO CHANGE
G. luminous
H. radiant
J. orange

19. A. NO CHANGE
B. watching the seagulls wheel and swoop, their
C. I watch the seagulls wheel and swoop. Their
D. the seagulls wheel and swoop. Their

20. F. NO CHANGE
G. Carney, the night security guard at the marina
H. Carney the night security guard at the marina,
J. Carney the night security guard at the marina

21. A. NO CHANGE
B. bay, itself,
C. bay itself,
D. bay itself

22. F. NO CHANGE
G. lights. In the middle
H. lights, in the center
J. lights in the center

23. A. NO CHANGE
B. is sitting
C. sets
D. sit

24. Given that all the choices are true, which one provides the most specific information about merchandise that can be found in the shop?
F. NO CHANGE
G. A rack of fishing rods covers one wall; shelves of reels, hooks, nets, and fishing line fill another.
H. The dark wood-paneled walls are jam-packed with equipment that would thrill any fishing enthusiast.
J. The shop offers gear for a range of different purposes.

25. A. NO CHANGE
B. straightened them
C. straightened those
D. straighten them

GO ON TO THE NEXT PAGE.

Practice ACT Tests

[5]

Next, I turn on the electric urn to heat water for hot tea, and I start a fresh pot of coffee. When I fill the bowl
26
of sugar cubes, take the lid off the powdered creamer, and add tea bags to the assortment in the basket on the counter I remove the cash drawer from the safe and put it in the cash register.

[6]

[1] Then, from the walk-in cooler, I drag bushels of bait clams to the counter. [2] I make sure the buckets of live herring, mullet, and shrimp are filled. [3] Since they're
27
sold by the baker's dozen, I fill Styrofoam containers with a bit of the grass and thirteen worms. [4] If it's a particularly nice day, or if the fish have been biting, I might prepare extra containers. [5] I pull out a large cardboard flat of worms packed in moist grass. 28

[7]

By this time, it's nearly six o'clock. I open the window blinds, unlock the front door, and greet the first customers with a smile. 29 If it's nippy outside, I offer them a complimentary cup of hot coffee or tea to help them start their day.

26. **F.** NO CHANGE
   G. As I fill
   H. Filling
   J. I fill

27. **A.** NO CHANGE
   B. live, herring, mullet,
   C. live, herring, mullet
   D. live herring mullet,

28. For the sake of the logic and coherence of this paragraph, Sentence 5 should be placed:
   F. where it is now.
   G. after Sentence 1.
   H. after Sentence 2.
   J. after Sentence 3.

29. If the writer were to delete the phrase "with a smile" from the preceding sentence, the sentence would primarily lose:
   A. information that contrasts the narrator's mood with that of the customers.
   B. a detail that describes the narrator's attitude toward the customers.
   C. a description that refers to a point made in the preceding paragraph.
   D. nothing at all, since this detail is clearly stated elsewhere in this paragraph.

Question 30 asks about the preceding passage as a whole.

---

30. Upon reviewing the essay and realizing that some key information has been left out, the writer composes the following sentence incorporating that information:

   I work at Stoney's Bait & Tackle Shop.

This sentence would most logically be placed after the last sentence in Paragraph:

   F. 1.
   G. 2.
   H. 3.
   J. 4.

GO ON TO THE NEXT PAGE.

PASSAGE III

A Few Words about Bats

The movie *Dracula*, featuring it's batlike title
<u>   </u>
                           31
character who feeds on human blood, is just one of many

sources of people's <u>ideas about bats that are flawed. The</u>
                                    32
facts about bats are <u>more interesting than</u> the falsehoods.
                            33
Just take three of the most common misconceptions about

<u>bats;</u> that they are dangerous to humans, that they are
  34
rodents, and that they cannot see.

In reality, only three of the more than 850 known

species of bats feed primarily on blood, and even

these do not draw nourishment from human blood;

<u>they bite cattle and horses in their sleep.</u> Most bats
                        35
eat insects; others feed on fruit, nectar, pollen, small

vertebrates, and fish.

Some people believe bats are <u>rodents; others</u> think
                                        36
bats are a kind of bird. Although winged, bats are not

related to birds, <u>because even if</u> a bat's small, furry body
                        37
may appear mouselike, bats are not rodents either. Rather,

bats are a unique order of mammals called <u>Chiroptera, the</u>
                                              38
only mammals that <u>truly flies.</u>
                        39
While some species of bats are blind, most are

not. However, bats that hunt at night use sound more

than sight to orient themselves in the dark. These bats

<u>sending out high-frequency sounds and using</u> the echoes
                      40
that bounce back from objects to locate their prey and to

navigate.

31. A. NO CHANGE
    B. with its
    C. based on its'
    D. who's

32. F. NO CHANGE
    G. ideas that are mistaken about bats.
    H. erroneous ideas about bats.
    J. mistaken ideas they have about bats.

33. A. NO CHANGE
    B. of more interest then
    C. the most interesting than
    D. more interesting then

34. F. NO CHANGE
    G. bats,
    H. bats
    J. bats:

35. A. NO CHANGE
    B. they bite sleeping cattle and horses.
    C. they bite cattle and horses when they are asleep.
    D. while asleep, they bite cattle and horses.

36. F. NO CHANGE
    G. rodents, others,
    H. rodents others
    J. rodents and others'

37. A. NO CHANGE
    B. whether
    C. and although
    D. seeing as

38. F. NO CHANGE
    G. Chiroptera, they are
    H. Chiroptera, so they are
    J. Chiroptera being

39. A. NO CHANGE
    B. is able to truly fly.
    C. can truly fly.
    D. has true flight ability.

40. F. NO CHANGE
    G. sending out high-frequency sounds and use
    H. sent out high-frequency sounds to use
    J. send out high-frequency sounds and use

GO ON TO THE NEXT PAGE.

In addition to being fascinating creatures, bats are useful to humans, especially farmers. [41] They consume beetles and moths that attack crops, reducing our reliance on chemical insecticides; in addition, bat droppings are useful for fertilizing fields and gardens.

There is one sad piece of news about bats: their habitats are being destroyed by humans. For example, bat caves are being disturbed or ruined as highways and housing developments are built. [42] As a consequence, several bat species face extinction. We should protect bats because, <u>though they might seem threatening,</u> they are an
43
important and beneficial part of life.

41. Given that all the following statements are true, which one provides the most relevant information at this point in the essay?

  A. Like all wild animals, bats may bite if handled.
  B. Bats pollinate plants, including fruits we eat.
  C. Some plants have developed special mechanisms to attract bats.
  D. Bats have eyes adapted for poor lighting conditions.

42. The writer is considering deleting the preceding sentence from this paragraph. If the writer made this deletion, the paragraph would primarily lose:

  F. information that distracts from the message about the extinction of some bat species.
  G. an example of ways readers can stop the destruction of bat habitats.
  H. scientific proof of the statement that bat habitats are being destroyed.
  J. evidence for the claim that bat habitats are being destroyed.

43. The writer wants to provide a phrase here that will tie the conclusion of the essay to its beginning. Which choice does that best?

  A. NO CHANGE
  B. though they mostly come out at night,
  C. though their habitats are vanishing,
  D. even if we rarely see them,

Questions 44 and 45 ask about the preceding passage as a whole.

---

44. The writer is considering deleting the last sentence of the first paragraph of the essay. If the writer were to make this deletion, the essay would primarily lose a statement that:

  F. introduces the organization of the next three paragraphs.
  G. summarizes points made earlier in the paragraph.
  H. provides a list of the kinds of creatures bats have been compared to.
  J. adds a much-needed touch of humor to the essay.

45. Suppose the writer's goal had been to write an essay focusing on the various ways in which people are causing the extinction of some bat species. Would this essay fulfill that goal?

  A. Yes, because the essay explains in detail that bats have many enemies, including humans, who pose the greatest threat of all to bat survival.
  B. Yes, because the essay focuses on the misconceptions people have about bats.
  C. No, because the essay primarily focuses on people's mistaken ideas about bats, not on ways in which people are causing the extinction of some bat species.
  D. No, because the essay indicates that not all bat species are at risk of becoming extinct, only the ones that feed on livestock.

GO ON TO THE NEXT PAGE.

PASSAGE IV

In Remembrance of a Student Hero

[1] When Mario Savio died in 1996, newspaper stories recounted the events that had put him in the national spotlight more than thirty years earlier. [2] In 1964, Savio was a philosophy major and a member of the executive committee of the Free Speech Movement at the University of California at Berkeley. [3] During the height of the United States presidential election campaign, the Free Speech Movement had organized to fight the university's decision to limit the activities of those groups on campus. [4] The son of working-class parents, Savio grew up in Queens, New York. [5] He had volunteered to do civil rights work in Mississippi, the twentieth state admitted to the Union, during the Freedom Summer of 1964 before returning to classes that fall. [6] Along with many others, Savio reacted fiercely when the university banned civil rights groups from setting up information tables on the campus plaza. [7] That stuff led to a student strike and a sit-in protest at the main administration building. [51]

46. Given that all the choices are true, which one most effectively introduces this sentence by describing what the Free Speech Movement was?
  F. NO CHANGE
  G. A coalition of civil rights groups and other political organizations,
  H. At the center of a conflict with university officials,
  J. Prompted by university action taken that fall,

47. A. NO CHANGE
  B. the state of Mississippi (also known as the Magnolia State),
  C. Mississippi, admitted to the Union in 1817,
  D. Mississippi

48. F. NO CHANGE
  G. 1964, before,
  H. 1964 before,
  J. 1964; before

49. A. NO CHANGE
  B. That ban
  C. Which
  D. It

50. F. NO CHANGE
  G. it became
  H. and was
  J. than

51. The writer has decided to divide this opening paragraph into two. The best place to add the new paragraph break would be at the beginning of Sentence:
  A. 4, because it would indicate that the essay is now going to focus on Savio's childhood.
  B. 4, because it would signal the essay's shift in emphasis back to Savio.
  C. 5, because it would indicate that the essay is now going to address Savio's experiences as a civil rights worker.
  D. 5, because it would signal the essay's shift from Savio's childhood to his adult life.

GO ON TO THE NEXT PAGE.

On December 2, 1964, Savio spoke insistently to
                                    ———————
                                        52

a countless group of protesters: "There is a time when the
  ——————————
        53

operation of the machine . . . makes you so sick at heart

that you can't take part . . . and you've got to make it

stop." That day, Savio and 800 other protesters were
       ————
        54

taken to jail in the largest mass arrest in California

history. Days later, the California Board of Regents

voted to override the university ban and granted full
                                 ———————
                                    55

speech rights on the Berkeley campus. [56]

The Free Speech Movement changed campus

life in the United States. It made a powerful case for the
                           ————
                            57

students' right to freedom of speech. It also popularized
                                      ——————
                                        58

the sit-in, as a protest tactic, became a model for student
    ———————————————————
            59

rallies and protests across the country. As for Mario Savio,

he went on to earn a master's degree in physics. He

52. Which choice would most clearly indicate that Savio succeeded in his appeal to the protesters?

   F. NO CHANGE
   G. emphatically
   H. compellingly
   J. excitably

53. **A.** NO CHANGE
   B. numerous group
   C. high volume
   D. large crowd

54. Which of the following alternatives to the underlined portion would be LEAST acceptable?

   F. Not long after,
   G. Besides,
   H. Soon,
   J. Then,

55. Which of the following alternatives to the underlined portion would be LEAST acceptable?

   A. ban, and this action
   B. ban, an action that
   C. ban and, thus,
   D. ban that

56. At this point, the writer is considering adding the following true statement:

> Appointed by the governor, the California Board of Regents is assigned to oversee that state's university system.

Should the writer add this sentence here?

   F. Yes, because it provides important background information concerning the vote.
   G. Yes, because it explains the makeup of this particular board to the reader.
   H. No, because it distracts the reader from the main point of this paragraph.
   J. No, because it does not provide specific enough information about the California Board of Regents.

57. **A.** NO CHANGE
   B. made for
   C. makes for
   D. makes

58. **F.** NO CHANGE
   G. For this reason, it
   H. However, it
   J. It thus

59. **A.** NO CHANGE
   B. sit-in as a protest tactic and
   C. sit-in, as a protest tactic, it
   D. sit-in as a protest tactic

GO ON TO THE NEXT PAGE.

then taught <u>mathematics and physics in high schools</u>
<u>and,</u> for his last six years, at Sonoma State University,

where he led protests against student fee increases.

Whether a student or a teacher, Savio applied the belief

that ordinary people banding together can make change

happen.

GO ON TO THE NEXT PAGE.

60. F. NO CHANGE
    G. then, taught, mathematics
    H. then taught mathematics,
    J. then, taught mathematics

PASSAGE V

Roberto Clemente in Right Field

[1]

Roberto Clemente, the Pittsburgh Pirates right

fielder from 1955 to 1972, was <u>one of baseballs most</u>

gifted athletes. He was <u>entitled</u> the National League

Batting Champion four times, the National League Most

Valuable Player (MVP) in 1966, and the World Series

<u>MVP in 1971.</u> In recognition of his fielding skills, he

was awarded twelve consecutive Gold Gloves. In 1973,

he was inducted into the Baseball Hall of Fame.

[2]

While Clemente's achievements in the sport

of baseball are <u>impressive. His</u> charity work off

the field has marked <u>himself</u> as one of the greatest

humanitarians in professional sports. Tragically, it was

during one of his goodwill missions that Clemente's life

61. A. NO CHANGE
    B. one, of baseball's
    C. one, of baseballs
    D. one of baseball's

62. F. NO CHANGE
    G. awarded
    H. named
    J. given

63. A. NO CHANGE
    B. in 1971 was awarded to Clemente.
    C. award in 1971 went to Clemente.
    D. award was given to him in 1971.

64. F. NO CHANGE
    G. impressive, but his
    H. impressive and his
    J. impressive, his

65. A. NO CHANGE
    B. him
    C. them
    D. itself

GO ON TO THE NEXT PAGE.

was cut short. In 1972, Clemente died in a plane crash
66

while delivering relief supplies to earthquake victims
67
in Nicaragua.

[3]

[1] At the time of his death, Clemente

was planning long-term humanitarian

projects, which were designed to last for years.
68

[2] A few years later, his wife Vera, fulfilled this
69
dream by founding the Roberto Clemente Ciudad

Deportiva (Sports City) in Puerto Rico. [3] Each year,

this 304-acre sports, counseling, and education center

provides thousands of Puerto Rican youths the chance

for a better life. [4] One of them was for children a sports
70

complex in his homeland. [71]

[4]

In 1993, Clemente's eldest son, Roberto Clemente Jr.,

established the Roberto Clemente Foundation. The

foundation's primary funding project, the RBI (Reviving

Baseball in the Inner City) Program, offers baseball,

softball, and educational opportunities for disadvantaged

Pittsburgh-area teenagers.

66. **F.** NO CHANGE
    G. perished in a deadly
    H. fatally perished in a
    J. died in a lethal

67. Which of the following alternatives to the underlined portion would NOT be acceptable?

    A. while he was delivering
    B. as he was delivering
    C. that was delivering
    D. as he delivered

68. **F.** NO CHANGE
    G. projects that would help others.
    H. projects of benefit to others.
    J. projects.

69. **A.** NO CHANGE
    B. later, his wife, Vera,
    C. later, his wife, Vera
    D. later his wife Vera,

70. The best placement for the underlined portion would be:

    F. where it is now.
    G. after the word *them.*
    H. after the word *complex.*
    J. after the word *homeland* (ending the sentence with a period).

71. For the sake of the logic and coherence of this paragraph, Sentence 4 should be placed:

    A. where it is now.
    B. before Sentence 1.
    C. after Sentence 1.
    D. after Sentence 2.

GO ON TO THE NEXT PAGE.

[5]

Clemente's example has also motivated major leaguers to participate in humanitarian projects. Since 1970, Major League Baseball has presented an award annual recognizing the player
                        72

who best exemplifies the principals of sportsmanship
                        73
and community service. In 1973, the award was renamed the Roberto Clemente Award.

[6]

While Clemente's exemplary baseball record remains fixed for the ages, the effects of his generosity continue to expand, as the story of his life is told to others.
                        74

72. F. NO CHANGE
   G. annually presented an award
   H. presented an award on an annually basis
   J. presented an annually award

73. A. NO CHANGE
   B. principals for
   C. principles in
   D. principles of

74. Which choice would best help this sentence to summarize key points made in the essay?
   F. NO CHANGE
   G. inspiring ballplayers and improving the lives of young people.
   H. and we can learn more about him in the Baseball Hall of Fame.
   J. regardless of whether the Pittsburgh team makes the playoffs or not.

> Question 75 asks about the preceding passage as a whole.

75. Upon reviewing notes for this essay, the writer comes across the following true statement:

> Recent recipients of this honor include Sammy Sosa, Tony Gwynn, and Curt Schilling.

If the writer were to use this sentence, the most logical place to add it would be at the end of Paragraph:

   A. 2.
   B. 4.
   C. 5.
   D. 6.

END OF TEST 1

STOP! DO NOT TURN THE PAGE UNTIL TOLD TO DO SO.

MATHEMATICS TEST
60 Minutes—60 Questions

DIRECTIONS: Solve each problem, choose the correct answer, and then fill in the corresponding oval on your answer document.

Do not linger over problems that take too much time. Solve as many as you can; then return to the others in the time you have left for this test.

You are permitted to use a calculator on this test. You may use your calculator for any problems you choose, but some of the problems may best be done without using a calculator.

Note: Unless otherwise stated, all of the following should be assumed.

1. Illustrative figures are NOT necessarily drawn to scale.
2. Geometric figures lie in a plane.
3. The word *line* indicates a straight line.
4. The word *average* indicates arithmetic mean.

---

1. On level ground, a vertical rod 12 feet tall casts a shadow 4 feet long, and at the same time a nearby vertical flagpole casts a shadow 12 feet long. How many feet tall is the flagpole?

   A. 4
   B. 8
   C. 12
   D. 20
   E. 36

2. The cost of a gym membership is a onetime fee of $140, plus a monthly fee of $40. Brendan wrote a $500 check to pay his gym membership for a certain number of months, including the onetime fee. How many months of membership did he pay for?

   F. 3
   G. 4
   H. 9
   J. 12
   K. 13

3. If $x = -5$, what is the value of $\frac{x^2 - 1}{x + 1}$?

   A. −6
   B. −4
   C. 4
   D. $5\frac{4}{5}$
   E. 19

4. A museum offers a 2-hour guided group tour. For groups with fewer than 25 people the cost is $9.25 per person; for groups with 25 people or more the cost is $8.50 per person. The 27 people in the 9:00 a.m. tour group each paid $9.25 in advance. What is the total refund that the museum owes the 9:00 a.m. group?

   F. $12.50
   G. $13.00
   H. $18.75
   J. $20.25
   K. $25.00

DO YOUR FIGURING HERE.

GO ON TO THE NEXT PAGE.

DO YOUR FIGURING HERE.

5. The 13-member math club needs to choose a student government representative. They decide that the representative, who will be chosen at random, CANNOT be any of the 3 officers of the club. What is the probability that Samara, who is a member of the club but NOT an officer, will be chosen?

   A. 0

   B. $\frac{1}{13}$

   C. $\frac{1}{10}$

   D. $\frac{3}{13}$

   E. $\frac{1}{3}$

6. What is the perimeter, in centimeters, of a rectangle with length 15 cm and width 6 cm ?

   F. 21
   G. 30
   H. 42
   J. 90
   K. 180

7. Tickets for a community theater production cost $6 each when bought in advance and $8 each when bought at the door. The theater group's goal is at least $2,000 in ticket sales for opening night. The theater group sold 142 opening-night tickets in advance. What is the minimum number of tickets they need to sell at the door on opening night to make their goal?

   A. 143
   B. 144
   C. 192
   D. 250
   E. 357

8. For what value of r is the equation $\frac{8}{12} = \frac{10}{r}$ true?

   F. 3
   G. 6
   H. 14
   J. 15
   K. 18

9. If $12(x - 11) = -15$, then $x = ?$

   A. $-\frac{49}{4}$

   B. $-\frac{13}{6}$

   C. $-\frac{5}{4}$

   D. $-\frac{1}{3}$

   E. $\frac{39}{4}$

GO ON TO THE NEXT PAGE.

10. In the figure below, A, D, C, and E are collinear. $\overline{AD}$, $\overline{BD}$, and $\overline{BC}$ are all the same length, and the angle measure of $\angle ABD$ is as marked. What is the degree measure of $\angle BCE$?

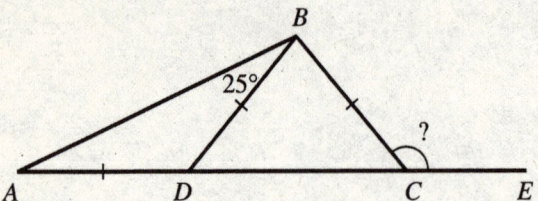

F. 50°
G. 100°
H. 105°
J. 130°
K. 160°

11. If $f(x) = 9x^2 + 5x - 8$, then $f(-2) = ?$

A. −54
B. −18
C. 18
D. 36
E. 38

12. What is the least common multiple of 30, 20, and 70 ?

F. 40
G. 42
H. 120
J. 420
K. 42,000

13. While doing a problem on his calculator, Tom meant to divide a number by 2, but instead he accidentally multiplied the number by 2. Which of the following calculations could Tom then do to the result on the calculator screen to obtain the result he originally wanted?

A. Subtract the original number
B. Multiply by 2
C. Multiply by 4
D. Divide by 2
E. Divide by 4

14. The 8-sided figure below is divided into 5 congruent squares. The total area of the 5 squares is 125 square inches. What is the perimeter, in inches, of the figure?

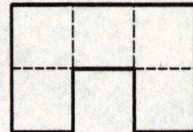

F. 25
G. 60
H. 80
J. 100
K. 125

GO ON TO THE NEXT PAGE.

DO YOUR FIGURING HERE.

15. In △*ABC*, ∠*A* measures greater than 43° and ∠*B* measures exactly 90°. Which of the following phrases best describes the measure of ∠*C* ?

    A. Greater than 47°
    B. Equal to 47°
    C. Equal to 60°
    D. Equal to 133°
    E. Less than 47°

16. Among the following arithmetic operations, which could the symbol ◊ represent given that the equation $(2 ◊ 1)^4 + (6 ◊ 3)^2 = 10$ is true?

    I. Addition
    II. Subtraction
    III. Division

    F. I only
    G. II only
    H. III only
    J. I and II only
    K. I, II, and III

17. One of the following is an equation of the linear relation shown in the standard (x,y) coordinate plane below. Which equation is it?

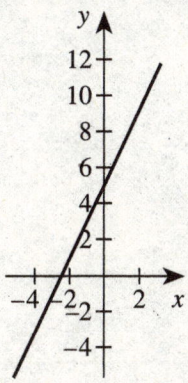

    A. $y = 5x$
    B. $y = 2x$
    C. $y = 5x + 2$
    D. $y = 2x - 5$
    E. $y = 2x + 5$

18. An integer, n, is added to 4. That sum is then multiplied by 8. This result is 10 less than twice the original integer. Which of the following equations represents this relationship?

    F. $8(n + 4) = 2n - 10$
    G. $8(n + 4) - 10 = 2n$
    H. $8(n + 4) = 10 - 2n$
    J. $n + 4 \times 8 = 2n - 10$
    K. $4 + 8 = 2n - 10$

GO ON TO THE NEXT PAGE.

DO YOUR FIGURING HERE.

19. Two workers were hired to begin work at the same time. Worker A's contract called for a starting salary of $20,000 with an increase of $800 after each year of employment. Worker B's contract called for a starting salary of $15,200 with an increase of $2,000 after each year of employment. If x represents the number of full years' employment (that is, the number of yearly increases each worker has received), which of the following equations could be solved to determine the number of years until B's yearly salary equals A's yearly salary?

   A. $20,000 + 800x = 15,200 + 2,000x$
   B. $20,000 + 2,000x = 15,200 + 800x$
   C. $(20,000 + 800)x = (15,200 + 2,000)x$
   D. $(2,000 + 800)x = 20,000 - 15,200$
   E. $(2,000 - 800)x = 20,000 + 15,200$

20. A ramp for loading trucks is 13 feet long and covers 12 feet along the level ground, as shown below. How many feet high is the highest point on the ramp?

   F. 1
   G. 2
   H. 4
   J. 5
   K. $6\frac{1}{4}$

21. The expression $7(x + 3) - 3(2x - 2)$ is equivalent to:

   A. $x + 1$
   B. $x + 15$
   C. $x + 19$
   D. $x + 23$
   E. $x + 27$

22. If $x + y = 32$, and $x - y = 12$, then $y = ?$

   F. 6
   G. 10
   H. 20
   J. 22
   K. 44

23. When $(2x - 3)^2$ is written in the form $ax^2 + bx + c$, where a, b, and c are integers, $a + b + c = ?$

   A. -17
   B. -5
   C. 1
   D. 13
   E. 25

GO ON TO THE NEXT PAGE.

DO YOUR FIGURING HERE.

24. What is the area, in square feet, of the figure below?

25 feet

5 feet

15 feet

15 feet

- F. 60
- G. 80
- H. 275
- J. 375
- K. 450

25. The table below gives the values of 2 functions, f and g, for various values of x. One of the functions expresses a linear relationship. What is the value of that function at $x = 4$?

x	$f(x)$	$g(x)$
−2	1.4	0.6
−1	1.2	0.9
0		
1	0.8	1.3
2	0.6	1.6
3		
4		

- A. 0.2
- B. 0.4
- C. 1.9
- D. 2.0
- E. 2.2

26. What is the slope of the line represented by the equation $6y - 14x = 5$?

- F. −14
- G. $\frac{5}{6}$
- H. $\frac{7}{3}$
- J. 6
- K. 14

27. What is the sum of the 2 solutions of the equation $x^2 + x - 12 = 0$?

- A. −12
- B. −4
- C. −1
- D. 0
- E. 3

GO ON TO THE NEXT PAGE.

DO YOUR FIGURING HERE.

28. Two similar triangles have perimeters in the ratio 3:5. The sides of the smaller triangle measure 3 cm, 5 cm, and 7 cm, respectively. What is the perimeter, in centimeters, of the larger triangle?

    F. 15
    G. 18
    H. 20
    J. 25
    K. 36

29. At a certain location, the low temperatures, in degrees Fahrenheit, for each of 7 consecutive days in January were −2°F, 4°F, −3°F, 1°F, 2°F, −5°F, and −6°F. What was the median of these low temperatures?

    A. −2°F
    B. −1°F
    C. 1°F
    D. 3°F
    E. 4°F

30. When asked his age, the algebra teacher said, "If you square my age, then subtract 23 times my age, the result is 50." How old is he?

    F. 23
    G. 25
    H. 27
    J. 46
    K. 50

31. The distance, d, an accelerating object travels in t seconds can be modeled by the equation $d = \frac{1}{2}at^2$, where a is the acceleration rate, in meters per second per second. If a car accelerates from a stop at the rate of 20 meters per second per second and travels a distance of 80 meters, about how many seconds did the car travel?

    A. Between 1 and 2
    B. Between 2 and 3
    C. Between 3 and 4
    D. 4
    E. 8

32. Let a, b, c, and d be distinct positive integers. What is the 4th term of the geometric sequence below?
    $$bcd, abc^2d, a^2bc^3d, \cdots$$

    F. a^3bc^4d
    G. $a^3b^2c^3d$
    H. $a^3b^2c^4d^2$
    J. a^4bc^6d
    K. a^4bc^9d

GO ON TO THE NEXT PAGE.

Use the following information to answer questions 33–35.

A survey in a study skills class asked the 20 students enrolled in the class how many hours (rounded to the nearest hour) they had spent studying on the previous evening. The 20 responses are summarized by the histogram below.

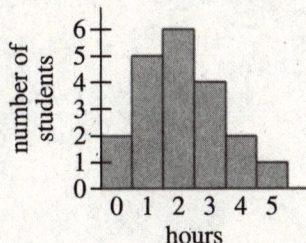

33. What fraction of the students responded that they had spent less than 3 hours studying?

A. $\frac{13}{100}$

B. $\frac{1}{5}$

C. $\frac{3}{10}$

D. $\frac{13}{20}$

E. $\frac{17}{20}$

34. The teacher decides to show the data in a circle graph (pie chart). What should be the measure of the central angle of the sector for 3 hours?

F. 18°
G. 20°
H. 36°
J. 72°
K. 90°

35. To the nearest tenth of an hour, what is the average number of hours for the 20 survey responses?

A. 2.0
B. 2.1
C. 2.3
D. 2.5
E. 3.0

GO ON TO THE NEXT PAGE.

DO YOUR FIGURING HERE.

36. For all $x > 21$, $\dfrac{(x^2 + 8x + 7)(x - 3)}{(x^2 + 4x - 21)(x + 1)} = ?$

   F. 1

   G. $\dfrac{9}{7}$

   H. $\dfrac{x-3}{x+3}$

   J. $\dfrac{2(x-3)}{x+1}$

   K. $-\dfrac{4(x-3)}{x+1}$

37. The bottom of the basket of a hot-air balloon is parallel to the level ground. One taut tether line 144 feet long is attached to the center of the bottom of the basket and is anchored to the ground at an angle of 72°, as shown in the figure below. Which of the following expressions gives the distance, in feet, from the center of the bottom of the basket to the ground?

   A. $\dfrac{144}{\cos 72°}$

   B. $\dfrac{144}{\sin 72°}$

   C. 144 tan 72°

   D. 144 cos 72°

   E. 144 sin 72°

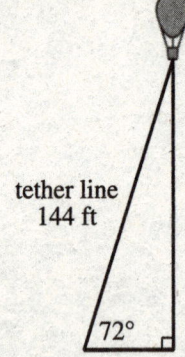

tether line
144 ft

72°

38. The coordinates of the endpoints of $\overline{GH}$, in the standard (x,y) coordinate plane, are $(-8,-3)$ and $(2,3)$. What is the x-coordinate of the midpoint of $\overline{GH}$?

   F. −6
   G. −3
   H. 0
   J. 3
   K. 5

39. On a map in the standard (x,y) coordinate plane, the towns of Arlington and Betelwood are represented by the points $(-2,-3)$ and $(-6,-7)$, respectively. Each unit on the map represents an actual distance of 10 miles. Which of the following is closest to the distance, in miles, between these 2 towns?

   A. 128
   B. 57
   C. 42
   D. 40
   E. 28

GO ON TO THE NEXT PAGE.

DO YOUR FIGURING HERE.

40. Which of the following statements is true about rational and/or irrational numbers?

   F. The product of any 2 irrational numbers is irrational.
   G. The quotient of any 2 irrational numbers is rational.
   H. The product of any 2 rational numbers is irrational.
   J. The quotient of any 2 rational numbers is irrational.
   K. The sum of any 2 rational numbers is rational.

41. For the complex number i and an integer x, which of the following is a possible value of i^x ?

   A. 0
   B. 1
   C. 2
   D. 3
   E. 4

42. Consider the equation $y = (x - 3)^2 + 2$ where x and y are both real numbers. The table below gives the values of y for selected values of x.

x	y
−6	83
−4	51
−2	27
0	11
2	3
4	3
6	11

   For the equation above, which of the following values of x gives the least value of y ?

   F. 1
   G. 2
   H. 3
   J. 4
   K. 5

43. The height and radius of the right circular cylinder below are given in meters. What is the volume, in cubic meters, of the cylinder?

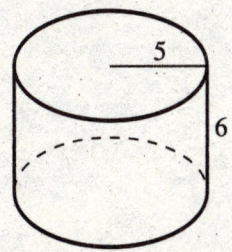

   A. 30π
   B. 31π
   C. 150π
   D. 180π
   E. 900π

GO ON TO THE NEXT PAGE.

44. Lines l_1 and l_2 intersect each other and 3 parallel lines, l_3, l_4, and l_5, at the points shown in the figure below. The ratio of the perimeter of $\triangle ABC$ to the perimeter of $\triangle AFG$ is 1:3. The ratio of DE to FG is 2:3. What is the ratio of AC to CE ?

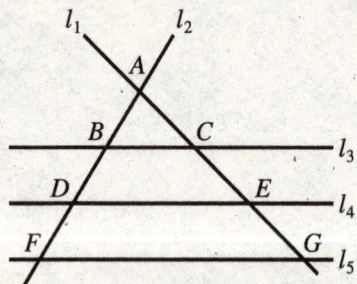

DO YOUR FIGURING HERE.

F. 1:1
G. 1:2
H. 1:3
J. 2:1
K. 3:1

45. A rocket lifted off from a launch pad and traveled vertically 30 kilometers, then traveled 40 kilometers at 30° from the vertical, and then traveled 100 kilometers at 45° from the vertical, as shown in the figure below. At that point, the rocket was how many kilometers above the height of the launch pad?

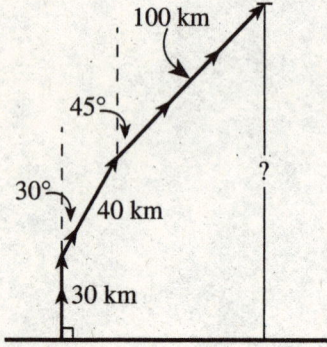

A. 100
B. 170
C. 190
D. $20\sqrt{3} + 50\sqrt{2}$
E. $30 + 20\sqrt{3} + 50\sqrt{2}$

46. In the standard (x,y) coordinate plane, what is the area of the circle $x^2 + y^2 = 16$?

F. 4π
G. 8π
H. 16π
J. 64π
K. 256π

GO ON TO THE NEXT PAGE.

DO YOUR FIGURING HERE.

47. In the standard (x,y) coordinate plane below, 1 side of a rectangle is on the x-axis, and the vertices of the opposite side of the rectangle are on the graph of the parabola $y = 6 - 2x^2$. Let a represent any value of x such that $0 < x < \sqrt{3}$. Which of the following is an expression in terms of a for the area, in square coordinate units, of any such rectangle?

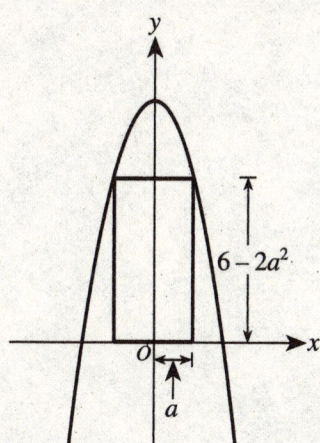

A. $-4a^3 + 12a$

B. $-2a^3 + 6a$

C. $-4a^2 + 4a + 12$

D. $-2a^2 + 2a + 6$

E. $4a^4 - 24a^2 + 36$

48. If n is a positive integer, which of the following expressions must be an odd integer?

F. 3^n

G. n^3

H. $3n$

J. $\frac{n}{3}$

K. $3 + n$

49. The value of $\log_5\left(5^{\frac{13}{2}}\right)$ is between which of the following pairs of consecutive integers?

A. 0 and 1

B. 4 and 5

C. 5 and 6

D. 6 and 7

E. 9 and 10

GO ON TO THE NEXT PAGE.

DO YOUR FIGURING HERE.

Use the following information to answer questions 50–52.

The table below shows the weekly sales totals (in thousands of dollars) for 4 departments at Pinky's Megamarket during the 5 most recent weeks. Data is missing due to a computer virus that infected the supermarket's database. The data in the table has been verified as being accurate.

Department	Week number				
	1	2	3	4	5
Meat	145	144	156	145	140
Produce	30				
Canned goods	54	62	69	75	
Dry goods	86	82		77	85

50. Which of the following is closest to the percent increase in meat department sales for Pinky's Megamarket from Week 2 to Week 3 ?

F. 1.1%
G. 6.0%
H. 7.7%
J. 8.3%
K. 12.0%

51. Prior to Week 3, the manager set the goal for meat department sales to average 150 thousand dollars per week from the beginning of Week 3 through the end of Week 6. To meet this goal, what must be the minimum meat department sales for Week 6, in thousands of dollars?

A. 146
B. 147
C. 156
D. 159
E. 170

52. The assistant manager recalls that produce department sales increased at a very high rate during the 5 weeks, due to a projected shortage of fruit. She says that for each week from Week 2 to Week 5, produce department sales increased 10% from the previous week. Which of the following values, in thousands of dollars, is closest to produce department sales for Week 5 ?

F. 48
G. 44
H. 42
J. 40
K. 33

GO ON TO THE NEXT PAGE.

53. A trigonometric function with equation $y = a \sin(bx + c)$, where a, b, and c are real numbers, is graphed in the standard (x,y) coordinate plane below. The *period* of this function $f(x)$ is the smallest positive number p such that $f(x + p) = f(x)$ for every real number x. One of the following is the period of this function. Which one is it?

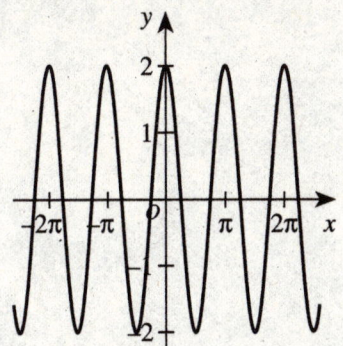

A. $\dfrac{\pi}{2}$

B. π

C. 2π

D. 4π

E. 2

54. The building below casts a shadow 24 yards long, and the angle of elevation from the tip of the shadow to the top of the building has a sine of $\dfrac{4}{5}$. What is the height of the building in yards?

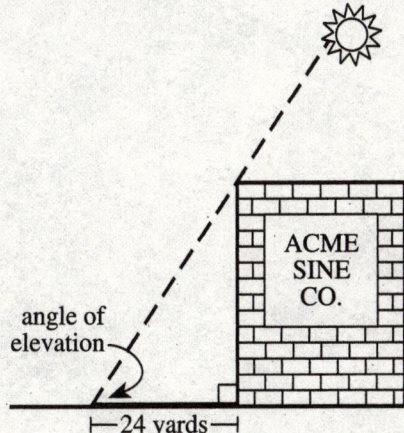

ACME SINE CO.

angle of elevation

⊢—24 yards—⊣

F. 14.4
G. 18.0
H. 19.2
J. 30.0
K. 32.0

55. Which of the following is an irrational number that is a solution to the equation $|x^2 - 12| - 4 = 0$?

A. 4

B. $\sqrt{2}$

C. $2\sqrt{2}$

D. $4\sqrt{2}$

E. $2\sqrt{3}$

GO ON TO THE NEXT PAGE.

56. The graph below shows the distance Malika is from a motion detector for a period of 10 seconds. A certain order of 3 of the following 5 actions describes Malika's movement in relation to the position of the motion detector. Which order is it?

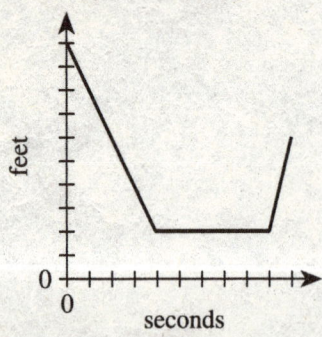

   I. Stands still for 5 seconds
  II. Walks away at 4 feet per second
 III. Walks toward at 4 feet per second
 IV. Walks away at 2 feet per second
  V. Walks toward at 2 feet per second

- **F.** I, II, V
- **G.** II, I, V
- **H.** III, I, IV
- **J.** IV, I, III
- **K.** V, I, II

57. As shown in the figure below, a clock has a minute hand that measures 5 cm from its tip to the center of the clock. To the nearest centimeter, what is the distance traveled by the tip of the minute hand between 2:10 p.m. and 5:30 p.m. ?

 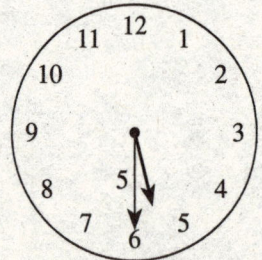

- **A.** 31
- **B.** 68
- **C.** 101
- **D.** 105
- **E.** 173

GO ON TO THE NEXT PAGE.

58. For φ, an angle whose measure is between 90° and 180°, $\tan \phi = -\frac{7}{24}$. Which of the following equals sin φ ?

F. $-\frac{24}{7}$

G. $-\frac{24}{25}$

H. $-\frac{7}{25}$

J. $\frac{24}{25}$

K. $\frac{7}{25}$

DO YOUR FIGURING HERE.

59. Consider all pairs of positive integers w and z whose sum is 5. For how many values of w does there exist a positive integer x that satisfies both $2^w = x$ and $x^z = 64$?

A. 0
B. 2
C. 4
D. 8
E. Infinitely many

60. A cube with edges 4 cm long is inscribed in a sphere, as shown below. What is the radius of the sphere, in centimeters?

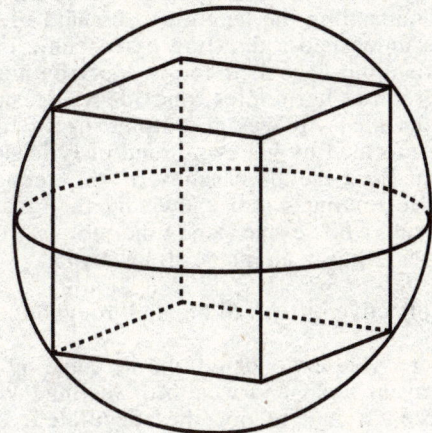

F. $2\sqrt{3}$
G. $2\sqrt{2}$
H. $4\sqrt{3}$
J. $4\sqrt{2}$
K. 2

END OF TEST 2

STOP! DO NOT TURN THE PAGE UNTIL TOLD TO DO SO.

DO NOT RETURN TO THE PREVIOUS TEST.

READING TEST
35 Minutes—40 Questions

DIRECTIONS: There are four passages in this test. Each passage is followed by several questions. After reading a passage, choose the best answer to each question and fill in the corresponding oval on your answer document. You may refer to the passages as often as necessary.

Passage I

PROSE FICTION: This passage is adapted from the novel *The Fisher King* by Paule Marshall (©2000 by Paule Marshall).

It was nearing the end of the second set, the jazz show winding down when Hattie heard Abe Kaiser at the microphone call Everett Payne's name. Heard his name and, to her surprise, saw him slowly stand up in
5 the bullpen up front. She hadn't seen him join the other local musicians, including Shades Bowen with his tenor sax, in what was called the bullpen, which was simply a dozen or so chairs grouped near the bandstand. The young locals gathered there each Sunday evening,
10 hoping for a chance to perform. Because toward the end of the final set, the custom was to invite one or two of them to sit in with the band. They sometimes even got to choose the tune they wanted to play.

This Sunday, Everett Payne, not long out of the
15 army, was the one being invited to sit in.

Breath held, Hattie watched him separate himself from the hopefuls and approach the stand, taking his time, moving with what almost seemed a deliberate pause between each step. The crowd waiting.

20 That was his way, Hattie knew. His body moving absentmindedly through space, his head, his thoughts on something other than his surroundings, and his eyes like a curtain he occasionally drew aside a fraction of an inch to peer out at the world. A world far less inter-
25 esting than the music inside his head.

She watched now as he slowly mounted the bandstand and conferred with the bassist and drummer, those two were all he would need. Then, without announcing the name of the tune he intended playing,
30 without in any way acknowledging the audience, he sat down at the piano and brought his hands—large hands, the fingers long and splayed and slightly arched—down on the opening bars of "Sonny Boy Blue."

"Sonny Boy Blue!" That hokey-doke tune!

35 Around her, the purists looked askance at each other from behind their regulation shades and slouched deeper in their chairs in open disgust.

At first, hokey though it was, he played the song straight through as written, the rather long introduction,
40 verse, and chorus. And he did so with great care, although at a slower tempo than was called for and with a formality that lent the Tin Pan Alley tune a depth and thoughtfulness no one else would have accorded it.

Quickly taking their cue from him, the bassist
45 reached for his bow, the drummer for his brushes, the two of them also treating the original as if it were a serious piece of music.

Everett Payne took his time paying his respects to the tune as written, and once that was done, he hunched
50 closer to the piano, angled his head sharply to the left, completely closed the curtain of his gaze, and with his hands commanding the length and breadth of the keyboard he unleashed a dazzling pyrotechnic of chords (you could almost see their colors), polyrhythms, seem-
55 ingly unrelated harmonies, and ideas—fresh, brash, outrageous ideas. It was an outpouring of ideas and feelings informed by his own brand of lyricism and lit from time to time by flashes of the recognizable melody. He continued to acknowledge the little simple-
60 minded tune, while at the same time furiously recasting and reinventing it in an image all his own.

A collective in-suck of breath throughout the club.

Where, Hattie wondered, did he come by the dazzling array of ideas and wealth of feeling? What was
65 the source? It had to do, she speculated, listening intently, with the way he held his head, angled to the left like that, tilted toward both heaven and earth. His right side, his right ear directed skyward, hearing up there, in the Upper Room among the stars Mahalia sang
70 about, a new kind of music: splintered, atonal, profane, and possessing a wonderful dissonance that spoke to him, to his soul-case. For him, this was the true music of the spheres, of the maelstrom up there. When at the piano, he kept his right ear tuned to it at all times, let-
75 ting it guide him, inspire him. His other ear? It remained earthbound, trained on the bedrock that for him was Bach and the blues.

Again and again he took them on a joyous, terrifying roller coaster of a ride it seemed to Hattie, and
80 when he finally deposited them on terra firma after close to twenty minutes, everyone in Putnam Royal

GO ON TO THE NEXT PAGE.

could only sit there as if they were in church and weren't supposed to clap. Overcome. Until finally Alvin Edwards lived on Decatur Street played trumpet
85 in the school band leaped to his feet and renamed him.

Alvin brought everyone up with him. Including the purists who normally refused to applaud even genius. They too stood up in languid praise of him.

1. It can reasonably be inferred from the passage that Shades Bowen:

   A. did not accompany Everett Payne as he played "Sonny Boy Blue."
   B. had been in the army with Everett Payne.
   C. was the oldest musician in the bullpen.
   D. did not usually allow the local musicians to play with the band.

2. The main purpose of the statement in line 62 is to:

   F. illustrate the high expectations the audience initially had for Everett Payne's performance.
   G. inform the reader of the audience's reaction to Everett Payne's performance.
   H. counteract the narrator's description of Everett Payne's performance.
   J. provide proof that Everett Payne was well known to the audience.

3. The passage most strongly suggests that the second set of the jazz shows at the club is:

   A. the final set.
   B. much longer than the first set.
   C. followed by a third set on Sunday nights.
   D. performed solely by the musicians in the bullpen.

4. Which of the following details is used in the passage to indicate how the purists in the audience initially reacted to Everett Payne's choice of music?

   F. The overall silence of the audience, including the purists
   G. The description of the audience's collective in-suck of breath
   H. The posture the purists assumed in their seats
   J. The fact that the purists stood up

5. According to the narrator, what did Hattie see Everett Payne do prior to playing "Sonny Boy Blue"?

   A. Move quickly from his seat to the bandstand
   B. Study the audience around him
   C. Confer with the bassist and the drummer
   D. Announce the name of the tune he was going to play

6. The passage initially portrays the purists most nearly as:

   F. knowledgeable and open minded.
   G. snobbish and intolerant.
   H. rational and well educated.
   J. inexperienced and uninhibited.

7. It can reasonably be inferred from the passage that Hattie believed Bach and the blues were the:

   A. musical influences that Everett Payne tried to avoid representing when he played piano.
   B. foundation of Everett Payne's inventive piano playing.
   C. true music of the heavens that inspired Everett Payne's creativity as a piano player.
   D. reason why Everett Payne's piano-playing abilities limited him to Tin Pan Alley tunes.

8. According to the passage, when Everett Payne first played "Sonny Boy Blue" straight through, he did so:

   F. more slowly than was intended by the composer.
   G. after it had been suggested by Abe Kaiser.
   H. against the wishes of the bassist and drummer.
   J. without following the original tune.

9. According to the passage, Hattie speculated that the source of Everett Payne's musical ideas and feelings during "Sonny Boy Blue" was in:

   A. the way he tilted his head.
   B. the simplemindedness of the song.
   C. his ability to play with great formality.
   D. his connection with the silent audience.

10. The narrator states that to Hattie, Everett Payne's performance was:

   F. overly slow and formal.
   G. deliberate yet absentminded.
   H. like a song played in a church.
   J. a roller coaster of a ride.

GO ON TO THE NEXT PAGE.

Passage II

SOCIAL SCIENCE: This passage is adapted from Richard Moe's article "Mindless Madness Called Sprawl," based on a speech he gave on November 30, 1996, in Fresno, California (©1996 by Richard Moe).

At the time he gave the speech, Moe was president of the National Trust for Historic Preservation.

Drive down any highway leading into any town in the country, and what do you see? Fast-food outlets, office parks and shopping malls rising out of vast barren plains of asphalt. Residential subdivisions
5 spreading like inkblots obliterating forests and farms in their relentless march across the landscape. Cars moving sluggishly down the broad ribbons of pavement or halting in frustrated clumps at choked intersections. You see communities drowning in a destructive, soul-
10 less, ugly mess called sprawl.

Many of us have developed a frightening form of selective blindness that allows us to pass by the appalling mess without really seeing it. We've allowed our communities to be destroyed bit by bit, and most of
15 us have shrugged off this destruction as "the price of progress."

Development that destroys communities isn't progress. It's chaos. And it isn't inevitable, it's merely easy. Too many developers follow standard formulas,
20 and too many government entities have adopted laws and policies that constitute powerful incentives for sprawl.

Why is an organization like the National Trust for Historic Preservation so concerned about sprawl?
25 We're concerned because sprawl devastates older communities, leaving historic buildings and neighborhoods underused, poorly maintained or abandoned. We've learned that we can't hope to revitalize these communities without doing something to control the sprawl that
30 keeps pushing further and further out from the center.

But our concern goes beyond that, because preservation today is about more than bricks and mortar. There's a growing body of grim evidence to support our belief that the destruction of traditional downtowns and
35 older neighborhoods—places that people care about—is corroding the very sense of community that helps bind us together as a people and as a nation.

One form of sprawl—retail development that transforms roads into strip malls—is frequently spurred
40 on by discount retailers, many of whom are now concentrating on the construction of superstores with more than 200,000 square feet of space. In many small towns, a single new superstore may have more retail space than the entire downtown business district. When
45 a store like that opens, the retail center of gravity shifts away from Main Street. Downtown becomes a ghost town.

Sprawl's other most familiar form—spread-out residential subdivisions that "leapfrog" from the urban
50 fringe into the countryside—is driven largely by the American dream of a detached home in the middle of a grassy lawn. Developers frequently claim they can build more "affordable" housing on the edge of town— but "affordable" for whom?

55 The developer's own expenses may be less, and the home buyer may find the prices attractive—but who picks up the extra costs of fire and police protection, new roads and new utility infrastructure in these out- lying areas? We all do, in the form of higher taxes for
60 needless duplication of services and infrastructure that already exist in older parts of our cities and towns.

People who say that sprawl is merely the natural product of marketplace forces at work fail to recognize that the game isn't being played on a level field. Gov-
65 ernment at every level is riddled with policies that man- date or encourage sprawl.

By prohibiting mixed uses and mandating inordi- nate amounts of parking and unreasonable setback requirements, most current zoning laws make it impos-
70 sible—even illegal—to create the sort of compact walkable environment that attracts us to older neighbor- hoods and historic communities all over the world. These codes are a major reason why 82 percent of all trips in the United States are taken by car. The average
75 American household now allocates more than 18 per- cent of its budget to transportation expenses, most of which are auto-related. That's more than it spends for food and three times more than it spends for health care.

80 Our communities should be shaped by choice, not by chance. One of the most effective ways to reach this goal is to insist on sensible land-use planning. The way we zone and design our communities either opens up or forecloses alternatives to the automobile. Municipali-
85 ties should promote downtown housing and mixed-use zoning that reduce the distances people must travel between home and work. The goal should be an inte- grated system of planning decisions and regulations that knit communities together instead of tearing them
90 apart. We should demand land-use planning that exhibits a strong bias in favor of existing communities.

11. The principal aim of the passage can best be classified as:

A. persuasive.
B. explanatory.
C. descriptive.
D. narrative.

GO ON TO THE NEXT PAGE.

12. Among the following quotations from the passage, the one that best summarizes what the author would like to see happen is:

    F. "laws and policies that constitute powerful incentives for sprawl" (lines 20–22).
    G. "the destruction of traditional downtowns" (line 34).
    H. "'affordable' housing on the edge of town" (line 53).
    J. "an integrated system of planning decisions and regulations" (lines 87–88).

13. The last paragraph differs from the first paragraph in that in the last paragraph the author:

    A. asks a question and then answers it.
    B. uses more statistics to support his arguments.
    C. incorporates more emotional language.
    D. offers solutions rather than stating a problem.

14. In the passage, the author answers all of the following questions EXCEPT:

    F. How long has sprawl been happening in U.S. cities?
    G. Is development synonymous with progress?
    H. What is one major reason that people in the United States use automobiles so much?
    J. What should communities do to combat sprawl?

15. The author states that one superstore may do all of the following EXCEPT:

    A. have more retail space than an entire downtown.
    B. lead to serious downtown renovations.
    C. make the downtown area into a ghost town.
    D. shift the center of gravity away from downtown.

16. The statistics cited by the author in the tenth paragraph (lines 67–79) are used to illustrate the concept that:

    F. allowing mixed uses of land leads to environmental destruction.
    G. current zoning laws help create a compact, walkable environment.
    H. land-use regulations now in effect increase the overall costs of transportation.
    J. Americans spend too much of their budgets on food and health care.

17. One form of sprawl the author describes is retail development that:

    A. adjoins existing downtown areas.
    B. utilizes historic buildings.
    C. turns roads into strip malls.
    D. promotes a sense of community around a superstore.

18. As it is used in line 51, the word *detached* most nearly means:

    F. objective.
    G. set apart.
    H. broken apart.
    J. taken away.

19. The author uses the statement "The game isn't being played on a level field" (line 64) most nearly to mean that:

    A. cities needlessly duplicate essential services.
    B. higher taxes for some people make their lives more difficult.
    C. marketplace forces are at work.
    D. governmental decisions influence marketplace forces.

20. The phrase *mixed uses* (line 67) most likely refers to:

    F. having large parking lots around even larger stores.
    G. preserving and restoring historic neighborhoods.
    H. ensuring that automobiles cannot be driven to the various local businesses.
    J. allowing one area to contain various types of development.

GO ON TO THE NEXT PAGE.

Passage III

HUMANITIES: This passage is adapted from the essay "My Life with a Field Guide" by Diana Kappel-Smith (©2002 by Phi Beta Kappa Society).

I was seventeen when it started. My family was on vacation, and one day we went on a nature walk led by a young man a few years older than I. Probably I wanted to get his attention—I'm sure I did—so I
5 pointed to a flower and asked, "What's that?"

"Hmmm? Oh, just an aster," he said.

Was there a hint of a sniff as he turned away? There was! It was just an aster and I was just a total ignoramus!

10 And I remember the aster. Its rays were a brilliant purple, its core a dense coin of yellow velvet. It focused light as a crystal will. It faced the sun; it was the sun's echo.

Later that day, a book with a green cover lay on
15 the arm of a chair under an apple tree. It was the same volume that our guide had carried as he marched us through the woods. The book had been left there, by itself. It was a thing of power. In the thin summer shadow of the tree, quivering, like a veil, the book was
20 revealed, and I reached for it. A FIELD GUIDE TO WILD FLOWERS—PETERSON & McKENNY, its cover said. Its backside was ruled like a measuring tape, its inside was full of drawings of flowers. By the end of that week I had my own copy. I have it still.

25 Over the next several years this field guide would become my closest companion, a slice of worldview, as indispensable as eyes or hands. I didn't arrive at this intimacy right away, however. This wasn't going to be an easy affair for either of us.

30 I'll give you an example of how it went. After I'd owned the Peterson's for about a week, I went on a hike with some friends up a little mountain, taking the book along. Halfway up the mountain, there by the trailside was a yellow flower, a nice opportunity to take my new
35 guide for a test drive. "Go on ahead!" I said to my hiking companions, "I'll be a minute . . ." Famous last words.

I had already figured out the business of the book's colored tabs. I turned in an authoritative way to
40 the Yellow part and began to flip through. By the time the last of my friends had disappeared up the trail, I'd arrived at a page where things looked right. Five petals? Yes. Pinnate leaves? Whatever. Buttercup? There are, amazingly, *eleven* buttercups. Who would
45 have thought? However hard I tried to make it so, my item was not one of them. Next page. Aha! this looked more like it. Bushy cinquefoil? Nope, leaves not *quiiite* right, are they? As the gnats descended, I noticed that there were six more pages ahead, each packed with
50 five-petaled yellow flowers—St. Johnsworts, loose-strifes, puccoons.

Why I persisted in carrying it around and consulting its crowded pages at every opportunity, I have no idea. The book was stubborn; well, I was stubborn, too;
55 that was part of it. And I had no choice, really, not if I wanted to *get in*. A landscape may be handsome in the aggregate, but this book led to the particulars, and that's what I wanted. A less complete guide would have been easier to start with, but more frustrating in the
60 end. A more complete book would have been impossible for me to use. So I persisted in wrestling with the Peterson's, and thus by slow degrees the crowd of plant stuff in the world became composed of individuals. As it did, the book changed: its cover was stained by
65 water and snack food, the spine grew invitingly lax, and some of the margins sprouted cryptic annotations.

By the time the next summer came, I had fully discovered the joy of the hunt, and every new species had its trophy of data—name and place and date—to be
70 jotted down. If I'd found a flower before, I was happy to see it again. I often addressed it with enthusiasm: *Hi there, Solidago hispida!* I discovered early on that a plant's Latin name is a name of power by which the plant can be uniquely identified among different spoken
75 tongues, across continents, and through time. The genus name lashes it firmly to its closest kin, while its species name describes a personal attribute—*rubrum* meaning red, *officinale* meaning medicinal, *odoratus* meaning smelly, and so on. It all makes such delightful
80 sense!

My friend Julie and I identified individual plants in our rambles, but from the particulars we began to know wholes. Bogs held one community, montane forests held another, and the plants they held in
85 common were clues to intricate dramas of climate change and continental drift. So from plant communities it followed that the grand schemes of things, when they came our way, arrived rooted in real place and personal experience: quaternary geology, biogeography,
90 evolutionary biology all lay on the road that we had begun to travel.

21. The passage is best described as being told from the point of view of someone who is:

   A. tracing her developing interest in identifying flowers and in the natural world.
   B. reexamining the event that led her to a lifelong fascination with asters.
   C. reviewing her relationships with people who have shared her interest in flowers.
   D. describing how her hobby of identifying flowers became a profitable career.

GO ON TO THE NEXT PAGE.

22. As portrayed by the author, the young man responded to her question about the flower with what is best described as:

    F. acceptance.
    G. surprise.
    H. condescension.
    J. anger.

23. What name, if any, does the author report assigning to the yellow flower she came across during a mountain hike?

    A. St. Johnswort
    B. Loosestrife
    C. Puccoon
    D. The passage doesn't name the flower.

24. Looking back at her early experiences with the Peterson's, the author most strongly implies that the guide was:

    F. daunting at first, but in retrospect preferable to either a more or a less complete guide.
    G. easy to use in the beginning, but more frustrating in the end than a more complete guide would have been.
    H. impossible for her to follow until she started pairing it with a different guide written for beginners.
    J. appealing initially until she realized how poorly illustrated its crowded pages were.

25. As it is used in line 56, the phrase *get in* most nearly means:

    A. arrive at a physical location.
    B. be chosen for group membership.
    C. truly understand the subject.
    D. be friendly with someone.

26. The passage best supports which of the following conclusions about Julie?

    F. She has more experience than the author has in identifying flowers.
    G. She owns a house that's close to either a bog or a montane forest.
    H. She sees value in understanding the various communities of plants.
    J. She stopped using the Peterson's as her primary source of flower information.

27. The author states that the Peterson's became her closest companion over a period of several:

    A. days.
    B. weeks.
    C. months.
    D. years.

28. In the context of the passage, the author's statement in lines 56–58 most nearly means that she:

    F. learned to understand landscapes by looking at their overall patterns rather than their details.
    G. found that landscapes lost their appeal the more she tried to understand them logically.
    H. hoped to paint attractive portraits of landscapes by paying careful attention to details.
    J. sought a deeper knowledge of landscapes through learning about their individual parts.

29. The details in lines 64–66 primarily serve to suggest the:

    A. poor craftsmanship the publishing company used in producing the Peterson's.
    B. transformation the author's copy of the Peterson's underwent as a result of heavy use.
    C. strange writing the author often encountered in reading the Peterson's.
    D. carelessness with which the author used the Peterson's, much to her later regret.

30. The author refers to *Solidago hispida* as an example of a flower that she:

    F. had great trouble identifying the first time she stumbled upon it.
    G. hopes to finally come across on one of her nature walks.
    H. was pleased to encounter again after she had learned to identify it.
    J. feels has an inappropriate name given the plant's characteristics.

Practice ACT Tests

GO ON TO THE NEXT PAGE.

Passage IV

NATURAL SCIENCE: This passage is adapted from the article "When Research Is a Snow Job" by Sarah Boyle (©2002 by National Wildlife).

The figure is beyond comprehension: Every year, 1,000,000,000,000,000,000,000,000 (1 septillion) snowflakes fall worldwide. As the crystals fall, they encounter different atmospheric conditions that produce
5 flakes with unique attributes. The more complex those conditions are, the more elaborate the crystals.

Kenneth Libbrecht is a physicist at the California Institute of Technology. Along with the work of scientists at the U.S. Department of Agriculture's Agricul-
10 tural Research Service (ARS), his research is uncovering new information about the magical world of snow crystals—information that has practical applications in such diverse areas as agriculture and the production of electricity.

15 Snow crystals are individual crystals—usually in a hexagonal form—while snowflakes are collections of two or more snow crystals. Beginning as condensed water vapor, a crystal typically grows around a nucleus of dust. Its shape depends on how the six side facets—
20 or faces—grow in relation to the top and bottom facets. If they grow relatively tall, the crystal appears column-like; if the side facets are short compared to the length of the bottom and top facets, the crystal looks platelike.

Currently Libbrecht is trying to crack the problem
25 of why the crystal facets' growth varies with temperature. He believes this may have something to do with the ice surface's "quasi-liquid" layer, which affects how water molecules stick to the surface.

By manipulating the temperature and humidity
30 within an incubation chamber (and by adding an electric current or various gases at times), Libbrecht creates "designer" snowflakes in his lab. Such experiments are helping him determine how crystals form.

William Wergin, a retired ARS research biologist,
35 and a colleague, Eric Erbe, were using scanning electron microscopy to look at biological problems relating to agriculture. To avoid the laborious procedure that using such equipment usually entails, the two scientists decided to freeze the tissue they were working with and
40 look at it in the frozen state.

"One day it happened to be snowing," says Wergin, "and we were looking for a specimen. We imaged some snowflakes and were very surprised to see what we did." It was the first time anyone had attempted to image snow crystals with scanning electron microscopy, which provides precise detail about the crystals' shape, structural features and metamorphosed conditions (crystals often change once on the ground depending on the surrounding environment).

Wergin called another ARS colleague, hydrologist Albert Rango, to see if the snow crystal magnifications

had any applications for his research. Rango now uses Wergin's electron microscopy data, along with microwave satellite data, in the Snowmelt Runoff
55 Model to predict the amount of water available in a winter snowpack. For western states such as Colorado, Montana, Utah and Wyoming, about 75 percent of the annual water supply comes from snowmelt. Snowmelt water is critical to crop irrigation and hydroelectric
60 power, as well as recreation and domestic water supplies, fisheries management and flood control.

Before employing the scanning electron microscopy results, the forecasted amounts of snowpack water were inaccurate whenever the size and shape of the
65 snow crystals varied much from the norm. "The more we know about crystals," notes Rango, "the easier it will be to use microwave satellite data for predictions of the snow water equivalent."

Currently, forecasts using the model are about
70 90 percent accurate. A 1980 study estimated that improving the prediction by 1 percent would save $38 million in irrigation and hydropower in the western United States.

Rango is also looking ahead at climate change pre-
75 dictions. "Following the estimates that have been made about what will happen by 2100, things are definitely warming up," he says. Temperature increases will likely result in a reduction in stream flow as overall snow accumulation decreases, winter precipitation runs
80 off as rain, and water evaporates at a quicker rate. The gap between water supply and demand will magnify even more, greatly increasing water's economic value, anticipates Rango.

Not only does the crystal research help gauge
85 snowmelt, it is also useful in predicting avalanches, designing artificial snow, and, perhaps in the near future, examining air pollution. "You can put snow in a scanning electron microscope and tell which elements are present, such as sulfur and nitrogen," says Wergin.
90 "You can then see what kind of pollution is in the area and possibly track the source."

31. It can reasonably be inferred from the passage that the information about the scientific study of snow is presented primarily to:

A. emphasize the importance of communication among scientists.
B. explain how snow crystal facets influence the snowpack in some western states.
C. showcase the varied uses of the scanning electron microscope.
D. demonstrate some of the practical applications of the study of snow crystals.

GO ON TO THE NEXT PAGE.

32. According to the passage, the use of scanning electron microscopy can save money by:

   F. encouraging scientists to make estimates of water requirements far into the future.

   G. allowing forecasters to predict more accurately the quantity of water in the snowpack.

   H. helping agricultural researchers to identify biological problems.

   J. increasing the water supply for Colorado, Montana, Utah, and Wyoming by 75 percent.

33. It can reasonably be inferred that the phrase *metamorphosed conditions* (lines 47–48) refers to the:

   A. temperature and humidity at which crystals form.

   B. process by which snow crystals develop from a speck of dust and water vapor.

   C. state of snow crystals after they reach the ground.

   D. major changes in environmental conditions.

34. According to the passage, the addition of electron microscopy data to the Snowmelt Runoff Model allows scientists using the model to include in their predictions detailed information about:

   F. microwave satellite data.

   G. structural variations of snow crystals.

   H. locations having the most snowfall.

   J. biological problems related to agriculture.

35. According to Rango, one reason that water's economic value is likely to increase by the year 2100 is that:

   A. more water will be polluted by then.

   B. less water will be wasted due to more accurate predictions of the water supply.

   C. the sulfur and nitrogen content in snow is likely to increase.

   D. predicted climate changes will reduce overall snow accumulation.

36. According to the passage, snowflakes have infinite variety because:

   F. enormous numbers of snow crystals fall worldwide.

   G. falling snow crystals meet with varied atmospheric conditions.

   H. snow crystals fall at various rates, creating unique snowflakes.

   J. complexities in the atmosphere slow snow crystal development.

37. The passage states that snowflakes differ from snow crystals in that snowflakes:

   A. grow around a nucleus of dust.

   B. combine to form snow crystals.

   C. grow in relation to top and bottom facets.

   D. are composed of more than one crystal.

38. The term *"designer" snowflakes* (line 32) refers directly to the fact that:

   F. no two snowflakes are alike.

   G. Libbrecht produces the snowflakes in his lab.

   H. snowflakes are part of the grand design of nature.

   J. Libbrecht's snowflakes exhibit special beauty.

39. As it is used in line 59, the word *critical* most nearly means:

   A. evaluative.

   B. faultfinding.

   C. vital.

   D. acute.

40. The passage states that research about snow crystals has helped scientists do all of the following EXCEPT:

   F. extract pollutants from snow.

   G. gauge snowmelt.

   H. design artificial snow.

   J. predict avalanches.

END OF TEST 3

STOP! DO NOT TURN THE PAGE UNTIL TOLD TO DO SO.

DO NOT RETURN TO A PREVIOUS TEST.

Practice ACT Tests

SCIENCE TEST

35 Minutes—40 Questions

DIRECTIONS: There are seven passages in this test. Each passage is followed by several questions. After reading a passage, choose the best answer to each question and fill in the corresponding oval on your answer document. You may refer to the passages as often as necessary.

You are NOT permitted to use a calculator on this test.

Passage I

Two measures of water quality are the number of *Escherichia coli* bacteria present and the *biotic index*, BI (a numerical value based on the type, diversity, and pollution tolerance of aquatic invertebrate animals). Both of these measures can be affected by water flow.

E. coli levels that are above 100 colonies formed per 100 mL of water indicate reduced water quality. Figure 1 shows the *E. coli* levels on 5 collection days at Sites 1 and 2 in a river.

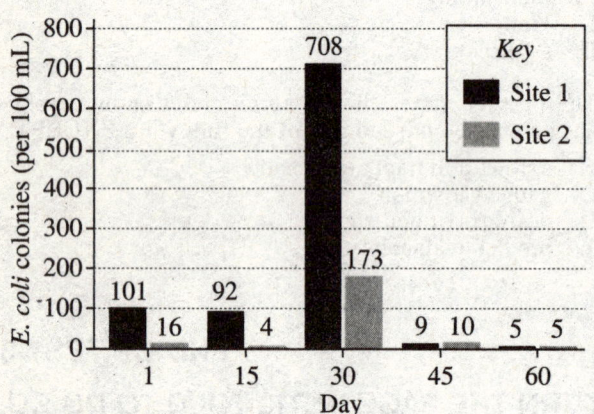

Figure 1

Table 1 shows how water quality rating varies with BI. Table 2 shows the average BI of each site during the collection period.

Table 1	
BI	Water quality rating
≥ 3.6	excellent
2.6 to 3.5	good
2.1 to 2.5	fair
1.0 to 2.0	poor

Table 2	
Location	Average BI
Site 1	6.3
Site 2	2.5

Figure 2 shows the water flow at each site on the 5 collection days.

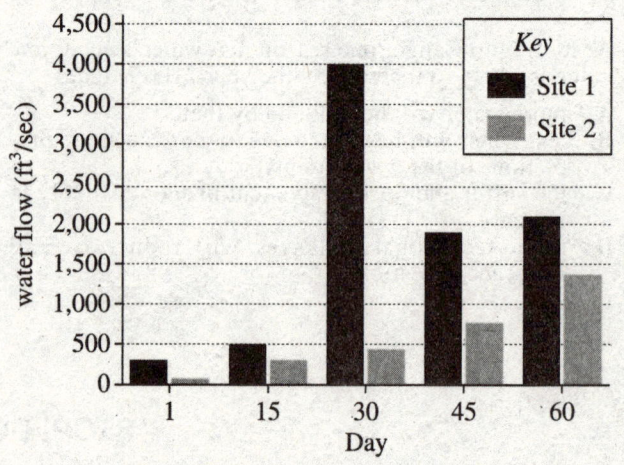

Figure 2

Figures adapted from Stephen C. Landry and Michele L. Tremblay, "State of the Upper Merrimack 1995–1997: A River Quality Report." ©2000 by Upper Merrimack River Local Advisory Committee.

1. If an *E. coli* level of over 400 colonies formed per 100 mL of water is unsafe for swimming, on which of the following collection days and at which site would it have been unsafe to swim?

A. Day 1 at Site 1
B. Day 30 at Site 1
C. Day 1 at Site 2
D. Day 30 at Site 2

GO ON TO THE NEXT PAGE.

2. Based on Figures 1 and 2, consider the average water flow and the average *E. coli* level for Site 1 and Site 2 over the collection period. Which site had the higher average water flow, and which site had the higher average *E. coli* level?

	Higher water flow	Higher *E. coli* level
F.	Site 1	Site 1
G.	Site 1	Site 2
H.	Site 2	Site 1
J.	Site 2	Site 2

3. As water quality improves, the number of *stone fly larvae* (a type of aquatic invertebrate) increases. Students hypothesized that more stone fly larvae would be found at Site 1 than at Site 2. Are the data presented in Table 2 consistent with this hypothesis?

A. Yes; based on BI, Site 1 had a water quality rating of good and Site 2 had a water quality rating of poor.

B. Yes; based on BI, Site 1 had a water quality rating of excellent and Site 2 had a water quality rating of fair.

C. No; based on BI, Site 1 had a water quality rating of poor and Site 2 had a water quality rating of good.

D. No; based on BI, Site 1 had a water quality rating of fair and Site 2 had a water quality rating of excellent.

4. Which set of data best supports the claim that Site 1 has *lower* water quality than Site 2 ?

F. Figure 1
G. Figure 2
H. Table 1
J. Table 2

5. Suppose large amounts of fertilizer from adjacent fields begin to enter the river at Site 1. The BI of this site will most likely change in which of the following ways? The BI will:

A. increase, because water quality is likely to increase.

B. increase, because water quality is likely to decrease.

C. decrease, because water quality is likely to increase.

D. decrease, because water quality is likely to decrease.

GO ON TO THE NEXT PAGE.

Passage II

Aluminum water-based paints (AWPs) contain aluminum (Al) flakes that give surfaces a shiny, metallic appearance. If the flakes corrode, a dull coating of aluminum hydroxide forms on them:

$$2Al + 6H_2O \rightarrow 2Al(OH)_3 + 3H_2$$

Table 1 shows the volume of H_2 gas produced over time (at 25°C and 1 atm) from 100 mL samples of freshly made AWPs 1–3 in 3 separate trials. AWPs 1–3 were identical except that each had a different concentration of DMEA, an AWP ingredient that increases pH.

	pH of AWP	Volume (mL) of H_2 produced by:			
AWP		Day 2	Day 4	Day 6	Day 8
1	8	4	33	81	133
2	9	21	187	461	760
3	10	121	1,097	2,711	4,480

Table 1

The AWP 3 trial was repeated 4 times, but for each trial, the sample had the same concentration of 1 of 4 corrosion inhibitors (see Figure 1).

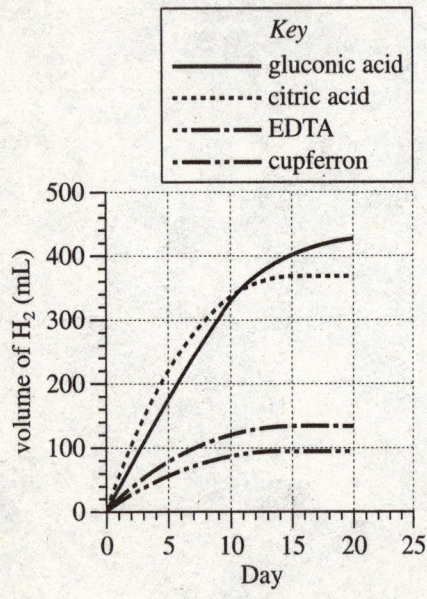

Figure 1

Figure 1 adapted from Bodo Müller, "Corrosion Inhibitors for Aluminum." ©1995 by Division of Chemical Education, Inc., American Chemical Society.

6. Based on Table 1, which of the following graphs best shows how the volume of H_2 produced by AWP 2 changed over time?

F.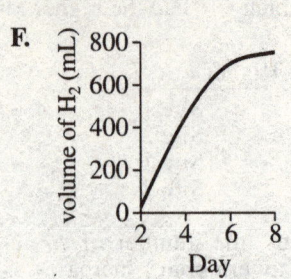

H.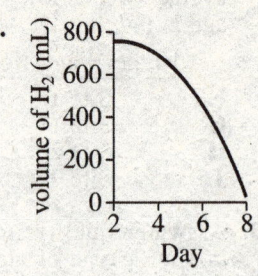

G.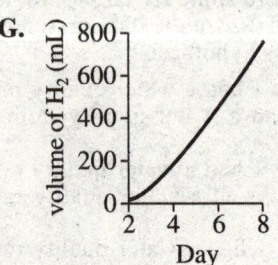

J.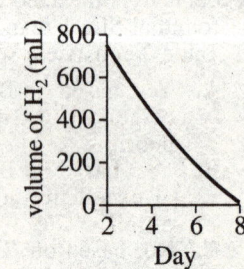

7. Based on Table 1, if the volume of H_2 produced by Day 10 from the AWP 1 sample had been measured, it would most likely have been:

A. less than 133 mL.
B. between 133 mL and 461 mL.
C. between 461 mL and 760 mL.
D. greater than 760 mL.

8. According to Table 1, what volume of H_2 was produced by AWP 1 from the time the volume was measured on Day 6 until the time the volume was measured on Day 8 ?

F. 52 mL
G. 81 mL
H. 133 mL
J. 214 mL

GO ON TO THE NEXT PAGE.

9. In the trials represented in Table 1 and Figure 1, by measuring the volume of H_2, the experimenters were able to monitor the rate at which:

A. H_2O is converted to Al.
B. Al is converted to H_2O.
C. Al is converted to $Al(OH)_3$.
D. $Al(OH)_3$ is converted to Al.

10. Consider the volume of H_2 produced by Day 2 from the AWP 3 sample that contained no corrosion inhibitor. Based on Table 1 and Figure 1, the AWP 3 sample containing EDTA produced approximately the same volume of H_2 by which of the following days?

F. Day 1
G. Day 4
H. Day 7
J. Day 10

Passage III

Students studied forces by using 2 identical platform scales, Scale A and Scale B, one of which is shown in Figure 1.

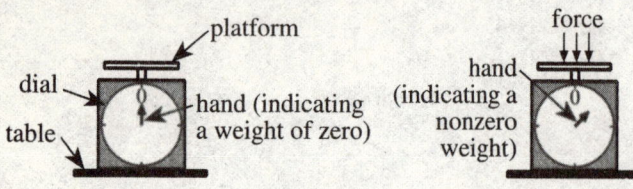

Figure 1

The weight of the platform of each scale was insignificant. When a force (such as that produced by a weight) was exerted on the surface of the platform, the hand rotated clockwise away from the zero point on the dial. The amount of rotation was directly proportional to the strength of the force.

Study 1

Prior to each of Trials 1–3, the students set the dial readings of both Scales A and B to zero. In each of these 3 trials, Scale A was stacked on top of Scale B (see Figure 2). In Trial 1, no weight was placed on the platform of Scale A; in Trial 2, a 5.0 newton (N) weight was placed on the platform of Scale A; and in Trial 3, a 10.0 N weight was placed on the platform of Scale A. The dial readings for the 3 trials are also shown in Figure 2.

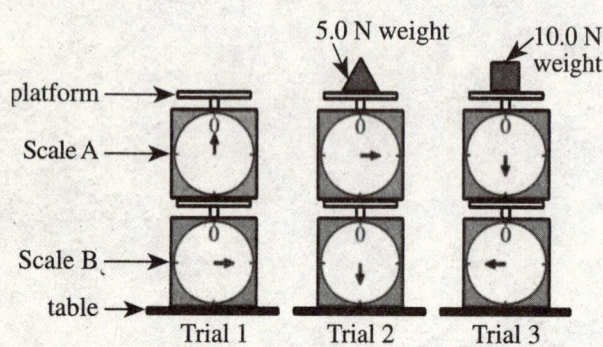

Figure 2

Study 2

The students placed a pencil on the platform of each scale and positioned on top of the pencils a board that spanned the 0.40 m distance between the 2 scales. Prior to each of Trials 4–6, the students set the dial readings of Scales A and B to zero (see Figure 3).

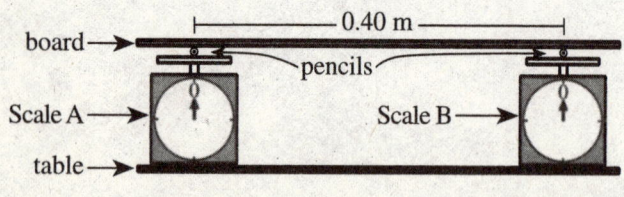

Figure 3

In each of these 3 trials, a 10.0 N weight was placed on the board at various distances from the pencil on Scale B (see Figure 4). In Trial 4, the weight was 0.10 m from the pencil; in Trial 5, the weight was 0.20 m from the pencil; and in Trial 6, the weight was 0.30 m from the pencil. The dial readings for the 3 trials are also shown in Figure 4.

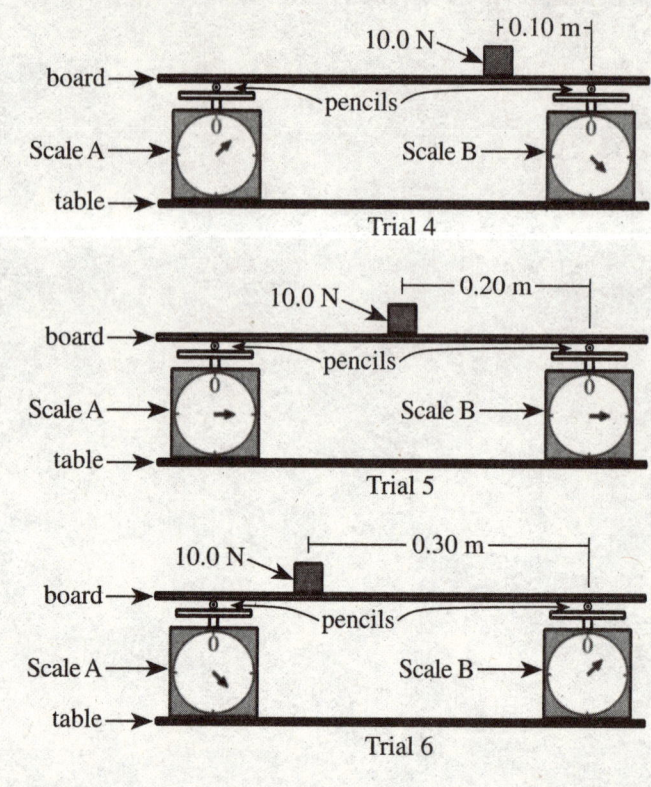

Figure 4

11. In which of the trials in Study 2, if any, was the force of the 10.0 N weight equally distributed between Scales A and B ?

A. Trial 4
B. Trial 5
C. Trial 6
D. None of the trials

12. Based on the results of Trials 1 and 2, Scale A and Scale B each weighed:

F. 2.5 N.
G. 5.0 N.
H. 7.5 N.
J. 10.0 N.

GO ON TO THE NEXT PAGE.

13. Assume that whenever a weight was placed on a scale's platform, a spring inside the scale was compressed. Assume also that the greater the added weight, the greater the amount of compression. Was the amount of potential energy stored in Scale A's spring greater in Trial 1 or in Trial 3 ?

  A. In Trial 1, because the amount of weight on the platform of Scale A was greater in Trial 1.
  B. In Trial 1, because the amount of weight on the platform of Scale A was less in Trial 1.
  C. In Trial 3, because the amount of weight on the platform of Scale A was greater in Trial 3.
  D. In Trial 3, because the amount of weight on the platform of Scale A was less in Trial 3.

14. In a new study, suppose Scale A were placed upside down atop Scale B, so that the platform of Scale A rested directly on the platform of Scale B. Which of the following drawings best represents the results that would most likely be obtained for this arrangement?

F. 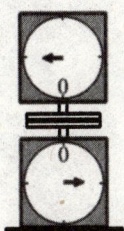   H.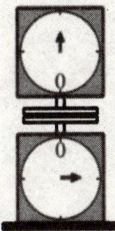

G. 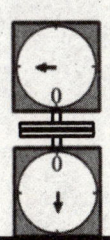   J.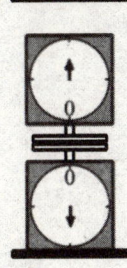

15. In Study 2, as the distance between the 10.0 N weight and the pencil on Scale B increased, the amount of force exerted on the surface of Scale B's platform:

  A. remained the same.
  B. increased only.
  C. decreased only.
  D. varied, but with no general trend.

16. Which of the following statements most likely describes an important reason for setting the dial readings of both scales to zero after Study 1, prior to each of Trials 4–6 ?

  F. To add the weights of the scales to each weight measurement
  G. To add the weights of the board and pencils to each weight measurement
  H. To subtract the weights of the scales from each weight measurement
  J. To subtract the weights of the board and pencils from each weight measurement

GO ON TO THE NEXT PAGE.

Passage IV

The *octane number* of a fuel is a measure of how smoothly the fuel burns in a gasoline engine. Lower octane fuels *knock* (explode) when burned, which lowers fuel efficiency and can cause engine damage. Heptane knocks considerably when burned and is given an octane number of 0. Isooctane knocks very little and is given an octane number of 100.

Different proportions of heptane and isooctane were mixed to obtain mixtures with octane numbers between 0 and 100 (see Table 1).

Table 1		
Volume of heptane (mL)	Volume of isooctane (mL)	Octane number
0	100	100
10	90	90
25	75	75
50	50	50
90	10	10
100	0	0

Experiment 1

A sample of each fuel mixture listed in Table 1 was burned in a test engine at an engine speed of 600 revolutions per minute (rpm). The number of knocks per minute was determined for each mixture. This was done so that an octane number could be assigned to any fuel by measuring its knock rate.

Experiment 2

Adding tetraethyllead (TEL) to a fuel changes its octane number. Different amounts of TEL were added to 1,000 mL samples of isooctane. Each fuel mixture was tested under the same conditions used in Experiment 1, and the measured knock rate was used to determine the octane number (see Figure 1).

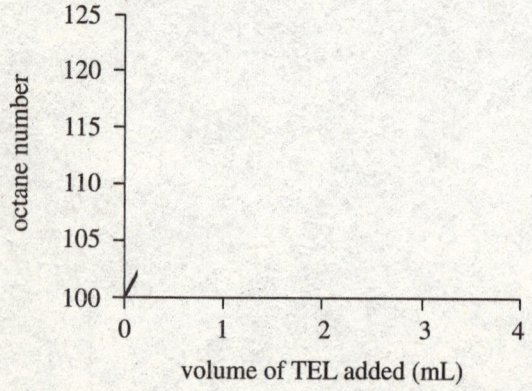

Figure 1

Experiment 3

The *engine octane requirement* (EOR) is the minimum octane number of a fuel required for an engine to operate without becoming damaged. Fuels A and B were burned separately in an engine at different speeds. Table 2 shows the octane number determined for each fuel at each engine speed and the known EOR of the engine at each speed.

Table 2			
Engine speed (rpm)	EOR	Octane number in engine of:	
		Fuel A	Fuel B
1,500	97.4	98.4	96.7
2,000	95.3	96.6	96.1
2,500	93.5	95.0	95.4
3,000	91.9	92.3	93.8
3,500	90.6	90.9	92.5

17. Based on Experiment 3, as engine speed increases, the minimum octane number of fuel required for an engine to operate without becoming damaged:

   A. increases only.
   B. decreases only.
   C. increases, then decreases.
   D. decreases, then increases.

18. Suppose a trial had been performed in Experiment 3 at an engine speed of 2,200 rpm. At this engine speed, which of the following sets of octane numbers would most likely have been determined for Fuel A and Fuel B ?

	Fuel A	Fuel B
F.	95.0	95.4
G.	96.1	95.8
H.	96.6	96.1
J.	97.6	96.4

GO ON TO THE NEXT PAGE.

19. Which of the following expressions is equal to the octane number of each fuel mixture listed in Table 1 ?

A. $\dfrac{\text{volume of isooctane}}{\text{volume of heptane}} \times 100$

B. $\dfrac{\text{volume of heptane}}{\text{volume of isooctane}} \times 100$

C. $\dfrac{\text{volume of isooctane}}{(\text{volume of heptane} + \text{volume of isooctane})} \times 100$

D. $\dfrac{\text{volume of heptane}}{(\text{volume of heptane} + \text{volume of isooctane})} \times 100$

20. Based on Table 1 and Experiment 2, if 3 mL of TEL were added to a mixture of 100 mL of heptane and 900 mL of isooctane, the octane number of the resulting fuel would most likely be:

F. less than 55.
G. between 55 and 90.
H. between 90 and 125.
J. greater than 125.

21. Which of the 2 fuels from Experiment 3 would be better to use in an engine that will run at all engine speeds between 1,500 rpm and 3,500 rpm ?

A. Fuel A, because its octane number was lower than the EOR at each of the engine speeds tested.
B. Fuel A, because its octane number was higher than the EOR at each of the engine speeds tested.
C. Fuel B, because its octane number was lower than the EOR at each of the engine speeds tested.
D. Fuel B, because its octane number was higher than the EOR at each of the engine speeds tested.

22. Based on Table 1, if 2 mL of heptane were mixed with 8 mL of isooctane, the octane number of this mixture would be:

F. 2.
G. 8.
H. 20.
J. 80.

GO ON TO THE NEXT PAGE.

Passage V

Introduction

Comets are complex mixtures of ices and dust that orbit the Sun. They can be classified by orbital period as either *long-period comets* or *short-period comets*.

Long-period comets have orbital periods of more than 200 yr and originate within our solar system in the *Oort Cloud*, a spherical shell of many icy bodies located at an average distance of 40,000 A.U. from the Sun (1 A.U. = average distance of Earth from the Sun). Long-period comets approach the Sun from all directions.

Short-period comets have orbital periods of 200 yr or less, and their orbital planes have *inclinations* 30° or less with respect to the *ecliptic plane*, the plane of Earth's orbit around the Sun. Portions of these planes are shown in Figure 1.

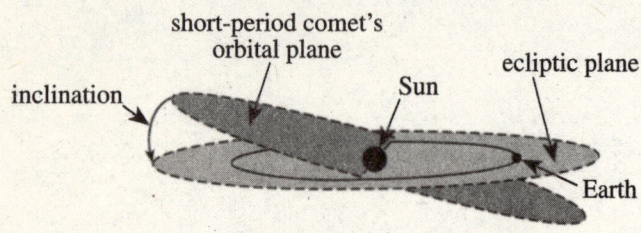

Figure 1

Two scientists present their viewpoints about the origin of short-period comets.

Scientist A

Short-period comets in our solar system originate within a thin ring-shaped region called the *Kuiper Belt* (KB). The KB has a small inclination with respect to the ecliptic plane and is located in the solar system between 30 A.U. and 50 A.U. from the Sun. The KB contains billions of icy bodies with diameters between 10 km and 30 km. These comet-size objects are too small to be clearly discerned at that distance with telescopes located on Earth's surface. Such telescopes have gathered indirect evidence, but not clear images, of much larger icy bodies that are part of the KB. The small inclinations of short-period comets' orbital planes with respect to the ecliptic plane are consistent with an origin in the KB. It has been discovered that other nearby stars have similar regions of icy bodies surrounding them.

Scientist B

The KB does not exist. Short-period comets were once long-period comets. Some long-period comets pass close enough to the giant planets (for example, Jupiter) to be influenced by the gravitational fields of the giant planets and are forced into orbits with orbital periods less than 200 yr. These altered orbits have orbital planes that have small inclinations with respect to the ecliptic plane. Also, most of the studied short-period comets have orbital planes with small inclinations with respect to the orbital planes of the giant planets, which, in turn, have small inclinations with respect to the ecliptic plane.

23. Which of the following generalizations about comets is most consistent with Scientist B's viewpoint?

   A. Long-period comets cannot become short-period comets.
   B. Short-period comets cannot become long-period comets.
   C. Long-period comets can become short-period comets.
   D. No long-period comets or short-period comets orbit the Sun.

24. Scientist A would most likely suggest that a new telescope more powerful than previous telescopes be used to search which of the following regions of space for objects in the KB ?

   F. The region 100,000 A.U. beyond our solar system
   G. The region 30 A.U. to 50 A.U. from the Sun at an angle of 90° with respect to the ecliptic plane
   H. The region 30 A.U. to 50 A.U. from the Sun at angles of 0° to 30° with respect to the ecliptic plane
   J. The region closely surrounding the planet Jupiter

25. Given the information about short-period comets in the introduction, which of the following inclinations with respect to the ecliptic plane would most likely NOT be observed for the orbital planes of short-period comets?

   A. 5°
   B. 15°
   C. 30°
   D. 45°

GO ON TO THE NEXT PAGE.

26. According to Scientist B, which of the following planets in our solar system is most likely capable of changing the orbit of a long-period comet over time?

F. Mercury
G. Earth
H. Mars
J. Saturn

27. Comet Halley currently has an orbital period of 76 yr. According to the information provided, Scientist B would most likely currently classify Comet Halley as a:

A. short-period comet that originated in the Oort Cloud.
B. short-period comet that originated in the KB.
C. long-period comet that originated in the Oort Cloud.
D. long-period comet that originated in the KB.

28. Based on Scientist A's viewpoint, the "much larger icy bodies" in the KB most likely have diameters of:

F. less than 10 km.
G. between 10 km and 20 km.
H. between 20 km and 30 km.
J. greater than 30 km.

29. Suppose a study of 1 nearby star revealed that it had no spherical shell of material similar to the Oort Cloud surrounding it. How would this discovery most likely affect the scientists' viewpoints, if at all?

A. It would weaken Scientist A's viewpoint only.
B. It would strengthen Scientist B's viewpoint only.
C. It would strengthen both scientists' viewpoints.
D. It would have no effect on either scientist's viewpoint.

GO ON TO THE NEXT PAGE.

Passage VI

Tomato plants grow poorly in high-salt environments. This effect is caused by 2 processes:

- A net movement of H_2O between the cytoplasm of the plants' cells and the environment via osmosis

- An increase in the cytoplasmic Na^+ concentration

The plant *Arabidopsis thaliana* carries a gene, *AtNHX1*. The product of this gene, *VAC*, facilitates uptake of cytoplasmic Na^+ by the plant's vacuoles.

A researcher created 4 genetically identical lines of tomato plants (L1–L4). An *AtNHX1* gene from *Arabidopsis thaliana* was isolated and 2 identical copies of this gene were incorporated into L1's genome. This process was repeated with L2 and L3 using a different *AtNHX1* allele for each line, so that L1, L2, and L3 had different genotypes for *AtNHX1*. The researcher then did an experiment.

Experiment

Fifty seedlings from each of the 4 lines were grown in 10 L of nutrient solution for 80 days. The 10 L nutrient solution contained H_2O, 12 g of fertilizer, and 3 g of NaCl. The nutrient solution was replaced every 5 days. After 80 days, average height, average mass (without fruit), and average fruit mass (per plant) were measured (see Table 1).

Table 1			
3 g of NaCl/10 L nutrient solution			
Line	Height (cm)	Mass (kg)	Fruit mass (kg)
L1	124	1.2	2.1
L2	128	1.2	2.0
L3	120	1.2	2.1
L4	124	1.2	2.0

This process was repeated except the 10 L nutrient solution contained 60 g of NaCl instead of 3 g of NaCl (see Table 2).

Table 2			
60 g of NaCl/10 L nutrient solution			
Line	Height (cm)	Mass (kg)	Fruit mass (kg)
L1	119	1.1	1.9
L2	121	1.1	1.9
L3	61	0.4	1.1
L4	63	0.5	1.0

The process was repeated again except the 10 L nutrient solution contained 120 g of NaCl instead of 3 g of NaCl (see Table 3).

Table 3			
120 g of NaCl/10 L nutrient solution			
Line	Height (cm)	Mass (kg)	Fruit mass (kg)
L1	118	1.0	1.8
L2	115	1.0	1.7
L3	34	0.2	0
L4	36	0.3	0

Tables 1–3 adapted from Hong-Xia Zhang and Eduardo Blumwald, "Transgenic Salt-Tolerant Tomato Plants Accumulate Salt in Foliage But Not in Fruit." ©2001 by Nature Publishing Group.

30. One plant produced no fruit and had a height of 21 cm. Which of the following most likely describes this plant?

   F. It was from L2 and was grown in a 10 L nutrient solution containing 60 g of NaCl.
   G. It was from L2 and was grown in a 10 L nutrient solution containing 120 g of NaCl.
   H. It was from L4 and was grown in a 10 L nutrient solution containing 60 g of NaCl.
   J. It was from L4 and was grown in a 10 L nutrient solution containing 120 g of NaCl.

31. During osmosis, water migrates through a semipermeable barrier. The osmosis referred to in the passage occurs through which of the following structures?

   A. Chromosomes
   B. Nuclear envelope
   C. Cell membrane
   D. Rough endoplasmic reticulum

GO ON TO THE NEXT PAGE.

32. For each line, as the concentration of salt in the nutrient solutions increased, average plant mass:

    F. increased only.
    G. decreased only.
    H. increased, then decreased.
    J. decreased, then increased.

33. Which of the following was an independent variable in the experiment?

    A. Whether a line received *AtNHX1*
    B. Whether a tomato plant was used
    C. Plant mass without fruit
    D. Plant height

34. Suppose the data for all of the plants were plotted on a graph with height on the *x*-axis and mass (without fruit) on the *y*-axis. Suppose also that the best-fit line for these data was determined. Which of the following would most likely characterize the slope of this line?

    F. The line would not have a slope, because the line would be vertical.
    G. The slope of the line would be zero.
    H. The slope of the line would be negative.
    J. The slope of the line would be positive.

35. The researchers included 1 of the 4 lines to serve as a control. This line was most likely which one?

    A. L1
    B. L2
    C. L3
    D. L4

GO ON TO THE NEXT PAGE.

Passage VII

When a temperature difference (ΔT) exists between the ends of an insulated metal rod (see Figure 1), heat flows from one end of the rod to the other. ($\Delta T = T_H - T_C$, where T_H and T_C represent the temperature of the hotter end and the colder end, respectively.)

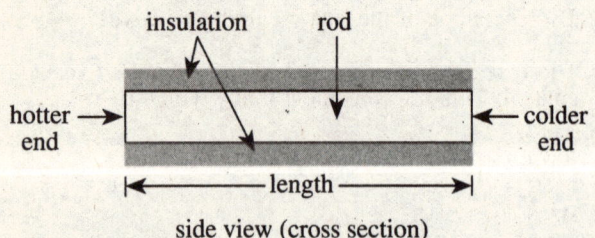

side view (cross section)

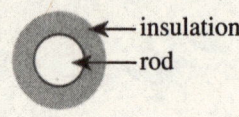

end view (cross section)

Figure 1

The rate at which heat flows is called the *heat transfer rate, R*.

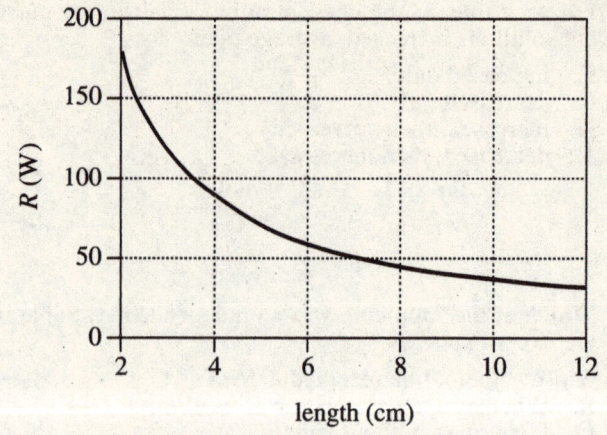

Figure 2

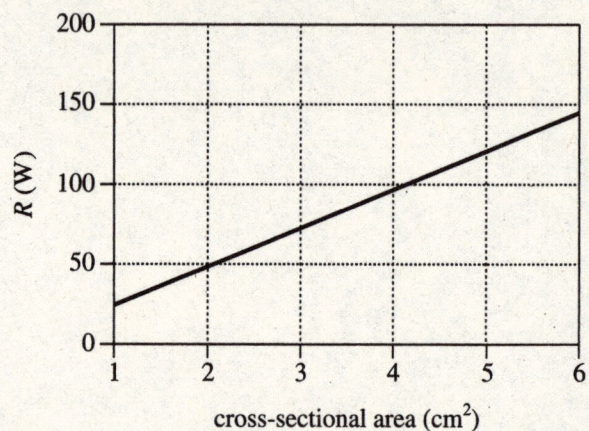

Figure 3

The following data apply to insulated copper rods. Table 1 gives R versus ΔT for a 5 cm long rod with a cross-sectional area of 3 cm². In Figure 2, R is plotted against length for rods having a ΔT of 30°C and a cross-sectional area of 3 cm². In Figure 3, R is plotted against cross-sectional area for 5 cm long rods with a ΔT of 30°C.

Table 1	
ΔT (°C)	R (W*)
10	24
20	48
30	71
40	95
50	118
*W = watt = joule/sec	

36. The data in the passage best support the hypothesis that the value of R decreases as which of the following properties of insulated copper rods increases?

   F. Length
   G. Cross-sectional area
   H. ΔT
   J. Radius

37. A and B are both insulated copper rods. Based on Figure 3, if B has the same length and ΔT as A, but B has double the cross-sectional area of A, the ratio of R for B to R for A will be:

   A. 1:4.
   B. 1:2.
   C. 2:1.
   D. 4:1.

GO ON TO THE NEXT PAGE.

38. For any of the rods described in the passage, most heat is transferred between the ends of the rod by which of the following processes?

     I. Radiation
     II. Convection
     III. Conduction

  F. I only
  G. II only
  H. III only
  J. I and II only

39. Which of the following arrangements of identical insulated copper rods, all having the same ΔT between the hotter end (H) and the colder end (C), will have the highest value of R ?

  A. H◯⬜C

  B. H◯⬜⬜C

  C. H◯⬜⬜⬜C

  D. H◯⬜⬜⬜⬜C

40. Based on the data in the passage, which of the following pairs of temperatures at the ends of identical insulated copper rods will result in the highest value of R ?

	T_H (°C)	T_C (°C)
F.	280	250
G.	280	260
H.	300	280
J.	310	300

END OF TEST 4

STOP! DO NOT RETURN TO ANY OTHER TEST.

Your Signature (do not print): _____

Print Your Name Here: _____

Your Date of Birth:
☐☐ – ☐☐ – ☐☐☐☐
Month   Day   Year

Form 4WT

The **ACT**® WRITING TEST BOOKLET

You must take the multiple-choice tests before you take the Writing Test.

Directions

This is a test of your writing skills. You will have thirty (30) minutes to write an essay in English. Before you begin planning and writing your essay, read the writing prompt carefully to understand exactly what you are being asked to do. Your essay will be evaluated on the evidence it provides of your ability to express judgments by taking a position on the issue in the writing prompt; to maintain a focus on the topic throughout the essay; to develop a position by using logical reasoning and by supporting your ideas; to organize ideas in a logical way; and to use language clearly and effectively according to the conventions of standard written English.

You may use the unlined pages in this test booklet to plan your essay. These pages will not be scored. *You must write your essay in pencil on the lined pages in the answer folder.* Your writing on those lined pages will be scored. You may not need all the lined pages, but to ensure you have enough room to finish, do NOT skip lines. You may write corrections or additions neatly between the lines of your essay, but do NOT write in the margins of the lined pages. *Illegible essays cannot be scored, so you must write (or print) clearly.*

If you finish before time is called, you may review your work. Lay your pencil down immediately when time is called.

DO NOT OPEN THIS BOOKLET UNTIL TOLD TO DO SO.

P.O. BOX 168
IOWA CITY, IA 52243-0168   **ACT**®

Practice Writing Test Prompt 4

As the amount of time students spend watching television increases, teachers debate whether television channels should be required to devote at least 20 percent of their programming to educational shows about topics such as science and history. Some teachers support this policy because they think television is an ideal teaching instrument with a very large and very receptive audience. Other teachers do not support this policy because they think what is considered educational by some could be considered merely entertaining by others. In your opinion, should television channels be required to devote at least 20 percent of their programming to educational shows?

In your essay, take a position on this question. You may write about either one of the two points of view given, or you may present a different point of view on this question. Use specific reasons and examples to support your position.

Use this page to *plan* your essay.
Your work on this page will *not* be scored.

If you need more space to plan,
please continue on the back of this page.

Use this page to *plan* your essay.
Your work on this page will *not* be scored.

You may wish to photocopy these sample answer document pages to respond to the practice ACT Writing Test.

Please enter the information at the right before beginning the Writing Test.

Use a soft lead No. 2 pencil only. Do NOT use a mechanical pencil, ink, ballpoint, or felt-tip pen.

WRITING TEST BOOKLET NUMBER

Print your 6-digit **Booklet Number** in the boxes at the right.

WRITING TEST FORM

Print your 3-character **Test Form** in the boxes above and fill in the corresponding oval at the right.

○ 1WT ○ 2WT ○ 3WT
○ 4WT ○ 5WT

Begin WRITING TEST here.

_____

_____

_____

_____

_____

_____

_____

_____

_____

_____

_____

_____

_____

_____

_____

_____

_____

_____

_____

_____

_____

If you need more space, please continue on the next page.

WRITING TEST

If you need more space, please continue on the next page.

WRITING TEST

If you need more space, please continue on the back of this page.

PLEASE DO NOT WRITE IN THIS AREA.

0876008

Practice ACT Tests

WRITING TEST

STOP here with the Writing Test.

Passage I

Question 1. The best answer is D because the phrase "Liv Arnesen of Norway and Ann Bancroft of Minnesota" forms the compound subject of the sentence, and there is no reason to put any punctuation between the two parts of this compound subject.

The best answer is NOT:

A because the comma after "Liv Arnesen of Norway" puts unnecessary and inaccurate punctuation between the two parts of the compound subject.

B because the commas after the women's names and after "of Norway" are unnecessary and break up the compound subject. If there were commas after both "of Norway" and "of Minnesota," this could be a correct alternative that treats the points of origin as extra information, but with the comma only before the prepositional phrase "of Minnesota" and not at the end, the sentence isn't correctly punctuated.

C because, as in B, the commas after the women's names are unnecessary and break up the compound subject. Additionally, the two prepositional phrases both have commas at the beginning and not at the end, creating an incorrectly punctuated sentence.

Question 2. The best answer is F because the previous sentence states that the women "became the first women to climb and ski across the continent of Antarctica," which means that they did finish the journey. This is the only choice that clearly indicates that the trip was finished (in 96 days).

The best answer is NOT:

G because "achieve" isn't the same thing as "complete." *Achieve* means to accomplish something or bring it about, but the word doesn't fit in this context; it is not an idiom in standard English to "achieve a trip."

H because *finalized* is similar in meaning to *complete*, but *finalize* is ordinarily used in the context of completing a transaction or a business deal and isn't used idiomatically in the context of "finalizing a trip" (unless it means finalizing the planning of a trip rather than the making of a trip). Also, "finalizing" takes place at the end of something, rather than over the course of 96 days.

J because *implemented* can mean to put a plan into effect, but it omits the information that the trip was necessarily finished or completed and so isn't an appropriate word choice in this context.

Question 3. The best answer is **B** because the comma after *Runway* sets off what follows it as an appositive (a word or phrase that refers to or explains the noun or noun phrase it follows). In this case, "Blue One Runway" is explained by the appositive "a solid-ice airstrip on the Atlantic coast of Antarctica."

The best answer is NOT:

A because the additional words *it is* make a second independent clause rather than the appositive described above, and the comma thus incorrectly joins two independent clauses and creates a comma splice.

C because when there is no comma after *Runway*, there is no punctuation to set off the appositive from the word that it explains or describes, which makes the sentence confusing.

D because the word *being* is unnecessary and not appropriate in standard written English; *which is*, or nothing at all (as in **B**), is appropriate at this point.

Question 4. The best answer is **J** because only a comma should be there to separate the introductory participial phrase, "Hiking unassisted up the 10,0000-foot-high Sygyn Glacier," and the main clause, "each woman pulled a sled that weighed more than 260 pounds." For clarity, the introductory phrase must be next to, or adjacent to, the subject of the clause that it modifies, "each woman."

The best answer is NOT:

F because the coordinating conjunction *and* is inappropriately placed between the introductory participial phrase, "Hiking unassisted up the 10,0000-foot-high Sygyn Glacier," and the main clause, "each woman pulled a sled that weighed more than 260 pounds." Coordinating conjunctions typically join two like structures (two phrases, two main clauses) rather than a phrase and a clause.

G because the subordinating conjunction *when* makes the main clause into a dependent clause. The resulting combination of introductory phrase and dependent clause is a sentence fragment (an incomplete sentence).

H because the subordinating conjunction *while* creates a sentence fragment in the same way as in **G**.

Question 5. The best answer is **B** because the details that are included in Sentence 5 expand on Sentence 4 by explaining what the things are that make the women's supplies weigh so much, and the list of supplies also gives an idea of what sort of things the women used on their trip, as **B** suggests.

The best answer is NOT:

A because there is no indication in the essay that each woman, though she pulled 260 pounds on her sled, was limited to this weight.

C because there is no indication in the passage that the women brought along more than they thought they would need; even though the sleds were heavy, the implication is that they brought what they needed.

D because the list of supplies in Sentence 5 in no way contradicts the information in Sentence 4 about the weight of the sleds. Rather, the information in Sentence 5 expands on what is said in Sentence 4.

Question 6. The best answer is J because "stretching for 1,000 miles" logically follows and continues the description of "a high, frozen desert." The underlined phrase makes sense in this location but not in the other locations.

The best answer is NOT:

F because although the phrase could be in this location to describe "the Polar Plateau," the phrase "stretching for 1,000 miles a high, frozen desert" makes no logical sense, at least without additional punctuation.

G because when the phrase "stretching for 1,000 miles" is placed at the beginning of the sentence, it would seem to modify the subject of the sentence "the adventurers" and imply that the adventurers stretched for 1,000 miles.

H because when the phrase is placed after the subject ("the adventurers stretching for 1,000 miles"), the sentence once again illogically implies that the adventurers stretched for 1,000 miles.

Question 7. The best answer is C because *blew* is the correct past tense form of the verb that correctly fits into the sentence and is parallel to the other past tense verb in the sentence, *sailed*. The rest of the paragraph is also written in the past tense.

The best answer is NOT:

A because *had blew* is an ungrammatical form of the verb. If it were an accurate past perfect verb form, it would say *had blown*, using the past participle *blown* rather than the past tense *blew*.

B because *blow* is the present tense form of the verb and doesn't fit logically into either the sentence or the paragraph, both of which are written in the past tense.

D because *blown* is the past participle, which cannot be used alone as a main verb but must be part of a verb phrase such as "had blown" or "was blown."

Question 8. The best answer is J because *these* is the only one of the four responses that, within the context of this sentence, doesn't logically refer to the two women. When *these* is placed into the sentence, it appears to refer to the strong winds ("The . . . strong winds blew daily, and these sailed 210 miles in just five days."). Therefore this is the LEAST acceptable alternative to *the team*.

The best answer is NOT:

F because *the two*, meaning Arnesen and Bancroft, is an acceptable alternative to *the team*.

G because the names of the two women, *Arnesen and Bancroft*, are also an acceptable alternative to *the team*.

H because *the women* also refers to Arnesen and Bancroft and is an acceptable alternative to *the team*.

Question 9. The best answer is D because the conjunctive adverb *however* appropriately sets up a contrast between the first week, when the wind blew daily, and the next five days, when there was very little wind.

The best answer is NOT:

A because *accordingly* suggests that one thing is a consequence of another. The wind ceasing to blow isn't a consequence of the wind blowing for a week, but rather a contrast with the previous week.

B because *otherwise* is used to imply that something might be the case under different circumstances (It's raining; otherwise, I would go with you), rather than to set up a contrast with a previous statement. It would not be idiomatic, or sound natural to a native speaker of English, to say, "For the next five days, otherwise, there was almost no wind."

C because *consequently*, just like *accordingly*, implies a cause-and-effect relationship between the wind blowing and the wind ceasing to blow, a relationship that makes no logical sense.

Question 10. The best answer is F because there is appropriately no punctuation between the two parts of the compound verb ("visited . . . and replenished") and the word *their* is the correct form of the third-person plural possessive pronoun (the food belonging to them).

The best answer is NOT:

G because the comma after *and* both separates the two parts of the compound verb and also is in an ungrammatical place following a coordinating conjunction. The correct form of the possessive pronoun is used, however.

H because the word *there* is the adverb meaning a place, rather than the required form of the third-person plural possessive pronoun.

J because the comma after *scientists* also separates the two parts of the compound verb. Additionally, the adverb form *there* is inappropriately used instead of the plural possessive *their*.

Question 11. The best answer is C because only the present participle *climbing* is needed to form an adjective phrase that relates back to the subject of the sentence, *they*.

The best answer is NOT:

A because the coordinating conjunction *and* ordinarily connects two similar structures, but this *and* inappropriately connects a main clause with a phrase ("while climbing over a 10,200-foot-high glacier named Titan Dome"), leaving the phrase as a dangling modifier separated from the subject it is supposed to modify.

B because adding the words *they climbed* after the comma creates a second main clause, thus creating a comma splice between two independent clauses.

D because although *to climb* almost works here—the women were outside in order to climb the glacier—it doesn't quite make sense because they weren't in bitter cold for the purpose of climbing the dome; rather, they were outside to climb the dome and it happened to be bitterly cold. C is a much clearer answer; D makes the reader stop to try to figure out what the writer meant.

Question 12. The best answer is J because only the coordinating conjunction *and* is needed here to join the two independent clauses.

The best answer is NOT:

F because "and during those last miles of the trip" is redundant (repetitive of a phrase already in the sentence, "the final few miles").

G because "and during those fortunate moments" refers generally to the wind being with the women for the last several miles, but this phrase is both somewhat redundant and unnecessarily wordy. The implication that the wind was fortunate because it enabled them to complete their trip and reach their goal is clearly there without being stated this explicitly.

H because the clause "so the wind carried them and" is redundant; it merely restates the idea in the words "the wind was with them."

Question 13. The best answer is B because although all the sentences are true and could work in the context of this paragraph, the women's main accomplishment, explained in the introductory paragraph and described throughout the essay, was to cross the Antarctic landmass. So B is the answer that most effectively and specifically emphasizes their accomplishment.

The best answer is NOT:

A because while it's true that this had been a long journey, this sentence is merely a comment on the trip rather than a description of the women's main accomplishment.

C because though the women were no doubt relieved to have safely descended Titan Dome, this additional information about how the women felt does not emphasize their main accomplishment as the question asks.

D because although mention of the women's last miles going by quickly is an interesting addition, this sentence fails to refer to the women's main accomplishment as the question asks.

Question 14. The best answer is J because the adverb *prudently* expresses the idea that it was prudent, or thoughtful and wise, for the women to call for a ski plane.

The best answer is NOT:

F because with the underlined portion in this location before "to airlift," *prudently* seems to refer to the ski plane as prudent, whereas only living beings can be prudent.

G because if the underlined portion is placed before *becoming*, it creates the phrase "prudently becoming stranded," which makes little sense. Becoming stranded would probably never be prudent.

H because if placed before the word *stranded*, the underlined portion would create the phrase "becoming prudently stranded," which is confusing in basically the same way as G.

Question 15. The best answer is **A** because if the final paragraph were deleted from the essay, the reader would not learn that the winds kept the women from safely skiing the last 460 miles to McMurdo Station.

The best answer is NOT:

B because the last paragraph doesn't explain why skiing to McMurdo Station was part of the women's original plan but only states that it was part of the original plan.

C because the final paragraph doesn't describe the weather conditions on the Ross Ice Shelf at various times of the year but only mentions the weather conditions at the particular time the women arrived there.

D because the last paragraph makes no mention of Arnesen and Bancroft's reaction to having to change their plan and be airlifted to McMurdo Station rather than skiing there.

Passage II

Question 16. The best answer is **H** because the word *but* sets up a contrast between the first independent clause and the second one, indicating that the narrator arrives thirty minutes earlier than the shop opens. It is grammatically correct to use a coordinating conjunction between two independent clauses.

The best answer is NOT:

F because having just a comma between the first independent clause and the second one creates a comma splice (two or more complete sentences separated only by a comma).

G because though it is often correct to set off a conjunctive adverb such as *however* with commas, when *however* comes between the two independent clauses in this sentence, it would need either a semicolon before it or else a period before it and a capital letter on *However* to create two separate sentences; the punctuation in G creates a comma splice.

J because when there is no punctuation at all following *morning*, the two independent clauses create a fused, or run-together, sentence.

Question 17. The best answer is **B** because it isn't logical to say that the sky becomes colorful "in order that" (so that) the sun begins to rise. Rather, the colorful sky happens simultaneously with the rising sun. So B is the LEAST acceptable alternative to the underlined portion, in which the word *as* indicates that the events described are simultaneous.

The best answer is NOT:

A because *at the same time* is a logical alternative to *as*, meaning simultaneously.

C because *while* is also a logical alternative to *as*, also meaning happening at the same time.

D because the coordinating conjunction *and* connects the clauses in a logical way, making this a reasonable alternative to *as* in the underlined portion. The comma is appropriate here after *ribbons* because the conjunction joins two independent clauses.

Question 18. The best answer is **J** because *orange* is the choice that is most consistent with the description elsewhere in this sentence, namely the "peach-and-melon-colored ribbons" in the sky. Both descriptions use color names that also are the names of fruit.

The best answer is NOT:

F because *solar* is both redundant—since *sun* and *solar* refer to the same thing, though one word is a noun and the other word is an adjective—and inconsistent with the other descriptions in the sentence.

G because though *luminous* can accurately be used to describe the sun, this description isn't consistent with the other descriptions in the sentence.

H because *radiant*, meaning "shining" or "glowing," could describe the sun but isn't similar to any other description in the sentence.

Question 19. The best answer is **C** because it is the only choice that provides the main subject and verb for the sentence, "I watch," and avoids creating a dangling modifier that doesn't refer logically to the subject of the sentence.

The best answer is NOT:

A because by creating a dangling modifier it inaccurately suggests that the seagulls, rather than the narrator, are "walking toward the docks."

B because it makes the subject of this sentence "their high-pitched cries," and both "walking toward the docks" and "watching the seagulls" would have to refer to "their high-pitched cries." Since high-pitched cries can neither walk nor watch, this would not be a logical choice. Once again, the problem is a dangling modifier.

D because it creates the same illogical and dangling modifier as in **A**, implying that the seagulls are walking toward the docks even as they are wheeling and swooping.

Question 20. The best answer is **F** because the noun phrase "the night security guard at the marina" is a nonrestrictive appositive that must be set off by commas from the noun it refers to, *Carney*.

The best answer is NOT:

G because it is missing the comma at the end of the appositive and creates an ambiguous and confusing sentence, with the name *Carney* seemingly just stuck into the middle of the sentence.

H because the comma between *Carney* and the appositive is missing, again creating a confusing sentence.

J because both commas around the appositive are missing, leaving a run-together subject that is confusing.

Question 21. The best answer is **C** because the most logical comparative description of the smell of the shop is "like the bay itself," with this phrase set off by commas. There is no need for a comma anywhere within the phrase.

The best answer is NOT:

A because, although the first part of the sentence could work ("The shop smells salty, like the bay,"), the rest of the sentence, "itself and the creaky oak floor is gritty with sand," becomes nonsensical.

B because there is no reason to set off the reflexive pronoun *itself* with commas.

D because since there is a comma at the beginning of the parenthetical phrase "like the bay itself," there must also be a comma at the end, following *itself*.

Question 22. The best answer is **G** because it appropriately divides the sentence into two complete sentences.

The best answer is NOT:

F because the lack of punctuation creates a fused, or run-together, sentence.

H because the comma after *lights* creates a comma splice.

J because, as in F, the lack of punctuation creates a fused, or run-together, sentence.

Question 23. The best answer is **D** because *sit* is the appropriate present tense plural verb to go with the plural subject *bins* and to match the other present tense verbs in the paragraph (for example, *smells, is, turn, straighten*).

The best answer is NOT:

A because *sits* is a singular verb, which doesn't agree with the plural subject, *bins*.

B because *is sitting* is a singular verb rather than a plural one; *are sitting* would be needed to agree with the subject. Also, there are no other present progressive verbs in the paragraph.

C because *sets* is a singular verb and because it is the wrong verb. *Set* is a transitive verb (a verb that takes a direct object), as in "Set the book on the table," whereas *sit* is an intransitive verb (one that doesn't need an object), as in "The book sits on the table."

Question 24. The best answer is **G** because it is the only choice that tells specifically what can be found for sale in the shop, as the question asks: fishing rods, reels, hooks, nets, and fishing line.

The best answer is NOT:

F because it refers to the equipment for sale only generally as "the wide variety of fishing equipment."

H because it describes the walls but not the merchandise, referring only to walls that are "jam-packed with equipment" but not mentioning anything specific.

J because it refers, again generally and not specifically, to "gear for a range of different purposes."

Question 25. The best answer is **A** because *straighten* is the appropriate present tense verb and *it* is the appropriate pronoun to refer to the singular noun *merchandise*. *Merchandise* is a collective noun, one that may seem to be plural since it can refer to many different things at the same time but that operates as a singular noun in English, as in "All the merchandise we have is new."

The best answer is NOT:

B because the verb *straightened* is in the past tense, whereas the rest of the paragraph is in the present tense, and the plural pronoun *them* doesn't refer correctly to the singular noun *merchandise*.

C because the verb *straightened*, as in **B**, is inappropriately in the past tense, and *those* is a plural pronoun instead of a singular one needed to refer to *merchandise*.

D because although *straighten* is the correct present tense verb, *them* is an inaccurately used plural pronoun.

Question 26. The best answer is **J** because it is the only choice that provides a subject and verb and creates a complete sentence.

The best answer is NOT:

F because it creates a sentence fragment. It has no main clause, but only a subordinate clause that begins with the subordinating conjunction *when*.

G because it creates a sentence fragment like that in **F**, except with the subordinating conjunction *as*.

H because it, too, creates a sentence fragment; this time there is a participial phrase where there should be a main clause.

Question 27. The best answer is **A** because it correctly punctuates the three items in a series ("live herring, mullet, and shrimp").

The best answer is NOT:

B because *live* is an adjective rather than an item in a series of nouns; the comma after *live* confusingly makes *live* appear to be a fourth item in the series.

C because it adds the same inappropriate comma between *live* and *herring* as does **B**.

D because the unpunctuated words *live herring mullet* (with a comma at the end of the phrase) are confusing and unclear; the lack of a comma between *herring* and *mullet* makes this seem to be one item rather than the first two items in a series.

Question 28. **The best answer is H** because Sentence 5 fits most logically and coherently after Sentence 2 and before Sentence 3. Sentence 5 first mentions the flat full of worms to be sold, and Sentence 3 refers to packing those worms into containers of thirteen worms apiece.

The best answer is NOT:

F because Sentence 5 is illogical in its original location. In this sentence order, the worms aren't brought out until after they have been divided into containers for sale back in Sentence 2.

G because although Sentence 5 could logically follow Sentence 1, it isn't logical to have Sentence 2, about herring, mullet, and shrimp, intervene between the introduction of the worms in Sentence 5 and their division into containers in Sentence 3.

J because it puts Sentence 3 and Sentence 5 adjacent to each other but in the wrong logical order. Sentence 5 needs to precede Sentence 3 for the sake of logic and coherence.

Question 29. **The best answer is B** because the phrase "with a smile," as B says, gives a detail that shows the narrator's attitude toward the customers.

The best answer is NOT:

A because the phrase characterizes only the narrator's attitude and contains no information that differentiates the narrator's mood from that of the customers.

C because the mention of the narrator's smile doesn't refer back to anything in the previous paragraph, which focuses on listing some of the things the narrator does to prepare the shop each morning.

D because it suggests that nothing would be lost if "with a smile" were deleted because this detail is clearly stated elsewhere in the paragraph; however, there is no other mention in the paragraph of the narrator's smile.

Question 30. **The best answer is F** because the sentence "I work at Stoney's Bait & Tackle Shop" fits logically at the end of Paragraph 1. The first sentence notes that most people in the narrator's town work in a job that has something to do with fishing and that the narrator is no different. The new sentence to be added explains what the narrator means in the first sentence and provides key information that helps all the rest of the essay to make sense.

The best answer is NOT:

G because the sentence to be added doesn't fit logically at the end of Paragraph 2, which describes how a typical early morning looks when the narrator is on the way to work.

H because the sentence to be added doesn't belong at the end of Paragraph 3, which tells about the night security guard and the narrator greeting each other as one leaves work and the other arrives. For the essay to make sense, the reader needs to know the information in the added sentence at a point earlier than this.

J because the sentence also doesn't fit well at the end of Paragraph 5, where it interrupts the description, given in both Paragraphs 5 and 6, of the many things the narrator does each morning to prepare the shop for its daily business.

Passage III

Question 31. The best answer is B because *its* is the correct singular possessive pronoun to agree with the noun phrase "The movie *Dracula*."

The best answer is NOT:

A because although the word *featuring* works fine in this context, the word *it's* is a contraction meaning "it is" rather than the singular possessive form *its* that is needed here.

C because while *based on* works in this context, the form of the word *its'* is incorrect (there is no plural possessive of the singular pronoun *its*).

D because *who's* is a contraction meaning "who is," which fits neither the meaning nor the sentence structure here.

Question 32. The best answer is H because it provides the clearest sentence structure.

The best answer is NOT:

F because its structure makes it ambiguous; it seems to imply that the bats, rather than the ideas, are flawed.

G because it is awkward and confusing; it could easily be clarified to "mistaken ideas about bats."

J because "people's mistaken ideas they have" is awkward and redundant.

Question 33. The best answer is A because it uses the correct comparative form "more interesting," and it uses the preposition *than* to introduce the second part of a comparison.

The best answer is NOT:

B because although "of more interest" works in this context, the adverb *then* is inaccurately used in place of the preposition *than*.

C because the comparison "the most interesting than" is grammatically flawed, using the superlative form *most* where the comparative form *more* is required.

D because although it uses the correct comparative words "more interesting," it includes the word *then* incorrectly.

Question 34. The best answer is J because the colon used in this choice appropriately introduces the list of the three most common misconceptions about bats.

The best answer is NOT:

F because the semicolon after *bats* leaves a long sentence fragment (the list of misconceptions about bats). Semicolons are appropriately used between two independent, closely related clauses and not to introduce a list.

G because the comma after *bats* runs the elements of this sentence together in a confusing manner and doesn't appropriately introduce the list of misconceptions.

H because the lack of any punctuation after *bats* makes this sentence confusing by failing to set off the list of misconceptions from the rest of the sentence.

Question 35. The best answer is B because its structure makes it the clearest choice, unambiguously stating that the cattle and horses are sleeping when the bats bite them.

The best answer is NOT:

A because the sentence is ambiguous in this form; it is unclear whether the cattle and horses or the bats are sleeping.

C because this sentence is ambiguous for the same reason as A; *they* in "when they are asleep" could refer either to the bats or to the cattle and horses.

D because, even more directly than A and C, this choice implies, illogically, that while the bats are asleep they bite cattle and horses.

Question 36. The best answer is F because separating two independent clauses or sentences that are closely related in content is an appropriate and effective use of a semicolon.

The best answer is NOT:

G because the comma after *rodents* creates a comma splice between two independent clauses and because the comma after *others* separates the subject of a main clause (*others*) and the verb in that clause, *think*.

H because the lack of any punctuation between the two independent clauses creates a run-together, or fused, sentence.

J because although using the coordinating conjunction *and* would be acceptable here, the apostrophe in *others'* introduces the plural possessive form, which is not appropriate here.

Question 37. The best answer is **C** because *and* is a coordinating conjunction used appropriately to connect the first independent clause ("bats are not related to birds") with the second independent clause ("bats are not rodents either"), and because *although* sets up the contrast expressed in the subordinate clause that introduces the second independent clause.

The best answer is NOT:

A because it creates an unclear sentence saying that bats are not related to birds because bats, although they appear mouselike, are not rodents.

B because *whether* doesn't fit logically into this sentence, making the meaning hard to interpret.

D because "seeing as" is too casual an expression for the context and does not connect the ideas here logically, and because the lack of the conjunction *and* creates a comma splice.

Question 38. The best answer is **F** because the comma after *Chiroptera* appropriately sets off the descriptive noun phrase that is in apposition to *Chiroptera*.

The best answer is NOT:

G because adding the words *they are* makes the part of the sentence following *Chiroptera* into an independent clause, and thus the comma after *Chiroptera* creates a comma splice.

H because the addition of the words *so they are* after *Chiroptera* creates an invalid claim of cause and effect; it isn't logical to say that because bats are called Chiroptera, they are the only mammals that can truly fly.

J because the phrase *Chiroptera being* makes the sentence unclear and confusing.

Question 39. The best answer is **C** because the verb *can . . . fly* agrees with the plural subject, *mammals*.

The best answer is NOT:

A because the singular verb *flies* doesn't agree with the plural subject, *mammals*.

B because the singular verb *is* doesn't agree with the plural subject, *mammals*.

D because the singular verb *has* doesn't agree with the plural subject, *mammals*.

Question 40. The best answer is **J** because it provides present tense main verbs (*send* and *use*) that are consistent with the rest of the paragraph.

The best answer is NOT:

F because participial verb forms (*sending* and *using*) result in a sentence fragment.

G because the two verb forms *sending* (participle) and *use* (present tense) are not parallel and create an ungrammatical sentence.

H because it places a past tense verb (*sent*) in the middle of a paragraph using present tense and because it confusingly uses the infinitive form of the verb *to use*.

Question 41. **The best answer is B** because to a paragraph about the ways in which bats are useful to humans, this sentence adds another relevant example: bats pollinate plants, including fruits that humans eat.

The best answer is NOT:

A because the fact that bats can bite when handled doesn't fit into a paragraph about how bats are useful to humans.

C because plants' development of mechanisms to attract bats is interesting information but not relevant at this point in the essay.

D because bats' eyes being adapted to poor lighting is information that isn't relevant to the discussion of bats' usefulness to humans.

Question 42. **The best answer is J** because the sentence that the writer is considering deleting contains specific examples (evidence) of ways that humans are destroying bat habitat, as claimed in the previous sentence—namely, by building highways and housing developments. If the sentence were deleted, this information would be lost.

The best answer is NOT:

F because the sentence under consideration identifies how bat habitat is being destroyed; the sentence adds to, rather than distracts from, the message about the possible extinction of some bat species.

G because the sentence under consideration contains no direct examples of ways readers can stop the destruction of bat habitats.

H because the sentence under consideration identifies ways that bat habitat is being destroyed but gives no scientific proof.

Question 43. **The best answer is A** because the opening paragraph discusses people's fears of and misconceptions about bats, so the phrase "though they might seem threatening" is the choice that best ties the conclusion of the essay to its beginning.

The best answer is NOT:

B because the phrase "though they mostly come out at night" doesn't relate as well as A to the opening of the essay about people's fears and misconceptions about bats.

C because the phrase "though their habitats are vanishing" doesn't relate to the fears and misconceptions that people have about bats that are mentioned at the beginning of the essay.

D because the phrase "even if we rarely see them" has little connection to the opening paragraph about people's fears and misconceptions about bats.

Question 44. The best answer is **F** because the last sentence of the essay's first paragraph lists three of the most common misconceptions humans have about bats, and each misconception is the topic of one of the following three paragraphs in the essay.

The best answer is NOT:

G because the last sentence of the first paragraph is introducing new ideas, not summarizing points made earlier.

H because listing misconceptions about bats, rather than kinds of creatures bats have been compared to, is the purpose of the last sentence of the first paragraph.

J because the last sentence of the first paragraph, listing misconceptions about bats, contains no humor.

Question 45. The best answer is **C** because the goal of focusing the essay on the various ways in which people are causing the extinction of some bat species was NOT met in this essay. There is a brief mention of the extinction of some species of bats in one paragraph, but the focus of the essay is on the mistaken ideas people have about bats.

The best answer is NOT:

A because it suggests inaccurately that the goal was met by the essay explaining in detail that humans pose the greatest threat to bats. However, the human threat to bats is only a small part of the essay.

B because it suggests inaccurately that the goal was met by the essay's focus on people's misconceptions about bats; but that is a different focus than the extinction of some bat species.

D because, although it states correctly that the goal of focusing on the various ways that humans cause the extinction of bats was NOT met in this essay, the reason given is inaccurate. The essay does indicate that not all bat species are at risk of becoming extinct, but there is no mention of the relationship between bats' extinction and their feeding on livestock, and this point is only tangential to the goal.

Passage IV

Question 46. The best answer is **G** because the question asks for the choice that introduces the sentence by describing the Free Speech Movement and **G** explains that the Free Speech Movement was composed of "a coalition of civil rights groups and other political organizations."

The best answer is NOT:

F because it mentions a different campaign occurring in the United States at this time, but it doesn't explain what the Free Speech Movement was.

H because it mentions the conflict between the Free Speech Movement and university officials but fails to describe the Free Speech Movement.

J because it hints at what caused the formation of the Free Speech Movement but doesn't describe what it was.

Question 47. The best answer is D because the only piece of relevant information given here is the location, Mississippi.

The best answer is NOT:

A because the fact that Mississippi was the twentieth state admitted to the Union is irrelevant in this essay.

B because Mississippi's being known as the Magnolia State is irrelevant in this essay.

C because it is irrelevant in the essay that Mississippi was admitted to the Union in 1817.

Question 48. The best answer is F because there is no need for any punctuation in this underlined portion. The four prepositional phrases in a row in this sentence work together to describe how Savio had spent his time: "in Mississippi during the Freedom Summer of 1964 before returning to classes that fall." Sometimes no punctuation is necessary.

The best answer is NOT:

G because *before* is confusingly and ungrammatically set off by commas from the preceding and following phrases, becoming kind of a floating word attached to nothing.

H because a comma is incorrectly placed between the preposition *before* and the object of the preposition, *returning*.

J because a semicolon is incorrectly placed between *1964* and *before*, leaving a sentence fragment following the semicolon.

Question 49. The best answer is B because the words *That ban* clearly refer to the ban, mentioned in the previous sentence, that the university had imposed on civil rights groups. This is the most specific choice, while all the other choices are unclear.

The best answer is NOT:

A because *That stuff* is vague and is too informal in tone.

C because beginning with *Which* turns the sentence into a relative clause and so into a sentence fragment rather than a complete sentence.

D because there is no clear referent for the pronoun *it* (nothing that explains exactly what *it* stands for in the sentence).

Question 50. The best answer is **F** because the coordinating conjunction *and* appropriately joins the two elements of the compound object in the sentence: "a student strike" and "a sit-in protest."

The best answer is NOT:

G because adding the words *it became* creates a second main clause that, because of the lack of punctuation, produces a fused, or run-together, sentence.

H because the statement created by the addition of **H**, "That ban led to a student strike and was a sit-in protest," doesn't make sense, saying that the ban *was* a sit-in protest.

J because the word *than* does not join the sentence elements meaningfully; "That ban led to a student strike than a sit-in protest" makes no sense.

Question 51. The best answer is **B** because Sentence 4 does return the discussion to Savio himself and shifts away from the emphasis in Sentence 3 on the Free Speech Movement.

The best answer is NOT:

A because although Sentence 4 is the right place to begin a new paragraph, the resulting paragraph doesn't focus on Savio's childhood but only mentions it briefly.

C because although Sentence 5 does discuss Savio's experience as a civil rights worker, that fact is noted as just one more step in his life story, not a shift in the focus of the essay. And beginning the new paragraph with Sentence 5 would leave Sentence 4, about Savio's being the son of working-class parents, stuck onto the end of paragraph that discusses the Free Speech Movement rather than at the beginning of a paragraph focused on Savio's life leading up to his involvement with the Free Speech Movement.

D because Sentence 5 doesn't shift the essay's focus from Savio's childhood to his adult life. One prior sentence (Sentence 4) mentions Savio's childhood, but with this one exception, the entire essay up to this point has already been about Savio's adult life. And, as in **C**, beginning the new paragraph with Sentence 5 strands Sentence 4.

Question 52. The best answer is **H** because *compellingly* means "convincingly," so this word choice most clearly suggests that Savio was successful in his appeal to the protesters. Also, this is the only choice that refers to Savio's effect on the listeners rather than on how he himself spoke or felt.

The best answer is NOT:

F because *insistently* would indicate that Savio spoke with persistence, but it doesn't imply that he was successful.

G because *emphatically* would indicate that Savio spoke forcefully and with lots of emphasis, but it doesn't imply success.

J because *excitably* would indicate that Savio was excited about what he was saying but would not imply he succeeded in his appeal.

Question 53. The best answer is D because *large crowd* is the most clear and logical way to say that many people were there.

The best answer is NOT:

A because *countless*, meaning "too many to be counted," is usually used with a plural noun, as in "she has countless friends" or "there are countless answers to this question." It doesn't fit with "group"—though it would be possible to say "there were countless people in the group."

B because *numerous group* doesn't work for the same reason as A; *numerous* means "many," and it too usually accompanies a plural noun, as in "he made numerous friends" or "they had planned numerous activities."

C because *high volume* means "holding a large capacity," and it usually refers to a container or a room or a space that can hold a lot of things or people; it isn't used to refer to the size of a group.

Question 54. The best answer is G because *Besides* is the only choice that doesn't refer to time. Customarily, *besides* is used to set up a contrast with something else, and here there is no contrast. The purpose of the introductory adverb or adverbial phrase is to locate the time at which this event happened, as the underlined portion, *That day*, does. Therefore, *Besides* is the LEAST acceptable alternative to *That day*.

The best answer is NOT:

F because *Not long after* refers logically to the time that Savio and others were taken to jail, so it is an acceptable alternative to *That day*.

H because *Soon* is another logical way to refer to how much time passed before Savio and others were taken to jail.

J because *Then* is also a time word, implying "next" or "soon," so it also works as a logical alternative to *That day*.

Question 55. The best answer is D because when the words *ban that* are inserted into the sentence, it becomes illogical; it would read, "Days later, the California Board of Regents voted to override the university ban that granted full speech rights on the Berkeley campus." We know from the first paragraph that the university had restricted free speech activities, so it makes no sense to suggest that the ban had *granted* full speech rights. This alternative makes no sense in the context of the essay and therefore is the LEAST acceptable.

The best answer is NOT:

A because it puts a comma after *ban* and adds a subject ("this action") to go with the second verb, thus creating two independent clauses joined by a coordinating conjunction; this choice keeps the original meaning, and so is an acceptable alternative.

B because it adds a subject ("an action") and a relative pronoun, *that*, to explain what it meant for the Regents to override the ban ("an action that granted full speech rights on the Berkeley campus"). B both maintains the original meaning and is grammatically correct, so it is an acceptable alternative.

C because it adds a conjunctive adverb, *thus*, properly set off by commas, for emphasis.

Question 56. The best answer is H because the sentence should not be added here. If it were added, it would distract readers from the main point of this paragraph, about how the protests led by Savio helped bring about a change in the speech rights policy at the Berkeley campus. It is already clear from the current last sentence in the paragraph that the California Board of Regents makes decisions regarding the Berkeley campus; it isn't necessary, in this context, to know that they are appointed by the governor or that they oversee other universities in California as well.

The best answer is NOT:

F because it says that the sentence should be added here to provide important background information. But the necessary information is already in the paragraph, and the extra information the sentence provides about the appointment and duties of the California Board of Regents is distracting and not important to this essay.

G because it says that the sentence should be added here to explain the makeup of the California Board of Regents. But the sentence does not do so, and even if it did, such an explanation would be irrelevant here.

J because although it notes correctly that the sentence should not be added here, the reason it gives isn't accurate. A sentence that gave even more specific information about the California Board of Regents would be even more distracting to the reader.

Question 57. The best answer is A because the past tense verb *made* is necessary to fit in with the rest of the paragraph and the essay, to relate a series of events that happened in the past.

The best answer is NOT:

B because *made for* is an expression meaning "had or caused an effect on" (for example, "The storms made for a long night"). Here, the expression is awkward and redundant ("It made for a powerful case for").

C because *makes for* has the same problems as B and is in the present tense, which isn't appropriate in this paragraph.

D because *makes* is in the present tense, which isn't appropriate in this paragraph.

Question 58. The best answer is F because the sentence mentions one additional effect of the Free Speech Movement, and therefore *also* is an appropriate word to use.

The best answer is NOT:

G because there is no reason given in this paragraph for why the Free Speech Movement popularized the sit-in, just a mention of the fact that it did so.

H because *however* is a word used to set up a contrast with something previously mentioned, and there is no contrast here, just some additional information.

J because the phrase *it thus* implies that a conclusion is being expressed on the basis of the previous text. But here, the popularization of the sit-in does not follow as a conclusion from the preceding sentence.

Question 59. The best answer is B because this is a case where no punctuation is best. The phrase "as a protest tactic" is necessary to define the sense in which the sit-in was popularized, and so the phrase should not be set off by commas as merely descriptive information would be. Also, the coordinating conjunction *and* is necessary to coordinate the compound predicate (*popularized* and *became*) in this sentence.

The best answer is NOT:

A because it sets off the defining phrase "as a protest tactic" by commas as though it were unnecessary information and because it omits the necessary coordinating conjunction *and*.

C because it has the same problem as A and, by adding the subject *it* to go with the verb *became*, creates a comma splice.

D because it appropriately leaves out commas around the phrase "as a protest tactic" but lacks a conjunction to connect the second part of the sentence to the first part, leaving a confusing and ungrammatical result.

Question 60. The best answer is F because this phrase needs no punctuation. There is no reason to follow the adverb *then* with a comma, to separate the verb *taught* from its direct object by a comma, or to break up the compound direct object, *mathematics and physics*, with a comma.

The best answer is NOT:

G because it contains two inappropriate commas, one after the adverb *then* and one between the verb (*taught*) and its direct object (*mathematics and physics*).

H because it has an inappropriate comma between two elements of the compound direct object.

J because it has an inappropriate comma after the adverb *then*.

Passage V

Question 61. The best answer is D because the possessive form of *baseball* (*baseball's*) is needed so that the phrase means "one of the most gifted athletes of baseball."

The best answer is NOT:

A because the plural *baseballs* rather than the possessive *baseball's* is used.

B because although the correct form of *baseball's* is used, there should not be a comma between a noun and the prepositional phrase that follows it and explains it ("one of baseball's most gifted athletes").

C because the plural *baseballs* instead of the possessive *baseball's* is used and because an inappropriate comma intervenes between the pronoun *one* and the adjoining prepositional phrase.

Question 62. The best answer is **H** because *named* is the only choice that fits exactly into this context. Clemente was "named the National League Batting Champion."

The best answer is NOT:

F because "he was entitled the National League Batting Champion" makes no sense. Clemente could be entitled *to* the championship, but he can't be "entitled the Champion."

G because Clemente could not be "awarded the National League Champion"; it would make sense to say he was awarded a championship, but not that he was awarded a champion.

J because Clemente could not be "given the Champion" (though he could be "given a championship").

Question 63. The best answer is **A** because the phrase "in 1971" is all that is needed to be parallel to the rest of the sentence. The verb in the sentence, *named*, applies to all three titles that Clemente won (National League Batting Champion, Nation League MVP, and World Series MVP).

The best answer is NOT:

B because the sentence already says that Clemente was named World Series MVP, so "was awarded to Clemente" is redundant and out of parallel with the rest of the sentence.

C because the information that the "World Series MVP award in 1971 went to Clemente" is redundant and out of parallel.

D because the information that the "World Series MVP award was given to him in 1971" is redundant and out of parallel.

Question 64. The best answer is **J** because the comma between *impressive* and *his* correctly separates the introductory subordinate clause from the main clause.

The best answer is NOT:

F because the period between *impressive* and *His* incorrectly punctuates the introductory clause beginning with *While* as though it were a complete sentence, resulting in a sentence fragment, "While Clemente's achievements in the sport of baseball are impressive."

G because the subordinator *While* and the coordinating conjunction *but* conflict, producing an uncoordinated sentence.

H because the subordinator *While* and the coordinating conjunction *and* conflict, producing an uncoordinated sentence that is further damaged by the lack of a comma after the introductory subordinate clause.

Question 65. The best answer is **B** because the word *him* is the appropriate pronoun to refer to Clemente.

The best answer is NOT:

A because the reflexive pronoun *himself* is incorrectly used here. Reflexive pronouns are used when the same person is doing and receiving the action (for example, "he gave himself a haircut"). In this case, the subject (charity work) is what marked Clemente; he did not "mark" himself.

C because *them* is the third-person plural pronoun, which doesn't have a logical antecedent here.

D because *itself* is a reflexive pronoun that should refer to a thing rather than to a person, and therefore does not work grammatically or logically here.

Question 66. The best answer is **F** because "died in a plane crash" is the most clear and concise way to give this information to the reader.

The best answer is NOT:

G because "perished in a deadly plane crash" is wordier than necessary and is redundant; if someone perishes in a plane crash, the crash is, by definition, "deadly."

H because "fatally perished" is redundant, with *fatally* and *perished* both referring to death.

J because the phrase "died in a lethal plane crash" is redundant.

Question 67. The best answer is **C** because the relative clause "that was delivering" grammatically refers to *crash*, making the sentence illogically say that the plane crash was delivering the relief supplies. This sentence structure is NOT an acceptable alternative to the underlined portion.

The best answer is NOT:

A because it is an acceptable alternative to the underlined portion: the addition of the words *he was* does not change the meaning nor disrupt the structure of the sentence.

B because *as he was* works equally well as *while* in the sentence structure.

D because using the simple past tense (*delivered*) here produces a grammatically correct and logical alternative to the underlined portion.

Question 68. The best answer is **J** because only the word *projects* is needed here. All the information in the other answers is repetitious.

The best answer is NOT:

F because "which were designed to last for years" pointlessly repeats the idea already expressed by *long-term*.

G because "that would help others" pointlessly repeats the idea already expressed by *humanitarian*.

H because "of benefit to others" pointlessly repeats the idea already expressed by *humanitarian*.

Question 69. The best answer is **B** because it appropriately sets off the introductory phrase with a comma and is correctly punctuated to indicate that Clemente's wife was named Vera (by setting the name off with commas).

The best answer is NOT:

A because it fails to set off the name *Vera* (here, a nonrestrictive appositive) from the noun *wife*.

C because it leaves out the comma after the name *Vera*, creating a confusing sentence: "A few years later, his wife, Vera fulfilled this dream" leaves unclear how the name *Vera* and *his wife* are related.

D because, by omitting a comma before *Vera* to indicate apposition, it ungrammatically separates the subject from the verb by a comma.

Question 70. The best answer is **H** because the logic of this sentence is to point out that one of the long-term projects Clemente's wife had established was "a sports complex for children," the one referred to in Sentence 3, and the sentence structure in **H** conforms to this logic.

The best answer is NOT:

F because "for children" in the phrase "was for children a sports complex" makes little sense and isn't standard English word order.

G because although the resulting clause almost makes sense ("One of them for children was a sports complex"), it is less clear than "a sports complex for children."

J because making the ending phrase of the sentence "in his homeland for children" indicates it is the homeland rather than the sports complex that is for children, which doesn't make sense.

Question 71. The best answer is **C** because the logic of the paragraph is that Sentence 4 should follow Sentence 1; Sentence 1 mentions the long-term humanitarian projects Clemente had been planning, and the pronoun *them* in Sentence 4 refers directly to these long-term humanitarian projects ("One of them was a sports complex for children in his homeland"). Then Sentence 2 appropriately follows Sentence 4 by describing this sports complex in more detail.

The best answer is NOT:

A because there is no logical referent for the pronoun *them* in Sentence 4 or in the previous two sentences, and the reader has to return to Sentence 1 to discover what is being referred to. With Sentence 4 where it is now, following Sentence 3, it sounds as though *them* refers to Puerto Rican youths, but this makes no sense in the context of Sentence 4.

B because beginning the paragraph with Sentence 4 would start with "One of them was a sports complex," leaving the reader wondering, "One of what?"

D because placing Sentence 4 after Sentence 2 puts Sentence 4's general statement of what was built after Sentence 2's specific description, exactly the opposite of how the paragraph should logically be organized.

Question 72. The best answer is G because it uses the correct form and placement of the adverb *annually*.

The best answer is NOT:

F because it places the adjective after the noun it would modify rather than in its correct position in front of the noun.

H because it places the adverb form *annually* illogically in front of the noun *basis*; this phrase, if correct, would use the adjective form and read "on an annual basis."

J because it uses the adverb form *annually* where the adjective form *annual* is required.

Question 73. The best answer is D because of the two often confused words *principals* and *principles*, the word that should be used here is *principles*, meaning fundamental rules. The preposition *of* is the one that is used most often with *principles*.

The best answer is NOT:

A because it uses *principals* in place of *principles*. *Principals*, in its plural form, can refer to important people, including principals of schools, or to sums of money that are invested. It cannot be used to mean the fundamental rules. The preposition *of* would be correct if used with the word *principles*.

B because it uses *principals* in place of *principles* and because the preposition *for* isn't idiomatic English.

C because although the correct word *principles* is used here, the phrase *principles in* is less idiomatic than the phrase *principles of*.

Question 74. The best answer is G because it best summarizes the effects of Clemente's generosity discussed in the essay: Clemente inspired ballplayers and improved the lives of young people.

The best answer is NOT:

F because although it is probably true that the effects of Clemente's generosity continue to spread as more people learn about his life, this choice doesn't summarize any key points made in the essay.

H because although we can learn more about Clemente in the Baseball Hall of Fame, this choice fails to summarize any of the points in the essay.

J because it is irrelevant to the points made in the essay.

Question 75. The best answer is C because the sentence to be added gives examples of people who have won an award, and Paragraph 5 is about the Roberto Clemente Award.

The best answer is NOT:

A because if this list of people were added at the end of Paragraph 2, they would be illogically listed for winning an award just after we learn that Clemente died in a plane crash.

B because Paragraph 4 is about the establishment of the Roberto Clemente Foundation and there is no mention of an award of any sort, so this would not be a logical place to add a list of award winners.

D because Paragraph 6 summarizes the legacy of Roberto Clemente, but it isn't a reasonable place to list the names of people who won an award not mentioned in this paragraph.

Question 1. **The correct answer is E.** You may want to make a sketch of this situation in your mind, or better yet, in the space in your test booklet. A sample sketch is shown below.

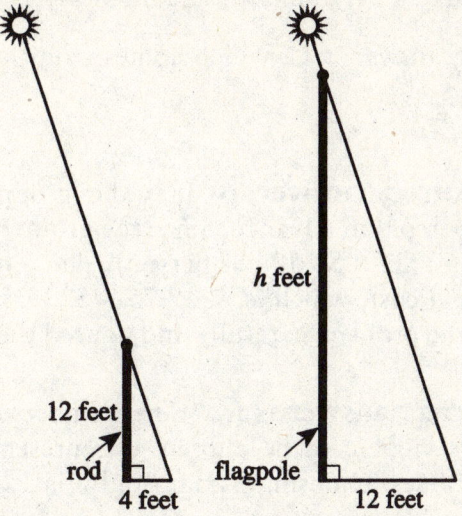

The vertical rod and the vertical flagpole each form a right angle with the level ground, resulting in 2 right triangles. The smaller right triangle (at left) is composed of the rod, the rod's shadow, and the line of sight of the Sun through the top of the rod. The larger right triangle (at right) is composed of the flagpole, the flagpole's shadow, and the line of sight of the Sun through the top of the flagpole. Since the angle of elevation of the Sun is the same for each triangle, the 2 triangles are similar by the *Angle-Angle Similarity* property. Using the ratios of corresponding sides of the similar triangles, the proportion $\frac{12}{h} = \frac{4}{12}$ is solved to find the height of the flagpole, $h = 36$ feet.

Common errors in this problem result from relying on an incorrect mental image or labeling the dimensions on the sketch incorrectly. If you chose **A**, you might have set up and solved the proportion $\frac{h}{12} = \frac{4}{12}$.

Question 2. **The correct answer is H.** After subtracting the onetime fee from the amount on Brendan's check ($500 − $140), the remaining $360 goes toward the amount spent on monthly fees. You can find the number of months of membership covered by the check by dividing the remaining $360 by the monthly fee of $40 per month, giving 9 months as the result.

You could also solve this problem by setting up and solving the equation $140 + 40m = 500$, where the expression $140 + 40m$ represents the cost of a gym membership for m months.

Question 3. **The correct answer is A.** Substituting –5 for x produces a numerator equal to $(-5)^2 - 1 = 25 - 1 = 24$ and a denominator equal to $-5 + 1 = -4$. Therefore, $\frac{x^2 - 1}{x + 1} = \frac{24}{-4} = -6$. The most common wrong answer is **C**, which comes from forgetting the negative sign in the given x-value: $\frac{5^2 - 1}{5 + 1} = \frac{24}{6} = 4$.

Question 4. **The correct answer is J.** The group of 27 people paid a total of $249.75 (27 × $9.25 per person) in advance. Since the group consisted of more than 25 people, the actual cost was $229.50 (27 × $8.50 per person). The refund is the difference between the amount paid and the actual cost, which is $249.75 – $229.50 = $20.25. If you chose **H**, you could have failed to read the problem carefully and figured the refund for a group of 25 people.

Question 5. **The correct answer is C.** The number of possible outcomes (that is, the total number of members eligible to be chosen as representative) is 13 – 3 = 10, and the number of favorable outcomes (choosing Samara only) is 1. The probability of the favorable outcomes is equal to $\frac{\text{the number of favorable outcomes}}{\text{the number of possible outcomes}}$. So, the probability of Samara being chosen as representative would be $\frac{1}{10}$. Careful reading is essential; if you chose **B**, you may have overlooked the words CANNOT and NOT.

Question 6. **The correct answer is H.** A rectangle has 2 pairs of congruent sides. So, the rectangle has 2 side measures of 15 cm and 2 side measures of 6 cm. The perimeter of the rectangle is equal to the sum of the 4 side measures, which is 15 + 15 + 6 + 6, or 2(15 + 6) = 42 cm. If you confused the formula for perimeter with the formula for area, you probably chose **J**, which was the most common incorrect answer.

Question 7. **The correct answer is B.** The amount collected from the sale of 142 tickets bought in advance is equal to ($6 per ticket)(142 tickets) = $852. The amount collected from the sale of d tickets bought at the door is equal to ($8 per ticket)($d$ tickets) = $8d$. The total amount collected from all ticket sales is $852 + 8d$. To determine the minimum number of tickets to produce $2,000 in ticket sales, you can set up an inequality: $852 + 8d \geq 2,000$. Subtracting 852 from both sides and then dividing by 8 produces the equivalent inequality $d \geq 143.5$. Keep in mind, however, that d must be a whole number of tickets, so you must select the whole number d to satisfy the inequality. This means you must round 143.5 *up* to obtain the correct answer. If you chose **A**, you probably rounded *down* to 143. If you chose **D**, you might have divided 2,000 by 8 without thinking carefully about what the numbers represent. If you chose **C** or **E**, you probably set up the inequality incorrectly.

Question 8. **The correct answer is J.** The proportion $\frac{8}{12} = \frac{10}{r}$ is true provided that the *cross product equation* $8r = 12(10)$ is true. Therefore, $r = \frac{120}{8} = 15$.

Question 9. **The correct answer is E.** Use of the *Distributive Property* gives the equivalent equation $12x - 132 = -15$. Adding 132 to both sides of the equation results in the equation $12x = 117$, implying that the solution is $x = \frac{117}{12}$, or $\frac{39}{4}$ when reduced to lowest terms. If you distributed 12 to *only* the first term, x, but forgot to distribute 12 to the second term, you probably got an answer of $-\frac{1}{3}$.

Question 10. **The correct answer is J.** The figure below illustrates the progression of angle measures found in determining the measure of ∠BCE.

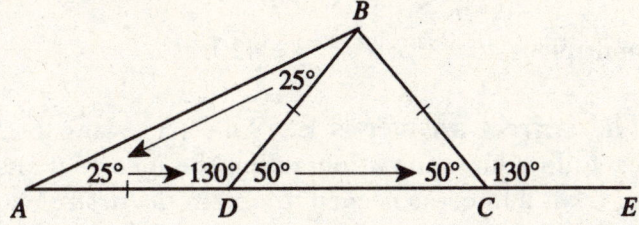

Because $\overline{BD} \cong \overline{AD}$, △ABD is isosceles, so its base angles are congruent. Therefore, $m\angle BAD = m\angle ABD = 25°$. Because the sum of the angle measures in △ABD must equal 180°, $m\angle ADB = 180° - (25° + 25°) = 130°$. Since ∠ADB and ∠BDC are a linear pair, $m\angle BDC = 180° - 130° = 50°$. Since $\overline{BD} \cong \overline{BC}$, △DBC is isosceles, so *its* base angles are congruent: $m\angle BCD = m\angle BDC = 50°$. Finally, ∠BCD and ∠BCE are a linear pair, so $m\angle BCE = 180° - 50° = 130°$.

Question 11. **The correct answer is C.** When you substitute –2 for x, you get $9(-2)^2 + 5(-2) - 8 = 9(4) + (-10) - 8 = 18$. If you chose **A**, you probably evaluated $9(-2)^2$ as –36. If you chose **E**, you probably evaluated $5(-2)$ as 10.

Question 12. The correct answer is J. One efficient way to solve this problem numericall is by listing the multiples of the largest of the 3 numbers (70) as a sequence and determinin whether or not each succeeding term in the sequence is a multiple of *both* 20 and 30.

70 (multiple of neither)
140 (multiple of 20 only)
210 (multiple of 30 only)
280 (multiple of 20 only)
350 (multiple of neither)
420 (multiple of both 20 and 30)

The first term in the sequence that is a multiple of both 20 and 30 is 420, which is the least common multiple of 20, 30, and 70. You can also find the least common multiple by expressing each of the 3 numbers as a product of primes (with exponents), listing all bases of exponential expressions shown, and choosing for each base listed the highest-valued exponent shown.

$$30 = 2^1 \times 3^1 \times 5^1$$
$$20 = 2^2 \times 5^1$$
$$70 = 2^1 \times 5^1 \times 7^1$$

The least common multiple is $2^2 \times 3^1 \times 5^1 \times 7^1 = 420$.

Question 13. The correct answer is E. You may want to choose an even integer as Tom's initial number, follow his steps in obtaining the *incorrect* answer, and then determine *what* operation using *what* number is needed to obtain the desired number. For example:

1) Choose the integer "6" as the initial number.
2) When Tom "accidentally multiplies the number by 2," he obtains an incorrect answer of 12.
3) Had Tom correctly divided the initial number by 2, he would have obtained 3 as the answer.
4) To convert his incorrect answer of 12 to the desired answer of 3, he must divide by 4.

You may want to confirm that E is the correct answer by choosing a different initial number and repeating the steps above.

Question 14.   The correct answer is G.   The 8-sided figure in the problem consists of 5 congruent squares whose areas total 125 square inches. Therefore, each congruent square has an area of $125 \div 5 = 25$ square inches, so each side of each square is $\sqrt{25} = 5$ inches long. The perimeter of the 8-sided figure is composed of 12 of these sides, each of length 5 inches, as shown in the figure below. Therefore, the 8-sided figure has a perimeter of $12 \times 5 = 60$ inches.

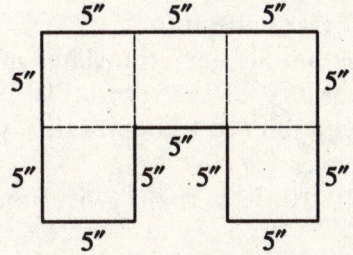

Question 15.   The correct answer is E.   You can solve this problem using the *Triangle Sum Theorem*. For any triangle, the sum of the measures of the 3 interior angles is 180°. So, for $\triangle ABC$, $m\angle A + m\angle B + m\angle C = 180°$. You are given that $m\angle B = 90°$. So $m\angle A + m\angle C = 90°$. Since $m\angle A > 43°$, that means that $m\angle C < 90° - 43° = 47°$.

You can also solve this problem using the following steps.

1)   Choose a measure for $\angle A$ that is greater than 43°, say 44°.
2)   This implies that $m\angle B = 180° - 90° - 44° = 46°$.
3)   This answer fits E.
4)   Choose a different measure for $\angle A$ (greater than 43°) to verify that E is the correct answer.

Question 16.   The correct answer is G.   For each operation given, you can determine whether the equation is true or false by substituting the operation symbol for ◊.

I.   Addition: $(2 + 1)^4 + (6 + 3)^2 = 3^4 + 9^2 = 81 + 81 = 162 \neq 10$ (false)
II.   Subtraction: $(2 - 1)^4 + (6 - 3)^2 = 1^4 + 3^2 = 1 + 9 = 10$ (true)
III.   Division: $(2 \div 1)^4 + (6 \div 3)^2 = 2^4 + 2^2 = 16 + 4 = 20 \neq 10$ (false)

The equation is true only when the subtraction sign is substituted for ◊.

Question 17.   The correct answer is E.   Each answer choice is a linear equation in *slope-intercept form*; that is, $y = mx + b$, where the value of m gives the slope of the line and the value of b gives the y-intercept of the line. Only the equation shown in E represents a line having a y-intercept ($b = 5$) that matches the value of the y-intercept indicated by the given graph.

Question 18. **The correct answer is F.** Translating sentences expressed in the English language into sentences expressed in the mathematical language of numbers and symbols is not unlike translating from, say, the English language to the Spanish language. English words, given in a certain context, can be represented by mathematical symbols as shown below.

1) "An integer, n, is *added* to 4" translates into "$4 + n$."
2) "That *sum* is then *multiplied* by 8" translates into "$(4 + n) \times 8$" or, equivalently, "$8(n + 4)$."
3) "*twice* the original integer" translates into "$2n$."
4) "10 *less than* twice the original integer" translates into "$2n - 10$." **Note:** The word *than* reverses the order in appearance of the terms "10" and "$2n$" when translated into the mathematical language. If you did not recognize this, you probably chose **H**, which was the most common incorrect answer.
5) "This result *is* ("equals") 10 less than twice the original integer" translates into "$8(n + 4) = 2n - 10$."

Question 19. **The correct answer is A.** For x years of full years' employment after being hired, Worker A's starting salary ($20,000) increases by $800 per year and Worker B's starting salary ($15,200) increases by $2,000 per year. After x years, Worker A's salary has increased by $800x$ and Worker B's salary has increased by $2,000x$. So, for x years of full years' employment after being hired, Worker A's yearly salary is represented by the expression $20,000 + 800x$ and Worker's B's salary is represented by the expression $15,200 + 2,000x$. These 2 yearly salaries are equal at the value of x for which the equation $20,000 + 800x = 15,200 + 2,000x$ is true.

Question 20. **The correct answer is J.** The figure shows a right triangle with 2 given side measures. To find the length of the third side, use the Pythagorean theorem, given below.

$$\text{(length of the hypotenuse)}^2 = \text{(length of one side of the triangle)}^2 + \text{(length of the other side of the triangle)}^2$$

In this problem, the 13-foot measure represents the length of the hypotenuse. So the formula above gives the equation $13^2 = 12^2 + x^2$, where x feet is the length of the missing side. To find x^2, subtract 12^2 from each side of the equation. The subtraction results in the equivalent equation $25 = x^2$, resulting in the solution $x = \pm 5$. Since the side length of a triangle must be positive, you can ignore the negative solution. If you chose **F**, you probably took the length of the hypotenuse and subtracted the length of the given leg, without applying the Pythagorean theorem at all. If you chose **G**, you probably *doubled* the lengths, rather than *squaring* them.

Question 21. **The correct answer is E.** To simplify this expression, use the *Distributive Property*: $7(x + 3) - 3(2x - 2) = 7x + (7)(3) + (-3)(2x) + (-3)(-2) = 7x + 21 + (-6x) + 6$. Then combine like terms to obtain $x + 27$. If you chose **B**, perhaps you forgot that $a - b = a + (-b)$, and so distributed 3 rather than -3 to the -2 term in $(2x - 2)$. If you chose **A**, perhaps you forgot to distribute the 7 and the -3 to the second term in each set of grouping symbols, setting $7(x + 3)$ equal to $7x + 3$ and $-3(2x - 2)$ equal to $-6x - 2$.

Question 22. **The correct answer is G.** Two common methods are often used in solving this system of equations.

Using the Substitution Method, you can convert the second equation into the equivalent equation $x = y + 12$, and then substitute $y + 12$ for x in the first equation to obtain $(y + 12) + y = 32$. From this it follows that $2y + 12 = 32$, so $2y = 20$, and $y = 10$.

Using the Addition Method, you can vertically align the 2 equations and add down, eliminating y.

$$\begin{array}{r} x + y = 32 \\ x - y = 12 \\ \hline 2x = 44 \end{array}$$

So $x = 22$, which implies that $22 + y = 32$, so $y = 10$.

Question 23. **The correct answer is C.** This problem tests your knowledge of how to square a binomial. The expression $(2x - 3)^2$ can be expanded into the $ax^2 + bx + c$ form using the *Distributive Property* as shown below.

$$(2x - 3)^2 = (2x - 3)(2x - 3) = (2x)(2x) + (2x)(-3) + (-3)(2x) +$$
$$(-3)(-3) = 4x^2 - 6x - 6x + 9 = 4x^2 - 12x + 9$$

When the coefficients of $4x^2 - 12x + 9$ are matched with the coefficients of $ax^2 + bx + c$, you can see that $a = 4$, $b = -12$, and $c = 9$, and $a + b + c = 4 + (-12) + 9 = 1$.

When you square a binomial, you must multiply 2 binomial expressions using the distributive property. Common errors result from reasoning that $(2x - 3)^2$ is equivalent to $(2x)^2 + (-3)^2$ or $(2x)^2 - (3)^2$, resulting in **B** or **D**.

Question 24.   **The correct answer is H.**   Two common approaches are often used in solving this problem.

In the first approach, the polygon can be divided into a 15 ft by 15 ft square and a 10 ft by 5 ft rectangle (see Figure 1 below). The area of the polygon is equal to the sum of the areas of the rectangle and the square, $(15)(15) + (10)(5) = 275$ square feet.

In the second approach, you take the rectangle formed by the 15 ft and 25 ft sides of the polygon and "cut away" a 10 ft by 10 ft square (see Figure 2 below). In this case, the area of the polygon is equal to the difference of the areas of the rectangle and the square $(15)(25) - (10)(10) = 275$ square feet.

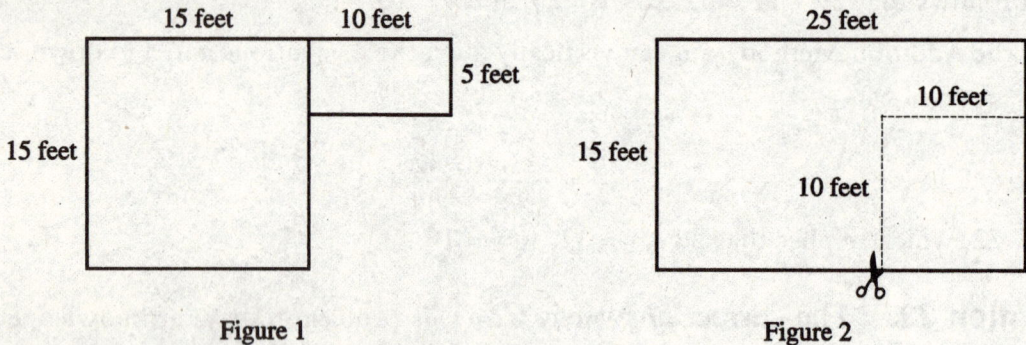

Figure 1   Figure 2

Question 25. The correct answer is A. You can solve this problem using a numerical approach. First, you must determine which of the 2 functions expresses a linear relationship, or equivalently, which of the 2 functions has a rate of change (slope) that is constant.

Between the x-values of -2 and -1, the rate of change for $f(x)$ is $\frac{1.2 - 1.4}{-1 - (-2)} = -0.2$, and the rate of change for $g(x)$ is $\frac{0.9 - 0.6}{-1 - (-2)} = 0.3$ (see the table below). Next, the possible values for $f(0)$ and $g(0)$ can be found by adding the respective rates of change to $f(-1)$ and $g(-1)$, respectively. The resulting values, $1.2 + (-0.2) = 1.0$ and $0.9 + 0.3 = 1.2$, are shown in boldface in the table.

By examining the rates of change of the 2 functions between the x-values of 0 and 1 (using the possible values for $f(0)$ and $g(0)$), you will find that the rate of change remains constant for $f(x)$, but the rate of change is not constant for $g(x)$. Therefore, $f(x)$ must be the function that expresses a linear relationship. When you add the rate of change for $f(x)$ to $f(2)$, and then to $f(3)$, you obtain the value of $f(4)$.

x	$f(x)$		$g(x)$	
-2	1.4	} rate of change $= -0.2$	0.6	} rate of change $= 0.3$
-1	1.2		0.9	
0	**1.0**	} rate of change $= -0.2$	**1.2**	} rate of change $= 0.1$
1	0.8		1.3	
2	0.6	} rate of change $= -0.2$	1.6	
3	**0.4**			
4	**0.2**			

Question 26. The correct answer is H. To find the slope, you can manipulate the equation $6y - 14x = 5$ algebraically in order to find its equivalent equation expressed in *slope-intercept form*, which is $y = mx + b$, where m is the slope and b is the y-intercept. The manipulations are shown below.

$$6y - 14x = 5 \Rightarrow 6y = 14x + 5 \Rightarrow y = \frac{14}{6}x + \frac{5}{6}$$

The slope of the line equals $\frac{14}{6}$, or $\frac{7}{3}$ when reduced to lowest terms.

Question 27. The correct answer is C. Three common techniques come to mind to solve this quadratic equation: factoring, completing the square, or the quadratic formula. If the expression opposite zero (in this case, $x^2 + x - 12$) looks simple, you should try factoring, as this method is generally quicker and less prone to calculation errors. (**Note:** Not all quadratic expressions will factor, so a minimal amount of time should be spent on factoring. If factoring is unsuccessful, you should move on to one of the other two techniques.) In this problem, factoring works easily. Since $x^2 + x - 12 = (x + 4)(x - 3)$, the quadratic is equal to 0 when $x + 4 = 0$ or $x - 3 = 0$, so $x = -4$ or $x = 3$. Therefore, the sum of the 2 solutions of the equation is $-4 + 3 = -1$.

Question 28. The correct answer is J. Similar triangles are triangles whose corresponding sides are proportional. The solution, x, is found by setting up the following proportion:

$$\frac{\text{the perimeter of the smaller triangle}}{\text{the perimeter of the larger triangle}} = \frac{3}{5} = \frac{(3 + 5 + 7)\text{ cm}}{x\text{ cm}}$$

To solve $\frac{3}{5} = \frac{15}{x}$ for x, cross multiply to obtain the equivalent equation $3x = 75$, and divide by 3 to obtain $x = 25$.

Question 29. The correct answer is A. To find the median, first rank the given data values from least to greatest (see the table below). When the number of data values is odd, the median is the middle-ranking value. Since there are 7 values given, the middle-ranking value is -2, shown in the shaded region of the table. If you forgot to rank the data, you probably chose C.

Rank	1st	2nd	3rd	4th	5th	6th	7th
Temperature (°F)	-6	-5	-3	-2	1	2	4

|←—3 values—→| | |←—3 values—→|

When the number of data values is even, the median is the average of the 2 middle-ranking data values. For example, the median of a list of 18 data values is the average of the 9th-ranking and 10th-ranking data values. In either case, even or odd, the number of data values less than or equal to the median equals the number of data values greater than or equal to the median.

Question 30.   The correct answer is G.   As in Question 18, you can use translation skills to set up an algebraic equation that, when solved, yields the solution to the problem.

1) Let the variable a represent the teacher's age.
2) "If you *square* my age" translates into "a^2."
3) "23 *times* my age" translates into "$23a$."
4) "then *subtract* 23 times my age" translates into "$a^2 - 23a$." Because the words *than* and *from* do not appear in the sentence, the order of the terms "a^2" and "$23a$" is NOT reversed when translated into mathematical language.
5) "the result is 50" translates into "$= 50$."

Therefore, the translation gives the equation $a^2 - 23a = 50$, which you may solve by subtracting 50 from both sides and factoring.

The equation $a^2 - 23a - 50 = 0$ is true, provided that $(a + 2)(a - 25) = 0$, which happens if $a = -2$ (but age cannot be negative) or $a = 25$.

Question 31.   The correct answer is B.   "If a car accelerates from a stop at the *rate* of 20 meters per second per second" implies that $a = 20$, and "travels a *distance* of 80 meters" implies that $d = 80$. Substituting these values into the equation $d = \frac{1}{2}at^2$ gives the equation $80 = \frac{1}{2}(20)t^2$, or equivalently, $80 = 10t^2$, or $8 = t^2$. Therefore $t = \sqrt{8} \approx 2.8$ seconds.

Question 32.   The correct answer is F.   Let r equal the common ratio for the geometric sequence. This means that each term is produced from the preceding one by multiplying by r. To determine r for this sequence, you may use the fact that the 1st term times r equals the 2nd term: $(bcd)r = abc^2d$. Therefore $r = \frac{abc^2d}{bcd} = ac$. The 4th term of the sequence is equal to the 3rd term times r: $(a^2bc^3d)r = (a^2bc^3d)ac = a^3bc^4d$.

Question 33.   The correct answer is D.   You must first determine from the frequency bar graph the number of students in the class responding that they spent 0, 1, or 2 hours studying on the previous evening. The bars in the graph indicate that 2 students studied 0 hours, 5 students studied 1 hour, and 6 students studied 2 hours. Therefore, the fraction of students in the class that responded they had spent less than 3 hours studying is equal to

$$\frac{\text{the number of students studying less than 3 hours}}{\text{the number of students in the class}} = \frac{2 + 5 + 6}{20} = \frac{13}{20}$$

If you chose B (the most common incorrect answer), perhaps you overlooked the phrase "less than" and selected the number of students studying exactly 3 hours as the numerator, obtaining the fraction $\frac{4}{20}$, or $\frac{1}{5}$.

Question 34. **The correct answer is J.** In the figure below, the shaded sector represents the 3-hour group.

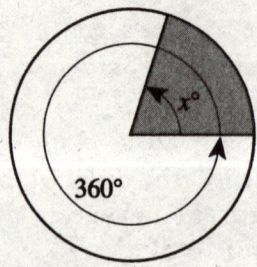

For this circle graph, the ratio $\dfrac{\text{the area of the shaded sector}}{\text{the area of the circle}}$ is equivalent to the ratio

$\dfrac{\text{the number of students in the 3-hour group}}{\text{the number of students in the class}}$. These ratios, in turn, are equivalent to the ratio

$\dfrac{\text{the measure of the central angle of the sector representing the 3-hour group}}{\text{the measure of the angle covered by 1 complete circle}}$. Letting the numerator of this

last ratio equal $x°$, and using the fact that the denominator of this ratio is $360°$,

you obtain the proportions $\dfrac{4}{20} = \dfrac{\text{the number of students studying 3 hours}}{\text{the number of students in the class}} = \dfrac{x°}{360°}$, so $x = 72$.

Question 35. **The correct answer is B.** Since this frequency bar graph gives the number of times each response was given, the frequency bar graph was constructed from the 20 data values below.

$$0, 0, 1, 1, 1, 1, 1, 2, 2, 2, 2, 2, 2, 3, 3, 3, 3, 4, 4, 5$$

The average number of hours for the 20 responses is equal to the average of the data values,

which is defined to be $\dfrac{\text{the sum of the data values}}{\text{the number of data values}}$.

This is equal to $\dfrac{0+0+1+1+1+1+1+2+2+2+2+2+2+3+3+3+3+4+4+5}{20}$, or equivalently,

$\dfrac{2(0) + 5(1) + 6(2) + 4(3) + 2(4) + 1(5)}{20} = \dfrac{42}{20} = 2.1$.

Question 36.   The correct answer is F. Because $(x^2 + 8x + 7) = (x + 7)(x + 1)$, you can factor the numerator further, into the product $(x + 1)(x + 7)(x - 3)$. Similarly, since $(x^2 + 4x - 21) = (x + 7)(x - 3)$, you can factor the denominator further, into the product $(x + 7)(x - 3)(x + 1)$. Then, as long as the denominator is not zero (that is, as long as x is not equal to -7, 3, or -1, which is guaranteed by the requirement that $x > 21$), you can write the given rational function

as $\frac{(x+1)(x+7)(x-3)}{(x+7)(x-3)(x+1)}$. Using the *Commutative Property for Multiplication*, the factors in the

numerator can be reordered, producing the equivalent expression $\frac{(x+7)(x-3)(x+1)}{(x+7)(x-3)(x+1)}$. Since the

numerator and denominator are equal, this rational expression is equal to 1.

Question 37.   The correct answer is E.   As shown in the figure below, the tether line, the level ground, and a line segment representing the altitude of the bottom of the basket form a right triangle.

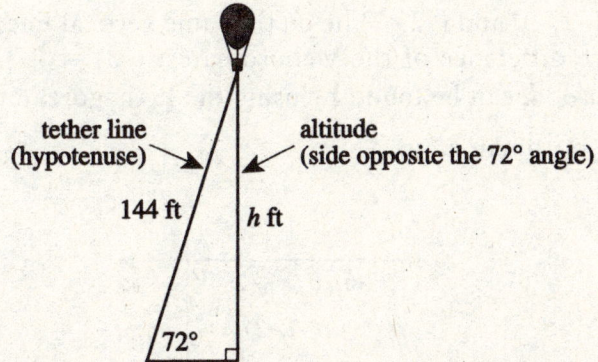

Let the length of the altitude equal h feet. You can use a trigonometric ratio to find h. The tether line forms the hypotenuse of the right triangle, and the line segment representing the altitude is the side opposite the 72° angle. Therefore the trigonometric ratio to be used with respect to the 72° angle is the sine ratio, which gives the equation below.

$$\sin 72° = \frac{\text{the length of the side opposite the 72° angle}}{\text{the length of the hypotenuse}} = \frac{h}{144}$$

Multiplying both sides of the equation $\frac{h}{144} = \sin 72°$ by 144 yields the value of h, which is 144 sin 72°.

Question 38.   **The correct answer is G.**   The midpoint of a line segment is the point halfway between the 2 endpoints of the line segment. A formula for finding the midpoint (x_m, y_m) of 2 points (x_1, y_1) and (x_2, y_2) in the standard (x, y) coordinate plane is

$$(x_m, y_m) = \left(\frac{x_1 + x_2}{2}, \frac{y_1 + y_2}{2} \right).$$ The x-coordinate of the midpoint, x_m, is the *average* of the x-coordinates

of the endpoints of the line segment. In the case of $\overline{GH}$, $x_m = \frac{x_1 + x_2}{2} = \frac{-8 + 2}{2} = -3$.

Question 39.   **The correct answer is B.**   You can find the distance, d, in coordinate units, between the 2 towns by using the *distance formula*. The distance between $(-2, -3)$ and $(-6, -7)$ is $d = \sqrt{(-2 - (-6))^2 + (-3 - (-7))^2} = \sqrt{4^2 + 4^2} = \sqrt{32}$ coordinate units.

You can also find d geometrically by envisioning the right triangle shown below in the standard (x, y) coordinate plane. Since $(-6, -7)$ and $(-2, -7)$ lie on the same horizontal line, the distance between them is equal to the positive difference of the x-coordinates: $(-2) - (-6) = 4$ coordinate units. Similarly, since $(-2, -3)$ and $(-2, -7)$ lie on the same vertical line, the distance between them is equal to the positive difference of the y-coordinates: $(-3) - (-7) = 4$ coordinate units. The length of the hypotenuse, d, can be found by using the Pythagorean theorem. Since $d^2 = 4^2 + 4^2$,

$d = \sqrt{4^2 + 4^2} = \sqrt{32}$ coordinate units.

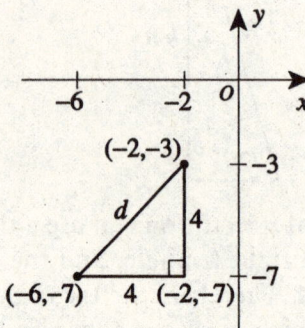

Since each unit on the map represents an actual distance of 10 miles, one can find the actual distance between the 2 towns by evaluating the expression ($\sqrt{32}$ coordinate units) × (10 miles per coordinate unit) ≈ 57 miles.

Question 40. **The correct answer is K.** In this problem, you are asked to choose the statement that is *always* true. You can approach this problem by attempting to find a *counterexample* for each statement: a specific example (such as a choice of values) for which the statement is false. You can find counterexamples for 4 of the 5 answer choices. Since the answer choices are statements about rational and irrational numbers, you will want to use irrational and rational numbers as counterexamples.

For **F**, the irrational numbers $\sqrt{2}$ and $\sqrt{8}$ are counterexamples because $(\sqrt{2})(\sqrt{8}) = \sqrt{16} = 4$, a *rational* number.

For **G**, the irrational numbers $\sqrt{14}$ and $\sqrt{2}$ are counterexamples because $\frac{\sqrt{14}}{\sqrt{2}} = \sqrt{7}$, an *irrational* number.

For **H**, the rational numbers 3 and 4 are counterexamples because $(3)(4) = 12$, a *rational* number.

For **J**, the irrational numbers 15 and 5 are counterexamples because $\frac{15}{5} = 3$, a *rational* number.

This leaves **K** as the one statement remaining. To be sure that it *must* be true, you may want to prove it.

The statement in **K** says that the sum of 2 rational number must a rational number. A rational number is any number that can be expressed as a fraction whose numerator and denominator are both integers. Testing simple examples may help you satisfy yourself that this is true: adding the rational numbers $\frac{1}{2}$ and $\frac{2}{3}$ produces $\frac{1(3) + 7(2)}{(2)(3)}$, or $\frac{7}{6}$, which is rational. In general, whenever a, b, c, and d are integers and b and d are nonzero, $\frac{a}{b} + \frac{c}{d} = \frac{ad + bc}{bd}$, which is rational since $ad + bc$ and bd are integers.

Question 41. **The correct answer is B.** By definition, $i^2 = -1$, so $i^4 = (i^2)^2 = (-1)^2 = 1$. Therefore, $i^x = 1$ for $x = 4$, so 1 is a possible value of i^x when x is an integer. More generally, when x is an integer, the only values of i^x possible are i, -1, $-i$, and 1, as shown in the table below.

...	i^{-3}	i^{-2}	i^{-1}	i^0	i^1	i^2	i^3	i^4	i^5	i^6	i^7	i^8	i^9	i^{10}	i^{11}	i^{12}	...
...	i	-1	$-i$	1	i	-1	$-i$	1	i	-1	$-i$	1	i	-1	$-i$	1	...

This rules out **A, C, D,** and **E**.

Question 42.   The correct answer is H.   The graph in the standard (x,y) coordinate plane that represents an equation of the form $y = a(x - h)^2 + k$ is a parabola. The minimum point of the parabola is at (h,k) when a is positive, and the maximum point is at (h,k) when a is negative. Here, $a = 1$, so a is positive. The graph representing $y = (x - 3)^2 + 2$ is a parabola with minimum point at $(3,2)$. So the minimum value of y is at $x = 3$.

You can also determine the correct answer by using the table shown in the problem. All parabolas represented by equations of the form $y = a(x - h)^2 + k$ have a vertical line of symmetry that contains the minimum (or maximum) point. Close examination of 2 pairs of points—$(0,11)$ and $(6,11)$, and $(2,3)$ and $(4,3)$—in the table (and on the parabola) show that each pair is symmetric with respect to the line $x = 3$, as shown in the figure below.

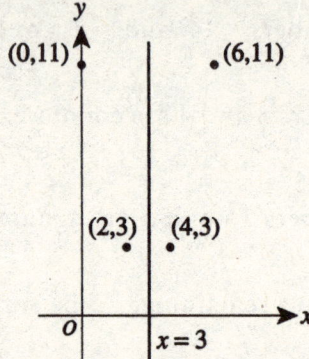

Question 43.   The correct answer is C.   The volume in cubic meters, V, of a right circular cylinder of radius r meters and height h meters is given by the formula $V = \pi r^2 h$. For the cylinder in this problem, $r = 5$ and $h = 6$. Therefore, $V = \pi(5^2)(6) = 150\pi$ cubic meters.

Question 44.   The correct answer is F.   The 3 triangles in the given figure ($\triangle ABC$, $\triangle ADE$, and $\triangle AFG$) can be shown to be similar by use of the *AA Similarity* property.

Since $\triangle ABC \sim \triangle AFG$, the phrase "The ratio of the perimeter of $\triangle ABC$ to the perimeter of $\triangle AFG$ is 1:3" implies that the ratio of AC to AG is 1:3. So if $AC = 1$ unit, then $AG = 3$ units (see Figure 1 below).

Since $\triangle ADE \sim \triangle AFG$, the phrase "The ratio of DE to FG is 2:3" implies that the ratio of AE to AG is 2:3. So if $AG = 3$ units, then $AE = 2$ units (see Figure 2 below).

This means that $AE = 2$ units when $AC = 1$ unit, implying that $CE = 1$ unit (see Figure 3 below). Therefore, the ratio of AC to CE is 1:1.

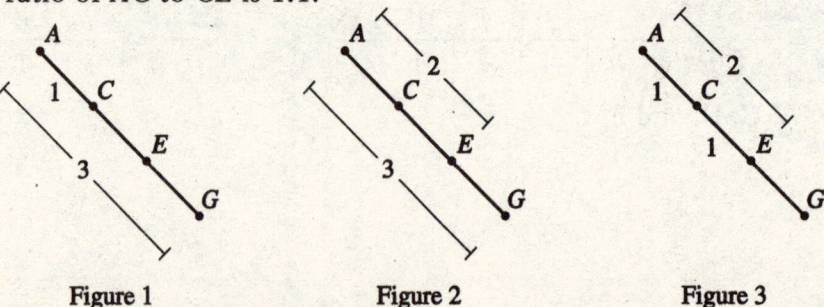

Figure 1   Figure 2   Figure 3

Question 45. The correct answer is E. Figure 1 below shows the 1st phase, when the rocket traveled vertically 30 kilometers.

Figure 2 below shows the 2nd phase, when the rocket traveled 40 km at 30° from the vertical. The 3 distances shown in Figure 2 are in the ratio $1:\sqrt{3}:2$, a characteristic of 30°-60°-90° triangles. The vertical distance covered in the 2nd phase is $20\sqrt{3}$ km.

Figure 3 below shows the 3rd phase, when the rocket traveled 100 km at 45° from the vertical. The 3 distances shown in Figure 3 are in the ratio $1:1:\sqrt{2}$, a characteristic of 45°-45°-90° triangles. The vertical distance covered in the 3rd phase is $50\sqrt{2}$ km.

Taking the sum of the vertical distances covered by each of the 3 phases gives the vertical distance of the rocket above the launch pad after the 3rd phase.

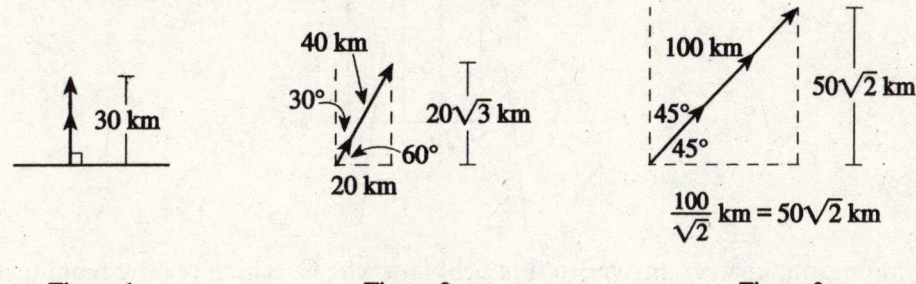

| Figure 1 | Figure 2 | Figure 3 |

Question 46. The correct answer is H. The general equation of a circle with radius r and center at (h,k) in the standard (x,y) coordinate plane is $(x - h)^2 + (y - k)^2 = r^2$. The area A of this circle is given by the formula $A = \pi r^2$. The equation $(x - 0)^2 + (y - 0)^2 = 4^2$ is equivalent to $x^2 + y^2 = 16$, meaning that the circle has a radius equal to 4 coordinate units. Therefore, $A = \pi(4^2) = 16\pi$ square coordinate units.

Question 47.   The correct answer is A. Because the parabola is symmetric about the y-axis, the variable a represents the distance of each of the 4 vertices of the rectangle from the y-axis. As a result, the rectangle will have a width of $a + a = (2a)$ coordinate units and a height of $(6 - 2a^2)$ coordinate units (see the figure below). The area of the rectangle is the product of the width and height: $(2a)(6 - 2a^2) = 12a - 4a^3 = (-4a^3 + 12a)$ coordinate units.

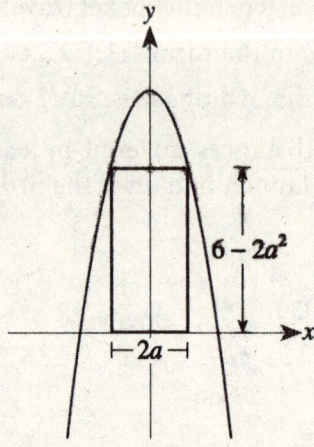

The most common incorrect answer to this problem was C, which results from using the formula for the perimeter of a rectangle.

Question 48.   The correct answer is F. You can solve this problem by finding counterexamples for 4 of the expressions, and then proving that the remaining expression must always be odd.

To find counterexamples, pick a positive integer value for n, like $n = 4$. When $n = 4$, G and H are *even* integers and J is not an integer. If you pick $n = 5$, K is an *even* integer.

For F, you can use the fact that the product of 2 odd integers is an odd integer. So, the product of any number of odd integers is an odd integer.

Since 3 is odd and $3^n = \underbrace{3 \times 3 \times 3 \times \ldots \times 3}_{n \text{ times}}$, 3^n is the product of n odd integers. Therefore, the value of 3^n is an odd integer.

Question 49. **The correct answer is D.** The value of $\log_5(5^{\frac{13}{2}})$ is found by solving the equation $\log_5(5^{\frac{13}{2}}) = x$. By definition of logarithm to the base 5, this equation is equivalent to the equation $5^x = 5^{\frac{13}{2}}$. The equation $5^x = 5^{\frac{13}{2}}$ is equivalent to the equation $x = \frac{13}{2}$, whose value is between 6 and 7.

Question 50. **The correct answer is J.** When comparing 2 values, an earlier value and a later value, finding the *percent increase* is equivalent to finding the percent of the earlier value that should be added to the earlier value to obtain the later value. In other words, you can first find the difference between the 2 values, and then answer the question, What percent is this difference of the earlier value? This procedure is summarized by the formula below.

$$\text{percent increase} = \frac{\text{later value} - \text{earlier value}}{\text{earlier value}} \times 100\%$$

Applying the formula to the problem gives percent increase $= \frac{156 - 144}{144} \times 100\% \approx 8.3\%$.

The most common incorrect answer was **F**, a choice that results from misinterpreting the percent increase as being the ratio of the later value to the earlier value $\left(\frac{156}{144} \approx 1.1\right)$.

Question 51. **The correct answer is D.** Let s = the meat sales, in thousands of dollars, for Week 6. You can find the correct answer by setting up and solving the algebraic sentence below. Note that because the problem asks for a *minimum*, this sentence is an inequality.

(Average weekly meat sales, in thousands, for Weeks 3 through 6) ≥ 150

So $\dfrac{\text{the sum of meat sales, in thousands, for Weeks 3, 4, 5, and 6}}{\text{the number of weeks}} \geq 150$

and $\dfrac{156 + 145 + 140 + s}{4} \geq 150$.

Multiplying both sides of the inequality by 4 gives $156 + 145 + 140 + s \geq 4(150)$, or equivalently, $441 + s \geq 600$. Subtracting 441 from both sides gives $s \geq 159$. The minimum possible value of s is 159.

To quickly verify the solution, you can calculate the average meat sales for the 4 weeks when the meat sales for Week 6 are \$159 thousand: $\dfrac{156 + 145 + 140 + 159}{4} = 150$.

Question 52.   **The correct answer is G.**   Increasing a value by 10% is the same as multiplying that value by (1 + 0.10) = 1.10. You can use this fact to calculate weekly produce department sales for Weeks 2 through 5, based upon a 10% increase from the previous week.

Week	Produce department sales (thousands of dollars)
2	30(1.10) = 33
3	33(1.10) = 36.3
4	36.3(1.10) = 39.93
5	39.93(1.10) = 43.923

The closest choice to produce department sales for Week 5 is 44. If you obtained the most common incorrect answer, **H**, you may have assumed that the weekly *dollar increase* (as opposed to the *percent increase*) was constant from week to week. Under this assumption, the increase from Week 1 to Week 2 would be 3 thousand dollars, and sales for the following weeks would increase as follows: 33 + 3 = 36 for Week 2 to Week 3, 36 + 3 = 39 for Week 3 to Week 4, and 39 + 3 = 42 for Week 4 to Week 5.

Question 53.   **The correct answer is B.**   The graph of any trigonometric function of the form $y = a \sin (bx + c)$ is cyclical. That is, the graph is composed of repeating, identical *cycles*. The shaded region in the graph below shows one such cycle. The *period* of the function is the width of the smallest interval of x on which one of these cycles appears. In the graph below, the period is the width of the shaded region, given by $2\pi - \pi = \pi$.

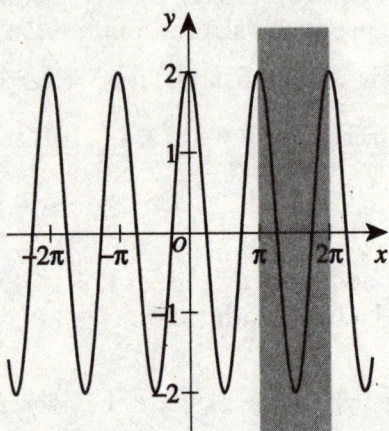

The period of $y = \sin x$ is 2π, which is **C**, the most common incorrect answer. If you chose **E**, you may have confused *period* with *amplitude*.

Question 54.   The correct answer is K. In this problem, the sine of the angle of elevation is given, suggesting that you should use the hypotenuse (the distance from the tip of the shadow to the top of the building) to find the length of the side opposite the angle of elevation (the height). What makes this problem more complex than the typical right-triangle trigonometry problem, however, is that the length of the side adjacent to the angle of elevation (and not the hypotenuse) is given. Therefore, the tangent ratio (the ratio using the opposite and adjacent sides) for the angle of elevation must be found.

Designate the angle of elevation as $\angle A$. Using the 3-4-5 right triangle shown below, you can

see that $\sin (\angle A) = \dfrac{4}{5} = \dfrac{\text{the length of the side opposite } \angle A}{\text{the length of the hypotenuse}}$, so that $\tan (\angle A) =$

$\dfrac{\text{the length of the side opposite } \angle A}{\text{the length of the side adjacent to } \angle A} = \dfrac{4}{3}$.

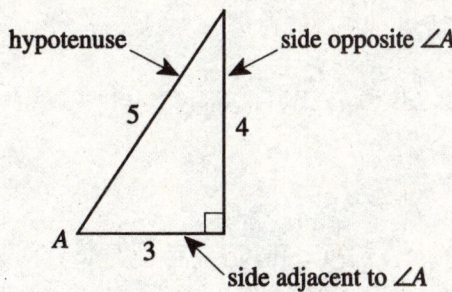

Therefore, $\tan (\angle A) = \dfrac{\text{the height of the building}}{\text{the length of the shadow}}$, so $\dfrac{4}{3} = \dfrac{\text{the height of the building}}{24}$, so that the height

of the building is $\dfrac{4}{3}(24)$, or 32 yards.

Question 55.   The correct answer is C. You should notice that $|x^2 - 12| - 4 = 0$ can be written as $|x^2 - 12| = 4$; so $x^2 - 12 = \pm 4$. Thus, either $x^2 = 12 - 4 = 8$, or $x^2 = 12 + 4 = 16$. Now $x^2 = 16$ when $x = \pm 4$, but both of these solutions are *rational*. When $x^2 = 8$, then $x = \pm\sqrt{8} = \pm 2\sqrt{2}$, and both of these solutions are *irrational*; of these, only $2\sqrt{2}$ is given as a choice.

Question 56.   The correct answer is K. The graph indicates there are changes of action at 4 seconds and 9 seconds. The endpoints on the graph and the points at which each change of action occurs can be used to calculate Malika's rates of movement in the time intervals 0 to 4 seconds, 4 to 9 seconds, and 9 to 10 seconds. The calculations are shown in the table below.

Time (seconds)	Distance from detector (feet)		
0	10	average rate $= \dfrac{(10-2)\text{ feet}}{(0-4)\text{ seconds}} = -2$ feet per second $\Rightarrow$	The distance between Malika and the detector is decreasing at a rate of 2 feet per second (Action V).
4	2		
4	2	average rate $= \dfrac{(2-2)\text{ feet}}{(4-9)\text{ seconds}} = 0$ feet per second $\Rightarrow$	The distance between Malika and the detector remains constant (Action I).
9	2		
9	2	average rate $= \dfrac{(2-6)\text{ feet}}{(9-10)\text{ seconds}} = 4$ feet per second $\Rightarrow$	The distance between Malika and the detector is increasing at a rate of 4 feet per second (Action II).
10	6		

Therefore the order of actions is V, I, II. In calculating the rates, be careful with the order of placement of the coordinates in the fractions, as this will affect the sign (positive or negative) of the rate. One such sign error results in H (the most common incorrect answer choice).

Question 57.   The correct answer is D. The distance traveled by the tip of the minute hand in 1 hour is equal to the circumference of the circle formed by the path of the tip, which is $2\pi \times$ radius $= 2\pi \times (5\text{ cm}) = 10\pi$ cm for this clock. The distance traveled by the tip in 20 minutes (or $\frac{20}{60} = \frac{1}{3}$ hour) is $\frac{1}{3} \times 10\pi = \frac{10}{3}\pi$ cm. Therefore the distance traveled by the tip of the minute hand in 3 hours and 20 minutes equals $\left(3(10\pi) + \frac{10}{3}\pi\right) \approx 105$ cm.

Question 58.   The correct answer is K.   The figure below shows the standard position of ϕ in the standard (x,y) coordinate plane. Note that since ϕ has a measure between 90° and 180°, the terminal side of the angle will be in Quadrant II. The angle θ shown in the figure is the *reference angle* for ϕ. The relationship between the tangent of ϕ and the tangent of its reference angle θ is given by $\tan \theta = |\tan \phi| = \frac{7}{24}$. By similarity, any right triangle having one vertical side, one side along the x-axis, and one side along the terminal side of ϕ will have a side length ratio of 7:24:25 and 1 angle measure of θ (as shown in the figure).

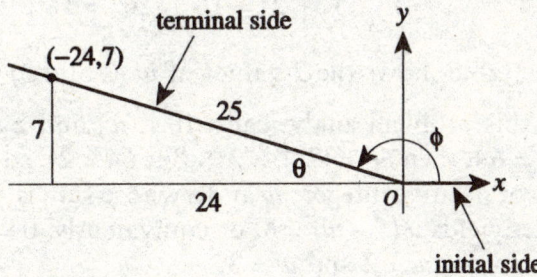

The right triangle having 1 vertex at $(-24,7)$ is shown in the figure. From this you can see that $\tan \theta = \frac{7}{24} = \frac{\text{the length of the side opposite } \theta}{\text{the length of the side adjacent to } \theta}$, and $\sin \theta = \frac{\text{the length of the side opposite } \theta}{\text{the length of the hypotenuse}} = \frac{7}{25}$. As in the case of the tangent, $\sin \theta = |\sin \phi|$, so $|\sin \phi| = \frac{7}{25}$. Since the sine values of all angles with measures between 90° and 180° are positive, $\sin \phi = \frac{7}{25}$.

Question 59. **The correct answer is B.** A numerical approach to the problem is shown in the table below. The table shows all possible pairs of values for w and z.

w	z	$2^w = x$	x^z
1	4	$2^1 = 2$	$2^4 = 16$
2	3	$2^2 = 4$	$4^3 = 64$
3	2	$2^3 = 8$	$8^2 = 64$
4	1	$2^4 = 16$	$16^1 = 16$

The shaded region in the table shows the 2 values of w (2 and 3) that satisfy both conditions.

You can also approach this problem analytically. If x, w, and z are positive integers such that $w + z = 5$, $2^w = x$, and $x^z = 64$, then $64 = (2^w)^z = 2^{wz}$. But $64 = 2^6$, so it must be true that $wz = 6$. So you need to find all pairs of positive integers w and z whose sum is 5 and product is 6. Substituting $5 - w$ for z in the product yields $w(5 - w) = 6$, or equivalently, $0 = w^2 - 5w + 6 = (w - 2)(w - 3)$. So, there are 2 solutions for w, $w = 2$ and $w = 3$.

Question 60. **The correct answer is F.** First, find the diameter of the sphere, which is equal to the length of the diagonal of the inscribed cube (represented by d in the figure below).

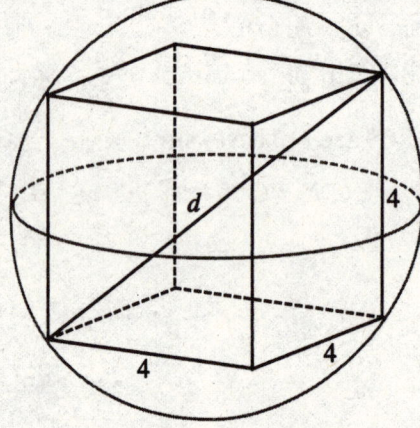

The length of the diagonal of any rectangular prism equals

$\sqrt{(\text{the length})^2 + (\text{the width})^2 + (\text{the height})^2}$. In the case of the cube shown in the figure,

$d = \sqrt{4^2 + 4^2 + 4^2} = \sqrt{3(4^2)} = 4\sqrt{3}$ cm. If you stopped at this point in the calculation, you

probably chose **H**, which was the most common incorrect answer. But the problem asks for the

radius of the sphere, which is $\frac{1}{2}(4\sqrt{3}) = 2\sqrt{3}$ cm.

Passage I

Question 1. The best answer is **A** because the passage identifies Shades Bowen as one of the other local musicians in the "bullpen" (lines 5–6) and goes on to state that, of those local musicians, Everett Payne "was the one being invited to sit in" (line 15) and play with the band that night. In this context, "the one" indicates that only Everett was sitting in, and no mention is made in the passage of any other musician sitting in.

The best answer is NOT:

B because while the passage indicates that Everett Payne is "not long out of the army" (lines 14–15), the passage makes no mention of Shades Bowen having been in the army as well.

C because while the passage refers to all the people in the "bullpen" as "young locals" (line 9), the passage makes no mention of Shades Bowen's age.

D because the passage states that Everett Payne joined Shades Bowen in the "bullpen" (lines 5–7) where "young locals gathered . . . each Sunday evening, hoping for a chance to perform" (lines 9–10). This indicates that Shades Bowen was a local musician himself, and there is no indication in the passage that Shades Bowen had any role in deciding which other local musicians were allowed to play with the band.

Question 2. The best answer is **G** because the statement in question (line 62) describes the audience's physical reaction to Everett Payne's performance. This performance is described in great detail in lines 48–61 as being impressive enough to warrant such a reaction.

The best answer is NOT:

F because the statement in question (line 62) refers to the audience's physical reaction to the improvisational passages that Payne played after he had taken his time "paying his respects to the tune as written" (lines 48–49). This indicates that the audience reaction was not based on "initial expectations" but rather on later developments in the playing of the song "Sonny Boy Blue."

H because the statement in question (line 62) supports, rather than counteracts, the narrator's description of Payne's performance.

J because there is no mention in the passage that anyone other than the narrator knows who Payne is.

Question 3. The best answer is **A** because the passage describes the jazz show as "winding down" (line 1) near the end of the second set. This implies the second set is the show's final set.

The best answer is NOT:

B because there is no description in the passage of the first set or of the length of either the first or the second set.

C because the narrator mentions that the show is "winding down" (lines 1–2), which suggests that there will be no third set.

D because the passage states that the jazz show is "nearing the end of the second set" (lines 1–2) when the musicians in the "bullpen" were called up to play. If the *entire* second set was performed solely by musicians from the "bullpen," then they would not be "called up to play" only toward the end of that set.

Question 4. **The best answer is H** because the passage states that when the purists first heard Payne's choice of music, they "slouched deeper in their chairs in open disgust" (lines 36–37).

The best answer is NOT:

F because while the passage mentions the silence following Payne's performance (lines 81–83), there is no specific mention of the audience reacting to Payne's choice of music with silence.

G because the audience's in-suck of breath (line 62) is in response to Payne's performance, not to his choice of music.

J because the purists stood up at the end of Payne's performance "in languid praise" (line 88) of Payne, not as a reaction to Payne's choice of music.

Question 5. **The best answer is C** because the narrator describes how she watched as Payne "slowly mounted the bandstand and conferred with the bassist and drummer" (lines 26–27).

The best answer is NOT:

A because Payne did not move quickly to the bandstand. Rather, the narrator describes him as moving with "a deliberate pause between each step" (lines 18–19).

B because the narrator describes Payne as sitting down to play "without in any way acknowledging the audience" (line 30).

D because the narrator says that Payne sat down at the piano "without announcing the name of the tune he intended playing" (lines 28–29).

Question 6. **The best answer is G** because the purists are described as reacting negatively to Payne because of his choice of song before even hearing him play (lines 35–37), suggesting intolerance. They are also described as normally refusing "to applaud even genius" (line 87), implying snobbishness.

The best answer is NOT:

F because while the term "purist" in the context of a jazz audience suggests that they may be knowledgeable about jazz music, the purists in this audience are described as reacting negatively to Payne because of his choice of song before even hearing him play (lines 35–37), suggesting that they are intolerant rather than open-minded.

H because the passage makes no mention of whether or not the purists are educated. Additionally, the purists are not portrayed as rational, as they normally refuse to acknowledge a praiseworthy performance (lines 86–87).

J because while the purists may be "uninhibited" in that they visibly react or do not react to performances as they please, the passage makes no mention of their "inexperience" regarding jazz. In fact, the opposite impression is created by the purists' initial disgust at the prospect of hearing a "hokey" (line 38), or old-fashioned, tune like "Sonny Boy Blue." Moreover, the term "purist" in general denotes someone devoted to the most essential or "pure" expression of a particular idea or practice, and such devotion usually indicates a deep familiarity with the object of their devotion rather than "inexperience."

Question 7. The best answer is **B** because the narrator refers to Bach and the blues as being the "bedrock" on which Payne had been trained (lines 76–77).

The best answer is NOT:

A because there is nothing in the passage to suggest that Everett did anything to avoid representing Bach and the blues when he played piano.

C because the narrator describes Bach and the blues as being "earthbound" (line 76) and "the bedrock" (line 76) of Payne's musical inspiration. Moreover, the narrator contrasts these influences, which Payne hears through "his other ear" (line 75) with "the true music of the spheres" (lines 72–73), which he hears through "his right ear directed skyward" (line 68).

D because the passage does not imply that Everett is limited to "Tin Pan Alley" tunes. Rather, the passage states that Everett "recast" and "reinvented" the Tin Pan Alley tune "Sonny Boy Blue" "in an image all his own" (lines 60–61).

Question 8. The best answer is **F** because the passage indicates that Payne first played the song "at a slower tempo than was called for" (line 41).

The best answer is NOT:

G because there is no indication in the passage that Payne spoke with anyone other than the bassist and the drummer.

H because while the passage states that Payne conferred with the bassist and the drummer (line 27), there is no mention in the passage that either the bassist or the drummer had any reaction to what Payne said to them.

J because when Payne first played "Sonny Boy Blue," he played the song "straight through as written" (line 39). The passage also states that throughout Payne's performance, he "continued to acknowledge the little simple-minded tune" (lines 59–60).

Question 9. The best answer is **A** because Hattie speculates that Payne's talent "had to do . . . with the way he held his head. . . . tilted" (lines 65–67).

The best answer is NOT:

B because the narrator never mentions the simplemindedness of the tune as being related to Payne's musical ideas and feelings. Rather, the characterization of "Sonny Boy Blue" as a "little simple-minded tune" (lines 59–60) creates a contrast between Payne's elaborate and inventive improvisations and the simple and overly familiar song that he chooses as a vehicle for those improvisations.

C because while the narrator mentions Payne's formality in playing through the parts of "Sonny Boy Blue" the first time (lines 42–43), the narrator does not identify this formality as the source of the musical ideas and feelings showcased in Payne's improvisations.

D because the passage makes no mention of any connection Payne feels with his audience. Rather, the passage states that Payne does not even acknowledge his audience before playing (line 30).

Question 10. The best answer is **J** because the passage states that Payne's performance seemed to Hattie "a joyous, terrifying roller coaster of a ride" (lines 78–79).

The best answer is NOT:

F because while the passage states that Payne's rendition of the song began slowly and formally (lines 41–43), the passage goes on to contrast this beginning with a lengthy improvisational section described in terms that indicate that Hattie found the performance as a whole anything but formal (lines 49–61).

G because there is no indication in the passage that Hattie considers Payne's musical performance absentminded. Instead, she describes his body "moving absentmindedly through space" as he approaches the bandstand to play (lines 20–21).

H because the narrator does not describe Payne's performance of "Sonny Boy Blue" as resembling a song played in church. Rather, she describes the audience reacting to Payne's performance "as if they were in church and weren't supposed to clap" (lines 82–83).

Passage II

Question 11. The best answer is **A** because the passage as a whole presents a cohesive argument that sprawl is both unpleasant and harmful (lines 9–10, 25–27, 33–37, 44–47, 59–61, 74–79), that its destructive effects are too often ignored (lines 11–16), that characterizations of sprawl as either inevitable or desirable are flawed (lines 17–19, 52–54, 62–66), that policies currently in place encourage sprawl to continue (lines 19–22, 67–74), and that there are a set of alternative policies which, if adopted, would resist sprawl and reduce these harmful effects (80–91). The overall effect of these linked propositions is to persuade the reader that a choice must be made between a proven harm and a beneficial alternative. Moreover, the language used to describe sprawl throughout the passage is consistently negative, including, for example, the initial identification of sprawl as a "destructive, soulless, ugly mess" (lines 9–10). In contrast to these descriptions, communities without sprawl are described as "places that people care about" (line 35) or characterized as representing a "compact walkable environment" (70–71). Drawing a contrast between attractive and unattractive descriptions, as this passage does, is a common tactic of persuasive rhetoric.

The best answer is NOT:

B because while the author explains what sprawl is, the main purpose of the passage is not merely to explain what sprawl is, but to argue for measures that would control sprawl and "knit communities together" (line 89).

C because while the author does describe sprawl throughout the passage, these descriptions are more often colorful and emotional than they are precise and exact. For example, sprawl is initially characterized as a "destructive, soulless, ugly mess" (lines 9–10). In contrast, communities without sprawl are described as "places that people care about" (line 35) or characterized as representing a "compact walkable environment" (70–71). Drawing a contrast between attractive and unattractive descriptions, as this passage does, is a common tactic of persuasive rather than descriptive rhetoric. Therefore the principal aim of the passage is persuasive rather than descriptive.

D because the passage does not tell a story. Rather, it informs the reader of a problem and urges the reader not only to see sprawl as a problem as well, but also to take measures to solve the problem.

Question 12. The best answer is **J** because after describing the effect of sprawl on communities, and criticizing policies that encourage sprawl, the author proposes the adoption of policies that discourage sprawl, such as "downtown housing and mixed-use zoning" (lines 85–86) and goes on to explain that "the goal should be an integrated system of planning decisions and regulations that knit communities together instead of tearing them apart" (lines 87–90). Therefore, in the context of the sentence in which it appears and in the context of the entire passage, the establishment of "an integrated system of planning decisions and regulations" is clearly something that the author would like to see happen.

The best answer is NOT:

F because the full sentence in question reads "Too many developers follow standard formulas, and too many government entities have adopted laws and policies that constitute powerful incentives for sprawl" (lines 19–22). The author's opposition to the laws in question is signaled within the sentence by the assertion that "too many government entities" enact them. In the context of the sentence in which it appears and in the context of the author's criticism of sprawl throughout the passage, the enactment of "laws . . . that provide powerful incentives for sprawl" is not something that the author would like to see happen.

G because "the destruction of traditional downtowns" (line 34) is presented as an end result of sprawl and as something which "is corroding the very sense of community that helps bind us together as a people and as a nation" (lines 35–37). In the context of the sentence in which it appears and in the context of the author's criticism of sprawl throughout the passage, "the destruction of traditional downtowns" is not something that the author would like to see happen.

H because the author explains that "'affordable' housing on the edge of town" (line 53) is only more affordable for developers (line 55) and that the construction of this housing, which is a familiar form of sprawl (lines 48–50), requires "higher taxes for needless duplication of services and infrastructure" (lines 59–60). In the context of the sentence in which it appears and in the context of the author's criticism of sprawl throughout the passage, the construction of housing like this is not something that the author would like to see happen.

Question 13. The best answer is **D** because in the first paragraph the author defines sprawl as a problem, while in the last paragraph, the author offers possible solutions to this problem, including "sensible land-use planning" (line 82), "mixed-use zoning" (lines 85–86), and "an integrated system of planning decisions and regulations" (lines 87–88).

The best answer is NOT:

A because the author does not ask a question at any point in the final paragraph. Rather, the author offers solutions to the problem explained throughout the passage.

B because the author mentions no specific statistics in the final paragraph.

C because the final paragraph does not incorporate more emotional language than the first. If anything, the opposite may be true. In the first paragraph, the author uses emotionally loaded language to encourage the reader to agree that the "destructive, soulless, ugly mess called sprawl" (lines 9–10) is a serious problem. In contrast, the last paragraph, while arguing that "our communities should be shaped by choice, not by chance" (lines 80–81), uses more precise and less emotional language to describe possible solutions to the problem of sprawl, such as "an integrated system of planning decisions and regulations" (lines 87–88). This less emotional language encourages the reader to agree that these solutions may be effective.

Question 14. The best answer is **F** because the passage makes no mention of how long the problem of sprawl has been happening in U.S. cities.

The best answer is NOT:

G because the author answers this question in lines 17–18: "Development that destroys communities isn't progress. It's chaos."

H because the author argues that current zoning laws, which make construction of a "walkable environment" impossible, "are a major reason why 82 percent of all trips taken in the United States are taken by car (lines 69–74).

J because the author offers solutions to the problem of what to do to combat sprawl in the final paragraph in the passage.

Question 15. The best answer is **B** because the passage does not support the idea that the opening of a superstore leads to downtown renovations. Rather, the passage states that, after a superstore opens in a small town, "downtown becomes a ghost town" (lines 46–47).

The best answer is NOT:

A because the author states that "in many small towns, a single new superstore may have more retail space than the entire downtown business district" (lines 42–44).

C because the author states that, after a superstore opens in a small town, "downtown becomes a ghost town" (lines 46–47).

D because the author states that, when a superstore opens in a small town, "the retail center of gravity shifts away from Main Street" (lines 45–46).

Question 16. The best answer is **H** because the statistics in question (lines 73–76) show that a significant majority of all trips taken in the United States are taken by car, and that American families spend a significant portion of their budget on transportation expenses. The author argues that these statistics regarding automobile transportation and its costs represent the effects of land use regulations that make it impossible to construct a "compact walkable environment" (lines 69–71).

The best answer is NOT:

F because the statistics in question (lines 73–76) do not support the idea that mixed-use zoning leads to environmental destruction. Rather, they show that a significant majority of all trips taken in the United States are taken by car, and that American families spend a significant portion of their budget on transportation. According to the author, the dependence on automobile transportation is a result of current zoning laws "prohibiting mixed uses" (line 67). Because this dependence on automobile transportation is associated with sprawl, which is associated with environmental destruction throughout the passage, the statistics in question support the argument that it is the prohibition of mixed-use zoning, rather than mixed-use zoning itself, that creates environmental destruction (line 67).

G because the statistics in question (lines 73–76) show that a significant majority of all trips taken in the United States are taken by car, and that American families spend a significant portion of their budget on transportation expenses. The author argues that these statistics regarding automobile transportation and its costs represent the effects of land-use regulations that make it impossible to construct a "compact walkable environment" (lines 69–71).

J because the statistics in question do not support the idea that Americans spend too much of their budgets on food and health care. Rather, the passage states that "the average American household now allocates more than 18 percent of its budget to transportation expenses" and that this is "more than it spends for food and three times more than it spends for health care" (lines 74–79). This strongly suggests that Americans spend too much on transportation, rather than suggesting that they spend too much on food and health care.

Question 17. The best answer is C because the passage refers to "retail development that transforms roads into strip malls" (lines 38–39).

The best answer is NOT:

A because the author discusses the type of sprawl that develops far away from town centers (line 30), not adjacent to them.

B because the author argues that the development of sprawl leads to the neglect of historic buildings in towns (lines 26–27), not that sprawl leads to the utilization of these buildings.

D because the author argues that the construction of superstores is part of a process whereby "the retail center of gravity shifts away from Main Street" and "downtown becomes a ghost town" (lines 45–47). This strongly suggests that superstores are associated with the destruction, rather than the promotion, of a sense of community in the towns in which they are constructed.

Question 18. The best answer is G because the sentence describes these "detached homes" as being located in "residential subdivisions that 'leapfrog' from the urban fringe into the countryside" (lines 49–50). Because *leapfrog* means that there is open space between that urban fringe and the subdivisions in question, this suggests that *detached* in this context refers to homes located in subdivisions that are "set apart" from urban areas.

The best answer is NOT:

F because while the word *detached* can indicate an objective point of view, *detached* is used in this context to describe a house (line 51), which cannot have a point of view.

H because the sentence describes these "detached homes" as being built in "residential subdivisions that 'leapfrog' from the urban fringe into the countryside" (lines 49–50). While the term *leapfrog* does suggest that the homes and the subdivisions in which they are located are separated from urban areas, there is no suggestion that the homes are mobile in any way and therefore have not been "broken apart" from anywhere or anything.

J because the sentence describes these "detached homes" as being located in "residential subdivisions that 'leapfrog' from the urban fringe into the countryside" (lines 49–50). While the term *leapfrog* does suggest that the homes and the subdivisions in which they are located are separated from urban areas, there is no suggestion that the homes are mobile in any way and therefore have not been "taken away" from anything or anywhere.

Question 19. The best answer is **D** because the statement in question is preceded by, and is intended to counter, the claim made by some people that "sprawl is merely the natural product of marketplace forces at work" (lines 62–63). Therefore, the author is arguing that people who make this claim "fail to recognize" (line 63) that those market forces are influenced by governmental decisions. The author's rhetoric here assumes that the reader will recognize "a level playing field" as a popular term for conditions governed purely by market forces, and will understand that a playing field that isn't "level" (line 64) refers to conditions where governmental decisions *do* influence market forces.

The best answer is NOT:

A because the "needless duplication of services and infrastructure" (line 60) referred to in the passage is identified as a *result* of sprawl, while the phrase "the game isn't being played on a level field" (line 64) is used to identify the influence of governmental decisions on market forces, and not market forces alone, as a *cause* of sprawl.

B because the "higher taxes" (line 59) referred to in the passage are identified as a *result* of sprawl, while the phrase "the game isn't being played on a level field" (line 64) is used to identify the influence of governmental decisions on market forces, and not market forces alone, as a *cause* of sprawl.

C because the phrase "the game isn't being played on a level field" (line 64) is used to identify the influence of governmental decisions on market forces, and not market forces alone, as a cause of sprawl. The author's rhetoric here assumes that the reader will recognize "a level playing field" as a popular term for conditions governed purely by market forces, and will understand that a playing field that "isn't level" (line 64) refers to conditions where governmental decisions do influence market forces.

Question 20. The best answer is **J** because the passage identifies zoning laws that prohibit "mixed uses" (line 67) as a primary cause of the separation of urban commercial zones and residential subdivisions described in the three paragraphs that immediately precede the sentence in question (lines 48–66). That separation of commercial and residential land use is contrasted, in the following sentences, with "the sort of compact walkable environment that attracts us to older neighborhoods and historic communities all over the world (lines 70–72). Therefore the term *mixed uses* can be understood as referring to zoning that allows one area to contain various types of development.

The best answer is NOT:

F because the passage identifies both large parking lots (lines 3–4) and large retail stores (lines 38–42) as being characteristic of sprawl, which is encouraged by the prohibition of "mixed uses" (line 67). Furthermore, parking lots and retail stores are both understood to be commercial uses of land, and therefore the phrase *mixed uses* is unlikely to refer to them.

G because while the passage states that the prohibition of "mixed uses" (line 67) makes it "impossible—even illegal—to create the sort of compact walkable environment that attracts us to older neighborhoods and historic communities" (lines 69–72), the term *mixed uses* itself is not directly associated with historic preservation in any way. Rather, *mixed uses* refers to the designation of land use as residential, commercial, or industrial under zoning laws.

H because while "mixed uses" (line 67) are understood within the context of the passage as encouraging the creation of a "walkable environment" (line 71), there is no association between the term *mixed uses* and the prohibition of driving or parking.

Passage III

Question 21. The best answer is A because the passage begins by with the narrator's description of an incident in which she first became interested in identifying flowers and in the natural world (lines 1–24), and the remainder of the passage describes how this early interest developed into a larger part of her life.

The best answer is NOT:

B because while the identification of an aster is part of the incident (lines 1–24) that leads to the narrator's lifelong interest in flowers and the natural world, there is no mention in the passage of the author having a lifelong fascination for asters in particular. Rather, the incident in question leads to a lifelong fascination with identifying flowers in general.

C because while the author briefly mentions hiking with companions (lines 31–32) and identifying flowers with a friend (lines 81–82), the primary focus of the passage is on the author's individual interest in flowers and how that interest developed.

D because the author does not discuss her career in the passage.

Question 22. The best answer is H because the author describes the young man's answer to her question as containing "the hint of a sniff" (line 7), which indicates that she detected disdain or condescension in the tone of the young man's answer.

The best answer is NOT:

F because there is nothing in the passage to suggest that the guide treated the author with acceptance. Rather, his reaction to her question about the flower is described as containing "the hint of a sniff" (line 7), which indicates disdain or condescension, qualities that are incompatible with acceptance.

G because there is no mention in the passage of the guide being surprised by the author's question. Rather, his reaction is described as containing "the hint of a sniff" (line 7), which indicates disdain or condescension and not surprise.

J because there is no mention in the passage of the guide becoming angry with the author. Rather, his reaction to her question about the flower is described as containing "the hint of a sniff" (line 7), which indicates disdain or condescension and not anger.

Question 23. The best answer is D because while the author describes her efforts to identify a yellow flower on a particular hike (lines 30–51), she does not name the flower in question. Rather, she uses the description of this incident to explain her developing "intimacy" (line 28) with the book *A Field Guide to Wild Flowers*.

The best answer is NOT:

A, B, or C because while the author mentions St. Johnswort, loosestrife, and puccoon as "five-petaled yellow flowers" (lines 50–51) similar to the one she is trying to identify, she does not identify the flower in question as St. Johnswort (A), loosestrife (B), or puccoon (C).

Question 24. The best answer is F because the author states that though daunting at first, the book was neither too frustrating as a more basic book would have become nor too daunting as a more complex one would have been (lines 58–61).

The best answer is NOT:

G because the author indicates that the book was not easy to use in the beginning. Rather, it was difficult for her, but she "persisted in wrestling" (line 61) with the book until it became easier.

H because the author makes no mention in the passage of any other guide she used.

J because the author makes no negative statements about the illustrations in the guide.

Question 25. The best answer is C because the sentence in question reads "I had no choice, really, not if I wanted to *get in*" (lines 55–56), and the surrounding sentences indicate that the matter she had no choice in was the use of the field guide, which "led to the particulars" (line 57), or deepened her understanding, of the landscape. Therefore, in this context, to "get in" to a subject can be understood as meaning to fully understand that subject.

The best answer is NOT:

A because the sentence in question reads "I had no choice, really, not if I wanted to *get in*" (lines 55–56), and there is no indication in the surrounding lines that the matter she has no choice in is her arrival in a specific location. Rather, she wants to figuratively, and not literally, arrive at a deeper understanding of the landscape, and she has no choice but to use the field guide in order to do so (lines 55–58).

B because the sentence in question reads "I had no choice, really, not if I wanted to *get in*" (lines 55–56), and there is no indication in the surrounding lines or the passage as a whole that the matter she has no choice in has anything to do with membership in any group. Rather, she wants to figuratively, and not literally, "get in" to a deeper understanding of the landscape, and she has no choice but to use the field guide in order to do so (lines 55–58).

D because the sentence in question reads "I had no choice, really, not if I wanted to *get in*" (lines 55–56), and there is no indication in the surrounding lines or the passage as a whole that the matter she has no choice in has anything to do with being friendly with someone. Rather, she wants to figuratively, and not literally, "get in" to a deeper understanding of the landscape, and she has no choice but to use the field guide in order to do so (lines 55–58).

Question 26. The best answer is H because the author states that she and Julie began to see that their understanding of plant communities was valuable because it led to a greater understanding of larger issues such as "climate change and continental drift" (lines 85–86).

The best answer is NOT:

F because there is no information in the passage about Julie's level of experience in identifying plant life.

G because there is no information in the passage about Julie owning a house near a bog.

J because there is no information in the passage about whether or not Julie used the Peterson's guide.

Question 27. The best answer is D because the author states that "over the next several years this field guide would become my closest companion" (lines 25–26), specifying that she measures the period in question in "years."

The best answer is NOT:

A because the author states that "over the next several years this field guide would become my closest companion" (lines 25–26), specifying "years" and not days as the way in which she measures the period in question.

B because the author states that "over the next several years this field guide would become my closest companion" (lines 25–26), specifying "years" and not weeks as the way in which she measures the period in question.

C because the author states that "over the next several years this field guide would become my closest companion" (lines 25–26), specifying "years" and not months as the way in which she measures the period in question.

Question 28. The best answer is J because the author's statement that "a landscape may be handsome in the aggregate, but this book led to the particulars, and that's what I wanted" (lines 56–58) contrasts the surface appeal of a landscape seen at a distance with the deeper knowledge of a landscape that only comes from familiarity with the "particulars," or individual parts, and specifies that this deeper knowledge of the landscape is what she sought.

The best answer is NOT:

F because the author's statement that "a landscape may be handsome in the aggregate, but this book led to the particulars, and that's what I wanted" (lines 56–58) specifies that she was more interested in the deeper knowledge of the landscape that comes from familiarity with the "particulars," or individual parts, than she was in an understanding of a landscape that might come from looking at its overall patterns.

G because while the passage does relate the way in which the field guide helps the author break landscapes down logically into their "particulars" (line 57), or individual parts, there is no indication that this made landscapes lose their appeal. Rather, she states that this kind of understanding was "what [she] wanted" (line 58) and that the logically ordered classifications in the field guide all made "such delightful sense" (lines 79–80).

H because there is no indication in the passage that the deeper understanding of landscapes that she sought through knowledge of their "particulars" (line 57), or individual parts, was in any way related to painting portraits of those landscapes.

Question 29. **The best answer is B** because the details in question describe the ways in which the field guide "changed" (line 64) as she figuratively, and not literally, "persisted in wrestling" (line 61) with it "by slow degrees" (line 62). In this context, these details indicate that this transformation occurred due to heavy use over a long period of time.

The best answer is NOT:

A because there is no indication that the transformation of the book described by the details in question (lines 64–66) takes place because of poor craftsmanship. Rather, the details in question describe the ways in which the field guide "changed" (line 64) as she, figuratively and not literally "persisted in wrestling" (line 61) with it "by slow degrees" (line 62). In this context, these details indicate that this transformation occurred due to heavy use over a long period of time.

C because the passage implies that the "cryptic annotations" (line 66) in the guide were made by the author herself.

D because the details in question describe the ways in which the field guide "changed" (line 64) as she, figuratively and not literally "persisted in wrestling" (line 61) with it "by slow degrees" (line 62). While this indicates that the book's condition was transformed due to heavy use, there is no specific indication of carelessness and no mention anywhere in the passage of any regret the author has regarding her use of the field guide.

Question 30. **The best answer is H** because the author mentions *Solidago hispida* in order to exemplify her practice of addressing flowers that she has encountered before by their Latin name after she has learned to identify them (lines 70–72).

The best answer is NOT:

F because the passage makes no mention of any trouble the author had initially identifying *Solidago hispida*.

G because the author mentions *Solidago hispida* as an example of a flower she has addressed in the past with great enthusiasm, meaning she has already come across the flower in her nature walks.

J because there is no indication anywhere in the passage that the author feels the name *Solidago hispida* is inappropriate. Rather, the author mentions *Solidago hispida* only in order to exemplify her practice of addressing flowers by their Latin name (lines 70–72).

Passage IV

Question 31. **The best answer is D** because the passage states that information gained from the study of snow crystals "has practical applications in such diverse areas as agriculture and the production of electricity" (lines 12–14). Specific details about these practical applications are presented in the final 5 paragraphs (lines 50–91) of the passage.

The best answer is NOT:

A because while the passage does mention the fact that scientists have communicated with each other in the course of studying snow crystals (lines 50–54), that communication is secondary to the main point of the passage, which is to explain the practical applications of such a study.

B because while the passage does discuss the role of snow crystal facets in the formation of snow crystals (lines 19–23) and also discusses the winter snowpack in some Western states (lines 56–61), the passage makes no specific connection between the snow crystal facets and the snowpack and does not indicate that either one is the primary reason for presenting information about the scientific study of snow.

C because while the passage does tell the story of the first time a scanning electron microscope was used in the scientific study of snow (lines 34–49), it tells this story in the context of presenting information about the practical applications of the scientific study of snow and does not explicitly discuss the varied uses of the scanning electron microscope.

Question 32. The best answer is G because the passage states that "before employing the scanning electron microscopy results, the forecasted amounts of snowpack water were inaccurate" (lines 62–64) and that "improving the prediction [of snowpack water] by 1 percent would save $38 million" in costs (lines 71–73). Because improving a prediction can be understood as making that prediction more accurate, this establishes a connection between the use of the scanning electron microscope and saving money.

The best answer is NOT:

F because while the passage mentions future predictions in the context of less snowfall expected (lines 75–80), those future predictions are not linked to any money saved.

H because as the passage states, the two scientists (who were looking at biological problems) froze the tissue they were using in order "to avoid the laborious procedure" (lines 37–38) that the use of scanning electron microscopes usually entailed. The passage does not state that the scientists were saving money by using these microscopes when looking for these biological problems.

J because while the passage states that snowmelt accounts for 75 percent of the annual water supply of these western states (lines 56–58), the passage mentions nothing about increasing the water supply of these states as a means of saving money.

Question 33. The best answer is C because the phrase in question is immediately followed by a statement in parentheses explaining that "crystals often change once on the ground depending on the surrounding environment" (lines 48–49). Since *metamorphosed* means "changed," and *conditions* and *environment* have similar meanings, we can read the parenthetical statement as clarifying the fact that *metamorphosed conditions* refers to the state of snow crystals after they reach the ground.

The best answer is NOT:

A because the passage does not establish a direct connection between the phrase *metamorphosed conditions* (lines 47–48) and the temperature and humidity at which crystals form. Rather, the phrase in question is immediately followed by a statement in parentheses explaining that "crystals often change once on the ground depending on the surrounding environment" (lines 48–49). Read in context, the parenthetical statement, which makes no mention of the temperature and humidity at which crystals form, can be understood as defining the term *metamorphosed conditions*.

B because the passage does not establish a direct connection between the phrase *metamorphosed conditions* (lines 47–48) and the process by which snow crystals develop from a speck of dust and water vapor. Rather, the phrase in question is immediately followed by a statement in parentheses explaining that "crystals often change once on the ground depending on the surrounding environment" (lines 48–49). Read in context, the parenthetical statement, which makes no mention of the formation of snow crystals, can be understood as defining the term *metamorphosed conditions*.

D because the phrase in question (lines 47–48) is immediately followed by a statement in parentheses explaining that "crystals often change once on the ground depending on the surrounding environment" (lines 48–49). This indicates that the phrase *metamorphosed conditions* refers to changes in the snowflake that occur as a result of changes in the environment, and not directly to changes in the environment.

Question 34. **The best answer is G** because the passage explains that "before employing the scanning electron microscopy results, the forecasted amounts of snowpack water were inaccurate whenever the size and shape of the snow crystals varied much from the norm" (lines 62–65). This indicates that the addition of scanning electron microscopy data allowed scientists using the model to include more detailed information about structural variations in snow crystals in their predictions, making those predictions more accurate.

The best answer is NOT:

F because the passage does not specify that the addition of scanning microscopy data allowed scientists using the Snowmelt Runoff Model to include more detailed information about microwave satellite data. Rather, the passage states that Albert Rango "now uses Wergin's electron microscopy data, along with microwave satellite data, in the Snowmelt Runoff Model to predict the amount of water available in a winter snowpack" (lines 52–56). This indicates that scanning electron microscopy data and microwave satellite data are used in conjunction with each other, not that one allows the inclusion of more detailed information about the other.

H because the passage makes no mention of electron microscopy in helping provide detailed information about locations having the highest amount of snowfall.

J because while the passage mentions that William Wergin and Eric Erbe were looking for biological problems related to agriculture (lines 34–37), there is no mention of biological problems in the discussion of the Snowmelt Runoff Model, which occupies the last 5 paragraphs of the passage (lines 50–91).

Question 35. **The best answer is D** because the passage states that, due to temperature increases, less snow will fall, thus "greatly increasing water's economic value" (lines 77–82).

The best answer is NOT:

A because while the passage mentions an increased ability to track water pollution via the use of crystal research (lines 90–91), the passage makes no mention of an increase of pollution as a cause of an increase in water's value.

B because the passage makes no mention of water conservation leading to an increase in water's value.

C because while the passage mentions the ability of scanning electron microscopes to detect sulfur and nitrogen in snow (lines 87–89), the passage makes no mention of a predicted increase in sulfur and nitrogen levels in snow.

Question 36. **The best answer is G** because the passage states that "as the crystals fall, they encounter different atmospheric conditions that produce flakes with unique attributes" (lines 3–5).

The best answer is NOT:

F because while the passage does state that 1 septillion snowflakes fall worldwide each year (lines 1–4) the passage does not make any connection between that enormous number and the infinite variety of snowflakes. Rather, the passage states that "as the crystals fall, they encounter different atmospheric conditions that produce flakes with unique attributes" (lines 3–5).

H because the passage makes no connection between the rate at which snowflakes fall and the infinite variety of snowflakes. Rather, the passage states that "as the crystals fall, they encounter different atmospheric conditions that produce flakes with unique attributes" (lines 3–5).

J because while the passage does state that more complex atmospheric conditions produce more elaborate and therefore more varied snow crystals (lines 5–6), the passage makes no connection between those complex atmospheric conditions and the speed at which snow crystals develop, and the passage makes no connection between the speed at which snow crystals develop and the infinite variety of snowflakes.

Question 37. **The best answer is D** because the passage states that "snowflakes are collections of two or more snow crystals" (lines 16–17).

The best answer is NOT:

A because the passage does not state that snowflakes grow around a nucleus of dust. Rather, the passage states that "snowflakes are collections of two or more snow crystals" (lines 16–17) and that a crystal "typically grows around a nucleus of dust" (lines 18–19).

B because the snowflakes do not combine to form snow crystals. Rather, according to the passage, the opposite is true: snow crystals combine to form snowflakes (lines 16–17).

C because while the passage states that the shape of a snow crystal "depends on how the six side facets—or faces—grow in relation to the top and bottom facets" (lines 19–20), there is no mention of any direct relation between top and bottom facets and the growth of snowflakes.

Question 38. **The best answer is G** because the passage specifies that the physicist Kenneth Libbrecht "creates 'designer' snowflakes in his lab" (lines 31–32).

The best answer is NOT:

F because the passage makes no connection between the term *"designer" snowflakes* (line 32) and the fact that no two snowflakes are alike. Rather, the passage specifies that the physicist Kenneth Libbrecht "creates 'designer' snowflakes in his lab" (lines 31–32).

H because the passage makes no mention of the grand design of nature. Rather, the passage specifies that the physicist Kenneth Libbrecht "creates 'designer' snowflakes in his lab" (lines 31–32).

J because while the passage does state that the physicist Kenneth Libbrecht "creates 'designer' snowflakes in his lab" (lines 31–32), the passage makes no mention of the beauty of Libbrecht's snowflakes.

Question 39. **The best answer is C** because the sentence in question states that "snowmelt water is critical to crop irrigation and hydroelectric power, as well as recreation and domestic water supplies, fisheries management and flood control" (lines 58–61). In context, this is understood to mean that snowmelt water is vital, or very important, to these processes and practices.

The best answer is NOT:

A because the sentence in question states that "snowmelt water is critical to crop irrigation and hydroelectric power, as well as recreation and domestic water supplies, fisheries management and flood control" (lines 58–61). In this context, *critical* cannot be read as meaning "evaluative" because snowmelt water cannot evaluate anything or anyone.

B because the sentence in question states that "snowmelt water is critical to crop irrigation and hydroelectric power, as well as recreation and domestic water supplies, fisheries management and flood control" (lines 58–61). In this context, *critical* cannot be read as meaning "faultfinding" because snowmelt water cannot find fault with anything or anyone.

D because the sentence in question states that "snowmelt water is critical to crop irrigation and hydroelectric power, as well as recreation and domestic water supplies, fisheries management and flood control" (lines 58–61). In context, the adjective *critical* is understood to mean that snowmelt water is vital, or very important, to these processes and practices. Although it is also an adjective and can sometimes be understood to mean vital or important, *acute* cannot be substituted for *critical* in this sentence because it would be neither grammatical nor logical to say "water is *acute* to crop irrigation."

Question 40. **The best answer is F** because while the passage does state that research about snow crystals has helped scientists to identify and possibly track the source of pollutants in snow (lines 90–91), the passage does not make any connection between research about snow crystals and the extraction of pollutants *from* snow.

The best answer is NOT:

G because one meaning of *gauge* is "to measure," and the term *snowmelt* refers to water generated by a melting snowpack; therefore, when the passage states that research about snow crystals has helped scientists to "predict the amount of water available in a winter snowpack" (lines 55–56), that statement means that research about snow crystals has helped scientists to gauge (measure) the probable amount of snowmelt. Lines 84–85 specifically state that "the crystal research help[s] gauge snowmelt."

H because the passage states that, in the process of conducting research about snow crystals, physicist Kenneth Libbrecht "creates 'designer' snowflakes in his lab" (lines 31–32).

J because the passage states that research about snow crystals "is also useful in predicting avalanches" (line 85).

Passage I

Question 1. The best answer is B. The question postulates that water is unsafe for swimming if there are over 400 *E. coli* colonies per 100 mL of water. Figure 1 shows that on Day 30 at Site 1 there were 708 *E. coli* colonies per 100 mL of water. Based on the criterion of the question, the water would have been unsafe for swimming only on Day 30 at Site 1.

The best answer is NOT:

A because Figure 1 shows that on Day 1 at Site 1 there were 101 *E. coli* colonies per 100 mL of water. The question postulates that water is unsafe for swimming if there are over 400 *E. coli* colonies per 100 mL of water. Based on this criterion, the water would have been safe for swimming on Day 1 at Site 1.

C because Figure 1 shows that on Day 1 at Site 2 there were 16 *E. coli* colonies per 100 mL of water. The question postulates that water is unsafe for swimming if there are over 400 *E. coli* colonies per 100 mL of water. Based on this criterion, the water would have been safe for swimming on Day 1 at Site 2.

D because Figure 1 shows that on Day 30 at Site 2 there were 173 *E. coli* colonies per 100 mL of water. The question postulates that water is unsafe for swimming if there are over 400 *E. coli* colonies per 100 mL of water. Based on this criterion, the water would have been safe for swimming on Day 30 at Site 2.

Question 2. The best answer is F. The average for a site is determined by summing the values for a site and then dividing by 5 (the number of collection days). Based on the data in Figure 1, the average number of *E. coli* colonies per 100 mL of water at Site 1 was (101 + 92 + 708 + 9 + 5)/5 = 183, and the average number of *E. coli* colonies per 100 mL of water at Site 2 was (16 + 4 + 173 + 10 + 5)/5 = 41.6. The average water flow at Sites 1 and 2 can be calculated in a similar fashion; however, it is easier to recognize that in Figure 2 the water flow at Site 1 was greater than the water flow at Site 2 on each of the 5 days. Thus, the sum of the values for Site 1 is greater than the sum of the values for Site 2, so the average water flow calculated for Site 1 would be greater than the average water flow calculated for Site 2. Therefore, Site 1 had the higher water flow and also the higher *E. coli* level.

The best answer is NOT:

G because based on the data in Figure 1, the average number of *E. coli* colonies per 100 mL of water at Site 2 is less than the average number of *E. coli* colonies per 100 mL of water at Site 1.

H because based on the data in Figure 2, the average water flow at Site 2 is less than the average water flow at Site 1.

J because based on the data in Figure 2, the average water flow at Site 2 is less than the average water flow at Site 1, and, according to Figure 1, the average number of *E. coli* colonies per 100 mL of water at Site 2 is less than the average number of *E. coli* colonies per 100 mL of water at Site 1.

Question 3. The best answer is B. Table 2 shows that the average BI at Sites 1 and 2 was 6.3 and 2.5, respectively. Table 1 shows that the water quality associated with a BI of 6.3 and a BI of 2.5 is excellent and fair, respectively. Thus, Site 1 would have more stonefly larvae than Site 2, which is consistent with the students' hypothesis.

The best answer is NOT:

A because although the data in Table 2 are consistent with the hypothesis, Site 1 had a water quality rating of excellent, not good, and Site 2 had a water quality rating of fair, not poor.

C because the data in Table 2 are consistent, rather than inconsistent, with the hypothesis. Site 1 had a water quality rating of excellent, not poor, and Site 2 had a water quality rating of fair, not good.

D because the data in Table 2 are consistent, rather than inconsistent, with the hypothesis. Site 1 had a water quality rating of excellent, not fair, and Site 2 had a water quality rating of fair, not excellent.

Question 4. The best answer is F. The passage states: "*E. coli* levels that are above 100 colonies formed per 100 mL of water indicate reduced water quality." Figure 1 shows that at Site 1 there were 2 days on which *E. coli* colonies per 100 mL of water were greater than 100: Day 1 and Day 30. In contrast, Figure 1 shows that at Site 2 there was only 1 day on which *E. coli* colonies per 100 mL of water were greater than 100: Day 30. Thus, Figure 1 supports the claim that Site 1 had a *lower* water quality than Site 2.

The best answer is NOT:

G because Figure 2 shows water flow data but does not provide any information about the relationship between water flow and water quality.

H because Table 1 does not provide any data about Site 1 or Site 2.

J because Table 2 shows that Site 1 has a higher average BI than does Site 2. Because Table 1 shows that water quality ratings are better when the BI is higher, Table 2 supports the conclusion that Site 1 has a *higher* water quality on average than Site 2. It does not support the conclusion that Site 1 has a *lower* water quality than Site 2.

Question 5. The best answer is D. The entry of large amounts of fertilizer at Site 1 will cause eutrophication (an increase in nutrients that leads to an overgrowth of algae, a decrease in dissolved oxygen, and a decrease in the number and diversity of aquatic invertebrate animals). Eutrophication decreases the water quality, which would be reflected in a decrease in the BI for Site 1, based on the information in Table 1.

The best answer is NOT:

A because eutrophication will decrease, not increase, the water quality at Site 1, resulting in a decrease, not an increase, in the BI for the site.

B because eutrophication will decrease the water quality at Site 1, resulting in a decrease, not an increase, in the BI for the site.

C because eutrophication will decrease, not increase, the water quality at Site 1, resulting in a decrease in the BI for the site.

Passage II

Question 6. The best answer is G. The data in Table 1 for the volume of H_2 produced by Days 2, 4, 6, and 8 from the AWP 2 sample are: 21 mL, 187 mL, 461 mL, and 760 mL, respectively. The graph in G has a curve including the coordinates (2,21), (4,187), (6,461), and (8,760), which correspond with the data for AWP 2 in Table 1.

The best answer is NOT:

F because the curve in this graph does not include the coordinates (4,187) and (6,461). Thus, this curve does not represent the data for AWP 2.

H or J because the curve in neither graph includes the coordinates (2,21), (4,187), (6,461), and (8,760). Thus, the curve in neither graph represents the data for AWP 2.

Question 7. The best answer is B. The data in Table 1 for the volume of H_2 produced by Days 2, 4, 6, and 8 from the AWP 1 sample are: 4 mL, 33 mL, 81 mL, and 133 mL, respectively. So, the volume of H_2 produced by AWP 1 increased over time. Between Days 2 and 4, 29 mL of H_2 was produced; between Days 4 and 6, 48 mL of H_2 was produced; and between Days 6 and 8, 52 mL of H_2 was produced. So, between Days 8 and 10, more than 52 mL of H_2 would most likely have been produced, but not as much as 328 mL of H_2. Thus, the volume of H_2 produced by Day 10 from the AWP 1 sample would most likely have been between 133 mL and 461 mL.

The best answer is NOT:

A because the volume of H_2 produced by Day 10 from the AWP 1 sample would more likely have been between 133 mL and 461 mL than it would have been less than 133 mL.

C the volume of H_2 produced by Day 10 from the AWP 1 sample would more likely have been between 133 mL and 461 mL than it would have been between 461 mL and 760 mL.

D the volume of H_2 produced by Day 10 from the AWP 1 sample would more likely have been between 133 mL and 461 mL than it would have been greater than 760 mL.

Question 8. The best answer is F. The data in Table 1 for the volume of H_2 produced by Days 6 and 8 from the AWP 1 sample are: 81 mL and 133 mL, respectively. Thus, from the time the volume was measured on Day 6 until the time the volume was measured on Day 8, the volume increased from 81 mL to 133 mL. So, the volume of H_2 produced by AWP 1 from the time the volume was measured on Day 6 until the time the volume was measured on Day 8 was equal to 133 mL minus 81 mL, or 52 mL.

The best answer is NOT:

G, H, or J because the volume of H_2 produced by AWP 1 from the time the volume was measured on Day 6 until the time the volume was measured on Day 8 was equal to 52 mL.

Question 9. The best answer is C. The chemical equation in the passage shows that Al and H_2O react to produce $Al(OH)_3$ and H_2. For every 6 molecules of H_2O consumed, 2 atoms of Al are converted to 2 units of $Al(OH)_3$, and 3 molecules of H_2 are produced. Thus, by measuring the volume of H_2 produced in the trials represented in Table 1 and Figure 1, the experimenters were able to monitor the rate at which Al is converted to $Al(OH)_3$.

The best answer is NOT:

A because Al and H_2O are reactants, so H_2O is not converted to Al.

B because Al and H_2O are reactants, so Al is not converted to H_2O.

D because Al is a reactant and $Al(OH)_3$ is a product, so Al is converted to $Al(OH)_3$. The single right arrow in the chemical equation indicates that the reaction does not occur in reverse.

Question 10. The best answer is J. Table 1 shows that the volume of H_2 produced by Day 2 from the AWP 3 sample that contained no corrosion inhibitor was 121 mL. Figure 1 shows the volume of H_2 produced by Days 1, 4, 7, and 10 from the AWP 3 sample containing EDTA. By Day 1, the volume was approximately 20 mL; by Day 4, the volume was approximately 65 mL; by Day 7, the volume was approximately 100 mL; and by Day 10, the volume was approximately 120 mL. Thus, the volume of H_2 produced by Day 2 from the AWP 3 sample that contained no corrosion inhibitor and the volume of H_2 produced by Day 10 from the AWP 3 sample containing EDTA were approximately the same.

The best answer is NOT:

F because the volume of H_2 produced by Day 1 from the AWP 3 sample containing EDTA was approximately 20 mL, which is approximately 100 mL less than 121 mL.

G because the volume of H_2 produced by Day 4 from the AWP 3 sample containing EDTA was approximately 65 mL, which is approximately 56 mL less than 121 mL.

H because the volume of H_2 produced by Day 7 from the AWP 3 sample containing EDTA was approximately 100 mL, which is approximately 20 mL less than 121 mL.

Passage III

Question 11. The best answer is B. In Trial 5, Scale A's hand pointed in the same direction as did Scale B's hand. Thus, the force of the 10.0 N weight was equally distributed between Scales A and B, and the forces on the 2 scales were equal.

The best answer is NOT:

A because in Trial 4, Scale A's hand was pointing in a different direction than was Scale B's hand. Thus, the forces on the 2 scales were not equal.

C because in Trial 6, Scale A's hand was pointing in a different direction than was Scale B's hand. Thus, the forces on the 2 scales were not equal.

D because in Trial 5, Scale A's hand was pointing in the same direction as was Scale B's hand. Thus, the forces on the 2 scales were equal. So there was, in fact, a trial in which the force of the 10.0 N weight was equally distributed.

Question 12. The best answer is G. Trials 1 and 2 allow one to make 2 observations: (1) In Trial 2, when the 5.0 N weight was placed on Scale A, Scale A's hand rotated one-fourth of the way around Scale A's dial. (2) In Trial 1, when Scale A was placed on Scale B, Scale B's hand rotated one-fourth of the way around Scale B's dial. The first observation shows that when a 5.0 N object was placed on either of the 2 identical scales, the hand of that scale rotated one-fourth of the way around the scale's dial. The second observation shows that Scale A weighed 5.0 N because when it was placed on Scale B, Scale B's hand rotated one-fourth of the way around Scale B's dial. Thus, these 2 identical scales each weigh 5.0 N.

The best answer is NOT:

F because if Scale A weighed 2.5 N, then when Scale A was placed on Scale B in Trial 1, Scale B's hand would have rotated one-eighth of the way around Scale B's dial.

H because if Scale A weighed 7.5 N, then when Scale A was placed on Scale B in Trial 1, Scale B's hand would have rotated three-eighths of the way around Scale B's dial.

J because if Scale A weighed 10.0 N, then when Scale A was placed on Scale B in Trial 1, Scale B's hand would have rotated one-half of the way around Scale B's dial.

Question 13. The best answer is C. In Trial 3, a 10.0 N weight was placed on Scale A. No weight was placed on Scale A in Trial 1. Scale A's hand rotated a greater distance in Trial 3 than in Trial 1. As rotation of the hand increased, compression of the spring increased. As compression of the spring increased, the amount of potential energy stored in the spring increased. Thus, compared to Trial 1, during Trial 3 the hand rotated more, so the spring compressed more, so more potential energy was stored in the spring.

The best answer is NOT:

A because Scale A's spring was not compressed in Trial 1, so the amount of potential energy stored in Scale A's spring did not increase. In contrast, a 10.0 N weight was placed on the platform of Scale A in Trial 3, so Scale A's spring was compressed, and the amount of potential energy stored in Scale A's spring did increase. In addition, the amount of weight on the platform of Scale A was less in Trial 1 than in Trial 3.

B because Scale A's spring was not compressed in Trial 1, so the amount of potential energy stored in Scale A's spring did not increase. In contrast, a 10.0 N weight was placed on the platform of Scale A in Trial 3, so Scale A's spring was compressed, and the amount of potential energy stored in Scale A's spring did increase.

D because the amount of weight on the platform of Scale A was *greater* in Trial 3 than in Trial 1. Thus, Scale A's spring was compressed more in Trial 3, and the potential energy stored in Scale A's spring was greater in Trial 3 than in Trial 1.

Question 14. The best answer is F. The results of Study 1 indicate that each scale weighs 5 N, and that for either scale, the pointer rotates 90° clockwise for every 5 N exerted on the scale's platform, starting from the "0" mark. When Scale A is upside down, its weight is supported by its platform; therefore Scale A's pointer will rotate 90° clockwise. When Scale A is placed atop Scale B, the weight of Scale A is also supported by Scale B; therefore Scale B's pointer will also rotate 90° clockwise. The only figure that shows each scale supporting 5 N of weight is F.

The best answer is NOT:

G because the figure indicates that Scale B is supporting 10 N of weight, not 5 N.

H because the figure indicates that Scale A is supporting 10 N of weight, not 5 N.

J because the figure indicates that each scale is supporting 10 N of weight, not 5 N.

Question 15. The best answer is C. Scale B's hand rotated a greater distance in Trial 4 than in Trial 5. Scale B's hand rotated a greater distance in Trial 5 than in Trial 6. Furthermore, the distance between the 10.0 N weight and the pencil was less in Trial 4 than in Trial 5. Likewise, the distance between the 10.0 N weight and the pencil was less in Trial 5 than in Trial 6. These observations support the following 2 conclusions: (1) When the force exerted on the surface of Scale B's platform was greatest (Trial 4), the distance between the weight and the pencil was least (0.10 m). (2) When the force exerted on the surface of Scale B's platform was least (Trial 6), the distance between the weight and the pencil was greatest (0.30 m). Thus, as the distance between the 10.0 N weight and the pencil on Scale B increased, the amount of force exerted on the surface of Scale B's platform decreased.

The best answer is NOT:

A because in Study 2, the amount of force exerted on the surface of Scale B's platform varied and this force was a function of the distance between the 10.0 N weight and the pencil on Scale B.

B because in Study 2, the force was greater when the distance was shorter. Thus, as the distance increased, the force did not increase, it decreased.

D because in Study 2, there was a general trend. The force was greater when the distance was shorter.

Question 16. The best answer is J. The students wanted to ensure that in Trials 4–6, the distance that each scale's hand rotated around the corresponding dial was a function of the force exerted by the 10.0 N weight. That is, they did not want to measure how the force exerted on the scale's platform was affected by the weight of the board or by the weight of the pencils. By setting the dial readings of both scales to zero, *after* the board and the pencils were positioned on the scales, the students ensured that the dial readings were a function of the force exerted by the 10.0 N weight. In other words, the weights of the board and pencils were subtracted from each weight measurement.

The best answer is NOT:

F or H because the weights of the scales did not affect the measured weights. Setting the dial readings of both scales to zero after Study 1 eliminated the weights of the board and pencils from the observed reading. It was not designed to eliminate the weights of the scales.

G because by setting the dial reading of both scales to zero after the board and pencils were placed on the scales, the weights of the board and pencils were *subtracted* from each weight measurement, not added.

Passage IV

Question 17. The best answer is B. According to Table 2, as engine speed increased from 1,500 rpm to 3,500 rpm, the EOR decreased from 97.4 to 90.6. An increase in engine speed was always accompanied by a decrease in the EOR. The EOR is the minimum octane number of a fuel required for an engine to operate without becoming damaged. Thus, as engine speed increases, the minimum octane number of a fuel required for an engine to operate without becoming damaged decreases only.

The best answer is NOT:

A, C, or D because according to Table 2, an increase in engine speed was always accompanied by a decrease in the EOR.

Question 18. The best answer is G. In Experiment 3, the octane number always decreased as engine speed increased for both Fuel A and Fuel B. So, the results of a trial performed at an engine speed of 2,200 rpm would most likely have been between the results of the trial performed at an engine speed of 2,000 rpm and the results of the trial performed at an engine speed of 2,500 rpm. For Fuel A, the octane numbers determined at engine speeds of 2,000 rpm and 2,500 rpm were 96.6 and 95.0, respectively. The octane number of 96.1 falls between these 2 values. For Fuel B, the octane numbers determined at engine speeds of 2,000 rpm and 2,500 rpm were 96.1 and 95.4, respectively. The octane number of 95.8 falls between these 2 values.

The best answer is NOT:

F, H, or J because at an engine speed of 2,200 rpm, the octane number determined for Fuel A would most likely have been less than 96.6 and greater than 95.0, and the octane number determined for Fuel B would most likely have been less than 96.1 and greater than 95.4.

Question 19. The best answer is C. Table 1 shows that the octane number of each fuel mixture is equal to the percent by volume of isooctane in the mixture. Thus, the octane number of each fuel mixture is equal to 100 times the volume of isooctane in the mixture divided by the sum of the volume of heptane and the volume of isooctane in the mixture.

The best answer is NOT:

A because the denominator of the fraction should be the sum of the volume of heptane and the volume of isooctane.

B because the numerator of the fraction should be the volume of isooctane and the denominator of the fraction should be the sum of the volume of heptane and the volume of isooctane.

D because the numerator of the fraction should be the volume of isooctane.

Question 20. The best answer is H. Table 1 shows that the octane number of a mixture of heptane and isooctane is equal to the percent by volume of isooctane in the mixture. A mixture of 100 mL of heptane and 900 mL of isooctane would be 10% heptane and 90% isooctane by volume. So, the octane number of this mixture would be 90. The passage states that adding TEL to a fuel changes the fuel's octane number. Experiment 2 shows that adding 3 mL of TEL to 1,000 mL of isooctane increased isooctane's octane number from 100 to 125. If 3 mL of TEL were added to a mixture of 100 mL of heptane and 900 mL of isooctane, the octane number of the resulting fuel would most likely be between 90 and 125.

The best answer is NOT:

F or G because the fuel is 10% heptane and 90% isooctane by volume and contains 3 mL of TEL. So, the octane number of the fuel would most likely exceed 90.

J because the fuel is 10% heptane and 90% isooctane by volume and contains 3 mL of TEL. So, the octane number of the fuel would most likely exceed 90, but not 125.

Question 21. The best answer is B. The octane number of a fuel should be equal to or higher than the minimum octane number of a fuel required for an engine to operate without becoming damaged, or the EOR. In Experiment 3, the slowest engine speed tested was 1,500 rpm and the fastest engine speed tested was 3,500 rpm. At all engine speeds tested in Experiment 3, the octane number of Fuel A was higher than the EOR. At an engine speed of 1,500 rpm, the octane number of Fuel B was lower than the EOR.

The best answer is NOT:

A because the octane number of Fuel A was higher than the EOR at each of the engine speeds tested.

C because the octane number of Fuel B was lower than the EOR only at an engine speed of 1,500 rpm.

D because the octane number of Fuel B was lower than the EOR at an engine speed of 1,500 rpm.

Question 22. The best answer is J. Table 1 shows that the octane number of a mixture of heptane and isooctane is equal to the percent by volume of isooctane in the mixture. A mixture of 2 mL of heptane and 8 mL of isooctane would be 20% heptane and 80% isooctane by volume. So, the octane number of this mixture would be 80.

The best answer is NOT:

F, G, or H because a mixture of heptane and isooctane that is 20% heptane and 80% isooctane by volume would have an octane number of 80.

Passage V

Question 23. The best answer is C. Scientist B states that short-period comets were once long-period comets. Thus, Scientist B believes that long-period comets can become short-period comets.

The best answer is NOT:

A because Scientist B states that short-period comets were once long-period comets. Thus, Scientist B would disagree with the generalization that long-period comets cannot become short-period comets.

B because Scientist B does not discuss whether short-period comets can become long-period comets. This generalization is neither consistent nor inconsistent with Scientist B's viewpoint.

D because the introduction states that comets orbit the Sun. Scientist B does not make any statements that contradict the notion that comets orbit the Sun.

Question 24. The best answer is H. Scientist A states that short-period comets originate within the KB, that the KB is 30 A.U. to 50 A.U. from the Sun, and that the KB has a small inclination with respect to the ecliptic plane. Telescopic evidence of the KB would support Scientist A's viewpoint. Thus, Scientist A would want to use the telescope to search the region of space that is 30 A.U. to 50 A.U. from the Sun and that has a small inclination with respect to the ecliptic plane, for example 0° to 30° with respect to the ecliptic plane.

The best answer is NOT:

F because Scientist A's viewpoint would be best supported by finding evidence of the KB. However, the KB is between 30 A.U. to 50 A.U. from the Sun. Searching regions of space that are 100,000 A.U. beyond our solar system would not help to establish the existence of the KB.

G because Scientist A's viewpoint would be best supported by finding evidence of the KB. Scientist A states that short-period comets originate within the KB. Scientist A also states that the KB has a small inclination with respect to the ecliptic plane. Thus, Scientist A would not predict that the KB would be found by searching regions of space that are at a 90° angle with respect to the ecliptic plane.

J because Scientist A's viewpoint would be best supported by finding evidence of the KB. Scientist A does not state that Jupiter is near the KB. Thus, it is unlikely that Scientist A would want to search regions near Jupiter for evidence of the KB.

Question 25. The best answer is D. The introduction states that short-period comets have orbital planes with inclinations of 30° or less. So, short-period comets should not have orbital planes with inclinations of 45° with respect to the ecliptic plane.

The best answer is NOT:

A, B, or C because the introduction states that short-period comets have orbital planes with inclinations of 30° or less; so, some short-period comets could have orbital planes with inclinations of 5° (A), 15° (B), or 30° (C) with respect to the ecliptic plane.

Question 26. The best answer is J. Scientist B says that long-period comets can become short-period comets when the long-period comets pass close enough to giant planets to be influenced by the gravitational fields of the giant planets. Of the 4 planets listed, Saturn is the only giant planet. So, of the 4 planets listed, Saturn would be the planet most likely to influence the orbit of a long-period comet.

The best answer is NOT:

F because Mercury is not a giant planet, so Mercury would be unlikely to influence the orbit of a long-period comet.

G because Earth is not a giant planet, so Earth would be unlikely to influence the orbit of a long-period comet.

H because Mars is not a giant planet, so Mars would be unlikely to influence the orbit of a long-period comet.

Question 27. The best answer is A. The introduction states that short-period comets have orbital periods of 200 yr or less and that long-period comets originate in the Oort Cloud. In addition, Scientist B states that the KB does not exist and that short-period comets were once long-period comets. Thus, because Comet Halley has an orbital period of 76 yr, it is by definition a short-period comet. Thus, Scientist B would most likely propose that it was once a long-period comet that originated in the Oort Cloud.

The best answer is NOT:

B or D because Scientist B states that the KB does not exist.

C because the Introduction states that long-period comets have orbital periods of more than 200 yr. So Comet Halley cannot be a long-period comet.

Question 28. The best answer is J. Scientist A states that the KB contains billions of comet-size icy bodies with diameters between 10 km and 30 km. Scientist A also states that there is telescopic evidence of larger icy bodies that are part of the KB. These larger icy bodies would have diameters greater than the comet-size icy bodies: that is, greater than 30 km.

The best answer is NOT:

F, G, or H because based on Scientist A's viewpoint, the larger icy bodies in the KB should have diameters that are greater than 30 km.

Question 29. The best answer is D. The 2 scientists do not disagree about the presence of the Oort Cloud. In addition, the finding that a nearby star lacked a spherical shell of material similar to the Oort Cloud would not affect the scientists' viewpoints.

The best answer is NOT:

A because this discovery would not affect Scientist A's viewpoint.

B because this discovery would not affect Scientist B's viewpoint.

C because this discovery would not affect Scientist A's or Scientist B's viewpoint.

Passage VI

Question 30. The best answer is J. Each line had a lower average fruit mass when it was grown in 120 g of NaCl/10 L of nutrient solution than when it was grown in 60 g of NaCl/10 L of nutrient solution, and Line 4 produced less fruit mass, on average, than did Line 2. Thus it is most likely that a plant that produced no fruit and had a height of only 21 cm came from Line 4 and that this plant was grown in 120 g of NaCl/10 L of nutrient solution.

The best answer is NOT:

F or G because Line 2 plants produced more fruit mass than did Line 4 plants.

H because Line 4 plants grown in 60 g of NaCl/10 L of nutrient solution produced more fruit mass than did Line 4 plants that were grown in 120 g of NaCl/10 L of nutrient solution.

Question 31. The best answer is C. The passage refers to osmosis occurring between the cytoplasm of the plants' cells and the environment, and the cell membrane separates the cytoplasm of the plants' cells and the environment.

The best answer is NOT:

A because the chromosomes do not separate the cytoplasm of the plants' cells and the environment.

B because the nuclear envelope does not separate the cytoplasm of the plants' cells and the environment.

D because the rough endoplasmic reticulum does not separate the cytoplasm of the plants' cells and the environment.

Question 32. **The best answer is G.** NaCl is a salt. In addition, for each line, average plant mass was greater in 3 g of NaCl/10 L of nutrient solution than in 60 g of NaCl/10 L of nutrient solution, and average plant mass was greater in 60 g of NaCl/10 L of nutrient solution than in 120 g of NaCl/10 L of nutrient solution. Thus, as the concentration of NaCl increased, average plant mass decreased only.

The best answer is NOT:

F, H, or J because average plant mass was greater in 3 g of NaCl/10 L of nutrient solution than in 60 g of NaCl/10 L of nutrient solution, and average plant mass was greater in 60 g of NaCl/10 L of nutrient solution than in 120 g of NaCl/10 L of nutrient solution. Thus, as the concentration of NaCl increased, average plant mass never increased.

Question 33. **The best answer is A.** The independent variable is the variable that is controlled by the experimenter. In the experiment, the experimenter determined whether or not each line received the *AtNHX1*.

The best answer is NOT:

B because all of the plants were tomato plants, so this factor was not varied.

C because the value of the plant mass without fruit was not directly controlled by the experimenter.

D because the value of the plant height was not directly controlled by the experimenter.

Question 34. **The best answer is J.** As height increased, mass increased. This results in a positive slope, because a positive change along the x-axis corresponds with a positive change along the y-axis.

The best answer is NOT:

F because the line would be vertical only if all of the points had the same x-value, but there was variability in plant height.

G because the line would have a slope of zero only if all of the points had the same y-value. However, there was variability in plant mass without fruit.

H because the line would have a negative slope only if as height increased, mass decreased. However, as height increased, mass increased.

Question 35. **The best answer is D.** The control line was the line that did not receive *AtNHX1*, and L4 did not receive *AtNHX1*.

The best answer is NOT:

A because the control line was the line that did not receive *AtNHX1*, and L1 received *AtNHX1*.

B because the control line was the line that did not receive *AtNHX1*, and L2 received *AtNHX1*.

C because the control line was the line that did not receive *AtNHX1*, and L3 received *AtNHX1*.

Passage VII

Question 36. The best answer is **F.** Figure 2 shows that as the length of the insulated copper rods increased from 2 cm to 12 cm, R continually decreased from about 175 W to about 40 W. In contrast, Figure 3 shows that as the cross-sectional area of the insulated copper rods increased from 1 cm² to 6 cm², R continually increased from about 30 W to about 145 W. Likewise, Table 1 shows that as ΔT increased from 10°C to 50°C, R continually increased from 24 W to 118 W. Since the radius of the insulated copper rods is directly proportional to the cross-sectional area of the insulated copper rods, as the radius of the insulated copper increased, R continually increased.

The best answer is NOT:

G because Figure 3 shows that as the cross-sectional area of the insulated copper rods increased from 1 cm² to 6 cm², R continually increased from about 30 W to about 145 W.

H because Table 1 shows that as ΔT increased from 10°C to 50°C, R continually increased from 24 W to 118 W.

J because the radius of the insulated copper rods is directly proportional to the cross-sectional area of the insulated copper rods, and Figure 3 shows that as the cross-sectional area of the insulated copper rods increased from 1 cm² to 6 cm², R continually increased from about 30 W to about 145 W.

Question 37. The best answer is **C.** Figure 2 shows that R is directly proportional to the cross-sectional area of the rods. Since the cross-sectional area of B is double the cross-sectional area of A, R for B will be twice as much as R for A. So the ratio of R for B to R for A will be 2:1.

The best answer is NOT:

A because Figure 2 shows that R is directly proportional to the cross-sectional area of the rods. Since the cross-sectional area of B is double the cross-sectional area of A, R for B will be twice as much as R for A. So the ratio of R for B to R for A will be 2:1, not 1:4.

B because Figure 2 shows that R is directly proportional to the cross-sectional area of the rods. Since the cross-sectional area of B is double the cross-sectional area of A, R for B will be twice as much as R for A. So the ratio of R for B to R for A will be 2:1, not 1:2.

D because Figure 2 shows that R is directly proportional to the cross-sectional area of the rods. Since the cross-sectional area of B is double the cross-sectional area of A, R for B will be twice as much as R for A. So the ratio of R for B to R for A will be 2:1, not 4:1.

Question 38. **The best answer is H.** In metal rods, heat is primarily transferred through conduction.

The best answer is NOT:

F because in metal rods, more heat is transferred through conduction than through radiation.

G because in metal rods, more heat is transferred through conduction than through convection.

J because in metal rods, more heat is transferred through conduction than through radiation and convection.

Question 39. **The best answer is A.** Figure 2 shows that as the length of the insulated copper rods increases, R decreases. So, the shortest rod will have the greatest R.

The best answer is NOT:

B because the insulated copper rod in A is shorter than the insulated copper rod in B.

C because the insulated copper rod in A is shorter than the insulated copper rod in C.

D because the insulated copper rod in A is shorter than the insulated copper rod in D.

Question 40. **The best answer is F.** Table 1 shows that as ΔT increases, R increases. In F, $\Delta T = 280°C - 250°C = 30°C$, which is greater than the ΔT in G, H, and J.

The best answer is NOT:

G because Table 1 shows that as ΔT increases, R increases. In G, $\Delta T = 280°C - 260°C = 20°C$, which is less than 30°C.

H because Table 1 shows that as ΔT increases, R increases. In H, $\Delta T = 300°C - 280°C = 20°C$, which is less than 30°C.

J because Table 1 shows that as ΔT increases, R increases. In J, $\Delta T = 310°C - 300°C = 10°C$, which is less than 30°C.

The ACT® *Sample Answer Sheet*

A NAME, MAILING ADDRESS, AND TELEPHONE
(Please print.)

Last Name   First Name   MI (Middle Initial)

House Number & Street (Apt. No.); or PO Box & No.; or RR & No.

City   State/Province   ZIP/Postal Code

Area Code   Number   Country

ACT, Inc.—Confidential Restricted when data present.

ALL examinees must complete block A – please print.

REGISTERED examinees **MUST** complete blocks **B, C, and D.** Find the MATCHING INFORMATION on your admission ticket and enter it EXACTLY the same way, even if any of the information is missing or incorrect. Fill in the corresponding ovals. If you do not complete these blocks to match your admission ticket EXACTLY, your scores will be **delayed up to 8 weeks**. Leave blocks E and F blank.

STANDBY examinees **MUST** complete blocks **B, D, and F.** Enter your information in blocks B and D and fill in the corresponding ovals. Leave block C blank. **For block E**, if you provided your SSN when you created your Web account or completed your standby folder, enter it here. The SSN will be used to help match this document to your registration information and will be included on reports to your college choices. If you did not provide it earlier, do not know it, or do not wish to provide it, leave block E blank. Be sure to fill in the oval in block F.

Do NOT mark in this shaded area.

B MATCH NAME
(First 5 letters of last name)

C MATCH NUMBER
(Registered examinees only)

D DATE OF BIRTH

	Month	Day	Year

Jan., Feb., March, April, May, June, July, Aug., Sept., Oct., Nov., Dec.

↓ STANDBY TESTING ONLY ↓

E SOCIAL SECURITY NUMBER
(Standby examinees only)

F STANDBY TESTING

Fill in the oval below ONLY if you turned in a standby registration at the test center today.

○ Yes, I am testing as a standby.

USE A SOFT LEAD NO. 2 PENCIL ONLY.
(Do NOT use a mechanical pencil, ink, ballpoint, correction fluid, or felt-tip pen.)

EXAMINEE STATEMENT AND SIGNATURE

1. Read the following **Statement:** By submitting this answer sheet, I agree to the terms and conditions set forth in the ACT registration booklet or website for this exam, including the arbitration and dispute remedy provisions. I understand that ACT owns the test questions and responses and affirm that I will not share any test questions or responses with anyone by any form of communication.

2. Copy the **Certification** shown below (only the text in italics) on the lines provided. Write in your normal handwriting.

   Certification: *I agree to the Statement above and certify that I am the person whose name and address appear on this form.*

   _____

   _____

   _____

   _____

3. Sign your name as you would any official document and enter today's date.

   Your Signature   Today's Date

ACT®
P.O. BOX 168, IOWA CITY, IOWA 52243-0168

Marking Directions: Mark only **one** oval for each question. Fill in response completely. Erase errors cleanly without smudging.

Correct mark: ○ ● ○ ○

Do NOT use these *incorrect* or *bad* **marks.**

Incorrect marks: ⊘ ⊗ ⊜ ◉
Overlapping mark: ○ ○ ◖ ○
Cross-out mark: ● ⊗ ○ ○
Smudged erasure: ○ ○ ◉ ○
Mark is too light: ◐ ○ ○ ○

BOOKLET NUMBER

① ① ① ① ① ①
② ② ② ② ② ②
③ ③ ③ ③ ③ ③
④ ④ ④ ④ ④ ④
⑤ ⑤ ⑤ ⑤ ⑤ ⑤
⑥ ⑥ ⑥ ⑥ ⑥ ⑥
⑦ ⑦ ⑦ ⑦ ⑦ ⑦
⑧ ⑧ ⑧ ⑧ ⑧ ⑧
⑨ ⑨ ⑨ ⑨ ⑨ ⑨
⓪ ⓪ ⓪ ⓪ ⓪ ⓪

FORM

Print your 3-character **Test Form** in the boxes above and fill in the corresponding oval at the right.

BE SURE TO FILL IN THE CORRECT FORM OVAL.

○ 1MC   ○ 2MC   ○ 3MC   ○ 4MC
○ 5MC

TEST 1

1 Ⓐ Ⓑ Ⓒ Ⓓ	14 Ⓕ Ⓖ Ⓗ Ⓙ	27 Ⓐ Ⓑ Ⓒ Ⓓ	40 Ⓕ Ⓖ Ⓗ Ⓙ	53 Ⓐ Ⓑ Ⓒ Ⓓ	66 Ⓕ Ⓖ Ⓗ Ⓙ
2 Ⓕ Ⓖ Ⓗ Ⓙ	15 Ⓐ Ⓑ Ⓒ Ⓓ	28 Ⓕ Ⓖ Ⓗ Ⓙ	41 Ⓐ Ⓑ Ⓒ Ⓓ	54 Ⓕ Ⓖ Ⓗ Ⓙ	67 Ⓐ Ⓑ Ⓒ Ⓓ
3 Ⓐ Ⓑ Ⓒ Ⓓ	16 Ⓕ Ⓖ Ⓗ Ⓙ	29 Ⓐ Ⓑ Ⓒ Ⓓ	42 Ⓕ Ⓖ Ⓗ Ⓙ	55 Ⓐ Ⓑ Ⓒ Ⓓ	68 Ⓕ Ⓖ Ⓗ Ⓙ
4 Ⓕ Ⓖ Ⓗ Ⓙ	17 Ⓐ Ⓑ Ⓒ Ⓓ	30 Ⓕ Ⓖ Ⓗ Ⓙ	43 Ⓐ Ⓑ Ⓒ Ⓓ	56 Ⓕ Ⓖ Ⓗ Ⓙ	69 Ⓐ Ⓑ Ⓒ Ⓓ
5 Ⓐ Ⓑ Ⓒ Ⓓ	18 Ⓕ Ⓖ Ⓗ Ⓙ	31 Ⓐ Ⓑ Ⓒ Ⓓ	44 Ⓕ Ⓖ Ⓗ Ⓙ	57 Ⓐ Ⓑ Ⓒ Ⓓ	70 Ⓕ Ⓖ Ⓗ Ⓙ
6 Ⓕ Ⓖ Ⓗ Ⓙ	19 Ⓐ Ⓑ Ⓒ Ⓓ	32 Ⓕ Ⓖ Ⓗ Ⓙ	45 Ⓐ Ⓑ Ⓒ Ⓓ	58 Ⓕ Ⓖ Ⓗ Ⓙ	71 Ⓐ Ⓑ Ⓒ Ⓓ
7 Ⓐ Ⓑ Ⓒ Ⓓ	20 Ⓕ Ⓖ Ⓗ Ⓙ	33 Ⓐ Ⓑ Ⓒ Ⓓ	46 Ⓕ Ⓖ Ⓗ Ⓙ	59 Ⓐ Ⓑ Ⓒ Ⓓ	72 Ⓕ Ⓖ Ⓗ Ⓙ
8 Ⓕ Ⓖ Ⓗ Ⓙ	21 Ⓐ Ⓑ Ⓒ Ⓓ	34 Ⓕ Ⓖ Ⓗ Ⓙ	47 Ⓐ Ⓑ Ⓒ Ⓓ	60 Ⓕ Ⓖ Ⓗ Ⓙ	73 Ⓐ Ⓑ Ⓒ Ⓓ
9 Ⓐ Ⓑ Ⓒ Ⓓ	22 Ⓕ Ⓖ Ⓗ Ⓙ	35 Ⓐ Ⓑ Ⓒ Ⓓ	48 Ⓕ Ⓖ Ⓗ Ⓙ	61 Ⓐ Ⓑ Ⓒ Ⓓ	74 Ⓕ Ⓖ Ⓗ Ⓙ
10 Ⓕ Ⓖ Ⓗ Ⓙ	23 Ⓐ Ⓑ Ⓒ Ⓓ	36 Ⓕ Ⓖ Ⓗ Ⓙ	49 Ⓐ Ⓑ Ⓒ Ⓓ	62 Ⓕ Ⓖ Ⓗ Ⓙ	75 Ⓐ Ⓑ Ⓒ Ⓓ
11 Ⓐ Ⓑ Ⓒ Ⓓ	24 Ⓕ Ⓖ Ⓗ Ⓙ	37 Ⓐ Ⓑ Ⓒ Ⓓ	50 Ⓕ Ⓖ Ⓗ Ⓙ	63 Ⓐ Ⓑ Ⓒ Ⓓ	
12 Ⓕ Ⓖ Ⓗ Ⓙ	25 Ⓐ Ⓑ Ⓒ Ⓓ	38 Ⓕ Ⓖ Ⓗ Ⓙ	51 Ⓐ Ⓑ Ⓒ Ⓓ	64 Ⓕ Ⓖ Ⓗ Ⓙ	
13 Ⓐ Ⓑ Ⓒ Ⓓ	26 Ⓕ Ⓖ Ⓗ Ⓙ	39 Ⓐ Ⓑ Ⓒ Ⓓ	52 Ⓕ Ⓖ Ⓗ Ⓙ	65 Ⓐ Ⓑ Ⓒ Ⓓ	

TEST 2

1 Ⓐ Ⓑ Ⓒ Ⓓ Ⓔ	11 Ⓐ Ⓑ Ⓒ Ⓓ Ⓔ	21 Ⓐ Ⓑ Ⓒ Ⓓ Ⓔ	31 Ⓐ Ⓑ Ⓒ Ⓓ Ⓔ	41 Ⓐ Ⓑ Ⓒ Ⓓ Ⓔ	51 Ⓐ Ⓑ Ⓒ Ⓓ Ⓔ
2 Ⓕ Ⓖ Ⓗ Ⓙ Ⓚ	12 Ⓕ Ⓖ Ⓗ Ⓙ Ⓚ	22 Ⓕ Ⓖ Ⓗ Ⓙ Ⓚ	32 Ⓕ Ⓖ Ⓗ Ⓙ Ⓚ	42 Ⓕ Ⓖ Ⓗ Ⓙ Ⓚ	52 Ⓕ Ⓖ Ⓗ Ⓙ Ⓚ
3 Ⓐ Ⓑ Ⓒ Ⓓ Ⓔ	13 Ⓐ Ⓑ Ⓒ Ⓓ Ⓔ	23 Ⓐ Ⓑ Ⓒ Ⓓ Ⓔ	33 Ⓐ Ⓑ Ⓒ Ⓓ Ⓔ	43 Ⓐ Ⓑ Ⓒ Ⓓ Ⓔ	53 Ⓐ Ⓑ Ⓒ Ⓓ Ⓔ
4 Ⓕ Ⓖ Ⓗ Ⓙ Ⓚ	14 Ⓕ Ⓖ Ⓗ Ⓙ Ⓚ	24 Ⓕ Ⓖ Ⓗ Ⓙ Ⓚ	34 Ⓕ Ⓖ Ⓗ Ⓙ Ⓚ	44 Ⓕ Ⓖ Ⓗ Ⓙ Ⓚ	54 Ⓕ Ⓖ Ⓗ Ⓙ Ⓚ
5 Ⓐ Ⓑ Ⓒ Ⓓ Ⓔ	15 Ⓐ Ⓑ Ⓒ Ⓓ Ⓔ	25 Ⓐ Ⓑ Ⓒ Ⓓ Ⓔ	35 Ⓐ Ⓑ Ⓒ Ⓓ Ⓔ	45 Ⓐ Ⓑ Ⓒ Ⓓ Ⓔ	55 Ⓐ Ⓑ Ⓒ Ⓓ Ⓔ
6 Ⓕ Ⓖ Ⓗ Ⓙ Ⓚ	16 Ⓕ Ⓖ Ⓗ Ⓙ Ⓚ	26 Ⓕ Ⓖ Ⓗ Ⓙ Ⓚ	36 Ⓕ Ⓖ Ⓗ Ⓙ Ⓚ	46 Ⓕ Ⓖ Ⓗ Ⓙ Ⓚ	56 Ⓕ Ⓖ Ⓗ Ⓙ Ⓚ
7 Ⓐ Ⓑ Ⓒ Ⓓ Ⓔ	17 Ⓐ Ⓑ Ⓒ Ⓓ Ⓔ	27 Ⓐ Ⓑ Ⓒ Ⓓ Ⓔ	37 Ⓐ Ⓑ Ⓒ Ⓓ Ⓔ	47 Ⓐ Ⓑ Ⓒ Ⓓ Ⓔ	57 Ⓐ Ⓑ Ⓒ Ⓓ Ⓔ
8 Ⓕ Ⓖ Ⓗ Ⓙ Ⓚ	18 Ⓕ Ⓖ Ⓗ Ⓙ Ⓚ	28 Ⓕ Ⓖ Ⓗ Ⓙ Ⓚ	38 Ⓕ Ⓖ Ⓗ Ⓙ Ⓚ	48 Ⓕ Ⓖ Ⓗ Ⓙ Ⓚ	58 Ⓕ Ⓖ Ⓗ Ⓙ Ⓚ
9 Ⓐ Ⓑ Ⓒ Ⓓ Ⓔ	19 Ⓐ Ⓑ Ⓒ Ⓓ Ⓔ	29 Ⓐ Ⓑ Ⓒ Ⓓ Ⓔ	39 Ⓐ Ⓑ Ⓒ Ⓓ Ⓔ	49 Ⓐ Ⓑ Ⓒ Ⓓ Ⓔ	59 Ⓐ Ⓑ Ⓒ Ⓓ Ⓔ
10 Ⓕ Ⓖ Ⓗ Ⓙ Ⓚ	20 Ⓕ Ⓖ Ⓗ Ⓙ Ⓚ	30 Ⓕ Ⓖ Ⓗ Ⓙ Ⓚ	40 Ⓕ Ⓖ Ⓗ Ⓙ Ⓚ	50 Ⓕ Ⓖ Ⓗ Ⓙ Ⓚ	60 Ⓕ Ⓖ Ⓗ Ⓙ Ⓚ

TEST 3

1 Ⓐ Ⓑ Ⓒ Ⓓ	8 Ⓕ Ⓖ Ⓗ Ⓙ	15 Ⓐ Ⓑ Ⓒ Ⓓ	22 Ⓕ Ⓖ Ⓗ Ⓙ	29 Ⓐ Ⓑ Ⓒ Ⓓ	36 Ⓕ Ⓖ Ⓗ Ⓙ
2 Ⓕ Ⓖ Ⓗ Ⓙ	9 Ⓐ Ⓑ Ⓒ Ⓓ	16 Ⓕ Ⓖ Ⓗ Ⓙ	23 Ⓐ Ⓑ Ⓒ Ⓓ	30 Ⓕ Ⓖ Ⓗ Ⓙ	37 Ⓐ Ⓑ Ⓒ Ⓓ
3 Ⓐ Ⓑ Ⓒ Ⓓ	10 Ⓕ Ⓖ Ⓗ Ⓙ	17 Ⓐ Ⓑ Ⓒ Ⓓ	24 Ⓕ Ⓖ Ⓗ Ⓙ	31 Ⓐ Ⓑ Ⓒ Ⓓ	38 Ⓕ Ⓖ Ⓗ Ⓙ
4 Ⓕ Ⓖ Ⓗ Ⓙ	11 Ⓐ Ⓑ Ⓒ Ⓓ	18 Ⓕ Ⓖ Ⓗ Ⓙ	25 Ⓐ Ⓑ Ⓒ Ⓓ	32 Ⓕ Ⓖ Ⓗ Ⓙ	39 Ⓐ Ⓑ Ⓒ Ⓓ
5 Ⓐ Ⓑ Ⓒ Ⓓ	12 Ⓕ Ⓖ Ⓗ Ⓙ	19 Ⓐ Ⓑ Ⓒ Ⓓ	26 Ⓕ Ⓖ Ⓗ Ⓙ	33 Ⓐ Ⓑ Ⓒ Ⓓ	40 Ⓕ Ⓖ Ⓗ Ⓙ
6 Ⓕ Ⓖ Ⓗ Ⓙ	13 Ⓐ Ⓑ Ⓒ Ⓓ	20 Ⓕ Ⓖ Ⓗ Ⓙ	27 Ⓐ Ⓑ Ⓒ Ⓓ	34 Ⓕ Ⓖ Ⓗ Ⓙ	
7 Ⓐ Ⓑ Ⓒ Ⓓ	14 Ⓕ Ⓖ Ⓗ Ⓙ	21 Ⓐ Ⓑ Ⓒ Ⓓ	28 Ⓕ Ⓖ Ⓗ Ⓙ	35 Ⓐ Ⓑ Ⓒ Ⓓ	

TEST 4

1 Ⓐ Ⓑ Ⓒ Ⓓ	8 Ⓕ Ⓖ Ⓗ Ⓙ	15 Ⓐ Ⓑ Ⓒ Ⓓ	22 Ⓕ Ⓖ Ⓗ Ⓙ	29 Ⓐ Ⓑ Ⓒ Ⓓ	36 Ⓕ Ⓖ Ⓗ Ⓙ
2 Ⓕ Ⓖ Ⓗ Ⓙ	9 Ⓐ Ⓑ Ⓒ Ⓓ	16 Ⓕ Ⓖ Ⓗ Ⓙ	23 Ⓐ Ⓑ Ⓒ Ⓓ	30 Ⓕ Ⓖ Ⓗ Ⓙ	37 Ⓐ Ⓑ Ⓒ Ⓓ
3 Ⓐ Ⓑ Ⓒ Ⓓ	10 Ⓕ Ⓖ Ⓗ Ⓙ	17 Ⓐ Ⓑ Ⓒ Ⓓ	24 Ⓕ Ⓖ Ⓗ Ⓙ	31 Ⓐ Ⓑ Ⓒ Ⓓ	38 Ⓕ Ⓖ Ⓗ Ⓙ
4 Ⓕ Ⓖ Ⓗ Ⓙ	11 Ⓐ Ⓑ Ⓒ Ⓓ	18 Ⓕ Ⓖ Ⓗ Ⓙ	25 Ⓐ Ⓑ Ⓒ Ⓓ	32 Ⓕ Ⓖ Ⓗ Ⓙ	39 Ⓐ Ⓑ Ⓒ Ⓓ
5 Ⓐ Ⓑ Ⓒ Ⓓ	12 Ⓕ Ⓖ Ⓗ Ⓙ	19 Ⓐ Ⓑ Ⓒ Ⓓ	26 Ⓕ Ⓖ Ⓗ Ⓙ	33 Ⓐ Ⓑ Ⓒ Ⓓ	40 Ⓕ Ⓖ Ⓗ Ⓙ
6 Ⓕ Ⓖ Ⓗ Ⓙ	13 Ⓐ Ⓑ Ⓒ Ⓓ	20 Ⓕ Ⓖ Ⓗ Ⓙ	27 Ⓐ Ⓑ Ⓒ Ⓓ	34 Ⓕ Ⓖ Ⓗ Ⓙ	
7 Ⓐ Ⓑ Ⓒ Ⓓ	14 Ⓕ Ⓖ Ⓗ Ⓙ	21 Ⓐ Ⓑ Ⓒ Ⓓ	28 Ⓕ Ⓖ Ⓗ Ⓙ	35 Ⓐ Ⓑ Ⓒ Ⓓ	

The **ACT**®

The ACT® *Sample Answer Sheet*

A NAME, MAILING ADDRESS, AND TELEPHONE
(Please print.)

Last Name   First Name   MI (Middle Initial)

House Number & Street (Apt. No.); or PO Box & No.; or RR & No.

City   State/Province   ZIP/Postal Code

Area Code   Number   Country

ACT, Inc.—Confidential Restricted when data present.

ALL examinees must complete block A – please print.

REGISTERED examinees **MUST complete blocks B, C, and D.** Find the MATCHING INFORMATION on your admission ticket and enter it EXACTLY the same way, even if any of the information is missing or incorrect. Fill in the corresponding ovals. If you do not complete these blocks to match your admission ticket EXACTLY, your scores will be **delayed up to 8 weeks.** Leave blocks E and F blank.

STANDBY examinees **MUST complete blocks B, D, and F.** Enter your information in blocks B and D and fill in the corresponding ovals. Leave block C blank. **For block E,** if you provided your SSN when you created your Web account or completed your standby folder, enter it here. The SSN will be used to help match this document to your registration information and will be included on reports to your college choices. If you did not provide it earlier, do not know it, or do not wish to provide it, leave block E blank. Be sure to fill in the oval in block F.

Do NOT mark in this shaded area.

B MATCH NAME
(First 5 letters of last name)

C MATCH NUMBER
(Registered examinees only)

D DATE OF BIRTH

	Month	Day	Year

↓ STANDBY TESTING ONLY ↓

E SOCIAL SECURITY NUMBER
(Standby examinees only)

F STANDBY TESTING

Fill in the oval below ONLY if you turned in a standby registration at the test center today.

○ Yes, I am testing as a standby.

USE A SOFT LEAD NO. 2 PENCIL ONLY.
(Do NOT use a mechanical pencil, ink, ballpoint, correction fluid, or felt-tip pen.)

EXAMINEE STATEMENT AND SIGNATURE

1. Read the following **Statement:** By submitting this answer sheet, I agree to the terms and conditions set forth in the ACT registration booklet or website for this exam, including the arbitration and dispute remedy provisions. I understand that ACT owns the test questions and responses and affirm that I will not share any test questions or responses with anyone by any form of communication.

2. Copy the **Certification** shown below (only the text in italics) on the lines provided. Write in your normal handwriting.

   Certification: *I agree to the Statement above and certify that I am the person whose name and address appear on this form.*

3. Sign your name as you would any official document and enter today's date.

Your Signature   Today's Date

ACT®

P.O. BOX 168, IOWA CITY, IOWA 52243-0168

Marking Directions: Mark only **one** oval for each question. Fill in response completely. Erase errors cleanly without smudging.

Correct mark: ⚪ ⚫ ⚪ ⚪

- -

Do NOT use these incorrect or bad marks.

Incorrect marks: ⊘ ⊗ ⊖ ⊙
Overlapping mark: ⚪ ⚪ ⚪ ⚫
Cross-out mark: ⚫ ⚫ ⚪ ⚪
Smudged erasure: ⚪ ⚪ ⚫ ⚪
Mark is too light: ⚫ ⚪ ⚪ ⚪

BOOKLET NUMBER

①	①	①	①	①	①
②	②	②	②	②	②
③	③	③	③	③	③
④	④	④	④	④	④
⑤	⑤	⑤	⑤	⑤	⑤
⑥	⑥	⑥	⑥	⑥	⑥
⑦	⑦	⑦	⑦	⑦	⑦
⑧	⑧	⑧	⑧	⑧	⑧
⑨	⑨	⑨	⑨	⑨	⑨
⓪	⓪	⓪	⓪	⓪	⓪

FORM

Print your 3-character **Test Form** in the boxes above and fill in the corresponding oval at the right.

BE SURE TO FILL IN THE CORRECT FORM OVAL.

⚪ 1MC   ⚪ 2MC   ⚪ 3MC   ⚪ 4MC
⚪ 5MC

TEST 1

1 Ⓐ Ⓑ Ⓒ Ⓓ	14 Ⓕ Ⓖ Ⓗ Ⓙ	27 Ⓐ Ⓑ Ⓒ Ⓓ	40 Ⓕ Ⓖ Ⓗ Ⓙ	53 Ⓐ Ⓑ Ⓒ Ⓓ	66 Ⓕ Ⓖ Ⓗ Ⓙ
2 Ⓕ Ⓖ Ⓗ Ⓙ	15 Ⓐ Ⓑ Ⓒ Ⓓ	28 Ⓕ Ⓖ Ⓗ Ⓙ	41 Ⓐ Ⓑ Ⓒ Ⓓ	54 Ⓕ Ⓖ Ⓗ Ⓙ	67 Ⓐ Ⓑ Ⓒ Ⓓ
3 Ⓐ Ⓑ Ⓒ Ⓓ	16 Ⓕ Ⓖ Ⓗ Ⓙ	29 Ⓐ Ⓑ Ⓒ Ⓓ	42 Ⓕ Ⓖ Ⓗ Ⓙ	55 Ⓐ Ⓑ Ⓒ Ⓓ	68 Ⓕ Ⓖ Ⓗ Ⓙ
4 Ⓕ Ⓖ Ⓗ Ⓙ	17 Ⓐ Ⓑ Ⓒ Ⓓ	30 Ⓕ Ⓖ Ⓗ Ⓙ	43 Ⓐ Ⓑ Ⓒ Ⓓ	56 Ⓕ Ⓖ Ⓗ Ⓙ	69 Ⓐ Ⓑ Ⓒ Ⓓ
5 Ⓐ Ⓑ Ⓒ Ⓓ	18 Ⓕ Ⓖ Ⓗ Ⓙ	31 Ⓐ Ⓑ Ⓒ Ⓓ	44 Ⓕ Ⓖ Ⓗ Ⓙ	57 Ⓐ Ⓑ Ⓒ Ⓓ	70 Ⓕ Ⓖ Ⓗ Ⓙ
6 Ⓕ Ⓖ Ⓗ Ⓙ	19 Ⓐ Ⓑ Ⓒ Ⓓ	32 Ⓕ Ⓖ Ⓗ Ⓙ	45 Ⓐ Ⓑ Ⓒ Ⓓ	58 Ⓕ Ⓖ Ⓗ Ⓙ	71 Ⓐ Ⓑ Ⓒ Ⓓ
7 Ⓐ Ⓑ Ⓒ Ⓓ	20 Ⓕ Ⓖ Ⓗ Ⓙ	33 Ⓐ Ⓑ Ⓒ Ⓓ	46 Ⓕ Ⓖ Ⓗ Ⓙ	59 Ⓐ Ⓑ Ⓒ Ⓓ	72 Ⓕ Ⓖ Ⓗ Ⓙ
8 Ⓕ Ⓖ Ⓗ Ⓙ	21 Ⓐ Ⓑ Ⓒ Ⓓ	34 Ⓕ Ⓖ Ⓗ Ⓙ	47 Ⓐ Ⓑ Ⓒ Ⓓ	60 Ⓕ Ⓖ Ⓗ Ⓙ	73 Ⓐ Ⓑ Ⓒ Ⓓ
9 Ⓐ Ⓑ Ⓒ Ⓓ	22 Ⓕ Ⓖ Ⓗ Ⓙ	35 Ⓐ Ⓑ Ⓒ Ⓓ	48 Ⓕ Ⓖ Ⓗ Ⓙ	61 Ⓐ Ⓑ Ⓒ Ⓓ	74 Ⓕ Ⓖ Ⓗ Ⓙ
10 Ⓕ Ⓖ Ⓗ Ⓙ	23 Ⓐ Ⓑ Ⓒ Ⓓ	36 Ⓕ Ⓖ Ⓗ Ⓙ	49 Ⓐ Ⓑ Ⓒ Ⓓ	62 Ⓕ Ⓖ Ⓗ Ⓙ	75 Ⓐ Ⓑ Ⓒ Ⓓ
11 Ⓐ Ⓑ Ⓒ Ⓓ	24 Ⓕ Ⓖ Ⓗ Ⓙ	37 Ⓐ Ⓑ Ⓒ Ⓓ	50 Ⓕ Ⓖ Ⓗ Ⓙ	63 Ⓐ Ⓑ Ⓒ Ⓓ	
12 Ⓕ Ⓖ Ⓗ Ⓙ	25 Ⓐ Ⓑ Ⓒ Ⓓ	38 Ⓕ Ⓖ Ⓗ Ⓙ	51 Ⓐ Ⓑ Ⓒ Ⓓ	64 Ⓕ Ⓖ Ⓗ Ⓙ	
13 Ⓐ Ⓑ Ⓒ Ⓓ	26 Ⓕ Ⓖ Ⓗ Ⓙ	39 Ⓐ Ⓑ Ⓒ Ⓓ	52 Ⓕ Ⓖ Ⓗ Ⓙ	65 Ⓐ Ⓑ Ⓒ Ⓓ	

TEST 2

1 Ⓐ Ⓑ Ⓒ Ⓓ Ⓔ	11 Ⓐ Ⓑ Ⓒ Ⓓ Ⓔ	21 Ⓐ Ⓑ Ⓒ Ⓓ Ⓔ	31 Ⓐ Ⓑ Ⓒ Ⓓ Ⓔ	41 Ⓐ Ⓑ Ⓒ Ⓓ Ⓔ	51 Ⓐ Ⓑ Ⓒ Ⓓ Ⓔ
2 Ⓕ Ⓖ Ⓗ Ⓙ Ⓚ	12 Ⓕ Ⓖ Ⓗ Ⓙ Ⓚ	22 Ⓕ Ⓖ Ⓗ Ⓙ Ⓚ	32 Ⓕ Ⓖ Ⓗ Ⓙ Ⓚ	42 Ⓕ Ⓖ Ⓗ Ⓙ Ⓚ	52 Ⓕ Ⓖ Ⓗ Ⓙ Ⓚ
3 Ⓐ Ⓑ Ⓒ Ⓓ Ⓔ	13 Ⓐ Ⓑ Ⓒ Ⓓ Ⓔ	23 Ⓐ Ⓑ Ⓒ Ⓓ Ⓔ	33 Ⓐ Ⓑ Ⓒ Ⓓ Ⓔ	43 Ⓐ Ⓑ Ⓒ Ⓓ Ⓔ	53 Ⓐ Ⓑ Ⓒ Ⓓ Ⓔ
4 Ⓕ Ⓖ Ⓗ Ⓙ Ⓚ	14 Ⓕ Ⓖ Ⓗ Ⓙ Ⓚ	24 Ⓕ Ⓖ Ⓗ Ⓙ Ⓚ	34 Ⓕ Ⓖ Ⓗ Ⓙ Ⓚ	44 Ⓕ Ⓖ Ⓗ Ⓙ Ⓚ	54 Ⓕ Ⓖ Ⓗ Ⓙ Ⓚ
5 Ⓐ Ⓑ Ⓒ Ⓓ Ⓔ	15 Ⓐ Ⓑ Ⓒ Ⓓ Ⓔ	25 Ⓐ Ⓑ Ⓒ Ⓓ Ⓔ	35 Ⓐ Ⓑ Ⓒ Ⓓ Ⓔ	45 Ⓐ Ⓑ Ⓒ Ⓓ Ⓔ	55 Ⓐ Ⓑ Ⓒ Ⓓ Ⓔ
6 Ⓕ Ⓖ Ⓗ Ⓙ Ⓚ	16 Ⓕ Ⓖ Ⓗ Ⓙ Ⓚ	26 Ⓕ Ⓖ Ⓗ Ⓙ Ⓚ	36 Ⓕ Ⓖ Ⓗ Ⓙ Ⓚ	46 Ⓕ Ⓖ Ⓗ Ⓙ Ⓚ	56 Ⓕ Ⓖ Ⓗ Ⓙ Ⓚ
7 Ⓐ Ⓑ Ⓒ Ⓓ Ⓔ	17 Ⓐ Ⓑ Ⓒ Ⓓ Ⓔ	27 Ⓐ Ⓑ Ⓒ Ⓓ Ⓔ	37 Ⓐ Ⓑ Ⓒ Ⓓ Ⓔ	47 Ⓐ Ⓑ Ⓒ Ⓓ Ⓔ	57 Ⓐ Ⓑ Ⓒ Ⓓ Ⓔ
8 Ⓕ Ⓖ Ⓗ Ⓙ Ⓚ	18 Ⓕ Ⓖ Ⓗ Ⓙ Ⓚ	28 Ⓕ Ⓖ Ⓗ Ⓙ Ⓚ	38 Ⓕ Ⓖ Ⓗ Ⓙ Ⓚ	48 Ⓕ Ⓖ Ⓗ Ⓙ Ⓚ	58 Ⓕ Ⓖ Ⓗ Ⓙ Ⓚ
9 Ⓐ Ⓑ Ⓒ Ⓓ Ⓔ	19 Ⓐ Ⓑ Ⓒ Ⓓ Ⓔ	29 Ⓐ Ⓑ Ⓒ Ⓓ Ⓔ	39 Ⓐ Ⓑ Ⓒ Ⓓ Ⓔ	49 Ⓐ Ⓑ Ⓒ Ⓓ Ⓔ	59 Ⓐ Ⓑ Ⓒ Ⓓ Ⓔ
10 Ⓕ Ⓖ Ⓗ Ⓙ Ⓚ	20 Ⓕ Ⓖ Ⓗ Ⓙ Ⓚ	30 Ⓕ Ⓖ Ⓗ Ⓙ Ⓚ	40 Ⓕ Ⓖ Ⓗ Ⓙ Ⓚ	50 Ⓕ Ⓖ Ⓗ Ⓙ Ⓚ	60 Ⓕ Ⓖ Ⓗ Ⓙ Ⓚ

TEST 3

1 Ⓐ Ⓑ Ⓒ Ⓓ	8 Ⓕ Ⓖ Ⓗ Ⓙ	15 Ⓐ Ⓑ Ⓒ Ⓓ	22 Ⓕ Ⓖ Ⓗ Ⓙ	29 Ⓐ Ⓑ Ⓒ Ⓓ	36 Ⓕ Ⓖ Ⓗ Ⓙ
2 Ⓕ Ⓖ Ⓗ Ⓙ	9 Ⓐ Ⓑ Ⓒ Ⓓ	16 Ⓕ Ⓖ Ⓗ Ⓙ	23 Ⓐ Ⓑ Ⓒ Ⓓ	30 Ⓕ Ⓖ Ⓗ Ⓙ	37 Ⓐ Ⓑ Ⓒ Ⓓ
3 Ⓐ Ⓑ Ⓒ Ⓓ	10 Ⓕ Ⓖ Ⓗ Ⓙ	17 Ⓐ Ⓑ Ⓒ Ⓓ	24 Ⓕ Ⓖ Ⓗ Ⓙ	31 Ⓐ Ⓑ Ⓒ Ⓓ	38 Ⓕ Ⓖ Ⓗ Ⓙ
4 Ⓕ Ⓖ Ⓗ Ⓙ	11 Ⓐ Ⓑ Ⓒ Ⓓ	18 Ⓕ Ⓖ Ⓗ Ⓙ	25 Ⓐ Ⓑ Ⓒ Ⓓ	32 Ⓕ Ⓖ Ⓗ Ⓙ	39 Ⓐ Ⓑ Ⓒ Ⓓ
5 Ⓐ Ⓑ Ⓒ Ⓓ	12 Ⓕ Ⓖ Ⓗ Ⓙ	19 Ⓐ Ⓑ Ⓒ Ⓓ	26 Ⓕ Ⓖ Ⓗ Ⓙ	33 Ⓐ Ⓑ Ⓒ Ⓓ	40 Ⓕ Ⓖ Ⓗ Ⓙ
6 Ⓕ Ⓖ Ⓗ Ⓙ	13 Ⓐ Ⓑ Ⓒ Ⓓ	20 Ⓕ Ⓖ Ⓗ Ⓙ	27 Ⓐ Ⓑ Ⓒ Ⓓ	34 Ⓕ Ⓖ Ⓗ Ⓙ	
7 Ⓐ Ⓑ Ⓒ Ⓓ	14 Ⓕ Ⓖ Ⓗ Ⓙ	21 Ⓐ Ⓑ Ⓒ Ⓓ	28 Ⓕ Ⓖ Ⓗ Ⓙ	35 Ⓐ Ⓑ Ⓒ Ⓓ	

TEST 4

1 Ⓐ Ⓑ Ⓒ Ⓓ	8 Ⓕ Ⓖ Ⓗ Ⓙ	15 Ⓐ Ⓑ Ⓒ Ⓓ	22 Ⓕ Ⓖ Ⓗ Ⓙ	29 Ⓐ Ⓑ Ⓒ Ⓓ	36 Ⓕ Ⓖ Ⓗ Ⓙ
2 Ⓕ Ⓖ Ⓗ Ⓙ	9 Ⓐ Ⓑ Ⓒ Ⓓ	16 Ⓕ Ⓖ Ⓗ Ⓙ	23 Ⓐ Ⓑ Ⓒ Ⓓ	30 Ⓕ Ⓖ Ⓗ Ⓙ	37 Ⓐ Ⓑ Ⓒ Ⓓ
3 Ⓐ Ⓑ Ⓒ Ⓓ	10 Ⓕ Ⓖ Ⓗ Ⓙ	17 Ⓐ Ⓑ Ⓒ Ⓓ	24 Ⓕ Ⓖ Ⓗ Ⓙ	31 Ⓐ Ⓑ Ⓒ Ⓓ	38 Ⓕ Ⓖ Ⓗ Ⓙ
4 Ⓕ Ⓖ Ⓗ Ⓙ	11 Ⓐ Ⓑ Ⓒ Ⓓ	18 Ⓕ Ⓖ Ⓗ Ⓙ	25 Ⓐ Ⓑ Ⓒ Ⓓ	32 Ⓕ Ⓖ Ⓗ Ⓙ	39 Ⓐ Ⓑ Ⓒ Ⓓ
5 Ⓐ Ⓑ Ⓒ Ⓓ	12 Ⓕ Ⓖ Ⓗ Ⓙ	19 Ⓐ Ⓑ Ⓒ Ⓓ	26 Ⓕ Ⓖ Ⓗ Ⓙ	33 Ⓐ Ⓑ Ⓒ Ⓓ	40 Ⓕ Ⓖ Ⓗ Ⓙ
6 Ⓕ Ⓖ Ⓗ Ⓙ	13 Ⓐ Ⓑ Ⓒ Ⓓ	20 Ⓕ Ⓖ Ⓗ Ⓙ	27 Ⓐ Ⓑ Ⓒ Ⓓ	34 Ⓕ Ⓖ Ⓗ Ⓙ	
7 Ⓐ Ⓑ Ⓒ Ⓓ	14 Ⓕ Ⓖ Ⓗ Ⓙ	21 Ⓐ Ⓑ Ⓒ Ⓓ	28 Ⓕ Ⓖ Ⓗ Ⓙ	35 Ⓐ Ⓑ Ⓒ Ⓓ	

The **ACT**®

080662

Practice Test 5

Today's Date: _____

Your Signature: _____

Print Your Name Here: _____

Your Date of Birth:

[ ][ ] – [ ][ ] – [ ][ ][ ][ ]
Month   Day   Year

Form 5MC

The **ACT**® 2011|2012

Directions

This booklet contains tests in English, Mathematics, Reading, and Science. These tests measure skills and abilities highly related to high school course work and success in college. *CALCULATORS MAY BE USED ON THE MATHEMATICS TEST ONLY.*

The questions in each test are numbered, and the suggested answers for each question are lettered. On the answer document, the rows of ovals are numbered to match the questions, and the ovals in each row are lettered to correspond to the suggested answers.

For each question, first decide which answer is best. Next, locate on the answer document the row of ovals numbered the same as the question. Then, locate the oval in that row lettered the same as your answer. Finally, fill in the oval completely. Use a soft lead pencil and make your marks heavy and black. *DO NOT USE INK OR A MECHANICAL PENCIL.*

Mark only one answer to each question. If you change your mind about an answer, erase your first mark thoroughly before marking your new answer. For each question, make certain that you mark in the row of ovals with the same number as the question.

Only responses marked on your answer document will be scored. Your score on each test will be based only on the number of questions you answer correctly during the time allowed for that test. You will NOT be penalized for guessing. *IT IS TO YOUR ADVANTAGE TO ANSWER EVERY QUESTION EVEN IF YOU MUST GUESS.*

You may work on each test ONLY when your test supervisor tells you to do so. If you finish a test before time is called for that test, you should use the time remaining to reconsider questions you are uncertain about in that test. You may NOT look back to a test on which time has already been called, and you may NOT go ahead to another test. To do so will disqualify you from the examination.

Lay your pencil down immediately when time is called at the end of each test. You may NOT for any reason fill in or alter ovals for a test after time is called for that test. To do so will disqualify you from the examination.

Do not fold or tear the pages of your test booklet.

**DO NOT OPEN THIS BOOKLET
UNTIL TOLD TO DO SO.**

ENGLISH TEST

45 Minutes—75 Questions

DIRECTIONS: In the five passages that follow, certain words and phrases are underlined and numbered. In the right-hand column, you will find alternatives for the underlined part. In most cases, you are to choose the one that best expresses the idea, makes the statement appropriate for standard written English, or is worded most consistently with the style and tone of the passage as a whole. If you think the original version is best, choose "NO CHANGE." In some cases, you will find in the right-hand column a question about the underlined part. You are to choose the best answer to the question.

You will also find questions about a section of the passage, or about the passage as a whole. These questions do not refer to an underlined portion of the passage, but rather are identified by a number or numbers in a box.

For each question, choose the alternative you consider best and fill in the corresponding oval on your answer document. Read each passage through once before you begin to answer the questions that accompany it. For many of the questions, you must read several sentences beyond the question to determine the answer. Be sure that you have read far enough ahead each time you choose an alternative.

PASSAGE I

Miami Time

My family is part of the Miami

tribe a Native American people, with strong
         1

ties to territory in present-day Ohio, Indiana,

and Illinois. Growing up in the Midwest, I often

heard my grandmother talk about "Miami time."

When she was doing something she loved, whether

it was making freezer jam or researching tribal history,
         2

she refused to be rushed in a hurry. "I'm on Miami time
         3

today," she would say. Conversely, if we were running

late for an appointment. She would chide us by saying,
         4

"Get a move on. We're not running on Miami time today,

you know."

1. A. NO CHANGE
   B. tribe, a Native American, people
   C. tribe, a Native American people
   D. tribe; a Native American people

2. At this point, the writer would like to provide a glimpse into the grandmother's interests. Given that all the choices are true, which one best accomplishes this purpose?
   F. NO CHANGE
   G. being actively involved in her pursuits,
   H. things I really hope she'll teach me one day,
   J. historical research as well as domestic projects,

3. A. NO CHANGE
   B. hurried or rushed.
   C. made to go faster or rushed.
   D. rushed.

4. F. NO CHANGE
   G. appointment; she
   H. appointment and she
   J. appointment, she

GO ON TO THE NEXT PAGE.

It was a difficult concept for me to grasp. My
grandmother tried to explain that "Miami time" referred to

those moments, when time seemed to slow down or stand

still. Recently, the meaning of her words started to sink in.

One morning, my son and I will inadvertently slip out of
the world measured in seconds, minutes, and hours, and
into one measured by curiosity and sensation.

[1] On a familiar trail near our house, I was pushing
Jeremy in his stroller and were thinking of the day ahead
and the tasks I had to complete. [2] Suddenly, he squealed
with pure delight and pointed toward a clearing. [3] There,
two does and three fawns stood watching us. [4] Five pairs
of ears flicked like antennae seeking a signal. [5] After a
few moments, the deer lowered their heads and began to
eat, as if they had decided we were harmless. [6] By then,
my son's face was full of wonder. ☐11

We spent the rest of the morning veering from the
trail to investigate small snatches of life. Lizards lazing
in the sun and quail rustled through grasses surprised us.

Wild blackberries melted on our tongues. For example, the
aroma of crushed eucalyptus leaves tingled in our noses.

---

5. Given that all the choices are true, which one provides
   the best opening to this paragraph?
   A. NO CHANGE
   B. I remember being late for a doctor's appointment
      one day.
   C. My grandmother lived with us, and as a result she
      and I became close over the years.
   D. My son asks me about my grandmother, whom he
      never met.

6. F. NO CHANGE
   G. moments when
   H. moments, as if
   J. moments, because

7. A. NO CHANGE
   B. spoken statements to my ears
   C. expressed opinions on the matter
   D. verbal remarks in conversation

8. F. NO CHANGE
   G. inadvertently slip
   H. are inadvertently slipping
   J. inadvertently slipped

9. A. NO CHANGE
   B. were having thoughts
   C. thinking
   D. DELETE the underlined portion.

10. F. NO CHANGE
    G. does, and three fawns
    H. does and three fawns,
    J. does and, three fawns

11. For the sake of the logic and coherence of this para-
    graph, Sentence 3 should be placed:
    A. where it is now.
    B. before Sentence 1.
    C. after Sentence 1.
    D. after Sentence 4.

12. F. NO CHANGE
    G. rustling
    H. were rustling
    J. DELETE the underlined portion.

13. A. NO CHANGE
    B. On the other hand, the
    C. Just in case, the
    D. The

GO ON TO THE NEXT PAGE.

By the time we found our way back to the car, the sun was high in the sky. We had taken three hours to complete a hike we usually finished in forty-five minutes. Yet the hike felt <u>shorter then</u> ever. As we drove off, I remembered
14
something else my grandmother used to say: "Miami time passes all too quickly."

14. F. NO CHANGE
    G. more shorter then
    H. the shortest than
    J. shorter than

> Question 15 asks about the preceding passage as a whole.

15. Suppose the writer's goal had been to write a brief essay conveying a personal experience with "Miami time." Would this essay successfully fulfill that goal?

    A. Yes, because it presents the narrator's firsthand experience of a morning spent in Miami time.
    B. Yes, because it reveals that after a conversation with the grandmother, the narrator decided to live in Miami time.
    C. No, because it shares the views of more than one person with regard to the meaning of Miami time.
    D. No, because the term "Miami time" belonged to the grandmother, not to the narrator.

PASSAGE II

Faith Ringgold's Quilting Bee

The artist Faith Ringgold has made a name for herself with her "story quilts," lively combinations of painting, quilting, and storytelling. Each artwork consists of a painting framed by quilted squares of fabric and story panels. One of these artworks, *The Sunflowers Quilting Bee at Arles*, depicts a scene of women at work on a quilt in a field of towering yellow <u>flowers that eight</u> African
16
American women sit around the quilt that covers their laps. Who are these people stitching among the flowers? What brings them so close that their shoulders touch?

16. F. NO CHANGE
    G. flowers and eight
    H. flowers. Eight
    J. flowers, eight

GO ON TO THE NEXT PAGE.

Thus, the answers to these questions can
___
17
be found in the artwork itself. Ringgold has told

the story of this gathering on two horizontal panels of text.
___
18
One panel is sewn into the piece's top border,

the other into it's bottom border. These eight
___
19

women the story explains, strove
___
20

in their various ways to support
___
21
the cause of justice in the world.

In reality, these women never met to piece togeth
___
22

a quilt. The scene comes out of the artists imagination
___
23
a statement of the unity of purpose that she perceives i

their lives. Sojourner Truth and Harriet Tubman fough

to abolish slavery and, later, was active in the crusade
___
24
for suffrage. Newspaper journalist Ida B. Wells

courageously spoke out for social and racial justice
___
25
in the late nineteenth and early twentieth centuries.
___
25

17. A. NO CHANGE
    B. Instead, the
    C. Furthermore, the
    D. The

18. F. NO CHANGE
    G. of this gathering the story on two horizontal panels of text.
    H. on two horizontal panels the story of this gathering of text.
    J. the story on two horizontal panels of text of this gathering.

19. A. NO CHANGE
    B. its'
    C. its
    D. their

20. F. NO CHANGE
    G. women, the story explains—
    H. women the story explains—
    J. women, the story explains,

21. The underlined phrase could be placed in all the following locations EXCEPT:
    A. where it is now.
    B. after the word *support*.
    C. after the word *cause*.
    D. after the word *world* (ending the sentence with a period).

22. F. NO CHANGE
    G. summary,
    H. addition,
    J. contrast,

23. A. NO CHANGE
    B. artist's imagination
    C. artists' imagination
    D. artists imagination,

24. F. NO CHANGE
    G. was actively engaged
    H. was engaged
    J. were active

25. Given that all the choices are true, which one provides the most relevant information at this point in the essay?
    A. NO CHANGE
    B. married Ferdinand Barnett, editor of the first Black newspaper in Chicago, the *Chicago Conservator*.
    C. wrote for newspapers in Memphis, New York City, and finally, Chicago.
    D. was born in Holly Springs, Mississippi, in 1862, the eldest of eight children.

GO ON TO THE NEXT PAGE.

Establishing her own hair products business, herself
in the first decade of the twentieth century,
__26__

millions of dollars were later bequeathed by Madam
C. J. Walker to charities and educational institutions.
__27__
Among the schools that benefited from this

generosity, were those that Mary McLeod Bethune
__28__
opened and ran in order to provide a better education

for Black students. And Fannie Lou Hamer, Ella Baker,

and Rosa Parks showed leadership and strength during the

civil rights movement, it happened in the 1950s and 1960s.
__29__
    In the artwork, Ringgold has surrounded these women

with bright sunflowers. The flowers seem to celebrate the

women's accomplishments and the beauty of their shared

vision. [30]

26. F. NO CHANGE
    G. business belonging to her
    H. business, herself,
    J. business

27. A. NO CHANGE
    B. Madam C. J. Walker later bequeathed millions of
       dollars to charities and educational institutions.
    C. charities and educational institutions later received
       millions of dollars from Madam C. J. Walker.
    D. millions of dollars were later bequeathed to chari-
       ties and educational institutions by Madam C. J.
       Walker.

28. F. NO CHANGE
    G. generosity; were
    H. generosity were
    J. generosity were:

29. A. NO CHANGE
    B. movement, it took place in
    C. movement, that happened in
    D. movement of

30. If the writer were to delete the preceding sentence, the
    essay would primarily lose:
    F. an interpretation of the artwork that serves to sum-
       marize the essay.
    G. a reflection on the women depicted in the artwork
       that compares them to Ringgold.
    H. a description of a brushwork technique that refers
       back to the essay's opening.
    J. an evaluation of Ringgold's artistic talent that
       places her in a historical context.

PASSAGE III

1902: A Space Odyssey

    Our technologically advanced times has allowed
__31__
filmmakers to create spectacular science fiction films to

intrigue us with worlds beyond our experience. Imagine

the excitement in 1902 when audiences first saw *Le Voyage*
__32__
dans la lune (A Trip to the Moon), a groundbreaking movie

produced by Georges Méliès.

31. A. NO CHANGE
    B. have allowed
    C. allows
    D. was allowing

32. F. NO CHANGE
    G. 1902, and when
    H. 1902, which
    J. 1902, where

GO ON TO THE NEXT PAGE.

[1] Undaunted, Méliès honed his photographic skills to tell fantasy stories instead. [2] Méliès, a French magician, was fascinated by the workings of the new motion picture camera. [3] Specializing in stage illusions, he thought the camera offered potential to expand its spectacular magic productions. [4] By 1895, he
___
33
was working with the new invention. [5] He found

out, however, that the public preferred live magic
___
34

acts to filmed versions. ☐35

Méliès's magician's eye led him to discover the basics of special effects. ☐36 He experimented with effects such as speeding up and slowing down the action, reversing it for backward movement, and superimposing images of fantastic creatures over real people. Using overhead

pulleys and trapdoors, he was able to do interesting things.
___
37
Aware of the popularity of Jules Verne's science fiction novels, Méliès saw exciting possibilities in filming a space odyssey. The interplanetary travel film that he created, *A Trip to the Moon*, had production costs of $4,000, highly excessively for its time. In this film, a space
___
38

capsule that is fired and thereby launched and projected
___
39
from a cannon lands in the eye of the Man in the Moon.

33. A. NO CHANGE
    B. their
    C. his
    D. it's

34. F. NO CHANGE
    G. out, however;
    H. out, however
    J. out however,

35. For the sake of the logic and coherence of this paragraph, Sentence 1 should be placed:
    A. where it is now.
    B. after Sentence 2.
    C. after Sentence 3.
    D. after Sentence 5.

36. The writer is considering deleting the preceding sentence from the essay. The sentence should NOT be deleted because it:
    F. describes Méliès's ability as a magician, which is important to understanding the essay.
    G. begins to explain the techniques of trick photography that Méliès eventually learned.
    H. creates a transition that provides a further connection between Méliès the magician and Méliès the filmmaker.
    J. indicates that Méliès's interest in learning about trick photography existed before his interest in magic.

37. Given that all the choices are true, which one would best conclude this sentence so that it illustrates Méliès's skill and inventiveness?
    A. NO CHANGE
    B. he used effects commonly seen in his stage productions.
    C. his actors could enter and leave the scene.
    D. he perfected eerie film entrances and exits.

38. F. NO CHANGE
    G. exceeding highly
    H. high excessively
    J. exceedingly high

39. A. NO CHANGE
    B. fired
    C. fired from and consequently projected
    D. fired and thereby propelled

GO ON TO THE NEXT PAGE.

In a strange terrain filled with hostile <u>creatures, the</u>
₄₀
space travelers experience many adventures. They

escape back to earth in the capsule by falling off the

edge of the <u>moon, landing</u> in the ocean, they bob
₄₁
around until a passing ship finally rescues them.

Producing the film long before

interplanetary explorations <u>had began,</u>
₄₂

Méliès could <u>arouse</u> his audience's
₄₃
curiosity with unconstrained fantasy.

<u>People are still going to theaters to see</u>
₄₄
<u>science fiction films.</u>
₄₄

40. F. NO CHANGE
   G. creatures, who they now realize live there,
   H. creatures, whom they are encountering,
   J. creatures who are found there,

41. A. NO CHANGE
   B. moon after landing
   C. moon. Landing
   D. moon, after landing

42. F. NO CHANGE
   G. would of begun,
   H. have began,
   J. had begun,

43. Which of the following alternatives to the underlined word would be LEAST acceptable?

   A. whet
   B. stimulate
   C. awaken
   D. disturb

44. Given that all the choices are true, which one would most effectively express the writer's viewpoint about Méliès's role in science fiction filmmaking?

   F. NO CHANGE
   G. This first space odyssey provided the genesis for a film genre that still packs theaters.
   H. Méliès made an important contribution to film-making many years ago.
   J. In Méliès's production even the film crew knew a lot about space.

Question 45 asks about the preceding passage as a whole.

---

45. Suppose the writer's goal had been to write a brief essay highlighting the contributions a single artist can make to a particular art form. Would this essay fulfill that goal?

   A. Yes, because the essay asserts that Méliès's work as a magician never would have succeeded without the contributions of the artists in the film industry.
   B. Yes, because the essay presents Méliès as a magician who used his talents and curiosity to explore and excel in the film world.
   C. No, because the essay focuses on the process of making science fiction films, not on a single artist's work.
   D. No, because the essay suggests that it took many artists working together to create the success that Méliès enjoyed.

GO ON TO THE NEXT PAGE.

PASSAGE IV

Nancy Drew in the Twenty-First Century

I thought the Nancy Drew mystery series had

went out of style. I was sure that girls growing up
___
46

today would have more up-to-date role models and my

generation's favorite sleuth would of been retired to the
___
47

library's dusty, back rooms. I was wrong.
___
48

Nancy Drew, the teenaged heroine of heaps of young
___
49

adult mystery novels, is alive and well and still on the job.
___
50

I know because my niece, Liana, and her friends were

reading that all summer long. By the time Liana went back
___
51

to school and had followed Nancy Drew on a safari to
___
52

solve *The Spider Sapphire Mystery* and had explored Incan
___
53

ruins for clues to *The Secret of the Crossword Cipher.*

With Nancy's help, Liana had read about different
___
54

places and various cultures all over the world.
___
54

46. **F.** NO CHANGE
    G. gone out of
    H. went from
    J. gone from

47. **A.** NO CHANGE
    B. would have been
    C. would of
    D. DELETE the underlined portion.

48. **F.** NO CHANGE
    G. libraries dusty,
    H. libraries dusty
    J. library's dusty

49. Which choice provides the most specific information?
    A. NO CHANGE
    B. a high number
    C. hundreds
    D. plenty

50. **F.** NO CHANGE
    G. novels, is alive,
    H. novels is alive,
    J. novels is alive

51. **A.** NO CHANGE
    B. the mysteries
    C. up on that
    D. it over

52. **F.** NO CHANGE
    G. school, she had
    H. school, having
    J. school, she

53. **A.** NO CHANGE
    B. solve:
    C. solve;
    D. solve,

54. Given that all the choices are true, which one best illustrates the variety of settings for the Nancy Drew mysteries and also expresses Liana's interest in these books?
    F. NO CHANGE
    G. Along with Nancy, Liana had many breathtaking adventures involving all sorts of colorful characters.
    H. With Nancy in the lead, Liana had chased suspects from Arizona to Argentina, from Nairobi to New York.
    J. Through her exposure to Nancy, Liana learned about many new places around the world.

Practice ACT Tests

GO ON TO THE NEXT PAGE.

When I was a girl in the 1960s,

my friends and I loved Nancy Drew. 55

We loved her loyal companions, her bravado, and

there was a love for her freedom to do what she wanted.
56

We also loved how smart she was and how pretty, how
57
confident and successful. We were surprised and delighted

that eighteen-year-old Nancy was so accomplished at so

many things. She was able to solve crimes, win golf
58
tournaments, kick bad guys in the shins, and impress her

father's distinguished clients. She did it all—and without

scuffing her shoes or losing her supportive boyfriend, Ned.

   Liana and her friends don't seem to care that Nancy is

pretty or popular. They laugh, mockingly I think, at

Nancy's friend Bess, who squeals at spiders. They prefer

her other girlfriend George, the judo expert and computer

whiz. They skip over the long descriptions of outfits and

fashion accessories. According to Liana, they just want to

get on with the story.

55. At this point, the writer is thinking about adding the following true statement:

> One of a number of series that have featured the young female detective, the Nancy Drew Mystery Story series was begun in 1930 and now totals 173 books.

Should the writer make this addition here?

A. Yes, because it supports statements about the longevity and popularity of this series.
B. Yes, because it helps to explain why the narrator "loved Nancy Drew."
C. No, because it distracts the reader from the main focus of this paragraph.
D. No, because it fails to include relevant information about the author of the series.

56. F. NO CHANGE
G. a love for her freedom to do what she wanted.
H. her freedom to do what she wanted.
J. the freedom to do as one wants.

57. Which of the following alternatives to the underlined portion would be LEAST acceptable?

A. furthermore
B. therefore
C. likewise
D. DELETE the underlined portion.

58. F. NO CHANGE
G. was capable of solving crimes,
H. was good at crime solving,
J. solved crimes,

GO ON TO THE NEXT PAGE.

Perhaps I am overly optimistic, but I'd like to believe that Liana's generation doesn't love Nancy Drew because she's a successful girl detective. They don't need to be reminded that girls can be successful they know that. What these girls need and love are the stories themselves:

those exciting adventure tales spiced with mystery.

59. A. NO CHANGE
    B. successful they already know
    C. successful; they know
    D. successful, knowing

60. Which choice most effectively supports the point being made in the first part of this sentence?
    F. NO CHANGE
    G. the answers to the mysteries of their lives.
    H. a strong role model for their generation.
    J. the ability to overcome obstacles.

PASSAGE V

Visiting Mars on a Budget

With its distinctive red tint and its polar ice caps, the planet Mars has fascinated humans for thousands of years. There were ancient Babylonian astronomers who associated Mars with their war god Negral, to twentieth-century science fiction writers whose works become best-sellers, this planet has often been a symbol of ill will and danger.

The United States has competed with other countries to explore space. By 2003, the National Aeronautics and

Space Administration (NASA) would of sent thirty

spacecraft to the red planet, speculation has been prompted that a human voyage may no longer be the stuff of fiction.

61. A. NO CHANGE
    B. When
    C. From
    D. Those

62. Given that all the choices are true, which one is most relevant to the statement that follows in this sentence?
    F. NO CHANGE
    G. with their wild imaginations about outer space,
    H. who penned spine-tingling stories of "little green men from Mars,"
    J. who created images of Mars in literature,

63. Given that all the choices are true, which one best leads from the preceding paragraph to the subject of this paragraph?
    A. NO CHANGE
    B. Today, such negative associations seem to be dissipating.
    C. In 1958, the United States founded an agency to run its space program.
    D. Earth and Mars are both planets in the inner solar system.

64. F. NO CHANGE
    G. had sent
    H. send
    J. have sent

65. A. NO CHANGE
    B. to which speculation has prompted
    C. prompting speculation
    D. which is speculation

GO ON TO THE NEXT PAGE.

Few would deny that the idea of a human mission to Mars
is exciting, who is ready to pay for such an expedition?

Recent reports suggest that the cost of a human

voyage to Mars could run as high as 100 billion dollars.

This is a startling number, especially in light of the fact

that the International Space Station, the most ambitious

NASA project yet, carried a projected price tag of "only"

17 billion dollars. In the end, NASA overspent on the

International Space Station. [68] One can only imagine

if the final price of a human voyage to Mars would be.

In contrast, the two Mars Rovers—

robotic spacecraft launched in 2003—carried

a combined price tag of less than one billion

dollars. These Rovers are sophisticated pieces of

technology, with the capacity and ability to examine soil

and rocks. Their equipment may answer questions that

have long been posed about the presence of water and life

on Mars.

66. **F.** NO CHANGE
    G. Maybe a few
    H. Although few
    J. Few, if any,

67. **A.** NO CHANGE
    B. yet
    C. yet:
    D. yet—

68. The writer is considering adding the following true information to the end of the preceding sentence (placing a comma after the word *Station*):

      with a final construction cost of almost 30 billion dollars.

Should the writer make this addition?

    F. Yes, because it strengthens the assertion made in this sentence by adding explicit detail.
    G. Yes, because it proves space flight will be more affordable in the future.
    H. No, because it weakens the point made in the paragraph about the cost of human flight to Mars.
    J. No, because it detracts from the essay's focus on the human experience in travel to Mars.

69. **A.** NO CHANGE
    B. what
    C. how
    D. DELETE the underlined portion.

70. Given that all the choices are true, which one most effectively describes what the Mars Rovers are?
    F. NO CHANGE
    G. which captured the imagination of the general public—
    H. the products described at length in the media—
    J. familiar to many who watched the news coverage at the time—

71. **A.** NO CHANGE
    B. genuine capacity
    C. potential capacity
    D. capacity

GO ON TO THE NEXT PAGE.

Sending machines unaccompanied by humans to Mars does drain some of the romance out of aging or older
72

visions of space travel. In other words, we need to keep in
73
mind that the right equipment can accomplish as much as any crew of scientists, if not more—such as a fraction of
74
the cost. Before any astronaut boards a spacecraft for that distant planet, the staggering expense of such a mission should be carefully considered. 75

72. **F.** NO CHANGE
   G. old age
   H. aging old
   J. age-old

73. **A.** NO CHANGE
   B. For that reason alone,
   C. In that time frame,
   D. Even so,

74. **F.** NO CHANGE
   G. at
   H. but only
   J. DELETE the underlined portion.

75. The writer is considering ending the essay with the following statement:

   > With the passage of time, humans will continue to gaze in awe toward the heavenly skies as a source of inspiration and mystery.

   Should the writer add this sentence here?

   A. Yes, because it captures the emotion that is the basis for the space exploration described in the essay.
   B. Yes, because it invites the reader to reflect on the insignificance of money in relation to the mystery of space.
   C. No, because it does not logically follow the essay's chronological history of people who traveled in space.
   D. No, because it strays too far from the essay's focus on Mars and the cost of sending humans there.

END OF TEST 1

STOP! DO NOT TURN THE PAGE UNTIL TOLD TO DO SO.

MATHEMATICS TEST
60 Minutes—60 Questions

DIRECTIONS: Solve each problem, choose the correct answer, and then fill in the corresponding oval on your answer document.

Do not linger over problems that take too much time. Solve as many as you can; then return to the others in the time you have left for this test.

You are permitted to use a calculator on this test. You may use your calculator for any problems you choose, but some of the problems may best be done without using a calculator.

Note: Unless otherwise stated, all of the following should be assumed.

1. Illustrative figures are NOT necessarily drawn to scale.
2. Geometric figures lie in a plane.
3. The word *line* indicates a straight line.
4. The word *average* indicates arithmetic mean.

---

1. If $\frac{3x}{2} + 12 = 4$, then $x = ?$

   DO YOUR FIGURING HERE.

   A. -8

   B. $-\frac{16}{3}$

   C. $\frac{4}{3}$

   D. $\frac{16}{3}$

   E. $\frac{32}{3}$

2. $2x^4 \cdot 5x^7$ is equivalent to:

   F. $7x^3$
   G. $7x^{11}$
   H. $10x^{11}$
   J. $7x^{28}$
   K. $10x^{28}$

3. Let $f(x) = \frac{x^2 + 12}{x - 6}$. What is the value of $f(10)$?

   A. 112
   B. 28
   C. 12
   D. 10
   E. 8

GO ON TO THE NEXT PAGE.

DO YOUR FIGURING HERE.

4. The 2 graphs shown below represent a car trip. The graph on the left shows the total distance as a function of time. The graph on the right shows the total number of gallons of gasoline used as a function of the total distance. Approximately how many gallons of gasoline were used during the first 2 hours of the trip?

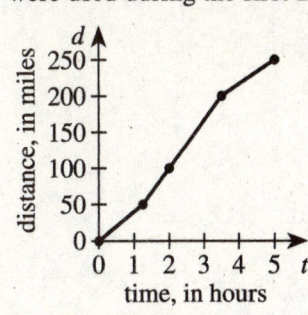 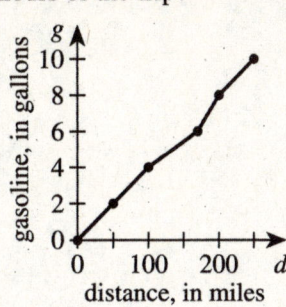

F. 2
G. 4
H. 8
J. 25
K. 100

5. What is the value of 442 + 325 + 287, rounded to the nearest hundred?

A. 700
B. 800
C. 900
D. 1,000
E. 1,100

6. A bus company always keeps 3 tires in stock for every bus it owns, plus an additional 30 tires in stock for emergencies. According to this policy, the bus company needs to have a total of 120 tires in stock. How many buses does the company own?

F. 30
G. 35
H. 40
J. 45
K. 50

7. For what value of x is the equation $2(x - 6) + x = 36$ true?

A. 24
B. 16
C. 14
D. 10
E. 8

GO ON TO THE NEXT PAGE.

DO YOUR FIGURING HERE.

8. Five points are shown on each of the 2 lines in the figure below. Point O is the intersection point of the 2 lines. Which of the following rays does NOT contain point O ?

F. $\overrightarrow{AB}$

G. $\overrightarrow{BD}$

H. $\overrightarrow{CD}$

J. $\overrightarrow{EF}$

K. $\overrightarrow{EG}$

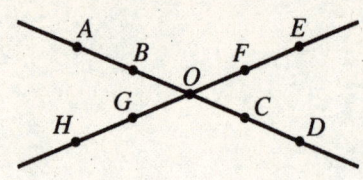

9. Let r, s, and t be positive integers such that $rs = 24$, $st = 36$, and $t = 3$. What is the value of r ?

A. 2
B. 4
C. 6
D. 8
E. 12

10. Mele earned scores of 75, 70, 92, 95, and 97 points (a total of 429 points) on the first 5 tests in Economics II. Solving which of the following equations for s gives the score he needs to earn on the 6th test to average exactly 85 points for all 6 tests?

F. $\dfrac{429}{5} + s = 85$

G. $\dfrac{429}{6} + s = 85$

H. $\dfrac{s + 429}{5} = 85$

J. $\dfrac{s + 429}{6} = 85$

K. $\dfrac{s + 429}{6} = \dfrac{85}{100}$

11. For how many whole numbers from 44 through 55 is the ones digit greater than the tens digit?

A. 3
B. 4
C. 5
D. 11
E. 12

12. The weight of a circular rod of a certain type is proportional to its length. A 15-foot circular rod of this type weighs 35 pounds. What is the weight, in pounds, of a 21-foot circular rod of this type?

F. 41
G. 44
H. 47
J. 49
K. 56

GO ON TO THE NEXT PAGE.

DO YOUR FIGURING HERE.

13. The vertices of a rectangle are $(-1,-2)$, $(4,-2)$, $(4,3)$, and $(-1,3)$. When the rectangle is graphed in the standard (x,y) coordinate plane below, what percent of the total area of the rectangle lies in Quadrant III ?

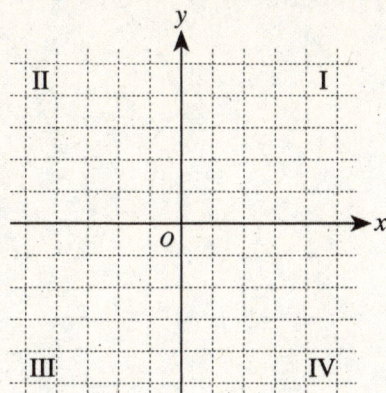

   A. 8%
   B. 12%
   C. 12.5%
   D. 32%
   E. 48%

14. Which of the following expressions is equivalent to the one given below?

$$\frac{3 + 7(x - 6)}{3(x - 6) + 10}$$

   F. $\frac{10}{13}$

   G. $\frac{7}{10}$

   H. $\frac{39}{8}$

   J. $\frac{7x - 39}{3x - 8}$

   K. $\frac{10x - 42}{13x - 18}$

15. In the standard (x,y) coordinate plane, an equation of a circle is $x^2 + y^2 = 81$. At what points does the circle intersect the y-axis?

   A. $(0, 1)$ and $(0, -1)$
   B. $(0, 9)$ and $(0, -9)$
   C. $(0, 18)$ and $(0, -18)$
   D. $(0, 27)$ and $(0, -27)$
   E. $(0, 81)$ and $(0, -81)$

16. Four points, A, B, C, and D, lie on a circle having a circumference of 17 units. B is 5 units counterclockwise from A. C is 3 units clockwise from A. D is 11 units clockwise from A and 6 units counterclockwise from A. What is the order of the points, starting with A and going clockwise around the circle?

   F. A, B, C, D
   G. A, B, D, C
   H. A, C, B, D
   J. A, C, D, B
   K. A, D, C, B

GO ON TO THE NEXT PAGE.

DO YOUR FIGURING HERE.

17. In 1985, the cost of clothing for a certain family was $620. In 1995, 10 years later, the cost of clothing for this family was $1,000. Assuming the cost increased linearly, what was the cost of this family's clothing in 1991 ?

   A. $908
   B. $848
   C. $812
   D. $810
   E. $772

18. For a math homework assignment, Karla found the area and perimeter of a room of her house. She reported that the area of her rectangular living room is 180 square feet and that the perimeter is 54 feet. When drawing a sketch of her living room the next day, she realized that she had forgotten to write down the dimensions of the room. What are the dimensions of Karla's living room, in feet?

   F.   9 by 20
   G. 10 by 18
   H. 12 by 15
   J. 14 by 13
   K. 16 by 11

19. If $1.056 \cdot 10^n = 0.0001056$, what is the value of n ?

   A. −7
   B. −4
   C. −3
   D.   4
   E.   7

20. The value of m is directly proportional to the value of p. When $m = 2$, $p = 6$. What is m when $p = 9$?

   F. $\frac{1}{3}$

   G. $\frac{4}{3}$

   H. 3

   J. 5

   K. 27

21. To park a car at a short-term parking lot costs $1.75 for the 1st hour or any part thereof, $1.50 for the 2nd hour or any part thereof, and $0.75 for each additional hour or any part thereof after the 2nd hour. Your ticket shows that you parked your car in this lot from 10:47 a.m. to 4:35 p.m. on the same day. What is the cost of parking your car, according to this ticket?

   (Note: Prices include all applicable sales tax.)

   A. $4.75
   B. $5.50
   C. $5.86
   D. $6.10
   E. $6.25

GO ON TO THE NEXT PAGE.

DO YOUR FIGURING HERE.

22. The degree measures of the interior angles of $\triangle ABC$, shown below, form an arithmetic sequence with common difference 10°. What is the first term of the sequence?

    F. 80°
    G. 60°
    H. 50°
    J. 40°
    K. 30°

23. Point B lies on $\overline{AC}$ between A and C. Point D is a point not on $\overline{AC}$ such that the measure of $\angle ABD$ is 38°. What is the measure of $\angle CBD$?

    A.   38°
    B.   52°
    C.   76°
    D. 128°
    E. 142°

24. Let $2x + 3y = 4$ and $5x + 6y = 7$. What is the value of $8x + 9y$?

    F. −10
    G. −1
    H.   2
    J.   7
    K. 10

25. Which of the following is the equation $3(x - y) = 5$ solved for y ?

    A. $y = x - \dfrac{5}{3}$

    B. $y = \dfrac{5}{3} - x$

    C. $y = 15 - x$

    D. $y = x - 15$

    E. $y = \dfrac{5}{3}x$

26. Which of the following statements is true about odd and/or even numbers?

    F. The sum of any 2 even numbers is odd.
    G. The sum of any 2 odd numbers is odd.
    H. The quotient of any 2 even numbers is odd.
    J. The quotient of any 2 even numbers is even.
    K. The product of any 2 odd numbers is odd.

GO ON TO THE NEXT PAGE.

DO YOUR FIGURING HERE.

27. A deck of cards for a children's game contains 10 red cards, 10 blue cards, and 10 yellow cards. The players take turns, each drawing a card at random from the deck and placing the card on the table. When it is the fourth player's turn, there are 3 yellow cards on the table. What is the probability that the fourth player will draw a yellow card?

   A. $\frac{7}{30}$

   B. $\frac{7}{27}$

   C. $\frac{1}{3}$

   D. $\frac{4}{10}$

   E. $\frac{7}{10}$

28. To win the student council election, a candidate must receive over 50% of the votes cast. There were 750 votes cast. Which of the following expressions is true about x, the minimum number of votes that a candidate must have received to win the election?

   F. $x < 375$
   G. $x = 375$
   H. $x > 375$
   J. $x < 376$
   K. $x > 376$

29. A machine part is diagrammed in the figure below with the dimensions given in inches. If the centers of the circles lie on the same line parallel to the bottom of the part, what is the distance, in inches, between the centers of the 2 holes in the machine part?

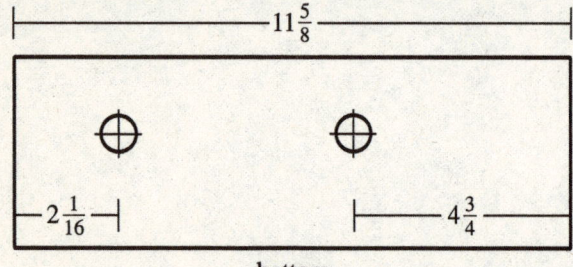

bottom

   A. $5\frac{3}{16}$

   B. $5\frac{1}{16}$

   C. 5

   D. $4\frac{13}{16}$

   E. $4\frac{3}{16}$

GO ON TO THE NEXT PAGE.

DO YOUR FIGURING HERE.

30. A father and his son are standing near to each other on level ground late one afternoon so that their shadows end at the same place. The father is 75 inches tall, the son is 50 inches tall, and the father's shadow is 120 inches long, as shown in the figure below. Which of the following is closest to the distance, d inches, between the father and his son?

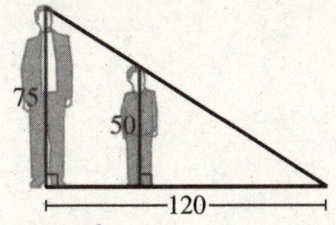

F. 25
G. 40
H. 60
J. 70
K. 80

31. In the standard (x,y) coordinate plane, what is the distance, in coordinate units, between $(-3,-2)$ and $(5,5)$?

A. $\sqrt{13}$
B. $\sqrt{15}$
C. $\sqrt{113}$
D. 5
E. 15

32. Chayton decides to save money in a savings account for a vacation. He deposits \$10 in his savings account the 1st month. Each month thereafter, the amount he deposits is \$10 more than the amount he deposited the previous month. Thus, Chayton's deposit is \$20 the 2nd month, \$30 the 3rd month, and so on. He makes his final deposit of \$360 the 36th month. What is the total amount of Chayton's 36 deposits?

F. \$ 710
G. \$1,850
H. \$6,300
J. \$6,480
K. \$6,660

33. One side of a triangle is 15 cm long, and another side is 28 cm long. Which of the following is a possible length, in centimeters, for the third side?

A. 2
B. 12
C. 31
D. 44
E. 52

34. The expression $\frac{2x+3}{12x^2}$ is equivalent to:

F. $\frac{1}{3}$

G. $\frac{1}{x}$

H. $\frac{1}{2x}$

J. $\frac{x+1}{2x^2}$

K. $\frac{1}{6x} + \frac{1}{4x^2}$

GO ON TO THE NEXT PAGE.

DO YOUR FIGURING HERE.

Use the following information to answer questions 35–37.

Ken baked, frosted, and decorated a rectangular cake for the last Math Club meeting. The cake was 3 inches high, 12 inches wide, and 16 inches long. He centered the cake on a piece of cardboard whose rectangular top surface had been covered with aluminum foil, as shown in the figure below.

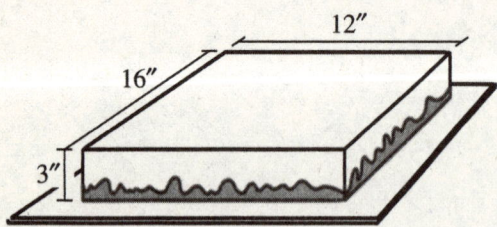

35. Ken used a piece of cardboard large enough to allow the cardboard to extend 2 inches beyond the cake on all sides. What is the area, in square inches, of the aluminum foil that is exposed on the top surface of the cardboard?

  A. 60
  B. 64
  C. 88
  D. 96
  E. 128

36. At the Math Club meeting, Principal Gonzales cut the entire cake into pieces. Each piece is 2 inches wide, 2 inches long, and 3 inches high. What is the number of pieces Principal Gonzales cut the cake into?

  F. 16
  G. 20
  H. 28
  J. 48
  K. 96

37. The Math Club will pay Ken $5.00 for preparing the cake and will also pay him for the cost of the cake mix at $1.73, the frosting mix at $2.67, and the sales tax of 5% on these 2 items. What is the total amount the Math Club will pay Ken?

  A. $4.67
  B. $9.40
  C. $9.45
  D. $9.62
  E. $9.87

GO ON TO THE NEXT PAGE.

DO YOUR FIGURING HERE.

38. Points *A* and *B* lie on the circle below, where central angle ∠*ACB* measures 110°. What is the measure of ∠*ABC* ?

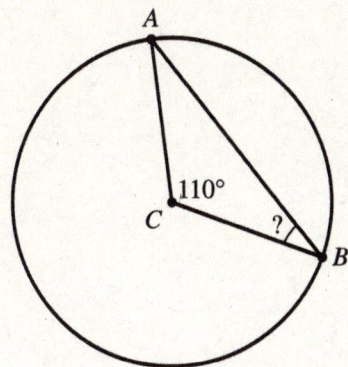

F. 35°
G. 40°
H. 45°
J. 55°
K. Cannot be determined from the given information

39. The graph below shows Allison's living expenses, which totaled $600, during September of her freshman year in college.

Allison's September Living Expenses

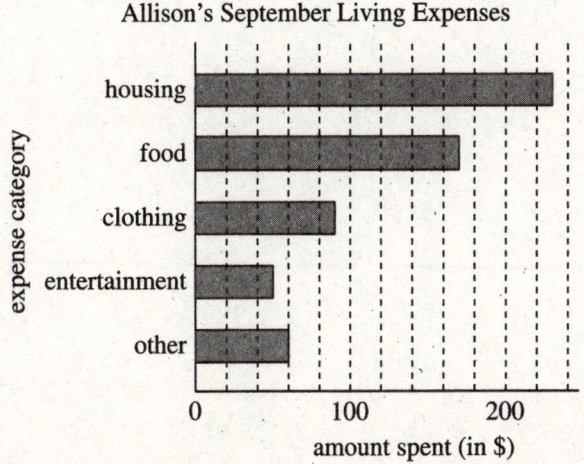

Trying to limit her spending, Allison decides that in October she could spend $60 less for food and $40 less for clothing. If she can accomplish this and the rest of her expenses are the same as they were in September, approximately what percent of Allison's October expenses will be for entertainment?

A. 5%
B. 8%
C. 10%
D. 17%
E. 20%

GO ON TO THE NEXT PAGE.

DO YOUR FIGURING HERE.

40. Nadia works exactly 40 hours each week and earns a minimum of $1,200 every 4 weeks. Her hourly rate of pay is determined by the job she is assigned and may vary. If x is Nadia's average hourly pay for a 4-week period, which of the following inequalities best describes x ?

  F. $x \leq \$\ 7.50$
  G. $x \geq \$\ 7.50$
  H. $x \leq \$\ 30.00$
  J. $x \geq \$\ 30.00$
  K. $x \geq \$120.00$

41. If x is any positive integer, then the sum of $8x$ and $13x$ is *always* divisible by which of the following?

  A.   5
  B.   8
  C. 13
  D. 21
  E. 104

42. The coordinates of the endpoints of $\overline{MN}$ in the standard (x,y) coordinate plane are $(-13,-4)$ and $(5,4)$. What is the x-coordinate of the midpoint of $\overline{MN}$?

  F. -8
  G. -4
  H.   0
  J.   4
  K.   9

43. The diagram of the roof for a new storage shed is shown below. Some lengths are given in meters, but the length of the vertical support, $\overline{BD}$, has been left off. Which of the following expressions gives the length, in meters, of $\overline{BD}$?

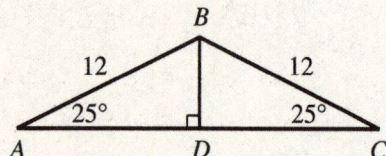

  A. $12 \sin 25°$

  B. $12 \tan 25°$

  C. $12 \cos 25°$

  D. $\dfrac{12}{\cos 25°}$

  E. $\dfrac{12}{\sin 25°}$

GO ON TO THE NEXT PAGE.

DO YOUR FIGURING HERE.

Use the following information to answer
questions 44–46.

In the figure below, △ACB is a right triangle with legs of
length a units and b units, where $0 < a < b$, and hypotenuse
of length c units. The triangles △YCA, △ZBA, and △XCB
are equilateral. The area of an equilateral triangle with
sides x units long is $\frac{\sqrt{3}}{4}x^2$ square units.

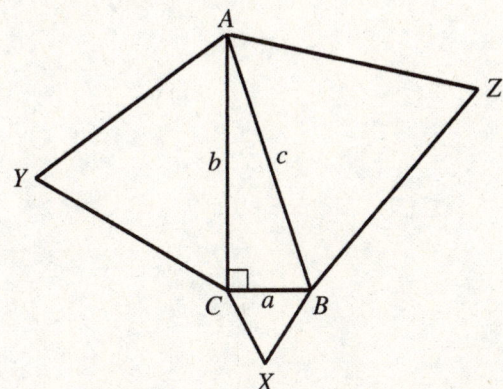

44. What is the perimeter of pentagon *AZBCY*, in units?

F. $a + b + 2c$
G. $a + 2b + 2c$
H. $a + 3b + 3c$
J. $2a + 2b + 2c$
K. $3a + 3b + 3c$

45. For all values of a and b such that $0 < a < b$, which of
the following lists the angles $\angle XCY$, $\angle CAZ$, and $\angle CBZ$
in order of their measures from *least* to *greatest*?

A. $\angle CBZ$, $\angle XCY$, $\angle CAZ$
B. $\angle CBZ$, $\angle CAZ$, $\angle XCY$
C. $\angle XCY$, $\angle CAZ$, $\angle CBZ$
D. $\angle CAZ$, $\angle CBZ$, $\angle XCY$
E. $\angle CAZ$, $\angle XCY$, $\angle CBZ$

46. If $b = 2a$, what is $\tan(\angle ABC)$?

F. 2

G. $\frac{1}{2}$

H. $\frac{1}{\sqrt{5}}$

J. $\frac{2}{\sqrt{5}}$

K. $\sqrt{5}$

GO ON TO THE NEXT PAGE.

DO YOUR FIGURING HERE.

47. The sum of 3 consecutive odd integers is k. In terms of k, what is the sum of the 2 smaller of these integers?

A. $\dfrac{2k}{3} - 2$

B. $\dfrac{2k}{3}$

C. $\dfrac{2k}{3} + 2$

D. $k - 2$

E. $k - 3$

48. The graph of $y = x^2$ is shown in the standard (x,y) coordinate plane below. For which of the following equations is the graph of the parabola shifted 3 units to the right and 2 units down?

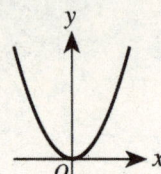

F. $y = (x + 3)^2 + 2$

G. $y = (x + 3)^2 - 2$

H. $y = (x - 2)^2 + 3$

J. $y = (x - 3)^2 + 2$

K. $y = (x - 3)^2 - 2$

49. Lucky found \$8.25 in pennies, nickels, dimes, and quarters while walking home from school one week. When she deposited this money in the bank, she noticed that she had twice as many nickels as pennies, 1 fewer dime than nickels, and 1 more quarter than nickels. How many quarters did Lucky find that week?

A. 3
B. 9
C. 16
D. 21
E. 26

50. The mean of 4 numbers is 32. The smallest of the 4 numbers is 5. What is the mean of the other 3 numbers?

F. $30\frac{3}{4}$

G. 32

H. 36

J. 41

K. $42\frac{2}{3}$

GO ON TO THE NEXT PAGE.

DO YOUR FIGURING HERE.

51. If the statement "If a cat is tricolor, then it is a female" were true, which of the following statements would also have to be true?

   A. "If a cat is a female, then it is tricolor."
   B. "If a cat is not a female, then it is tricolor."
   C. "If a cat is not a female, then it is not tricolor."
   D. "If a cat is not tricolor, then it is a female."
   E. "If a cat is not tricolor, then it is not a female."

52. What is the set of all the values of b that satisfy the equation $\left(x^3\right)^{4-b^2} = 1$ for all nonzero values of x ?

   F. $\{0\}$
   G. $\{2\}$
   H. $\{4\}$
   J. $\{-\sqrt{7}, \sqrt{7}\}$
   K. $\{-2, 2\}$

53. Which of the following trigonometric functions is equivalent to the function $g(x) = \sin x \sec x$?

   (Note: $\sec x = \dfrac{1}{\cos x}$)

   A. $f(x) = \cos x$
   B. $f(x) = \cot x$
   C. $f(x) = \csc x$
   D. $f(x) = \sin x$
   E. $f(x) = \tan x$

54. The table below gives some (x,y) pairs that satisfy a linear relationship. What does z equal?

x	y
-2	-7
2	5
0	-1
-3	z

   F. -10
   G. -8
   H. -7
   J. -2
   K. 0

55. The volume of a right circular cylinder with a height of 6 cm is 150π cubic centimeters. What is the lateral surface area, in square centimeters, of this cylinder?

   (Note: For a right circular cylinder with radius r and height h, the lateral surface area is $2\pi rh$ and the volume is $\pi r^2 h$.)

   A. 25π
   B. 36π
   C. 50π
   D. 60π
   E. 110π

GO ON TO THE NEXT PAGE.

56. Whenever w is an integer greater than 1, $\log_w \dfrac{w^2}{w^6} = ?$

DO YOUR FIGURING HERE.

   F. -4

   G. -3

   H. $-\dfrac{1}{3}$

   J. $\dfrac{1}{3}$

   K. 3

57. Amal's teacher assigned each student in class to draw a trapezoid using a segment of the line $y = x$ as one side. The interior of Amal's trapezoid is shown shaded in the standard (x,y) coordinate plane below. The equations of the lines that intersect to form the trapezoid are also shown.

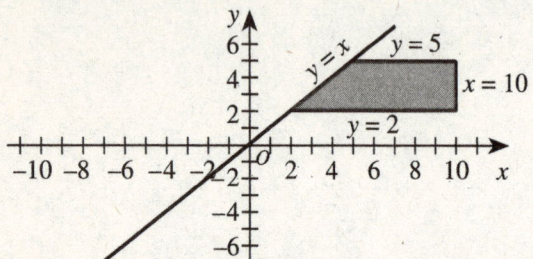

The next part of the assignment was to reflect the trapezoid across the x-axis and write a set of inequalities defining the reflected trapezoid and its interior. Which of the following sets of inequalities should Amal have written?

   A. $x \le 10,\quad 2 \le y \le 5,\quad y \le x$
   B. $x \le 10,\quad -5 \le y \le -2,\quad y \ge -x$
   C. $x \le 10,\quad -5 \le y \le -2,\quad y \le -x$
   D. $x \le -10,\quad 2 \le y \le 5,\quad y \le -x$
   E. $x \le -10,\quad -5 \le y \le -2,\quad y \ge x$

58. In the standard (x,y) coordinate plane below, an angle is shown whose vertex is the origin. One side of this angle with measure θ passes through $(4,-3)$, and the other side includes the positive x-axis. What is the cosine of θ ?

   F. $-\dfrac{4}{3}$

   G. $-\dfrac{3}{4}$

   H. $-\dfrac{3}{5}$

   J. $\dfrac{4}{5}$

   K. $\dfrac{5}{4}$

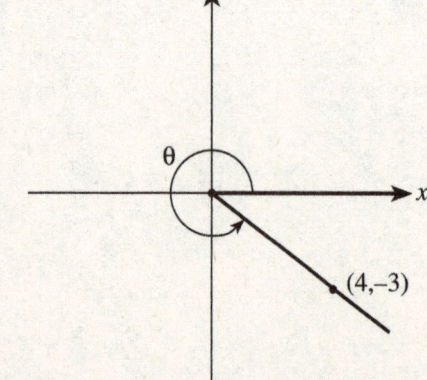

GO ON TO THE NEXT PAGE.

59. Triangle $\triangle ABC$ has vertices $A(8,2)$, $B(0,6)$, and $C(-3,2)$. Point C can be moved along a certain line, with points A and B remaining stationary, and the area of $\triangle ABC$ will not change. What is the slope of that line?

DO YOUR FIGURING HERE.

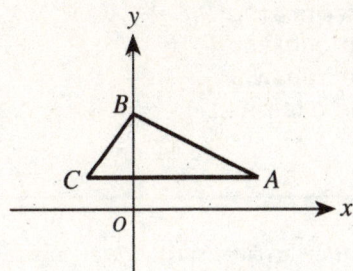

A. $-\dfrac{1}{2}$

B. $-\dfrac{3}{4}$

C. 0

D. $\dfrac{4}{3}$

E. 2

60. Let the function $f(a,b)$ be defined as $f(a,b) = b^2 - a$. For all x and y, $f\big((x^2 + y^2),(x - y)\big) = ?$

F. $2y^2$

G. 0

H. $-2y^2$

J. $-2xy + 2y^2$

K. $-2xy$

END OF TEST 2

STOP! DO NOT TURN THE PAGE UNTIL TOLD TO DO SO.

DO NOT RETURN TO THE PREVIOUS TEST.

Practice ACT Tests

READING TEST
35 Minutes—40 Questions

DIRECTIONS: There are four passages in this test. Each passage is followed by several questions. After reading a passage, choose the best answer to each question and fill in the corresponding oval on your answer document. You may refer to the passages as often as necessary.

Passage I

PROSE FICTION: This passage is adapted from the novel *Winter Wheat* by Mildred Walker (©1944 by Harcourt, Brace and Company, Inc.).

The setting is the northern prairies of Montana in 1940.

September is like a quiet day after a whole week of wind. I mean real wind that blows dirt into your eyes and hair and between your teeth and roars in your ears after you've gone inside. The harvesting is done and the
5 wheat stored away and you're through worrying about hail or drought or grasshoppers. The fields have a tired peaceful look, the way I imagine a mother feels when she's had her baby and is just lying there thinking about it and feeling pleased.

10 It was hot, though, like a flash-back to July. I was glad we weren't cooking for harvest hands. There wasn't any fire in the stove and everything was spick-and-span because I had just washed the dinner dishes. Mom was out having another look for the turkeys that
15 were always wandering off. Dad was lying on the couch in the other room waiting for the noon broadcast of wheat prices to come on. We had to sell our wheat this month and not hold it over; that is, we did if I was going to the university that fall. It might go higher
20 along toward Christmas, but we couldn't wait for that.

The house was so quiet I could hear Mom calling the turkeys down by the barn. Dad told Mom not to bother, they'd come back by themselves, but Mom worried if anything was lost or left unlocked.

25 "When I've got something, I take care of it," she always said.

I washed some cucumbers while I was waiting. They were bright-green and shiny in the water. I used to play they were alligators when I was a child. Then I
30 fenced them in with my hand and poured off the water into the kettle on the stove. When you have to carry every drop of water you use half a mile, you don't throw away any.

And then it began. I knew before Dad turned it up.
35 The voice of the man who announces the wheat prices is as familiar to me as Dad's. It's different from anybody's voice around Gotham—more like one of those

city voices that broadcasts the war news. That voice touches us here, and all the ranches spread out over the
40 prairies between the Rockies and the Mississippi. It touches all the people in Clark City, thirty miles from here, who live on the ranchers, even though they try to forget it.

"Here is your Grain Market Broadcast for today:
45 Spring and Winter . . . up two."

I could add two to yesterday's price, so I didn't have to hear any more, but I listened out of habit and because I love to hear it.

"One heavy dark Northern Spring . . . fifty-two."
50 The words came so fast they seemed to roll downhill. Nobody ever calls it all that; it's just spring wheat, but I like the words. They heap up and make a picture of a spring that's slow to come, when the ground stays frozen late into March and the air is raw, and the skies
55 are sulky and dark. The "Northern" makes me feel how close we are to the Rockies and how high up on the map, almost to Canada.

"One dark hard Winter . . . fifty-three."

It's just winter wheat to the people who raise it,
60 only to me it means more than that. It means all the winter and all the cold and the tight feeling of the house in winter, but the rich secret feeling I have, too, of treasure in the ground, growing there for us, waiting for the cold to be over to push up strong and green. They
65 sound like grim words without any comfort to them, but they have a kind of strength all their own.

"Durum, Flax, and Rye . . . up one." The broadcast ran on. Mom came in while I was standing there listening.

70 "Wheat's up," I told her.

Mom nodded. She stood there untying her bandanna and I watched her as though I didn't know her face better than my own. Mom's is a quiet face with a broader forehead than mine and dark brows and eyes
75 and a wide mouth. She doesn't show in her face what she thinks or feels—that's why people in Gotham think she's hard to know—but when she laughs, the laughter goes deeper down in her eyes than anybody's I know.

GO ON TO THE NEXT PAGE.

I look more like Dad. He is tall and thin and has
80 light hair and blue eyes and his face shows what he
thinks or feels. I am strong like Mom, though, and I
like working in the fields better than in the house.

Dad clicked off the radio and came out to the
kitchen. "Well, we'll go over and tell Bailey we're
85 going to sell. Fifty-three is good enough. Come on,
Ellen, you can drive me over."

I took off my apron and was running across to the
barn for the pickup before Dad had taken his hat from
behind the door. I felt so excited I couldn't walk
90 soberly.

Glory, it was hot! I had the doors of the truck tied
open with a piece of rope so the air could rush through,
but it felt hot enough to scorch my bare ankles, and the
heat of the engine came up through the rubber soles of
95 my sneakers.

1. The point of view from which the passage is told is
best described as that of a young woman who:

A. is unsure whether she would like to attend college
in the fall but is aware that she will have the
option.
B. had made plans to go to college in the fall but is
now convinced that the high cost to attend will
prevent her from going.
C. had assumed that she would go to college in the
fall but is now considering working on the family
ranch for a year instead.
D. is anxiously anticipating attending college in the
fall but is aware of the conditions that could affect
her plans.

2. The passage most strongly suggests that the narrator's
family grows:

F. wheat only.
G. wheat and rye only.
H. wheat, rye, and durum only.
J. wheat, rye, durum, and flax.

3. The passage does NOT mention which of the following
as something that at least one member of the family
monitors carefully?

A. The turkeys
B. Land disputes in Gotham
C. How water is used
D. Wheat price fluctuations

4. The narrator describes her mom as having all of the
following EXCEPT:

F. facial features that differ from those of the narra-
tor's dad.
G. a strength that the narrator identifies with.
H. a noticeable sense of worry over the current year's
wheat prices.
J. a commitment to caring for her belongings.

5. As it is used the first time in line 34, the word *it* most
precisely refers to:

A. the radio.
B. one of the city voices that broadcasts the war
news.
C. the narrator's dad's voice.
D. the noon broadcast of wheat prices.

6. The narrator's statement in lines 75–78 most nearly
means that she believes her mom is:

F. a somewhat moody person who is often difficult
for the narrator and her dad to understand.
G. an expressive person who is known for laughing
openly and deeply.
H. a serious person who rarely interacts with most of
the people of Gotham.
J. a warm person who is not well understood by
people in Gotham.

7. As it is used in line 2, the word *real* most nearly
means:

A. factual.
B. positive.
C. established.
D. powerful.

8. Which of the following does the narrator NOT directly
identify as a threat to the wheat crop?

F. Grasshoppers
G. Wind
H. Hail
J. Drought

9. As it is used in line 30, the word *fenced* can reasonably
be said to mean all of the following EXCEPT:

A. shut.
B. penned.
C. committed.
D. held.

10. When the narrator's dad tells her that he has decided to
sell the current crop of wheat, the narrator reacts to the
news with a feeling of excitement that:

F. she tries to hide from him.
G. consumes her.
H. is paired with discontent.
J. is tinged with guilt.

GO ON TO THE NEXT PAGE.

Passage II

SOCIAL SCIENCE: This passage is adapted from the article "Virtually Rebuilt, A Ruin Yields Secrets" by Sam Lubell (©2002 by The New York Times Company).

Everyone knows that the Roman Colosseum is an architectural marvel. Built so that thousands of people could be ushered in and out in minutes, it is a testament to the genius of Roman engineering. Or is it? By recon-
5 structing the building with three-dimensional computer modeling and then virtually "walking through" it, researchers have discovered dark, narrow upper hallways that probably hemmed in spectators, slowing their movement to a crawl.

10 Such three-dimensional modeling is turning some of archaeology's once-established truths on their heads. Because 3-D software can take into account the building materials and the laws of physics, it enables scholars to address construction techniques in ways
15 sometimes overlooked when they are working with two-dimensional drawings.

The Colosseum, a vast four-story oval arena, was built from around A.D. 70 to 80. It once held as many as 50,000 spectators. Earthquakes and the ravages of
20 time have destroyed much of the building, but an impressive amount, including most of its facade, still stands.

Dean Abernathy, a doctoral student who helped reconstruct the Colosseum, confronted the issue of the
25 third-level hallways. His model drew on the findings of a team of experts on Roman architecture assembled by the University of California at Los Angeles who had studied similar amphitheaters, drawings of the Colosseum and records of the building's construction and
30 expansion. The team also examined what was left of the upper hallways, an area that had previously been all but closed to researchers.

Bernard Frischer, a classics professor at UCLA and director of its Cultural Virtual Reality Lab, said
35 that researchers have generally held that the entire Colosseum was a masterpiece of circulation, with people able to enter and leave in as little as 10 minutes. After touring the virtual Colosseum, now he is not so sure. "Most scholars just never focused on the problem
40 of circulation throughout the building," he said. "They assumed that each of the floors was going to look like the bottom," which is spacious and well lighted.

Such reconstructions have challenged traditional thinking about other sites as well. Analysis of UCLA
45 models suggests that the Roman Senate may have been poorly ventilated and lighted and had inferior acoustics. The models also raised some new questions about the Temple of Saturn, whose design may have been altered centuries after its construction.

50 Samuel Paley, a classics professor at the State University of New York at Buffalo, and members of the virtual reality lab there have worked with a design company that specializes in archaeological visualizations to produce virtual models of several Assyrian palaces.
55 Moving through a simulation of the northwest palace of Ashur-Nasir-Pal II of Assyria, an ancient site in modern-day Iraq, he caught a glimpse of three leaf bas-relief sculptures in a row. The sculptures, which depicted a ritual involving the king, courtiers and pro-
60 tective gods, could be viewed as a single, isolated tableau only from his position on the threshold of the throne room—as was evidently the intention of the palace's designers. When Paley described his finding at a lecture, "the room went absolutely silent," he said. "I
65 think people realized right then that this is a useful technology that helps them see things in a different way."

Some experts hesitate to rely on such modeling, saying that it can gloss over the realities of the past.
70 Kenneth Kolson, deputy director of the division of research programs for the National Endowment for the Humanities, said that virtual images conveyed a "false sense of integrity and purity." He added, "Those images, especially the stunningly seductive ones,
75 convey as much or more about our own values and cultural aspirations as about the ancients."

Even Frischer and other scholars who have embraced interactive 3-D modeling caution that their reconstructions can never be accepted as fact, partly
80 because new information is always surfacing. "We're working the stuff out," said Mark Wilson Jones, a member of the UCLA committee of Roman architecture experts and a lecturer in architecture. "Nothing's ever final." One advantage of using digital models, scholars
85 say, is that they can easily be updated with new findings.

Fikret Yegul, a professor of architectural history at the University of California at Santa Barbara, acknowledges that computer modeling can shed new light on
90 the past. Still, he questions some of the theories of the team of experts assembled by UCLA. "VR models can never be seen as the last word," he said. "They are only another perspective."

11. The main function of the first paragraph is to:
   A. state then question a widely held notion about the Colosseum.
   B. praise the Colosseum as an architectural and engineering marvel.
   C. show how people in ancient times moved quickly in and out of the Colosseum.
   D. point out a flaw in the design and construction of the Colosseum and how it was later corrected.

GO ON TO THE NEXT PAGE.

12. The passage indicates that in its research on the Colosseum, the UCLA-assembled team of Roman architecture experts made use of all of the following sources of information EXCEPT:

    F. the remains of a part of the Colosseum usually inaccessible to researchers.

    G. records of the Colosseum's construction and expansion.

    H. studies of amphitheaters similar to the Colosseum.

    J. models of the Colosseum made from clay.

13. Frischer attributes the theory that "the entire Colosseum was a masterpiece of circulation" (lines 35–36) directly to:

    A. flawed experiments yielding incorrect results.

    B. misleading computer models.

    C. erroneous data about the building's bottom floor.

    D. false assumptions left unquestioned by most scholars.

14. The author describes the Roman Senate and the Temple of Saturn as two buildings that:

    F. have yet to be studied by UCLA researchers.

    G. are being reevaluated thanks to computer modeling.

    H. underwent design changes long after their construction.

    J. featured inferior ventilation, lighting, and acoustics.

15. As Paley relates it, the lecture audience's reaction to his finding about an Assyrian palace is best described as:

    A. stunned amazement.

    B. silent contempt.

    C. mild concern.

    D. feigned interest.

16. In the context of the eighth paragraph (lines 68–76), the statement in lines 73–76 most nearly means that:

    F. computer models reveal a great deal about the values and culture of the ancient world.

    G. because they reflect modern ideas, computer models risk obscuring the ancient past.

    H. modern people have aspirations similar to those of the people of the ancient world.

    J. through their images, the ancients vividly conveyed their values and hopes.

17. When Mark Wilson Jones talks about "working the stuff out" (line 81), he is most likely referring to:

    A. correcting errors in computer models as new data emerge.

    B. eliminating serious flaws in the software used to make computer models.

    C. ending the conflict between supporters and critics of computer modeling.

    D. integrating architecture and archaeology into his classroom lectures.

18. The author most likely places the words "walking through" in quotation marks in line 6 to:

    F. reveal the speed at which ancient Romans moved through the Colosseum's upper hallways.

    G. suggest that tourist visits to the Colosseum in Rome are best done at a leisurely pace.

    H. warn readers that researchers are just beginning to develop computer models of the Colosseum.

    J. stress that researchers' tours of the reconstructed Colosseum are actually taken via computer.

19. According to the passage, which of the following is true about the present state of the Colosseum?

    A. As a result of earthquakes, little of the Colosseum's facade remains.

    B. Impressively, the Colosseum remains unaffected by the passage of time.

    C. Much of the Colosseum has been destroyed, but a notable amount is still standing.

    D. The Colosseum's facade remains intact, but the rest of the structure has been destroyed.

20. The passage mentions which of the following as a strength of using computer models in archaeology?

    F. They cost relatively little to produce.

    G. They can easily be updated with new findings.

    H. They entertain and inform the public.

    J. They encourage improvements in technology.

GO ON TO THE NEXT PAGE.

Passage III

HUMANITIES: This passage is adapted from the article "India Resounding in New York" by Jon Pareles (©2004 by The New York Times Company).

When *Bombay Dreams*, the musical about making it in the Indian film capital known as Bollywood, was imported from London to Broadway in 2004, it introduced some listeners to the madcap eclecticism of *filmi*,
5 the song-and-dance numbers that punctuate Bollywood's sprawling musicals. But Broadway was the last
to know about the rendezvous of Indian and Western
music. The profound improvisations of South Asian
classical music have long been welcome in New York
10 City's concert halls. Jazz musicians have been absorbing ideas and collaborating with Indian musicians at
least since the 1960's. Hip-hop has latched on to Indian
rhythms. In New York's clubs, the sounds of Bollywood and other South Asian fusions have been drawing
15 crowds for years.

As often happens, the music follows demograph-
ics. In the 1960's, a change in immigration law brought
a wave of white-collar Indians and Pakistanis and
Bangladeshis to the United States. Now their sons and
20 daughters are establishing their place in the arts as well
as in the wider American economy, and they are
making sense of a musical upbringing that is likely to
include Bollywood tunes alongside hip-hop, Western
classical music, Indian classical music, rock and jazz.

25 For South Asian and Asian-American musicians,
producers and disc jockeys who have been building
their own scene in New York, the latest East-West
hybrids are not just occasion for musical connections
and experiments. They are also affirmations of an iden-
30 tity that grows ever more complex and cosmopolitan.
Vijay Iyer, a pianist who brings his Indian background
to jazz, said: "Making music is very much aligned with
activism and sociopolitical cultural work, and that actually is something that does unite this community. It's
35 not just making music to be cool or look hip or be sexy,
but actually to make a difference in the world. Especially in New York, that's a mobilizing force for the
South Asian community."

The New York wave of South Asian music was
40 preceded by influential South Asian hybrids from England. The documentary *Mutiny: Asians Storm British
Music* details the way established Indian and Pakistani
communities in London confronted racism with music.
In the 1970's and 80's, bands in London merged Indian
45 elements—notably a 4/4 Punjabi beat called bhangra—
with other music that connoted resistance, like punk,
reggae and hip-hop. And in the 1990's, studio wizards
came up with styles that became known as Asian
Underground, which swirled together South Asian
50 music with the beats and textures of electronica.

The music traveled to New York at such parties as
DJ Rekha's Basement Bhangra. "It's very urban, very
New York, and that's what makes it exciting," Rekha

said. "We play big-room hip-hop and a little bit of
55 dancehall as well as bhangra, and the music has gotten
a lot more intense. The drums are more pronounced; the
production is much better. The music has come of age."
Regular visitors include groups of young South Asians
who participate in intercollegiate bhangra dance com-
60 petitions around the country.

AR Rahman, who wrote the songs for *Bombay
Dreams*, is one of the top modern *filmi* composers, but
also one of the most Western-flavored. Through the
decades, *filmi* have tossed together everything from
65 electro to salsa to surf music to funk with vocals that
hint at ancient Indian traditions; there's a daring shamelessness to the way they steal from and one-up their
sources.

Iyer has collaborated with disc jockeys and Indian
70 classical musicians as well as jazz improvisers. His
own compositions and arrangements reach deep into
both the labyrinthine harmonies of modern jazz and the
rhythmic cycles of Indian music. Iyer grew up in
Rochester, New York, surrounded by American culture
75 as much as by the Indian music his parents had brought
with them. "I went to hundreds of Indian music concerts," he said. "Without trying to pretend that I'm an
expert on it, because that's something you have to
devote your whole life to, it's a second language that
80 something in my heart was really drawing me toward. It
was really about trying to make sense of who I am. I'm
not trying to recapitulate Indian music or pretend that
I'm playing Indian music.

"It's very trendy right now to be associated with
85 all things South Asian," Iyer said. "I don't know how
long that's going to last. But I can't escape it; this is
what I am. And I'm going to be with this forever."

---

21. The passage devotes the LEAST attention to which of
the following topics?

A. The people making and promoting music influenced by South Asia

B. The growing influence of South Asian music on
the American music scene

C. The plot of *Bombay Dreams* and how it makes use
of song-and-dance numbers

D. The significance of the latest East-West musical
hybrids for some South Asians and Asian Americans

22. Which of the following developments does the passage
indicate occurred first chronologically?

F. *Bombay Dreams* has its U.S. premiere.

G. London bands merge Indian elements with punk,
reggae, and hip-hop.

H. Studio wizards develop the styles known as Asian
Underground.

J. The Basement Bhangra party starts in New York.

GO ON TO THE NEXT PAGE.

23. In the passage, who most directly expresses the opinion that South Asian musical hybrids have matured musically?

A. Iyer
B. Rekha
C. Rahman
D. Iyer's parents

24. Viewed in the context of the passage, the words *daring shamelessness*, *steal*, and *one-up* (lines 66–67) are most likely intended by the author to convey a tone of:

F. scorn.
G. alarm.
H. indifference.
J. appreciation.

25. Information about and quotations from Iyer in the passage best support the conclusion that he:

A. emphasizes modern jazz harmonies over Indian rhythms in his compositions and arrangements.
B. considers himself an expert in Indian music after having attended hundreds of concerts where such music was played.
C. is just now starting to explore American culture after years of studying the Indian music of his parents.
D. finds Indian music personally and professionally rewarding though he doesn't feel he understands it fully.

26. The passage claims that collaborations between jazz and Indian musicians:

F. began no later than the 1960s but may have occurred earlier as well.
G. started before the 1960s, the decade that saw the most collaborations.
H. ended in the 1960s when hip-hop began using Indian rhythms.
J. couldn't have started before the 1960s, the decade jazz was born.

27. In describing white-collar South Asians who immigrated to the United States in the 1960s, the author characterizes their children's musical upbringing as generally being:

A. shaped by a variety of Indian and Western musical forms.
B. focused primarily on classical traditions from India and the West.
C. directed mainly toward American musical styles, such as rock and jazz.
D. influenced first by Bollywood tunes, then later by classical music.

28. The quotation in lines 32–38 most strongly stresses the role of music making in:

F. maintaining a hip image in the South Asian community.
G. bringing people together to promote change in the world.
H. uniting New Yorkers in a love of South Asian music.
J. improving the quality of entertainment throughout the world.

29. The passage states that the documentary *Mutiny* deals with how:

A. Indian and Pakistani communities first became established in London.
B. influential South Asian musical hybrids came to London from India and Pakistan.
C. established Indian and Pakistani communities in London used music to confront racism.
D. London's Indian and Pakistani residents came to appreciate the 4/4 bhangra beat.

30. The passage identifies Rahman as being both:

F. hugely popular with audiences and greatly underrated by music critics.
G. highly successful as a *filmi* composer and strongly influenced by Western music.
H. interested in modern *filmi* and dedicated to preserving Indian musical traditions.
J. fond of electro and salsa and uncomfortable with surf music and funk.

GO ON TO THE NEXT PAGE.

Passage IV

NATURAL SCIENCE: This passage is adapted from the article "A Mystery Squid Found Lurking at Ocean Bottom" by Carol Kaesuk Yoon (©2001 by The New York Times Company).

In a finding that has thrilled deep-sea scientists and put squid experts in a tizzy, researchers have reported the discovery of a bizarre squid reaching 23 slimy feet in length lurking the oceans' depths all
5 across the globe. In *Science* magazine, an international team of researchers documents eight sightings of the creatures. At rest, the beasts look something like a pair of elephant ears atop bent, threadlike arms resembling moon-landing gear. Scientists still have not captured
10 the animals, which were seen near the sea floor in the Atlantic, Pacific and Indian Oceans and the Gulf of Mexico at crushing depths, one to three miles below the surface.

"It occurred to me that these things were showing
15 up all over the place in deep water," said Dr. Mike Vecchione, a squid biologist with the National Oceanic and Atmospheric Administration and the lead author of the *Science* paper. "For this large, highly visible animal to be common in the largest ecosystem on earth and for
20 us to know nothing about it seems fairly remarkable."

Unlike the 60-foot-long giant squids, however, these new squids have never washed up on shore or been found in the stomachs of whales. Researchers say that is not surprising because they are probably too del-
25 icate to survive such passage without disintegrating or being eaten. Not even the giant squid, *Architeuthis*, has been seen alive in its natural deep-sea habitat.

Scientists calculate that the deep sea—the lightless zone of the ocean that includes everything below
30 3,000 feet—encompasses more than 90 percent of the earth's biosphere. The skin of habitat on land is minis-cule in comparison. Yet because the ocean's depths are dangerous and expensive to explore, very little is known about the deep sea—so little that even a big,
35 common creature can go undetected.

"It's just a fantastic finding," said Dr. J. Frederick Grassle, the director of the Institute of Marine and Coastal Sciences at Rutgers University. "I've made a lot of dives in submersibles and never seen anything
40 like these. It's remarkable that there have been so many sightings recently."

Perhaps most remarkable is that researchers could piece the sightings together at all. Dr. Vecchione said all the squids were spotted incidentally, by scientists or
45 oil company workers looking for something else on the ocean floor. The chance observations occurred over the last 13 years. Dr. Vecchione said the first videotape he saw of one of these animals was made not for science, but for love, by a man aboard an oil exploration vessel
50 using a remotely operated submersible. When the sub-mersible came across the squid, the man filmed it, because his girlfriend was interested in marine biology.

"It was just pure luck," Dr. Vecchione said. Once aware of the new squid, he began learning of the other
55 observations.

The squids are unusual in a number of ways, including their excessively long arms held in a unique bent stance, their large fins and their apparent lack of concern with the proximity of the submersibles. When
60 observed, the squids were mostly hanging in the water, gently waving their fins to hold their position, arms dangling beneath them. Unlike most squids, which have two long tentacles and eight shorter arms, the new squid's arms and tentacles are indistinguishably long.

65 "It's a very exciting animal," said Dr. Clyde Roper, a zoologist at the National Museum of Natural History at the Smithsonian Institution. "This animal probably doesn't weigh more than 25 to 50 pounds. Most of its length is in these very, very thin, tendrilous
70 appendages."

Without specimens in hand, it is impossible for scientists to say whether the squids represent one or more species. The animals remain unnamed. The mys-tery squids are most similar to small, young squids dis-
75 covered several years ago near Hawaii and California that had large fins and long, slender arms. Dr. Vecchione speculated that the new squids might eat small crustaceans that they grabbed with what scientists suspected were sticky arms. "One of the squids actually
80 got its arms stuck on a submersible, and it had trouble letting go," he said. "I think what it has are many really tiny suckers on it."

Dr. Ron O'Dor, a senior scientist at the Census of Marine Life, says the new finding proves how far biolo-
85 gists have to go in understanding the deep sea. "We'll be exploring essentially unknown territory," Dr. O'Dor said. Even as scientists undertook more detailed stud-ies, he said much would remain unseen because any animal too fast or too smart to be caught in the lights of
90 submersibles would remain out of view.

31. The passage implies that for researchers, the biggest obstacle to learning more about the new squid is(are) the:

A. reluctance of the squid to approach submersibles or to be filmed.

B. uncertainty over how many different species the squid represents.

C. declining number of sightings of the squid in recent years.

D. risks and costs imposed by the squid's remote habitat.

GO ON TO THE NEXT PAGE.

32. The language of the first paragraph is most likely intended to convey a sense of:

    F. excitement generated by an intriguing discovery.
    G. confusion over a newly encountered species.
    H. skepticism about an allegedly important finding.
    J. enthusiasm for the practical benefits of a research study.

33. Which of the following statements best summarizes the comments in the passage from O'Dor?

    A. Deep-sea exploration is wasteful because so much of the ocean will remain unseen.
    B. Biologists are getting close to a full understanding of the deep sea.
    C. New submersibles will be needed to study the ocean's smart, fast creatures.
    D. A great deal about the deep sea is unknown and will likely stay that way.

34. According to the passage, *Architeuthis* is a name for:

    F. both the giant squid and its close relative, the new squid.
    G. both the giant squid and its distant relative, the new squid.
    H. the giant squid only.
    J. the new squid only.

35. The passage states that the giant squid has yet to be:

    A. found washed up on shore.
    B. found in the stomach of a whale.
    C. seen alive in its natural habitat.
    D. reported on in *Science* magazine.

36. The author refers to "the skin of habitat on land" (line 31) primarily to:

    F. contend that researchers should look underground rather than underwater for new animal species.
    G. emphasize the vastness of deep-sea habitat in contrast to land habitat.
    H. suggest that land habitats are just as worthy of study as ocean habitats.
    J. point out that much deep-sea research could be performed more safely and cheaply on land.

37. Within the passage, Grassle's statement in the fifth paragraph (lines 36–41) serves mainly to:

    A. emphasize the value and uniqueness of the discovery of the new squid.
    B. offer an urgent call for more submersible-based studies of the new squid.
    C. reveal that he spends most of his time as a researcher making dives in submersibles.
    D. explain the role the Institute of Marine and Coastal Sciences has in squid research.

38. In the passage, Vecchione claims that all of the sightings of the new squid were made:

    F. intentionally by scientists looking specifically for the squid.
    G. intentionally by scientists hoping to find several new species of marine life.
    H. unintentionally by scientists or oil company workers searching for something else.
    J. unintentionally by oil company workers exploring the ocean floor with submersibles.

39. It can most reasonably be inferred that the word *love* in line 49 refers to the man's love for:

    A. the new squid.
    B. marine biology.
    C. another person.
    D. submersibles.

40. The passage characterizes the idea that the new squid eats small crustaceans obtained with sticky arms as:

    F. a fact verified by examination of tiny suckers on the squid's arms.
    G. a fact supported by the study of similar squids found near Hawaii and California.
    H. an opinion founded on videotaped images of the squid's mouth and teeth.
    J. an opinion based in part on an incident involving one of the squids and a submersible.

END OF TEST 3

STOP! DO NOT TURN THE PAGE UNTIL TOLD TO DO SO.

DO NOT RETURN TO A PREVIOUS TEST.

Practice ACT Tests

SCIENCE TEST

35 Minutes—40 Questions

DIRECTIONS: There are seven passages in this test. Each passage is followed by several questions. After reading a passage, choose the best answer to each question and fill in the corresponding oval on your answer document. You may refer to the passages as often as necessary.

You are NOT permitted to use a calculator on this test.

Passage I

When a substance dissolves in H_2O, heat is either absorbed from or given off to the solution. Experiments were done in which a known mass of a solute was added to a known mass of H_2O at a known initial temperature (T_i) in a closed, insulated container. When the maximum temperature change of the solution had occurred, the final temperature (T_f) was recorded. The maximum temperature change (ΔT) was then calculated as follows:

$$\Delta T = T_f - T_i$$

Figures 1 and 2 show the results for lithium chloride (LiCl) and ammonium nitrate (NH_4NO_3), respectively. In each trial, all of the solute completely dissolved.

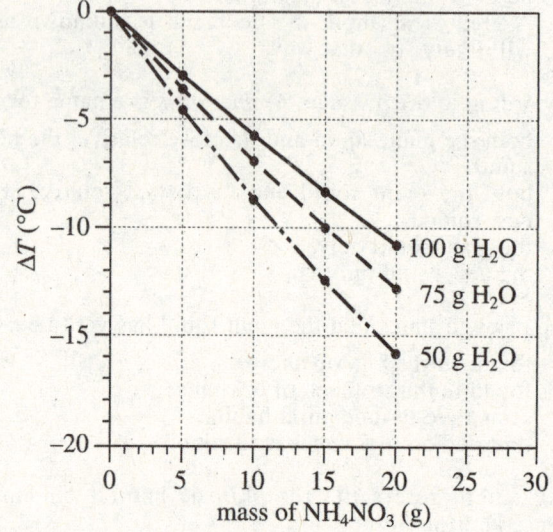

Figure 2

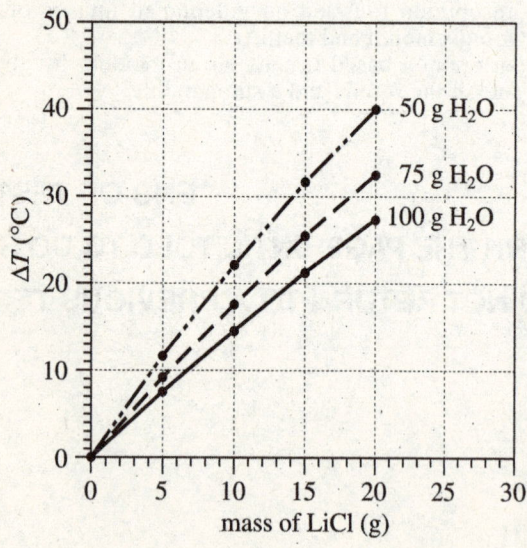

Figure 1

1. Based on Figure 1, when 5 g of LiCl was added to 50 g of H_2O, the temperature:

   A. decreased, because heat was removed from the solution.
   B. decreased, because heat was added to the solution.
   C. increased, because heat was removed from the solution.
   D. increased, because heat was added to the solution.

GO ON TO THE NEXT PAGE.

2. Consider the trials represented in Figure 1 involving 20 g of LiCl. From trial to trial, as the LiCl concentration in the resulting solutions increased, the ΔT that was observed:

   F. increased only.
   G. increased, then decreased.
   H. decreased only.
   J. decreased, then increased.

3. If an additional trial had been done in which 25 g of LiCl had been added to 75 g of H_2O, ΔT would most likely have been:

   A. less than 20°C.
   B. between 20°C and 30°C.
   C. between 30°C and 40°C.
   D. greater than 40°C.

4. According to Figure 2, when 5 g of NH_4NO_3 was added to 100 g of H_2O, the temperature of the solution:

   F. decreased, because ΔT was positive.
   G. decreased, because ΔT was negative.
   H. increased, because ΔT was positive.
   J. increased, because ΔT was negative.

5. Based on Figures 1 and 2, which of the following combinations of a solute and H_2O at a known T_i would produce the greatest *increase* in temperature?

   A. 2 g of LiCl added to 5 g of H_2O
   B. 2 g of LiCl added to 10 g of H_2O
   C. 2 g of NH_4NO_3 added to 5 g of H_2O
   D. 2 g of NH_4NO_3 added to 10 g of H_2O

GO ON TO THE NEXT PAGE.

Practice ACT Tests

Passage II

During prophase I of meiosis, homologous chromosomes frequently exchange segments in a process called *crossing over*. As a result, genes on homologous chromosomes recombine, forming new allele combinations along chromosomes (see Figure 1).

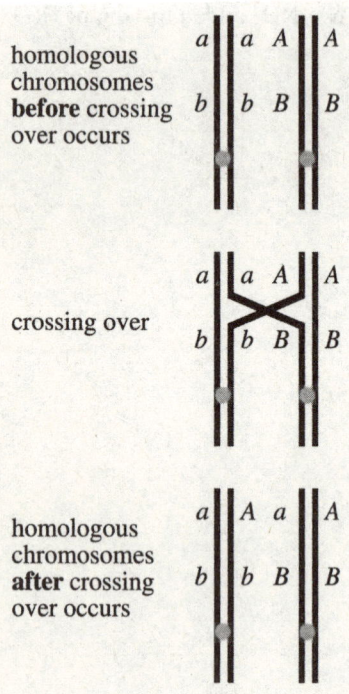

homologous chromosomes **before** crossing over occurs

crossing over

homologous chromosomes **after** crossing over occurs

Figure 1

Because the frequency of recombination (RF) increases as the *map distance* (distance along a chromosome, in *map units* [mu]) between 2 genes increases, RF can be used to estimate the map distance between genes on a chromosome. However, as the map distance between 2 genes increases, the probability of multiple crossovers increases. Multiple crossovers decrease the apparent RF between 2 genes, resulting in RF values that underestimate map distance. To compensate for this effect, researchers use a mapping function to better estimate the map distance between 2 genes based on their RF (see Figure 2).

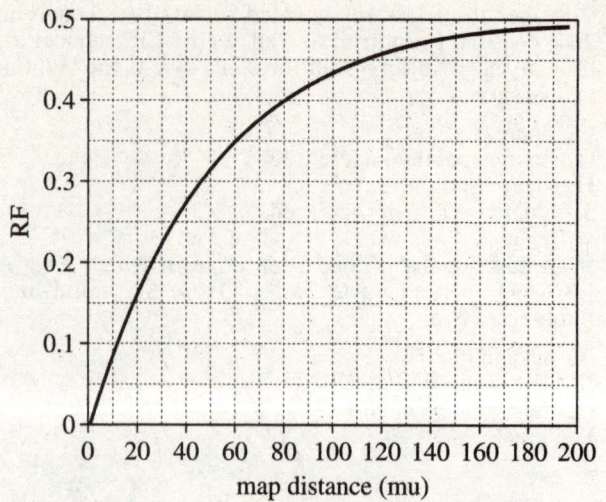

Figure 2

Four researchers performed a series of experiments to determine the RF for various pairs of genes on a chromosome. They then used the mapping function to determine the map distance between each pair. The results appear in Table 1.

Table 1		
Genes	RF	Map distance (mu)
A and B	0.165	20
B and C	0.226	30
A and D	0.122	14

Each of the 4 researchers then proposed a model that is consistent with the results in Table 1. Each model shows how the genes might be located along the chromosome (see Figure 3). Each model correctly assumes the lengths of the genes are short enough that they can be ignored when calculating the map distance between genes.

Researcher	Model
1	D A B C
2	A DB C
3	DC A B
4	C A DB

Figure 3

Later, a fifth researcher working with the same chromosome and the same genes determined that the RF for Genes A and C is 0.091.

GO ON TO THE NEXT PAGE.

6. All 4 models agree on the map distance between which of the following pairs of genes?

F. Genes A and B
G. Genes A and C
H. Genes B and D
J. Genes C and D

7. According to Figure 2, if 2 genes are separated by 70 mu, the RF of those 2 genes is most likely closest to which of the following?

A. 0.377
B. 0.477
C. 0.577
D. 0.677

8. If Researcher 2's model is correct and an additional gene, Gene G, is 8 mu from Gene B and 14 mu from Gene D, then Gene G is most likely between:

F. Genes A and B.
G. Genes A and D.
H. Genes B and C.
J. Genes B and D.

9. The result of the mapping experiment performed by the fifth researcher for Genes A and C is consistent with the models proposed by which 2 researchers?

A. Researchers 1 and 3
B. Researchers 1 and 4
C. Researchers 2 and 3
D. Researchers 3 and 4

10. Based on the information provided, crossing over occurs during the process that leads directly to the formation of which of the following?

F. Neurons
G. Skin cells
H. Erythrocytes
J. Gametes

11. Which researcher's model proposes that Genes C and D are separated by 64 mu?

A. Researcher 1's
B. Researcher 2's
C. Researcher 3's
D. Researcher 4's

12. Genes R and T are separated by 10 mu on 1 chromosome. An organism has alleles R and T on 1 chromosome and alleles r and t on the homologous chromosome. If a single crossover occurred between these 2 genes as shown in Figure 1, the genotype of Genes R and T for the 2 chromatids involved in the crossover would be:

F. Rt and rT.
G. RT and rt.
H. Rr and Tt.
J. RR and TT.

Passage III

Pore water is water in the pores of subsurface material. Pore water chemistry in 2 wetlands—a *fen* and a *bog*—was studied during a 1990 summer drought and again the next summer, which had normal rainfall. The primary water supplies for fens and bogs are, respectively, groundwater and rainfall. Figure 1 shows the methane (CH_4) gas concentration in the pore water at various depths in the fen and the bog. Figures 2 and 3 show the pore water *conductivity* (which is directly proportional to the concentration of dissolved ions) and pH at various depths in the fen and the bog, respectively. Also shown are the locations of the water table, the *peat* (partially decomposed plant material) layer, and the mineral soil layer.

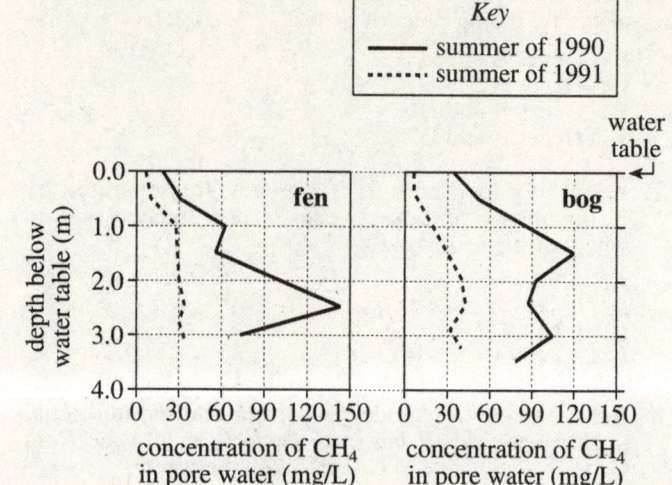

Figure 1

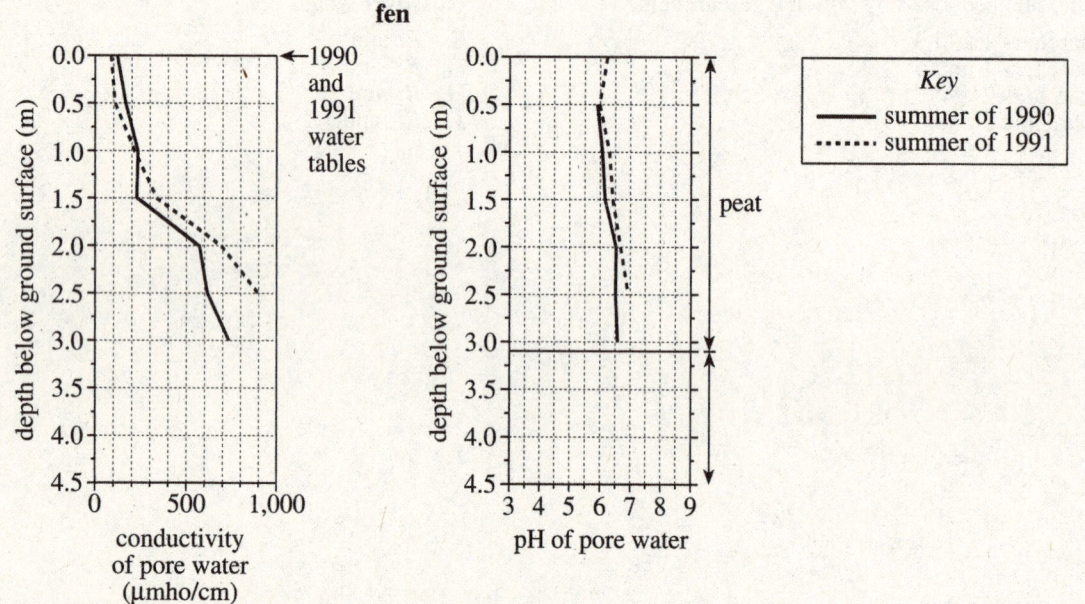

Note: Mineral soil is composed mainly of mineral matter.

Figure 2

GO ON TO THE NEXT PAGE.

bog

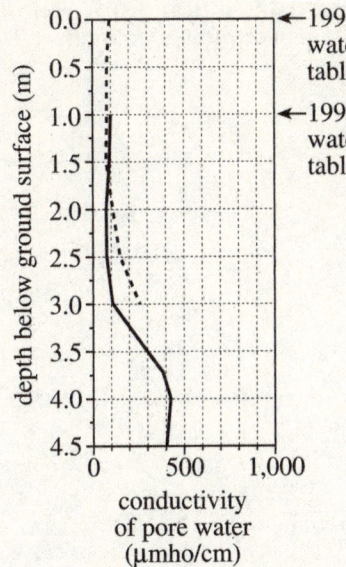

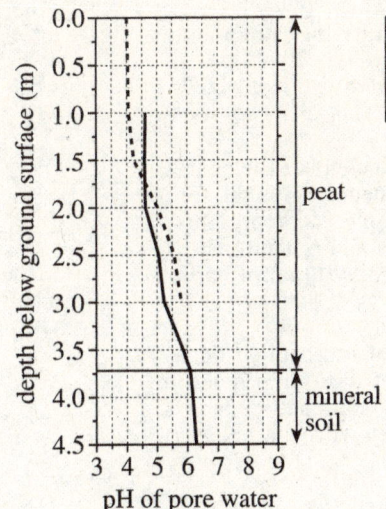

Note: Mineral soil is composed mainly of mineral matter.

Figure 3

Figures adapted from Edwin Romanowicz, Donald Siegel, and Paul Glaser, "Hydraulic Reversals and Episodic Methane Emissions During Drought Cycles in Mires." ©1993 by the Geological Society of America.

13. According to Figure 2, the conductivity of fen pore water in 1990 at a depth of 2.5 m was closest to which of the following?

A. 350 μmho/cm
B. 475 μmho/cm
C. 600 μmho/cm
D. 725 μmho/cm

14. Based on Figure 2, if the pH of pore water in the fen at a depth of 2.7 m had been measured in the summer of 1991, it would most likely have been closest to which of the following?

F. 4.0
G. 5.5
H. 7.0
J. 8.5

15. Which of the following is the most likely explanation for the difference in the depth of the bog water table in the 2 years?

A. The amount of groundwater discharged to the bog was higher during the drought, and therefore the bog received more water than normal.
B. The amount of groundwater discharged to the bog was higher during the drought, and therefore the bog received less water than normal.
C. The amount of rainfall received by the bog was higher during the drought, and therefore the bog received more water than normal.
D. The amount of rainfall received by the bog was lower during the drought, and therefore the bog received less water than normal.

16. If the data in Figures 2 and 3 are typical of fens and bogs in general, one would most likely make which of the following conclusions about the peat layer in a fen and in a bog?

F. The peat layer in both a fen and a bog is completely above the water table at all times.
G. The peat layer in both a fen and a bog is completely below the water table at all times.
H. The peat layer in a fen is thicker than the peat layer in a bog.
J. The peat layer in a fen is thinner than the peat layer in a bog.

17. According to Figure 1, the average concentration of CH_4 over the depths from 0.0 m to 3.0 m was higher during the summer of:

A. normal rainfall than during the summer of drought in both wetlands.
B. normal rainfall than during the summer of drought in the fen only.
C. drought than during the summer of normal rainfall in both wetlands.
D. drought than during the summer of normal rainfall in the bog only.

GO ON TO THE NEXT PAGE.

Passage IV

Atomic nuclei can be represented by the combination of symbols

$$^A_Z X$$

where Z is the number of protons in a nucleus of Element X, and A (equal to Z plus the number of neutrons) is the mass number of the same nucleus. For example, $^{12}_6C$ represents a nucleus of carbon containing 6 protons and 6 neutrons; $^{14}_6C$ represents a nucleus of a different *isotope* (type) of carbon that contains 6 protons and 8 neutrons.

Atomic nuclei undergo 3 types of radioactive decay. Particles emitted during the 3 types of decay are listed in Table 1. Figure 1 shows a sequence of radioactive decays, called the *uranium series*, that begins with the decay of $^{238}_{92}U$.

	Table 1	
Type of radioactive decay	Particle emitted	Symbol of emitted particle
Alpha	helium nucleus	^4_2He
Beta	electron	e^-
Gamma	gamma ray photon	γ

element

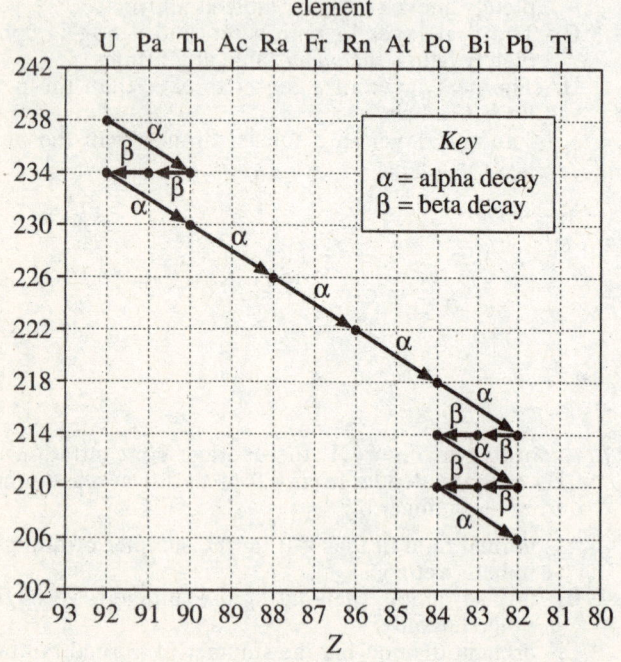

Figure 1

18. Which of the following symbols correctly represents the isotope of radium (Ra) that is part of the radioactive decay sequence plotted in Figure 1 ?

F. $^{88}_{226}Ra$

G. $^{226}_{226}Ra$

H. $^{88}_{88}Ra$

J. $^{226}_{88}Ra$

19. How many neutrons, if any, does a nucleus of the isotope of helium listed in Table 1 contain?

A. 0
B. 1
C. 2
D. 3

20. Based on Figure 1, if a nucleus of $^{230}_{90}Th$ underwent beta decay, which of the following nuclei would be produced?

F. $^{230}_{230}Pa$

G. $^{230}_{91}Pa$

H. $^{230}_{91}Th$

J. $^{91}_{231}Th$

GO ON TO THE NEXT PAGE.

21. A sample of spent nuclear reactor fuel contains a mixture of a uranium isotope, $^{235}_{92}U$, and a plutonium isotope, $^{239}_{94}Pu$. Based on Table 1 and Figure 1, if one of the isotopes is produced by the radioactive decay of the other isotope, which of the following best explains how the mixture was formed?

A. $^{235}_{92}U$ underwent alpha decay, producing $^{239}_{94}Pu$.

B. $^{239}_{94}Pu$ underwent alpha decay, producing $^{235}_{92}U$.

C. $^{235}_{92}U$ underwent beta decay, producing $^{239}_{94}Pu$.

D. $^{239}_{94}Pu$ underwent beta decay, producing $^{235}_{92}U$.

22. Suppose the $^{4}_{2}He$ nucleus emitted during an alpha decay and the e^{-} emitted during a beta decay have the same kinetic energy. Which of the 2 particles is moving at the higher speed?

F. The $^{4}_{2}He$ nucleus, because it is more massive than the e^{-}.

G. The $^{4}_{2}He$ nucleus, because it is less massive than the e^{-}.

H. The e^{-}, because it is more massive than the $^{4}_{2}He$ nucleus.

J. The e^{-}, because it is less massive than the $^{4}_{2}He$ nucleus.

GO ON TO THE NEXT PAGE.

Passage V

Size exclusion chromatography (SEC) is used to separate the components of a solution of polymer molecules. In SEC a sample solution of polymer molecules is injected into a flow of solvent. The sample is then carried through a column filled with beads that contain microscopic pores (see Figure 1).

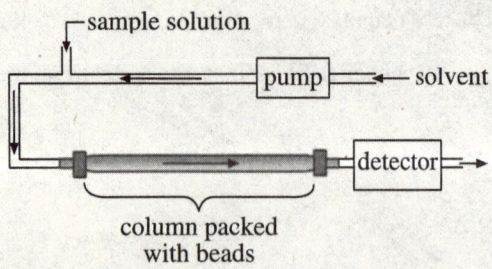

sample solution
pump ← solvent
detector
column packed
with beads

Figure 1

Smaller molecules easily diffuse into the pores. Larger molecules do not as easily diffuse into the pores, or are larger than the pores. Therefore, smaller molecules spend more time in the column than do larger molecules, causing the components of the mixture to separate. As solvent containing a component of the mixture exits the column through the detector, a peak is plotted versus time (starting from injection). The portion of solvent corresponding to a peak is called a *fraction*. The time corresponding to the top of a peak is the fraction's *retention time* (RT). The RT corresponds to the *average molecular mass* (AMM) of the molecules in that fraction. The shape of the peak reflects the distribution of molecular masses of the molecules in the fraction.

Experiment 1

Polystyrene is a polymer made up of identical subunits. Five types of polystyrene (P1–P5) were dissolved together in a solvent. The AMM of P1–P5 is given in Table 1. The range of molecular masses for each of P1–P5 was ±100 amu of the AMM.

Table 1	
Polystyrene	AMM (amu*)
P1	800
P2	4,000
P3	10,000
P4	50,000
P5	200,000
*amu = atomic mass unit	

A sample of the solution was injected into an SEC apparatus. Each fraction was analyzed as it exited the apparatus (see Figure 2).

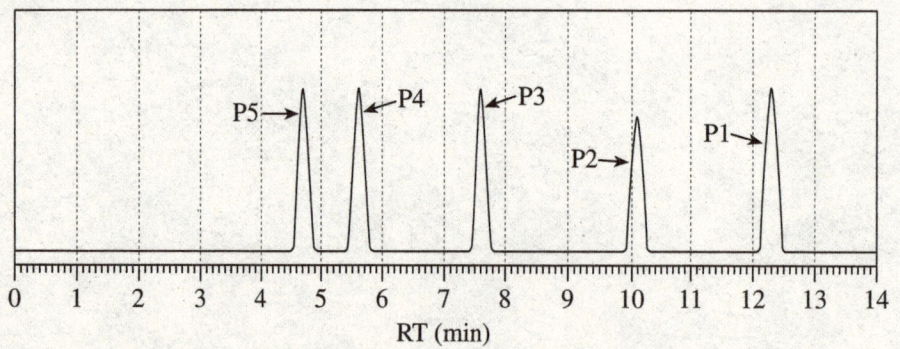

RT (min)

Figure 2

GO ON TO THE NEXT PAGE.

Experiment 2

Chemists used 3 different methods to synthesize polystyrenes, forming polystyrene mixtures M1, M2, and M3, respectively. Each of M1–M3 was then analyzed as in Experiment 1 (see Figure 3).

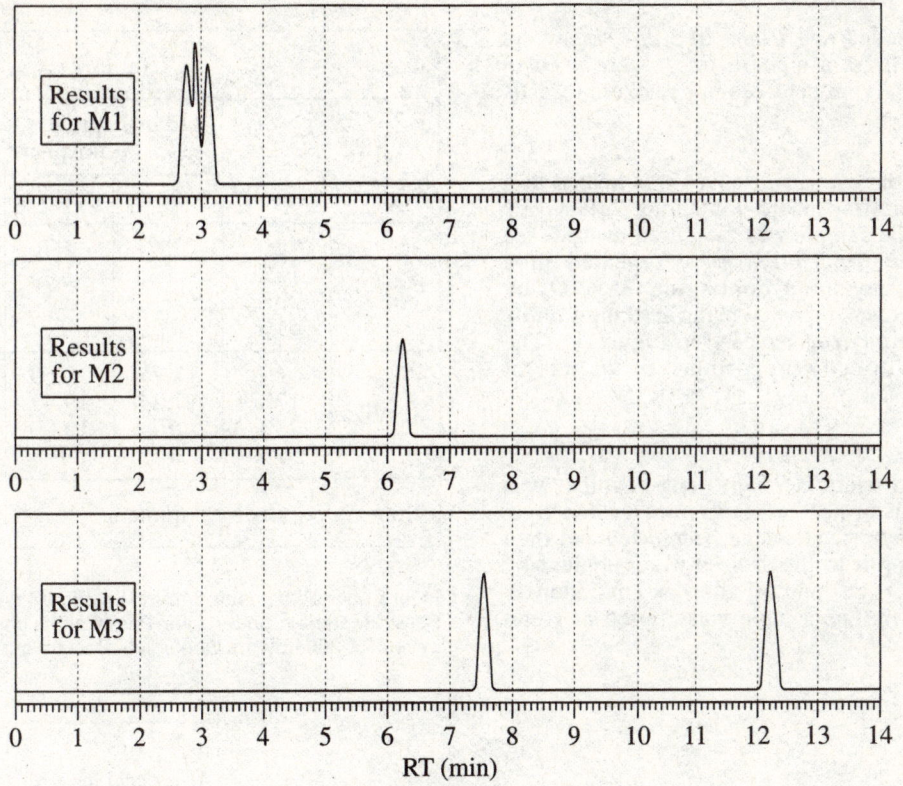

Figure 3

23. Based on the results of Experiments 1 and 2, M3 is most likely which polymer(s) from Experiment 1 ?

A. P1 only
B. A mixture of P1 and P3 only
C. A mixture of P3 and P5 only
D. A mixture of P2, P4, and P5 only

24. In Experiment 1, the molecules of which of the following polymers spent the longest amount of time in the column?

F. P1
G. P2
H. P4
J. P5

25. Based on the results of Experiments 1 and 2, which of the following ranks P4, P5, and M2 from smallest AMM to largest AMM ?

A. P4, P5, M2
B. P5, M2, P4
C. M2, P4, P5
D. M2, P5, P4

26. In Experiment 1, on average, did P3 molecules or P4 molecules more easily diffuse into the pores of the beads while in the column of the SEC apparatus?

F. P3 molecules, because they have a larger AMM.
G. P3 molecules, because they have a smaller AMM.
H. P4 molecules, because they have a larger AMM.
J. P4 molecules, because they have a smaller AMM.

27. In which, if any, of the mixtures synthesized for Experiment 2 is the average mass of the molecules in the mixture most likely greater than 200,000 amu ?

A. M1
B. M2
C. M3
D. Neither M1, M2, nor M3

28. How does the number of molecules in a 1 g sample of P2 compare to the number of molecules in a 1 g sample of P4 ? The number of P2 molecules is:

F. less, because P2 has a larger AMM than does P4.
G. less, because P2 has a smaller AMM than does P4.
H. greater, because P2 has a larger AMM than does P4.
J. greater, because P2 has a smaller AMM than does P4.

GO ON TO THE NEXT PAGE.

Passage VI

Two studies examined how forest fires would have burned during the late Paleozoic era, when Earth's atmosphere contained an elevated O_2 content of more than 21% by volume.

Araucaria tree leaves and *Pinus* tree *dowels* (wood pieces) and needles, all from modern trees, were used in the studies to most closely model trees in Paleozoic forests.

Study 1

A 10 mg sample of *Araucaria* leaves was heated at a rate of 40°C/min in an atmosphere containing 21% O_2 by volume. The mass of the sample was measured every 2 sec during heating. These procedures were repeated in a second trial in an atmosphere containing 35% O_2 by volume. Then each trial was repeated using a 10 mg sample of paper instead of *Araucaria* leaves (see Figure 1). The rate of mass loss was directly proportional to the rate of combustion.

Study 2

In each of several trials, a 75 cm long chamber was filled either with dowels or needles, both from a *Pinus* tree. Each sample of dowels or needles had been dried and then soaked in water to bring it to the desired water content by weight. A mixture of O_2 gas and N_2 gas was continuously supplied to the chamber. The sample was ignited at 1 end of the chamber.

For any trial in which the sample burned completely, the flame spread rate was recorded. Those trials represented conditions under which a forest fire would have burned out of control. A *failed burn* (F) was recorded for any trial in which the fire in the chamber extinguished itself before the sample burned completely (see Table 1).

	Table 1				
		Flame spread rate (cm/min) in an atmosphere containing:			
Water content of:		16% O_2	21% O_2	28% O_2	35% O_2
Dowels	2%	2.48	2.76	3.92	5.00
	12%	F	1.45	2.49	3.09
	23%	F	F	F	2.73
	61%	F	F	F	F
Needles	2%	18.75	20.69	37.50	39.30
	12%	17.24	19.43	22.61	28.08
	23%	F	15.00	18.22	22.86
	61%	F	F	F	F
Note: % O_2 was by volume.					

Figure and table adapted from Richard Wildman et al., "Burning of Forest Materials under Late Paleozoic High Atmospheric Oxygen Levels." ©2004 by the Geological Society of America.

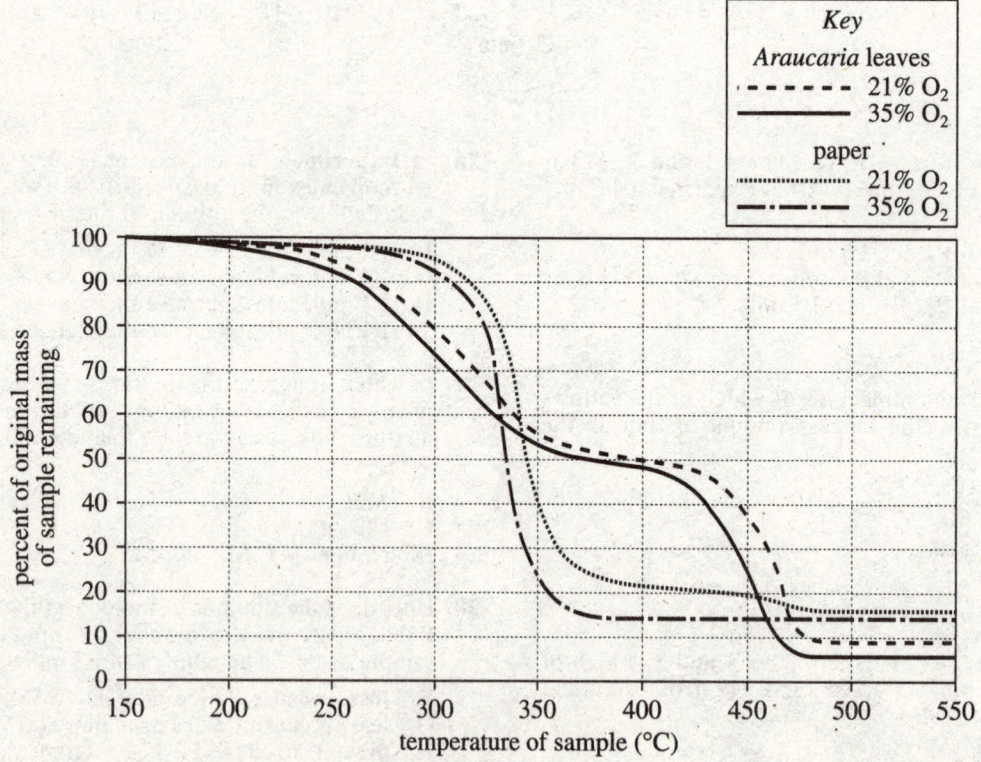

Figure 1

GO ON TO THE NEXT PAGE.

 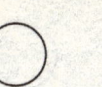 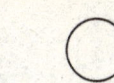

29. According to the results of Study 2, as O_2 content increased from 16% to 35%, the flame spread rate for dowels having a water content of 2%:

   A. increased only.
   B. increased, then decreased.
   C. decreased only.
   D. decreased, then increased.

30. According to the results of Study 1, the sample of *Araucaria* leaves heated in an atmosphere containing 35% O_2 lost mass most rapidly over which of the following temperature ranges?

   F. 275°C to 325°C
   G. 325°C to 375°C
   H. 375°C to 425°C
   J. 425°C to 475°C

31. Suppose that the needles and wood of a type of tree that existed in the late Paleozoic era and closely resembled modern *Pinus* trees had water contents above 65% by weight. Based on Study 2, would a tree of that type have burned completely in an atmosphere containing 28% O_2 by volume and in an atmosphere containing 35% O_2 by volume, respectively?

	28% O_2	35% O_2
A.	No	Yes
B.	No	No
C.	Yes	No
D.	Yes	Yes

32. Suppose that in an additional trial in Study 2, needles having a water content of 10% by weight had been burned in an atmosphere containing 28% O_2 by volume. Based on the results of Study 2, the flame spread rate recorded for that trial would most likely have been:

   F. less than 18.22 cm/min.
   G. between 18.22 cm/min and 22.61 cm/min.
   H. between 22.61 cm/min and 37.50 cm/min.
   J. greater than 37.50 cm/min.

33. Consider a Paleozoic forest fire burning out of control in a stand of trees that closely resembled modern *Pinus* trees. Based on the results of Study 2 for an atmosphere containing 28% O_2 and an atmosphere containing 35% O_2, is it more likely that the *crown fire* (fire spreading through the live foliage of trees) or the *surface fire* (fire spreading through the trees just above the ground) would have spread faster?

   A. The crown fire, because the flame spread rates for needles were much lower than the corresponding rates for dowels.
   B. The crown fire, because the flame spread rates for needles were much higher than the corresponding rates for dowels.
   C. The surface fire, because the flame spread rates for needles were much lower than the corresponding rates for dowels.
   D. The surface fire, because the flame spread rates for needles were the same as the corresponding rates for dowels.

34. In Study 1, the paper sample heated in an atmosphere containing 21% O_2 had lost approximately what percent of its original mass by the time the temperature reached 350°C ?

   F. 20%
   G. 40%
   H. 60%
   J. 80%

GO ON TO THE NEXT PAGE.

Passage VII

Students studied the trajectories of a baseball launched under a variety of conditions.

Study 1

On a flat plain during a windless day, students launched a baseball using the launcher shown in Figure 1.

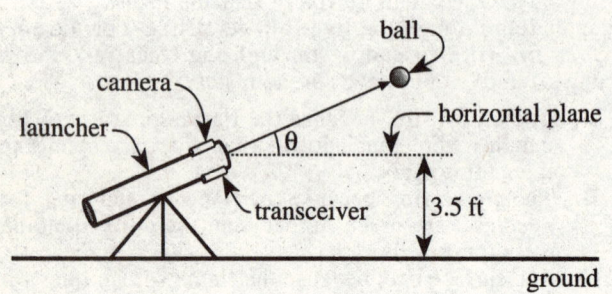

Figure 1

A camera mounted on the launcher always pointed in the direction of the ball's launch. A radar *transceiver* (transmitter-receiver) was also mounted on the launcher.

As the ball moved along its path, Angle θ, which is defined in Figure 1, continuously varied. The variation in θ was monitored by the camera, which recorded the ball's image in its viewfinder every 0.5 sec after launch until the ball landed. For each recorded image, θ was found (see Figure 2).

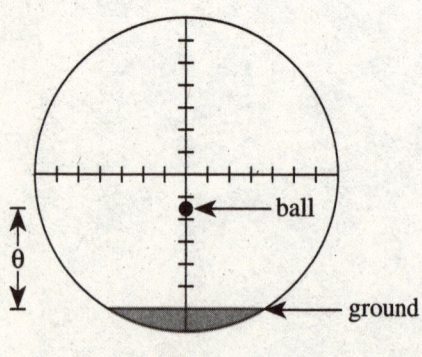

Figure 2

In addition, every 0.5 sec after launch, the transceiver emitted a radar pulse, part of which was reflected back to the transceiver by the ball. The round-trip travel time of each pulse was recorded and then used to determine the distance, D, between the transceiver and the ball (see Figure 3).

Figure 3

Using D and θ, the students found the ball's height, H, and distance, R, at the end of each 0.5 sec interval. H was plotted versus R, and a smooth curve was fitted to the data points.

This procedure was followed for launches of the ball at speeds of 80 mph, 90 mph, 100 mph, 110 mph, and 120 mph. For each launch speed, the ball was launched at $\theta = 35°$. The curves representing the 5 launch speeds were connected by lines drawn through the data points representing H and R for time = 2 sec, 3 sec, 4 sec, and 5 sec after launch (see Figure 4).

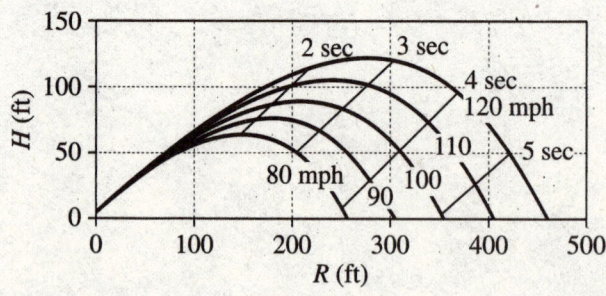

Figure 4

Figure 4 adapted from Robert K. Adair, *The Physics of Baseball*, 3rd ed. ©2002 by Robert K. Adair.

GO ON TO THE NEXT PAGE.

Study 2

Using a mathematical model, the students calculated *H* and *R* at 0.5 sec intervals for the same ball launched under the same conditions as in Study 1, except that they assumed that air was absent. The results are plotted in Figure 5.

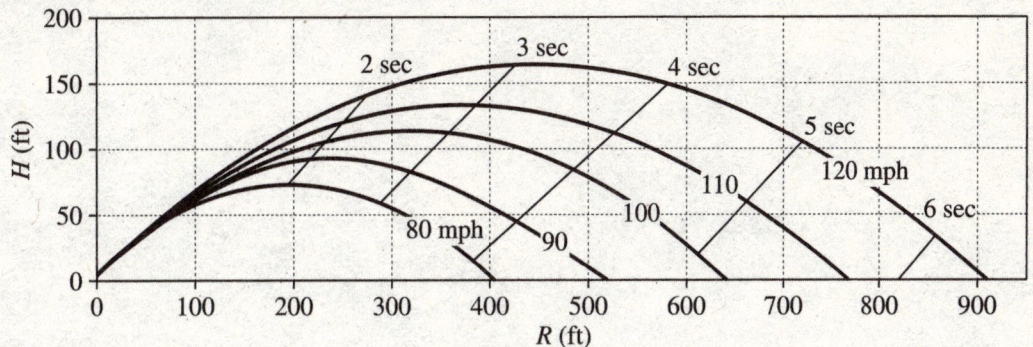

Figure 5

35. Suppose the ball were launched at 35° in the absence of air from a height of 3.5 ft. Based on Figure 5, the ball would land approximately how many feet farther from the launcher if it were launched at 100 mph than if it were launched at 90 mph ?

A.   50 ft
B.   100 ft
C.   500 ft
D.   600 ft

36. While the ball was in flight, how frequently did the camera record the ball's image?

F.   One time per second
G.   Two times per second
H.   Three times per second
J.   Four times per second

37. Fenway Park, home of baseball's Boston Red Sox, has a wall in left field that is 37 ft high. The distance measured along the left field line from home plate to the bottom of the wall is 310 ft. Assume that, on a windless day, a ball identical to the one used in Experiment 1 leaves a bat at an initial height of 3.5 ft above the ground, at an angle of 35° with respect to the horizontal, and flies straight along the left field line. The ball will fly over the wall if the ball leaves the bat at which of the speeds given in Figure 4 ?

A.   120 mph only
B.   110 mph or 120 mph only
C.   100 mph, 110 mph, or 120 mph only
D.   Any of the speeds given in Figure 4

38. Based on Figure 4, as the launch speed was increased, how did *H* and *R* at 3 sec after launch vary?

	$\underline{H}$	$\underline{R}$
F.	increased	increased
G.	increased	decreased
H.	decreased	increased
J.	decreased	decreased

39. Based on Figure 5, if the ball were launched in the absence of air from a height of 3.5 ft at 120 mph and θ = 35°, how long would the ball most likely be in flight from the moment it was launched to the moment it landed?

A.   Between 4 sec and 5 sec
B.   Between 5 sec and 6 sec
C.   Between 6 sec and 7 sec
D.   Between 7 sec and 8 sec

40. Based on Figure 3, if c represents the speed of light, how long did it take each radar pulse to make the round-trip between the transceiver and the ball?

F. $2\dfrac{D}{c}$

G. $\dfrac{R}{c}$

H. $2\dfrac{c}{D}$

J. $\dfrac{c}{R}$

END OF TEST 4

STOP! DO NOT RETURN TO ANY OTHER TEST.

072954   **Practice Writing Test Prompt 5**

Your Signature (do not print): _____

Print Your Name Here: _____

Your Date of Birth:

☐☐ – ☐☐ – ☐☐☐☐

Month   Day   Year

Form 5WT

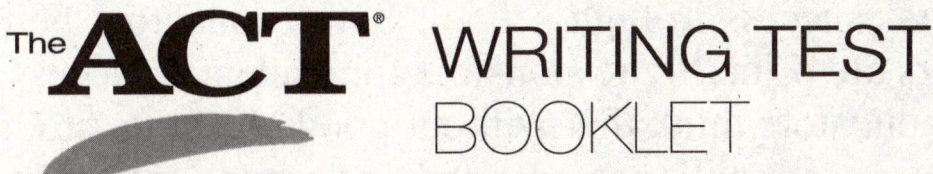

The ACT® WRITING TEST BOOKLET

You must take the multiple-choice tests before you take the Writing Test.

Directions

This is a test of your writing skills. You will have thirty (30) minutes to write an essay in English. Before you begin planning and writing your essay, read the writing prompt carefully to understand exactly what you are being asked to do. Your essay will be evaluated on the evidence it provides of your ability to express judgments by taking a position on the issue in the writing prompt; to maintain a focus on the topic throughout the essay; to develop a position by using logical reasoning and by supporting your ideas; to organize ideas in a logical way; and to use language clearly and effectively according to the conventions of standard written English.

You may use the unlined pages in this test booklet to plan your essay. These pages will not be scored. *You must write your essay in pencil on the lined pages in the answer folder.* Your writing on those lined pages will be scored. You may not need all the lined pages, but to ensure you have enough room to finish, do NOT skip lines. You may write corrections or additions neatly between the lines of your essay, but do NOT write in the margins of the lined pages. *Illegible essays cannot be scored, so you must write (or print) clearly.*

If you finish before time is called, you may review your work. Lay your pencil down immediately when time is called.

DO NOT OPEN THIS BOOKLET UNTIL TOLD TO DO SO.

P.O. BOX 168
IOWA CITY, IA 52243-0168   **ACT**®

Practice Writing Test Prompt 5

Educators often debate who is primarily responsible for students' success in high school. Some educators believe that teachers are primarily responsible for students' success because these educators think that without good teaching, students will not learn and will not succeed in school. Other educators believe that the students themselves are primarily responsible for their success because these educators think that students must be personally motivated and willing to actively participate in learning if they are to succeed in school. In your opinion, who is primarily responsible for students' success in high school?

In your essay, take a position on this question. You may write about either one of the two points of view given, or you may present a different point of view on this question. Use specific reasons and examples to support your position.

Use this page to *plan* your essay.
Your work on this page will *not* be scored.

If you need more space to plan,
please continue on the back of this page.

**Use this page to *plan* your essay.
Your work on this page will *not* be scored.**

You may wish to photocopy these sample answer document pages to respond to the practice ACT Writing Test.

Please enter the information at the right before beginning the Writing Test.

Use a soft lead No. 2 pencil only. Do NOT use a mechanical pencil, ink, ballpoint, or felt-tip pen.

WRITING TEST BOOKLET NUMBER

Print your 6-digit **Booklet Number** in the boxes at the right.

WRITING TEST FORM

Print your 3-character **Test Form** in the boxes above and fill in the corresponding oval at the right.

○ 1WT ○ 2WT ○ 3WT
○ 4WT ○ 5WT

Begin WRITING TEST here.

If you need more space, please continue on the next page.

WRITING TEST

If you need more space, please continue on the next page.

WRITING TEST

If you need more space, please continue on the back of this page.

PLEASE DO NOT WRITE IN THIS AREA.

0876008

Practice ACT Tests

WRITING TEST

STOP here with the Writing Test.

ENGLISH · PRACTICE TEST 5 · EXPLANATORY ANSWERS

Passage I

Question 1. The best answer is C because the comma after *tribe* sets off what follows as a nonrestrictive appositive that describes what "the Miami tribe" is: "a Native American people with strong ties to territory in present-day Ohio, Indiana, and Illinois."

The best answer is NOT:

A because it is missing the comma needed after *tribe* to set off the following nonrestrictive appositive from the noun *tribe* and because it places an unnecessary and confusing comma between the noun *people* and the series of prepositional phrases starting with *with strong ties* that follows and describes *people*.

B because it pointlessly separates with a comma the adjective *Native American* from the noun *people*.

D because it misuses the semicolon. The semicolon inappropriately implies that what will follow is an independent clause, as in "My family is part of the Miami tribe; we are a Native American people . . . ."

Question 2. The best answer is F because "making freezer jam or researching tribal history" gives the most specific and vivid glimpse of what the grandmother was interested in.

The best answer is NOT:

G because "being actively involved in her pursuits" is vague and doesn't suggest what those pursuits are.

H because "things I really hope she'll teach me one day" gives no suggestion of what those things are.

J because "historical research as well as domestic projects" offers only a general notion of the interests that are more pointedly described in **F**.

Question 3. The best answer is D because the word *rushed* by itself is sufficient to express the idea "urged to hasten."

The best answer is NOT:

A because the word *rushed* and the phrase *in a hurry* are redundant.

B because the words *hurried* and *rushed* are redundant.

C because the phrase *made to go faster* and the word *rushed* are redundant.

Question 4. The best answer is J because a comma is appropriate between the long introductory adverbial clause "if we were running late for an appointment" and the sentence's main clause, which begins with "she."

The best answer is NOT:

F because placing a period after the word *appointment* makes the introductory adverbial clause (subordinated by the conjunction *if*) into a sentence fragment and obscures how the ideas are related.

G because placing a semicolon after the word *appointment* makes the introductory adverbial clause into a sentence fragment and obscures how the ideas are related.

H because the coordinating conjunction *and* should not be used to join two unequal sentence elements, such as a subordinate clause and a main clause, as would be the case here.

Question 5. The best answer is **A** because it opens this paragraph with a general statement about the concept of Miami time and serves as the most logical link between the preceding paragraph and the subject of this paragraph.

The best answer is NOT:

B because the reference to the doctor's appointment is only loosely related to the end of the preceding paragraph and to the subject of this paragraph, which is defining and describing the concept of Miami time.

C because the general reference to the relationship between the narrator and the grandmother is only loosely related to the subject of this paragraph, which is defining and describing the concept of Miami time.

D because the general reference to the son being curious about and having never met the grandmother is only loosely related to the subject of this paragraph, which is defining and describing the concept of Miami time.

Question 6. The best answer is **G** because the dependent clause "when time seemed to slow down or stand still" is necessary information to explain which moments are being referred to and thus should not be set off from the rest of the sentence by a comma.

The best answer is NOT:

F because the comma between the words *moments* and *when* identifies the information in the dependent clause "when time seemed to slow down or stand still" as unnecessary information when, in fact, the clause is vital to defining the moments of Miami time.

H because the comma between the words *moments* and *as if* identifies the information in the dependent clause "as if time seemed to slow down or stand still" as unnecessary information and because the conjunction *as if* does not appropriately link the ideas in this sentence.

J because the comma between the words *moments* and *because* identifies the information in the dependent clause "because time seemed to slow down or stand still" as unnecessary information and because the conjunction *because* does not appropriately link the ideas in this sentence.

Question 7. The best answer is **A** because the word *words* by itself is a sufficient, clear, and appropriate way to refer to what the grandmother had said.

The best answer is NOT:

B because the phrase "spoken statements to my ears" is clumsy, wordy, and overly formal for the tone of the essay.

C because the phrase "expressed opinions on the matter" is wordy and overly formal for the tone of the essay.

D because the phrase "verbal remarks in conversation" is wordy, redundant, and overly formal for the tone of the essay.

Question 8. The best answer is J because the past tense verb *slipped* appropriately describes an event that occurred in the past and is consistent with the other past tense verbs used throughout the essay.

The best answer is NOT:

F because the verb *will slip* describes a past event in future tense.

G because the verb *slip* describes a past event in present tense.

H because the verb *are slipping* describes a past event in present progressive tense.

Question 9. The best answer is C because *thinking* is the second half of a compound verb (*was pushing and . . . thinking*). The words *I was* are implied in front of *thinking*.

The best answer is NOT:

A because the plural verb *were thinking* doesn't agree with the singular subject *I*.

B because the plural verb *were having thoughts* doesn't agree with the singular subject *I*.

D because deleting the underlined portion would leave the second part of the sentence without a verb ("I was pushing Jeremy in his stroller and of the day ahead . . .").

Question 10. The best answer is F because no punctuation should interrupt the compound subject "two does and three fawns" or separate it from the rest of the sentence.

The best answer is NOT:

G because it places an unnecessary comma between parts of the compound subject.

H because it places an unnecessary comma between the compound subject and the verb *stood*.

J because it places an unnecessary comma between parts of the compound subject.

Question 11. The best answer is A because Sentence 3, which introduces the deer, fits logically between Sentence 2's reference to Jeremy squealing and pointing at the clearing and Sentence 4's reference to the movement of the deers' ears.

The best answer is NOT:

B because the word *there* in Sentence 3 would have no logical antecedent, leaving unclear where the deer are. Also, the setting for the paragraph, revealed in Sentence 1 ("a familiar trail near our house"), would not yet have been established.

C because the narration in the first part of the paragraph involves a surprise: the pair are out for a walk (Sentence 1), then Jeremy suddenly squeals and points (Sentence 2), and then the surprise is explained (Sentence 3). Placing the revelation in Sentence 3 before what happens in Sentence 2 removes the surprise.

D because the word *there* in Sentence 3 would have no logical antecedent in Sentence 4, leaving unclear what *there* refers to. Also, the more general introduction to the deer in Sentence 3 ("two does and three fawns") should occur before the more specific reference to the deer in Sentence 4 ("five pairs of ears").

Question 12. The best answer is G because the word *rustling* is parallel in form to *lazing* earlier in the sentence. Together, these two words help form the compound subject of the verb *surprised* ("Lizards lazing . . . and quail rustling . . . surprised us").

The best answer is NOT:

F because *rustled* isn't parallel in form to *lazing* earlier in the sentence, and this lack of parallelism creates an ungrammatical sentence ("Lizards lazing in the sun and quail rustled through grasses surprised us").

H because *were rustling* isn't parallel in form to *lazing* earlier in the sentence, and this lack of parallelism creates an ungrammatical sentence ("Lizards lazing in the sun and quail were rustling through grasses surprised us").

J because deleting the underlined portion creates an ungrammatical, nonsensical sentence ("Lizards lazing in the sun and quail through grasses surprised us").

Question 13. The best answer is D because no transition word or phrase is necessary here to make the sentence part of a list of sensory experiences the narrator and son had: seeing lizards and quail, eating wild blackberries, and smelling crushed eucalyptus leaves.

The best answer is NOT:

A because the phrase "For example" illogically suggests that the aroma of crushed eucalyptus leaves is an example of the taste of wild blackberries rather than being the third item in a list of sensory experiences.

B because the phrase "On the other hand" illogically suggests that the aroma of crushed eucalyptus leaves is somehow in opposition to the taste of wild blackberries rather than being the third item in a list of sensory experiences.

C because the phrase "Just in case" makes no sense in this context, as it is unclear what smelling the aroma of crushed eucalyptus leaves would be designed to prevent.

Question 14. The best answer is J because *shorter than* is the correct comparative form to use to contrast how long the three-hour hike seemed to take with how long the normal-length hike usually seemed.

The best answer is NOT:

F because the adverb *then* is incorrectly used instead of the preposition *than* to introduce the second part of the comparison.

G because *more shorter* is an incorrectly formed comparative term and because the adverb *then* is incorrectly used instead of the preposition *than* to introduce the second part of the comparison.

H because *shortest* is a superlative term used here incorrectly to compare two things.

Question 15. The best answer is **A** because most of the essay narrates a hike that took a long time but seemed short, the rhetorical aim being to illustrate one of the narrator's personal experiences with Miami time as that concept is defined in the early part of the essay.

The best answer is NOT:

B because while the essay has met the goal specified in the question, which was to convey a personal experience with Miami time, the reason given here is inaccurate. The essay doesn't reveal whether the narrator decided to live in Miami time, nor is it clear that one can actually choose to live always in Miami time.

C because the essay has met the goal specified in the question, which was to convey a personal experience with Miami time. That the grandmother's view of Miami time is represented doesn't detract from the fact that the essay still relates the narrator's personal experience.

D because the essay has met the goal specified in the question, which was to convey a personal experience with Miami time. It is unclear what it would mean for the term *Miami time* to *belong* to the grandmother. The essay indicates that the narrator and the grandmother came to share a similar sense of Miami time.

Passage II

Question 16. The best answer is **H** because the meaning here is clearest when the ideas are divided into two sentences, with the first sentence giving a general description of the artwork and the second describing the eight women in the artwork more specifically.

The best answer is NOT:

F because the relative pronoun *that* should be used to connect an adjectival clause to a main clause, not two main clauses. *That* in this position would logically refer to the immediately preceding noun, *flowers*, which makes no sense here.

G because the coordinating conjunction *and* creates a rambling sentence in which it's difficult to tell where one thought ends and the next begins, especially without a comma before *and*.

J because using only the comma after *flowers* to join two independent clauses creates a comma splice.

Question 17. The best answer is **D** because no transition word is necessary here to link the two questions posed at the end of the essay's first paragraph with the answers that unfold beginning in the second paragraph.

The best answer is NOT:

A because the word *thus* illogically suggests that the fact that the answers to the questions posed at the end of the essay's first paragraph can be found in the artwork itself is a result of the questions being posed.

B because the word *instead* illogically sets up a contrast between the questions posed at the end of the essay's first paragraph and the fact that the answers can be found in the artwork itself.

C because the word *furthermore* illogically suggests that something additional but similar to the questions posed at the end of the essay's first paragraph is coming next (mostly likely, more questions), when, in fact, the essay switches to discussing the answers to the questions.

Question 18. The best answer is **F** because the word order creates a clear, understandable sentence.

The best answer is NOT:

G because the placement of the phrase "the story" creates a nonsensical statement.

H because the placement of the phrase "of text" creates a nonsensical expression ("this gathering of text").

J because the placement of the phrase "on two horizontal panels of text" divides the phrase "the story" from the prepositional phrase that describes the story, "of this gathering."

Question 19. The best answer is **C** because *its* is the correct form of the singular possessive pronoun and agrees with its singular antecedent, understood to be the noun *piece*.

The best answer is NOT:

A because *it's* is a contraction meaning "it is" rather than the singular possessive pronoun *its*, which is needed here.

B because *its'* is an incorrect form of the singular possessive pronoun *its*, which is needed here.

D because *their* is the plural possessive pronoun, which doesn't agree with its singular antecedent, understood to be the noun *piece*.

Question 20. The best answer is **J** because the interposed explanatory phrase "the story explains" is properly set off from the rest of the sentence by two commas, indicating that the phrase could be omitted without changing the basic meaning of the sentence.

The best answer is NOT:

F because the interposed explanatory phrase "the story explains" is not preceded by a comma, which would be needed to set the phrase off properly from the rest of the sentence.

G because the interposed explanatory phrase "the story explains" is improperly set off from the rest of the sentence by a comma before the phrase and a dash after the phrase. Either two commas or two dashes would be appropriate, but not one of each.

H because the interposed explanatory phrase "the story explains" is not preceded by a dash, which would be needed to set the phrase off properly from the rest of the sentence.

Question 21. The best answer is C because placing the underlined portion after the word *cause* is the only one of the four choices that wouldn't be acceptable. This placement of the phrase "in their various ways" divides the phrase "the cause" from the prepositional phrase that describes the cause, "of justice." Therefore, all of the choices would be acceptable EXCEPT C.

The best answer is NOT:

A because keeping the underlined portion where it is now creates a clear and correct sentence in English.

B because placing the underlined portion after the word *support* creates a clear and correct sentence in English.

D because placing the underlined portion after the word *world* (and before the period) creates a clear and correct sentence in English.

Question 22. The best answer is F because the rest of the paragraph explains that the women depicted in the artwork lived at different times and so couldn't have sat together and made a quilt.

The best answer is NOT:

G because the phrase "in summary" illogically suggests that the sentence summarizes the preceding text, which it does not do.

H because the phrase "in addition" illogically suggests that the sentence directly adds to the preceding text, which it does not do.

J because the phrase "in contrast" illogically suggests that the sentence provides a direct contrast to the preceding text, which it does not do.

Question 23. The best answer is B because Ringgold is the only artist being referred to at this point; the singular possessive form of the noun, *artist's*, is therefore required.

The best answer is NOT:

A because *artists* is a plural noun, not the singular possessive form of the noun, *artist's*, that is required.

C because *artists'* is a plural possessive form of the noun, not the singular possessive form, *artist's*, that is required.

D because the phrase "artists imagination" uses the plural form of the noun *artists* instead of the singular possessive, *artist's*, that is required, and because D includes an unnecessary comma after *imagination*.

Question 24. The best answer is J because the plural verb *were* agrees with the plural compound subject, "Sojourner Truth and Harriet Tubman."

The best answer is NOT:

F because the singular verb *was* doesn't agree with the plural "Sojourner Truth and Harriet Tubman."

G because the singular verb *was* doesn't agree with the plural "Sojourner Truth and Harriet Tubman."

H because the singular verb *was* doesn't agree with the plural "Sojourner Truth and Harriet Tubman."

Question 25. The best answer is **A** because information about Wells speaking out for social and racial justice is highly relevant, given that the paragraph focuses on the causes championed by the women, including Wells, depicted in Ringgold's artwork.

The best answer is NOT:

B because information about the man Wells married is only marginally relevant to the topic of the paragraph: the historical reality behind Ringgold's artwork.

C because information about which newspapers Wells wrote for isn't as relevant to the topic of the paragraph as the information in **A**.

D because information about Wells's birthplace, birth year, and siblings is only marginally relevant to the topic of the paragraph.

Question 26. The best answer is **J** because the word *business* is sufficient, together with the words *her own* earlier in the sentence, to indicate that Madame C. J. Walker established her own business.

The best answer is NOT:

F because the intensive pronoun *herself* is awkward and redundant with *her own* and because the comma between the noun *business* and the intensive *herself* is unnecessary and confusing.

G because the phrase *belonging to her* is awkward and redundant with *her own*.

H because the intensive pronoun *herself* is awkward and redundant with *her own* and because an intensifier, even when appropriate in a sentence, doesn't need to be set off by commas from the rest of the sentence.

Question 27. The best answer is **B** because this sentence structure makes "Madam C. J. Walker" the subject of the sentence, which is necessary in order to have the introductory participial phrase "establishing her own hair products business in the first decade of the twentieth century" refer clearly to Walker.

The best answer is NOT:

A because this sentence structure makes the introductory participial phrase a dangling modifier that refers to *millions of dollars*, which doesn't make sense.

C because this sentence structure makes the introductory participial phrase a dangling modifier that refers to *charities and educational institutions*, which doesn't make sense.

D because this sentence structure makes the introductory participial phrase a dangling modifier that refers to *millions of dollars*, which doesn't make sense.

Question 28. The best answer is H because no punctuation is warranted in this underlined portion. "Among the schools that benefited from this generosity" is an introductory adverbial phrase that, because it immediately precedes the verb it modifies, should not be set off by a comma. Had the sentence elements been arranged in the more typical subject-verb-object order ("Those [schools] that Mary McLeod Bethune opened and ran in order to provide a better education for Black students were among the schools that benefited from this generosity"), it would've been more obvious that no internal punctuation is required.

The best answer is NOT:

F because the comma after the word *generosity* is an unwarranted break between the prepositional phrase and the verb it modifies.

G because the semicolon after the word *generosity* creates two inappropriate sentence fragments, as neither what precedes nor what follows the semicolon is an independent clause.

J because the colon after the word *were* is unwarranted; what follows the colon is neither a series, a list, an explanation, nor a clarification.

Question 29. The best answer is D because the phrase "movement of" creates a clear, complete sentence, with the preposition *of* heading the phrase *of the 1950s and 1960s*.

The best answer is NOT:

A because "movement, it happened in" forms a second independent clause in the sentence joined to the original independent clause by only a comma, creating a comma splice.

B because "movement, it took place in" forms a second independent clause in the sentence joined to the original independent clause by only a comma, creating a comma splice.

C because "movement, which happened in" forms a second independent clause in the sentence joined to the original independent clause by only a comma, creating a comma splice.

Question 30. The best answer is F because the sentence under consideration interprets what the flowers represent ("seem to celebrate") and makes a concluding reference to the main focus of the essay ("the women's accomplishments and the beauty of their shared vision").

The best answer is NOT:

G because the sentence under consideration makes no comparison of Ringgold to the women depicted in the artwork.

H because the sentence under consideration says nothing about a brushwork technique.

J because the sentence under consideration offers no evaluation of Ringgold's artistic talent, only an interpretation of what the flowers represent ("seem to celebrate").

Passage III

Question 31. The best answer is **B** because the plural present perfect verb *have allowed* agrees with the plural subject *times* and indicates appropriately that the creation of spectacular science fiction films continues.

The best answer is NOT:

A because the singular present perfect verb *has allowed* doesn't agree with the plural subject *times*.

C because the singular verb *allows* doesn't agree with the plural subject *times*.

D because the singular past progressive verb *was allowing* doesn't agree with the plural subject *times* and incorrectly indicates that the creation of spectacular science fiction films ended in the past.

Question 32. The best answer is **F** because the relative adverb *when* is appropriately used to follow a time expression (*in 1902*); no punctuation is needed.

The best answer is NOT:

G because the coordinating conjunction *and* treats a dependent clause ("when audiences first saw . . . ") as a second independent clause, creating a nonsensical sentence.

H because the relative pronoun *which* logically refers to *1902*, both implying that audiences first saw the year 1902 (rather than first seeing a groundbreaking movie) and creating a garbled sentence.

J because the relative adverb *where* doesn't fit logically, since *1902* refers to time rather than place.

Question 33. The best answer is **C** because *his* is the appropriate masculine singular pronoun to refer to the male magician Méliès.

The best answer is NOT:

A because the singular pronoun *its* refers to things, not people, and would illogically refer to the camera.

B because the plural pronoun *their* has no logical antecedent in the sentence.

D because *it's* is a contraction meaning "it is," which makes no sense in the sentence.

Question 34. The best answer is **F** because when a conjunctive adverb such as *however* is used in the middle of a sentence, it needs to be set off by commas.

The best answer is NOT:

G because the semicolon after the word *however* creates an abbreviated main clause ("he found out, however;") followed by a sentence fragment ("that the public preferred live magic acts to filmed versions").

H because the phrase "out, however" lacks the comma after the word *however* needed to set off the conjunctive adverb from the rest of the sentence.

J because the phrase "out however," lacks the comma after the word *out* needed to set off the conjunctive adverb from the rest of the sentence.

Question 35. The best answer is **D** because Sentence 1 explains what Méliès did after he was *undaunted* by the discovery that people didn't like filmed magic acts (Sentence 5). He began *instead* to tell fantasy stories.

The best answer is NOT:

A because keeping Sentence 1 where it is now would weaken the logic and coherence of the paragraph. The paragraph would begin with a reference to Méliès being *undaunted* and turning to fantasy stories *instead* before Méliès had been formally described in Sentence 2 and before the incident that caused him to turn away from filmed magic acts had been related (Sentences 3 to 5).

B because placing Sentence 1 after Sentence 2 would weaken the logic and coherence of the paragraph. The words *undaunted* and *instead* in Sentence 1 would make no sense, as there's nothing in Sentence 2 to suggest that Méliès had met with any problems.

C because placing Sentence 1 after Sentence 3 would weaken the logic and coherence of the paragraph. The words *undaunted* and *instead* in Sentence 1 would make no sense, as there's nothing in Sentences 2 or 3 to suggest that Méliès had met with any problems.

Question 36. The best answer is **H** because the sentence under consideration should NOT be deleted; it creates a transition between the preceding paragraph, about Méliès the magician, and this paragraph, which focuses on Méliès's exploration of special film effects.

The best answer is NOT:

F because the sentence under consideration mentions Méliès's "magician's eye" but doesn't otherwise describe his ability as a magician.

G because the sentence under consideration mentions "the basics of special effects" but doesn't begin to explain any of the techniques of trick photography.

J because the sentence under consideration doesn't indicate "that Méliès's interest in learning about trick photography existed before his interest in magic." The preceding paragraph, in fact, describes Méliès's interests as beginning with magic, then moving into filmmaking.

Question 37. The best answer is **D** because perfecting "eerie film entrances and exits" is a specific example of Méliès's skill and inventiveness.

The best answer is NOT:

A because the clause "he was able to do interesting things" is vague and doesn't give any specific illustration of Méliès's skill and inventiveness.

B because the clause "he used effects commonly seen in his stage productions" doesn't suggest that Méliès was skillful or inventive; it suggests that the best Méliès could do as a filmmaker was to copy himself.

C because "his actors could enter and leave the scene" shifts the focus away from Méliès to his actors, which doesn't effectively highlight Méliès's skill and inventiveness, and because relative to **D**, **C** is imprecise.

Question 38. The best answer is **J** because the phrase "exceedingly high" appropriately uses the adverb *exceedingly* in front of the adjective it modifies, *high*, which in turn modifies the noun *costs*.

The best answer is NOT:

F because an adjective is needed to modify the noun *costs*, whereas the phrase "highly excessively" consists of two adverbs.

G because an adjective is needed to modify the noun *costs*, whereas the phrase "exceeding highly" consists of a participle and an adverb.

H because the phrase "high excessively" reverses conventional word order.

Question 39. The best answer is **B** because the verb *fired* is sufficient to indicate the action clearly.

The best answer is NOT:

A because the words *fired*, *launched*, and *projected* mean essentially the same thing in this context, making the phrasing redundant.

C because the words *fired* and *projected* mean essentially the same thing in this context, making the phrasing redundant.

D because the words *fired* and *propelled* mean essentially the same thing in this context, making the phrasing redundant.

Question 40. The best answer is **F** because the noun *creatures* is sufficient to indicate clearly what the terrain was filled with.

The best answer is NOT:

G because the clause "who they now realize live there" adds only wordiness to the sentence, which already strongly implies that the space travelers realize that the hostile creatures they encounter live in the strange terrain.

H because the clause "whom they are encountering" adds only wordiness to the sentence, which already clearly indicates that the space travelers encounter hostile creatures in the strange terrain.

J because the clause "who are found there" adds only wordiness to the sentence, which already clearly indicates that hostile creatures are found in the strange terrain.

Question 41. **The best answer is C** because for clarity this sequence of events should be divided into two sentences, the first indicating that the travelers fall off the edge of the moon to escape, and the second establishing that the travelers land in the ocean and are eventually rescued.

The best answer is NOT:

A because using only a comma after the word *moon* to join two independent clauses creates a comma splice. (Alternatively, it's possible to see the error here as a comma splice created by the comma after the word *ocean*.)

B because the phrase "moon after landing" creates a fused sentence. (Alternatively, it's possible to see the error here as a comma splice created by the comma after the word *ocean*, with the sentence then suggesting illogically that the space travelers fell off the edge of the moon after landing in the ocean.)

D because using only a comma after the word *moon* to join two independent clauses creates a comma splice. (Alternatively, it's possible to see the error here as a comma splice created by the comma after the word *ocean*.)

Question 42. **The best answer is J** because the past perfect verb *had begun* is made up of the past tense form *had* and the past participle *begun*. Past perfect is called for here since Méliès produced *A Trip to the Moon* long before interplanetary explorations had taken place.

The best answer is NOT:

F because *had began* is an improperly formed past perfect verb that uses the past tense form *began* instead of the past participle *begun*.

G because *would of begun* is an improperly formed verb that uses the word *of* instead of *have*.

H because *have began* is an improperly formed present perfect verb that uses the past tense form *began* instead of the past participle *begun*. (Even if the present perfect verb had been formed properly, it still wouldn't work in this context since past perfect is needed to indicate that producing *A Trip to the Moon* occurred before interplanetary explorations had taken place.)

Question 43. **The best answer is D** because *disturb* is the only one of the four alternatives that, in the context of the sentence, can't reasonably be used as a substitute for the underlined word (*arouse*). "Disturb his audience's curiosity" is neither a conventional expression in Standard English nor an appropriate innovation here. Therefore, *disturb* is the LEAST acceptable alternative to *arouse*.

The best answer is NOT:

A because the word *whet*, meaning here to stimulate or excite curiosity, is an acceptable, idiomatically appropriate alternative to the word *arouse*.

B because the word *stimulate*, meaning here to encourage or increase curiosity, is an acceptable, idiomatically appropriate alternative to the word *arouse*.

C because the word *awaken*, meaning here to stir up or stimulate curiosity, is an acceptable, idiomatically appropriate alternative to the word *arouse*.

Question 44. The best answer is **G** because the writer's assertion that *A Trip to the Moon* "provided the genesis for a film genre"—science fiction—"that still packs theaters" is both specific and consistent with the writer's point, made throughout the essay, that Méliès produced a landmark movie.

The best answer is NOT:

F because the assertion that "People are still going to theaters to see science fiction films" has no clear tie to Méliès's role in science fiction filmmaking.

H because the assertion that "Méliès made an important contribution to filmmaking many years ago" is vague and doesn't clearly express the writer's viewpoint about Méliès's role in science fiction filmmaking.

J because the assertion that "In Méliès's production even the film crew knew a lot about space" shifts the focus away from Méliès's own role in science fiction filmmaking.

Question 45. The best answer is **B** because the essay fulfills the specified goal by focusing on a single artist, Méliès, and explaining how he used his talents as a magician and filmmaker to produce the landmark film *A Trip to the Moon* and thereby inaugurated the genre of science fiction films.

The best answer is NOT:

A because while the essay fulfills the goal specified in the question, which was to highlight the contributions a single artist can make to a particular art form, the essay doesn't assert that Méliès's work as a magician never would have succeeded without the contributions of the artists in the film industry. Instead, the essay indicates that Méliès was a successful magician prior to having any association with film and filmmaking.

C because the essay fulfills the goal specified in the question and because the main focus of the essay is on a single artist, Méliès, and a specific film, *A Trip to the Moon*, not on the general process of making science fiction films.

D because the essay fulfills the goal specified in the question and because the essay doesn't suggest that it took many artists working together to create Méliès's success. Rather, the essay stresses Méliès's accomplishments as a magician and his central role in creating the film *A Trip to the Moon*.

Passage IV

Question 46. The best answer is **G** because the past perfect verb *had gone* is made up of the past tense form *had* and the past participle *gone*. Past perfect is called for here because if the Nancy Drew mystery series had gone out of style, it would have occurred prior to the events narrated here in past tense ("I thought . . ."). Furthermore, "gone out of style" is a conventional, idiomatic expression indicating that something has become unfashionable.

The best answer is NOT:

F because *had went* is an improperly formed past perfect verb that uses the past tense form *went* instead of the past participle *gone*.

H because *had went* is an improperly formed past perfect verb that uses the past tense form *went* instead of the past participle *gone* and because "went from style" isn't a conventional, idiomatic expression in standard English.

J because "gone from style" isn't a conventional, idiomatic expression in standard English.

Question 47. The best answer is B because the context calls for the auxiliary verb *would* to express the presumption expressed by "I was sure" (and to parallel *would have* earlier in the sentence) and calls for the present perfect verb *have been retired* in the passive voice to indicate the idea that the "sleuth" received the action of being "retired" to the library's back rooms.

The best answer is NOT:

A because *would of been* is an improperly formed verb that uses the word *of* instead of *have*.

C because *would of* is an improperly formed verb that uses the word *of* instead of *have*.

D because deleting the underlined portion leaves just the simple past tense verb *retired*, which isn't parallel to the other verb in the sentence, *would have*.

Question 48. The best answer is J because the possessive form of the word *library* (*library's*) is needed to indicate "the dusty back rooms of the library" and because no comma is needed between the words *dusty* and *back* since *back rooms* functions as a single unit (a compound noun) and *dusty* and *back* aren't coordinate adjectives.

The best answer is NOT:

F because the comma between *dusty* and *back* is unnecessary since *back rooms* functions as a single unit (a compound noun) and *dusty* and *back* aren't coordinate adjectives. (You couldn't say "the library's dusty *and* back rooms," for example.)

G because the plural form *libraries* is incorrectly used in place of the possessive form *library's* and because the comma between *dusty* and *back* is unnecessary since *back rooms* functions as a single unit (a compound noun) and *dusty* and *back* aren't coordinate adjectives.

H because the plural form *libraries* is incorrectly used in place of the possessive form *library's*.

Question 49. The best answer is C because of the four choices, the word *hundreds* provides the most specific information about the number of Nancy Drew novels in existence.

The best answer is NOT:

A because the word *heaps* is vague and too informal for the style and tone of the essay.

B because the phrase *a high number* is vague.

D because the word *plenty* is vague.

Question 50. The best answer is F because the comma after the word *novels* is needed to finish setting off the nonrestrictive appositive *the teenaged heroine of hundreds of young adult mystery novels* from *Nancy Drew*, the noun the appositive describes.

The best answer is NOT:

G because the comma after the word *alive* is unnecessary since the list of adjectives *alive and well and still on the job* is already linked by the coordinating conjunction *and*.

H because a comma is needed after the word *novels* to finish setting off the nonrestrictive appositive *the teenaged heroine of hundreds of young adult mystery novels* from *Nancy Drew*, the noun the appositive describes, and because the comma after the word *alive* is unnecessary since the list of adjectives *alive and well and still on the job* is already linked by the coordinating conjunction *and*.

J because a comma is needed after the word *novels* to finish setting off the nonrestrictive appositive *the teenaged heroine of hundreds of young adult mystery novels* from the noun *Nancy Drew*.

Question 51. The best answer is B because the phrase "the mysteries" makes clear that the girls were reading Nancy Drew novels all summer long.

The best answer is NOT:

A because the pronoun *that* has no clear, logical antecedent. Though *that* is obviously intended to refer to the Nancy Drew novels the girls were reading all summer long, *that* is singular while *novels* is plural.

C because the pronoun *that* has no clear, logical antecedent. Though *that* is obviously intended to refer to the Nancy Drew novels the girls were reading all summer long, *that* is singular while *novels* is plural. Furthermore, "reading up on that" is an idiomatic phrase but one that doesn't work in this context. To "read up on" something means to learn about a topic, not to read a number of novels for pleasure.

D because "Liana and her friends were reading it over all summer long" is confusing. First, we again have to ask what they were reading, since *it* doesn't logically refer to anything in the preceding sentence. Then "over all summer long" is a redundant phrase, with *over* being an extra, or superfluous, word.

Question 52. The best answer is G because the main clause of the sentence must have a subject (*she*) and a verb (*had followed*), and the verb must be in past perfect tense to indicate that Liana had already read the Nancy Drew novels *The Spider Sapphire Mystery* and *The Secret of the Crossword Cipher* before she went back to school.

The best answer is NOT:

F because *school and had* leaves no main clause, creating an inappropriate sentence fragment.

H because *school, having* leaves no main clause, creating an inappropriate sentence fragment.

J because *school, she* creates an inappropriate verb tense shift. The words *By the time* and *went back* signal that the past perfect verb *had followed*, rather than the simple past form *followed*, is needed to indicate that Liana had already read the Nancy Drew novels *The Spider Sapphire Mystery* and *The Secret of the Crossword Cipher* before she went back to school.

Question 53. The best answer is **A** because no punctuation is warranted between the verb *solve* and its direct object, "*The Spider Sapphire Mystery.*"

The best answer is NOT:

B because the colon between *solve* and "*The Spider Sapphire Mystery*" is unnecessary and confusing.

C because the semicolon between *solve* and "*The Spider Sapphire Mystery*" is unnecessary and confusing.

D because the comma between *solve* and "*The Spider Sapphire Mystery*" is unnecessary and confusing.

Question 54. The best answer is **H** because this sentence names some specific settings for the Nancy Drew novels (Arizona, Argentina, Nairobi, New York) and uses the verb *had chased*, which suggests that Liana was so caught up in what she was reading that she felt like she was solving the mysteries along with Nancy Drew.

The best answer is NOT:

F because this sentence refers generally to "different places and various cultures all over the world" but doesn't specify any settings for the Nancy Drew novels and because the verb *had read* doesn't make clear that Liana was particularly interested in the novels.

G because this sentence refers generally to "many breathtaking adventures involving all sorts of colorful characters" but doesn't specify any settings for the Nancy Drew novels.

J because this sentence refers generally to "many new places around the world" but doesn't specify any settings for the Nancy Drew novels and because the phrases *through her exposure to* and *learned about* don't make clear that Liana was particularly interested in the novels.

Question 55. The best answer is **C** because the proposed sentence, concerning how many books are in one of the series featuring Nancy Drew, shouldn't be added at this point in the essay because it distracts the reader from the main point of the paragraph, which is about why the narrator and her childhood friends loved Nancy Drew so much.

The best answer is NOT:

A because while the proposed sentence does attest to the longevity and popularity of the Nancy Drew Mystery Story series, the sentence is out of place and largely irrelevant at this point in a paragraph mainly about the place Nancy Drew held in the narrator's childhood and that of her friends.

B because the proposed sentence, with its facts and figures, addresses the history of the Nancy Drew Mystery Story series, not why the narrator loved Nancy Drew, which is why the sentence is out of place and largely irrelevant at this point in a paragraph mainly about the place Nancy Drew held in the narrator's childhood and that of her friends.

D because while the proposed sentence shouldn't be added at this point, adding in information about the author of the Nancy Drew Mystery Story series would only make the sentence more out of place and irrelevant, given that the paragraph is mainly about the place Nancy Drew held in the narrator's childhood and that of her friends.

Question 56. The best answer is **H** because "her freedom to do what she wanted" is clear and is parallel with "her loyal companions" and "her bravado," used earlier in the sentence to identify two other things the narrator and her friends loved about Nancy Drew.

The best answer is NOT:

F because "there was a love for her freedom to do what she wanted" is not parallel with the two similar structures in the sentence ("her loyal companions," "her bravado") and is awkward, wordy, and redundant with "we loved."

G because "a love for her freedom to do what she wanted" is not parallel with the two similar structures in the sentence ("her loyal companions," "her bravado") and is awkward and redundant with "we loved."

J because "the freedom to do as one wants" is not parallel with the two similar structures in the sentence ("her loyal companions," "her bravado") and because the impersonal and rather formal pronoun *one* is stilted and out of place in a sentence focused on Nancy Drew's qualities.

Question 57. The best answer is **B** because the word *therefore* is the only one of the four alternatives that, in the context of the sentence, can't reasonably be used as a substitute for the underlined portion (*also*). *Therefore* introduces something that is a result of something else, but *also* only signals the addition of one or more things. Thus, *therefore* is the LEAST acceptable alternative to *also*.

The best answer is NOT:

A because the word *furthermore*, meaning "in addition," is an acceptable alternative to the word *also*, as the two mean essentially the same thing in this context.

C because the word *likewise*, meaning "in a similar manner," is an acceptable alternative to the word *also*, as the two mean essentially the same thing in this context.

D because deleting the underlined portion doesn't change the meaning of the sentence much if at all. Even without the word *also*, the sentence is clearly adding to the list of qualities that the narrator and her friends loved about Nancy Drew.

Question 58. The best answer is F because the phrase "was able to solve crimes" effectively sets up a grammatically parallel list of notable things Nancy Drew was able to do: "solve crimes," "win golf tournaments," "kick bad guys in the shins," and "impress her father's distinguished clients."

The best answer is NOT:

G because the phrase "was capable of solving crimes" doesn't set up a parallel list of notable things Nancy Drew was able to do, as *solving* isn't parallel with *win*, *kick*, and *impress*, nor is it standard to say that Drew "was capable of . . . win golf tournaments," and so on.

H because the phrase "was good at crime solving" doesn't set up a parallel list of notable things Nancy Drew was able to do, as *solving* isn't parallel with *win*, *kick*, and *impress*, nor is it standard to say that Drew "was good at . . . win golf tournaments," and so on.

J because the phrase "solved crimes" doesn't set up a parallel list of notable things Nancy Drew was able to do, as *solved* isn't parallel with *win*, *kick*, and *impress*.

Question 59. The best answer is C because the semicolon after the word *successful* is appropriately used to divide this sentence into two closely related independent clauses.

The best answer is NOT:

A because the lack of appropriate punctuation and/or a conjunction between the words *successful* and *they* creates a fused sentence.

B because the lack of appropriate punctuation and/or a conjunction between the words *successful* and *they* creates a fused sentence.

D because *successful, knowing* creates a confusing, possibly redundant sentence, as it's not clear who knows what.

Question 60. The best answer is F because the phrase "those exciting adventure tales spiced with mystery" effectively supports the point in the first part of the sentence that what the girls in Liana's generation "need and love" is entertaining fiction ("the stories themselves").

The best answer is NOT:

G because the phrase "the answers to the mysteries of their lives" suggests that what the girls in Liana's generation "need and love" are stories that teach the girls about themselves, whereas "the stories themselves," used in the first part of the sentence, suggests that what the girls really want is entertaining fiction.

H because the phrase "a strong role model for their generation" suggests that what the girls in Liana's generation "need and love" are stories that inspire them, whereas "the stories themselves," used in the first part of the sentence, suggests that what the girls really want is entertaining fiction. The preceding two sentences in the paragraph also make the point that girls today don't need a "successful girl detective" as a role model.

J because the phrase "the ability to overcome obstacles" clumsily suggests that what the girls in Liana's generation "need and love" are stories that show a "successful girl detective" rising above adversity, whereas "the stories themselves," used in the first part of the sentence, suggests that what the girls really want is entertaining fiction. The preceding two sentences in the paragraph also make the point that girls today don't need a "successful girl detective" as a role model.

Passage V

Question 61. The best answer is C because the preposition *from* effectively sets up the long introductory phrase "From ancient Babylonian astronomers . . . to twentieth-century science fiction writers" that begins the sentence.

The best answer is NOT:

A because the words *there were* introduce another independent clause into the sentence, resulting in ungrammatical and confusing sentence structure.

B because the subordinating conjunction *when* creates a nonsensical introductory phrase and an ungrammatical sentence.

D because the adjective *those* creates a nonsensical introductory phrase and an ungrammatical sentence.

Question 62. The best answer is H because the clause "who penned spine-tingling stories of 'little green men from Mars'" is the most relevant to helping make the point that Mars "has often been a symbol of ill will and danger."

The best answer is NOT:

F because the fact that there are twentieth-century science fiction writers "whose works become best-sellers" isn't relevant to making the point that Mars "has often been a symbol of ill will and danger."

G because the comment that there are twentieth-century science fiction writers who have "wild imaginations about outer space" is too vague to help explain why Mars "has often been a symbol of ill will and danger."

J because the fact that there are twentieth-century science fiction writers "who created images of Mars in literature" doesn't say anything specific about the nature of those images or help explain why Mars "has often been a symbol of ill will and danger."

Question 63. The best answer is B because this sentence effectively ties together the bad reputation Mars has often had ("such negative associations"), described in the preceding paragraph, and the more recent interest in robotic and human missions to Mars, discussed in this paragraph.

The best answer is NOT:

A because this sentence about the United States competing with other countries to explore space is only loosely relevant to the topic of this paragraph, which is recent interest in robotic and human missions to Mars, and is unconnected to the topic of the preceding paragraph, Mars's impact on thought and culture.

C because this sentence about which year the United States founded its space agency is loosely relevant to the topic of this paragraph, which is recent interest in robotic and human missions to Mars, but is unconnected to the topic of the preceding paragraph, Mars's impact on thought and culture.

D because this sentence about Earth and Mars being planets in the inner solar system offers textbook-style information that is only loosely related to the topic of this paragraph, which is recent interest in robotic and human missions to Mars, and the topic of the preceding paragraph, Mars's impact on thought and culture.

Question 64. The best answer is **G** because the past perfect tense verb *had sent* is made up of the past tense form *had* and the past participle *sent*. Past perfect is called for here to indicate that one event in the past (NASA sending its thirtieth spacecraft to Mars) took place before another past event ("By 2003").

The best answer is NOT:

F because *would of sent* is an improperly formed verb that uses the word *of* instead of *have*.

H because the present tense verb *send* is inappropriate given that a past perfect verb is needed to make clear that NASA had already sent its thirtieth spacecraft to Mars "by 2003."

J because the present perfect tense verb *have sent* is inappropriate given that a past perfect verb is needed to make clear that NASA had already sent its thirtieth spacecraft to Mars "by 2003."

Question 65. The best answer is **C** because the participial phrase *prompting speculation* modifies in a clear way the preceding clause: by sending thirty spacecraft to Mars by 2003, NASA had led people to think seriously about the possibility of a human mission to Mars.

The best answer is NOT:

A because the subject *speculation* and the verb *has been prompted* begin a second independent clause joined to the first by only the comma after the word *planet*, creating a comma splice.

B because the words *to which speculation has prompted* create a confusing and ungrammatical construction, partly because *speculation has prompted* isn't a conventional, idiomatic expression and partly because the pronoun *which* has no logical antecedent.

D because the words *which is speculation* create a confusing construction because the pronoun *which* has no logical antecedent.

Question 66. The best answer is **H** because the phrase "Although few" begins a subordinate introductory clause that is set off from the sentence's main clause with a comma, resulting in a complete and logical sentence.

The best answer is NOT:

F because the lack of a subordinating conjunction in front of the word *Few* turns the introductory clause into an independent clause joined to the sentence's main clause by only the comma after the word *exciting*. The result is a comma splice.

G because the lack of a subordinating conjunction in front of the words *Maybe a few* turns the introductory clause into an independent clause joined to the sentence's main clause by only the comma after the word *exciting*. The result is a comma splice.

J because the lack of a subordinating conjunction in front of the words *Few, if any,* turns the introductory clause into an independent clause joined to the sentence's main clause by only the comma after the word *exciting*. The result is a comma splice.

Question 67. The best answer is **A** because the nonrestrictive appositive "the most ambitious NASA project yet" is nonessential explanatory information that needs to be set off by commas from the rest of the sentence.

The best answer is NOT:

B because a comma is needed after the word *yet* to finish setting off the nonrestrictive appositive "the most ambitious NASA project yet" from the rest of the sentence.

C because a comma, not a colon, is needed after the word *yet* to finish setting off the nonrestrictive appositive "the most ambitious NASA project yet" from the rest of the sentence.

D because a comma, not a dash, is needed after the word *yet* to finish setting off the nonrestrictive appositive "the most ambitious NASA project yet" from the rest of the sentence. While a pair of dashes could have been used to set off the nonrestrictive appositive, the writer uses a comma after the word *Station*, so parallelism requires that a second comma follow the word *yet*.

Question 68. The best answer is **F** because the information should be added to the sentence, as the explicit detail about the amount of money actually spent on constructing the space station—nearly double the already high projected cost of $17 billion—strengthens the sentence's assertion that "NASA overspent on the International Space Station."

The best answer is NOT:

G because while the information should be added to the sentence, nothing in the information suggests, let alone proves, that space flight will be more affordable in the future.

H because the information would strengthen, rather than weaken, the point made in the paragraph about the high cost of human flight to Mars. If the actual cost of constructing the International Space Station was almost double the projected cost, it's reasonable to worry about the accuracy of the already high projections of the cost of sending humans to Mars. Thus, the information should be added to the sentence.

J because the essay's focus isn't on the human experience in travel to Mars but rather on the costs of manned and unmanned missions to the planet. The information isn't a digression but instead strengthens the point made in the paragraph about the high cost of human flight to Mars. Thus, the information should be added to the sentence.

Question 69. The best answer is **B** because *what* is the logical introductory word in the noun clause functioning as the direct object of the verb *imagine*, resulting in "what the final price of a human voyage to Mars would be." Turning this clause around reinforces the idea that *what* is the best answer: "The final price of a human voyage to Mars would be *what*?"

The best answer is NOT:

A because *if* is an illogical introductory word in the noun clause functioning as the direct object of the verb *imagine*. Turning the clause around makes this clear: "The final price of a human voyage to Mars would be *if*?"

C because *how* is an illogical introductory word in the noun clause functioning as the direct object of the verb *imagine*. Turning the clause around makes this clear: "The final price of a human voyage to Mars would be *how*?"

D because deleting the underlined portion results in an illogical, incomplete-sounding sentence: "One can only imagine the final price of a human voyage to Mars would be."

Question 70. The best answer is F because "robotic spacecraft launched in 2003" offers an effective description of the Mars Rovers.

The best answer is NOT:

G because "which captured the imagination of the general public" doesn't offer any specific description of the Mars Rovers.

H because "the products described at length in the media" doesn't offer any specific description of the Mars Rovers.

J because "familiar to many who watched the news coverage at the time" doesn't offer any specific description of the Mars Rovers.

Question 71. The best answer is D because the word *capacity* is sufficient to refer to the capability of the Mars Rovers to examine soil and rocks.

The best answer is NOT:

A because the words *capacity* and *ability* are redundant, as they mean basically the same thing in this context.

B because the adjective *genuine* in the phrase *genuine capacity* creates a confusing expression, as *genuine* suggests there might be some doubt about the Rovers' capability; but no doubts have been raised.

G because the phrase *potential capacity* is a confusing expression, as *potential* suggests there might be some conditions or limits on the Rovers' capability; but no conditions or limits have been mentioned.

Question 72. The best answer is J because *age-old*, which means having been around for a long time, is a conventional, idiomatic expression that makes sense in this context.

The best answer is NOT:

F because the words *aging* and *older* are redundant, as they mean basically the same thing in this context. "Aging or older visions" is also not likely what the writer intends to say here, as the writer suggests in the essay that there's a timeless appeal to the notion of human spaceflight.

G because *old age* creates a silly expression (*old age visions*) that implies that visions of human space travel are held only by old people.

H because *aging old* creates a nonsensical expression (*aging old visions*).

Question 73. The best answer is **D** because the phrase "Even so," meaning "despite that," effectively signals the contrast between the preceding sentence, which says that using only machines to explore Mars may take some of the romance out of space travel, and this sentence, which says that we nevertheless need to remember that the right machines can do as much as if not more than humans can and at a fraction of the cost.

The best answer is NOT:

A because the phrase "In other words" incorrectly indicates that this sentence restates or summarizes the preceding sentence. Instead, this sentence offers a contrast to the preceding one.

B because the phrase "For that reason alone" incorrectly indicates that this sentence offers a consequence following from a circumstance identified in the preceding sentence. Instead, this sentence offers a contrast to the preceding one.

C because the phrase "In that time frame" makes no sense in context, as no time frame is indicated in the preceding sentence. Instead, this sentence offers a contrast to the preceding one.

Question 74. The best answer is **G** because the word *at* creates a conventional, idiomatic expression ("at a fraction of the cost") that makes sense in the context of the writer identifying an additional consideration (machines doing as much as, if not more than, humans *and* at a much lower cost).

The best answer is NOT:

F because the phrase *such as* creates a nonsensical expression ("such as a fraction of the cost").

H because the phrase *but only* is missing the word *at* that would make it a conventional, idiomatic expression ("but only *at* a fraction of the cost") and because *but* suggests a contrast with what precedes it in the sentence when what follows is an additional consideration (machines doing as much as, if not more than, humans *and* at a much lower cost). (The writer here might have used *at only*, for example, but not *but only*.)

J because deleting the underlined portion creates a nonsensical expression. "A fraction of the cost" suggests that what precedes it in the sentence identifies a cost (e.g., ". . . less than one billion dollars—a fraction of the cost [of a human mission]"), but this isn't the case.

Question 75. The best answer is **D** because concluding the essay with the proposed sentence would blur the essay's focus on Mars and the cost of sending humans there.

The best answer is NOT:

A because although the proposed sentence may capture the emotion that is the basis for the space exploration described in the essay, the sentence is out of place as a conclusion to an essay mainly focused on the expense of a human mission to Mars.

B because although the proposed sentence may invite the reader to reflect on the insignificance of money in relation to the mystery of space, the sentence is out of place as a conclusion to a paragraph and essay on the expense of a human mission to Mars.

C because while the proposed sentence shouldn't be added at this point, the essay doesn't contain a chronological history of people who traveled in space.

Question 1. The correct answer is B. Using the *Subtraction Property of Equality*, you can subtract 12 from both sides of the given equation to obtain $\frac{3x}{2} = -8$. Next, using the *Multiplication Property of Equality*, you can multiply both sides of this equation by 2 to obtain $3x = -16$. Finally, using the *Division Property of Equality*, you can divide both sides by 3 and get the equation $x = -\frac{16}{3}$.

Question 2. The correct answer is H. A natural first step in simplifying the expression $2x^4 \cdot 5x^7$ is to use the *Commutative Property for Multiplication* and *Associative Property for Multiplication* to rearrange the terms in the product. This produces the equivalent expression $(2 \cdot 5)x^4 x^7$, which is equal to $10x^4 x^7$. By the rules of exponents, $10x^4 x^7 = 10x^{4+7} = 10x^{11}$.

In this solution method, you *multiply* the integer coefficients and *add* the exponents. If you chose **K**, you probably multiplied in both cases, and if you chose **G**, you probably added in both cases.

Question 3. The correct answer is B. Finding the value of $f(10)$ is equivalent to finding the value of $\frac{x^2 + 12}{x - 6}$ when $x = 10$. Substituting 10 for x gives $\frac{10^2 + 12}{10 - 6} = \frac{100 + 12}{10 - 6} = \frac{112}{4} = 28$.

Question 4. The correct answer is G. As shown in the time-distance graph below at left, 2 hours on the horizontal axis corresponds to 100 miles on the vertical axis. This means the car traveled a distance of 100 miles during the first 2 hours. Since both graphs represent the same car on the same trip, the vertical axis in the graph at left is identical to the horizontal axis in the distance-gallons graph at right. So the 100-mile mark on the vertical axis at left corresponds to the 100-mile mark on the horizontal axis at right, as shown in the figure. In the graph at right, 100 miles corresponds to 4 gallons. This means that when the car traveled 100 miles, it used 4 gallons of gasoline, or equivalently, during the first 2 hours of the trip, the car used 4 gallons of gasoline.

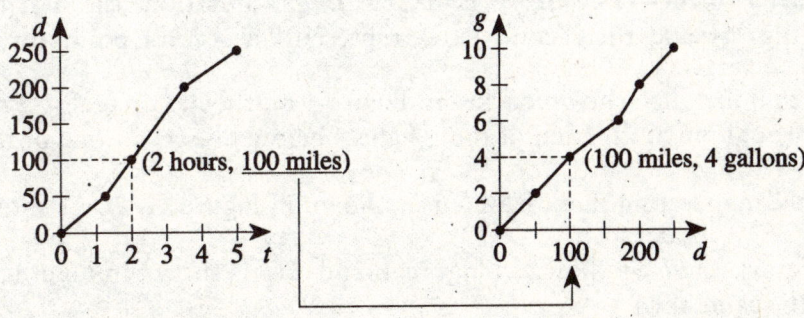

Question 5. The correct answer is E. The sum of 442 + 325 + 287 is 1,054. Since the value of the digit in the tens place is greater than or equal to 5, the digit 0 in the hundreds place increases to 1 when the sum is rounded to the nearest hundred. So the sum, rounded to the nearest hundred, is 1,100.

Question 6. The correct answer is F. Let the variable b represent the number of buses owned by the company. The company "keeps 3 tires in stock for every bus it owns, plus an additional 30 tires," so the total number of tires in stock is equal to $(3b + 30)$. Therefore, the solution to the equation $3b + 30 = 120$ gives the number of buses the company owns. Subtracting 30 from both sides if the equation gives $3b = 90$, and dividing by 3 gives $b = 30$.

You can quickly check this answer: the company "keeps 3 tires in stock" for *each of the 30 buses* it owns, "plus an additional 30 tires" means the company has $3(30) + 30 = 120$ tires in stock.

Question 7. The correct answer is B. You can solve this equation by following these steps:

By the *Distributive Property* $2(x - 6) + x = 36$ is equivalent to $2x - 12 + x = 36$. (If you chose **C**, the most common incorrect answer, you probably forgot to distribute the 2 to the 6.)

Combining like terms on the left side of the equation $2x - 12 + x = 36$ results in $3x - 12 = 36$. (If you chose **A**, you may have forgotten the term x on the left-hand side.)

Adding 12 to both sides of $3x - 12 = 36$ results in $3x = 48$. (If you subtracted 12 from both sides, you probably chose **E**.)

Finally, dividing both sides of $3x = 48$ by 3 leads to the solution $x = 16$.

You can quickly verify the solution by substituting 16 for x in the expression $2(x - 6) + x$ to obtain $2(16 - 6) + 16 = 2(10) + 16 = 20 + 16 = 36$.

Question 8. The correct answer is H. In ray notation, the first letter represents the endpoint of the ray and the second letter represents a second point through which the ray passes. For example, $\overrightarrow{AD}$ (shown darker in Figure 1 on the next page) is a ray with endpoint A that passes through point D. Each of the 5 figures below illustrates one of the 5 given rays with respect to the 2 intersecting lines. Ray $\overrightarrow{AB}$ is shown in Figure 1, $\overrightarrow{BD}$ is shown in Figure 2, $\overrightarrow{CD}$ is shown in Figure 3, $\overrightarrow{EF}$ is shown in Figure 4, and $\overrightarrow{EG}$ is shown in Figure 5. ($\overrightarrow{EF}$ and $\overrightarrow{EG}$ are 2 names for the same ray.)

MATHEMATICS · PRACTICE TEST 5 · EXPLANATORY ANSWERS

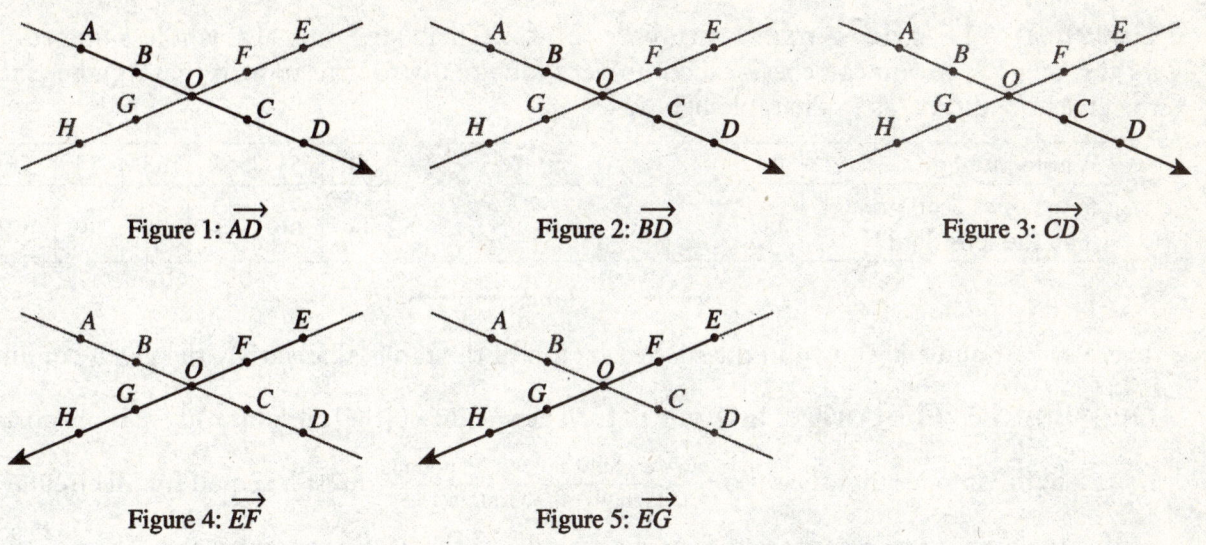

Figure 1: $\overrightarrow{AD}$ Figure 2: $\overrightarrow{BD}$ Figure 3: $\overrightarrow{CD}$

Figure 4: $\overrightarrow{EF}$ Figure 5: $\overrightarrow{EG}$

From the 5 figures it can be seen that only $\overrightarrow{CD}$ does not contain point O.

Question 9. The correct answer is A. To solve this system of equations, you can work backward, substituting $t = 3$ into the equation $st = 36$ to obtain the equation $3s = 36$. Dividing both sides by 3 produces $s = 12$. Working backward once more, substitute $s = 12$ into the equation $rs = 24$ to obtain the equation $12r = 24$. Dividing both sides by 12 gives the solution: $r = 2$.

Question 10. The correct answer is J. Let s represent the score on the 6th test. Then the average score on the 6 tests is equal to $\dfrac{75 + 70 + 92 + 95 + 97 + s}{6}$, or equivalently $\dfrac{s + 429}{6}$. Be sure to read carefully: the average is 85 *points*, not *percent*. Interpreting the average as a percent leads to **K** (the most common incorrect answer), rather than the correct answer of $\dfrac{s + 429}{6} = 85$.

Question 11. **The correct answer is C.** There are only 12 whole numbers from 44 through 55, so you can check each number individually to determine if that number satisfies the given condition, as in the table below.

Whole number	44	45	46	47	48	49	50	51	52	53	54	55
Is the ones digit greater than the tens digit?	no	yes	yes	yes	yes	yes	no	no	no	no	no	no

←————5 values————→

There are 5 numbers, shown in the shaded region of the table, that satisfy the given condition.

Question 12. **The correct answer is J.** "The weight of [the] circular rod . . . is proportional to its length" implies that the ratio $\dfrac{\text{the weight of the rod, in pounds}}{\text{the length of the rod, in feet}}$ must be equal for all circular rods of this type. Let w represent the weight, in pounds, of the 21-foot circular rod. Then, $\dfrac{35\text{ pounds}}{15\text{ feet}}$ must equal $\dfrac{w\text{ pounds}}{21\text{ feet}}$, which gives the equation $\dfrac{35}{15} = \dfrac{w}{21}$. So $(35)(21) = 15w$, and $w = \dfrac{(35)(21)}{15} =$ 49 pounds.

Question 13. **The correct answer is A.** As shown in the figure below, the given vertices form a 5-unit-by-5-unit rectangle (or square), which has an area of $5 \times 5 = 25$ square coordinate units. The portion of that square lying in Quadrant III is shown in the figure as the 2-unit-by-1-unit shaded rectangle, which has an area of $2 \times 1 = 2$ square coordinate units. Therefore, the

percent of the total area of the square lying in Quadrant III $= \dfrac{\text{the area of the shaded rectangle}}{\text{the area of the square}} \times 100\% = \dfrac{2}{25} \times 100\% = 8\%$.

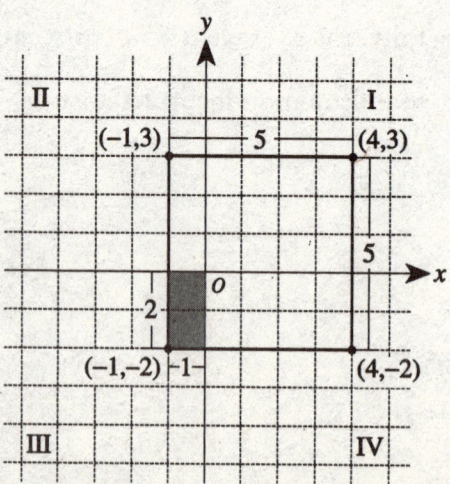

Question 14. The correct answer is J. The rational expression given in the problem can be simplified by following the steps shown below.

$$\frac{3+7(x-6)}{3(x-6)+10} = \frac{3+7x-42}{3x-18+10} = \frac{7x-39}{3x-8}$$

If you chose F, perhaps you thought that the $x-6$ in the numerator and the $x-6$ in the denominator could be "cancelled," producing $\frac{3+7}{3+10}$. But this can only be done when $x-6$ appears as a common *factor* of both numerator and denominator.

Question 15. The correct answer is B. You can approach this problem analytically or graphically.

In the analytic approach, you must find all points on the y-axis of the form $(0,y)$ that also lie on the circle. The possible values of y are the solutions to the equation $0^2 + y^2 = 81$, or $y^2 = 81$, so $y = \pm 9$.

In the graphical approach, the equation $x^2 + y^2 = 81$ $\left(\text{or } (x-0)^2 + (y-0)^2 = 9^2 \right)$ represents a circle of radius 9 that is centered at $(0,0)$, as shown in the standard (x,y) coordinate plane below. The desired points must be 9 coordinate units from $(0,0)$ on the y-axis. These points are at $(0, 0+9)$ and $(0, 0-9)$.

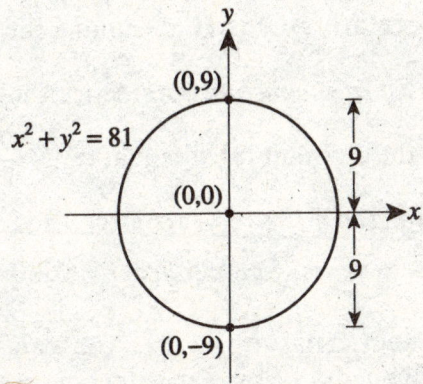

Question 16. The correct answer is J. You can approach this problem by drawing a series of sketches that represent the characteristics of the 4 points on the circle.

Since "B is 5 units counterclockwise from A," draw B on a circle so that the point is approximately $\frac{1}{3}$ (about $\frac{5}{17}$) of the distance counterclockwise around the circle (see Figure 1 below).

Since "C is 3 units clockwise from A," draw C on the circle so that the point is approximately $\frac{1}{5}$ (about $\frac{3}{17}$) of the distance counterclockwise around the circle (see Figure 2 below).

Since "D is 11 units clockwise from A and 6 units counterclockwise from A," draw D on the circle so that the point is 6 units from A in a counterclockwise direction, or just beyond B (which lies 5 units from A). Since the clockwise distance is also from A, this distance could be ignored when sketching (see Figure 3 below).

Figure 4 shows the final order of points, A, C, D, B, going clockwise around the circle.

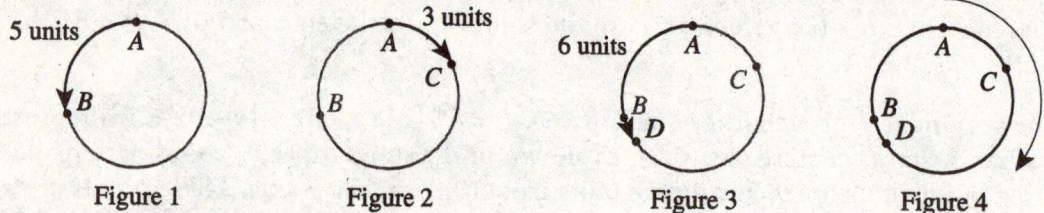

Figure 1   Figure 2   Figure 3   Figure 4

Question 17. The correct answer is B. Assuming the cost increased *linearly* is equivalent to assuming the cost increased *at a constant rate*. Since the cost of the clothing increased from $620 to $1,000 in 10 years, the constant rate is equal to $\frac{\$1,000 - \$620}{10 \text{ years}}$, or $38 per year. Therefore, the cost of the family's clothing in 1991 (6 years after 1985) is:

$$\$620 + (6 \text{ years})(\$38 \text{ per year}) = \$620 + \$228 = \$848.$$

Question 18. The correct answer is H. You can solve this problem numerically by considering all of the possible pairs of integer values representing the width and length of the room for which the area equals 180 ft². Then you can find the pair of values for which the perimeter equals 54 ft (that pair is 12 ft and 15 ft in the shaded region of the table below).

Width (ft)	1	2	3	4	5	6	9	10	12
Length (ft)	180	90	60	45	36	30	20	18	15
Area (ft²)	180	180	180	180	180	180	180	180	180
Perimeter (ft)	362	184	126	98	82	72	58	56	54

You can also approach this problem analytically by solving the system of equations $2w + 2l = 54$ and $wl = 180$, which result from using the perimeter and the area formulas, respectively.

Notice that $2w + 2l = 54$ is equivalent to $w + l = 27$, and solving $wl = 180$ for l gives $l = \frac{180}{w}$.

Substituting this value for l, you obtain $w + \frac{180}{w} = 27$; multiplying both sides by w and then subtracting $27w$ from both sides leads to $w^2 - 27w + 180 = 0$. Factoring the quadratic gives the equivalent equation $(w - 12)(w - 15) = 0$, with solutions $w = 12$ or $w = 15$; the corresponding solutions for l are $\frac{180}{w} = 15$ and $\frac{180}{w} = 12$.

You may notice that the work involved in factoring is essentially the same work required in the numerical method, so the analytical method is a little less efficient. You may also notice that the system of equations is symmetric in w and l, so that the solutions for *either w or l* give the dimensions of the living room.

Question 19. The correct answer is B. The decimal number D in this problem is shown in its *scientific notation* form, $D = A \cdot 10^n$, where n is an integer and $1 \le A < 10$. When D is greater than 1, n is positive. When D is between 0 and 1, n is negative. Therefore, in the case where $D = 0.0001056$, n is negative since D is between 0 and 1.

The absolute value of n represents the number of decimal places the decimal point in D must be moved to obtain the value of A (that is, the value such that $1 \le A < 10$). For the decimal number 0.0001056, the decimal point must be moved 4 decimal places to obtain the value $A = 1.056$, as shown below. Since the absolute value of n is 4 and n is negative, n must equal -4.

0.0001.056

4 places

Question 20. The correct answer is H. Because the value of m is *directly proportional* to the value of p, there is a constant K such that $m = Kp$. Substituting $m = 2$ and $p = 6$, you can see that $2 = 6K$, so $K = \frac{1}{3}$. So m and p are related by the equation $m = \frac{1}{3}p$; substituting $p = 9$, you obtain $m = \frac{1}{3}(9) = 3$.

When the value of m is *directly proportional* to the value of p, you can also solve the proportion $\frac{m}{p} = \frac{2}{6} = \frac{x}{9}$ for x in order to obtain the correct answer.

Question 21. The correct answer is E. Let the variable t represent the number of hours that a car is parked at this short-term parking lot. The phrase "the cost is for t hours or *any part thereof*" means that when one parks at the lot for t hours, the cost will be for the whole number of hours, n, nearest to and greater than or equal to t. For example, when you park a car at the lot for 9 hours and 45 minutes, $t = 9\frac{45}{60}$, and $n = 10$, so the cost is for 10 hours.

In this problem, the car has been parked at the lot for 5 hours and 52 minutes. Therefore, $t = 5\frac{52}{60}$ and $n = 6$. So the cost for parking the car is the sum of $1.75 (the cost for the 1st hour), $1.50 (the cost for the 2nd hour), and $0.75(n - 2) = \$0.75(6 - 2) = \$3.00$ (the additional cost, which excludes the 1st and 2nd hours), which is $1.75 + $1.50 + $3.00 = $6.25.

Question 22. The correct answer is H. Let a_n be the value of the nth term of an arithmetic sequence. Then $a_n = a_1 + d(n - 1)$, where d is the *common difference* of the sequence ($d = a_{n+1} - a_n$). For example, if an arithmetic sequence has terms $a_{12} = 46$ and $a_{13} = 53$, then $d = a_{13} - a_{12} = 53 - 46 = 7$.

For the sequence given in this problem, $a_2 = a_1 + 10(2 - 1) = a_1 + 10$ and $a_3 = a_1 + 10(3 - 1) = a_1 + 20$. The fact that a_1, a_2, and a_3 represent the degree measures of the interior angles of $\triangle ABC$ implies that $a_1 + a_2 + a_3 = 180°$. Substituting for a_2 and a_3 yields $a_1 + (a_1 + 10) + (a_1 + 20) = 180$, or equivalently, $3a_1 + 30 = 180$. Solving for a_1 yields $a_1 = 50$, so $a_2 = 60$ and $a_3 = 70$. You can quickly check that these are correct: $a_1 + a_2 + a_3 = 50 + 60 + 70 = 180$.

Question 23. The correct answer is E. As in many geometry problems, you may find it helpful to draw one or more sketches to represent the situation.

Figure 1 shows Point B lying on $\overline{AC}$ between A and C.

Figure 2 shows Point D, a point not on $\overline{AC}$.

Figure 3 shows that the measure of $\angle ABD$ is 38°.

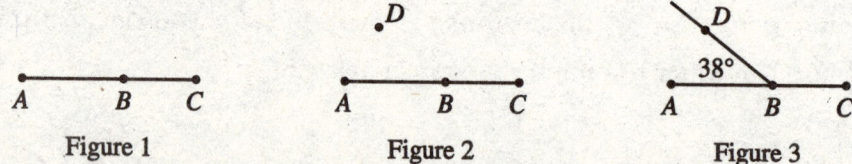

Figure 1   Figure 2   Figure 3

Using Figure 3, you can see that $\angle ABD$ and $\angle CBD$ form a linear pair. Therefore, $m\angle ABD + m\angle CBD = 180°$, so $38° + m\angle CBD = 180°$, which means that $m\angle CBD = 142°$.

Question 24. The correct answer is K. To determine the value of $8x + 9y$, find the solution (x,y) to the system of 2 equations given in the problem. This system can be solved using an elimination method. First, determine which of the 2 variables would be easiest to eliminate. For this system, eliminating the y-variable would be easier. In order to eliminate the y-variable, the y-coefficients in each equation (or equivalent equation) must be opposite numbers (-6 and 6 would be the best choice). Therefore, all terms in the upper equation should be multiplied by -2 (Step 1 below) to form an equivalent equation with -6 as the y-coefficient. Now the 2 equations have y-coefficients of -6 and 6, respectively, so adding the equations will eliminate the y-variable (Step 2 below).

$$
\begin{array}{ccccc}
 & & \textbf{Step 1} & & \textbf{Step 2} \\
2x + 3y = 4 & & -2(2x + 3y) = \ -2(4) & & -4x - 6y = \ -8 \\
5x + 6y = 7 & \Rightarrow & 5x + 6y = \ 7 & \Rightarrow & \underline{5x + 6y = \ \ \ 7} \\
 & & & & x \ \ \ = \ -1
\end{array}
$$

Substituting into either of the 2 initial equations produces an equation that can be solved for y; for example, letting $x = -1$ in $2x + 3y = 4$ gives $2(-1) + 3y = 4$. Solving for y, $-2 + 3y = 4$, so $3y = 6$. Therefore, $y = 2$.

Substituting $x = -1$ and $y = 2$ into $8x + 9y$ yields $8(-1) + 9(2) = -8 + 18 = 10$.

Question 25. The correct answer is A. By the *Distributive Property*, you can substitute $3x - 3y$ for $3(x - y)$ in the given equation to obtain $3x - 3y = 5$. To isolate the y-term, you can then subtract $3x$ from both sides to obtain the equivalent equation $-3y = -3x + 5$. Finally, multiplying both sides by $-\frac{1}{3}$ produces $y = -\frac{1}{3}(3x + 5)$. Using the *Distributive Property* again, $-\frac{1}{3}(3x + 5) = (-\frac{1}{3})(-3)x + (-\frac{1}{3})(5) = x - \frac{5}{3}$, so that $y = x - \frac{5}{3}$. If you chose **B** (the most common incorrect answer), you may have multiplied by $\frac{1}{3}$ instead of $-\frac{1}{3}$ in the last step.

Question 26. The correct answer is K. You can identify the one true statement by trying to find counterexamples for as many of the given statements as you can. As soon as you have counterexamples for 4 statements, the remaining statement should be true.

The pair of even numbers 4 and 6 is a counterexample for the statements given in **F**, **H**, and **J**:

   $6 + 4 = 10$, which is *even*
   $6 \div 4 = 1.5$, which is neither *even* nor *odd*

The pair of odd numbers 3 and 5 is a counterexample for the statement given in **G**:

   $3 + 5 = 8$, which is *even*

The remaining statement given in **K** is a well-known property of odd numbers. If you are not familiar with this property, however, you can convince yourself that it is true by trying it out on several pairs of odd numbers.

Question 27. The correct answer is B. The probability that the fourth player will draw a

yellow card = $\dfrac{\text{the number of yellow cards } \textit{left} \text{ in the deck after the first 3 draws}}{\text{the numbers of cards of all colors } \textit{left} \text{ in the deck after the first 3 draws}} = \dfrac{10-3}{10+10+10-3} = \dfrac{7}{27}$. If

you didn't take into account the 3 yellow cards that were previously drawn, you probably chose **A** or

C, the most common incorrect answers.

Question 28. The correct answer is H. Careful reading is essential. Because a candidate must receive *over* 50% of the votes cast, it follows that, in order to win, the candidate must receive *greater than* $0.50(750) = 375$ votes. So, in particular, $x > 375$.

In fact, x is exactly 376. Since $x = 376$ is not an answer choice, you must determine which choice is true when 376 is substituted for x.

Question 29. The correct answer is D. Let x (shown in the figure below) represent

the distance between the centers of the 2 holes. Since the 3 segments with lengths $2\frac{1}{16}$ inches,

x inches, and $4\frac{3}{4}$ inches are collinear, the sum of their lengths must be $11\frac{5}{8}$. Therefore,

$x = 11\frac{5}{8} - 2\frac{1}{16} - 4\frac{3}{4} = \frac{93}{8} - \frac{33}{16} - \frac{19}{4} = \frac{186}{16} - \frac{33}{16} - \frac{76}{16} = \frac{77}{16} = 4\frac{13}{16}$ inches.

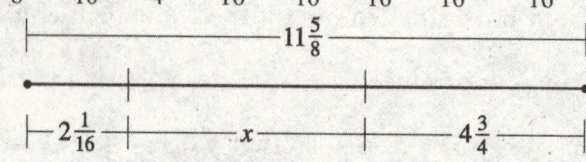

Question 30. The correct answer is G. The figure below shows 2 separate right triangles, one for the father's shadow and one for the son's, where s represents the length of the son's shadow. The 2 triangles are similar by the *AA (Angle-Angle) Similarity* property. Therefore, the ratios of the 3 pairs of corresponding sides must be equal. By solving the proportion $\frac{75}{50} = \frac{120}{s}$, it follows that $s = 80$.

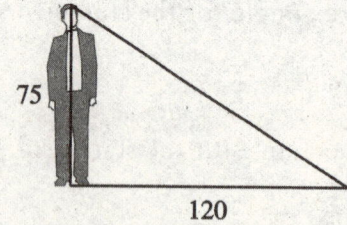

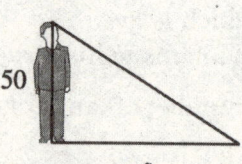

As shown in the figure below, the sum of d and s is 120. Therefore, $d = 120 - 80 = 40$ inches.

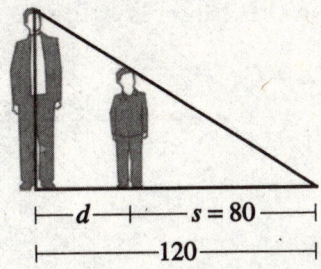

Question 31. The correct answer is C. Analytically, the distance d between 2 points (x_1, y_1) and (x_2, y_2) can be found by using the *distance formula*: $d = \sqrt{(x_2 - x_1)^2 + (y_2 - y_1)^2}$.

Therefore, the distance d between $(-3, -2)$ and $(5, 5)$ is $d = \sqrt{(5 - (-3))^2 + (5 - (-2))^2} = \sqrt{8^2 + 7^2} = \sqrt{113}$ coordinate units.

Alternatively, the distance d can be found graphically by use of the Pythagorean theorem on the right triangle shown below in the standard (x, y) coordinate plane: $d^2 = 8^2 + 7^2 = 113$, so $d = \sqrt{113}$.

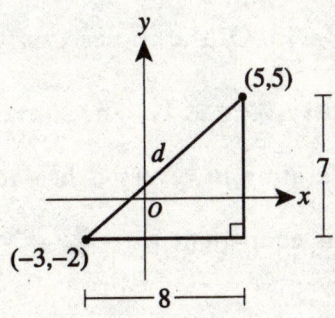

Question 32. The correct answer is K. From the table below, you can see that the amounts Chayton deposited each month form the *arithmetic sequence* 10, 20, 30, 40, ⋯, 360 with common difference $d = 10$.

Month	1st	2nd	3rd	4th	⋯	35th	36th
Amount deposited ($)	10	20	30	40	⋯	350	360

The total amount of Chayton's 36 deposits is the sum of these amounts, $10 + 20 + 30 + \cdots + 360$, an *arithmetic series* of 36 terms. The *partial sum S* of an arithmetic series of n terms with 1st term a_1 and common difference d is given by the formula $S = \dfrac{n(2a_1 + d(n-1))}{2}$. Here, $n = 36$, $a_1 = 10$, and $d = 10$, so the partial sum $10 + 20 + 30 + \cdots + 360$ is equal to $\dfrac{36(2(10) + 10(36-1))}{2}$, which simplifies to $\dfrac{36(20 + 350)}{2} = \dfrac{36(370)}{2} = \dfrac{13,320}{2} = \$6,660$.

Question 33. The correct answer is C. Two extreme cases for the triangle described in the problem, $\triangle ABC$, are shown in the 2 figures below.

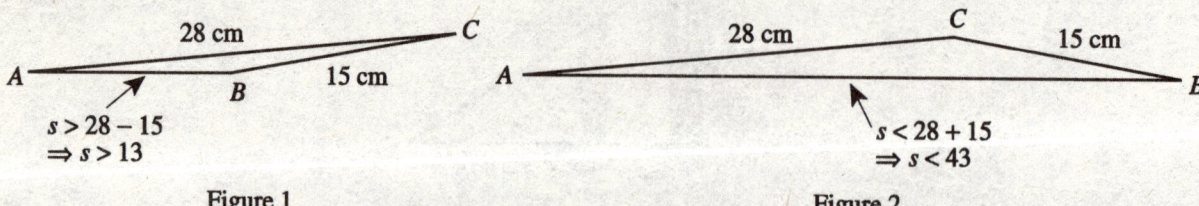

Figure 1   Figure 2

Figure 1 shows the case where the length s of $\overline{AB}$ nears its lower limit. When $s = 28 - 15 = 13$, $\overline{AB}$ and $\overline{BC}$ are collinear. Therefore, no triangle can be formed from points A, B, and C. But when s has a value just slightly greater than 13, $\overline{AB}$ and $\overline{BC}$ are no longer collinear, and can form a triangle as in Figure 1. So Figure 1 illustrates one condition for s that must be met, $s > 13$.

Figure 2 shows the case where the side length s of $\overline{AB}$ nears its upper limit. When $s = 28 + 15 = 43$, $\overline{AB}$ and $\overline{BC}$ are again collinear. Therefore, no triangle can be formed from points A, B, and C. But when s is just slightly less than 43, $\overline{AB}$ and $\overline{BC}$ are no longer collinear, and can form a triangle as in Figure 2. So Figure 2 illustrates another condition for s that must be met, $s < 43$.

Therefore, s must satisfy $13 < s < 43$. Of the choices, only 31 meets that condition.

Question 34. The correct answer is K. The sum of any 2 rational expressions $\frac{a}{c}$ and $\frac{b}{c}$ is given by $\frac{a}{c} + \frac{b}{c} = \frac{a+b}{c}$. Operating in reverse, the rational expression $\frac{a+b}{c}$ can be written as the sum $\frac{a}{c} + \frac{b}{c}$. So, $\frac{2x+3}{12x^2}$ is equivalent to $\frac{2x}{12x^2} + \frac{3}{12x^2}$. Factoring each denominator and simplifying produces $\frac{2x}{2x(6x)} + \frac{3}{3(4x^2)} = \frac{1}{6x} + \frac{1}{4x^2}$.

Because the expression $2x + 3$ in the numerator is a sum, you CANNOT find an equivalent expression by cancelling the terms 2, $2x$, or 3, with $12x^2$. This type of error leads to the two most common incorrect answers: $\frac{2x+3}{12x^2} = \frac{1+2}{6x} = \frac{1}{2x}$, which is **H**, and $\frac{2x+3}{12x^2} = \frac{x+3}{6x^2} = \frac{x+1}{2x^2}$, which is **J**.

Had the numerator been a *product* rather than a *sum*, as in $\frac{2x(3)}{12x^2}$, then cancellation of 2, 3, and x with $12x^2$ would have been acceptable.

Question 35. The correct answer is E. Since the cardboard extends 2 inches beyond the cake on all sides, the cardboard forms a rectangle whose length and width are each 4 inches longer than the length and width of the rectangular cake, as shown in the figure below. The area of aluminum foil that is exposed (the shaded region in the figure) equals the area of the foil covering the entire cardboard surface (or area of the cardboard) minus the area of the foil covered by the cake. So the area, in square inches, of aluminum foil exposed equals $20(16) - 16(12)$ $= 320 - 192 = 128$.

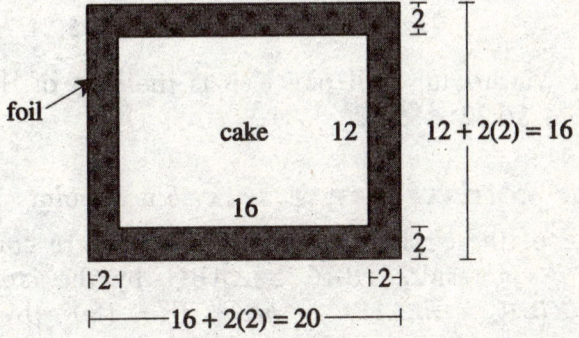

Question 36. The correct answer is J. The figure below shows the cake after it has been cut. The "length" of the cut cake is (16 inches) ÷ (2 inches per piece) = 8 pieces. The "width" of the cut cake is (12 inches) ÷ (2 inches per piece) = 6 pieces. Since the cake has 6 rows each containing 8 pieces, the cake was cut into $6(8) = 48$ pieces.

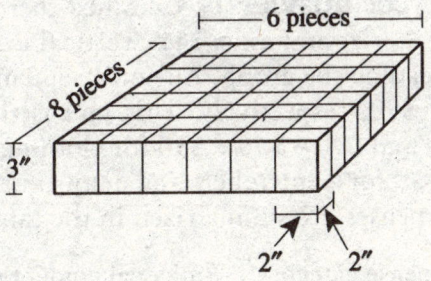

Question 37. The correct answer is D. The table below lists all expenses for Ken's cake that were given in the problem.

	Expenses for cake	cost
items purchased {	Cake preparation	$5.00
	Cake mix	$1.73
	Frosting mix	$2.67
	Tax on items purchased	$0.05(\$1.73 + \$2.67) = \$0.22$

The total amount the Math Club will pay Ken is the sum of the costs shown in the table, $\$5.00 + \$1.73 + \$2.67 + \$0.22 = \$9.62$.

Question 38. The correct answer is F. Since points A and B lie on the circle, $\overline{CA}$ and $\overline{CB}$ are radii of the circle. All radii of a circle are congruent; therefore, $\triangle ABC$ is an isosceles triangle. As a result, $\angle BAC \cong \angle ABC$, by the *Isosceles Triangle Base Angles Theorem*. Because $m\angle BAC + m\angle ABC + m\angle ACB = 180°$ (by the *Angle Sum Theorem*), $m\angle ABC + m\angle ABC + m\angle ACB = 180°$ (by substituting $m\angle ABC$ for $m\angle BAC$). Thus $2(m\angle ABC) + 110° = 180°$; so $2(m\angle ABC) = 70°$, or equivalently, $m\angle ABC = 35°$.

You may check this answer by substituting the angle measures into the *Angle Sum Theorem*: $m\angle BAC + m\angle ABC + m\angle ACB = 35° + 35° + 110° = 180°$.

Question 39. The correct answer is C. Since there are 5 evenly spaced vertical grid lines for every $100 on the horizontal axis, each vertical grid line has an incremental value of $\$100 \div 5 = \$20$. Then, by reading the graph, Allison's September expenses for food and clothing are found to be $170 and $90, respectively. This means that in October she plans to spend $\$170 - \$60 = \$110$ for food and $\$90 - \$40 = \$50$ for clothing. The remaining expenses projected for October are the same as for September, and may be read from the bar graph. Allison's projected October living expenses are summarized in the table below.

Expense category	Projected amount spent (in $)
Housing	230
Food	110
Clothing	50
Entertainment	50
Other	60
Total	500

Therefore, the amount spent for entertainment will account for $\frac{50}{500} \times 100\% = 10\%$ of Allison's projected October expenses.

Question 40. The correct answer is G. Nadia's minimum earnings for 4 weeks (or $4 \times 40 = 160$ hours) are $1,200. Therefore, her *minimum* hourly rate of pay (or the *minimum* value of x) for those 160 hours is $\frac{\$1,200}{160 \text{ hours}} = \$7.50$ per hour. Therefore, $x \geq \$7.50$.

To verify that the correct inequality symbol is $\geq$ (not $\leq$), try testing a number—say 1,600—representing earnings greater than $1,200. Then $\frac{\$1,600}{160 \text{ hours}} = \$10$ per hour $\geq \$7.50$ per hour.

Question 41. The correct answer is D. Let S represent the sum of $8x$ and $13x$. Then $S = 8x + 13x = 21x$, so $\frac{S}{21} = x$. Since x is a positive integer, S must be divisible by 21.

Question 42. The correct answer is G. The midpoint of a segment with endpoints (x_1, y_1) and (x_2, y_2) in the standard (x, y) coordinate plane is $\left(\frac{x_1 + x_2}{2}, \frac{y_1 + y_2}{2} \right)$. Therefore, the x-coordinate of the midpoint of $\overline{MN}$ is $\frac{-13 + 5}{2} = -\frac{8}{2} = -4$.

Question 43. The correct answer is A. For right triangle $\triangle ABD$ shown below, the length of the hypotenuse is given, and you must calculate the length of the side opposite $\angle A$. The sine ratio relates these 2 lengths:

$$\sin(\angle A) = \frac{\text{the length of the side opposite } \angle A}{\text{the length of the hypotenuse}}$$

So $\sin 25° = \frac{BD}{12}$ and $BD = 12 \sin 25°$.

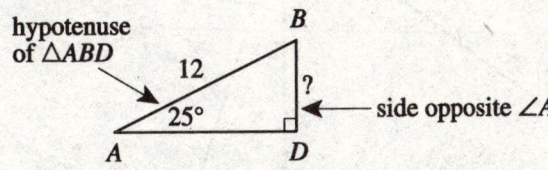

Question 44. The correct answer is G. Since triangles △YCA and △ZBA are equilateral, $AC = CY = YA = b$ units and $AB = BZ = ZA = c$ units. The figure below shows pentagon AZBCY with its side measures, in units, included.

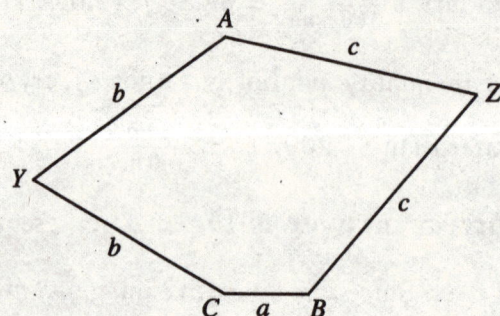

The perimeter of pentagon $AZBCY = AZ + ZB + BC + CY + YA = c + c + a + b + b = a + 2b + 2c$.

Question 45. The correct answer is D. The key to solving this problem is knowing that since $a < b$, the length of side $\overline{BC}$ in △ABC is less than the length of side $\overline{AC}$ in △ABC. Therefore, by the *Triangle Inequality*, $m\angle CAB < m\angle ABC$. Also, the acute angles ($\angle CAB$ and $\angle ABC$) of right triangle △ABC are complementary angles (their sum equals 90°).

The solution must work for *all* measures of complementary angles $\angle CAB$ and $\angle ABC$ for which $m\angle CAB < m\angle ABC$. But an example will serve to illustrate the general case. Suppose $m\angle CAB = 20°$ and $m\angle ABC = 70°$. As shown in the figure below, all 3 equilateral triangles must have interior angle measures of 60°, regardless of the measures of $\angle CAB$ and $\angle ABC$.

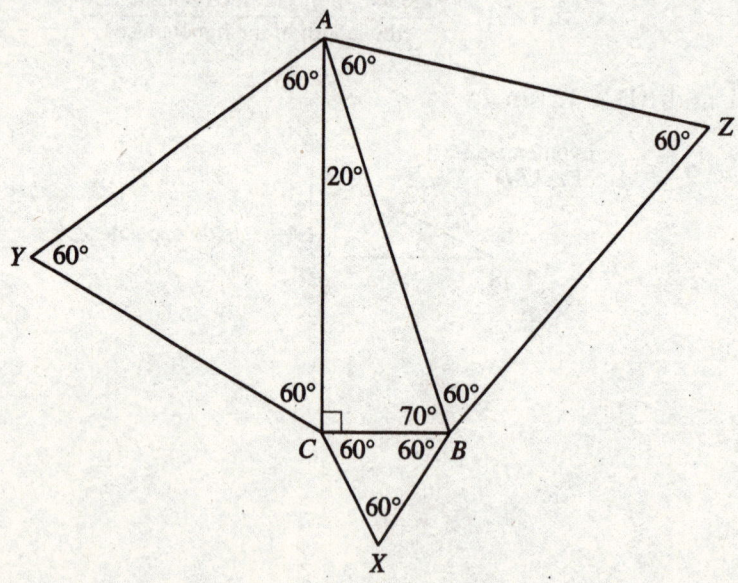

From the figure, you can see that $m\angle XCY = 360° - (60° + 90° + 60°) = 150°$, $m\angle CAZ = 20° + 60° = 80°$, and $m\angle CBZ = 70° + 60° = 130°$. In this case (as in all cases), you can see that $m\angle CAZ < m\angle CBZ < m\angle XCY$.

Question 46. **The correct answer is F.** From $\triangle ABC$ shown below, $\tan(\angle ABC) =$
$\dfrac{\text{the length of the side opposite } \angle ABC}{\text{the length of the side adjacent to } \angle ABC} = \dfrac{2a}{a} = 2.$

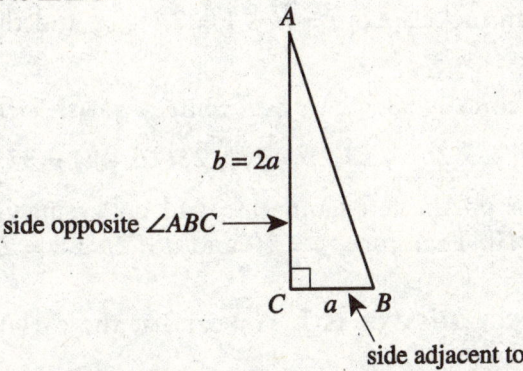

Question 47. **The correct answer is A.** If you let x represent the 1st odd integer, then $(x + 2)$ represents the 2nd odd integer and $(x + 4)$ represents the 3rd odd integer. Therefore,

$k = x + (x + 2) + (x + 4) = 3x + 6$, so $k - 6 = 3x$, and $x = \dfrac{k}{3} - 2$. The sum of the 2 smaller odd

integers is $x + (x + 2) = 2x + 2$. Substituting for x gives $= 2\left(\dfrac{k}{3} - 2\right) + 2 = \dfrac{2k}{3} - 4 + 2 = \dfrac{2k}{3} - 2$.

Question 48. **The correct answer is K.** One can approach this problem graphically or analytically.

Using the graphical approach, you may recall the general equation of the parabola with vertex (h,k) in the standard (x,y) coordinate plane: $y = a(x - h)^2 + k$. The equation of the parabola shown in the graph is $y = x^2$, with vertex at $(0,0)$ and $a = 1$. When the graph of $y = x^2$ is shifted 3 units to the right and 2 units down, a is still equal to 1, but the vertex of the parabola moves to $(0 + 3, 0 - 2) = (3,-2) = (h,k)$. Therefore, the equation of the parabola after the shift is $y = a(x - h)^2 + k = 1(x - 3)^2 + (-2)$; that is, $y = (x - 3)^2 - 2$.

Using the analytical approach, you may recall that for any function f, the graph of $y = f(x - a) + b$ in the standard (x,y) coordinate plane is the graph of $y = f(x)$ translated a units to the right and b units up. Likewise, the graph of $y = f(x - a) + (-b) = f(x - a) - b$ is the graph of $y = f(x)$ translated a units to the right and b units down.

So the graph of $y = f(x)$ translated 3 units to the right and 2 units down is the graph of $y = f(x - 3) - 2$. In this problem, $f(x) = x^2$, so $f(x - 3) - 2 = (x - 3)^2 - 2$.

Question 49. The correct answer is D. Let p = the number of pennies, n = the number of nickels, d = the number of dimes, and q = the number of quarters. Each of these variables can be expressed in terms of a common variable—in this case, p.

Lucky had p pennies, so the value of the pennies was p cents. Because she had twice as many nickels as pennies, $n = 2p$, and the value of the nickels was $5(2p)$ cents. She had 1 fewer dime than nickels, so $d = n - 1 = 2p - 1$, and the value of the dimes was $10(2p - 1)$ cents. Finally, she had 1 more quarter than nickels, so $q = n + 1 = 2p + 1$, and the value of the quarters was $25(2p + 1)$ cents.

Since the total value of the coins is \$8.25, or 825 cents, p satisfies the equation below.

$$p + 5(2p) + 10(2p - 1) + 25(2p + 1) = 825$$

Multiplying out each factor on the left-hand side and collecting like terms, you can see that $81p + 15 = 825$, so $81p = 810$. Therefore, $p = 10$ and $q = 2p + 1 = 2(10) + 1 = 21$ quarters.

Question 50. The correct answer is J. You can use the variables x, y, and z, to represent the 3 unknown numbers. Since the mean of the 4 numbers (the 3 unknown numbers and 5) is 32, it follows that $\frac{x + y + z + 5}{4} = 32$. So $x + y + z + 5 = 128$, and therefore $x + y + z = 123$. From this you may conclude that the mean of the 3 unknown numbers, $\frac{x + y + z}{3}$, is $\frac{123}{3}$, or 41.

Question 51. The correct answer is C. The statement given in the problem is a conditional statement, "If P, then Q," where P is the statement "A cat is tricolor" and Q is the statement "A cat is female." You may recall that a conditional statement and its *contrapositive*—"If *not Q*, then *not P*"—are logically equivalent. In particular, whenever a given conditional statement is true, so is its contrapositive.

So the contrapositive of the conditional statement given in this problem—"If a cat is not a female, then it is not tricolor"—must be true.

Question 52. The correct answer is K. You can begin by noticing that, by the rules of exponents, $(x^3)^{4-b^2}$ is equal to $x^{3(4-b^2)}$. Therefore, $x^{3(4-b^2)}$ is equal to 1. Recalling that $x^0 = 1$, it follows that $(x^3)^{4-b^2} = x^0$. Since x^0 is the *only* power of x equal to 1, it follows that $3(4-b^2) = 0$. This last equation is true provided that $4 - b^2 = 0$; so $b^2 = 4$, or equivalently, $b = \pm 2$.

If you chose **G** (the most common incorrect answer), you probably forgot that 4 has a negative square root. If you chose **H** (the second most common incorrect answer), perhaps you solved for b^2 instead of b.

Question 53. The correct answer is E. In this problem, the Note gives the identity $\sec x = \frac{1}{\cos x}$. You may then substitute $\frac{1}{\cos x}$ for $\sec x$ in the definition of $g(x)$ to see that $g(x) = (\sin x)\left(\frac{1}{\cos x}\right) = \frac{\sin x}{\cos x}$. Then you must recall the identity $\frac{\sin x}{\cos x} = \tan x$ to see that $f(x) = \tan x$ is equivalent to $g(x)$. If you chose **B** or **C**, you may have confused the identity for $\tan x$ with the identity for $\cot x$ (which equals $\frac{\cos x}{\sin x}$) or $\csc x$ (which equals $\frac{1}{\sin x}$).

Question 54. The correct answer is F. Since the (x,y) pairs satisfy a linear relationship, the rate of change of y with respect to x is constant. In order to more easily determine this rate of change, you can rearrange the (x,y) pairs in the table so that the x-values are in ascending order, as shown below. It can be seen from the calculations on the (x,y) pairs with given coordinates that the constant rate of change equals 3.

x	y	Rate of change
-3	z	
-2	-7	$\dfrac{-1-(-7)}{0-(-2)} = \dfrac{6}{2} = 3$
0	-1	$\dfrac{5-(-1)}{2-0} = \dfrac{6}{2} = 3$
2	5	

To find z, you can use the rate of change, the pair $(-3,z)$, and the pair $(-2,-7)$ to set up and solve the equation $\frac{z-(-7)}{-3-(-2)} = 3$, or equivalently, $\frac{z+7}{-1} = 3$. Solving $z + 7 = -3$ gives $z = -10$.

Question 55. The correct answer is D. You could use the formula for the volume of a right circular cylinder to find the radius r, in centimeters. Since the volume is 150π cubic centimeters and the height is 6 centimeters, it follows that $150\pi = \pi r^2(6)$. Dividing both sides by 6π and simplifying, $r^2 = \frac{150}{6} = 25$. Since r must be positive, $r = 5$. Substituting this value for r, along with h, into the formula for the lateral surface area gives $2\pi rh = 2\pi(5)(6) = 60\pi$ square centimeters.

Question 56. The correct answer is F. Let $x = \frac{w^2}{w^6}$. Using the properties of exponents, $\frac{w^2}{w^6} = w^{2-6} = w^{-4}$, so $x = w^{-4}$. The expression $\log_w x$ equals the exponent to which w must be raised to produce x (if $a = b^c$, then $\log_b a = c$). Since $x = w^{-4}$, that exponent is -4.

Question 57. The correct answer is B. In the standard (x,y) coordinate plane, the reflection across the x-axis of a point (a,b) is $(a,-b)$ and the reflection across the x-axis of a line $y = cx + d$ is $y = -cx + d$. The vertices of Amal's original trapezoid are the intersection points of the lines forming the trapezoid and have coordinates $(2,2)$, $(5,5)$, $(10,5)$, and $(10,2)$. Therefore, the vertices of the reflection of Amal's trapezoid across the x-axis are $(2,-2)$, $(5,-5)$, $(10,-5)$, and $(10,-2)$. The reflection of the trapezoid, its shaded interior, and its sides (segments on the lines $y = -2$, $y = -5$, $x = 10$, and $y = -x$) are shown in the figure below.

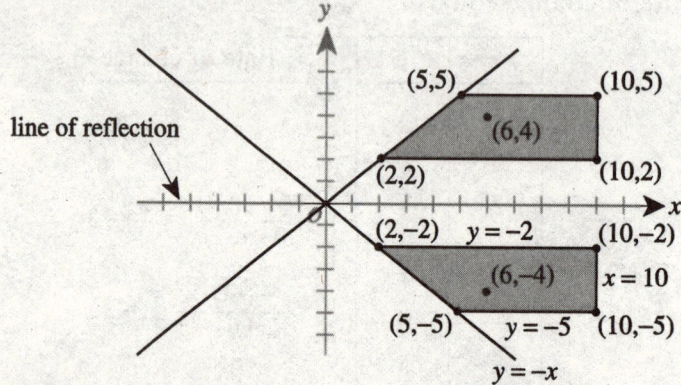

You can see from looking at the figure that the points in the interior of the reflected trapezoid satisfy the inequalities $x \le 10$ and $-5 \le y \le -2$. Determining which inequality these same points satisfy, $y \le -x$ or $y \ge -x$, is not as apparent. You can see which of the 2 inequalities fits by first choosing a specific point in the interior of the reflected trapezoid, say $(6,-4)$, and then testing to see which inequality is satisfied by $x = 6$ and $y = -4$.

The inequality $y \leq -x$ is equivalent to $-4 \leq -6$, a false statement. The inequality $y \geq -x$ is equivalent to $-4 \geq -6$, a true statement.

Therefore, points (x,y) in the reflected trapezoid must satisfy the inequality $y \geq -x$, together with the inequalities $x \leq 10$ and $-5 \leq y \leq -2$.

Question 58. The correct answer is J. The figure below shows the 3-4-5 right triangle with sides formed by the x-axis, the vertical line through $(4,-3)$, and the terminal side of θ. The angle, α, formed by the terminal side and the x-axis is called the *reference angle* of θ.

The relationship between θ and α is $\cos \alpha = |\cos \theta|$. From the figure, you can see that $\cos \alpha =$

$\dfrac{\text{the length of the side adjacent to } \angle\alpha}{\text{the length of the hypotenuse}} = \dfrac{4}{5} = |\cos \theta|$. Since the terminal side of θ lies in Quadrant IV,

$\cos \theta$ is positive. Therefore, $\cos \theta = \dfrac{4}{5}$.

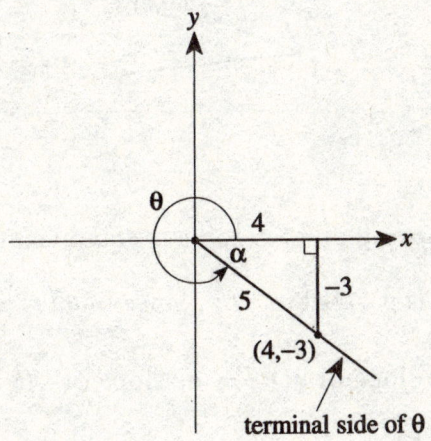

Question 59. The correct answer is A. Since points A and B are stationary, the side $\overline{AB}$ of $\triangle ABC$ will not change in length or direction. The *altitude* of $\triangle ABC$ with respect to side $\overline{AB}$ is the segment having one endpoint at point C that is perpendicular to $\overleftrightarrow{AB}$. The area of $\triangle ABC$, in square coordinate units, can be found using the formula below.

$$\text{area} = \tfrac{1}{2}(AB)(\text{the length of the altitude from } C \text{ to } \overline{AB})$$

Since the length AB must remain constant, the altitude from C of any new triangle whose area is equal to that of the original $\triangle ABC$ must have the same length. Three of these new triangles (and their altitudes from C) are shown in the figures below.

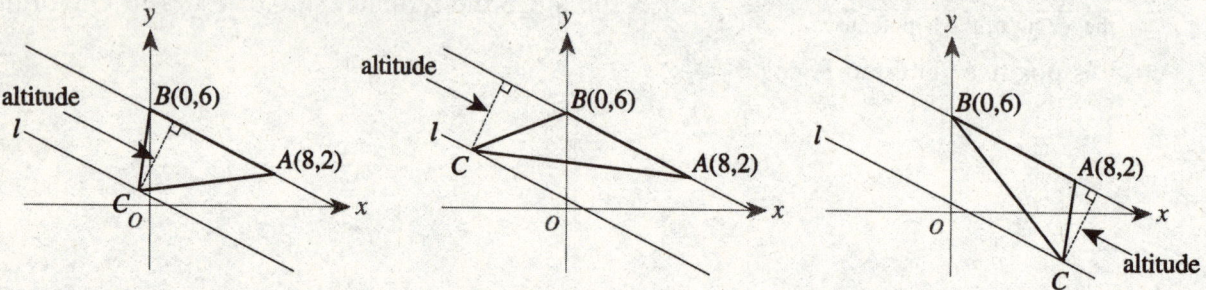

For all altitudes from the moving point C to have equal lengths, C must lie on the line l (shown in each figure), where line l is parallel to $\overleftrightarrow{AB}$. Since line l is parallel to $\overleftrightarrow{AB}$, the lines must have equal slopes. Therefore, the slope of line l = the slope of $\overleftrightarrow{AB} = \dfrac{6-2}{0-8} = \dfrac{4}{-8} = -\dfrac{1}{2}$.

Question 60. The correct answer is K. To find $f\big((x^2+y^2),(x-y)\big)$, you can substitute x^2+y^2 for a and $x-y$ for b in the equation $f(a,b) = b^2 - a$.

$$
\begin{aligned}
f\big((x^2+y^2),(x-y)\big) &= (x-y)^2 - (x^2+y^2)\\
&= (x^2 - 2xy + y^2) - (x^2+y^2)\\
&= x^2 - 2xy + y^2 - x^2 - y^2\\
&= -2xy.
\end{aligned}
$$

Choices **G**, **H**, and **J** were each as popular, if not more popular, than the correct answer. Each of these 3 incorrect answers is the result of committing one or both of the following errors: expanding $(x-y)^2$ as $x^2 - y^2$ without including the middle term $(-2xy)$; and writing $-(x^2+y^2)$ as $-x^2 + y^2$ and forgetting to distribute the minus sign to y^2.

Passage I

Question 1. The best answer is D because the narrator knows that her being able to attend college depends on the price and sale of wheat from the family's crop (lines 17–19).

The best answer is NOT:

A because the passage makes no mention of the narrator being "unsure" of her plans to attend college.

B because the passage makes no mention of the high cost of college. The only "cost" the passage mentions is that of wheat as it is announced on the radio.

C because, while the narrator states that she likes "working in the fields better than in the house" (lines 81–82), the passage makes no mention of the narrator considering working on the family ranch in lieu of attending college.

Question 2. The best answer is F because after the radio announcer announces the price of spring and winter wheat (lines 44–45), the narrator says she "didn't have to hear any more" (lines 46–47), implying that wheat was the only crop with which the family needed be concerned.

The best answer is NOT:

G because the narrator states that she "didn't have to hear" (lines 46–47) the part of the broadcast that "ran on" (lines 67–68) after the wheat prices were announced, suggesting that the prices of other crops were superfluous to her family's finances because they grow only wheat, not wheat and rye.

H because the narrator states that she "didn't have to hear" (lines 46–47) the part of the broadcast that "ran on" (lines 67–68) after the wheat prices were announced, suggesting that the prices of other crops were superfluous to her family's finances because they grow only wheat, not wheat, rye, and durum.

J because the narrator states that she "didn't have to hear" (lines 46–47) the part of the broadcast that "ran on" (lines 67–68) after the wheat prices were announced, suggesting that the prices of other crops were superfluous to her family's finances because they grow only wheat, not wheat, rye, durum, and flax.

Question 3. The best answer is B because the passage makes no mention of land disputes (or any disputes) in Gotham.

The best answer is NOT:

A because the passage states that the narrator's mother went out to look for the turkeys that had wandered off (lines 14–15), indicating that the narrator's mother monitors the turkeys.

C because the passage states that the narrator pours the cucumber wash water into the kettle on the stove (lines 27–31). This indicates that the narrator carefully monitors water use, because "when you have to carry every drop of water you use half a mile, you don't throw away any" (lines 31–33).

D because the passage describes the narrator and her father listening to the radio broadcast and, according to the narrator, "the voice of the man who announces the wheat prices is as familiar to me as Dad's" (lines 35–36). This indicates that the narrator and her father regularly monitor fluctuations in the price of wheat by listening to the radio broadcasts.

Question 4. The best answer is **H** because the narrator's mother did *not* show signs of worry. Rather, the narrator states that her mother "doesn't show in her face what she thinks or feels" (lines 75–76).

The best answer is NOT:

F because the narrator discusses how her mother's facial features differ from her father's (line 74, line 80) and how she herself more closely resembles her father (lines 79–81).

G because the narrator states, "I am strong like Mom" (line 81).

J because the narrator explicitly states that her mother does have a commitment to caring for her belongings and remembers her mother saying, "when I've got something, I take care of it" (lines 25–26).

Question 5. The best answer is **D** because the line in question, which reads "And then it began. I knew it before Dad turned it up," is preceded by the explanation that the narrator's father (lines 16–17) and the narrator (lines 17–20; line 27) were waiting for the noon broadcast of wheat prices to begin.

The best answer is NOT:

A because *it* appears twice in line 34, the first time as a reference to the report ("and then it began") and the second time as a reference to the radio ("I knew before Dad turned it up").

B because the narrator and her father are not listening to the war news. Rather, the narrator compares the voice of the announcer of the wheat prices to "one of those city voices that broadcasts the war news" (lines 37–38).

C because the narrator's father does not speak in the passage until later after the broadcast has ended (lines 84–86).

Question 6. The best answer is **J** because the narrator explains that while her mother is capable of much feeling, as evidenced by her laughter, the people of Gotham "think she's hard to know" (lines 76–77) because she doesn't often show in her face what she thinks or feels.

The best answer is NOT:

F because the passage makes no mention of the narrator's mother as being a moody person, only that her feelings don't often show in her face.

G because, while the narrator mentions that her mother's laugh "goes deeper down in her eyes than anybody's" (line 78), the passage makes no mention of anyone other than the narrator knowing this fact. Rather, the narrator states that the people of Gotham "think [her mother is] hard to know" (lines 76–77).

H because the passage does not specify whether the narrator's mother interacts often or rarely with the people of Gotham.

Question 7. The best answer is D because the narrator, in using the word *real* in line 2 of the passage, is describing a strong and powerful wind, the kind of wind that "blows dirt into your eyes and hair" (lines 2–3), as differentiated from an "ordinary" or a "mild" wind.

The best answer is NOT:

A because the narrator does not use the word *real* to indicate a comparison between factual and fictional winds. Rather she uses the word to emphasize the strength of the wind.

B because the narrator makes no judgment of the wind being either positive or negative. She is merely stating its strength by the use of the word *real*.

C because, while the narrator does describe the wind as both powerful and long-lasting, the description of the wind's power ("that blows dirt into your eyes and hair," lines 2–3) follows first after *real* in the sentence, emphasizing power over duration as a defining quality of a "real" wind.

Question 8. The best answer is G because, although the narrator does mention a strong wind (lines 2–4), she does not identify wind as being a threat to the wheat crop.

The best answer is NOT:

F, H, or J because the narrator states that when the harvesting is done, there are no more worries about "hail or drought or grasshoppers" (lines 4–6).

Question 9. The best answer is C because the narrator states that she "fenced in" cucumbers with her hands (line 30), and the word *committed* has no meaning similar to physically holding something in place, which is the meaning that the context here indicates the narrator intends to convey.

The best answer is NOT:

A because the word *shut* has the connotation of holding or blocking something in, which is the meaning the author intended through the use of the word *fenced* (line 30).

B because the word *penned* has the connotation of holding or blocking something in, which is the meaning the author intended through the use of the word *fenced* (line 30).

D because, like *shut* and *penned*, the word *held* has the connotation of holding or blocking something in, which is the meaning the author intended through the use of the word *fenced* (line 30).

Question 10. The best answer is G because the narrator describes herself "running across to the barn" (lines 87–88) because she "felt so excited [she] couldn't walk soberly" (lines 89–90). This suggests the narrator was completely caught up in and consumed by her excitement.

The best answer is NOT:

F because the narrator's description of herself as "running across to the barn" (lines 87–88) strongly suggests that she was not trying to hide her excitement from her father.

H because the passage makes no mention of any feelings of discontent on the narrator's part.

J because there is nothing in the passage to suggest the narrator feels guilty about anything.

Passage II

Question 11. The best answer is A because the passage first states the commonly held belief that the Colosseum is a "testament to the genius of Roman engineering" (lines 3–4), but goes on to question the validity of this belief, stating that researchers have found evidence to the contrary (lines 4–9).

The best answer is NOT:

B because while the first paragraph of the passage states that the Colosseum is commonly believed to be an architectural marvel (lines 1–2), this paragraph also states that there is reason to doubt this belief (lines 4–9).

C because the passage refers to "dark, narrow upper hallways that probably hemmed in spectators, slowing their movement to a crawl" (lines 7–9).

D because the passage makes no mention of any later correction of what might have been flaws in the Colosseum's design.

Question 12. The best answer is J because the passage makes no mention of the UCLA team using models made out of clay as a source of information about the Colosseum.

The best answer is NOT:

F because the passage states that researchers examined "what was left of the upper hallways, an area that had previously been all but closed to researchers" (lines 30–32).

G because the passage states that researchers used "records of the building's construction and expansion" as part of their research (lines 29–30).

H because the passage states that the UCLA team had "studied similar amphitheaters" (lines 27–28).

Question 13. The best answer is D because the passage explains that past scholars "never focused" on the circulation problem and that scholars had "assumed" that the different floors of the Colosseum had all looked alike (lines 39–42).

The best answer is NOT:

A because the passage makes no mention of any flawed experiments conducted by scholars.

B because while the passage mentions misleading computer models (lines 72–73), these flawed models are mentioned as a criticism of virtual reality models in general, not as an explanation for the theory of the Colosseum being a "masterpiece of circulation" (lines 35–36).

C because there is no mention in the passage of any false data concerning the Colosseum's bottom floor; the passage only mentions that this bottom floor was previously the only floor studied by scholars, and that scholars had previously made the assumption that all the Colosseum floors had looked the same (lines 39–42).

Question 14. The best answer is **G** because the passage mentions the Roman Senate and the Temple of Saturn as two sites about which "traditional thinking" has been challenged by computer "reconstructions" (lines 43–44).

The best answer is NOT:

F because the sixth paragraph (lines 43–49) specifically identifies the Roman Senate and the Temple of Saturn as sites about which "traditional thinking" has been challenged by "analysis of the UCLA models."

H because while the passage does state that the design of the Temple of Saturn "may have been altered centuries after its construction" (lines 48–49), the passage does not confirm this as a fact and makes no mention of any changes to the design of the Roman Senate.

J because while the passage does say that "analysis of UCLA models suggests that the Roman Senate may have been poorly ventilated and lighted and had inferior acoustics" (lines 44–46), the use of the words *suggests* and *may have* indicate that this is speculation rather than established fact. Moreover, while the passage goes on to say that "models also raised some new questions about the Temple of Saturn" (lines 47–48), it does not state as speculation or established fact that the Temple of Saturn featured inferior lighting, ventilation, and acoustics.

Question 15. The best answer is **A** because Paley states that when he announced his findings about the place of Ashur-Nasir-Pal II at a lecture, "the room went absolutely silent" (line 64). The sudden, physical nature of the audience's reaction to Paley's announcement indicates stunned amazement.

The best answer is NOT:

B because Paley interprets the audience's silence as a positive reaction, indicating a sudden realization of the usefulness of computer models, rather than contempt.

C because the sudden silence of the audience suggests a reaction stronger than one of "mild concern."

D because the sudden, physical reaction of the audience suggests real, not feigned, interest in Paley's findings.

Question 16. The best answer is **G** because the statement in question (lines 73–76), by explaining that modern technology conveys "as much or more about our own values and cultural aspirations as about the ancients" (lines 75–76), exemplifies the view that computer modeling "can gloss over the realities of the past" (line 69).

The best answer is NOT:

F because the statement in question (lines 73–76) specifically says that the "seductive images" conveyed by virtual models tell us "as much or more about our own values and cultural aspirations as about the ancients."

H because the statement in question (lines 73–76) makes no comparison between the values of "the ancients" and those of modern people.

J because the statement in question (lines 73–76) makes an argument about what images created by virtual reality models do and do not tell us about "the ancients," and makes no mention of what images created by the ancients ("their images") tell us.

Question 17. The best answer is **A** because Jones's statement (line 81) immediately follows and confirms an assertion that "even Frischer and other scholars who have embraced interactive 3–D modeling caution that their reconstructions can never be accepted as fact, partly because new information is always surfacing" (lines 77–80).

The best answer is NOT:

B because the passage makes no mention of any "serious flaws" in the software used to make computer models, only that the models require frequent updating because "new information is always surfacing" (line 80).

C because Jones's comment (line 81) is related to the need to constantly update computer models, not to the disagreement between supporters and critics of computer models.

D because the passage makes no mention of the content of Jones's classroom lectures other than that he is a "lecturer in architecture" (line 83).

Question 18. The best answer is **J** because the quotation marks indicate that the scientists were not literally and physically *walking through* the Colosseum. Rather, they are navigating through the computer-generated model of the Colosseum, as signaled by the use of the adverb *virtually* (line 6) directly preceding the phrase *walking through*.

The best answer is NOT:

F because in the sentence in question (lines 4–9) *walking through* describes the virtual passage of researchers through a 3–D model of the Colosseum's upper hallway, rather than the physical passage of ancient Romans through the upper hallway of the actual Colosseum.

G because the passage makes no suggestion as to how tourists should walk through the Colosseum.

H because the purpose of first paragraph of the passage is not to question the validity of computer-generated models or warn readers about them. Rather, the first paragraph questions previously held assumptions about the Colosseum's structure, assumptions that are being challenged via use of technology that allows researchers to virtually "walk through" the structure (line 6).

Question 19. The best answer is **C** because the passage states that "an impressive amount, including most of [the Colosseum's] facade, still stands" (lines 20–22).

The best answer is NOT:

A because the passage states that "most of [the Colosseum's] facade" (line 21) still stands.

B because the Colosseum was not unaffected by time. Rather, the passage states that "earthquakes and the ravages of time have destroyed much of the building" (lines 19–20).

D because while the passage states that "most of [the Colosseum's] facade" remains intact (lines 21–22), the use of the word *most* implies that a portion of the Colosseum's facade did not remain intact. In addition, the passage states that an impressive amount of the Colosseum, *including* most of the facade, had remained intact. This indicates that the "rest" of the Colosseum (the part other than the facade) had not been entirely destroyed.

Question 20. The best answer is **G** because the passage states specifically that "one advantage of using digital models . . . is that they can easily be updated with new findings" (lines 84–86).

The best answer is NOT:

F because the passage makes no mention of the cost of producing computer-generated models.

H because the passage does not discuss whether or not computer-generated models are entertaining to the public.

J because the passage does not mention whether or not computer-generated models encourage other improvements in technology.

Passage III

Question 21. The best answer is **C** because the passage only mentions the plot of *Bombay Dreams* in the first paragraph, where there are only two lines dedicated to it (lines 1–2).

The best answer is NOT:

A because the passage devotes significant attention to the people making and promoting music influenced by South Asia, starting with the discussion of pianist Vijay Iyer (line 31) and continuing throughout.

B because the influence of South Asian music on American music is a major theme of the passage, introduced in the first paragraph with the statement that "Broadway was the last to know about the rendezvous of Indian and Western music" (lines 6–8) and continuing throughout.

D because the significance of these musical hybrids to some South Asians and Asian Americans is an important topic in the passage. This topic is introduced by the third paragraph (lines 25–38) and revisited for emphasis in the seventh (lines 69–83) and eighth (lines 84–87) paragraphs.

Question 22. The best answer is **G** because the passage states that "the New York wave of South Asian music was preceded by influential South Asian hybrids from England" (lines 39–41), where London-based bands merged Indian musical elements into other musical genres in the 1970s (lines 44–45). The developments cited in other answers occurred after the 1970s.

The best answer is NOT:

F because the passage specifies that the Broadway musical *Bombay Dreams* opened in 2004 (line 3).

H because the passage states that the styles of the Asian Underground were developed in the 1990s (lines 47–49).

J because the passage specifies that the Basement Bhangra parties featured the music of the Asian Underground, which had "traveled to New York" from London (line 51), and that the styles of the Asian Underground were not developed until the 1990s (lines 47–49).

Question 23. The best answer is **B** because in discussing the Basement Bhangra music, which is one of the South Asian musical hybrids, Rekha states specifically that "the music has come of age" (line 57).

The best answer is NOT:

A because Iyer makes no statement in the passage about the maturity of the South Asian musical hybrids.

C because while Rahman is identified as "one of the top modern *filmi* composers" (line 62), he is not quoted in the passage, and no mention is made regarding his opinion of the maturity of the musical hybrids.

D because Iyer's parents are only mentioned in the passage as having brought Indian music with them to America (lines 75–76). They are not quoted in the passage, and no mention is made of their opinion of the maturity of the musical hybrids.

Question 24. The best answer is **J** because in the sentence in question (lines 66–67) *daring* places the potentially negative connotations of *shamelessness* in a positive light, while *one-up* suggests that *filmi* composers make inventive use of the musical styles that they figuratively and not literally "steal" from a wide variety of sources. In context, these potentially negative terms convey an appreciation for *filmi* music.

The best answer is NOT:

F because while the words *steal* and *one up* have negative connotations, the author is using them to express admiration for the way that *filmi* incorporates different sources (lines 66–67).

G because there is no evidence anywhere in the passage that the author feels alarmed by the fact that *filmi* incorporates other sources into it.

H because the words in question are words with strong connotations, which do not support a tone of "indifference."

Question 25. The best answer is **D** because while Iyer expresses his appreciation for Indian music throughout the passage, and incorporates it into the music that he plays (lines 31–32), he does so "without trying to pretend that I'm an expert on it, because that's something you have to devote your whole life to" (lines 77–79).

The best answer is NOT:

A because while the passage states that Iyer's music incorporates both jazz and Indian music, the passage makes no mention of Iyer emphasizing one genre over the other.

B because Iyer states in the passage that he is *not* an expert on Indian music (lines 77–78).

C because Iyer is not just beginning to explore American culture; rather, the passage states that Iyer grew up "surrounded by American culture" (line 74).

Question 26. The best answer is F because the passage states that "jazz musicians have been absorbing ideas and collaborating with Indian musicians at least since the 1960's" (lines 10–12). The use of the phrase *at least* indicates that these collaborations began no later than the 1960s but may have occurred earlier as well.

The best answer is NOT:

G because the passage makes no mention of the 1960s being the decade that saw the most collaborations between Indian musicians and Western jazz musicians.

H because the passage does not say that the collaborations between Western jazz musicians and Indian musicians ended in the 1960s and does not suggest that hip-hop began using Indian rhythms in the 1960s.

J because the passage does not state in which decade jazz was born and does not claim that no collaborations between Western jazz musicians and Indian musicians could have occurred before the 1960s.

Question 27. The best answer is A because the author describes the musical upbringing of the children of the white-collar South Asians as likely including a variety of Indian and Western musical forms, such as "Bollywood tunes alongside hip-hop, Western classical music, Indian classical music, rock and jazz" (lines 23–24).

The best answer is NOT:

B because the author does not describe the likely musical upbringing of the children of white-collar south Asian immigrants of the 1960s as being more focused on one musical form than another.

C because the author does not describe the likely musical upbringing of the children of white-collar south Asian immigrants of the 1960s as being directed more toward one musical style or another.

D because the author does not limit the description of the musical influences on the children of South Asian immigrants of the 1960s to only Bollywood tunes and classical music, and does not state that any one influence preceded another.

Question 28. The best answer is G because in the section in question (lines 32–38) Iyer states that "making music is very much aligned with activism" (lines 32–33), and that music can "make a difference in the world" (line 36).

The best answer is NOT:

F because Iyer states that the role of music making is "not just making music to be cool or look hip" (line 35).

H because Iyer makes no mention of uniting New Yorkers in a love of South Asian music. Rather, his message is a larger one regarding the relationship between music, activism, and New York's South Asian community (lines 36–38).

J because Iyer's statement is about the ability of music making to "make a difference in the world" (line 36) and makes no explicit reference to improving the quality of entertainment in the world.

Question 29. The best answer is C because the passage states that the documentary *Mutiny: Asians Storm British Music* "details the way established Indian and Pakistani communities in London confronted racism with music" (lines 42–43).

The best answer is NOT:

A because the passage makes no mention of how Indian and Pakistani communities first became established in London.

B because, while the passage states that influential South Asian musical hybrids came to New York from England (lines 39–41, line 51), it does not say that those hybrids came to London from India and Pakistan. Rather, it states that those hybrids formed in London from Indian elements and "other music that connoted resistance, like punk, reggae and hip-hop" (lines 46–47).

D because, while the passage does mention the appreciation for and use of the bhangra beat in London (line 45), it does not specify that this appreciation was specifically or solely attributable to Indian and Pakistani residents, and the passage makes no mention of *Mutiny: Asians Storm British Music* dealing with an appreciation for this beat.

Question 30. The best answer is G because the passage identifies Rahman as being "one of the top modern *filmi* composers, but also one of the most Western-flavored" (lines 62–63).

The best answer is NOT:

F because the passage makes no mention of a critical response to Rahman's work.

H because the passage makes no mention of Rahman having an interest in preserving Indian musical traditions. Rather, he is described as being one of the most "Western-flavored" (line 63) of the *filmi* composers.

J because while the passage mentions that *filmi* composers have incorporated elements of electro, salsa, surf music, and funk into their work (lines 64–65), there is no mention of Rahman's opinion of these genres.

Passage IV

Question 31. The best answer is D because the passage states explicitly that "because the ocean's depths are dangerous and expensive to explore, very little is known about the deep sea" (lines 32–34). This indicates that the risks and costs imposed by the squid's remote habitat are the biggest obstacles to learning more about the new squid.

The best answer is NOT:

A because the newly discovered squid is not reluctant to approach submersibles. Rather, the passage notes the squid's "apparent lack of concern with the proximity of the submersibles" (lines 58–59).

B because the uncertainty about how many species the new squid sightings represent (lines 71–73) stems from a larger problem of not having specimens in hand to study due to the risks and costs imposed by the squid's remote habitat.

C because there is no decline in the number of sightings of the new squid. To the contrary, the passage states "it's remarkable that there have been so many sightings recently" (lines 40–41).

Question 32. The best answer is **F** because in the first paragraph the author uses words such as *thrilled* (line 1) and phrases like *in a tizzy* (line 2) to convey a strong sense of excitement at the discovery of the new squid.

The best answer is NOT:

G because there is nothing in the first paragraph to suggest confusion on the part of either the author or on the part of the researchers who made the sightings of the squid.

H because there is nothing in the author's language conveying skepticism. Rather, the author's language supports the notion that the discovery of the squid is of great importance.

J because the first paragraph describes enthusiastic responses to the discovery of the "bizarre" squid (line 3) and not responses to a research study or enthusiasm for practical results.

Question 33. The best answer is **D** because O'Dor states that in studying the deep sea, scientists are exploring "unknown territory" (line 86) and that "much would remain unseen" (line 88) despite this exploration.

The best answer is NOT:

A because there is nothing in O'Dor's statement to suggest he feels deep-sea exploration is wasteful.

B because O'Dor does not feel that scientists are coming close to understanding the deep sea. To the contrary, O'Dor states that the new finding "proves how far biologists have to go in understanding the deep sea" (lines 84–85).

C because O'Dor makes no mention of the need for new submersibles, only that some creatures might be "too fast or too smart" (line 89) to be seen by submersibles.

Question 34. The best answer is **H** because the passage identifies *Architeuthis* as the name for the giant squid (lines 26–27) and states that the new squids "remain unnamed" (line 73).

The best answer is NOT:

F because the passage identifies *Architeuthis* as the name for the giant squid (lines 26–27), states that the new squids "remain unnamed" (line 73), and does not identify the new squid as a close relative of the giant squid.

G because the passage identifies *Architeuthis* as the name for the giant squid (lines 26–27), states that the new squids "remain unnamed" (line 73), and does not specify whether the new squid is a close or distant relative of the giant squid.

J because the passage states that the new squids "remain unnamed" (line 73) and specifically identifies *Architeuthis* as the name for the giant squid (lines 26–27).

Question 35. The best answer is C because the passage states that "not even the giant squid. . . has been seen alive in its natural deep-sea habitat" (lines 26–27).

The best answer is NOT:

A because the passage states that the new squid, unlike the giant squid, has "never washed up on shore or been found in the stomachs of whales" (lines 22–23). This indicates that giant squids have washed up on shore.

B because the passage states that the new squid, unlike the giant squid, has "never washed up on shore or been found in the stomachs of whales" (lines 22–23). This indicates that giant squids have been found in the stomachs of whales.

D because the passage does not mention whether or not the giant squid has been reported on in *Science* magazine.

Question 36. The best answer is G because the full sentence in question reads "The skin of habitat on land is miniscule in comparison" (lines 31–32). This sentence is preceded by the statement "Scientists calculate that the deep sea . . . encompasses more than 90 percent of the earth's biosphere" (lines 28–31). Taken together, these two statements indicate a contrast between a vast deep-sea habitat and a comparatively smaller surface habitat.

The best answer is NOT:

F because the author makes no argument in the passage that researchers should look underground rather than underwater for new animal species. On the contrary, the author emphasizes the importance of the discovery of the new squid.

H because the author mentions land habitats (line 31) in order to establish, by comparison, the enormity of the deep sea. The passage makes no argument regarding the validity of the study of land habitats.

J because the author only mentions land habitats (line 31) in order to establish, by comparison, the enormity of the deep sea. The passage does state that "the ocean's depths are dangerous and expensive to explore" (lines 32–34) but makes no mention of the relative cost or safety of doing deep-sea research, or any research, on land.

Question 37. The best answer is A because Grassle's use of the words *fantastic* (line 36) and *remarkable* (line 40) to describe the sightings suggests that he feels the discovery of the squid is something valuable. In addition, he says that although he has made many dives, he has "never seen anything like these [squids]" (lines 39–40), implying the uniqueness of sightings of the new squid.

The best answer is NOT:

B because while Grassle states that he has "made a lot of dives in submersibles" (lines 38–39), he does not make any appeal for an increase in submersible-based studies.

C because while Grassle says he has "made a lot of dives in submersibles" (lines 38–39), he does not suggest that this is how he spends most of his time as a researcher.

D because while he is identified by the author as the director of the Institute of Marine and Coastal Sciences (lines 37–38), Grassle makes no statement about the role of this institute in squid research.

Question 38. The best answer is H because according to Vecchione, "all the squids were spotted incidentally, by scientists or oil company workers looking for something else on the ocean floor" (lines 44–46).

The best answer is NOT:

F because according to Vecchione, all of the sightings of the new squid were "by scientists or oil company workers looking for something else on the ocean floor" (lines 44–46). Therefore the sightings were not made intentionally as part of a search specifically for the new squid.

G because the passage states the squid was discovered "incidentally" (line 44), not intentionally by scientists hoping to find new marine life.

J because the passage states that the sightings were by oil company workers *and* scientists (lines 44–46), not just by oil company workers.

Question 39. The best answer is C because the passage states that the videotape of the new squid was taken "for love, by a man aboard an oil exploration vessel" (line 49) who took the film "because his girlfriend was interested in marine biology" (line 52). In this context, love for another person, specifically the man's girlfriend, is what prompted the filming.

The best answer is NOT:

A because the passage states that the videotape of the new squid was taken "for love, by a man aboard an oil exploration vessel" (line 49) who took the film "because his girlfriend was interested in marine biology" (line 52). Therefore the love that prompted the filming was the love he felt for his girlfriend. Although there is much enthusiasm about the discovery of the new squid in the passage, there is no mention of any person feeling love for the new squid.

B because the passage states that the videotape of the new squid was taken "for love, by a man aboard an oil exploration vessel" (line 49) who took the film "because his girlfriend was interested in marine biology" (line 52). Although the man's girlfriend is described as having an interest in marine biology, neither she nor the man in question is described as feeling love for marine biology.

D because the passage makes no mention of any love the man has for submersibles. The passage merely mentions that the man was "aboard an oil exploration vessel using a remotely operated submersible" (lines 49–50) when he sighted and videotaped the new squid.

Question 40. The best answer is **J** because according to the passage "Dr. Vecchione speculated that the new squids might eat small crustaceans that they grabbed with what scientists suspected were sticky arms" (lines 76–79). The words *speculated* and *suspected* indicate that this is a matter of informed opinion and not settled fact. The passage goes on to explain that the basis for this opinion is an incident where one of the new squids "got its arms stuck on a submersible, and it had trouble letting go" (lines 80–81).

The best answer is NOT:

F because there is no mention in the passage of any examination revealing tiny suckers on the new squid's arms, and because the words *speculated* and *suspected* in Vecchione's statements about the squid's eating habits (lines 76–82) indicate informed opinion on his part rather than verified fact.

G because there is no mention of any study of similar squids found near Hawaii and California, and because the words speculated and suspected in Vecchione's statements about the squid's eating habits (lines 76–82) indicate informed opinion on his part rather than verified fact.

H because the passage makes no mention of the new squid's mouth or teeth. Rather, Vecchione supports his speculation regarding the new squid's eating habits with an anecdote about an incident involving one of the squids and a submersible (lines 76–82).

Passage I

Question 1. The best answer is D. Figure 1 shows that when 5 g of LiCl was added to 50 g of H_2O, ΔT was approximately 12°C. Because ΔT equals T_f minus T_i, a ΔT of approximately 12°C indicates that the temperature of the solution increased by approximately 12°C. Thus, heat was added to the solution.

The best answer is NOT:

A or **B** because a ΔT of approximately 12°C indicates that the temperature of the solution increased; it did not decrease.

C because an increase in the temperature of the solution indicates that heat was added to the solution. If heat had been removed from the solution, the temperature of the solution would have decreased.

Question 2. The best answer is F. In Figure 1, for 20 g of LiCl, as the mass of H_2O decreased from 100 g to 75 g to 50 g, ΔT increased from approximately 27°C to approximately 33°C to 40°C. A solution containing 100 g of H_2O and 20 g of LiCl has a lower LiCl concentration than does a solution containing 75 g of H_2O and 20 g of LiCl because the solution containing 100 g of H_2O and 20 g of LiCl has fewer grams of LiCl per gram of H_2O. Likewise, a solution containing 75 g of H_2O and 20 g of LiCl has a lower LiCl concentration than does a solution containing 50 g of H_2O and 20 g of LiCl. Thus, as the mass of H_2O decreased, the LiCl concentration in the solutions increased, and as the mass of H_2O decreased, ΔT increased. So, as the LiCl concentration in the solutions increased, the ΔT that was observed increased only.

The best answer is NOT:

G, H, or **J** because as the mass of the H_2O decreased, the LiCl concentration in the solutions increased and ΔT increased only; ΔT never decreased.

Question 3. The best answer is C. For a given mass of H_2O, as the mass of LiCl increased, ΔT increased. To estimate ΔT in an additional trial in which 25 g of LiCl had been added to 75 g of H_2O, the line in Figure 1 for 75 g H_2O will need to be extrapolated from. When this line is extrapolated to 25 g of LiCl, the value of ΔT is approximately 38°C, which is between 30°C and 40°C.

The best answer is NOT:

A or **B** because as the mass of LiCl increased, ΔT increased. ΔT in the trial in which 20 g of LiCl was added to 75 g of H_2O was approximately 33°C. So, ΔT in a trial in which 25 g of LiCl had been added to 75 g of H_2O would most likely have been greater than 33°C.

D because extrapolating from the line for 75 g H_2O in Figure 1 out to 25 g of LiCl gives an estimate of 38°C for ΔT.

Question 4. The best answer is G. According to Figure 2, when 5 g of NH_4NO_3 was added to 100 g of H_2O, ΔT was approximately –3°C. Because ΔT equals T_f minus T_i, a ΔT of approximately –3°C indicates that the temperature of the solution decreased by approximately 3°C.

The best answer is NOT:

F because ΔT was negative.

H because the temperature of the solution decreased and ΔT was negative.

J because the temperature of the solution decreased.

Question 5. The best answer is A. Figure 1 shows that as the ratio of grams of LiCl to grams of H_2O increased, ΔT increased. For a given mass of LiCl, as the mass of H_2O decreased, ΔT increased. Similarly, for a given mass of H_2O, as the mass of LiCl increased, ΔT increased. Each LiCl and H_2O combination in Figure 1 produced an increase in temperature, and the LiCl and H_2O combination with the highest ratio of grams of LiCl to grams of H_2O produced the greatest increase in temperature. Figure 2 shows that as the ratio of grams of NH_4NO_3 to grams of H_2O increased, ΔT decreased. For a given mass of NH_4NO_3, as the mass of H_2O decreased, ΔT decreased. Similarly, for a given mass of H_2O, as the mass of NH_4NO_3 increased, ΔT decreased. Each NH_4NO_3 and H_2O combination in Figure 2 produced a decrease in temperature. Thus, a combination of LiCl and H_2O with the highest ratio of grams of LiCl to grams of H_2O would produce the greatest increase in temperature.

The best answer is NOT:

B because adding 2 g of LiCl to 10 g of H_2O would result in a lower ratio of grams of LiCl to grams of H_2O than would adding 2 g of LiCl to 5 g of H_2O.

C because adding 2 g of NH_4NO_3 to 5 g of H_2O would produce a decrease in temperature.

D because adding 2 g of NH_4NO_3 to 10 g of H_2O would produce a decrease in temperature.

Passage II

Question 6. The best answer is F. All of the models are consistent with the data in Table 1, and Table 1 lists a map distance of 20 mu for Genes A and B. Table 1 does not provide a map distance for Genes A and C, Genes B and D, or Genes C and D, and, based on the information provided in Figure 3, all of the models do not agree on the distance between the genes in each of these gene pairs. The figure below shows the model proposed by each researcher along with the map distances listed in Table 1 (black lines and text) and estimates of the map distances between Genes A and C, Genes B and D, and Genes C and D that can be made using the information in Table 1 and Figure 3 (gray lines and text).

Researcher	Model
1	D—14 mu—A——20 mu——B———30 mu———C 34 mu · 50 mu · 64 mu
2	6 mu A—14 mu—D—B———30 mu———C 20 mu · 36 mu · 50 mu
3	4 mu 10 mu D—C——A——20 mu——B 14 mu · 30 mu · 34 mu
4	10 mu 6 mu C———A—14 mu—D—B 20 mu · 30 mu · 24 mu

The best answer is NOT:

G because Researcher 1's model and Researcher 2's model estimate that the map distance between Genes A and C is 50 mu, but Researcher 3's model and Researcher 4's model estimate that the map distance between Genes A and C is 10 mu.

H because Researcher 1's model and Researcher 3's model estimate that the map distance between Genes B and D is 34 mu, but Researcher 2's model and Researcher 4's model estimate that the map distance between Genes B and D is 6 mu.

J because Researcher 1's model estimates that the map distance between Genes C and D is 64 mu, Researcher 2's model estimates that the map distance between Genes C and D is 36 mu, Researcher 3's model estimates that the map distance between Genes C and D is 4 mu, and Researcher 4's model estimates that the map distance between Genes C and D is 24 mu.

Question 7. The best answer is A. In Figure 2, the *x*-axis is map distance and the *y*-axis is RF. A map distance of 70 mu corresponds to an RF of 0.377 because the line in Figure 2 passes through the coordinates (70,0.377).

The best answer is NOT:

B because in Figure 2, the line does not pass through the coordinates (70,0.477).

C because in Figure 2, the line does not pass through the coordinates (70,0.577).

D because in Figure 2, the line does not pass through the coordinates (70,0.677).

Question 8. The best answer is H. Based on Researcher 2's model, for Gene G to be a greater map distance from Gene D than from Gene B, it must be located to the right, based on the orientation of the genes in Figure 3, of Gene B. Furthermore, based on Table 1 and Figure 3, the estimated map distance between Genes D and B is 6 mu (see figure below). Thus, to be 8 mu from Gene B and 14 mu from Gene D, Gene G must be 8 mu to the right of Gene B, which is between Gene B and Gene C in Researcher 2's model. (Note that chromosomes do not really have right and left ends. This convention has been used only to help visualize the location of Gene G with respect to the orientation of the genes as they are shown in Figure 3.)

Researcher	Model
2	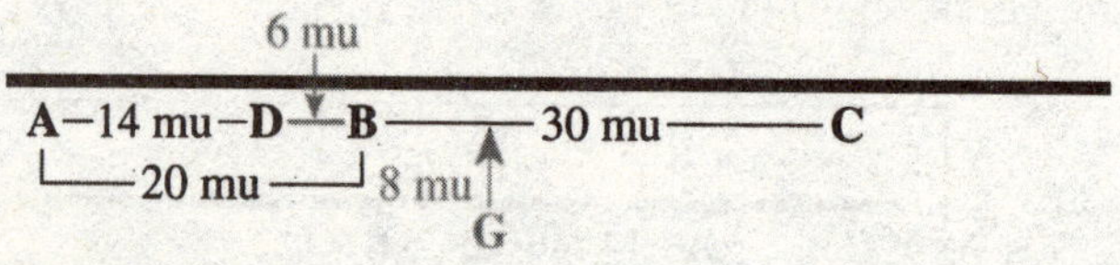 6 mu A—14 mu—D—B———— 30 mu ———— C └—— 20 mu ——┘ 8 mu↑ G

The best answer is NOT:

F, G, or J because Gene G must be to the "right" of Gene B, as described above.

Question 9. **The best answer is D.** Figure 2 shows that an RF of 0.091 corresponds to a map distance of approximately 10 mu. Based on Table 1 and Figure 3, Researcher 3's model and Researcher 4's model propose that Genes A and C are separated by 10 mu. Both models propose that Gene A is between Genes B and C; therefore, if the map distance between Genes B and C is 30 mu and the map distance between Genes A and B is 20 mu, the map distance between Genes A and C is estimated to be 10 mu (see figure below). In contrast, Researcher 1's model and Researcher 2's model estimate that Genes A and C are separated · by 50 mu: the 20 mu between Genes A and B plus the 30 mu between Genes B and C (see figure below).

Researcher	Model
1	D A——20 mu——B————30 mu————C ————50 mu————

2	A D B————30 mu————C
	     ——20 mu——
	             —————50 mu—————

3	10 mu ↓ D C——A——20 mu——B ————30 mu————
4	10 mu ↓ C——A D B ——20 mu—— ————30 mu————

The best answer is NOT:

A or **B** because Researcher 1's model proposes that Genes A and C are separated by 50 mu, which is not consistent with an RF of 0.091.

C because Researcher 2's model proposes that Genes A and C are separated by 50 mu, which is not consistent with an RF of 0.091.

Question 10. The best answer is J. The passage states that crossing over occurs during meiosis, and meiosis is the process by which gametes (sperm and eggs) are formed.

The best answer is NOT:

F because meiosis does not directly result in the formation of neurons; mitosis produces neurons.

G because meiosis does not directly result in the formation of skin cells; mitosis produces skin cells.

H because meiosis does not directly result in the formation of erythrocytes; mitosis produces erythrocytes.

Question 11. The best answer is A. Researcher 1's model proposes that the map distance between Genes D and C is equal to the map distance between Genes D and A plus the map distance between Genes A and B plus the map distance between Genes B and C. According to Table 1, this distance is 14 mu + 20 mu + 30 mu = 64 mu.

The best answer is NOT:

B because Researcher 2's model proposes that the map distance between Genes D and C is less than the map distance between Genes A and C. According to Researcher 2's model, the map distance between Genes A and C equals the map distance between Genes A and B plus the map distance between Genes B and C. According to Table 1, the map distance between Genes A and B plus the map distance between Genes B and C is 20 mu + 30 mu = 50 mu. So Researcher 2's model proposes that the map distance between Genes D and C is less than 50 mu.

C because Researcher 3's model proposes that the map distance between Genes D and C is less than the map distance between Genes D and A. According to Table 1, the map distance between Genes D and A is 14 mu. So Researcher 3's model proposes that the map distance between Genes D and C is less than 14 mu.

D because Researcher 4's model proposes that the map distance between Genes D and C is less than the map distance between Genes C and B. According to Table 1, the map distance between Genes C and B is 30 mu. So Researcher 4's model proposes that the map distance between Genes D and C is less than 30 mu.

Question 12. The best answer is F. The example shown in Figure 1 involves the 2 chromatids that carry Genes A and B. Each chromatid is represented by a single line. One chromatid has the alleles *a* and *b*; the other chromatid has the alleles *A* and *B*. Figure 1 shows these chromatids crossing over. It then shows the result: One chromatid has the alleles *A* and *b*; the other chromatid has the alleles *a* and *B*. This question refers to an analogous situation. To predict the result, redraw Figure 1, but replace each *A* with an *R*, each *a* with an *r*, each *B* with an *T*, and each *b* with an *t*. The result is that 1 of the chromatids participating in the crossover will have the alleles *R* and *t*, and the other chromatid participating in the crossover will have the alleles *r* and *T*.

The best answer is NOT:

G because this arrangement of alleles corresponds to the chromatids before the crossing over occurred.

H or J because each chromatid will not have 2 copies of Gene R or 2 copies of Gene T.

Passage III

Question 13. **The best answer is C.** In the graph on the left in Figure 2, the x-axis is conductivity of pore water and the y-axis is depth below ground surface. The solid line in this graph shows the data for the summer of 1990. Thus, a depth below ground surface of 2.5 m corresponds to a conductivity of pore water closest to 600 μmho/cm.

The best answer is NOT:

A because the graph shows that the conductivity of pore water at a depth below ground surface of 2.5 m was closest to 600 μmho/cm, not closest to 350 μmho/cm.

B because the graph shows that the conductivity of pore water at a depth below ground surface of 2.5 m was closest to 600 μmho/cm, not closest to 475 μmho/cm.

D because the graph shows that the conductivity of pore water at a depth below ground surface of 2.5 m was closest to 600 umho/cm, not closest to 725 μmho/cm.

Question 14. **The best answer is H.** In the graph on the right in Figure 2, the x-axis is pH of pore water and y-axis is depth below ground surface. The dashed line in this graph shows the data for the summer of 1991. Extrapolating this line to a depth below ground surface of 2.7 m results in a pH between 7.0 and 7.2. Thus, of the 4 options provided, 7.0 is closest to the predicted pH between 7.0 and 7.2.

The best answer is NOT:

F because 7.0 is closer to the predicted pH between 7.0 and 7.2 than is 4.0.

G because 7.0 is closer to the predicted pH between 7.0 and 7.2 than is 5.5.

J because 7.0 is closer to the predicted pH between 7.0 and 7.2 than is 8.5.

Question 15. **The best answer is D.** The information in the passage indicates that the primary water supply for a bog is rainfall. This explains why the depth below ground surface of the water table was greater in 1990 than in 1991. That is, in 1990, there was a drought, so the bog received less water from its primary water supply source: rainfall. So the water table was not as high.

The best answer is NOT:

A or B because the primary water supply for a bog is rainfall, not groundwater discharge. Thus, the difference in rainfall between 1990 and 1991 would have had little, if any, effect on the bog's water table depth.

C because during a drought the amount of rainfall received by the bog would have been less than normal.

Question 16. The best answer is J. Figure 2 shows that the peat had a thickness of approximately 3.1 m in the fen, and Figure 3 shows that the peat had a thickness of approximately 3.7 m in the bog. Thus, the peat layer was thinner in the fen than in the bog.

The best answer is NOT:

F or G because Figure 3 shows that in 1990, portions of the bog peat layer were above, at, and below the water table.

H because Figure 2 shows that the peat had a thickness of approximately 3.1 m in the fen, and Figure 3 shows that the peat had a thickness of approximately 3.7 m in the bog. Thus, the peat layer was thinner in the fen than in the bog; it was not thicker in the fen than in the bog.

Question 17. The best answer is C. In both graphs shown in Figure 1, for any given depth between 0.0 m and 3.0 m, the concentration of CH_4 in pore water was greater in the summer of 1990 than in the summer of 1991. Because the passage states that there was a drought in 1990, the passage supports the conclusion that over a depth of 0.0 m to 3.0 m, the average concentration of CH_4 in pore water was greater during the drought than during the summer of normal rainfall. This observation was seen in both the fen and the bog.

The best answer is NOT:

A or B because Figure 1 shows that the average concentration of CH_4 in pore water was greater during the summer of 1990 than during the summer of 1991.

D because Figure 1 shows that the average concentration of CH_4 in pore water was greater during the drought than during the summer of 1991 in both the fen and the bog, not in the bog only.

Passage IV

Question 18. The best answer is J. In Figure 1, Z is shown on the x-axis and A is shown on the y-axis. The isotope of radium (Ra) shown in Figure 1 has a Z of 88 and an A of 226. Based on the passage, the value for A appears as a superscript to the left of the symbol abbreviation and the value for Z appears as a subscript to the left of the symbol abbreviation. Thus the correct symbol for this isotope of radium is $^{226}_{88}\text{Ra}$.

The best answer is NOT:

F because the value that appears as a superscript to the left of the symbol abbreviation should be the value for A (226 in this question) and the value that appears as a subscript to the left of the symbol abbreviation should be the value for Z (88 in this question). In F, these values are reversed.

G because the value that appears as a superscript to the left of the symbol abbreviation should be the value for A (226 in this question) and the value that appears as a subscript to the left of the symbol abbreviation should be the value for Z (88 in this question). In G, the value of A is found in both of these positions.

H because the value that appears as a superscript to the left of the symbol abbreviation should be the value for A (226 in this question) and the value that appears as a subscript to the left of the symbol abbreviation should be the value for Z (88 in this question). In H, the value of Z is found in both of these positions.

Question 19. The best answer is C. In Table 1, the isotope of helium is abbreviated as ^4_2He, so A is 4 and Z is 2. A is the number of protons plus the number of neutrons. Z is the number of protons. Thus, the number of neutrons is equal to the A minus Z, or 2.

The best answer is NOT:

A because the number of neutrons is equal to the A minus Z, or 2, not 0.

B because the number of neutrons is equal to the A minus Z, or 2, not 1.

D because the number of neutrons is equal to the A minus Z, or 2, not 3.

Question 20. The best answer is G. Figure 1 shows that when an element undergoes beta (β) decay, A remains constant and Z increases by 1. Thus, if an element having an A = 230 and a Z = 90 undergoes beta decay, the new element produced will have an A = 230 and a Z = 91. Figure 1 shows an isotope of Pa that has an A = 230 and a Z = 91 and that this isotope is produced via beta decay of $^{230}_{90}Th$.

The best answer is NOT:

F because Z will equal 91, not 230.

H because the element that has a Z of 91 is Pa, not Th.

J because Z will equal 91, not 231, A will equal 230, not 91, and the element that has Z of 91 is Pa, not Th.

Question 21. The best answer is B. Table 1 and Figure 1 show that when an element undergoes alpha (α) decay, A decreases by 4 and Z decreases by 2. Thus, if $^{239}_{94}Pu$ underwent alpha decay, it would become $^{235}_{92}U$.

The best answer is NOT:

A because Table 1 and Figure 1 show that when an element undergoes alpha (α) decay, A decreases by 4 and Z decreases by 2. Thus, if $^{235}_{92}U$ underwent alpha decay, it would become $^{231}_{90}Th$. It would not become $^{239}_{94}Pu$.

C because Figure 1 shows that when an element undergoes beta (β) decay, A remains constant and Z increases by 1. Thus, if $^{235}_{92}U$ underwent beta decay, it would become $^{235}_{93}Np$. It would not become $^{239}_{94}Pu$.

D because Figure 1 shows that when an element undergoes beta (β) decay, A remains constant and Z increases by 1. Thus, if $^{239}_{94}Pu$ underwent beta decay, it would become $^{239}_{95}Am$. It would not become $^{235}_{92}U$.

Question 22. The best answer is J. The kinetic energy (KE) of a particle is given by: KE = $\frac{1}{2}mv^2$, where m is the particle's mass, and v is the particle's velocity. The question states that the KE of the helium nucleus is equal to the KE of the electron. Therefore, because a helium nucleus has a much greater mass than an electron, the electron must have the greater velocity.

The best answer is NOT:

F because if the helium nucleus were moving faster than the electron, the helium nucleus would have far more KE than the electron, contradicting the premise of the question.

G because a helium nucleus is far more massive than an electron.

H because an electron is far less massive than a helium nucleus.

Passage V

Question 23. The best answer is B. Figure 3 shows 2 peaks for M3, one at 7.6 min and the other at 12.2 min. Figure 2 shows the peak for P3 at 7.6 min and the peak for P1 at 12.3 min. Thus, M3 was most likely a mixture of P1 and P3 only.

The best answer is NOT:

A because in Figure 3, M3 has a peak at 7.6 min and a peak at 12.2 min. Figure 2 shows the peak for P3 at 7.6 min. Thus, M3 most likely contained P3 also.

C because Figure 2 shows the peak for P5 at 4.7 min. In Figure 3, M3 has a peak at 7.6 min and a peak at 12.2 min, but no peak at 4.7 min.

D because Figure 2 shows the peaks for P2, P4, and P5 at 10.1 min, 5.6 min, and 4.7 min, respectively. In Figure 3, M3 has a peak at 7.6 min and a peak at 12.2 min, but no peak at 10.1 min, 5.6 min, or 4.7 min.

Question 24. The best answer is F. The molecules that spent the longest amount of time in the column were those of the polymer that had the longest RT. Figure 2 shows that P1 is the polymer with the longest RT.

The best answer is NOT:

G because Figure 2 shows that P1 had a longer RT than did P2, so P1 molecules spent more time in the column than did P2 molecules.

H because Figure 2 shows that P1 had a longer RT than did P4, so P1 molecules spent more time in the column than did P4 molecules.

J because Figure 2 shows that P1 had a longer RT than did P5, so P1 molecules spent more time in the column than did P5 molecules.

Question 25. The best answer is C. The passage states that smaller molecules spend more time in the column than do larger molecules. In Figure 2, the peaks for P4 and P5 are at 5.6 min and 4.7 min, respectively. In Figure 3, the peak for M2 is at 6.2 min. Because M2 has a longer RT than do P4 and P5, M2 exited the column after P4 and P5. This indicates that M2 has a smaller AMM than do P4 and P5. Similarly, because P4 has a longer RT than does P5, P4 exited the column after P5. This indicates that P4 has a smaller AMM than does P5. Table 1 shows that P4 has an AMM of 50,000 amu and P5 has an AMM of 200,000 amu. Thus, the correct ranking of the 3 polymers, from smallest AMM to largest AMM, is: M2, P4, P5.

The best answer is NOT:

A, B, or D because among the 3 polymers, M2 has the smallest AMM, P4 has the next largest AMM, and P5 has the largest AMM.

Question 26. The best answer is G. The passage states that smaller molecules more easily diffuse into the pores of the beads than do larger molecules. Smaller molecules have a smaller AMM than do larger molecules. Table 1 shows that P3 has an AMM of 10,000 amu and P4 has an AMM of 50,000 amu. Because P3 has a smaller AMM than does P4, P3 molecules more easily diffused into the pores of the beads than did P4 molecules. This conclusion is supported by Figure 2, which shows that P3 has a longer RT than does P4. P3 molecules spent more time in the column of the SEC apparatus than did P4 molecules, so P3 exited the column after P4.

The best answer is NOT:

F because P3 molecules have a smaller AMM than do P4 molecules.

H because the passage states that smaller molecules more easily diffuse into the pores of the beads than do larger molecules. Thus, P4 molecules did not diffuse more easily into the pores of the beads.

J because P4 molecules have a larger AMM than do P3 molecules. The passage states that smaller molecules more easily diffuse into the pores of the beads than do larger molecules. Thus, P4 molecules did not diffuse more easily into the pores of the beads.

Question 27. The best answer is A. The passage states that smaller molecules spend more time in the column than do larger molecules. According to Figure 2, P5 has an RT of 4.7 min. Table 1 shows that P5 has an AMM of 200,000 amu. A polymer with an AMM greater than 200,000 amu would have an RT shorter than 4.7 min. Of the 3 mixtures tested in Experiment 2, only M1 has components with RTs shorter than 4.7 min. As Figure 3 shows, the peaks for M1 are at approximately 3.0 min. Thus, the average mass of the molecules in M1 is most likely greater than 200,000 amu.

The best answer is NOT:

B because Figure 3 shows that the peak for M2 is at 6.2 min, so the average mass of the molecules in M2 is most likely less than 200,000 amu.

C because Figure 3 shows that the peaks for M3 are at 7.6 min and 12.2 min, so the average mass of the molecules in M3 is most likely less than 200,000 amu.

D because Figure 3 shows that the peaks for M1 are at approximately 3.0 min, so the average mass of the molecules in M1 is most likely greater than 200,000 amu.

Question 28. The best answer is J. Table 1 shows that P2 has an AMM of 4,000 amu and P4 has an AMM of 50,000 amu. Thus, P2 molecules have less average mass than do P4 molecules. Because P2 molecules have less average mass than do P4 molecules, more P2 molecules are required to make up a 1 g of sample of P2 and fewer P4 molecules are required to make up a 1 g sample of P4. So, the number of P2 molecules in a 1 g sample of P2 is greater than the number of P4 molecules in a 1 g sample of P4.

The best answer is NOT:

F because P2 has a smaller AMM than does P4 and the number of P2 molecules in a 1 g sample of P2 is greater than the number of P4 molecules in a 1 g sample of P4.

G because the number of P2 molecules in a 1 g sample of P2 is greater than the number of P4 molecules in a 1 g sample of P4.

H because P2 has a smaller AMM than does P4.

Passage VI

Question 29. The best answer is A. According to Table 1, for dowels having a water content of 2%, the flame spread rate was 2.48 cm/min in 16% O_2, 2.76 cm/min in 21% O_2, 3.92 cm/min in 28% O_2, and 5.00 cm/min in 35% O_2. Thus, as the O_2 content increased from 16% to 35%, the flame spread rate for dowels with a water content of 2% only increased.

The best answer is NOT:

B, C, or D because as the O_2 content increased from 16% to 35%, the flame spread rate for dowels with a water content of 2% never decreased.

Question 30. The best answer is J. The solid curve in Figure 1 shows that from 425°C to 475°C, the *Araucaria* leaves heated in an atmosphere containing 35% O_2 lost approximately 40% of the original mass of sample. In contrast, from 275°C to 325°C, the *Araucaria* leaves heated in an atmosphere containing 35% O_2 lost approximately 20%; from 325°C to 375°C, the *Araucaria* leaves heated in an atmosphere containing 35% O_2 lost approximately 15%; and from 375°C to 425°C, the *Araucaria* leaves heated in an atmosphere containing 35% O_2 lost approximately 7%.

The best answer is NOT:

F because Figure 1 shows that from 425°C to 475°C, the *Araucaria* leaves heated in an atmosphere containing 35% O_2 lost approximately 40% of the original mass of sample. In contrast, from 275°C to 325°C, the *Araucaria* leaves heated in an atmosphere containing 35% O_2 lost approximately 20%.

G because Figure 1 shows that from 425°C to 475°C, the *Araucaria* leaves heated in an atmosphere containing 35% O_2 lost approximately 40% of the original mass of sample. In contrast, from 325°C to 375°C, the *Araucaria* leaves heated in an atmosphere containing 35% O_2 lost approximately 15%.

H because Figure 1 shows that from 425°C to 475°C, the *Araucaria* leaves heated in an atmosphere containing 35% O_2 lost approximately 40% of the original mass of sample. In contrast, from 375°C to 425°C, the *Araucaria* leaves heated in an atmosphere containing 35% O_2 lost approximately 7%.

Question 31. The best answer is B. Table 1 shows that when the *Pinus* wood pieces (dowels) with a water content of 61% were ignited, the fire in the chamber extinguished itself before the sample burned completely. This occurred when the atmosphere contained 16% O_2, 21% O_2, 28% O_2, and 35% O_2. Likewise, Table 1 shows that when the *Pinus* needles with a water content of 61% were ignited, the fire in the chamber extinguished itself before the sample burned completely. This occurred when the atmosphere contained 16% O_2, 21% O_2, 28% O_2, and 35% O_2. Given these results, if a tree that resembled modern *Pinus* trees and had a water content greater than 65% was ignited in an atmosphere that contained 28% O_2 or that contained 35% O_2, then it is most likely the tree would not have burned completely.

The best answer is NOT:

A because based on Table 1, if a tree that resembled modern *Pinus* trees and had a water content greater than 65% was ignited in an atmosphere that contained 35% O_2, then it is most likely the tree would not have burned completely.

C because based on Table 1, if a tree that resembled modern *Pinus* trees and had a water content greater than 65% was ignited in an atmosphere that contained 28% O_2, then it is most likely the tree would not have burned completely.

D because based on Table 1, if a tree that resembled modern *Pinus* trees and had a water content greater than 65% was ignited in an atmosphere that contained 28% O_2 or that contained 35% O_2, then it is most likely the tree would not have burned completely.

Question 32. The best answer is H. Based on Table 1, if needles having a water content of 10% had been burned in an atmosphere containing 28% O_2, then the flame rate would have been between the flame rate that was observed when needles having a water content of 2% had been burned in an atmosphere containing 28% O_2 and the flame rate that was observed when needles having a water content of 12% had been burned in an atmosphere containing 28% O_2. When needles with a 2% water content were burned in 28% O_2, the flame rate was 37.50 cm/min. When needles with a 12% water content were burned in 28% O_2, the flame rate was 22.61 cm/min. So if needles with a 10% water content had been burned in 28% O_2, the flame rate would most likely have been greater than 22.61 cm/min and less than 37.50 cm/min.

The best answer is NOT:

F or G because the flame rate would most likely have been greater than 22.61 cm/min.

J because the flame rate would most likely have been less than 37.50 cm/min.

Question 33. The best answer is B. In Study 2, for a given water content, flame rates were greater for needles than for dowels. So, the burn rate would have been greater in the crown, which contains needles, than along the surface, which contains wood.

The best answer is NOT:

A because Table 1 shows that the flame rates for needles were greater than the flame rates for dowels.

C or D because Table 1 shows that the flame rates for needles were greater than the flame rates for dowels (wood pieces), and the crown fire would have consumed needles, while the surface fire would have consumed wood pieces.

Question 34. The best answer is H. In Figure 1, the x-axis is degrees Celsius and the y-axis is percent of the original mass of the sample that was remaining. The dotted line represents paper heated in an atmosphere containing 21% O_2. Thus, when the temperature reached 350°C, 40% of the sample mass remained. If 40% of the sample mass remained, then 60% of the sample mass had been consumed.

The best answer is NOT:

F because when the temperature reached 350°C, 40% of the sample mass remained, so 60% of the sample mass had been consumed, not 20%.

G because when the temperature reached 350°C, 40% of the sample mass remained, so 60% of the sample mass had been consumed, not 40%.

J because when the temperature reached 350°C, 40% of the sample mass remained, so 60% of the sample mass had been consumed, not 80%.

Passage VII

Question 35. The best answer is B. Figure 5 shows that a ball launched at 100 mph would travel 630 ft, while a ball launched at 90 mph would travel 520 ft. Thus, if the ball were launched at 100 mph, it would have traveled about 100 ft farther than if it were launched at 90 mph. Note that Figure 5 is a mathematical model that corresponds to the conditions listed in the question: a launch angle of 35°, a launch height of 3.5 ft, and the absence of air.

The best answer is NOT:

A, C, or D because Figure 5 shows that a ball launched at 100 mph would travel 630 ft, while a ball launched at 90 mph would travel 520 ft.

Question 36. The best answer is G. The passage states that the camera recorded the ball's image every 0.5 sec. Thus, during a 1 sec interval, the camera recorded the ball's image twice.

The best answer is NOT:

F because the ball's image was recorded 2 times per second, not 1 time per second.

H because the ball's image was recorded 2 times per second, not 3 times per second.

J because the ball's image was recorded 2 times per second, not 4 times per second.

SCIENCE · PRACTICE TEST 5 · EXPLANATORY ANSWERS

Question 37. The best answer is C. The ball would need to be 37 ft above the ground after it had traveled 310 ft. Figure 4 shows the height of each ball after it had traveled 310 ft. In Figure 4, the *y*-axis is height (*H*), in ft, and the *x*-axis is distance, in ft, along the ground that the ball would have traveled (*R*). For the 5 speeds tested—80, 90, 100, 110, and 120 mph—the ball was at a height of at least 37 ft when it was launched at 100, 110, and 120 mph. When the ball was launched at a speed of 80 mph, the ball did not travel 310 ft. When the ball was launched at a speed of 90 mph, the ball appears to have traveled less than 310 ft, but even if it had reached 310 ft, its height at this time would have been lower than 37 ft. Thus, only those balls launched at 100, 110, and 120 mph would have cleared the left field wall.

The best answer is NOT:

A because Figure 4 shows that a ball launched at 100 mph would have been over 50 ft above the ground when it had traveled the necessary 310 ft. Figure 4 also shows that a ball launched at 110 mph would have been almost 100 ft above the ground when it had traveled the necessary 310 ft.

B because Figure 4 shows that a ball launched at 100 mph would have been over 50 ft above the ground when it had traveled the necessary 310 ft.

D because Figure 4 shows that a ball launched at 80 mph would not have traveled 310 ft.

Question 38. The best answer is F. In Figure 4, at 3 sec, as launch speed increases from 80 mph to 120 mph, both *H* and *R* increase continually. For example, with a launch speed of 80 mph, at 3 sec, *R* is approximately 200 ft and *H* is approximately 50 ft; with a launch speed of 100 mph, at 3 sec, *R* is approximately 250 ft and *H* is approximately 80 ft; and with a launch speed of 120 mph, at 3 sec, *R* is approximately 300 ft and *H* is approximately 120 ft.

The best answer is NOT:

G because in Figure 4, at 3 sec, as launch speed increases from 80 mph to 120 mph, *R* increases continually.

H because in Figure 4, at 3 sec, as launch speed increases from 80 mph to 120 mph, *H* increases continually.

J because in Figure 4, at 3 sec, as launch speed increases from 80 mph to 120 mph, both *H* and *R* increase continually.

Question 39. The best answer is C. Figure 5 shows that if the ball were launched in the absence of air from a height of 3.5 ft at 120 mph and θ = 35°, its height after 4, 5, and 6 sec would be approximately 150 ft, 110 ft, and 35 ft, respectively. If its arc is extrapolated out, it would hit the ground before it had traveled for 7 sec. Thus, it would likely be in flight for between 6 and 7 sec.

The best answer is NOT:

A because Figure 5 shows that it would still be in air after 5 sec.

B because Figure 5 shows that it would still be in air after 6 sec.

D because Figure 5 shows that it would hit the ground in less than 7 sec.

Question 40. The best answer is F. D is the distance the radar pulse would travel from the transceiver to the ball. It would then travel this same distance (D) on its return path from the ball back to the transceiver. So it would have to travel $2D$. To determine how long it would take to travel $2D$, the distance is divided by the speed that the radar pulse travels: c. As a concrete example, consider the following: light travels approximately 980,000,000 ft/sec. If the radar pulse hit the ball when the ball was 250 ft from the transceiver, then the radar pulse would have to travel a total of 500 ft. The time required to travel 500 ft would be calculated by dividing 500 ft by 980,000,000 ft/sec. That is it would take about 5×10^{-7} sec for the radar pulse to travel from the transceiver to the ball and then back to the transceiver.

The best answer is NOT:

G or J because R is the distance along the ground, not the distance from the transceiver to the ball. The distance from the transceiver to the ball is D. As shown in Figure 3, R is less than D.

H because to calculate time, distance is divided by speed.

Chapter 5: Interpreting Your ACT Test Scores

This chapter will help you learn as much as possible from your performance on the practice tests. You will also learn how to use the ACT scores you'll receive when you take the actual ACT. In particular, this chapter tells you exactly what kind of score information is best to use to find out:

- how your performance compares to that of other college-bound students

- what your areas of relative strength and weakness are

- how to identify areas where you might want to get additional instruction in order to be better prepared for college

When scoring each practice test and reviewing your scores, it's important to remember your scores on the practice tests are only *estimates* of the scores that you will obtain on an actual form of the ACT. If your score isn't as high as you expected, it could mean a number of things. Maybe you need to review important content and skills. Maybe you should work a little faster when taking the test. Perhaps you simply weren't doing your best work on the test. Or maybe you need to take more challenging courses to be better prepared. Keep in mind that a test score is just one indicator of your level of academic knowledge and skills. You know your own strengths and weaknesses better than anyone else, so keep them in mind as you evaluate your performance.

Scoring Your Practice Test

On each of the four multiple-choice tests (English, Mathematics, Reading, and Science), the number of questions you answer correctly is called a "raw" score. It's easy to figure out your raw scores for the practice tests in this book: Simply count up all your correct answers for each test using the scoring keys provided at the end of this chapter. Then you can convert your raw scores into "scale" scores using the conversion charts available at the end of this chapter. Scale scores are the scores that ACT reports to students, high schools, colleges, and scholarship agencies. One of the reasons ACT uses scale scores is to adjust for small differences occurring among different versions of the ACT tests. After you've converted your raw scores for the practice tests to scale scores, you'll want to convert your scale scores to percentile ranks. Percentile ranks, which are explained in the following pages, are useful for interpreting your scores relative to the scores of others who have taken the ACT.

If you took the optional practice Writing Test, the Six-Point Holistic Scoring Rubric on page 141 should be used to judge what rating your essay should receive (1–6). It is difficult to be objective about one's own work, and you have not had the extensive training provided to actual readers of the ACT Writing Test. However, it is to your advantage to read your own writing critically. Becoming your own editor helps you grow as a writer and as a reader. So it makes sense for you to evaluate your own practice essay. That having been said, it may also be helpful for you to give your practice essay to another reader to get another perspective: perhaps that of a classmate, a parent, or an English teacher, for example. To rate your essay, you and your reader should read the scoring rubric on page 141 and the examples on pages 123–140, and then assign your practice essay a score of 1 through 6. Your Writing Test subscore should be based on **two** ratings, so you may either multiply your own rating times two, or sum your rating and another reader's ratings to calculate your subscore (2–12) for your practice Writing Test. To calculate your Combined English/Writing scale score, use the charts and procedures available at the end of this chapter. Finally, convert your Writing Test subscore and Combined English/Writing scale score to percentile ranks using the procedures described. Percentile ranks allow you to compare your Writing Test subscore and Combined English/Writing scale score to those of others who have taken the ACT Writing Test.

Understanding Your ACT Test Results

How ACT Scores Your Multiple-Choice Tests

How does ACT determine the scores it reports for students taking the ACT multiple-choice tests? The first step is to do exactly what you are about to do for your practice tests: count the number of questions you answered correctly to determine your raw score. There's no deduction for incorrect answers.

Next, these raw scores are converted to scale scores—scores that have the same meaning for all versions of the ACT. The scale scores range from 1 (low) to 36 (high) for each of the four individual tests and for the Composite score, which is the average of the four test scores.

ACT also computes subscores for areas within the English, Reading, and Mathematics Tests. The subscores range from 1 (low) to 18 (high). Because the four multiple-choice test scores are computed independently of the subscores for the tests, the sum of the subscores for a particular test won't necessarily equal the score for that test. For example, the two subscores for the Reading Test won't necessarily add up to the overall score for the Reading Test.

How ACT Scores Your Writing Test

How does ACT determine the scores it reports for students taking the ACT Writing Test? Under true scoring conditions, two trained raters score each Writing Test essay based on the Six-Point Holistic Scoring Rubric, which can be found on page 141. These raters are trained by reading examples of papers at each score point and by scoring many practice papers. During actual scoring, score differences between the two raters of more than one point will be evaluated by a third trained rater to resolve discrepancies. This method is designed to be as objective and impartial as possible. Each rater gives the essay a score on a scale from 1 (low) to 6 (high). The score is based on the overall elements of the writing. The scores given by the two raters are then added together, yielding a Writing subscore ranging from 2 to 12.

ACT also computes a Combined English/Writing scale score by using the same chart and procedure you used in scoring your practice Writing Test. This Combined score is reported on a scale of 1–36.

Test Scores Are Just Estimates

No test, including the ACT, can precisely measure educational achievement. As a result, we estimate the amount of imprecision, or error, in test scores. One estimate for this error is called the "standard error of measurement." On the ACT, the standard error of measurement (SEM) is about 2 points for each of the multiple-choice test scores and subscores and about 1 point for the Composite score.

Because of the imprecision of test scores, it's best to think of each of your ACT scores as a range of scores rather than as a precise number. The SEM can be used to estimate ranges for your scores. To do this, just add the SEM to, and subtract it from, each of your scores. For example, if your score on the English Test is 22, your level of English skills and knowledge probably lies somewhere in the interval of 20 to 24 (22 plus or minus 2).

Following is an example of the way test scores are shown on *The ACT® Plus Writing Student Report*:

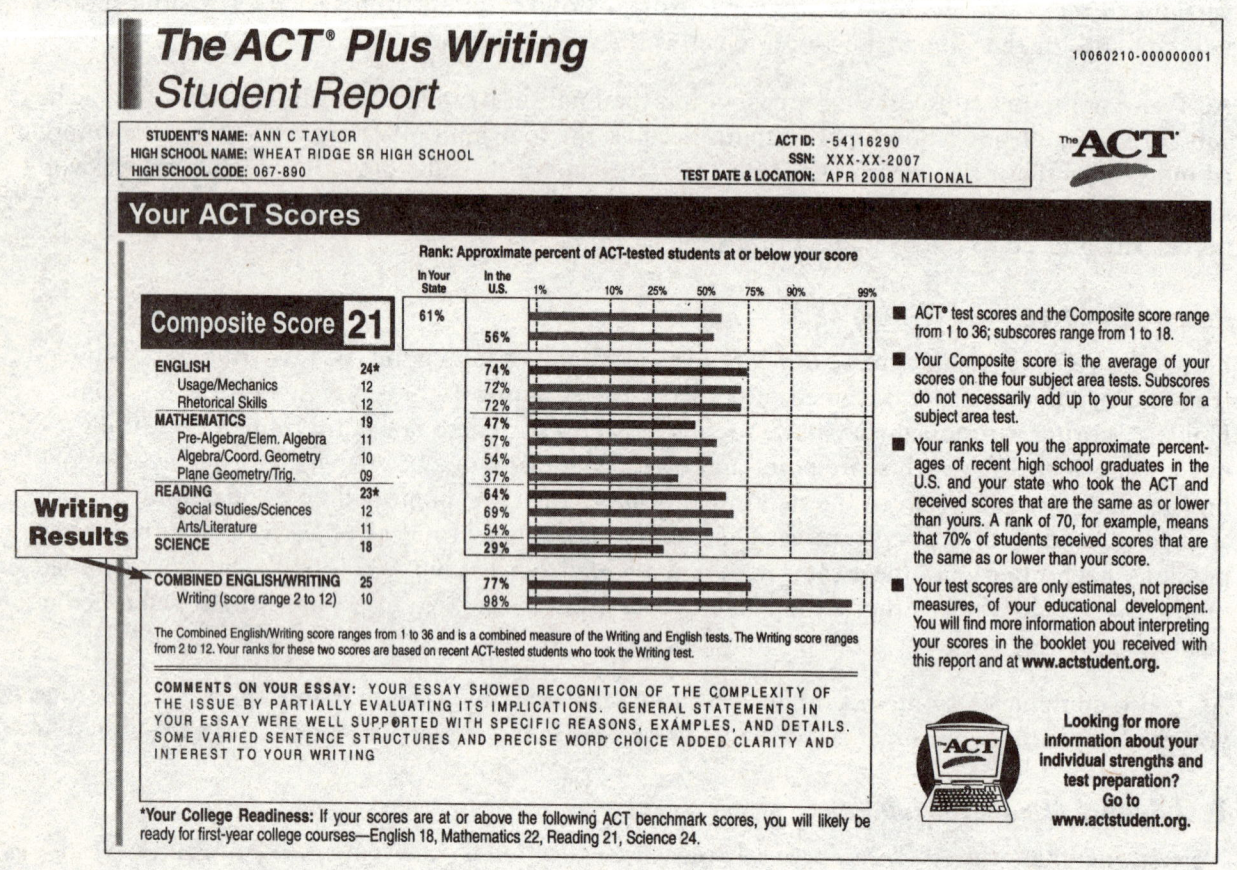

Using Ranks to Interpret Your Scores

In the example above, the imaginary Ann C. Taylor is given two different kinds of scores, scale scores and ranks, to describe her performance in the different test areas. Ranks are one way to interpret ACT test scores. A score's rank shows the percent of recent high school graduates who took the ACT and who scored *at* or *below* that score. In the example, Ann's ACT Composite score is 21. If you look to the right of that score, you'll see 61%. This number—the state rank for Ann's Composite score—means that 61% of ACT-tested students in Ann's state had ACT Composite scores that were the same as or lower than Ann's Composite score. Next to the right is 56%. This number—the national rank for Ann's Composite score—means that 56% of ACT-tested students nationwide had ACT Composite scores that were the same as or lower than Ann's Composite score. Test scores and percentile ranks are only estimates of Ann's level of academic skills and knowledge.

Comparing Your Test Scores to Each Other

Another way to interpret your ACT test scores is by comparing them to each other using the ranks. You may find it interesting, for example, to compare your ranks for the Science and Mathematics Tests to your ranks for the Reading and English Tests. Perhaps you've felt more comfortable and successful in some subject areas than in others. Making comparisons among your ACT test ranks can be especially helpful as you make decisions about the courses you will take in high school and college. A high rank in a particular area may indicate a good chance of success in related college majors and careers. A low rank may indicate that you need to develop your skills more in that area.

It's important to know that scale scores from the different individual tests can't be directly compared to each other. If you earn scores of 23 on the ACT English and Mathematics Tests, for example, this doesn't necessarily mean that your levels of skill and knowledge in English are the same as they are in mathematics. The percentile ranks corresponding to the scores—not the scores themselves—are probably best for making comparisons among subject areas.

Comparing Your Scores to Your High School Grades

After you take the ACT and receive your student report, you'll want to compare your scores to your high school grades using the ranks. Are your highest grades and highest ACT test scores in the same content areas? If so, you might want to consider college majors that would draw on your areas of greatest strength. On the other hand, if your grades and scores differ, talk with your counselor about possible reasons for the differences.

Comparing Your Scores to Those of Enrolled First-Year College Students

Another way to understand your ACT test scores is by comparing them to the scores of students enrolled at colleges or universities you're interested in attending. This information can be very useful as you make decisions about applying for college. Keep in mind that admissions offices use a number of measures—including high school grades, recommendations, and extracurricular activities—to determine how students are likely to perform at their schools. Still, knowing that your ACT test scores are similar to those of students already enrolled at a college or university you're considering may make you more confident in applying for admission there. A chart in the *ACT Student Report* will help you compare your ACT scores to those of first-year students at the schools you indicate when you register for the ACT. See the sample chart for Ann C. Taylor on the following page.

Your College Reports

At your direction, your scores from this test date are being reported to the colleges shown below. College planning information is provided for the first four choices you listed when you registered or tested. (Fifth and sixth choices, if any, appear just above your first choice.) Your GPA was calculated from the grades you reported. To view additional college planning information or to send additional reports, visit www.actstudent.org.

College Name and Code	What is the profile of enrolled 1st-year students at this college?			Is the program of study you prefer offered?	What are the approximate annual tuition and fees?		What percent of 1st-year students receive financial aid based on:	
	High School Class Rank	ACT Composite Score	High School Grade Point Average		In-state	Out-of-state	Need?	Merit?
UNIVERSITY OF OMEGA 9521 OMEGA CO 800/498-6068 www.omega.edu	Majority in top 50%	Middle 50% between 18–24	2.76	Yes: 4-Yr. Degree	$5,600	$12,000	67%	20%
ALPHA UNIVERSITY 9059 UNIVERSITY CENTER IA 319/337-1000 www.alpha.edu	Majority in top 25%	Middle 50% between 21–26	3.12	Yes: 4-Yr. Degree	$9,000	$15,000	85%	27%
BETA COMMUNITY COLLEGE 6866 CLARKSTON CO 800/498-6481 www.betacc.edu	Majority in top 75%	Middle 50% between 16–21	2.49	Yes: Program Avail	$4,000	$4,000	58%	18%
MAGNA COLLEGE 8905 PLAINVIEW OH 800/525-6926 www.magna.edu	Majority in top 50%	Middle 50% between 21–26	2.71	Yes: 4-Yr. Degree	$8,500	$16,000	90%	35%

Your Information ➤

Your Class Rank	Your Composite Score	Your Calculated GPA	Your Selected Major
TOP 25%	21	3.29	BUSINESS & MGMT, GEN

Check with colleges for recent changes in information.   A dash (—) indicates information was not provided or could not be calculated.   *Comprehensive fee including room and board.   © 2008 by ACT, Inc. All rights reserved.

Using College Readiness Standards™ to Help You Understand Your ACT Scores

After you calculate your scores, you may wonder what your test scores *really* mean. In other words, what do your test scores tell you about your knowledge and skills in English, math, reading, and science? One way to understand this is to consider your scores from the perspective of what students who have that score are likely to know and be able to do. ACT developed the College Readiness Standards™ to tell you exactly that.

What Are College Readiness Standards?

The College Readiness Standards are sets of statements that describe what students are *likely* to know and be able to do in each content area based on their scores on each of the tests (English, Mathematics, Reading, Science, and Writing). The statements serve as score descriptors and reflect a progression of skills and knowledge in a particular content area. The College Readiness Standards are reported in terms of score range, so that the statements describe the knowledge and skills that students *typically* demonstrate who score in these different score ranges on the multiple-choice tests: 13–15, 16–19, 20–23, 24–27, 28–32, 33–36. A score of 1–12 indicates the student is most likely beginning to develop the knowledge and skills described in the 13–15 score range for that particular test. For the Writing Test, which is scored on a different scale, the score ranges are 3–4, 5–6, 7–8, 9–10, and 11–12. A score below 3 does not permit useful generalizations about the student's writing abilities. All the College Readiness Standards are cumulative, meaning that students typically can also demonstrate the skills and knowledge described in the score ranges below the range in which they scored.

How Can the College Readiness Standards Help You?

The purpose of the College Readiness Standards is to help you and others better understand what your ACT scores indicate about the knowledge and skills you likely have, and what areas might need further development for you to be better prepared for college.

Because the College Readiness Standards provide statements that describe what you are *likely* to know and be able to do, you can use that information to help zero in on what specific things you should do to further develop your college readiness. If, for example, you scored in the 16–19 range on the English Test, you might infer that you are likely able to do and know the skills and knowledge described in the 13–15 and in the 16–19 range. You might choose to take a closer look at the Standards in the 20–23 and higher score ranges to see what courses to take, or what instruction you might want to get, to develop those particular areas in order to be better prepared for college. In other words, you can use the College Readiness Standards to help you select courses and instruction that will focus on preparing you for college.

College Readiness Benchmarks

Your College Readiness

ACT has identified the minimum score needed on each ACT test to indicate a 50% chance of obtaining a B or higher or about a 75% chance of obtaining a C or higher in the corresponding first-year college course. Each of your scores that is at or above the benchmark for that subject area is marked with an asterisk (*) on your score report.

ACT Test	ACT Benchmark Score	College Course
English	18	English Composition
Math	22	Algebra
Reading	21	Social Sciences/Humanities
Science	24	Biology

To increase your college readiness, consider taking additional rigorous coursework before you enter college. When you meet with your academic advisor to plan your first-year college courses, select courses that are appropriate for your academic background and reflect your planned curriculum. On the ACT Writing Test, ACT's research to date suggests that examinees with a Writing subscore of 7 or higher possess sufficient general writing skills to be ready for college-level writing assignments.

College Readiness Standards — English		
Topic Development in Terms of Purpose and Focus	**Organization, Unity, and Coherence**	**Word Choice in Terms of Style, Tone, Clarity, and Economy**
13–15	Use conjunctive adverbs or phrases to show time relationships in simple narrative essays (e.g., *then*, *this time*)	Revise sentences to correct awkward and confusing arrangements of sentence elements Revise vague nouns and pronouns that create obvious logic problems
16–19 Identify the basic purpose or role of a specified phrase or sentence Delete a clause or sentence because it is obviously irrelevant to the essay	Select the most logical place to add a sentence in a paragraph	Delete obviously synonymous and wordy material in a sentence Revise expressions that deviate from the style of an essay
20–23 Identify the central idea or main topic of a straightforward piece of writing Determine relevancy when presented with a variety of sentence-level details	Use conjunctive adverbs or phrases to express straightforward logical relationships (e.g., *first*, *afterward*, *in response*) Decide the most logical place to add a sentence in an essay Add a sentence that introduces a simple paragraph	Delete redundant material when information is repeated in different parts of speech (e.g., "alarmingly startled") Use the word or phrase most consistent with the style and tone of a fairly straightforward essay Determine the clearest and most logical conjunction to link clauses
24–27 Identify the focus of a simple essay, applying that knowledge to add a sentence that sharpens that focus or to determine if an essay has met a specified goal Delete material primarily because it disturbs the flow and development of the paragraph Add a sentence to accomplish a fairly straightforward purpose such as illustrating a given statement	Determine the need for conjunctive adverbs or phrases to create subtle logical connections between sentences (e.g., *therefore*, *however*, *in addition*) Rearrange the sentences in a fairly uncomplicated paragraph for the sake of logic Add a sentence to introduce or conclude the essay or to provide a transition between paragraphs when the essay is fairly straightforward	Revise a phrase that is redundant in terms of the meaning and logic of the entire sentence Identify and correct ambiguous pronoun references Use the word or phrase most appropriate in terms of the content of the sentence and tone of the essay
28–32 Apply an awareness of the focus and purpose of a fairly involved essay to determine the rhetorical effect and suitability of an existing phrase or sentence, or to determine the need to delete plausible but irrelevant material Add a sentence to accomplish a subtle rhetorical purpose such as to emphasize, to add supporting detail, or to express meaning through connotation	Make sophisticated distinctions concerning the logical use of conjunctive adverbs or phrases, particularly when signaling a shift between paragraphs Rearrange sentences to improve the logic and coherence of a complex paragraph Add a sentence to introduce or conclude a fairly complex paragraph	Correct redundant material that involves sophisticated vocabulary and sounds acceptable as conversational English (e.g., "an aesthetic viewpoint" versus "the outlook of an aesthetic viewpoint") Correct vague and wordy or clumsy and confusing writing containing sophisticated language
33–36 Determine whether a complex essay has accomplished a specific purpose Add a phrase or sentence to accomplish a complex purpose, often expressed in terms of the main focus of the essay	Consider the need for introductory sentences or transitions, basing decisions on a thorough understanding of both the logic and rhetorical effect of the paragraph and essay	Delete redundant material that involves subtle concepts or that is redundant in terms of the paragraph as a whole

College Readiness Standards — English (continued)

	Sentence Structure and Formation	Conventions of Usage	Conventions of Punctuation
13–15	Use conjunctions or punctuation to join simple clauses Revise shifts in verb tense between simple clauses in a sentence or between simple adjoining sentences	Solve such basic grammatical problems as how to form the past and past participle of irregular but commonly used verbs and how to form comparative and superlative adjectives	Delete commas that create basic sense problems (e.g., between verb and direct object)
16–19	Determine the need for punctuation and conjunctions to avoid awkward-sounding sentence fragments and fused sentences Decide the appropriate verb tense and voice by considering the meaning of the entire sentence	Solve such grammatical problems as whether to use an adverb or adjective form, how to ensure straightforward subject-verb and pronoun-antecedent agreement, and which preposition to use in simple contexts Recognize and use the appropriate word in frequently confused pairs such as *there* and *their*, *past* and *passed*, and *led* and *lead*	Provide appropriate punctuation in straightforward situations (e.g., items in a series) Delete commas that disturb the sentence flow (e.g., between modifier and modified element)
20–23	Recognize and correct marked disturbances of sentence flow and structure (e.g., participial phrase fragments, missing or incorrect relative pronouns, dangling or misplaced modifiers)	Use idiomatically appropriate prepositions, especially in combination with verbs (e.g., *long for*, *appeal to*) Ensure that a verb agrees with its subject when there is some text between the two	Use commas to set off simple parenthetical phrases Delete unnecessary commas when an incorrect reading of the sentence suggests a pause that should be punctuated (e.g., between verb and direct object clause)
24–27	Revise to avoid faulty placement of phrases and faulty coordination and subordination of clauses in sentences with subtle structural problems Maintain consistent verb tense and pronoun person on the basis of the preceding clause or sentence	Ensure that a pronoun agrees with its antecedent when the two occur in separate clauses or sentences Identify the correct past and past participle forms of irregular and infrequently used verbs and form present-perfect verbs by using *have* rather than *of*	Use punctuation to set off complex parenthetical phrases Recognize and delete unnecessary commas based on a careful reading of a complicated sentence (e.g., between the elements of a compound subject or compound verb joined by *and*) Use apostrophes to indicate simple possessive nouns Recognize inappropriate uses of colons and semicolons
28–32	Use sentence-combining techniques, effectively avoiding problematic comma splices, run-on sentences, and sentence fragments, especially in sentences containing compound subjects or verbs Maintain a consistent and logical use of verb tense and pronoun person on the basis of information in the paragraph or essay as a whole	Correctly use reflexive pronouns, the possessive pronouns *its* and *your*, and the relative pronouns *who* and *whom* Ensure that a verb agrees with its subject in unusual situations (e.g., when the subject-verb order is inverted or when the subject is an indefinite pronoun)	Use commas to set off a nonessential/nonrestrictive appositive or clause Deal with multiple punctuation problems (e.g., compound sentences containing unnecessary commas and phrases that may or may not be parenthetical) Use an apostrophe to show possession, especially with irregular plural nouns Use a semicolon to indicate a relationship between closely related independent clauses
33–36	Work comfortably with long sentences and complex clausal relationships within sentences, avoiding weak conjunctions between independent clauses and maintaining parallel structure between clauses	Provide idiomatically and contextually appropriate prepositions following verbs in situations involving sophisticated language or ideas Ensure that a verb agrees with its subject when a phrase or clause between the two suggests a different number for the verb	Use a colon to introduce an example or an elaboration

College Readiness Standards — Mathematics

	Basic Operations & Applications	Probability, Statistics, & Data Analysis	Numbers: Concepts & Properties	Expressions, Equations, & Inequalities
13–15	Perform one-operation computation with whole numbers and decimals Solve problems in one or two steps using whole numbers Perform common conversions (e.g., inches to feet or hours to minutes)	Calculate the average of a list of positive whole numbers Perform a single computation using information from a table or chart	Recognize equivalent fractions and fractions in lowest terms	Exhibit knowledge of basic expressions (e.g., identify an expression for a total as $b + g$) Solve equations in the form $x + a = b$, where a and b are whole numbers or decimals
16–19	Solve routine one-step arithmetic problems (using whole numbers, fractions, and decimals) such as single-step percent Solve some routine two-step arithmetic problems	Calculate the average of a list of numbers Calculate the average, given the number of data values and the sum of the data values Read tables and graphs Perform computations on data from tables and graphs Use the relationship between the probability of an event and the probability of its complement	Recognize one-digit factors of a number Identify a digit's place value	Substitute whole numbers for unknown quantities to evaluate expressions Solve one-step equations having integer or decimal answers Combine like terms (e.g., $2x + 5x$)
20–23	Solve routine two-step or three-step arithmetic problems involving concepts such as rate and proportion, tax added, percentage off, and computing with a given average	Calculate the missing data value, given the average and all data values but one Translate from one representation of data to another (e.g., a bar graph to a circle graph) Determine the probability of a simple event Exhibit knowledge of simple counting techniques	Exhibit knowledge of elementary number concepts including rounding, the ordering of decimals, pattern identification, absolute value, primes, and greatest common factor	Evaluate algebraic expressions by substituting integers for unknown quantities Add and subtract simple algebraic expressions Solve routine first-degree equations Perform straightforward word-to-symbol translations Multiply two binomials
24–27	Solve multi-step arithmetic problems that involve planning or converting units of measure (e.g., feet per second to miles per hour)	Calculate the average, given the frequency counts of all the data values Manipulate data from tables and graphs Compute straightforward probabilities for common situations Use Venn diagrams in counting	Find and use the least common multiple Order fractions Work with numerical factors Work with scientific notation Work with squares and square roots of numbers Work problems involving positive integer exponents Work with cubes and cube roots of numbers Determine when an expression is undefined Exhibit some knowledge of the complex numbers	Solve real-world problems using first-degree equations Write expressions, equations, or inequalities with a single variable for common pre-algebra settings (e.g., rate and distance problems and problems that can be solved by using proportions) Identify solutions to simple quadratic equations Add, subtract, and multiply polynomials Factor simple quadratics (e.g., the difference of squares and perfect square trinomials) Solve first-degree inequalities that do not require reversing the inequality sign
28–32	Solve word problems containing several rates, proportions, or percentages	Calculate or use a weighted average Interpret and use information from figures, tables, and graphs Apply counting techniques Compute a probability when the event and/or sample space are not given or obvious	Apply number properties involving prime factorization Apply number properties involving even/odd numbers and factors/multiples Apply number properties involving positive/negative numbers Apply rules of exponents Multiply two complex numbers	Manipulate expressions and equations Write expressions, equations, and inequalities for common algebra settings Solve linear inequalities that require reversing the inequality sign Solve absolute value equations Solve quadratic equations Find solutions to systems of linear equations
33–36	Solve complex arithmetic problems involving percent of increase or decrease and problems requiring integration of several concepts from pre-algebra and/or pre-geometry (e.g., comparing percentages or averages, using several ratios, and finding ratios in geometry settings)	Distinguish between mean, median, and mode for a list of numbers Analyze and draw conclusions based on information from figures, tables, and graphs Exhibit knowledge of conditional and joint probability	Draw conclusions based on number concepts, algebraic properties, and/or relationships between expressions and numbers Exhibit knowledge of logarithms and geometric sequences Apply properties of complex numbers	Write expressions that require planning and/or manipulating to accurately model a situation Write equations and inequalities that require planning, manipulating, and/or solving Solve simple absolute value inequalities

College Readiness Standards — Mathematics (continued)

	Graphical Representations	**Properties of Plane Figures**	**Measurement**	**Functions**
13–15	Identify the location of a point with a positive coordinate on the number line		Estimate or calculate the length of a line segment based on other lengths given on a geometric figure	
16–19	Locate points on the number line and in the first quadrant	Exhibit some knowledge of the angles associated with parallel lines	Compute the perimeter of polygons when all side lengths are given Compute the area of rectangles when whole number dimensions are given	
20–23	Locate points in the coordinate plane Comprehend the concept of length on the number line Exhibit knowledge of slope	Find the measure of an angle using properties of parallel lines Exhibit knowledge of basic angle properties and special sums of angle measures (e.g., 90°, 180°, and 360°)	Compute the area and perimeter of triangles and rectangles in simple problems Use geometric formulas when all necessary information is given	Evaluate quadratic functions, expressed in function notation, at integer values
24–27	Identify the graph of a linear inequality on the number line Determine the slope of a line from points or equations Match linear graphs with their equations Find the midpoint of a line segment	Use several angle properties to find an unknown angle measure Recognize Pythagorean triples Use properties of isosceles triangles	Compute the area of triangles and rectangles when one or more additional simple steps are required Compute the area and circumference of circles after identifying necessary information Compute the perimeter of simple composite geometric figures with unknown side lengths	Evaluate polynomial functions, expressed in function notation, at integer values Express the sine, cosine, and tangent of an angle in a right triangle as a ratio of given side lengths
28–32	Interpret and use information from graphs in the coordinate plane Match number line graphs with solution sets of linear inequalities Use the distance formula Use properties of parallel and perpendicular lines to determine an equation of a line or coordinates of a point Recognize special characteristics of parabolas and circles (e.g., the vertex of a parabola and the center or radius of a circle)	Apply properties of 30°-60°-90°, 45°-45°-90°, similar, and congruent triangles Use the Pythagorean theorem	Use relationships involving area, perimeter, and volume of geometric figures to compute another measure	Evaluate composite functions at integer values Apply basic trigonometric ratios to solve right-triangle problems
33–36	Match number line graphs with solution sets of simple quadratic inequalities Identify characteristics of graphs based on a set of conditions or on a general equation such as $y = ax^2 + c$ Solve problems integrating multiple algebraic and/or geometric concepts Analyze and draw conclusions based on information from graphs in the coordinate plane	Draw conclusions based on a set of conditions Solve multistep geometry problems that involve integrating concepts, planning, visualization, and/or making connections with other content areas Use relationships among angles, arcs, and distances in a circle	Use scale factors to determine the magnitude of a size change Compute the area of composite geometric figures when planning or visualization is required	Write an expression for the composite of two simple functions Use trigonometric concepts and basic identities to solve problems Exhibit knowledge of unit circle trigonometry Match graphs of basic trigonometric functions with their equations

College Readiness Standards — Reading

	Main Ideas and Author's Approach	Supporting Details
13–15	Recognize a clear intent of an author or narrator in uncomplicated literary narratives	Locate basic facts (e.g., names, dates, events) clearly stated in a passage
16–19	Identify a clear main idea or purpose of straightforward paragraphs in uncomplicated literary narratives	Locate simple details at the sentence and paragraph level in uncomplicated passages Recognize a clear function of a part of an uncomplicated passage
20–23	Infer the main idea or purpose of straightforward paragraphs in uncomplicated literary narratives Understand the overall approach taken by an author or narrator (e.g., point of view, kinds of evidence used) in uncomplicated passages	Locate important details in uncomplicated passages Make simple inferences about how details are used in passages
24–27	Identify a clear main idea or purpose of any paragraph or paragraphs in uncomplicated passages Infer the main idea or purpose of straightforward paragraphs in more challenging passages Summarize basic events and ideas in more challenging passages Understand the overall approach taken by an author or narrator (e.g., point of view, kinds of evidence used) in more challenging passages	Locate important details in more challenging passages Locate and interpret minor or subtly stated details in uncomplicated passages Discern which details, though they may appear in different sections throughout a passage, support important points in more challenging passages
28–32	Infer the main idea or purpose of more challenging passages or their paragraphs Summarize events and ideas in virtually any passage Understand the overall approach taken by an author or narrator (e.g., point of view, kinds of evidence used) in virtually any passage	Locate and interpret minor or subtly stated details in more challenging passages Use details from different sections of some complex informational passages to support a specific point or argument
33–36	Identify clear main ideas or purposes of complex passages or their paragraphs	Locate and interpret details in complex passages Understand the function of a part of a passage when the function is subtle or complex

Descriptions of the ACT Reading Passages

Uncomplicated Literary Narratives refers to excerpts from essays, short stories, and novels that tend to use simple language and structure, have a clear purpose and a familiar style, present straightforward interactions between characters, and employ only a limited number of literary devices such as metaphor, simile, or hyperbole.

More Challenging Literary Narratives refers to excerpts from essays, short stories, and novels that tend to make moderate use of figurative language, have a more intricate structure and messages conveyed with some subtlety, and may feature somewhat complex interactions between characters.

Complex Literary Narratives refers to excerpts from essays, short stories, and novels that tend to make generous use of ambiguous language and literary devices, feature complex and subtle interactions between characters, often contain challenging context-dependent vocabulary, and typically contain messages and/or meanings that are not explicit but are embedded in the passage.

College Readiness Standards — Reading (continued)

	Sequential, Comparative, and Cause-Effect Relationships	Meanings of Words	Generalizations and Conclusions
13–15	Determine when (e.g., first, last, before, after) or if an event occurred in uncomplicated passages Recognize clear cause-effect relationships described within a single sentence in a passage	Understand the implication of a familiar word or phrase and of simple descriptive language	Draw simple generalizations and conclusions about the main characters in uncomplicated literary narratives
16–19	Identify relationships between main characters in uncomplicated literary narratives Recognize clear cause-effect relationships within a single paragraph in uncomplicated literary narratives	Use context to understand basic figurative language	Draw simple generalizations and conclusions about people, ideas, and so on in uncomplicated passages
20–23	Order simple sequences of events in uncomplicated literary narratives Identify clear relationships between people, ideas, and so on in uncomplicated passages Identify clear cause-effect relationships in uncomplicated passages	Use context to determine the appropriate meaning of some figurative and nonfigurative words, phrases, and statements in uncomplicated passages	Draw generalizations and conclusions about people, ideas, and so on in uncomplicated passages Draw simple generalizations and conclusions using details that support the main points of more challenging passages
24–27	Order sequences of events in uncomplicated passages Understand relationships between people, ideas, and so on in uncomplicated passages Identify clear relationships between characters, ideas, and so on in more challenging literary narratives Understand implied or subtly stated cause-effect relationships in uncomplicated passages Identify clear cause-effect relationships in more challenging passages	Use context to determine the appropriate meaning of virtually any word, phrase, or statement in uncomplicated passages Use context to determine the appropriate meaning of some figurative and nonfigurative words, phrases, and statements in more challenging passages	Draw subtle generalizations and conclusions about characters, ideas, and so on in uncomplicated literary narratives Draw generalizations and conclusions about people, ideas, and so on in more challenging passages
28–32	Order sequences of events in more challenging passages Understand the dynamics between people, ideas, and so on in more challenging passages Understand implied or subtly stated cause-effect relationships in more challenging passages	Determine the appropriate meaning of words, phrases, or statements from figurative or somewhat technical contexts	Use information from one or more sections of a more challenging passage to draw generalizations and conclusions about people, ideas, and so on
33–36	Order sequences of events in complex passages Understand the subtleties in relationships between people, ideas, and so on in virtually any passage Understand implied, subtle, or complex cause-effect relationships in virtually any passage	Determine, even when the language is richly figurative and the vocabulary is difficult, the appropriate meaning of context-dependent words, phrases, or statements in virtually any passage	Draw complex or subtle generalizations and conclusions about people, ideas, and so on, often by synthesizing information from different portions of the passage Understand and generalize about portions of a complex literary narrative

Uncomplicated Informational Passages refers to materials that tend to contain a limited amount of data, address basic concepts using familiar language and conventional organizational patterns, have a clear purpose, and are written to be accessible.

More Challenging Informational Passages refers to materials that tend to present concepts that are not always stated explicitly and that are accompanied or illustrated by more—and more detailed—supporting data, include some difficult context-dependent words, and are written in a somewhat more demanding and less accessible style.

Complex Informational Passages refers to materials that tend to include a sizable amount of data, present difficult concepts that are embedded (not explicit) in the text, use demanding words and phrases whose meaning must be determined from context, and are likely to include intricate explanations of processes or events.

College Readiness Standards — ACT Writing Test

	Expressing Judgments	Focusing on the Topic	Developing a Position
3–4	Show a little understanding of the persuasive purpose of the task but neglect to take or to maintain a position on the issue in the prompt Show limited recognition of the complexity of the issue in the prompt	Maintain a focus on the general topic in the prompt through most of the essay	Offer a little development, with one or two ideas; if examples are given, they are general and may not be clearly relevant; resort often to merely repeating ideas Show little or no movement between general and specific ideas and examples
5–6	Show a basic understanding of the persuasive purpose of the task by taking a position on the issue in the prompt but may not maintain that position Show a little recognition of the complexity of the issue in the prompt by acknowledging, but only briefly describing, a counterargument to the writer's position	Maintain a focus on the general topic in the prompt throughout the essay	Offer limited development of ideas using a few general examples; resort sometimes to merely repeating ideas Show little movement between general and specific ideas and examples
7–8	Show understanding of the persuasive purpose of the task by taking a position on the issue in the prompt Show some recognition of the complexity of the issue in the prompt by • acknowledging counterarguments to the writer's position • providing some response to counter-arguments to the writer's position	Maintain a focus on the general topic in the prompt throughout the essay and attempt a focus on the specific issue in the prompt Present a thesis that establishes focus on the topic	Develop ideas by using some specific reasons, details, and examples Show some movement between general and specific ideas and examples
9–10	Show clear understanding of the persuasive purpose of the task by taking a position on the specific issue in the prompt and offering a broad context for discussion Show recognition of the complexity of the issue in the prompt by • partially evaluating implications and/or complications of the issue, and/or • posing and partially responding to counter-arguments to the writer's position	Maintain a focus on discussion of the specific topic and issue in the prompt throughout the essay Present a thesis that establishes a focus on the writer's position on the issue	Develop most ideas fully, using some specific and relevant reasons, details, and examples Show clear movement between general and specific ideas and examples
11–12	Show clear understanding of the persuasive purpose of the task by taking a position on the specific issue in the prompt and offering a critical context for discussion Show understanding of the complexity of the issue in the prompt by • examining different perspectives, and/or • evaluating implications or complications of the issue, and/or • posing and fully discussing counter-arguments to the writer's position	Maintain a clear focus on discussion of the specific topic and issue in the prompt throughout the essay Present a critical thesis that clearly establishes the focus on the writer's position on the issue	Develop several ideas fully, using specific and relevant reasons, details, and examples Show effective movement between general and specific ideas and examples

College Readiness Standards — ACT Writing Test (continued)

	Organizing Ideas	**Using Language**
3–4	Provide a discernible organization with some logical grouping of ideas in parts of the essay Use a few simple and obvious transitions Present a discernible, though minimally developed, introduction and conclusion	Show limited control of language by • correctly employing some of the conventions of standard English grammar, usage, and mechanics, but with distracting errors that sometimes significantly impede understanding • using simple vocabulary • using simple sentence structure
5–6	Provide a simple organization with logical grouping of ideas in parts of the essay Use some simple and obvious transitional words, though they may at times be inappropriate or misleading Present a discernible, though underdeveloped, introduction and conclusion	Show a basic control of language by • correctly employing some of the conventions of standard English grammar, usage, and mechanics, but with distracting errors that sometimes impede understanding • using simple but appropriate vocabulary • using a little sentence variety, though most sentences are simple in structure
7–8	Provide an adequate but simple organization with logical grouping of ideas in parts of the essay but with little evidence of logical progression of ideas Use some simple and obvious, but appropriate, transitional words and phrases Present a discernible introduction and conclusion with a little development	Show adequate use of language to communicate by • correctly employing many of the conventions of standard English grammar, usage, and mechanics, but with some distracting errors that may occasionally impede understanding • using appropriate vocabulary • using some varied kinds of sentence structures to vary pace
9–10	Provide unity and coherence throughout the essay, sometimes with a logical progression of ideas Use relevant, though at times simple and obvious, transitional words and phrases to convey logical relationships between ideas Present a somewhat developed introduction and conclusion	Show competent use of language to communicate ideas by • correctly employing most conventions of standard English grammar, usage, and mechanics, with a few distracting errors but none that impede understanding • using some precise and varied vocabulary • using several kinds of sentence structures to vary pace and to support meaning
11–12	Provide unity and coherence throughout the essay, often with a logical progression of ideas Use relevant transitional words, phrases, and sentences to convey logical relationships between ideas Present a well-developed introduction and conclusion	Show effective use of language to clearly communicate ideas by • correctly employing most conventions of standard English grammar, usage, and mechanics, with just a few, if any, errors • using precise and varied vocabulary • using a variety of kinds of sentence structures to vary pace and to support meaning

College Readiness Standards — Science

	Interpretation of Data	Scientific Investigation	Evaluation of Models, Inferences, and Experimental Results
13–15	Select a single piece of data (numerical or nonnumerical) from a simple data presentation (e.g., a table or graph with two or three variables; a food web diagram) Identify basic features of a table, graph, or diagram (e.g., headings, units of measurement, axis labels)		
16–19	Select two or more pieces of data from a simple data presentation Understand basic scientific terminology Find basic information in a brief body of text Determine how the value of one variable changes as the value of another variable changes in a simple data presentation	Understand the methods and tools used in a simple experiment	
20–23	Select data from a complex data presentation (e.g., a table or graph with more than three variables; a phase diagram) Compare or combine data from a simple data presentation (e.g., order or sum data from a table) Translate information into a table, graph, or diagram	Understand the methods and tools used in a moderately complex experiment Understand a simple experimental design Identify a control in an experiment Identify similarities and differences between experiments	Select a simple hypothesis, prediction, or conclusion that is supported by a data presentation or a model Identify key issues or assumptions in a model
24–27	Compare or combine data from two or more simple data presentations (e.g., categorize data from a table using a scale from another table) Compare or combine data from a complex data presentation Interpolate between data points in a table or graph Determine how the value of one variable changes as the value of another variable changes in a complex data presentation Identify and/or use a simple (e.g., linear) mathematical relationship between data Analyze given information when presented with new, simple information	Understand the methods and tools used in a complex experiment Understand a complex experimental design Predict the results of an additional trial or measurement in an experiment Determine the experimental conditions that would produce specified results	Select a simple hypothesis, prediction, or conclusion that is supported by two or more data presentations or models Determine whether given information supports or contradicts a simple hypothesis or conclusion, and why Identify strengths and weaknesses in one or more models Identify similarities and differences between models Determine which model(s) is(are) supported or weakened by new information Select a data presentation or a model that supports or contradicts a hypothesis, prediction, or conclusion
28–32	Compare or combine data from a simple data presentation with data from a complex data presentation Identify and/or use a complex (e.g., nonlinear) mathematical relationship between data Extrapolate from data points in a table or graph	Determine the hypothesis for an experiment Identify an alternate method for testing a hypothesis	Select a complex hypothesis, prediction, or conclusion that is supported by a data presentation or model Determine whether new information supports or weakens a model, and why Use new information to make a prediction based on a model
33–36	Compare or combine data from two or more complex data presentations Analyze given information when presented with new, complex information	Understand precision and accuracy issues Predict how modifying the design or methods of an experiment will affect results Identify an additional trial or experiment that could be performed to enhance or evaluate experimental results	Select a complex hypothesis, prediction, or conclusion that is supported by two or more data presentations or models Determine whether given information supports or contradicts a complex hypothesis or conclusion, and why

Science College Readiness Standards are measured in the context of science topics students encounter in science courses. These topics may include:

Life Science/Biology	Physical Science/Chemistry, Physics	Earth & Space Science
• Animal behavior • Animal development and growth • Body systems • Cell structure and processes • Ecology • Evolution • Genetics • Homeostasis • Life cycles • Molecular basis of heredity • Origin of life • Photosynthesis • Plant development, growth, structure • Populations • Taxonomy	• Atomic structure • Chemical bonding, equations, nomenclature, reactions • Electrical circuits • Elements, compounds, mixtures • Force and motions • Gravitation • Heat and work • Kinetic and potential energy • Magnetism • Momentum • The Periodic Table • Properties of solutions • Sound and light • States, classes, and properties of matter • Waves	• Earthquakes and volcanoes • Earth's atmosphere • Earth's resources • Fossils and geological time • Geochemical cycles • Groundwater • Lakes, rivers, oceans • Mass movements • Plate tectonics • Rocks, minerals • Solar system • Stars, galaxies, and the universe • Water cycle • Weather and climate • Weathering and erosion

Reviewing Your Performance on the Practice Tests

After you have determined your scores, consider the following as you evaluate how you did on the practice tests.

- **Did you run out of time before you completed a test?** If so, read the sections in this book on pacing yourself. Perhaps you need to adjust the way you used your time in responding to the questions. It is to your advantage to answer every question and pace yourself so that you can do so. **Remember, there is no penalty for guessing.**

- **Did you spend too much time trying to understand the directions to the tests?** If so, study the directions for each test again thoroughly. The directions in the practice test are exactly like the directions that will appear in your test booklet on the test day. Make sure you understand them now, so you won't have to spend too much time studying them when you take the actual test.

- **Review the questions that you missed.** Did you select a response that was an incomplete answer or that did not directly respond to the question being asked? Use the explanatory answers following each practice test to help you identify any mistakes you may have made, and to learn how to avoid making those mistakes again.

  Did a particular type of question confuse you? Did the questions you missed come from a particular subscore area? In reviewing your responses to the practice test, check to see whether a particular type of question or a particular subscore area was more difficult for you or took more of your time.

Get All the Information You Can

Your *ACT Student Report* will provide additional information to help you understand your ACT test results and use them in making important decisions about college and exploring possible future careers. You'll also want to review the booklet *Using Your ACT Results* available on the website. This booklet not only lists activities designed to help you identify and explore career options, but also includes other practical information.

As you approach decisions about college and careers, be sure to take advantage of all the assistance you can find. Talk to your parents, counselors, and teachers; visit your local library; and write directly to colleges in which you're interested. The more you can find out about all the educational options available to you and the level of your academic skills and knowledge (using such information as your ACT test results), the better prepared you'll be to make informed college and career choices.

Scoring Keys and Conversion Tables

Practice Test 1

Scoring Your Multiple-Choice Practice Test

To score your multiple-choice practice test, follow these eight steps:

STEP 1. Write a "1" in the blank for each English Test question that you answered correctly. An example is provided in the box below:

	Key	Subscore Area*		Your answer was
		UM	RH	
1.	A			Incorrect
2.	J		1	Correct
3.	B		1	Correct
4.	G			Incorrect

English Scoring Key Practice Test 1

	Key	Subscore Area*			Key	Subscore Area*			Key	Subscore Area*	
		UM	RH			UM	RH			UM	RH
1.	C	___		26.	F		___	51.	C		___
2.	G	___		27.	D		___	52.	F		___
3.	A	___		28.	J			53.	B	___	
4.	F	___		29.	B	___		54.	F		___
5.	C		___	30.	J	___		55.	D	___	
6.	G	___		31.	B	___		56.	F		___
7.	C	___		32.	J	___		57.	B	___	
8.	F	___		33.	C	___		58.	G	___	
9.	D		___	34.	F	___		59.	C	___	
10.	J		___	35.	D		___	60.	J	___	
11.	B	___		36.	G		___	61.	D	___	
12.	J	___		37.	B		___	62.	H	___	
13.	B	___		38.	G	___		63.	D	___	
14.	H	___		39.	A	___		64.	G		___
15.	C	___		40.	F	___		65.	A		___
16.	H		___	41.	A	___		66.	F		___
17.	B	___		42.	J	___		67.	D		___
18.	J	___		43.	C		___	68.	G		___
19.	B	___		44.	J		___	69.	A		___
20.	J		___	45.	A	___		70.	F		___
21.	D		___	46.	J	___		71.	C		___
22.	F	___		47.	B	___		72.	H	___	
23.	A	___		48.	H	___		73.	C	___	
24.	H		___	49.	A	___		74.	H		___
25.	C	___		50.	J		___	75.	D		___

* UM = Usage/Mechanics
RH = Rhetorical Skills

STEP 2. Add up the numbers in each subscore area and enter them in the appropriate blanks in the shaded box below:

> **Number Correct (Raw Score) for:**
>
> Usage/Mechanics (UM) Subscore Area (40 questions)   _____
>
> Rhetorical Skills (RH) Subscore Area (35 questions)   _____
>
> Total Number Correct for English Test (UM + RH; 75 questions)   _____

STEP 3. Compute your total number correct for the English Test by adding the numbers you entered in Step 2. Write this total in the appropriate blank in the shaded box above. This is your raw score.

STEP 4. Repeat Steps 1 through 3 for the ACT Mathematics, Reading, and Science Tests using the scoring keys on the following pages. Note that the Science Test doesn't have subscores, so determine your raw score for that test simply by adding up the number of "1s" you entered.

Mathematics ▪ Scoring Key ▪ Practice Test 1

Key		EA	AG	GT		Key		EA	AG	GT
1.	E	—				31.	B		—	
2.	H		—			32.	J	—		
3.	A		—			33.	B			—
4.	J	—				34.	K			—
5.	D	—				35.	D		—	
6.	J			—		36.	J	—		
7.	A	—				37.	C			—
8.	F	—				38.	K			—
9.	C		—			39.	B			—
10.	H		—			40.	K			—
11.	C		—			41.	E			—
12.	K	—				42.	F			—
13.	D	—				43.	E	—		
14.	H		—			44.	G	—		
15.	C	—				45.	E		—	
16.	H	—				46.	G			—
17.	E		—			47.	D		—	
18.	J		—			48.	J		—	
19.	A	—				49.	D		—	
20.	H			—		50.	F	—		
21.	A			—		51.	A		—	
22.	H		—			52.	H			—
23.	B		—			53.	B			—
24.	G			—		54.	J			—
25.	D			—		55.	A		—	
26.	H			—		56.	K		—	
27.	B	—				57.	A		—	
28.	G			—		58.	F		—	
29.	B			—		59.	A	—		
30.	G			—		60.	K			—

* EA = Pre-Algebra/Elementary Algebra
AG = Intermediate Algebra/Coordinate Geometry
GT = Plane Geometry/Trigonometry

Number Correct (Raw Score) for:

Pre-Alg./Elem. Alg. (EA) Subscore Area (24 questions) _____

Inter. Alg./Coord. Geom. (AG) Subscore Area (18 questions) _____

Plane Geom./Trig. (GT) Subscore Area (18 questions) _____

Total Number Correct for Math Test (EA + AG + GT; 60 questions) _____

Reading ■ Scoring Key ■ Practice Test 1

	Key	Subscore Area* SS	AL		Key	Subscore Area* SS	AL		Key	Subscore Area* SS	AL
1.	A		___	15.	C	___		29.	B		___
2.	G		___	16.	G	___		30.	H		___
3.	B		___	17.	D	___		31.	B	___	
4.	F		___	18.	J	___		32.	F	___	
5.	C		___	19.	A	___		33.	D	___	
6.	J		___	20.	J	___		34.	G	___	
7.	D		___	21.	B			35.	D	___	
8.	J		___	22.	F		___	36.	H	___	
9.	C		___	23.	C		___	37.	B	___	
10.	H		___	24.	H		___	38.	F	___	
11.	B		___	25.	D		___	39.	D	___	
12.	F	___		26.	F		___	40.	H	___	
13.	A	___		27.	D		___				
14.	F	___		28.	G		___				

* SS = Social Studies/Sciences
AL = Arts/Literature

Number Correct (Raw Score) for:

Studies/Sciences (SS) Subscore Area (20 questions) _____

Arts/Literature (AL) Subscore Area (20 questions) _____

Total Number Correct for Reading Test (SS + AL; 40 questions) _____

Science Scoring Key Practice Test 1

	Key			Key			Key	
1.	B	___	15.	A	___	29.	B	___
2.	J	___	16.	H	___	30.	F	___
3.	D	___	17.	D	___	31.	C	___
4.	J	___	18.	J	___	32.	H	___
5.	B	___	19.	B	___	33.	A	___
6.	G	___	20.	F	___	34.	F	___
7.	D	___	21.	C	___	35.	C	___
8.	F	___	22.	G	___	36.	J	___
9.	C	___	23.	A	___	37.	B	___
10.	J	___	24.	J	___	38.	J	___
11.	C	___	25.	B	___	39.	A	___
12.	F	___	26.	G	___	40.	F	___
13.	A	___	27.	C	___			
14.	J	___	28.	H	___			

Number Correct (Raw Score) for:

Total Number Correct for Science Test (40 questions) _____

STEP 5. On each of the four tests, the total number of correct responses yields a raw score. Use the conversion table on the following page to convert your raw scores to scale scores. For each of the four tests, locate and circle your raw score or the range of raw scores that includes it in the conversion table. Then, read across to either outside column of the table and circle the scale score that corresponds to that raw score. As you determine your scale scores, enter them in the blanks provided on page 880. The highest possible scale score for each test is 36. The lowest possible scale score for any of the four tests is 1.

STEP 6. Compute your Composite score by averaging the four scale scores. To do this, add your four scale scores and divide the sum by 4. If the resulting number ends in a fraction, round it off to the nearest whole number. (Round down any fraction less than one-half; round up any fraction that is one-half or more.) Enter this number in the appropriate blank on page 880. This is your Composite score. The highest possible Composite score is 36. The lowest possible Composite score is 1.

Scale Score Conversion Table
Practice Test 1

Scale Score	Raw Score				Scale Score
	English	Mathematics	Reading	Science	
36	75	60	39–40	40	36
35	74	58–59	38	39	35
34	73	57	37	–	34
33	72	56	36	38	33
32	71	55	35	–	32
31	70	53–54	34	37	31
30	69	52	33	–	30
29	67–68	50–51	32	36	29
28	66	48–49	31	35	28
27	64–65	46–47	30	33–34	27
26	63	44–45	28–29	32	26
25	61–62	41–43	27	30–31	25
24	59–60	39–40	26	29	24
23	57–58	37–38	25	27–28	23
22	54–56	35–36	23–24	26	22
21	52–53	33–34	22	24–25	21
20	49–51	30–32	21	22–23	20
19	46–48	27–29	20	21	19
18	43–45	24–26	19	18–20	18
17	40–42	20–23	18	17	17
16	38–39	17–19	17	15–16	16
15	35–37	14–16	15–16	14	15
14	33–34	12–13	14	12–13	14
13	31–32	9–11	12–13	11	13
12	29–30	8	9–11	10	12
11	26–28	6–7	8	8–9	11
10	24–25	5	6–7	7	10
9	21–23	4	5	6	9
8	17–20	3	–	5	8
7	14–16	–	4	4	7
6	11–13	2	–	3	6
5	9–10	–	3	2	5
4	6–8	–	2	–	4
3	5	1	–	1	3
2	3–4	–	1	–	2
1	0–2	0	0	0	1

STEP 7. Now convert your seven raw subscores to scale subscores using the table below. For each of the seven subscore areas, locate and circle either the raw score or the range of raw scores that includes it in the table. Then read across to either outside column of the table and circle the scale subscore that corresponds to that raw subscore. As you determine your scale subscores, enter them in the blanks on page 880. The highest possible scale subscore is 18. The lowest possible scale subscore is 1.

Scale Subscore Conversion Table
Practice Test 1

Scale Subscore	English		Mathematics			Reading		Scale Subscore
	Usage/ Mechanics	Rhetorical Skills	Pre-Alg./ Elem. Alg.	Inter. Alg./ Coord. Geom.	Plane Geom./ Trigonometry	Soc. Studies/ Sciences	Arts/ Literature	
18	40	35	23–24	18	18	20	19–20	18
17	38–39	34	22	17	–	18–19	18	17
16	37	33	21	–	16–17	17	17	16
15	36	31–32	20	15–16	15	15–16	16	15
14	34–35	30	19	14	14	14	15	14
13	33	28–29	18	12–13	12–13	13	14	13
12	31–32	26–27	17	10–11	10–11	12	13	12
11	29–30	23–25	15–16	9	8–9	11	12	11
10	27–28	21–22	14	7–8	6–7	9–10	11	10
9	25–26	18–20	12–13	6	5	8	10	9
8	23–24	15–17	10–11	4–5	4	7	–	8
7	20–22	13–14	8–9	–	3	6	8–9	7
6	18–19	11–12	6–7	3	2	5	7	6
5	16–17	9–10	4–5	2	–	4	5–6	5
4	13–15	7–8	3	–	–	3	4	4
3	10–12	5–6	2	1	1	2	3	3
2	6–9	3–4	1	–	–	1	2	2
1	0–5	0–2	0	0	0	0	0–1	1

STEP 8. Use the table on page 881 to determine your estimated percentile ranks (percent at or below) for each of your scale scores. In the far left column of the table, circle your scale score for the English Test (from page 878). Then read across to the percentile rank column for that test; circle or put a check mark beside the corresponding percentile rank. Use the same procedure for the other three tests (from page 878) and for the subscore areas (from page 879). You may find it easier to use the right-hand column of scale scores for your Science Test and Composite scores. As you mark your percentile ranks, enter them in the blanks provided below. You may also find it helpful to compare your performance with the national mean (average) score for each of the four tests, the subscore areas, and the Composite as shown at the bottom of the table.

Your Multiple-Choice Test Scores
Practice Test 1

	Your Scale Score (Steps 5 & 6)	Your Scale Subscore (Step 7)	Your Percentile Rank (Step 8)
English	_____		_____
Usage/Mechanics (UM)		_____	_____
Rhetorical Skills (RH)		_____	_____
Mathematics	_____		_____
Pre-Algebra/Elem. Algebra (EA)		_____	_____
Inter. Algebra/Coord. Geometry (AG)		_____	_____
Plane Geometry/Trigonometry (GT)		_____	_____
Reading	_____		_____
Social Studies/Sciences (SS)		_____	_____
Arts/Literature (AL)		_____	_____
Science	_____		_____
Sum of scores	_____		
Composite score (sum ÷ 4)	_____		

National Distributions of Cumulative Percents for ACT Test Scores
ACT-Tested High School Graduates from 2008, 2009, and 2010

Score	ENGLISH	Usage/Mechanics	Rhetorical Skills	MATHEMATICS	Pre-Algebra/Elem. Alg.	Alg./Coord. Geometry	Plane Geometry/Trig.	READING	Soc. Studies/Sciences	Arts/Literature	SCIENCE	COMPOSITE	Score
36	99			99				99			99	99	36
35	99			99				99			99	99	35
34	99			99				99			99	99	34
33	97			98				97			99	99	33
32	96			97				95			98	98	32
31	95			96				93			98	97	31
30	93			95				91			97	96	30
29	91			93				88			95	94	29
28	89			91				85			94	91	28
27	86			88				81			91	88	27
26	83			84				78			88	84	26
25	79			79				74			84	80	25
24	74			74				70			77	74	24
23	69			68				66			71	69	23
22	63			62				60			64	62	22
21	57			57				54			56	55	21
20	50			52				48			48	48	20
19	43			47				41			38	41	19
18	37	99	99	41	99	99	99	35	99	99	30	34	18
17	33	96	99	34	96	99	99	30	97	97	23	27	17
16	28	93	97	25	91	98	98	25	93	91	18	21	16
15	23	88	92	14	86	95	95	19	88	85	14	15	15
14	18	83	86	06	80	92	90	14	82	77	10	10	14
13	14	78	79	02	74	83	82	10	76	70	07	06	13
12	11	71	71	01	66	75	73	06	69	64	05	03	12
11	08	64	60	01	58	65	63	03	60	56	03	01	11
10	05	56	49	01	49	52	52	01	51	46	01	01	10
09	03	44	37	01	39	36	38	01	40	38	01	01	09
08	02	35	27	01	31	23	25	01	29	30	01	01	08
07	01	26	18	01	20	13	15	01	18	22	01	01	07
06	01	19	11	01	08	08	09	01	10	15	01	01	06
05	01	12	07	01	03	05	06	01	05	09	01	01	05
04	01	07	04	01	01	02	03	01	02	04	01	01	04
03	01	03	01	01	01	01	02	01	01	01	01	01	03
02	01	01	01	01	01	01	01	01	01	01	01	01	02
01	01	01	01	01	01	01	01	01	01	01	01	01	01
Mean	20.6	10.2	10.6	21.0	11.0	10.5	10.5	21.4	10.8	10.9	20.9	21.1	
S.D.	6.3	3.9	3.3	5.3	3.6	2.9	3.1	6.2	3.5	3.9	5.0	5.1	

Note: These norms are the source of national norms, for multiple-choice tests, printed on ACT score reports during the 2010–2011 testing year. Sample size: 4,463,185.

Scoring Your Practice Writing Test Essay

To score your practice Writing Test essay, follow these seven steps:

STEP 1. Use the guidelines on the Six-Point Holistic Scoring Rubric (page 141) to score your essay. Because many papers do not fit the exact description at each score point, the rubric says: "Papers at each level exhibit *all* or *most* of the characteristics in the descriptors." To score your paper, read it and try to determine which paragraph in the rubric best describes *most* of the characteristics of your essay.

STEP 2. Because your Writing Test subscore is the sum of **two** readers' ratings of your essay, you should multiply your own 1–6 rating from Step 1 above by 2. Or, have both you and someone else read and score your practice essay and add those ratings together. In either case, record the total in the blank in Step 4 below and also in the blank labeled "Your Subscore" on page 884.

STEP 3. Locate your scale score for the English Test on page 880 and enter it here: _____.

STEP 4. Enter your Writing Test subscore from Step 2 here: _____.

STEP 5. Use the table on page 883 to find your Combined English/Writing scale score.

- First, circle your ACT English Test score in the left column.

- Second, circle your ACT Writing Test subscore at the top of the table.

- Finally, follow the English Test Score row across and the Writing Test Subscore row down until the two meet. Circle the Combined score where the two columns meet. (For example, if an English Test score were 19 and a Writing Test subscore were 6, the Combined English/Writing scale score would be 18.)

STEP 6. Using the number you circled on page 883, write your Combined English/Writing scale score on page 884. (The highest possible Combined English/Writing scale score is 36 and the lowest possible scale score is 1.)

Combined English/Writing Scale Scores

English Test Score	Writing Test Subscore										
	2	3	4	5	6	7	8	9	10	11	12
1	1	2	3	4	5	6	7	8	9	10	11
2	2	3	4	5	6	6	7	8	9	10	11
3	2	3	4	5	6	7	8	9	10	11	12
4	3	4	5	6	7	8	9	10	11	12	13
5	4	5	6	7	8	9	10	11	12	12	13
6	5	6	7	7	8	9	10	11	12	13	14
7	5	6	7	8	9	10	11	12	13	14	15
8	6	7	8	9	10	11	12	13	14	15	16
9	7	8	9	10	11	12	13	13	14	15	16
10	8	9	9	10	11	12	13	14	15	16	17
11	8	9	10	11	12	13	14	15	16	17	18
12	9	10	11	12	13	14	15	16	17	18	19
13	10	11	12	13	14	14	15	16	17	18	19
14	10	11	12	13	14	15	16	17	18	19	20
15	11	12	13	14	15	16	17	18	19	20	21
16	12	13	14	15	16	17	18	19	20	20	21
17	13	14	15	16	16	17	18	19	20	21	22
18	13	14	15	16	17	18	19	20	21	22	23
19	14	15	16	17	18	19	20	21	22	23	24
20	15	16	17	18	19	20	21	21	22	23	24
21	16	17	17	18	19	20	21	22	23	24	25
22	16	17	18	19	20	21	22	23	24	25	26
23	17	18	19	20	21	22	23	24	25	26	27
24	18	19	20	21	22	23	23	24	25	26	27
25	18	19	20	21	22	23	24	25	26	27	28
26	19	20	21	22	23	24	25	26	27	28	29
27	20	21	22	23	24	25	26	27	28	28	29
28	21	22	23	24	24	25	26	27	28	29	30
29	21	22	23	24	25	26	27	28	29	30	31
30	22	23	24	25	26	27	28	29	30	31	32
31	23	24	25	26	27	28	29	30	30	31	32
32	24	25	25	26	27	28	29	30	31	32	33
33	24	25	26	27	28	29	30	31	32	33	34
34	25	26	27	28	29	30	31	32	33	34	35
35	26	27	28	29	30	31	31	32	33	34	35
36	26	27	28	29	30	31	32	33	34	35	36

STEP 7. Use the table on page 885 to determine your estimated percentile rank (percent at or below) for your Writing Test subscore and your Combined English/Writing scale score. In the far left column of the table on page 885, circle your Combined English/Writing scale score. Then read across to the percentile rank column headed "Combined English/Writing"; circle or put a check mark beside the corresponding percentile rank. Use the same procedure for your Writing Test subscore, this time using the column headed "Writing." As you mark your percentile ranks, enter them in the blanks provided in the table below. You may also find it helpful to compare your performance with the national mean (average) score for the Combined English/Writing scale score and the Writing Test subscore as shown at the bottom of the table on page 885.

Your Writing Test Scores
Practice Test 1

	Your Subscore (Step 2)	Your Scale Score (Steps 5 & 6)	Your Percentile Rank (Step 7)
Writing	_____		_____
Combined English/Writing		_____	_____

National Distributions of Cumulative Percents for ACT Writing Test Scores

ACT-Tested High School Graduates from 2008, 2009, and 2010

Score	Combined English/Writing	Writing
36	99	
35	99	
34	99	
33	99	
32	99	
31	98	
30	95	
29	93	
28	90	
27	87	
26	84	
25	79	
24	74	
23	69	
22	61	
21	55	
20	46	
19	40	
18	34	
17	28	
16	23	
15	18	
14	14	
13	10	
12	07	99
11	05	99
10	03	99
09	02	93
08	01	84
07	01	49
06	01	35
05	01	10
04	01	06
03	01	02
02	01	01
01	01	
Mean	20.8	7.2
S.D.	5.6	1.6

Note: These norms are the source of the Writing Test norms printed on the ACT score reports of students who took the optional Writing Test during the 2010–2011 testing year. Sample size: 2,454,255.

Scoring Keys and Conversion Tables

Practice Test 2

Scoring Your Multiple-Choice Practice Test

To score your multiple-choice practice test, follow these eight steps:

STEP 1. Write a "1" in the blank for each English Test question that you answered correctly. An example is provided in the box below:

	Key	Subscore Area*		Your answer was
		UM	RH	
1.	A			Incorrect
2.	J		1	Correct
3.	B		1	Correct
4.	G			Incorrect

English ■ Scoring Key ■ Practice Test 2

	Key	Subscore Area*			Key	Subscore Area*			Key	Subscore Area*	
		UM	RH			UM	RH			UM	RH
1.	A			26.	F			51.	C		
2.	G			27.	D			52.	J		
3.	C			28.	G			53.	D		
4.	H			29.	D			54.	H		
5.	B			30.	F			55.	D		
6.	J			31.	A			56.	H		
7.	C			32.	H			57.	A		
8.	J			33.	A			58.	H		
9.	B			34.	J			59.	D		
10.	F			35.	B			60.	F		
11.	D			36.	F			61.	A		
12.	F			37.	C			62.	H		
13.	A			38.	H			63.	B		
14.	G			39.	D			64.	J		
15.	D			40.	F			65.	A		
16.	F			41.	C			66.	F		
17.	B			42.	G			67.	C		
18.	F			43.	D			68.	J		
19.	B			44.	G			69.	B		
20.	G			45.	C			70.	F		
21.	B			46.	F			71.	B		
22.	H			47.	C			72.	G		
23.	D			48.	J			73.	D		
24.	H			49.	A			74.	J		
25.	D			50.	G			75.	D		

* UM = Usage/Mechanics
RH = Rhetorical Skills

STEP 2. Add up the numbers in each subscore area and enter them in the appropriate blanks in the shaded box below:

Number Correct (Raw Score) for:	
Usage/Mechanics (UM) Subscore Area (40 questions)	_____
Rhetorical Skills (RH) Subscore Area (35 questions)	_____
Total Number Correct for English Test (UM + RH; 75 questions)	_____

STEP 3. Compute your total number correct for the English Test by adding the numbers you entered in Step 2. Write this total in the appropriate blank in the shaded box above. This is your raw score.

STEP 4. Repeat Steps 1 through 3 for the ACT Mathematics, Reading, and Science Tests using the scoring keys on the following pages. Note that the Science Test doesn't have subscores, so determine your raw score for that test simply by adding up the number of "1s" you entered.

Mathematics ■ Scoring Key ■ Practice Test 2

	Key	EA	AG	GT			Key	EA	AG	GT
1.	C	—				31.	E			—
2.	J	—				32.	G			—
3.	B	—				33.	D		—	
4.	H	—				34.	F		—	
5.	A	—				35.	B			—
6.	F	—				36.	F			—
7.	C			—		37.	E		—	
8.	K			—		38.	G		—	
9.	B	—				39.	D		—	
10.	K	—				40.	G	—		
11.	C	—				41.	B	—		
12.	K	—				42.	F	—		
13.	C	—				43.	D		—	
14.	H			—		44.	G			—
15.	C			—		45.	E	—		
16.	H		—			46.	J			—
17.	C			—		47.	B	—		
18.	H			—		48.	G			—
19.	E	—				49.	A			—
20.	G		—			50.	K		—	
21.	B			—		51.	D			—
22.	H		—			52.	H			—
23.	A	—				53.	D		—	
24.	K		—			54.	K			—
25.	C	—				55.	D		—	
26.	F			—		56.	J			—
27.	D			—		57.	A	—		
28.	J			—		58.	J		—	
29.	B	—				59.	A		—	
30.	K	—				60.	F	—		

* EA = Pre-Algebra/Elementary Algebra
AG = Intermediate Algebra/Coordinate Geometry
GT = Plane Geometry/Trigonometry

Number Correct (Raw Score) for:

Pre-Alg./Elem. Alg. (EA) Subscore Area (24 questions) _____

Inter. Alg./Coord. Geom. (AG) Subscore Area (18 questions) _____

Plane Geom./Trig. (GT) Subscore Area (18 questions) _____

Total Number Correct for Math Test (EA + AG + GT; 60 questions) _____

Reading ■ Scoring Key ■ Practice Test 2

	Key	Subscore Area* SS	AL
1.	D		
2.	F		___
3.	B		___
4.	H		___
5.	D		___
6.	H		___
7.	B		___
8.	H		___
9.	A		___
10.	G		___
11.	B		___
12.	F	___	
13.	A	___	
14.	H	___	

	Key	Subscore Area* SS	AL
15.	C	___	
16.	F		
17.	B	___	
18.	H	___	
19.	D	___	
20.	F	___	
21.	A		
22.	H		___
23.	C		___
24.	J		___
25.	D		___
26.	F		___
27.	D		___
28.	F		___

	Key	Subscore Area* SS	AL
29.	B		___
30.	G		___
31.	B		
32.	F	___	
33.	C	___	
34.	J	___	
35.	D		
36.	H	___	
37.	B	___	
38.	F	___	
39.	B	___	
40.	J	___	

* SS = Social Studies/Sciences
AL = Arts/Literature

Number Correct (Raw Score) for:

Social Studies/Sciences (SS) Subscore Area (20 questions) _____

Arts/Literature (AL) Subscore Area (20 questions) _____

Total Number Correct for Reading Test (SS + AL; 40 questions) _____

Science ■ Scoring Key ■ Practice Test 2

	Key			**Key**			**Key**	
1.	B	____	15.	B	____	29.	D	____
2.	F	____	16.	F	____	30.	F	____
3.	A	____	17.	A	____	31.	C	____
4.	H	____	18.	J	____	32.	F	____
5.	D	____	19.	A	____	33.	A	____
6.	G	____	20.	J	____	34.	J	____
7.	D	____	21.	C	____	35.	B	____
8.	F	____	22.	H	____	36.	J	____
9.	C	____	23.	C	____	37.	B	____
10.	G	____	24.	G	____	38.	H	____
11.	C	____	25.	D	____	39.	C	____
12.	H	____	26.	G	____	40.	J	____
13.	D	____	27.	B	____			
14.	G	____	28.	J	____			

Number Correct (Raw Score) for:

Total Number Correct for Science Test (40 questions)   _____

STEP 5. On each of the four tests, the total number of correct responses yields a raw score. Use the conversion table on the following page to convert your raw scores to scale scores. For each of the four tests, locate and circle your raw score or the range of raw scores that includes it in the conversion table. Then, read across to either outside column of the table and circle the scale score that corresponds to that raw score. As you determine your scale scores, enter them in the blanks provided on page 893. The highest possible scale score for each test is 36. The lowest possible scale score for any of the four tests is 1.

STEP 6. Compute your Composite score by averaging the four scale scores. To do this, add your four scale scores and divide the sum by 4. If the resulting number ends in a fraction, round it off to the nearest whole number. (Round down any fraction less than one-half; round up any fraction that is one-half or more.) Enter this number in the appropriate blank on page 893. This is your Composite score. The highest possible Composite score is 36. The lowest possible Composite score is 1.

Scale Score Conversion Table
Practice Test 2

Scale Score	Raw Score				Scale Score
	English	Mathematics	Reading	Science	
36	75	60	39–40	40	36
35	74	59	38	39	35
34	73	58	37	38	34
33	71–72	57	36	37	33
32	70	55–56	35	36	32
31	69	54	33–34	–	31
30	67–68	52–53	32	35	30
29	65–66	50–51	30–31	34	29
28	64	48–49	29	33	28
27	62–63	45–47	27–28	31–32	27
26	59–61	43–44	26	30	26
25	57–58	40–42	25	29	25
24	55–56	38–39	23–24	27–28	24
23	52–54	36–37	22	25–26	23
22	50–51	34–35	21	24	22
21	47–49	33	20	22–23	21
20	45–46	31–32	18–19	20–21	20
19	42–44	28–30	17	19	19
18	40–41	26–27	16	17–18	18
17	38–39	23–25	15	15–16	17
16	35–37	20–22	14	14	16
15	32–34	17–19	13	13	15
14	29–31	14–16	12	11–12	14
13	27–28	12–13	10–11	10	13
12	25–26	9–11	8–9	9	12
11	24	7–8	7	7–8	11
10	22–23	6	6	6	10
9	20–21	5	5	5	9
8	16–19	4	4	4	8
7	13–15	–	–	3	7
6	11–12	3	3	–	6
5	8–10	2	–	2	5
4	6–7	–	2	–	4
3	4–5	1	1	1	3
2	3	–	–	–	2
1	0–2	0	0	0	1

STEP 7. Now convert your seven raw subscores to scale subscores using the table below. For each of the seven subscore areas, locate and circle either the raw score or the range of raw scores that includes it in the table. Then read across to either outside column of the table and circle the scale subscore that corresponds to that raw subscore. As you determine your scale subscores, enter them in the blanks on page 893. The highest possible scale subscore is 18. The lowest possible scale subscore is 1

Scale Subscore Conversion Table
Practice Test 2

Scale Subscore	Raw Scores							Scale Subscore
	English		Mathematics			Reading		
	Usage/ Mechanics	Rhetorical Skills	Pre-Alg./ Elem. Alg.	Inter. Alg./ Coord. Geom.	Plane Geom./ Trigonometry	Soc. Studies/ Sciences	Arts/ Literature	
18	40	35	23–24	18	18	20	19–20	18
17	38–39	33–34	22	17	–	18–19	17–18	17
16	36–37	32	21	16	17	16–17	16	16
15	34–35	30–31	20	15	15–16	15	15	15
14	32–33	28–29	19	13–14	14	13–14	14	14
13	31	26–27	18	12	12–13	12	13	13
12	29–30	24–25	16–17	10–11	10–11	11	11–12	12
11	27–28	22–23	15	9	9	10	10	11
10	24–26	20–21	14	8	7–8	9	9	10
9	22–23	17–19	12–13	6–7	6	8	8	9
8	20–21	15–16	10–11	5	5	6–7	7	8
7	17–19	13–14	8–9	4	4	5	6	7
6	15–16	11–12	6–7	3	–	–	5	6
5	13–14	10	5	–	3	4	4	5
4	10–12	8–9	3–4	2	–	3	3	4
3	8–9	5–7	2	1	2	2	2	3
2	5–7	3–4	1	–	1	–	1	2
1	0–4	0–2	0	0	0	0–1	0	1

STEP 8. Use the table on page 881 to determine your estimated percentile ranks (percent at or below) for each of your scale scores. In the far left column of the table, circle your scale score for the English Test (from page 891). Then read across to the percentile rank column for that test; circle or put a check mark beside the corresponding percentile rank. Use the same procedure, for the other three tests (from page 891) and for the subscore areas (from page 892). You may find it easier to use the right-hand column of scale scores for your Science Test and Composite scores. As you mark your percentile ranks, enter them in the blanks provided below. You may also find it helpful to compare your performance with the national mean (average) score for each of the four tests, the subscore areas, and the Composite as shown at the bottom of the table.

Your Multiple-Choice Test Scores
Practice Test 2

	Your Scale Score (Steps 5 & 6)	Your Scale Subscore (Step 7)	Your Percentile Rank (Step 8)
English	━━━━		━━━━
Usage/Mechanics (UM)		_____	_____
Rhetorical Skills (RH)		_____	_____
Mathematics	━━━━		
Pre-Algebra/Elem. Algebra (EA)		_____	_____
Inter. Algebra/Coord. Geometry (AG)		_____	_____
Plane Geometry/Trigonometry (GT)		_____	_____
Reading	━━━━		━━━━
Social Studies/Sciences (SS)		_____	_____
Arts/Literature (AL)		_____	_____
Science	━━━━		━━━━
Sum of scores	━━━━		
Composite score (sum ÷ 4)	━━━━		

Scoring Your Practice Writing Test Essay

To score your practice Writing Test essay, follow these seven steps:

STEP 1. Use the guidelines on the Six-Point Holistic Scoring Rubric (page 141) to score your essay. Because many papers do not fit the exact description at each score point, the rubric says: "Papers at each level exhibit *all* or *most* of the characteristics in the descriptors." To score your paper, read it and try to determine which paragraph in the rubric best describes *most* of the characteristics of your essay.

STEP 2. Because your Writing Test subscore is the sum of **two** readers' ratings of your essay, you should multiply your own 1–6 rating from Step 1 above by 2. Or, have both you and someone else read and score your practice essay and add those ratings together. In either case, record the total in the blank in Step 4 below and also in the blank labeled "Your Subscore" on page 896.

STEP 3. Locate your scale score for the English Test on page 893 and enter it here: _____.

STEP 4. Enter your Writing Test subscore from Step 2 here: _____.

STEP 5. Use the table on page 895 to find your Combined English/Writing scale score.

- First, circle your ACT English Test score in the left column.

- Second, circle your ACT Writing Test subscore at the top of the table.

- Finally, follow the English Test Score row across and the Writing Test Subscore row down until the two meet. Circle the Combined score where the two columns meet. (For example, if an English Test score were 19 and a Writing Test subscore were 6, the Combined English/Writing scale score would be 18.)

STEP 6. Using the number you circled on page 895, write your Combined English/Writing scale score on page 896. (The highest possible Combined English/Writing scale score is 36 and the lowest possible scale score is 1.)

English Test Score	Writing Test Subscore										
	2	3	4	5	6	7	8	9	10	11	12
1	1	2	3	4	5	6	7	8	9	10	11
2	2	3	4	5	6	6	7	8	9	10	11
3	2	3	4	5	6	7	8	9	10	11	12
4	3	4	5	6	7	8	9	10	11	12	13
5	4	5	6	7	8	9	10	11	12	12	13
6	5	6	7	7	8	9	10	11	12	13	14
7	5	6	7	8	9	10	11	12	13	14	15
8	6	7	8	9	10	11	12	13	14	15	16
9	7	8	9	10	11	12	13	13	14	15	16
10	8	9	9	10	11	12	13	14	15	16	17
11	8	9	10	11	12	13	14	15	16	17	18
12	9	10	11	12	13	14	15	16	17	18	19
13	10	11	12	13	14	14	15	16	17	18	19
14	10	11	12	13	14	15	16	17	18	19	20
15	11	12	13	14	15	16	17	18	19	20	21
16	12	13	14	15	16	17	18	19	20	20	21
17	13	14	15	16	16	17	18	19	20	21	22
18	13	14	15	16	17	18	19	20	21	22	23
19	14	15	16	17	18	19	20	21	22	23	24
20	15	16	17	18	19	20	21	21	22	23	24
21	16	17	17	18	19	20	21	22	23	24	25
22	16	17	18	19	20	21	22	23	24	25	26
23	17	18	19	20	21	22	23	24	25	26	27
24	18	19	20	21	22	23	23	24	25	26	27
25	18	19	20	21	22	23	24	25	26	27	28
26	19	20	21	22	23	24	25	26	27	28	29
27	20	21	22	23	24	25	26	27	28	28	29
28	21	22	23	24	24	25	26	27	28	29	30
29	21	22	23	24	25	26	27	28	29	30	31
30	22	23	24	25	26	27	28	29	30	31	32
31	23	24	25	26	27	28	29	30	30	31	32
32	24	25	25	26	27	28	29	30	31	32	33
33	24	25	26	27	28	29	30	31	32	33	34
34	25	26	27	28	29	30	31	31	32	33	34	35
35	26	27	28	29	30	31	31	32	33	34	35
36	26	27	28	29	30	31	32	33	34	35	36

Combined English/Writing Scale Scores

STEP 7. Use the table on page 885 to determine your estimated percentile rank (percent at or below) for your Writing Test subscore and your Combined English/Writing scale score. In the far left column of the table on page 885, circle your Combined English/Writing scale score. Then read across to the percentile rank column headed "Combined English/Writing"; circle or put a check mark beside the corresponding percentile rank. Use the same procedure for your Writing Test subscore, this time using the column headed "Writing." As you mark your percentile ranks, enter them in the blanks provided in the table below. You may also find it helpful to compare your performance with the national mean (average) score for the Combined English/Writing scale score and the Writing Test subscore as shown at the bottom of the table on page 885.

Your Writing Test Scores
Practice Test 2

	Your Subscore (Step 2)	Your Scale Score (Steps 5 & 6)	Your Percentile Rank (Step 7)
Writing	_____		_____
Combined English/Writing		_____	_____

Scoring Keys and Conversion Tables

Practice Test 3

Scoring Your Multiple-Choice Practice Test

To score your multiple-choice practice test, follow these eight steps:

STEP 1. Write a "1" in the blank for each English Test question that you answered correctly. An example is provided in the box below:

	Key	Subscore Area*		Your answer was
		UM	RH	
1.	A			Incorrect
2.	J		1	Correct
3.	B		1	Correct
4.	G			Incorrect

English ■ Scoring Key ■ Practice Test 3

	Key	Subscore Area*				Key	Subscore Area*				Key	Subscore Area*	
		UM	RH				UM	RH				UM	RH
1.	B		___		26.	J	___			51.	B	___	
2.	H	___			27.	B	___			52.	H	___	
3.	A	___			28.	J	___			53.	B	___	
4.	F	___			29.	A	___			54.	J	___	
5.	C	___			30.	G		___		55.	C		___
6.	H		___		31.	D		___		56.	G		___
7.	D		___		32.	F		___		57.	C	___	
8.	F	___			33.	A		___		58.	H	___	
9.	D		___		34.	G		___		59.	D	___	
10.	J	___			35.	C		___		60.	F	___	
11.	B	___			36.	J		___		61.	C	___	
12.	J	___			37.	D		___		62.	G		___
13.	A	___			38.	G		___		63.	A		___
14.	J	___			39.	D		___		64.	G		___
15.	D		___		40.	F		___		65.	A		___
16.	H		___		41.	D		___		66.	G		___
17.	A		___		42.	F		___		67.	D	___	
18.	H	___			43.	C		___		68.	G	___	
19.	A	___			44.	J	___			69.	A	___	
20.	H		___		45.	C		___		70.	J		___
21.	A	___			46.	J		___		71.	A	___	
22.	G	___			47.	C		___		72.	J	___	
23.	D	___			48.	F		___		73.	C	___	
24.	F		___		49.	B		___		74.	F	___	
25.	C	___			50.	G		___		75.	B	___	

* UM = Usage/Mechanics
RH = Rhetorical Skills

STEP 2. Add up the numbers in each subscore area and enter them in the appropriate blanks in the shaded box below:

Number Correct (Raw Score) for:	
Usage/Mechanics (UM) Subscore Area (40 questions)	_____
Rhetorical Skills (RH) Subscore Area (35 questions)	_____
Total Number Correct for English Test (UM + RH; 75 questions)	_____

STEP 3. Compute your total number correct for the English Test by adding the numbers you entered in Step 2. Write this total in the appropriate blank in the shaded box above. This is your raw score.

STEP 4. Repeat Steps 1 through 3 for the ACT Mathematics, Reading, and Science Tests using the scoring keys on the following pages. Note that the Science Test doesn't have subscores, so determine your raw score for that test simply by adding up the number of "1s" you entered.

Mathematics ■ Scoring Key ■ Practice Test 3

#	Key	EA	AG	GT		#	Key	EA	AG	GT
1.	E	—				31.	E		—	
2.	H	—				32.	K			—
3.	D	—				33.	A			
4.	H	—				34.	G	—		
5.	E			—		35.	A			
6.	F			—		36.	K			—
7.	D	—				37.	C			
8.	H	—				38.	H			—
9.	B			—		39.	C			—
10.	H	—				40.	K	—		
11.	D	—				41.	B			—
12.	K	—				42.	J			—
13.	D	—				43.	D			—
14.	K	—				44.	K	—		
15.	B	—				45.	B			—
16.	G		—			46.	F			—
17.	A	—				47.	E			
18.	K		—			48.	G		—	
19.	D		—			49.	D			—
20.	F		—			50.	F			
21.	E	—				51.	A			
22.	J		—			52.	H	—		
23.	C	—				53.	B		—	
24.	G		—			54.	F			
25.	D		—			55.	A			
26.	G	—				56.	F	—	—	
27.	B	—				57.	D			—
28.	J		—			58.	H			—
29.	B		—			59.	B	—		
30.	H			—		60.	J	—		

* EA = Pre-Algebra/Elementary Algebra
AG = Intermediate Algebra/Coordinate Geometry
GT = Plane Geometry/Trigonometry

Number Correct (Raw Score) for:

Pre-Alg./Elem. Alg. (EA) Subscore Area (24 questions) _____

Inter. Alg./Coord. Geom. (AG) Subscore Area (18 questions) _____

Plane Geom./Trig. (GT) Subscore Area (18 questions) _____

Total Number Correct for Math Test (EA + AG + GT; 60 questions) _____

Reading ■ Scoring Key ■ Practice Test 3

	Key	Subscore Area* SS	AL
1.	C		____
2.	J		____
3.	A		____
4.	F		____
5.	B		____
6.	G		____
7.	D		____
8.	H		____
9.	B		____
10.	H		____
11.	B		____
12.	J	____	
13.	A	____	
14.	F	____	

	Key	Subscore Area* SS	AL
15.	C	____	
16.	G	____	
17.	D	____	
18.	J	____	
19.	A	____	
20.	H	____	
21.	A	____	
22.	J		____
23.	D		____
24.	J		____
25.	C		____
26.	H		____
27.	B		____
28.	H		____

	Key	Subscore Area* SS	AL
29.	D		____
30.	F		____
31.	D	____	
32.	H	____	
33.	A	____	
34.	H	____	
35.	A	____	
36.	F	____	
37.	C	____	
38.	G	____	
39.	D	____	
40.	G	____	

* SS = Social Studies/Sciences
AL = Arts/Literature

Number Correct (Raw Score) for:

Social Studies/Sciences (SS) Subscore Area (20 questions) ____

Arts/Literature (AL) Subscore Area (20 questions) ____

Total Number Correct for Reading Test (SS + AL; 40 questions) ____

Science ▪ Scoring Key ▪ Practice Test 3

	Key			Key			Key
1.	D	____	15.	B	____	29.	C
2.	F	____	16.	H	____	30.	H
3.	B	____	17.	C	____	31.	A
4.	H	____	18.	G	____	32.	J
5.	D	____	19.	B	____	33.	D
6.	J	____	20.	J	____	34.	G
7.	D	____	21.	A	____	35.	A
8.	F	____	22.	G	____	36.	J
9.	A	____	23.	B	____	37.	C
10.	H	____	24.	F	____	38.	G
11.	C	____	25.	C	____	39.	A
12.	J	____	26.	G	____	40.	G
13.	A	____	27.	D	____		
14.	J	____	28.	G	____		

Number Correct (Raw Score) for:

Total Number Correct for Science Test (40 questions) _____

STEP 5. On each of the four tests, the total number of correct responses yields a raw score. Use the conversion table on the following page to convert your raw scores to scale scores. For each of the four tests, locate and circle your raw score or the range of raw scores that includes it in the conversion table. Then, read across to either outside column of the table and circle the scale score that corresponds to that raw score. As you determine your scale scores, enter them in the blanks provided on page 904. The highest possible scale score for each test is 36. The lowest possible scale score for any of the four tests is 1.

STEP 6. Compute your Composite score by averaging the four scale scores. To do this, add your four scale scores and divide the sum by 4. If the resulting number ends in a fraction, round it off to the nearest whole number. (Round down any fraction less than one-half; round up any fraction that is one-half or more.) Enter this number in the appropriate blank on page 904. This is your Composite score. The highest possible Composite score is 36. The lowest possible Composite score is 1.

Scale Score Conversion Table
Practice Test 3

Scale Score	Raw Score				Scale Score
	English	Mathematics	Reading	Science	
36	75	60	38–40	39–40	36
35	74	59	37	38	35
34	72–73	58	36	37	34
33	71	57	35	36	33
32	70	56	34	35	32
31	69	55	33	–	31
30	67–68	53–54	32	34	30
29	65–66	51–52	31	33	29
28	63–64	48–50	29–30	31–32	28
27	61–62	45–47	28	30	27
26	58–60	42–44	27	29	26
25	55–57	40–41	26	28	25
24	53–54	37–39	24–25	26–27	24
23	50–52	36	23	25	23
22	48–49	34–35	22	23–24	22
21	45–47	33	21	22	21
20	42–44	31–32	20	20–21	20
19	40–41	29–30	19	18–19	19
18	37–39	26–28	18	17	18
17	35–36	23–25	17	15–16	17
16	33–34	20–22	16	14	16
15	30–32	16–19	14–15	13	15
14	28–29	13–15	13	11–12	14
13	26–27	11–12	11–12	10	13
12	24–25	9–10	9–10	9	12
11	22–23	7–8	7–8	8	11
10	20–21	6	6	7	10
9	18–19	5	5	5–6	9
8	15–17	4	–	4	8
7	13–14	3	4	–	7
6	10–12	–	3	3	6
5	8–9	2	–	2	5
4	6–7	–	2	–	4
3	4–5	1	–	1	3
2	2–3	–	1	–	2
1	0–1	0	0	0	1

STEP 7. Now convert your seven raw subscores to scale subscores using the table below. For each of the seven subscore areas, locate and circle either the raw score or the range of raw scores that includes it in the table. Then read across to either outside column of the table and circle the scale subscore that corresponds to that raw subscore. As you determine your scale subscores, enter them in the blanks on page 904. The highest possible scale subscore is 18. The lowest possible scale subscore is 1.

Scale Subscore Conversion Table
Practice Test 3

Scale Subscore	Raw Scores							Scale Subscore
	English		Mathematics			Reading		
	Usage/ Mechanics	Rhetorical Skills	Pre-Alg./ Elem. Alg.	Inter. Alg./ Coord. Geom.	Plane Geom./ Trigonometry	Soc. Studies/ Sciences	Arts/ Literature	
18	39–40	35	24	18	18	19–20	19–20	18
17	37–38	34	22–23	–	–	17–18	18	17
16	35–36	32–33	21	–	16–17	16	17	16
15	33–34	30–31	19–20	16–17	14–15	14–15	16	15
14	31–32	28–29	18	15	12–13	13	15	14
13	30	26–27	17	13–14	11	12	14	13
12	28–29	23–25	16	12	9–10	11	13	12
11	25–27	21–22	15	10–11	8	10	12	11
10	23–24	18–20	13–14	8–9	7	8–9	11	10
9	21–22	16–17	12	7	6	7	10	9
8	19–20	14–15	10–11	5–6	5	6	9	8
7	17–18	12–13	8–9	4	4	5	8	7
6	15–16	11	6–7	–	–	4	7	6
5	12–14	9–10	4–5	3	3	3	5–6	5
4	10–11	7–8	3	2	–	–	4	4
3	8–9	5–6	2	–	2	2	2–3	3
2	5–7	3–4	1	1	1	1	1	2
1	0–4	0–2	0	0	0	0	0	1

STEP 8. Use the table on page 881 to determine your estimated percentile ranks (percent at or below) for each of your scale scores. In the far left column of the table, circle your scale score for the English Test (from page 902). Then read across to the percentile rank column for that test; circle or put a check mark beside the corresponding percentile rank. Use the same procedure for the other three tests (from page 902) and for the subscore areas (from page 903). You may find it easier to use the right-hand column of scale scores for your Science Test and Composite scores. As you mark your percentile ranks, enter them in the blanks provided below. You may also find it helpful to compare your performance with the national mean (average) score for each of the four tests, the subscore areas, and the Composite as shown at the bottom of the table.

Your Multiple-Choice Test Scores
Practice Test 3

	Your Scale Score (Steps 5 & 6)	Your Scale Subscore (Step 7)	Your Percentile Rank (Step 8)
English	_____		_____
Usage/Mechanics (UM)		_____	_____
Rhetorical Skills (RH)		_____	_____
Mathematics	_____		_____
Pre-Algebra/Elem. Algebra (EA)		_____	_____
Inter. Algebra/Coord. Geometry (AG)		_____	_____
Plane Geometry/Trigonometry (GT)		_____	_____
Reading	_____		_____
Social Studies/Sciences (SS)		_____	_____
Arts/Literature (AL)		_____	_____
Science	_____		_____
Sum of scores	_____		
Composite score (sum ÷ 4)	_____		

Scoring Your Practice Writing Test Essay

To score your practice Writing Test essay, follow these seven steps:

STEP 1. Use the guidelines on the Six-Point Holistic Scoring Rubric (page 141) to score your essay. Because many papers do not fit the exact description at each score point, the rubric says: "Papers at each level exhibit *all* or *most* of the characteristics in the descriptors." To score your paper, read it and try to determine which paragraph in the rubric best describes *most* of the characteristics of your essay.

STEP 2. Because your Writing Test subscore is the sum of **two** readers' ratings of your essay, you should multiply your own 1–6 rating from Step 1 above by 2. Or, have both you and someone else read and score your practice essay and add those ratings together. In either case, record the total in the blank in Step 4 below and also in the blank labeled "Your Subscore" on page 907.

STEP 3. Locate your scale score for the English Test on page 904 and enter it here: _____.

STEP 4. Enter your Writing Test subscore from Step 2 here: _____.

STEP 5. Use the table on page 906 to find your Combined English/Writing scale score.

- First, circle your ACT English Test score in the left column.

- Second, circle your ACT Writing Test subscore at the top of the table.

- Finally, follow the English Test Score row across and the Writing Test Subscore row down until the two meet. Circle the Combined score where the two columns meet. (For example, if an English Test score were 19 and a Writing Test subscore were 6, the Combined English/Writing scale score would be 18.)

STEP 6. Using the number you circled on page 906, write your Combined English/Writing scale score on page 907. (The highest possible Combined English/Writing scale score is 36 and the lowest possible scale score is 1.)

Combined English/Writing Scale Scores											
English Test Score	Writing Test Subscore										
	2	3	4	5	6	7	8	9	10	11	12
1	1	2	3	4	5	6	7	8	9	10	11
2	2	3	4	5	6	6	7	8	9	10	11
3	2	3	4	5	6	7	8	9	10	11	12
4	3	4	5	6	7	8	9	10	11	12	13
5	4	5	6	7	8	9	10	11	12	12	13
6	5	6	7	7	8	9	10	11	12	13	14
7	5	6	7	8	9	10	11	12	13	14	15
8	6	7	8	9	10	11	12	13	14	15	16
9	7	8	9	10	11	12	13	13	14	15	16
10	8	9	9	10	11	12	13	14	15	16	17
11	8	9	10	11	12	13	14	15	16	17	18
12	9	10	11	12	13	14	15	16	17	18	19
13	10	11	12	13	14	14	15	16	17	18	19
14	10	11	12	13	14	15	16	17	18	19	20
15	11	12	13	14	15	16	17	18	19	20	21
16	12	13	14	15	16	17	18	19	20	20	21
17	13	14	15	16	16	17	18	19	20	21	22
18	13	14	15	16	17	18	19	20	21	22	23
19	14	15	16	17	18	19	20	21	22	23	24
20	15	16	17	18	19	20	21	21	22	23	24
21	16	17	17	18	19	20	21	22	23	24	25
22	16	17	18	19	20	21	22	23	24	25	26
23	17	18	19	20	21	22	23	24	25	26	27
24	18	19	20	21	22	23	23	24	25	26	27
25	18	19	20	21	22	23	24	25	26	27	28
26	19	20	21	22	23	24	25	26	27	28	29
27	20	21	22	23	24	25	26	27	28	28	29
28	21	22	23	24	24	25	26	27	28	29	30
29	21	22	23	24	25	26	27	28	29	30	31
30	22	23	24	25	26	27	28	29	30	31	32
31	23	24	25	26	27	28	29	30	30	31	32
32	24	25	25	26	27	28	29	30	31	32	33
33	24	25	26	27	28	29	30	31	32	33	34
34	25	26	27	28	29	30	31	32	33	34	35
35	26	27	28	29	30	31	31	32	33	34	35
36	26	27	28	29	30	31	32	33	34	35	36

STEP 7. Use the table on page 885 to determine your estimated percentile rank (percent at or below) for your Writing Test subscore and your Combined English/Writing scale score. In the far left column of the table on page 885, circle your Combined English/Writing scale score. Then read across to the percentile rank column headed "Combined English/Writing"; circle or put a check mark beside the corresponding percentile rank. Use the same procedure for your Writing Test subscore, this time using the column headed "Writing." As you mark your percentile ranks, enter them in the blanks provided in the table below. You may also find it helpful to compare your performance with the national mean (average) score for the Combined English/Writing scale score and the Writing Test subscore as shown at the bottom of the table on page 885.

Your Writing Test Scores
Practice Test 3

	Your Subscore (Step 2)	Your Scale Score (Steps 5 & 6)	Your Percentile Rank (Step 7)
Writing	_____		_____
Combined English/Writing		_____	_____

Scoring Keys and Conversion Tables

Practice Test 4

Scoring Your Multiple-Choice Practice Test

To score your multiple-choice practice test, follow these eight steps:

STEP 1. Write a "1" in the blank for each English Test question that you answered correctly. An example is provided in the box below:

	Key	Subscore Area*		Your answer was
		UM	RH	
1.	A			Incorrect
2.	J		1	Correct
3.	B		1	Correct
4.	G			Incorrect

English ▪ Scoring Key ▪ Practice Test 4

	Key	Subscore Area*				Key	Subscore Area*				Key	Subscore Area*	
		UM	RH				UM	RH				UM	RH
1.	D				26.	J				51.	B		
2.	F				27.	A				52.	H		
3.	B				28.	H				53.	D		
4.	J				29.	B				54.	G		
5.	B				30.	F				55.	D		
6.	J				31.	B				56.	H		
7.	C				32.	H				57.	A		
8.	J				33.	A				58.	F		
9.	D				34.	J				59.	B		
10.	F				35.	B				60.	F		
11.	C				36.	F				61.	D		
12.	J				37.	C				62.	H		
13.	B				38.	F				63.	A		
14.	J				39.	C				64.	J		
15.	A				40.	J				65.	B		
16.	H				41.	B				66.	F		
17.	B				42.	J				67.	C		
18.	J				43.	A				68.	J		
19.	C				44.	F				69.	B		
20.	F				45.	C				70.	H		
21.	C				46.	G				71.	C		
22.	G				47.	D				72.	G		
23.	D				48.	F				73.	D		
24.	G				49.	B				74.	G		
25.	A				50.	F				75.	C		

* UM = Usage/Mechanics
RH = Rhetorical Skills

STEP 2. Add up the numbers in each subscore area and enter them in the appropriate blanks in the shaded box below:

Number Correct (Raw Score) for:

Usage/Mechanics (UM) Subscore Area (40 questions)   _____

Rhetorical Skills (RH) Subscore Area (35 questions)   _____

Total Number Correct for English Test (UM + RH; 75 questions)   _____

STEP 3. Compute your total number correct for the English Test by adding the numbers you entered in Step 2. Write this total in the appropriate blank in the shaded box above. This is your raw score.

STEP 4. Repeat Steps 1 through 3 for the ACT Mathematics, Reading, and Science Tests using the scoring keys on the following pages. Note that the Science Test doesn't have subscores, so determine your raw score for that test simply by adding up the number of "1s" you entered.

Mathematics ■ Scoring Key ■ Practice Test 4

	Key	Subscore Area* EA	AG	GT			Key	Subscore Area* EA	AG	GT
1.	E			___		31.	B	___		
2.	H	___				32.	F		___	
3.	A	___				33.	D	___		
4.	J	___				34.	J			___
5.	C	___				35.	B			___
6.	H			___		36.	F			___
7.	B		___			37.	E		___	
8.	J	___				38.	G		___	
9.	E	___				39.	B		___	
10.	J			___		40.	K	___		
11.	C		___			41.	B		___	
12.	J	___				42.	H		___	
13.	E	___				43.	C			___
14.	G			___		44.	F			___
15.	E			___		45.	E			___
16.	G	___				46.	H		___	
17.	E	___				47.	A		___	
18.	F	___				48.	F	___		
19.	A	___				49.	D		___	
20.	J			___		50.	J	___		
21.	E	___				51.	D	___		
22.	G		___			52.	G	___		
23.	C	___				53.	B			___
24.	H			___		54.	K			___
25.	A		___			55.	C		___	
26.	H		___			56.	K		___	
27.	C	___				57.	D			___
28.	J		___			58.	K			___
29.	A	___				59.	B		___	
30.	G	___				60.	F			___

* EA = Pre-Algebra/Elementary Algebra
AG = Intermediate Algebra/Coordinate Geometry
GT = Plane Geometry/Trigonometry

Number Correct (Raw Score) for:	
Pre-Alg./Elem. Alg. (EA) Subscore Area (24 questions)	_____
Inter. Alg./Coord. Geom. (AG) Subscore Area (18 questions)	_____
Plane Geom./Trig. (GT) Subscore Area (18 questions)	_____
Total Number Correct for Math Test (EA + AG + GT; 60 questions)	_____

Reading ■ Scoring Key ■ Practice Test 4

Subscore Area*

	Key	SS	AL
1.	A		
2.	G		
3.	A		
4.	H		
5.	C		
6.	G		
7.	B		
8.	F		
9.	A		
10.	J		
11.	A		
12.	J		
13.	D		
14.	F		

Subscore Area*

	Key	SS	AL
15.	B		
16.	H		
17.	C		
18.	G		
19.	D		
20.	J		
21.	A		
22.	H		
23.	D		
24.	F		
25.	C		
26.	H		
27.	D		
28.	J		

Subscore Area*

	Key	SS	AL
29.	B		
30.	H		
31.	D		
32.	G		
33.	C		
34.	G		
35.	D		
36.	G		
37.	D		
38.	G		
39.	C		
40.	F		

* SS = Social Studies/Sciences
  AL = Arts/Literature

Number Correct (Raw Score) for:

Studies/Sciences (SS) Subscore Area (20 questions) _____

Arts/Literature (AL) Subscore Area (20 questions) _____

Total Number Correct for Reading Test (SS + AL; 40 questions) _____

Science ▪ Scoring Key ▪ Practice Test 4

	Key			Key			Key	
1.	B	____	15.	C	____	29.	D	____
2.	F	____	16.	J	____	30.	J	____
3.	B	____	17.	B	____	31.	C	____
4.	F	____	18.	G	____	32.	G	____
5.	D	____	19.	C	____	33.	A	____
6.	G	____	20.	H	____	34.	J	____
7.	B	____	21.	B	____	35.	D	____
8.	F	____	22.	J	____	36.	F	____
9.	C	____	23.	C	____	37.	C	____
10.	J	____	24.	H	____	38.	H	____
11.	B	____	25.	D	____	39.	A	____
12.	G	____	26.	J	____	40.	F	____
13.	C	____	27.	A	____			
14.	F	____	28.	J	____			

Number Correct (Raw Score) for:

Total Number Correct for Science Test (40 questions) ____

STEP 5. On each of the four tests, the total number of correct responses yields a raw score. Use the conversion table on the following page to convert your raw scores to scale scores. For each of the four tests, locate and circle your raw score or the range of raw scores that includes it in the conversion table. Then, read across to either outside column of the table and circle the scale score that corresponds to that raw score. As you determine your scale scores, enter them in the blanks provided on page 915. The highest possible scale score for each test is 36. The lowest possible scale score for any of the four tests is 1.

STEP 6. Compute your Composite score by averaging the four scale scores. To do this, add your four scale scores and divide the sum by 4. If the resulting number ends in a fraction, round it off to the nearest whole number. (Round down any fraction less than one-half; round up any fraction that is one-half or more.) Enter this number in the appropriate blank on page 915. This is your Composite score. The highest possible Composite score is 36. The lowest possible Composite score is 1.

Scale Score Conversion Table
Practice Test 4

Scale Score	Raw Score				Scale Score
	English	Mathematics	Reading	Science	
36	75	59–60	40	39–40	36
35	72–74	57–58	–	38	35
34	71	56	39	37	34
33	70	54–55	38	–	33
32	69	53	37	36	32
31	68	51–52	–	35	31
30	66–67	50	36	34	30
29	65	49	35	33	29
28	64	47–48	34	32	28
27	62–63	45–46	33	31	27
26	60–61	42–44	32	29–30	26
25	58–59	40–41	31	27–28	25
24	56–57	38–39	30	26	24
23	53–55	35–37	29	24–25	23
22	51–52	33–34	27–28	22–23	22
21	47–50	32	26	20–21	21
20	44–46	30–31	24–25	18–19	20
19	41–43	28–29	22–23	17	19
18	39–40	26–27	21	15–16	18
17	37–38	22–25	19–20	14	17
16	34–36	18–21	17–18	13	16
15	31–33	14–17	15–16	12	15
14	29–30	10–13	13–14	11	14
13	27–28	8–9	11–12	10	13
12	25–26	7	9–10	9	12
11	23–24	5–6	8	8	11
10	20–22	4	6–7	7	10
9	17–19	–	–	5–6	9
8	15–16	3	5	4	8
7	12–14	–	4	–	7
6	10–11	2	3	3	6
5	7–9	–	–	2	5
4	6	1	2	–	4
3	4–5	–	–	1	3
2	2–3	–	1	–	2
1	0–1	0	0	0	1

STEP 7. Now convert your seven raw subscores to scale subscores using the table below. For each of the seven subscore areas, locate and circle either the raw score or the range of raw scores that includes it in the table. Then read across to either outside column of the table and circle the scale subscore that corresponds to that raw subscore. As you determine your scale subscores, enter them in the blanks on page 915. The highest possible scale subscore is 18. The lowest possible scale subscore is 1.

Scale Subscore Conversion Table
Practice Test 4

Scale Subscore	Raw Scores							Scale Subscore
	English		Mathematics			Reading		
	Usage/ Mechanics	Rhetorical Skills	Pre-Alg./ Elem. Alg.	Inter. Alg./ Coord. Geom.	Plane Geom./ Trigonometry	Soc. Studies/ Sciences	Arts/ Literature	
18	38–40	35	23–24	18	18	20	20	18
17	37	34	22	17	17	19	19	17
16	35–36	32–33	21	16	15–16	18	–	16
15	34	30–31	20	15	14	17	18	15
14	32–33	29	19	13–14	13	16	17	14
13	31	27–28	18	11–12	11–12	15	16	13
12	29–30	25–26	17	10	10	14	15	12
11	27–28	22–24	15–16	8–9	9	13	14	11
10	24–26	20–21	14	7	7–8	11–12	12–13	10
9	21–23	17–19	12–13	6	6	10	11	9
8	19–20	15–16	10–11	5	5	8–9	10	8
7	17–18	13–14	7–9	4	4	6–7	8–9	7
6	14–16	12	5–6	3	3	5	7	6
5	12–13	10–11	4	–	2	4	5–6	5
4	9–11	8–9	3	2	–	3	4	4
3	7–8	5–7	2	1	1	2	2–3	3
2	4–6	3–4	1	–	–	1	1	2
1	0–3	0–2	0	0	0	0	0	1

STEP 8. Use the table on page 881 to determine your estimated percentile ranks (percent at or below) for each of your scale scores. In the far left column of the table, circle your scale score for the English Test (from page 913). Then read across to the percentile rank column for that test; circle or put a check mark beside the corresponding percentile rank. Use the same procedure for the other three tests (from page 913) and for the subscore areas (from page 914). You may find it easier to use the right-hand column of scale scores for your Science Test and Composite scores. As you mark your percentile ranks, enter them in the blanks provided below. You may also find it helpful to compare your performance with the national mean (average) score for each of the four tests, the subscore areas, and the Composite as shown at the bottom of the table.

Your Multiple-Choice Test Scores
Practice Test 4

	Your Scale Score (Steps 5 & 6)	Your Scale Subscore (Step 7)	Your Percentile Rank (Step 8)
English	_____		_____
Usage/Mechanics (UM)		_____	_____
Rhetorical Skills (RH)		_____	_____
Mathematics	_____		_____
Pre-Algebra/Elem. Algebra (EA)		_____	_____
Inter. Algebra/Coord. Geometry (AG)		_____	_____
Plane Geometry/Trigonometry (GT)		_____	_____
Reading	_____		_____
Social Studies/Sciences (SS)		_____	_____
Arts/Literature (AL)		_____	_____
Science	_____		_____
Sum of scores	_____		
Composite score (sum ÷ 4)	_____		

Scoring Your Practice Writing Test Essay

To score your practice Writing Test essay, follow these seven steps:

STEP 1. Use the guidelines on the Six-Point Holistic Scoring Rubric (page 141) to score your essay. Because many papers do not fit the exact description at each score point, the rubric says: "Papers at each level exhibit *all* or *most* of the characteristics in the descriptors." To score your paper, read it and try to determine which paragraph in the rubric best describes *most* of the characteristics of your essay.

STEP 2. Because your Writing Test subscore is the sum of **two** readers' ratings of your essay, you should multiply your own 1–6 rating from Step 1 above by 2. Or, have both you and someone else read and score your practice essay and add those ratings together. In either case, record the total in the blank in Step 4 below and also in the blank labeled "Your Subscore" on page 918.

STEP 3. Locate your scale score for the English Test on page 915 and enter it here: _____.

STEP 4. Enter your Writing Test subscore from Step 2 here: _____.

STEP 5. Use the table on page 917 to find your Combined English/Writing scale score.

- First, circle your ACT English Test score in the left column.

- Second, circle your ACT Writing Test subscore at the top of the table.

- Finally, follow the English Test Score row across and the Writing Test Subscore row down until the two meet. Circle the Combined score where the two columns meet. (For example, if an English Test score were 19 and a Writing Test subscore were 6, the Combined English/Writing scale score would be 18.)

STEP 6. Using the number you circled on page 917, write your Combined English/Writing scale score on page 918. (The highest possible Combined English/Writing scale score is 36 and the lowest possible scale score is 1.)

Combined English/Writing Scale Scores											
English Test Score	Writing Test Subscore										
	2	3	4	5	6	7	8	9	10	11	12
1	1	2	3	4	5	6	7	8	9	10	11
2	2	3	4	5	6	6	7	8	9	10	11
3	2	3	4	5	6	7	8	9	10	11	12
4	3	4	5	6	7	8	9	10	11	12	13
5	4	5	6	7	8	9	10	11	12	12	13
6	5	6	7	7	8	9	10	11	12	13	14
7	5	6	7	8	9	10	11	12	13	14	15
8	6	7	8	9	10	11	12	13	14	15	16
9	7	8	9	10	11	12	13	13	14	15	16
10	8	9	9	10	11	12	13	14	15	16	17
11	8	9	10	11	12	13	14	15	16	17	18
12	9	10	11	12	13	14	15	16	17	18	19
13	10	11	12	13	14	14	15	16	17	18	19
14	10	11	12	13	14	15	16	17	18	19	20
15	11	12	13	14	15	16	17	18	19	20	21
16	12	13	14	15	16	17	18	19	20	20	21
17	13	14	15	16	16	17	18	19	20	21	22
18	13	14	15	16	17	18	19	20	21	22	23
19	14	15	16	17	18	19	20	21	22	23	24
20	15	16	17	18	19	20	21	21	22	23	24
21	16	17	17	18	19	20	21	22	23	24	25
22	16	17	18	19	20	21	22	23	24	25	26
23	17	18	19	20	21	22	23	24	25	26	27
24	18	19	20	21	22	23	23	24	25	26	27
25	18	19	20	21	22	23	24	25	26	27	28
26	19	20	21	22	23	24	25	26	27	28	29
27	20	21	22	23	24	25	26	27	28	28	29
28	21	22	23	24	24	25	26	27	28	29	30
29	21	22	23	24	25	26	27	28	29	30	31
30	22	23	24	25	26	27	28	29	30	31	32
31	23	24	25	26	27	28	29	30	30	31	32
32	24	25	25	26	27	28	29	30	31	32	33
33	24	25	26	27	28	29	30	31	32	33	34
34	25	26	27	28	29	30	31	32	33	34	35
35	26	27	28	29	30	31	31	32	33	34	35
36	26	27	28	29	30	31	32	33	34	35	36

STEP 7. Use the table on page 885 to determine your estimated percentile rank (percent at or below) for your Writing Test subscore and your Combined English/Writing scale score. In the far left column of the table on page 885, circle your Combined English/Writing scale score. Then read across to the percentile rank column headed "Combined English/Writing"; circle or put a check mark beside the corresponding percentile rank. Use the same procedure for your Writing Test subscore, this time using the column headed "Writing." As you mark your percentile ranks, enter them in the blanks provided in the table below. You may also find it helpful to compare your performance with the national mean (average) score for the Combined English/Writing scale score and the Writing Test subscore as shown at the bottom of the table on page 885.

Your Writing Test Scores
Practice Test 4

	Your Subscore (Step 2)	Your Scale Score (Steps 5 & 6)	Your Percentile Rank (Step 7)
Writing	_____		_____
Combined English/Writing		_____	_____

Scoring Keys and Conversion Tables

Practice Test 5

Scoring Your Multiple-Choice Practice Test

To score your multiple-choice practice test, follow these eight steps:

STEP 1. Write a "1" in the blank for each English Test question that you answered correctly. An example is provided in the box below:

	Key	Subscore Area*		Your answer was
		UM	RH	
1.	A	_____		Incorrect
2.	J		1	Correct
3.	B		1	Correct
4.	G	_____		Incorrect

English ■ Scoring Key ■ Practice Test 5

	Key	Subscore Area*				Key	Subscore Area*				Key	Subscore Area*	
		UM	RH				UM	RH				UM	RH
1.	C				26.	J				51.	B		
2.	F				27.	B				52.	G		
3.	D				28.	H				53.	A		
4.	J				29.	D				54.	H		
5.	A				30.	F				55.	C		
6.	G				31.	B				56.	H		
7.	A				32.	F				57.	B		
8.	J				33.	C				58.	F		
9.	C				34.	F				59.	C		
10.	F				35.	D				60.	F		
11.	A				36.	H				61.	C		
12.	G				37.	D				62.	H		
13.	D				38.	J				63.	B		
14.	J				39.	B				64.	G		
15.	A				40.	F				65.	C		
16.	H				41.	C				66.	H		
17.	D				42.	J				67.	A		
18.	F				43.	D				68.	F		
19.	C				44.	G				69.	B		
20.	J				45.	B				70.	F		
21.	C				46.	G				71.	D		
22.	F				47.	B				72.	J		
23.	B				48.	J				73.	D		
24.	J				49.	C				74.	G		
25.	A				50.	F				75.	D		

* UM = Usage/Mechanics
  RH = Rhetorical Skills

STEP 2. Add up the numbers in each subscore area and enter them in the appropriate blanks in the shaded box below:

Number Correct (Raw Score) for:	
Usage/Mechanics (UM) Subscore Area (40 questions)	_____
Rhetorical Skills (RH) Subscore Area (35 questions)	_____
Total Number Correct for English Test (UM + RH; 75 questions)	_____

STEP 3. Compute your total number correct for the English Test by adding the numbers you entered in Step 2. Write this total in the appropriate blank in the shaded box above. This is your raw score.

STEP 4. Repeat Steps 1 through 3 for the ACT Mathematics, Reading, and Science Tests using the scoring keys on the following pages. Note that the Science Test doesn't have subscores, so determine your raw score for that test simply by adding up the number of "1s" you entered.

Mathematics ▪ Scoring Key ▪ Practice Test 5

	Key	Subscore Area* EA	AG	GT			Key	Subscore Area* EA	AG	GT
1.	B	___				31.	C	___		
2.	H	___				32.	K	___		
3.	B		___			33.	C			
4.	G		___			34.	K		___	
5.	E	___				35.	E			___
6.	F	___				36.	J			___
7.	B	___				37.	D	___		
8.	H			___		38.	F			___
9.	A	___				39.	C		___	
10.	J	___				40.	G		___	
11.	C	___				41.	D		___	
12.	J	___				42.	G		___	
13.	A			___		43.	A			___
14.	J		___			44.	G			___
15.	B		___			45.	D			___
16.	J			___		46.	F			___
17.	B	___				47.	A	___		
18.	H			___		48.	K		___	
19.	B	___				49.	D		___	
20.	H			___		50.	J		___	
21.	E	___				51.	C		___	
22.	H		___			52.	K		___	
23.	E		___			53.	E		___	
24.	K		___			54.	F			___
25.	A	___				55.	D			___
26.	K	___				56.	F		___	
27.	B	___				57.	B			___
28.	H	___				58.	J			___
29.	D	___				59.	A	___		
30.	G			___		60.	K	___		

* EA = Pre-Algebra/Elementary Algebra
AG = Intermediate Algebra/Coordinate Geometry
GT = Plane Geometry/Trigonometry

Number Correct (Raw Score) for:	
Pre-Alg./Elem. Alg. (EA) Subscore Area (24 questions)	___
Inter. Alg./Coord. Geom. (AG) Subscore Area (18 questions)	___
Plane Geom./Trig. (GT) Subscore Area (18 questions)	___
Total Number Correct for Math Test (EA + AG + GT; 60 questions)	___

Reading ■ Scoring Key ■ Practice Test 5

	Key	Subscore Area* SS	AL		Key	Subscore Area* SS	AL		Key	Subscore Area* SS	AL
1.	D			15.	A	___		29.	C		___
2.	F			16.	G	___		30.	G		___
3.	B			17.	A	___		31.	D	___	
4.	H			18.	J	___		32.	F	___	
5.	D			19.	C	___		33.	D	___	
6.	J			20.	G	___		34.	H	___	
7.	D			21.	C		___	35.	C	___	
8.	G			22.	G		___	36.	G	___	
9.	C			23.	B		___	37.	A	___	
10.	G			24.	J		___	38.	H	___	
11.	A	___		25.	D		___	39.	C	___	
12.	J	___		26.	F		___	40.	J	___	
13.	D	___		27.	A		___				
14.	G	___		28.	G		___				

* SS = Social Studies/Sciences
  AL = Arts/Literature

Number Correct (Raw Score) for:

Studies/Sciences (SS) Subscore Area (20 questions) _____

Arts/Literature (AL) Subscore Area (20 questions) _____

Total Number Correct for Reading Test (SS + AL; 40 questions) _____

Science ■ Scoring Key ■ Practice Test 5

	Key			Key			Key	
1.	D	___	15.	D	___	29.	A	___
2.	F	___	16.	J	___	30.	J	___
3.	C	___	17.	C	___	31.	B	___
4.	G	___	18.	J	___	32.	H	___
5.	A	___	19.	C	___	33.	B	___
6.	F	___	20.	G	___	34.	H	___
7.	A	___	21.	B	___	35.	B	___
8.	H	___	22.	J	___	36.	G	___
9.	D	___	23.	B	___	37.	C	___
10.	J	___	24.	F	___	38.	F	___
11.	A	___	25.	C	___	39.	C	___
12.	F	___	26.	G	___	40.	F	___
13.	C	___	27.	A	___			
14.	H	___	28.	J	___			

Number Correct (Raw Score) for:

Total Number Correct for Science Test (40 questions) ___

STEP 5. On each of the four tests, the total number of correct responses yields a raw score. Use the conversion table on the following page to convert your raw scores to scale scores. For each of the four tests, locate and circle your raw score or the range of raw scores that includes it in the conversion table. Then, read across to either outside column of the table and circle the scale score that corresponds to that raw score. As you determine your scale scores, enter them in the blanks provided on page 926. The highest possible scale score for each test is 36. The lowest possible scale score for any of the four tests is 1.

STEP 6. Compute your Composite score by averaging the four scale scores. To do this, add your four scale scores and divide the sum by 4. If the resulting number ends in a fraction, round it off to the nearest whole number. (Round down any fraction less than one-half; round up any fraction that is one-half or more.) Enter this number in the appropriate blank on page 926. This is your Composite score. The highest possible Composite score is 36. The lowest possible Composite score is 1.

Scale Score Conversion Table
Practice Test 5

Scale Score	Raw Score				Scale Score
	English	Mathematics	Reading	Science	
36	75	58–60	40	38–40	36
35	73–74	56–57	–	37	35
34	72	54–55	39	36	34
33	71	52–53	38	35	33
32	70	51	37	34	32
31	69	50	36	33	31
30	68	49	34–35	32	30
29	66–67	47–48	33	31	29
28	65	45–46	32	30	28
27	63–64	43–44	31	29	27
26	61–62	41–42	30	28	26
25	58–60	39–40	29	26–27	25
24	56–57	37–38	28	24–25	24
23	53–55	35–36	26–27	23	23
22	50–52	34	25	21–22	22
21	47–49	32–33	23–24	20	21
20	44–46	31	22	18–19	20
19	42–43	29–30	20–21	16–17	19
18	40–41	26–28	19	15	18
17	37–39	23–25	18	14	17
16	35–36	18–22	16–17	13	16
15	32–34	14–17	15	12	15
14	30–31	11–13	13–14	11	14
13	28–29	9–10	12	10	13
12	26–27	7–8	10–11	9	12
11	24–25	6	8–9	8	11
10	22–23	5	7	7	10
9	19–21	4	6	5–6	9
8	16–18	3	5	4	8
7	13–15	–	–	–	7
6	11–12	2	4	3	6
5	8–10	–	3	2	5
4	6–7	1	2	–	4
3	4–5	–	–	1	3
2	3	–	1	–	2
1	0–2	0	0	0	1

STEP 7. Now convert your seven raw subscores to scale subscores using the table below. For each of the seven subscore areas, locate and circle either the raw score or the range of raw scores that includes it in the table. Then read across to either outside column of the table and circle the scale subscore that corresponds to that raw subscore. As you determine your scale subscores, enter them in the blanks on page 926. The highest possible scale subscore is 18. The lowest possible scale subscore is 1.

Scale Subscore Conversion Table
Practice Test 5

Scale Subscore	Raw Scores							Scale Subscore
	English		Mathematics			Reading		
	Usage/ Mechanics	Rhetorical Skills	Pre-Alg./ Elem. Alg.	Inter. Alg./ Coord. Geom.	Plane Geom./ Trigonometry	Soc. Studies/ Sciences	Arts/ Literature	
18	39–40	35	23–24	17–18	18	20	20	18
17	38	34	22	16	17	19	19	17
16	36–37	32–33	21	15	15–16	18	17–18	16
15	35	30–31	20	14	14	17	16	15
14	34	28–29	19	12–13	12–13	16	15	14
13	32–33	26–27	18	11	11	14–15	–	13
12	30–31	23–25	17	10	10	13	14	12
11	28–29	21–22	16	9	9	12	12–13	11
10	25–27	18–20	14–15	7–8	7–8	10–11	11	10
9	23–24	16–17	13	6	6	9	10	9
8	21–22	14–15	10–12	5	5	7–8	9	8
7	19–20	12–13	7–9	4	4	6	8	7
6	16–18	11	5–6	–	3	4–5	7	6
5	14–15	9–10	4	3	–	3	6	5
4	12–13	7–8	3	2	2	–	4–5	4
3	9–11	5–6	2	–	1	2	3	3
2	6–8	3–4	1	1	–	1	1–2	2
1	0–5	0–2	0	0	0	0	0	1

STEP 8. Use the table on page 881 to determine your estimated percentile ranks (percent at or below) for each of your scale scores. In the far left column of the table, circle your scale score for the English Test (from page 924). Then read across to the percentile rank column for that test; circle or put a check mark beside the corresponding percentile rank. Use the same procedure for the other three tests (from page 924) and for the subscore areas (from page 925). You may find it easier to use the right-hand column of scale scores for your Science Test and Composite scores. As you mark your percentile ranks, enter them in the blanks provided below. You may also find it helpful to compare your performance with the national mean (average) score for each of the four tests, the subscore areas, and the Composite as shown at the bottom of the table.

Your Multiple-Choice Test Scores
Practice Test 5

	Your Scale Score (Steps 5 & 6)	Your Scale Subscore (Step 7)	Your Percentile Rank (Step 8)
English	▬▬▬		▬▬▬
Usage/Mechanics (UM)		___	___
Rhetorical Skills (RH)		___	___
Mathematics	▬▬▬		▬▬▬
Pre-Algebra/Elem. Algebra (EA)		___	___
Inter. Algebra/Coord. Geometry (AG)		___	___
Plane Geometry/Trigonometry (GT)		___	___
Reading	▬▬▬		▬▬▬
Social Studies/Sciences (SS)		___	___
Arts/Literature (AL)		___	___
Science	▬▬▬		▬▬▬
Sum of scores	▬▬▬		
Composite score (sum ÷ 4)	▬▬▬		

Scoring Your Practice Writing Test Essay

To score your practice Writing Test essay, follow these seven steps:

STEP 1. Use the guidelines on the Six-Point Holistic Scoring Rubric (page 141) to score your essay. Because many papers do not fit the exact description at each score point, the rubric says: "Papers at each level exhibit *all* or *most* of the characteristics in the descriptors." To score your paper, read it and try to determine which paragraph in the rubric best describes *most* of the characteristics of your essay.

STEP 2. Because your Writing Test subscore is the sum of **two** readers' ratings of your essay, you should multiply your own 1–6 rating from Step 1 above by 2. Or, have both you and someone else read and score your practice essay and add those ratings together. In either case, record the total in the blank in Step 4 below and also in the blank labeled "Your Subscore" on page 929.

STEP 3. Locate your scale score for the English Test on page 926 and enter it here: _____.

STEP 4. Enter your Writing Test subscore from Step 2 here: _____.

STEP 5. Use the table on page 928 to find your Combined English/Writing scale score.

- First, circle your ACT English Test score in the left column.

- Second, circle your ACT Writing Test subscore at the top of the table.

- Finally, follow the English Test Score row across and the Writing Test Subscore row down until the two meet. Circle the Combined score where the two columns meet. (For example, if an English Test score were 19 and a Writing Test subscore were 6, the Combined English/Writing scale score would be 18.)

STEP 6. Using the number you circled on page 928, write your Combined English/Writing scale score on page 929. (The highest possible Combined English/Writing scale score is 36 and the lowest possible scale score is 1.)

Combined English/Writing Scale Scores										
English Test Score	Writing Test Subscore									
	2	3	4	5	6	7	8	9	10	11	12
1	1	2	3	4	5	6	7	8	9	10	11
2	2	3	4	5	6	6	7	8	9	10	11
3	2	3	4	5	6	7	8	9	10	11	12
4	3	4	5	6	7	8	9	10	11	12	13
5	4	5	6	7	8	9	10	11	12	12	13
6	5	6	7	7	8	9	10	11	12	13	14
7	5	6	7	8	9	10	11	12	13	14	15
8	6	7	8	9	10	11	12	13	14	15	16
9	7	8	9	10	11	12	13	13	14	15	16
10	8	9	9	10	11	12	13	14	15	16	17
11	8	9	10	11	12	13	14	15	16	17	18
12	9	10	11	12	13	14	15	16	17	18	19
13	10	11	12	13	14	14	15	16	17	18	19
14	10	11	12	13	14	15	16	17	18	19	20
15	11	12	13	14	15	16	17	18	19	20	21
16	12	13	14	15	16	17	18	19	20	20	21
17	13	14	15	16	16	17	18	19	20	21	22
18	13	14	15	16	17	18	19	20	21	22	23
19	14	15	16	17	18	19	20	21	22	23	24
20	15	16	17	18	19	20	21	21	22	23	24
21	16	17	17	18	19	20	21	22	23	24	25
22	16	17	18	19	20	21	22	23	24	25	26
23	17	18	19	20	21	22	23	24	25	26	27
24	18	19	20	21	22	23	23	24	25	26	27
25	18	19	20	21	22	23	24	25	26	27	28
26	19	20	21	22	23	24	25	26	27	28	29
27	20	21	22	23	24	25	26	27	28	28	29
28	21	22	23	24	24	25	26	27	28	29	30
29	21	22	23	24	25	26	27	28	29	30	31
30	22	23	24	25	26	27	28	29	30	31	32
31	23	24	25	26	27	28	29	30	30	31	32
32	24	25	25	26	27	28	29	30	31	32	33
33	24	25	26	27	28	29	30	31	32	33	34
34	25	26	27	28	29	30	31	32	33	34	35
35	26	27	28	29	30	31	31	32	33	34	35
36	26	27	28	29	30	31	32	33	34	35	36

STEP 7. Use the table on page 885 to determine your estimated percentile rank (percent at or below) for your Writing Test subscore and your Combined English/Writing scale score. In the far left column of the table on page 885, circle your Combined English/Writing scale score. Then read across to the percentile rank column headed "Combined English/Writing"; circle or put a check mark beside the corresponding percentile rank. Use the same procedure for your Writing Test subscore, this time using the column headed "Writing." As you mark your percentile ranks, enter them in the blanks provided in the table below. You may also find it helpful to compare your performance with the national mean (average) score for the Combined English/Writing scale score and the Writing Test subscore as shown at the bottom of the table on page 885.

Your Writing Test Scores
Practice Test 5

	Your Subscore (Step 2)	Your Scale Score (Steps 5 & 6)	Your Percentile Rank (Step 7)
Writing	_____		_____
Combined English/Writing		_____	_____

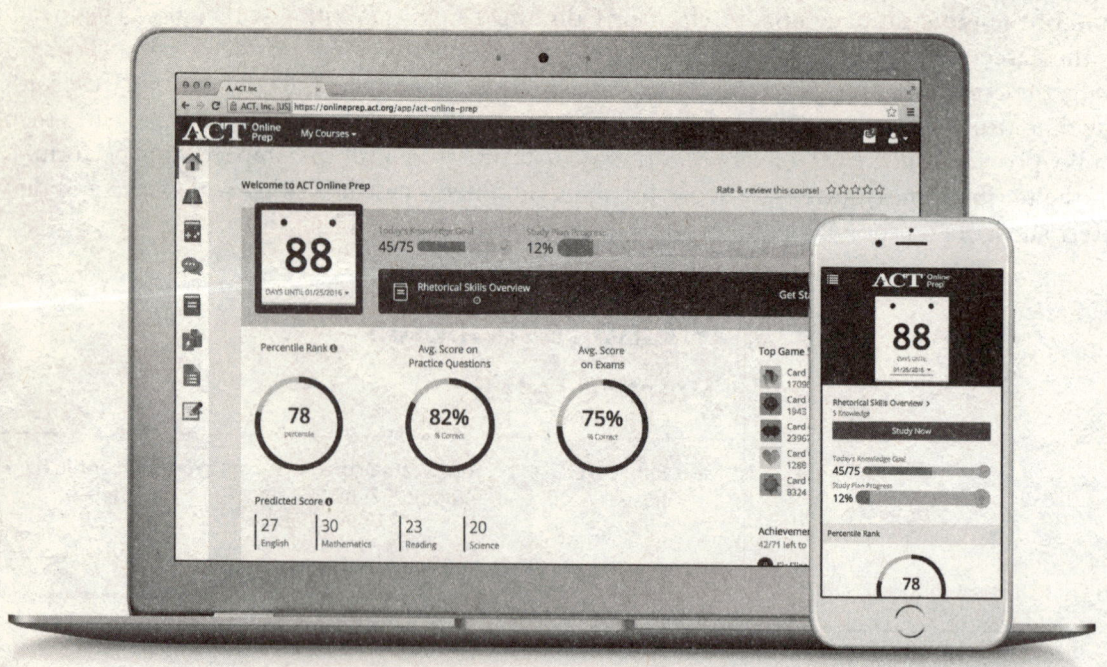

Get the edge you seek with
ACT Online Prep™!

- Prepare anywhere, anytime at your pace—online and with our mobile app

- Follow learning plans customized especially for you

- See questions from previous ACT tests and take a full-length practice test

To learn more and order the program, visit
www.actstudent.org/onlineprep.